LeBlonds'

1-2-3/G HANDBOOK for Presentation Manager

LeBlonds'

1-2-3/G HANDBOOK for Presentation Manager

The LeBlond Group

Geoffrey T. LeBlond

William B. LeBlond

Laura D. Mann

BANTAM BOOKS

TORONTO • NEW YORK • LONDON • SYDNEY • AUCKLAND

LeBlonds' 1-2-3/G Handbook for Presentation Manager
A Bantam Book/November 1990

ISBN 0-553-34995-3

Published simultaneously in the United States and Canada

Bantam Books are published by Bantam Books, a division of Bantam Doubleday Dell Publishing Group, Inc. Its trademark, consisting of the words "Bantam Books" and the portrayal of a rooster, is Registered in U.S. Patent and Trademark Office and in other countries. Marca Registrada, Bantam Books, 666 Fifth Avenue, New York, New York 10103.

PRINTED IN THE UNITED STATES OF AMERICA

0 9 8 7 6 5 4 3 2 1

4 Cutting and Pasting Data 293

5 File Management 379

FOREWORD

Chuck Sullivan
Senior Product Manager for Lotus 1-2-3
Lotus Development Corporation

It was 1983. I was working as an analyst for a Fortune 500 company. I produced budgets, forecasts, and analysis upon analysis (such is the job of an analyst). Needless to say, I spent a lot of time crunching numbers, mostly by hand, using a pencil, paper, and a calculator. Expending hour upon hour, day upon day, repetitiously working and reworking numbers was not exactly the pinnacle of my career aspirations. I figured that in the modern era of 1983, with high technology beginning to flourish, there must be a better way to work with numbers—perhaps using a computer. Although I worked in a company with a myriad of "data processing" systems, there were none, per se, that helped me, personally, to do my job better. Oh, we had rooms full of mainframes, minis, and other computer systems which were used to run the business ... but none of these directly helped me.

Then we got an IBM Personal Computer (PC) and a copy of Lotus 1-2-3. It was ostensibly purchased by the Vice President of Management Information Systems (MIS) as a research project (he was getting nervous about PCs starting to pop up on people's desks around the company). For the most part, our gleaming new PC sat around gathering dust as the MIS people tried to figure out what to do with it. Unauthorized personnel were not allowed to use it. Through some fancy statesmanship and pleading, I was given access to the new PC. I was to learn about it in order to see if it could help improve the productivity of our business staff.

Back in 1983, there wasn't a heck of a lot of help to be had for novice PC users. You were given a box full of computer parts and some software manuals and told, "Get to it!" So there I was, with a beautiful bouncing baby PC and a daunting-looking manual entitled "Lotus 1-2-3. Spreadsheet. Graphics. Information Management. Plus." According to everything I'd heard, somewhere in this innocent but unapproachable mass of technology were the productivity improvements I and my company sought.

By staying late at nights and coming in weekends to work on the PC, I had soon mastered the Herculean tasks of starting it up and running the sample

BASIC programs. I dabbled with Lotus 1-2-3, but for the most part the techniques for tapping into its power escaped me. I went through the tutorial program, and that at least got me started with 1-2-3. However, my attempts to become a 1-2-3 master by reading the Lotus manual usually ended up with my falling asleep or playing cards on the train with the person in the next seat. What I needed was some help in learning how to "use" 1-2-3.

So I sought out a friend in another department, who had already experienced the rites of passage and was a recognized PC guru. As I explained my situation, he began to grin. Then, in a manner reminiscent of Obi Won Canobie granting Luke Skywalker "the Force," he loaned me a tattered, yet obviously revered, book call *Using 1-2-3*. The authors, Doug Cobb and Geoffrey LeBlond, he explained, were the Jedi Warriors of 1-2-3, the undisputed experts. "Read this book," he said. "Then come back to see me if you need some more help."

The book *Using 1-2-3* helped to change my life. Its easy reading approach and wealth of how-to tips soon helped me master first the basics and then later the finer arts of Lotus 1-2-3. It took me step by step through the fundamentals and intricacies of 1-2-3, using and building upon real-life examples. By reading *Using 1-2-3*, I was quickly able to master Lotus 1-2-3. My personal productivity increased tremendously. One time-consuming regular report I prepared, which was jam-packed with numbers and calculations, was reduced from a week-long monthly task to four hours, from start to finish.

Before long, I was the new 1-2-3 Guru—an important development in my career. I was assigned to help put together the company's new forecasting system in 1-2-3. A promotion to PC Manager soon followed. And in 1984, I was offered a new job in an exciting young company—Lotus Development Corporation. Improving my personal productivity with Lotus 1-2-3 (with the help of *Using 1-2-3*) had led directly to the new career opportunities I desired. Why Lotus 1-2-3? What was so special about it?

Lotus 1-2-3- was (and is, as you learn by reading *LeBlonds' 1-2-3/G Handbook for Presentation Manager*) a revolutionary product. It was the first software package designed specifically for and to take advantage of the new IBM Personal Computer. It combined, for the first time in any single program, the three functions most commonly used by people who work with numbers: an electronic spreadsheet for performing calculations; business graphics for presenting your work; and database tools for managing your data. It was fast and powerful and, perhaps most importantly, it was fun to use. Lotus 1-2-3 became a phenomenon. Almost overnight, it changed forever the way people work with numbers. No more drudgery and repetitive pounding on a calculator as you scribble new numbers or erase a mistake from your report. Just set up a spreadsheet with all the calculations and let 1-2-3 do the work.

It was a phenomenon in the marketplace as well, the most successful software product ever, and the example against which all other programs are measured. Since its initial introduction in 1983, 1-2-3 has been improved, or upgraded, several times, with each new release adding more power and flexibility than the previous one. Currently, there are several versions of 1-2-3 available for both PC users and users of a wide range of other systems. These include 1-2-3 Release 2.2 for 8088-based PCs running MS-DOS; 1-2-3 Release 3.1 for 80286- and 80386-based PCs running DOS or DOS/Windows 3.0; 1-2-3 for Sun and UNIX System V; 1-2-3 for DEC VAX and All-in-One; and 1-2-3/M for IBM System 370 mainframes.

One of the newest and most advanced members of the Lotus 1-2-3 family—and of particular interest to readers of this book—is 1-2-3/G for OS/2 Presentation Manager. The first of a new generation of Lotus spreadsheets, 1-2-3/G was designed specifically to exploit the graphical capabilities and user interface of OS/2 PM. It offers the full benefits of a graphical interface, including a What-You-See-Is-What-You-Get (WYSIWYG) display, full mouse support, windowing, pull-down menus, and dialog boxes.

1-2-3/G provides many advanced spreadsheet features such as a true three-dimensional worksheet, file linking, a relational database that can dynamically access external data sources like a central database, enhanced charting, and presentation-quality output. In addition, 1-2-3/G includes Solver, an advanced goal-seeking technology for answering sophisticated "what-if" problems.

1-2-3/G was designed to provide 1-2-3 users an easy migration to OS/2 and Presentation Manager, and to preserve their investment in 1-2-3 applications and experience. By capitalizing on the new graphical capabilities of OS/2 Presentation Manager and the power of Lotus 1-2-3, 1-2-3/G offers users the best of both worlds—1-2-3 and a graphical user interface.

Users of 1-2-3/G can expect the same high level of support that 1-2-3 users have come to expect over the years. Support for 1-2-3 users comes in many forms. Lotus provides a variety of services for its users, including six months of access to a toll-free premium support hot line, courseware for learning how to use Lotus products, and *Lotus Magazine*, a publication chock full of tips and techniques for using Lotus products.

In addition, users of 1-2-3/G and other Lotus products benefit from a healthy aftermarket of products and services designed to assist them in learning and using these products. Independent Lotus Authorized Training Centers are located in over 150 locations throughout the United States and Canada. Third-party software developers produce a wide array of add-on products and turn-key spreadsheet applications for 1-2-3.

And of course, once again Geoffrey LeBlond is there, this time with his brother Bill, providing an excellent new book designed to assist both new and experienced 1-2-3 users in learning how to take advantage of 1-2-3/G. Over the years, Geoffrey and I have worked on several new versions of 1-2-3 and books to support them. Geoffrey is one of a handful of 1-2-3 experts who regularly work with Lotus in the design and testing of these new 1-2-3s. His experience with 1-2-3—and his ability to represent 1-2-3 users and their needs—is routinely relied upon by Lotus—to both our benefit and to yours, the user of 1-2-3 and the reader of Geoffrey's books.

I hope you enjoy reading *LeBlond's 1-2-3/G Handbook for Presentation Manager.*

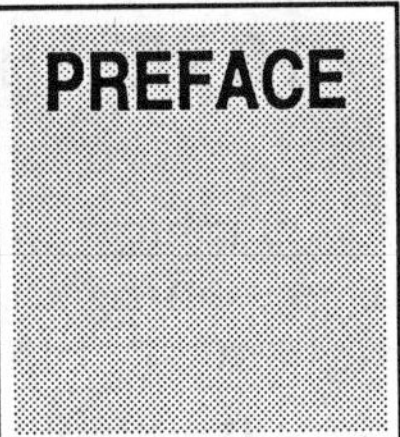

PREFACE

I first saw 1-2-3 in the spring of 1983. I was an M.B.A. student at the time in search of a summer job. Que Corporation, then a fledgling publishing company, was looking for a writer with some PC experience (a rare commodity at the time) to help coauthor a book about this new, though as yet scarcely known, spreadsheet program.

Previous to that summer, Doug Cobb, an editor at Que (now the president of the Cobb Group, a Louisville-based publisher of software newsletters), happened to have an office in the same building as Lotus Development in Cambridge, Massachusetts. Since Doug had gotten an early copy of 1-2-3 and had been working with it for several months, he knew his way around the program pretty well. He also showed me several of the tricks and techniques that would soon become the lingua franca of the business world.

The program Doug and I were looking at was an early test copy, but it was clear that it was something quite special. The ease with which you could enter complex formulas and instantly get results made the financial modeling programs I was using look arcane. And although I had seen VisiCalc running on an Apple computer, 1-2-3's speed on the IBM PC, and its intuitiveness, put it in a league all its own. We knew we were on to something.

During that summer Doug and I wrote *Using 1-2-3* for Que, which became an instant bestseller. In a few short years, it sold well over a million copies as 1-2-3's sales skyrocketed and became the stuff of industry lore.

Ever since that summer I have been working continuously with 1-2-3 in one way or another. I have written several books about it and started a software company to develop add-in software for it. Most recently, our company, The LeBlond Group, has completed books on 1-2-3 Release 2.2 and Release 3.

In many ways, my interest in 1-2-3/G is part of my ongoing interest in 1-2-3. But after working with 1-2-3/G for several months, I have to say that it is much more than that. 1-2-3/G represents something quite extraordinary. Like its early forefather, Release 1, 1-2-3/G represents a significant leap in spreadsheet power.

WHY WE WROTE THIS BOOK

1-2-3/G ushers in a new era of the graphical spreadsheet. As you are no doubt aware, Microsoft preceded Lotus in offering a graphical spreadsheet; PC Excel has been around for several years now. But there's a fundamental difference between the two products. 1-2-3/G retains the familiar feel and many of the same keystrokes as previous releases of 1-2-3. It's difficult to overestimate the importance of this because it brings the millions of 1-2-3 users into the graphical world. In fact, if you are familiar with 1-2-3, it *really is easy* to get started with 1-2-3/G. On the other hand, learning to use Excel is to start anew, not a very inviting prospect to an experienced 1-2-3 user.

Nevertheless, 1-2-3/G has many more features than any spreadsheet on the market, some of them quite complicated. In fact, it can take several months to learn how to take advantage of all of 1-2-3/G's features and their nuances. Because most business people simply don't have this kind of time, we decided to help shorten the learning curve by writing this book. We've cut away at the periphery to really get at the heart of 1-2-3/G. We've also provided many useful examples to help you make sense of all the new features.

ABOUT THIS BOOK

This book is designed to be the most comprehensive guide to 1-2-3/G available. If you are a new user, you will find all you need in the early chapters to get going quickly in an easy-to-read style. If you are an intermediate or advanced 1-2-3 user, you'll find many tips and techniques that are specially tailored to help further your knowledge and make the most of 1-2-3/G.

In *LeBlonds' 1-2-3/G Handbook*, we've made a special effort to fill in where the documentation leaves off. For example, we've included extensive sections on cutting and pasting data, managing the desktop, and creating macros. And these are just a few of the areas where we have endeavored to fill in the gaps.

Special Assistance for Knowledgeable 1-2-3 Users

One of the dilemmas in writing a book about 1-2-3/G is the variety of backgrounds that the audience for such a book brings with it. While some readers may have little or no 1-2-3 experience, others may be quite advanced.

To help new users, we've covered all the basics in the early chapters of the book. Even if you are familiar with 1-2-3, you are bound to find these early chapters helpful for learning how to use 1-2-3/G's new graphical environment, such as navigating with the mouse, moving between multiple worksheets and files, and the like.

In addition, we have adopted a few conventions to help those already familiar with 1-2-3 get directly to the information they need about 1-2-3/G. For example, at the start of each chapter is a section called "What's New." These sections give experienced users some quick insight into what's new in the product and where to go in the chapter to get detailed information.

We've also marked several notes in the book as "Note for Release 2 Users" and "Note for Release 2 and 3 Users." So, if you are familiar with 1-2-3, you'll find these notes helpful because they point out differences between 1-2-3/G and previous releases of 1-2-3, especially where those differences can create potential pitfalls.

WHAT'S COVERED IN THIS BOOK

This book is organized into 13 chapters and 2 appendices that cover the full range of 1-2-3/G.

Chapter 1, "1-2-3/G Basics," discusses many of the most prominent features of 1-2-3/G. By reading this chapter, you'll have all the basics you need to use the spreadsheet portion of 1-2-3/G.

Chapter 2, "Managing the Desktop," describes how to work with windows on the 1-2-3/G Desktop. For example, it describes how to move and resize windows. It also describes how to place multiple files on the desktop and group those files under different desktop names.

Chapter 3, "Formatting Worksheets," describes how to improve the appearance and layout of your worksheets. For example, you'll learn how to format cells, change fonts, insert and delete columns and rows, and protect worksheets.

Chapter 4, "Cutting and Pasting Data," discusses the commands you use to edit your 1-2-3/G worksheets. Topics include how to use the Copy and Move commands to place data in other cells and how to use the Edit commands to edit your worksheets using the clipboard.

Chapter 5, "File Management," covers all of 1-2-3/G's File commands. For example, you'll learn how to use File Open, which lets you open multiple files on the 1-2-3/G desktop, and File Retrieve, which lets you replace the current file with a file on disk.

Chapter 6, "Functions," is a reference chapter on all the @functions available in 1-2-3/G. Functions are organized by category for easy reference.

Chapter 7, "Graphs," describes a full range of topics related to 1-2-3/G's graphics capability. For example, you'll learn how to use the Graph commands to automatically create graphs as well as how to use the Graph Tool to enhance your graphs to suit your needs.

Chapter 8, "Printing," examines all the topics related to printing in 1-2-3/G. For example, you'll learn how to print output to a printer, how to create ASCII files for use by other programs, and how to combine worksheets and graphs on the same printed page.

Chapter 9, "Data Management," describes how to create a database in 1-2-3/G and how to use the Data commands to organize and query it. Other topics include how to sort a database and how to search a database for information, such as a certain last name or an order number. This chapter also describes how to access external databases with the new DataLens drivers.

Chapter 10, "Creating Macros," describes how to use 1-2-3/G's macro facility and includes many useful examples to increase your understanding. It also describes how to use the Keystroke Editor to replay keystrokes and save them as macros.

Chapter 11, "The Macro Programming Language," is a reference to 1-2-3/G's macro programming commands. You'll learn how to use these commands to create sophisticated macro programs of your own design.

Chapter 12, "Networking 1-2-3/G," explains how to take advantage of 1-2-3/G's built-in networking features. For example, you'll learn how to use 1-2-3/G's file reservation system to manage files in shared directories on a network. You'll also learn how to seal your files to protect sensitive areas and settings.

Chapter 13, "The Backsolver and Solver," describes how to use the Backsolver and Solver to solve what-if problems in your worksheets. This chapter includes several examples to help you identify when the Backsolver or the Solver is most appropriate.

Appendix A, "Customizing 1-2-3/G," describes how you can set up 1-2-3/G to take advantage of your unique operating environment. For example, it describes how to change 1-2-3/G's default settings and how to add the 1-2-3/G title to the Start Programs window (in OS/2 1.1) or the Group window (in OS/2 1.2).

Appendix B, "The 1-2-3/G Character Set," lists the characters in the 1-2-3/G character set. It also shows you how to produce 1-2-3/G characters whether or not they are on your keyboard.

CONVENTIONS

Throughout this book, certain conventions are used to make the text easier to understand. An example of each convention follows:

- Commands appear as they do on the screen, for example, Range Erase.
- User input appears as you would enter it from the keyboard. When it appears within the main body of the text, it is bolded, for example, "enter **+A2+B5**." Otherwise, it is set off from regular text as in the following:

```
+A2+B5
```

- Keys appear in caps, for example, INS or ESC. When two or more keys must be pressed simultaneously, those keys are separated by hyphens; for example, ALT-F2.

- File names, range names, and functions appear in capitals, as in "the FEATURES.WG1 file," "the range name TOTAL_SALES," and the "the @DSUM function."
- This book includes many tips which are set off from the rest of the text to make them easily identifiable, as in the following:

Tip: Selecting function keys with the mouse

> You can also select a function key by using the mouse. To do so, however, you must first activate the on-screen function key template so that it appears at the bottom of the desktop.

IN CONCLUSION

1-2-3/G is a significant new product. It is the first spreadsheet program to bring the power and familiarity of 1-2-3 to the graphical environment of OS/2. At the same time, 1-2-3/G has many more features than any other spreadsheet program available. Because of its breadth and complexity, learning to use 1-2-3/G can be especially challenging.

In this book we've made a special effort to give you the real substance behind 1-2-3/G. At the same time, we believe we've written the most comprehensive and useful book on the topic. We hope our enthusiasm for 1-2-3/G passes on to you.

Geoffrey LeBlond

1-2-3/G Basics

1-2-3/G is a graphical version of the highly popular 1-2-3 spreadsheet program that is designed specifically for OS/2 and Presentation Manager (PM). Although other spreadsheets are available for OS/2, 1-2-3/G is the only one to bring the familiar "feel" of earlier versions of 1-2-3 to a graphical user interface (GUI).

As a Presentation Manager application, 1-2-3/G incorporates many of the features of a graphical user interface, such as WYSIWYG (what you see is what you get) display, windowing, mouse support, dialog boxes, pulldown menus, and presentation-quality output. In addition, 1-2-3/G adds several new features to the GUI interface, like font previews in dialog boxes and cascade menus that give it a special look all its own.

This chapter teaches you the basics of 1-2-3/G. You will learn how to navigate in worksheets using the mouse and keyboard. You'll also learn how to use menus, dialog boxes, and many other features of 1-2-3/G's graphical interface. Along the way you'll learn several new terms associated with 1-2-3/G, such as "cascade menu" and "collection." When you've completed this chapter, you'll have all the basic tools you need to perform worksheet-related tasks in 1-2-3/G.

What's New

If you are familiar with 1-2-3, you will find working with 1-2-3/G quite comfortable because you can use many of the same keystrokes you already know. For example, nearly all of 1-2-3 Release 2.2's most commonly used commands are identical in 1-2-3/G. In addition, 1-2-3/G incorporates many of 1-2-3 Release 3's features, including 3-dimensional (3-D) worksheets, file linking, access to external databases through DataLens drivers, and network support.

As you would expect, 1-2-3/G has many new features that are by-products of a graphical user interface, such as mouse support, WYSIWYG, fonts, and colors. In addition, it has many enhancements to 1-2-3's familiar capabilities, including the following that you will read about in this chapter:

- **3–D worksheets:** Every 1-2-3/G worksheet file has 256 worksheets. Unlike 1-2-3 Release 3, you do not have to insert the additional worksheets in the file; they are always present.
- **New range features:** Like 1-2-3 Release 3, 1-2-3/G allows you to specify 3–D ranges that span multiple worksheets. In addition, you can have collections, which are groups of discontiguous ranges that 1-2-3/G treats like a range.
- **GUI selection order:** You can also use a GUI selection order; that is, you can select a range and then apply a command or action to it.
- **New key sequences for navigating and selecting:** 1-2-3/G has many new keys sequences for navigating in and between worksheets. It also has new sequences for selecting rows, columns, worksheets, and entire worksheet files.
- **New function and accelerator keys:** 1-2-3/G has many new function keys that you can press in combination with CTRL and ALT. You can also place a function key template on the screen and select function keys with the mouse.
- **Multilevel undo:** 1-2-3/G has a powerful undo feature that lets you reverse up to 20 previous commands or actions.
- **Search and replace:** In 1-2-3/G, you can use the Range Search command to search and replace characters in labels or formulas. You can search through 2–D and 3–D ranges and collections.
- **A Note utility:** 1-2-3/G has a powerful new note utility for annotating cells and named ranges. You can attach up to four notes to each cell or named range.
- **Help utility:** 1-2-3/G has a new Help utility that is far more comprehensive than in any previous release of 1-2-3.

PRESENTATION MANAGER TERMINOLOGY

If you are new to a graphical user interface, it is helpful to learn some Presentation Manager terminology before you embark on the task of learning 1-2-3/G. Table 1–1 shows some common terms used throughout this book.

TABLE 1–1 Common Presentation Manager Terms

Term	Explanation
Click	Press the mouse button (usually the leftmost one) and release it.
Click on	Move the mouse pointer to an area on the desktop and press the mouse button.
Double-click	Press the mouse button twice in succession.
Dialog box	A message in an on-screen box.
Drag	Keep the mouse button pressed (the leftmost one) while moving the mouse.
Elevator button	The box in a scroll bar that you can drag to adjust the viewing area of the window.
Grab	Move the mouse pointer to an area on the desktop where the mouse pointer changes shape.
Insertion point	A flashing vertical bar indicating where text is inserted when you type (also called the cursor).
Maximize	Enlarge a window to its full screen size.
Minimize	Reduce the window to an icon on the desktop.
Point	Move the mouse until the tip of the mouse pointer rests on what you want to point to.
Scroll bar	The narrow bar near the edge of a window that lets you view information that won't fit in a window.

THE DESKTOP

In 1-2-3/G, your work is displayed in an area known as the *Desktop*. You can place worksheets or graphs on the Desktop and arrange them as you please. You can also save the current arrangement of worksheets and graphs in a desktop file.

There are four main parts to the Desktop—the Title bar, the Menu bar, the Control line, and the Work area. Figure 1–1 shows the different elements of the Desktop. The sections that follow describe these areas in more detail.

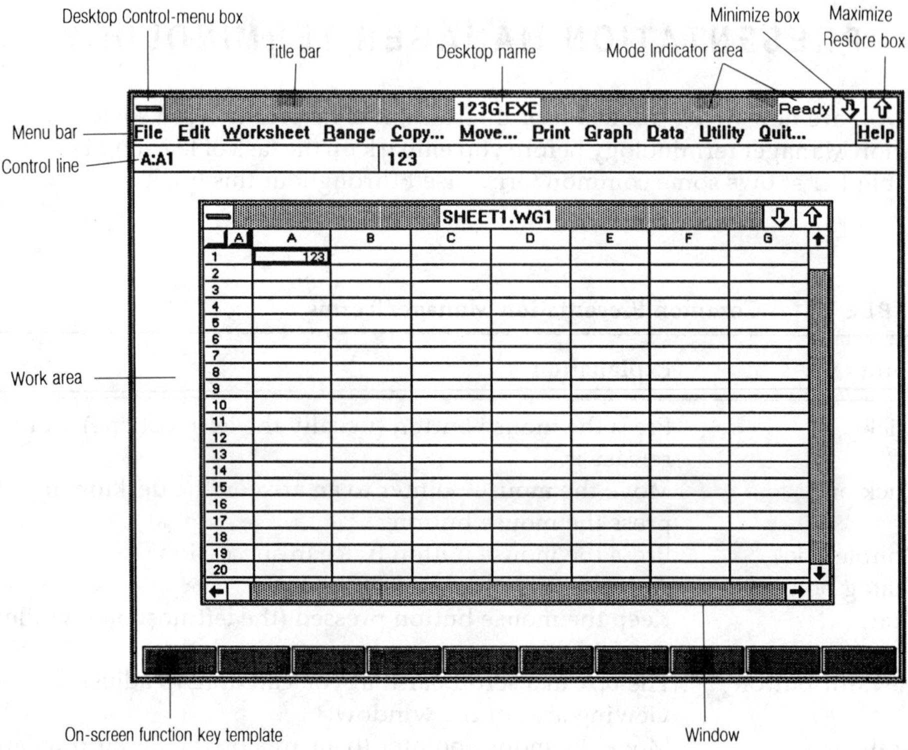

FIGURE 1–1 Elements of the Desktop

The Title Bar

The Title bar is the first line of the Desktop and has the following five parts:

- **Desktop Control-menu box:** When you click on this box or press ALT-SPACEBAR, 1-2-3/G displays the *Desktop Control menu*. You can use this menu to control the size and placement of the Desktop on the screen. You can also use it to access the OS/2 Task Manager as well as various 1-2-3/G windows and utilities. (See Chapter 2, "Managing the Desktop," for a complete description of the Desktop Control menu.)
- **Desktop name:** If you have assigned a desktop file name, that name appears in this area of the Title bar following "1-2-3/G.EXE." When you first start using 1-2-3/G, however, you are unlikely to have a Desktop file name. (See Chapter 2 for information on Desktop filenames.)
- **Mode indicator area:** This is the area of the screen where mode indicators appear. Mode indicators provide information about the state that 1-2-3/G is in (see "Mode Indicators" later).

- **Minimize box:** When you click on this box, the 1-2-3/G Desktop is reduced to an icon. (You can achieve the same effect by selecting Minimize from the Desktop Control menu.) If, after minimizing the Desktop, you want to restore it to its previous size, double-click on the Desktop icon (see Chapter 2 for more details).
- **Maximize/Restore box:** You can click on this box to expand the Desktop to occupy the entire screen and, afterward, to restore the desktop to its previous size. (Select Maximize or Restore from the Desktop Control menu to achieve the same effect.)

The Menu Bar

The *Menu bar* appears on the second line of the Desktop. The Menu bar has two components, or sections. The first section contains the main menu for the tool or utility that is currently active. In Figure 1-1, the active tool is a worksheet. Therefore, the Worksheet Tool menu is displayed.

Note

Selecting menu items is covered later in this chapter under "Menus." However, you can select a menu item by clicking on its name with your mouse. Alternatively, you can select a menu item with the keyboard. To do this, press MENU (F10) or ALT to activate the menu. Then, type the first letter of the menu item, or use the arrow keys to highlight it and press ENTER.

The second section of the Menu bar contains the Help box. This box appears at the far right of the Menu bar. By clicking on it, or pressing HELP (F1), you can get context-sensitive help for 1-2-3/G (see "Getting Help" later).

The Control Line

The *Control line* occupies the third line of the Desktop. This line is used for entering and editing data in worksheets. When a worksheet window is active, as in Figure 1-1, the Control line shows the current cell address on the left and the contents of the cell on the right.

The Work Area

The *Work area* is the entire area of the Desktop below the first three lines. It is the area where you place worksheet and graph windows as well as where 1-2-3/G displays dialog boxes and utilities (the Help window is an example of a utility). You'll spend most of your time working in this area of the Desktop.

At the foot of the Work area is the *On-screen function key template* (see Note below). This template shows the names of the function keys you can use with the active window. If you press SHIFT, ALT, or CTRL, the template changes to show the names of the function keys you can use in combination with those keys. (See "Function and Accelerator Keys" later for more on 1-2-3/G's function keys.)

Note

> The on-screen function key template does not appear when you first start 1-2-3/G. You must activate it by using the Utility User-Settings Preferences command. This same command affects whether you can see on screen the state of the CAPSLOCK, NUM LOCK, and SCROLL LOCK keys. (See Appendix A, "Customizing 1-2-3/G," for more on the User-Settings Preferences command.)

TOOLS AND UTILITIES

The windows that appear within the Work area are divided into two groups—tool windows and utility windows. In general, *tool windows* are for entering and displaying data. There are two types of tool windows in 1-2-3/G—worksheet and graph. When you start 1-2-3/G for the first time, a worksheet window appears on the screen. The majority of this chapter covers how to work with the worksheet window. You'll read about the graph window in Chapter 7, "Graphs."

Utility windows, on the other hand, help you analyze data. They are not used for entering data. 1-2-3/G offers the following utility windows:

- **Keystroke Editor:** This utility records every keystroke you make in 1-2-3/G and lets you replay those keystrokes directly or place them in a macro. See Chapter 10, "Creating Macros," for more on the Keystroke Editor.
- **Note:** The Note utility lets you attach notes of up to 512 characters in length to an individual cell or a range name (see "Cell Notes" later).
- **Solver:** This utility lets you perform complex "what if" analysis on problems that have several possible answers. For example, suppose you have determined that your company must reach a certain profit figure in the upcoming year, and you want to know the best mix of sales and marketing expenses needed to reach the chosen figure. You can use the Solver utility to determine the "best" answer, as well as several other possible answers. See Chapter 13, "The Backsolver and Solver," for more information.

- **Print Preview:** The Print Preview utility lets you preview your printed material on screen before sending it to the printer. See Chapter 8, "Printing," for more information.

WINDOWS

When you look at a tool or utility in 1-2-3/G, you are viewing it through a rectangular area on the desktop known as a *window*. By placing windows on the desktop, you can view several different tools and utilities at once. For example, you can view a graph in one window and a worksheet in another. Alternatively, you can view two worksheets in two different windows. In fact, you can have up to 16 windows open at once in 1-2-3/G.

Figure 1–2 shows the elements of a 1-2-3/G window. They are described as follows:

- **Border:** Each 1-2-3/G window is surrounded by a border that appears highlighted when the window is active. You can change the size of the window by moving the mouse pointer to the border, at which point the pointer changes to a double-headed arrow. This means that you can grab the window

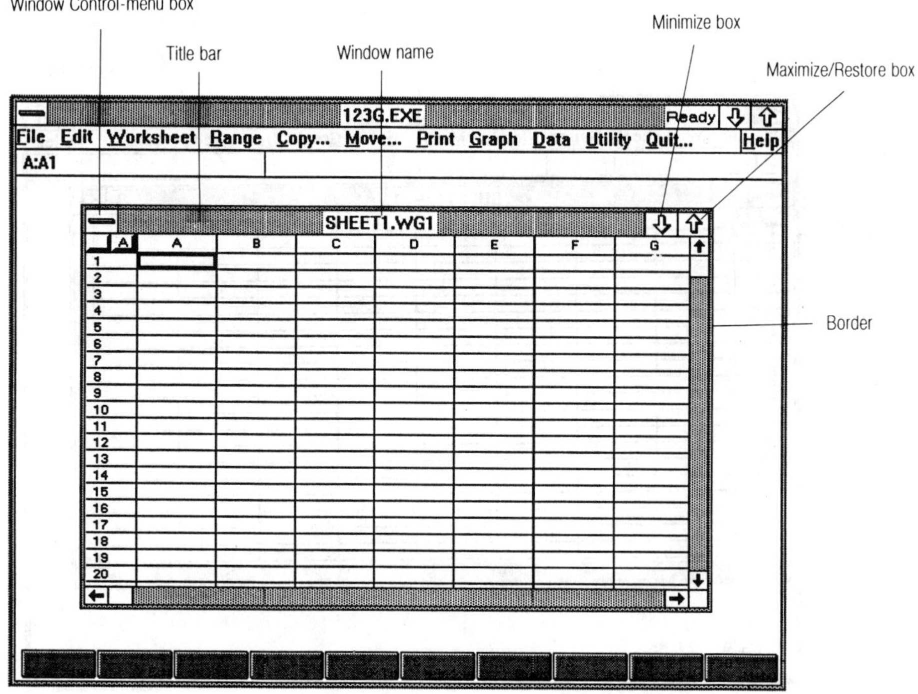

FIGURE 1–2 Elements of a window

border and adjust the size of the window (see Chapter 2, "Managing the Desktop," for more information).

- **Minimize box:** When you click on this box, the window is reduced to an icon. (You can achieve the same effect by selecting Minimize from the Window Control menu.) If, after minimizing the window, you want to restore it to its previous size, double-click on the Window icon (see Chapter 2).
- **Maximize/Restore box:** You can click on this box to expand the window to occupy the entire Desktop and, afterward, to restore the window to its previous size. (Select Maximize or Restore from the Window Control menu to achieve the same effect.) See Chapter 2 for more information.
- **Title bar:** The first line of the window shows the Window Control-menu box, window name (usually a data file or utility name), Minimize box, and Maximize/Restore box.
- **Window name:** This area of the Title bar shows the current worksheet or graph filename or the active utility name, depending on the contents of the window.
- **Window Control-menu box:** When you click on this box or press ALT- — (minus), 1-2-3/G displays the *Window Control menu*. You can use this menu to control the size and placement of a window on the Desktop (see Chapter 2).

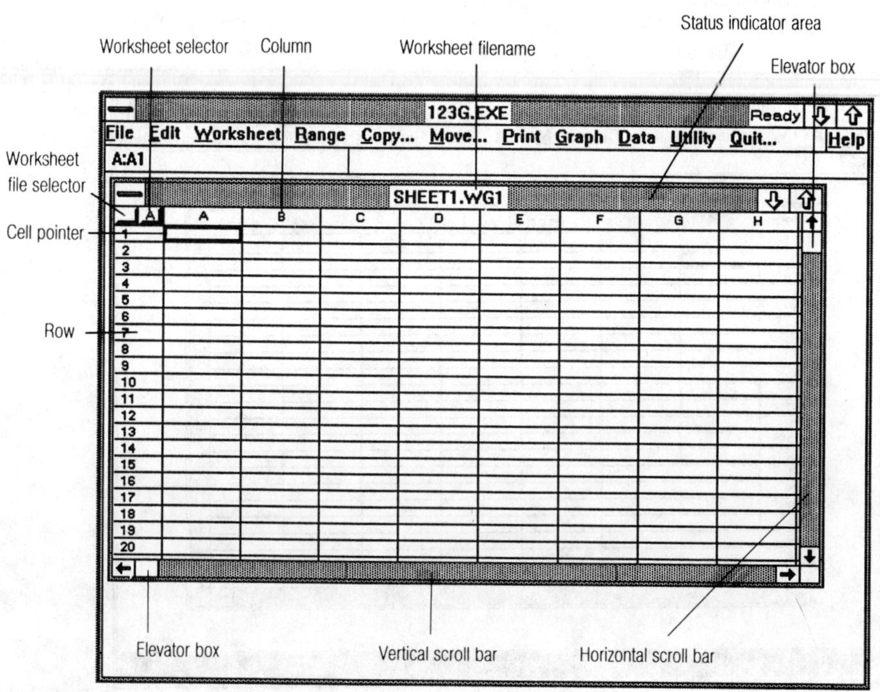

FIGURE 1–3 Elements of a worksheet window

THE WORKSHEET

As mentioned, when you first start 1-2-3/G, a worksheet window appears on the screen. This is quite natural because the worksheet is the tool you will use most often in 1-2-3/G to perform your work. Figure 1–3 shows the unique elements of a worksheet window.

The worksheet is divided into columns labeled with letters across the top, and rows labeled with numbers. Like a piece of graph paper, the intersection of the columns and rows form a series of small boxes known as *cells*. Each cell starts out empty and fills when you enter data in it.

The point at which a column and a row meet defines the location of a cell. The combination of the column letter and row number is the *cell address*, such as A9 or CA11. The column letter is always specified first, followed by the row number. You are always located at some cell address called the *current cell address*. The current cell address matches the location of the *cell pointer*, a black outline surrounding the current cell.

The worksheet area that appears within a window is actually a view onto a much larger worksheet space. In fact, a 1-2-3/G worksheet has 256 columns and 8192 rows. (The lower rightmost cell in a worksheet is IV8192.) The worksheet area that appears on your screen is limited by the size of the window. You can expand and contract the size of the window (see Chapter 2, "Managing the Desktop"), but you can still see only a small portion of the worksheet at any one time. Later on you'll learn how to shift the contents of the window to view different parts of the worksheet.

Unlike prior releases of 1-2-3, a single 1-2-3/G worksheet file contains 256 worksheets. Think of these worksheets as individual sheets of paper stacked one behind the other in your computer's memory. You can use each worksheet separately, or you can link worksheets together, lending a 3–dimensional (3–D) aspect to 1-2-3/G. Here are some of the advantages of having multiple-worksheet files:

- Rather than shoehorn everything into one large worksheet, as was required in previous releases of 1-2-3, you can now easily divide your work into smaller, more natural segments and place them in different worksheets. For example, you can place a spreadsheet in one worksheet, a database in another, and macros in a third.
- You can more easily consolidate information. For example, suppose you want to consolidate departmental budgets. You can place each budget in a separate worksheet and link them all to a single master worksheet using formulas. Then, when you make a change to one of the departmental worksheets, you can easily see the effect on the master worksheet.
- Data in one worksheet is protected from other worksheets. That is, you can change one worksheet at any time without moving, reformatting, or accidentally erasing data in other worksheets in the file.

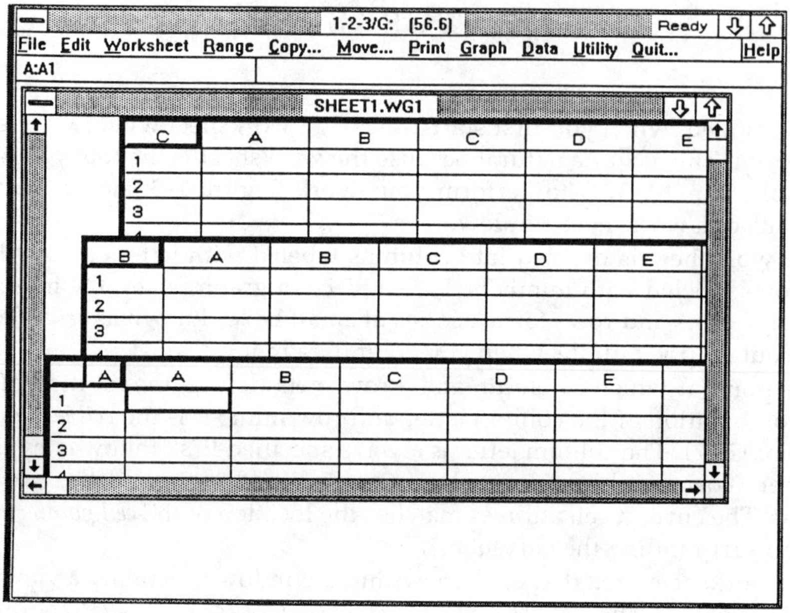

FIGURE 1–4 **Worksheets A, B, and C**

When you first start 1-2-3 only a single worksheet appears in the window. This is the top worksheet. You can see the next worksheet in the file by pressing CTRL-PGUP. Pressing CTRL-PGDN moves the cell pointer back to the previous worksheet in the stack. The worksheets are named A through IV. Each worksheet is the same size, 256 columns by 8192 rows. The worksheet in which the cell pointer is sitting is called the *current worksheet*.

Figure 1–4 shows three worksheets—A, B, and C—in a file called SHEET1.WG1 (the filename appears in the title bar at the top of the window). Worksheet A is the current worksheet. You can view three worksheets at once using the Worksheet Window Perspective command. To move between worksheets in perspective view, press CTRL-PGUP or CTRL-PGDN. To return 1-2-3/G to a single worksheet within a window, you use the Worksheet Window Clear command. (See Chapter 2 for more information on how to view more than one worksheet at a time.)

Because there are multiple worksheets in a file, you must precede the cell address with a worksheet letter followed by a colon. For example, the cell address B:C6 refers to the second worksheet, third column, and sixth row, and the cell address C:C6 refers to the same cell address in the next worksheet. This method of cell referencing is called *full cell addressing*. You do not have to use a full cell address, though, when you reference a cell that is in the current worksheet; instead you can use *abbreviated cell addressing*—where you reference only the column and row—for example, A7. You'll learn more about this in "Entering Formulas" later in this chapter.

To further complicate matters, you can have more than one worksheet file active in memory at a time. To load a new file into memory without erasing any existing files, you use the File New command. To load an existing file from disk into memory without erasing any existing files, you use the File Open command. Chapter 2, "Managing the Desktop," discusses how to load and work with multiple files in memory.

CELL INFORMATION

At various sites on the desktop you can see information about the location and contents of the current cell and its settings. As mentioned, the Control line (the third line of the Desktop), shows the current cell address on the left of the line. For example, in Figure 1–5, the current cell address is A:A1. Notice that this matches the location of the cell pointer and that the address appears as a worksheet letter followed by a colon, a column letter, and row number.

To the right of the cell address on the Control line is the *contents box*. This part of the Control line serves as a window into which you can enter and edit information that is ultimately added to the worksheet. In Figure 1–5 the contents of cell A:A1 is the number 345. Had the cell contained a label entry (text), such as Sales, the entry would be preceded by a *label prefix*, for example, 'Sales. Later on in this chapter you will learn more about label prefixes.

Below the Control line, in the Title bar for the window, you can see the current cell's protection status, *U* for unprotected or *PR* for protected. In Figure 1–5, cell A:A1 is unprotected. If the cell is protected, you cannot change its value.

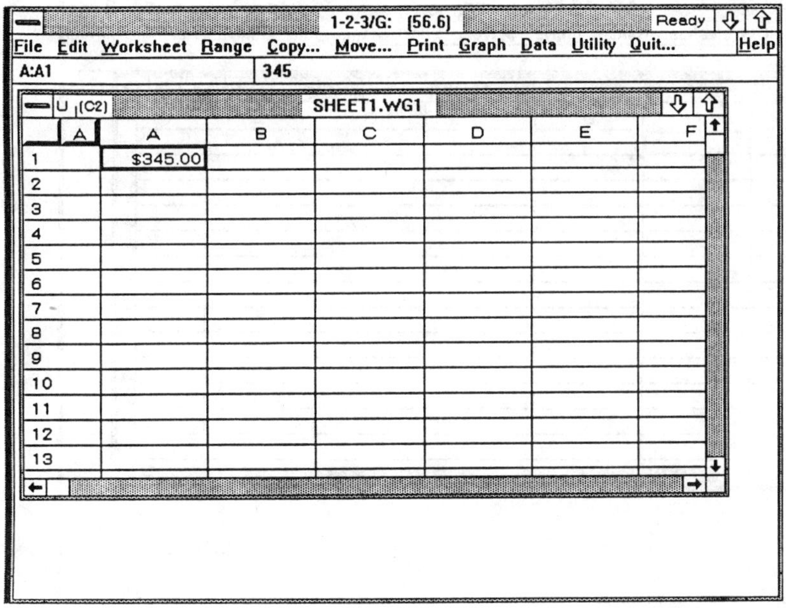

FIGURE 1–5 An example of cell information

For the protection status to appear in the Control line, global protection must be turned on (with Worksheet Global Protection Enable—see Chapter 3, "Formatting the Worksheet"), or the cell must have been explicitly unprotected (with Range Unprotect—see Chapter 3 here also).

To the right of the protection status, you may see the cell's format in parentheses. The *format* controls how a value (number or formula) displays in a cell (see Chapter 3). In the current example, the cell is formatted for Currency, two decimal places. The cell's format shows in the Control line only if it is changed from the default format for the entire worksheet.

INDICATORS

1-2-3/G has two types of indicators, status and mode indicators. Mode indicators appear on the right-hand side of the Desktop's Title bar. Status indicators, on the other hand, appear on the right-hand side of the Window's Title bar. Figure 1–6 shows the locations of 1-2-3/G indicators.

Mode Indicators

Mode indicators provide information about what 1-2-3/G is doing. When 1-2-3/G is idle—waiting for input—the mode indicator shows Ready. When something is going on, the mode indicator changes from Ready to some other single keyword indicating an activity or condition. Table 1–2 shows the different mode keywords and what each means.

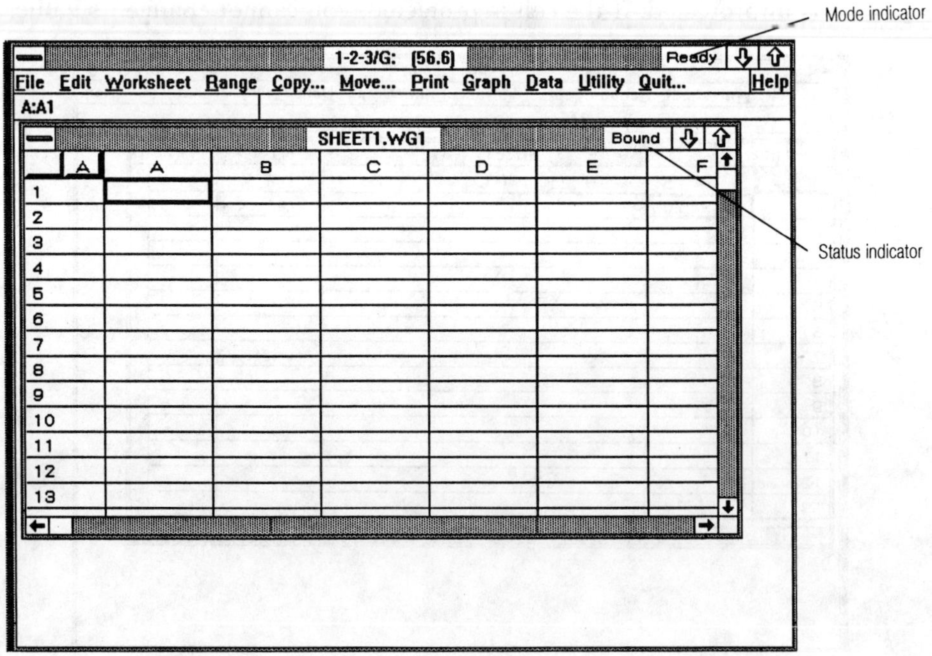

FIGURE 1–6 Mode and status indicators

Table 1–2 Mode Indicators

Keyword	Description
Edit	You pressed EDIT (F2) to edit a cell entry, or made an error entering a formula.
Find	You selected Data Query Find to find database records matching certain criteria, and 1-2-3/G has located such a record. Pressing QUERY (F7) to repeat the latest Data Query Find also causes 1-2-3/G to show this indicator.
Group	Worksheets in the active file are grouped; you selected Worksheet Global Group Enable (or pressed SHIFT-F7).
Label	You are entering a label (text).
Link	You used the Data External command to link to an external database and the link needs to be refreshed (updated).
Menu	You pressed / (slash), ALT, or MENU (F10) to access 1-2-3/G's main menu. 1-2-3/G also shows this indicator when a dialog box is active, indicating that you can move the pointer between other choices in a group.
Msg	1-2-3/G is displaying a warning or some other message.
Point	You are being prompted to specify a range in response to a command; or you are currently entering a formula by highlighting a cell or range.
Ready	1-2-3 is waiting for input.
SST	A macro is running in single-step mode and has paused for input. This indicator also appears when you run keystrokes in the Keystroke Editor in single-step mode.
Step	You pressed STEP (ALT-F2) to execute a macro one step at a time (single-step mode). This indicator also appears when you run keystrokes in the Keystroke Editor in single-step mode.
Value	You are entering a value (a number or a formula).
Wait	1-2-3 is busy—it's either completing a command or recalculating the worksheet.

Status Indicators

Status indicators are linked to a key that you press to put the system in a particular state, such as End or Bound. They can also warn about a particular system condition that may need your attention, such as Calc or Circ. Table 1–3 describes 1-2-3/G's various status indicators and the activity that is associated with each of them.

Table 1–3 Status Indicators

Indicator	Description
Bound	You selected BOUND (SHIFT-F4) to restrict cell-pointer movement to a specific selection (a range or collection).
Calc	The worksheet is set for manual recalculation, and it needs recalculating; press CALC (F9).
Circ	1-2-3 has detected a circular reference (a formula that refers to itself); use the Worksheet Status command to see the first cell involved in the circular reference.
Cmd	1-2-3 is pausing while running a macro.
End	You pressed END and 1-2-3 is waiting for the next key; press a cursor movement key (see Table 1–7) or END to cancel.
Input	You selected the Range Input command (see Chapter 3).
RO	The active file has read-only status. You can make changes to the file, but you cannot save it under its current name.

FUNCTION AND ACCELERATOR KEYS

Function keys and *Accelerator keys* are assigned to common tasks you want 1-2-3/G to perform. Many are simply shortcuts to menu commands. Others perform tasks you cannot perform in any other way. In 1-2-3/G, you can use F1 through F11 alone or in conjunction with the SHIFT, ALT, or CTRL. These are the names assigned to the different combinations:

Key	Alone	SHIFT	CTRL	ALT
F1	HELP			COMPOSE
F2	EDIT	TRACE		STEP
F3	NAME	OPTIONS		RUN
F4	ABS	BOUND	CLOSE WINDOW	CLOSE DESKTOP
F5	GOTO			
F6	WINDOW	HIDE	NEXT WINDOW	
F7	QUERY	GROUP		
F8	TABLE	DETACH		
F9	CALC			
F10	MENU			
F11	HELP INDEX	MAIN INDEX		

Table 1–4 shows the different activities assigned to 1-2-3/G's function and accelerator keys. Note that some keys work only in a particular mode, or work differently depending on the mode. For those keys, the table also shows the mode in parentheses. Each of these keys is explained fully in appropriate chapters of this book.

Tip: Selecting function keys with the mouse

You can also select a function key by using the mouse. To do so, however, you must first activate the on-screen function key template so that it appears at the bottom of the desktop (see Figure 1–1). To do this, select the Utility User Settings Preferences command and turn on the Function key display box. (This same command affects whether you can see on-screen the state of the CAPSLOCK, NUM LOCK, and SCROLL LOCK keys.) Once the on-screen function key template is displayed, select a function key by clicking on it in the template. If you press SHIFT, ALT, or CTRL, the template changes to show the names of the function keys that you can click after holding down one of those keys.

Table 1–4 Function and Accelerator Keys

Key	Name	Description
F1	HELP	Displays 1-2-3/G's Help window containing context-sensitive help.
F2	EDIT	Switches to Edit mode letting you edit a cell entry (Ready mode only).
F3	NAME	Displays a list of named ranges from which to choose (Point mode); if you type +—/ ^ (or * then press NAME, 1-2-3 displays a list of range names in the worksheet (Value mode); if you type @ then press NAME, 1-2-3/G displays a list of available @functions from which to choose.
F4	ABS	Toggles a cell or range address from relative, to absolute, to mixed (Point and Edit modes).
F5	GOTO	Positions the cell pointer at a given cell address, the

Continued on page 16

Table 1-4 Function and Accelerator Keys *(continued)*

Key	Name	Description
		upper-left corner cell of a named range, another worksheet in the same file, or another open file (Ready mode).
F6	WINDOW	Moves between two windows you have set up with Worksheet Window Horizontal or Vertical (Ready mode).
F7	QUERY	Repeats last Data Query Extract or Find command (Ready mode); toggles between Find and Ready mode during Data Query Find (Find mode).
F8	TABLE	Repeats last Data Table command (Ready mode).
F9	CALC	Recalculates all formulas in the worksheet, except formulas that reference files on disk (Ready mode); converts a formula to its current value (Value and Edit modes).
F10	MENU	Activates the menu.
F11	Help Index	When the Help Window is active, displays an index of Help topics for the active tool or utility.
ALT-F1	COMPOSE	Creates LCS characters (Ready and Edit modes); see Appendix B for more information.
ALT-F2	STEP	Toggles Step mode on and off; Step mode lets you run a macro or keystrokes in the Keystroke Editor a single step at a time.
ALT-F3	RUN	Displays a list of range names from which you can select a macro to run.
ALT-F4	Close Desktop	Closes the Desktop and ends 1-2-3/G.
ALT- — (minus)	Display Window Control menu	Displays the Window Control menu for the current window.

Continued on Page 17

Table 1-4 Function and Accelerator Keys *(continued)*

Key	Name	Description
ALT-BACK-SPACE	UNDO	Reverses the last change you made.
ALT-SPACE-BAR	Desktop Control menu	Displays the Desktop Control menu.
ALT-ESC	Next application	Activates the next Presentation Manager application.
CTRL-F4	Close window	Closes the active window.
CTRL-F6	Activate window	Activates the next open window on the Desktop.
CTRL-. (period)	Anchor	Anchors a selection.
CTRL-ESC	Task Manager	Activates the Task Manager.
CTRL-INS	Copy	Copies data to the clipboard (Ready mode)
DEL	Clear	Deletes the current selection permanently (BEWARE!).
SHIFT-F2	Trace	Opens the Trace window (for debugging macros).
SHIFT-F3	Options	Displays the options dialog box for Copy and Range Erase (same as selecting the Options icon with the mouse—see Chapter 4, "Cutting and Pasting Data").
SHIFT-F4	BOUND	Toggles Bound on and off; Bound restricts cell-pointer movement to a specific selection.
SHIFT-F6	HIDE	Toggles hidden columns, rows, and worksheets on and off.

Continued on page 18

Table 1–4 Function and Accelerator Keys *(continued)*

Key	Name	Description
SHIFT-F7	GROUP	Toggles Group mode on and off.
SHIFT-F8	DETACH	Detaches and attaches the cell pointer (see "Selecting Cells, Ranges, and Collections").
SHIFT-F11	Main Index	When the Help Window is active, takes you to the Main Help index
SHIFT-DEL	Cut	Moves data into the clipboard.
SHIFT-ENTER	Confirm	Confirms the selection in a dialog box.
SHIFT-ESC	Cancel	Cancels a dialog box.
SHIFT-INS	Paste	Moves data from the clipboard to the location of the cell pointer (you can also paste to graphs, notes, and other windows)

GETTING HELP

As mentioned, you can access 1-2-3/G's context-sensitive help anytime you need to. *Context-sensitive* means that 1-2-3/G tries to guess what you need based on what you are doing. You can access Help in any of the following ways:

- Pressing HELP (F1).
- Clicking on the HELP (F1) function key on the on-screen template, provided you have activated the template.
- Clicking on the Help box that appears in the Menu bar (available in Ready or Menu mode only).

1-2-3/G then displays the Help window, as in Figure 1–7. Items that you can get further help on appear in red and are known as *hot-text items*. You can use the keys in Table 1–5 or the mouse movements in Table 1–6 to navigate in the

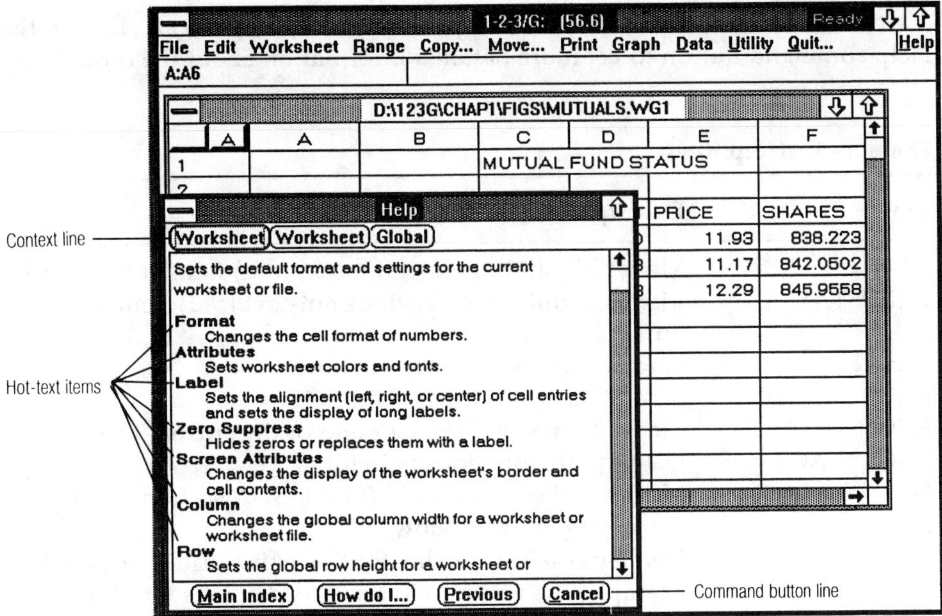

Figure 1–7 The Help window

Help window. If you are using a mouse to navigate through Help, be aware that the mouse pointer turns into a question mark when it is located on a hot-text item. To select a hot-text item with the mouse, simply click on it.

To eliminate the Help window from the screen, perform any of the following:

- Press ESC or C.
- Double-click on the Window Control-menu box.
- Select Close from the Help window's Window Control menu.

Tip: Closing a window with the mouse

The easiest way to close a window with the mouse in 1-2-3/G is to double-click on the Window Control menu box. You can also close 1-2-3/G (or any other PM application) by double-clicking on the Desktop Control-menu box. See Chapter 2, "Managing the Desktop," for more on opening and closing windows.

Note that when an error message appears in 1-2-3/G, you can click on the Help command button to get more detailed information about the error.

Table 1-5 Help Keys

Key	Description
TAB or →	Moves highlight to next hot-text (red) item or text button.
SHIFT-TAB or ←	Moves highlight to previous hot-text (red) item or text button.
↑ and ↓	Scrolls text up or down one line.
PGUP or PGDN	Scroll text up or down one screen.
HOME or END	Moves to the beginning or end of the current topic.
BACKSPACE or P	Displays the previous help topic.
H	Moves to the "How do I" (task based) section of Help.
ESC or C	Closes the Help window.
F11 or M	Displays the Help index for the active utility or tool; for example, if a graph tool is active, displays the Help index for graph.
SHIFT-F11	Displays the main index for all of Help, regardless of the active window type
F9	Displays help for valid keys for the active tool or utility.
Underlined letter	Chooses a command button—the shortcut for selecting a command; for example, *M* selects the Main Index command button.

Table 1-6 Help Mouse Navigation

Clicking on	Does this
Hot-text item	Displays help for that item.
Previous command button	Displays the previous Help topic.
Main command button	Displays the Help index for the active utility or tool; for example, if a graph tool is active, displays the Help index for graph.
Cancel command button	Closes the Help window (you can also double-click on the Window Control-menu box to cancel Help).
How do I command button	Moves to the "How do I" (task based) section of Help.
Scroll bar	Scrolls text up and down on the screen (see "Scroll Bars" later).

MOVING WITHIN A WORKSHEET

Before you can enter data into the cells that make up the worksheet area, you must move the cell pointer to where the information belongs. When you first start 1-2-3/G, the cell pointer is sitting in cell A:A1. To make an entry in another cell, you must move the cell pointer to that cell. 1-2-3/G offers a variety of ways to navigate within a worksheet window using the mouse or the keyboard. As you work with 1-2-3/G, you are likely to use a combination of the mouse and the keyboard to navigate in a worksheet window.

Moving with the Mouse

Because 1-2-3/G takes full advantage of Presentation Manager's graphical user interface, navigating with the mouse is especially easy. The sections that follow describe the basic mouse movements.

Moving to a Cell within the Window

When a cell appears within the current worksheet window, the easiest way to move to that cell in 1-2-3/G is to place the mouse pointer on the cell and click on it. 1-2-3/G immediately shifts the cell pointer to that cell, and you can enter or edit information in that cell.

Scrolling with the Mouse

Because a worksheet contains 256 columns by 8192 rows, a worksheet window cannot possibly display all the cells at once. To view other areas of the worksheet, you must scroll the window. *Scrolling* involves using the vertical and horizontal scroll bars that border the worksheet window, as in Figure 1–8.

You can scroll in any of the following ways with the mouse:

- To scroll up or down a row at a time, click on the top or bottom arrow in the Vertical scroll bar. You can scroll continuously by pointing to the top or bottom arrow and holding down the mouse button. Figure 1–9 shows how the window in Figure 1–8 appears after you scroll down a row.
- To scroll left or right a column at a time, click on the right or left arrow in the Horizontal scroll bar. You can scroll continuously by pointing to the left or right arrow and holding down the mouse button.
- To scroll up or down a windowful of rows, click above or below the elevator box in the Vertical scroll bar.
- To scroll left or right a windowful of columns, click to the left or right of the elevator box in the Horizontal scroll bar.
- To scroll to a precise row, drag the elevator box in the Vertical scroll bar up or down. 1-2-3/G shows the current row location in the Control line (the third line of the Desktop) as you go.

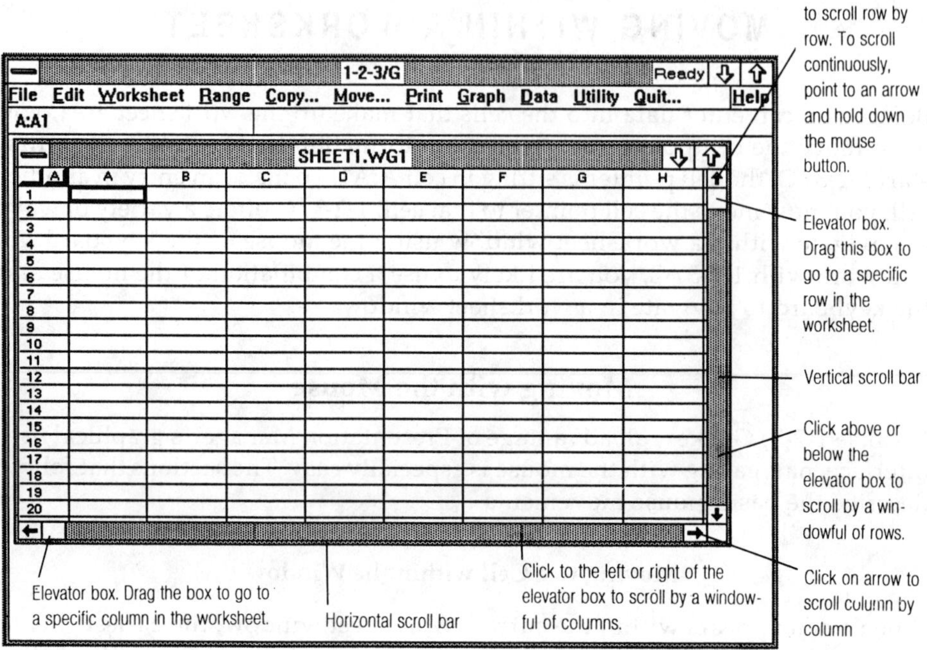
1-2-3/G
Ready
File Edit Worksheet Range Copy... Move... Print Graph Data Utility Quit... Help
A:A1
SHEET1.WG1
Click on an arrow to scroll row by row. To scroll continuously, point to an arrow and hold down the mouse button.
Elevator box. Drag this box to go to a specific row in the worksheet.
Vertical scroll bar
Click above or below the elevator box to scroll by a windowful of rows.
Click on arrow to scroll column by column
Elevator box. Drag the box to go to a specific column in the worksheet.
Horizontal scroll bar
Click to the left or right of the elevator box to scroll by a windowful of columns.

Figure 1–8 Scroll bars

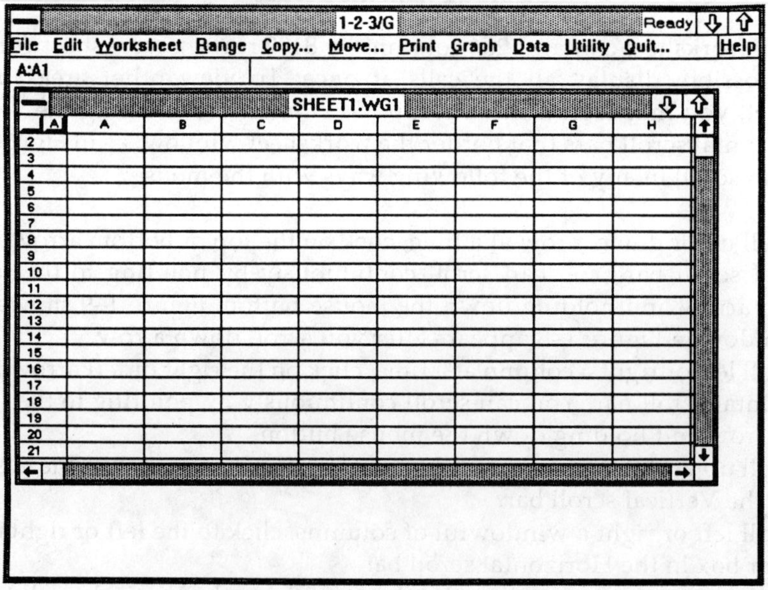

Figure 1–9 How Figure 1-8 appears after clicking the bottom arrow in the Vertical scroll bar

- To scroll to a precise column, drag the elevator box in the Horizontal scroll bar left or right. 1-2-3/G shows the current column location in the Control line as you go.
- To scroll to the *home position,* cell A1, drag the elevator box in the Vertical scroll bar all the way to the top and in the Horizontal scroll bar all the way to the left.

Note

When you scroll using the mouse, the cell pointer may no longer appear within the window. Instead it stays with the original cell it resided in before you started scrolling. For example, in Figure 1–9, the cell pointer does not appear on the screen because it remains with cell A:A1 (you can tell the cell pointer location by the address in the Control line, A:A1 in Figure 1–9). To move the cell pointer into the window, simply point to a cell anywhere within the window and click on it.

Tip: Returning to the point of origin after scrolling the screen

Suppose you have used the mouse to scroll to a new position in the worksheet far from your original point of origin; but when you arrive there, you decide you want to return to where you started from. Because the cell pointer remains with the original cell it resided in before you started scrolling, that cell's address still appears in the Control line. You can return the window to that address by pressing GOTO (F5), typing the cell address (for example, **C5**), and pressing ENTER. 1-2-3/G shifts the window to the requested cell. Although using GOTO (F5) is one way to return to the original address, there is another easier way. By pressing one of the arrow keys (→, ←, ↑, or ↓), you can have 1-2-3/G shift the window to a cell immediately adjacent to your original point of origin. You can then press the opposite arrow key to return to the original cell. For example, if you press → immediately after scrolling, press ← to return to the original cell.

Moving with the Keyboard

Because of its character-based heritage, 1-2-3/G has many powerful keys for navigating in the worksheet. Table 1–7 lists those keys and how each works.

Moving with the keyboard is slightly different from moving with the mouse. The differences arise because when you use the keys to navigate, 1-2-3/G always moves the cell pointer, and it may or may not scroll the window contents. (As you'll soon see, 1-2-3/G only scrolls the window when you move the cell pointer beyond the edge of the worksheet window.) When you navigate with the keyboard, the cell pointer always remains in view.

Table 1–7 Cell Pointer Movement Keys

Key	Description
←	Moves the cell pointer left one column.
→	Moves the cell pointer right one column.
↑	Moves the cell pointer up one row.
↓	Moves the cell pointer down one row.
CTRL-← or SHIFT-TAB	Moves the cell pointer left one windowful.
CTRL → or TAB	Moves the cell pointer right one windowful.
HOME	Moves the cell pointer to cell A1 in the current worksheet.
END ←, END →, END ↑, END ↓	When followed by an arrow key, moves the cell pointer in the direction of the arrow to the next filled cell that is followed or preceded by a blank cell.
END HOME	Moves the cell pointer to the lower right corner of the active area in the current worksheet.
PGDN	Moves the cell pointer down one windowful.
PGUP	Moves the cell pointer up one windowful.
CTRL-PGUP	Moves the cell pointer to the next worksheet.
CTRL-PGDN	Moves the cell pointer to the previous worksheet.
CTRL-HOME	Returns the cell pointer to cell A:A1 from any worksheet in the file.
END CTRL-HOME	Moves the cell pointer to the last cell containing data in the last worksheet.
END CTRL-PGUP	Moves the cell pointer forward through worksheets to the intersection of a blank and nonblank cell.
END CTRL-PGDN	Moves the cell pointer backward through worksheets to the intersection of a blank and nonblank cell.

The Arrow Keys

The arrow keys move the cell pointer a single cell at a time. For example, with the cell pointer located in cell A:A1, as in Figure 1–8, if you press ↓, the cell pointer moves to cell A:A2. If you then press →, the cell pointer shifts to cell A:B2. Pressing ↑ shifts the cell pointer to cell A:B1. Finally, pressing ← returns the cell pointer to cell A:A1.

Moving the Window Around the Worksheet

As mentioned, when you press an arrow key to navigate in the worksheet, 1-2-3/G moves the cell pointer to an adjacent cell, but it may or may not scroll the window. Only when you move beyond the edge of the window does 1-2-3/G scroll the window contents so that it always keeps the cell pointer in view.

The way that 1-2-3/G scrolls the screen when you move beyond the edge of the window depends on many factors, including the size of the window, the number of columns and rows, and the like. As an example, suppose your 1-2-3/G desktop contains the worksheet window in Figure 1–8 with the cell pointer in cell A:A1, and you press → until the cell pointer resides in cell A:H1. If you press → an additional time to move beyond the edge of the window, 1-2-3/G updates the screen to bring all of column I into view and moves the cell pointer to cell I1 (column A no longer appears on the screen). Now suppose you press ↓ to move the cell pointer to cell I20, and press ↓ one more time to move beyond the edge of the window. 1-2-3/G scrolls the screen so that it appears as in Figure 1–10.

Moving the Cell Pointer a Windowful at a Time

1-2-3/G has four keys for moving the cell pointer around the worksheet a windowful at a time: PGUP, PGDN, CTRL-→ (or TAB), and CTRL-← (or SHIFT-TAB). These keys are convenient for moving around a worksheet in large steps.

The PGUP and PGDN keys let you move the cell pointer up and down a windowful of rows at a time. For example, suppose you have the worksheet window in Figure 1–8, which shows just over 20 full rows, and the cell pointer is located in cell A:A1. If you press PGDN, 1-2-3/G shifts the cell pointer down 20 rows and displays cell A:A21 in the upper-left corner. If you press PGDN a second time, 1-2-3/G shifts the cell pointer down to cell A:A41. If you then press PGUP, 1-2-3/G shifts the cell pointer back up to cell A:A21. Press it a second time, and 1-2-3/G returns the cell pointer to cell A:A1.

To move horizontally a windowful of columns at a time, you use the CTRL-→ and CTRL-← commands. (Pressing TAB is identical to pressing CTRL-→, and pressing SHIFT-TAB is identical to pressing CTRL-←.) For example, starting with the worksheet window in Figure 1–8, if you press CTRL-→, 1-2-3/G shifts the cell pointer eight columns to the right and displays cell A:I1 in the upper-left

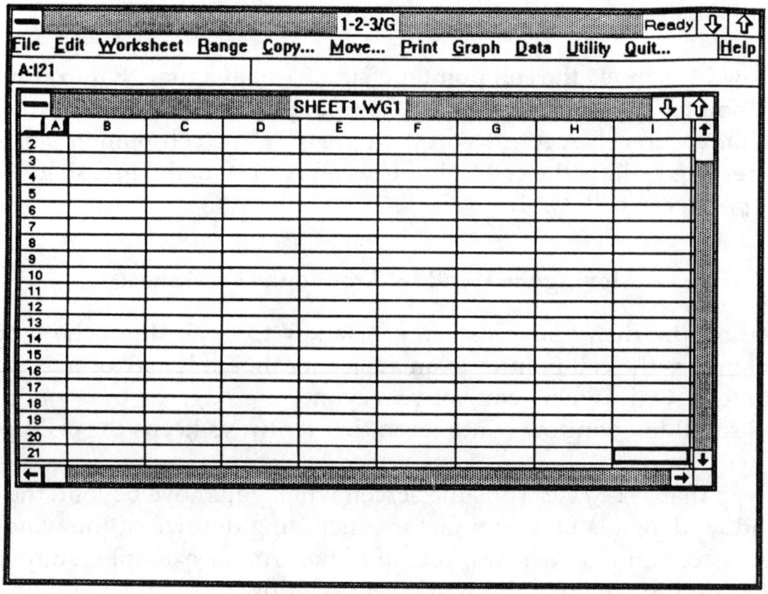

FIGURE 1–10 **Result of moving beyond the edge of the window**

corner. If you then press CTRL-←, 1-2-3/G shifts the cell pointer eight columns to the left, returning the cell pointer to cell A:A1.

The END Key

The END key lets you move the cell pointer to the end of a range of cells. When you press END, 1-2-3/G waits until you press an arrow key before moving the cell pointer in the direction of the arrow. 1-2-3/G then places the cell pointer at the next filled cell (a cell that contains data or a label prefix) that is followed or preceded by a blank cell. If 1-2-3/G does not encounter a filled cell, it places the cell pointer at the worksheet boundary.

For example, suppose you have the worksheet in Figure 1–11, and you press END→. 1-2-3/G moves the cell pointer to cell C2 (the last nonblank cell in the direction of he arrow). If you press END→ again, 1-2-3/G moves the cell pointer to cell E2 (the first nonblank cell in the direction of the arrow). Press END→ a third time, and 1-2-3/G moves the cell pointer to cell F2 (the last nonblank cell). Press END→ the fourth time, and 1-2-3/G moves the cell pointer to IV2 (the worksheet boundary).

The HOME Key

Pressing HOME moves the cell pointer to cell A1 in the current worksheet. Cell A1 is known as the *home position* in a worksheet.

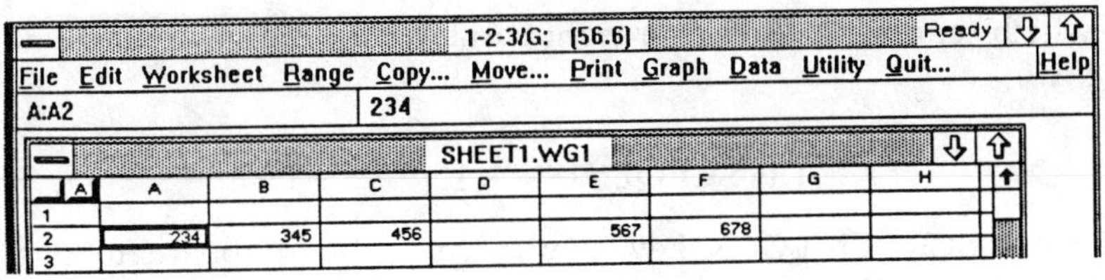

FIGURE 1–11 **The effect of the END key**

Pressing HOME can be quite convenient when it is your intent to move to the home position. However, it is not uncommon to press HOME inadvertently while moving around the worksheet. Unfortunately, there is no convenient key combination to return the cell pointer to its previous position after accidentally pressing HOME. You will likely have to use PGDN, CTRL-→, and other key combinations or mouse movements to return the cell pointer to its previous position. Alternatively, you can select GOTO (F5), type the appropriate cell address, and press ENTER.

The END HOME Combination

The END HOME key combination moves the cell pointer to the lower-right corner of the active area in the current worksheet. In previous releases of 1-2-3/G, the *active area* is a rectangular block that encompasses every entry in the worksheet, including formatted cells that are blank. However, in 1-2-3/G the active area is the area between cell A1 and the lowest and rightmost cell in the worksheet that contains data; formatted cells that are blank are not included.

For example, suppose you have the worksheet in Figure 1–12 in which the only entry is in cell G8. If you press END HOME, 1-2-3/G moves the cell pointer

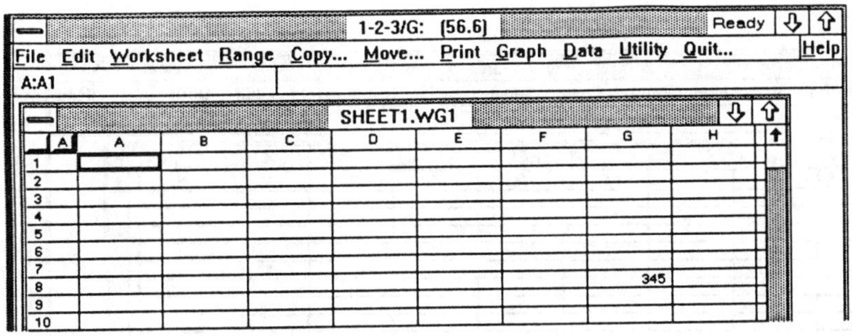

FIGURE 1–12 **A worksheet with a single entry in cell G8**

to cell G8 which represents the lower right corner of the active area, as shown in Figure 1–13.

The SCROLL LOCK Key

By pressing the SCROLL LOCK key, you can use the keyboard to scroll a worksheet window in the same way you use the mouse to scroll the window. For example, suppose you have the worksheet in Figure 1–8, and you press SCROLL LOCK followed by ↓. 1-2-3/G shifts the screen so that it appears as shown in Figure 1–9. Notice that this is exactly the same as using the mouse to click on the bottom arrow in the Vertical scroll bar. The screen scrolls down one line, but the cell pointer does not move from its original position of cell A1.

Note to Release 2 and Release 3 Users

1-2-3/G's behavior when you press SCROLL LOCK is slightly different than in earlier releases of 1-2-3. In Release 2, for example, when you press a key that would cause the cell pointer to shift beyond the edge of the worksheet window, 1-2-3 shifts the location of the cell pointer to keep it in view. In 1-2-3/G, however, the cell pointer always remains in its original position regardless of your keystrokes.

MOVING BETWEEN WORKSHEETS

As mentioned, a single 1-2-3/G worksheet file contains 256 worksheets. To allow you to move between worksheets, Lotus has incorporated special mouse movements and keyboard sequences into 1-2-3/G. These are described in the

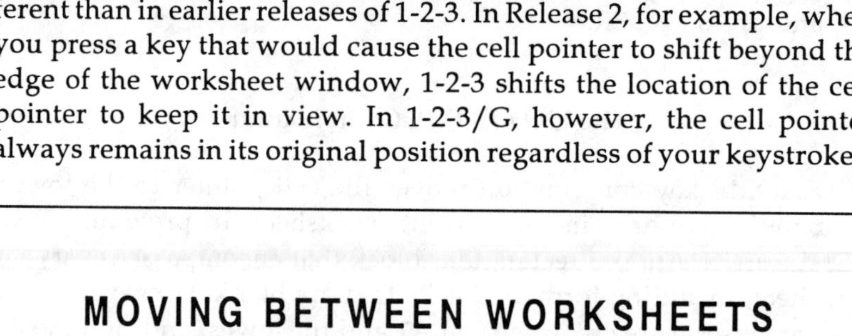

FIGURE 1–13 The effect of END HOME

following sections. See "Selecting Cells, Ranges, and Collections" for more information on moving between worksheets in separate worksheet files.

With the Mouse

Although a single 1-2-3/G worksheet file has 256 worksheets, when you first start 1-2-3/G, only a single worksheet appears in the window. Before you can move between worksheets using the mouse, you must display more than one worksheet within the window. To do so, you shift the window to perspective mode using the Worksheet Window Perspective command. Figure 1–14 shows an example of perspective mode with 3 worksheets (the default).

Once the worksheet window is set for perspective mode, you can then scroll within individual worksheets using the Horizontal and Vertical scroll bars in the same fashion as for a single worksheet, and select cells by clicking on them. Note that when you scroll the screen using the Horizontal or Vertical scroll bars, 1-2-3/G synchronizes the scrolling in all worksheets in the window. For example, if you click on the bottom arrow in the Vertical scroll bar, 1-2-3/G scrolls all the worksheets down one row. To scroll the worksheets independently, you must use the Worksheet Window Unsync command (see Chapter 2, "Managing the Desktop," for more information).

In addition to the Horizontal and Vertical scroll bars, Lotus has provided an additional scroll bar for scrolling between worksheets, the *Worksheet scroll bar*. This bar appears on the lefthand side of the window in Figure 1–14. Note that the Worksheet scroll bar only appears when the window is set for perspective mode.

You can use the Worksheet scroll bar in any of the following ways:

- To scroll up or down a worksheet at a time, click on the top or bottom arrow in the Worksheet scroll bar. Figure 1–15 shows how the window in Figure 1–14 appears after you click on the top arrow. Notice that the worksheets that appear within the window have changed from A, B, and C to B, C, and D. You can scroll continuously between worksheets by pointing to the top or bottom arrow and holding down the mouse button.
- To scroll to a precise worksheet, drag the elevator box in the Worksheet scroll bar up or down. 1-2-3/G shows the current worksheet location in the Control line (the third line of the Desktop) in place of the current cell address as you go.
- To scroll to the first worksheet in the file, drag the elevator box in the Worksheet scroll bar all the way to the bottom.

With the Keyboard

Like 1-2-3 Release 3, 1-2-3/G has special key sequences for moving between multiple worksheets. You can use these keys regardless of whether 1-2-3/G is in perspective mode.

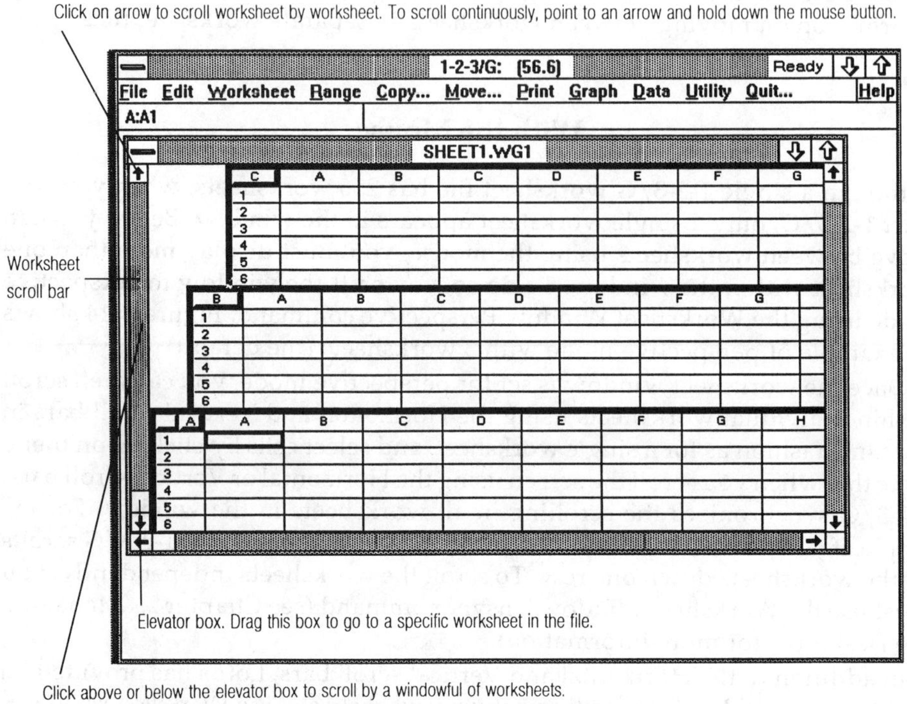

Click on arrow to scroll worksheet by worksheet. To scroll continuously, point to an arrow and hold down the mouse button.

Worksheet scroll bar

Elevator box. Drag this box to go to a specific worksheet in the file.

Click above or below the elevator box to scroll by a windowful of worksheets.

Figure 1–14 Viewing worksheets in perspective mode

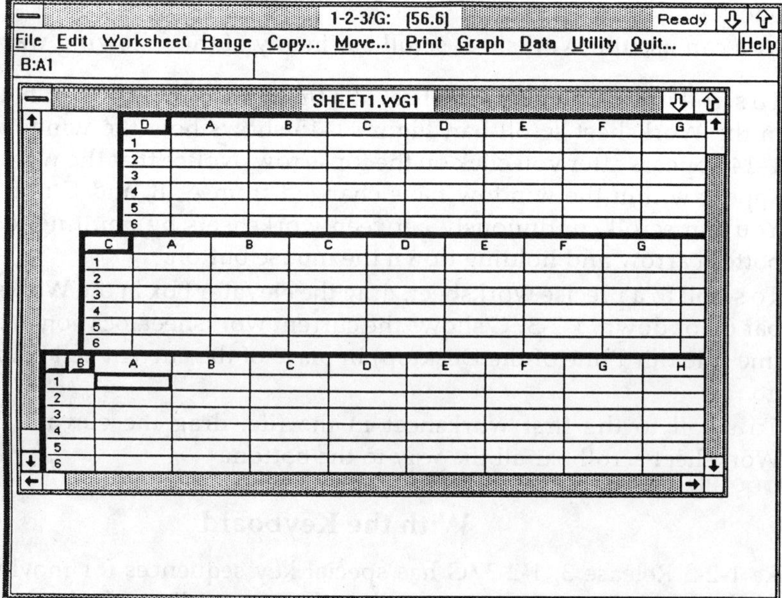

Figure 1–15 Scrolling between worksheets with the mouse

Moving Forward and Backward—CTRL-PGUP and CTRL-PGDN

As mentioned earlier, the key sequences for moving forward and backward through worksheets are CTRL-PGUP and CTRL-PGDN. When you move to a new worksheet by means of either key, 1-2-3/G remembers the cell pointer's previous position in each worksheet. For example, suppose that the last time you were in worksheet C, the cell pointer was located in cell C5. If you are in cell B4 of worksheet A and you press CTRL-PGUP twice, the cell pointer again comes to rest in cell C5 of worksheet C.

The First and Last Active Cell—CTRL-HOME and END CTRL-HOME

In 1-2-3/G and all previous releases of 1-2-3, HOME takes you to cell A1, and END HOME takes you to the last active (nonblank) cell in a worksheet. Like 1-2-3 Release 3, 1-2-3/G offers two equivalent keys for navigating in three-dimensional space: CTRL-HOME and END CTRL-HOME.

Pressing CTRL-HOME takes you to cell A:A1, regardless of which worksheet contains the cell pointer. On the other hand, when you press END CTRL-HOME, 1-2-3/G takes you to the last active cell containing data in the last worksheet.

The Next Filled Cell—END CTRL-PGUP and END CTRL-PGDN

As you know, the END → key sequence takes you across a single worksheet and locates the cell pointer in the next filled cell that is followed or preceded by a blank cell. If 1-2-3/G does not encounter a blank cell, it takes you all the way across a given row to the last column in the worksheet. END → and its companion key sequences END ←, END ↑, and END ↓ are handy tools for jumping across a worksheet to find needed information.

Like 1-2-3 Release 3, 1-2-3/G has two additional key sequences, END CTRL-PGUP and END CTRL-PGDN, which perform similar functions in three-dimensional worksheet space. For example, if you enter END CTRL-PGUP, 1-2-3/G takes you forward through multiple worksheets to the next filled cell which is followed or preceded by a blank cell. If 1-2-3/G does not encounter a filled cell in one of the worksheets in the file, it moves the cell pointer all the way to the last worksheet in the file.

For example, if the cell pointer is in cell A1 of worksheet A (A:A1) when you press END CTRL-PGUP, 1-2-3/G takes you forward through multiple worksheets to the first worksheet with data in cell A1. The cell pointer will then come to rest in cell A1 of that worksheet. However, if 1-2-3 does not find a worksheet that has data in cell A1, it will take you to the last worksheet in the file (cell IV:A1)

Conversely, END CTRL-PGDN takes you backward through worksheets to the next filled cell followed or preceded by a blank cell. If a filled cell is not found in one of the worksheets in the file, END CTRL-PGDN takes you all the way to the first worksheet in the file.

JUMPING TO CELLS

When you are working with a complex worksheet that has many cell entries, using the mouse and pointer-movement keys to move around the worksheet can be quite cumbersome. The problem grows even worse when you are using multiple worksheets in a file, not to mention multiple worksheet files in memory.

To speed up navigation, 1-2-3/G provides the GOTO (F5) key that lets you jump to a specific cell within a worksheet. You can also use it to move between worksheets and between files.

> **Note**
>
> You can also use 1-2-3/G's new Range Goto command to access the dialog box in Figure 1–16. In fact, the GOTO (F5) key and the Range Goto command are identical.

When you press GOTO (F5) or select the Range Goto command, 1-2-3/G presents the dialog box in Figure 1–16, and displays the address of the current selection in the Range(s) box (the current selection is A:A1 in Figure 1–16). To jump to a specific cell or worksheet, you can type any of the following in the Range(s) text box and press ENTER:

- **An abbreviated cell address, such as J32:** 1-2-3/G takes you directly to cell J32 in the current (same) worksheet, as shown in Figure 1–17. Notice that when you use GOTO and the cell is not in view, 1-2-3/G places the cell in the upper-left corner of the window and locates the cell pointer in that cell. However, when the cell is already in view, 1-2-3/G places the cell pointer in the cell without shifting the window contents.
- **A full cell address, such as D:A10**: 1-2-3/G takes you directly to worksheet D, cell A10, of the current worksheet file.
- **A worksheet letter followed by a colon, such as D:** 1-2-3/G takes you to cell A1 of worksheet D in the current worksheet file.
- **A range name:** 1-2-3/G takes you to the top left cell in the range. You can also select from among the range names that appear in the list box (see "Named Ranges" below).
- **A filename in double angle brackets, such as <<BUDGET1>>**: When you type the file name and press ENTER, 1-2-3/G searches the files that are open on the desktop to find that name. If the file is not open, 1-2-3/G issues an error message. However, if the file is open, 1-2-3/G displays the range names from that file, if any, in the list box below. Select the range name you want by double-clicking on it, or by using the arrow keys to highlight it and

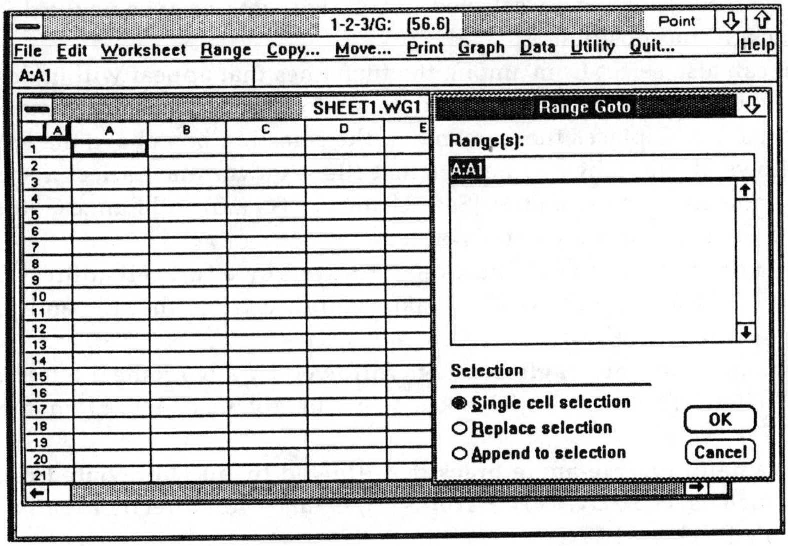

FIGURE 1–16 The GOTO (F5) and Range Goto dialog box

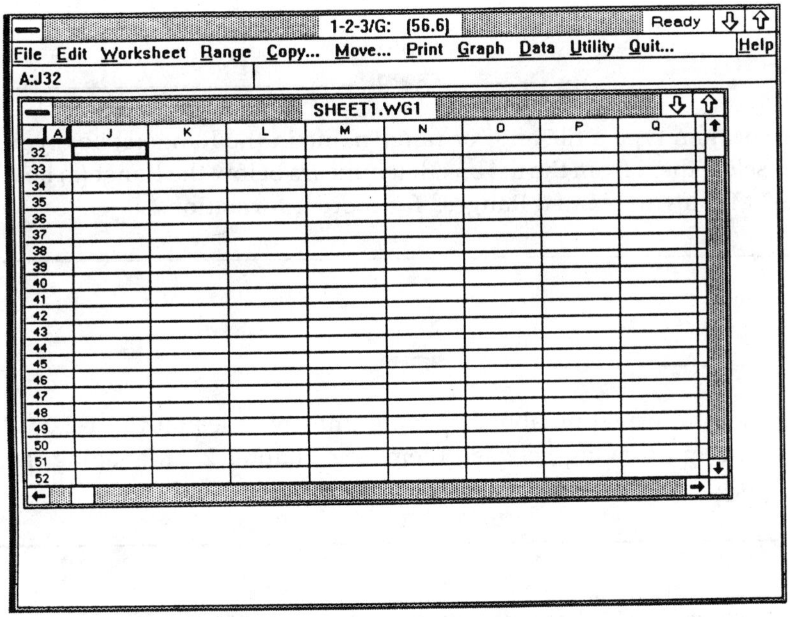

FIGURE 1–17 After jumping to cell J32

pressing ENTER. 1-2-3 moves to the top left cell of the range you selected. The BUDGET.WG1 file then becomes the currently active file. The worksheet file in which you originally selected GOTO (F5) remains open on the desktop in a background position.

You can also select from among the filenames that appear within double-angle brackets (<< >>) in the list box. If you double-click on a filename in the list box, 1-2-3/G places the filename in the selection box above the list box and shows all the range names for that file. You can then select a specific range name to go to in that file. [See "Using GOTO (F5) and Range Goto with Named Ranges" for more details on this.]

- **A filename in double-angle brackets followed by a full cell address, such as <<BUDGET1>>E:B20:** 1-2-3/G takes you directly to that file and places the cell pointer in cell E:B20.
- **A filename in double-angle brackets followed by a worksheet letter, such as <<BUDGET1>>E:** 1-2-3/G takes you directly to cell E:A1 in the file BUDGET1.WG1.
- **A filename in double-angle brackets followed by an abbreviated cell address, such as <<BUDGET1>>A10:** 1-2-3/G takes you directly to cell A:A10 in the file BUDGET1.WG1.
- **A filename in double-angle brackets followed by a range name, such as <<BUDGET1>>SALES**: 1-2-3/G takes you directly to that file and places the cell pointer in the first cell of the range named SALES.

Note

> Rather than type a file and/or range name in the Range(s) box, you can select them from the list box that appears below the Range(s) box. See "Moving to Named Ranges" for more information.

Note

> For more information about opening multiple files on the 1-2-3/G desktop and moving between them, see Chapter 2, "Managing the Desktop."

Besides using GOTO (F5) and Range Goto to jump to specific cells, you can also use them to select ranges or collections of cells. See "Using GOTO (F5) and Range Goto with Selections" later for a complete description.

MENUS

As you know, whenever you start 1-2-3/G, the Menu bar appears on the second line of the Desktop. It is through this Menu bar that you can generate graphs, print data, save files, and perform many other powerful operations that 1-2-3/G is known for. There are two types of menus in 1-2-3/G: pulldown and cascade.

- **Pulldown:** When you select a command from the Menu bar, 1-2-3/G typically shows the items related to that command in a pulldown menu. For example, Figure 1–18 shows the Edit pulldown menu.
- **Cascade:** If an item in a pulldown menu has related commands, an arrow (▶) appears to the right of that item. If you then select the item in the pulldown menu, the related items appear in a cascade menu. Items in cascade menus may also have arrows indicating additional cascade menus are available.

As with almost every operation in 1-2-3/G, you can use the mouse or the keyboard (or a combination of the two) to access 1-2-3/G's menus. Here are some common conventions for 1-2-3/G menus:

- **Grayed text:** When an item is not accessible at the current moment, it appears grayed. For example, when you first start 1-2-3/G and access the Edit menu to manipulate data in the clipboard, the Paste command usually appears gray because there is nothing in the clipboard at the start of a session.
- **Arrow (▶):** Indicates that a command has related items available in a cascade menu.
- **Ellipses (. . .):** When ellipses appear after a menu item, selecting that item from the menu will produce a dialog box or a Control line that prompts you for information.
- **Underlined letters:** Each item in a menu has an underlined letter indicating that you can select that item by typing the underlined letter on the keyboard. For example, to select the Edit menu from the Menu bar, press / (slash) followed by *E*. The / selects the main menu and E the Edit menu.
- **Accelerator keys:** Many menu items show a key sequence to the right of an item. Pressing this key sequence has the same effect as selecting the command. For example, as Figure 1–18 shows, selecting ALT-BACKSPACE is the same as selecting the Edit Undo command.
- **Horizontal lines:** These lines separate related commands in a pulldown or cascade menu.

Accessing Menus with the Mouse

To access 1-2-3/G's main menu with the mouse, simply click on any command in the Menu bar. Once you've clicked on a command, that command appears highlighted; and if a pulldown menu is available, the first item on the pulldown menu also appears highlighted. In addition, 1-2-3/G displays a capsule description of the highlighted item on the first line of the Desktop. After you've accessed the menu, you can then select an item from within a pulldown or cascade menu by clicking on it as well. Table 1–8 shows how you can use the mouse with menus.

When using the mouse to access 1-2-3/G's menus, one of the easiest ways to see all the available menu choices and their associated capsule descriptions is to drag the menu pointer from one menu item to the next (press and hold down the left mouse button and keep it down as you move the mouse). When you reach the item you want, release the button to select the menu choice and issue the command. If you want to bail out of the menu without selecting a command, simply release the mouse button outside the menu area.

Accessing Menus with the Keyboard

To access 1-2-3/G's Menu bar with the keyboard, you can press slash (/), ALT, or F10 (MENU). None of these keys affects the data contained in the current cell. To leave the main menu and return to the worksheet, press ESC (or CTRL-BREAK). See Table 1–9.

When you access the Menu bar, a rectangular pointer called the *command pointer* highlights a command. A capsule description of the highlighted command appears in the first line of the Desktop.

Worksheet Command Summary

The commands that appear on the Menu bar depend on the active tool. For example, when you first start 1-2-3/G, the worksheet tool is active, and its commands appear in the Menu bar. When the graph tool is active a different set of commands appear in the Menu bar. The commands that appear within the Menu bar for a given tool are known as that tool's *main menu*.

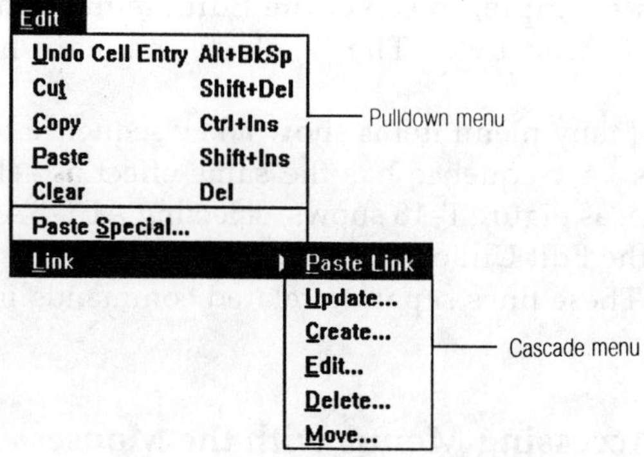

Figure 1–18 Pulldown and cascade menus

Table 1-8 Mouse Clicks in Menus

Click On	Result
A menu option	Activates the main menu.
Desktop Control-menu box	Activates the Desktop Control Menu (see Chapter 2).
Window Control-menu box	Activates the Window Control Menu for the given window (see Chapter 2).
Highlighted menu option	Chooses that option.
Elsewhere on the screen	Cancels the entire command.

Table 1-9 Menu-related Keys

Key	Result
/, ALT, or F10	Activates the main menu.
ALT-SPACEBAR	Activates the Desktop Control menu (see Chapter 2).
ALT- — (minus)	Activates the Window Control menu for theactive window (see Chapter 2).
CTRL-BREAK	Cancels a command entirely.
END	Moves to the last command in a pulldown or cascade menu.
ENTER	Chooses the highlighted menu option.
ESC	Leaves the menu if at the main menu; goes to the previous level when at any other level in the command hierarchy.
HOME	Moves the pointer to the first command in a menu.
←	Moves the pointer left one command in the Menu bar.
→	Moves the pointer right one command in the Menu bar.
↑	Moves the pointer up one command in a pulldown or cascade menu.
↓	Moves the pointer down one command in a pulldown or cascade menu.
Underlined letter	Chooses a menu item; the shortcut for selecting a command.

The commands in the Worksheet's Menu bar are briefly described as follows:

- **File:** Opens, saves, and prints worksheet files. The section "Saving and Retrieving Files" later in this chapter discusses how to save and restore your work, and Chapter 5 discusses file management in detail. The File menu is common to all Presentation Manager applications.
- **Edit:** Cuts and copies to the clipboard; also lets you undo previous commands. The "Undo" section in this chapter discusses how to undo commands, and Chapter 4 discusses all the different aspects of cutting and pasting data. The Edit menu is common to all Presentation Manager applications.
- **Worksheet:** Changes the global settings (defaults) that affect the worksheet display and format. The Worksheet command actually affects many 1-2-3/G activities and is discussed throughout this book.
- **Range:** Manipulates cell ranges and their data. The Range Name, Range Goto, and Range Search commands are covered in this chapter in "Naming Ranges," "Selecting Ranges and Collections," and "Searching for Data." All the other Range commands are covered in Chapter 3.
- **Copy:** Copies one range or collection to another. Chapter 4 covers the Copy command in detail.
- **Move:** Moves one range or collection to another. Chapter 4 covers this command.
- **Print:** Prints worksheet ranges to a printer or file. Chapter 8 discusses this command as well as the File Print command.
- **Graph:** Creates graphs of worksheet data. Chapter 7 discusses how to use this command to view your information in graphic format.
- **Data:** Provides you with access to 1-2-3/G's database management facility, including access to external databases. It is described in Chapter 9.
- **Utility:** Gives you access to many 1-2-3/G's utilities including Note, Solver, and Keystroke Editor. The Note utility allows you to attach notes to cells and is described later in this chapter. Solver allows you to solve problems in the worksheet and is described in Chapter 13, "The Backsolver and Solver." The Keystroke Editor captures the keystrokes you make in 1-2-3/G and allows you to copy them to the worksheet for use as a macro. This utility is described in Chapter 10, "Creating Macros."
- **Quit:** Takes you out of 1-2-3/G permanently and returns you to the Start Programs window (or the next successive OS/2 application). This chapter discusses how to exit 1-2-3.

Canceling a Command

Suppose you have selected a command and then decide that you do not want to use the command after all. You can cancel a command with the mouse or the keyboard.

Note

> You can also access 1-2-3/G's Help system from the Menu bar. With the keyboard, press / (slash), ALT, or F10 (MENU) to access the main menu then press H (for the Help menu item). To access Help with the mouse, simply click on the Help box. See "Getting Help" above for more information.

With the Mouse

If you change your mind about your choice of a command, you can cancel the command by using the mouse in any of the following ways:

- Click anywhere outside the menu, and 1-2-3/G will return you to the worksheet. Clicking on a blank area of the Desktop is best, so that you don't inadvertently select something else in the window.
- Click on another command to select it instead. This technique will not work when 1-2-3/G is displaying a dialog box or prompting you for input in the Control line.
- If a dialog box is active, you must click on the appropriate command button (usually Cancel or No) to cancel the dialog box and its associated command.
- If 1-2-3/G is prompting you for input in the Control line, click on the Cancel icon which resembles an X, if it is available. For example, Figure 1–19 shows the Copy command's Cancel icon (see Chapter 4 for more details on this).

With the Keyboard

To cancel a command by using the keyboard, and return to the worksheet in Ready mode, press CTRL-BREAK. You can use this sequence from anywhere within 1-2-3/G's command hierarchy, even from within a dialog box. For example, suppose you select the Utility User Settings Preferences command, and when you see the command's dialog box, you decide you've chosen the wrong command. If you press CTRL-BREAK, 1-2-3/G removes the command's dialog box from the screen and returns you to the worksheet.

To exit the current command level and return to the previous command level, press ESC. If you are at the main menu level, ESC returns you to the worksheet in Ready mode, just like CTRL-BREAK does from any where with the command hierarchy.

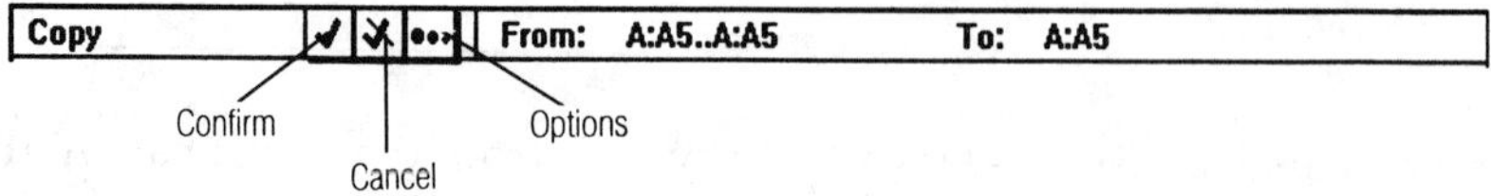

Figure 1–19 The Copy command's icons

DIALOG BOXES

1-2-3/G displays a dialog box when it needs additional information to carry out a command. A dialog box contains areas where you enter information; there are different kinds of areas depending on what kind of information is needed. Figures 1–20 and 1–21 show some sample dialog boxes.

Here are some definitions and descriptions of the different areas that a dialog box may have:

- **Text box** is where you type information. The text you type appears to the left of the insertion point, a flashing vertical line. When you type text, it pushes any existing text to the right. An example of a text box appears in Figure 1–20.
- **List box** contains the names of available choices—in Figure 1–20, for example, the names of files and directories on the disk. Files in a dialog box are listed in alphabetical order by filename. The parent directory (one level up) is indicated by two periods (..). The list box has vertical scroll bars when all the available items don't fit in the list box.
- **The Title bar** shows the name of the command you used to activate the dialog box. For example, the File Retrieve command was used to activate the dialog box in Figure 1–20. To move the dialog box on the desktop, grab the title bar and drag it to a new location.
- **Command buttons** generally carry out or cancel commands when they are chosen; these buttons have labels—OK and Cancel, for example—to indicate what the buttons do. For example, clicking on the OK command button carries out the action of the dialog box. Conversely, clicking on the Cancel command button cancels the dialog box. As you can see, the dialog boxes in both Figure 1–20 and 1–21 contain command buttons.
- **Option buttons** are circular and let you select options for a particular command. In a group of option buttons, only one option at a time can be selected. The dialog boxes in both Figure 1–20 and 1–21 contain option buttons.
- **Check boxes** are square and let you turn an option on or off. An X appears in the box when you turn an item on. In a group of options with check boxes,

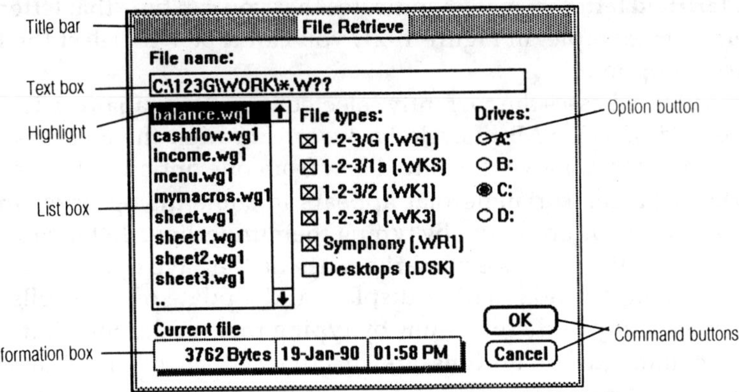

Figure 1–20 The File Retrieve dialog box

several options can be selected at the same time. The dialog boxes in both Figure 1–20 and 1–21 contain check boxes.

- **Information boxes** display information about a file, including the size, date of creation, and time of creation. For example, the dialog box in Figure 1–20 contains an information box.

Conventions within a Dialog Box

A 1-2-3/G dialog box maintains certain conventions to indicate what options and items you can choose in a dialog box and how you can choose them.

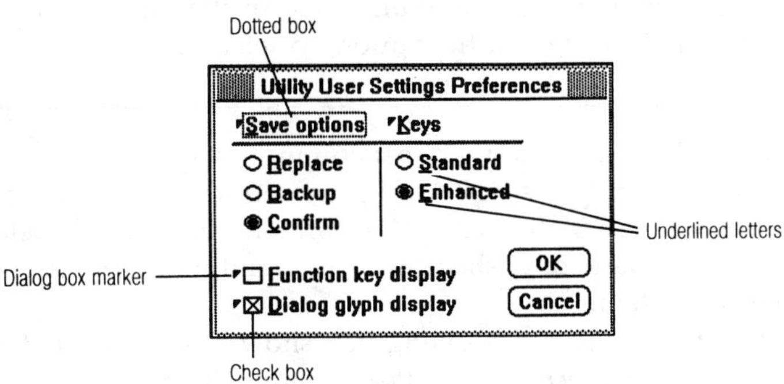

Figure 1–21 The Utility User Settings Preferences dialog box

- An **underlined letter** in an item indicates that you can type that letter to select the item. For example, in Figure 1–21, you can type *F* to select the Function key display option.
- A **dotted box** indicates the currently selected item. You can press TAB to cycle forward and SHIFT-TAB to cycle backward through the available options, and, in the process, move the dotted box from one option to the next.
- A **marker** is a small triangle that appears in some dialog boxes indicating which options you can choose by typing their underlined letter. For example, in Figure 1–21, the presence of markers beside the Save options, Keys, Function key display, Dialog marker display, and Update options tells you that you can select any of these options by typing their underlined letter.
- **Grayed commands or options** are inactive, which means that you can't currently use them.
- A **highlight** in a list box indicates the currently selected item. To choose the highlighted item in a list box and leave the dialog box in the process, double-click on the item in the list box, or press ENTER.

Selecting Items within a Dialog Box

If you're using the mouse, you can easily select any item within a dialog box by clicking on it. For example, to choose an option from a group of option buttons, you move the pointer to the option and click the left mouse button. Likewise, to turn a check box on or off, you move the pointer to the check box and click on the item.

Note

> When you are using the mouse, you can click anywhere on an option to select it. For example, you do not have to click precisely on the check box to turn an option on or off. You can click anywhere on the option, including the text of the option, to select it.

If you're using the keyboard, the most common way to move from item to item in a dialog box is by pressing TAB. To move through the dialog box in the opposite direction, press SHIFT-TAB. You can tell the currently selected item because it has a box made of dashed lines surrounding it. You can then press ENTER to select the item.

In addition, if the items in the dialog box show underlined letters in their names, you can use the *direct-access method* to move directly to them. Press and hold down the ALT key, then press the underlined letter in the item name. For example, in Figure 1–21, you can move directly to the Keys option from any other option by pressing ALT-K. This method is a handy alternative to pressing

Table 1–10 Dialog Box Keys

Key	Action
TAB or SHIFT-TAB	Moves the dotted box from one choice to the next or previous choice.
ALT-Underlined letter	Moves directly to the item with the underlined letter.
SPACEBAR	Selects an option button or turns a check box on or off; you can also type its underlined letter.
ENTER	Selects the next choice in the dialog box; if the next choice is the last choice in the dialog box, confirms the dialog box.
SHIFT-ENTER	Confirms the dialog box.
CTRL-BREAK	Cancels a dialog box.
DEL	Turns a check box off.
ESC	Selects the previous choice in the dialog box; if the previous choice is the first choice, cancels the dialog box.
←, →, ↑, and ↓	Moves the dotted box another item within a group.
Underlined letter	Selects an option button or turns a check box on or off.

TAB to sequentially move through the components of a dialog box, in order to activate the one you want.

Table 1–10 shows the keys you can use to select items in a dialog box.

Selecting Items within a List Box

When a dialog box contains a list box, you can select an item from the list box using the mouse or the keyboard. If you're using the mouse, you can highlight an item from a list box by moving the pointer to the item and clicking the left mouse button. To choose the item from the list box and leave the dialog box in the process, double-click on the item.

In addition, when a list box contains a scroll bar, you can drag the elevator button up or down. You can also drag the highlight up or down. Either way, 1-2-3/G updates the list as you go. In some instances, however, when the items in the list box are too few to require scrolling, the scroll bar appears gray (meaning you cannot select it) instead of black (active). When this is the case, you are limited to moving the highlight with either the keyboard or the mouse.

If you're using the keyboard, you can use the ↑ and ↓ keys to move up and down in the list. As you move in a list box, the item you move to is highlighted, to show that it is selected.

The HOME key moves to the top of the list and selects the first item. The END key moves to the bottom of the list and selects the last item.

You can use the PGUP and PGDN keys to move within a list box. These keys will move the list up or down by "page"—that is, as much as will fit in the visible portion of the list box at one time.

Tip: Speed selection in a list box

When 1-2-3/G shows items in a list box, the quickest way to select an item in a large list is by typing its first letter. For example, if you use the File Retrieve command to display the dialog box in Figure 1–20, you can select the MYMACROS.WG1 filename from within the list box by typing *M* twice. The first time you type *M*, 1-2-3/G locates the highlight at the first name in the list box that begins with "M," which in this case is MENU.WG1. When you type *M* a second time, 1-2-3/G moves the highlight to the next item in the list box that begins with "M," MYMACROS.WG1. This technique is especially helpful for locating filenames in large directories.

Editing the Contents of a Text Box

Table 1–11 shows the keys you can use to edit text in a text box. A good way to test the behavior of these keys is to access a command that displays a text box—for example, the Print Printer Options Header command—and enter some sample text. For example, try these steps:

1. Select the Printer Printer Options Header command.
2. Enter **This is a test** (or some other text) in the text box.
3. Test the following keys: HOME, END, →, ←, CTRL-→, CTRL-←, END, BACKSPACE, and DEL.
4. When you are finished testing keys, select the Cancel control button to eliminate the text box entry.

If you are using the mouse, you can move the insertion point in a text box by moving the pointer to where you want the insertion point to be and clicking the left mouse button. To highlight text in a text box, simply move the pointer where you want to begin highlighting, press the left mouse button, and drag the mouse over the text.

Using the Clipboard to Edit the Contents of a Text Box

Suppose you have typed some text into a text box and then decide that you want to rearrange the order of the words. For example, imagine that you have mistakenly entered **Sales December** in the Print Printer Options Header text

Table 1-11 Keys for Editing a Text Box

Key	Action
←	Moves the insertion point left one character.
→	Moves the insertion point right one character.
BACKSPACE	Deletes the character to the left of the insertion point.
END	Moves to the end of the text.
HOME	Moves to the start of the text.
CTRL-→	Moves the insertion point right five characters.
CTRL-←	Moves the insertion point left five characters.
DEL	Deletes the character to the right of the insertion point or deletes highlighted characters.
SHIFT-←	Highlights the character to the left of the insertion point.
SHIFT-→	Highlights the character to the right of the insertion point.
SHIFT-END	Highlights all the characters from the insertion point to the end of the text
SHIFT-HOME	Highlights all the characters from the insertion point to the beginning of the text
SHIFT-DEL	Deletes all the highlighted characters and copies them to the clipboard; you can use SHIFT-INS to paste the characters back into the text line in another location.

box, and you want to swap the order of the words to read "December Sales." You can use the clipboard to save yourself some typing.

Begin by moving the insertion point to the start of the text. Press HOME or click just in front of the *S* in "Sales." Next, press SHIFT-→ six times to highlight "Sales " (make sure to highlight the blank space following the *s*) or press the left mouse button and drag the mouse over the text. Press SHIFT-DEL to delete the highlighted characters and copy them to the clipboard. Press END to locate the cursor at the end of "December" or click just to the right of the *r* in "December." Next, press SPACEBAR to add a blank space at the end of the text. Finally, paste the deleted characters back into the text box at the end of the entry by pressing SHIFT-INS. Your entry now reads "December Sales."

SHIFT-DEL and SHIFT-INS are shortcuts for the Edit Cut and Edit Paste commands. See Chapter 4, "Cutting and Pasting Data," for a complete discussion of all the Edit commands and ways you can use the clipboard in 1-2-3/G.

ENTERING DATA IN WORKSHEET CELLS

To enter data in a worksheet cell, first position the cell pointer at the cell where you want to put the data. You can then enter a number or label in the cell simply by typing it and pressing ENTER. For example, to place the number 123 in cell A1, type **123** and press ENTER. Figure 1–22 shows what your screen will look like.

1-2-3/G determines the type of cell entry you are making by the first character you type. If you type a number, 1-2-3/G assumes you are entering a number, and if you type a letter, 1-2-3/G assumes you are entering a label.

There are two types of cell entries: values and labels. Values are number and formula entries and labels are text entries. The mode indicator changes to Value or Label based on 1-2-3/G's assessment of the type of entry you are making.

Confirming an Entry

There are many ways to confirm an entry after you have finished typing it, depending on how you want to move the cell pointer afterward. Confirming an entry transfers it from the Control line (the third line of the Desktop) to the current cell. The simplest way to confirm an entry with the keyboard is to press ENTER. The simplest way with the mouse is to click on the Confirm icon (✔) in the Control line (see Figure 1–23). Confirming an entry in either of these ways

1-2-3/G: [56.6] Ready
File Edit Worksheet Range Copy... Move... Print Graph Data Utility Quit... Help
A:A1 123
SHEET1.WG1
A A B C D E F G H
1 123
2
3
4

FIGURE 1–22 Entering 123 in a cell

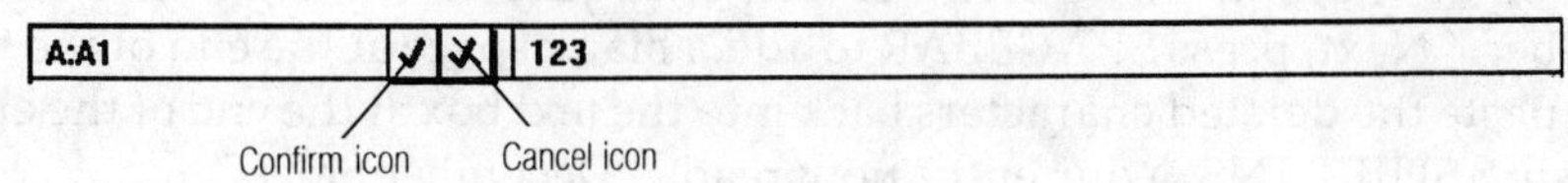

FIGURE 1–23 The Confirm and Cancel icons

places the entry in the current cell and leaves the cell pointer in its original position.

Another convenient way to confirm a cell entry is to use an arrow key, which places the entry in the current cell and moves the cell pointer one cell in the direction of the arrow. For example, suppose you want to enter a column of numbers, moving downward as you go. You can use ↓ to confirm each cell entry and move the cell pointer down a cell. Figure 1–24 shows what happens when you type **123** in cell A1, press ↓, type **234** in cell A2, and press ↓ again.

You can actually use any of the movement keys to confirm a cell entry, including ↓, ↑, →, ←, CTRL-→, CTRL-←, PGUP, PGDN, HOME, END, CTRL-PGUP, and CTRL-PGDN.

Besides using the keyboard, you can also use the mouse to confirm a cell entry and move to another cell in the process. For example, suppose you want to enter a number in cell A1 then move to cell C1 to make another entry. To do so, you begin by typing the number for cell A1, then click on cell C1. 1-2-3/G immediately enters the number in cell A1 and moves the cell pointer to cell C1. Besides clicking on a cell, you can also click on the scroll bar to confirm the current entry and move to a new cell in the process.

Note

> If you make a mistake when entering data in a cell, 1-2-3/G usually issues an error message and puts you in Edit mode. Making changes in Edit mode is discussed in detail under "Editing Cell Entries" later in this chapter.

Changing Cell Entries Before Confirming Them

Suppose you start making a cell entry and then decide that you want to change it before confirming it. You can use any of the following keys:

- **BACKSPACE:** removes the character to the left of the insertion point.

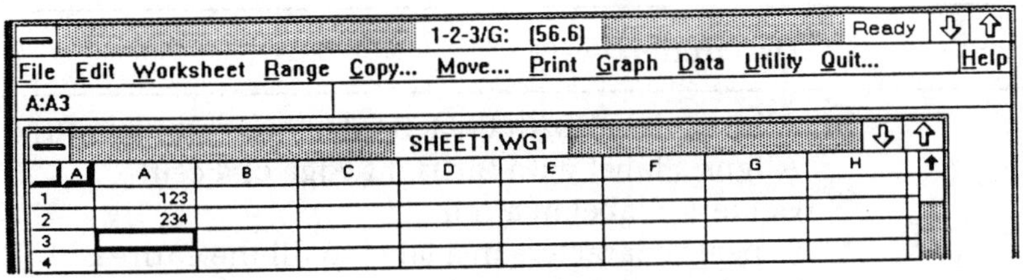

1-2-3/G: [56.6] Ready

File Edit Worksheet Range Copy... Move... Print Graph Data Utility Quit... Help

A:A3

SHEET1.WG1

A	A	B	C	D	E	F	G	H
1	123							
2	234							
3								
4								

FIGURE 1–24 Using ↓ to confirm cell entries

- **ESC:** Cancels the entry entirely and returns you to the worksheet in Ready mode.
- **EDIT (F2):** Accesses Edit mode (see "Editing Cell Entries" later).

If you are using the mouse, you can do any of the following to change a cell entry before confirming it:

- Change the position of the insertion point in the entry by moving the pointer to where you want the insertion point to be located and clicking the left mouse button.
- Highlight part of the entry by moving the pointer to where you want to begin highlighting, pressing the left mouse button, and dragging the mouse over the text. You can then delete the highlighted text by pressing DEL.
- Click on the Cancel icon in the Control line (see Figure 1–23) to cancel the cell entry and return to the worksheet in Ready mode.

Labels

A *label* is a text entry. For example, in Figure 1–25, the various titles and asset names are all labels. The maximum length of a label (or any other 1-2-3/G cell entry) is 512 characters.

Label Prefixes and Alignment

All labels begin with a *label prefix*. A label prefix determines how the text is aligned in the cell. Table 1–12 shows 1-2-3/G's label prefixes and describes their effect on alignment. Figure 1–26 shows some examples of how label prefixes affect a label's position in the cell.

For the most part, when you enter a label in 1-2-3/G, you do not enter a label prefix. Instead you rely on 1-2-3/G to automatically supply it for you. When you begin a cell entry with a letter or a blank space, 1-2-3/G assumes you are entering a label and supplies the default label prefix, typically ' for left align-

Table 1–12 Label Prefixes

Character	Description
'	Aligns a label with the left edge of a cell (default).
"	Aligns a label with the right edge of a cell.
^	Centers a label in a cell.
\	Repeats characters in a label to fill the entire cell.
|	Displays a label on screen but doesn't print it.

1-2-3/G: [56.6] Ready

File Edit Worksheet Range Copy... Move... Print Graph Data Utility Quit... Help

A:A3 'Current Assets:

FIG1-25.WG1

	A	B	C	D	E	F	G	H
1	Perkerson Supply Company--Balance Sheet							
2								
3	Current Assets:							
4	Cash							
5	Accounts Receivable							
6	Inventory							
7	Total Current Assets							
8								
9	Noncurrent Assets:							
10	Land							
11	Buildings and Machinery							
12	Less Accumulated Depreciation							
13	Total Noncurrent Assets							
14	Total Assets							
15								
16								

FIGURE 1–25 Some sample labels

ment. For example, when you type **Income** in cell B1 of Figure 1–26 and press ENTER, 1-2-3/G automatically inserts the default label prefix at the beginning of your entry and displays it in the contents box. In fact, you can check the label prefix of any label by moving the cell pointer to that cell and viewing the special character which precedes the text in the contents box.

When you begin a text entry with a number or a numeric symbol (see "Values" later), you must enter the label prefix first. Otherwise, 1-2-3/G will assume you've made an error. For example, suppose you want to enter the title "12/90 Sales" in a worksheet. If you type **12/90 Sales** and press ENTER, 1-2-3/G

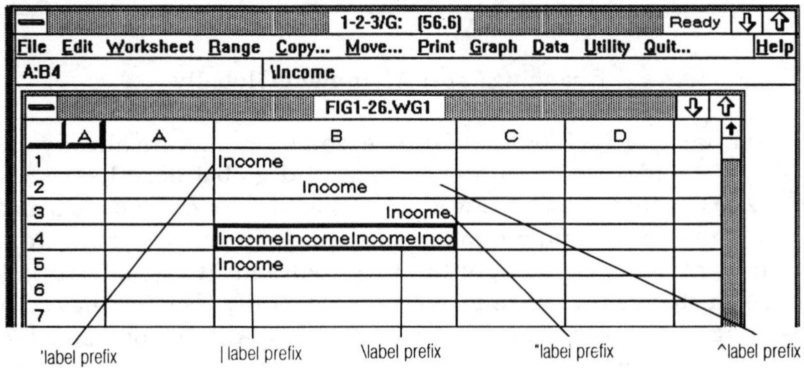

FIGURE 1–26 Label prefixes and their effect on alignment

displays the error message "Not a valid expression" because it assumes you are entering a value since you started the entry with a number. After you clear the error message from the screen, 1-2-3/G puts you in EDIT mode so you can correct the error. To fix this entry, press HOME (or click just before the "1") to move the insertion point to the start of the entry (see "Editing Cell Entries" later). You can then insert a label prefix in front of the first character, and 1-2-3/G will then accept the entry as a label. For example, to right align the label in the cell, insert a double quote (") at the start of the entry. The entry now reads **"12/90 Sales**.

Telephone numbers, social security numbers, and street addresses are all examples of text entries for which you will have to enter a label prefix. For example, suppose you want to enter the social security number "272–45–7865" in the current cell as a label. To do this, type a label prefix (') before entering the numbers. Otherwise, 1-2-3/G will enter a negative number in the cell. In most cases, however, you can rely on 1-2-3/G to supply the label prefix for you.

Tip: Changing the label prefix

Suppose you have entered a label in a cell and then decide that you want to change its alignment. Rather than enter Edit mode and manually insert a label prefix, an easier way is to use the Range Label Labels command. (For example, to center a label in a cell, you use the Range Label Labels Center command.) What's more, even if you know before entering a label that you will want to use a different label prefix than the default, you will still find it easier to enter the label relying on 1-2-3/G to supply the default prefix, and then use the Range Label Labels command to change the alignment afterward. See Chapter 3, "Formatting Worksheets," for more on this command.

Changing Label Alignment Globally

When you start 1-2-3/G for the first time, some settings are already made for you. These include 1-2-3/G's user settings and global defaults. *User settings* affect 1-2-3/G's use of fonts as well as its startup directory names and tools, hardware preferences, and international settings. In general, these are settings that you want 1-2-3/G to apply to every tool and utility and during every session. You change user settings through the Utility User Settings command. User settings are covered in detail in Appendix A, "Customizing 1-2-3/G." They are also discussed at various places throughout the remainder of this book.

Global defaults, on the other hand, affect the settings for the current worksheet or file. These settings include the default format, worksheet colors and fonts,

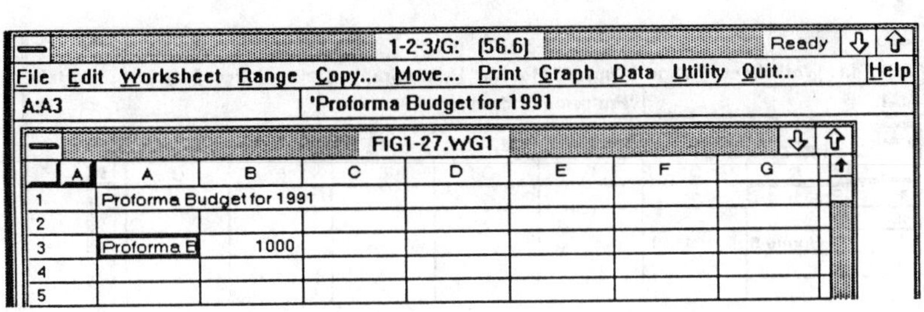

FIGURE 1–27 Long labels

column width, label and number alignment, and the like. To change global defaults, you use the Worksheet Global command.

To change the global default for label alignment, you use the Worksheet Global Label Labels command. If, for example, you want to change the default label prefix from ' (left alignment) to " (right alignment), you use the Worksheet Global Label Labels Right command. Chapter 3, "Formatting the Worksheet," discusses how to change the default label alignment (and other global defaults) in more detail.

Long Labels

Occasionally you will enter a label into a worksheet that is too long to fit within the current column. When this happens, the label extends into the next column to the right. When a label does this, it is known as a *long label.* When you enter data into the cell immediately to the right of a long label, any text that extends into that cell disappears from view. However, if you move the cell pointer back to the cell where you entered the long label, you will notice that the long label is still there in the contents box—1-2-3/G simply truncates it when it is displayed in the cell. For example, in Figure 1–27, cell A1 shows a long label. Cell A3 contains the same label, but 1-2-3/G cuts it off because of the entry that was made in cell B3.

You can expand the width of column A in Figure 1–27 to display more of the label. Chapter 3 explains how to do this as well as how to change the default width of all the columns in the worksheet.

If you prefer that 1-2-3/G always cut off long labels so that they never extend beyond their own column, you can use the Worksheet Global Label Cell display Short labels command. Figure 1–28 shows the effect. See Chapter 3 for more on this command.

Repeating Characters

To fill a cell with a label, you use the \ label prefix. That is, 1-2-3/G repeats the characters in a label as many times as will fit in the cell. One of the most common

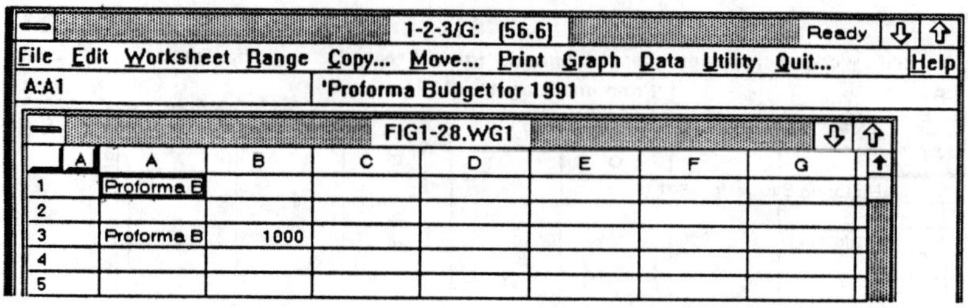

1-2-3/G: [56.6] Ready

File Edit Worksheet Range Copy... Move... Print Graph Data Utility Quit... Help

A:A1 'Proforma Budget for 1991

FIG1-28.WG1

A	A	B	C	D	E	F	G
1	Proforma B						
2							
3	Proforma B	1000					
4							
5							

FIGURE 1–28 The effect of choosing short labels

uses for repeating characters is to underline cells and create dividers between cells. For example, if you type \=, 1-2-3/G repeats the equal sign enough times to fill the cell, as in Figure 1–29. You can use * and \- to create a similar effect. Figure 1–30 shows how you can create a divider between cells by placing \- in a series of contiguous cells.

Note

There are other more aesthetic ways to underline (and double underline) an entry than by placing repeating characters in the next cell down below the entry. One way is to change the font of the entry to an underlined font using the Range Attributes Font command. Another way is to create a border along the bottom edge of the cell using the Range Attributes Border command. See Chapter 3, "Formatting the Worksheet," for more information on these commands.

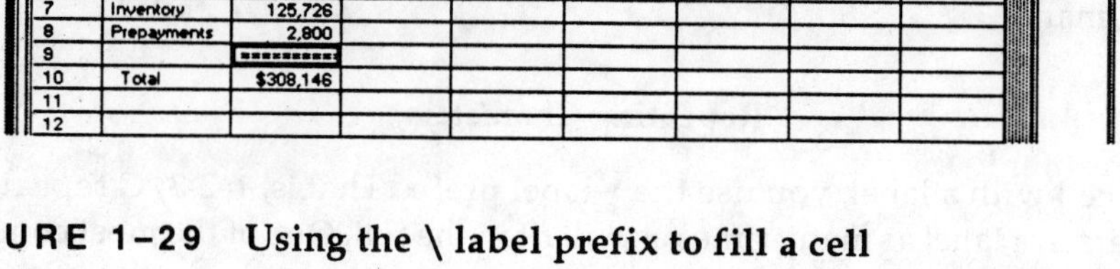

1-2-3/G: [56.6] Ready

File Edit Worksheet Range Copy... Move... Print Graph Data Utility Quit... Help

A:B9 \=

FIG1-29.WG1

A	A	B	C	D	E	F	G	H
1	Specialty Stores, Inc.							
2								
3	Current Assets:							
4	Cash	$24,000						
5	Securities	12,500						
6	A/R	143,120						
7	Inventory	125,726						
8	Prepayments	2,800						
9		==========						
10	Total	$308,146						
11								
12								

FIGURE 1–29 Using the \ label prefix to fill a cell

1-2-3/G: (56.6) Ready

File Edit Worksheet Range Copy... Move... Print Graph Data Utility Quit... Help

A:B5

FIG1-30.WG1

A	A	B	C	D	E	F	G	H
1				ABC Company				
2				Operating Expenses				
3								
4		Jan-91	Feb-91	Mar-91	Apr-91	May-91	Jun-91	
5		----------	----------	----------	----------	----------	----------	
6	Salaries	$173,400	$183,804	$194,832	$206,522	$218,914	$232,048	
7	Benefits	$12,138	$12,866	$13,638	$14,457	$15,324	$16,243	
8	Rent	$5,833	$5,833	$5,833	$5,833	$5,833	$5,833	
9	Insurance	$1,458	$1,458	$1,458	$1,458	$1,458	$1,458	
10	Legal	$1,276	$1,404	$1,544	$1,698	$1,868	$2,055	
11	Accounting	$1,914	$2,105	$2,316	$2,548	$2,802	$3,083	
12	Consulting	$4,607	$4,837	$5,079	$5,333	$5,600	$5,880	
13	Supplies	$1,926	$1,965	$2,004	$2,044	$2,085	$2,126	
14	Telephone	$3,202	$3,330	$3,463	$3,602	$3,746	$3,896	
15	Advertizing	$7,456	$7,829	$8,220	$8,631	$9,063	$9,516	
16	Miscellaneous	$2,000	$2,000	$2,000	$2,000	$2,000	$2,000	
17		==========	==========	==========	==========	==========	==========	
18	Total	$215,211	$227,432	$240,389	$254,127	$268,693	$284,139	
19								
20								
21								

FIGURE 1–30 **Creating a divider between cells with \-**

Values

A *value* is a number or formula that begins with one of the numbers 0 through 9 or one of these numeric symbols: + — (. @ # $. When you enter a number or one of the numeric symbols, the mode indicator changes to Value.

Numbers

Numbers have the following entry restrictions in 1-2-3/G:

- They can range from 1^{-99} to 1^{99}.
- They cannot include spaces.
- You can enter them in scientific notation (for example, 1.23E09 or 123E-06).
- You can enter them with or without commas, or another thousands separator (see NOTE below).
- They can begin with the $ symbol (see NOTE below).

- You can enter them as percentages, as long as the % follows the number (for example, 24%).

Note

> If you include commas or dollar signs when entering numbers, 1-2-3/G will discard them, unless you have set 1-2-3/G for automatic formatting (you used the Range Format Automatic command). See Chapter 3 for information on formatting worksheets.

When you enter a number, 1-2-3/G assumes the number is positive. To enter a negative number precede the number with a minus sign (from the numeric keypad) or a hyphen.

Note

> The cell format determines how a value is displayed in the worksheet. You change the cell format using the Range Format command. For example, to format a cell to show a dollar sign, commas between thousands, and two decimal places, you use the Range Format Currency 2 command (see Chapter 3, "Formatting Worksheets"). You can format a cell either before or after you enter data in it.

In its default state, 1-2-3/G right aligns numeric values. You can, however, change the alignment using the Worksheet Global Label Values command (see Chapter 3).

Numeric entries are accurate to 18 decimal places of precision in 1-2-3/G. If you are using 1-2-3/G for business applications, it is unlikely that this will concern you because business applications are rarely so precise. However, if you are using 1-2-3/G for scientific or engineering purposes, you may find this information of value. You can change 1-2-3/G's level of precision using the Range Attributes Precision command.

Table 1–13 Formula Symbols

Symbol	Description
+	Positive number or addition in a numeric formula
-	Negative value or subtraction in a numeric formula
*	Multiplication in a formula
/	Division in a formula
@	String following this symbol is an @function name
.	Decimal point in a formula
(	Precedes @function arguments or changes order of precedence
)	Closes an @function or changes order of precedence
#	Starts or ends a logical operator (for example, #AND#)
>	Greater than logical operator
<	Less than logical operator
=	Equal to logical operator
<>	Not equal to
$	Starts absolute reference (for example, $A$4)
&	String concatenation

Formulas

A formula is an entry that performs a calculation. You can enter four different types of formulas in 1-2-3/G: numeric, string, logical, and @function. Table 1–13 shows the special characters you can use when entering formulas. See "Entering Formulas" for a description of how to use these characters in formulas.

Long Values

When a value is too wide to fit within its column, it is known as a *long value.* 1-2-3/G treats long values differently than long labels. Rather than showing what it can within the column or extending the value into adjacent blank cells, 1-2-3/G displays asterisks, as in Figure 1–31.

Here are the precise rules that 1-2-3/G follows for displaying long values:

- When the format of the cell is General (the default), 1-2-3/G displays the integer portion of the entry, if it can. (If it can show more than the integer portion, it will.) If the integer portion is too wide, 1-2-3/G shows the entry in scientific notation. If the column is still too narrow to display the entry in scientific notation, 1-2-3/G displays asterisks.
- When you have assigned a format other than General (for example, Currency, as in Figure 1–31), 1-2-3/G displays asterisks.

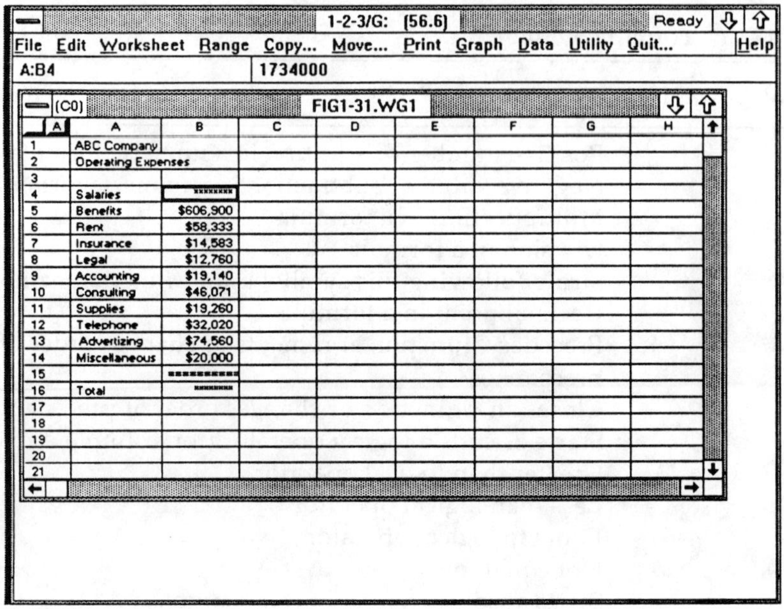

1-2-3/G: [56.6] Ready

File Edit Worksheet Range Copy... Move... Print Graph Data Utility Quit... Help

A:B4 1734000

(C0) FIG1-31.WG1

A	A	B	C	D	E	F	G	H
1	ABC Company							
2	Operating Expenses							
3								
4	Salaries	********						
5	Benefits	$606,900						
6	Rent	$58,333						
7	Insurance	$14,583						
8	Legal	$12,760						
9	Accounting	$19,140						
10	Consulting	$46,071						
11	Supplies	$19,260						
12	Telephone	$32,020						
13	Advertizing	$74,560						
14	Miscellaneous	$20,000						
15		==========						
16	Total	********						
17								
18								
19								
20								
21								

FIGURE 1–31 **Long value displayed as asterisks**

To change 1-2-3/G's display so that you can see the entire long value, you must widen the column. If you are using the mouse, move the pointer within the column border to the gridline separating two columns. (You'll know you're there when the pointer changes to a two-headed arrow.) Next, drag the column border to the right to widen the column (drag it left if you've gone too far). If you are using the keyboard, select the Worksheet Column Set width command. Press the → key to increase the number of places the column displays until the entire value is shown (press ← if you have gone too far). Press ENTER to complete the command. Chapter 3 discusses setting column widths in more detail.

Dates

1-2-3/G has a special numbering system for handling dates. Each date from January 1, 1900 to November 21, 9999, has been assigned a sequential number, starting with 1 and ending with 2958425. For example, the date number for January 21, 1990 is 32894. These numbers are called *date numbers*.

Here are two ways to enter dates:

- Enter the assigned date number.

- Use the @DATE function to calculate the date number, a much easier alternative than trying to discern the proper date number to enter. The format of the function is

```
@DATE(year,month,day).
```

Just as soon as you have entered a date in a cell, you must change the cell's format so that you can interpret the date. To do this, you use the Range Format Date command. For example, Figure 1–32 shows how you can use the @DATE function to enter the date for January 21, 1990. The cell has been formatted with the Range Format Date 4 command. (See Chapter 3 for more on date formats.)

Note to Release 2 and 3 Users

In previous releases, you may recall that 1-2-3's sequential date numbering system ended with 73050, for December 31, 2099. Notice that Lotus has significantly increased the number of days in 1-2-3/G's date numbering system.

Times

1-2-3/G also uses a sequential numbering system for times. Each time from midnight to 11:59.59 P.M. has been assigned a decimal number from .000000 to .999999. These are known as *time numbers*.

Here are two ways to enter times:

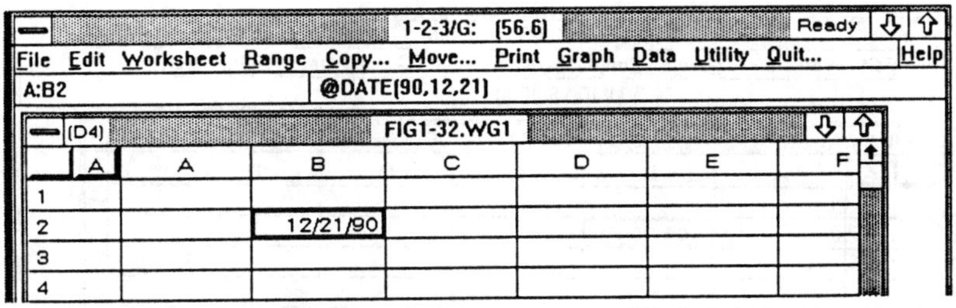

FIGURE 1–32 Date formatted with Range Format Date/Time 4

- Enter the decimal number assigned to the time
- Enter the @TIME function to calculate the time number, a much easier alternative than trying to discern the proper time number to enter. The format of the function is

```
@TIME(hour,minutes,seconds).
```

As with dates, just as soon as you enter a time number in a cell, you must format it in order to be able to read it. The command for formatting times is also Range Format Date/Time. For example, Figure 1–33 shows the @TIME function you use for entering the time for 6:30 P.M. The cell was formatted using the Range Format Date/Time 7 command.

Combined Date/Time Entries

Dates and times are actually part of the same sequential numbering system. To see how this works, place the @NOW function in a cell. @NOW returns the combined date and time number for the current date and time. For example, if you enter the @NOW function in a cell at 6:40 P.M. on January 21, 1990, 1-2-3/G shows the combined date/time number which appears in cell B1 of Figure 1–34. The integer portion is the date, and the decimal portion the time.

You can format the combined date/time number in cell A:B1 of 1–34 to display either a date or a time. For example, cell A:B3 illustrates what happens when you format the cell containing this number with the Range Format Date/Time 4 command. 1-2-3/G uses the integer portion of the value and displays a date in the cell. On the other hand, cell A:B5 shows the same date/time number formatted with the Range Format Date/Time 7 command. In this case, 1-2-3/G uses the decimal portion of the value and displays the current time in the cell.

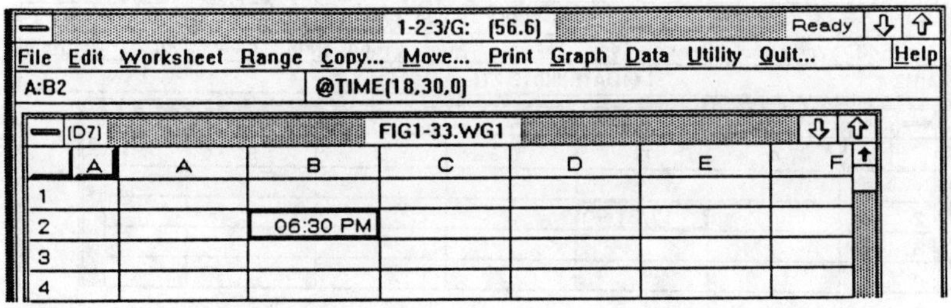

FIGURE 1–33 Time formatted with Range Format Date/Time 7

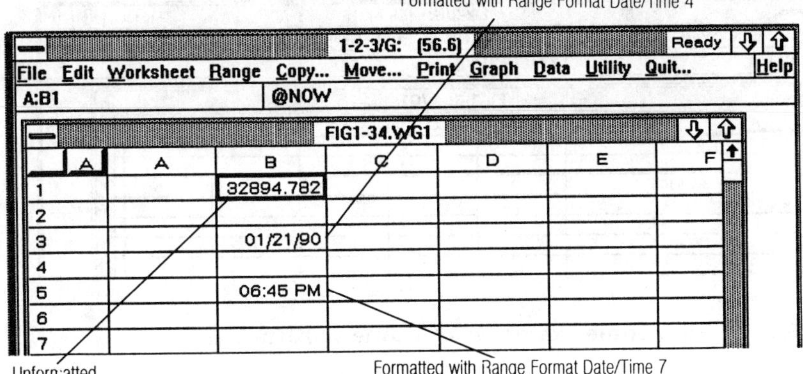

FIGURE 1–34 A combined date/time number

ENTERING FORMULAS

Up to this point you have entered only labels and numbers in the worksheet. Although labels and numbers are a necessary part of every worksheet, you can only get a sense of 1-2-3/G's calculative power by using formulas.

As mentioned, 1-2-3/G has four types of formulas: numeric, string, logical, and @function. The sections that follow describe each type.

Numeric Formulas

Numeric formulas perform calculations on numbers. The simplest kinds of calculations are the same as those you would perform on a four-function calculator, including addition, subtraction, multiplication, and division. Examples of more complicated calculations you can perform with numeric formulas are determining the internal rate of return of a series of unequal cash flows or calculating the standard deviation of a sample population.

The best way to get a feel for how numeric formulas work is to try entering some simple examples. Begin by moving the cell pointer to cell C1, typing **28+60+31**, and pressing ENTER to confirm the entry. 1-2-3/G automatically calculates the result and displays the number 119 in the cell. Notice that when you enter a formula in 1-2-3/G, the formula appears in the contents box, and the result appears in the cell.

Next, try entering the following formulas. Your screen should look like Figure 1–35.

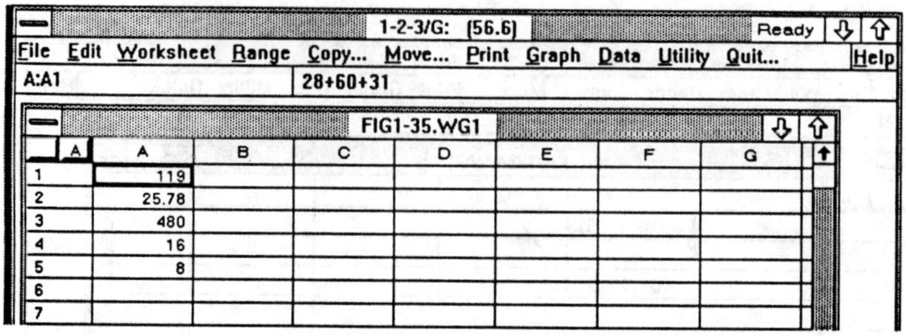

FIGURE 1–35 Some examples of numeric formulas

Cell	You enter	Cell displays
A2	55.52–29.74	25.78
A3	16*30	480
A4	256/16	16
A5	2^3	8

As you can see, simple numeric formulas use the following mathematical operators: + (plus) for addition,—(minus) for subtraction, * (asterisk) for multiplication, / (slash) for division, and ^ (caret) for exponentiation.

Using Cell References

Rather than using literal numbers in your formulas, a more common use of formulas is to refer to other cells using cell references. By referencing other cells, you can have your formulas use the contents of those cells in calculations. When you change the contents of a referenced cell, the value of using cell references becomes apparent. 1-2-3/G instantly recalculates your formula and displays the result. You can use this process to play *what if*, one of the most important aspects of using a spreadsheet like 1-2-3/G. On the other, if you use literal numbers in your formulas, the formulas are static. Only when you edit one of the numbers in the formula does its value change.

To reference another cell in a formula, simply place that cell's address in the formula preceded by a numeric operator, typically + — (. or $. (If you forget the numeric operator, 1-2-3/G will assume you are entering a label.) For example, imagine you have the number 10 in cell A1 and the number 20 in cell B1. With the cell pointer in cell C1, you enter the formula **+A1+B1**. When you press ENTER to confirm this formula, 1-2-3/G calculates the value 30 in cell C1. If you then change the value in cell A1 from 10 to 20, 1-2-3/G immediately updates C1 and shows 40 in that cell. Thus, you have created a dynamic situation in which the value of cell C1 depends upon the value of cells A1 and B1.

You can apply this simple principle of one cell depending on another to evaluate everyday business problems. For example, suppose you want to create a model that evaluates sales for a small company over several months. The sales from one month to the next is dependent on a growth factor. When you change the growth factor, the dollar volume for sales in each month changes upward or downward accordingly. What follows is a description of how you might go about setting up just such a model.

Figure 1–36 shows a likely framework for the sales/growth factor model. It contains the following labels and numbers:

Cell	You Enter
A:A1	Growth rate
A:A2	.09
A:A5	Sales
A:B1	Starting Sales
A:B2	100
A:B4	^Jan
A:C4	^Feb
A:D4	^Mar

If you move the cell pointer to cell A:B5, type **+A:B2**, and press ENTER, 1-2-3/G enters the value from cell A:B2 into cell A:B5, which shows the result 100, as in Figure 1–37. After entering the formula, you'll notice that 1-2-3/G automatically creates an abbreviated cell address. That is, it removes the worksheet reference—the formula now reads +B2. 1-2-3/G uses an abbreviated

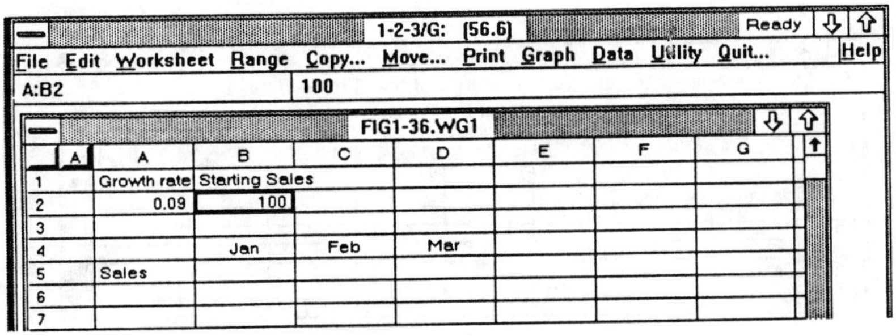

1-2-3/G: [56.6] Ready

File Edit Worksheet Range Copy... Move... Print Graph Data Utility Quit... Help

A:B2 100

FIG1-36.WG1

A	A	B	C	D	E	F	G
1	Growth rate	Starting Sales					
2	0.09	100					
3							
4		Jan	Feb	Mar			
5	Sales						
6							
7							

FIGURE 1–36 A simple worksheet

1-2-3/G: (56.6) Ready

File Edit Worksheet Range Copy... Move... Print Graph Data Utility Quit... Help

A:D5 +C5*(1+A2)

FIG1-37.WG1

A	A	B	C	D	E	F	G
1	Growth rate	Starting Sales					
2	0.09	100					
3							
4		Jan	Feb	Mar			
5	Sales	100	109	118.81			
6							
7							

FIGURE 1–37 Numeric formulas with cell references

cell address because the cell you are referencing resides in the same worksheet. Therefore, the worksheet portion of the reference is unnecessary.

If you then move the cell pointer to cell A:C5 and enter **+B5*(1+A2)**, you are indicating to 1-2-3/G that you want to multiply the value in cell A:B5 by 1 plus the value in cell A:A2. (Notice that because you are referencing cells in the current worksheet, you can use abbreviated cell addresses.) 1-2-3/G shows the result, 109, in cell A:C5. Then, if you enter the formula **+C5*(1+A2)** in cell A:D5, your worksheet will appear as in Figure 1-37.

Now, suppose you want to see the effect that changing the growth rate will have on your formulas. Move the cell pointer to cell A2 and enter **.15** in that cell. 1-2-3/G immediately updates the worksheet to reflect the change, as shown in Figure 1-38. Notice how the sales figures have increased.

The formulas you have entered thus far have been quite simple. As you can imagine, however, 1-2-3/G formulas can be quite complex with many operators and cell references. The only limitation you have in entering formulas in

1-2-3/G Ready

File Edit Worksheet Range Copy... Move... Print Graph Data Utility Quit... Help

A:D5 +C5*(1+A2)

FIG1-38.WG1

A	A	B	C	D	E	F	G	H
1	Growth rate	Starting sales						
2	0.15	100						
3								
4		Jan	Feb	Mar				
5	Sales	100	115	132.25				
6								
7								

FIGURE 1–38 The effect of changing the value in cell A2

1-2-3/G is that they cannot exceed the maximum cell entry length of 512 characters.

Pointing

When you want to enter a cell address in a formula, you do not have to type the entry. Instead you can specify the cell address by *pointing*. Besides being easier, pointing has the distinct advantage that it helps prevent errors in your formulas. You can point to a cell using the keyboard or the mouse.

For example, suppose you want to create a formula in cell A:E5 that totals the monthly sales figures in Figure 1–38. The formula you want to create is +A:B5+A:C5+A:D5. To create the formula by pointing with the keyboard, start with the cell pointer located in A:E5 and type +. Next, press the ← key. 1-2-3/G moves the cell pointer to cell A:D5 and appends its address to the end of the formula in the contents box. The formula now reads +A:D5. Then, as you move the cell pointer in the worksheet, the cell address follows your movement (from +A:D5 to +A:C5 and +A:C5 to +A:B5). After moving the cell pointer to cell A:B5, type + to accept that cell address as part of the formula. 1-2-3/G immediately moves the cell pointer back to cell A:E5 (the original cell), and the formula now reads +A:B5+. You can then move the cell pointer left two cells to append the address A:C5 to the formula. Type + a second time, and the formula now reads +A:B5+A:C5+. Move the cell pointer one cell to the left and press ENTER to complete the formula. Your worksheet should now look like Figure 1–39.

Pointing with the mouse is even easier than pointing with the keyboard. To point with the mouse while creating a formula, you simply click on the cell you want.

For example, to create the same formula outlined above using the mouse, place the cell pointer in A:E5 and type +. Next, move the mouse pointer to cell A:B5 and click on that cell. 1-2-3/G appends that cell's address to the end of the formula, which now reads +A:B5. Type + to accept that cell address as part of the formula. 1-2-3/G returns the cell pointer to cell A:E5, and the formula now reads +A:B5+. Repeat the same steps for cells A:C5 and A:D5. When your formula reads +A:B5+A:C5+A:D5, press ENTER.

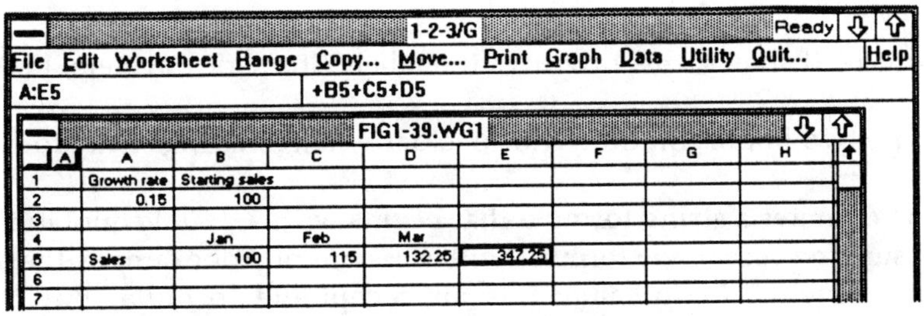

1-2-3/G Ready

File Edit Worksheet Range Copy... Move... Print Graph Data Utility Quit... Help

A:E5 +B5+C5+D5

FIG1-39.WG1

A	A	B	C	D	E	F	G	H
1	Growth rate	Starting sales						
2	0.15	100						
3								
4		Jan	Feb	Mar				
5	Sales	100	115	132.25	347.25			
6								
7								

FIGURE 1–39 Creating a formula by pointing to cells

For more information on selecting cell addresses, see "Selecting Cells, Ranges, and Collections" later.

Absolute and Relative References

There are three different types of cell addresses in 1-2-3/G formulas—relative, absolute, and mixed. These affect how the Copy and Edit Paste commands work when you copy a formula to another cell.

Thus far, you have used only relative cell addresses in your formulas. When you use the Copy command to copy this kind of formula to another location in a worksheet file, 1-2-3/G changes the references relative to the worksheet, column, and row location of the destination cell. With absolute cell references, however, 1-2-3/G does not change the references in any way when you copy them; they are identical in the source and destination cells. Mixed cell references are a combination of relative and absolute. That is, part of the cell reference changes when you copy the formula and part does not.

You use the $ symbol to indicate an absolute reference in 1-2-3/G. An example absolute reference is $A:$A$1, and a relative reference is A:A1. Examples of mixed cell references are $A:$A1, $A:A$1, and A:A$1.

When you enter a cell address in a formula, you can press ABS(F4) to cycle the cell address from relative to absolute, to mixed, and back to relative again. See Chapter 4, "Cutting and Pasting Data," for a detailed discussion of absolute and relative cell addressing, as well as a variety of other topics related to the Copy and Edit Paste commands.

String Formulas

String formulas use the string operator, & (ampersand), to create labels. The & symbol is a *concatenation* operator. It tells 1-2-3/G to concatenate, or string together, two labels. For example, the formula +"1-2-3/G " & "Handbook" produces the string *1-2-3/G Handbook.* As another example, suppose cell C1 contains the label "Strategic Partners, Inc." and cell C2 contains the label "Cash Flow." You can concatenate the two labels together by placing the following formula in an empty cell:

```
+C1&"—"&C2
```

As Figure 1-40 shows, this produces the label "Strategic Partners, Inc.—Cash Flow."

Here are two important things to consider when entering string formulas:

- When you enter a string formula that begins with a double quotation mark, make sure to precede the formula with a + symbol. For example, the formula +"Preventive"&" Maintenance" is an acceptable formula. But "Preventive"&"Maintenance" (without the starting +) is not; 1-2-3/G regards this as a right-aligned label, because of the initial quotation mark.

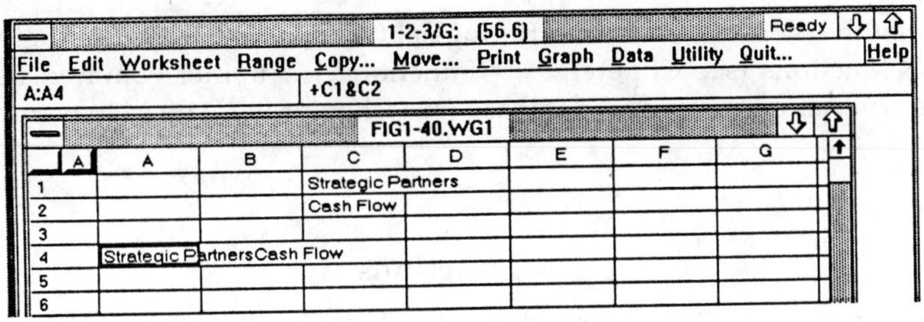

FIGURE 1–40 A string formula example

- You cannot use the & symbol to concatenate strings and numbers. For example, if cell A4 contains the number 90, and you place the formula +"Budget 19"&A4 in a cell, the formula will not work; it returns the value ERR (see "Error Values" later). If you want to combine a string and number together, you must convert the number to a string using the @STRING function. For example, the formula +"Budget 19"&@STRING(A4,0), when cell A4 contains the number 90, will produce the string "Budget 1990." See "@Functions" later for more. In addition, see the section "Combining a Value with a String into One Label" in Chapter 6.

Logical Formulas

Logical formulas compare two values or labels in a worksheet and produce a logical result, either 1 (true) or 0 (false). You use logical operators to compare the values in a logical formula. Table 1–14 shows 1-2-3/G's logical operators.

For example, if you place the formula +B2>=1000 in a cell, 1-2-3/G displays a 1 (true) if the value in cell B2 is greater than or equal to 1,000. If the value is less than 1,000, 1-2-3/G displays a 0 (false).

Table 1–14 Logical Operators

Operator	Definition
=	Equal to
<	Less than
>	Greater than
<=	Less than or equal to
>=	Greater than or equal to
<>	Not equal to
#AND#	Both condition 1 AND condition 2
#OR#	Either condition 1 OR condition 2
#NOT#	NOT condition 1

One of the most common uses for logical formulas is to perform logical tests in @IF functions (see Chapter 6, "@Functions"). Another common use is to create criteria for querying a database (see Chapter 9, "Data Management").

@Functions

Another type of 1-2-3/G formula is the @function. An *@function* is a built-in formula that performs some type of calculation. For example, one of 1-2-3/G's most frequently used mathematical @functions is @SUM, which totals a range of values. Chapter 6 describes how to use the @SUM function and all of 1-2-3/G's other @functions.

Figure 1–41 shows how you can use the @SUM function to total a column of expenses. To sum the cells in the range B6 to B16, you enter the formula @SUM(B6..B16) in cell A:B18. Imagine how tedious it would be to create a formula that sums the cells in the range if you were limited to using only the + operator!

Figure 1–42 shows another example of @SUM, one which totals the expenses for all the months in the quarter (the range B18..D18). This @SUM function actually derives its result by totaling all the @SUM functions at the foot of each column.

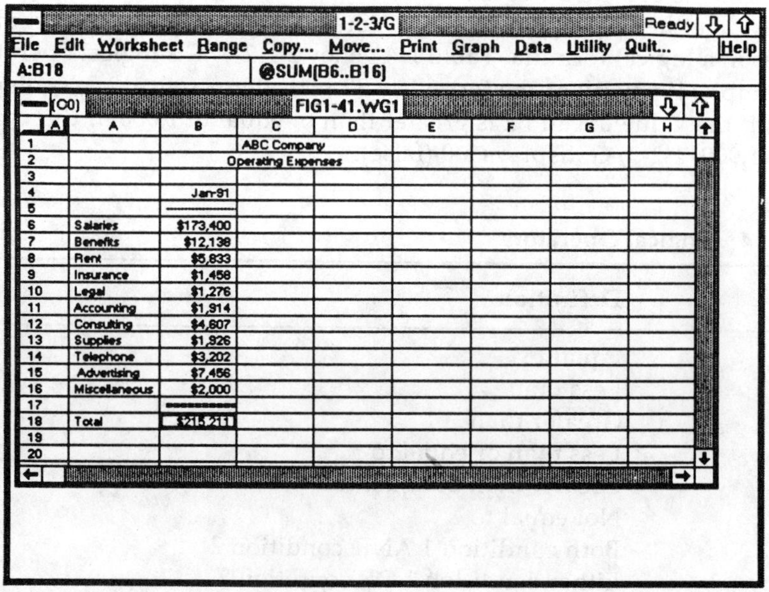

1-2-3/G Ready

File Edit Worksheet Range Copy... Move... Print Graph Data Utility Quit... Help

A:B18 @SUM(B6..B16)

(C0) FIG1-41.WG1

A	A	B	C	D	E	F	G	H
1			ABC Company					
2		Operating Expenses						
3								
4		Jan-91						
5								
6	Salaries	$173,400						
7	Benefits	$12,138						
8	Rent	$5,833						
9	Insurance	$1,458						
10	Legal	$1,276						
11	Accounting	$1,914						
12	Consulting	$4,607						
13	Supplies	$1,926						
14	Telephone	$3,202						
15	Advertising	$7,456						
16	Miscellaneous	$2,000						
17								
18	Total	$215,211						
19								
20								

FIGURE 1–41 The @SUM function

1-2-3/G Ready

File Edit Worksheet Range Copy... Move... Print Graph Data Utility Quit... Help

A:E18 @SUM(B18..D18)

(C0) FIG1-42.WG1

A	A	B	C	D	E	F	G	H
1			ABC Company					
2			Operating Expenses					
3								
4		Jan-91	Feb-91	Mar-91	Q1			
5		----------	----------	----------	----------			
6	Salaries	$173,400	$183,804	$194,832	$552,036			
7	Benefits	$12,138	$12,866	$13,638	$38,643			
8	Rent	$5,833	$5,833	$5,833	$17,500			
9	Insurance	$1,458	$1,458	$1,458	$4,375			
10	Legal	$1,276	$1,404	$1,544	$4,224			
11	Accounting	$1,914	$2,106	$2,316	$6,335			
12	Consulting	$4,607	$4,837	$5,079	$14,524			
13	Supplies	$1,926	$1,965	$2,004	$5,894			
14	Telephone	$3,202	$3,330	$3,463	$9,995			
15	Advertising	$7,456	$7,829	$8,220	$23,505			
16	Miscellaneous	$2,000	$2,000	$2,000	$6,000			
17		==========	==========	==========	==========			
18	Total	$215,211	$227,432	$240,389	$683,031			
19								
20								

FIGURE 1–42 **Another example of @SUM**

Error Values

Occasionally you will enter a formula that will yield ERR rather than a label or value. This means that 1-2-3/G cannot decipher the underlying formula. There are many reasons why this might occur. Here are some of the more common ones:

- You are dividing by zero. For example, suppose you have the formula +B1/B2 in cell B3, and B2 is blank. Cell B3 displays ERR.
- When you moved or copied data to a new location, you obscured a range boundary. For example, suppose you have the formula @SUM(C1..C10) in cell C11, and you use the Move command to move the contents of cell C2 to cell C1. Cell C11 shows ERR because 1-2-3/G cannot adjust the formula and therefore replaces the range reference with @ERR; the formula now reads @SUM(@ERR). See Chapter 4, "Cutting and Pasting Data," for more on the Move command.
- You have deleted a row or column using the Worksheet Delete Row or Column command and in the process have obscured a formula. For example, suppose you have the formula +A2+B2+C2 in cell D2. If you delete column

B, cell D2 displays ERR. See Chapter 3, "Formatting Worksheets," for more on the Worksheet Delete Row and Column commands.

Order of Precedence

As you know, operators perform mathematical, string, or logical operations in formulas. Because you can have any number of operators in a formula, 1-2-3/G needs a way to determine which ones to evaluate first. The sequence in which 1-2-3/G evaluates operators is known as the *order of precedence.* Table 1–15 shows 1-2-3/G operators and their order of precedence. Operators with lower numbers are evaluated first. For example, the formula 3+5*2 evaluates to 13 because * (multiplication) has a higher order of precedence than + (addition). Operators with the same precedence number are evaluated from left to right.

You can override 1-2-3/G's order of precedence by using parentheses. For example, the formula 2*3+10 evaluates to 16, but the formula 2*(3+10) evaluates to 26.

Table 1–15 Order of Precedence

Order	Operator	Operation
1	^	Exponentiation
2	-	Negative
2	+	Positive
3	*	Multiplication
3	/	Division
4	+	Addition
4	-	Subtraction
5	=	Equal to test
5	<>	Not equal to test
5	<	Less than test
5	>	Greater than test
5	<=	Less than or equal to test
5	>=	Greater than or equal to test
6	#NOT#	Logical NOT test
7	#AND#	Logical AND test
7	#OR#	Logical OR test
7	&	String concatenation

EDITING CELL ENTRIES

You can easily modify a cell entry in a 1-2-3/G worksheet using the keyboard or the mouse. Most editing requires a combination of the two.

Editing with the Mouse

To modify the contents of a cell using the mouse, begin by moving the cell pointer to the cell containing the information you want to change. Then, move the mouse pointer to the contents box and click on the location where you want to make the change. 1-2-3/G enters Edit mode (the mode indicator changes from Ready to Edit) and places the insertion point, also called the cursor (a flashing vertical bar), at the location you've chosen. You can then type additional information or press DEL to delete information. Press ENTER to confirm your changes and place the edited entry in the current cell.

Tip: Editing a cell by double-clicking

> You can also edit a cell by double-clicking on it. 1-2-3/G immediately places you in Edit mode and locates the cursor at the end of the entry in the contents box.

To confirm your change, click on the confirm icon or press ENTER. You can also click on another cell or use one of the pointer movement keys. (See "Confirming an Entry" above.)

If you want to erase the entire entry while in Edit mode and begin again, press ESC. You can then type a new entry from scratch and confirm it. Pressing ESC a second time returns you to Ready mode and cancels all the changes you made while in Edit mode, leaving your original cell entry intact.

For example, suppose you have entered **Marketing Porposal** in cell A2 and you want to correct your errant spelling. After moving the cell pointer to cell A2, click just before the first *o* to enter Edit mode. 1-2-3/G displays the insertion point just before the *o*. Press DEL to remove the *o* then press → to move the insertion point to the right one character. Type *o* and the entry now appears as 'Marketing Proposal. Press ENTER, or click on the confirm icon, to confirm the entry and return to Ready mode.

Table 1-16 Edit Mode Keys

Key	Action
←	Moves the cursor left one character.
→	Moves the cursor right one character.
↓	Moves the cursor down one line, provided the contents span more than one line.
↑	Moves the cursor up one line, provided the contents span more than one line.
BACKSPACE	Deletes the character to the left of the cursor.
DEL	Deletes one character to the right of the cursor. In Ready mode, deletes the contents of the current cell..
CTRL-→	Moves the cursor right five characters.
CTRL-←	Moves the cursor left five characters.
END	Moves the cell pointer to the end of the entry.
HOME	Moves the cursor to the start of the entry.
ESC	Erases the entry from the contents box and starts over. Type a new entry and press ENTER to confirm it. Or, press ESC again to leave Edit mode and return to worksheet with the original entry intact.

Editing with the Keyboard

To modify the contents of a cell using the keyboard, move the cell pointer to the cell you want to change and press EDIT (F2). 1-2-3/G enters Edit mode and places the cursor at the end of the entry in the contents box. To make a change, use the keys in Table 1–16.

For example, imagine once again that you have entered the misspelled label **Marketing Porposal** in cell A2. To correct the error, move the cell pointer to A2 and press EDIT (F2). 1-2-3/G places the cursor at the end of 'Marketing Porposal in the contents box. Press CTRL-← once then ← twice to locate the cursor under the *o*. Press DEL to remove the *o*. The contents box now reads 'Marketing Prposal. Next, press → then type *o*. The entry now appears as 'Marketing Proposal. Press ENTER to confirm the entry.

Notes on Editing Cells

Here are some things to consider when editing cell entries:

- The quickest way to delete the current cell entry from Ready mode is to press DEL (see Chapter 4, "Cutting and Pasting Data").
- If you want to convert a formula to its literal value, press CALC (F9) while in Edit mode. For example, suppose you have the formula @SUM(A1..A3) in

cell A4 and its result is 50. If you move the cell pointer to A4, press EDIT (F2) to enter Edit mode and then press CALC (F9), 1-2-3/G shows 50 in the contents box. You can then press ENTER to confirm the entry and place it in the worksheet.

- If, while making a cell entry for the first time, you want to enter Edit mode, press EDIT (F2) at any time. You can then use any of the cursor-movement keys in Table 1–16.
- If you make an error while entering data in a cell, 1-2-3/G issues an error message, such as "Illegal number in formula" or "Not a valid expression," and automatically places you in Edit mode after you clear the error. Often the cursor will be located directly below the invalid part of the entry, giving you a good indication of where to start editing.
- While in Edit mode, you can enter Point mode at any time by pressing EDIT (F2) a second time. While in Point mode, you can use the mouse or any of the cursor-movement keys to point to a selection (see "Pointing" above).

Tip: Deleting, moving, and copying several characters at once

Suppose you are in Edit mode and you want to delete part of an entry and leave the rest of the entry intact. For example, suppose you have the entry '1991 Expenses, and you want to delete the year from the label. The easiest way to do this is to move the mouse pointer to just before the *1* in 1990 and press the left mouse button. Then, while holding the button, drag the mouse over the word and release the button when you reach the end of the word. The year now appears highlighted in the contents box. Press DEL to delete the highlighted text from the entry.

You can also delete a block of characters using the keyboard. To highlight a block of text, press and hold down SHIFT then press any of the arrow keys. For example, to highlight a block of five characters, press and hold down SHIFT then press → five times. You can then press DEL to delete the characters from the entry.

If you want to move a block of characters in an entry, you can use the clipboard. (The clipboard is shared by all Presentation Manager applications and is simply a place where you can store data temporarily and then reuse it if you want.) Highlight the text as outlined above then press SHIFT-DEL to cut the highlighted text to the clipboard; "cutting" deletes the highlighted text and places a copy in the clipboard. To place the text in another location in the entry, move the insertion point to the desired location and press SHIFT-INS. (You can even move the cell pointer to another cell.) 1-2-3/G pastes the entry from the clipboard to the new location.

To copy a block of highlighted characters to another location, press CTRL-INS. This leaves the highlighted characters intact but places a copy in the clipboard. Move the insertion point to another location and press SHIFT-INS to paste the entry into the new location. You can also move the cell pointer to a new cell before pressing SHIFT-INS to paste the entry. See Chapter 3, "Cutting and Pasting Data," for more information.

RANGES

Many commands you select in 1-2-3/G act on a range. For example, if you select the Move command, 1-2-3/G asks you to supply a range to move from and a range to move to.

A *range* is a rectangular block of contiguous cells. It can be as small as a single cell or as large as the entire worksheet file. Figure 1–43 shows some sample ranges. For example, cells A:A2, A:A3, A:B2, and A:B3 taken together constitute

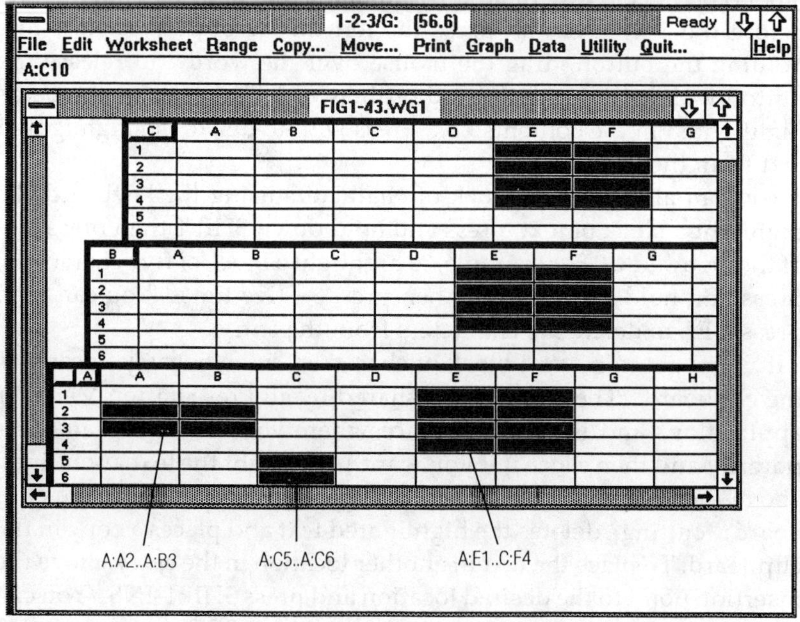

FIGURE 1–43 Some sample ranges

a range. Cells A:C5 and A:C6 are also a range. In addition, because ranges can span multiple worksheets, the highlighted block beginning in cell A:E1 and extending backward through worksheets to cell C:F4 is also a range. In 3-D space, you can think of ranges as "cubes" of data. A range cannot encompass multiple worksheet files, however.

A range is made up of two cell addresses representing diagonally opposite corners. For example, the range A:A2..A:B3 encompasses cells A:A2, A:A3, A:B2, and A:B3 in Figure 1-43. Likewise, the range A:E1..C:F4 represents the 3-D range on the right-hand side of the figure.

You can use ranges with commands or with formulas. For example, suppose you want to select the 2-D range A:A2..A:B3 in preparation for a command. To select the range with the keyboard, perform the following steps:

1. Move the cell pointer to cell A:A2.
2. Press and hold down the SHIFT key. This *anchors* the cell pointer in the current cell. Cell A:A2 is now known as the *anchor cell* because it contains the anchored cell pointer. [You can press CTRL-. (period) rather than holding down the SHIFT key to anchor the cell pointer.]
3. Press → followed by ↓. This moves the *free cell*, the cell diagonally opposite the cell pointer, to cell A:B3.
4. Release the SHIFT key.

TIP: Specifying ranges that span multiple columns, rows, or worksheets

When specifying a range that spans entire rows or columns, you do not need to designate two diagonally opposite corners. For example, to specify a range that spans all the cells in rows 2 and 3 of worksheet A, you can use A:2..A:3. Of course, you could also use the designation A:A2..A:IV3 to accomplish the same thing. Likewise, B:A..B:B specifies a range that spans all of the cells in columns A and B of worksheet B, as does B:A1..B:B8192.

To specify a range that spans entire worksheets, you need only enter the worksheet letters, each one followed by a colon. For example, the range A:..C: spans all the cells in worksheets A, B, and C. Likewise the range A:..IV: spans all the cells in the entire worksheet file.

The range now appears highlighted in the worksheet. You can now select any command that requires a range, and 1-2-3/G will automatically apply the command to your selection.

To cancel the range selection, press ESC or move the cell pointer to another cell. See "Canceling a Range or Collection" below for more details. For other ways to select a range see "Selecting Cells, Ranges, and Collections" later in this chapter.

Suppose you want to select the 3–D range A:E1..C:F4 in Figure 1–43. Perform the following:

1. Select the Worksheet Window Perspective command to place the worksheet file in Perspective mode (this step is optional).
2. Move the cell pointer to cell A:E1.
3. Press CTRL-. (period) to anchor the cell pointer.
4. Use the arrow keys to highlight the range A:E1..A:F4.
5. Press CTRL-PGUP twice to expand the range to worksheets B and C.
6. Press ENTER to complete the selection. (If you don't press ENTER, 1-2-3/G will not know you are finished highlighting the last range.)

The range now appears highlighted. To return the window to a single worksheet, select the Worksheet Window Clear command. To cancel the 3–D range, move the cell pointer or press ESC.

COLLECTIONS

A *collection* is an assortment of discontiguous ranges that is treated as a single entity. The ranges you include in a collection can be from the same worksheet, different worksheets, or even different worksheet files. For example, all the ranges that appear in Figure 1–43 can be treated as a collection.

You can use a collection in place of a range in almost every 1-2-3/G command that calls for a range. Before you can use a collection in a formula, however, you must name the collection (see "Naming Ranges and Collections" later).

To select a collection, you must detach the cell pointer from the current range. To do this, press DETACH (SHIFT-F8) or click the right mouse button. After pressing DETACH, you can then move the cell pointer to another location and add another cell or range to the collection. (You can also edit any cell without canceling the current selection.)

For example, suppose you want to select a collection that includes all the ranges in Figure 1–43. To select the collection using the keyboard, perform the following steps:

1. Select the Worksheet Window Perspective command to place the worksheet file in Perspective mode (this step is optional).
2. Select the 2–D range A:A2..A:B3 as outlined in "Ranges" above.
3. Press DETACH (SHIFT-F8). This frees the cell pointer for movement.

Note

Because DETACH (SHIFT-F8) is a toggle key, the cell pointer remains free until you press DETACH again.

4. Move the cell pointer to cell A:C5.
5. Press and hold down the SHIFT key while you press ↓ to move the cell pointer to cell A:C6.
6. Release the SHIFT key.
7. Move the cell pointer to A:E1.
8. Press CTRL-. (period) to anchor the cell pointer.
9. Use the arrow keys to highlight the range A:E1..A:F4.
10. Press CTRL-PGUP twice to expand the range to worksheets B and C.
11. Press ENTER to complete this last selection. (If you don't press ENTER, 1-2-3/G will not know you have completed highlighting the last 3–D range and will continue to expand the highlight as you move the cell pointer.)

The collection is now complete. If you set the window for Perspective mode, you can return it to a single worksheet by selecting the Worksheet Window Clear command. To cancel the collection, move the cell pointer to another cell or press ESC.

Note

A collection can have ranges from more than one worksheet file. To use the collection with a command, however, all the worksheet files must be open. This is not normally a problem, unless you select a collection and then close a file.

Note

> For information on selecting collections with the mouse, see the next section entitled "Selecting Cells, Ranges, and Collections."

To enter a collection in response to a command, type the ranges and cells that make up the collection one after another, separated by commas. For example, suppose you want to format a collection of ranges that includes A:A1..A:A9, A:C1..A:10, and A:G11..A:G12 as currency with two decimal places ($1,234.56). Select the Range Format Currency 2 command, and type

```
A:A1..A:A9,A:C1..A:10,A:G11..A:G12
```

in the Range(s) text box. (You can also highlight the ranges in the worksheet; see the next section.)

As mentioned, a range can extend across more than one worksheet, but it cannot extend between files. To get around this problem, you can link files using formulas. For example, to sum the range A:A1..A:B3 from the worksheet file ACCT.WG1, you could enter the formula @SUM(<<ACCT.WG1>>A:A1..A:B3) in a cell in the current worksheet. (If the ACCT.WG1 file is not open, 1-2-3/G places ERR in the cell.) See Chapter 2, "Managing the Desktop," for more on linking files.

SELECTING CELLS, RANGES, AND COLLECTIONS

Suppose you have identified a cell or group of cells that you want to select before using a command. This section tells you all you need to know to make the selection, whether you are selecting a cell, range, or collection. Because this section is all-inclusive, you may want to skim it the first time through and refer back to it later when you need to.

As you read this section, keep in mind the following rules about the selection process:

- You can make a selection before or after you choose a command.
- If you make a selection before choosing a command, your choice remains selected even after the command is completed, unless of course the command

eliminates the selection from the window (for example, the Worksheet Erase command eliminates the selection because it erases the entire worksheet).

Selecting with the Mouse

This section gives the steps for selecting cells, ranges, and collections with the mouse. It also describes how to select entire rows or columns, entire worksheets, and entire files.

To Select a Cell

As you know, to select a cell with the mouse, you simply move the mouse pointer to that cell and click on it. 1-2-3/G moves the cell pointer to that cell (see "Moving with the Mouse" above).

To Select a Two-Dimensional Range

To select the 2–D range with the mouse, for example A:B3..A:B5 in Figure 1–44, perform the following:

1. Move the mouse pointer to one corner of the range (anchor cell), for example, cell A:B3.
2. Press and hold down the left button.

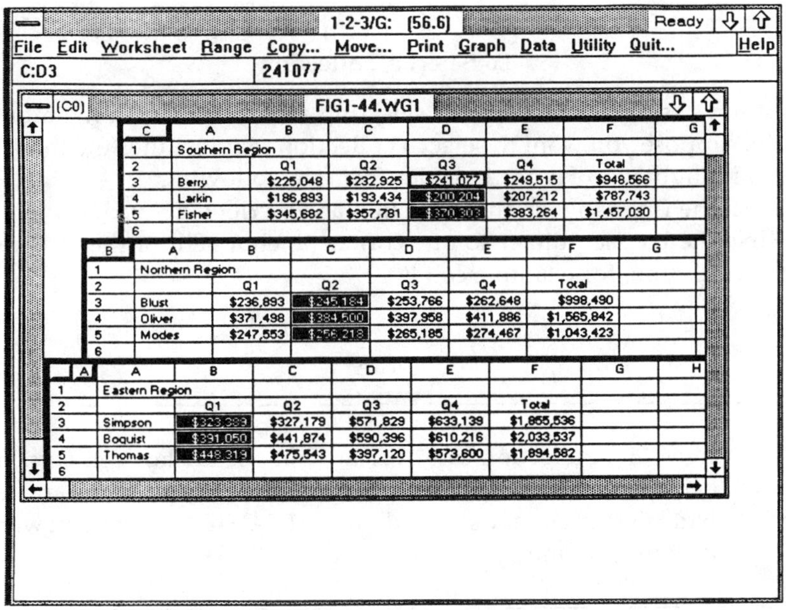

FIGURE 1–44 Selecting 2–D ranges with the mouse

3. Drag the pointer to the diagonally opposite corner (free cell)—in this example cell A:B5—and release the mouse button.

Note

> If the diagonally opposite corner cell of the range does not appear within the current worksheet window, move the mouse pointer to the edge of the window in the direction of the desired cell, and 1-2-3/G will scroll the contents of the window in that direction.

Note

> You cannot select a 3–D range with the mouse. Select a collection of 2–D ranges instead, or use the keyboard.

To Select a Collection

This section describes the steps for selecting a collection with the mouse. For example, suppose you want to select a collection that includes the three ranges that are highlighted in Figure 1–44. Perform the following:

1. Select the first range in the collection as described above.
2. Move the mouse pointer to one corner (anchor cell) of the next range in the collection, for example cell B:C3.

Note

> The ranges in a collection can overlap, but the anchor cell *must* be outside the previously selected range. (If you do not place the anchor cell outside the previously selected range, 1-2-3/G assumes you want to adjust your previously selected range.)

3. Press and hold down the right mouse button.
4. Drag the pointer to the diagonally opposite corner, in this case B:C5, and release the button.
5. Repeat the steps 2 through 4 for all the remaining ranges in the collection. In the current example, repeat the steps for the range C:D3..C:D5.

Note

> You can add cells from another worksheet file to a collection by activating the worksheet file and selecting a range just as you would in the current worksheet file (see Chapter 2, "Managing the Desktop," for more on activating open worksheet files). In addition, before a command or formula can use a collection, all of the worksheet files that contain ranges within the collection must be open.

To Select an Entire Row or Column

To select an entire row, click on the box surrounding the row number in the worksheet frame. To select an entire column, click on the box surrounding the column letter at the top of the worksheet frame.

For example, suppose you want to select all of row 1 in worksheet A of Figure 1–44. Click on the box surrounding that row's number in worksheet A's frame.

To Select a Range of Rows or Columns

To select a range of rows, drag the mouse pointer across the boxes surrounding the row numbers in the worksheet frame. For example, to select rows 2, 3, and 4 in worksheet A of Figure 1–44, drag the mouse pointer across the row number boxes in worksheet A's frame.

To select a range of columns, drag the mouse pointer across the boxes surrounding the column letters in the worksheet frame.

To Select an Entire Worksheet

To select an entire worksheet at once, click on the Worksheet selector button that appears in the upper-left corner of the worksheet frame. The Worksheet selector button contains the worksheet letter followed by a colon. 1-2-3/G highlights the entire worksheet.

To Select an Entire Worksheet File

To select the entire worksheet file, click on the Worksheet file selector button. This is the blank button located just to the left of worksheet A's Worksheet selector button in the upper-left corner of the worksheet frame. 1-2-3/G highlights all the worksheets in the file.

Selecting with the Keyboard

This section describes how to make selections with the keyboard. It also describes how to select entire rows or columns, entire worksheets, and entire files.

To Select a Cell

As mentioned, you select a cell with the keyboard by moving the cell pointer to that cell using any of the navigation keys (see "Moving with the Keyboard" above).

To Select a Two-Dimensional Range

The easiest way to select a 2–D range with the keyboard is to use the SHIFT key. For example, suppose you want to select the range A:C3..A:C5. Perform the following.

1. Use the navigation keys to move the cell pointer to one corner (anchor cell) of the range. Cell A:C3 is a good choice in the current example.
2. Press and hold down the SHIFT key to anchor the cell pointer in the current cell.
3. Use the navigation keys to move to the diagonally opposite corner (free cell). In the current example, press ↓ twice to move the free cell to A:C5. 1-2-3/G highlights the range as you go.

Note

You can also select a range by pressing CTRL-. (period) to anchor the cell pointer in the current cell, then use the navigation keys to move to the diagonally opposite corner cell. Press ENTER to complete your selection.

To Select a Three-Dimensional Range

To select a 3–D range with the keyboard, you must use the CTRL-. (period) to first anchor the cell pointer. For example, suppose you want to select the range A:B3..C:F5 in Figure 1–44. Perform the following:

1. Use the navigation keys to move the cell pointer to one corner (anchor cell) of the range, cell A:B3 in this example.
2. Press CTRL-. (period) to anchor the cell pointer at the current cell.
3. Use the navigation keys to move to the diagonally opposite corner of the range within the same worksheet. In the current example, press END → then END ↓ to locate the cell pointer at cell A:F5.
4. Press CTRL-PGUP (or CTRL-PGDN) as many times as necessary to expand the highlight to multiple worksheets. In the current example, press CTRL-PGUP twice to expand the highlight to worksheet C. The entire range A:B3..C:F5 should now be highlighted on your screen.
5. Complete the selection by pressing ENTER.

To Select a Collection

This section describes the steps for selecting a collection with the keyboard. For example, suppose you want to select all the ranges that are highlighted in Figure 1–44. Perform the following:

1. Select the first range in the collection as described above in "To Select a 2–D Range."
2. Press DETACH (SHIFT-F8). 1-2-3/G frees the cell pointer for movement. (The cell pointer remains free until you press DETACH again.)
3. Move the cell pointer to a corner (anchor cell) of the next range in the collection. For the current example, move the cell pointer to cell B:C3 by pressing CTRL-PGUP then →.

Note

> The ranges in a collection can overlap, but the anchor cell *must* be outside the previously selected range.

4. Press and hold down the SHIFT key while you move the cell pointer to the diagonally opposite corner of the range. In the current example, hold

down the SHIFT key while you press ↓ 3 times to move the cell pointer to B:C5. Then release the SHIFT key.

5. Repeat the steps 3 through 4 for each range in the collection. In the current example, repeat the steps to add the range C:D3..C:D5 to the collection.

To Select an Entire Row or Column

To select an entire row with the keyboard, move the cell pointer to any cell in that row and press SHIFT-ALT-← or SHIFT-ALT-→. To select an entire column, move the cell pointer to any cell in the column and press SHIFT-ALT-↑ or SHIFT-ALT-↓.

Note

When selecting an entire row or column, do not press an arrow key on the numeric keypad—1-2-3/G will not recognize it. You must press an arrow on the separate arrow key keypad.

For example, suppose you want to select row 2 in worksheet A. After moving the cell pointer to any cell in that worksheet and row, press SHIFT-ALT-← or SHIFT-ALT-→. 1-2-3/G highlights the entire row in the worksheet.

To Select a Range of Rows or Columns

To select a range of rows with the keyboard, move the cell pointer to any cell in the first or last row of the range and press SHIFT-ALT-← or SHIFT-ALT-→. (1-2-3/G highlights the current row.) Then, while releasing ALT, but continuing to hold down the SHIFT key, press ↑ or ↓ to add additional rows to the range. 1-2-3/G highlights entire rows as you go.

To select a range of columns, move the cell pointer to any cell in the first or last column of the range and press SHIFT-ALT-↑ or SHIFT-ALT-↓. Then, while releasing the ALT key but continuing to hold down the SHIFT key, press ← or → to add additional columns to the range.

Note

> When selecting a range of rows or columns, do not press an arrow key on the numeric keypad—1-2-3/G will not recognize it. You must press an arrow on the separate arrow key keypad.

To Select an Entire Worksheet

To select an entire worksheet with the keyboard, place the cell pointer in any cell in the worksheet and perform either of the following:

- Press SHIFT-ALT then HOME.
- Press SHIFT-ALT then ↑ or ↓ to select an entire column and continue to hold down the SHIFT and ALT keys. Then select ← or → to select the entire worksheet.

1-2-3/G highlights the current worksheet.

Note

> When selecting an entire worksheet with the keyboard, do not press the HOME or arrow keys on the numeric keypad; if you do, 1-2-3/G will ignore the keypress. Make sure you press these keys on the nonnumeric (gray) keypad.

To Select an Entire Worksheet File

To select the entire worksheet file with the keyboard, press SHIFT-ALT then HOME twice, once to select the current worksheet and the second time to select the entire worksheet file. 1-2-3/G highlights all the worksheets in the file.

Note

> When selecting an entire worksheet file with the keyboard, do not press the HOME key on the numeric keypad; if you do, 1-2-3/G will ignore the key press. Make sure you press the HOME key on the nonnumeric (gray) keypad.

Adding a Range from Another Worksheet File

Suppose you make a selection in one worksheet file and then decide to add a range from another worksheet file to form a collection. After opening the second worksheet file with the File Open command, you can then select a range from that file, just as you would within the current worksheet file. For example, if you are using the mouse, press the right button and drag the pointer across the range. If you are using the keyboard, press ALT-SPACEBAR to activate the Desktop Control menu. Next, select the Window command followed by the appropriate filename from the cascade menu. You can then move the cell pointer to a corner of the range, press the SHIFT key, and move the free cell to the diagonally opposite corner. (See Chapter 2, "Managing the Desktop," for more details on moving between files.)

Modifying a Range Selection

Suppose you have made a range selection and you later decide that you want to increase or decrease its size. This section describes how to modify a selection with the mouse or the keyboard.

With the Mouse

If you have already selected a range and then decide to change its size using the mouse, you can modify the range by clicking on a cell inside the range with the right mouse button. 1-2-3/G assigns the free cell to the cell you've chosen. Then, by holding down the button, you can drag the corner of the range to a new location. Release the button when you arrive at your desired location.

For example, imagine you have chosen the range A:B6..A:D16, as in Figure 1–45, but you then decide to press DETACH (SHIFT-F8) to free the cell pointer so that you can move the cell pointer to another location in the worksheet to do some editing. At this point, you decide that you want to return to the selected range and increase its size to encompass all the numbers in the worksheet. You click on cell A:D16 (the lower-right cell in the range) with the right mouse button, and while continuing to hold down the button, you drag diagonally to cell A:D18. Your screen then looks like Figure 1–46.

Note

The steps for modifying a range in a collection are the same as those outlined here for modifying an independent range, whether you are using the keyboard or the mouse.

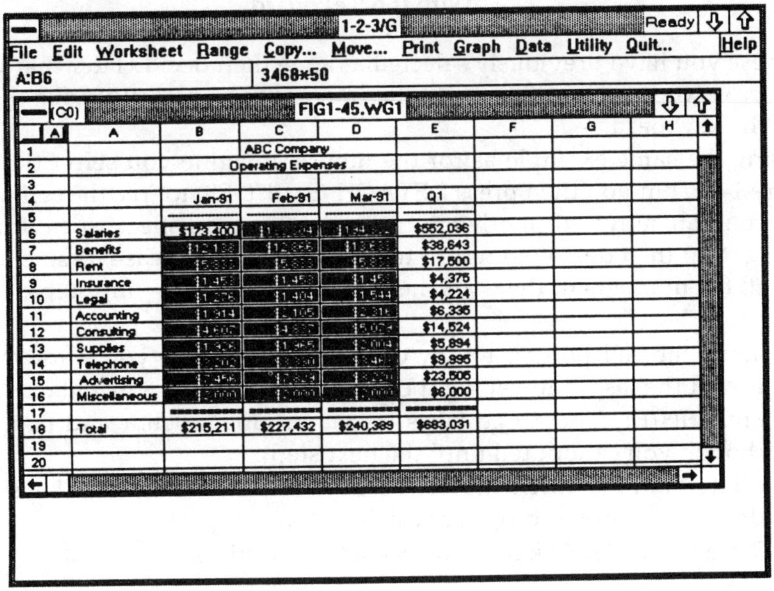

FIGURE 1–45 A selected range

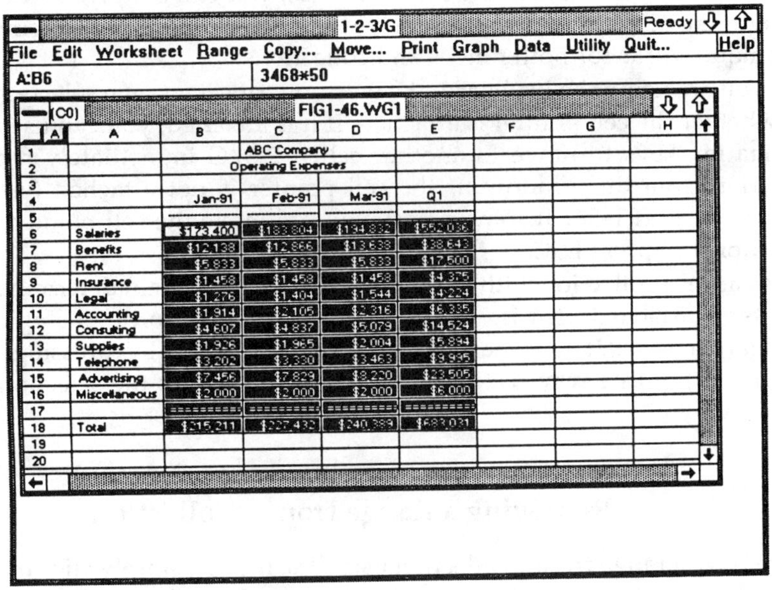

FIGURE 1–46 After expanding the range

With the Keyboard

Suppose you have previously selected a range then decide later that you want to increase or decrease the size of the range. You can easily make the change with the keyboard.

Using the same example as for the mouse, imagine you select the range in Figure 1–45, but you then press DETACH (SHIFT-F8) to free the cell pointer so that you can move to another location in the worksheet to perform some editing. You then decide to return to the range and increase its size to encompass all the numbers in the worksheet. Perform the following steps:

1. Move the cell pointer to any cell inside the range you want to modify, except the last or lower-right cell (cell A:D16 in the current example).
2. Press SHIFT. The range takes on the original anchor and free cells (although you cannot tell until the next step).
3. While holding down the SHIFT key, use the navigation keys to move down two rows and right one column.
4. Release the SHIFT key to complete the selection.

Your screen now looks like Figure 1–46.

Canceling a Range or Collection

Suppose you select a range or collection but then decide to cancel your selection. To cancel the selection with the mouse, you can simply click on any cell outside the selection. 1-2-3/G removes the selection from the window. This technique works for both ranges and collections.

If you are using the keyboard, the way you cancel a range selection depends on whether the cell pointer is attached. If it is attached, you can use any of the navigation keys to move to another cell; 1-2-3/G immediately removes the selection from the window. If the cell pointer is not attached (you pressed DETACH, SHIFT-F8, at some point), you can move the cell pointer inside the selection and press ESC.

To cancel a collection with the keyboard, you must again determine if the cell pointer is attached. If it is, you can cancel the collection by using any of the navigation keys. If it is not attached, then attach it by pressing DETACH (SHIFT-F8). Either way, 1-2-3/G immediately removes the selection from the window.

Removing a Range from a Collection

To remove a range from a collection using the mouse, simply click on the range with the right button. To remove the range with the keyboard, move the cell pointer inside the range and press ESC.

USING GOTO (F5) OR RANGE GOTO WITH SELECTIONS

In 1-2-3/G, Lotus has significantly enhanced the power of the GOTO (F5) key to make it easier to select ranges and collections. This section describes the many ways you can use GOTO (F5) and its counterpart, the Range Goto command, to make selections.

Replacing or Appending to a Selection

As you know, you can use GOTO (F5) or the Range Goto command to jump to a specific location in the current worksheet file or to another worksheet file in memory. You can also use GOTO (F5) and Range Goto to replace or append to a selection.

For example, Figure 1–47 shows a typical dialog box that appears when you press GOTO (F5) after selecting the range A:B6..A:D16 in the worksheet. Suppose you want to *append* the range A:B18..A:D18 to the current selection. To do this, type the range you want to append in the Range(s) text box—in this case **B18..D18**—or select it in the worksheet using the mouse or the keyboard. (As soon as you begin typing or pointing, 1-2-3/G will remove the reference to the current selection from the text box.) Next, click on the "Append to selection" button. Your screen now looks like Figure 1–48. To complete the operation, press ENTER, or click on the OK button. The collection

```
A:B6..A:D16,A:B18..A:D18
```

now appears highlighted in the worksheet.

As another example, suppose you want to use GOTO (F5) or the Range Goto command to *replace* the current selection with a new collection that includes the ranges A1..A4, B1..C5, and D6..D8. To replace the current selection with a new selection, begin by typing the new selection (in this case, **A1..A4,B1..C5,D6..D8**) in the Range(s) text box (you can also highlight them in the worksheet if you prefer). Then, click the Replace selection button in the dialog box and press ENTER. 1-2-3/G displays the newly highlighted collection in the worksheet.

Note

> You can also enter range names in response GOTO (F5). See "Naming Ranges and Collections."

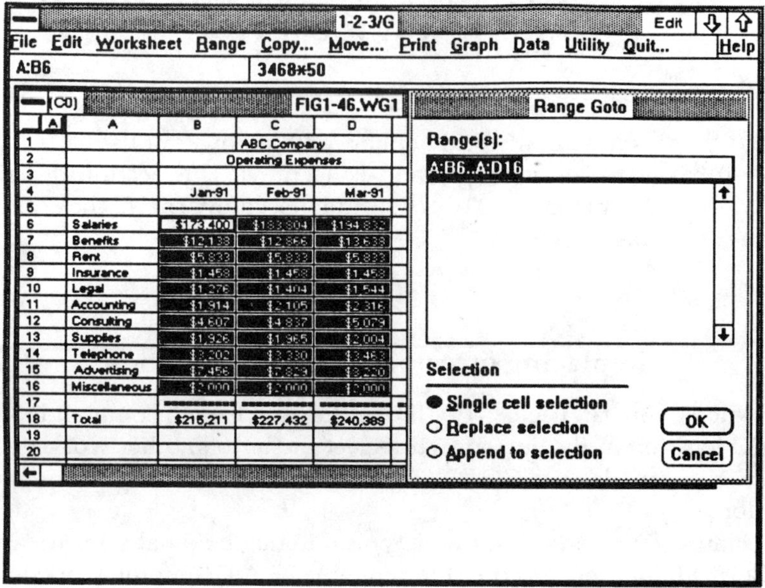

FIGURE 1–47 The GOTO (F5) and Range Goto dialog box

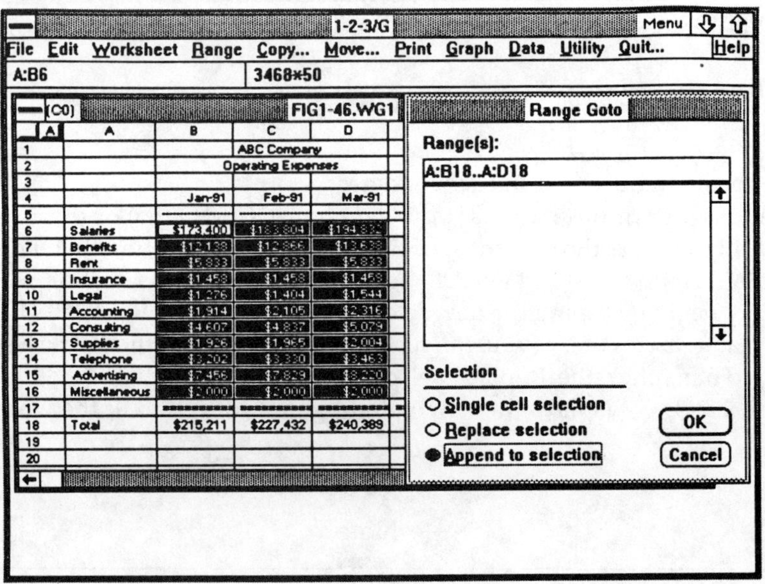

FIGURE 1–48 Appending the range A:B18..A:D18 to the current selection

Because you can accomplish all the above by using the mouse and/or the keyboard, you may be wondering, why would I ever use GOTO (F5) or the Range Goto command when selecting ranges. There are two important reasons:

- Using GOTO (F5) and Range Goto is much easier than using key sequences when selecting entire rows or columns, ranges of rows or columns, entire worksheets, or entire worksheet files.
- In 1-2-3/G macros, the only way to select entire rows or columns, ranges of rows or columns, entire worksheets, or entire worksheet files is by using GOTO (F5) or Range Goto. You cannot use mouse movements or key sequences in these situations (see Chapter 10, "Creating Macros," for more details).

When GOTO (F5) Is Easier than Key Sequences

Here are the cases when using GOTO (F5) or the Range Goto command is easier than using key sequences for selecting ranges or collections:

- **Selecting an Entire Row or Column:** To select an entire row, enter the row number in the Range(s) text box. For example, to select row 1 of the current worksheet, simply enter 1 in the box. Then, click on the Replace selection button and press ENTER. To select an entire column, such as column B of worksheet C, type **C:B** in the Range(s) text box. Of course, you can also append an entire row or column to the current selection by clicking on the Append to selection button.
- **Selecting a Range of Rows or Columns:** To select a range of rows, enter the row numbers separated by periods in the Range(s) text box. For example, to select rows 2 through 6 of the current worksheet, simply enter **2..6**. Then, click on the Replace selection button and press ENTER. To select a range of columns, such as column A through C of worksheet D, type **D:A..D:C** in the Range(s) text box.
- **Selecting an Entire Worksheet:** To select an entire worksheet, enter the worksheet letter followed by a colon in the Range(s) text box. For example, to select worksheet B, type **B:**, click on the Replace selection button, and press ENTER. To select a range of worksheets, for example, worksheets B through D, type **B:..D:**.
- **Selecting an Entire Worksheet File:** To select an entire worksheet file, type the filename in double angle brackets, for example, **<<SALES91>>** (the .WG1 extension is optional). Then, click on the Replace selection button, and press ENTER.

SPECIFYING RANGES DURING COMMANDS

The techniques outlined in the previous sections for selecting ranges can be used in preparation for a command. However, you can also use most of these same techniques to select or modify a range *during* a command.

In Chapter 3 you'll learn about the Range Format command. This command is typical of commands that use ranges and will be used as an example here. This command allows you to change the appearance of numbers in the worksheet. For example, you might use this command to format a cell as Currency 2. With this format, the number that appears in the cell will be displayed with a leading dollar sign, thousands separated by commas, and two places after the decimal. For example, the number 1000 is displayed as $1,000.00. When you select the Range Format command, 1-2-3/G displays the dialog box in Figure 1–49.

Of immediate concern in Figure 1–49 is the Range(s) text box. Most commands that use ranges display a dialog box that contains a text box entitled either Range(s) or a similar name. This text box contains the range or collection to which the command will be applied. If you select a range or collection before selecting a command, the Range(s) text box displays that selection. If you do not make a selection before entering a command, the Range(s) text box shows the selection that defines the current position of the cell pointer.

You can modify the selection that appears in the Range(s) text box for the current command. In fact, 1-2-3/G always gives you an opportunity to do so. For example, if you select the Range Format command, 1-2-3/G displays the dialog box in Figure 1–49. You can then select Currency from the "Category" list box and 1-2-3/G will display the "Decimal places" text box, prompting you for the number of places after the decimal (the default is 2). After you make an

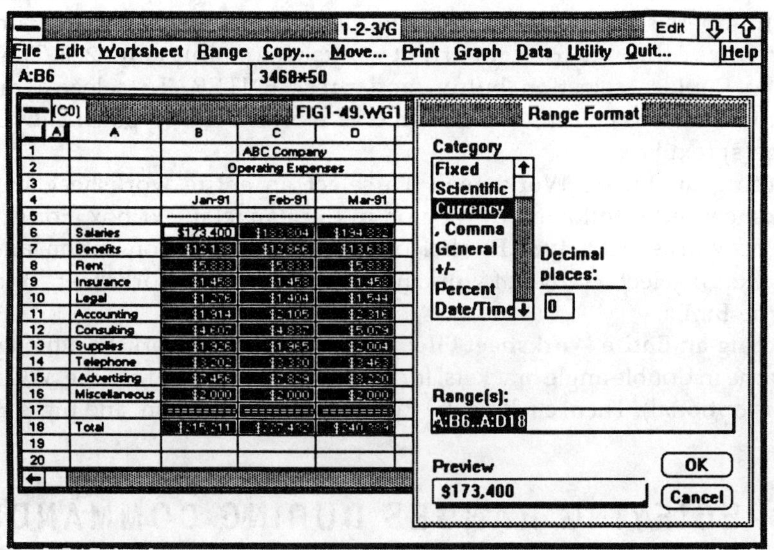

FIGURE 1–49 Range Format is typical of commands that use ranges

entry or confirm the current one in the "Decimal places" text box, 1-2-3/G activates the Range(s) text box, asking you to confirm the current selection before completing the command.

To change the range in the Range(s) text box, you must activate the text box. However, you do not need to sequentially execute the steps in a command to reach the Range(s) text box. In fact, you can activate the text box at any time by pressing TAB to move to it, by pressing ALT-R, or by clicking on the text box. Once the Range(s) text box is activated, you can use any of the following techniques to change the current selection:

- Type a new range, for example A:B6..A:D18, or a collection, for example A:B6..AD18,A:B100..A:D110. As you start typing, 1-2-3/G clears the Range(s) text box to make room for your new entry. (You do not need to include both of the periods in a range specification. For example, the range specification A:B6.A:D18 will work every bit as well as A:B6..A:D18).
- Press any arrow key. 1-2-3/G shrinks the size of the dialog box to display only the Range(s) text and enters POINT mode. However, the current selection remains highlighted in the worksheet and the cell pointer is anchored at this time. You can use the arrow keys to expand or contract the current selection. Or, you can press ESC or BACKSPACE to free the cell pointer (unanchor it). You can then use the arrow keys to move the cell pointer to the beginning of a new range. Next, press period (.) to anchor the cell pointer and use the arrow keys to expand the cell pointer to highlight a new range. When you're ready, press ENTER. 1-2-3/G applies the command to the new range you've selected.
- You can also use the arrow key method to specify a collection. For example, if you press ↓, 1-2-3/G returns you to the worksheet in POINT mode. Press ESC or BACKSPACE to free the cell pointer. Move the cell pointer to a new location, press period (.) to anchor it, and highlight a new range. Then press comma (,). 1-2-3/G returns you to the dialog box. Press ↓ again to return to the worksheet and use the same procedure outlined previously to add a new range to the collection.
- Click the left mouse button on any cell in the worksheet and hold the mouse button down. 1-2-3/G shrinks the size of the dialog box to display only the Range(s) text box. Drag the mouse to highlight a new range and release, 1-2-3/G returns you to the dialog box and shows the new range in the Range(s) text box.
- You can also use the mouse method to build a collection. To do this, click the left mouse button on the worksheet and drag to highlight a new range. When you're ready, release the mouse button. 1-2-3/G returns you to the dialog box and displays the new range you've selected in the Range(s) text box. Now, click and hold the *right* mouse button on any cell in the worksheet. 1-2-3/G adds a comma (,) to the current range specification and shrinks the dialog box to display only the Range(s) text box. Drag to highlight an additional range

for the collection and release. 1-2-3/G returns to the dialog box and displays the new selection in the Range(s) text box.

When you are using the keyboard to modify the current selection in the Range(s) text box, much depends on whether the cell pointer is anchored or unanchored for the command you are using. If only a single cell is included in the current selection, the cell pointer may, or may not, be anchored for a particular command. For example, when you select the Range Format command with only a single cell included in the current selection, the cell pointer is anchored. If the Range(s) text box is active, and you press ↓, 1-2-3/G will expand the current selection to include the cell immediately below the cell pointer. To free the cell pointer to highlight a new range, you must press ESC or BACKSPACE.

Note

> If a multiple-cell range is selected, the cell pointer is always anchored, regardless of the command you select.

On the other hand, the cell pointer is not anchored for commands such as File Print, Print Worksheet, Data Fill, and Data Sort. If a single cell is selected when you enter one of the commands, you can select the Range(s) text box and press any arrow key to return to the worksheet. When you arrive in the worksheet the cell pointer is not anchored, and you can move it anywhere you want, without selecting a range. To anchor the cell pointer in order to select a range, press (.) and use the arrow keys to expand the highlight accordingly.

Tip: Checking a range during a command

> You can use the period (.) key to check the corners of a range during a command. For example, when you select the Range Format command, 1-2-3/G displays the Range Format dialog box. The current selection is displayed in the Range(s) text box. To see what is included in the current selection, activate the Range(s) text box and press period. 1-2-3/G returns you to the worksheet. Press period (.) again. 1-2-3/G moves clockwise to the next corner cell in the current selection. Each time you press period, 1-2-3/G moves clockwise to the next corner in the range. You can use this technique to get an indication of what is included in the current selection before you confirm it for the current command.

NAMING RANGES AND COLLECTIONS

Thus far, all the ranges and collections that you have seen have included cell addresses, such as A:A1..A:B3 (range) and A:A10..B:20,A:A30..B:40 (collection). 1-2-3/G lets you assign names to ranges and collections and to use those names in commands and formulas. The advantage of using range and collection names is that they are much easier to remember than cell addresses.

Creating a Named Range or Collection

To create a named range or collection, you use the Range Name Create command. 1-2-3/G then shows a dialog box as in Figure 1–50. (If this is the first range or collection name in the worksheet file, you won't see any names in the list box.)

You can enter a name of up to 15 characters in the Range name text box (see "Range Name Rules"). After you type a name, for example **LEGAL**, and press TAB or ENTER, 1-2-3/G highlights the current selection in the Range(s) text box. You can then accept the selection or enter a new one using the techniques outlined in the previous section.

For example, Figure 1–51 shows how your screen appears after you enter the name LEGAL and select the range A:B10..A:D10. Press ENTER or click on the OK button to complete the command. You can then use the range or collection name in place of cell addresses in your formulas. For example, entering the formula @SUM(LEGAL) in a worksheet is now equivalent to entering @SUM(A:B10..A:D10).

Note to Release 2.2 Users

In 1-2-3 Release 2.2, when you create a range name such as LEGAL, 1-2-3 immediately substitutes that name in all your existing formulas in place of cell addresses. For example, @SUM(B10..D10) automatically becomes @SUM(LEGAL). In 1-2-3/G, however, no substitution takes place. Instead, 1-2-3/G uses a range name only when you explicitly enter that name in a formula. This does not affect your formulas in the least. They will continue to reference the correct range.

As you review the list box in Figure 1–51, notice that the type of range name appears in parentheses following the range name. Three types of names appear in the list: Range, which identifies a range name; Coll, which identifies a collection; and, in addition, 1-2-3/G displays Ref when a range name refers to another worksheet file. Further, although it does not appear in the list in Figure 1–51, there is a fourth type of range name, Undef. The Undef abbreviation

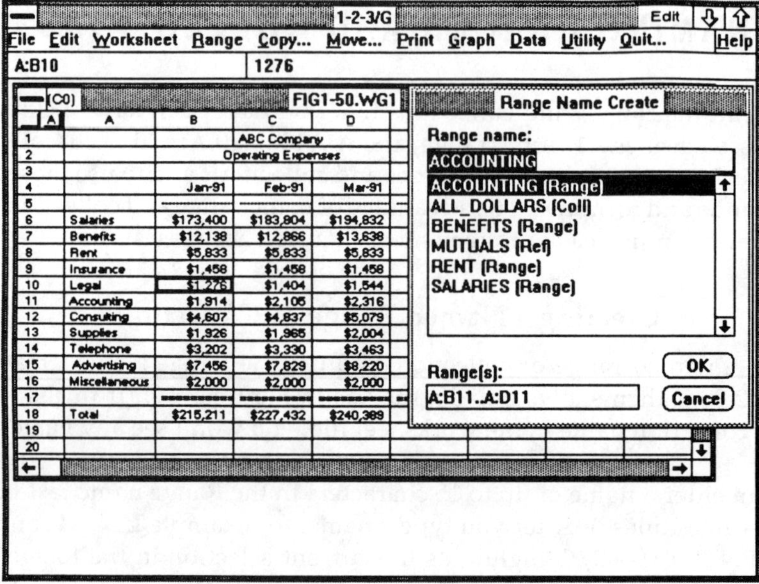

FIGURE 1–50 The Range Name Create dialog box

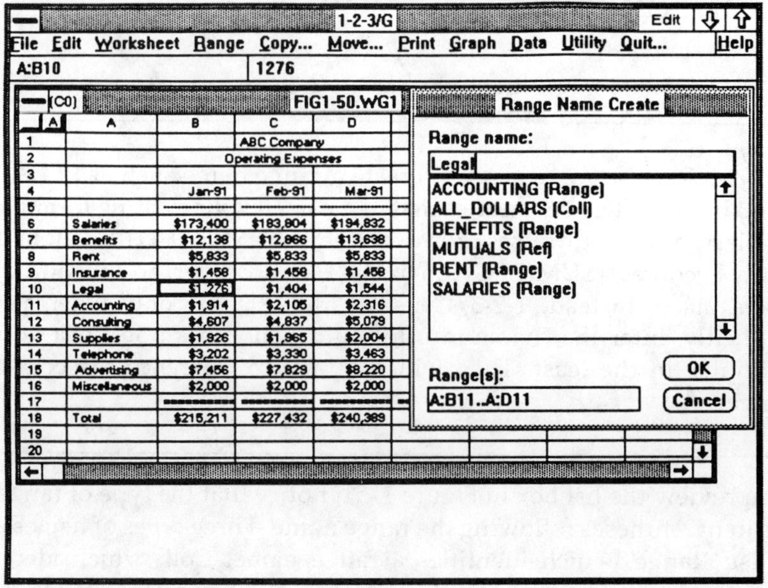

FIGURE 1–51 The Range Name list box

indicates an undefined range name, which is a range name without cell coordinates. See "Using Undefined Range Names" later in this chapter for more information on this.

Because two worksheet files are involved, setting up a Ref type range name bears a bit more explanation. For example, imagine you have the worksheet file in Figure 1–51 open on the desktop along with another worksheet file called MUTUALS.WG1. (See Chapter 2 for more about opening multiple files on the desktop.) To set up a range name in the current file (Figure 1–51) that refers to a range in the MUTUAL.WG1 files, select the Range Name Create command. 1-2-3/G displays the Range Name Create dialog box and prompts you for a range name. Type the name **MUTUALS**, or another name of your choosing, and press ENTER. 1-2-3/G activates the Range(s) text box prompting you for a range to apply the name to.

With the Range(s) text box active, click on the title bar of the MUTUALS.WG1 file to activate it and highlight the range A:B10..A:D10 in that file. 1-2-3/G places the file and range reference <<MUTUALS.WG1>>A:B10..A:D10 in the Range(s) text box. Finally, press ENTER to complete the Range Name Create command. 1-2-3/G returns to READY mode in the worksheet file shown in Figure 1–51. At that point, you can enter the formula @SUM(MUTUALS) in any cell in the file in Figure 1–51 and 1-2-3/G will record the sum of the values in the range A:B10..A:B16 of the MUTUALS.WG1 file in that cell.

Note

> For a complete explanation of using file references, for example <<MUTUALS.WG1>>, to refer to ranges in other files, see Chapter 2, "Managing the Desktop."

Range Name Rules

Here are some general rules that apply to creating range names:

- Range names can be up to 15 characters in length. If you enter a name that is longer than 15 characters, 1-2-3/G issues an error message warning you that the name you've chosen is too long.
- You can include spaces, periods, underscores, or any other LCS character (see Appendix B) in a range name, but it is wise to avoid characters such as +—* / & > < @ and #, which may cause you (and 1-2-3/G) to confuse a range name that resembles formulas with actual formulas.
- Do not use a number as the first character of a range name. If you do, 1-2-3/G will not allow you to use that range name in a formula. If you try, 1-2-3/G will issue an error message.

- Do not assign names that resemble cell addresses, row numbers, or column letters. For example, if you assign names such as Q1, 1990, and BT, 1-2-3/G will assume you mean a cell address, a row, and column letter when you enter these addresses in formulas.
- @Function names (such as @AVG) and macro key names (such as GOTO) are also inappropriate for range names (see Chapter 6 and Chapter 10).

Using Named Ranges

Once you have named a range or collection, you can use that name in place of cell addresses when you enter formulas and when you respond to commands. For example, if you have assigned the name CASH_FLOW to the range A:A1..A:H50, you can use that name for the print range when you use the Print Printer command to print the data in your worksheet.

When a named range defines a single cell, you can use the name anywhere you would use a cell address in a formula, for example, +Q1_SALES/4 or +COGS/AVG_PRICE. When a name defines a multiple-cell range or a collection, you can use the name in place of a range or collection, for example, @SUM(FEB_EXPENSES) or @MIN(SALES_89_AND_90). As mentioned, you must name a collection before you can use it in a formula.

Note

If you use a multiple-cell range or collection in a formula where 1-2-3/G expects a single-cell range, that formula evaluates to ERR.

Tip:Using range names with GOTO (F5) and Range Goto

When you press GOTO (F5) or select the Range Goto command to jump to a location in the worksheet file, 1-2-3/G displays a dialog box that includes a list of range names in the current worksheet, as in Figure 1–52. When you highlight a range name and press ENTER, or double-click on the name, 1-2-3/G moves the cell pointer to the first cell in the range.

If you have more than one file in memory (you used the File Open command), 1-2-3/G shows the names of the other files in double-angle brackets (<< >>) at the top of the range name list. For example, in Figure 1–52, the file MUTUALS.WG1 is also active in memory. To see the named ranges in that file, highlight <<MUTUALS.WG1>> in the list and press ENTER, or double-click on the name. 1-2-3/G displays a list of range names in that file and the names of other active files. Highlight the range name you want to jump to and press

ENTER, or double-click on the name, and 1-2-3/G moves the cell pointer to the first cell in the range in that file.

Using Undefined Ranges

In 1-2-3/G, you can use *undefined range names* in your formulas. An undefined range name is one that has no defined cell coordinates. If you enter a formula with an undefined range name in it, 1-2-3/G lets you complete the formula, but the formula evaluates to ERR until you define the range name using the Range Name Create command.

For example, suppose you enter the formula +TOTAL_SALES/12, but you haven't yet defined TOTAL_SALES. The formula evaluates to ERR until you use the Range Name Create command to assign a cell address to TOTAL_SALES.

The advantage of using undefined range names is that you can create formulas using undefined names, and then supply the coordinates later. Without having to stop and define each range name before using it, you can be much more fluid in developing your worksheets.

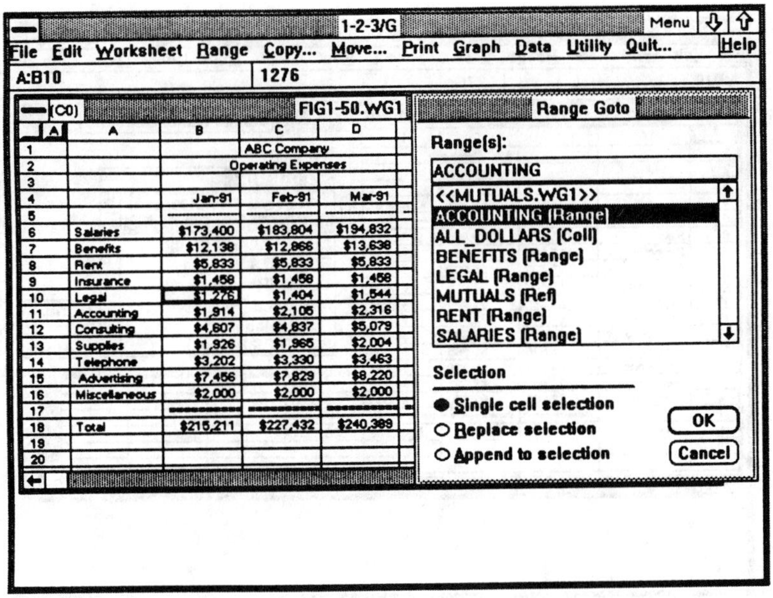

FIGURE 1–52 Using GOTO (F5) and Range Goto with range names

In 1-2-3/G, you can also create an undefined range name by breaking the link between a range name and its cell coordinates. To do this, you use the Range Name Undefine command. When you select this command, your screen appears as in Figure 1–53. 1-2-3/G displays in the list box the names of defined ranges in the current worksheet file and the names of other active files appear in double-angle brackets (<< >>). To undefine a range name, highlight its name in the list box and press ENTER or click on the OK button. When you undefine a range name, 1-2-3/G unlinks the range name from its cell coordinates, and the formulas containing the range name now evaluate to ERR, both in the current file or in other active files.

To undefine a range name in another active file, highlight the name of the file that contains the range name and press ENTER, or double-click on the filename. 1-2-3/G displays a list of defined range names in that file, along with the names of other active files. Highlight the range name you want to undefine and press ENTER, or double-click on the name, and 1-2-3/G undefines the name in that file. The formulas in that file that contain the range name now evaluate to ERR, both in that file and in other active files.

Using NAME (F3)

Suppose you are building a formula, and you want to use a range name in the formula. In 1-2-3/G, you can paste a range name in a formula by pressing NAME (F3) and selecting the range name from the list. For example, Figure

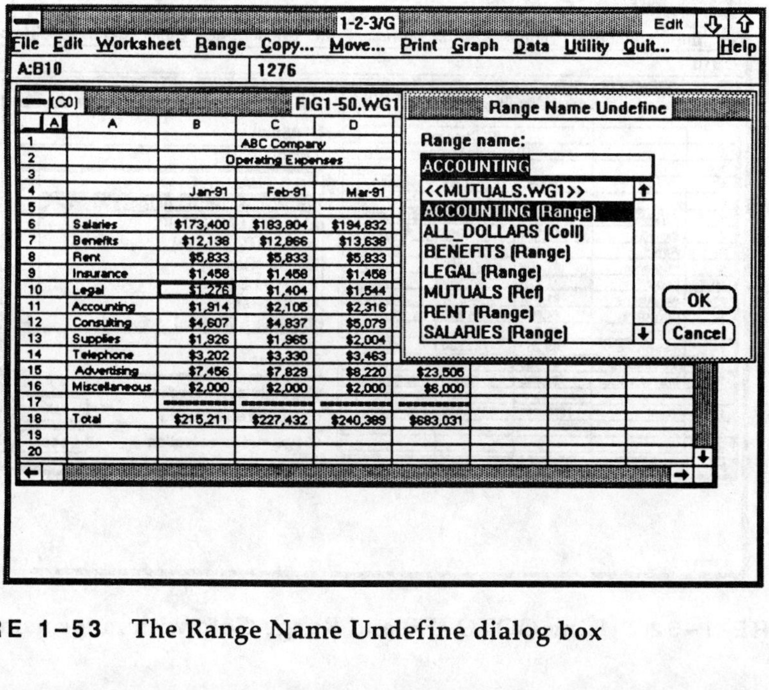

FIGURE 1–53 The Range Name Undefine dialog box

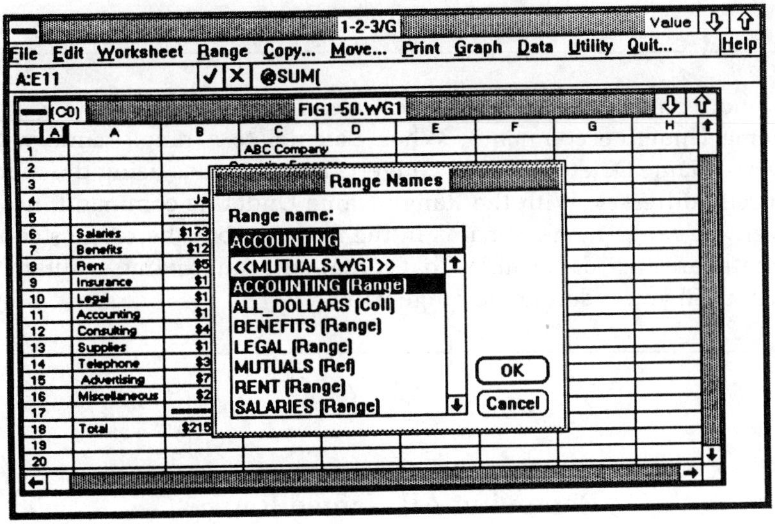

FIGURE 1–54 Selecting a named range

1–54 shows a typical example of what your screen looks like when you type @SUM and press NAME (F3). To select a name to paste into your formula, highlight the name in the list and press ENTER, or double-click on the name. 1-2-3/G appends the name to the end of your formula.

Changing Named Ranges

If you have assigned a name to a range or collection but decide later that you want to change its assigned coordinates, select the Range Name Create command. When 1-2-3/G displays a list of range names, highlight the name you want to change. As you move the highlight through the list box, 1-2-3/G shows the dimensions of the range or collection in the Range(s) text box. Enter the new dimensions you want in the Range(s) text box and press ENTER or click on the OK button.

Deleting Named Ranges

To remove a single range name from the range name list, use the Range Name Delete command. When you select this command, 1-2-3/G displays a list of range names in a dialog box similar to the one in Figure 1–54. Highlight a name in the list and press ENTER.

Note

Do not confuse the Range Name Delete command with the Range Name Undefine command. When you delete a range name with Range Name Delete, 1-2-3/G converts any formulas using the name to cell addresses. With the Range Name Undefine command, however, the range name remains in the formula, but the range's coordinates are erased. Formulas that contain the range name evaluate to ERR until you redefine the range name.

Removing All Named Ranges

Once in a while, you may want to remove all the named ranges in the current worksheet file and start over with a clean slate. The Range Name Reset command deletes all the named ranges in the current worksheet file. For formulas that contain range names, 1-2-3/G substitutes cell coordinates in place of the names. For example, if a formula reads @SUM(LEGAL) before the command and the range name LEGAL is assigned to A:B10..A:D10, the formula reads @SUM(A:B10..A:D10) after the command.

There is no confirmation step for the Range Name Reset command. Once you select the command, the range names in the current worksheet file are gone. If you want to reverse the effect of the Range Name Reset command, press ALT-BACKSPACE to activate undo and restore the range names to the worksheet file.

Inserting a Range Name Table into a Worksheet

Imagine that you have created several ranges and collections in a worksheet file, and you're having trouble remembering what cell coordinates you've assigned them to. You can place a list of the current range and collection names in the worksheet using the Range Name Table command. When you execute this command, 1-2-3/G inserts a table in the worksheet that lists each range and collection name in alphabetical order, followed by its cell coordinates and type—either Range (for ranges) or Coll (for collections). (Undefined range names do not appear in the table.) For example, Figure 1–55 shows some typical results from selecting the Range Name Table command and choosing cell A:H1 as the starting location for the table. Note that columns H and I were widened in order to see the full width of the entries that 1-2-3/G made in the worksheet (see Chapter 3, "Formatting the Worksheet," for information on widening columns).

When you use the Range Name Table command, be sure to choose a starting location that has enough empty cells below it to accommodate the table. When 1-2-3/G places the table in the worksheet, it does not stop if any data is in the way—you can easily overwrite needed information. If you face this problem, press ALT-BACKSPACE to activate undo and reverse the effect of the Range Name Table command.

Using Labels to Name Ranges

You can use the Range Name Labels command to define range names for single-cell ranges using the labels in contiguous cells. When you select the command, 1-2-3/G presents a dialog box with the following menu options: Right, Left, Up, Down, and Intersect. If you want to use the labels in a column of cells to name the cells to the left or right, you select Left or Right. Likewise, if you want to use the labels in a row of cells to name the cells above or below, you use Up or Down. You use the Intersect option when you want to combine the labels from the first row and column of a range to name the cells within the range.

For example, suppose you want to use the labels in column A of Figure 1–56 to name the dollar amounts in column B. When you select the Range Name

1-2-3/G: (56.6) Ready

File Edit Worksheet Range Copy... Move... Print Graph Data Utility Quit... Help

A:H1 'ACCOUNTING

(D1) FIG1-53.WG1

A	H	I	J	K	L	M
1	ACCOUNTING	A:B11..A:D11	Range			
2	ADVERTISING	A:B15..A:D15	Range			
3	ALL DOLLARS	A:B6..A:E16,A:B18..A:E18	Coll			
4	BENEFITS	A:B7..A:D7	Range			
5	CONSULTING	A:B12..A:D12	Range			
6	INSURANCE	A:B9..A:D9	Range			
7	LEGAL	A:B10..A:D10	Range			
8	MISCELLANEOUS	A:B16..A:D16	Range			
9	RENT	A:B8..A:D8	Range			
10	SALARIES	A:B6..A:D6	Range			
11	SUPPLIES	A:B13..A:D13	Range			
12	TELEPHONE	A:B14..A:D14	Range			
13						
14						
15						
16						
17						
18						
19						
20						
21						

FIGURE 1–55 Some sample results from the Range Name Table command

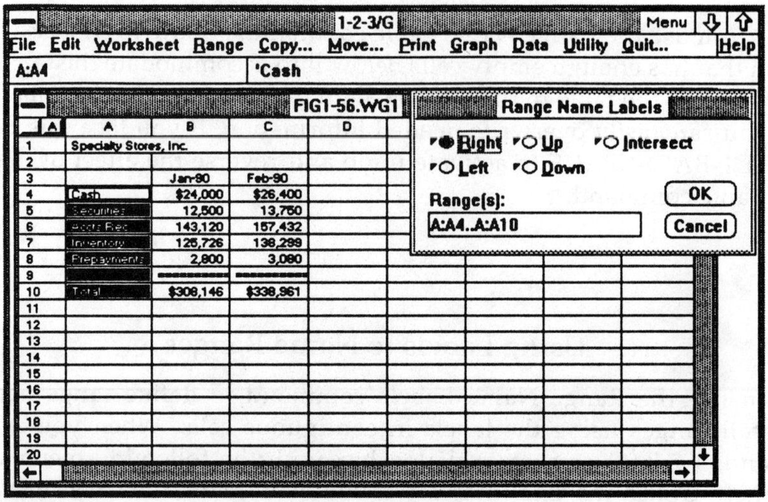

FIGURE 1–56 **Using the Range Name Labels Right command to define single-cell ranges**

Labels command, 1-2-3/G displays a dialog box like the one in the figure. Choose the Right command, then select the range A:A3..A:A9 in the Range(s) text box. Press ENTER or click on the OK icon to complete the command. 1-2-3/G creates the following range names:

Range name	Cell
CASH	A:B5
SECURITIES	A:B6
ACCTS REC	A:B7
INVENTORY	A:B8
PREPAYMENTS	A:B9

In 1-2-3/G, you can use the Intersect option to define range names by combining the asset names in column A of Figure 1–56 with the dates (labels) in row 3. To do this, select the Range Name Labels Intersect command, specify the range A:A3..A:C10 in the Range(s) text box, and press ENTER. Here are the range names that 1-2-3/G creates:

Range name	Cell
JAN-90_CASH	A:B4
JAN-90_SECURITI	A:B5
JAN-90_ACCTS RE	A:B6
JAN-90_INVENTOR	A:B7
JAN-90_PREPAYME	A:B8
JAN-90_TOTAL	A:B10
IFEB-90_CASH	A:C4
FEB-90_SECURITI	A:C5
FEB-90_ACCTS RE	A:C6
FEB-90_INVENTOR	A:C7
FEB-90_PREPAYME	A:C8
FEB-90_TOTAL	A:C10

Notice that 1-2-3/G automatically truncates range names that would exceed the 15-character limit.

USING BOUND TO RESTRICT POINTER MOVEMENT

By pressing BOUND (SHIFT-F4), you can restrict cell pointer movement to a specific area within a worksheet file. The area that movement is limited to is determined by your current selection when you press BOUND. Although BOUND is most commonly used with macros, it is mentioned here to give you an idea of how you might use it to automate the process of entering data in a worksheet file.

Before you press BOUND (SHIFT-F4), you should begin by selecting a range or collection that you want to limit cell pointer movement to. For example, Figure 1–57 shows a simple worksheet for entering checking account information. Because you want to limit pointer movement to the date, amount, and remark columns, you select the collection A:B2..A:C10,A:E2..A:E10.

Once you have selected the collection, you press BOUND (SHIFT-F4) to limit pointer movement to the appropriate columns. When you press BOUND, 1-2-3/G displays BOUND for the status indicator. In addition, if the cell pointer is detached, as in Figure 1–57, 1-2-3/G places the cell pointer in the top left visible cell of the last range you highlighted for the collection. If the cell pointer is attached, it remains in its current position. At this point, you can use the cell pointer movement keys outlined in Table 1–17 to move within the collection.

Here are some important points to remember about cell pointer movement when BOUND is on:

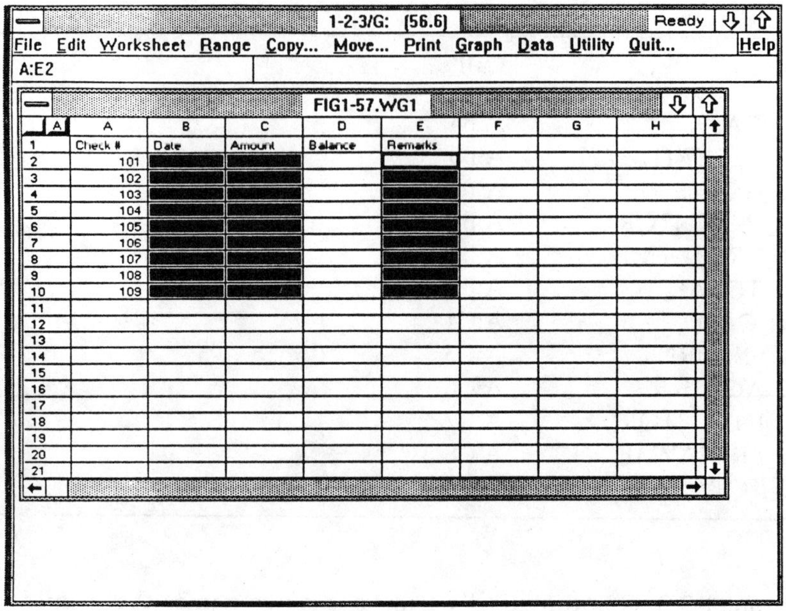

FIGURE 1–57 **Before pressing BOUND (SHIFT-F4) to restrict cell pointer movement**

- Movement is row by row within the selection. For example, if the cell pointer is located in cell A:B2 (the first cell) of Figure 1–57, pressing → or ENTER causes the cell pointer to move to the cell immediately to the right, cell A:C2. Pressing either key again causes the cell pointer to move to cell A:B3.
- If you are moving within a range and you reach the beginning or end of the range, the cell pointer moves to the opposite end of the range.
- If you are moving within a collection and you reach the end of a range (for example, A:C10 in Figure 1–57), the cell pointer moves to the beginning of the next range (A:E2). If the cell pointer reaches the first or last cell of the collection, it moves to the opposite end of the collection.

Here are some restrictions that apply when BOUND is on:

- You cannot detach the cell pointer with DETACH (SHIFT-F8).
- If, while you are editing a cell, you enter Point mode (for example, you use the Move command to copy a cell to another location), you can move outside of the current selection. When pointing ends, however, you are once again restricted to moving with the current selection.

Note

> BOUND (SHIFT-F4) is a toggle key. After pressing BOUND once to restrict cell pointer movement, press it again to free the cell pointer. You can also free the cell pointer by clicking on any cell outside the current selection or pressing GOTO (F5).

Table 1-17 BOUND (SHIFT-F4) Movement Keys

Key	Action
→ or ENTER	Moves to the next cell, row by row.
← or SHIFT-ENTER	Moves to the previous cell, row by row.
↓ or ↑	Moves the cell pointer up or down a row in the current column.
TAB or SHIFT-TAB	Moves clockwise or counterclockwise to the next corner of the current range.
HOME	Moves to the first cell of the current range.
CTRL-HOME	Moves to the first cell of the first range in a collection.
PGDN	Moves to the first cell in the next range in a collection.
PGUP	Moves to the last cell in the previous range in a collection.
CTRL-PGDN or CTRL-PGUP	Moves to the same cell in the next or previous worksheet in a 3-D range.

ANNOTATING YOUR WORKSHEETS

As you use 1-2-3/G, you'll soon find that remembering the assumptions that go into your worksheets can be quite difficult. To help get around this problem, 1-2-3/G includes the Note utility, which allows you to attach notes to cells and ranges. The Note utility operates in its own window. Therefore, you can print your worksheets without printing your notes. In 1-2-3/G, you can attach notes of up to 512 characters in length to cells and named ranges. Each cell or range name can have up to four notes.

Note

> You cannot attach notes to a cell address or to a collection, even if you have named the collection.

To create, edit, delete, and list notes, you use the Utility Note command. When you select this command, 1-2-3/G displays the Note utility, as shown in Figure 1–58. Notice that when the Note utility is active, 1-2-3/G displays a new menu in the Menu bar. The sections that follow describe how to use Note utility menu options as well as all the other elements of the Note utility window.

Creating and Editing Notes

To enter a new note for a cell, begin by selecting the cell in the worksheet. Next, choose the Utility Note command followed by the Note option. 1-2-3/G displays a blank text box for you to enter a new note. At this point, you can type the note and move within the text box using the keys outlined in "Editing the Contents of a Text Box" above.

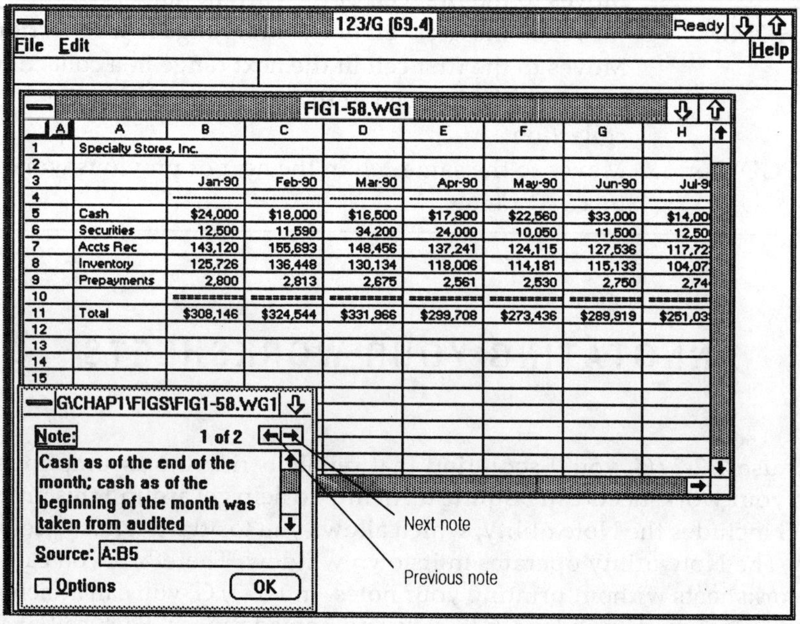

FIGURE 1–58 The Note utility with a sample note for cell A:B5

Suppose you want to attach another note to a cell. The arrow icons above the top right edge of the Note text box let you use the mouse to cycle through the notes attached to a cell. For example, to move from one note to the next, click on the → icon identified in Figure 1–58. To return to the previous note, click on the ← icon. If you are using the keyboard, press PGUP to go to the next note and PGDN to return to the previous note.

Note

> When you attach a note to a cell, 1-2-3/G displays an *N* at the left of the Window's Title bar when you locate the cell pointer on the cell. Note that the *N* does not appear when the Note utility is active.

If you want to view the notes for another cell, choose the Source option and select the cell in the worksheet. For example, suppose you want to view the notes for cell A:B7. If you are using the keyboard, select the Source option then move the cell pointer to that cell. 1-2-3/G instantly shows the first note for the cell in the Notes text box. If you are using the mouse, select the Source option and click on the cell to see its notes.

Entering a note for a named range is nearly identical to entering a note for a cell. After selecting Utility Note, choose the Source option and enter the range name in the Source text box. 1-2-3/G then displays a blank text box for you to enter text. To see the notes for another range, enter its name in the Source text box.

Accepting or Canceling Notes

If you have completed entering your cell notes, select the OK button to return to the worksheet. 1-2-3/G removes the Note utility from the screen.

If, on the other hand, you have entered a note but decide that you don't want to keep the note, perform any of the following:

- Press ESC as many times as are necessary to return to the worksheet.
- Press CTRL-BREAK.
- Select Close from the Window Control menu. You activate the Window Control menu with the mouse by clicking on the icon resembling a space bar in the upper left corner of the window. To activate the menu using the keyboard, press ALT- — (minus).
- Press CTRL-F4

Tip:Using name (F3) to select a range name for attaching a note

When you want to enter or edit a range name note, you can have 1-2-3/G automatically enter the range name for you in the Source text box. Begin by selecting the Utility Note Source command. Next, press NAME (F3) to see a list of range names in the current worksheet file. Highlight a range name from the list and press ENTER, or click on the OK button. 1-2-3/G copies the range name to the Source text box. You can then enter or edit the range name note as you normally would.

Expanding the Note Utility

By selecting the Options command in the Note utility, you can have 1-2-3/G instantly expand the utility to list all the cells and range names that have notes attached to them. For example, Figure 1–59 shows how the screen appears when you click on the Options box to expand the Note utility in Figure 1–58. Notice that part of each note appears to the right of the cell address in the list. If a cell or range name has more than one note attached to it, 1-2-3/G displays one entry in the list for each note. For example, in Figure 1–59, cell A:B5 has two notes attached to it and, therefore, has two entries in the list.

To browse through notes in the current file, you move the highlight through the list. 1-2-3/G changes the contents of the Note text box as you go. For example, if you click on the note for cell A:C6 in the list in Figure 1–59, 1-2-3/G displays the note for that cell in the Note text box.

Note

Because 1-2-3/G lists your notes in alphabetical order, range notes usually appear after cell notes. Thus, to see your range notes, you may need to scroll to the bottom of the notes list, as in Figure 1–60.

Deleting a Note

To delete a cell or range note, highlight the note in the list and select Options, if you haven't done so already, and then select the Delete command button. 1-2-3/G instantly removes the note from the list. If you have entered more than

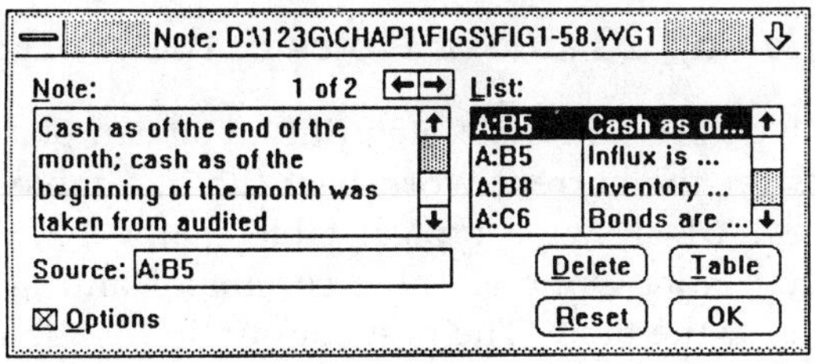

FIGURE 1–59 Note utility expanded

one note for a cell or range name and you delete one of its notes, any notes that follow the deleted note are shifted up by one.

Note

If you accidentally delete a note, you press ALT-BACKSPACE to use the undo feature to restore the note.

Deleting all Notes in the Worksheet File

To delete all the cell and range notes in the current worksheet file, select the Reset option from the Note utility. When you select this option, 1-2-3/G displays a Yes/No confirmation box informing you that all notes in the current file will be deleted. If you select Yes, 1-2-3/G clears all the notes in the notes list, and you cannot restore them with undo.

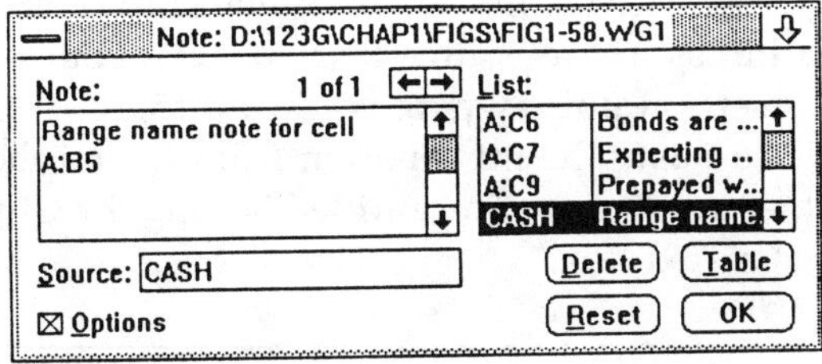

FIGURE 1–60 A range name note

Placing a Table of Notes in the Worksheet

By using the Table option in the Note utility, you can place a list of all the cell and range notes for the current worksheet file in a table in a worksheet. For example, Figure 1-61 shows a typical table that 1-2-3/G creates when you choose the Utility Note Options Table command and select cell A:J1 as the starting location for the table. The first column in the table contains either the cell address or the range name to which the note is attached. (Column J was widened in order to see the full width of the range names. See Chapter 3, "Formatting the Worksheet," for information on widening columns.) The second column in the table contains the cell and range notes themselves in the form of long labels.

Leaving the Note Utility Temporarily

Suppose you are entering a cell note in the text box and you decide to temporarily leave the Note utility to return to the worksheet to check on the contents of a cell or do some editing. If you select a cell in the worksheet, 1-2-3/G inactivates the Note utility. To reactivate the Note utility and complete your cell note, click anywhere in the Note utility window or press NEXT WINDOW (CTRL-F6) to move to it. If you are using the keyboard, select the Window command from the Desktop Control menu and choose the Note utility from the cascade menu. (You activate the Window Control menu with the keyboard by pressing ALT-SPACEBAR. See Chapter 2 for more on managing windows.)

TIP: Editing notes using the clipboard

You can use the clipboard to edit your cell and range notes. For example, suppose you have attached a note to a cell and then decide that you want to move part of the text to another cell note. To cut text from the note and place it in the clipboard, highlight the text in the text box and press SHIFT-DEL. Then, move to the target note (enter the new cell address in the Source text box). To complete the operation, place the insertion point where you want to insert the text, and press SHIFT-INS to paste the information from the clipboard to the target note. See the previous section entitled "Using the Clipboard to Edit the Contents of a Text Box."

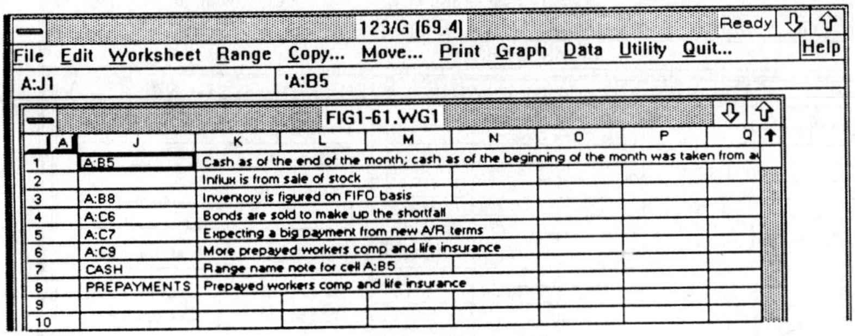

	J	K
1	A:B5	Cash as of the end of the month; cash as of the beginning of the month was taken from a
2		Influx is from sale of stock
3	A:B8	Inventory is figured on FIFO basis
4	A:C6	Bonds are sold to make up the shortfall
5	A:C7	Expecting a big payment from new A/R terms
6	A:C9	More prepayed workers comp and life insurance
7	CASH	Range name note for cell A:B5
8	PREPAYMENTS	Prepayed workers comp and life insurance

FIGURE 1–61 Creating a list of cell and range name notes

SEARCHING AND REPLACING DATA

In 1-2-3/G, you can use the Range Search command to search for characters in cells that contain labels or formulas. You can search through a single- or multiple-worksheet range or collection. You can even search across multiple files, provided all the files are active in memory.

When you choose the Range Search command, 1-2-3/G displays a dialog box as in Figure 1–62. For the Range(s) box, make a selection using the techniques outlined in "Selecting Ranges and Collections" above. For example, to search all of worksheet A, click on the Worksheet selector button, or type **A:** in the text box. To search the entire worksheet file, click on the worksheet file selector button, or type **A:..IV:**.

In the Search for box, enter the string to search for. The string can be either text or numbers, but it cannot exceed 512 characters.

Note

> 1-2-3/G does not perform a case-sensitive search unless you turn off the Any case check box.

Next, enter the search type. Select one of the following based on the data you want to search:

- **Formulas:** Searches cells with formulas for the search string (the default)
- **Labels:** Searches cells with labels for the search string

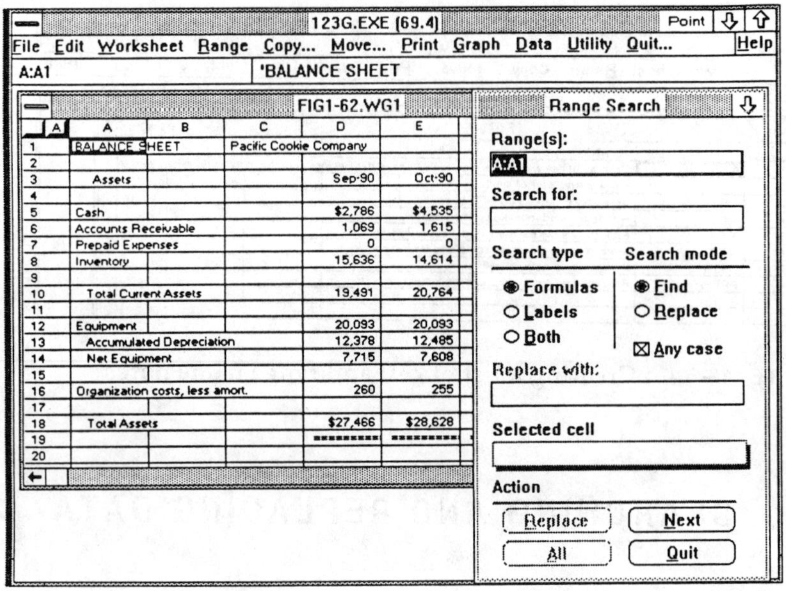

FIGURE 1–62 The Range Search dialog box

- **Both:** Searches cells with labels or formulas for the search string

After selecting a search type, choose a search mode—Find or Replace. If you select Find, you can have 1-2-3/G start the search by selecting Next from the Action buttons. 1-2-3/G searches the range you selected and when it finds a cell that contains the search string, it displays the address and contents of the cell in the Selected cell box. It also moves the cell pointer to that cell. To search for the next occurrence of the search string, select the Next button again. If 1-2-3/G does not find the search string in the remainder of the search range, it displays a "No more matching strings" error message box. Pressing ESC or ENTER, or clicking on the OK button, returns 1-2-3/G to Ready mode, leaving the cell pointer where the search ended.

If you select Replace for the search mode, enter a replace string in the Replace with text box. Next, select one of the following Action buttons:

- **Replace:** Replaces the current occurrence of search string with the replace string and searches for the next occurrence of the search string.
- **All:** Replaces all occurrences of the search string with the replace string in the remainder of the search range.
- **Next:** Searches for the next occurrence of the search string *without* replacing the contents of the current occurrence

- **Quit:** Returns to Ready mode without replacing the search string, and places the cell pointer in the cell containing the search string.

If 1-2-3/G is in Replace mode and it reaches the end of the search range without finding the search string, it responds as it does in Find mode. That is, it displays a "No more matching strings" error message. To return to Ready mode, press ESC or ENTER, or click on the OK button. This leaves the cell pointer where the search concluded.

Note

You can easily undo the effect of replacing a search string. After completing the Range Search command, press ALT-BACKSPACE to activate undo. 1-2-3/G undoes any replacements you may have made. Be aware, however, that it does not return the cell pointer to its original position.

Table 1–18 shows some examples of the kinds of search strings 1-2-3/G can find and replace. If you use Range Search to replace all or part of a formula, be sure to check the results of the command. 1-2-3/G does not stop to warn you when replacing a formula results in ERR. By taking a moment to check the results of the command, you may save yourself significant work later.

Although 1-2-3/G's Range Search command is more powerful than in any previous release of 1-2-3, it is still incapable of performing some standard search tasks. Here is a list of some of the things that 1-2-3/G's Range Search cannot do:

- **Search backward:** You can only search forward in 1-2-3/G.
- **Search for numbers that are not included in formulas:** 1-2-3/G can search labels and formulas, but it cannot search values. Therefore, it cannot find a value, such as the number 100, when it is alone in a cell.
- **Search for formula results:** 1-2-3/G cannot find a value or label that is the result of a formula. For example, suppose you place the formula @SUM(B1..B4) in cell B5, and it displays the value 100. You then enter a search string of 100. When 1-2-3/G searches through the worksheet, it encounters the formula @SUM(B1..B4) in cell B5, not 100, and skips over the cell.

Table 1–18 Some Sample Search and Replace Strings

String type	Search string	Replace string
Character strings	A/R	Accounts Receivable
Numbers in label form	1990	'1991
Range names	CASHOUT	CASHIN
Range addresses	A10..C:A10	REVENUES
Parts of formulas	@CELL	@CELLPOINTER
	+C6+.025	+C6+POINTS
Whole formulas	+C:D4	+C:D5
	+A10+B:A10+C:A10	@SUM(A10..B:A10)

SAVING AND RETRIEVING FILES

When you have completed your work on the current worksheet file, you must decide whether you want to save the file so that you can access it again later. Because 1-2-3/G does not automatically save the file for you, if you erase the current worksheet file or leave 1-2-3/G without saving it, your changes to the file are lost. This is actually convenient when you have made changes to a worksheet file and you don't want to save them. However, the majority of the time you will want to save your work.

To save a file in 1-2-3/G, you use the File Save command. When you select this command, 1-2-3/G displays a dialog box as in Figure 1–63.

As you've undoubtedly noticed by now, when you start 1-2-3/G for the first time, it automatically assigns the name SHEET.WG1 to the first worksheet file and displays the name in the title bar at the top of the window. If you create another new file with the File New command, 1-2-3/G assigns it the name SHEET1.WG1. The next new file is assigned the name SHEET2.WG1, and so on.

When you select the File Save command, rather than accept the filename that 1-2-3/G automatically assigns, you can enter your own more descriptive filename in the File name text box. If, on the other hand, you retrieved the current worksheet file from disk using the File Retrieve command, 1-2-3/G displays the existing file name in the File name text box. Use this filename to overwrite the old version of the worksheet file on disk, or enter a new filename if you want to preserve the old version of the file.

When you press ENTER, or click on the OK button, 1-2-3/G saves the file to disk. To use the file again, use the File Retrieve command (to load the file into memory and replace any existing files) or the File Open command (to load the

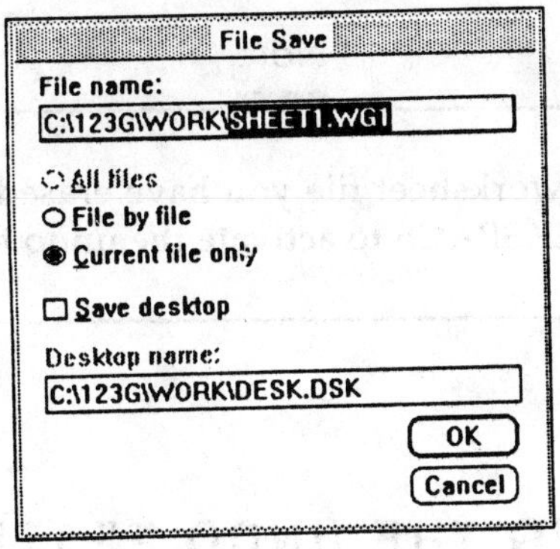

File Save
File name:
C:\123G\WORK\SHEET1.WG1
All files
File by file
Current file only
Save desktop
Desktop name:
C:\123G\WORK\DESK.DSK
OK
Cancel

FIGURE 1–63 The File Save dialog box

file into memory without replacing any existing files) and select the file name from the list that appears. Chapter 2, "Managing the Desktop," describes how to work with multiple files in memory. In addition, Chapter 5, "File Management," discusses all the File commands in detail.

ERASING AN ENTIRE WORKSHEET FILE

Suppose you have completed work on a worksheet file and you want to erase the file from the desktop and begin working on a new file. To erase the worksheet file in the active window, you use the Worksheet Erase command. When you select this command, 1-2-3/G displays the Worksheet Erase dialog box, which asks whether you want to delete all views on the file. Select Yes if you want to clear the worksheet file from memory. (1-2-3/G displays a confirmation box if you have made changes to the file that you have not saved.) Select No if you want to cancel the command and return to Ready mode.

When you erase a worksheet file with Worksheet Erase, 1-2-3/G clears the file from memory, including all of its range names, graph settings, print settings, and the like. It then displays the next available filename in the active window. The new file has all default settings.

Although Worksheet Erase clears a file from memory, it does not remove it from disk. To erase a file from disk, use the File Erase command (see Chapter 5, "File Management").

Note

You can restore a worksheet file you have erased from memory by pressing ALT-BACKSPACE to activate the undo feature.

USING THE UNDO FEATURE

1-2-3/G has a multilevel undo feature that lets you reverse the effect of previous commands or actions. You access the undo feature by selecting the Edit Undo command or by pressing ALT-BACKSPACE—the shortcut for the Edit Undo command. This applies to all cell entries, commands, and changes to settings.

For example, suppose you place a formula in a cell and then press ALT-BACKSPACE. 1-2-3/G removes the formula from the cell and returns the worksheet to the way it was before you entered the formula.

As another example, suppose you select the Worksheet Erase Yes command to erase the entire worksheet, then decide that you want to undo the erasure. If you select Edit Undo, 1-2-3/G restores the erased worksheet to the Desktop the way it was before you use the Worksheet Erase command.

You can choose Undo up to 20 times in succession to undo previous commands or actions. Each time you activate undo, 1-2-3/G undoes the next previous command or action.

Note

If you attempt to select Undo when a dialog box is open, 1-2-3/G beeps and disregards your action. If, after completing your work in the dialog box, you select Undo, 1-2-3/G reverses all the settings you made in the dialog box.

Actions That 1-2-3/G Cannot Undo

Although 1-2-3/G's Undo is significantly more powerful than in any previous version of 1-2-3, there are still certain commands and actions that it cannot undo.

TIP: The advantage of using Edit Undo over ALT-BACKSPACE

There is one important advantage to using the Edit Undo command over the ALT-BACKSPACE shortcut. Unlike ALT-BACKSPACE, when you select Edit Undo, 1-2-3/G displays to the right of the Undo command the name (or an abbreviation) of the last command or action you performed, as in Figure 1–64. This lets you verify whether you want to reverse the previous action. When you are undoing several commands or actions in succession, it helps to know exactly what you are undoing. If you are using ALT-BACKSPACE, you don't have this luxury.

- Navigation actions. For example, if you move the cell pointer or scroll the screen, 1-2-3/G cannot undo the action. This includes mouse movements.
- Selection of cells, ranges, collections, or worksheets.
- Recalculating the worksheet by pressing CALC (F9) when recalculation is set to manual (see "Recalculation").
- GOTO (F5) or Range Goto.
- Worksheet Global Default.
- Data stored in the clipboard during an Edit command (see Chapter 4, "Cutting and Pasting Data," for an explanation of the clipboard).
- Edit Link commands.
- Print menu commands.
- Graph menu commands.
- Desktop and Window Control commands.
- Utility User Settings and Utility Macro commands.
- All commands that affect external files but do not affect the active worksheet file. These commands include, for example, Data External

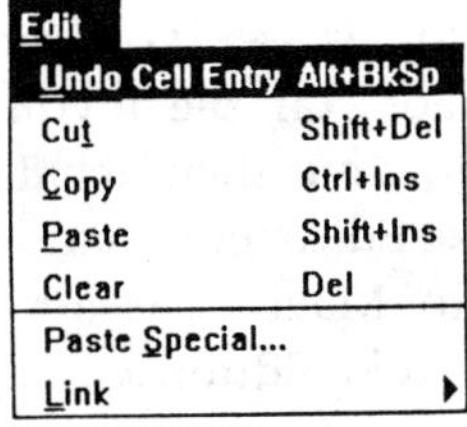

FIGURE 1–64 The Edit Undo command

Modify; Data External Create, Delete, and Use; File New or File Open for graph files; File Erase, File Print, File Utility, File Admin Links-Refresh, and File Save. If you save a file under a new name, however, just prior to undoing the save, 1-2-3/G reopens the original file with a RO (read only) indicator, indicating read only status. (This means that you can change the file but you cannot save it under its current name; you must save it under another name instead.)

- If you attempt to undo a File Save command, the overwritten file saved on disk is not restored.
- If you attempt to undo a Worksheet Erase command, 1-2-3/G issues an error message about the file's reservation, but will allow you to reopen the file with RO (read only) status. Because of these restrictions, undoing a Worksheet Erase command is possible, but you must save it under a new name in order to recover your work.
- Undo does not restore information to the Clipboard. For example, if you undo the Edit Cut, Edit Paste, or Edit Paste special commands, the information is restored to the worksheet, but not the Clipboard.

Note

If you undo a File Directory command, 1-2-3/G undoes the File Directory command for all tools on the desktop and restores the default directory.

Tip: Reversing the effect of Undo

Undo is not a toggle key. In other words, if you change your mind about what you just undid, you cannot select Undo again to reverse the effect. However, in some cases, you can use the Keystroke Editor to recover the lost data. For example, if you select Undo once to undo a cell entry you just made, but then decide that you want the entry back, select the Keystroke Editor command from the Desktop Control menu (or from the Utility Macros cascade menu). 1-2-3/G displays the contents of the Keystroke Editor window that still contains your cell entry. From this point, the steps are different whether you are using the mouse or the keyboard.

- With the mouse, highlight the keystrokes you want to recover by clicking on the first character and dragging the mouse to the end of the desired key sequence.
- With the keyboard, press ← as many times as necessary to locate the cursor at the start of the keystrokes you want to copy. Next, to highlight the keystrokes you want to copy, select SHIFT-→ until you reach the end of the sequence.

Select the Run Go command to execute the highlighted key sequence. 1-2-3/G recovers your cell entry.

Turning Undo Off

When you first start 1-2-3/G, the undo feature is on. You can, however, turn undo off to reclaim additional memory for your work. You turn undo off by using the Worksheet Global Default Set Undo Disable command. To save this setting on a permanent basis, select the Update control button from the Worksheet Global Default dialog box. To turn undo back on, you use the Worksheet Global Default Set Undo Enable command.

RECALCULATION

As you know, when you enter a formula in a worksheet that refers to other cells, 1-2-3/G automatically updates the formula when you change the entries in the other cells. This updating of formulas is known as *recalculation*.

In the early releases of 1-2-3, prior to Releases 2.2 and 3, the entire worksheet was recalculated every time you made an entry. This is not a problem when a worksheet is small and has only a few formulas. But when a worksheet is large with many complex formulas, the process of recalculating the entire worksheet can be quite time-consuming. What's more, while 1-2-3 was busy recalculating your worksheet, you could not use your computer. It wasn't uncommon to make a change in a large formula-intensive model late in the day, and have to leave the computer running all night so that you could see the updated worksheet in the morning.

Like other recent versions of 1-2-3, 1-2-3/G gets around these problems by using *minimal* and *background recalculation*. With minimal recalculation, you can add or edit a cell in 1-2-3/G, and only the cells that are affected by the entry are recalculated. 1-2-3/G also recalculates in the background while you continue to do your work. In 1-2-3/G, you can view and edit your worksheets, even leave 1-2-3/G to work on another OS/2 application, while 1-2-3/G recalculates.

1-2-3/G's minimal and background recalculation occur automatically, and you cannot control them. However, there are certain aspects of 1-2-3/G's recalculation that you can control. You can, for example, govern when recalculation takes place. That is, you can set recalculation to occur automatically or you can initiate it manually. In addition, you can control the order in which 1-2-3/G recalculates cells. The three available settings are natural, columnwise, and rowwise.

You control all of 1-2-3/G's recalculation settings using the Worksheet Global Manual Recalc command. Figure 1–65 shows the dialog box that appears when you select this command. You can also view the current recalculation settings using the Worksheet Status command.

Controlling When Recalculation Takes Place

Like previous releases of 1-2-3, there are two settings for controlling when recalculation takes place: Automatic and Manual. Automatic recalculation means that 1-2-3/G automatically recalculates the worksheet file whenever you make an entry in one cell that affects an entry in another. This is the default method of recalculation in 1-2-3/G.

Although automatic recalculation is fine for most worksheet files, there are times when it is not what you want. Consider the case when you have a large worksheet with many complex formulas that take a lot of time to recalculate. To avoid having 1-2-3/G recalculate your worksheet automatically each time you make a change to your data, you can set 1-2-3/G for manual recalculation. Then, when you have finished entering all your new data, you can press CALC (F9) to have 1-2-3/G recalculate all your formulas all at once.

Here's an example that illustrates how manual recalculation works. Starting with a blank worksheet, suppose you enter **50** in cell B2 and **20** in cell B3. Next, you enter the formula **+B2*B3** in cell B5. As expected, when you complete the formula, 1-2-3/G displays the value 1000. To change the recalculation method from automatic to manual, choose the Worksheet Global Manual Recalc com-

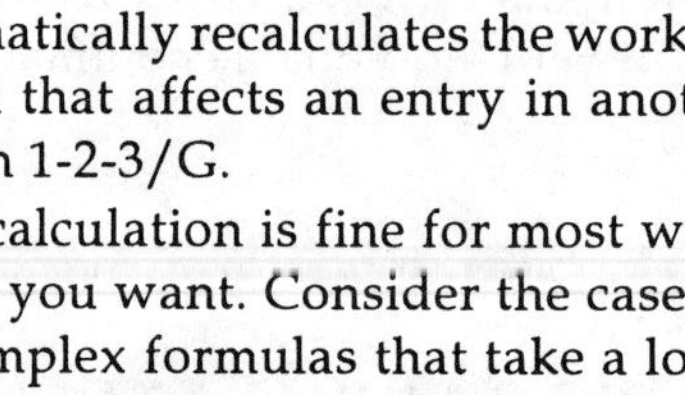

FIGURE 1–65 The Worksheet Global Manual Recalc Dialog box

mand and select the Manual option. Next, enter **30** in cell B3. Your screen now appears as in Figure 1–66.

Notice that a Calc indicator appears in the upper-right corner of the Worksheet window's Title bar. 1-2-3/G has detected a change in the worksheet file and is informing you that you must press CALC (F9) to recalculate the worksheet. In addition, the formula in cell B5 still has its original value, 1000, even though it should read 1500.

Now, suppose you press CALC (F9) to recalculate the worksheet. Figure 1–67 shows the results. Notice that the Calc indicator is no longer present and that the formula in cell B5 now reads 1500.

Note

Changing the recalculation settings with the Worksheet Global Manual Recalc command affects all the worksheets in the current file.

Order of Recalculation

There are three ways to control the order of recalculation in 1-2-3/G: natural, columnwise, and rowwise. Natural order is the default order that 1-2-3/G uses to recalculate your formulas. It begins with the most fundamental formulas in the worksheet—those that must be recalculated first before any other formulas that depend on them can be recalculated. Then, it recalculates the next most fundamental formulas, and so on until all the formulas in the worksheet have been recalculated. You can think of the way natural order or recalculation works as an inverted pyramid, with the most fundamental formulas forming the broad top with the most dependent formulas at the bottom.

To get a better understanding of how natural order of recalculation works, suppose you make the following entries in a blank worksheet:

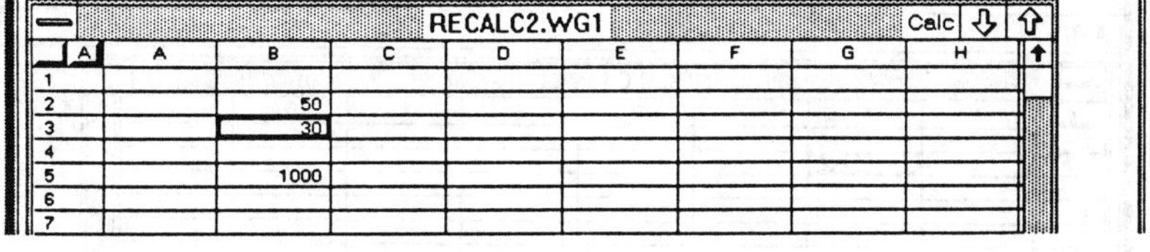

FIGURE 1–66 After setting a worksheet for manual recalculation

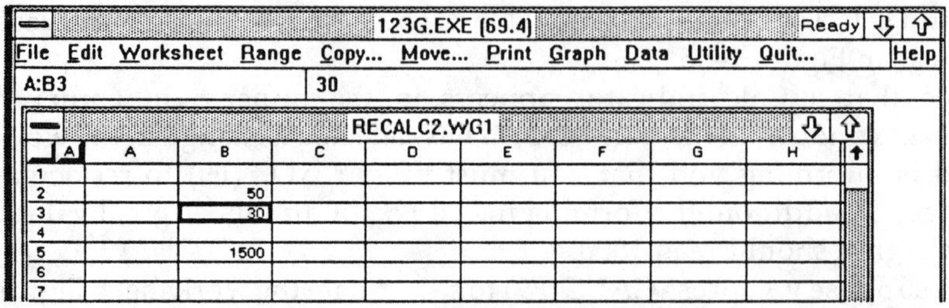

FIGURE 1–67 After pressing CALC (F9) to recalculate the worksheet

Cell	You enter
B1	100
B2	+B1+B3
B3	+B1+B4
B4	400

Figure 1–68 shows how your screen appears. Consider how 1-2-3/G recalculates the worksheet when you enter a new value in cell B4. It begins by recalculating the formula in cell B3 first, even though it is not the first formula in the worksheet. Then it recalculates the formula in cell B2, which depends on the result of the formula in B3.

In case you want to control the recalculation order, the Worksheet Global Manual Recalc command lets you change from natural to columnwise or rowwise order. When you select columnwise recalculation, 1-2-3/G begins recalculating at cell A:A1 and works its way down column A cell by cell until

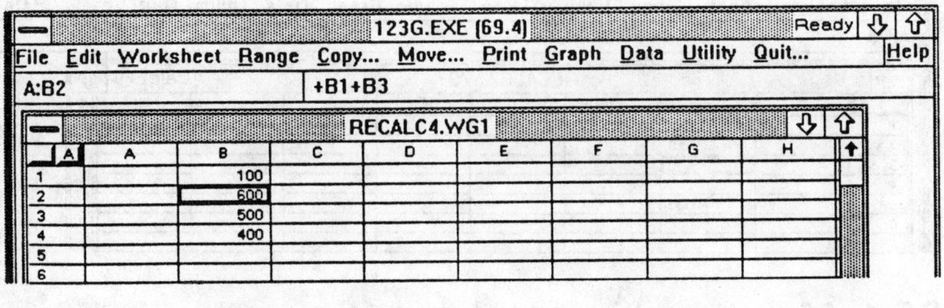

FIGURE 1–68 The benefit of natural recalculation

it reaches the last filled cell in the worksheet. It then moves to column B and works its way down that column, and so on. When it finishes recalculating worksheet A it moves to worksheet B, then to C, and so on until it has recalculated all the worksheets in the file. Rowwise recalculation is similar to columnwise, except that 1-2-3/G recalculates in a rowwise fashion, beginning in cell A:A1 and working its way through the entire worksheet file.

With most worksheet files, it doesn't matter whether you have set 1-2-3/G for natural, columnwise, or rowwise recalculation. The results are the same regardless. However, when a worksheet has a *forward reference,* columnwise and rowwise recalculation can yield incorrect results while natural recalculation does not.

A forward reference occurs when a cell's formula refers to another cell that is lower in the worksheet. For example, in Figure 1–68 the formula in cell B2 includes a forward reference because it refers to cell B3. A forward reference also occurs in 3–D space when a cell's formula refers to a worksheet that comes afterward in the file—for example, when a cell in worksheet A refers to a cell in worksheet B.

When a worksheet has a forward reference and you are using columnwise or rowwise recalculation, you can usually get 1-2-3/G to reflect the proper results for all formulas by pressing CALC (F9) twice. (Occasionally, you may need to press CALC more than twice.) You can also get the same outcome by setting the iteration count to 2 (or more) with the Iterations option of the Worksheet Global Recalc Manual command.

Circular References

A *circular reference* occurs when you place a formula in a cell whose value depends on that same cell. Circular references are usually the result of an error, but sometimes they are intentional.

The simplest form of circular reference occurs when a formula refers to itself. For example, imagine that you make the following cell entries in which the formula in cell A1 refers to itself:

Cell	You enter
A1	+A1+A2
A2	200

Figure 1–69 shows that 1-2-3/G displays a Circ indicator in the upper-right corner of the Worksheet window indicating that you have a circular reference.

1-2-3/G is incapable of resolving many circular references; the simple circular reference just discussed is one example. On the other hand there are some circular references that 1-2-3/G can resolve, provided you increase the iteration count (see "Resolving Intentional Circular References," later).

Eliminating Mistaken Circular References

Suppose you have inadvertently entered a circular reference and you want to eliminate it from your worksheet file. When you select the Worksheet Status command, 1-2-3/G shows you the location of a cell involved in the circular reference. For example, Figure 1–70 shows how the Worksheet Status dialog box appears when you enter the circular reference in Figure 1–69. Notice the "Circular ref:" setting in the Recalculation area of the dialog box which shows that cell A:A1 is the problem cell.

When you locate the problem cell, fixing the circular reference is often as simple as changing an erroneous cell reference. However, when a worksheet file has many complicated formulas and references, it can be quite difficult to correct the problem, even when you know one of the problem cells. For example, imagine that your worksheet file contains the following formulas:

Cell	Formula
A:A6	+C:A6
A:C3	+B:C3–@SUM(C:B5..C:B15)
B:A3	+A:A6/A:A103
C:A6	+B:A3

In this case, sorting out the cause of the circular reference can be quite difficult because you have several formulas involved, some of whose references are not involved in the circle. What's more, the Worksheet Status command

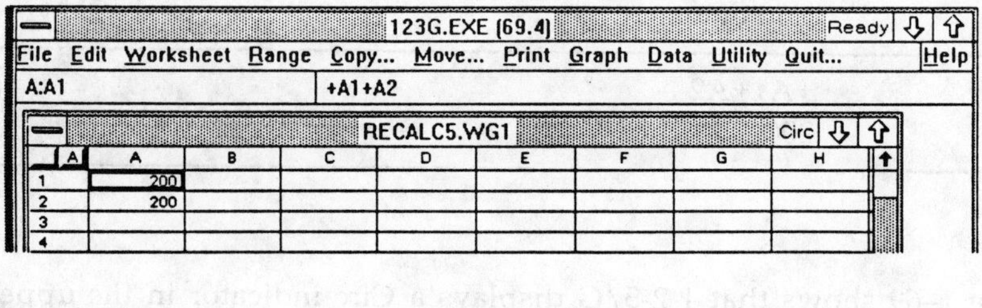

FIGURE 1–69 **The Circ indicator informs you of a circular reference**

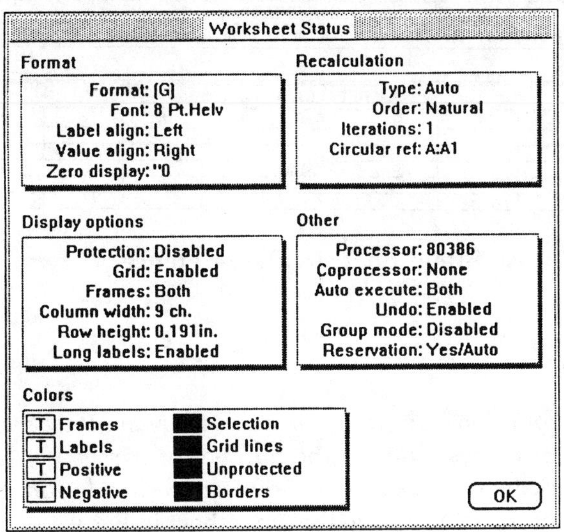

FIGURE 1–70 Worksheet Status shows circular references

shows only the first cell involved in the circular reference, cell A:A6, and this may not be the actual problem cell.

What is your best course of action? About all you can do is try to chase down each cell that is involved in the circular reference chain. In the example above, you would try to find all those cells that reference cell A:A6. You would then try to find all the cells that reference other cells that eventually lead you back to cell A:A6.

As you can imagine, it is easy to get involved in a wild goose chase when trying to correct a circular reference. Nevertheless, 1-2-3/G does offer the Range Search command, which can help you significantly in locating and correcting circular references. For example, in the previous example formulas, you can use the Range Search command to search for all those cells in the worksheet file that reference cell A:A6.

Resolving Intentional Circular References

Occasionally you will enter an intentional circular reference that you want 1-2-3/G to resolve. When this is the case, 1-2-3/G must recalculate the worksheet file more than once. The simplest way to increase the number of times 1-2-3/G recalculates a worksheet file is to use the Worksheet Global

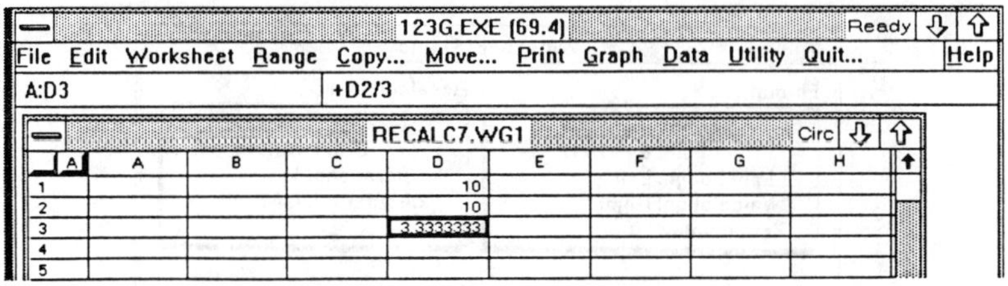

FIGURE 1–71 **An intentional circular reference**

Manual Recalc command and enter a number in the Iterations text box. The number you enter corresponds to the number of passes you want 1-2-3/G to make on the worksheet file before it completes recalculation.

For example, suppose you have the worksheet in Figure 1–71, which has the following formulas involved in an intentional circular reference:

Cell	Formula
A:D1	10
A:D2	+A:D1+A:D3
A:D3	+A:D2/3

When you first enter the formulas, cell A:D2 equals 10 and cell A:D3 equals 3.3333333.

For 1-2-3/G to resolve the circular reference, you must increase the number of passes it makes on the worksheet file before it completes recalculation. To do this, begin by selecting the Worksheet Global Manual Recalc command. Next, when 1-2-3/G displays the dialog box in Figure 1–65, select the Iterations option and enter a number between 1 and 50 (the default is 1), corresponding to the number of iterations you want 1-2-3/G to make when you press CALC (F9) to recalculate the worksheet. For the current example, type **15** and press ENTER or click on the OK button.

Figure 1–72 shows what happens to the formulas when you press CALC (F9) to recalculate the worksheet. With each iteration, 1-2-3/G comes closer to resolving the circular reference. Still, even after the fifteenth iteration, the formulas have not yet converged on the final correct values, 15 for cell A:D2 and 5 for cell A:D3. To have 1-2-3/G converge on these values, press CALC (F9) again to have 1-2-3/G recalculate the worksheet 15 more times.

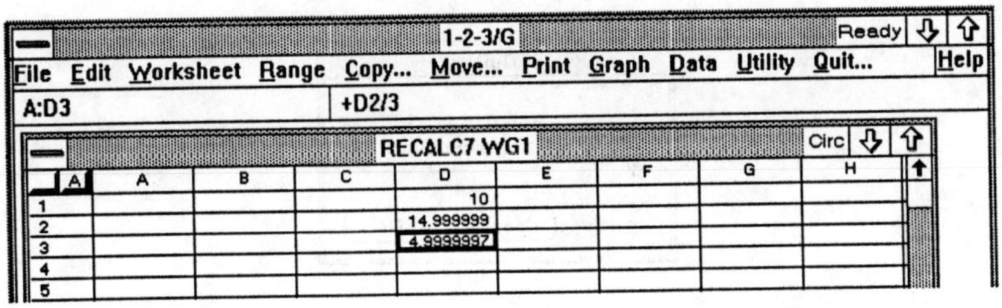

FIGURE 1–72 Results of each iteration after setting the iteration count to 15 and pressing CALC (F9)

Iteration number	A:D1	A:D2	A:D3
1	10	10	3.3333333
2	10	13.333333	4.4444444
3	10	14.444444	4.8148148
4	10	14.814815	4.9382716
5	10	14.938272	4.9794239
6	10	14.979424	4.9931413
7	10	14.993141	4.9977138
8	10	14.997714	4.9992379
9	10	14.999238	4.9997460
10	10	14.999746	4.9999153
11	10	14.999915	4.9999718
12	10	14.999972	4.9999906
13	10	14.999991	4.9999969
14	10	14.999997	4.9999990
15	10	14.999999	4.9999997

QUITTING 1-2-3/G

To quit 1-2-3/G and close all open windows, select Quit from the Worksheet menu. When you select this command, 1-2-3/G presents the dialog box in Figure 1–73. Selecting No returns you to 1-2-3/G. If you select Yes, 1-2-3/G checks to see if you have made any changes to the files in memory and displays the Close Window dialog box in Figure 1–74 for each file that you have modified

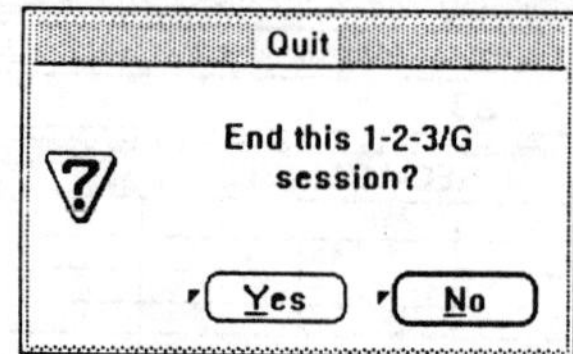

FIGURE 1–73 The Quit dialog box

but not saved. If you want to close an active file without saving it, select No. Be aware, however, that if you select No, everything in the file that is unsaved will be lost, and you will not get a second chance to reconsider.

If you want to quit 1-2-3/G without seeing the Quit dialog box, perform either of the following:

- Select Close from the Desktop Control menu.
- Press ALT-F4.

1-2-3/G takes you directly to the Close Window dialog box for each file.

LEAVING 1-2-3/G TEMPORARILY

Rather than quit 1-2-3/G altogether, you may simply want to leave 1-2-3/G running but move to another application. The ways to exit 1-2-3/G temporarily are

- Press ALT-ESC to access the next application.
- Press CTRL-ESC to access the Task Manager.
- Select Task Manager from the Desktop Control menu if you are using OS/2 Version 1.1 or Switch to if you are using OS/2 Version 1.2.

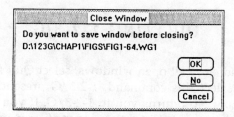

Close Window
Do you want to save window before closing?
D:\123G\CHAP1\FIGS\FIG1-64.WG1
OK
No
Cancel

FIGURE 1–74 The Close Window dialog box

- Minimize the 1-2-3/G desktop and select another application (see Chapter 2, "Managing the Desktop," for more information).

Here are some of the ways you can return to 1-2-3/G from another application:

- Press ALT-ESC as many times as necessary to cycle back to 1-2-3/G.
- Press CTRL-ESC to access the Task Manager and select 1-2-3/G from the list.
- If you have minimized the 1-2-3/G desktop, restore it by double-clicking on the 1-2-3/G icon (see Chapter 2 for other ways to restore 1-2-3/G).

SUMMARY

In this chapter, you learned how to move within a worksheet, navigate between worksheets, enter data, and create formulas. You also learned the fundamentals of how to use commands, work with ranges and collections, make selections, and annotate your worksheets. Finally, you learned how to search for data, use undo, control recalculation, save and retrieve files, and exit 1-2-3/G.

You now have all the skills you need to create simple worksheet models. But there is much more to know before you can take advantage of 1-2-3/G's full power. In the next chapter you'll learn how to manage the 1-2-3/G desktop to suit your needs, one of the most important aspects of mastering 1-2-3/G.

CHAPTER

2

Managing the Desktop

From the Presentation Manager desktop you can run multiple applications at the same time, each in its own window. What's more, you can move from one window to the next, performing operations that are specific to the application in each window.

Like Presentation Manager, 1-2-3/G provides its own desktop. On this desktop, you can have multiple tools (worksheets and graphs) or utilities (Solver, Note, etc.) open and available for your use at the same time. Just as Presentation Manager confines each application to its own window, 1-2-3/G confines each tool or utility to its own window. Further, 1-2-3/G allows you to move from one window to the next, performing operations that are specific to the window you're in. And, although you can save the contents of each window separately, you can also save a record of the windows currently on the desktop under a single desktop name. That way, you can open the same desktop in a future 1-2-3/G session and have all your files placed back on the desktop, each in their respective windows, just as you left them.

This chapter shows you how to organize and manage multiple windows on the 1-2-3/G desktop. Initially, however, this chapter concentrates on giving you the skills you'll need to manage a single window. For example, you'll learn how to change the size of a window, move it to a new location, or reduce it to an icon. You'll also learn how to split a worksheet window so that you can display different parts of the same worksheet, or multiple worksheets, in the same window.

Once you've mastered the skills associated with a single window, this chapter shows you how to work with multiple files on the desktop. For example, you'll learn how to open multiple windows containing different worksheet files or graphs and to move back and forth between those windows. You'll also learn how to rearrange windows to have them appear stacked (one on top of the other) or tiled (side by side). In addition, you'll learn how to link worksheet files together, and you'll learn how to specify commands so that they affect ranges in different files.

Once you've learned how to create and manage multiple files on the desktop, this chapter teaches you how to group those files under different desktop names. For example, you'll learn how to save the current desktop and open it again in a future session. You'll also learn how to copy a desktop from one directory to another, how to archive a desktop, and how to get information about files included in a particular desktop.

What's New

Most of the commands and techniques discussed in this chapter have to do with managing windows in a Graphical User Interface (GUI) environment. Therefore, virtually everything in this chapter is new to 1-2-3.

On the other hand, if you're an experienced Presentation Manager or Microsoft Windows user, you won't find many things in this chapter that are terribly new. For example, you already know how to change the size of a window, move it, maximize it to occupy the entire screen, reduce it to an icon, and so on. However, 1-2-3/G's scheme for managing multiple files on the desktop and grouping files into different desktops still bears your attention. These operations involve commands and techniques that are unique to 1-2-3/G.

If you're an experienced 1-2-3 Release 2 or 3 user, you'll find that some familiar features have been enhanced. For example, you may already know how to use the Worksheet Window command to split the current worksheet either horizontally or vertically into two panes. This allows you to simultaneously view and edit divergent portions of a worksheet. However, in 1-2-3/G, you can view different worksheets in each window pane. You can also use the Worksheet Window command to view up to five consecutive worksheets at the same time.

Further, if you have a copy of Release 2.2 or 3, you'll find the file-linking feature in 1-2-3/G remarkably similar to these previous releases. For example, to refer by formula to data in another worksheet file from the current worksheet, you need only enclose the name of the file in double-angle brackets << >> followed by a range name or address from that file, for example +<<C:\MARKET\SALES>>A:A100. Additionally, unlike Releases

2.2 of 1-2-3, you can include such a file reference in even your most complex formulas.

In addition to linking files by using formulas, 1-2-3/G also allows you to link files by using the Edit Link command. Like formula links, this powerful new command allows you to use information from other files in the current file. However, the Edit Link command takes advantage of Presentation Manager's Dynamic Data Exchange (DDE) protocol to form the links. This means you can link a 1-2-3/G worksheet to a 1-2-3/G graph, and vice versa, or you can link either of these to a file created by another Presentation Manager application that supports DDE.

CONTROLLING A SINGLE WINDOW

The 1-2-3/G desktop usually fills your entire screen, as shown in Figure 2-1. As you know, the first three lines of the desktop include the Title bar, the Menu bar, and the Control line. The balance of the 1-2-3/G desktop, beneath these three lines, is called the Work area. Within the Work area, 1-2-3/G displays the

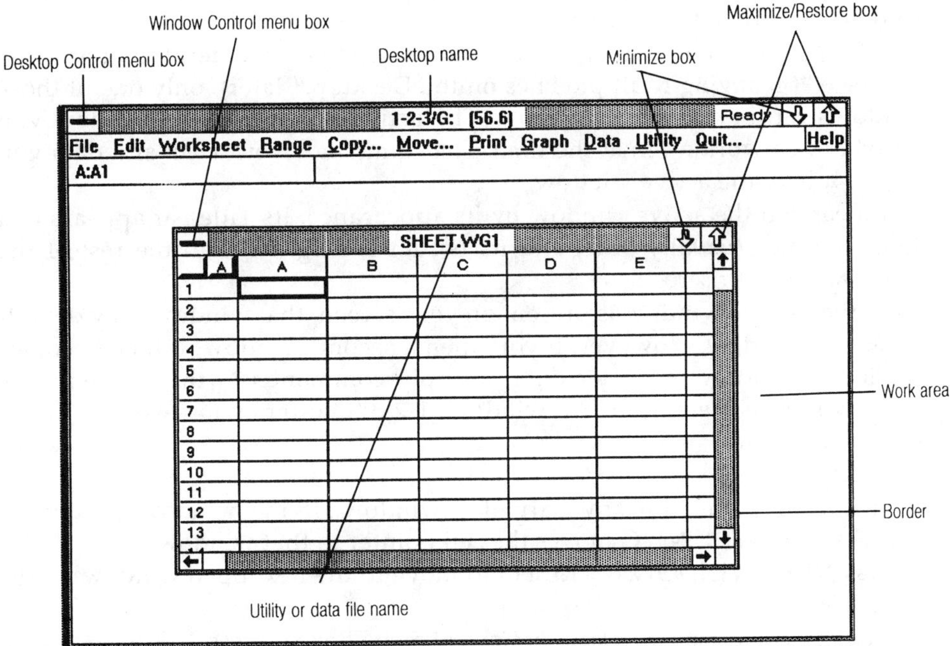

FIGURE 2-1 The 1-2-3/G desktop with a single window displayed

tools or utilities currently open on the desktop. Each tool or utility appears in its own window.

A window is a rectangular region of your screen through which you view a 1-2-3/G tool, such as a worksheet or graph, or a utility, such as Solver or Note. For example, Figure 2–1 shows the 1-2-3/G desktop with a single window in the Work area. This window contains a worksheet file. The Title bar for the window displays the name of the tool or utility it contains. For example, the window in Figure 2–1 contains a worksheet file called SHEET.WG1.

1-2-3/G allows you to control the display of your windows in several ways. For example, you can move a window from one part of the Work area to another. You can also change the size of a window by making it taller or wider. Or, you can *maximize* a window so that it occupies the entire Work area. Finally, you can *minimize* a window, reducing it to an icon (a small picture that represents the window). The sections that follow show you how to do each of these things.

Activating a Window

Before you can change the size or position of a window or apply commands to it, you must *activate* the window. Activating a window is simply a matter of selecting a particular window from among the other windows currently open on the desktop. This informs 1-2-3/G that you want your commands and actions to apply to that window.

Although you can have up to 16 windows open on the desktop at any one time (see "Managing Multiple Files on the Desktop," later), only one of those windows can be the *active* window. The active window is the window you happen to be working in at the time. The commands you select and data you enter apply to the active window.

You can tell the active window by its appearance. Its Title bar appears in a different color (usually blue) and its border is brighter than the rest of the windows on your screen.

If only a single window is present on your screen, that window is by default the active window. However, if you open a second window, it then becomes the active window. To enter data or apply commands in the first window again, you must reactivate the window. 1-2-3/G offers you several ways to activate a window:

- Click your mouse on any part of a window. If the window contains a worksheet tool, 1-2-3/G moves the cell pointer to that window.
- Press NEXT WINDOW (CTRL-F6) to move to the next open window on the desktop.
- Click your mouse on the Desktop Control menu box, or press ALT-SPACEBAR, to display the Desktop Control menu. Next, select Window from that menu. 1-2-3/G displays a list of open windows on the desktop. (The currently active

window has a check mark next to its name.) Select the name of the window you wish to activate.

Note

> The Desktop Control menu is discussed in more detail in the sections that follow.

Changing the Size of a Window

You can change the size of a window with either your mouse or your keyboard. Both methods are discussed in this section.

With the Mouse

Imagine you want to change the size of the window shown in the Work area of Figure 2–1. To do this with your mouse, begin by moving the mouse pointer to the right border of the window. The shape of the mouse pointer changes to a horizontal double arrow. Click your left mouse button to grab the border and drag it to the right to widen the window or to the left to make the window thinner. Then, release the mouse button. 1-2-3/G changes the width of the window accordingly. You can perform this same operation on the left border of the window.

To change the height of the window in Figure 2–1, move the mouse pointer to the top or bottom border of the window. The shape of the mouse pointer changes to a vertical double arrow. Click and drag the border up or down to the desired height and then release your mouse button. 1-2-3/G changes the height of the window accordingly.

You can also change the size of a window by clicking your mouse on the window's corners. For example, if you move the mouse pointer to the upper-left corner of a window, its shape is transformed into a diagonal double arrow. You can then click and drag the corner to the desired position. As you do this, the top and left borders of the window are simultaneously expanded or contracted as needed. When you release the mouse button, both the height and width of the window are changed. This same procedure can be used on the upper-right, bottom-left, or bottom-right corners of a window.

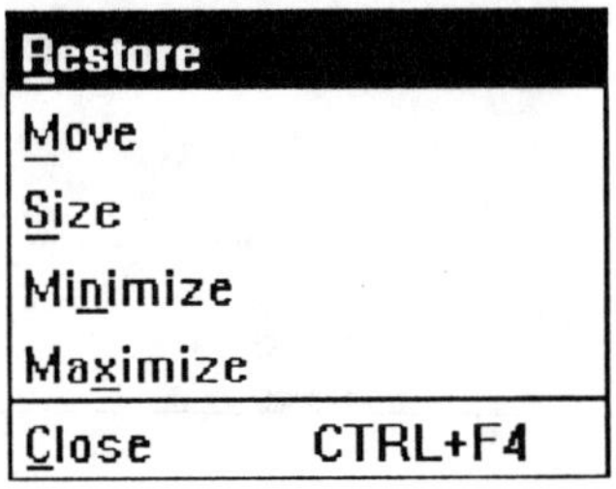

Restore	
Move	
Size	
Minimize	
Maximize	
Close	CTRL+F4

FIGURE 2-2 The Window Control menu.

With the Window Control Menu

You can also adjust the size of a window by using the Window Control menu shown in Figure 2–2. To access this menu, click on the Window Control menu box located in the upper-left corner of the current window. Alternatively, you can press ALT— (ALT-MINUS) to display the Window Control menu. Then, select Size from the Window Control menu. Next, press an arrow key that points to the border you want to adjust. For example, to adjust the top border, press ↑. Then, press ↑ again to move the top border up or ↓ to move the top border down. To complete the job, press ENTER. 1-2-3/G changes the height of the window accordingly. You can use this same technique to point to and adjust the bottom, left, and right borders of a window.

Note

The Window Control menu is common to every window on the 1-2-3/G desktop. Regardless of whether you open a tool, such as a worksheet or graph file, or a utility, such as Note or Solver, the window for that tool or utility will have a Window Control menu. You access the Window Control menu for each window using the techniques just described. What's more, the options available from the Window Control menu are the same for all 1-2-3/G windows.

Changing the Size of the Desktop

You can also change the size of the 1-2-3/G desktop. To do this, you use the same techniques as just described for changing the size of a single window in the Work area. For example, notice in Figure 2–1 that the desktop has borders just like a Work area window. What's more, when you move the mouse pointer to the edge of the desktop or to one of its corners, the shape of the mouse pointer becomes a double arrow. You can then click and drag an edge or corner to resize the entire 1-2-3/G desktop.

As an alternative to resizing the desktop with your mouse, you can use the Desktop Control menu. To access the Desktop Control menu, either click on the Desktop Control menu box (upper-left corner of the desktop), or press ALT-SPACEBAR. 1-2-3/G displays the menu shown in Figure 2–3.

To change the size of the desktop, select Size from the Desktop Control menu. Next, select an arrow key that points to the border you want to adjust. For example, to adjust the top border of the desktop, press ↑. Then, press ↓ to move the top border down or ↑ to move the top border up. To complete the job, press ENTER. 1-2-3/G changes the height of the desktop accordingly. You can use this same technique to point to and adjust the bottom, left, and right borders of the desktop.

When you decrease the size of the 1-2-3/G desktop, you'll notice that the Presentation Manager screen can be seen behind 1-2-3/G. Thus, it may be said that the 1-2-3/G desktop itself is really just a big window through which you view 1-2-3/G.

Note

> Notice that the first five options in the Desktop Control menu in Figure 2–3 exactly match those of the Window Control menu shown earlier in Figure 2–2. These five options allow you to control the size and position of the desktop window in the same way that the first five options in the Window Control menu allow you to control the size and position of a single tool window.

Maximizing a Window

1-2-3/G also allows you to resize a window to occupy the entire desktop Work area. This is referred to as maximizing a window. To do this, click on the Window Control menu box, or press ALT– (ALT-MINUS) to display the Window Control menu shown in Figure 2–2. Then select Maximize. 1-2-3/G increases the size of the current window to occupy the entire Work area as shown in Figure 2–4.

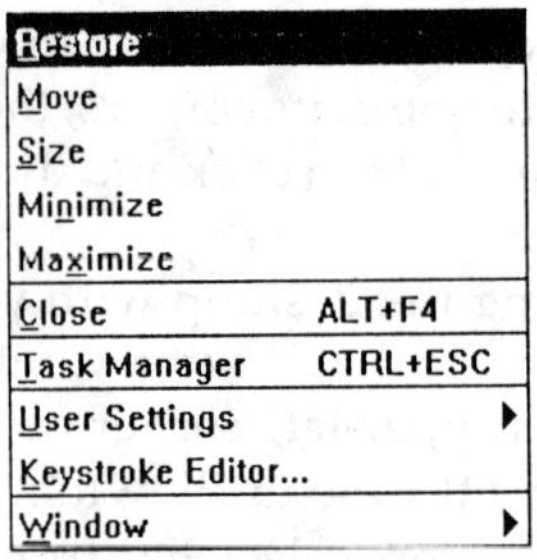

Restore
Move
Size
Minimize
Maximize
Close ALT+F4
Task Manager CTRL+ESC
User Settings ▸
Keystroke Editor...
Window ▸

FIGURE 2-3 The Desktop Control menu

There are two alternatives to using the Window Control to maximize a window. Both apply only if you're using a mouse. The first alternative is to click a single time on the Maximize/Restore box located in the upper-right corner of the window. This box contains a single ↑ as shown in Figure 2-1. (Once the window is maximized, the Maximize/Restore box will contain both an ↑ and

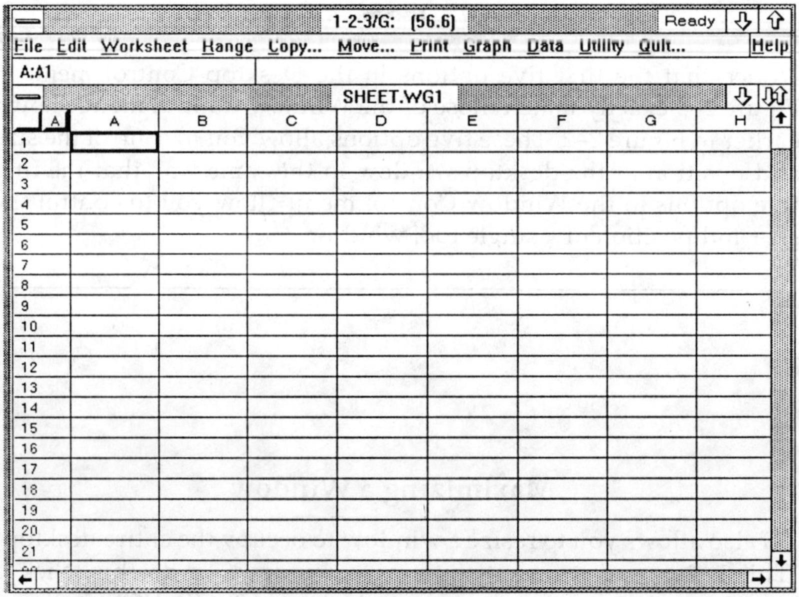

1-2-3/G: (56.6) Ready
File Edit Worksheet Range Copy... Move... Print Graph Data Utility Quit... Help
A:A1
SHEET.WG1
A | A B C D E F G H
1 2 3 4 5 6 7 8 9 10 11 12 13 14 15 16 17 18 19 20 21

FIGURE 2-4 A worksheet window maximized to occupy the entire desktop Work area

a ↓.) The second alternative for maximizing a window is to double-click on the Title bar for the window. Using either of these alternatives has the same effect as clicking on the Maximize option in the Window Control menu.

Tip: Restoring a maximized window

Notice that the Maximize/Restore box in Figure 2–4 contains both an ↑ and a ↓ after the window has been maximized. When you click on the Maximize/Restore box in Figure 2–4, 1-2-3/G will restore the window to its original size and location. Alternatively, you can double-click on the window's Title bar. See "Restoring a Window" later in this section for more details.

You can also maximize the 1-2-3/G desktop. For example, imagine you have reduced the size of the desktop window such that it does not occupy the entire screen. You can maximize the desktop window to once again occupy the entire screen by using any one of the following methods:

- Activate the Desktop Control menu by clicking on the Desktop Control menu box, or pressing ALT-SPACEBAR, and select Maximize.
- Click on the Maximize/Restore box located in the upper-right corner of the desktop window. This box contains a single ↑.
- Double-click on the Title bar for the desktop.

Reducing a Window to an Icon

Figure 2–5 shows a window that has been reduced to an icon (a small picture that represents the window). The icon for the window is located on the lower-left corner of Figure 2–5. The process of reducing a window to an icon is referred to as minimizing a window. You can minimize the current window by using either of two methods. With your mouse, click on the Minimize box located in the upper-right corner of the window, located just to the left of the Maximize/Restore box. Alternatively, you can click on the Window Control menu box, or press ALT- (ALT-MINUS) to display the Window Control menu. Next, select Minimize from that menu. Using either method minimizes the current window to an icon, as in Figure 2–5.

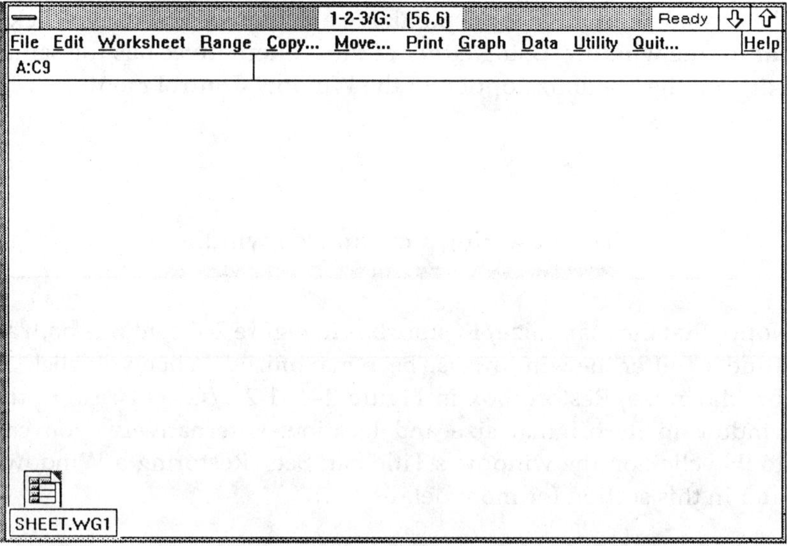

FIGURE 2-5 **A worksheet window reduced to an icon**

Note

> When you minimize a window, its contents are still in active memory. Therefore, you can apply commands to that window, provided it is the active window, even though you've reduced it to an icon.

You can also minimize the 1-2-3/G desktop. You can do this in one of two ways. First, you can click your mouse on the Minimize box located in the upper-right corner of the desktop, immediately to the left of the Maximize/Restore box. Alternatively, you can click on the Desktop Control menu box, or press ALT-SPACEBAR, to display the Desktop Control menu. Then, select Minimize from this menu. In either case, the 1-2-3/G desktop is minimized to an icon on the Presentation Manager desktop. Your screen should look similar to Figure 2–6. See the next section, "Restoring a Window," for details.

Restoring a Window

Once you've minimized or maximized a window, you can quickly restore it to its original size and position. 1-2-3/G offers you several ways to do this.

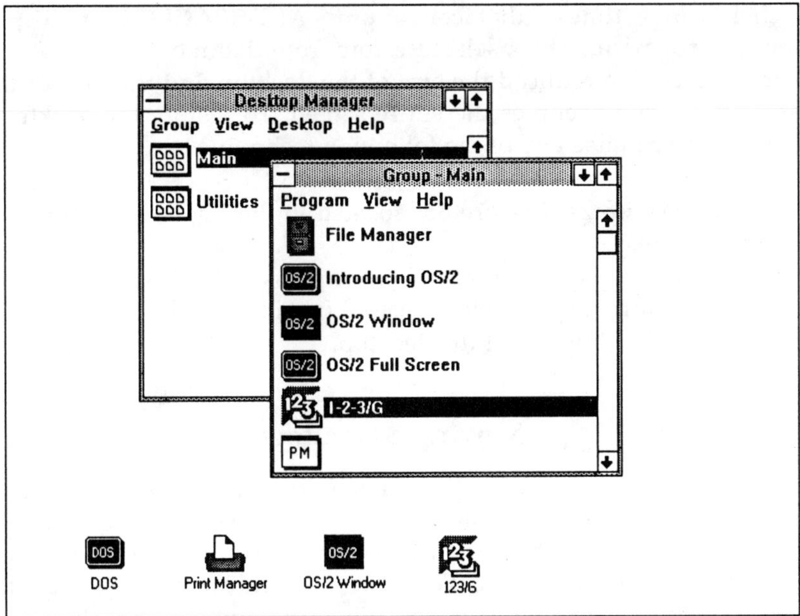

FIGURE 2-6 The Presentation Manager screen after the 1-2-3/G desktop has been minimized

Imagine for a moment that you have minimized a window (reduced it to an icon), as shown in Figure 2–5. To redisplay this window, simply double-click your mouse on the icon. 1-2-3/G restores the window to its former size and location. Alternatively, you can click once on the icon, or press ALT-- (ALT-MINUS) to display the Window Control menu. Select Restore from this menu to have 1-2-3/G restore the window to its former size and location.

On the other hand, imagine for a moment that you have maximized a window so that it occupies the entire screen. To restore this window to its former size, you have three choices:

- Click on the Maximize/Restore box located in the upper-right corner of a maximized window. You can tell the window has been maximized when the Maximize/Restore box contains both an ↑ and a ↓.
- Click on the Window Control menu box, or press ALT— (ALT-MINUS) to display the Window Control menu. Select Restore from that menu.
- Click twice on the Title bar of a maximized window.

You can use most of the same techniques to restore the 1-2-3/G desktop. For example, imagine you've minimized the 1-2-3/G desktop to an icon, as shown in Figure 2–6. To restore the 1-2-3/G desktop, click twice on the icon. Alternatively, click a single time on that icon, or press ALT-SPACEBAR, to display the Desktop Control menu. Then, select Restore from that menu.

Or, imagine you've reduced the size of the desktop and then maximized it, so that it once again occupies the entire screen. To restore the desktop to its former size, you can use any of the following techniques:

- Click on the Maximize/Restore box located in the upper-right corner of the desktop window.
- Click on the Desktop Control menu box, or press ALT-SPACEBAR to display the Desktop Control menu. Select Restore from that menu.
- Click twice on the Title bar of the desktop.

Moving a Window

You can move a window by using the mouse or by using the keyboard. To move a window with the mouse, click on the window's Title bar and hold your mouse button down. Then, drag the window to another location on the desktop and release your mouse button. 1-2-3/G moves the window to a new location.

Alternatively, you can click on the Window Control menu box, or press ALT-- (ALT-MINUS) to display the Window Control menu. Then, select Move from that menu. Next, use the arrow keys or your mouse to move the window in the direction that you want. To complete the job, press ENTER or click your mouse button. 1-2-3/G moves the window to the new location.

If you've reduced a window to an icon (minimized it), you can move the icon. To do this, click your mouse button on the icon and hold it down. Then, drag the icon to another location on the desktop and release the mouse button. Or, if you click a single time on the icon, or press ALT-- (ALT-MINUS), 1-2-3/G displays the Window Control menu. Select Move from this menu. Then, use the arrow keys, or your mouse, to move the icon to new location. To complete the job, press ENTER or click your mouse.

You can also move the 1-2-3/G desktop. To do this, click your mouse on the Title bar for the desktop and drag it to any location you want and release. Alternatively, click on the Desktop Control menu box, or press ALT-SPACEBAR, to display the Desktop Control menu. Select Move from this menu. Next, use the arrow keys, or your mouse, to move the desktop in any direction you want. To complete the move, press ENTER or click your mouse button.

If you've reduced the desktop to an icon, you can move this icon by using the same techniques as you would for a window icon. For example, you can click on the desktop icon, hold your mouse button down, and drag the icon to any location on the Presentation Manager desktop. When you've got the icon where you want it, release your mouse button. On the other hand, if you click on the desktop icon a single time, or press ALT-ESC as needed to make 1-2-3/G the active application, the Desktop Control menu is displayed. Select Move from this menu and use the arrow keys or your mouse to move the icon to a new location. Complete the move by pressing ENTER or by clicking your mouse.

Closing a Window

To remove a window from the desktop, you must close it. To close the active window, you can use any of the following techniques:

- Double-click on the Window Control menu box.
- Click once on the Window Control menu box, or press ALT— (ALT-MINUS), to display the Window Control menu. Then, select Close from that menu.
- Press CTRL-F4.

If the contents of the active window have not been saved, or you've made changes since you opened the window, 1-2-3/G will prompt you to save the window before closing it. To do this, 1-2-3/G displays the Close Window box shown in Figure 2–7. To save the active window's contents before closing it, select the OK command button. To close the window without saving its contents, select the NO command button. To cancel the Close operation and leave the window on the desktop, select Cancel.

As an alternative to selecting Quit to end 1-2-3/G, you can close the Desktop window. The techniques for closing the desktop are very similar to those used to close a tool window. For example, you can do any of the following:

- Double-click twice on the Desktop Control menu box.
- Click once on the Desktop Control menu box to display the Desktop Control menu. Select Close from that menu.
- Press ALT-F4.

As you might imagine, if the contents of one or more windows on the desktop have not as yet been saved, or if you've made changes to one or more windows since you opened them, 1-2-3/G prompts you to save your changes before closing the desktop. To do this, 1-2-3/G displays the Close Window dialog box for each new window as well as for each modified window. To save the contents of a window, select the OK command button. To avoid saving the contents of a window, select the NO command button.

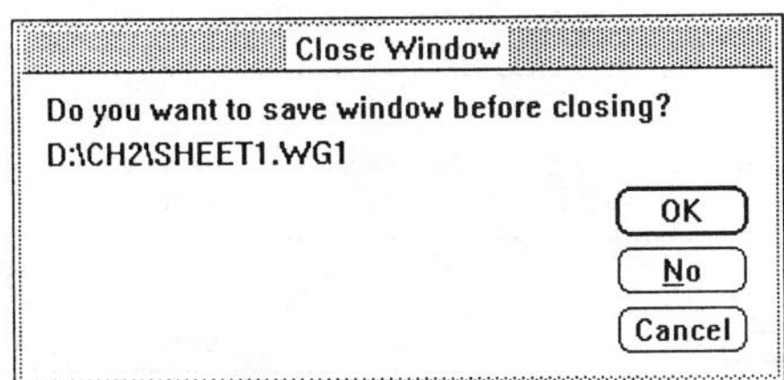

FIGURE 2-7 The Close Window dialog box

To cancel the closing of the desktop and leave the remaining open windows on the desktop, select Cancel.

SPLITTING A WORKSHEET WINDOW

1-2-3/G offers several methods you can use to split a window containing a worksheet file. Splitting windows allows you to better view the contents of a single worksheet or of several worksheets at once. For example, you can split a window vertically or horizontally into two *panes* and view different parts of the same worksheet or even different worksheets in each pane. Or, you can set up a window to display portions of up to five consecutive worksheets stacked one behind the other, sloping upward to the right. This is referred to as a *perspective* view. Perspective view can be particularly handy when you are setting up a multiple worksheet model that requires three-dimensional ranges.

Splitting Windows Horizontally

Figure 2–8 shows a worksheet window that has been split horizontally into two panes. Notice that the top pane of the window shows a view of the range

1-2-3/G: [56.6] Ready

File Edit Worksheet Range Copy... Move... Print Graph Data Utility Quit... Help

A:A107 'Gross Profit

FIG2-8.WG1

A	A	B	C	D	E	F
1		Qtr. End	Qtr. End	Qtr. End	Qtr. End	Year End
2		03/31/92	06/30/92	09/30/92	12/31/92	12/31/92
3	============	==========	==========	==========	==========	==========
4	Net Sales	$85,000	$72,700	$78,900	$101,350	$337,950
5						
6	Direct Material	$27,625	$27,263	$22,487	$34,966	$112,340
7	Direct Labor	$12,750	$10,905	$11,835	$15,203	$50,693
8						
9	Direct Costs	$40,375	$38,168	$34,322	$50,168	$163,032
10						
11	Gross Profit	$44,625	$34,533	$44,579	$51,182	$174,918
12						

A	A	B	C	D	E	F
100	Net Sales	100%	100%	100%	100%	100%
101						
102	Direct Material	33%	38%	29%	35%	33%
103	Direct Labor	15%	15%	15%	15%	15%
104						
105	Direct Costs	48%	52%	44%	50%	48%
106						
107	Gross Profit	52%	48%	57%	51%	52%

FIGURE 2-8 A worksheet window split horizontally

A1..F12 of worksheet A and the bottom pane shows a view of the range A100..F108 of the same worksheet. Thus, you can use horizontal windows to view, compare, and edit vastly divergent parts of the same worksheet at the same time.

1-2-3/G allows you to split a window horizontally either by using your mouse or by using the keyboard. The sections that follow discuss both methods.

With the Mouse

To split a window horizontally using your mouse, begin by moving the mouse pointer into any column frame at the top of the worksheet. (Column frames contain the column letters.) Position the mouse pointer toward the top of the column frame until it is transformed into a vertical double arrow. (The vertical double arrow will appear black on a color screen.) Next, click your left mouse button and hold it down. 1-2-3/G displays a white dotted line across the column frames. Then, drag the dotted white line downward until it reaches the bottom border of the row where you want to split the window. For example, if you want to split the window at row 12, as in Figure 2–8, drag the dotted line to the bottom border of row 12. Finally, release your mouse button. 1-2-3/G splits the window and displays a second set of column frames (column letters), creating two panes through which you may view the current worksheet.

Note

> When creating horizontal panes with the mouse, make sure you move the dotted line outside the row of column frames. Otherwise, 1-2-3/G issues the error massage "Cannot create panes—not enough room."

When you first split a worksheet window horizontally, the cell pointer remains in the top pane. To move back and forth between horizontal windows, press WINDOW (F6). For example, when you press WINDOW (F6) the first time, 1-2-3/G moves the cell pointer to the bottom pane. Or, you can click your mouse pointer on any cell in the bottom pane. To return to the top pane again, press WINDOW (F6) or click your mouse on any cell in the top pane.

You can move the window containing the cell pointer to another area of the same worksheet, or to a different worksheet in the same file. To do this, simply move the cell pointer as you normally would. As you do, 1-2-3/G moves the window pane along with the cell pointer.

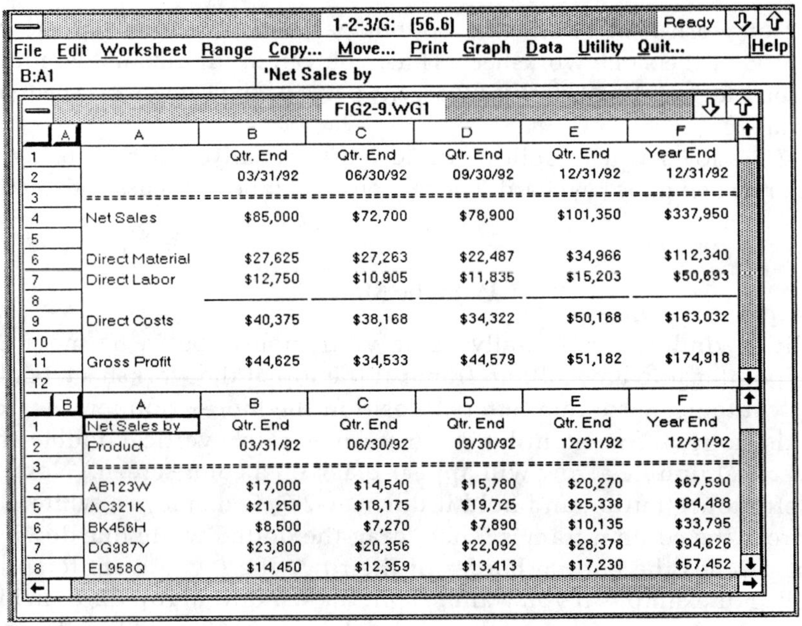

1-2-3/G: [56.6] Ready

File Edit Worksheet Range Copy... Move... Print Graph Data Utility Quit... Help

B:A1 'Net Sales by

FIG2-9.WG1

A	A	B	C	D	E	F
1		Qtr. End	Qtr. End	Qtr. End	Qtr. End	Year End
2		03/31/92	06/30/92	09/30/92	12/31/92	12/31/92
3	=============	=========	=========	=========	=========	=========
4	Net Sales	$85,000	$72,700	$78,900	$101,350	$337,950
5						
6	Direct Material	$27,625	$27,263	$22,487	$34,966	$112,340
7	Direct Labor	$12,750	$10,905	$11,835	$15,203	$50,693
8						
9	Direct Costs	$40,375	$38,168	$34,322	$50,168	$163,032
10						
11	Gross Profit	$44,625	$34,533	$44,579	$51,182	$174,918
12						

B	A	B	C	D	E	F
1	Net Sales by	Qtr. End	Qtr. End	Qtr. End	Qtr. End	Year End
2	Product	03/31/92	06/30/92	09/30/92	12/31/92	12/31/92
3	=============	=========	=========	=========	=========	=========
4	AB123W	$17,000	$14,540	$15,780	$20,270	$67,590
5	AC321K	$21,250	$18,175	$19,725	$25,338	$84,488
6	BK456H	$8,500	$7,270	$7,890	$10,135	$33,795
7	DG987Y	$23,800	$20,356	$22,092	$28,378	$94,626
8	EL958Q	$14,450	$12,359	$13,413	$17,230	$57,452

FIGURE 2-9 Different worksheets displayed in horizontal window panes

With horizontal window panes, the rows displayed in the pane that do not contain the cell pointer remain static on your screen. For example, notice in Figure 2–8 that rows 1 through 12 remain in view in the top pane while the bottom pane, the pane that contains the cell pointer, has been moved to display rows 100 through 108 in the same worksheet.

Figure 2–9 shows what happens when you press CTRL-PGUP to move the cell pointer to worksheet B. Notice that the bottom pane, the window pane with the cell pointer, now shows a view of worksheet B while the top pane still shows rows 1 through 12 of worksheet A.

Initially, when you split a window horizontally, 1-2-3/G synchronizes column scrolling between the two window panes. In other words, the same columns always appear in both the top and bottom panes. However, you can desynchronize the scrolling of worksheets within window panes so that different columns appear within horizontal window panes. See "Unsynchronizing Panes" later in this section for more details.

With the Keyboard

To split the active window horizontally using your keyboard, you use the Worksheet Window command. When you select this command, 1-2-3/G displays the Worksheet Window dialog box shown in Figure 2–10. To split

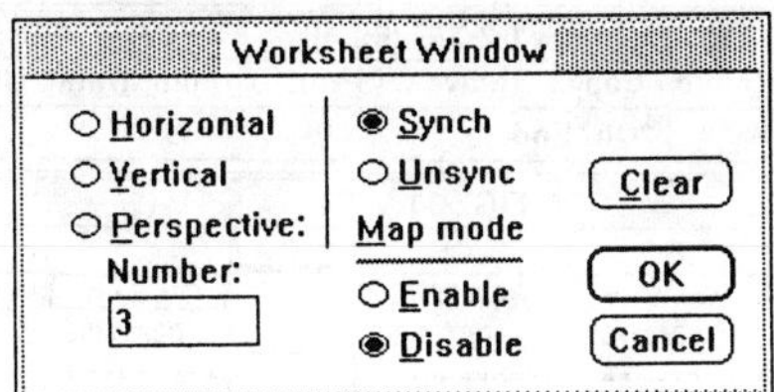

FIGURE 2-10 **The Worksheet Window dialog box**

the currently active worksheet window horizontally, select the Horizontal command button. This causes the current worksheet to be split horizontally at the location of the cell pointer.

Before issuing for the Worksheet Window Horizontal command, it is helpful to position the cell pointer below the row where you want to split the window. For example, if you want to split the current window at row 12, as shown in Figure 2–8, position the cell pointer in row 13. Next, select the Worksheet Window command to display the dialog box in Figure 2–10. Next, select Horizontal. To complete the command, select the OK command button, or press ENTER. 1-2-3/G splits the active window into two horizontal panes at the location of the cell pointer.

Note

> There must be at least one row between the cell pointer and the top of the worksheet when you use the Worksheet Window Horizontal command. If not, 1-2-3/G will beep and ignore the command.

Splitting Windows Vertically

You can also split a worksheet window into two vertical panes using either your mouse or the keyboard. Figure 2–11 shows an example of a worksheet window split into two vertical panes.

With the Mouse

To split a worksheet window into two vertical panes using your mouse, begin by positioning the mouse pointer inside any row frame (row frames contain the row numbers). Gradually move the mouse pointer to the left of the row frame

1-2-3/G (69.4) Ready

File Edit Worksheet Range Copy... Move... Print Graph Data Utility Quit... Help

A:J1 ^Qtr. End

FIG2-11.WG1

A	A	B	C	A	J	K	L
1		Qtr. End	Qtr. End	1	Qtr. End	Qtr. End	Qtr. End
2		03/31/92	06/30/92	2	03/31/93	06/30/93	09/30/93
3	============	===========	===========	3	=========	=========	==========
4	Net Sales	$85,000	$72,700	4	$98,000	$101,700	$107,000
5				5			
6	Direct Material	$27,625	$27,263	6	$23,765	$38,138	$40,125
7	Direct Labor	$12,750	$10,905	7	$14,700	$15,255	$16,050
8				8			
9	Direct Costs	$40,375	$38,168	9	$38,465	$53,393	$56,175
10				10			
11	Gross Profit	$44,625	$34,533	11	$59,535	$48,308	$50,825
12				12			
13	Operating Expenses:			13			
14	Salaries	$24,000	$28,000	14	$26,000	$30,000	$26,000
15	Advertising	$3,000	$3,000	15	$3,000	$3,000	$3,000
16	Supplies	$1,500	$1,500	16	$1,500	$1,500	$1,500
17	Phone	$1,200	$1,200	17	$1,200	$1,200	$1,200
18	Rent	$6,000	$6,000	18	$6,000	$6,000	$6,000
19	Insurance	$900	$900	19	$900	$900	$900
20	Depreciation	$3,000	$3,000	20	$3,000	$3,000	$3,000
21				21			
22	Total	$39,600	$43,600	22	$41,600	$45,600	$41,600

FIGURE 2-11 **A worksheet window split vertically**

until its shape is transformed into a horizontal double arrow. (This horizontal double arrow will appear black on a color screen.) Next, click your left mouse button and hold it down. 1-2-3/G displays a vertical dotted white line across the row frames. Drag the dotted white line to the right until it reaches the right border of the column where you want to split the screen. For example, if you want to split the window vertically at column C, as in Figure 2-11, drag the dotted white line to the right border of column C. When you're ready, release your mouse button. 1-2-3/G splits the active window into two vertical panes at the location you designated and displays a new set of row frames to mark the split.

Note

When creating vertical panes with the mouse, make sure you move the dotted line outside the column of row frames. Otherwise, 1-2-3/G issues the error massage "Cannot create panes—not enough room."

The same rules apply for moving within vertical windows as for horizontal windows. For example, you can move the cell pointer back and forth between vertical windows by pressing WINDOW (F6) or you can click your mouse on any cell in either pane. What's more, you can move the pane containing the cell pointer to another area of the same worksheet, or to a different worksheet in the same file, simply by moving the cell pointer to that location.

When you move within vertical window panes, 1-2-3/G keeps the same rows in view in both panes. For example, notice in Figure 2–11 that rows 1 through 22 are shown in both the left and right panes. If you press PGDN, or click your mouse on the vertical scroll bar, 1-2-3/G continues to show the same rows in both window panes. Conversely, if you scroll to the right or left, the columns shown in the two panes may vary. For example, Figure 2–11 shows columns A, B, and C of worksheet A in the left panes, and columns J, K, and L of the same worksheet in the right pane.

Note

> You can desynchronize window scrolling for vertical windows to display different rows in the left and the right panes. See "Unsynchronizing Panes" later in this section for details on how to do this.

With the Keyboard

You can also split the current window into two vertical panes using your keyboard. To do this, you use the Worksheet Window Vertical command. In preparation for this command, it is helpful to position the cell pointer in the column immediately to the right of where you want to split the window. For example, to split the window at column C as in Figure 2–11, place the cell pointer in column D. Next, select the Worksheet Window command. 1-2-3/G displays the Worksheet Window dialog box shown in Figure 2–10. Select the Vertical option button from this dialog box. To complete the command, select the OK command button, or press ENTER. 1-2-3/G splits the screen vertically at the location of the cell pointer.

Note

> There must be at least one column between the cell pointer and the left worksheet border when you select the Worksheet Window Vertical command. Otherwise, 1-2-3/G will beep and ignore the command.

Perspective View

Perspective view allows you to view portions of up to five consecutive worksheets at the same time. The worksheets appear stacked, one behind the other, with equal portions of each worksheet displayed. Figure 2–12 shows an example of perspective view displaying three worksheets at once. Perspective view can be very helpful when you're pointing to three-dimensional ranges either during commands or while entering formulas.

To create a display like the one in Figure 2–12, you must use the Worksheet Window command. When you enter this command, 1-2-3/G displays the Worksheet Window dialog box shown in Figure 2–10. From this dialog box, select the Perspective option button. Next type in a number from 2 to 5, indicating the number of worksheets you want displayed. (If you do not provide a number, 1-2-3/G automatically displays three worksheets in perspective view.) To complete the command, select the OK command button or press ENTER. 1-2-3/G returns you to the currently active window and displays the number of consecutive worksheets you specified.

1-2-3/G always displays consecutive worksheets in perspective view. The worksheet containing the cell pointer is used as the starting position for the Worksheet Window Perspective command. For example, imagine you have the cell pointer located in worksheet A. You then select the Worksheet Window Perspective command and specify three worksheets. 1-2-3/G displays work-

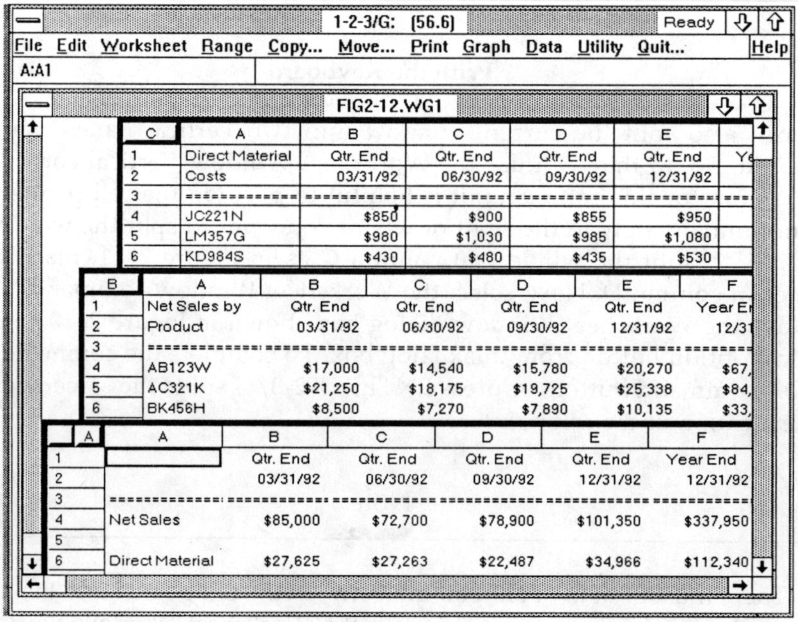

1-2-3/G: (56.6) Ready

File Edit Worksheet Range Copy... Move... Print Graph Data Utility Quit... Help

A:A1

FIG2-12.WG1

C	A	B	C	D	E	
1	Direct Material	Qtr. End	Qtr. End	Qtr. End	Qtr. End	Y
2	Costs	03/31/92	06/30/92	09/30/92	12/31/92	
3	============	===========	===========	===========	===========	===
4	JC221N	$850	$900	$855	$950	
5	LM357G	$980	$1,030	$985	$1,080	
6	KD984S	$430	$480	$435	$530	

B	A	B	C	D	E	F
1	Net Sales by	Qtr. End	Qtr. End	Qtr. End	Qtr. End	Year E
2	Product	03/31/92	06/30/92	09/30/92	12/31/92	12/3
3	============	===========	===========	===========	===========	======
4	AB123W	$17,000	$14,540	$15,780	$20,270	$67,
5	AC321K	$21,250	$18,175	$19,725	$25,338	$84,
6	BK456H	$8,500	$7,270	$7,890	$10,135	$33,

A	A	B	C	D	E	F
1		Qtr. End	Qtr. End	Qtr. End	Qtr. End	Year End
2		03/31/92	06/30/92	09/30/92	12/31/92	12/31/92
3	============	===========	===========	===========	===========	===========
4	Net Sales	$85,000	$72,700	$78,900	$101,350	$337,950
5						
6	Direct Material	$27,625	$27,263	$22,487	$34,966	$112,340

FIGURE 2-12 Perspective view

sheets A, B, and C in the current window. If you subsequently press CTRL-PGUP three times, or click on the worksheet scroll bar three times, 1-2-3/G advances the cell pointer to worksheet D and displays worksheets B, C, and D in the current window.

Note

When 1-2-3/G is displaying a perspective view, you cannot use the Worksheet Window command to split the current window horizontally or vertically. Conversely, you cannot create a perspective view while either the Worksheet Window Horizontal or Vertical command is in effect. In either case, you must clear the current Worksheet Window setting before establishing a new one. See "Clearing Worksheet Window Settings" later in this chapter for details on how to clear horizontal or vertical windows.

Initially, 1-2-3/G synchronizes the scrolling of all panes in perspective view. That way, the same portions of each worksheet are always displayed on your screen. However, you can desynchronize scrolling so that different portions of each worksheet are displayed. See "Unsynchronizing Panes" in the next section for details on how to do this.

Unsynchronizing Panes

Initially, when you split the current worksheet window using your mouse or the Worksheet Window command, 1-2-3/G synchronizes the scrolling of window panes as follows:

- **Horizontal:** The same columns always appear in both the top and bottom window panes.
- **Vertical:** The same rows always appear in the left and right windows.
- **Perspective view:** The same portions of each worksheet are always displayed.

When you desynchronize the scrolling of window panes, however, you can view different columns in horizontal window panes, different rows in vertical panes, and different portions of each worksheet in perspective view.

To desynchronize window scrolling, select the Worksheet Window command to display the Worksheet Window dialog box. Then, select the Unsync

1-2-3/G: [56.6] Ready

File Edit Worksheet Range Copy... Move... Print Graph Data Utility Quit... Help

A:G107

(P0) FIG2-13.WG1

A	A	B	C	D	E	F
1		Qtr. End	Qtr. End	Qtr. End	Qtr. End	Year End
2		03/31/92	06/30/92	09/30/92	12/31/92	12/31/92
3	=============	===========	===========	===========	===========	===========
4	Net Sales	$85,000	$72,700	$78,900	$101,350	$337,950
5						
6	Direct Material	$27,625	$27,263	$22,487	$34,966	$112,340
7	Direct Labor	$12,750	$10,905	$11,835	$15,203	$50,693
8		————	————	————	————	————
9	Direct Costs	$40,375	$38,168	$34,322	$50,168	$163,032
10						
11	Gross Profit	$44,625	$34,533	$44,579	$51,182	$174,918
12						

A	B	C	D	E	F	G
100	100%	100%	100%	100%	100%	
101						
102	33%	38%	29%	35%	33%	
103	15%	15%	15%	15%	15%	
104	————	————	————	————	————	
105	48%	52%	44%	50%	48%	
106						
107	52%	48%	57%	51%	52%	

FIGURE 2-13 The Worksheet Window Unsync command desynchronizes window scrolling

option button. To complete the command, select the OK command button, or press ENTER. From then on, the scrolling of window panes is confined to the pane containing the cell pointer. Panes without the cell pointer remain static on your screen. To resynchronize windows (the default), select the Synch option button.

Figure 2-13 shows an example of the effect that using the Worksheet Window Unsync command can have on horizontal window panes. Notice that the columns displayed in the top and bottom window do not match. This was done by moving the cell pointer to the bottom pane and then beyond the right edge of the current window. The top window remains static and does not scroll with the movement of the cell pointer. The same is true with vertical window panes; the pane with cell pointer moves while the pane without the cell pointer remains static. With a perspective view, you can move around the worksheet containing the cell pointer while the worksheets that do not contain the cell pointer remain static on your screen.

Notice further in Figure 2-13 that an additional horizontal scroll bar has been added to the display. If you compare this screen shot to Figures 2-8 and 2-9, you'll notice this scroll bar does not appear there. This scroll bar allows you to use your mouse to scroll horizontally in whichever window pane currently contains the cell pointer. Conversely, when you desynchronize vertical windows, 1-2-3/G adds an additional vertical scroll bar, allowing you to use your mouse to scroll vertically in the window that contains the cell pointer.

Map View

You can also use the Worksheet Window command to display a compressed view of your worksheets. This compressed view is referred to as *map* view. This term is somewhat descriptive in that it allows you to zoom out on your worksheet and see more of it than you normally can. Thus, you can get a bird's eye view, or map, of the layout and organization of your data. Unfortunately, the view is not WYSIWYG (what you see is what you get). Instead, 1-2-3/G sets all column widths to two characters in the smallest font available. Further, 1-2-3/G displays a plus sign (+) in cells with formulas, a pound sign (#) in cells with values, and a backslash (\) in cells with labels. In addition, the background of cells with labels appears red, the background of cells with values appears blue, and the background of cells with formulas appears green. Figure 2–14 shows an example of map view.

To turn map view on, select the Worksheet Window command to display the Worksheet Window dialog box. Next, select "mode" Map and select the Enable option button. To complete the command, select the OK command

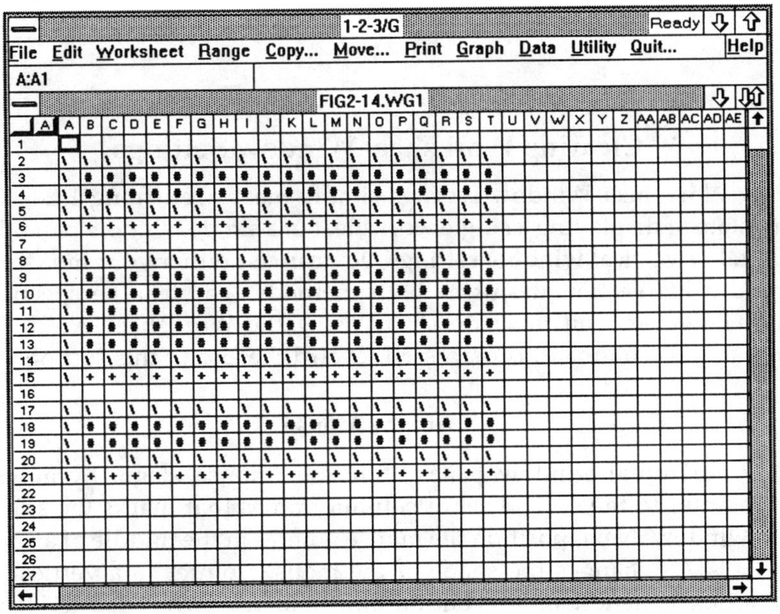

FIGURE 2-14 Map view

button, or press ENTER. 1-2-3/G returns you to the current window and displays its contents in map view. To disable map view, use the Disable option button.

Map view does not change the contents of your worksheet cells in any way. Further, map view does not disable the functionality of 1-2-3/G. For example, you can still use commands and move around the worksheet entering and editing data. Existing data appears in the Control Line when you move the cell pointer onto its cell.

Map view can be helpful for scanning your worksheets to make sure there are no incorrect entries. For example, you can check to see that you have not entered a value where a formula should be. Or, you can find and edit cells that contain a label prefix without any label contents. Additionally, you can take a look at the overall organization of your data.

Tip: Printing in map view

If you print a range while in map view, 1-2-3/G sends the map view characters to your printer. Thus, you can create a printed map of your worksheet. See Chapter 8, "Printing," for details on how to print a worksheet.

Clearing Worksheet Window Settings

Clearing Worksheet Window settings simply means returning 1-2-3/G to its default state of displaying a single worksheet in a single window pane. To clear horizontal or vertical window settings, you can use either your mouse or your keyboard. This section discusses both methods. To clear perspective-view settings, however, you must do so by using the Worksheet Window Clear command. This command is discussed toward the end of this section.

With the Mouse

To clear horizontal window panes with your mouse, begin by moving the mouse pointer to the second set of column frames that marks the split in the current window. Next, position the mouse pointer in the middle of any column frame. 1-2-3/G changes the shape of the mouse pointer to a vertical double arrow. Click your left mouse button and hold it down. 1-2-3/G displays a dotted line across the second set of column frames. Drag the dotted line upward until it meets the top set of column frames, or downward until it meets the scroll bar, and release your mouse button. 1-2-3/G presents a message box with the message "This action will clear panes." To clear the horizontal window panes, select the OK command button from this message box, or press ENTER. To cancel the operation altogether, select the Cancel command button or press ESC.

Clearing vertical window panes with your mouse is very similar to clearing horizontal window panes. To clear vertical panes, move the mouse pointer to the second set of row frames that marks the vertical split in the current window. Next, position the mouse pointer in the middle of any row frame. 1-2-3/G changes the shape of the mouse pointer to a horizontal double arrow. Click you left mouse button and hold it down. 1-2-3/G displays a vertical dotted line to access the second set of row frames. Drag the dotted line to your left until it meets the first set of row frames at the left of the window, or to the right until it meets the scroll bar, and release the mouse button. 1-2-3/G displays the message box that says "This action will clear panes." To clear the vertical panes, select the OK command button from the message box, or press ENTER. To cancel the operation, select the Cancel command button or press ESC.

With the Keyboard

To clear horizontal panes, vertical panes, or perspective view window settings, select the Worksheet Window command. 1-2-3/G displays the Worksheet Window dialog box. Select the Clear command button from this dialog box. 1-2-3/G clears the current horizontal, vertical, or perspective view window settings and returns you to the current worksheet.

You must clear the current Worksheet Window settings before you establish new ones. For example, when 1-2-3/G is displaying vertical window panes, you cannot use the Worksheet Window command to split the current window horizontally or to create a perspective view. Instead, you must clear the current vertical window setting first and then establish the new horizontal or perspective view settings.

DISPLAYING WORKSHEET TITLES

Many worksheets have entries in the first few columns and rows that identify their contents. For example, Figure 2–15 shows an example expense worksheet where the type of expense is listed in column A and the account number for that expense is listed in column B. Along the top row of the worksheet, the months in which those expenses are incurred are shown. Unfortunately, when you move the cell pointer beyond the edge of the worksheet window, some or all of these titles disappear from view.

However, 1-2-3/G allows you to freeze selected columns and/or rows along the top and/or left edges of the current worksheet. The columns and/or rows you select remain static and in view at all times, regardless of where you move the cell pointer in the current worksheet. For example, Figure 2–16 shows the

1-2-3/G (69.4) Ready

File Edit Worksheet Range Copy... Move... Print Graph Data Utility Quit... Help

A:C3 900

(F0) FIG2-15.WG1

A	A	B	C	D	E	F	G
1	EXPENSES:	ACCT	Jan-92	Feb-92	Mar-92	Apr-92	May-92
2							
3	Insurance	801	900	900	900	900	900
4	Legal/Accounting	802	2500	0	2500	0	2500
5	Salaries	803	37000	37000	41000	37000	37000
6	Payroll Tax	804	4181	4181	4633	4181	4181
7	Office Supplies	805	1100	1100	1100	1100	1100
8	Rent	806	2100	2100	2100	2100	2100
9	Telephone	807	450	450	450	450	450
10	Advertising	808	12000	12000	12000	12000	12000
11	Tradeshows	809	0	6500	0	6500	0
12	Miscellaneous	810	500	500	500	500	500
13	Travel	811	1600	0	1600	0	1600
14	Repairs	812	500	500	500	500	500
15	Postage	813	750	750	750	750	750
16	Printing	814	300	300	300	300	300
17	Equipment	815	1250	0	1250	0	1250
18	Amortization	816	600	600	600	600	600
19	Depreciation	817	700	700	700	700	700
20	Benifits	818	4500	4500	4500	4500	4500
21	Interest	819	450	450	450	450	450
22	Bank Charges	820	135	135	135	135	135

FIGURE 2-15 A sample worksheet with column and row titles

1-2-3/G (69.4) Ready

File Edit Worksheet Range Copy... Move... Print Graph Data Utility Quit... Help

A:H23 0

(F0) FIG2-16.WG1

A	A	B	D	E	F	G	H
1	EXPENSES:	ACCT	Feb-92	Mar-92	Apr-92	May-92	Jun-92
2							
5	Salaries	803	37000	41000	37000	37000	37000
6	Payroll Tax	804	4181	4633	4181	4181	4181
7	Office Supplies	805	1100	1100	1100	1100	1100
8	Rent	806	2100	2100	2100	2100	2100
9	Telephone	807	450	450	450	450	450
10	Advertising	808	12000	12000	12000	12000	12000
11	Tradeshows	809	6500	0	6500	0	6500
12	Miscellaneous	810	500	500	500	500	500
13	Travel	811	0	1600	0	1600	0
14	Repairs	812	500	500	500	500	500
15	Postage	813	750	750	750	750	750
16	Printing	814	300	300	300	300	300
17	Equipment	815	0	1250	0	1250	1250
18	Amortization	816	600	600	600	600	600
19	Depreciation	817	700	700	700	700	700
20	Benifits	818	4500	4500	4500	4500	4500
21	Interest	819	450	450	450	450	450
22	Bank Charges	820	135	135	135	135	135
23	Property Tax	821	0	0	3700	0	0
24	Consulting	822	3000	3000	3000	3000	3000

FIGURE 2-16 Worksheet Titles freezes columns and rows

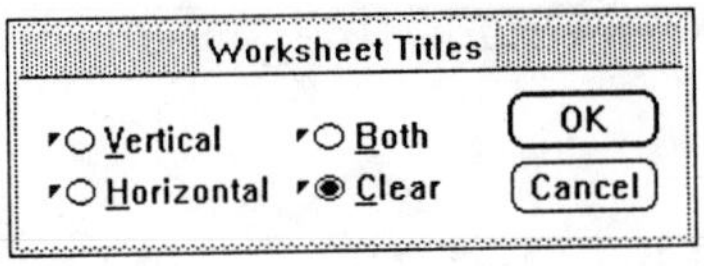

Worksheet Titles

Vertical Both OK

Horizontal Clear Cancel

FIGURE 2-17 The Worksheet Titles dialog box

same worksheet as in Figure 2–15 after columns A and B and row 1 have been frozen. Notice that although the cell pointer has been moved beyond the edge of the worksheet window, the appropriate column and row titles for the expense table remain in view.

To freeze selected columns and/or rows, you use the Worksheet Titles command. When you enter this command, 1-2-3/G displays the Worksheet Titles dialog box shown in Figure 2–17. To freeze rows above the location of the cell pointer, you use the Horizontal option button. To freeze columns to the left of the cell pointer, you use the Vertical option button. To freeze both the rows above and the columns to the left of the cell pointer, select the Both option button. To clear the current Worksheet Titles settings, select the Clear option button.

Positioning of the cell pointer before issuing the Worksheet Titles command is an important factor. 1-2-3/G uses the location of the cell pointer to determine which columns and/or rows to freeze. The sections that follow discuss this in more detail.

Freezing Rows

To freeze one or more rows so that they are always displayed along the top edge of the worksheet, begin by positioning the cell pointer one row below the rows you want to freeze. For example, to freeze row 1 of the current worksheet, place the cell pointer in row 2. Next, select the Worksheet Titles command and select Horizontal. To complete the command, select the OK command button, or press ENTER. 1-2-3/G returns you to the current worksheet. When you move the cell pointer below the bottom edge of the worksheet window, the contents of row 1 remain constantly in view.

Freezing Columns

To freeze one or more columns so that they are always displayed along the left edge of the current worksheet, position the cell pointer one column to the right of the columns you want to freeze. For example, to freeze columns A and B, place the cell pointer in column C. Next, select the Worksheet Titles command and select the Vertical option button. Complete the command by selecting the OK command button or by pressing ENTER. 1-2-3/G returns you to the current worksheet. When you move the cell pointer beyond the right edge of the worksheet window, the contents of columns A and B remain constantly in view.

Freezing Both Rows and Columns

To freeze both rows and columns, position the cell pointer one row below and one column to the right of the columns you want to freeze. For example, to freeze rows 1 and 2 as well as columns A and B of the current worksheet, position the cell pointer in cell C3. Then, select the Worksheet Titles command and select Both from the Worksheet Titles dialog box. Complete the command by selecting the OK command button or by pressing ENTER. 1-2-3/G returns you to the current worksheet. From then on, regardless of where you move the cell pointer in the current worksheet, the contents of rows 1 and 2 and columns A and B remain constantly in view.

Tips on Worksheet Titles

When you freeze columns and/or rows with Worksheet Titles, cell pointer movement is restricted to cells outside the title area. For example, imagine you freeze columns A and B as well as rows 1 and 2 with the Worksheet Titles Both command. When you press HOME after completing this command, 1-2-3/G moves the cell pointer to cell C3, not cell A1. What's more, if you attempt to move the mouse pointer into any cell in columns A or B or rows 1 or 2, the mouse pointer takes on a grayed shading and clicking your mouse button has no effect.

To move the cell pointer into a frozen column or row, you must press GOTO (F5) or select the Range Goto command to display the Range Goto dialog box. Next, type a range name or address within the title area. To complete the command, select the OK command button, or press ENTER. 1-2-3/G moves the cell pointer to the range you specified within the title area.

When you move the cell pointer into the title area, 1-2-3/G temporarily displays a double image of the rows and columns included in the title area. You can then move the cell pointer within the title area to enter and edit data. When you complete editing, press PGDN followed by PGUP or CTRL- → followed by CTRL- ← to move the cell pointer beyond the edge of the worksheet window and then back again. 1-2-3/G once again displays a single image of the title area, and cell pointer movement is restricted to cells outside the title area.

The Worksheet Titles command applies only to the current worksheet. To establish Worksheet Title settings in another worksheet, you must move the cell pointer to that worksheet and enter the command there.

You must have at least one column to the left and/or one row above the cell pointer when you use the Worksheet Titles command. Otherwise, 1-2-3/G issues an error message. For example, imagine you select the Worksheet Titles Horizontal command with the cell pointer in cell A1 of the current worksheet.

1-2-3/G issues an error message because a row does not exist above the location of the cell pointer.

Note

If you attempt to include hidden columns, rows, or worksheets within the title area, 1-2-3/G issues an error message.

MANAGING MULTIPLE FILES ON THE DESKTOP

As mentioned, you can have up to 16 windows open on the desktop at any one time, each containing a different worksheet file, graph file, or utility. For example, Figure 2–18 shows a view of multiple windows open on the 1-2-3/G desktop.

The advantage to the desktop approach is that it allows you to assemble all the tools you need in one place. For example, you can create new files as you need them, or you can open existing files on the desktop and draw on the data in those files. When a file is no longer needed or appropriate, you can replace it with another file or remove it from the desktop altogether. Finally, if you need one or more utilities such as Note or Keystroke Editor to augment your work, you can open those utilities on the desktop as they are needed. See "Adding Tools and Utilities to the Desktop" later for more details on this.

Although you can have multiple windows open on the desktop at any one time, only one of those windows can be active. The active window is the one you happen to be working in at the time. Most of the commands you select and data you enter apply only to the currently active window. To activate another window you must move to that window. See "Moving Between Windows" later in this chapter for details.

1-2-3/G also provides commands that allow you to rearrange multiple windows on your screen. For example, you can choose from a tiled (side by side) arrangement, as shown in Figure 2–18, or you can choose a stacked arrangement (one worksheet stacked behind the other). See "Tiling and Stacking" windows later in this chapter for more details on this.

In general, when you open multiple worksheet files on the desktop, those files exist in memory independently of one another. However, 1-2-3/G allows you to link one file to another. To do this, you can build a formula in one worksheet file that refers to data in another worksheet in another file. See "Linking Worksheet Files with Formulas" for details on this. You can also link

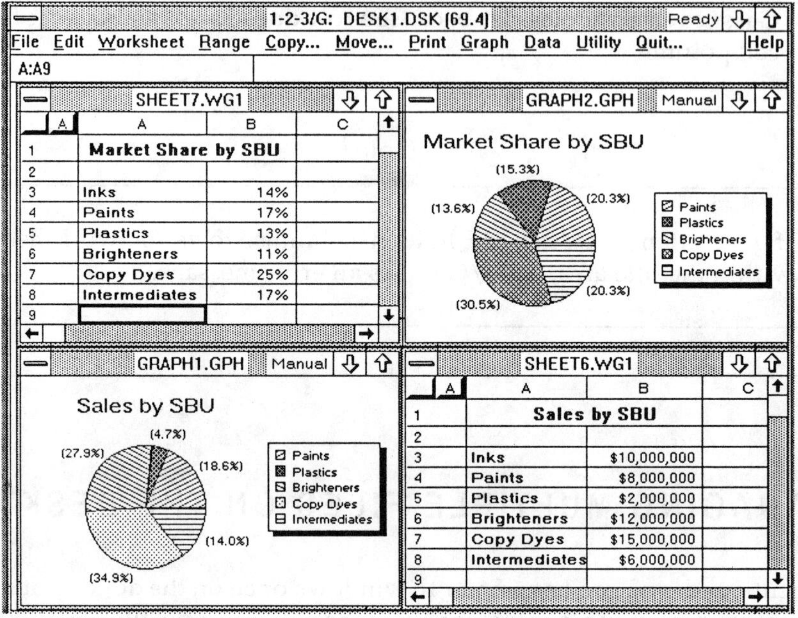

FIGURE 2-18 **Multiple windows open on the desktop**

files by using the Edit command. See "Linking Files With the Edit Command" for more on this.

You can also select commands in the current worksheet file and apply them to ranges in other worksheet files. For example, you can copy or move information from one worksheet file to another. Or, you can enter commands in the current worksheet that apply to worksheets located in other open files. See "Specifying Ranges in Different Files" later in this chapter for more on this topic.

1-2-3/G also allows you to open multiple copies of the same worksheet or graph file on the desktop. Each copy of the file is referred to as a *view* of that file. When you make a change in one view of the file, the other open views of the file are updated to reflect the change. See "Creating Multiple Views of the Same File" later in this chapter for details on how to do this.

Adding Tools and Utilities to the Desktop

This section provides an overview of commands and techniques that you can use to create new files, open existing files, and replace files on the 1-2-3/G desktop. This section also discusses what happens when you close a window with multiple files open on the desktop. Finally, this section briefly discusses 1-2-3/G's available utilities and how you can open them on the desktop.

Creating a New File on the Desktop

To create a new file on the desktop, you use the File New command. When you select this command, 1-2-3/G displays the dialog box in Figure 2–19. You can use this dialog box to add a window to the current desktop that contains either a new worksheet file or a new graph file. At the top of the File New dialog box is a text box entitled "Create window." In this text box, 1-2-3/G displays a default file name. You can accept this default file name, or you can type in one of your own.

The default file name displayed by 1-2-3/G depends on your selection in the list box below entitled "Tool names." In this list box, 1-2-3/G displays the types of tools you can elect to create. At present, the choices are Worksheet or Graph. If you select Worksheet, 1-2-3/G displays a default file name of SHEET.WG1. For each new worksheet file you create in a directory, 1-2-3/G adds a numeric digit to the default file name. 1-2-3/G increases this digit by one for each new file you create. For example, the default name for the second worksheet file you create is SHEET1.WG1, the third SHEET2.WG1, and so on. For graph files, the first default file name is GRAPH.GPH, the second GRAPH1.GPH, the third GRAPH2.GPH, and so on.

Once you've selected the name for the new file and the type of tool you wish to create, you can complete the File New command by selecting the OK command button, or by pressing ENTER. 1-2-3/G places an additional window on the current desktop and opens the type of file you selected within that window under the name you specified. The new window then becomes the active window. Any commands you select or data you enter apply to the new window. Any windows already on the desktop remain there in the background. To apply commands or enter data in one of those windows, you must activate that window by moving to it. See "Moving between Windows" later for details.

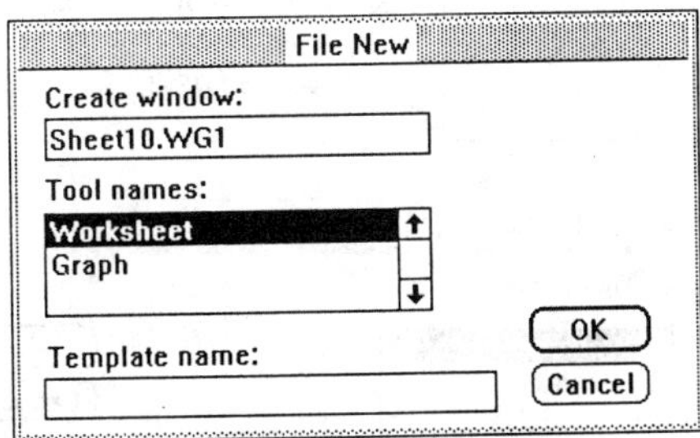

FIGURE 2-19 The File New dialog box

Note

For a complete discussion of the File New command, see Chapter 5, "File Management." For a complete discussion of graph windows and how to use them to create graphs that visually display your data, see Chapter 7, "Graphs."

Opening an Existing File on the Desktop

To open an existing file on the desktop, you use the File Open command. When you select this command, 1-2-3/G displays the dialog box in Figure 2–20. You can use this dialog to open an existing 1-2-3/G worksheet, graph, or desktop file. (See "Opening an Existing Desktop" later in this chapter for more details on this.)

At the top of the File Open dialog box is a text box entitled "File name." Ultimately, this text box will contain the name of the file you wish to open on the desktop. You can type in a drive, path, and filename of your own or you can select a file to open from the list box below. To complete the File Open command, select the OK command button, or press ENTER. 1-2-3/G adds a new window to the desktop and opens the file you specified inside that window. The new window then becomes the active window. Any windows already open on the desktop remain open in the background.

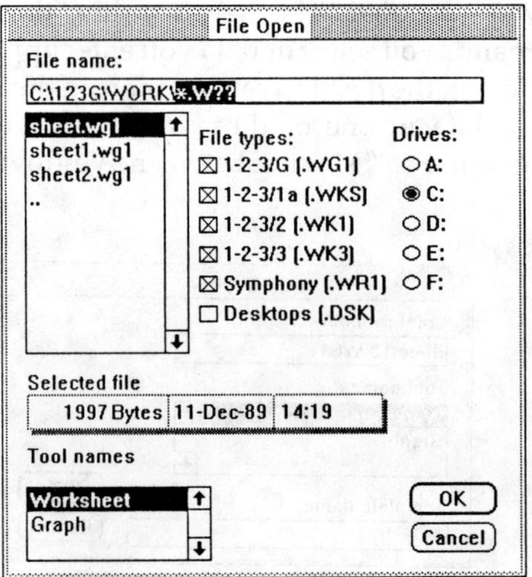

FIGURE 2-20 **The File Open dialog box**

As mentioned, instead of typing a full path and filename in the "File name" text box, you can select a filename from the list box located below. The contents of this list box are determined by the drive and directory information displayed in the "File name" text box. Initially, 1-2-3/G displays the drive and path for the current directory in the "File name" text box. This is followed by a wild-card file extension that matches the file type of the currently active window.

For example, if the active window contains a worksheet file, and the current directory is C:\123G\WORK\, 1-2-3/G displays C:\123G\WORK*.W?? in the "File name" text box. This causes the worksheet files in the current directory to appear in the list box immediately beneath. (The filenames appear in alphabetical order by file extension.) On the other hand, if the active window contains a graph file, 1-2-3/G displays a *.GPH wild-card file extension in the File name text box and displays the graph files in the current directory. To display the files on another drive and/or directory in the list box, simply edit the drive and/or directory that appears in the "File name" text box.

To select a file to open from the File name list box, simply double-click on the name of that file in the list box. Alternatively, you can click once, or use the arrow keys to move the highlight to the filename you want. When you're ready, press ENTER, or select the OK command button. 1-2-3/G opens the file you specified and places it in its own window on the desktop. The newly opened window then becomes the active window. Any windows already open on the desktop remain open in the background.

The File Open dialog box contains a number of other convenient features that can help you in selecting an existing file to open on the desktop. For a complete discussion of these features, as well as the File Open command, see Chapter 5, "File Management."

Replacing a File on the Desktop

To replace a file on the desktop with another existing file from disk, you use the File Retrieve command. This command closes the currently active file and replaces it with the file you select. However, if you've made changes to the currently active file since you loaded it into memory, 1-2-3/G prompts you to save your changes prior to replacing the active file. If you have more than one view (copy) of the active file open (see "Opening Multiple Views of the Same File" later), 1-2-3/G displays an error message when you attempt to replace the file. If you still want to replace the file, you must first close other open views so that only one copy of the file is open in the desktop.

When you select the File Retrieve command, 1-2-3/G displays the dialog box in Figure 2–21. (The use of this dialog box is similar to the File Open dialog box shown earlier in Figure 2–20.) At the top of the dialog box is a text box entitled "File name." Ultimately, this text box will contain the name of the file that will replace the currently active file. You can type the drive, path, and filename for the replacement file in this text box and complete the File Retrieve command by pressing ENTER or by selecting the OK command button. 1-2-3/G closes the currently active file and replaces it with the file you specified. If you made changes to the currently active file, however, 1-2-3/G allows you to save your changes prior to replacing the file. The replacement file then becomes the new active file.

Instead of typing a filename in the File name text box, you can select a replacement file name from the list box below. When you first enter the File Retrieve command, the "File name" text box contains the drive and path for the current directory followed by a wild-card file extension (*.W?? or *.GPH). The wild-card extension shown depends on whether the currently active window contains a worksheet or a graph file. The wild-card extension determines whether 1-2-3/G displays worksheet or graph files in the list box below. To display the files on another drive and/or directory in the list box, simply edit the drive and/or path displayed in the "File name" text box and press ENTER. To select a file to replace the currently active file from the list box, you can use any of the following methods:

- Double-click on a displayed filename in the list box.
- Click once on a displayed filename, or press ↓ to move the highlight to a displayed filename and select the OK command button or press ENTER.

Whichever of these methods you use, 1-2-3/G replaces the active file with the file you selected.

The File Retrieve dialog box contains a number of other convenient features that can help you in selecting a replacement file. For a complete discussion of these features, as well as the File Retrieve command, see Chapter 5, "File Management."

Opening Multiple Views of the Same File

1-2-3/G also allows you to open more than one view (copy) of the same worksheet or graph file on the desktop at the same time. To do this, simply use the File Open command to open as many copies of the file as you need. Each view of the file is placed in its own window. To indicate a second view of the file is open, 1-2-3/G displays a 2 in parentheses (2) after the file-name in the window title bar. This parenthetical number indicates that this is the second view of the file. For each additional copy you open, 1-2-3/G increases this number by one for that particular window.

1-2-3/G only allows you to save one version of a given worksheet or graph file in each directory. Therefore, when you make a change to the data or settings in one open view of a file, all other open views are immediately updated for that change. Further, if you use the File Retrieve command to replace a view of the file, 1-2-3/G issues the error message "Cannot change the filename—more than one view of the file is open." Once again, this prevents you from saving two versions of the same file in the same directory. Finally, when you use the File Save command to save a file with several open views, only a single copy of that file is saved to disk.

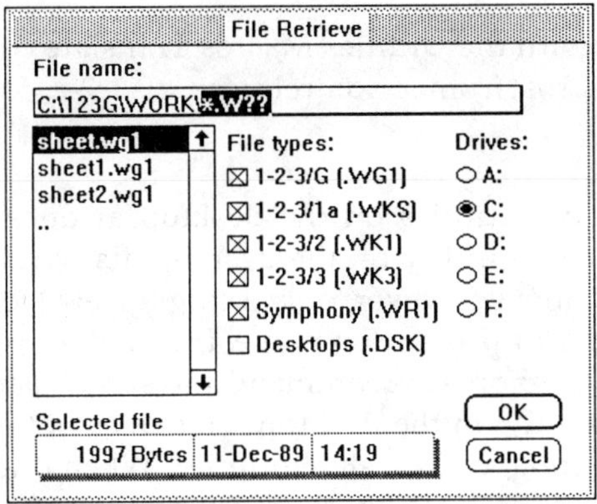

FIGURE 2-21 **The File Retrieve dialog box**

Opening Utilities on the Desktop

As mentioned in Chapter 1, 1-2-3/G provides a number of utilities that you can use to augment your work. These utilities include the following:

- **Note:** Accessed with the Utility Note command, Note allows you to attach up to four notes to a worksheet cell (Chapter 1).
- **Solver:** Accessed with the Utility Solver command, Solver allows you to perform what-if analysis with your worksheet models (Chapter 13).
- **Keystroke Editor:** Accessed with the Utility Macros Keystroke Editor command or by selecting Keystroke Editor from the Desktop Control menu, the Keystroke Editor allows you to capture keystrokes and play them back or place them in the worksheet for use in macros (Chapter 10).
- **Print Preview:** Accessed by selecting the "Screen preview" check box available in either the Print Printer or File Print Print Worksheet dialog boxes, Print Preview allows you to preview a document before it is printed (Chapter 8).

1-2-3/G also includes some other minor utilities that do not remain on the desktop. That is, they disappear from the desktop when you finish using them. These utilities include the following:

- **Backsolver:** Accessed with Utility Backsolver, it allows you to perform what-if analysis in reverse (Chapter 13).
- **Debug:** Accessed with the Utility Macros Debug command, it allows you to execute macros a step at a time and trace macro command execution to highlight errors (Chapter 10).

- **Translate:** Accessed with the Utilities Macros Translate command, it allows you to translate macros from prior releases of 1-2-3 for use in 1-2-3/G (Chapter 10).

You can open multiple utilities on the desktop at once, each in its own window. When you open a utility on the desktop, its window automatically becomes the active window. However, only a single view (copy) of each utility can be present on the desktop at any one time. If you attempt to open a second view of a utility, 1-2-3/G ignores the command and simply activates the present view of the utility currently on the desktop. This does not present a problem with the Backsolver, Debug, or Translate utilities. When one of these applications is active, you cannot move to another window or enter a command until either the utility is finished running or until you cancel it, thus removing it from the desktop.

Common Menus

Each tool or major utility offered by 1-2-3/G has its own main menu. That menu appears in the menu bar at the desktop when you activate the tool or utility. However, consistent with its Graphical User Interface (GUI) design, 1-2-3/G offers two menu options that are common to most tools and utilities, the File and Edit menu options.

The File menu is present for all tools and utilities. This menu allows you to create new files, open existing files, change the current directory, or manage the desktop (archive it, copy it, and so on) from whatever tool or utility you happen to be using. Some tools or utilities may add options to the File menu, and, in some tools and utilities, the options in the File menu may appear grayed, meaning that you cannot select them. The use of the File menu is discussed at length in Chapter 5, "File Management."

The Edit menu, on the other hand, is present in all tools and utilities except Solver. The Edit menu gives you access to the Presentation Manager clipboard. Using this menu, you can copy data to the Presentation Manager clipboard and then paste that data into other 1-2-3/G tools or utilities. For example, you might want to copy and paste data between two worksheet files or between a worksheet and a graph window.

The Edit menu also allows you to create a link between worksheet windows or between a graph and a worksheet window. That way, you can reference data from another file in the current file. You can also use the Edit command to form a link between a graph or worksheet window and a file created by another Presentation Manager application that supports the DDE (Dynamic Data Exchange) message protocol. As is the case with the File menu, some tools and utilities may add options to the Edit menu, and some may remove options altogether. What's more, in some tools and utilities the options in the Edit menu may appear grayed, meaning you cannot select them. The use of the Edit menu to copy and paste data between files is discussed at length in Chapter 4,

"Cutting and Pasting Data." The use of the Edit menu to link one file to another is discussed later in this chapter under "Linking Files."

Closing Windows on the Desktop

As mentioned earlier in this chapter, you can close a window on the desktop in several ways. However, when you have multiple windows open on the desktop, closing the active window has the effect of activating the next window on the desktop. As you may recall, you can close the currently active window by using any of the following techniques:

- Double-click on the Window Control menu box for the window.
- Click once on the Window Control menu box, or press ALT-- (ALT-MINUS), to display the Window Control menu. Then, select Close from that menu.
- Press CTRL-F4.

If the contents of the active window have not been saved, or if you've made changes since you opened the window, 1-2-3/G will prompt you to save the window before closing it. It does this by displaying the Close Window dialog box. To save the active window's contents before closing it, select the OK command button from this dialog box. To close the window without saving its contents, select the NO command button. To cancel the Close operation and leave the window on the desktop, select Cancel.

Note

> If only a single window is open on the desktop, and you close it, 1-2-3/G's main menu is removed from the menu bar at the top of your screen. It is replaced by a single command, File. However, this command gives you access to the File Open and File New commands discussed earlier. These commands allow you to open an existing file or create a new file.

Moving between Windows

As mentioned, regardless of how many windows you have open on the desktop, only one of those windows can be active. The active window is the window you happen to be working in at the time. The menu names in the Desktop menu bar and the data you enter apply only to that window.

You can tell the active window by its appearance. Its title bar appears in different color than the rest of the windows on the desktop and its border appears brighter.

If only a single window is present on the desktop, that window is by default the active window. However, when you add a window to the desktop by creating a new worksheet or graph file or by opening an existing file or a utility, the window containing that file or utility then becomes the active window. To apply commands and enter data in another window, you must move to that window. 1-2-3/G offers you several ways to move between windows.

- Click your mouse on any part of a window. If the window contains a worksheet tool, 1-2-3/G moves the cell pointer to that window.
- Press NEXT WINDOW (CTRL-F6) to move to the next open window on the desktop. In fact, pressing CTRL-F6 repeatedly will cycle you through all the open windows on the desktop.
- Click your mouse on the Desktop Control menu box, or press ALT-SPACEBAR, to display the Desktop Control menu. Next, select Window from that menu. 1-2-3/G displays a list of open windows on the desktop. (The currently active window has a check mark next to its name.) Select the name of the window you wish to activate.
- Press GOTO (F5) or select the Range Goto command. In either case, 1-2-3/G displays the Range Goto dialog box. You can use this dialog box to jump to a range address or range name either in the currently active worksheet file or in another open worksheet file. See Chapter 1 for a detailed explanation of the Range Goto and GOTO (F5).

A window can still be active even though you've minimized it (reduced it to an icon). For example, when you press NEXT WINDOW (CTRL-F6) to move to the next window, 1-2-3/G will still activate the next window, even if it is an icon. Similarly, clicking on an icon serves to activate the window that icon represents. Therefore, you can apply commands to a window, even though it has been minimized.

Tiling and Stacking Windows

With multiple windows on the desktop, you are constantly faced with the challenge of arranging those windows on your screen so that you see their contents. 1-2-3/G offers a partial solution to this problem by providing internal commands that allow you to stack and tile windows.

With a stacked window arrangement, each window on the desktop is adjusted to the same size, and they appear stacked (one behind the other) with the title bar of each window exposed. The currently active window is placed at the front of the stack. That way, you can easily see the name of each window currently on the desktop and you can move quickly to a specific window simply by clicking on its title bar. Figure 2–22 shows an example of stacked windows.

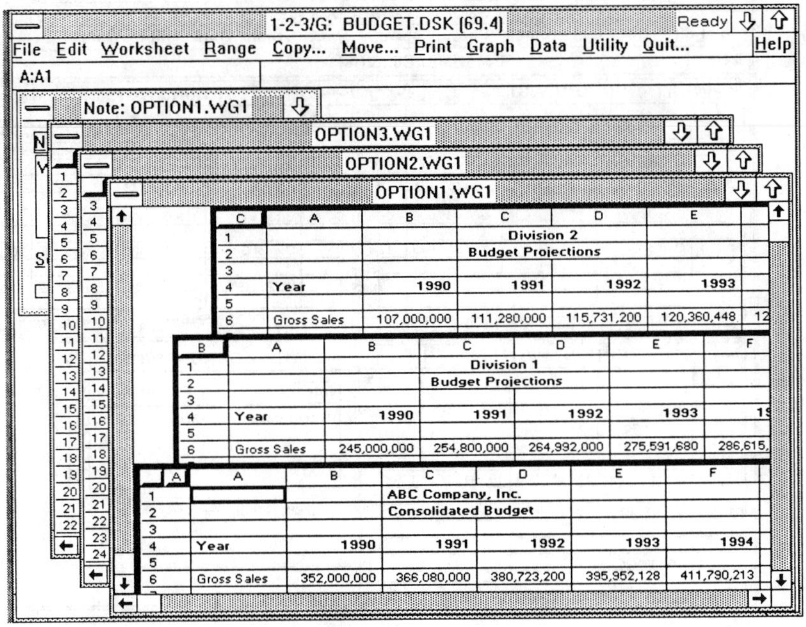

FIGURE 2-22 Stacked windows

With a tiled window arrangement, the windows appear side-by-side, much like a tiled floor. 1-2-3/G adjusts the size of each window as necessary so that a section of each window on the desktop is displayed. The currently active window is placed in the upper-left corner of the desktop. Figure 2–23 shows an example of tiled windows. Tiling windows is helpful when you want to view the contents of two or more windows at the same time.

To tile or stack windows, click on the Desktop Control menu box, or press ALT-SPACEBAR, to display the Desktop Control menu. Select the Window option from that menu. 1-2-3/G presents a cascade menu with two options, Stack and Tile, followed by a list of window names currently open on the desktop. To stack the windows on the desktop, select Stack. 1-2-3/G arranges all the windows on the desktop in a stack, placing the active window at the front of the stack. To tile the windows on the desktop, select the Tile option. 1-2-3/G arranges the windows on the desktop in a tiled fashion, placing the currently active window in the upper-left corner of your screen.

LINKING FILES

1-2-3/G allows you to link files either by using formulas or by using the Edit Link command. Linking allows you to reference data in other files in the current

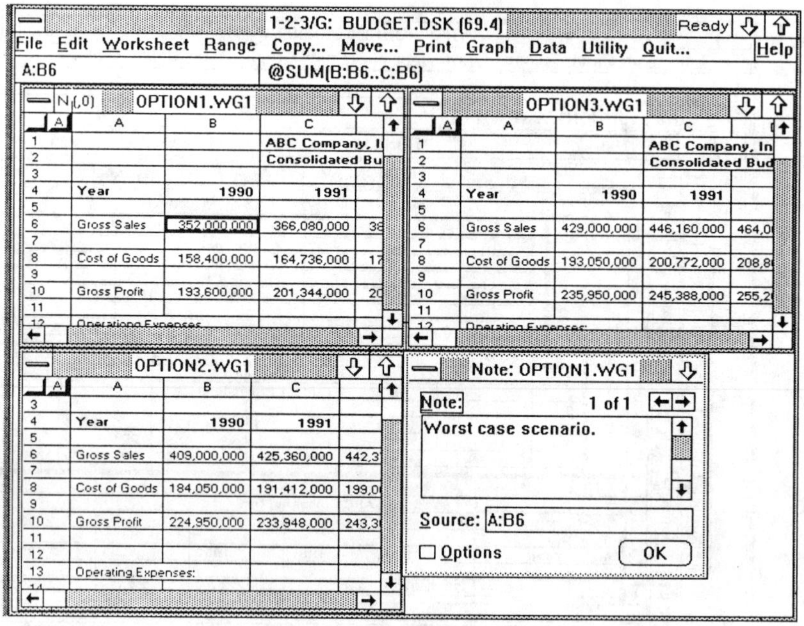

FIGURE 2-23 **Tiled windows**

file. Both forms of linking are dynamic. That is, when you change the data in the *source* file—the file referenced by the link—the *destination* file—the file containing the link—is automatically updated for the change. However, linking files with formulas is restricted to worksheet files only. On the other hand, you can use the Edit Link command to link one 1-2-3/G worksheet file to another or to link a 1-2-3/G worksheet file to a 1-2-3/G graph file. In addition, you can use the Edit Link command to link a 1-2-3/G worksheet and/or graph file to a file created by another Presentation Manager Application that supports DDE (Dynamic Data Exchange). Both methods of linking files are discussed in the sections that follow.

Linking Worksheet Files with Formulas

1-2-3/G allows you to build formulas in the current worksheet file that refer to data in other worksheet files. When you create such a formula, 1-2-3/G actually forms a link between the destination file (the file containing the formula) and the source file (the file containing the data to which the formula refers). The source file can be open on the desktop or on disk.

To create a link formula in the current worksheet file, you use a file reference. File references can be used in any formula in place of an ordinary cell address. To create a file reference, you enclose the name of the file to be linked in double-angle brackets << >> and follow this with a range name or address from that file. For example, to link the single cell range A:A10 in a file named SALES.WG1 located in the current directory to the currently active file, you can use the following formula in any cell in the current active file: **+<<SALES.WG1>>A:A10**. 1-2-3/G copies the data from cell A:A10 of SALES.WG1 to the current cell in the current worksheet file.

If you are a 1-2-3 Release 2.2 or 3 user, you'll notice that the linking scheme in 1-2-3/G is very similar to those releases. However, in Release 2.2, you are limited to single-cell linking, as shown in the previous example. That is, you can only reference the contents of a single cell in another file. However, in Release 3.0 and 1-2-3/G you can reference multiple-cell ranges in other files. For example, you might use the following formula:

@SUM(<<SALES.WG1>>A:A1..A:A10)

From the current worksheet file, you can link to files that are open on the desktop as well as to files on disk. However, when you link two files that are currently open on the desktop, 1-2-3/G updates the destination file automatically whenever the data in the source file changes. For example, imagine you have two files open on the desktop, MARKET.WG1 and SALES.WG1. The MARKET.WG1 file contains the formula +<<SALES.WG1>>A:A10 in cell A:A1 and is therefore the destination file. When the contents of cell A:A10 in the source file, SALES.WG1, are changed, the link formula in cell A:A1 of the MARKET.WG1 file is updated for that change automatically.

1-2-3/G updates your links whenever you load a worksheet file into memory. For example, imagine you have linked the two files, MARKET.WG1 and SALES.WG1, as described in the previous paragraph. You then save both files to disk and leave 1-2-3/G. In a subsequent session, you make changes to the SALES.WG1 file (the source file). The next time you load the MARKET.WG1 file (the destination file) into memory, its link formula referencing SALES.WG1 is automatically updated to reflect the changes to SALES.WG1, even though the SALES.WG1 remains closed on disk.

Tip: Use drive and path identifiers in link formulas

It is always a good idea to include a drive and/or directory path in the file reference section of your link formulas. That way, 1-2-3/G will always be able to find the source file, even when you change the current directory. If 1-2-3/G cannot find the file referenced in a link formula, 1-2-3/G will display ERR in the cell when you load the file containing that link formula into memory. For example, if the file SALES.WG1 is located in a directory named ACCT23 on drive C, use the formula +<<C:\ACCT23\ SALES.WG1>>A:A10 instead of +<<SALES.WG1>>A:A10.

Note

You can change the current directory by using either the File Directory command or the User Settings Directories Working directory command, available from either the Desktop Control menu or the Utility menu. See Chapter 5, "File Management," for details on these commands.

You can use a file and range reference in place of a range name or address in virtually any formula. For example, you can use a file and range reference with a function like @SUM, as in @SUM(<<C:\SALES.WG1>>A:A1..A:A10). You can either type in the file and range reference manually, or you can enter POINT mode and select it. To use POINT mode, however, both files must be open on the desktop.

Figure 2-24 shows an example of how you might use a link formula to consolidate information from several worksheet files into the current file. Three files are shown on the desktop in Figure 2-24, HOST.WG1, DEPT3.WG1, and DEPT4.WG1. Cell A:B5 of the HOST.WG1 file (on the left side of Figure 2-24)

1-2-3/G: LINK.DSK (69.4) Ready

File Edit Worksheet Range Copy... Move... Print Graph Data Utility Quit... Help

A:B5 +<<DEPT3.WG1>>A:B5+<<DEPT4.WG1>>A:B5

(,0) HOST.WG1

A	A	B	C
1		Consolidated Budge	
2			
3		Jan-92	Feb-9
4	Direct Costs:		
5	Direct Labor	270,000	277,80
6	Direct Materials	486,000	500,04
7	Total	756,000	777,84
8			
9	Overhead - Fixed		
10	Building Rent	39,000	39,00
11	Depreciation, machinery	11,320	11,32
12	Supervisory Salaries	71,500	71,50
13	Total	121,820	121,82
14			
15	Overhead - Variable		
16	Indirect Labor	13,000	12,00
17	Indirect Materials	6,000	5,50
18	Maintainance	7,000	8,20
19	Power and Lights	4,400	5,50
20	Total	30,400	31,20
21			
22	Totals	908,220	930,86
23			
24			
25			
26			
27			

DEPT3.WG1

A	A	B	C
1		Department 3 -- Bud	
2			
3		Jan-92	Feb-9
4	Direct Costs:		
5	Direct Labor	120,000	124,80
6	Direct Materials	216,000	224,64
7	Total	336,000	349,44
8			
9	Overhead - Fixed		
10	Building Rent	21,000	21,00
11	Depreciation, machinery	6,750	6,75
12	Supervisory Salaries	37,000	37,00

DEPT4.WG1

A	A	B	C
1		Department 4 -- Bud	
2			
3		Jan-92	Feb-9
4	Direct Costs:		
5	Direct Labor	150,000	153,00
6	Direct Materials	270,000	275,40
7	Total	420,000	428,40
8			
9	Overhead - Fixed		
10	Building Rent	18,000	18,00
11	Depreciation, machinery	4,570	4,57
12	Supervisory Salaries	24,500	24,50

FIGURE 2-24 Linking files on the desktop

contains the formula +<<DEPT3.WG1>>A:B5+<<DEPT4.WG1>>A:B5. You can enter this formula manually, or you can construct it by using POINT mode. To construct this formula by using POINT mode, perform the following steps:

1. Move the cell pointer to cell A:B5 of the HOST.WG1 file and press +. 1-2-3/G enters POINT mode.
2. Click on cell A:B5 of the DEPT3.WG1 window, or press CTRL-F6 (NEXT WINDOW) to move to the DEPT3.WG1 window and highlight cell A:B5. 1-2-3/G now shows +<<DEPT3.WG1>>A:B5 in the Control Line.
3. Press + again. 1-2-3/G returns the cell pointer to the HOST.WG1 window and remains in POINT mode. 1-2-3/G now displays +<<DEPT3.WG1>>A:B5+ in the Control Line.
4. Click on cell A:B5 of the DEPT4.WG1 window, or press NEXT WINDOW (CTRL-F6) twice to move to the DEPT4.WG1 window and highlight cell A:B5. 1-2-3/G now shows +<<DEPT3.WG1>>A:B5+<<DEPT4>>A:B5 in the Control Line.
5. Complete the formula by pressing ENTER.

Note

While constructing a link formula with POINT mode, when you point to a range in another file that is stored in a directory other than the current directory, 1-2-3/G appends the complete filename, including its drive and path to the file, to your link formula.

As mentioned you can also use range names in place of range addresses in link formulas. You can either type in the range name or you can select it by pressing NAME (F3) to display a list of files, and their range names, currently on the desktop.

To select from a list of range names, press any operator (+, -, *, /, (, or ^) that causes 1-2-3/G to enter POINT mode. Then, press NAME (F3). 1-2-3/G displays the Range Names dialog box shown in Figure 2–25. Initially, this dialog box displays only the names of the files currently open on the desktop. To select a displayed file name, click on it, or highlight it and press ENTER. 1-2-3/G places the filename in text box above and encloses it in double-angle brackets << >>. In addition, the range names for that file are now displayed in the list box. To select a range name to add to the file reference, click on it and select the OK command button, or highlight it and press ENTER. 1-2-3/G appends the file and range name reference to your formula, returns you to the active window,

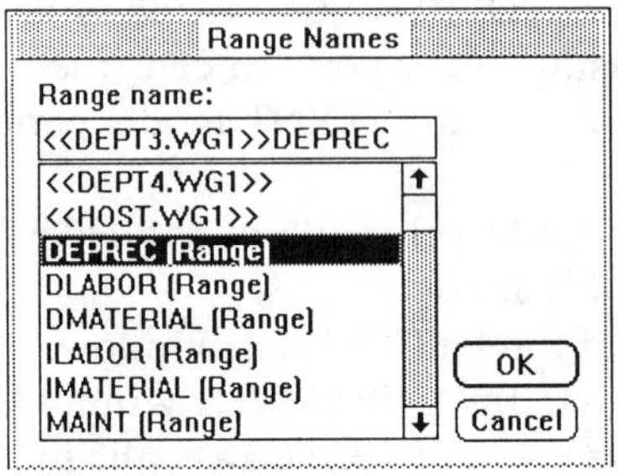

Range Names
Range name:
<<DEPT3.WG1>>DEPREC
<<DEPT4.WG1>>
<<HOST.WG1>>
DEPREC (Range)
DLABOR (Range)
DMATERIAL (Range)
ILABOR (Range)
IMATERIAL (Range)
MAINT (Range)
OK
Cancel

FIGURE 2-25 The Range Names dialog box

and remains in POINT mode. At this point, you can continue adding to the formula or you can complete it by pressing ENTER.

If a range name is unique among the files in memory, you can use a wild-card file reference, <<?>>, in your link formula followed by the range name. When you do this, 1-2-3/G searches all the files currently open on the desktop to find that range name. For example, if the range name JAN_LABOR is unique to all the files in memory, you can use the reference <<?>>JAN_LABOR in a formula to refer to that range.

When you use a wild-card file reference <<?>> followed by a range name in a link formula, the file containing that range name must be present in memory. Otherwise, 1-2-3/G assumes the range name is undefined and returns ERR in the cell containing the formula. What's more, in subsequent 1-2-3/G sessions, when you load the file containing that formula onto the desktop, the file containing the range name must also be loaded. Otherwise, 1-2-3/G will not be able to find the range name and will return ERR in the cell.

You can also create forward references with link formulas. For example, imagine you have three worksheet files on the desktop SHEET1.WG1, SHEET2.WG1, AND SHEET3.WG1. In cell A:A1 of SHEET2.WG1 you have the formula +<<SHEET3>>A:A1. In cell A:A1 of SHEET1.WG1, you have the formula +<<SHEET2>>A:A1. 1-2-3/G uses the link formula in cell A:A1 of SHEET1.WG1 to get the value from call A:A1 of SHEET2.WG1, which gets it value from cell A:A1 of SHEET3.WG1. You can do the same thing using named ranges or named collections.

When you copy link formulas from one area of the worksheet to another, 1-2-3/G adjusts the range references in the formula relative to cell A1 in the source file. For example, imagine you have the formula +<<SALES>>A:A10 in cell A:A1 of the current file. You then copy that formula to cell A:A2 of the current file, or to another file. The copied formula in cell A:A2 reads +<<SALES>>A:A11, because it has been adjusted to reflect its new position relative to cell A1 in the source file. The same thing will happen with a range name. To avoid this adjustment, you can use an absolute reference in the formula, as in +<<SALES.WG1>>$A:$A$10 or +<<BUDGET.WG1>>$JAN_LABOR. See Chapter 4, "Cutting and Pasting Data," for more on copying formulas as well as using absolute references.

When you move data referenced by a link formula, 1-2-3/G updates the link formula. For example, imagine you have the formula +<<SALES.WG1>>A:A10 in a cell in the current file. Imagine further that you move the contents of cell A:A10 in the SALES.WG1 file to cell A:B100 in the file MARKET.WG1 located on the C:\ACCT23 directory. The link formula in the original file is now updated to read +<<C:\ACCT23\MARKET>>+A:B100. For information on how to move data from one location to another, see Chapter 4 "Cutting and Pasting Data."

Moving Formula Link References

1-2-3/G allows you to change the source references for link formulas in the current worksheet file to refer to another worksheet file. To do this, you use the File Admin Move-Links command. This command is only available if link formulas exist in the current worksheet file.

When you select the File Admin Move-Links command, 1-2-3/G displays the dialog box in Figure 2-26. At the top of this dialog is a text box entitled "Destination file." This text box always contains the name of the current file. You cannot change the contents of this text box. Beneath this are two other text boxes, "Current source" and "New source," each with its own list box. The "Current source" text box, and its corresponding list box, shows the names of all worksheet files, both open and on disk, that are referred to by link formulas in the current file. The "New source" text box, and its corresponding list box, shows the names of all open worksheet files as well as the names of worksheet files on disk in the current directory.

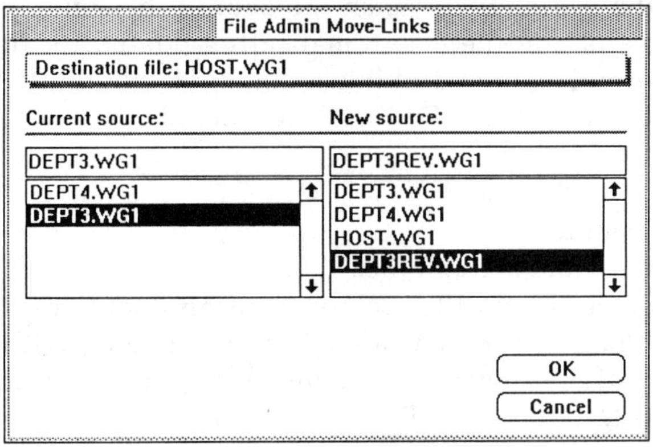

FIGURE 2-26 The File Admin Move-Links dialog box

To change the source references for link formulas in the current file, specify the name of the source file you want to move the links from in the "Current source" text box. You can type in the name of the source file, or you can select it from the list box below. To specify a file to move the link references to, use the "New source" text box. You can either type in the name of the appropriate worksheet file, or you can select it from the list box below. To complete the File Admin Move-Links command, select the OK command button, or press ENTER. 1-2-3/G updates the link formulas in the current worksheet file. All references to the old source file are replaced with references to the same ranges in the new source file.

The File Admin Move-Links command can save you time and effort. For example, imagine you've created link formulas in the current worksheet file that consolidate departmental budget data from several other worksheet files. However, one of the departments has seen fit to dramatically revise its budget. Further, this department has submitted a new worksheet file with the same structure, but under a different file name. Rather than manually revise all your link formulas in the current file, you can use the File Admin Move-Links command to change the appropriate references in your link formulas to refer to the new file.

Linking Files with Edit Link

You can also link files by using the Edit Link command. This command is available from either the Worksheet Tool menu or from the Graph Tool menu. The Edit Link command performs basically the same function in either Tool. However, this section focuses on using the Edit Link command from the Worksheet Tool menu to link 1-2-3/G worksheet files to other files. Using the Edit Link command from the Graph Tool menu to link graph files to other files is discussed in Chapter 7, "Graphs."

Similar to linking files with formulas, the Edit Link command allows you to create a link in one file (the destination file) that refers to information in another file (the source file). When the data in the source file changes, the data in the destination file is automatically updated for the change. However, unlike formulas, the Edit Link command is not limited to linking only worksheet files. In fact, the Edit Link command can be used to link any of the following:

- Two worksheet files.
- A worksheet file and a graph file.
- A worksheet file and a file created with another Presentation Manager application that supports Dynamic Data Exchange (DDE).
- A graph file and a file created with another Presentation Manager application that supports Dynamic Data Exchange (DDE).

The Edit Link command allows you to open up a one-way door either between two 1-2-3/G files or between a file created by 1-2-3/G and a file created by another Presentation Manager application. This passageway is only open to Presentation Manager applications that support the Dynamic Data Exchange (DDE) protocol. 1-2-3/G is one such application.

DDE allows applications to communicate with one another through a messaging system. Because of this messaging system, you can create dynamic links between files created by the same or different Presentation Manager applications. For example, you might link a Presentation Manager word processor file to a 1-2-3/G graph file. That way, the 1-2-3/G graph is displayed in the file created by the word processor. In turn, that graph file may be linked to numbers that are located in a 1-2-3/G worksheet file. When you change the numbers in the 1-2-3/G worksheet file, both the 1-2-3/G graph file and the file created by the word processor product are updated for the change.

In addition to supporting DDE, 1-2-3/G also takes advantage of the Presentation Manager *clipboard*. The clipboard is essentially an area of your computer's memory in which Presentation Manager can store information temporarily. The clipboard is available to all Presentation Manager applications. With this design, data can be copied between different 1-2-3/G tools as well as Presentation Manager applications. For example, as you'll see in Chapter 4, you can use the Edit Copy command to copy information from a worksheet into the clipboard and then use the Edit Paste command to paste that information into either another worksheet, a graph, or a 1-2-3/G utility. However, applications cannot communicate through the clipboard. Therefore, the information copied from one 1-2-3/G tool or utility to another through the clipboard is static in nature.

Note

> When you copy data from a 1-2-3/G worksheet file into the clipboard, the data is copied along with its location (file and range). As you'll soon see, the Edit Link command allows you to use the information in the clipboard to create links between worksheet files.

Creating Links

To link two worksheet files, you use the Edit Link Create command. In order for this command to work, however, both files must be open on the desktop. You cannot use Edit Link Create to link to files on disk. Additionally, the Edit Link Create command can only be used to create links in the currently active file. Therefore, make sure that the file in which you want to create the link is the active file (contains the cell pointer).

In preparation for the Edit Link command, move the cell pointer to the cell in the active file that will contain the link. Then, select the Edit Link command. When you select this command, 1-2-3/G displays the dialog box in Figure 2-27. At the top of this dialog box is an information box entitled "Destination file." In this box, 1-2-3/G displays the name of the currently active file. For example, in Figure 2-27 the filename STMT92.WG1 appears in this text box. This same file appears as the active file in Figure 2-28. The contents of "Destination file" box is for your information only—you cannot edit the contents of this box.

Beneath the "Destination file" information box is another text box entitled "Source file and item." This text box, and its accompanying list box, lets you specify a filename and range to link to the current file. Initially the text box is empty. However, in the list box below, 1-2-3/G lists the names of available source files that you can link to the currently active file. For example, in Figure 2-27, the names of the open worksheet files shown in Figure 2-28 are displayed. (The names of files created by 1-2-3/G are displayed in upper-case letters. Files created by other Presentation Manager Applications are displayed in lower case.)

To select a range in another worksheet file to link to the current file, specify the name of that file followed by a range from that file in the "Source file and item" text box. You can use any of the following methods to do this:

- Type the filename enclosed in double-angle brackets << >> followed by a range address or range name from that file. For example, Figure 2-27 shows

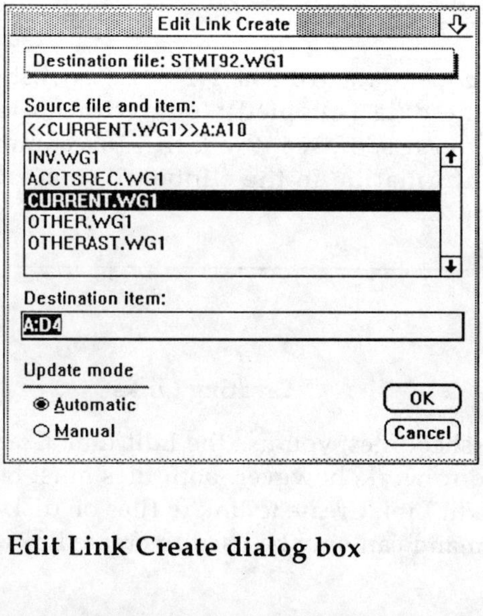

Edit Link Create

Destination file: STMT92.WG1

Source file and item:

<<CURRENT.WG1>>A:A10

INV.WG1
ACCTSREC.WG1
CURRENT.WG1
OTHER.WG1
OTHERAST.WG1

Destination item:

A:D4

Update mode

◉ Automatic
○ Manual

OK
Cancel

FIGURE 2-27 **The Edit Link Create dialog box**

the entry <<CURRENT>>A:A10 in the "Source file and item" text box. To confirm your selection, press ENTER.

- Click on the title bar of the window that contains the source file, or press NEXT WINDOW (CTRL-F6) to move the cell pointer to that window. 1-2-3/G shrinks the Edit Link Create dialog box and displays only the "Source file and item" text box containing the name of the window you selected in double-angle brackets. Select the range you want to link to from that file and press ENTER.
- Click on the name of a file in the list box, to move the highlight to that file name. 1-2-3/G displays the file name in the "Source file and item" text box. Click on the end of the file entry in the "Source file and item" text box and type the range address or range name from that file. Complete your selection by pressing ENTER.

Once you specify an entry in the "Source file and item" text box, 1-2-3/G activates the "Destination item" text box. Use this text box to specify the location of the link in the currently active file. Initially, this box displays the address of the current selection in the active file. For example, in Figure 2–27, the range address A:D4 appears in the "Destination item" text box. As you may have noticed, this corresponds to location of the cell pointer in Figure 2–28. You can accept this range, edit it, or highlight a new range. You can also press NAME (F3) to display a list of named ranges in the current file and make a selection from this list.

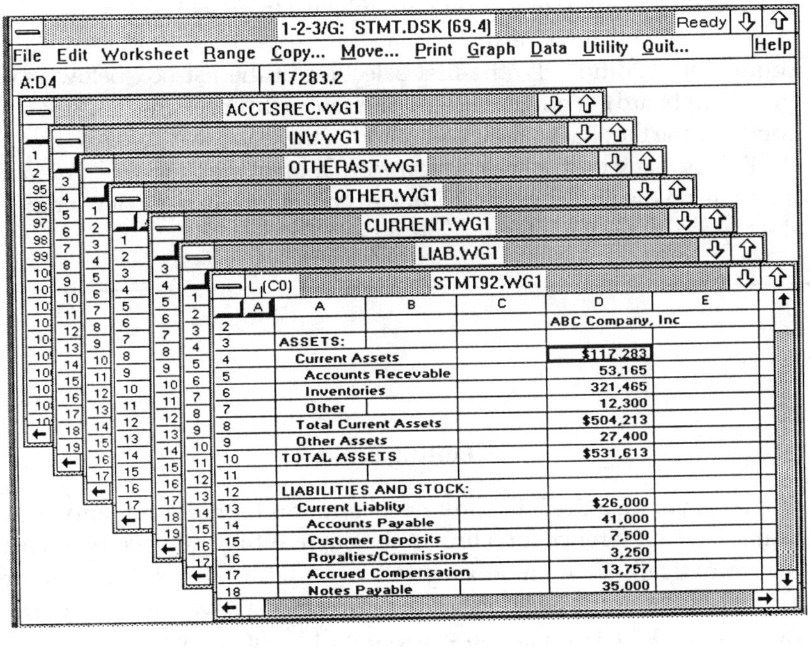

FIGURE 2-28 Multiple open files linked to the active file

Before you complete the Edit Link Create command, you can specify the method for updating the link. To do this, select from either the "Automatic" or "Manual" option buttons in the "Update mode" section of the Edit Link Create dialog box. If you select "Automatic" (the default), the destination file will be updated whenever the data in the source file changes. If you select "Manual," links in the destination file are only updated when you select the Edit Link Update command. See "Updating Links Manually" later in this chapter for more details on using the Edit Link Update command.

To complete the Edit Link Create command,select the OK command button, or press ENTER. 1-2-3/G forms a link between the destination and source files. Data from the range you selected in the source file is copied to the range you selected in the destination file. Additionally, 1-2-3/G displays an L at the far left of the worksheet window title bar, indicating the current cell contains a link.

Note

Initially, the "Source file and item" text box appears empty, provided the Presentation Manager clipboard does not contain data. However, if you used the Edit Copy or Edit Cut commands to copy data to the clipboard, 1-2-3/G displays the contents of the clipboard (filename and range) in the "Source file and item" text box when you select the Edit Link Create command. Additionally, the first selection in the list box below reads (from clipboard). You can accept this entry by pressing ENTER and complete the Edit Link Create command in the usual way. 1-2-3/G creates the link by using the file and range information in the clipboard. For more about using the Edit Copy and Edit Cut commands to copy or cut data to the clipboard, see Chapter 4, "Cutting and Pasting Data."

Editing Links

To edit a link, you use the Edit Link Edit command. This command allows you to edit the source reference for a link in the current file and specify whether that link is automatically or manually updated. As with Edit Link Create, the Edit Link Edit command applies only to the currently active file. Therefore, make sure that the file whose links you want to edit is the active file.

When you select the Edit Link Edit command, 1-2-3/G displays the dialog box in Figure 2–29. At the top of this dialog box, 1-2-3/G displays the name of

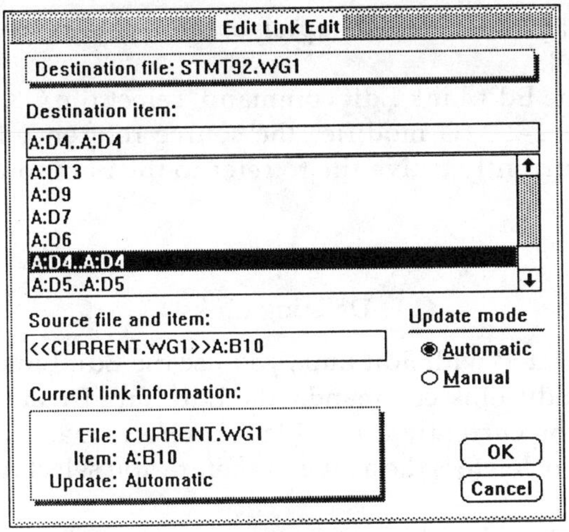

FIGURE 2-29 The Edit Link Edit dialog box

the currently active file in an information box entitled "Destination file." As you might imagine, you cannot edit the contents of this box.

Beneath the "Destination file" information box, 1-2-3/G displays another text box, and an accompanying list box, entitled "Destination item." This list box contains all the range addresses or range names in the current file that contain links to ranges in other files. To select a link to edit, click on the appropriate range address or name, or press ↓ to highlight it and press ENTER.

When you select a link to edit, 1-2-3/G updates the remaining components of the Edit Link Edit dialog box to reflect the nature of the link. For example, the "Source file and item" text box is activated and shows the current source file and range of the link. The "Update mode" section shows whether the link is automatically or manually updated. Also, the "Current link information" box shows information about the link you've selected.

To specify a new source file and range for the selected link, use the "Source file and item text" box. You can either edit the contents of this box, click your mouse on the title bar of an open window and select a range from that file, or press CTRL-NEXT WINDOW (CTRL-F6)) to move to other open windows and select a range to link.

Before completing the Edit Link Edit command, you can use the "Automatic" or "Manual" option buttons in the "Update mode" section to specify an update method for the link. If you select "Automatic" (the default), 1-2-3/G automatically updates the selected link whenever the data in the source file changes. On the other hand, if you select "Manual," 1-2-3/G only updates the link when you use the Edit Link Update command. See "Updating Links Manually" later in this chapter for more details on using the Edit Link Update command.

To complete the Edit Link Edit command, select the OK command button or press ENTER. 1-2-3/G modifies the source reference for the range you selected in the currently active file to refer to the new source file and range you specified.

Deleting Links

To delete links created with Edit Link, you use the Edit Link Delete command. Similar to other Edit Link commands, the Edit Link Delete command applies only to links in the currently active file. Therefore, make sure the file whose link(s) you want to delete is the active file before you select the Edit Link Delete command.

When you select the Edit Link Delete command, 1-2-3/G displays the dialog box shown in Figure 2–30. At the top of this box, the name of the currently active file appears in an information box entitled "Destination file." The contents of this box are solely for your information and cannot be edited.

Beneath the "Destination file" box are two option buttons, "All links" and "Selected links." To delete all the links in the currently active file, select "All links." To delete only a single link, choose "Selected link." If you choose "Selected link," then choose the link you want to delete from the list box below. This list box shows all the range addresses and range names in the currently active file that contain links. When you make a selection from this list, 1-2-3/G displays information about the link in the "Current link information" box below. This box displays the source file

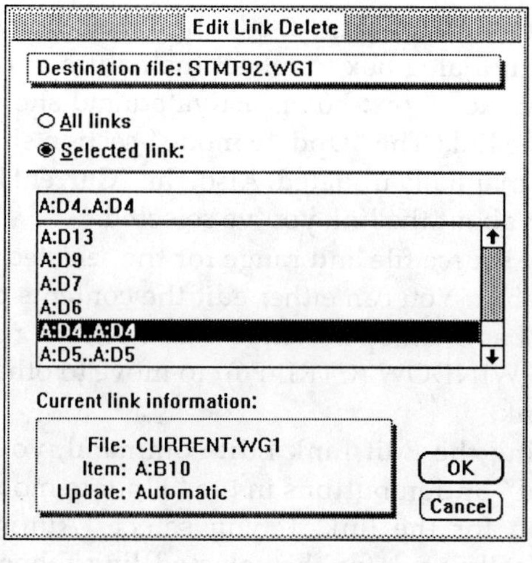

Edit Link Delete

Destination file: STMT92.WG1

All links

Selected link:

A:D4..A:D4

A:D13
A:D9
A:D7
A:D6
A:D4..A:D4
A:D5..A:D5

Current link information:

File: CURRENT.WG1
Item: A:B10
Update: Automatic

OK

Cancel

FIGURE 2-30 **The Edit Link Delete dialog box**

and range referenced by the link as well as the method of update, Automatic or Manual.

To complete the Edit Link Delete command, select the OK command button, or press ENTER. 1-2-3/G deletes the link(s) you specified. When you delete a link, 1-2-3/G only deletes the link relationship between the source and destination file. The range in the currently active file that was the destination for the link retains its value as of the last time the link was updated.

Moving Links

You can also change the source reference for links in the active file from one source file to another. To do this, you use the Edit Link Move command. You can also use this command to delete links in the currently active file that refer to a specific source file.

In preparation for the Edit Link Move command, make sure the file that contains the links (the destination file) is active. Then, select the Edit Link Move command. When you select this command, 1-2-3/G displays the dialog box in Figure 2–31. At the top of this dialog box, the name of the currently active file appears in an information box entitled "Destination file." Similar to the other Edit Link dialog boxes, the "Destination file" box is for information only; you cannot edit its contents.

Beneath the "Destination file" box, two other text boxes appear, "Current source" and "New source." Both text boxes have an accompanying list box. The "Current source" text box identifies the source file to which the links in the active file currently refer. In this box, specify the source file you want to move the links from. You can type in the filename or select it from the list box below. The "New source" text box identifies the file you want to use as the new source for the links. You can type the name of this file in the "New source" text box or you can select it from the list box below.

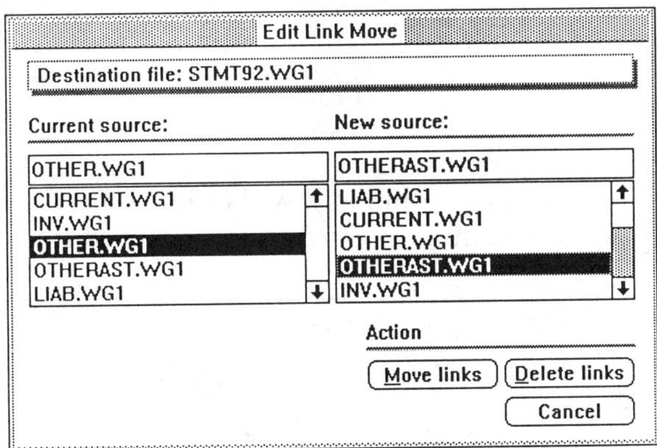

FIGURE 2-31 The Edit Link Move dialog box

To move or delete links, select from either the "Move links" or "Delete links" command buttons in the "Action section" of the Edit Link Move dialog box. If you select "Move links," 1-2-3/G moves the appropriate links from the file specified in the "Current source" text box to the file specified in the "New source" text box. When the links are moved, they refer to the same ranges in the new source file as they did in the old source file. On the other hand, if you select "Delete links," 1-2-3/G deletes links that refer to the file you specified in the "Current source" text box. If both the "Current source" text box and the "New source" text box contain the same file name, you can only delete links, not move them.

Pasting Links

You can use the Edit Link Paste Link command to create a link in the currently active file that uses data stored in the clipboard. In Chapter 4 you'll learn about the Edit Copy and Edit Cut commands that allow you to copy or move data from a worksheet to the clipboard. You can then use the Edit Paste command to copy that information from the clipboard to a range in the current worksheet or another worksheet in either the same file or another file. However, when you copy information to the clipboard with Edit Copy or Edit Cut, 1-2-3/G also copies the location (filename and range) for that data to the clipboard as well. The Edit Link Paste Link command allows you to use this location information to create a link in the current file that refers to the range from which the data was originally copied.

To use the Edit Link Paste Link command, begin by moving the cell pointer to the worksheet cell in which you want to establish the link. Then, select the Edit Link Paste Link command. 1-2-3/G reads the information in the clipboard and sets up a link between the worksheet file from which that data was copied and the current worksheet file. Once the link is formed, 1-2-3/G copies the information from the source worksheet into the current worksheet, starting at the location of the cell pointer. From that point on, the data in the current worksheet is automatically updated whenever the data in the source worksheet changes.

Note

> The Edit Link Paste Link command will only work when you have already copied data to the clipboard from a valid source file.

Updating Links Manually

As you may recall from earlier in this section, you can specify a manual update mode when you create a link with Edit Link Create or when you edit a link with

Edit Link Edit. Specifying a manual update mode allows you to control when your links are updated. To update the manual mode links in the current file, you use the Edit Link Update command. This command lets you update all of the links in the current file, or just selected ones. Before you select this command, however, make sure the file containing the manual links you want to update is the active file.

When you select the Edit Link Update command, 1-2-3/G displays the dialog box in Figure 2–32. At the top of the dialog box is an information box entitled "Destination file." 1-2-3/G displays the name of the currently active file in this box. This box is for your information only; you cannot edit its contents.

Beneath the "Destination file" text box are two option buttons, "All links" and "Selected links." If you select "All links" (the default), 1-2-3/G updates all manual links in the currently active file. To update only a specific link, choose "Selected links." Then, select the range address or range name that contains that link from the list box below. To do this, click on the appropriate range address or range name or press ↓ to move the highlight to it. When you select a link, 1-2-3/G displays information about the source of that link in the "Current link information" box below. To complete the Edit Link Update command, select the OK command button, or press ENTER. 1-2-3/G updates the manual link(s) you selected.

Linking Other Presentation Manager Applications to 1-2-3/G

As mentioned, 1-2-3/G takes advantage of Presentation Manager's DDE (Dynamic Data Exchange) messaging system. This messaging system lets you create links in 1-2-3/G files that reference data in files created by other Presen-

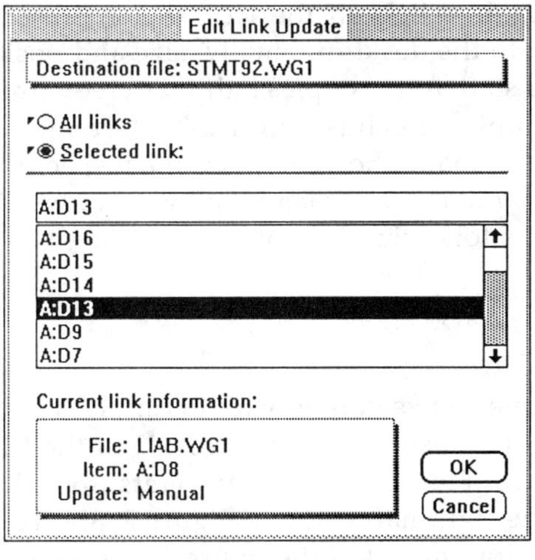

FIGURE 2-32 The Edit Link Update dialog box

tation Manager (PM) applications that support DDE. Conversely, you can also create links in files from other PM applications that reference data in 1-2-3/G files. As of the writing of this book, however, 1-2-3/G was one of the few Presentation Manager applications available. Therefore, to show you how to set up a cross-application link, it will be necessary to use multiple instances (two copies) of 1-2-3/G.

Note

> The example that follows shows you the commands and techniques you'll need to create a link from within a 1-2-3/G worksheet file that references another PM application file. To create a link in another PM application file that references a 1-2-3/G file, you must do so from within that application. Additionally, because that application may use an entirely different procedure for creating links, you must refer to the documentation that came with that application.

Figure 2–33 shows two instances (copies) of 1-2-3/G open on the Presentation Manager desktop. You can do this yourself, provided your computer has the memory, and provided you read the early part of this chapter, which describes how to size and position windows. To set up the configuration in Figure 2–33, simply start 1-2-3/G and minimize it to an icon. Then, start 1-2-3/G again. Presentation Manager loads a second copy of 1-2-3/G. Size and position the window containing the second copy of 1-2-3/G to occupy half the screen (the right half). Next, double-click on the icon that represents the first copy of 1-2-3/G to restore it to the desktop. Finally, size and position the window for this copy of 1-2-3/G so that it occupies half the screen (the left half).

To create a cross-application link with 1-2-3/G, you use the Edit Link Create command. For this command, however, you must specify a file reference that includes an *application* name, a *filename*, and a *range* within that file. This file reference will take the following format:

```
<<application|file-name>>range
```

The following example shows you how to do this.

Imagine you want to create a link in cell A:B5 of the file COPY_1.WG1 (on the left-hand side of Figure 2–33) that refers to cell A:B19 in the file COPY_2.WG1 (on the right-hand side of Figure 2–33). To do this, click on the first copy of 1-2-3/G (on the left of the figure) or press ALT-ESC to move to it. Then, move the cell pointer to cell A:B5 in the COPY-1.WG1 file and select the

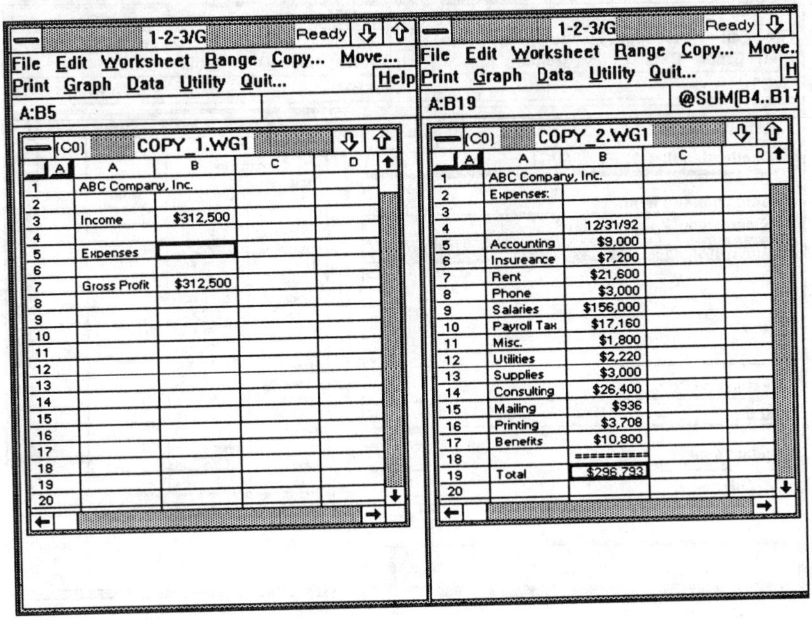

FIGURE 2-33 **Two copies of 1-2-3/G open on the desktop**

Edit Link Create command. 1-2-3/G displays the Edit Link Create dialog box as shown in Figure 2–34.

In the "Source file and item" list box, 1-2-3/G displays the names of other files open on the 1-2-3/G desktop, if any, and the names of other PM application files to which you can link. For example, in Figure 2–34, 1-2-3/G shows the name <<lotus | COPY_2.WG1>>. The first part of this name, before the vertical bar, is the name of the application. The second part of this name, after the vertical bar, identifies a file that is open for that application (COPY_2.WG1), which you can link. To link to this application and file, click on it in the list box. 1-2-3/G displays the selection in the "Source file and item" text box. Next, click the mouse twice at the very end of this entry. Then, type **A:B19** (the range in the COPY_2.WG1 file). Press ENTER to confirm this entry. 1-2-3/G activates the "Destination item" text box.

The "Destination item" text box should already contain the cell address A:B5. If not, type the address or click on this cell in the COPY_1.WG1 file. To complete the Edit Link Create command, select the OK command button or press ENTER. 1-2-3/G creates the link and copies the data from cell A:B19 of the COPY_2.WG1 file in the second instance of 1-2-3/G (on the right) to cell A:B5 in the COPY_1.WG1 file in the first instance of 1-2-3/G (on the left). Your screen now looks like Figure 2–35.

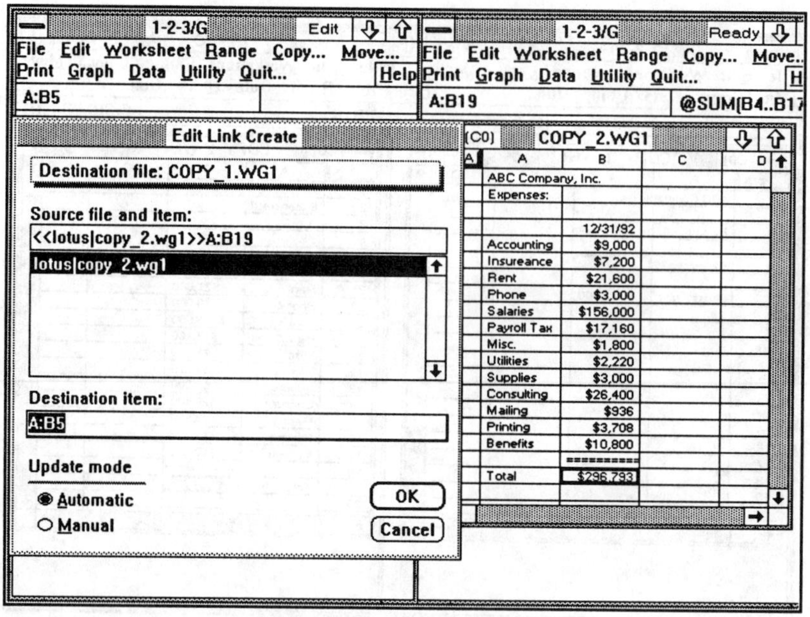

FIGURE 2-34 The Edit Link Create dialog box

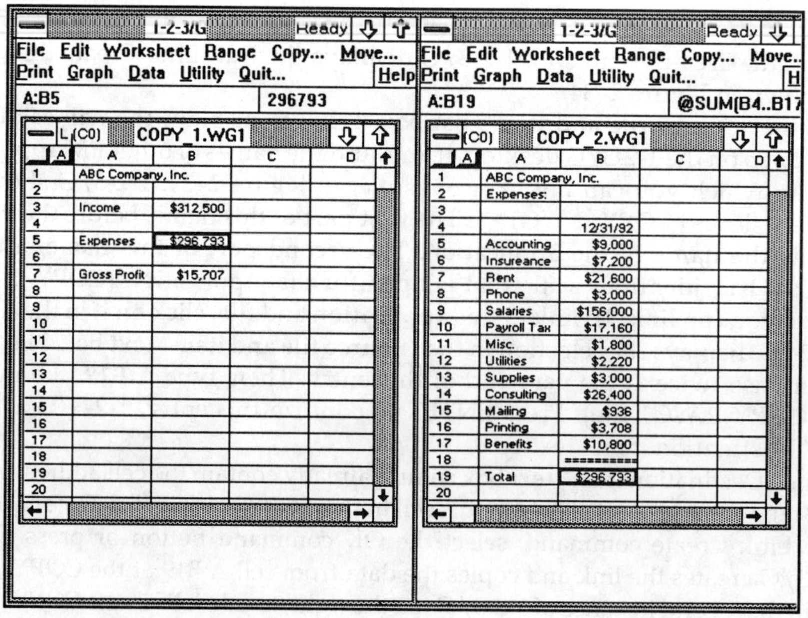

FIGURE 2-35 One file linked to another

SPECIFYING RANGES IN DIFFERENT FILES FOR COMMANDS

In 1-2-3/G you select a command in one worksheet file and have it apply to another worksheet file. For example, you can select the Range Format command in the currently active worksheet file and specify a range address or range name for that command that is located in another open worksheet file.

To specify a range in another worksheet file for a 1-2-3/G command, you use the same file and range referencing scheme that you use for link formulas. For example, the filename must be enclosed in double-angle brackets << >> followed by a range name or address from that worksheet file. You can specify a file and range specification for a command by using any of the following techniques:

- Type in the file and range specification in the Range(s) text box during the command.
- Highlight a range or collection from another file before or during a command.
- Press NAME (F3) during a command to select from a list of files and their range names currently open on the desktop.

Figure 2-36 shows an example of how you might apply the Range Format command across worksheet files. The figure shows two files currently open on

1-2-3/G: SELECT.DSK [69.4] Point
File Edit Worksheet Range Copy... Move... Print Graph Data Utility Quit... Help
A:A1

(G) ACTIVE.WG1

A	A	B	C	D
1		Accounts Receivable		
2				
3	Customer	Invoice	Date	Amount
4	10123	9623	01/10/92	$9,889.00
5	10129	9635	01/22/92	$9,895.00
6	10137	9647	02/03/92	$9,903.00
7	10130	9659	02/15/92	$9,896.00
8	10189	9671	02/27/92	$9,955.00
9	10214	9683	03/10/92	$9,980.00
10	10304	9695	03/22/92	$10,070.00
11	10259	9707	04/03/92	$10,025.00
12	10348	9719	04/15/92	$10,114.00
13	10415	9731	04/27/92	$10,181.00
14	10337	9743	05/09/92	$10,103.00
15	10371	9755	05/21/92	$10,137.00
16	10281	9767	06/02/92	$10,047.00
17	10191	9779	06/14/92	$9,957.00
18	10068	9791	06/26/92	$9,834.00
19				
20	Total			$149,986.00
21				
22				
23				
24				
25				
26				

INACTIVE.WG1

A	A	B	C	D
1		Accounts Payable		
2				
3	Vendor	Date	Terms	Amount
4	1049	06/02/92	N30	7968
5	1055	06/04/92	N30	7974
6	1063	06/06/92	N30	7982
7	1056	06/08/92	N30	7975
8	1115	06/10/92	N30	8034
9	1140	06/12/92	N30	8059
10	1230	06/14/92	N30	8149
11	1185	06/16/92	N30	8104
12	1274	06/18/92	N30	8193
13	1341	06/20/92	N30	8260
14	1263	06/22/92	N30	8182
15	1297	06/24/92	N30	8216
16	1207	06/26/92	N30	8126
17	1117	06/28/92	N30	8036
18	1994	06/30/92	N30	7913
19				
20	Total			121171
21				

Range Format
<<INACTIVE.WG1>>A:D4..A:D20

FIGURE 2-36 Selecting ranges in a nonactive worksheet file

the desktop. For purposes of illustration, the two files have been named ACTIVE.WG1 and INACTIVE.WG1, respectively. The active file is ACTIVE.WG1 (on the left side of Figure 2–36) and it contains the cell pointer. To apply the Range Format command to the range A:D4..A:D20 of the INACTIVE.WG1 file, perform the following steps:

1. From any cell in the ACTIVE.WG1 worksheet file, select the Range Format command. 1-2-3/G displays the Range Format dialog box. Select a format type, for example Currency, and specify the number of decimal places you desire.
2. Press TAB to move the cursor to the Range(s) box, or Click on that box. From there, you can:

   - Type in **<<INACTIVE.WG1>>A:D4..A:D20**.
   - Press NEXT WINDOW (CTRL-F6) to move the cell pointer to the INACTIVE.WG1 window and highlight the range A:D4..A:D20. 1-2-3/G places <<INACTIVE.WG1>>A:D4..A:D20 in the Range(s) box.
   - Click on any exposed portion of the INACTIVE.WG1 window. 1-2-3/G reduces the size Range Format dialog box as shown in Figure 2–36. Next, click and drag to highlight the range A:D4..A:D20 in the usual way. 1-2-3/G places <<INACTIVE.WG1>>A:D4..A:D20 in the Range(s) box.

3. Complete the Range Format command either by pressing ENTER or by selecting the OK command button. 1-2-3/G formats the range A:D4..A:D20 in the INACTIVE.WG1 file and returns the cell pointer to its original position in the ACTIVE.WG1 file.

You can also specify range names located in other files for use with commands by typing them in during a command or by pressing NAME (F3) to display a list of available range names. For example, imagine that range A:D4..A:D20 of the INACTIVE.WG1 file, shown in the previous example, is defined by the range name ACCT_PAY. The file ACTIVE.WG1 is once again the active file. To use the ACCT_PAY range name with the Range Format command, begin by selecting the command to display the Range Format dialog box. Specify the format type and number of decimal places you want. Next, press TAB to move the cursor to the Range(s) box. Once there, you can either type in **<<INACTIVE>>ACCT_PAY**, or press NAME (F3) to display the Range Names dialog box shown in Figure 2–37.

When you press NAME (F3) during a command to display the Range Names dialog box, 1-2-3/G shows you a list of worksheet files currently open on the

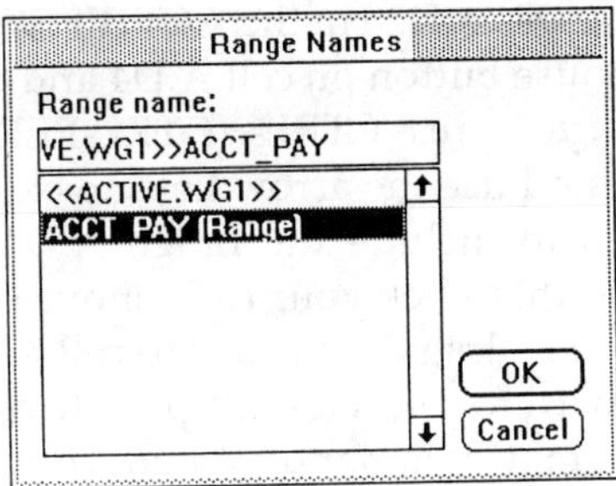

FIGURE 2-37 **Selecting range names in nonactive files**

NOTE

> If a range name is unique among the worksheet files currently on the desktop, you can use a wild-card file reference, <<?>>, during a command. For example, building on the previous example, you can enter **<<?>>ACCT_PAY** in the Range(s) text box of the Range Format dialog box. 1-2-3/G will search for this range throughout the worksheet files currently on the desktop and apply the Range Format command to it.

desktop. To select a range name from this dialog box, begin by selecting a filename, in this case INACTIVE.WG1. When you do this, 1-2-3/G places that filename in the text box at the top of the dialog box and displays a list of range names available in that file. Select ACCT_PAY from this list. To complete the selection of the range name, select the OK command button, or press ENTER. 1-2-3/G returns you to the Range Format dialog box and places <<INACTIVE>>ACCT_PAY in its Range(s) text box. From there, you can complete the Range Format command in the usual way.

You can also specify a multiple-file collection for a command. For example, imagine you have the two worksheet files ACTIVE.WG1 and INACTIVE.WG1 currently open on the desktop, as shown in Figure 2–36. Imagine further that you want to apply the Range Format command to the range A:D4..A:D20 in both files at the same time. To do this, you specify a collection that includes this range in both files. You can specify this collection either before or during the Range Format command. For example, to specify the collection before entering the Range Format command, perform the following:

1. Highlight the range A:D4..A:D20 in the ACTIVE.WG1 file. To do this, you can click your left mouse button on cell A:D4 and drag downward to cell A:D20. Alternatively, you press CTRL-. (CTRL-PERIOD) to anchor the cell pointer on cell A:D4 and use the arrow keys to expand the highlight.
2. Extend the collection to include the range A:D4..A:D20 of the INACTIVE.WG1 file. To do this, click your right mouse button on cell A:D4 of the INACTIVE.WG1 file, drag downward to cell A:D20, and release. (You cannot use the keyboard to select a multiple-file collection.)
3. Select the Range Format command. When you select this command, 1-2-3/G displays the Range format dialog box. The Range(s) text box contains the following range specifications:

```
<<ACTIVE.WG1>>A:D4..A:D20,<<INACTIVE.WG2>>A:D4..A:D20
```

4. Complete the Range Format command by selecting the OK command button, or by pressing ENTER. 1-2-3/G simultaneously applies the Range Format command to the range A:D4..A:D20 in both the ACTIVE.WG1 and INACTIVE.WG1 worksheet files.

MANAGING MULTIPLE DESKTOPS

You can create more than one desktop. That is, you can assign a filename to the current desktop and save it to disk. You can then load that same desktop into memory at a later time. When you do, all the same tools and utilities that were present on the desktop when you saved it are again recalled to your screen. Thus, you can create different desktops containing the tools you need for different jobs. What's more, the same worksheet or graph files can be used on different desktops. Therefore, you can share information from the same files across your various desktops.

1-2-3/G also provides commands that allow you to manage your various desktops. For example, you can archive a desktop to another directory on your hard disk. That way, you can make changes to one or more files on a desktop and still have a backup copy of the original, should the need arise. In addition, you can copy an entire desktop to another hard-disk directory. Finally, 1-2-3/G provides a command that allows you to get information about files that are included in a desktop.

Saving the Desktop

1-2-3/G allows you save the current status of the desktop to a *desktop file* (a file with a .DSK extension). Desktop files are not data files. Instead, desktop files include the following:

- The names and disk locations of the files currently open on the desktop. This includes worksheet and graph files as well as any utilities you may have open.
- The relative size, position, and status of all open windows
- The links that exist between files

Thus, desktop files are purely configuration files. They do not contain the contents of any worksheet or graph windows. These must be saved to disk separately. However, once you have saved the status of the current desktop to a desktop file, you need only open that file again to have 1-2-3/G load all those same files and utilities and place them back on the desktop just as you left them.

To save the contents of the current desktop, you use the File Save command. When you enter this command, 1-2-3/G displays the dialog box shown in Figure 2–38. If more than one file is currently open on the desktop, 1-2-3/G displays **All Modified** in the "File name" text box at the top of File Save dialog box. Otherwise, if only a single file is open, 1-2-3/G displays the name of that file. Immediately beneath the File name text box are three option buttons and a check box. These perform the following functions:

- **All Files:** Saves all new and modified worksheet and graph file windows currently open on the desktop. This is the default with multiple open files.
- **File by file:** Saves open files one at a time. Use this option to save only selected files.
- **Current file only:** Saves only the currently active file.
- **Save desktop:** Saves the current desktop configuration to a desktop file. This check box appears with an X when multiple files are open on the desktop. To avoid creating a desktop file, remove the X from this box by clicking on it or by pressing TAB to move to it and then pressing the space bar. If only a single file is open, this box appears without an X.

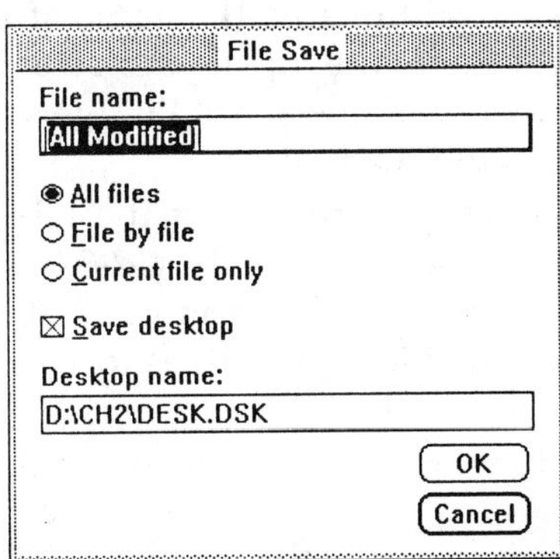

FIGURE 2-38 **The File Save dialog box**

The "Desktop name" text box, located at the bottom of the File Save dialog box, allows you to specify a name for a desktop file. Initially, 1-2-3/G suggests a default file name in this box. For the first desktop filename in the current directory, 1-2-3/G suggests DESK.DSK. For the second new desktop file in a directory, 1-2-3/G suggests DESK1.DSK, for the third DESK2.DSK, and so on. You can accept this filename or type in one of your own. However, make sure you use the .DSK extension.

After filling in the File Save dialog box, you can complete the File Save command by selecting the OK command button, or by pressing ENTER. 1-2-3/G begins saving the open files on the desktop, and, if the "Save desktop" box appears checked, 1-2-3/G also creates a desktop file under the name you specified. If any open files already exist on disk, 1-2-3/G displays a Save Window dialog box for each open window. This box contains three command buttons, Replace, Backup, and Cancel. The buttons have the following effects:

- **Replace:** Replaces the file on disk with the file in memory.
- **Backup:** Copies the existing file on disk to the current backup directory, usually C:\123G\BACKUP. The original file on disk is then replaced with the file from memory. You can change the default backup directory with the User Settings Directories command, available from either the Desktop Control or Utility menus.
- **Cancel:** Cancels the File Save command.

Opening an Existing Desktop

Once you've saved a desktop file, you can reopen it again by using the File Open command. You may recall this command was discussed earlier in this chapter in the context of opening individual files. However, when you open an existing desktop file, 1-2-3/G adds the windows associated with that file to those already on the desktop. Additionally, the name of the desktop file appears in the 1-2-3/G desktop title bar at the top of your screen. The windows associated with that desktop file are sized and placed in the same positions as when you originally saved the desktop file to disk.

To open an existing desktop file, select the File Open command. 1-2-3/G displays the File Open dialog box. Initially, 1-2-3/G does not display the names of desktop files in the current directory in the "File name" list box. However, you can use any of the following techniques to select a desktop filename:

- Type in the drive, directory, and file name of the desktop file in the "File name" text box.
- Place an X in the "Desktops (.DSK)" check box in the "File types" section of the File Open dialog box. This causes 1-2-3/G to add the names of desktop files located in the current directory to the list in the "File name" list box.

Once an X appears in the "Desktops (.DSK)" check, you can use any of the following techniques to see a list of desktop files located in other directories:

- Edit the drive or directory in the "File name" text box.
- Select a new drive from the available option buttons in the "Drives" section of the dialog box. 1-2-3/G shows you files from the last directory used on the drive you select.
- Select the two dots (..) from the "File name" list box to display the files and subdirectories that are associated with the directory that is one level closer to the root directory.

To select a particular desktop file name from the list box, you can double-click on it, click on it once and select OK, or press ↓ to highlight it and press ENTER. Whichever method you use, 1-2-3/G opens the desktop file you selected. Its windows are then added to the windows already open on the desktop.

If a desktop file is already open when you open a second existing desktop file, 1-2-3/G adds the windows for the second desktop file to those of the first. However, the name of the first desktop file continues to appear in the title bar at the top of your screen. Thus, the integrity of both desktop files is lost. If you save the 1-2-3/G desktop at this point, the windows from both desktop files will be saved under a single name. To preserve the integrity of both the desktop files, you must save only individual files as needed.

As you might imagine, you can open an individual file that is part of a desktop file without having to open the whole desktop file. To do this, use the File Open command as you normally would to select only the name of the individual file. See "Opening an Existing File on the Desktop" earlier in this chapter for more details on opening individual files.

Note

If an individual file associated with a particular desktop file is already open when you open its desktop file, 1-2-3/G does not open a second view (copy) of the individual file. Instead, 1-2-3/G only opens the remaining files included in the desktop file. The size and position of the remaining windows is determined by the desktop file. However, the size and position of the window containing the individual preopened window is not affected. What's more, any changes you may have made to the individual preopened file are preserved.

Replacing the Desktop

You can replace the currently open desktop with another existing desktop by using the File Retrieve command. When you replace one desktop with another, all open windows, regardless of their origin, are closed, before the windows associated with the replacement desktop file are loaded. If you've made changes to any of the open windows, however, 1-2-3/G prompts you to save the contents of each modified window, prior to closing it. It does this by displaying the Close Window dialog box for each modified window. You can select from OK to save the modified file, No to avoid saving the file, or Cancel to cancel the File Retrieve command altogether.

When you select the File Retrieve command, 1-2-3/G displays the File Retrieve dialog box. Initially, 1-2-3/G does not display the names of desktop files in the current directory in the File name list box. However, you can use any of the following techniques to select a desktop filename:

- Type in the drive, directory, and filename of the desktop file in the "File name" text box.
- Place an X in the "Desktops (.DSK)" check box in the "File types" section of the File Retrieve dialog box. This causes 1-2-3/G to add the names of desktop files located in the current directory to the list in the "File name" list box.

Once an X appears in the "Desktops (.DSK)" check box, you can use any of the following techniques to see a list of desktop files located in other directories:

- Edit the drive or directory in the "File names" text box.
- Select a new drive from the available option buttons in the "Drives" section of the dialog box.
- Select the two dots (..) from the "File name" list box to display the files and subdirectories that are associated with the directory that is one level closer to root directory.

To select a particular desktop filename from the list box, you can double-click on it, click on it once and select OK, or press ↓ to highlight it and press ENTER. Whichever method you use, 1-2-3/G closes any windows currently open, prompting you to save changes to those windows if necessary. The files associated with the replacement desktop are then opened and its name appears in the title bar at the top of your screen.

You can replace an individual file that is part of a desktop file without having to replace the whole desktop file. To do this, you use the File Retrieve to select only the name of the individual file, rather than the desktop file name. See "Replacing a File on the Desktop" earlier in this chapter for more details.

If one or more individual files included in a replacement desktop file are already open when you use File Retrieve, 1-2-3/G leaves those files open on the desktop. That way, any changes you may have made to those files prior to retrieving the replacement desktop are preserved. However, the windows for those individual preopened files are restored to the same size, position, and status as when you originally saved the replacement desktop file to disk. Any open windows that are not associated with the replacement desktop file, however, are closed.

Clearing the Desktop

To clear the desktop of all open windows, you use the File Utility New Desktop command. This command closes all open files and utilities and leaves the desktop empty. Figure 2-39 shows the results of the File Utility New Desktop command.

Notice in Figure 2-39 that despite the fact that the desktop is empty, the File command remains displayed in the desktop menu bar. That way, you can create a new file or open an existing file or desktop.

If you've made no changes to any open files since you last saved them to disk, the File Utility New Desktop command clears the desktop without any confirmation. However, if you have a desktop file open, and you've made changes to any of its windows or data files, or added any windows, 1-2-3/G prompts you to save the desktop prior to closing it. It does this by displaying the Close Desktop dialog box shown in Figure 2-40. To save the desktop before closing, select the OK command button. To close the desktop without saving it, select No. To cancel the File Utility New Desktop command altogether, select Cancel.

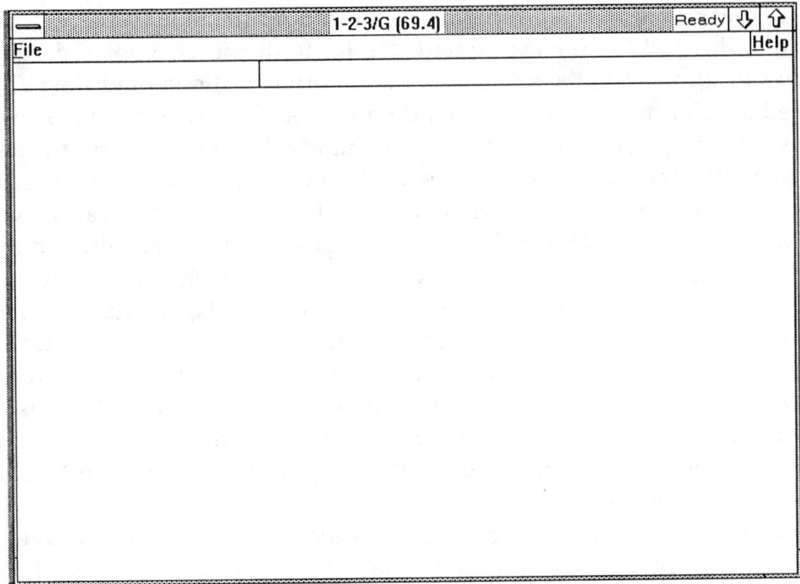

FIGURE 2-39 An empty desktop

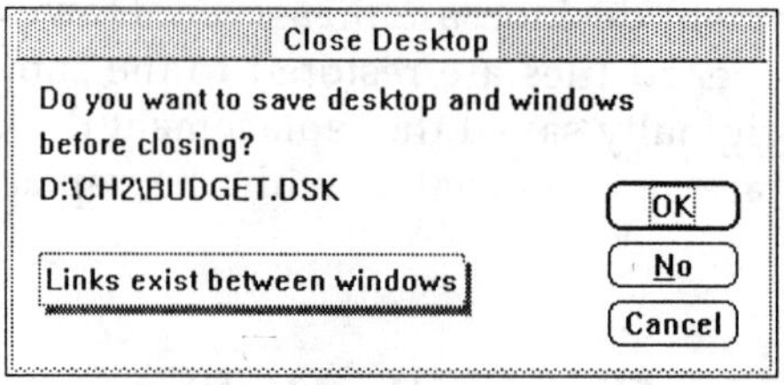

Close Desktop
Do you want to save desktop and windows before closing?
D:\CH2\BUDGET.DSK
OK
No
Cancel
Links exist between windows

FIGURE 2-40 **The Close Desktop dialog box**

If only individual files are open on the desktop, and you've made no changes to those files since they were last saved to disk, the File Utility New Desktop command clears the desktop without a confirmation. However, if you've made any changes to data or settings, 1-2-3/G prompts you to save each modified window before clearing the desktop. It does this by displaying the Close Window dialog box for each modified window. From this dialog box, you can select OK to save the file before closing it, No to close the window without saving it, or Cancel to cancel the File Utility New Desktop command and avoid closing further windows.

Copying the Desktop

1-2-3/G also allows you to copy a desktop file, and all its associated worksheet and/or graph files, to another directory on your hard disk or to a diskette. The original files remain where they are and are not affected. However, the new version of the desktop file is updated to refer to the newly copied data files in the new location. What's more, any links between the copied data files are updated to refer to the newly copied data files in the new location. The ability to copy a desktop in this way may come in handy if you need to use the desktop data on another computer or if you want to reorganize your hard disk.

To copy a desktop file and its associated data files to a new location, you use the File Utility Copy Desktop command. When you select this command, 1-2-3/G displays the dialog box shown in Figure 2–41. As you might imagine, the "From" and "To" text boxes at the top of this dialog box identify the location you want to copy from and the location you want to copy to. Both text boxes use the list box located beneath the "From" text box. Initially, the "From" box lists the current drive and directory followed by *.DSK. Thus, all files with a .DSK extension in the current directory are shown in the list box below. Either type in the desktop filename you want to copy, or select it from the list box below by double-clicking on it.

To select a location and filename to copy to, press TAB to move to the "To" text box. Initially, 1-2-3/G displays the current drive and directory in this box. You can type in a new drive, directory, and .DSK file name or you can select it by double-clicking on it in the list box below. You can

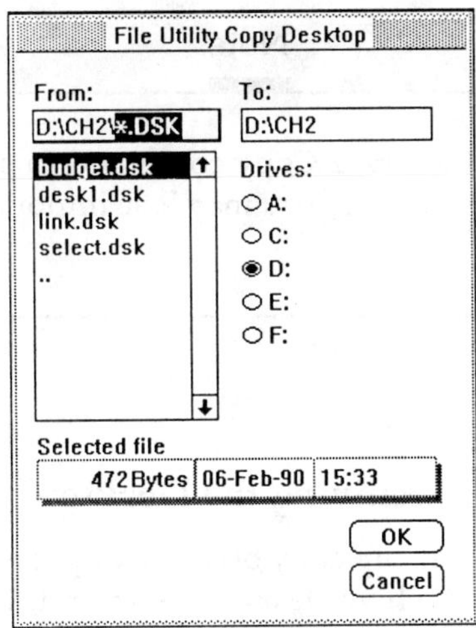

FIGURE 2-41 The File Utility Copy Desktop dialog box

also use the option buttons in the "Drives" section to have 1-2-3/G list the contents of the last directory used on each drive. Additionally, you can specify any filename you want for a copied desktop file, provided you use the .DSK file extension. If you do not provide this extension, 1-2-3/G will do so for you.

To complete the File Utility Copy Desktop command, select the OK command button, or press ENTER. 1-2-3/G copies the desktop file you specified in the "From" text box, along with all its associated worksheet and/or graph files, to the new location. The names of the worksheet and/or graph files remain the same. However, the desktop file is given the name you specified in the "To" text box.

Caution

The File Utility Copy Desktop command creates a new standalone version of a desktop file and its associated data files in a new location. When you make changes to the original desktop file or data files, the copies are not updated.

Note

> Do not use the DOS or OS/2 Copy command to copy a desktop file from one location to another. You may lose important information in the desktop file.

Archiving the Desktop

You can archive (create a backup copy of) a desktop file, and its associated data files, by using File Utility Archive Desktop command. This command performs the same function as the File Utility Copy Desktop in one respect. That is, it copies a desktop file and its associated data files to a new location. However, in this case, the desktop file is **not** updated to refer to the newly copied data files in the new location. Instead, the desktop file continues to refer to the original data files in their original locations. Thus, this command creates a static backup copy of desktop file and its associated data files. However, you can use this backup copy to restore the original desktop to its former state, should the need arise.

When you select the File Utility Archive Desktop command, 1-2-3/G displays the dialog box in Figure 2–42. At the top of this dialog box are two text boxes, "From" and "To." The "From" text box identifies the location and filename you want to copy from, and the "To" text box identifies the location and file name you want to copy to. Both text boxes use the list box located beneath the "From"

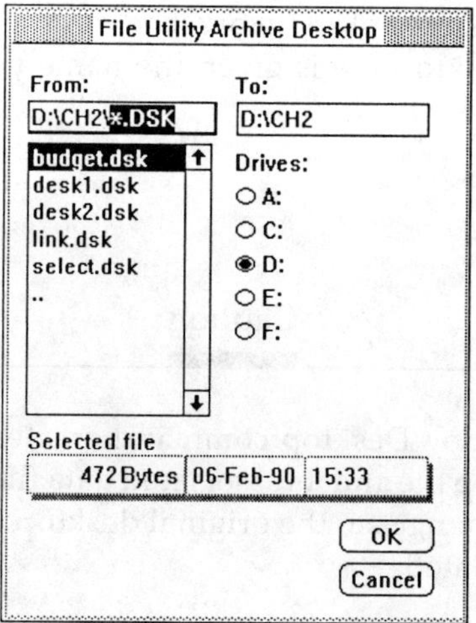

FIGURE 2-42 The File Utility Archive Desktop dialog box

text box. Initially, the "From" box lists the current drive and directory followed by *.DSK. Thus, all files with a .DSK extension in the current directory are shown in the list box below. You can select a filename from this list or you can type in a drive, directory, and filename of the desktop file you want to archive. To see a list of desktop files in directories other than the current directory, you can edit the drive and path in the "From" text box or you can select from the available "Drives" options buttons.

To select a drive, directory, and filename to archive to, press TAB to move to the "To" text box. Initially, 1-2-3/G displays the current drive and directory in this box as well. You can type in a new drive, directory and .DSK file name or you can select it using the list box or "Drives" options buttons below. The "To" text box will be updated for your selection. Although you can specify any filename you want for an archived desktop file, make sure you use the .DSK file extension. If you do not provide this extension, 1-2-3/G will do so for you.

To complete the File Utility Archive Desktop command, select the OK command button, or press ENTER. 1-2-3/G copies the desktop file you specified in the "From" text box, along with all its associated worksheet and/or graph files, to the drive and/or directory you specified in the "To" text box. The names of the associated worksheet and/or graph files remain the same. However, the desktop file is given the name you specified in the "To" text box.

Restoring the Desktop

To restore an archived desktop, you use the File Utility Restore Desktop command. This command allows you to copy an archived version of a desktop file to the directory of your choosing. The archived data files that are associated with that particular desktop file, however, are always copied back to the directory in which they were originally created.

When you select the File Utility Restore Desktop command, 1-2-3/G displays the dialog box shown in Figure 2–43. The "From" text box at the top of this dialog box allows you to specify the directory and name under which the archived desktop file and its associated data files are stored. Initially, however, this box shows the current drive and directory followed by *.DSK, causing the desktop files in the current directory to appear in the list box below. To select a desktop to restore, type in the appropriate drive, directory, and desktop filename in the "From" text box. Alternatively, you can select a desktop filename using the list box and/or Drives options buttons below. The "From" text box will be updated for your selection.

The "To" text box, on the other hand, identifies the directory where you want the desktop file copied, as well as the name you want to use for the restored desktop file. You can use the same desktop filename that appears in the "From" text box, or you can change it. You can also specify a different drive and directory for the restored desktop file. However, the archived data files associated with the desktop file will always be copied back to the directory in

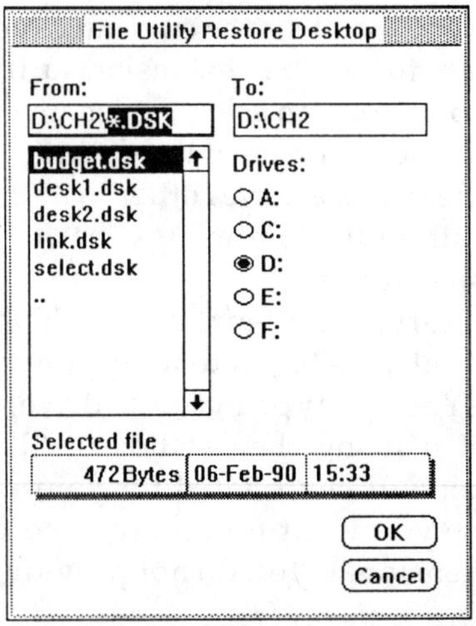

File Utility Restore Desktop

From: D:\CH2*.DSK

To: D:\CH2

budget.dsk
desk1.dsk
desk2.dsk
link.dsk
select.dsk
..

Drives:
A:
C:
D:
E:
F:

Selected file
472Bytes | 06-Feb-90 | 15:33

OK
Cancel

FIGURE 2-43 The File Utility Restore Desktop dialog box

which they were originally created. To specify a destination drive, directory, and filename, press TAB to move to the "To" text box. You can then type the appropriate information in the "To" text box, or you can select an existing drive, directory, and filename from the list box below.

To complete the File Utility Restore Desktop command, select the OK command button, or press ENTER. 1-2-3/G copies the desktop file specified in the "From" text box to the directory and under the name specified in the "To" text box. The archived data files associated with the desktop file name in the "From" box are restored to the directory in which they were originally created.

Getting Information about a Desktop File

To get information about the files included in a particular desktop file, you use the File Utility View Desktop command. When you select this command, 1-2-3/G displays the dialog box in Figure 2–44. The "File name" text box at the top of this dialog box allows you to specify the name of a desktop file about which you want information. Initially, however, this box shows the current drive and directory followed by *.DSK, causing the names of desktop files in the current directory to appear in the list box below. You can type in the drive, directory, and name of the desktop file you want information about, or you can use the list box and "Drives" option buttons below to select a filename. Once the appropriate filename appears in the File name text box, select the "View..." command button. 1-2-3/G displays the dialog box in Figure 2–45.

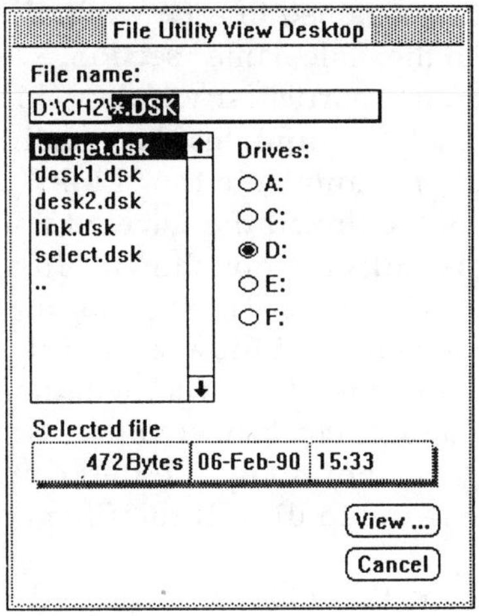

FIGURE 2-44 **The File Utility View Desktop dialog box**

The dialog box in Figure 2-45 contains information about the data files and utilities included in the desktop file you specified. The name of the desktop file you selected appears in the title bar of the dialog box. Beneath the title bar, the "Window name" section shows the name of each window in the desktop file.

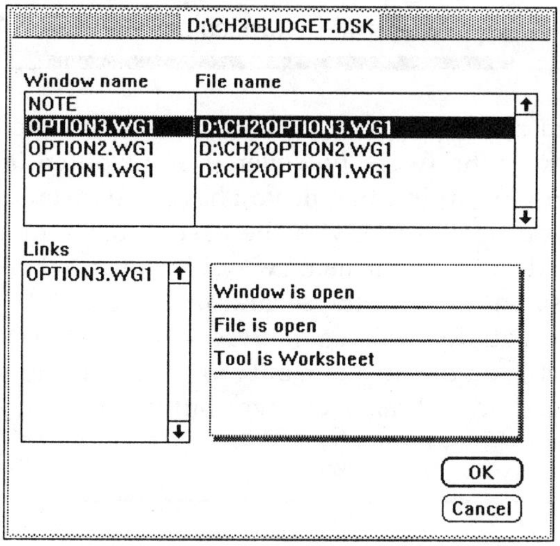

FIGURE 2-45 **The File Utility View Desktop information box**

Adjacent to the "Window name" section, the "File name" section shows the full path and name for the file contained in each window. If a window contains a utility, nothing appears in the "File name" section.

To get information about a particular window, highlight the name of the window. When you do, 1-2-3/G updates the remaining components of the dialog box accordingly. For example, in the "Links" list box below, 1-2-3/G lists the files to which you've linked the selected window by using the Edit Link command. (Formula links are not shown.) In addition, to the right of the "Links" box there are four slots. The top slot identifies the status of the window whether it is the active window or simply an open window. The second slot identifies the status of the file, whether it is open or not. The third slot indicates which tool, Worksheet versus Graph, was used to create the file, and the fourth slot shows any file description you may have specified when you saved the file to disk. If the file is password protected, no description appears.

To get information about the windows included in another desktop file, select the Cancel command button; or press ESC to return to the File Utility View desktop dialog box. To return to the currently active window, select the OK command button.

Note

See Chapter 5, "File Management," for more on how to use the File Save command to save a file with a password and/or a description.

Tip: Multiple instances of 1-2-3/G

You can open more than one copy of 1-2-3/G on the Presentation Manager desktop. Be aware, however, of some potential file-sharing limitations. For example, imagine you have two instances of 1-2-3/G running. If you open a file with the first instance of 1-2-3/G, it is placed on the desktop in the usual way. However, when you attempt to open the same file with the second instance of 1-2-3/G, you are informed that you do not have the reservation for that file. You can still open the file on the desktop, but only as a read-only file. That is, you look at the file and make changes but you cannot save it under the same name.

SUMMARY

In this chapter you learned the commands and techniques you'll need to manage the 1-2-3/G desktop. For example, you now know how to control your windows. That is, you know how to change the size of a window to make it appear smaller or larger, and you can move it from one location to another. You also know how to maximize a window to have it occupy the entire desktop, and you can quickly restore that window to its original size. You also know how to reduce a window to an icon (minimize it), or remove it from the desktop altogether.

This chapter also showed you commands and techniques that you can use to better display the data in your worksheet windows. For example, you now know how to use the Worksheet Window command to split the current window horizontally or vertically and display divergent parts of the same worksheet, or different worksheets, at the same time. You also know how to create a perspective view that allows you to look at portions of up to five different worksheets at the same time. In addition, you also know how to freeze columns and rows along the left and top borders of a worksheet window so that the appropriate titles are always displayed for each column and row.

This chapter also provides you with an introduction to managing multiple files on the desktop. For example, you now know how to add new files to the desktop, open existing files, or replace a file on the desktop. You also know how to move back and forth between windows to apply commands that are specific to each window. In addition, you're aware of 1-2-3/G's commands that allow you stack and tile windows on the desktop. You also know how to link files with formulas and you can specify ranges in different files for commands.

Toward the end of this chapter you learned the commands and techniques you'll need to create and manage multiple desktops. For example, you now know how to create a desktop file that contains a record of the files currently open on the desktop. You also know to use that file to quickly load that same set of files back onto the desktop. Thus, you can group sets of related files to perform specific functions.

You also know how to manage desktop files. That is, you can now copy a selected desktop from one directory to another under a different name. You can also archive a desktop and restore it, if necessary. Finally, you know how to get information about the files included in a specific desktop.

CHAPTER

3

Formatting Worksheets

Formatting allows you to control the appearance of your data both on screen as well as when it's printed. To format data, you assign a particular type of format to the cell that contains it. For example, imagine you have the number 100 in a cell. You can make that number appear with a leading dollar sign and two decimal places—for example, $100.00—simply by formatting the cell that contains it. Once the cell is formatted in this way, you can enter a completely new number, such as 123.4, and 1-2-3/G will display it and print it as $123.40. A discussion of 1-2-3/G's available cell formats and how to apply them is covered later in this chapter under "Formatting Cells."

Formatting can mean other things as well. For example, you can choose whether a label or value appears flush left, flush right, or centered in a cell. See "Aligning Data in Cells" later for more details. Or, you can control the appearance of cells that contain or evaluate to zero. For example, you can choose to display a zero, a blank cell, or a label of your own design. See "Formatting the Display of Zeros" for coverage of this topic.

In 1-2-3/G, you can also assign attributes to worksheet cells, to make their entries stand out. For example, you can select different type styles and sizes as well as choose from bold, underline, or italics. You can also have cells and entries displayed in different colors, and you can create borders (outlines) that surround cell entries. See "Assigning Cell Attributes" for more details on this topic.

Formatting can also mean working with columns, rows, and worksheets. For example, you can increase or decrease column widths or row heights. You can also insert new columns or rows into the current worksheet and insert new worksheets into the current file. Thus, you can improve the appearance and layout of your data as well as make room for additional data. This topic is discussed at length under "Working with Columns, Rows, and Worksheets."

Finally, formatting includes protecting the data in your worksheets. If you're preparing a worksheet for use by others, you can hide confidential or extraneous data from view. You can also prevent data entry to the worksheet or limit it to certain cells that you select. A discussion of this topic appears under "Protecting Your Worksheets."

What's New

For the experienced 1-2-3 user who is upgrading from 1-2-3 Release 2 or 3, this section gives you a brief description of some of the new formatting commands included in 1-2-3/G. Each of these commands is discussed at length in the chapter.

The Range Format command has some new options. For example, the User option lets you create user-defined cell formats using 1-2-3/G's new Format Description Language. For example, you can display a value in a social security number format, 272–44–8765, or a phone number, (408) 476–2239. The new (Parens) option displays all numbers in a selected range in parentheses. The new Automatic option, carried forward from Release 3, formats cells for you automatically based on what your entry looks like. For example, when you enter $123.12, 1-2-3/G formats the cell as Currency with two displayed decimal places. The Range Format command also includes a Label option. When you format a range with this option, all your entries, including numbers and formulas, are formatted as labels. See "Formatting Cells" for descriptions of these new Range Format options.

1-2-3/G includes a new command, Range Attributes. This command allows you to format the labels and numbers in a range in one of 20 different font styles you've installed for Presentation Manager. For example, you can choose to have the data in a range displayed and printed in 14-point Times Roman font. You can also add bolding, underlining, or italics if you want. Range Attributes also lets you assign colors to the contents and background of cells. For example, you can elect to have all negative numbers displayed in red on a blue background. Further, this command lets you build borders around the edges of cells. Thus, you can call attention to selected cells or build boxes around your data. See "Assigning Cell Attributes" for details on this command.

The Range Label command has been enhanced. You can now change the alignment of both labels and numeric values in their cells. See "Aligning Data in Cells" for a description of this command.

The Worksheet Column command has been enhanced. It now has a Fit largest option, which allows you to set the width for one or more columns based on the longest entry in each column. See "Adjusting Column Widths" for more details.

A new command, Worksheet Row, allows you to adjust the height of rows from 0 to 10 inches. You can also hide rows with this command. See "Adjusting Row Heights" later in this chapter for information on how to use this command.

The Worksheet Insert command has been enhanced so that you can insert part of a column, row, or worksheet. Conversely, the Worksheet Delete command now allows you to delete part of a row, column, or worksheet. See "Inserting Columns, Rows, and Worksheets" and "Deleting Columns, Rows, and Worksheets" for an update.

The Worksheet Global Group command, carried forward from Release 3, allows you to group the worksheets in a file. When you make a change to the settings or formatting in one worksheet, the other worksheets in the group take on the same settings and formatting. See "Grouping Worksheets" for more about this command.

A new command, Worksheet Global Screen Attributes, allows you to assign colors to different objects in the worksheet window. For example, you can assign colors to cell foreground and background. You can also remove the worksheet grid as well as the worksheet frame. See "Changing Screen Attributes" for a complete description of this command.

FORMATTING CELLS

1-2-3/G allows you to choose from among 14 different cell formats for displaying your data. For example, one of the more commonly used format types for values is Currency 2, meaning Currency with two displayed decimal places. This causes a leading dollar ($) sign to be are displayed in front of the value, thousands separated by commas, and two places always displayed after the decimal. Therefore, the value 1000 is entered as 1000 but is displayed and printed as $1,000.00. A brief description of each of 1-2-3/G's format types appears later in this section along with some tips about using each format.

Range versus Global Formatting

When you start 1-2-3/G, each cell in a new worksheet is automatically assigned 1-2-3/G's default General format (described later). This format affects only the display of numbers and is rather plain in appearance. There are no commas to separate thousands and you have no control over the number of places displayed after the decimal. For example, if you type the number 100.00, 1-2-3/G truncates the trailing zeros after the decimal and displays it as 100. To display numbers in a different format, you must format the cells that contain those numbers.

1-2-3/G allows you to format worksheet cells in the following ways:

- **Individually:** One cell at a time.
- **As a range:** Multiple adjacent cells, including three-dimensional ranges spanning multiple worksheets.
- **As a collection:** Separate ranges in the same worksheet, different worksheets in the same file, or worksheets in different files.
- **Globally:** The entire current worksheet.

To format a single cell, range, or collection, you use the Range Format command. To format the entire current worksheet, you use the Worksheet Global Format command. Both commands offer the same cell formatting options. A discussion of how to use each command follows later in this section.

In general, when you format a cell with Range Format, it overrides the current global setting for the worksheet, which is set with Worksheet Global Format. For example, imagine you format the cells in column B of the current worksheet as Currency 2. Next, you use the Worksheet Global Format command to change the global format for the entire worksheet. The cells in Column B remain formatted as Currency 2. Furthermore, if you use the Range Format command again to format another range of cells in the same worksheet, those cells will take on the new format you assign.

Once you format some or all of the cells in a worksheet, you need only save the file that contains that worksheet to save your formatting. The next time you load the file into memory, your data is again displayed using the range and global format settings you previously specified.

The Range Format Command

Figures 3-1 and 3-2 show a before and after view of the effect that the Range Format command can have on your worksheet. Figure 3-1 shows an excerpt from a balance sheet in which the numbers in Column E appear as they were entered, in 1-2-3/G's default General format. Note the rather plain appearance of the numbers. Figure 3-2, on the other hand, shows the same numbers after formatting. The numbers in cells A:E6 and A:E12 have been formatted as

1-2-3/G Ready

File Edit Worksheet Range Copy... Move... Print Graph Data Utility Quit... Help

A:E12 @SUM(E6..E10)

FIG3-1.WG1

A	A	B	C	D	E	F
1		Capitola Computers, Inc.				
2			Balance Sheet			
3						
4	ASSETS:					
5						
6	Cash				32555.55	
7	Accounts Receivable				104326.2	
8	Inventory				233518.48	
9	Equipment				78321.94	
10	Accumulated Depreciation				55425.29	
11						
12	Total Assets				504147.46	
13						

FIGURE 3–1 **A sample worksheet with numbers in 1-2-3/G's default General Format**

Currency 2, and the numbers in the range A:E7..A:E10 have been formatted as Comma 2. Note the improvement in appearance and readability of the data.

To use the Range Format command, you must select one or more ranges in your worksheet(s) to which the command will apply. As you know, you can do this either before or during the command.

The example that follows takes you through a typical Range Format session to show you how you might format the range A:E6..A:E12 in Figure 3–1 so that

1-2-3/G Ready

File Edit Worksheet Range Copy... Move... Print Graph Data Utility Quit... Help

A:E12 @SUM(E6..E10)

(C2) FIG3-2.WG1

A	A	B	C	D	E
1		Capitola Computers, Inc.			
2			Balance Sheet		
3					
4	ASSETS:				
5					
6	Cash				$32,555.55
7	Accounts Receivable				104,326.20
8	Inventory				233,518.48
9	Equipment				78,321.94
10	Accumulated Depreciation				55,425.29
11					
12	Total Assets				$504,147.46
13					

FIGURE 3–2 **The same worksheet as in Figure 3–1 after formatting the range A:E6..A:E12 with Range Format**

it appears as in Figure 3–2. The range A:E7..A:E10 will be formatted first as a single range. Next, you'll format cells A:E6 and A:E12 as a collection.

To format the values in the range A:E7..A:E10 of Figure 3–1, perform the following:

1. Click and hold down the left button of your mouse on cell A:E7 and drag down to highlight the range A:E7..A:E10.

Note

> If you're using a keyboard, move the cell pointer to cell A:E7 and press CTRL-. (CTRL-PERIOD) to anchor the cell pointer. Then, press ↓ three times.

2. Select Range Format. 1-2-3/G displays the Range Format dialog box shown in Figure 3–3.

The Range Format Dialog Box contains a list box titled "Category," a text box titled "Range(s)," and an information box titled "Preview." The "Category" box lists the format types available for your selection. (Each format type is explained later in detail.) The "Range(s)" text box shows the current selection (the

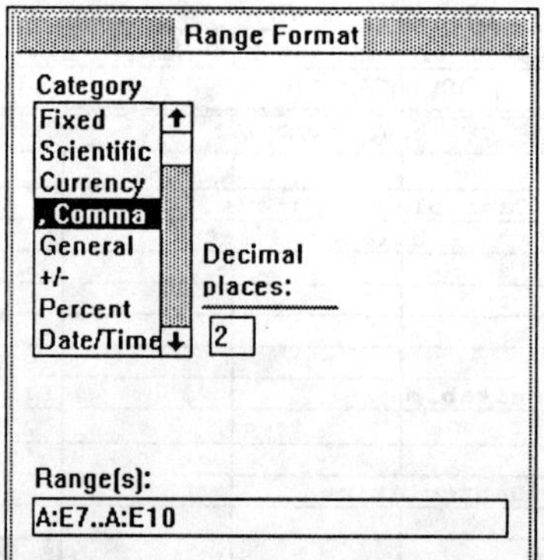

FIGURE 3–3 The Range Format dialog box

range in the worksheet that will be affected by the command). The "Preview" box shows you what effect your format selection will have on the data in your worksheet.

3. Select , *Comma* from the "Category" list box. If the Comma selection does not appear in the box, use the scroll bar at the right side of the "Category" box to scroll through the selections in the box until it does. Then click once on Comma. 1-2-3/G prompts you for the number of places you wish to have appear after the decimal and displays 2 as the default. Accept this default for now.

Note

If you're using the keyboard, use the arrow keys to locate the highlight on ", Comma" and press ENTER. (You can also type "c" to select the Comma format.) Press ENTER again to confirm the two places after the decimal.

4. Notice the Range(s) box. It should contain the range A:E7..A:E10. If it does not, press TAB to get to the Range(s) box, or click on it, and do one of the following:

    - Type in the correct range address. When you start typing, 1-2-3/G clears the Range(s) text box to make room for your entry.
    - If you're using the mouse, click on the Minimize arrow that now appears in the upper-right corner of the dialog box. This reduces the size of the dialog box to show only the Range(s) box and returns you to the current worksheet in POINT mode. Next, click and hold down the left mouse button on cell A:E7, drag down to highlight the range A:E7..A:E10, and release. Finally, restore the Range Format dialog box by clicking on the Maximize/Restore box in its upper-right corner.
    - As an alternative keyboard method, press ↓. 1-2-3/G reduces the size of the Range Format dialog box to show only the "Range(s)" box and returns to the worksheet in POINT mode. Press ESC to free the cell pointer and then use the arrow keys to move the cell pointer to cell A:E7. Press . (period) to anchor the cell pointer, press ↓ three times to highlight the range A:E7..A:E10, and press ENTER. 1-2-3/G formats the range as Comma with two decimal places.

5. If you used the mouse in this procedure, 1-2-3/G returns you to the Range Format dialog box. Select the OK command button or press ENTER to

complete the Range Format command. 1-2-3/G formats the range A:E7..A:E10 as Comma with two displayed places after the decimal and returns you to the worksheet.

Tip for Release 2 and 3 Users

The following steps will achieve the same results as in the above example:

1. Locate the cell pointer on cell A:E7.
2. Select /Range Format Currency.
3. Press ENTER to confirm two decimal places.
4. Press ↓ three times.
5. Press ENTER.

To finish formatting the worksheet in Figure 3–1, you'll format cells A:E6 and A:E12 as a collection in Currency 2 format, as follows:

1. Click the left button of your mouse on cell A:E6 to make it the current selection. Then, click the right mouse button on cell A:E12. You have now created a collection that includes cells A:E6 and A:E12.

Note

To perform step 1 with your keyboard, use the arrow keys to move the cell pointer to cell A:E6 and press DETACH (SHIFT-F8) to detach the cell pointer. This marks the end of the first range in the collection and frees the cell pointer to allow you to highlight another range. Next, use the arrow keys to move the cell pointer to cell A:E12 and leave it there. This marks the second part of the collection.

2. Select the Range Format command. 1-2-3/G displays the Range Format dialog box shown in Figure 3–3.
3. Select "Currency" from the "Category" list box and confirm that two decimal places are to be displayed, as we did in step 3 of the previous example.

4. Note the Range(s) box. It should contain the range address A:E6,A:E12..A:E12. The comma (,) separates the two distinct ranges in the collection, A:E6 and A:E12..A:E12. If the Range(s) box does not contain the correct range addresses, press TAB to get to the Range(s) box, or click on it, and do one of the following:

   - Type in the correct range addresses separated by a comma. When you start typing, 1-2-3/G clears the "Range(s)" text box to make room for your entry.
   - With the mouse, click on the ↓ that now appears in the upper-right corner of the dialog box. This reduces the size of the dialog box to show only the "Range(s)" text box and returns you to the worksheet in POINT mode. Click the left mouse button on cell A:E6 and the right button on A:E12. Finally, restore the Range Format dialog box by clicking on the Maximize/Restore box that now appears in the upper-right corner of the down-sized dialog box.
   - As an alternative keyboard method, press ↓. 1-2-3/G reduces the size of the dialog box to show only the "Range(s) text box and returns you to the worksheet in POINT mode. Press ESC to free the cell pointer. Move to cell A:E6 and press , (comma). 1-2-3/G returns you to the dialog box. Press ↓ again to return to the worksheet. Highlight cell A:E12 and press ENTER. 1-2-3/G formats the collection as Currency with two decimal places.
   - As another alternative keyboard method, press ↓. 1-2-3/G reduces the size of the dialog box to show only the "Range(s) text box and returns you to the worksheet in POINT mode. Press ESC to free the cell pointer. Move to cell A:E6 and press DETACH (SHIFT-F8). Press ↓ to move the cell pointer to cell A:E12 and press ENTER. 1-2-3/G formats the collection as Currency with two decimal places.

5. If you used the mouse in this procedure, 1-2-3/G returns you to the Range Format dialog box. Click on the OK command button or press ENTER to complete the Range Format command. 1-2-3/G formats the collection as Currency with two decimal places.

Tip: You can format a cell before you enter data

You can specify a given format for a cell either before or after you enter data in the cell.

Selecting Decimal Display

When you select one of the 1-2-3/G's number formats including Fixed, Scientific, Currency, Comma, or Percent, from the Range Format dialog box, 1-2-3/G displays the "Decimal places" text box, prompting you to select the number of places to be displayed after the decimal. The default is two places, as shown in Figure 3-3. However, you can select from 0 to 15 places to be displayed after the decimal. To change the number of displayed decimal places, click on the current number in the "Decimal places" text box, or press TAB to move to the "Decimal places" text box, and type in a new number from 0 to 15.

Formatting Does Not Affect Cell Contents

When you format a cell using either Range Format or Worksheet Global Format, it is the underlying cell that is formatted, not the value within the cell. Thus, the contents of the cell are not affected. In fact, 1-2-3/G continues to display the cell's stored value in the Control Line at the top of your screen, and uses that value in all calculations.

Rounding

Depending on the number of decimal places you select for a number format, 1-2-3/G may appear to round the value in a cell. For example, if you have the value 123.125 in a cell, and you format the cell as Currency 2, 1-2-3/G will display and print $123.13.

Because 1-2-3/G may round the decimal display of a number in a cell, your subtotals may not appear to match the sum of the parts. For example, adding two cells that both contain 123.123, displayed as 123.12, appears to equal 246.25. Thus, the total does not appear to match the sum of its parts. To solve this problem, you can use the @ROUND function covered in Chapter 6, "Functions." This function allows you to specify the number of decimal places used in calculations. As an alternative to the @ROUND function, you can use the Range Attributes Precision command to control the number of decimal places used in calculations within a given range. See "Setting Decimal Precision" under "Assigning Cell Attributes" later in this chapter for more details on the Range Attributes Precision command.

Column Widths and Cell Formatting

The width of the current column also affects the display of numbers. The width, in characters, of the current column determines the width of all cells in that column. If the current cell is not wide enough to display all the digits in a number, 1-2-3/G will either round the decimal portion of the value or display asterisks (*) in the cell. In general, the width of a cell in characters must be equal to or exceed the number of characters in the formatted value, to avoid rounding or asterisks.

For example, imagine you enter the value 123.123456 (10 characters) in cell A:A1 of a fresh worksheet. Imagine further that the width of column A is set to nine characters, the default. 1-2-3/G rounds the display of the decimal portion of the value and shows 123.12346 in the cell. However, increasing the width of column A to 10 characters will cause the value to be displayed as entered.

Or, imagine you enter the value 10000000 (8 characters) in cell A:A1 of a fresh worksheet. Next, you format cell A:A1 as Currency 2. Thus, 10000000 becomes $10,000,000.00, requiring a 14-character display. 1-2-3/G displays asterisks (********) in the cell, because the width of the formatted value exceeds that of the cell. To display the value as formatted, you must increase the width of column A, and thus cell A:A1, to at least 14 characters.

Note

For a complete discussion of how to increase, or decrease, the width of columns in your worksheets, see "Adjusting Column Widths" under "Working with Columns, Rows, and Worksheets" later in this chapter.

The Worksheet Global Format Command

If you intend to use a particular cell format frequently in a given worksheet, you can save yourself time and effort by formatting the entire worksheet ahead of time. To do this, you use the Worksheet Global Format command.

The Worksheet Global Format command offers the same formatting options as the Range Format command. However, your selection of a format type affects all the cells in the worksheet, except those you've already formatted with the Range Format command. What's more, any cells you subsequently format with Range Format override the current global setting. Thus, you can use the Worksheet Global Format command to establish a global format for the worksheet as a whole, and then use the Range Format command to format smaller ranges of cells as the need arises.

The procedure for using the Worksheet Global Format command is very similar to that of the Range Format. However, it is not necessary to select a range to which the command will apply. By default, the command will apply to the worksheet that contains the cell pointer. When you enter the Worksheet Global Format command, 1-2-3/G displays a dialog box similar to the Range Format dialog box shown in Figure 3-3. Simply select the format type you want from the "Category" list box, specify the number of desired decimal places, if prompted, and either press ENTER or click on the OK command button to complete the command.

The Worksheet Global Format command applies only to the worksheet that contains the cell pointer. Therefore, to apply a new global format to another worksheet in the same file, or a different file, you must move the cell pointer to that worksheet. Then use the Worksheet Global Format command.

Tip: Formatting more than one worksheet

You can apply a single Worksheet Global Format command to more than one worksheet at a time by grouping the worksheets. To do this, you use the Worksheet Global Group command. See "Grouping Worksheets" later in this chapter for more details on this command.

Unfortunately, you cannot save a Worksheet Global Format setting for use with all of your new worksheet files. However, when you create new worksheet files with the File New command, you can specify another worksheet file that will be used as a *template* for creating the new file. A template file is simply another worksheet file that is used as a model for the new file. All the format settings and data from that file are used when creating the new file. This option is described briefly later in this section under "Using Template Files." It is also described in detail in Chapter 5, "File Management," under "Creating New Files."

Determining Cell Format

To determine the current format for a specific cell, move the cell pointer to that cell and look at the left-hand side of the Title Bar of the current worksheet window. 1-2-3/G shows an abbreviation for the cell's format enclosed in parentheses. For example, Figure 3–4 shows the cell pointer on cell A:A1, which contains the number 123 formatted as Fixed 2. Therefore the abbreviation (F2) appears in the Title Bar of the worksheet window, just to the right of the Window Control box. In this case, the F stands for Fixed format and the 2 stands for the number of places displayed after the decimal. In general, the number following the letter increases as the number of decimal places increases. Therefore, the Fixed 3 format abbreviation would be (F3), and so on. However, there are exceptions to this. For example, (D4) stands for Date 4, which has the form MM/DD/YY. In some cases, no number follows the letter, for example (A) for

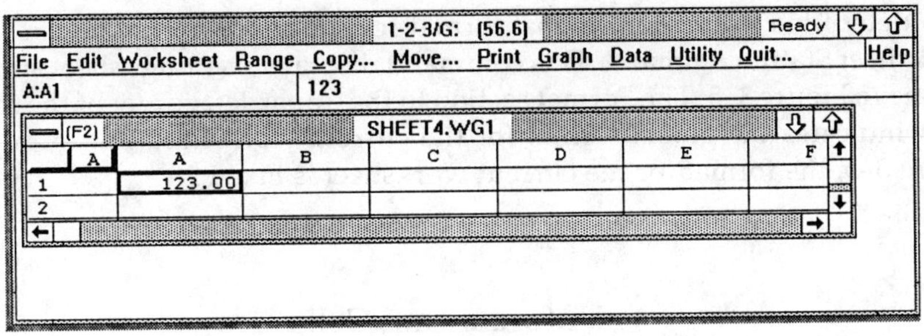

FIGURE 3–4 A cell's format is displayed in the title bar of the worksheet window

Automatic or (H) for Hidden. The following table shows some typical cell format abbreviations:

Abbreviation	Cell Format	Example Display
(F2)	Fixed 2	1000.00
(S2)	Scientific 2	1.23E+02
(,2)	Comma 2	1,000.00
(G)	General	1000)
(+)	Bar Format (+/–)	+
(P2)	Percent 2	10.00%
(D4)	Date/Time 4	12/21/92
(D7)	Date/Time 7	12:58 PM
(A)	Automatic	Not applicable
(T)	Text	@SUM(A:A1..A:A10)
(L)	Label	'123
(H)	Hidden	
(())	Parens	(123)
(U)	User defined	Not applicable

Note

If the format of the current cell is the same as the global format for the current worksheet, 1-2-3/G does not display a format abbreviation in the Title Bar.

To determine the current global format for the worksheet, you can use the Worksheet Status command. This command displays a settings sheet similar to the one in Figure 3–5. The Format section in the upper-left corner of the settings sheet indicates the global format for the current worksheet. For example, in Figure 3–5, the format for the current worksheet is Fixed 2.

Unformatting Cells

You can reset a range of cells to match the current global setting by using the Range Format Reset command. To do this, simply highlight a range of cells in the usual manner and select Range Format. 1-2-3/G displays the Range Format dialog box. Next, select Reset from the "Category" list box and press ENTER, or click your mouse on the OK command button. 1-2-3/G formats the cells you've selected to match the global format for the current worksheet, which is set with the Worksheet Global Format command.

1-2-3/G's Cell Format Types

A brief description of each of 1-2-3/G's cell format types follows, along with some tips on using them. Keep in mind that the cell format types that follow can be applied to ranges, including three-dimensional ranges, or to collections of cells by using the Range Format command. These same formats can be

Worksheet Status

Format
Format: (F2)
Font: 10 Pt.Courier
Label align: Left
Value align: Right
Zero display: '0

Recalculation
Type: Auto
Order: Natural
Iterations: 1
Circular ref:

Display options
Protection: Disabled
Grid: Enabled
Frames: Both
Column width: 9 ch.
Row height: 0.235in.
Long labels: Enabled

Other
Processor: (Unknown)
Coprocessor: None
Auto execute: Both
Undo: Enabled
Group mode: Disabled
Reservation: Yes/Auto

Colors
T Frames
T Labels
T Pos values
T Neg values
Selection
Grid lines
Unprotected
Borders

OK

FIGURE 3–5 The Worksheet Status settings sheet

applied to the entire current worksheet by using the Worksheet Global Format command.

Fixed

The Fixed format affects numbers only, and it allows you to fix the number of places displayed after the decimal point. You can select from 0 to 15 places after the decimal. Decimal values are displayed with a leading zero, and negative values are displayed with a leading minus sign (-). To enter a negative value, precede it with a minus sign (-). Some examples of Fixed format follow:

Cell Entry	Format Type	Display
123123.123	Fixed 2	123123.12
123123.123	Fixed 3	123123.123
–123.123	Fixed 2	–123.12

For example, imagine you have a formula in the current cell that evaluates to 10567.678. To format the cell containing this formula as Fixed with two decimal places, select the Range Format command. 1-2-3/G displays the Range Format dialog box. Select "Fixed" from the "Category" list box. 1-2-3/G displays the "Decimal places" text box, prompting you to select the number of decimal places, and displays 2 as the default. Accept the default number for decimal places and confirm the current range in the Range(s) text box by selecting the OK command button. 1-2-3/G completes the Range Format command and displays 10567.68 in the current cell. As an alternative to selecting the OK command button when 1-2-3/G prompts you for the number of decimal places, you can press ENTER twice, once to confirm the number of decimal places and again to confirm the current range and complete the Range Format command.

Scientific

Scientific format allows you to display values in scientific notation. This format is useful when particularly large numbers are involved. This format displays numbers in powers of 10 with an exponent from -99 to +99 and you can choose from 0 to 15 decimal places. For example, the number 10,000 is really 10 to the power of 4, or 10x10x10x10. Some examples of Scientific format follow:

Cell Entry	Format Type	Display
10000	Scientific 2	1.00E+04
123123	Scientific 2	1.23E+15
–123	Scientific 2	-1.23E+02

Currency

The Currency format displays a currency symbol ($) in front of values, separates thousands with commas, and allows you to choose from 0 to 15 places to appear after the decimal. Decimal values are displayed with a leading zero, and negative values are enclosed in parentheses. Some examples follow:

Cell Entry	Format Type	Display
123123.123	Currency 2	$123,123.12
–123.125	Currency 2	($123.13)

You can use the User Settings International command available from the Utility menu or the Desktop Control menu to modify the display of the Currency format. For example, you can specify a new default currency symbol or have the currency symbol follow, instead of precede, a value. You can also have negative values preceded by a simple minus sign (-) instead of enclosed in parentheses (the default). See "International Formats" later in this section for details on how to use the User Settings International command to modify the display of Currency format.

, (Comma)

The , Comma format displays values with commas to separate hundreds, thousands, millions, and so on. You can specify from 0 to 15 places after the decimal. A leading zero is displayed in front of decimal values and negative numbers are displayed in parenthesis (( )). Some examples of the comma format follow:

Cell Entry	Format Type	Display
123123.123	, Comma 2	123,123.12
-123.123	, Comma 2	(123.12)

You can modify the display of the Comma format by using the User Settings International command available from either the Utility menu or the Desktop Control menu. For example, you can choose a separator character other than the comma. You can also choose to have negative numbers preceded by a minus sign (-) for the ", Comma" format, instead of enclosed in parentheses. See "International Formats" later in this section for more about how to use the User Setting International command to modify the display of the Comma format.

General

General format is the default format assigned to all the cells in a new worksheet file. The General format does not allow you to control the number of places to be displayed after the decimal point, there are no commas to separate thousands, and it does not provide trailing zeros after a decimal. Further, negative values are preceded only by a minus sign (-).

Column widths also affect the display of values in General format. When the number of digits to the *left* of the decimal point causes the value to exceed the width of the current cell, 1-2-3/G displays the value in Scientific format. For example, imagine you enter the number 1231231231 (10 digits) in the current cell. Imagine further that the current column-width setting is nine characters (the default). 1-2-3/G displays the value as 1.23E+09. On the other hand, if the number of digits to the *right* of the decimal causes a value to exceed the width of the cell, 1-2-3/G rounds the decimal portion of the value. For example, imagine you enter the value 123123.125 (nine digits and a decimal) in a cell with a nine-character width. 1-2-3/G displays the value as 123123.13.

+/- Horizontal Bar Format

The Horizontal Bar format (+/-) portrays numbers as a series of plus signs (+), minus signs (–), or as a period. All numbers are rounded to the closest whole number. Positive numbers are shown as plus symbols. For example, the number 3 appears as +++. Negative numbers are portrayed as minus signs (–). For example, the number –3 appears as– – –. Finally, decimal values between 1 and -1 are shown as a period. For example, the number .45 appears as . (period). Additional examples of Horizontal Bar format follow:

Cell Entry	Format Type	Display
5	+/-	+++++
-7	+/-	-------
-.25	+/-	.

Percent

The Percent format causes numbers to be displayed as percentages. The number appears as if it were multiplied by 100 with a trailing percent sign (%). The Percent format allows from 0 to 15 places to be displayed after the decimal. Some examples of Percent format follow:

Cell Entry	Format Type	Display	Stored as
1	Currency 2	100.00%	1
.5	Currency 2	50.00%	.5
-.66666	Currency 3	-66.666	-.66666

Date/Time

You can use the Date/Time format to format cells containing date and/or time values. You can choose from one of five date formats or one of four time formats. See "Date and Time Formats" later in this section for a complete discussion of how to format date and time values.

Automatic

The Automatic format automatically formats a cell based on how your entry appears. For example, the entry $123.12 is interpreted as Currency 2, and the cell is automatically formatted in that fashion. As another example, the entry 123.12 is interpreted as Fixed 2, and the cell is formatted as such. Thus, the Automatic format can save you time by formatting cells at the point of entry.

When you format a range as Automatic, existing numbers within the range are assigned a General format. From that point on, all new entries are formatted based on their appearance. The Automatic format responds to Comma, Currency, Fixed, Percent, or Scientific entries. In addition, many date and time entries are supported. When you make any entry in the form of Date 1 (DD-MMM-YY), Date 2 (DD-MMM), Date 3 (MMM-YY), Date 4 (MM/DD/YY), or any time format, 1-2-3/G places the correct date or time value in the cell and formats it accordingly.

The Automatic format is also useful for entering labels. Any entry whose first character causes 1-2-3/G to enter LABEL mode is given a label prefix (') and stored in the cell as a label. What's more, if a number is entered followed by a space or another nonnumeric character, 1-2-3/G gives the entry a label prefix and stores it in the cell as a label. For example, if you make the entry **221 Sevilla Drive,** the space following the initial number causes the entry to be interpreted as a label. Finally, if you enter a formula that is invalid by 1-2-3/G's standards, the entry is given a label prefix and stored as a label. For example, imagine you make the entry **@SUM)A:A1..A:A10)**. Since the first paren in the formula is backward 1-2-3/G stores the entry as '@SUM)A:A1..A:A10). To turn the entry into a formula, select the Range Format Reset command and specify the address of the current cell in the Range(s) text box. Select OK to complete the command. Next, press EDIT (F2) to place the entry in the Control Line, correct the error, remove the label prefix, and press ENTER.

Note

Once the Automatic format causes a cell to be formatted in a certain way, the cell retains that format for future entries. To change the format for the cell, you must use the Range Format command to specify a new format. For example, if you make the entry **$123.12,** 1-2-3/G automatically formats the cell as Currency 2, and displays $123.12. If you subsequently make the entry 123.12 (Fixed 2), 1-2-3/G continues to display $123.12 (Currency 2) in the cell.

Text

The Text format causes formulas to be displayed as labels. However, the formulas are still active and perform their prescribed calculations. Any existing numbers in cells within the formatted range take on a General format. For example, if you enter the formula **123*123** in a cell, 1-2-3/G displays 123*123. However, all formulas that refer to the cell use the number 15,129—the result of the formula. Text format can be useful when you want to examine a formula's components or when you're teaching someone else how to use 1-2-3/G.

Label

Label format causes all entries, both labels and numbers, to be formatted as labels. All existing numbers within the formatted range take on the default General format. For example, if you make the entry 100.00, 1-2-3/G stores '100.00 in the cell and displays it as a label. Therefore, the entry cannot be used in calculations. The Label format can be useful for data entry to a database field where all entries must be in the form of a label. See Chapter 9, "Data Management," for more about using databases with 1-2-3/G.

Note

When a range is formatted as Label, removing the label prefix in front of a numeric entry has no effect. That is, when you press ENTER after removing the label prefix, 1-2-3/G once again stores the entry to the cell as a label. To use the entry as a number, you must use the Range Format command and specify a number format for the cell, or use the Range Format Reset command to match the format of the cell to that of the current worksheet. Then remove the label prefix or make a new entry.

Hidden

The Hidden format causes the contents of a cell to disappear from view. What's more, the data in a hidden cell does not print. However, the entry is still there and can be used in calculations. The Hidden format can be useful when you're preparing or printing a worksheet for use by others and you wish to hide extraneous or confidential data.

Tip: The contents of hidden cells appear in the control line

When you format a range as Hidden, the data in the cell disappears from view. However, when you move the cell pointer to the cell, the entry is displayed in the Control Line. To hide the entry totally from view, you must protect the worksheet. To protect a worksheet, you use the Worksheet Global Protection command. This command is discussed toward the end of this chapter under "Protecting Your Worksheets."

To redisplay the contents of a hidden cell, you have two choices. You can either use the Range Format Reset command to reset the format for the cell to match the current global format, or you can use the Range Format command to establish a new format for the cell.

(Parens)

You can use the (Parens) format to specify that all numbers within a given range or worksheet be enclosed within parentheses. When you select this format from either the Range Format or Worksheet Global Format dialog box, 1-2-3/G prompts you with No/Yes command-button menu. If you select Yes, 1-2-3/G encloses all numbers within parentheses. To differentiate negative numbers, 123/G uses a leading minus sign (-123).

User

The User format allows you to design your own custom formats to display numbers. You can select "User" from the "Category" list box for either the Range Format or Worksheet Global Format command. 1-2-3/G shows you a list of previously defined user formats from which you can select, as well as an empty box in which you can create a new user-defined format. To create a user-defined format, you must use 1-2-3/G's Format Description Language. For a complete discussion of how to create user-defined formats and apply them, see "Creating User-Defined Formats" later in this section.

Date and Time Formats

As mentioned earlier, 1-2-3/G allows you to choose from five different formats to display dates and four different formats to display times. However, to display either a date or a time in a cell, you must first enter a date value, a time value, or a combined date/time value in that cell. For a complete discussion about date and time values, see Chapter 1, "123/G Basics."

To format a date and/or time value to display a date or time, you use the Range Format command and select "Date/Time" from the "Category" list box. When you select "Date/Time," a list box titled "Format" appears, as shown in Figure 3–6. From this list box, 1-2-3/G allows you to select from one of nine Date/Time formats. However, as you can see from Figure 3–6, only the first eight format options are initially displayed. You must scroll the list box to see the last option.

The first five choices in the "Format" list box (Date 1 through Date 5) are used to format the display of date values to display dates. The last four choices (6 though 9) are used to format the display of times values to display times.

Figure 3–6 also shows the results of using each of the Date/Time format options (1 through 9) to format the @NOW function. The @NOW function calculates a combined date/time value for the current date and time by using you computer's system clock. In Figure 3–6, the @NOW functions are located

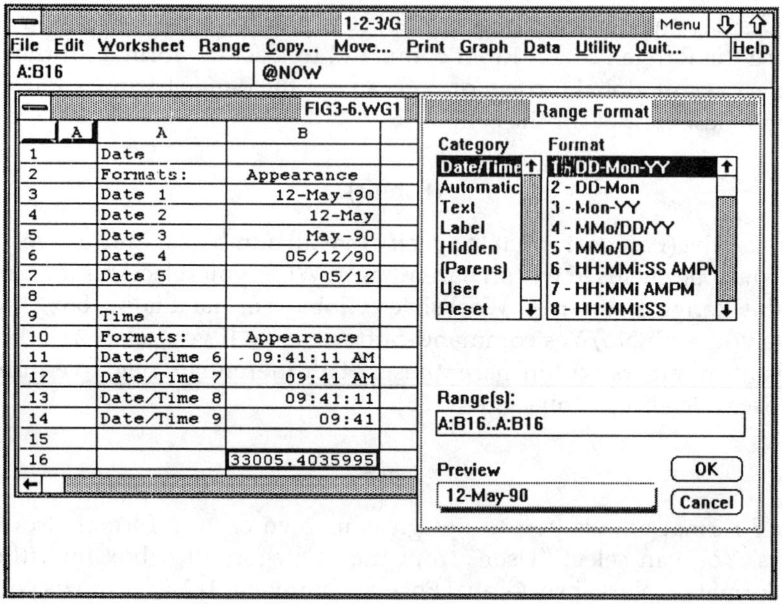

FIGURE 3–6 **Choosing date and time formats**

in column B and were entered as of May 12, 1990 at 9:41 AM and approximately 11 seconds. Each format type is identified by a label in an adjacent cell in column A.

The Date formats (Date 1 through Date 5) are shown in the range A:B3..A:B7 of Figure 3–6. The Date 4 and Date 5 formats, referred to as Long Int'l and Short Int'l, respectively, have a default display as shown in Figure 3–6. However, you can modify the display of these two date formats by using the Utility User Settings International command covered later under "International Formats."

1-2-3/G's available time formats (Date/Time 6 through Date/Time 9) are shown in the range A:B9..A:B12 of Figure 2–6. The convention of calling the time formats Date/Time 6 through Date/Time 9 may seem peculiar to you at first. However, it is in keeping with 1-2-3/G's date and time numbering scheme, in which the integer portion of a value is used to represent the date and the decimal portion of that same value is used to represent the time.

Similar to the date formats Date 4 and Date 5, the time formats Date/Time 8 and Date/Time 9 are referred to as Long Int'l and Short Int'l, respectively. Date/Time 8 and Date/Time 9 have the default display shown in Figure 3–6. Both the Date/Time 8 and Date/Time 9 formats are displayed in 24-hour (military) time format as the default. However, the display of these two formats can be changed through the Utility User Setting International command. See

"International Formats" later in this section for more details on how to modify the display of these time formats.

Column widths can have an impact on the display of dates and times. For example, Date/Time 6 has an 11-character format, and requires an 11-character column width in order to be displayed. If the width of the current column is nine characters (the default), 1-2-3/G displays asterisks in the cell. To display the time properly, you must widen the column. See "Working with Column, Rows, and Worksheets" later in this chapter for details on how to set column widths.

Creating User-Defined Formats

As mentioned earlier, you can create your own user-defined formats for values, including date and time values. To do this, you use a special language called the Format Description Language. This language is composed of a series of special symbols that allow you to build a "picture" of the format you want. These symbols are combined to form a *format string*. To create a format string that describes your new format, you must enter either the Range Format or Worksheet Global Format command and select "User" from the "Category" list box.

Figure 3–7 shows an example of what your screen looks like when you select "User" from the Range Format dialog box. Notice that a list box titled "Format" appears. In this list box, 1-2-3/G lists any user-defined formats you may have defined thus far for that worksheet file. Each format type appears in a slot. There are 64 slots in all and the first 26 slots are marked "a" through "z." If you have not defined a format for a specific slot, 1-2-3/G displays Undefined in that slot. For example, slot "h" in Figure 3–7 is undefined. Beneath the "Format" list box is a text box titled "User format." It is in this text box that you enter the format string that describes your user-defined format.

To define a new user-defined format, first select a slot marked "Undefined" from the "Format" list box. 1-2-3/G moves the cursor to the "User format" text box and you can begin typing in the format string that describes your new format. When you're finished, press ENTER. 1-2-3/G activates the "Range(s)" text box. Accept or modify the current selection in this box in the usual way and press ENTER, or select the OK command button, to complete the Range Format command. 1-2-3/G formats the range you've selected using your new user-defined format.

To format the currently selected range using a previously defined user format, simply select the appropriate slot for that format from the "Format" list box. In the "Preview" text box at the bottom of the screen, 1-2-3/G shows you an example of what the format will look like in the worksheet. Complete the Range Format command as you normally do.

To change a previously defined user format, select the slot for that format from the "Format" list box. 1-2-3/G places the format string for that particular format in the "User format" text box. Press TAB to move the "User format" text

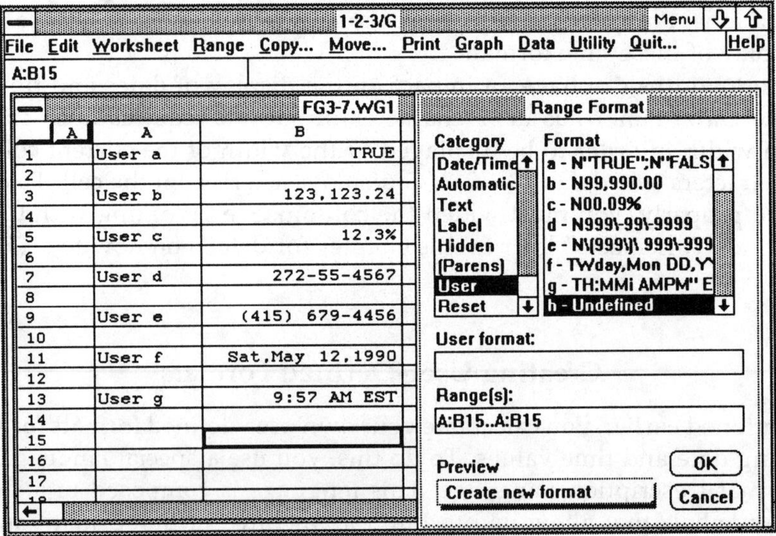

FIGURE 3–7 Selecting Range Format User

box, or click on it. Make the necessary modifications and select the OK command button. 1-2-3/G records your modification in the appropriate slot and formats the current selection with the modified format.

The sections that follow show you how to use the symbols in the Format Description Language to create format strings for user-defined formats. There are three symbol groups from which you can choose to build format strings: Number, General, and Date/Time. The tables that follow show you the symbols contained within each group along with a description of the function they perform. Following each table are some examples of user-defined formats for that group.

Number Format Symbols

The following table contains the Number format symbols. To signify to 1-2-3/G that you are creating a number format, begin the format with N or n.

Symbol	Description
N or n	Begins a number format.
0	(Zero). A numeric digit is always displayed. If the number you enter does not have a digit in this position, 1-2-3/G will display a zero here.

Symbol	Description
9	Displays a numeric digit, provided there is one. If not, nothing is displayed.
%	Displays the number as a percentage. The number appears as if multiplied by 100 with a trailing percent sign.
, (comma)	Displays a comma between thousands. The comma occupies a single space. If you specify another thousands separator with Utility User Settings International Number format, that separator will be used.
. (period)	Signifies a decimal. The decimal occupies one space. If you specify another decimal separator with Utility User Settings International Number format, that separator will be used.
; (semicolon)	Separates one format from another in the same format string, e.g., Format1;Format2. When two formats are included in the same format string, the first applies to numbers greater than or equal to zero and the second to numbers less than zero. When three formats are included in the same format string, the first applies to numbers greater than zero, the second applies to zero, and the third to numbers less than zero.
E- or e-	Inserts an E or e and displays the number in Scientific format. A minus sign is displayed in front of negative exponents. At least one 0 or 9 must follow this symbol. If the exponent contains more digits than there are 0's or 9's following the E, those digits will be displayed.
E+ or e+	Inserts an E or e and displays the number in Scientific format. A minus sign (-) is displayed in front of negative exponents and a plus sign (+) in front of positive exponents. At least one 0 or 9 must follow this symbol. If the exponent contains more digits than there are 0's or 9's following the E, those digits will be displayed.
Currency	You can also place currency symbols, for example $, at the beginning or end of number format strings. For example, n$9,999.99.

Number Format Examples

The following table shows some examples of number format strings and their effect on the display of various numbers.

Format String	Number Entry	Displayed as
N99,999.00	1231.235	1,123.24
N99,000.09	12	012.0
N00.09%	.123	12.3%
N0.0E+00	123	1.2E+02
N99,900.09;N-0.09	-12	-12.0
N990.00;Nzero;N(0.00)	123	123.00
N990.00;Nzero;N(0.00)	0	zero
N990.00;Nzero;N(0.00)	-123	(123)
N$9,999	1231.235	$1,231

General Format Symbols

The following table shows you the General format symbols for the Format Description Language. The General format symbols can be used with either Number format strings or Date/Time format strings (covered later).

Symbol	Description
\	Displays the character following the backslash within the format. (The backslash itself is not displayed.) To show a backslash, you must use two backslashes (\\).
*	Repeats the character following the asterisk as necessary to fill that part of the cell not occupied by the number. If the number occupies the entire cell, the character following the asterisk is not displayed.
" "	Include the text string within the double quotes as part of the number's format.

General Format Examples

The following table shows some examples of how you might use the General format symbols to format numbers.

Format String	Number Entry	Displayed as
N999\-99\-9999	272554567	272–55–4567
N\(999\)\ 999\-9999	4156794456	(415) 679–4456
N*$9,990.00	12.34	$$$12.34 (with a column width of nine characters)
N99,990.00" LBS."	123	123.00 LBS.
TMM\/DD\/YY	32881	01/08/90
TH:MM AMPM" EST"	.625	3:00 PM EST

Date/Time Symbols

The following table shows you the Date/Time format symbols for the Format Description Language. To signify to 1-2-3/G that you are creating a Date/Time format, begin the format with T or t.

Symbol	Description
T or t	Begins a Date/Time format string.
m or M or Mo or MO	Displays the month as a one- or two-digit number, for example 1–12.
mm or MM or mmo or MMO	Displays the month as a two-digit number, for example 01–12.
mon	Displays the month as three characters in lower case, for example jan-dec.
Mon	Displays the month as three characters with the first letter capitalized, for example Jan-Dec.
MON	Displays the month as three characters with all letters capitalized, for example JAN-DEC.
month	Displays the month spelled out in lower case, for example january-december.
Month	Displays the month spelled out with the first letter capitalized, for example January-December.
MONTH	Displays the month spelled out in upper case, for example JANUARY-DECEMBER.
d	Displays the day as a one- or two-digit number, for example 1–31.
dd	Displays the day as a two-digit number, for example 01–31.
wday	Displays the day as three characters in lower case, for example mon-sun.

continued on page 234

Symbol	Description *(continued)*
Wday	Displays the day as three characters with the first letter capitalized, for example Mon-Sun.
WDAY	Displays the day as three characters in upper case, for example MON-SUN.
weekday	Displays the day spelled out in lower case, for example monday-sunday.
Weekday	Displays the day spelled out with the first letter capitalized, for example Monday-Sunday.
WEEKDAY	Displays the day spelled out in upper case, for example MONDAY-SUNDAY.
YY or yy	Displays the year's last two digits, for example 89, 90, and so on.
YYYY	Displays all four digits in the year, for example 1991.
h	Displays the hour as one or two digits in 12-hour format, for example 1–12.
hh	Displays the hour as two digits in 12-hour format, for example 01–12.
H	Displays the hour as one or two digits in 24-hour format, for example 0–23.
HH	Displays the hour as two digits in 24-hour format, for example 00–23.
m or M or mi or MI	Displays the minute as one or two digits, for example 1–59.
mm or MM or mmi or MMI	Displays the minute as two digits, for example 01–59.
S or s	Displays the second as one or two digits, for example 1–59.
SS or ss	Displays the second as two digits, for example 01–59.
ampm or AMPM	Displays am or AM for times between midnight and noon and pm or PM for times between noon and midnight.
ap or AP	Displays a or A for times between midnight and noon and p or P for times between noon and midnight.

Date/Time Examples

The following table shows examples of Date/Time symbols used in format strings to format various date and time values. Notice that all date or time format strings must begin with T or t.

Format String	Number Entry	Displayed as
TMonth d, yyyy	32881	January 8, 1990
TWday	32881	Mon
TWeekday	2881	Monday
TWday, Month d, yyyy	32881	Mon, January 8, 1990
TH:MM AMPM	625	3:00 PM
TMon d, yyyy, H:MM AMPM	32881.625	Jan 8, 1990, 3:00 PM

International Formats

Both the Desktop Control menu and the Utility menu offer a User Settings International menu option. Either command gives you access to the settings sheet shown in Figure 3–8. This settings sheet allows you to change the way that many of 1-2-3/G's default formats are displayed. This applies to conventional numbers as well as date and/or time values.

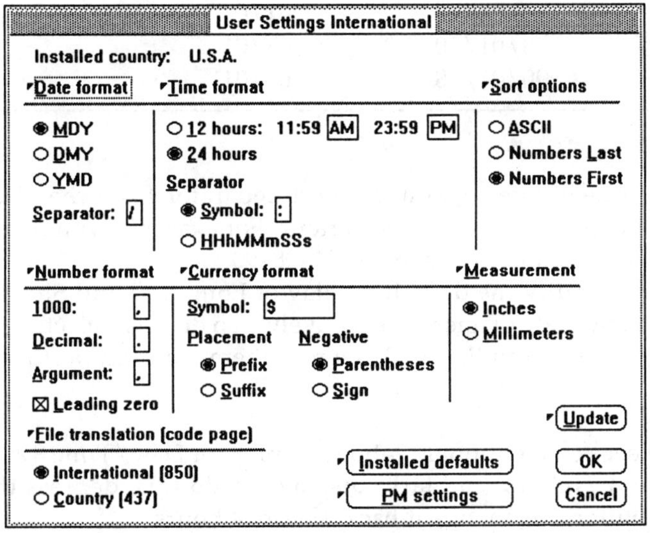

FIGURE 3–8 The Utility User Settings International settings sheet

Note

> When you make a change to 1-2-3/G's default settings by using either the Desktop User Settings International or Utility User Settings International command, you can save those changed settings for use in future 1-2-3/G sessions. To do this, select the "Update" command button in the lower-right corner of the User Settings International dialog box.

International Dates and Times

You can use the settings sheet in Figure 3–8 to modify the display of Long Int'l and Short Int'l Dates (Date 4 and Date 5, respectively). You can also modify the character used to separate months, days, and years. To modify the display of Date 4 and Date 5 formats, select Utility User Settings International to display the settings sheet in Figure 3–8. Next, select "Date format." Then, select one of the three available command buttons. The following table shows the effect of each choice on the display of Date 4 and Date 5.

Choice	Date 4	Date 5
MDY	01/08/90	01/08
DMY	08/01/90	08/01
YMD	90/01/08	08/01

To specify a new date separator, select Separator from the "Date format" section. Then, type in a new date separator. For example, you might type in a dash (-) so that dates are displayed as 01–08–90.

You can also modify the default display of Long Int'l and Short Int'l Times (Date/Time 8 and Date/Time 9, respectively). To do this, select "Time format" from the settings sheet in Figure 3–8. From there, you can perform any of the following:

- You can select a conventional 12–hour display for Date/Time 8 and 9, instead of the default 24–hour (military) display. To do this, depress the 12 hours command button. To change it back, select 24 hours.
- If you selected 12 hours, you can also change the default AM and PM suffixes. Normally, 1-2-3/G displays AM for times between midnight and noon. To change this, select 11:59 and type in a suffix of your own. Additionally,

1-2-3/G displays PM for times between noon and midnight. To change this, select 23.59 and type in a new suffix.

- To specify a new character to separate hours, minutes and seconds in time formats, select Separator, select the Symbol option, and type in a new symbol. Or, select the HHhMMmSSs option to have times displayed as 10h30m51s.

International Number and Currency Formats

You can use the "Number format" section of the International settings sheet in Figure 3–8 to change the default symbols used in number formats. When you select "Number format," you can perform any of the following:

- **Change the symbol used as a thousands separator in number formats.** To do this, select 1000 and type in a new thousands separator. The symbols accepted by 1-2-3/G are the comma (,), the period (.), the apostrophe ('), or a blank space. The thousands separator must differ from the decimal separator.
- **Change the symbol used as a decimal in number formats.** To do this, select Decimal and type in a new character—for example, a comma (,)—instead of the default period. The decimal symbol you select must differ from the thousands separator.
- **Change the argument separator used in 1-2-3/G macros and @functions.** Symbols accepted by 1-2-3/G as an argument separator are the comma (,), the period (.), and semi-colon (;). The argument separator cannot be the same as the decimal symbol.
- **Remove the leading zero from formats that display a leading zero, such as Comma and Currency.** For example, the default display of a decimal value in Currency 2 format is $0.20. Removing the leading zero displays $.20. To remove the leading zero from these formats, click or press the space bar on the Leading zero check box. This removes the X from the box.

You can use the Currency section of the settings sheet in Figure 3–8 to modify the display of numbers in Currency format. When you select Currency from the settings sheet, you can perform any of the following:

- **Change the default currency symbol.** To do this, select Symbol and type in any currency symbol you want, up to five characters. You can enter any characters in the Lotus Character Set (LCS), including characters that do not appear on your keyboard. To do this, you can use COMPOSE sequences. For example, you can press COMPOSE (ALT-F1) followed by L= to enter the British pound symbol (£). For more about the Lotus Character Set and the use of COMPOSE sequences to enter characters, see Appendix B.
- **Change the placement of the currency symbol;** that is, place it before or after the number. To have the currency symbol appear after the number, select

Suffix. To have the currency symbol appear in front of the number (the default), select Prefix.

- **Have negative numbers in Currency and Comma format appear with a leading minus (-) sign,** instead of enclosed in parentheses (the default). To have a leading minus sign appear, select Sign.

Using Template Files for Formatting

1-2-3/G allows you to use one file as a *template* for creating another. All data and settings, including formatting, in the template file are used to create the new file. Thus, the new file you create is essentially a mirror image of the old file, but with a new name of your choosing. If you have a particularly complex formatting scheme in an old file that you want reuse in a new file, without having to reenter all the formatting information again, try using the old file as a template to create the new file.

As you'll learn in Chapter 5, you create a new file by using the File New command. When you enter this command, 1-2-3/G shows you the File New dialog box shown in Figure 3–9. The dialog box features a text box titled "Create window" in which you will enter the name of your new file. It also features a list box titled "Tool name" from which you will select the tool that you wish to create, in this case Worksheet. Finally, the File New dialog box includes a text box titled "Template Name." In this text box you can type in the path and name of an existing file to use as a template to create the new file. Normally, 1-2-3/G lists the file DEFAULT.WG1 in this box. However, you can type in any path and filename you like. When you complete the File New command, 1-2-3/G will create the new file by using the file you specified as a template. For more on the File New command, see Chapter 5, "File Management."

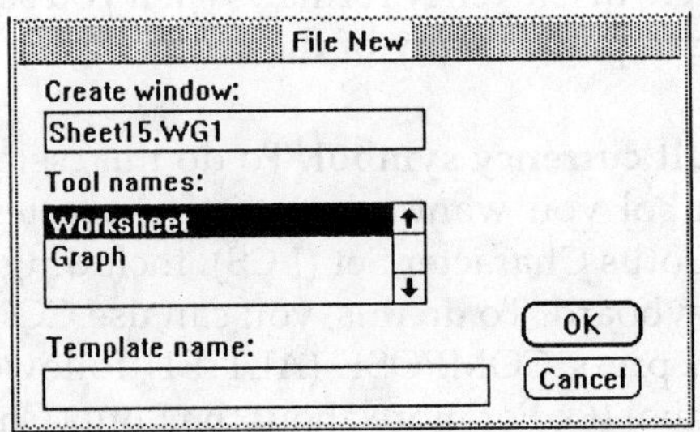

FIGURE 3–9 The File New dialog box

Tip: Use a startup worksheet to save formatting time

If you have a specific worksheet format that you intend to use each time you start 1-2-3/G, you can save that formatting in a worksheet file. You can then have 1-2-3/G load that file automatically each time you start the program. To do this, you use the User Settings Startup command from either the Utility menu or the Desktop Control menu. This command allows you to select a specific file to be opened each time you start 1-2-3/G. For additional information on this command see Appendix A, "Customizing 1-2-3/G."

ASSIGNING CELL ATTRIBUTES

1-2-3/G also allows you to assign attributes to cells to make their contents stand out from the rest of your worksheet. For example, you can assign a different *font* (type size and style) to a cell. You can also enhance that font with bold, underlining, italics, or a combination thereof. Or, you can build borders around the edges of cells to outline their contents. You can also assign foreground and background colors to cells based on their contents. For example, you can have all negative numbers appear in red with a blue background.

In addition to assigning fonts, borders, and colors to cells, you can also specify decimal precision. Decimal precision refers to the number of decimal places that 1-2-3/G uses in calculations. Although ordinarily 1-2-3/G retains the original value of the cell, it will, if necessary, round the decimal portion of the number for purposes of calculations.

Assigning Fonts

1-2-3/G allows you to format your data—both numbers and labels—in various fonts. Fonts are essentially styles of type, or *type faces,* that come in various sizes. For example, Figure 3–10 shows you the default fonts initially available from 1-2-3/G. Notice that there are only four basic type faces, but each comes in a variety of sizes.

The size of a type face is measured in *points.* (A point represents about 1/72 of an inch.) Each size of a particular type face represents a separate font. For example, 1-2-3/G offers four type faces: Helvetica, Courier, Times Roman, and System Proportional, as shown in Figure 3–10. These type faces come in various point sizes. For example, the Helvetica and Times Roman type faces come in 8,

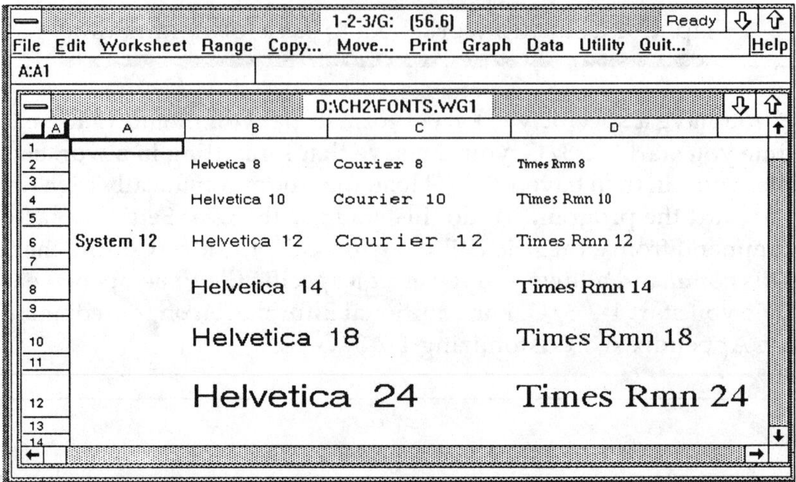

FIGURE 3–10 The default fonts available in 1-2-3/G

10, 12, 14, 18, and 24 point sizes. Thus, six Helvetica fonts and six Times Roman fonts are available. The Courier type face comes in 8, 10, and 12 point sizes, for a total of three fonts; and the System Proportional type face comes in a single 12–point size.

The default font used by 1-2-3/G when you start the system for the first time is Helvetica 8. This font is very small and thus difficult to read. As you read the balance of this section, you'll learn not only how to format your data so that it is displayed in a larger font, but also how to save that setting for future 1-2-3/G sessions.

Note

> The default 1-2-3/G font set just described is provided by OS/2, not 1-2-3/G. You can add your own fonts to 1-2-3/G's repertoire of fonts, if you so desire, but you must install those fonts in your OS2/DLL directory first. See Appendix A "Customizing 1-2-3/G" for information on how to install fonts.

Assigning Fonts to Ranges

To assign a font attribute to a range of cells, you use the Range Attribute Font command. When you enter this command, 1-2-3/G displays the Range Attributes Font dialog box shown in Figure 3–11. This dialog box allows you to select a particular font that will be used to display and print the currently selected range. It also allows you to apply additional attributes such as bolding, underlining, italics, and strikeout to the display of that font. The following paragraphs describe each component of the Range Attribute Font dialog box and how it is used to format a range of data.

The "Fonts" list box displays all the fonts currently available for 1-2-3/G. This list box contains 20 available slots for font names (labeled a through t). You'll notice in Figure 3–11, however, that only five slots (a through e) are initially displayed. Notice as well that the "Fonts" list box is split in half vertically. The fonts on the left are used to display your data on screen. The fonts on the right are used to print your data. In most cases, the font name on the left matches the font name on the right. However, there are some slots where the two differ. Thus, you can display your data in one font and print it in another.

To select a font to apply to the currently selected range, simply click on the abbreviation for that font in the left column of the "Fonts" list box, or highlight it and press ENTER. Selecting a font from the left column for your screen display automatically selects the corresponding printer font for that slot.

Note

You can rearrange as well as add to the fonts listed in the "Fonts" list box for both the (screen) and (printer) columns. That way, you can place your more commonly used font choices at the top of the list or add new ones. See "Changing the Default Font Set" later in this section for more details on how to do this.

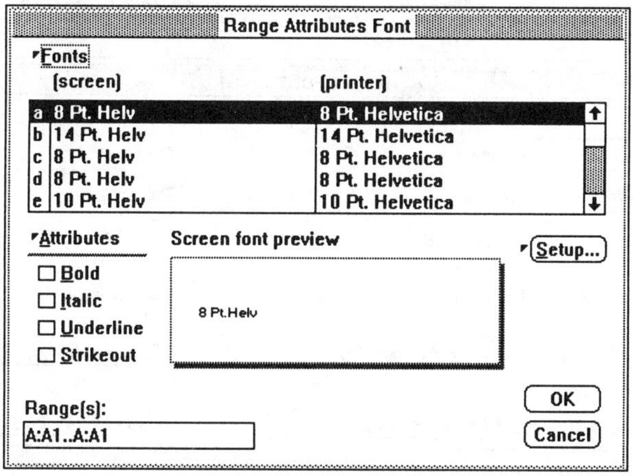

Range Attributes Font

Fonts

	(screen)	(printer)
a	8 Pt. Helv	8 Pt. Helvetica
b	14 Pt. Helv	14 Pt. Helvetica
c	8 Pt. Helv	8 Pt. Helvetica
d	8 Pt. Helv	8 Pt. Helvetica
e	10 Pt. Helv	10 Pt. Helvetica

Attributes — Screen font preview — Setup...

- ☐ Bold
- ☐ Italic
- ☐ Underline
- ☐ Strikeout

8 Pt.Helv

Range(s): A:A1..A:A1

OK

Cancel

FIGUREs 3–11 The Range Attributes Font dialog box

Note

As you review the contents of the "Fonts" list box, you'll notice that all 20 slots (a through t) contain font names. It should be noted, however, that initially 1-2-3/G only offers the 16 fonts shown in Figure 3–10. Four of the slots in the list box are repeats.

As soon as you select a font for the current range, the impact of your choice is displayed in the "Screen font preview" information box. This box gives you an indication of what your data will look like in the worksheet.

You can also assign additional attributes such as bolding, underlining, italics, or strikeout to a font. To do this, you use the "Attributes" section of the Range Attributes Font dialog box. This section contains four check boxes arranged vertically. Initially, all four check boxes are blank. To select an attribute, simply click your left mouse button on the check box so that an X appears in the box. If you're using your keyboard, press TAB to move to the item and press the space bar to select it. Any selection you make applies to the currently selected font in the "Fonts" list box. As soon as you make a selection, your choice is reflected in the "Screen font preview" information box. You can assign either a single attribute or multiple attributes to a font, as shown in Figure 3–12.

The Range(s) box indicates the range to which your font and attribute selections will apply. Using the techniques described earlier in this chapter under

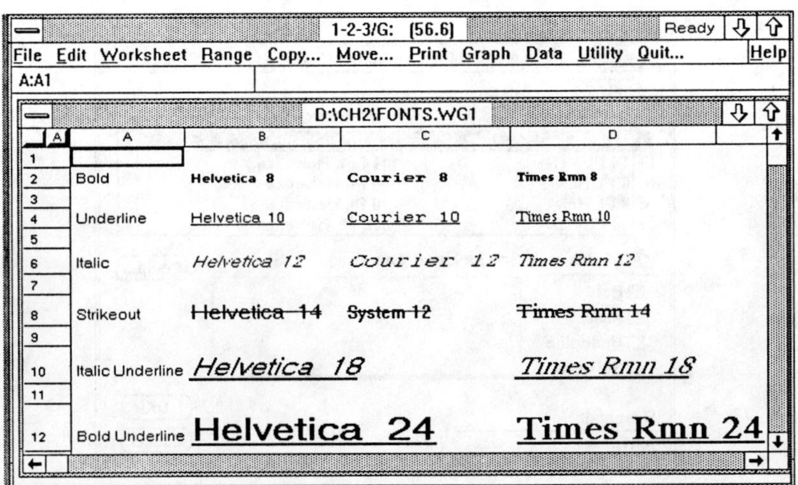

FIGURE 3–12 Various fonts with multiple attributes

"Formatting Cells," you can accept the current range selection or edit it with either the keyboard or the mouse. To complete the Range Attributes Font command, select the OK command button. 1-2-3/G assigns the font and attributes you specified to the select range.

If you specify a multiple-cell range before selecting the Range Attributes Font command, the "Attributes" check boxes appear grayed. This gray color is a 1-2-3/G convention indicating that different attributes may have already been assigned to some or all of the cells in that range. Further, those attributes will not be changed. However, you may add to the attributes that already exist.

For example, imagine you've already assigned a Bold attribute to the range A:A1..A:F10 in the current worksheet. Next, you highlight the range A:A1..A:F20 and select the Range Attributes Font command. 1-2-3/G displays the Range Attributes Font dialog box with the "Attributes" check boxes grayed. Now, suppose you select the "Italic" check box. When you select this check box, its color changes to white. Select it again to place an X in the box. When you select OK to complete the command, the Range A:A1..A:F10 appears as Bold-Italic and the range A:A11..A:F20 as Italic only.

THE EFFECT OF FONTS ON ROW HEIGHTS If you assign a font to a cell that exceeds the height of the cell, 1-2-3/G automatically increases the height of the cell to accommodate the larger font. In fact, the height of all the cells in the entire row are automatically adjusted to accommodate the largest font in any cell within the row.

This automatic adjustment of row heights may cause the spacing of rows of data elsewhere in your worksheet to appear uneven. However, you can manually adjust the height of rows to override the automatic adjustment. See "Adjusting Row Heights" later under "Working with Columns, Rows, and Worksheets" for details on how to manually adjust row heights.

Assigning Fonts to Worksheets

You can also assign a font to all the cells in an entire worksheet. To do this, you use the Worksheet Global Attributes Font command. When you select this command, 1-2-3/G shows you the Worksheet Global Attributes Font dialog box. This dialog box matches the Range Attributes Font dialog box shown in Figure 3–11 in all respects except one—there is no Range(s) box. Instead, the screen and printer fonts you select and the attributes you assign apply to all the cells in the current worksheet.

If you've already assigned fonts to some cells in the worksheet by using the Range Attributes Font command, the Worksheet Global Attributes Font command has no effect on those cells. Further, if you subsequently use the Range Attributes Font to format additional cells, the settings you make override the current global setting within that range.

When you select a global format for the worksheet, 1-2-3/G adjusts the row height for all the cells in the worksheet to accommodate the new font selection.

This may cause more or fewer rows in the worksheet to be displayed in the same size window

The Worksheet Global Attributes Font command affects only the current worksheet. If you wish to apply a font to another worksheet in the same file or another file, you must move to that worksheet and use the Worksheet Global Attributes Font command there.

Changing the Default Font Set

You can rearrange and add to the list of default fonts used by the Range Attributes Font command and the Worksheet Global Attributes Font command. Once you change the default font set for a particular worksheet file, you need only save that file to preserve your changes. The next time you open the file, those same font choices will be available for your selection.

CHANGING FONTS FOR RANGE ATTRIBUTE FONT To rearrange or add to the default fonts for the Range Attribute Font command, select the command to display the Range Attribute Font dialog box. Then select the "Setup" command button. When you select "Setup," 1-2-3/G displays the Range Attributes Font Setup dialog box shown in Figure 3-13.

At the top of the Setup dialog box, 1-2-3/G displays the "Fonts" list box as it is currently set up for the Range Attributes Font command. To change a font, first select the slot from the "Fonts" list box that you want to change. For example, if you wish to change slot "a," highlight slot a, as shown in Figure

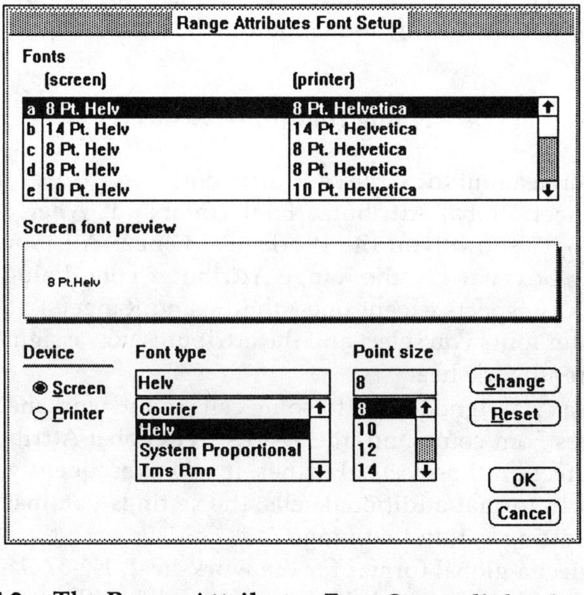

FIGURE 3-13 The Range Attributes Font Setup dialog box

3–13. Next, select whether you want to change the screen or printer font. To do this, select from either the "Screen" or "Printer" option buttons in the "Device" section of the dialog box. If you select "Screen," 1-2-3/G will change the font listed on the left side of the slot. On the other hand, if you select "Printer," 1-2-3/G will change the font listed on the right side of the slot.

Once you select a device (screen or printer), 1-2-3/G displays a list of fonts that are available for that device in the "Font type" list box. If you selected "Screen," 1-2-3/G displays the fonts you've installed for Presentation Manager. (See Appendix A "Customizing 1-2-3/G" for information on font installation.) On the other hand, if you select "Printer," 1-2-3/G shows a list of fonts supported by the current printer driver. If you have more than one printer driver installed, 1-2-3/G uses the current printer driver. The current printer driver is determined by the setting for the File Print Destination command. See Chapter 8, "Printing," for more on this command. (See Appendix A, "Customizing 1-2-3/G," for information about installing printer drivers.)

To choose a font for a particular device, select its name from the "Font types" list box. When you make a selection from this box, 1-2-3/G shows you the point sizes available for that font in the "Point size" list box. Select from this box the point size you want for the font you select in the "Font type" list box. When you're ready, select the "Change" command button. 1-2-3/G places the font you selected in the slot you selected in the "Fonts" list box. To complete the command, select the OK command button or press ENTER. 1-2-3/G records the change and returns you to the Range Attributes Font dialog box. Your font changes now appear in the "Fonts" list box.

Note

If you want, you can select several screen and printer fonts for different slots before selecting the Change command button to update the slots.

When you make a change to the "Fonts" list box and then save the file, your new settings are saved along with the file. If you use the file again on the same desktop, or a different desktop, the font listing changes you selected are preserved.

To cancel a change, select the Range Attributes Font Setup command to display the Setup dialog box. Then highlight the slot you want to cancel. Next, select the Reset command button. 1-2-3/G replaces the screen and printer fonts in the slot you selected with the current default fonts for that slot.

Note

> If you change the font for slot "a," the data in all your worksheet in the currently active file will be displayed using that font.

CHANGING FONTS FOR WORKSHEET GLOBAL ATTRIBUTE FONT To rearrange or add to the fonts for the Worksheet Global Attribute Font command, enter the command, and select the Setup command button. 1-2-3/G displays the Worksheet Global Attribute Font Setup dialog box. This dialog box is exactly like the Range Attributes Font Setup dialog box shown in Figure 3–13. To change the fonts listed in the "Fonts" dialog box, you use the same procedures just described under "Changing Fonts for the Range Format Command."

Choosing Colors

1-2-3/G also allows you to assign specific colors to the contents and background of cells in a range or a worksheet. You can assign a foreground and background color attribute to any of the following:

- All cells.
- Cells that contain labels.
- Cells that contain negative numbers.
- Cells that contain positive numbers.

To assign color attributes to a range of cells, you use the Range Attributes Color command. To assign color attributes to all the cells in the current worksheet, you use the Worksheet Global Attributes Color command. As you might imagine, when you enter either one of these commands, 1-2-3/G displays a dialog box that allows you to select color attributes. For example, Figure 3–14 shows the Range Attributes Color dialog box.

The top portion of the Range Attributes Color dialog box is divided into two sections, Text and Background. Any selection you make from the "Text" section applies to text (numbers, labels, formulas, and so forth) that appears in a cell. The "Background" section applies to the cell itself. Both sections offer an identical set of option buttons: "All," "Labels," "Positive," and "Negative," When you choose "All," all the cells in the currently selected range will be assigned the color you subsequently select. "Labels" applies only to labels, "Positive" applies only to cells with positive numbers, and "Negative" applies only to cells with negative numbers.

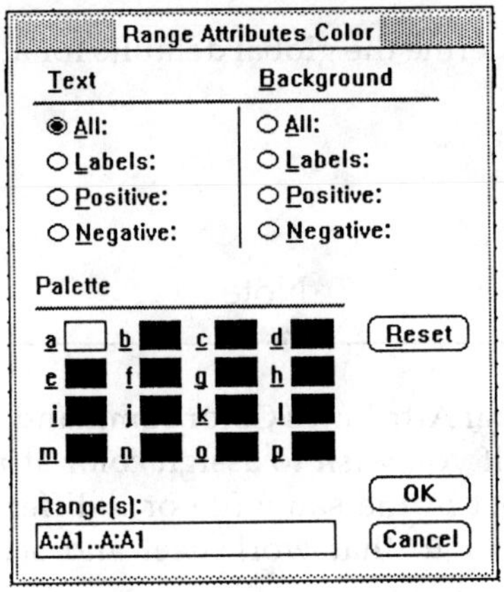

Range Attributes Color

Text | Background
All: | All:
Labels: | Labels:
Positive: | Positive:
Negative: | Negative:

Palette

a b c d
e f g h
i j k l
m n o p

Reset

Range(s):
A:A1..A:A1

OK
Cancel

FIGURE 3–14 The Range Attributes Color dialog box

The "Palette" section of the Range Attributes Color dialog box contains the colors 1-2-3/G has to offer. This section of the dialog box is aptly named. It works like an artist's palette.

To assign a color attribute, first select from the "Text" or "Background" menu. For example, imagine you want to have all negative numbers in the currently selected range appear in red on a blue background. To do this, select the "Negative" option button from the "Text" section. Next, move down to the "Palette" section and click on the box that is colored red (box e), or type **e**. 1-2-3/G places a small red box next to the "Negative" option in the "Text" section of the dialog box. To select a blue background color for negative cells, select the "Negative" option button from the "Background" section of the dialog box. Next, select the blue box (box g) from the "Palette" section. To complete the command, select the OK command button or press ENTER. 1-2-3/G formats all cells in the range that contain or evaluate to a negative number with red numbers on a blue background.

To reset an option in the "Text" or "Background" section to match the current global color setting, first select the appropriate option and then select the "Reset" command button. When you select "Reset," 1-2-3/G returns the option you selected to match the current global setting. Moreover, 1-2-3/G places an R next to the option, indicating that it has been reset.

To assign global color attributes to all the cells in the current worksheet, select the Worksheet Global Attributes Color command. 1-2-3/G displays the Worksheet Global Attributes Color dialog box. This dialog box looks very similar to the Range Attributes Color dialog box shown in Figure 3–14, and you use it in exactly the same way. However, the Worksheet Global Attributes Color dialog box does not have a Range(s) box or a "Reset" command button. Since the selections you make define the global defaults for all cells in the worksheet, these are unnecessary.

Note

> The Worksheet Global Attributes Color command applies only to the current worksheet. If you wish to assign color attributes to the cells in another worksheet in the same file or a different file, you must move the cell pointer to that worksheet and select the command there.

Creating Cell Borders

You can create borders that surround the cells in a range. You can also display cell borders inside a range. To do either, you use the Range Attributes Border command. When you select this command, 1-2-3/G displays the Range Attributes Border dialog box shown in Figure 3–15.

The top section of the Range Attributes Border dialog box is divided into two sections, "Frame" and "Inside,". The "Frame" section is useful when you want to control cell borders that surround or "frame" a range. The effects of using each of its option buttons are shown in the range A:B3..A:B11 of Figure 3–16. These option buttons have the following effects on the currently selected range:

- **All:** Show lines along all exterior edges.
- **Right:** Place lines along the right edge only.
- **Left:** Place lines along the left edge only.
- **Top:** Place lines along the top edge only.
- **Bottom:** Place lines along the bottom edge only.

On the other hand, the "Inside" section of the Range Attributes Border dialog box allows you to display cell borders within a range. The effects of using each of these options to format a multiple cell range is shown in the range A:E3..A:E15 of Figure 3–16. Each of these options has the following effect for the cell borders in the currently selected range:

- **All:** Creates borders within all cells.
- **Horiz:** Creates horizontal borders only.
- **Vert:** Creates vertical borders only.

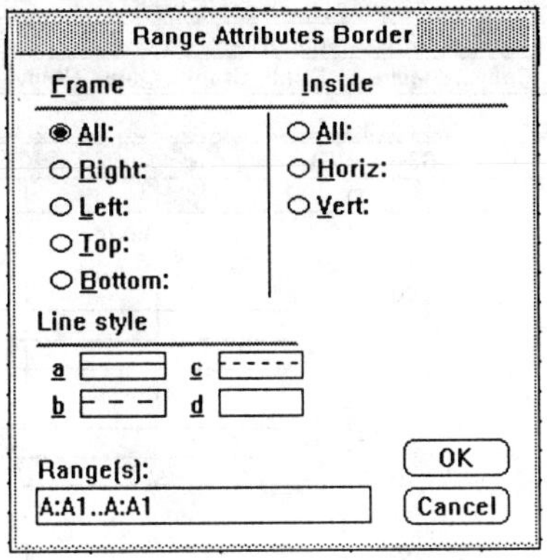

Range Attributes Border

Frame: All: / Right: / Left: / Top: / Bottom:

Inside: All: / Horiz: / Vert:

Line style: a, b, c, d

Range(s): A:A1..A:A1

OK / Cancel

FIGURE 3–15 The Range Attributes Border dialog box

Note

To show you the effects of the Range Attributes Border command, the grid lines were removed from Figure 3–16. You can do this yourself by using the Worksheet Global Screen Attributes Settings command and removing the X from the "Grid lines" check box. See "Changing Screen Attributes" at the end of this chapter for more details on this command.

To select a line style to apply to the current "Frame" or "Inside" option, use the "Line-style" section of the Range Attributes Border dialog box. As you can see in Figure 3–15, this section allows you to choose from three line styles: (a) a solid line, (b) a sparse dashed line, or (c) a dense dashed line. The fourth option (d) is blank. Use this option to remove cell borders.

Figure 3–16 also shows an example of how you might use a frame of cell borders. A frame of cell borders appears around the multiple cell range A:B13..A:B14. The dense dashed-line style was chosen. To frame these cells yourself, begin by selecting the range A:B13..A:B14. Next, select Range Attributes Border to display the dialog box in Figure 3–15. By default, the All option button in the "Frame" section is selected for you. Therefore, you need only select option (c), the dense dashed line, from the "Line-style" section and then click on the OK command button. 1-2-3/G places a frame of cell borders around the range A:B13..A:B14.

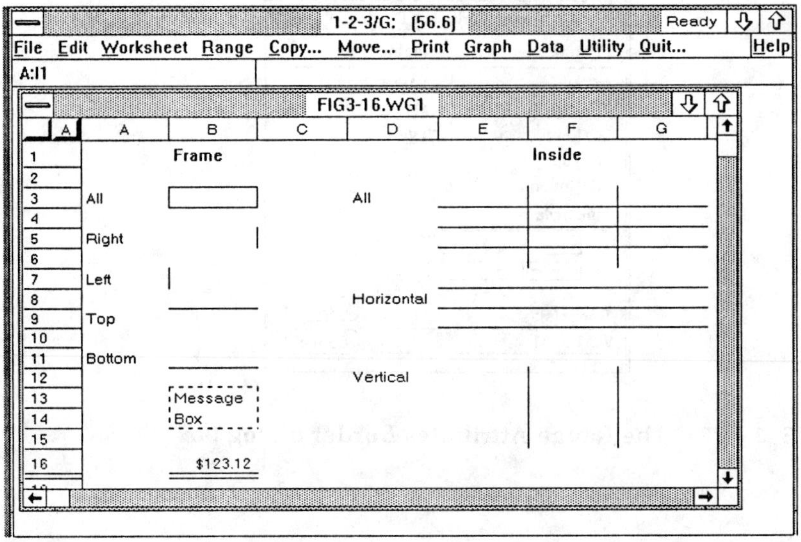

FIGURE 3–16 Range Attributes Border examples

Note

> When you specify cell borders for adjacent ranges, there may be conflicts because of overlapping borders. Borders on the right edge of a range override those on the left edge of an adjacent range located immediately to the right. Moreover, borders along the bottom edge of a range override those along the top edge of an adjacent range located immediately below.

Setting Decimal Precision

You can use the Range Attributes Precision command to set the decimal precision for a range of cells. Although the cells in the range continue to retain their original values, 1-2-3/G rounds the values in the range to the number of decimal places you specify for calculation purposes.

When you enter the Range Attributes Precision command, 1-2-3/G displays the dialog box in Figure 3–17. The default is "Full precision." However, you can select "Limit precision" and type in a number from 0 to 15, representing the number of places you want used in calculations. To complete the command,

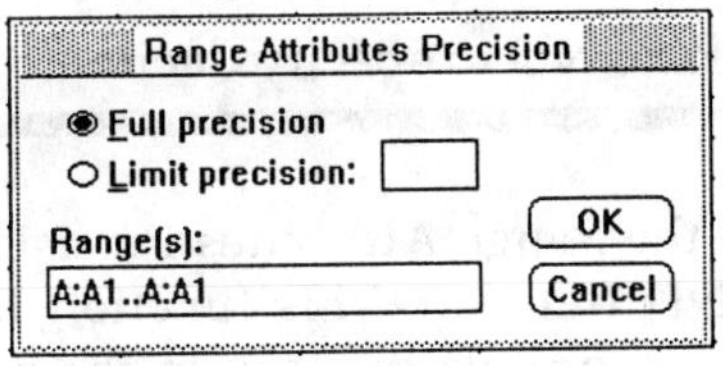

Range Attributes Precision

◉ Full precision
○ Limit precision: [ ]

Range(s):
A:A1..A:A1

OK
Cancel

FIGURE 3–17 The Range Attributes Precision dialog box

Tip: Creating double underlines

The Range Attributes Border command allows you to create double underlines. For example, the number in cell A:B16 of Figure 3–16 has a double underline. To do this yourself, select cell A:B16 and use the Range Attributes Border Frame Bottom command to place a solid line along the bottom of the cell. Next, perform the same operation to create a bottom border for a blank cell immediately beneath cell A:B17. Finally, decrease the height of row 17 until the bottom borders in cell A:B16 and A:B17 come close to converging. See "Adjusting Row Heights" later in this chapter under "Working with Columns, Rows, and Worksheets" for information on how to decrease the height of rows in the worksheet.

click on the OK command button or press ENTER. 1-2-3/G limits the decimal precision for the currently selected range to the number of places you specified.

To return a range to the default of calculating with full decimal precision, begin by selecting the range. Next, select Range Attributes Precision Full precision and then select OK or press ENTER. 1-2-3/G returns the currently selected range to full decimal precision.

When you specify limited decimal precision, the effects of your formatting may have an impact elsewhere in the worksheet. For example, imagine cell A:A1 contains the value 9.56 and that you have formatted that cell with a decimal precision of zero. Imagine further that the formula +A:A1*10 resides in cell A:A100, outside the formatted range. That formula will yield a value of 100. If you then return cell A:A1 to full decimal precision, the formula in cell A:A100 yields 95.6.

Tip:Use @ROUND to specify decimal precision

As an alternative to the Range Attributes Precision command, you can use the @ROUND function. This function limits the decimal precision of a value or formula in a cell to the number of decimal places you specify. See Chapter 6, "Functions," for more on the @ROUND function.

ALIGNING DATA IN CELLS

You can use the Range Label command to control the alignment of data in cells. This applies to labels, numbers, or formulas formatted to display as text (using the Range Format Text command). This command also allows you to format the display of long labels (labels that exceed the width of the current cell).

When you select the Range Label command, 1-2-3/G displays the dialog box shown in Figure 3-18. This dialog box is divided into three sections. The first section, "Labels," affects the alignment of labels in the currently selected range. The "Values" section affects the alignment of numbers. The "Cell Display" section, discussed later, affects the display of long labels.

The first three option buttons for both "Labels" and "Values" sections perform the same function for their respective entries. As you can see in Figure 3-19, the "Left" option aligns labels and/or values flush left, the "Right" option aligns labels and/or values flush right, and the "Center" option centers the entry in the cell. The "Fill" option button is only available for labels. It causes the label to be repeated until it fills the cell. The "Global" option resets the display of labels and/or values to match the current global setting, which is set with Worksheet Global Label.

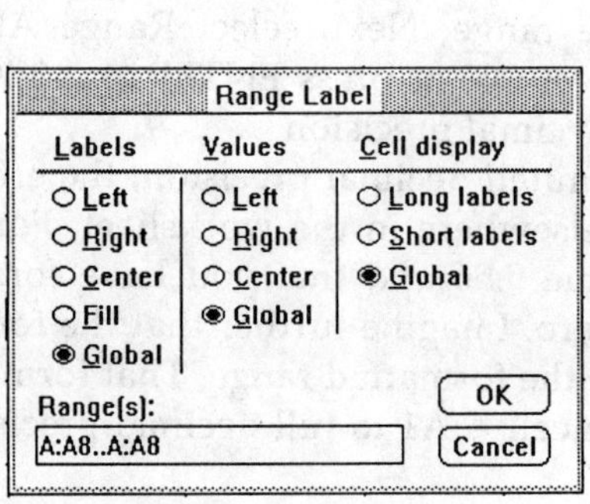

Range Label

Labels	Values	Cell display
Left	Left	Long labels
Right	Right	Short labels
Center	Center	Global
Fill	Global	
Global		

Range(s): A:A8..A:A8

OK

Cancel

FIGURE 3-18 **The Range Label dialog box**

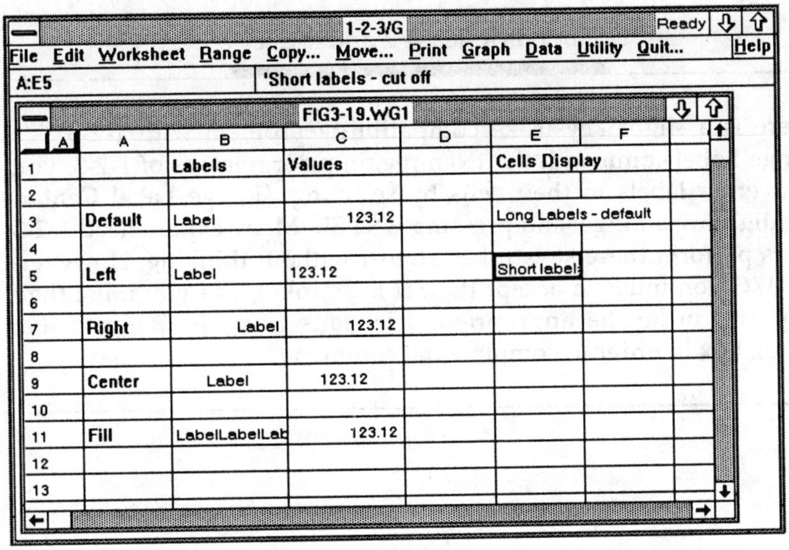

1-2-3/G Ready

File Edit Worksheet Range Copy... Move... Print Graph Data Utility Quit... Help

A:E5 'Short labels - cut off

FIG3-19.WG1

A	A	B	C	D	E	F
1		Labels	Values		Cells Display	
2						
3	Default	Label	123.12		Long Labels - default	
4						
5	Left	Label	123.12		Short label	
6						
7	Right	Label	123.12			
8						
9	Center	Label	123.12			
10						
11	Fill	LabelLabelLab	123.12			
12						
13						

FIGURE 3–19 Range Label examples

The "Cell Display" section of the Range Label dialog box applies strictly to the display of long labels (labels whose length exceeds the width of the cell). Normally, long labels are allowed to spill over into an adjacent cell located immediately to the right, provided that the cell is blank. For example, Figure 3–19 shows a long label displayed in cell A:E3 that spills over into cell A:F3. However, if you select "Short labels" from the "Cell Display" section, 1-2-3/G displays only that portion of the label that will fit in the cell. An example of such a label appears in cell A:E5 of Figure 3–19.

Note

> In general, a cell must be set wider than the entry it contains for the Range Label command to have any visible effect. If the label, value, or formula already fills the cell, 1-2-3/G has no room to move the entry left or right. However, the cell is still formatted for the alignment you selected. If you subsequently place a shorter entry in the cell, it will take on the alignment you specified.

Tip: For Release 2 and 3 Users

There is a slight keystroke compatibility problem with 1-2-3/G's Range Label command. For example, in prior releases of 1-2-3, you can center labels in their cells by selecting /Range Label Center, highlighting a range, and pressing ENTER. Many experienced 1-2-3 users perform these keystrokes almost without thinking. However, 1-2-3/G continues to accept the /rl keystrokes, but you must then stop and make the appropriate selections from the Range Label dialog box in order to complete the command.

Note

As is the case with most of the Worksheet Global commands, the Worksheet Global Label command applies only to the current worksheet (the worksheet containing the cell pointer). To set a global label alignment in another worksheet in the same file, or in a different file, you must move the cell pointer to that worksheet and enter the command there.

You can also select a global alignment for labels, values, and formulas formatted as text for the entire current worksheet. To do this, you use the Worksheet Global Label command. This command displays a dialog box almost exactly like the Range Label dialog box in Figure 3–18. However, the selections you make apply to all the cells in the worksheet, except those cells you've already formatted with the Range Label command.

FORMATTING THE DISPLAY OF ZEROS

In 1-2-3/G, you can format the display of cells that contain or evaluate to zero. As you know, 1-2-3/G normally displays a zero in such cells. However, you

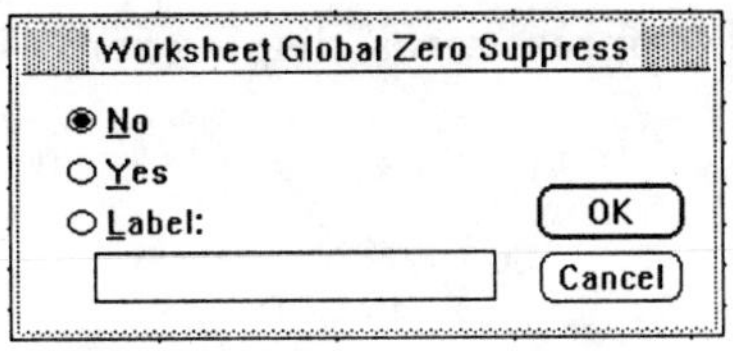

FIGURE 3–20 The Worksheet Global Zero Suppress dialog box

can suppress the display of zeros and have the cell appear blank, or you can elect to have 1-2-3/G display a label of your own design.

To format the display of zeros for the current worksheet, you use the Worksheet Global Zero Suppress command. When you select this command, 1-2-3/G displays the dialog box in Figure 3–20. Notice that the dialog box contains three command buttons, No, Yes, and Label. No (the default) causes zeros to be displayed as zeros. The Yes option causes 1-2-3/G to suppress the display of zeros and have blank cells appear. Label allows you to enter a label of up to 512 characters that will be displayed in place of zeros. If you select this option, type in a label of your choice. 1-2-3/G will display that label as right justified in cells that contain or evaluate to zero. You can control the alignment of that label by using a label prefix such as ', ^, ", or \, just as you would for any label in the worksheet.

You can also control the display of cells that contain or evaluate to zero within a range of cells that you select. To do this, you use the Range Zero Suppress command. When you enter this command, 1-2-3/G displays the dialog box in Figure 3–21.

Notice that the dialog box in Figure 3–21 differs slightly from the Worksheet Global Zero dialog box in that it does not allow you to specify a label to be displayed in cells that contain or evaluate to zero. Instead, it contains three option buttons, Yes, No, and Default. If you select Yes, 1-2-3/G will override the current global setting, if necessary, and suppress the display of zeros, displaying a blank cell. If you select No, 1-2-3/G will once again override the current global setting, if necessary, and display zeros in cells. Finally, if you select Default, 1-2-3/G will use the global setting for the worksheet, set with Worksheet Global Zero Suppress. Depending on the current setting for this

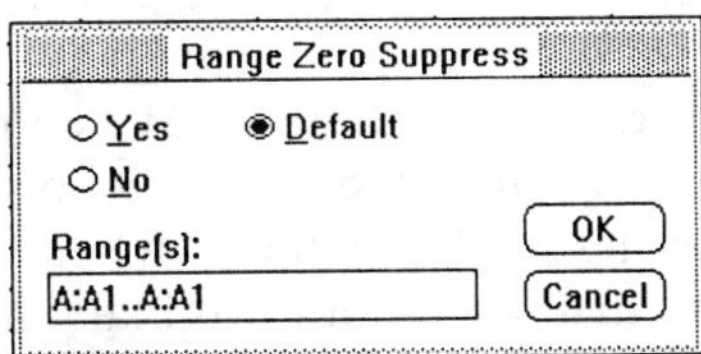

FIGURE 3–21 The Range Zero Suppress dialog box

command, 1-2-3/G will suppress zeros, display zeros, or display a custom label in place of zeros.

Caution

When you suppress the display of cells that contain or evaluate to zero, the cell appears blank until you move the cell pointer onto the cell and view the Control Line. If you're not careful, you may accidentally assume the cell is blank and enter new data into it, or worse, erase its contents. To avoid this, you can protect such cells from data entry altogether. To do this, however, you must protect your worksheet. In general, you protect a worksheet by using the Worksheet Global Protection Enable command. See "Protecting Your Worksheet" later in this chapter for more details.

WORKING WITH COLUMNS, ROWS, AND WORKSHEETS

This section shows you commands and techniques that you can use to work with columns, rows, and worksheets. For example, you'll learn how to adjust (increase and decrease) the width of columns and the height of rows. You'll also learn how to insert columns and rows into a worksheet, and to insert new worksheets into the middle of a file. Using the techniques provided you can change the layout of your data and make room for additional data. Finally, you'll learn how to eliminate unneeded columns, rows, and worksheets altogether.

Adjusting Column Widths

One of the first problems you encounter while entering data into the worksheet is insufficient column widths. By now, you've probably entered a number and formatted it, only to have 1-2-3/G display asterisks (********) in the cell, indicating an insufficient cell width. Or, you may have entered a long label (a label that is wider than its cell). In this case, 1-2-3/G borrows some display space from the adjacent cells to the right. However, when you make an entry in one of those adjacent cells, the display of your original long label is cut off. You can solve both of these problems by increasing the width of the cell that contains the entry.

The width of cells is determined by the width of the column that contains them. Therefore, to increase or decrease the width of cells, you must increase or decrease the width of the column.

By default, 1-2-3/G measures column widths in characters. Generally speaking, a cell's width must be at least as wide as the entry it contains to fully display the entry. For example, imagine the current column-width setting is nine characters, the default. You then enter the number 100000 in a cell in that column. 1-2-3/G accepts this six-character entry with no problem. However, you now format the value as Currency 2 so that it is displayed as $100,000.00 (11 characters). 1-2-3/G now displays asterisks (*********) in the cell. To display this entry, you need to increase the width of the current column.

The size of the current font for the cell can also affect the display of a numeric entry. For example, imagine the font for the current cell is Helvetica 8 Point and the entry is fully displayed. However, now imagine you change the font for the cell to Helvetica 10 Point, requiring additional display space. This may cause 1-2-3/G to display asterisks (*) in the cell.

Although 1-2-3/G measures column widths in characters as the default, as you'll soon see, you can also state column widths in hundredths of characters. For example, you can create a column that is 11.625 characters wide. Or, you can have 1-2-3/G measure column widths in inches.

Using the Mouse

The easiest and most productive way to increase or decrease the width of a single column or a group of adjacent columns is with your mouse. To adjust the width of a single column, column A for example, begin by moving your mouse pointer to the right side of the block at the top of the column that contains the column letter. Then gradually move the mouse pointer to the right until it reaches the divider that separates column A from column B. When you reach the divider, the shape of the mouse pointer changes to a horizontal double arrow. Now click the left button of your mouse and drag the edge of the column to your right. You'll notice as you click and drag that the edge of the column becomes a dotted line. You'll also notice that the cell address in the Control Line is replaced by the width of the current column in characters, which increases as you drag. When the column reaches the desired width, release your mouse button. 1-2-3/G adjusts the column width accordingly.

To increase the width of a range of adjacent columns, first click and drag your mouse to select a range that includes a single cell from each of the adjacent columns. Then, perform the procedure described in the previous paragraph to adjust the width of any one of the selected columns. As you adjust the width of a single column, the balance of the columns in the selection are adjusted to the same width.

To adjust the width of a group of nonadjacent columns, first create a collection that includes the columns you want to adjust. For example, imagine you want to adjust the width of columns A, C, and E to the same width. To do this, click your left mouse button on cell A:A1. Then, click your right mouse button on cell A:C1 and again on cell A:E1. Finally, adjust the width of a single column, for example, column E. Columns A and C are adjusted to the same width.

Using the Worksheet Column Command

You can also increase or decrease the width of one or more columns by using the Worksheet Column command. This command allows you to set the width of all the columns in the current selection. When you select Worksheet Column, 1-2-3/G displays the dialog box in Figure 3–22.

To change the width of the columns in the current selection, select the "Set width" option button. Next, press TAB to move to the adjacent text box and type in a number from 1 to 512, representing the width in characters you want for the column(s) that you are adjusting. Or, you can press → to increase the column width or ← to decrease it. To complete the command, click on the OK command button or press ENTER.

To reset the width of the columns in the current selection to match the current global column width for the worksheet, select "Reset width" from the Worksheet Column dialog box. 1-2-3/G resets the width of the columns in the current selection to match the current global column width, which is set with the Worksheet Global Column command (see the next section).

To set the width for a range of columns based on the longest entry in each column, select the "Fit largest" command button from the Worksheet Column dialog box. When you select this option, 1-2-3/G scans each column in the current selection to determine the longest entry. It then sets the width of each column wide enough to fully display the longest value and/or label in that column.

The "Fit largest" option only works for existing entries. If you make an entry at a later time that exceeds the current column width, you must use the Worksheet Column Fit largest command again to accommodate that entry.

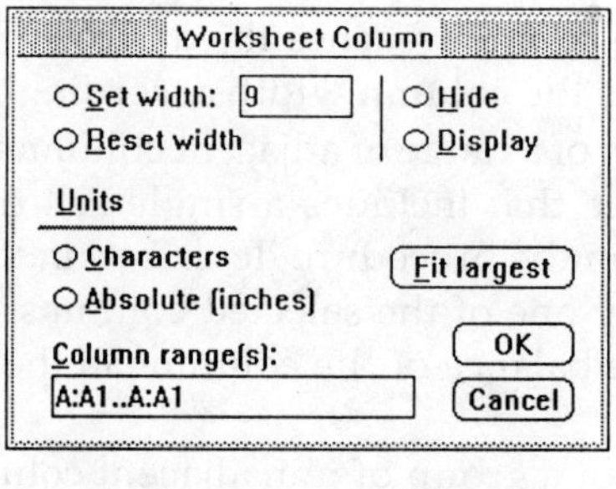

FIGURE 3–22 The Worksheet Column dialog box

Note

> If you specify a three-dimensional range before using the "Fit largest" option, 1-2-3/G adjusts the appropriate column widths in all the worksheets that are included in the range.

Use the "Units" section of the Worksheet Column dialog box to change the unit of measure for column widths from characters to inches, or millimeters (depending on the Utility User Settings International Units setting). To have column widths measured in inches (or millimeters) instead of characters, select "Absolute (inches)." Once you select this option, you can use the "Set width" option above to set the width of columns in inches, up to three decimal places. For example, you can set a column width of 1.476 inches.

Measuring column widths in inches can be helpful when printing. That way, you can accurately estimate how many columns of data you can fit horizontally on a specific paper size.

Using the Worksheet Global Column Command

You can also set a global column width for all the columns in the current worksheet. To do this, you use the Worksheet Global Column command. When you select this command, 1-2-3/G displays the Worksheet Global Column dialog box. This dialog box is much simpler than the Worksheet Column dialog box in Figure 3–22. However, it provides a text box which allows you to specify a global column width for all the columns in the worksheet. And, like the Worksheet Column dialog box, the Worksheet Global Column dialog box also has a "Units" section that allows you to choose between "Characters" and "Absolute (inches)."

Hiding Columns

You can use the Worksheet Column command to hide entire columns of your worksheet from view. To do this, select the "Hide" option button from the Worksheet Column dialog box shown in Figure 3–22. To complete the Worksheet Column command, select the OK command button, or press ENTER. 1-2-3/G hides all the columns in the current selection from view. The remaining columns in the worksheet are shifted over to close up the space. For example, if the cell pointer is located on a cell in column B, and you select Worksheet Column Hide, 1-2-3/G hides column B from view, and column C now appears next to column A.

You can still use the cells in hidden columns. For example, you can refer to the cells of a hidden column in your formulas and commands. To apply commands to cells in hidden columns, simply type the appropriate cell address in the Range(s) box of the dialog box that is associated with the command you happen to be using. Additionally, when you can activate the Range(s) text box, 1-2-3/G redisplays hidden columns in a worksheet. The hidden columns are marked by an asterisk (*) next to the column letter. You can then select a range that includes the hidden column and enter your command. Or, while composing a formula, you can press HIDE (SHIFT-F6) to expose hidden columns. You can then compose the formula by pointing to cells in hidden columns. To rehide the columns, press HIDE (SHIFT-F6) again.

Note

You cannot use GOTO (F5) or the Range Goto command to go to cells in hidden columns.

To bring the columns out of hiding permanently, select Worksheet Column to access the dialog box in Figure 3–22. [When you select Worksheet Column, all hidden columns are temporarily redisplayed. The hidden columns are marked by an asterisk (*) next to the column letter.] Then select the "Display" option button. When you complete the command, any hidden columns in the current selection are redisplayed.

You can also hide columns by using your mouse. To do this, move your mouse pointer to the right edge of the box surrounding the column's letter. The shape of the mouse pointer changes to horizontal double arrow. Next, click your left mouse button to grab the edge of the column and drag it to the left until the column is removed from view. Release the mouse button to have 1-2-3/G hide the column. (In effect, you have just assigned a width of 0 characters to that column.) If you now press HIDE (SHIFT-F6), 1-2-3/G will display the column with an asterisk (*) next to its column letter, indicating that it is a hidden column. Press HIDE (SHIFT-F6) again to rehide the column. To permanently redisplay this column, you must use the Worksheet Column Display command.

Note

If more than one column is included in the current selection when you use your mouse to hide a single column, all the columns in the current selection are hidden.

Tip: Hidden columns do not print

When you hide one or more columns included within a print range, 1-2-3/G ignores those hidden columns when printing. You can use this technique to exclude confidential or extraneous data from your printouts. You can also use it to have two nonadjacent columns appear next to each other in your printed report.

Adjusting Row Heights

1-2-3/G allows you to change the height of rows in your worksheet. You can do this in two ways: with your mouse or by using commands.

1-2-3/G measures row heights in inches (or millimeters, depending on the Utility User Settings International Units setting). You can adjust rows from 0 to 10 inches high.

Using the Mouse

To adjust the height of a row with your mouse, begin by moving the mouse pointer to the bottom edge of the box that contains the row number. The shape of the mouse pointer changes to a vertical double arrow. Click the left mouse button to grab the bottom edge of the row. Then, drag downward to increase the height of the row, or upward to decrease it. When you've got the row to the size you want, release your mouse button. 1-2-3/G adjusts the height of the row accordingly.

As you click and drag the bottom edge of a row upward or downward, 1-2-3/G replaces the current cell address in the Control Line with the height of the row in inches. When you release your mouse button, 1-2-3/G removes the row height and replaces it with the current cell address again.

Note

If more than one row is included in the current selection when you use your mouse to adjust a single row height, all the rows in the current selection are adjusted to the same height.

Using the Worksheet Row Command

You can adjust row heights by using the Worksheet Row command. When you select this command, 1-2-3/G displays the dialog box shown in Figure 3–23.

To change the height of the rows in the current selection, select "Set height." Then press TAB to move to the adjacent text box. Type in a number from 0 to 10 inches. You can specify up to three decimal places, if you want. For example, to specify a row height that is two-thirds of an inch tall, type **.666**. Or, you can press ↑ to decrease the row height number or ↓ to increase it. To complete the command, select the OK command button or press ENTER.

To reset the height of the row(s) in the current selection to match the global setting for the worksheet, select "Reset height" from the Worksheet Row dialog box. To complete the command, select the OK command button or press ENTER. 1-2-3/G adjusts the heights of the row(s) in the current selection to match the global row-height setting, set with Worksheet Global Row.

Using the Worksheet Global Row Command

To specify a global height setting for all the rows in the current worksheet, you use the Worksheet Global Row command. When you enter this command, 1-2-3/G displays the Worksheet Global Row dialog box. This dialog box contains a single text box, titled "Global height," which allows you to type in a global height for all rows in the worksheet in inches. To complete the command, select the OK command button or press ENTER. 1-2-3/G adjusts the height of all the rows in the worksheet, except those you've already set with the Worksheet Row command to the new global row-height setting.

Hiding Rows

1-2-3/G allows you to hide one or more rows. Like hidden columns, hidden rows are not displayed on your screen, nor do they print. You can hide rows either with your mouse or by using the Worksheet Row command.

To hide a row with your mouse, move the mouse pointer to the bottom edge of the box that contains the row number. The shape of the mouse pointer changes into a vertical double arrow. Click the left mouse button to grab the bottom edge of the row. Next, drag the bottom edge of the row upward until it meets the bottom edge of the row above and release your mouse button.

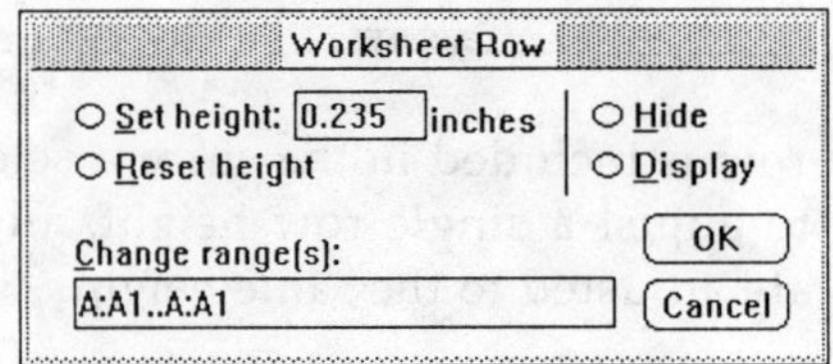

FIGURE 3–23 **The Worksheet Row dialog box**

Note

As is the case with most of the Worksheet Global commands, the Worksheet Global Row command applies only to the current worksheet (the worksheet containing the cell pointer). To set a global row height in another worksheet in the same file, or in a different file, you must move the cell pointer to that worksheet and enter the command there.

1-2-3/G hides the row from view. (In effect, you have just set the height of the row to 0 inches.) To see the row, press HIDE (SHIFT-F6). HIDE redisplays hidden rows and columns. Your hidden rows are redisplayed and are marked by an asterisk (*) next to the row number. To rehide the rows, press HIDE (SHIFT-F6) again.

You can also hide the row(s) included in the current selection by using the Worksheet Row command. When you enter this command, 1-2-3/G displays the dialog box shown in Figure 3–23. Select the "Hide" option from the dialog box. To complete the command, select the OK command button or press ENTER. To redisplay the hidden rows, select Worksheet Row again. 1-2-3/G redisplays all hidden rows in the worksheet and shows you the Worksheet Row dialog box. Select Display from the dialog box. To complete the command, select the OK command button or press ENTER.

As you can with hidden columns, you can refer to the data in hidden rows in commands and formulas. When you do this, however, you may find it helpful to press HIDE (SHIFT-F6) to temporarily redisplay the hidden rows. That way, you can select the cells in hidden rows as part of a range before issuing a command. On the other hand, when you activate the Range(s) text box during a command, 1-2-3/G temporarily redisplays hidden rows. You can then point to cells in those rows with your keyboard or mouse. Or, while composing formulas, you can enter POINT mode and point to the cells in hidden rows. When you're finished, press HIDE (SHIFT-F6) again to rehide the rows.

Note

As with hidden columns, you cannot use GOTO (F5) or the Range Goto command to go to cells in hidden rows.

Inserting Columns, Rows, and Worksheets

To insert new columns or rows into your worksheets, or to insert new worksheets into the current file, you use the Worksheet Insert command. When you enter this command, 1-2-3/G displays the dialog box in Figure 3–24. The sections that follow show you how to use this dialog box.

Inserting Columns

To insert columns into the current worksheet, begin by locating the cell pointer where you want the new columns inserted. For example, imagine you want to insert a new column B into the worksheet in Figure 3–25. To do this, position the cell pointer in any cell in column B. Next, enter the Worksheet Insert command to display the dialog box in Figure 3–24 and select Column. To complete the command, select the OK command button or press ENTER. 1-2-3/G inserts a new column B to the left of the cell pointer and shifts the remaining columns in the worksheet to the right. Your worksheet now looks like Figure 3–26.

To insert more than one column, enter the Worksheet Insert Column command as you normally would. Then, press TAB to move to the Number text box and type in the number of new columns you want inserted. Alternatively, if you include more than one adjacent column in the current selection before entering the Worksheet Insert Column command, 1-2-3/G shows that number of columns in the Number text box. When you complete the command, 1-2-3/G inserts a new column for each highlighted column. The new columns are inserted to the left of the first cell in the current selection.

If you want, you can insert partial columns. That is, instead of inserting whole columns that shift other whole columns in the worksheet to the right, only part of a column is inserted. This causes information only in selected rows to be shifted to the right. To insert a partial column, highlight only that part of a column where you want new cells inserted. Next, select the Worksheet Insert

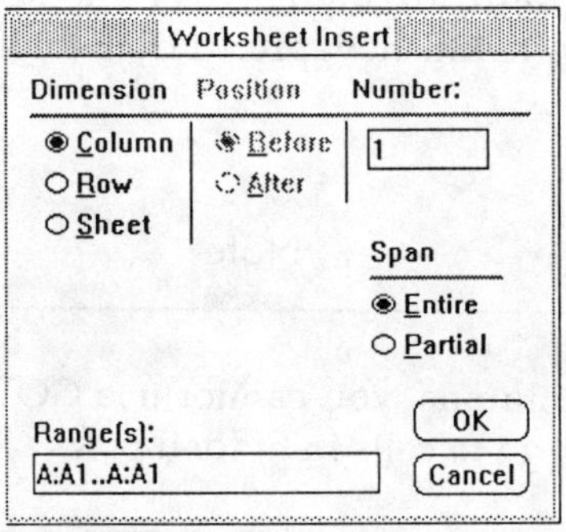

Worksheet Insert
Dimension Position Number:
Column Before 1
Row After
Sheet
Span
Entire
Partial
Range(s): OK
A:A1..A:A1 Cancel

FIGURE 3–24 The Worksheet Insert dialog box

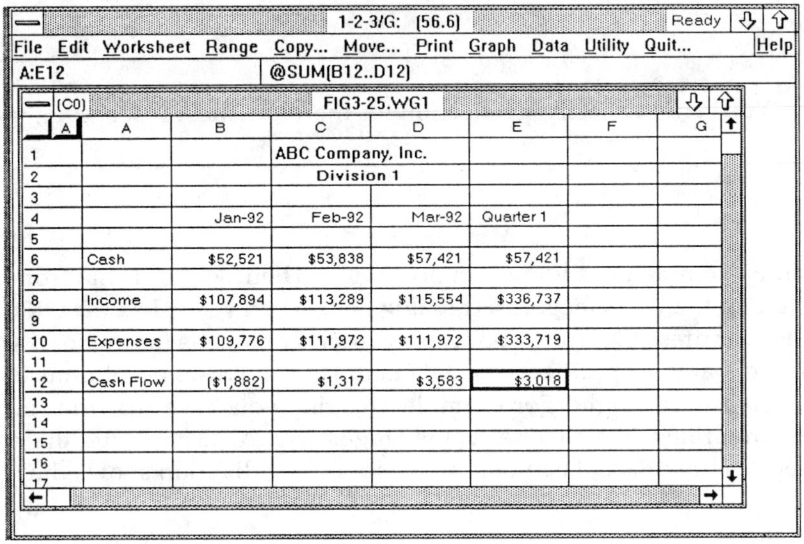

1-2-3/G: (56.6) Ready

File Edit Worksheet Range Copy... Move... Print Graph Data Utility Quit... Help

A:E12 @SUM(B12..D12)

(C0) FIG3-25.WG1

A	A	B	C	D	E	F	G
1			ABC Company, Inc.				
2			Division 1				
3							
4		Jan-92	Feb-92	Mar-92	Quarter 1		
5							
6	Cash	$52,521	$53,838	$57,421	$57,421		
7							
8	Income	$107,894	$113,289	$115,554	$336,737		
9							
10	Expenses	$109,776	$111,972	$111,972	$333,719		
11							
12	Cash Flow	($1,882)	$1,317	$3,583	$3,018		
13							
14							
15							
16							
17							

FIGURE 3–25 A sample worksheet

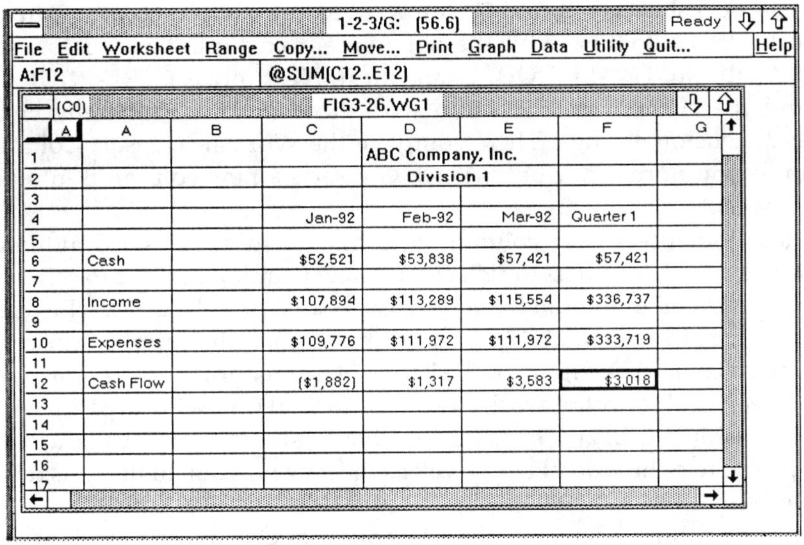

1-2-3/G: (56.6) Ready

File Edit Worksheet Range Copy... Move... Print Graph Data Utility Quit... Help

A:F12 @SUM(C12..E12)

(C0) FIG3-26.WG1

A	A	B	C	D	E	F	G
1				ABC Company, Inc.			
2				Division 1			
3							
4			Jan-92	Feb-92	Mar-92	Quarter 1	
5							
6	Cash		$52,521	$53,838	$57,421	$57,421	
7							
8	Income		$107,894	$113,289	$115,554	$336,737	
9							
10	Expenses		$109,776	$111,972	$111,972	$333,719	
11							
12	Cash Flow		($1,882)	$1,317	$3,583	$3,018	
13							
14							
15							
16							
17							

FIGURE 3–26 The Worksheet Column command is used to insert a new column B

Note

You cannot specify a collection for the Worksheet Insert command.

Column command as you normally would. Then, select Partial from the Span section of the Worksheet Insert dialog box. When you select the OK command button, or press ENTER, 1-2-3/G only inserts new cells for the rows within the column that you specified. The data in those same rows in columns to the right is shifted to the right. For example, imagine you have the first four cells in column A filled. You then select the range A:A2..A:A3 and enter the Worksheet Insert Column Partial command. The following diagram shows the results:

Before Column A	After Column A	After Column B
1	1	
2		2
3		3
4	4	

You can also insert columns into more than one worksheet at a time. For example, imagine you're working with a model that includes three worksheets—worksheets A, B, and C. You want to insert a new column B in all three worksheets. To do this, move the cell pointer to column B in worksheet A and press CTRL-. (CTRL-PERIOD) to anchor it. Next, press CTRL-PGUP twice to expand the current selection into worksheets B and C, thereby creating a three-dimensional range. Then, complete the Worksheet Insert Column command as you normally would. 1-2-3/G inserts a new column B into all three worksheets.

When you insert new columns into a worksheet, 1-2-3/G automatically updates existing formulas to reflect their new position relative to cell A:A1. For example, the cell pointer in Figure 3–25 is located on cell A:E12, which contains the formula @SUM(B12..D12). This formula sums the numbers in row 12 of columns B, C, and D. Figure 3–26 shows the same formula after a new column B has been added to the worksheet. The formula, now located in cell A:F12, reads @SUM(C12..E12). Thus, 1-2-3/G has updated the formula to reflect its new position in the worksheet as well as the new position of the cells referenced by the formula.

Inserting columns can have the effect of expanding multiple-cell range references in your formulas. When you insert a column between the first and last cell of an existing range, 1-2-3/G expands the range reference in your formula. For example, imagine you have the formula @SUM(A1..F1) in cell A:G10. This formula sums the numbers in row 1 of columns A through F. You then insert a new column B into the worksheet. The formula, now located in cell A:H10, reads @SUM(A1..G1); the range reference in the formula has been expanded to include an additional column. In the event the range reference in the original formula was defined by a range name, that range name would also be redefined to include the additional column.

Inserting new columns can also expand three-dimensional ranges. When you insert a column into the last worksheet of a three dimensional range, the new column may cause the lower-right anchor cell of the range to be shifted to the right. This in turn increases the range's size not only in the last worksheet, but also in the other worksheets included in the range. For example, imagine for the sake of argument that you have a named range called TITLES. The specifications for that range are A:A4..C:E5. Thus, the TITLES range encompasses A4..E5 in worksheets A, B, and C of the current file. If you insert a new column B in worksheet C, the TITLES range specification becomes A:A4..C:F5, meaning that it now includes the range A4..F5 in all three worksheets.

Inserting Rows

To insert rows into the worksheet, you use the Row option from the Worksheet Insert dialog box. To insert a single row into the worksheet, row 2 for example, start by moving the cell pointer to the row where you want the new row inserted. (1-2-3/G always inserts new rows immediately above the first cell in the current selection.) Enter the Worksheet Insert command to display the dialog box in Figure 3–24 and select "Row." To complete the command, select the OK command button or press ENTER. 1-2-3/G inserts a new row 2 and shifts the data in the rest of the worksheet one row downward. That is, the data that was in row 2 is now located in row 3, row 3's data is now in row 4, and so on.

To insert more than one row into a worksheet, position the cell pointer where you want the new rows inserted. Select the Worksheet Insert Row command and press TAB to get to the Number text box. Replace the number 1 (the default) with the number of new rows you want inserted. Complete the command by selecting OK or pressing ENTER. Alternately, you can select a range that includes a single cell from multiple adjacent rows before you enter the Worksheet Insert Row command. That way, when you subsequently enter the command, the Number text box includes the number of rows you specified. When you complete the command, 1-2-3/G inserts the specified number of rows immediately above the first row in your selection.

You can also insert rows into more than one worksheet at a time. For example, imagine you are working with a three-worksheet model that includes worksheets A, B, and C. All three worksheets need a new row 2. To do this, locate the cell pointer in any cell of row 2 in worksheet A. Press CTRL-. (CTRL-PERIOD) to anchor the cell pointer in the first worksheet. Then press

CTRL-PGUP twice to expand the selection into worksheets B and C. Finally, enter the Worksheet Insert Row command. When you complete the command, 1-2-3/G inserts a new row 2 for worksheets A, B, and C.

1-2-3/G also allows you to insert partial rows. That is, instead of inserting whole new rows that cause the rest of the rows in the worksheet to be shifted downward, only part of a row is inserted. Therefore, only cells in selected columns are shifted downward. To insert part of a row, begin by selecting that portion of the row where you want the new cells inserted. Then, enter the Worksheet Insert command and select Partial from the Span section of the Worksheet Insert dialog box. For example, imagine you have rows 1, 2, and 3 of columns A, B, C, and D of the current worksheet filled with numbers. You then select the range B1..C1 and use the Worksheet Insert Row Partial command. The following diagram shows the results.

	Before				**After**			
Column	A	B	C	D	A	B	C	D
Row 1	1	1	1	1	1			1
Row 2	2	2	2	2	2	1	1	2
Row 3	3	3	3	3	3	2	2	3
Row 4						3	3	

Caution

When you insert partial rows, only selected columns of data are shifted downward. This may cause a mismatch of data elsewhere in your worksheet. For example, your row titles may no longer be in the same row as the numbers to which they refer.

As you might expect, when you insert new rows into the worksheet, 1-2-3/G updates all the range specifications in your existing formulas. For example, imagine you have the formula +A1 in cell A:A10 of the current worksheet. You then insert a new row 1 into that worksheet. The formula, now in cell A:A11, reads +A2. If the original cell A1 was defined by a range name, that range name now refers to cell A2 in all your formulas.

Inserting rows into the middle of a multiple-cell range referenced in a formula increases the size of that range. For example, imagine you have the formula @SUM(A1..A10) in cell A:A12 of the current worksheet. This formula sums the numbers in rows one through 10 of column A. You then insert a new row 2 into the worksheet. The formula, now in cell A:A13, reads @SUM(A1..A11).

Inserting rows can increase the size of three-dimensional ranges as well. This only happens when you insert rows into the last worksheet of a three-dimensional range. The new rows may cause the lower-right anchor cell of the three-dimensional range to be shifted downward, causing the size of the range to increase not only in the last worksheet but in all the other worksheets included in the range. For example, imagine you have a named range called TITLES that includes the range A:A1..C:C4. Thus, this range includes the range A1..C4 in worksheet A, B, and C of the current file. You then insert a new row 2 in worksheet C, causing the lower-right anchor cell of the TITLES range, C:C4, to be moved downward to cell C:C5. The TITLES range name now refers to the range A:A1..C:C5.

Inserting Worksheets

Occasionally, you may find it necessary to insert a new worksheet into a file. For example, imagine you are working on a cash flow projection for your company that includes three divisions. You've decided to place the projection for each division in its own worksheet. In fact, you've got the Division 1 and Division 3 worksheets done. These are located in worksheets A and B, respectively, of the current file. However, now you need to insert a consolidation worksheet at the front of the file as well as a new worksheet for Division 2, located between the Division 1 and 3 worksheets. To insert these new worksheets, you'll use the Worksheet Insert Sheet command.

To insert a worksheet at the front of the file, locate the cell pointer in worksheet A. Then, enter the Worksheet Insert command to display the Worksheet Insert dialog box. Select Sheet from the dialog box. 1-2-3/G activates the Position section of the dialog box. Select the Before option button, so that 1-2-3/G will insert the new worksheet in front of the current worksheet. To complete the command, select the OK command button, or press ENTER. 1-2-3/G inserts a new worksheet (as worksheet A), places the cell pointer in cell A1 of that worksheet, and shifts the rest of the worksheets in the file back by one. So, the original worksheet A becomes worksheet B, worksheet B becomes worksheet C, and so on. Figure 3–27 shows an example of what your screen might look like after you've entered some data in the new worksheet A.

Note

To make your screen show four stacked worksheets as in Figure 3–27, use the Worksheet Window Perspective command and specify a four-worksheet display.

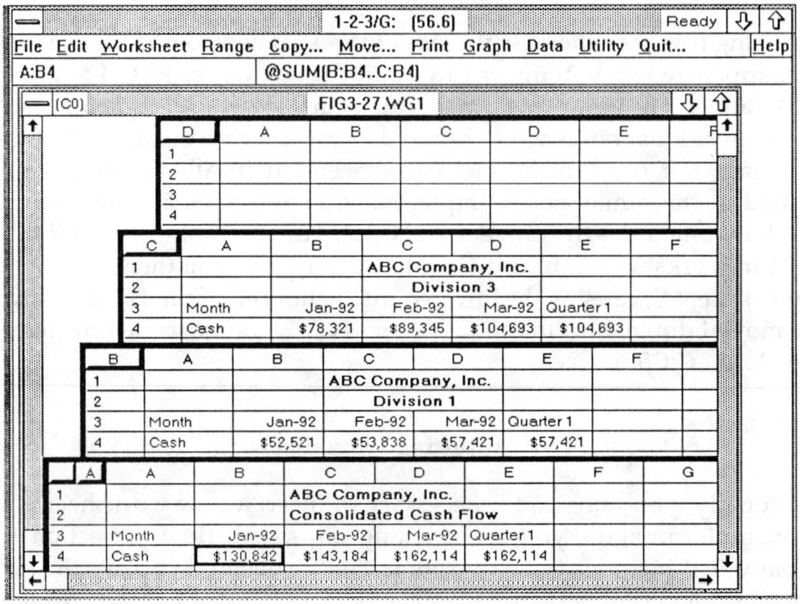

1-2-3/G: (56.6) Ready

File Edit Worksheet Range Copy... Move... Print Graph Data Utility Quit... Help

A:B4 @SUM(B:B4..C:B4)

(C0) FIG3-27.WG1

D	A	B	C	D	E
1					
2					
3					
4					

C	A	B	C	D	E	F
1			ABC Company, Inc.			
2			Division 3			
3	Month	Jan-92	Feb-92	Mar-92	Quarter 1	
4	Cash	$78,321	$89,345	$104,693	$104,693	

B	A	B	C	D	E	F
1			ABC Company, Inc.			
2			Division 1			
3	Month	Jan-92	Feb-92	Mar-92	Quarter 1	
4	Cash	$52,521	$53,838	$57,421	$57,421	

A	A	B	C	D	E	F	G
1			ABC Company, Inc.				
2			Consolidated Cash Flow				
3	Month	Jan-92	Feb-92	Mar-92	Quarter 1		
4	Cash	$130,842	$143,184	$162,114	$162,114		

FIGURE 3–27 Worksheet Insert Sheet Before inserts a new worksheet A at the front of a file

To insert a new worksheet for Division 2 in the model in Figure 3–27, press CTRL-PGUP to move the cell pointer to worksheet B (the Division 1 worksheet). Enter the Worksheet Insert command again and select the Sheet option. 1-2-3/G activates the Position section of the Worksheet Insert dialog box. This time, select the After option. That way, 1-2-3/G will insert the new worksheet behind the current one. To complete the command, select the OK command button or press ENTER. 1-2-3/G inserts a new worksheet C into the file, moves the cell pointer to cell A1 of that worksheet, and shifts the rest of the worksheets in the file back by one. Your screen now looks like Figure 3–28.

You can also insert more than one worksheet at a time. To do this, enter the Worksheet Insert command to display the Worksheet Insert dialog box. Then, select Sheet to activate the Position section of the dialog box. Select from Before or After and press TAB to move to the Number text box. Replace the 1 (the default) with the number of worksheets you want inserted before or after the current worksheet. To complete the command, select the OK command button or press ENTER. Alternatively, prior to selecting Worksheet Insert, you can select a three-dimensional range that includes a single cell from more than one adjacent worksheet, one worksheet for each new worksheet you want to insert. That way, when you enter the Worksheet Insert command, the Number text box is already updated for the number of worksheets you want to insert. The new worksheets will be inserted either before or after the first worksheet in your three-dimensional range.

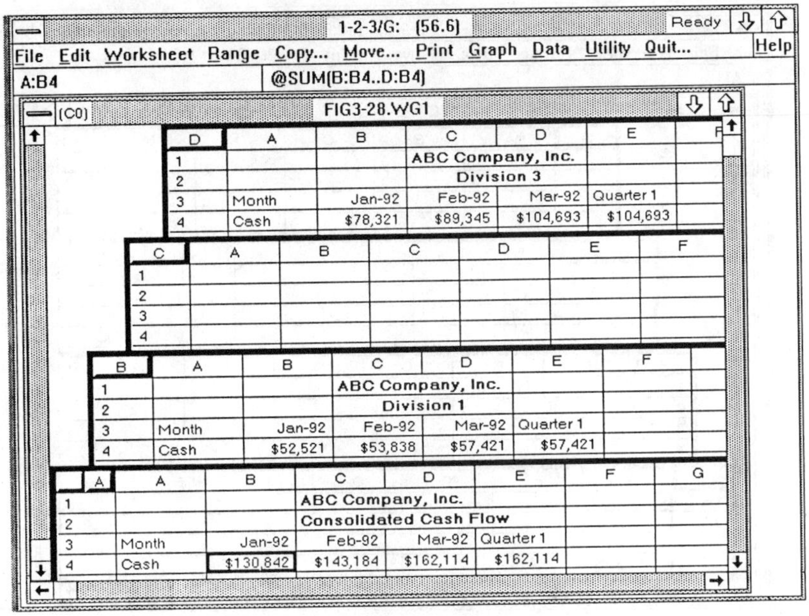

FIGURE 3–28 **Worksheet Insert Sheet After inserts a new worksheet C**

You can also insert part of a worksheet. That is, instead of inserting an entire new worksheet and causing all the worksheets in the file to be shifted backward, only part of a new worksheet is inserted. Therefore, only a selected block of cells in each worksheet is shifted back.

To insert a partial worksheet into a file, begin by selecting a rectangular range of cells in the current worksheet. Then, select the Worksheet Insert command to display the Worksheet Insert dialog box. Next, select the Sheet option, choose from Before or After, and then select the Partial option. Finally, select the OK command button, or press ENTER to complete the command. 1-2-3/G inserts new cells in the current worksheet, as defined by the current selection, and pushes the original contents of those cells backward or forward through worksheets as needed.

For example, imagine you have three worksheets in a file, worksheet A, B, and C. Imagine further that you have filled the range A:A1..A:C3 with numbers. You then select the range A:A1..A:B2 and select the Worksheet Insert Sheet Before Partial command. Figure 3–29 shows the results.

As you might imagine, when you insert new worksheets into a file, 1-2-3/G automatically updates the range names and addresses in your existing formulas. For example, imagine you have the formula +C:A1 in cell A:A1 of the current file. You then insert a new worksheet C, causing the original worksheet C to become worksheet D. The formula in cell A:A1 now reads +D:A1.

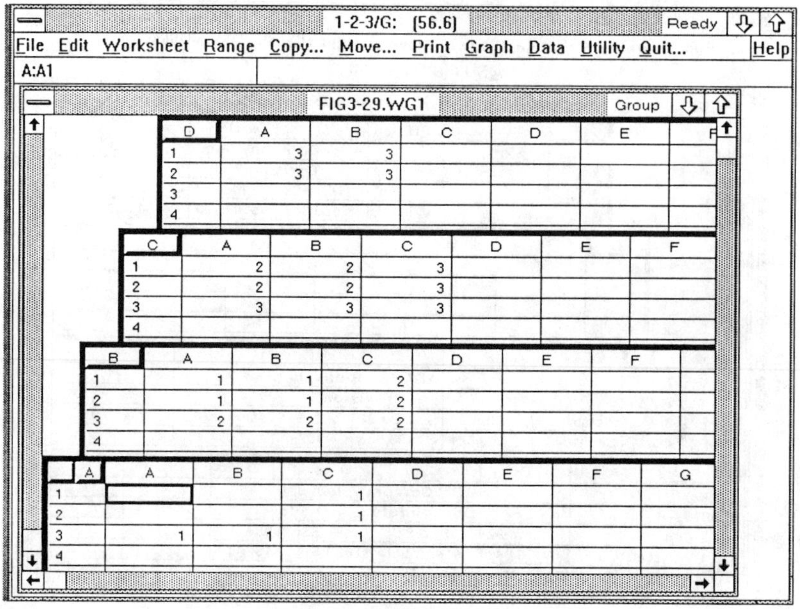

FIGURE 3–29 **A new partial worksheet is inserted into a file**

Inserting a worksheet into the middle of a three-dimensional range causes the range to increase in size. For example, notice in Figure 3–27 that cell A:B4 contains the formula @SUM(B:B4..C:B4), which sums cells B4 in worksheets B and C. Figure 3–28 shows that same formula after a new worksheet, worksheet C, has been inserted into the file. The formula in cell A:B4 now reads @SUM(B:B4..D:B4); its range has been expanded to accommodate the additional worksheet.

Deleting Columns, Rows, and Worksheets

To delete columns, rows, or worksheets, you use the Worksheet Delete command. When you select the Worksheet Delete command, 1-2-3/G displays the dialog box in Figure 3–30.

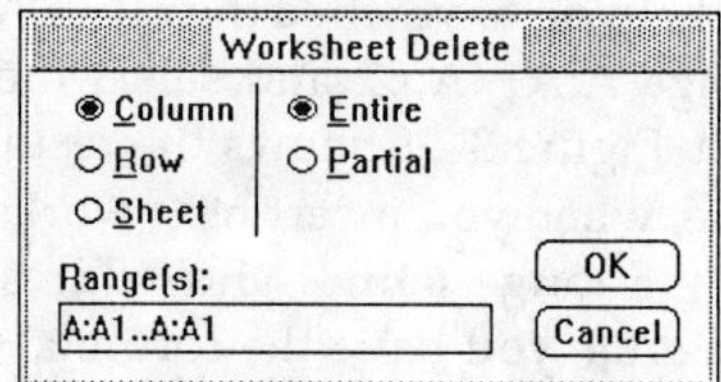

FIGURE 3–30 **The Worksheet Delete dialog box**

Note

Use the Worksheet Delete command with care. Otherwise, you might delete valuable data. If you change your mind after using the command, press ALT-BACKSPACE immediately to activate the Undo feature and reclaim the lost data.

Deleting Columns

To delete one or more columns from the current worksheet, select a range that includes a single cell from one or more adjacent columns that you want to delete. (You cannot specify a collection for the Worksheet Delete command.) Enter the Worksheet Delete command and select Column from the dialog box in Figure 3–24. To complete the command, select the OK command button or press ENTER. 1-2-3/G deletes the column(s) you specified. Any data in those columns is deleted as well. 1-2-3/G then closes up the space occupied by those columns by shifting data in the remaining columns of the worksheet to the left.

You can also delete columns in more than one worksheet at a time. To do this, select a three-dimensional range that includes adjacent columns from more than one worksheet. For example, to delete columns A, B, and C of worksheets, A, B, and C of the current file, begin by moving the cell pointer to cell A:A1. Press CTRL-. (CTRL-PERIOD) to anchor it and then use the arrow keys to expand to select the range A:A1..A:C1. Next, press CTRL-PGUP twice to expand the cell pointer into worksheets B and C. Finally, enter the Worksheet Delete Column command. When you complete the command, 1-2-3/G deletes columns A, B, and C from worksheets A, B, and C of the current file. Data in the remaining columns of the worksheet is shifted to the left to close up the space.

1-2-3/G also allows you to delete part of a column. To do this, highlight a rectangular range of cells that you want deleted from one or more adjacent columns. Next, enter the Worksheet Delete Column command and select the Partial option button. When you complete the command, 1-2-3/G deletes the cells in the columns you specified. Data located in columns to the right of the deleted cells are shifted to the left to close up the space. For example, imagine you have rows 1 through 4 of columns A through D filled with numbers. You then use the Worksheet Delete Column Partial command to delete the range A2..B3. The diagram at the top of the following page shows the results.

Use caution when deleting columns in the worksheet. If you delete a column containing data referenced by a formula elsewhere in your worksheet, that formula evaluates to ERR. For example, imagine you have the formula @SUM(B1..B20) in cell F20, which sums rows 1 through 20 in column B. If you delete column B, the formula in cell A:F20 evaluates to ERR. In addition, if the range B1..B20 is defined by a range name, 1-2-3/G undefines the range name

	Before				After			
	A	B	C	D	A	B	C	D
Row 1	1	2	3	4	1	2	3	4
Row 2	1	2	3	4	3	4		
Row 3	1	2	3	4	3	4		
Row 4	1	2	3	4	1	2	3	4

when you delete column B. All formulas that use the range name both in the current file and other files, now evaluate to ERR.

If you delete a column from within a multiple-cell range, 1-2-3/G shrinks the range. Formulas and commands that use the range now refer to the new smaller range. For example, imagine you have the formula @SUM(B10..G10) in cell H10, which sums row 10 of columns B through H. Then suppose you use the Worksheet Delete Column command to delete column C. 1-2-3 updates the formula, now in cell G10, to read @SUM(B10..F10). In the same example, if the range B10..G10 is defined by a range name, the range name is redefined to B10..F10 when column C is deleted. Any formulas or commands that use the range name now refer to the new smaller range.

Deleting Rows

To delete rows, you use the Worksheet Delete Row command. To prepare for the command, select a range that includes a single cell from one or more of the adjacent rows you want to delete. (You cannot specify a collection for this command.) Then enter the Worksheet Delete command and select Row. Complete the command by selecting the OK command button or pressing ENTER. 1-2-3/G deletes the rows in the current selection. The data in those rows are deleted as well. Data located in rows beneath the current selection are shifted upward to close up the space.

Caution

> Similar to deleting columns, when you delete a row containing data or a named range used by formulas located elsewhere in your worksheets, those formulas evaluate to ERR. Or if you delete a row within a multiple-cell range or range name, 1-2-3/G reduces the size of the range accordingly. Formulas or commands that reference the range now refer to the new smaller range.

You can also delete rows from more than one worksheet at a time. To do this, specify a three-dimensional range that includes one or more adjacent rows either prior to or during the Worksheet Delete Row command.

1-2-3/G also allows you to delete part of a row. To do this, begin by highlighting a range of adjacent cells in a row. Then, select the Worksheet Delete Row command and select Partial from the Worksheet Delete dialog box. 1-2-3/G deletes the cells in the current selection, and shifts the data in columns located beneath the current selection upward. For example, imagine you have rows 1 through 4 of columns A through D of the current worksheet filled with numbers. You then use the Worksheet Delete Row Partial command to delete the range B2..C3. The following diagram shows the results.

	Before				**After**			
	A	B	C	D	A	B	C	D
Row 1	1	1	1	1	1	3	3	1
Row 2	2	2	2	2	2	4	4	2
Row 3	3	3	3	3	3			3
Row 4	4	4	4	4	4			4

Tip:Deleting rows from macros

When deleting rows, be careful that you do not inadvertently delete a line from one of your macros. This will undoubtedly cause an error in the macro, or worse, cause two macros to converge such that one begins as the other is ending. To avoid this, try locating your macros out of harm's way in a separate worksheet.

Deleting Worksheets

To delete one or more worksheets, you use the Worksheet Delete Sheet command. To prepare for this command, select a single cell from one or more worksheets in the current file. If you specify multiple worksheets for deletion, make sure you specify a three-dimensional range that includes consecutive worksheets. (You cannot specify a collection for the Worksheet Delete command.) Next, enter the Worksheet Delete command and select Sheet from the Worksheet Delete dialog box. To complete the command, select the OK command button or press ENTER. 1-2-3/G deletes the worksheets in the current selection and closes up the space by shifting data from other worksheets forward.

Caution

As you might imagine, when you delete a worksheet containing data used by formulas in other worksheets, those formulas evaluate to ERR. If the worksheet contains named ranges, those range names become undefined. Formulas using those range names now evaluate to ERR. Or if you delete a worksheet that is included in a three-dimensional range, 1-2-3/G reduces the size of the range. Formulas and commands that use the range now refer to the new, smaller range. If the three-dimensional range is defined by a range name, 1-2-3/G redefines the range name to reference the smaller range. Formulas using that range name are updated accordingly.

You can also use the Worksheet Delete Sheet command to delete part of a worksheet. To do this, select those cells from one or more worksheets that you wish to delete. Then enter the Worksheet Delete Sheet command and select the Partial option. Complete the command in the usual way. 1-2-3/G deletes the cells in the current selection and shifts that same range of cells in other worksheets forward through worksheets as necessary. For example, imagine you have the range A1..D4 of worksheets A, B, and C filled with numbers. You then select the range A:B1..A:C2 and enter the Worksheet Delete Partial command. Figure 3–31 shows the results.

GROUPING WORKSHEETS

In 1-2-3/G you can assign two or more worksheets to a group. When worksheets are grouped, you can make a settings change in one of the worksheets and the other worksheets in the group will receive the same settings change. To form a worksheet group, you use the Worksheet Global Group command. Alternatively, you can press GROUP (SHIFT-F7). Whichever method you choose, 1-2-3/G displays the dialog box in Figure 3–32.

Group mode can be extremely convenient when you want to assign similar formatting to multiple worksheets. For example, suppose you have a situation similar to the one shown in Figure 3–33. This figure shows three worksheets (A, B, and C). Notice that worksheet A has different column widths, cell formatting, and so on than do worksheets B and C. To assign the formatting in worksheet A to worksheets B and C, begin by selecting a three-dimensional range that includes all three worksheets (A:A1..C:C1). For example, move the cell pointer to cell A:A1 and press CTRL-. (CTRL-PERIOD) to anchor it. Then

1-2-3/G: (56.6) Ready

File Edit Worksheet Range Copy... Move... Print Graph Data Utility Quit... Help

A:A1 1

FIG3-31.WG1

C	A	B	C	D	E	F
1	3			3		
2	3			3		
3	3	3	3	3		
4	3	3	3	3		
5						
6						

B	A	B	C	D	E	F
1	2	3	3	2		
2	2	3	3	2		
3	2	2	2	2		
4	2	2	2	2		
5						
6						

A	A	B	C	D	E	F	G
1	1	2	2	1			
2	1	2	2	1			
3	1	1	1	1			
4	1	1	1	1			
5							
6							

FIGURE 3–31 The Worksheet Delete Sheet Partial command is used to delete part of a worksheet

press CTRL-PGUP twice to expand the highlight into worksheets B and C. Next, select the Worksheet Global Group command, or press GROUP (SHIFT-F7). 1-2-3/G displays the dialog box in Figure 3–32. Select Enable from this dialog box. Then select the Copy command button. 1-2-3/G copies the settings and formatting from worksheet A to the other worksheets in the group (worksheets B and C). A GROUP mode indicator is then displayed in the title bar of the worksheet window. Your screen now looks like Figure 3–34.

To return to working strictly on worksheet A again, press GROUP (SHIFT-F7) to remove the GROUP mode indicator from the title bar of the worksheet window. Then press ESC to cancel the current three-dimensional range selection and return

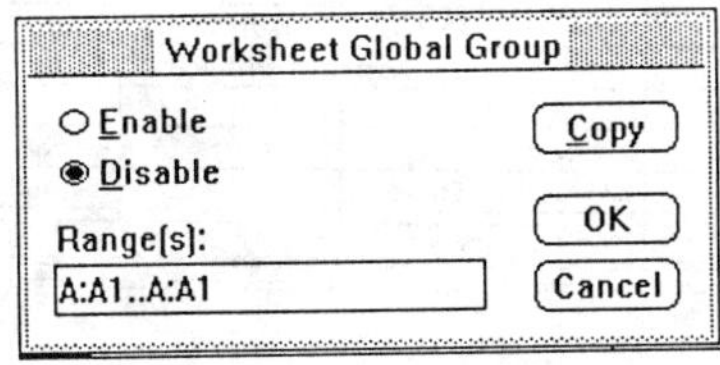

FIGURE 3–32 The Worksheet Global Group dialog box

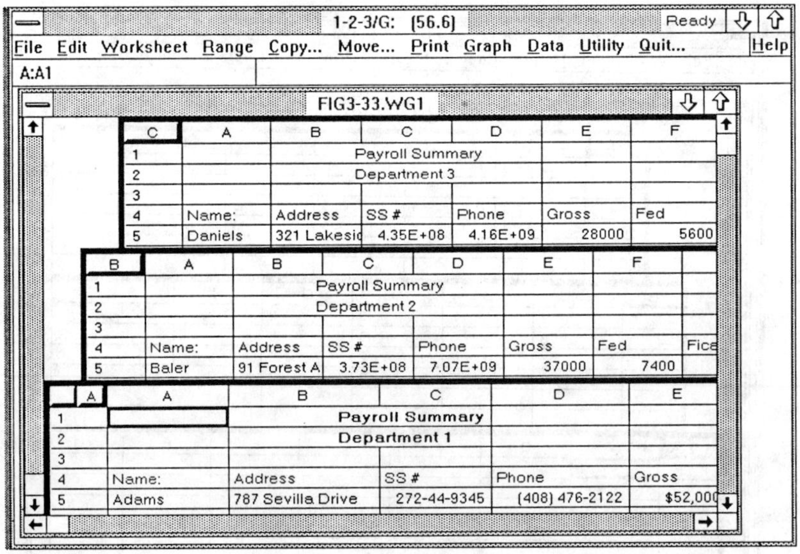

FIGURE 3–33 The formatting in worksheet A is different than in worksheets B and C

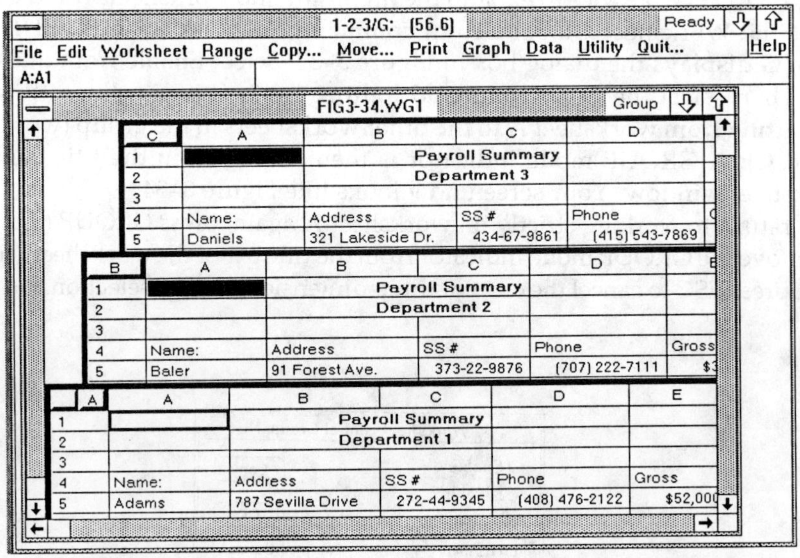

FIGURE 3–34 The Worksheet Global Group command transfers settings and formats from worksheet A to worksheets B and C

the cell pointer to worksheet A. You can now perform any command in any worksheet in the group without affecting the other worksheets in the group.

Suppose, however, that you now wish to have a command apply to all the worksheets in the group. Press GROUP (SHIFT-F7) again. 1-2-3/G enters GROUP mode and displays the GROUP mode indicator in the worksheet window title bar. In addition, 1-2-3/G sets up a three-dimensional range that spans the same cells in all the worksheets in the group. Thus, when you enter a command, it applies to all the worksheets in the group. For example, if you use the Worksheet Insert command to insert a new row 2 in worksheet A, a new row 2 is also added to the other worksheets in the group. To disable GROUP mode, select the Worksheet Global Group Disable command.

Note

When 1-2-3/G enters GROUP mode, it automatically establishes a three-dimensional range. You can press ESC to clear the range, but when you attempt to anchor the cell pointer by clicking your mouse or pressing CTRL-. (CTRL-PERIOD), 1-2-3/G automatically sets up the three-dimensional range again. To highlight a range in an individual worksheet, you must press GROUP (SHIFT-F7) to turn GROUP mode off, or disable GROUP mode by using the Worksheet Global Group Disable command.

Tip:Use GROUP mode to apply global commands

Normally, Worksheet Global commands apply only to the worksheet in which you enter them. The other worksheets in the file are not affected. However, in GROUP mode, any Worksheet Global command entered in the current worksheet also applies to the other worksheets included in the group.

PROTECTING YOUR WORKSHEETS

If you're preparing a worksheet file for use by others, you should be aware of 1-2-3/G's worksheet protection features. 1-2-3/G allows you to protect your worksheets by limiting data entry to cells that you select. You can also hide specific ranges or entire worksheets from view. Thus, your users need not see extraneous or confidential information.

Turning Protection On and Off

Think of each cell in a worksheet as having an ON/OFF switch for protection. When the protection switch for a cell is ON, you cannot enter data into the cell. However, when the protection switch is set to OFF, you can use the cell as you normally would.

1-2-3/G's worksheet protection scheme requires that you protect all the cells in the worksheet first. Then, to allow data entry to selected cells, you turn protection off just for those cells.

To protect the current worksheet, you use the Worksheet Global Protection command. When you enter this command, 1-2-3/G displays the dialog box in Figure 3–35. Select the Enable option from this dialog box. To complete the command, select the OK command button or press ENTER. 1-2-3/G protects the current worksheet by disallowing data entry in all its cells. A PR indicator is displayed at the left side of the title bar for the worksheet window. To disable global protection, select the Disable option from the Worksheet Global Protection dialog box.

To unprotect selected cells in a protected worksheet, you use the Range Unprotect command and select a range, or collection, to which the command will apply. (This command does not have a dialog box.) 1-2-3/G unprotects the range you selected and allows data entry to the cells within that range. A U indicator is displayed at the left side of the worksheet window title bar, indicating that the current cell is unprotected. When you make an entry to an unprotected cell, 1-2-3/G displays the entry in green on a color screen. If you attempt to enter data outside the unprotected areas of a protected worksheet, 1-2-3/G issues an error message.

Note

Normally 1-2-3/G displays data in unprotected cells as green on a color screen. However, you can use the Worksheet Global Screen Attributes Unprotected text command to select a different display color. See "Changing Screen Attributes" later in this chapter for more details on this command.

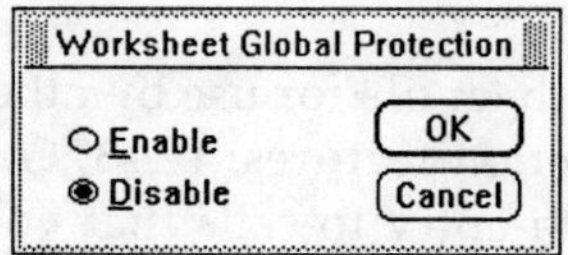

FIGURE 3–35 The Worksheet Global Protection dialog box

If, after unprotecting a range of cells, you decide you want to reprotect selected cells within that unprotected area, you can use the Range Protect command. To do this, enter the command and select a range to which it applies. (This command does not have a dialog box.) 1-2-3/G re-enables protection for the cells you selected.

Note

> Enabling global protection for the current worksheet is an excellent way to protect your macros in that worksheet. However, if those macros change the contents of any cells in the worksheet, make sure those cells are unprotected. Otherwise, 1-2-3/G will issue an error message when you run the macro.

The Worksheet Global Protection command applies only to the current worksheet. Therefore, if you wish to turn on global protection in another worksheet, you must move to that worksheet and apply the command there. Alternatively, if you wish to protect a series of consecutive worksheets, you can select a three-dimensional range, or activate GROUP mode, and then select the Worksheet Global Protection Enable command.

When you enable protection for a worksheet, 1-2-3/G disallows the use of some commands for that worksheet. For example, you cannot use the Worksheet Insert command to insert columns, rows, or partial worksheets. You can, however, insert new worksheets into the file, even though the worksheets surrounding the new worksheet are protected. Similarly, you cannot use the Worksheet Delete command to delete columns, rows, or partial worksheets. You can, however, delete unprotected worksheets in the file. Finally, you cannot use the Worksheet Page Break command to insert page breaks, and you cannot use the Range Justify command to justify a range of text.

You can, however, use those commands in a protected worksheet that do not affect its contents. For example, you can use the Range Attributes or Range Format command. These commands simply alter the appearance of the data in a cell without changing its contents. You can also use the Worksheet Windows and Worksheet Titles command. These commands simply affect the way your worksheets are displayed and do not change its contents in any way.

Tip: Enhancing global protection

In most cases, enabling global protection is sufficient to keep someone from tampering with your worksheet. However, if you're dealing with knowledgeable users, you risk someone disabling global protection (selecting Worksheet Global Protection Disable). To avoid this, you can use the File Admin Seal command. This command seals the current settings for a file with a password. See Chapter 12, "Networking 1-2-3/G," for more on this command. Incidentally, don't let the networking label put you off. The File Admin Seal command is ideal for use in a single-user environment.

Creating a Custom Input Form

Using the Range Input command, you can limit cell pointer movement to unprotected cells in a specific area of the worksheet. Thus, you can create the appearance of a customized fill-in-the-blank form where data entry is limited to only certain cells in that form.

Note

The Range Input command is normally used within an interactive macro to present a form for data entry. You can also use the {FORM} advanced macro command to create custom data entry forms. In fact, the {FORM} command gives you more control over user input than does the Range Input command. For more about using macros, see Chapter 10, "Creating Macros," and Chapter 11, "Advanced Macro Commands."

In preparation for the Range Input command, you must create your data entry form and then unprotect cells within that form. For example, Figure 3–36 shows a custom form ready for use. Within this form, the Range Unprotect command has been used to unprotect cells in the ranges A:B4..A:B7, A:B9..A:B10, A:B12, A:B14, and A:B16.

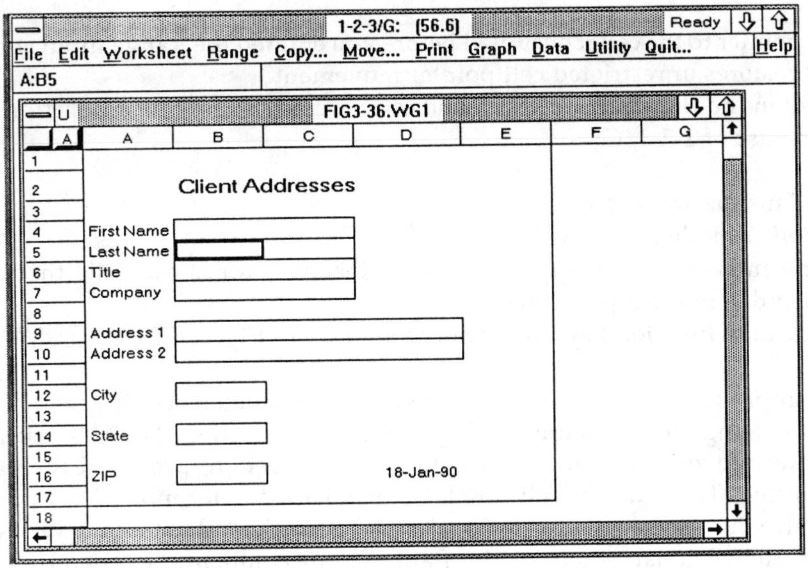

FIGURE 3–36 The Range Input command is used to activate a custom form.

Note

After typing in the text, the following commands were used to prepare the input form in Figure 3–36: Range Attributes Border Frame All for ranges A1..E17, B4..C7, B9..D10, B12, B14, and B16. Range Attributes Border Inside Horizontal for ranges B4..C7 and B9..D10. Range Attributes Font for cell B2 to specify a 14-point Helvetica font.

When you're ready, select Range Input. 1-2-3/G prompts you to specify a range for the command. Select the range that includes your entire input form (A:A1..A:E17 in Figure 3–36). 1-2-3/G moves the input form to the upper-left corner of the current window and places the cell pointer in the first unprotected cell of that form. To enter data into the form, start typing. When you complete the entry for the first cell, use the arrow keys to move to the next unprotected cell. If the next unprotected cell is not immediately adjacent to the current cell, 1-2-3/G skips over cells as needed to jump to the next unprotected cell. To complete data entry, press ESC, ENTER, or CTRL-BREAK. 1-2-3/G returns the cell pointer to the cell it occupied before you entered the Range Input command and restores unrestricted cell pointer movement.

When the Range Input command is active, the following restrictions apply to the use of 1-2-3/G:

- All menus are disabled.
- POINT mode is disabled.
- The mouse pointer appears grayed (inactive) for those cells that are not included in the input range.
- The only function keys you can use are HELP (F1), EDIT (F2), and ABS (F4).

If appropriate, you can select either a collection or a three-dimensional range for the Range Input command. If you select a collection, 1-2-3/G restricts cell pointer movement to the cells within that collection, provided they are unprotected. The order of cell pointer movement is determined by the order in which you selected the individual ranges for the collection. If you select a three-dimensional range for the Range Input command, or a collection that includes multiple worksheets, you cannot use CTRL-PGUP or CTRL-PGDN to move between worksheets. Instead, simply press the arrow keys to move from one cell to the next in the input range. 1-2-3/G will do the jumping from worksheet to worksheet for you.

Tip: Use BOUND (Shift-F4) to restrict movement

If you're simply interested in confining cell pointer movement to a specific area of the worksheet, use BOUND (SHIFT-F4) instead of Range Input. To use BOUND, begin by selecting a range or collection in the worksheet. Then press BOUND (SHIFT-F4). Cell pointer movement is now restricted to the range(s) you specified. However, 1-2-3/G's menus are still active, and you can enter POINT mode with the mouse or keyboard to build formulas. To free the cell pointer, press BOUND (SHIFT-F4) again. For a complete discussion of BOUND, see Chapter 1, "1-2-3/G Basics."

Hiding Worksheets

1-2-3/G also allows you to hide entire worksheets from view. That way, extraneous or confidential data is removed from sight. To hide one or more worksheets, you use the Worksheet Hide command. When you select this command, 1-2-3/G displays the dialog box in Figure 3–37.

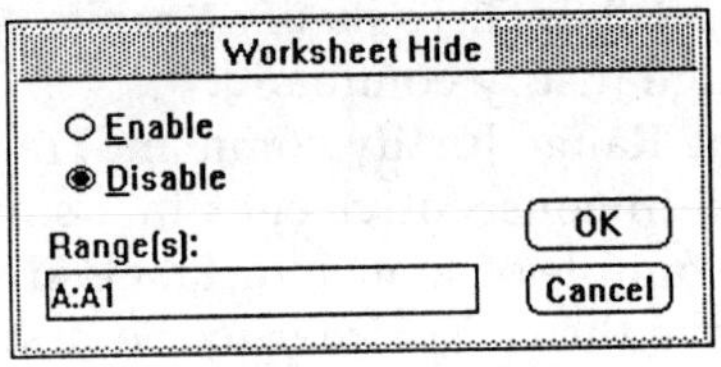

FIGURE 3–37 The Worksheet Hide dialog box

Before issuing the Worksheet Hide command, select a range or collection that includes a single cell from the worksheets you want to hide. Then select the Worksheet Hide command to display the dialog box in Figure 3–37 and select the Enable option. To complete the command, select the OK command button or press ENTER. 1-2-3/G hides the worksheet(s) in the current selection in the Range(s) text box completely from view. For example, if you hide worksheet B, worksheet C now appears after worksheet A.

While a worksheet is hidden, you cannot move to that worksheet or point to its data by entering POINT mode during commands. You can, however, refer to its cell addresses in commands and formulas. What's more, the formulas, macros, etc., in that hidden worksheet are still functional.

To display hidden worksheets, press HIDE (SHIFT-F6). HIDE causes 1-2-3/G to redisplay hidden worksheets, columns, and rows. The hidden worksheets are marked by an asterisk (*) next to the worksheet letter. You can then move to the hidden worksheets and point to their data during commands. To return those worksheets to hiding, press HIDE (SHIFT-F6) again.

To redisplay hidden worksheets permanently, select the Worksheet Hide command again. 1-2-3/G redisplays all hidden worksheets with asterisks (*) next to their column letters and shows you the Worksheet Hide dialog box. Select the Disable option and specify in the Range(s) text box a range or collection that includes a single cell from those worksheets you want to redisplay. Select OK or press ENTER to complete the command. 1-2-3/G redisplays all hidden worksheets in the current selection.

JUSTIFYING A RANGE OF LONG LABELS

1-2-3/G is by no means a word processor. However, you can justify a series of long labels located in a single column to fit within a specified width. The result is a paragraph-like arrangement of text. Thus, you can dash out a short memo without having to leave 1-2-3/G. To justify a range of long labels to a specified width, you use the Range Justify command.

In preparation for the Range Justify command, make sure you have a series of long labels arranged in consecutive cells in a single column. For example, Figure 3–38 shows an example of some long labels arranged in consecutive cells in column A. Next, move the cell pointer to the first label in that column (cell A:A1). Then, enter the Range Justify command. 1-2-3/G prompts you for a justify range. Select a row of cells that defines the width you want for the labels, or type in its range name. For example, if you want the labels to fit within the width of Columns A, B, and C, select the range A:A1..A:C1. To complete the command, press ENTER. 1-2-3/G rearranges the words in your long labels to fit within the justify range you specified, wrapping portions of those labels to the next row, if necessary. To complete the job, 1-2-3/G left aligns the justified labels and gives each of them a label prefix of ' (apostrophe). Your screen should look like Figure 3–39.

As you can see from Figure 3–39, the width of cells in the justify range ultimately determines the length of your justified labels. For example, if you increase or decrease the width of columns A, B, and C in Figure 3–39, you would get different results. However, keep in mind that the maximum width allowed for any label in 1-2-3/G is 512 characters.

When you execute the Range Justify command, 1-2-3/G continues justifying labels in the current column until it encounters either a blank cell or a numeric value. At that point, 1-2-3/G stops justification and assigns each of the affected cells in the column the same cell format and protection status as the first cell in the column.

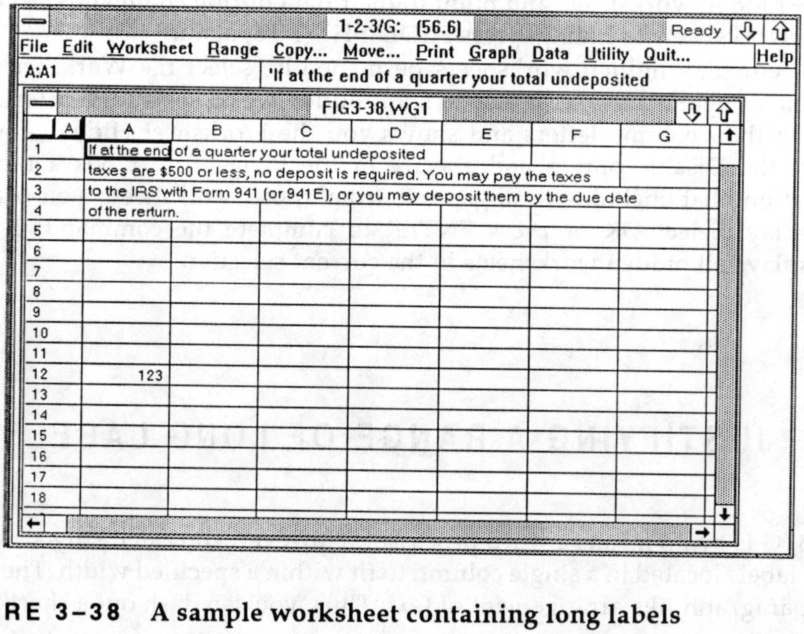

1-2-3/G: (56.6) Ready
File Edit Worksheet Range Copy... Move... Print Graph Data Utility Quit... Help
A:A1 'If at the end of a quarter your total undeposited
FIG3-38.WG1
A B C D E F G
1 If at the end of a quarter your total undeposited
2 taxes are $500 or less, no deposit is required. You may pay the taxes
3 to the IRS with Form 941 (or 941E), or you may deposit them by the due date
4 of the rerturn.
12 123

FIGURE 3–38 **A sample worksheet containing long labels**

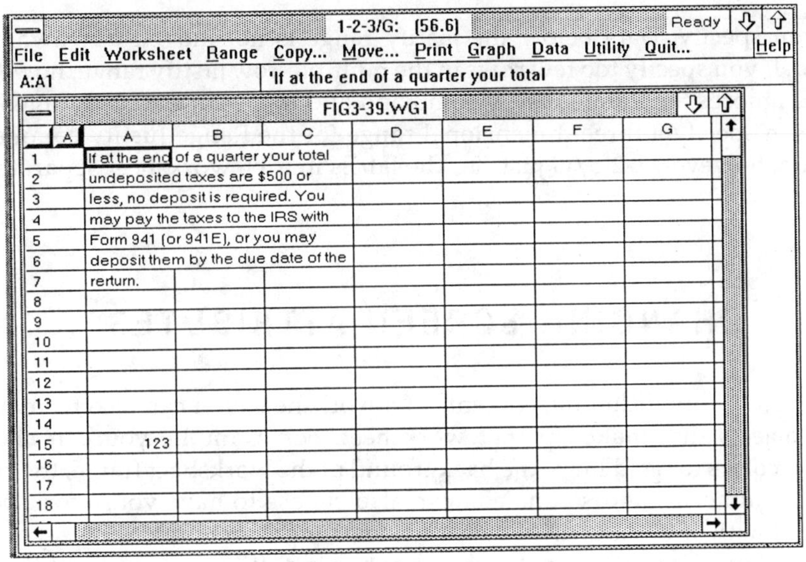

1-2-3/G: (56.6) Ready

File Edit Worksheet Range Copy... Move... Print Graph Data Utility Quit... Help

A:A1 'If at the end of a quarter your total

FIG3-39.WG1

A	A	B	C	D	E	F	G
1	If at the end of a quarter your total						
2	undeposited taxes are $500 or						
3	less, no deposit is required. You						
4	may pay the taxes to the IRS with						
5	Form 941 (or 941E), or you may						
6	deposit them by the due date of the						
7	rerturn.						
8							
9							
10							
11							
12							
13							
14							
15	123						
16							
17							
18							

FIGURE 3–39 Range Justify is used to used to justify long labels within a specific width

The previous example shows you how to use the Range Justify command with a single-row justify range. When you use a single row justify range, 1-2-3/G uses additional rows, if necessary, to fit the labels within the width you specified. If additional rows are required, data below the justified labels is pushed downward. For example, notice in Figure 3–38 that a number, 123, resides in cell A:A12. That same number resides in cell A:A15 of Figure 3–39. The number has been pushed downward, because three additional rows were required to justify the labels within the specified width. Conversely, if fewer rows are required, 1-2-3/G shifts the data below the justified labels upward.

You can also specify a multiple-row justify range for the Range Justify command. When you do, 1-2-3/G confines the justification to the number of

Note

Be careful not to include formulas formatted as text (formatted with Range Format Text) within the justify range for the Range Format command. If you do, 1-2-3/G treats those formulas as if they were pure labels and justifies them. Therefore, the formulas will no longer function.

rows you specify. Data below the justify range is not moved downward or upward. If you specify too few rows in the multiple-row justify range, however, 1-2-3/G ignores the Range Justify command and issues an error message.

You can specify a three-dimensional range for the Range Justify command. If you do, however, 1-2-3/G justifies the labels in each worksheet separately.

CHANGING SCREEN ATTRIBUTES

In addition to formatting the contents of a worksheet, you can also format the screen objects that make up that worksheet. For example, you can choose different colors for grid lines, the background of the worksheet frame, the color of text within cells, and so on. You can also choose to have your worksheets displayed with or without grid lines. To change these screen attributes, you use the Worksheet Global Screen Attributes command. When you enter this command, 1-2-3/G displays the dialog box in Figure 3–40.

Note

None of the screen attribute settings changes you make with Worksheet Global Screen Attributes will affect your printed output.

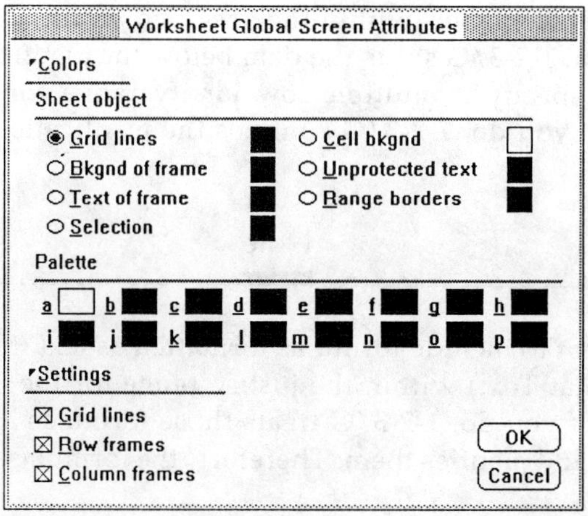

Worksheet Global Screen Attributes

Colors

Sheet object

Grid lines
Bkgnd of frame
Text of frame
Selection
Cell bkgnd
Unprotected text
Range borders

Palette

a b c d e f g h
i j k l m n o p

Settings

Grid lines
Row frames
Column frames

OK
Cancel

FIGURE 3–40 The Worksheet Global Screen Attributes dialog box

To change the color of a particular screen object, select the option for that object from the Sheet object section of the dialog box in Figure 3–40. Then, select a color for that screen object from the Palette section. For example, to have the background color of all the cells in the worksheet appear blue, select the "Cell bkgnd" option from the Sheet object section. Then select the blue color block (block g) from the Palette section. To complete the command, select the OK command button or press ENTER. 1-2-3/G returns you to the current worksheet and displays all the cells in the worksheet with a blue background.

To cancel the display of grid lines or the worksheet frame for the current worksheet, use the Settings section of the Worksheet Global Screen Attributes dialog box. For example, to remove all grid lines from the worksheet, click on the "Grid lines" check box, or press the space bar, to remove the X from the box. To remove the left part of the worksheet frame that contains row numbers, remove the X from the "Row frames" check box. To remove the display of the top section of the worksheet frame that contains the column letters, remove the X from the "Column frames" check box.

Note

When you elect to cancel the display of the worksheet grid with Worksheet Global Screen Attributes, cell borders you've set with Range Attributes Border are not affected.

FORMATTING EXAMPLES

This section contains two examples that use many of the formatting commands outlined in this chapter. The commands required to create each example are provided for you. We hope these examples will serve to show you some of the special display effects you can achieve with 1-2-3/G and spur your creativity as you build your own worksheet displays.

Figure 3–41 shows an example that you might display at the start of a session. To create this graphic yourself, perform the following steps:

1. In cell C8 enter the label **Welcome to 1-2-3/G**.
2. Select Range Attributes Font. Select font option o (24 Pt. Times Rmn) from the Fonts list box. Select both Bold and Italic from the Attributes section. Select OK.

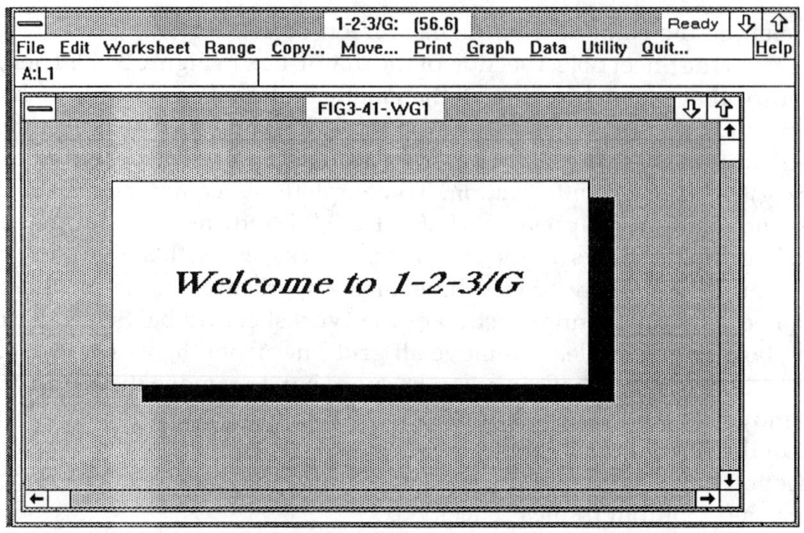

FIGURE 3–41 **An example graphic**

3. Select the range B4..G12 and select Range Attributes Border Frame All and select the solid line style (a) from the Line-style section. Select OK.
4. Move the cell pointer to cell B4 and select Worksheet Column Set width and type in **2**,. meaning 2 characters. Select OK.
5. Leave the cell pointer in cell B4 and select Worksheet Row Set height and type in **.2**, meaning 2/10 of an inch. Select OK.
6. Move the cell pointer to cell H13 and select Worksheet Column Set width and type in **1.5** characters. Select OK.
7. Leave the cell pointer in cell H13 and select Worksheet Row Set height and type in **.2**, meaning 2/10 of an inch. Select OK.
8. Select the range A1..I21 and select Range Attributes Color Background All and select the gray color block (block b) from the Palette section. Select OK.
9. Select the range H13..H5 and select Range Attributes Color Background All and select the black color block (block d) from the Palette section. Select OK.
10. Select the range C13..G13 and select Range Attributes Color Background All and select the black color block (block d) from the Palette section. Select OK.
11. Select the range B4..G12 and select Range Attributes Color Background All and select the white color block (block a) from the Palette section. Select OK.
12. Select Worksheet Global Screen Attributes and remove the X's from the "Grid lines," "Row frames," and "Column frames" check boxes. Select OK.

Figure 3–42 shows an example invoice. To create this form yourself, perform the following steps:

1. Use the Range Attributes Border Frame All command and select a solid line style (Line style a) for the following ranges, B2..C4, B6..C8, B10..G17.
2. Move the cell pointer to cell B5 and select Worksheet Row Set Height and type in **.175** for the row height. Select OK.
3. Use the Worksheet Column Set width command to set the width of column D to 15 characters and column F to 5 characters.
4. Select the range B10..B17 and select Range Attributes Border Frame Right and select a solid line style (Line style a). Select OK.
5. Select the range B10..G10 and select Range Attributes Border Frame Bottom and select a solid line style (Line style a). Select OK.
6. Select the range E11..G17 and select Range Attributes Border Inside All and select a solid line style (Line style a). Select OK.
7. Select the range E11..E17 and select Range Attributes Border Frame Left and select a solid line style (Line style a). Select OK.
8. Select the range G18..G20 and select Range Attributes Border Frame All and select a solid line style (Line style a). Then select Inside Horiz and select a solid line style (Line style a). Select OK.
9. Fill in the text for the invoice as it appears in Figure 3–42.

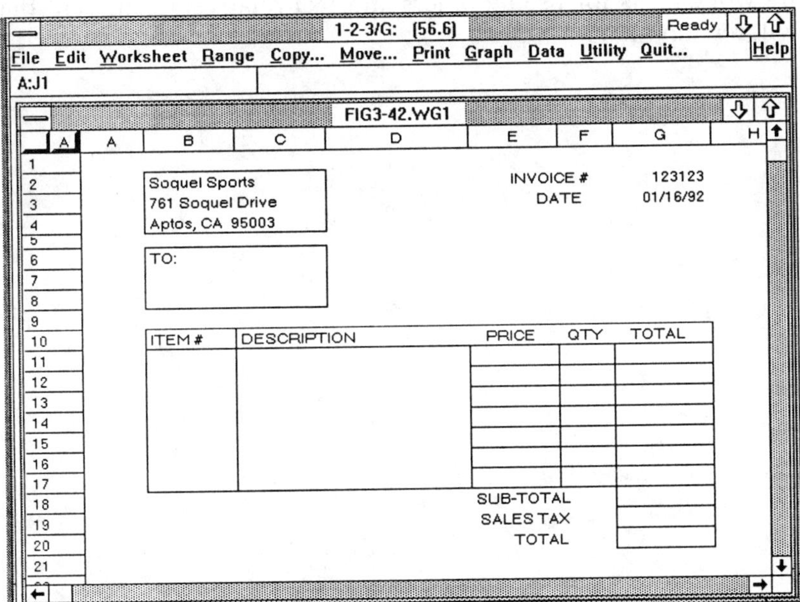

FIGURE 3–42 A sample invoice

SUMMARY

In this chapter you learned about virtually every aspect of formatting worksheets. For example, you know how to use the Range Format command to assign formats to cells so that 1-2-3/G always displays the data in those cells in a certain way.

You also know how to use the Range Attributes command to apply attributes to cells. For example, you can now have your data displayed in different fonts. You can also assign bolding, underlining, or italics to those fonts. Further, you know how to assign colors to different cells based on their contents, and you can create borders to frame the edges of selected cells.

You've acquired other skills as well. For example, you can use the Range Label command to change the alignment of data in cells, and you know how to use the Range Zero Suppress command to control the display of cells that contain zero.

This chapter also showed you some commands and techniques you can use to manage columns, rows, and worksheets. For example, you can now use the Worksheet Insert command to insert columns, rows, and worksheets where needed. Thus, you can improve the appearance and layout of your data. Further, you know how to delete columns, rows, and worksheets when needed.

You also know how to use the Worksheet Global Group command to group worksheets. Thus, you can standardize formatting and settings across worksheets.

Finally, you now know how to protect your worksheets. Thus, you can prepare worksheets for use by others and feel relatively confident that your data will remain intact.

CHAPTER

4

Cutting and Pasting Data

After entering data in a 1-2-3/G worksheet file, you will almost invariably find that it is not positioned exactly where you want it. You may also find that you need to copy the data to another location, or perhaps remove it from the worksheet file altogether.

All these operations fit the category of cutting and pasting data. And as you might expect, 1-2-3/G offers many powerful commands for cutting and pasting within and between worksheets. For example, you can use the Copy command to duplicate data in another worksheet, even when that worksheet resides in a separate file. You can use the Move command to move data from one location to another without modifying it. And with the Range Erase or Edit Clear commands, you can delete data in worksheets. 1-2-3/G also has special commands for copying formulas as values (Range Value) and transposing data from a columnwise to a rowwise orientation or vice versa (Range Transpose).

In addition, you can cut and paste using the clipboard. You access the clipboard through the Edit menu, which is available from nearly every 1-2-3/G tool and utility. You can also use the clipboard to share data with other programs, such as SideKick for Presentation Manager.

What's New

1-2-3/G adds many new features to the familiar 1-2-3 commands Range Erase, Move, Copy, Range Value, and Range Transpose. Here are some examples:

- Many of these commands now include Confirm (✓) and Cancel (X) icons in the Control line to make them easier to use with a mouse. By clicking on the Cancel (X) icon, you can abort the command. Conversely, by clicking on the confirm (✓) icon, you can complete a command. Some commands, like Copy, also include an Options (. . .) icon in the Control line which lets you access a dialog box to set options for the command.
- As you know, you can use the Range Erase command to erase the contents of a cell or range. However, you can now use this command to erase the contents of a collection or even entire worksheets. In addition, the new Range Erase Options dialog box lets you control whether you erase values, settings, or both. What's more, the Edit Clear command (and its shortcut DEL) now provides an alternative method to Range Erase for erasing information.
- You can now use the Move command to move information from cells, ranges, or worksheets (even an entire worksheet file) to a new location either in the current worksheet file or in another open worksheet file. In addition, when you move information between open files, you can, in the process, establish links between those files.
- The Copy command now copies information in a cell, range, collection, or even entire worksheets. It also allows you to copy information between two open files. In addition, 1-2-3/G has a new Copy Options dialog box that allows you to specify the contents, settings, and types of data that are copied.
- You can now use the Range Value command with a single cell, 2-D and 3-D ranges, collections, or even entire worksheets—and, in the process, convert formulas to values and labels only. Like the other cut and paste commands, you can even use the Range Value command between open files.
- The Range Transpose command now transposes 2-D and 3-D information in rows, columns, and ranges. In addition, the Range Transpose Options dialog box now allows you to specify the type of 2-D or 3-D transposition.

Like other Presentation Manager applications, 1-2-3/G provides an Edit menu for cutting and pasting information through the clipboard. Here are some highlights of the Edit commands:

- The Edit Cut and Copy commands allow you to cut or copy information to the clipboard. You can then use the Edit Paste and Paste Special commands to paste (copy) this information to another location in the same worksheet, another worksheet, or another file. You can also use these commands to cut and paste to other 1-2-3/G tools (such as the Note Utility) or to other Presentation Manager applications.

- When you use the Edit Paste Special command to paste data, a dialog box exactly like the Copy Options dialog box appears that allows you to choose which contents, settings, and types of data are copied from the clipboard.
- The Edit Link Create command allows you to establish a "live" link between 1-2-3/G and another open worksheet file, or an open file created in another Presentation Manager application. Using the other Edit Link options, you can then update, edit, delete, or move these links. These topics are all discussed in Chapter 2, "Managing the Desktop," and in Chapter 7, "Graphs."
- The Edit Undo command allows you to reverse your previous actions. See Chapter 1, "1-2-3/G Basics," for a complete description.

ERASING

Once you enter information in 1-2-3/G, you will want to be able to delete it. Using 1-2-3/G's Range Erase command, you can erase the contents of a cell, range, or collection, even entire worksheets.

In its normal state, the Range Erase command performs the following:

- Erases the contents of a range you specify.
- Leaves intact any settings and attributes, including format and alignment settings. Notes are also left intact.

In previous releases of 1-2-3, Range Erase also erases the contents of a range and leaves its settings intact. Now, by using 1-2-3/G's new Range Erase Options dialog box, you can choose to erase *both* the contents and the settings of your range, thereby returning the range to its global settings. You can also use this dialog box to erase just the settings of your range and leave the information intact. This dialog box is discussed in detail below.

As with 1-2-3/G's other cut and paste commands, you can specify the range you want to erase either *before* or *during* the Range Erase command. See Chapter 1 for more information on selecting ranges.

You cannot erase information and settings in protected cells. Rather, you must first unprotect these cells before you can use the Range Erase command. However, you can erase information in hidden areas without first redisplaying the hidden information.

Tip: Using DEL instead of range erase

1-2-3/G offers an easier way to erase information without even accessing the Main menu. Using the keyboard or mouse, select a range then simply press DEL, a shortcut for the Edit Clear command. The contents of each cell in the range is erased, but all attributes, notes, formats, and other settings remain intact. This new method of erasing is easier to use than the Range Erase command when you want to keep a range's settings intact. (See "The Erasing with Edit Clear" command for more information.)

When you select the Range Erase command, Confirm (✓), Cancel (X), and Options (. . .) icons are now displayed in the Control line, as shown in Figure 4–1. Click on the Cancel (X) icon at any time during the Range Erase command to abort the operation. Click on the Confirm (✓) icon at the end of the Range Erase command to complete the operation. By clicking on the Options (. . .) icon, you can access the Range Erase Options dialog box to select what 1-2-3/G erases within cells.

Erasing a Range

Suppose you have the spreadsheet shown in Figure 4–2. You want to erase the information in the range A:B3..A:E4, which contains the 1990 quarterly sales estimates for two product lines. Just use the following procedure:

1. Locate the cell pointer in cell A:B3. This is the upper-left corner of the range you want to erase.
2. Select the Range Erase command. 1-2-3/G displays the prompt "Enter:", followed by the current selection in the form of a range, A:B3..A:B3.
3. Use any of the following methods to specify the range you want to erase, A:B3..A:E4:

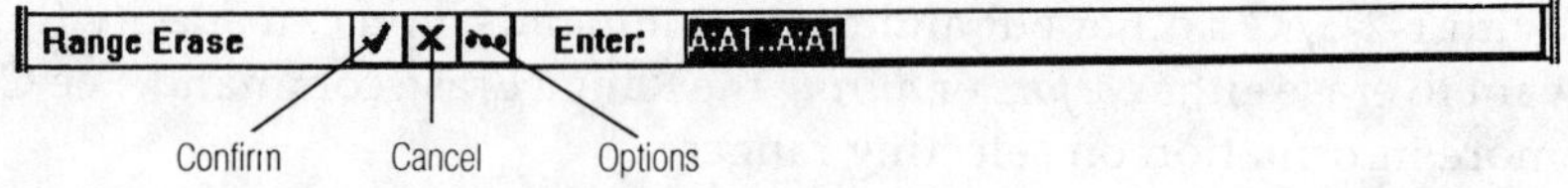

FIGURE 4–1 The Range Erase Control line

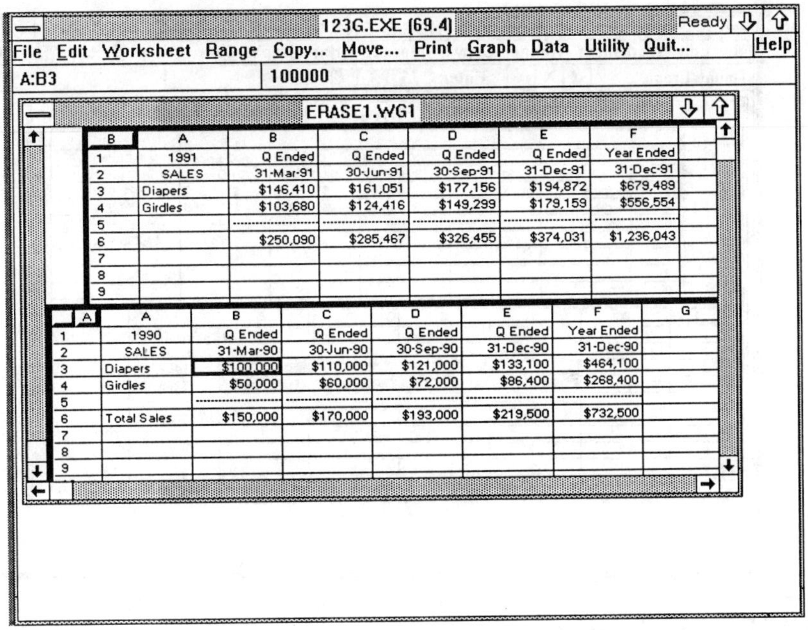

123G.EXE (69.4) Ready

File Edit Worksheet Range Copy... Move... Print Graph Data Utility Quit... Help

A:B3 100000

ERASE1.WG1

B	A	B	C	D	E	F
1	1991	Q Ended	Q Ended	Q Ended	Q Ended	Year Ended
2	SALES	31-Mar-91	30-Jun-91	30-Sep-91	31-Dec-91	31-Dec-91
3	Diapers	$146,410	$161,051	$177,156	$194,872	$679,489
4	Girdles	$103,680	$124,416	$149,299	$179,159	$556,554
5						
6		$250,090	$285,467	$326,455	$374,031	$1,236,043
7						
8						
9						

A	A	B	C	D	E	F	G
1	1990	Q Ended	Q Ended	Q Ended	Q Ended	Year Ended	
2	SALES	31-Mar-90	30-Jun-90	30-Sep-90	31-Dec-90	31-Dec-90	
3	Diapers	$100,000	$110,000	$121,000	$133,100	$464,100	
4	Girdles	$50,000	$60,000	$72,000	$86,400	$268,400	
5							
6	Total Sales	$150,000	$170,000	$193,000	$219,500	$732,500	
7							
8							
9							

FIGURE 4–2 A sample worksheet file

- Type in **A:B3..A:E4** or **B3..E4**. Notice that you can use an abbreviated cell address if the cell pointer is located in the same worksheet as the range you want to erase.
- Highlight the range using the keyboard. Since the cell pointer is anchored in cell A:B3, press ↓ once and → three times.
- Highlight the range using the mouse. Click on cell A:B3 as the beginning of your range. Keeping the left button depressed, drag the mouse so that the range A:B3..A:E4 is highlighted.

As shown in Figure 4–3, the range A:B3..A:E4 is now highlighted and displayed in the Control line.

4. Press ENTER, or click on the Confirm (✓) icon in the Control line.

The results of this erase operation are displayed in Figure 4–4. The range A:B3..A:E4 is now empty. Notice that in worksheet B, the projected sales figures now appear as $0's because they reference cells in the erased range in worksheet A.

Only the contents of these cells are erased, not the formats and other settings. However, you can now erase both the contents and settings of a range using 1-2-3/G's new Range Erase Options dialog box discussed later.

123G.EXE (69.4) — Point

File Edit Worksheet Range Copy... Move... Print Graph Data Utility Quit... Help

Range Erase ✓ X ••• Enter: A:B3..A:E4

ERASE1.WG1

B	A	B	C	D	E	F
1	1991	Q Ended	Q Ended	Q Ended	Q Ended	Year Ended
2	SALES	31-Mar-91	30-Jun-91	30-Sep-91	31-Dec-91	31-Dec-91
3	Diapers	$146,410	$161,051	$177,156	$194,872	$679,489
4	Girdles	$103,680	$124,416	$149,299	$179,159	$556,554
5						
6		$250,090	$285,467	$326,455	$374,031	$1,236,043
7						
8						
9						

A	A	B	C	D	E	F	G
1	1990	Q Ended	Q Ended	Q Ended	Q Ended	Year Ended	
2	SALES	31-Mar-90	30-Jun-90	30-Sep-90	31-Dec-90	31-Dec-90	
3	Diapers	$100,000	$110,000	$121,000	$133,100	$464,100	
4	Girdles	$50,000	$60,000	$72,000	$86,400	$268,400	
5							
6	Total Sales	$150,000	$170,000	$193,000	$219,500	$732,500	
7							
8							
9							

FIGURE 4–3 Erasing a range

123G.EXE (69.4) — Ready

File Edit Worksheet Range Copy... Move... Print Graph Data Utility Quit... Help

A:B3

ERASE1.WG1

B	A	B	C	D	E	F
1	1991	Q Ended	Q Ended	Q Ended	Q Ended	Year Ended
2	SALES	31-Mar-91	30-Jun-91	30-Sep-91	31-Dec-91	31-Dec-91
3	Diapers	$0	$0	$0	$0	$0
4	Girdles	$0	$0	$0	$0	$0
5						
6		$0	$0	$0	$0	$0
7						
8						
9						

A	A	B	C	D	E	F	G
1	1990	Q Ended	Q Ended	Q Ended	Q Ended	Year Ended	
2	SALES	31-Mar-90	30-Jun-90	30-Sep-90	31-Dec-90	31-Dec-90	
3	Diapers					$0	
4	Girdles					$0	
5							
6	Total Sales	$0	$0	$0	$0	$0	
7							
8							
9							

FIGURE 4–4 After the Range Erase command

Erasing an Entire Worksheet

Erasing an entire worksheet is easy in 1-2-3/G. Suppose you want to erase all of the information in worksheet B in Figure 4–2. Assuming the cell pointer is located in cell A:A1, do the following:

1. Select the Range Erase command. 1-2-3/G displays the prompt "Enter:", followed by the current selection in the form of a range, A:A1..A:A1.
2. Designate worksheet B as your range to be erased using any of the following methods:

   - Type **B:**.
   - Highlight the worksheet using the keyboard. Since the cell pointer is anchored in cell A:A1, press ESC to free the cell pointer, then press CTRL-PGUP to locate the cell pointer in B:B1. Now press ALT-SHIFT-HOME. (Make sure you press the HOME key on the nonnumeric (gray) keypad. Otherwise, 1-2-3/G will ignore your keypress. See Chapter 1 for more information on selecting an entire worksheet.)
   - Highlight the worksheet using the mouse. Click on the Worksheet selector button in the top left-hand corner of worksheet B. Worksheet B is now highlighted and B: is displayed in the Control line.

3. Press ENTER, or click on the Confirm (✓) icon in the Control line.

When the Range Erase command has completed, all information in worksheet B is erased. However, the settings, including any formats, attributes, and notes remain intact.

Caution

> Do not confuse the Worksheet Erase command with the Range Erase command. The Worksheet Erase command removes the entire worksheet *file* from memory, not just specific ranges or worksheets. The original file on disk, however, is not affected.

Erasing Back-to-Back Worksheets

When you erase back-to-back worksheets, such as worksheets B and C, you specify your range differently depending on whether you use the keyboard or the mouse. For example, suppose the cell pointer is located in B:B1. When you select the Range Erase command, specify your range to be erased in any of the following ways:

- Type **B:..C:**.
- Using the keyboard, specify the continuous range B:..C:. Press ALT-SHIFT-HOME to select worksheet B as the beginning of your range. Then press CTRL-SHIFT-PGUP so that both worksheets B and C are highlighted.
- Using the mouse, specify the collection B:,C:. Click on worksheet B's Worksheet selector button. Then, using the right mouse button, click on worksheet C's Worksheet selector button.

Both worksheets B and C are highlighted. Press ENTER, or click on the Confirm (✓) icon in the Control line to complete the command.

The Range Erase Options Dialog Box

As mentioned, 1-2-3/G contains a new Range Erase Options dialog box that lets you control what is erased within cells. To display this dialog box, select the Range Erase command, then click on the Options (. . .) icon in the Control line, or press SHIFT-F3. Figure 4–5 shows the dialog box that appears. You can activate the Range Erase Options dialog box at any time during the Range Erase command.

The Range Erase Options dialog box offers two options, Values and Settings. You can specify the following combinations:

- Values (the default)
- Settings
- Values and Settings

After completing a Range Erase command, the Range Erase Options dialog box always reverts to the Values option. If you cancel the dialog box by pressing ESC, or by clicking on the cancel button, the dialog box also reverts to Values.

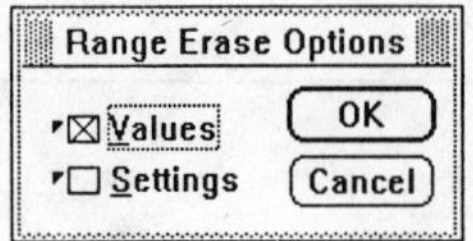

FIGURE 4–5 The Range Erase Options dialog box

Values

The Values option is the default setting of the Range Erase dialog box. When this option is on, only the contents of cells are erased.

Suppose you have the value .2 in a cell formatted as Percent with 0 decimal places, as shown in Table 4–1. The value is displayed as 20%. However, your global value format is Currency, 2 decimal places. When you select the Values option during the Range Erase command, the cell containing this value is blanked, but it is still formatted as Percent. If you enter the value 5 in this cell, as in Table 4–1, it is displayed as 500%.

Now suppose you have right-aligned the label Expenses, as shown in Table 4–1. The global label alignment is centered. When you specify the Values option during the Range Erase command, the cell containing this label is blanked. However, the cell retains its label alignment setting. As shown in Table 4–1, when you enter the label "More Expenses" in this cell, it is still right-aligned.

Settings

By selecting the Settings option by itself, you can erase only the settings of cells, while retaining the information in those cells. The Settings option erases:

- All settings, including formats, label alignment, and protection, returning the cells to global settings.
- Notes that reference the erased cells.
- Attributes, such as colors, fonts, borders, and precision, returning the cells to the global attribute settings.

You must select the Settings option for each range you erase.

TABLE 4–1 Using the Range Erase Options Dialog Box

Before Range Erase	Range Erase Option Used	After Range Erase	After Entering New Data
20%	Values		500.00%
20%	Settings		$0.20
20%	Values and Settings		$5.00
Expenses	Values		More Expenses
Expenses	Settings	Expenses	
Expenses	Values and Settings		More Expenses

Table 4–1 shows what happens when you select the Settings option and cancel the Values option in the Range Erase dialog box. Notice that the cell still contains the value .2, but the value is displayed using the global cell format, Currency, 2 decimal places. A cell containing the label "Expenses" would still contain this label. However, the label would now be center-aligned, which is the global setting for label alignment.

Note

If you only want to return a cell's format and label alignment to their global settings, use the Range Format Reset command instead of the Range Erase command.

Values and Settings

When you select both the Values and Settings options, both the contents and settings of cells are erased. Because 1-2-3/G always reverts to the Values option only, you must deliberately choose the Settings option for each selection you erase.

As shown in Table 4–1, when you select both options, cells containing the value .2 and the label Expenses are now blank and revert to their global settings—a numeric format of Currency and center alignment. If you now enter the value 5 in this cell, it is displayed as $5.00. If you enter the label "More Expenses," it is displayed center-aligned.

Erasing with Edit Clear

The Edit Clear command performs the same function as the Range Erase command. That is, it erases the contents of a selection and leaves its formats and other settings intact. The shortcut for this command is DEL.

Unlike the other Edit commands, Edit Clear does not use the clipboard. Therefore, information that resides in the clipboard is unaffected when you use this command.

Note

To erase both the contents *and* settings of a range, use the Range Erase Options dialog box discussed above.

There are certain restrictions to using the Edit Clear command. For example, you cannot use Edit Clear to erase any of the following:

- A collection.
- A worksheet, if you use the Worksheet selector button.
- A worksheet file, if you use the Worksheet file selector button.
- A column or row, if you select the box surrounding the column letter or row number.

Rather, you must specify a range with Edit Clear.

An Example

Suppose you have the worksheet in Figure 4–2, and you want to erase the range A:B3..A:E4. Begin by highlighting the range you want to erase, A:B3..A:E4, using the keyboard or a mouse. Next, select the Edit Clear command, or just press DEL. The contents in the range A:B3..A:E4 are erased, as shown in Figure 4–4. However, the formats and other settings remain intact.

Notes on Range Erase and Edit Clear

Keep in mind the following when you use the Range Erase and Edit Clear commands:

- You can cancel Range Erase or Edit Clear at any time during the command by either pressing ESC until you return to the Main menu, pressing CTRL-BREAK, or (in the case of Range Erase only) by clicking on the new Cancel (X) icon in the Control line.
- If you erase information you need using the Range Erase or Edit Clear command, simply press ALT-BACKSPACE immediately after the command to undo the erasure. (See Chapter 1 for a complete discussion of the undo feature.)
- To ensure that you do not erase any hidden information, press HIDE (SHIFT-F6). Hidden information will then be displayed. (To rehide information, press HIDE again.) You can also protect hidden information before you select the Range Erase command (see Chapter 3).
- If you erase the contents of a cell that a string formula references, you change the results of that string formula. 1-2-3/G assigns a value of 0 to a blank cell, and a string formula referencing that cell will return ERR. See "String Formulas" in Chapter 1 for further details.
- To erase an entire worksheet from a file and move other worksheets up to fill in the gap, use the Worksheet Delete Sheet command. Likewise, to erase an entire row or column from a worksheet and have the other rows or columns move to fill the gap, use the Worksheet Delete Row or Column command (see Chapter 3).

- To erase an entire worksheet file, use the Worksheet Erase command (see Chapter 1).

MOVING

Moving information is one of the easiest operations to master in 1-2-3/G. You can use the Move command to move information in a cell, range, or even an entire worksheet to another location in a worksheet file. You cannot move a collection. Rather, you must move each range separately. You also cannot use the Move command to move a column to a row, or a row to a column. Instead, use the Range Transpose command discussed later in this chapter. You can, however, use 1-2-3/G's Move command to move information from one file to another file.

1-2-3/G's Move command performs the following:

- Moves information in one location to a new location. Any existing information in the new location is eliminated.
- Moves formats, attributes, protection status, and other settings to the new location. Notes are moved as well.
- Blanks the contents of the original location, which returns to its global attribute, format, and other settings.

In 1-2-3/G, you can move information from a protected area of your file. However, the destination range (the range you are moving the data to) must be unprotected. See "Protecting Your Worksheets" in Chapter 3 for more on protecting and unprotecting ranges in worksheets.

You can also move information from or to a hidden area. When you select the Move command, 1-2-3/G redisplays hidden rows, columns, or worksheets. The hidden areas are marked by an asterisk (*) next to the row number, column letter, or worksheet letter. You can then use the Move command as you normally would. See Chapter 2 for more on hiding rows, columns, or worksheets.

Note

> Moving information with the Move command produces the same result as using the Edit Cut (SHIFT-DEL) and Edit Paste (SHIFT-INS) commands. However, the Edit Cut command is used to move the information from the worksheet to the Clipboard. Then, the Edit Paste is used to copy the information from the Clipboard to one or more new locations. (See "Editing Information" later in this chapter.) However, the Move command does not affect the Clipboard.

The Move command now includes Confirm (✓) and Cancel (X) icons in the Control line. Click on the Cancel (X) icon at any time during a Move command to abort the operation. Click on the Confirm (✓) icon at the end of the Move command to complete the operation.

Moving Information within a File

Suppose you have created the worksheet in Figure 4–6, and you want to move the information in the range A:C2..A:C7 to the range B:D2..B:D7. Perform the following:

1. Locate the cell pointer in the upper-left cell of the range you want to move, A:C2.
2. Select the Move command. 1-2-3/G displays a "From:" prompt in the Control line followed by the current selection in the form of a range, A:C2..A:C2.
3. Specify the information you want to move, the range A:C2..A:C7. Use any of the following methods:

   - Type **A:C2..A:C7**, or just **C2..C7**.

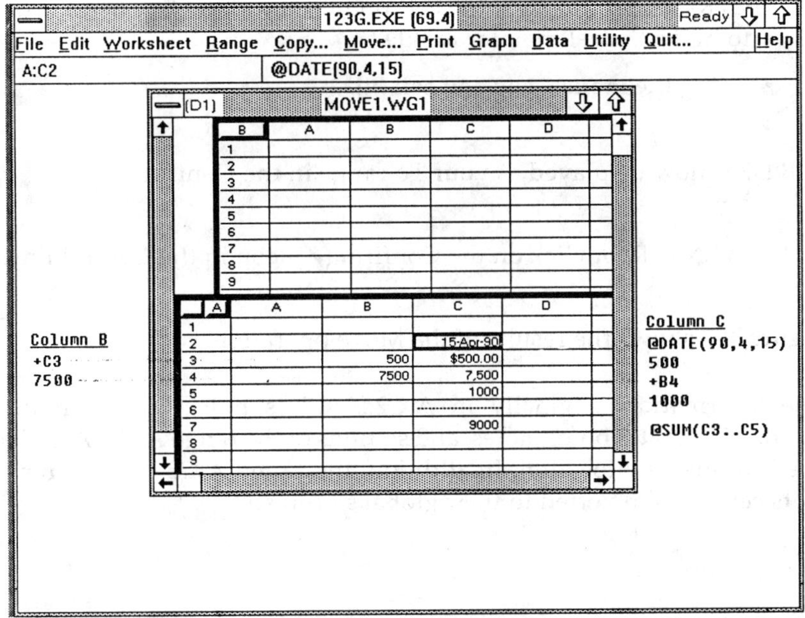

FIGURE 4–6 Before moving information to another worksheet

- Highlight the range using the keyboard. Since the cell pointer is already anchored in cell A:C2, press END then ↓.
- Highlight the range using the mouse. Click on cell A:C2, and keeping the left button depressed, drag the pointer down the column until the range A:C1..A:C7 is highlighted.The From range A:C2..A:C7 is now displayed in the Control line.

The From range A:C2..A:C7 is now displayed in the Control line.

4. Press ENTER, or click to the right of the "To:" prompt. (You cannot use the Confirm (✓) icon during this step.) 1-2-3/G shifts to the "To:" prompt, which displays the first cell in the current selection, in this case A:C2.
5. Specify the location in your file where you want to move the information to, B:D2..B:D7. When you specify a To range, you need to provide only a single cell address. 1-2-3/G uses this cell as the upper-left corner of your To range and moves the information in your From range while maintaining its size and shape. Use any of the following methods to specify cell B:D2:

- Type **B:D2**.
  - Use the keyboard to highlight the cell. After you specify your From range, the cell pointer is unanchored in cell A:C2. Press CTRL-PGUP to move the cell pointer to cell B:C1. Then press → to move the cell pointer to B:D2.
  - Using the mouse, click on cell B:D2.

Cell B:D2 is now displayed as your To range in the Control line.

6. Press ENTER, or click on the Confirm (✓) icon in the Control line.

Figure 4-7 shows the results of the Move operation.

The information originally in A:C2..A:C7 is now located in the range B:D2..B:D7. The attributes, notes, and settings of the range A:C2..A:C7 have also moved to this new location. In addition, the range A:C2..A:C7 is now empty and its cells have reverted to their global settings.

Move Command Notes

Keep in mind the following when you use 1-2-3/G's Move command:

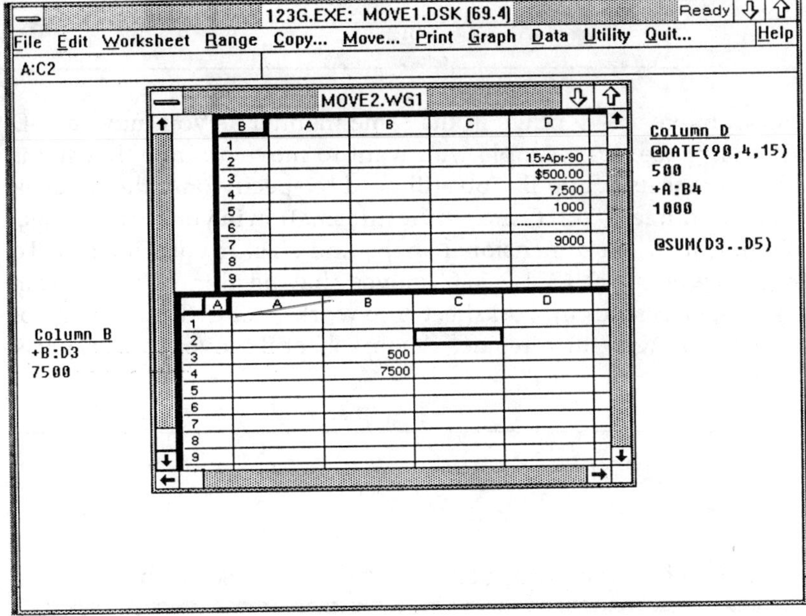

FIGURE 4–7 After moving information to another worksheet

- You can cancel the Move command at any time by pressing ESC until you return to the Main menu, by pressing CTRL-BREAK, or by clicking on the new Cancel (X) icon in the Control line.
- You cannot use the mouse to move a 3–D range. This stems from the fact that you cannot use the mouse to highlight a 3–D range in the first place. Instead you must use the keyboard to highlight a 3–D range.
- You cannot specify a collection for the Move command. That is, you cannot use the mouse to highlight various ranges from different worksheets and then use the Move command to move those ranges. Instead, try using the keyboard to select a 3–D range that includes the information you want to move and then use the Move command.
- If you inadvertently write over existing information using the Move command, simply press ALT-BACKSPACE immediately after completing the command to cancel the move.
- When you move an entire column, row, or worksheet, 1-2-3/G does not move any settings associated with the row, column, or worksheet. For example, it does not move the row height, column width, or global protection setting.
- To insert a new worksheet in file and move the other worksheets back to make room, use the Worksheet Insert Sheet command. Likewise, to insert a new column or row in a worksheet and move the other columns or rows to make room, use the Worksheet Insert Row or Column command (see Chapter 3).

Note

You can move a 3–D range in the same manner as you move a 2–D range. Suppose, for example, you want to move a range that spans both worksheets A and B. You still need to specify only the first cell in your To range. 1-2-3/G moves the information in your From range, including its three-dimensional shape and size. If you choose a To range in worksheet C, 1-2-3/G moves that portion of your From range which resides in worksheet A to worksheet C. That portion of your From range which resides in worksheet B moves to worksheet D.

Tip: Specifying a FROM or TO range before selecting move

You can now specify the From *or* To range *before* selecting the Move command. 1-2-3/G automatically displays the current selection following the "From:" prompt and the first cell of the selection following the "To:" prompt.

For example, suppose you have the worksheet in Figure 4–6 and you want to move the range A:C2..A:C7 to another location. You begin by selecting the range A:C2..A:C7 using the keyboard or the mouse (see "Selecting Cells, Ranges, and Collections" in Chapter 1). You then select the Move command. 1-2-3/G displays the current selection, A:C2..A:C7, following the "From:" prompt. You can accept the selection or enter a new one. After you press ENTER or click on the "To:" prompt, 1-2-3/G displays the first cell of the current selection (not the complete selection) following that prompt. Again, you can accept the suggestion or change it. When you complete the Move command, the current selection remains highlighted in the worksheet.

How the Move Command Affects Cell References

As the examples in Figures 4–6 and 4–7 show, when you use the Move command to move formulas, 1-2-3/G automatically adjusts the cell references within those formulas. The way the cell references are adjusted depends on their location.

Here are the general rules:

- 1-2-3/G automatically adjusts cell references that refer to moved cells. These references are adjusted regardless of whether they are located inside or outside of the moved range.
- Cell references that are located either inside or outside of a moved range that refer to unmoved cells are not affected.

For example, in Figure 4–6 cell A:C7 contains the formula @SUM(C3..C5), referencing cells C3, C4, and C5 in worksheet A. Yet, as Figure 4–7 shows, when you move this formula to cell B:D7, it changes to @SUM(D3..D5), which refers to cells D3, D4, and D5 in worksheet B. 1-2-3/G adjusted the formula in B:D7 to take into account the new location of the cells it references. The value returned in B:D7 of Figure 4–6, 9000, is the same value returned in A:C7 of Figure 4–7.

As another example, before the Move command cell A:B3 contains the formula +A:C3 and returns the value 500 (Figure 4–6). After the Move command, the contents of cell A:B3 did not move, but the contents of the cell it refers to, cell A:C3, did move. Therefore, 1-2-3/G automatically adjusts the formula in cell A:B3 to +B:D3, the new location of the contents previously in A:C3. Notice in Figure 4–7 that cell A:B3 still contains the same value, 500.

Finally, cell A:C4 in Figure 4–6 contains the formula +B4, which returns the value 7,500. After the Move command, cell B:D4 now contains this formula and its resulting value. Therefore, even though the contents of cell A:C4 were moved, the cell it refers to, cell A:B4, did not move. Thus, the formula, which now resides in cell B:D4, was unaffected by the Move operation.

Problems with Move

Here are some common problems you may encounter when you use the Move command:

- Writing over cells that are referenced in formulas will cause those formulas to return ERR.
- Moving a cell that defines a range, that is, the upper-left or lower-right corner cell of a range, modifies the range.

Each of these situations is discussed below.

Writing Over Cell References

As you know, 1-2-3/G's Move command writes over any existing information in the To range. After the Move command, any formulas that refer to this erased information now return ERR.

For example, suppose your worksheet contains the following formulas and values:

Cell	Contents	Result
A1	+B1	5
B1	5	5
C1	10	10

Suppose you then use the Move command to move the contents of cell C1 to cell B1, writing over the original contents of cell B1. Here are the results:

Cell	Contents	Result
A1	+@ERR	ERR
B1	10	10
C1		

Notice that the formula in cell A1 no longer refers to cell B1, but that 1-2-3/G has replaced the reference with @ERR. Thus, cell B1 now displays ERR.

In a similar manner, when you move the contents of one cell on top of another cell that is used as the upper-left or lower-right corner of a range, formulas that refer to that range evaluate to ERR. For example, suppose you have the worksheet in Figure 4–8. Notice that the formula in cell A:B7 is @SUM(B3..B5). Suppose you then use the Move command to move the contents of cell C3 to cell B3. Figure 4–9 shows the results. Notice that the formula in cell B7 is now @SUM(@ERR). 1-2-3/G replaces the range reference with @ERR because the original reference was obscured when you performed the move.

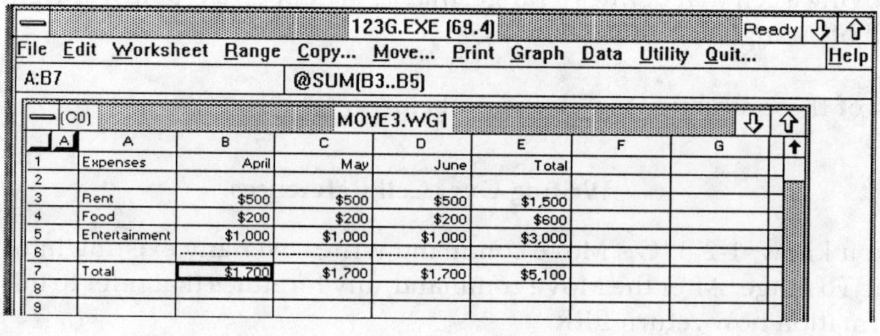

FIGURE 4–8 A sample worksheet that includes a range reference

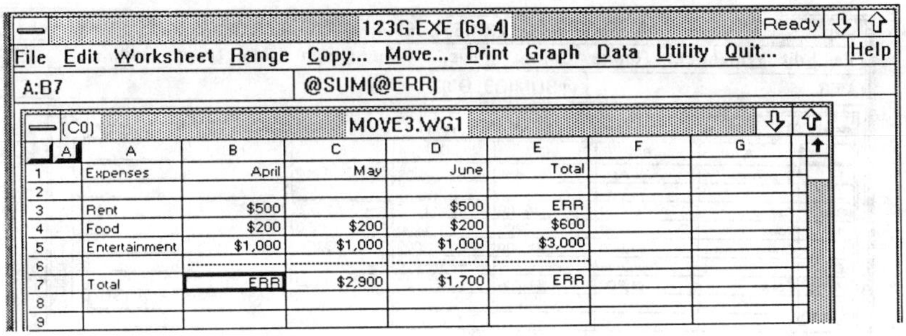

123G.EXE (69.4) Ready

File Edit Worksheet Range Copy... Move... Print Graph Data Utility Quit... Help

A:B7 @SUM(@ERR)

(C0) MOVE3.WG1

A	A	B	C	D	E	F	G
1	Expenses	April	May	June	Total		
2							
3	Rent	$500		$500	ERR		
4	Food	$200	$200	$200	$600		
5	Entertainment	$1,000	$1,000	$1,000	$3,000		
6							
7	Total	ERR	$2,900	$1,700	ERR		
8							
9							

FIGURE 4–9 The effect of moving data onto the first (or last) cell of a range referenced in a formula

Moving a Cell Within a Referenced Range

When you move information into or out of cells that are in the middle of a range referenced in a formula, that formula is not affected. However, when you move the contents of the upper-left or lower-right corner of a range which is referenced in a formula, you change the size of the range in the formula.

For example, suppose you have the worksheet in Figure 4–10. Cell E3 contains the formula @SUM(B3..D3), which is the quarterly total for Rent. Cells E4 and E5 also contain formulas that sum the monthly totals for Food and Entertainment. Cell B7 contains the formula @SUM(B3..B5), the total monthly expenditures in column B. Cells C7, D7, and E7 also sum the expenses in each column.

Now, imagine you use the Move command to move the contents of cell C4 to cell G4. Figure 4–11 shows the results. Cell E4 still contains the formula @SUM(B4..D4), but returns the value $400 because cell C4 is now blank. Similarly, cell C7, which still contains the formula @SUM(C3..C5) now returns the value $1,500 since cell C4 is blank. These formulas are not affected because cell C4 is in the *middle* of the range each formula references. Of course, the values returned by these formulas are affected because the range's contents have changed.

Let's look at an example where you move the contents of the upper-left or lower-right corner of a range which is referenced in a formula. Suppose you have the same example in Figure 4–10. Notice that cell E3 contains the formula @SUM(B3..D3) and that cell D3 denotes the lower-right corner of the range in the formula. Now, suppose you move the range D1..D7 to column G, beginning in cell G1. Figure 4–12 shows the results. Notice that cell E3 now contains the formula @SUM(B3..G3) which returns $3,000. The range reference within the formula has grown to match the new location of the corner cell. In a similar manner, the size of the range in the formula @SUM(B3..D3) would also change if you moved the upper-left corner cell in the range reference, cell B3.

123G.EXE (69.4) Ready

File Edit Worksheet Range Copy... Move... Print Graph Data Utility Quit... Help

A:E3 @SUM(B3..D3)

(C0) MOVE3.WG1

A	A	B	C	D	E	F	G
1	Expenses	April	May	June	Total		
2							
3	Rent	$500	$500	$500	$1,500		
4	Food	$200	$200	$200	$600		
5	Entertainment	$1,000	$1,000	$1,000	$3,000		
6							
7	Total	$1,700	$1,700	$1,700	$5,100		
8							
9							

FIGURE 4–10 A sample worksheet

Note

1-2-3/G also expands or contracts the size of a named range in the same manner when you move the contents of the cell that defines the upper-left or lower-right corner of the named range.

Moving Information to Another File

As in Release 3, you can use 1-2-3/G's Move command to move information between open files. For example, suppose you have two open files on the desktop, MOVE3.WG1 and BUDGET.WG1, as shown in Figure 4–13. You want to move the information in the range A:A1..A:E7 of MOVE3.WG1 to the same position in BUDGET.WG1. Perform the following steps:

1. With the cell pointer located in cell A:A1 of MOVE3.WG1, select the Move command. 1-2-3/G displays the current selection in the form of a range, A:A1..A:A1, following the "From:" prompt.
2. Specify the From range as A:A1..A:E7 using any of the following methods:

123G.EXE (69.4) Ready

File Edit Worksheet Range Copy... Move... Print Graph Data Utility Quit... Help

A:E4 @SUM(B4..D4)

(C0) MOVE4.WG1

A	A	B	C	D	E	F	G
1	Expenses	April	May	June	Total		
2							
3	Rent	$500	$500	$500	$1,500		
4	Food	$200		$200	$400		$200
5	Entertainment	$1,000	$1,000	$1,000	$3,000		
6							
7	Total	$1,700	$1,500	$1,700	$4,900		
8							
9							

FIGURE 4–11 After moving a cell in the *middle* of a range reference

123G.EXE (69.4) Ready

File Edit Worksheet Range Copy... Move... Print Graph Data Utility Quit... Help

A:E3 @SUM(B3..G3)

(C0) MOVE3.WG1 Circ

A	A	B	C	D	E	F	G
1	Expenses	April	May		Total		June
2							
3	Rent	$500	$500		$3,000		$500
4	Food	$200	$200		$1,200		$200
5	Entertainment	$1,000	$1,000		$6,000		$1,000
6							
7	Total	$1,700	$1,700		$10,200		$1,700
8							
9							

FIGURE 4–12 **After moving the lower-right corner cell that *defines* a range**

- Type **A:A1..A:E7**, or just **A1..E7**.
- Highlight the range using the keyboard. Since the cell pointer is already anchored in cell A1, keep pressing → and ↓ until the range A:A1..A:E7 is highlighted.
- Highlight the range using the mouse. In MOVE3, click on cell A:A1, and keeping the left button depressed, drag the pointer across the worksheet so that the range A:A1..A:E7 is highlighted.

The From range is now displayed in the Control line as A:A1..A:E7.

123G.EXE: D:\123G\CHAP4\FIGS\FIG4-13.DSK (69.4) Ready

File Edit Worksheet Range Copy... Move... Print Graph Data Utility Quit... Help

A:A1 'Expenses

MOVE3.WG1

A	A	B	C	D	E	F	G
1	Expenses	April	May	June	Total		
2							
3	Rent	$500	$500	$500	$1,500		
4	Food	$200	$200	$200	$600		
5	Entertainment	$1,000	$1,000	$1,000	$3,000		
6							
7	Total	$1,700	$1,700	$1,700	$5,100		
8							
9							
10	Income	$1,500	$2,200	$1,900	$5,600		
11	Expenses	$1,700	$1,700	$1,700	$5,100		
12	Net Cash	($200)	$500	$200	$500		

BUDGET.WG1

A	A	B	C	D	E	F	G
1							
2							
3							
4							
5							
6							
7							
8							
9							
10							
11							

FIGURE 4–13 **Two windows on the desktop**

3. Press ENTER or click to the right of the "To:" prompt. 1-2-3/G shifts to the "To:" prompt, which displays the current selection, A:A1.
4. Specify the location you want to move the information to, A:A1..A:E7 of BUDGET.WG1. You need only specify the first cell in the range, cell A:A1. Use any of the following methods:

   - Type in the path and filename enclosed in double-angle brackets (the .WG1 extension is optional), followed by the cell address, as in **<<BUDGET.WG1>>A:A1**.
   - Highlight the cell using the keyboard. Press NEXT WINDOW (CTRL-F6) to move to the next window on the desktop, in this case BUDGET.WG1. 1-2-3/G moves the cell pointer to cell A:A1 of BUDGET.WG1.
   - Highlight the cell using the mouse. Click on cell A:A1 in BUDGET.WG1.

The To range is displayed as <<BUDGET.WG1>>A:A1 in the Control line. (If BUDGET.WG1 is not located in current directory, 1-2-3/G displays a pathname preceding the filename in the Control line.)

5. Press ENTER or click on the Confirm (✓) icon in the Control line to complete the command.

Figure 4–14 shows the results. The information originally in A:A1..A:E7 of MOVE3.WG1 is now located in the range A:A1..A:E7 in BUDGET.WG1. As you might expect, the attributes, notes, and settings of this range have also moved to the new location in BUDGET.WG1. In MOVE3.WG1, the range A:C1..A:E7 is now blank and all its cells have reverted to their global settings.

The Effect on Cell References

What happens to cell references when you move them from one file to another? Again, it depends on where the cell references are in relation to the range you move. For example, before the Move command, cell C3 in MOVE3.WG1 contains the formula +B3. After the Move command, cell C3 in BUDGET.WG1 now contains the formula +B3. Because the formula maintained its same relative position within the worksheet when it was moved to BUDGET.WG1, its cell reference is unaffected.

On the other hand, even though cell B11 of MOVE3.WG1 did not move, it is still affected by the Move command. In Figure 4–13, this cell contains the formula +B7. After the Move command, however, the information originally in cell B7 of MOVE3.WG1 is now located in cell B7 of BUDGET.WG1. As shown in Figure 4–14, 1-2-3/G automatically adjusts the formula in cell B11 of MOVE3.WG1 to +<<C:\123G\WORK\BUDGET.WG1>>A:B7. The files

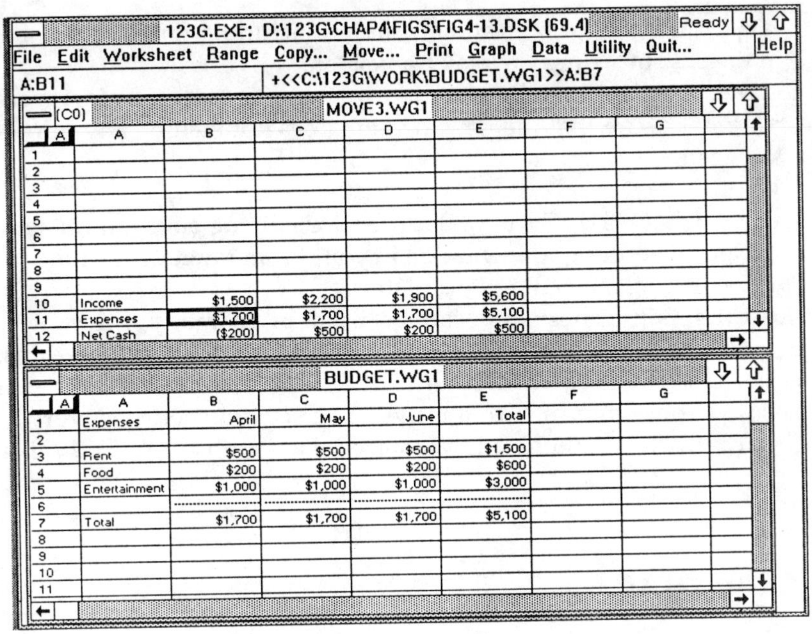

A	A	B	C	D	E	F	G
1	Expenses	April	May	June	Total		
2							
3	Rent	$500	$500	$500	$1,500		
4	Food	$200	$200	$200	$600		
5	Entertainment	$1,000	$1,000	$1,000	$3,000		
6							
7	Total	$1,700	$1,700	$1,700	$5,100		
8							
9							
10							
11							

FIGURE 4–14 After moving a range from MOVE3.WG1 to BUDGET.WG1

MOVE3.WG1 and BUDGET.WG1 are now linked. If the information in cell B7 of BUDGET.WG1 changes, the value in cell B11 of MOVE3.WG1 will also reflect the change. (See Chapter 2 for more on linking files.)

COPYING

The Copy command is one of 1-2-3/G's most versatile commands. It copies information from a source (From) range to a destination (To) range in the same or different worksheet file. The From range can be any of the following:

- a single cell.
- a 2–D or 3–D range.
- a collection (a combination of single cells, 2–D, and/or 3–D ranges).
- entire worksheets.

In its default state, the Copy command performs the following:

- Copies data to the To range exactly as it exists in the From range, including the same labels, values, formulas, and notes.

- Copies the same cell formats and attributes, including fonts, colors, borders, and (in the case of values) levels of precision.
- Writes over any existing information in your To range. Before you copy information, be sure that the new location does not include any information that you need.

However, by using 1-2-3/G's new Copy Options dialog box, you can choose to copy only specific types of information in your From range to the new location (see "The Copy Options Dialog Box," later).

Because the Copy command can be used in so many ways, it can be difficult to understand. Therefore, it is presented here in two sections. This first section covers the basic mechanics of the Copy command—for example, how to copy from one range to another. The second section covers how to copy formulas, which includes how to use relative, absolute, and mixed cell addressing.

Note

> Copying information with the Copy command produces the same result as using the Edit Copy (CTRL-INS) command followed by Edit Paste (SHIFT-INS). However, the Edit Copy command copies the information from the worksheet to the clipboard. You can then use Edit Paste to copy (paste) the information from the clipboard to one or more locations. See "Using the Clipboard to Cut and Paste," later in this chapter.

When you select the Copy command, Confirm (✓), Cancel (X), and Options (. . .) icons are now displayed in the Control line, as shown in Figure 4–15. Click on the Cancel (X) icon at any time during the Copy command to abort the operation. Click on the Confirm (✓) icon at the end of the Copy command to complete the operation. By clicking on the Options (. . .) icon, you can access the Copy Options dialog box to gain more control over what is copied between cells.

FIGURE 4–15 The Copy Control line

Note

As with 1-2-3/G's other cut and paste commands, you can make a selection before using the Copy command. 1-2-3/G automatically applies the entire selection to the From range and the current cell pointer location to the To range. (See Chapter 1 for more on selecting cells.)

Copying a Single Cell

Suppose you have the worksheet in Figure 4–16 and you want to copy the value 32.5 in cell A1 to another location. Regardless of the destination you specify, you always specify a single-cell From range the same way. Perform the following steps:

1. Starting with the cell pointer in cell A:A1, select the Copy command. 1-2-3/G displays a "From:" prompt, followed by the current selection in the form of a range, A:A1..A:A1.
2. Confirm this cell as your From range in either of the following ways:

   - Press ENTER.
   - Using the mouse, click to the right of the "To:" prompt. (You cannot use the Confirm (✓) icon in the Control line during this step.)

   1-2-3/G now prompts you for a To range. You can copy the information in one cell to any of the following locations:

   - Another cell in the same worksheet or a different worksheet.
   - A range in the same worksheet, a different worksheet, or multiple worksheets.

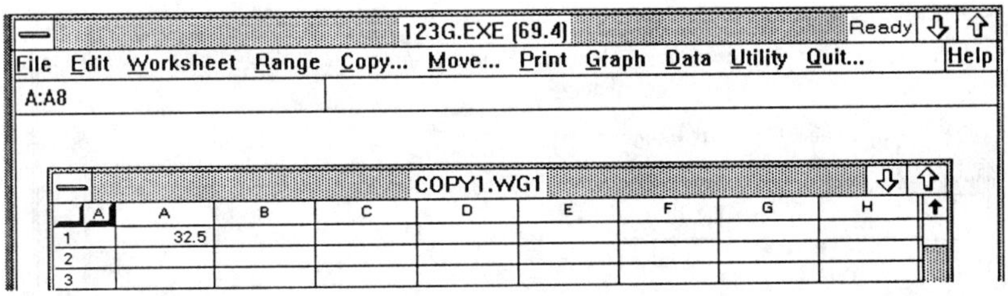

123G.EXE (69.4) Ready
File Edit Worksheet Range Copy... Move... Print Graph Data Utility Quit... Help
A:A8
COPY1.WG1

A	A	B	C	D	E	F	G	H
1	32.5							
2								
3								

FIGURE 4–16 A sample worksheet

- A collection in the same worksheet, a different worksheet, or multiple worksheets.

Copying to a Single Cell

The most basic form of copy operation copies the information in one cell to another cell within the same worksheet. Returning to the example in Figure 4–16, suppose you want to copy the value in cell A:A1, 32.5, to cell A:C1.

After you have specified your From range, A:A1, 1-2-3/G prompts you for a To range, followed by the current location of the cell pointer, cell A:A1. Use any of the following methods to specify your To range, A:C1:

- Type **A:C1**, or just **C1**.
- Use the keyboard to highlight the cell. After you specify your From range, the cell pointer is unanchored in A:A1. Press → twice to position the cell pointer in cell A:C1.
- Use the mouse to click on A:C1.

The single-cell To range A:A3..A:A3 is now displayed in the Control line. Press ENTER or click on the Confirm (✓) icon in the Control line to complete the operation.

1-2-3/G copies the value 32.5 in cell A:A1 to cell A:C1, as shown in Figure 4–17. It also copies the settings of this cell, including the format and attributes.

Copying to a Range, Collection, or Worksheet

You can also copy the information in cell A:A1 of Figure 4–16 to a location that contains more than one cell, including any of the following:

- A range.
- A collection.
- An entire worksheet (or worksheets).

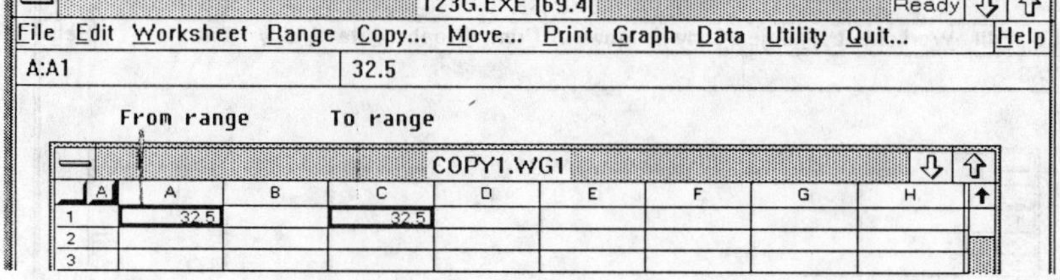

FIGURE 4–17 Copying a single cell to a single cell

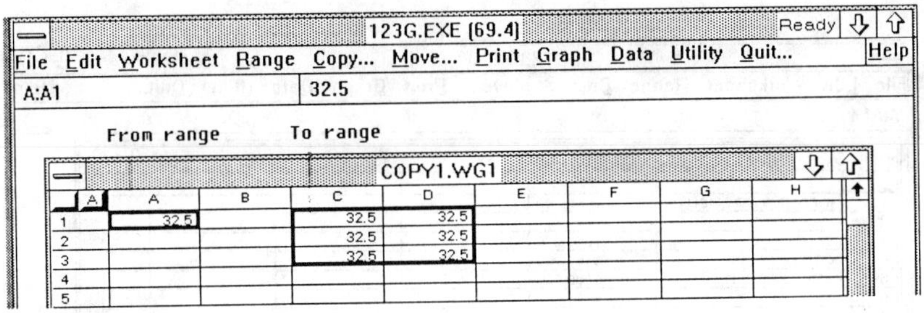

A	A	B	C	D	E	F	G	H
1	32.5		32.5	32.5				
2			32.5	32.5				
3			32.5	32.5				
4								
5								

FIGURE 4–18 Copying a single cell to a range

In all cases the results will be the same. 1-2-3/G copies the information in cell A:A1 to *each* cell in your To range. (For information on copying between files, see "Copying between Files" later in this chapter.)

For example, imagine you have the worksheet in Figure 4–16 and you want to copy the information in cell A:A1 to the range A:C1..A:D3. After you specify your From range, A:A1, use any of the following methods to specify your To range, A:C1..A:D3:

- Type **A:C1..A:D3**, or just **C1..D3**.
- Highlight the range using the keyboard. Press → twice to move the cell pointer to cell A:C1. Then press . (period) to anchor the cell pointer in A:C1. Now press ↓ twice and → once to highlight the range A:C1..A:D3.
- Highlight the range using the mouse. Click on cell C:C1, and keeping the left button depressed, drag the pointer so that the range A:C1..A:D3 is highlighted.

The To range A:C1..A:D3 is now displayed in the Control line. To complete the Copy command, press ENTER or click on the Confirm (✓) icon in the Control line.

1-2-3/G copies the value 32.5 to *all* cells in the range A:C1..A:D3, as shown in Figure 4–18. It also copies the settings of cell A:A1, including the format and attributes, to all the cells in this range.

Copying a Two-Dimensional Range

In many instances, you will use the Copy command to copy a two-dimensional range to another location. For example, suppose you want to copy the 2–D range in A:A1..A:B5 of Figure 4–19. Regardless of the To range you specify, the

123G.EXE (69.4) Ready

File Edit Worksheet Range Copy... Move... Print Graph Data Utility Quit... Help

A:A14

COPY7.WG1

A	A	B	C	D	E
1	INCOME STATEMENT	31-Mar-90			
2					
3	SALES	$500,000			
4	COGS	$150,000			
5	GROSS PROFIT	$350,000			
6					
7					

FIGURE 4–19 A sample worksheet

manner in which you specify a two-dimensional From range is always the same. Just use the following procedure:

1. Position the cell pointer in cell A:A1 and select the Copy command. 1-2-3/G displays the prompt "From:", followed by the current selection in the form of a range, A:A1..A:A1.
2. Specify your From range, A:A1..A:B5, using any of the following methods:

   - Type in the range **A:A1..A:B5** or **A1..B5**.
   - Highlight the range using the keyboard. Since the cell pointer is anchored in cell A:A1, simply press → once, then ↓ four times to highlight the range A:A1..A:B5.
   - Highlight the range using the mouse. Click on A:A1, then keeping the left button depressed, drag the pointer so that the range A:A1..A:B5 is highlighted.

   The From range A:A1..A:B5 is now displayed in the Control line.

3. Press ENTER, or click to the right of the "To:" prompt. (You cannot use the Confirm (✓) icon in the Control line during this step.)

When you use 1-2-3/G's Copy command to copy a range, you can copy it to any of the following:

- A range within the same worksheet.
- A range in a different worksheet.
- Ranges in multiple worksheets.

The way you choose each of these different locations within the same file is discussed below. Copying to another file is discussed under "Copying between Files," later in this chapter.

Note

> Because the Copy command writes over any existing information in your To range, make sure you scan the area surrounding the range before performing the copy. Of course, if the Copy command should overwrite some important information, you can press ALT-BACKSPACE to restore your work.

Copying to a Range in the Same Worksheet

The easiest multicell copy operation is when you copy a two-dimensional range to a range of equal size and shape within the same worksheet. For example, suppose you want to copy the information in the range A:A1..A:B5 in Figure 4–19 to the range A:D1..A:E5.

After you have specified your From range A:A1..A:B5 as described above, 1-2-3/G prompts you for your To range. Simply specify the upper-left cell in your To range, which is where you want the information in the upper-left cell of your From range to be copied to. (If you specify a larger To range, 1-2-3/G ignores all but the upper-left cell.)

In the current example, you want the information in cell A:A1 to be copied to cell A:D1. Use any of the following methods to specify this To range:

- Type **A:D1** or just **D1**.
- Use the keyboard to highlight the cell. After you specify your From range, the cell pointer is unanchored in cell A:A1. Press → twice to position the cell pointer in cell A:D1.
- Use the mouse to click on A:D1.

The To selection A:D1 is now displayed in the Control line. To complete the Copy command, either press ENTER, or click on the Confirm (✓) icon in the Control line.

1-2-3/G copies information and the settings in the range A:A1..A:B5 to the range A:D1..A:E5, as shown in Figure 4–20. All of the formats and attributes (in this example, the Date and Currency formatting) are also copied to this location. Notice, however, that the column width settings are not copied. To see the full width of the long labels in column D, you must widen the column (see Chapter 3).

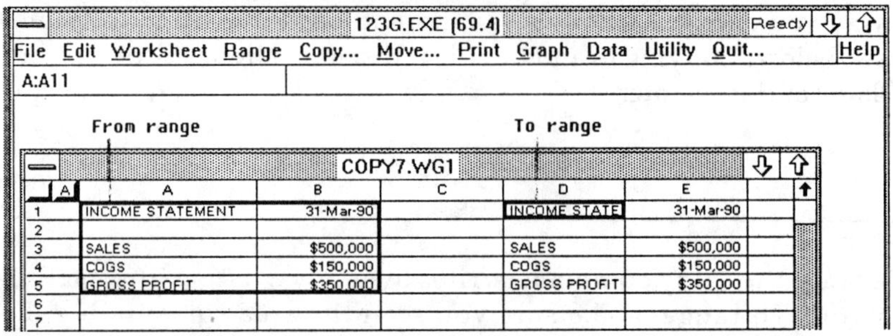

123G.EXE [69.4] Ready

File Edit Worksheet Range Copy... Move... Print Graph Data Utility Quit... Help

A:A11

From range   To range

COPY7.WG1

A	A	B	C	D	E
1	INCOME STATEMENT	31-Mar-90		INCOME STATE	31-Mar-90
2					
3	SALES	$500,000		SALES	$500,000
4	COGS	$150,000		COGS	$150,000
5	GROSS PROFIT	$350,000		GROSS PROFIT	$350,000
6					
7					

FIGURE 4–20 **Copying a range within the same worksheet**

Note

By specifying a collection for your To range, you can have 1-2-3/G copy your From range to more than one location at a time. For example, to have 1-2-3/G copy the range in Figure 4–19 to both A:D1..A:E5 and A:G1..H5, specify the collection D1,G1 for your To range.

Copying to a Range in Another Worksheet

Now suppose you want to copy the information in the range A:A1..A:B5 in Figure 4–19 to the range B:A1..B:B5. As in the previous example, you only have to specify the upper-left cell of your To range, B:A1. Use any of the following methods:

- Type **B:A1**.
- Use the keyboard. After you specify your From range, the cell pointer is unanchored in A:A1. Press CTRL-PGUP to move the cell pointer to cell B:A1.
- Use the mouse to click on cell B:A1.

The To Range B:A1 is now displayed in the Control line. To complete the Copy command, either press ENTER or click on the Confirm (✓) icon in the Control line.

Figure 4–21 shows the results of this Copy operation. All the information in the range A:A1..A:B5, including formats and other settings, is copied to the range B:A1..B:B5.

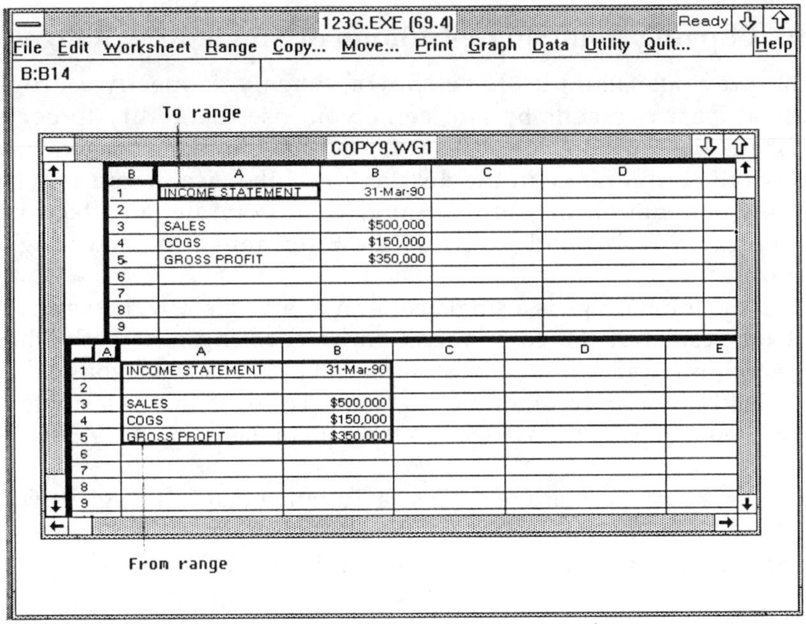

FIGURE 4–21 Copying a range to another worksheet

Note

In Figure 4–21, column A of worksheet B was widened to display the full width of the long labels. You can also use the Worksheet Global Group Command to keep the column widths consistent in worksheets A and B.

Copying to Multiple Worksheets

Suppose you want to copy the information in the range A:A1..A:B5 of Figure 4–19 to the same position in worksheets B *and* C (that is, to the range B:A1..B:B5 and C:A1..C:B5). After selecting the Copy command, begin by specifying your From range, A:A1..A:B5, in the usual fashion. Then, when 1-2-3/G prompts you for a To range, perform either of the following:

- Specify the range B:B1..C:C1.
- Specify the collection B:B1,C:B1.

1-2-3/G then copies the range A:A1..A:B5 to *both* worksheets B and C.

Copying from Single-Column or Single-Row Ranges

As the previous examples have shown, when you specify a From range that is at least two cells by two cells, you lose the ability to control the size of the destination range. That is, 1-2-3/G mimics the same size and shape of the From range in the destination. Likewise, if you specify more than one destination in your To range—for example, a collection— 1-2-3/G mimics the size and shape of the From range in each range in the collection.

When the From range is a single column or a single row, however, you can affect the results of the copy operation by choosing differently shaped To ranges. For example, Figure 4–22 shows what happens when you select a From range that is a single column, A1..A3, and a To range that is a single cell, C1. As you would expect, 1-2-3/G copies the data in the range A1..A3 to the range C1..C3.

Suppose, however, that you choose a To range that is a single row, such as E1..G1. 1-2-3/G copies the information in the range A1..A3 three times, to columns E, F, and G, all beginning in row 1. Figure 4–22 shows these results as well.

Conversely, Figure 4–23 shows what happens when you select a From range of A1..C1 in Figure 4–23 and a To range of E1..E3. 1-2-3/G copies the information in the From range three times, to rows 1, 2, and 3, all beginning in column E.

Note

> To copy the values or labels in a column and transpose them to a row (or in a row and transpose them to a column), use the Range Transpose command discussed later in this chapter.

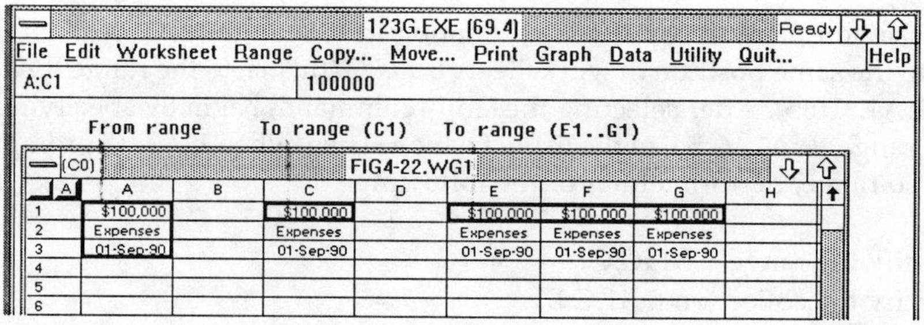

FIGURE 4–22 Copying to a single cell then a single column

123G.EXE (69.4) Ready

File Edit Worksheet Range Copy... Move... Print Graph Data Utility Quit... Help

A:A1 100000

From range To range

(C0) FIG4-23.WG1

A	A	B	C	D	E	F	G	H
1	$100,000	Expenses	01-Sep-90		$100,000	Expenses	01-Sep-90	
2					$100,000	Expenses	01-Sep-90	
3					$100,000	Expenses	01-Sep-90	
4								
5								
6								

FIGURE 4–23 Copying to a single row

Tip: Copying repetitively

As in previous releases, 1-2-3/G has a little-known quirk that you can take advantage of to copy information repetitively. For example, suppose you have created the form in Figure 4–24, and you want to copy this pattern down the length of your worksheet. (Notice that the grid lines have been removed to show that cell borders have been set. Use the Worksheet Global Screen Attributes Settings Grid lines command to control grid lines. See Chapter 3.)

There are two tricks to copying repetitively. First, specify your From range as the entire area of the worksheet you want the headings to be copied to. For example, if you want to copy the pattern in A:A1..A:H3 to A:A1..A:H20, specify your From range as A:A1..A:H20. Second, specify your To range as a single cell, but within your From range. If you want your heading to be repeated beginning in cell A:A4, specify your To range as A:A4. The result of this copy operation is shown in Figure 4–25. Notice that the heading is copied over and over within the From range you specified.

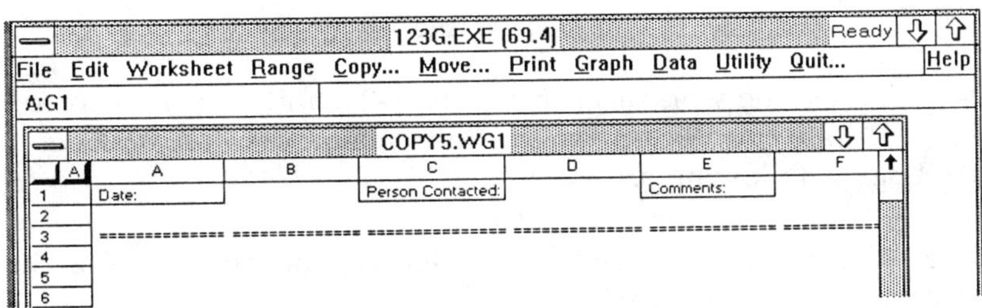

FIGURE 4–24 A sample form

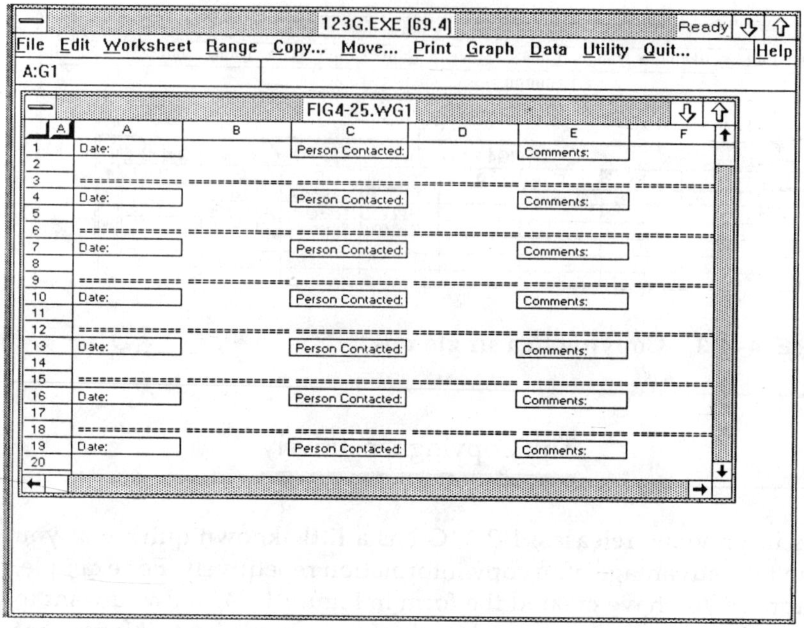

FIGURE 4–25 The results of copying repetitively

Copying a Collection

As mentioned, you can use the Copy command to copy a collection in 1-2-3/G. As you know, a collection is a group of noncontiguous ranges that is treated as a single entity. Each range in a collection can be from the same worksheet, different worksheets, or even different worksheet files (see Chapter 1 for more on collections).

Why would you use a collection with the Copy command? The advantage is that you can simultaneously copy selected ranges, yet keep the relationship (spacing) between those ranges intact. In previous editions of 1-2-3, you had to copy each range separately.

An Example

Suppose you have the worksheet in Figure 4–26, and you want to copy the collection A:B1..A:F2,A:A3..A:A5 so that the contents of cell A:B1 are copied to cell A:B8. Use the following procedure:

1. Locate the cell pointer in the upper-left cell in the first range in your collection, in this case, cell A:B1.
2. Select the Copy command. 1-2-3/G displays the "From:" prompt, followed by the current selection in the form of a range, A:B1..A:B1.

123G.EXE (69.4) Ready

File Edit Worksheet Range Copy... Move... Print Graph Data Utility Quit... Help

A:B1 "Q Ended

COPY12.WG1

A	A	B	C	D	E	F	G
1		Q Ended	Q Ended	Q Ended	Q Ended	Year Ended	
2	SCENARIO 1	31-Mar-90	30-Jun-90	30-Sep-90	31-Dec-90	31-Dec-90	
3	Sales	$500,000	$800,000	$500,000	$200,000	$2,000,000	
4	COGS	$250,000	$400,000	$250,000	$100,000	$1,000,000	
5	Gross Profit	$250,000	$400,000	$250,000	$100,000	$1,000,000	
6							
7							
8							

FIGURE 4–26 A sample worksheet

3. Specify your From range as a collection using any of the following methods:

    - Type in **A:B1..A:F2,A:A3..A:A5** or just **B1..F2,A3..A5**.
    - Use the keyboard to highlight the collection. Since the cell pointer is anchored in cell A:B1, press END then →, followed by ↓. The range A:B1..A:F2 is now highlighted. Press DETACH (SHIFT-F8) to detach the cell pointer from this range. Next, move the cell pointer to cell A:A3 and while holding down the SHIFT key, press ↓ twice so that the range A:A3..A:A5 is also highlighted.
    - Use the mouse to highlight the collection. Click on cell A:B1, and keeping the left button depressed, drag the pointer so that the range A:B1..A:F2 is highlighted. Next, using the right mouse button, click on cell A:A3, and keeping the button depressed, drag the pointer so that the range A:A3..A;A5 is also highlighted.

The From collection A:B1..A:F2,A:A3..A:A5 is now displayed in the Control line and highlighted on your screen.

4. Press ENTER or click to the right of the To prompt in the Control line. (You cannot use the Confirm (✓) icon during this step.)
5. Specify your To range. Note that when you are copying a collection, you need to specify only a single cell address, the upper-left cell of the first range in collection. Use any of the following methods to specify your To range as cell A:B8:

    - Type **A:B8** or simply **B8**.
    - Use the keyboard to highlight A:B8.
    - Use the mouse to click on cell A:B8.

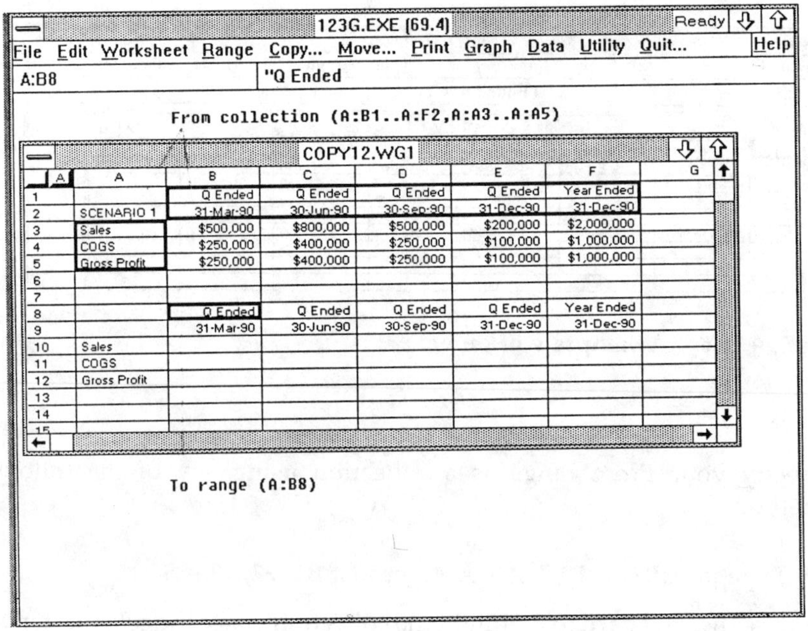

123G.EXE (69.4) Ready

File Edit Worksheet Range Copy... Move... Print Graph Data Utility Quit... Help

A:B8 "Q Ended

From collection (A:B1..A:F2,A:A3..A:A5)

COPY12.WG1

A	A	B	C	D	E	F	G
1		Q Ended	Q Ended	Q Ended	Q Ended	Year Ended	
2	SCENARIO 1	31-Mar-90	30-Jun-90	30-Sep-90	31-Dec-90	31-Dec-90	
3	Sales	$500,000	$800,000	$500,000	$200,000	$2,000,000	
4	COGS	$250,000	$400,000	$250,000	$100,000	$1,000,000	
5	Gross Profit	$250,000	$400,000	$250,000	$100,000	$1,000,000	
6							
7							
8		Q Ended	Q Ended	Q Ended	Q Ended	Year Ended	
9		31-Mar-90	30-Jun-90	30-Sep-90	31-Dec-90	31-Dec-90	
10	Sales						
11	COGS						
12	Gross Profit						
13							
14							

To range (A:B8)

FIGURE 4–27 Copying a 2–D collection within a worksheet

The To range A:B8 is now displayed in the Control line. To complete the Copy command, either press ENTER, or click on the Confirm (✓) icon in the Control line. The results of this copy operation are displayed in Figure 4–27.

Another Example

As another example, suppose you want to copy the same collection as in the previous example, A:B1..A:F2,A:A3..A:A5, but you want to copy this collection to both worksheets B and C, beginning in cell B1 in each worksheet (Figure 4–28). To do so, you must specify a 3–D To range.

You specify a 3–D To range differently, depending on whether you use the keyboard or the mouse. After you have selected the From collection A:B1..A:F2,A:A3..A;A5 as described above, 1-2-3/G prompts you for a To range, followed by the current location of the cell pointer, A:B1. As in the previous example, you must specify the upper-left cell of the To range, but in this case, you must specify it for each worksheet where you want the collection copied. Specify the To range using any of the following methods:

- Type in the range **B:B1..C:B1**. Notice that this is a continuous range spanning both worksheets B and C.
- Use the keyboard to specify the range B:B1..C:B1. After you specify your From range, the cell pointer is unanchored in cell A:B1. Press CTRL-PGUP to locate

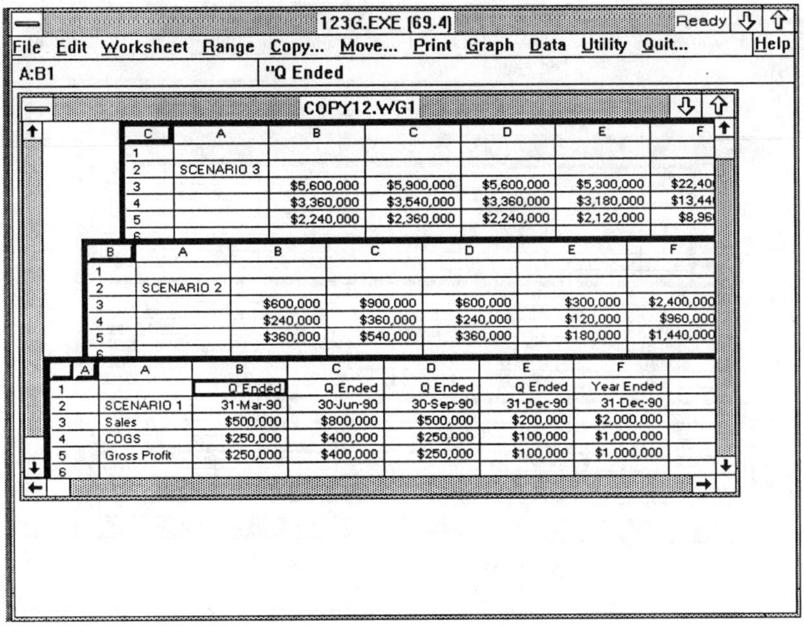

123G.EXE (69.4) Ready

File Edit Worksheet Range Copy... Move... Print Graph Data Utility Quit... Help

A:B1 "Q Ended

COPY12.WG1

C	A	B	C	D	E	F
1						
2	SCENARIO 3					
3		$5,600,000	$5,900,000	$5,600,000	$5,300,000	$22,40
4		$3,360,000	$3,540,000	$3,360,000	$3,180,000	$13,44
5		$2,240,000	$2,360,000	$2,240,000	$2,120,000	$8,96

B	A	B	C	D	E	F
1						
2	SCENARIO 2					
3		$600,000	$900,000	$600,000	$300,000	$2,400,000
4		$240,000	$360,000	$240,000	$120,000	$960,000
5		$360,000	$540,000	$360,000	$180,000	$1,440,000

A	A	B	C	D	E	F
1		Q Ended	Q Ended	Q Ended	Q Ended	Year Ended
2	SCENARIO 1	31-Mar-90	30-Jun-90	30-Sep-90	31-Dec-90	31-Dec-90
3	Sales	$500,000	$800,000	$500,000	$200,000	$2,000,000
4	COGS	$250,000	$400,000	$250,000	$100,000	$1,000,000
5	Gross Profit	$250,000	$400,000	$250,000	$100,000	$1,000,000
6						

FIGURE 4–28 The sample worksheet file set for perspective mode

the cell pointer in cell B:B1, then press . (period) to anchor the cell pointer in that cell. Next, press CTRL-PGUP again and the cell pointer is now located in cell C:B1. The 3–D range B:B1..C:B1 is highlighted and is displayed in the Control line.

- Use the mouse to specify your To range as a collection. Click on cell B:B1, then using the right mouse button, click on cell C:B1. The To collection B:B1,C:B1 is now displayed in the Control line.

To complete the Copy command, either press ENTER, or click on the Confirm (✓) icon in the Control line.

Figure 4–29 shows the results of the copy operation. Notice that 1-2-3/G has copied the collection twice, to both worksheet B and worksheet C. In both cases, it has maintained the relationship (space) between each range in the collection.

Copying a Three-Dimensional Range

You can also use the Copy command to copy information in 3–D ranges (ranges spanning more than one worksheet). For example, suppose you have the

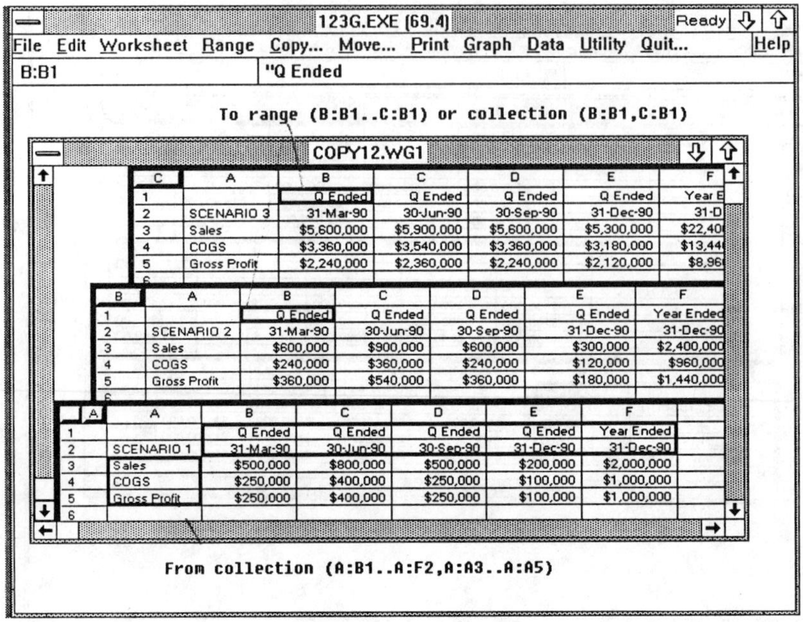

123G.EXE (69.4) Ready

File Edit Worksheet Range Copy... Move... Print Graph Data Utility Quit... Help

B:B1 "Q Ended

To range (B:B1..C:B1) or collection (B:B1,C:B1)

COPY12.WG1

C	A	B	C	D	E	F
1		Q Ended	Q Ended	Q Ended	Q Ended	Year E
2	SCENARIO 3	31-Mar-90	30-Jun-90	30-Sep-90	31-Dec-90	31-D
3	Sales	$5,600,000	$5,900,000	$5,600,000	$5,300,000	$22,40
4	COGS	$3,360,000	$3,540,000	$3,360,000	$3,180,000	$13,44
5	Gross Profit	$2,240,000	$2,360,000	$2,240,000	$2,120,000	$8,96

B	A	B	C	D	E	F
1		Q Ended	Q Ended	Q Ended	Q Ended	Year Ended
2	SCENARIO 2	31-Mar-90	30-Jun-90	30-Sep-90	31-Dec-90	31-Dec-90
3	Sales	$600,000	$900,000	$600,000	$300,000	$2,400,000
4	COGS	$240,000	$360,000	$240,000	$120,000	$960,000
5	Gross Profit	$360,000	$540,000	$360,000	$180,000	$1,440,000

A	A	B	C	D	E	F
1		Q Ended	Q Ended	Q Ended	Q Ended	Year Ended
2	SCENARIO 1	31-Mar-90	30-Jun-90	30-Sep-90	31-Dec-90	31-Dec-90
3	Sales	$500,000	$800,000	$500,000	$200,000	$2,000,000
4	COGS	$250,000	$400,000	$250,000	$100,000	$1,000,000
5	Gross Profit	$250,000	$400,000	$250,000	$100,000	$1,000,000
6						

From collection (A:B1..A:F2,A:A3..A:A5)

FIGURE 4–29 **After copying a 2–D collection to worksheets B and C**

worksheets in Figure 4–30, and you want to copy the values in the 3–D range A:A1..B:B4 to the range C:A1..D:B4. Perform the following:

1. With the cell pointer located in cell A:A1, select the Copy command. 1-2-3/G displays the prompt "From:", followed by the current selection in the form of a range, A:A1..A:A1.
2. Specify your From range A:A1..B:B4 using any of the following methods:

- Type in the 3–D range **A:A1..B:B4**.
- Highlight the range using the keyboard. Since the cell pointer is anchored in A:A1, press END then ↓ followed by →. The range A:A1..A:B4 is now highlighted. Next, press CTRL-PGUP so that the 3–D range A:A1..B:B4 is highlighted. The From range A:A1..B:B4 is now displayed in the Control line.
- Highlight the range using the mouse. You must specify your From range as a collection. Click on A:A1, then drag the pointer so that the range A:A1..A:B4 is highlighted. Next, using the right mouse button, click on B:A1, then drag the pointer so the range B:A1..B:B4 is also highlighted. The From collection A:A1..A:B4,B:A1..B:B4 is now displayed in the Control line.

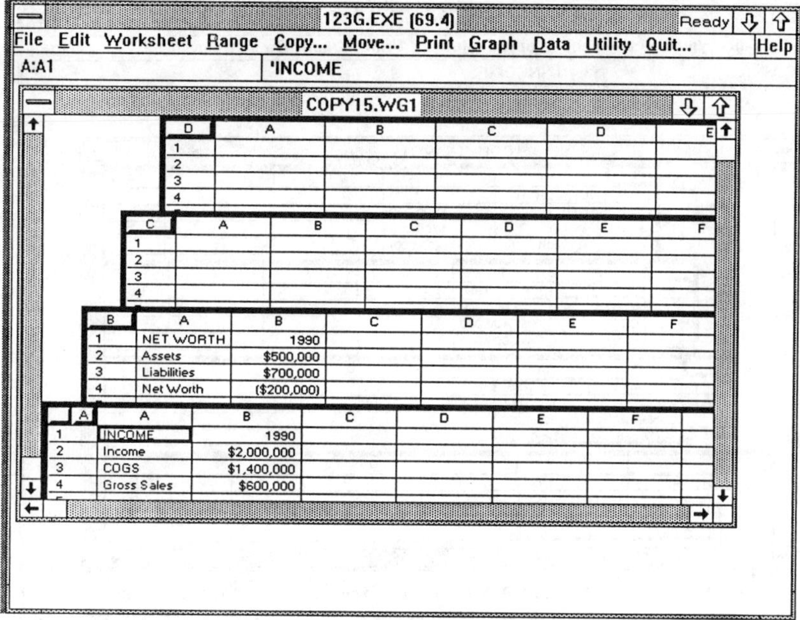

FIGURE 4–30 **Some sample worksheets**

3. Press ENTER, or click to the right of the To prompt. (You cannot use the Confirm (✓) icon in the Control line during this step.)
4. Specify your To range. Remember, you only have to specify the upper-left cell of your To range, C:C1. Use any of the following methods:

   - Type **C:C1**.
   - Use the keyboard to highlight the cell. Press CTRL-PGUP twice to locate the cell pointer in cell C:C1.
   - Use the mouse to click on cell C:C1.

   The To range C:C1 is now displayed in the Control line.

5. Press ENTER or click on the Confirm (✓) icon in the Control line.

Figure 4–31 shows the results. Notice that even in three-dimensional space, 1-2-3/G duplicates the size and shape of your From range in your To range.

Copying Entire Worksheets

You can also use 1-2-3/G's Copy command to copy multiple worksheets simultaneously. For example, suppose you want to copy worksheets A and B

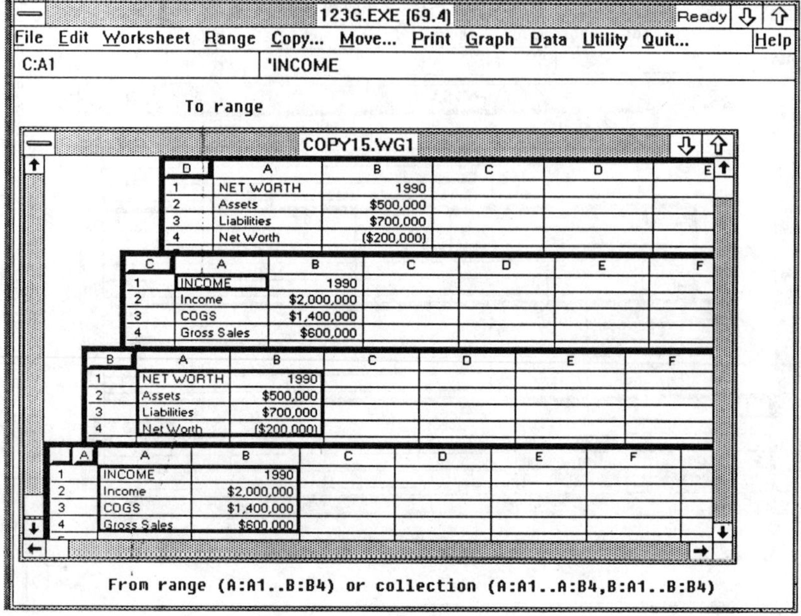

FIGURE 4–31 **After copying a 3-D range**

in Figure 4–30 to worksheets C and D. You would perform the same steps as those in the previous example, except that in step 2 you specify your From range, worksheets A and B, using any of the following methods:

- Type in the collection **A:,B:** or the continuous range **A:..B:**.
- Highlight a continuous range using the keyboard. Press ALT-SHIFT-HOME (make sure to use the HOME on the gray keypad). Worksheet A is now highlighted. Press CTRL-SHIFT-PGUP to highlight both worksheets A and B. The From range A:..B: is now displayed in the Control line.
- Highlight a collection using the mouse. Click on the Worksheet selector button in the top-left corner of worksheet A. Worksheet A is now highlighted. Then, using the right mouse button, click on the Worksheet selector button for worksheet B. Both worksheets A and B are now highlighted and the From collection A:,B: appears in the Control line.

In addition, when specifying your To range in step 4, you need to select only the first cell in your To range, cell A:C1. Use any of the following methods:

- Type **C:A1** or **C:** (to select all of worksheet C).
- Highlight the cell using the keyboard. Press CTRL-PGUP twice to position the cell pointer in C:A1.

- Use the mouse to click on cell C:A1.

When you complete the copy operation, the results will be identical to those in the previous example (Figure 4–31).

Note

> You can also use the Copy command to copy noncontinuous worksheets. For example, suppose you want to copy worksheets A and C to worksheets D and F. Specify your From range as the collection A:,C:. Specify your To range as D:A1 or D: (worksheet D). Remember, 1-2-3/G copies the relationship between ranges in a collection. So 1-2-3/G copies worksheet A to worksheet D, and worksheet C to worksheet F. Worksheet E is unaffected.

Copying between Files

As in Release 3, you can use 1-2-3/G's Copy command to copy information between files. You can copy a single cell, a 2–D or 3–D range, a collection, or a worksheet to another file. You can even copy an entire worksheet file to another file.

Note to Release 2 Users

> In Release 2, recall that you cannot use the Copy command to copy information between files. Instead you must use the /File Combine command to copy information from a file on disk to the file in memory. However, with 1-2-3/G's Copy command, copying between files is much simpler and less prone to error.

Let's look at the example in Figure 4–32. The left-hand window contains the file EXPENSES.WG1. Suppose you want to copy all the information in worksheet A of EXPENSES.WG1 to worksheet A of BUDGET.WG1, the file in the right-hand window. Use the following procedure:

1. Starting with the cell pointer located in cell A:A1 of EXPENSES.WG1, select the Copy command. The "From:" prompt is displayed followed by the current selection in the form of a range, A:A1..A:A1.
2. Specify your To range, worksheet A of EXPENSES.WG1, using any of the following methods:

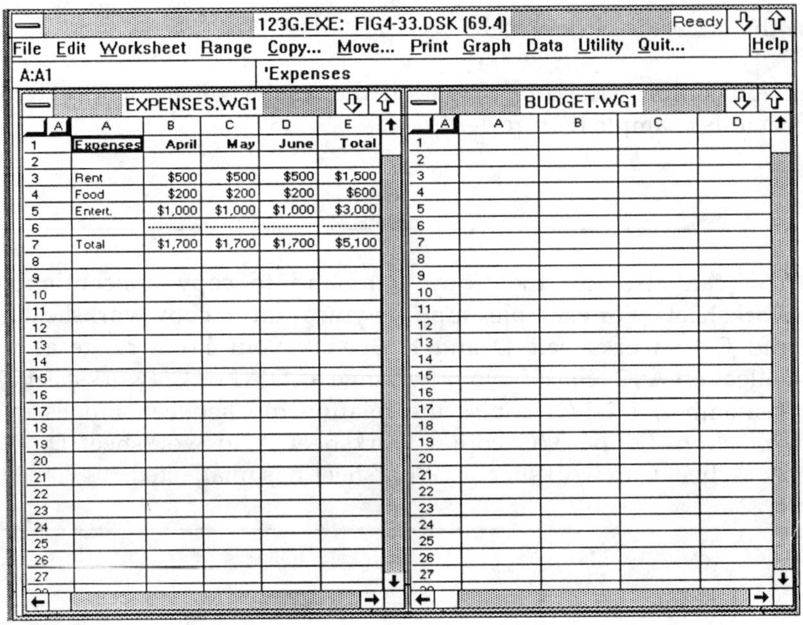

123G.EXE: FIG4-33.DSK [69.4] Ready

File Edit Worksheet Range Copy... Move... Print Graph Data Utility Quit... Help

A:A1 'Expenses

EXPENSES.WG1

A	A	B	C	D	E
1	Expenses	April	May	June	Total
2					
3	Rent	$500	$500	$500	$1,500
4	Food	$200	$200	$200	$600
5	Entert.	$1,000	$1,000	$1,000	$3,000
6		----------	----------	----------	----------
7	Total	$1,700	$1,700	$1,700	$5,100

BUDGET.WG1

FIGURE 4–32 Two files on the Desktop

- Type **A:**.
- Using the keyboard, simply press ALT-SHIFT-HOME (make sure you use the HOME key on the gray keypad).
- Using the mouse, click on the Worksheet selector button for worksheet A.

Worksheet A is now highlighted and A: is now displayed following the "From:" prompt in the Control line.

3. Press ENTER, or click to the right of the "To:" prompt.
4. Specify your To range, cell A:A1 of BUDGET.WG1. Use any of the following methods:

- Type in the filename enclosed in double-angle brackets (the extension is optional) followed by the cell reference, <BUDGET.WG1>A:A1.
- Using the keyboard, press NEXT WINDOW (CTRL-F6) to move the cell pointer to cell A:A1 of BUDGET.WG1.
- Using the mouse, click on cell A:A1 in BUDGET.WG1.

Worksheet A in BUDGET is now highlighted and the To range is displayed as <BUDGET.WG1>A1: in the Control line.

5. Press ENTER, or click on the Confirm (✓) icon in the Control line.

Figure 4–33 shows the results. Copying information to another file produces the same results as copying information within a file. That is, the Copy command copies all formulas in your From range in EXPENSES.WG1 to your To range in BUDGET.WG1. All the settings, attributes, and notes are copied as well.

Note

In the previous example, when you copy worksheet A from one file to the other, 1-2-3/G does not copy the associated column width settings. For example, in Figure 4–33 notice how the column widths vary between the two worksheet files. In fact, whenever you copy an entire column, row, worksheet, and/or worksheet file, 1-2-3/G does not normally copy any of the associated attributes and settings—column widths, row heights, global worksheet settings, and the like. If you want to copy these settings to the To range, select the All attributes copied option from the Copy Options dialog box.

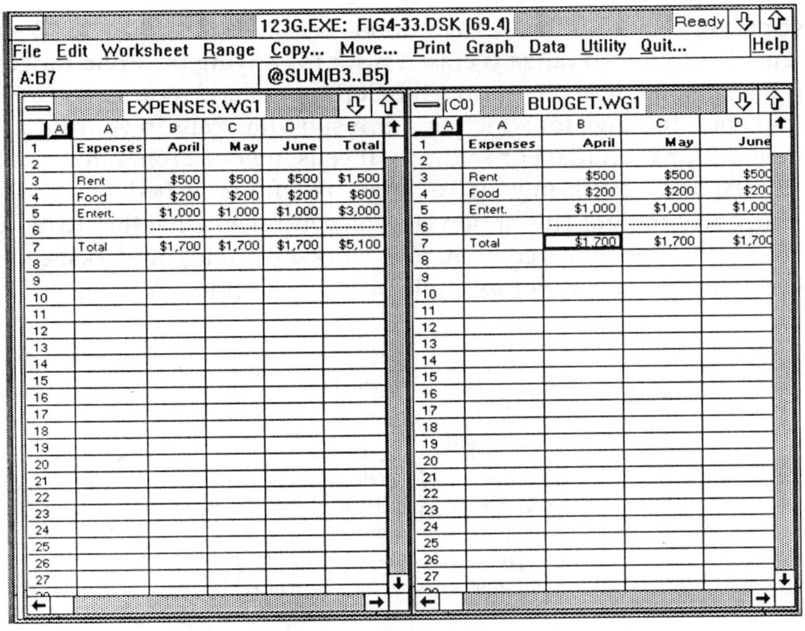

FIGURE 4–33 After copying information between two open files

The Copy Options Dialog Box

As mentioned, you can use the Copy Options dialog box to specify what types of information are copied between your From and To ranges. To display this dialog box, select the Copy command, then click on the Options (. . .) icon in the Control line, or press SHIFT-F3. Your screen appears as in Figure 4–34.

If you do not use the Copy Options dialog box, 1-2-3/G's Copy command copies formulas, values, labels, formats, attributes, and notes of all of the cells in your From range to your To range. It also writes over any information in your To range.

However, by using the new Copy Options dialog box, you can now choose any of the following options to gain more control over what elements are copied:

- **Type of entry:** Lets you choose the type of cell entries that are copied from your From range—labels, numbers, and/or formulas. In its default state, 1-2-3/G copies all of these entries.
- **Contents:** Lets you choose the contents that the cells in your To range receive—formulas, values, notes, and/or settings. For example, by turning off the Formulas option and leaving the Values option on, you can have 1-2-3/G copy values in place of formulas (which produces the same result as the Range Value command). As another example, by turning off the Notes option, you can prevent 1-2-3/G from copying to the To range any notes you may have created for the From range cells. The default setting is to copy all contents—formulas, values, notes, and settings.
- **Destination cleared:** When this option is selected (the default), all existing information in the To range is erased prior to copying the From range to the To range. If you cancel this option, the Copy command writes over only those cells in your To range for which the corresponding cells in your From range contain information (data or settings). If cells in your From range are blank, the corresponding cells in your To range are left untouched.
- **All attributes copied:** This option lets you control whether the attributes and settings associated with a column, row, worksheet, and/or worksheet file are copied to the To range. For example, when this option is selected, and you

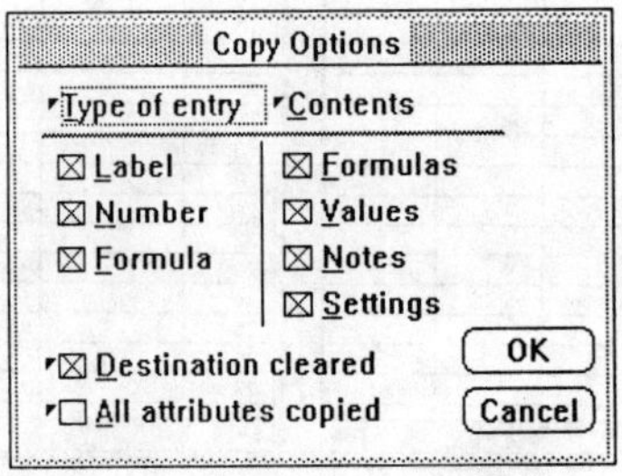

Copy Options
Type of entry | Contents
☒ Label | ☒ Formulas
☒ Number | ☒ Values
☒ Formula | ☒ Notes
☒ Settings
☒ Destination cleared — OK
☐ All attributes copied — Cancel

FIGURE 4–34 The Copy Options dialog box

copy an entire column to a new location, the column width setting is also copied. The default is not to copy any of these settings and attributes.

Each of these Options is discussed in more detail below.

You can activate the Copy Options dialog box at any time during the Copy command. After completing a Copy command, the Copy Options dialog box always reverts to the default settings shown in Figure 4–34. If you cancel the dialog box by pressing ESC, or by clicking on the cancel button, the dialog box also reverts to these default settings.

The Type of Entry Option

Typically, when you copy information using 1-2-3/G's Copy command, you automatically copy all cells in your From range to your To range. However, the Type of entry options in the Copy Options dialog box allow you to limit 1-2-3/G's copying to certain types of cell entries. The Type of entry options you can select are Label, Number, and/or Formula.

For example, suppose you have the worksheet in Figure 4–35. Column A contains labels, values, and formulas. Now let's turn off each of the Type of entry options in turn, and compare the results to the entries in column A.

First, the entries in column A were copied to column C with the Label option turned off (only the Number and Formula options were selected).

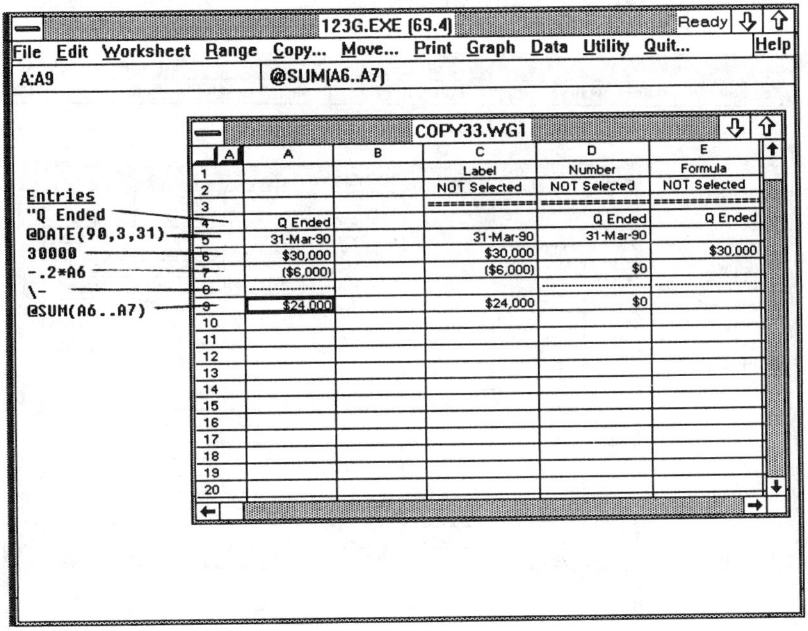

123G.EXE (69.4) Ready

File Edit Worksheet Range Copy... Move... Print Graph Data Utility Quit... Help

A:A9 @SUM(A6..A7)

COPY33.WG1

Entries
"Q Ended
@DATE(90,3,31)
30000
-.2*A6
\-
@SUM(A6..A7)

	A	B	C	D	E
1			Label	Number	Formula
2			NOT Selected	NOT Selected	NOT Selected
3			============	============	============
4	Q Ended			Q Ended	Q Ended
5	31-Mar-90		31-Mar-90	31-Mar-90	
6	$30,000		$30,000		$30,000
7	($6,000)		($6,000)	$0	
8	------------			------------	------------
9	$24,000		$24,000	$0	

FIGURE 4–35 Effect of the Type of entry option in the Copy Options dialog box

Notice that all the entries in the From range were copied to the To range except the labels "Q Ended" in cell A4 and "\-" in cell A8.

Next, the entries were copied to column D with the Number option turned off (only the Label and Formula options were selected). Notice that all entries in From range were copied to the To range, except the value $30,000 in cell A6. As a result, while the formulas in cells A7 and A9 were copied to column D, they now return 0 because they reference cell D6, which is now blank.

Finally, the entries were copied to column E with the Formula option turned off (only the Label and Number options were selected). Notice that the @DATE function in cell A5 was not copied to column E because 1-2-3/G considers it a formula. Likewise, the formulas in cells A7 and A9 were not copied.

The Contents Option

As mentioned, when you copy information using 1-2-3/G's Copy command and you do not use the Copy Options dialog box, you automatically copy all cell contents in your From range to your To range. However, by accessing the Contents options in the Copy Options dialog box, you can choose the type of contents that the cells in your To range receive. The Contents options you can select are Formulas, Values, Notes, and/or Settings options.

For example, suppose you have made the entries in column A of the worksheet in Figure 4-36. Notice that just as in the previous example, column A contains labels, values, and formulas. Columns C, D, E, and F show what

123/G (69.4) Ready

File Edit Worksheet Range Copy... Move... Print Graph Data Utility Quit... Help

A:C9 24000

COPY34.WG1

Entries		A	B	C	D	E	F
	1			Formulas	Values	Settings	Notes
	2			NOT Selected	NOT Selected	NOT Selected	NOT Selected
	3			===========	===========	===========	===========
"Q Ended	4	Q Ended		Q Ended		Q Ended	Q Ended
@DATE(90,3,31)	5	31-Mar-90		31-Mar-90	31-Mar-90	32963	31-Mar-90
30000	6	$30,000		$30,000		30000	$30,000
-.2*A6	7	($6,000)		($6,000)	$0	-6000	($6,000)
\-	8	----------		----------			----------
@SUM(A6..A7)	9	$24,000		$24,000	$0	24000	$24,000

FIGURE 4–36 Selecting different Contents options

happens when you turn off each of the Contents options in turn and copy the entries in column A to each column.

The entries in column A were first copied to column C with only the Formula option turned off (Values, Notes, and Settings were selected). Notice in the Control line that only the result of the formula in cell A9 was copied from cell A9 to cell C9; it has been changed from a formula into a value.

If you unselect the Copy Options Contents Formulas option, any formulas in the From range are *converted* into the resulting values in the To range. This produces a different result than when you turn off the Copy Options Type of entry Formula selection, which does not copy any formulas in the From range to the Destination range.

Note

> Selecting the Contents option from the Copy Options dialog box performs the same function as the Range Value command discussed later in this chapter. 1-2-3/G copies values and labels to the To range, not their underlying formulas.

Next, column D shows the results when only the Value option is turned off (Formulas, Notes, and Settings were selected). Notice that the value $30,000 in cell A6 was not copied to column D; neither were the labels "Q Ended" and "\-". The formulas in cells A7 and A9 were copied but now return 0 because they reference cell D6, which is now blank. This produces the same result as when you unselect both the Copy Options Type of Entry Label and Number selections.

Column E shows the results when the Settings option was turned off (only Formulas, Values, and Notes were selected). All the information in column A has been copied to column E. However, all settings (including attributes) have returned to their global settings. For example, the label "Q Ended" is now left-aligned. The date value 32963 is displayed instead of the formatted date "31-Mar-90." All values have returned to the General format, the global value format.

Finally, column F shows what happens when only the Notes option is turned off (only Formulas, Values, and Settings were selected). Again, all the information and settings in column A have been copied to column F. However, any notes for the cells in A:A4..A:A9 have not been copied to the cells in A:F4..A:F9.

The Destination Cleared Option

Normally, 1-2-3/G's Copy command writes over any existing information in the To range. You can now control this through the Destination cleared option in the Copy Options dialog box. As Figure 4–34 shows, in its default state, the Destination cleared option is selected.

To see the effects of the Destination cleared option, suppose you have the worksheet in Figure 4–37, and you want to copy the range A1..B9 to the ranges D1..E9 and G1..H9. Notice that both of these destination ranges already contain existing information. Some of this information, such as the labels "INCOME," "STATEMENT," and "DATE," are in cells that are blank in the range A1..B9.

Figure 4–38 shows the results of copying with the Destination cleared option on and off. First, the range A1..B9 was copied to D1..E9 with the Destination cleared option turned on (the default). Notice that all of the information in the To range is overwritten when 1-2-3/G copies the From range to this destination.

Next, the range A1..B9 was copied to G1..H9 with the Destination clear option turned off. Notice that the nonblank cells—the cells that contain information—in the From range write over the existing information in the To range. However, the information in the To range in cells G1, G2, and G4 is left intact, since the corresponding cells in the From range, A1, A2, and A4 are blank. As you can tell, 1-2-3/G does not write over the existing information in the To range when the cells in the From range are blank.

The All Attributes Copied Option

When you use 1-2-3/G's Copy command to copy an entire column to another column, 1-2-3/G does not normally copy the column width setting—the To column keeps its original column width. Likewise, when you copy an entire

123G.EXE (69.4) Ready

File Edit Worksheet Range Copy... Move... Print Graph Data Utility Quit... Help

A:A1

COPY35.WG1

A	A	B	C	D	E	F	G	H
1				INCOME			INCOME	
2				STATEMENT			STATEMENT	
3								
4		Q Ended		DATE	Q Ended		DATE	Q Ended
5		31-Mar-90			31-Dec-90			31-Dec-90
6	Sales	$30,000		Q Sales	$100,000		Q Sales	$100,000
7	COGS	($6,000)		cogs	($20,000)		cogs	($20,000)
8		----------			----------			----------
9	Gross Profit	$24,000		Profit	$80,000		Profit	$80,000
10								
11								
12								
13								
14								
15								
16								
17								
18								
19								
20								

FIGURE 4–37 Turning off Destination cleared in the Copy Options dialog box

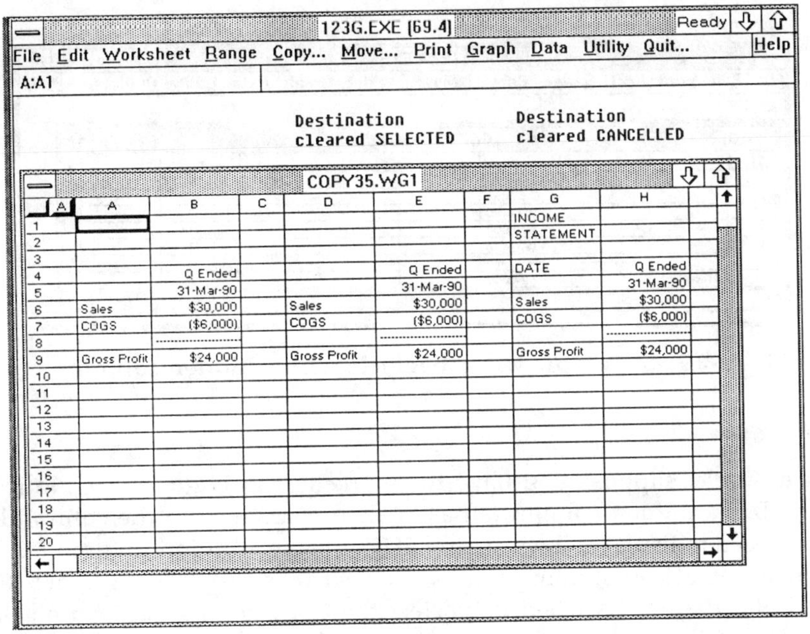

123G.EXE [69.4] Ready

File Edit Worksheet Range Copy... Move... Print Graph Data Utility Quit... Help

A:A1

Destination cleared SELECTED   Destination cleared CANCELLED

COPY35.WG1

A	A	B	C	D	E	F	G	H
1							INCOME	
2							STATEMENT	
3								
4		Q Ended			Q Ended		DATE	Q Ended
5		31-Mar-90			31-Mar-90			31-Mar-90
6	Sales	$30,000		Sales	$30,000		Sales	$30,000
7	COGS	($6,000)		COGS	($6,000)		COGS	($6,000)
8								
9	Gross Profit	$24,000		Gross Profit	$24,000		Gross Profit	$24,000

FIGURE 4–38 After turning Destination cleared on and off in the Copy Options dialog box

row to another location, 1-2-3/G does not normally copy the row height. In fact, whenever you copy an entire column, row, worksheet, or worksheet file, 1-2-3/G does not usually copy any of the associated settings or attributes to the To location.

However, you can now use the All attributes copied option in the Copy Options dialog box to control whether 1-2-3/G copies column, row, worksheet, and worksheet file settings and attributes. Some example settings and attributes are row height, column width, hidden status, global numeric format, global screen attributes, and global label alignment.

Note

For the All attributes copied option to have any effect on the Copy command, you must select an *entire* row, column, worksheet, or worksheet file for the To range. If you select anything less, for example, A:A1..A:A8191 rather than A:A1..A:A8192 or A:A, 1-2-3/G ignores this option.

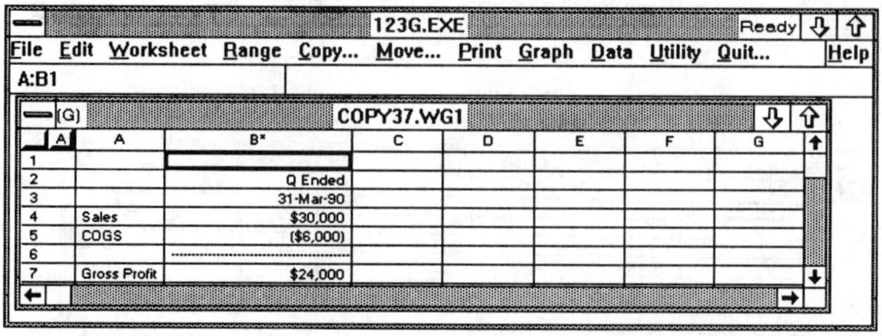

123G.EXE Ready

File Edit Worksheet Range Copy... Move... Print Graph Data Utility Quit... Help

A:B1

(G) COPY37.WG1

A	A	B*	C	D	E	F	G
1							
2		Q Ended					
3		31-Mar-90					
4	Sales	$30,000					
5	COGS	($6,000)					
6		------------------------					
7	Gross Profit	$24,000					

FIGURE 4–39 **A sample worksheet file with a hidden column**

For example, suppose you have the worksheet in Figure 4–39. Notice that column B is a hidden column (an asterisk appears next to the column letter) that has been redisplayed by pressing SHIFT-F6. In addition, column B's width is 20, while all other columns in the worksheet are set to the default of 9. Figure 4–40 shows the results when you select the Copy command, turn on the All attributes copied option in the Copy Options dialog box, and copy column B to D. Notice that as a result of the copy operation, column D now has a column width of 20 and is also a hidden column. (If you press SHIFT-F6 to rehide hidden information, columns B and D will disappear from view.)

Notes on the Copy Command

Keep in mind the following when you use 1-2-3/G's Copy command:

- You can cancel the Copy command at any time during a copy operation. Either press ESC until you return to the Main menu, press CTRL-BREAK, or click on the new Cancel (X) icon in the Control line.

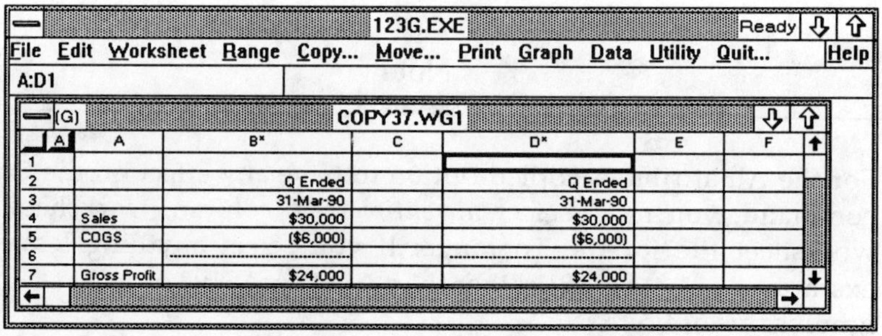

123G.EXE Ready

File Edit Worksheet Range Copy... Move... Print Graph Data Utility Quit... Help

A:D1

(G) COPY37.WG1

A	A	B*	C	D*	E	F
1						
2		Q Ended		Q Ended		
3		31-Mar-90		31-Mar-90		
4	Sales	$30,000		$30,000		
5	COGS	($6,000)		($6,000)		
6		------------------------		------------------------		
7	Gross Profit	$24,000		$24,000		

FIGURE 4–40 **After copying column B to D with the All attributes copied option selected**

- If you should overwrite important information using the Copy command, simply press ALT-BACKSPACE immediately after completing the copy operation to activate 1-2-3/G's Undo feature and cancel the completed command.
- To ensure that you do not write over any hidden information, press SHIFT-F6 before using the Copy command to redisplay hidden information. After completing the Copy command, press SHIFT-F6 again to rehide this information. Of course, you can copy information from or to hidden areas without redisplaying the hidden information, but you run the risk of overwriting it.
- You can copy information and properties from protected cells if the destination range is unprotected. However, to copy information to protected cells, you must first unprotect these cells before you can use the Copy command (see Chapter 3).
- If you want to copy information to another tool on the desktop, say to a graph window or the Note Utility, use the Edit commands instead of Copy. See "Using the Clipboard to Cut and Paste," later.

COPYING FORMULAS

By far the most powerful feature of the Copy command is its ability to copy formulas. This is one of the most time-saving features in 1-2-3/G. However, to maintain accuracy in your worksheet and to efficiently use the Copy command, it is necessary to have an in-depth understanding of how 1-2-3/G copies formulas.

As you know, a formula in 1-2-3/G usually contains at least one cell reference, such as +B1. When you copy a formula to another location in your worksheet, or to another worksheet file, 1-2-3/G automatically adjusts the cell references within the formula to account for the formula's new position. 1-2-3/G adjusts cell references in a formula differently, depending on the type of cell references you have. In 1-2-3/G, you can use any of the following types of cell references:

- relative
- absolute
- mixed

To fully understand how 1-2-3 copies formulas, it is first necessary to understand how 1-2-3 copies each type of cell reference.

Relative References

Without knowing it, most of the formulas you create in 1-2-3/G use relative references. This is the default form of cell referencing in 1-2-3/G. For example, the formula 55+C1+@SUM(A1..A3) contains four relative references—a relative reference to cell C1, and relative references to cells A1, A2, and A3 in the range A1..A3.

How does relative addressing work in 1-2-3/G? When you copy a formula containing a relative address, 1-2-3/G automatically adjusts these cell references *relative* to the new location of the formula.

An Example of Two-Dimensional Relative Referencing

Suppose you have the worksheet in Figure 4–41, and you want to copy the formula in cell B6, @SUM(B3..B4), to the range C6..E6. This formula totals the cells in column B immediately above its location, cell B6. Notice that this formula includes relative references to cells B3 and B4. Select the Copy command, specify your From range as cell B6, and your To range as C6..F6. The results are shown in Figure 4–42.

If you look at the formula for cell C6 in the Control line, you'll notice that it is similar to the original formula in cell B6, except that 1-2-3/G has automatically adjusted the cell references relative to the formula's new location. In fact, 1-2-3/G has adjusted all the formulas in the To range as follows:

C6: @SUM(C3..C4)
D6: @SUM(D3..D4)
E6: @SUM(E3..E4)

123G.EXE (69.4) Ready

File Edit Worksheet Range Copy... Move... Print Graph Data Utility Quit... Help

A:B6 @SUM(B3..B4)

COPY20.WG1

A	A	B	C	D	E
1		Q Ended	Q Ended	Q Ended	Q Ended
2		31-Mar-90	30-Jun-90	30-Sep-90	31-Dec-90
3	Sales	$30,000	$25,000	$50,000	$90,000
4	COGS	($6,000)	($5,000)	($10,000)	($18,000)
5					
6	Gross Profit	$24,000			

FIGURE 4–41 **A sample worksheet with relative references**

123G.EXE [69.4] Ready

File Edit Worksheet Range Copy... Move... Print Graph Data Utility Quit... Help

A:C6 @SUM(C3..C4)

COPY20.WG1

A	A	B	C	D	E	F	G
1		Q Ended	Q Ended	Q Ended	Q Ended		
2		31-Mar-90	30-Jun-90	30-Sep-90	31-Dec-90		
3	Sales	$30,000	$25,000	$50,000	$90,000		
4	COGS	($6,000)	($5,000)	($10,000)	($18,000)		
5							
6	Gross Profit	$24,000	$20,000	$40,000	$72,000		

FIGURE 4–42 After copying a formula with relative references across columns

In each case, 1-2-3/G has adjusted the cell references by leaving the row number constant and increasing the column letter by one for each column in the To range.

As another example, imagine you have the worksheet in Figure 4–43. Notice in the Control line that cell F3 contains the formula @SUM(B3..E3), with relative references to the cells in the range B3..E3. Now let's copy this formula to cells F4 and F6. Select the Copy command and specify your From range as cell B6 and your To range as the collection F4, F6. The results are shown in Figure 4–44.

Notice in the Control line that the formula in cell F4 is @SUM(B4..E4). As in the previous example, 1-2-3/G has adjusted the cell references in the formula relative to its new location, cell F4. However, in this case, because you have copied down a row, 1-2-3/G has left the column letter constant and adjusted the row component of each reference. Likewise, 1-2-3/G has adjusted the formula in cell F6 to @SUM(B6..E6).

An Example with Three-Dimensional Relative Referencing

What happens to a formula that contains relative references when you copy it from one worksheet to another? 1-2-3/G adjusts any cell references in the same manner as for two-dimensional referencing, except it also adjusts the worksheet component.

123G.EXE (69.4) Ready

File Edit Worksheet Range Copy... Move... Print Graph Data Utility Quit... Help

A:F3 @SUM(B3..E3)

(C0) COPY23.WG1

A	A	B	C	D	E	F	G
1		Q Ended	Q Ended	Q Ended	Q Ended	Yr Ended	
2		31-Mar-90	30-Jun-90	30-Sep-90	31-Dec-90	31-Dec-90	
3	Sales	$30,000	$25,000	$50,000	$90,000	$195,000	
4	COGS	($6,000)	($5,000)	($10,000)	($18,000)		
5							
6	Gross Profit	$24,000	$20,000	$40,000	$72,000		
7							
8							
9							
10							
11							
12							
13							
14							
15							
16							
17							
18							
19							
20							

FIGURE 4–43 Another sample worksheet with relative references

123G.EXE (69.4) Ready

File Edit Worksheet Range Copy... Move... Print Graph Data Utility Quit... Help

A:F4 @SUM(B4..E4)

(C0) COPY23.WG1

A	A	B	C	D	E	F	G
1		Q Ended	Q Ended	Q Ended	Q Ended	Yr Ended	
2		31-Mar-90	30-Jun-90	30-Sep-90	31-Dec-90	31-Dec-90	
3	Sales	$30,000	$25,000	$50,000	$90,000	$195,000	
4	COGS	($6,000)	($5,000)	($10,000)	($18,000)	($39,000)	
5							
6	Gross Profit	$24,000	$20,000	$40,000	$72,000	$156,000	
7							
8							
9							
10							
11							
12							
13							
14							
15							
16							
17							
18							
19							
20							

FIGURE 4–44 After copying a formula with relative references down column F

For example, suppose you have the worksheets in Figure 4–45. Worksheet A contains projected sales for 1990, worksheet B for 1991, and worksheet C for 1992. (Notice that worksheet A is the same worksheet shown in Figure 4–44.)

Imagine that you copy the formula in cell A:F4 to cell B:F4. Figure 4–46 shows the results. As shown in the Control line, the formula in cell B:F4 is @SUM(B4..E4), which is the same formula as in A:F4. Nevertheless, this formula references cells in worksheet B, not worksheet A. 1-2-3/G has adjusted the worksheet component of the cell references.

As another example, suppose cell B:C3 contains the formula +B3. (Notice that both cells B:B3 and B:C3 display the value $100,000.) Figure 4–47 shows what happens when you copy this formula to cell C:D4. Notice in the Control line that cell C:D4 now contains the formula +C4. 1-2-3/G has adjusted each component of the relative cell reference by one unit (one worksheet, one column, and one row).

Problems with Relative References

By using the Copy command with relative references, you can easily copy a formula in one location to many other locations in a worksheet file, saving yourself substantial time and effort in the process. However, if you copy relative references incorrectly, you can also create errors.

123G.EXE (69.4) Ready

File Edit Worksheet Range Copy... Move... Print Graph Data Utility Quit... Help

A:F4 @SUM(B4..E4)

COPY30.WG1

C	A	B	C	D	E	F
1		Q Ended	Q Ended	Q Ended	Q Ended	Yr Ended
2		31-Mar-92	30-Jun-92	30-Sep-92	31-Dec-92	31-Dec-92
3	Sales	$250,000	$500,000			
4	COGS	($50,000)	($100,000)			
5		----------	----------			
6		$200,000	$400,000			

B	A	B	C	D	E	F
1		Q Ended	Q Ended	Q Ended	Q Ended	Yr Ended
2		31-Mar-91	30-Jun-91	30-Sep-91	31-Dec-91	31-Dec-91
3	Sales	$100,000	$100,000	$90,000	$200,000	$490,000
4	COGS	($20,000)	($20,000)	($18,000)	($40,000)	
5		----------	----------	----------	----------	----------
6	Gross Profit	$80,000	$80,000	$72,000	$160,000	$392,000

A	A	B	C	D	E	F	G
1		Q Ended	Q Ended	Q Ended	Q Ended	Yr Ended	
2		31-Mar-90	30-Jun-90	30-Sep-90	31-Dec-90	31-Dec-90	
3	Sales	$30,000	$25,000	$50,000	$90,000	$195,000	
4	COGS	($6,000)	($5,000)	($10,000)	($18,000)	($39,000)	
5		----------	----------	----------	----------	----------	
6	Gross Profit	$24,000	$20,000	$40,000	$72,000	$156,000	

FIGURE 4–45 Some sample worksheets with formulas that contain relative addresses

123G.EXE (69.4) Ready

File Edit Worksheet Range Copy... Move... Print Graph Data Utility Quit... Help

B:F4 @SUM(B4..E4)

COPY30.WG1

C	A	B	C	D	E	F
1		Q Ended	Q Ended	Q Ended	Q Ended	Yr Ended
2		31-Mar-92	30-Jun-92	30-Sep-92	31-Dec-92	31-Dec-92
3	Sales	$250,000	$500,000			
4	COGS	($50,000)	($100,000)			
5		------	------			
6		$200,000	$400,000			

B	A	B	C	D	E	F
1		Q Ended	Q Ended	Q Ended	Q Ended	Yr Ended
2		31-Mar-91	30-Jun-91	30-Sep-91	31-Dec-91	31-Dec-91
3	Sales	$100,000	$100,000	$90,000	$200,000	$490,000
4	COGS	($20,000)	($20,000)	($18,000)	($40,000)	($98,000)
5		------	------	------	------	------
6	Gross Profit	$80,000	$80,000	$72,000	$160,000	$392,000

A	A	B	C	D	E	F	G
1		Q Ended	Q Ended	Q Ended	Q Ended	Yr Ended	
2		31-Mar-90	30-Jun-90	30-Sep-90	31-Dec-90	31-Dec-90	
3	Sales	$30,000	$25,000	$50,000	$90,000	$195,000	
4	COGS	($6,000)	($5,000)	($10,000)	($18,000)	($39,000)	
5		------	------	------	------	------	
6	Gross Profit	$24,000	$20,000	$40,000	$72,000	$156,000	

FIGURE 4–46 After copying a formula with relative references to another worksheet

123G.EXE (69.4) Ready

File Edit Worksheet Range Copy... Move... Print Graph Data Utility Quit... Help

C:D4 +C4

COPY30.WG1

C	A	B	C	D	E	F
1		Q Ended	Q Ended	Q Ended	Q Ended	Yr Ended
2		31-Mar-92	30-Jun-92	30-Sep-92	31-Dec-92	31-Dec-92
3	Sales	$250,000	$500,000			
4	COGS	($50,000)	($100,000)	($100,000)		
5		------	------			
6		$200,000	$400,000			

B	A	B	C	D	E	F
1		Q Ended	Q Ended	Q Ended	Q Ended	Yr Ended
2		31-Mar-91	30-Jun-91	30-Sep-91	31-Dec-91	31-Dec-91
3	Sales	$100,000	$100,000	$90,000	$200,000	$490,000
4	COGS	($20,000)	($20,000)	($18,000)	($40,000)	($98,000)
5		------	------	------	------	------
6	Gross Profit	$80,000	$80,000	$72,000	$160,000	$392,000

A	A	B	C	D	E	F	G
1		Q Ended	Q Ended	Q Ended	Q Ended	Yr Ended	
2		31-Mar-90	30-Jun-90	30-Sep-90	31-Dec-90	31-Dec-90	
3	Sales	$30,000	$25,000	$50,000	$90,000	$195,000	
4	COGS	($6,000)	($5,000)	($10,000)	($18,000)	($39,000)	
5		------	------	------	------	------	
6	Gross Profit	$24,000	$20,000	$40,000	$72,000	$156,000	

FIGURE 4–47 After copying a formula with a relative reference between worksheets

For example, suppose you have the worksheet in Figure 4–48 in which you have entered all the projected sales figures for January in column B. Because you predict that sales will increase by 1% each month for January through June, you place the monthly growth factor in cell C3. You then plan to build a formula, which you will then copy to the range C7..G9, that references this monthly growth factor.

You begin by entering the formula +B7*(1+C3) in cell C7 and formatting the cell for Comma, with 0 decimal places, as shown in Figure 4–48. Notice that this formula adds the growth factor in cell C3 to one and multiplies the result by the projected figure for women's pants sales for January in cell B7.

To copy the formula in cell C7 to the rest of the range, C7..G9, you select the Copy command, specify C7 as the FROM range, and C7..G9 as the To range. Figure 4–49 shows the results.

Because the formula contains a relative reference to cell C3, 1-2-3/G adjusts that reference when you copy the formula. As you can tell, the results are not at all what you want because, for example, the formula in cell D7 is +C7*(1+D3), and cell D3 does not refer to the growth factor.

However, 1-2-3/G does provide a solution to this problem. You can copy the formula B7*(1+C3) anywhere in your worksheet, while maintaining the cell reference C3, by using *absolute* addressing.

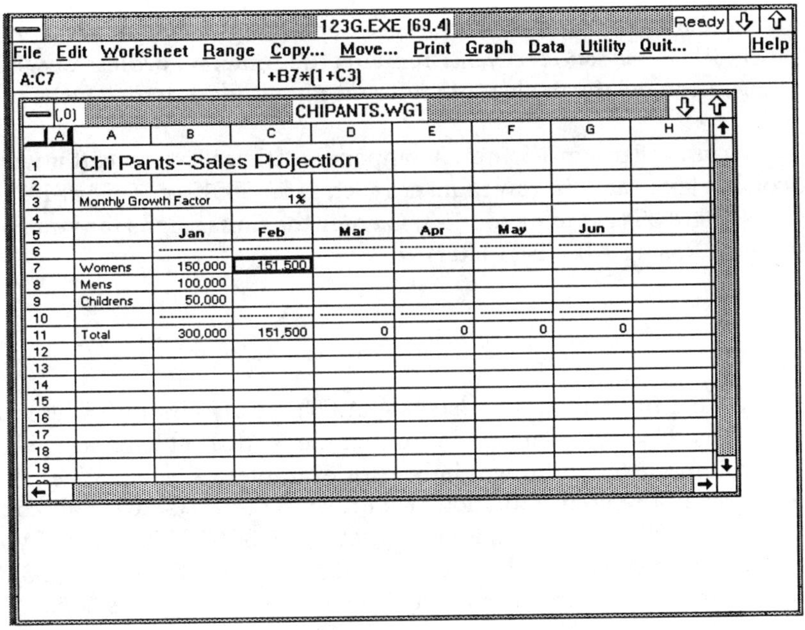

123G.EXE (69.4) Ready

File Edit Worksheet Range Copy... Move... Print Graph Data Utility Quit... Help

A:C7 +B7*(1+C3)

(,0) CHIPANTS.WG1

	A	B	C	D	E	F	G	H
1	Chi Pants--Sales Projection							
2								
3	Monthly Growth Factor		1%					
4								
5		Jan	Feb	Mar	Apr	May	Jun	
6		----------	----------	----------	----------	----------	----------	
7	Womens	150,000	151,500					
8	Mens	100,000						
9	Childrens	50,000						
10		----------	----------	----------	----------	----------	----------	
11	Total	300,000	151,500	0	0	0	0	
12								
13								
14								
15								
16								
17								
18								
19								

FIGURE 4–48 An inappropriate use of a relative cell reference

123G.EXE (69.4) Ready

File Edit Worksheet Range Copy... Move... Print Graph Data Utility Quit... Help

A:D7 +C7*(1+D3)

(,0) CHIPANTS.WG1

A	A	B	C	D	E	F	G	H
1	Chi Pants--Sales Projection							
2								
3	Monthly Growth Factor		1%					
4								
5		Jan	Feb	Mar	Apr	May	Jun	
6		----------	----------	----------	----------	----------	----------	
7	Womens	150,000	151,500	151,500	151,500	151,500	151,500	
8	Mens	100,000	100,000	100,000	100,000	100,000	100,000	
9	Childrens	50,000	50,000	50,000	50,000	50,000	50,000	
10		----------	----------	----------	----------	----------	----------	
11	Total	300,000	301,500	301,500	301,500	301,500	301,500	
12								
13								
14								
15								
16								
17								
18								
19								

FIGURE 4–49 **After copying the invalid formula across columns**

Absolute References

Whereas a relative cell reference changes depending on where you copy it in a worksheet file, an *absolute reference* remains the same, regardless of where you copy it. You can create an absolute reference in either of two ways:

- By typing in a dollar sign before each component of the cell reference (the worksheet, the column letter, and the row number), such as $A:$B$10 or $C:$AZ$105.
- By pressing ABS (F4) to have 1-2-3/G enter the dollar signs for you automatically (see "Using ABS (F4)" later).

Note

To make a full cell address (such as A:C7) a truly absolute reference, you must place a dollar sign in front of the worksheet letter as well as the column letter and row number (for example, $A:$C$7). When you copy such a reference to another worksheet, 1-2-3/G keeps all components of the reference the same (that is, $A:$C$7). However, if you copy the reference to the same worksheet (worksheet A), 1-2-3/G converts the reference to an abbreviated cell address (that is, $C$7).

An Example

Figure 4–50 shows an example of how you might use an absolute reference. Notice that the formula in cell C7 is identical to the one in Figure 4–48 except that the reference to cell C3 is absolute. Figure 4–51 shows what happens when you copy this formula to the range C7..G9. Notice in the Control line that the formula for cell D7 contains the same absolute reference to cell C3 as the original formula in cell C7. Compare these results to those in Figure 4–49, where cells C7 and D7 contain relative references to cell C3.

A Running Totals Example

Another typical use of absolute references is when you want to create *running totals* using the @SUM function. Running totals is simply a balance at the end of each time period equal to the current period balance plus the accumulated balance for prior periods. A typical running totals is a checkbook balance. Running totals are also typically kept for balance sheet items such as retained earnings and accumulated depreciation.

For example, say you have the depreciation expense worksheet in Figure 4–52, and you want to keep a running or year-to-date total of accumulated depreciation. Your beginning balance for accumulated depreciation from the prior year is $150,000 in cell B10.

123G.EXE (69.4) Ready

File Edit Worksheet Range Copy... Move... Print Graph Data Utility Quit... Help

A:C7 +B7*(1+$C$3)

(,0) CHIPANTS.WG1

A	A	B	C	D	E	F	G	H
1	Chi Pants--Sales Projection							
2								
3	Monthly Growth Factor		1%					
4								
5		Jan	Feb	Mar	Apr	May	Jun	
6								
7	Womens	150,000	151,500					
8	Mens	100,000						
9	Childrens	50,000						
10								
11	Total	300,000	151,500	0	0	0	0	
12								
13								
14								
15								
16								
17								
18								
19								

FIGURE 4–50 After entering an absolute reference in a formula

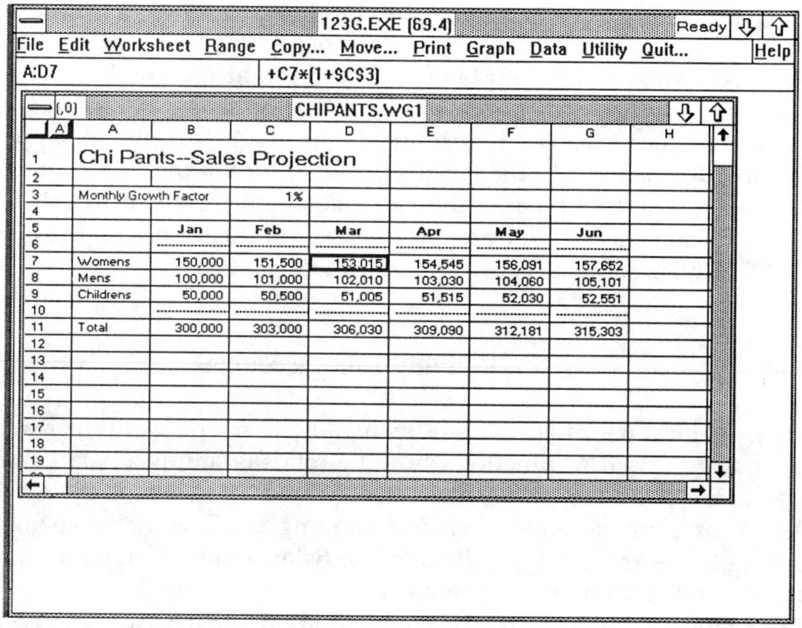

123G.EXE (69.4) Ready

File Edit Worksheet Range Copy... Move... Print Graph Data Utility Quit... Help

A:D7 +C7*(1+$C$3)

(,0) CHIPANTS.WG1

A	A	B	C	D	E	F	G	H
1	Chi Pants--Sales Projection							
2								
3	Monthly Growth Factor		1%					
4								
5		Jan	Feb	Mar	Apr	May	Jun	
6		--------	--------	--------	--------	--------	--------	
7	Womens	150,000	151,500	153,015	154,545	156,091	157,652	
8	Mens	100,000	101,000	102,010	103,030	104,060	105,101	
9	Childrens	50,000	50,500	51,005	51,515	52,030	52,551	
10		--------	--------	--------	--------	--------	--------	
11	Total	300,000	303,000	306,030	309,090	312,181	315,303	
12								
13								
14								
15								
16								
17								
18								
19								

FIGURE 4–51 Copying a formula with a relative reference

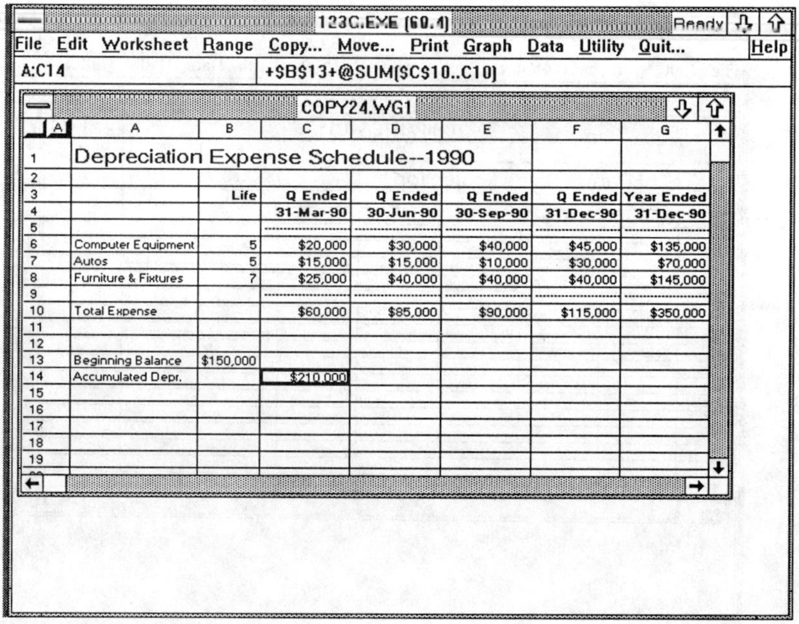

123G.EXE (69.4) Ready

File Edit Worksheet Range Copy... Move... Print Graph Data Utility Quit... Help

A:C14 +$B$13+@SUM($C$10..C10)

COPY24.WG1

A	A	B	C	D	E	F	G
1	Depreciation Expense Schedule--1990						
2							
3		Life	Q Ended	Q Ended	Q Ended	Q Ended	Year Ended
4			31-Mar-90	30-Jun-90	30-Sep-90	31-Dec-90	31-Dec-90
5			--------	--------	--------	--------	--------
6	Computer Equipment	5	$20,000	$30,000	$40,000	$45,000	$135,000
7	Autos	5	$15,000	$15,000	$10,000	$30,000	$70,000
8	Furniture & Fixtures	7	$25,000	$40,000	$40,000	$40,000	$145,000
9			--------	--------	--------	--------	--------
10	Total Expense		$60,000	$85,000	$90,000	$115,000	$350,000
11							
12							
13	Beginning Balance	$150,000					
14	Accumulated Depr.		$210,000				
15							
16							
17							
18							
19							

FIGURE 4–52 Using absolute references in the first cell of a running total

To create the running total using absolute references, begin by entering **+$B$13+@SUM($C$10..C10)** in cell C14, as displayed in the Control line of Figure 4–52. Notice that the range reference, $C$10..C10, contains both an absolute and relative reference. Next, use the Copy command to copy this formula from C14 to the range D14..F14.

The results of the copy operation are displayed in Figure 4–53. Notice in the Control line that the formula in cell F14 is +$B$13+@SUM($C$10..F10). As you can see, the relative portion of the range reference has changed as you copied the formula across the worksheet. However, the references to cells B13 and C10 do not change.

Mixed References

A *mixed reference,* as its name implies, uses components of both relative and absolute referencing in the same cell address. To create a mixed reference, you place a dollar sign in front of the appropriate component of the cell reference that you want to remain fixed—the worksheet letter, the column letter, and/or the row number. For example, the cell reference A:A$1 keeps the row component constant when you copy the reference to another cell but lets the worksheet and column letters vary. On the other hand, the mixed reference $A:$A1 keeps the worksheet and column components constant but lets the row vary.

123G.EXE [69.4] Ready

File Edit Worksheet Range Copy... Move... Print Graph Data Utility Quit... Help

A:F14 +$B$13+@SUM($C$10..F10)

COPY24.WG1

A	A	B	C	D	E	F	G
1	Depreciation Expense Schedule--1990						
2							
3		Life	Q Ended	Q Ended	Q Ended	Q Ended	Year Ended
4			31-Mar-90	30-Jun-90	30-Sep-90	31-Dec-90	31-Dec-90
5							
6	Computer Equipment	5	$20,000	$30,000	$40,000	$45,000	$135,000
7	Autos	5	$15,000	$15,000	$10,000	$30,000	$70,000
8	Furniture & Fixtures	7	$25,000	$40,000	$40,000	$40,000	$145,000
9							
10	Total Expense		$60,000	$85,000	$90,000	$115,000	$350,000
11							
12							
13	Beginning Balance	$150,000					
14	Accumulated Depr.		$210,000	$295,000	$385,000	$500,000	
15							
16							
17							
18							
19							

FIGURE 4–53 After copying the running total formula across the row.

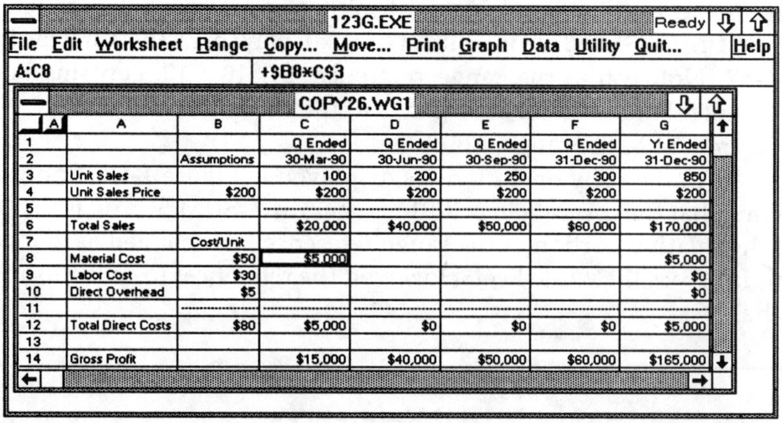

123G.EXE Ready

File Edit Worksheet Range Copy... Move... Print Graph Data Utility Quit... Help

A:C8 +$B8*C$3

COPY26.WG1

A	A	B	C	D	E	F	G
1			Q Ended	Q Ended	Q Ended	Q Ended	Yr Ended
2		Assumptions	30-Mar-90	30-Jun-90	30-Sep-90	31-Dec-90	31-Dec-90
3	Unit Sales		100	200	250	300	850
4	Unit Sales Price	$200	$200	$200	$200	$200	$200
5			----------	----------	----------	----------	----------
6	Total Sales		$20,000	$40,000	$50,000	$60,000	$170,000
7		Cost/Unit					
8	Material Cost	$50	$5,000				$5,000
9	Labor Cost	$30					$0
10	Direct Overhead	$5					$0
11		----------	----------	----------	----------	----------	----------
12	Total Direct Costs	$80	$5,000	$0	$0	$0	$5,000
13							
14	Gross Profit		$15,000	$40,000	$50,000	$60,000	$165,000

FIGURE 4–54 A sample worksheet with 2–D mixed cell references

Like absolute references, you can create mixed cell references by typing in the dollar signs or by pressing ABS (F4) key to have 1-2-3/G insert the dollar signs for you automatically (see "Using ABS (F4)" later).

Figure 4–54 shows an example of how you might use mixed cell references in a financial model. This model calculates direct costs based on the number of units sold. For each quarter, direct material, labor, and overhead are projected by multiplying the number of units sold by the cost per unit. The formula +$B8*C$3 in cell C8 computes the direct material cost for the quarter ended March 30, 1990. To calculate the remaining direct costs, you copy this formula to the range C8..F10.

The first reference, $B8, tells 1-2-3/G that you always want to refer to the values in column B. In other words, as you copy the formula down columns and across rows, you want the column reference to remain "frozen" but the row reference to vary. On the other hand, in the second reference, C$3, you want the row reference to remain frozen, but the column reference to vary.

Figure 4–55 shows the results when you copy the formula in cell C8 to the remainder of the range. As you review the results, notice in the Control line that the formula in cell F10 is +$B10*F$3. Because the column in the first reference is frozen, 1-2-3/G only adjusted the row during the copy process. Likewise, since the row is frozen in the second reference, 1-2-3/G only adjusted the column reference.

Using ABS (F4)

Rather than typing $ signs, you can use the ABS (F4) key to create absolute and mixed references in your formulas. You can use ABS when you are typing a reference (Value mode), pointing to a reference (Point mode), or editing a formula (Edit mode).

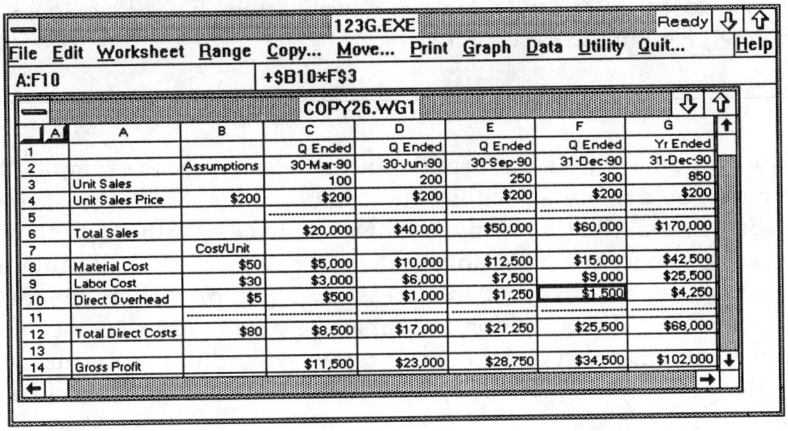

123G.EXE — Ready

File Edit Worksheet Range Copy... Move... Print Graph Data Utility Quit... Help

A:F10 +$B10*F$3

COPY26.WG1

A	A	B	C	D	E	F	G
1			Q Ended	Q Ended	Q Ended	Q Ended	Yr Ended
2		Assumptions	30-Mar-90	30-Jun-90	30-Sep-90	31-Dec-90	31-Dec-90
3	Unit Sales		100	200	250	300	850
4	Unit Sales Price	$200	$200	$200	$200	$200	$200
5							
6	Total Sales		$20,000	$40,000	$50,000	$60,000	$170,000
7		Cost/Unit					
8	Material Cost	$50	$5,000	$10,000	$12,500	$15,000	$42,500
9	Labor Cost	$30	$3,000	$6,000	$7,500	$9,000	$25,500
10	Direct Overhead	$5	$500	$1,000	$1,250	$1,500	$4,250
11							
12	Total Direct Costs	$80	$8,500	$17,000	$21,250	$25,500	$68,000
13							
14	Gross Profit		$11,500	$23,000	$28,750	$34,500	$102,000

FIGURE 4–55 The results of using mixed cell references

Suppose, for example, you want to enter a simple formula in cell B2 that contains an absolute reference to cell A1. To enter the formula by pointing, begin by placing the cell pointer in cell B2 and type +. Next, press ← and ↑ to highlight cell A1, or simply click on cell A1. 1-2-3/G enters Point mode, and the formula appears as +A:A1 in the Control line. To change the cell reference, to an absolute reference, press ABS (F4). 1-2-3/G automatically converts the reference to read +$A:$A$1 in the Control line. To accept the formula and place it in cell B1, you press ENTER or click on the Confirm (✓) icon in the Control line.

Rather than pressing ENTER, however, suppose you press ABS (F4) again—1-2-3/G converts the formula to read +$A:A$1, a mixed cell reference. Press ABS again, and the formula reads +$A:$A1, another form of mixed reference. In fact, by pressing ABS (F4) repeatedly, you can cycle through the following choices of cell references:

Press ABS (F4)	Formula	Cell Address	Worksheet	Column	Row
Once	+$A:$A$1	Absolute	Fixed	Fixed	Fixed
Twice	+$A:A$1	Mixed	Fixed	Changes	Fixed
Three times	+$A:$A1	Mixed	Fixed	Fixed	Changes
Four times	+$A:A1	Mixed	Fixed	Changes	Changes
Five times	+A:$A$1	Mixed	Changes	Fixed	Fixed
Six times	+A:A$1	Mixed	Changes	Changes	Fixed
Seven times	+A:$A1	Mixed	Changes	Fixed	Fixed
Eight times	+A:A1	Relative	Changes	Changes	Changes

Of course, to accept a cell reference simply press ENTER, or click on the Confirm (✓) icon in the Control line.

Using ABS (F4) in Edit Mode

Suppose you have entered a formula, but later decide, for example, that you want to change a reference within the formula to an absolute or mixed reference. You can use ABS (F4) while in Edit mode to change the type of reference. To enter Edit mode, begin by moving the cell pointer to the cell containing the formula you want to change. Next, press EDIT (F2) or click on the formula in the contents box. Then, position the cursor below the cell reference you want to change (anywhere on or by the cell reference will do). You can then press ABS (F4) repeatedly to cycle through the eight combinations of absolute, mixed, and relative references.

For example, say you have the formula +A1+A2 in a cell, and you want to convert the relative reference to cell A1 to an absolute reference. You begin by pressing EDIT (F2) to enter Edit mode, then press HOME to move to the start of the formula. Next, press ABS (F4), and 1-2-3/G changes the formula to read +$A:$A$1+A2. Press ENTER to complete the formula and place it in the cell. Of course, if you want you can press ABS (F4) as many times as you like to cycle through the available reference choices.

Using ABS (F4) with Range References

Like its predecessors, 1-2-3/G behaves differently when you use ABS (F4) with range references. Suppose, for example, you enter the formula @SUM(A1..A3), and you press ABS (F4) before you confirm the entry. The formula changes to @SUM($A:$A$1..$A:$A$3), converting both beginning and ending addresses of the range reference to absolute references. If you press ABS (F4) again, the formula reads @SUM($A:A$1..$A:A$3), and so on. Because 1-2-3/G converts both addresses in tandem, you will need to manually insert or delete the dollar signs if you want one range reference to read differently from another.

Using ABS (F4) with Range Names

Using ABS (F4) with range names is problematic. For example, suppose you have assigned the range name DIRECT_COSTS to the range A:A3..A:A10, and you enter the formula @SUM(DIRECT_COSTS) in another cell. Suppose you then want to convert the reference to DIRECT_COSTS in the formula to an absolute range reference. You begin by pressing EDIT (F2) (or clicking on the entry in the contents box) to enter Edit mode. When you press ABS (F4) to convert the reference to an absolute reference, 1-2-3/G shows @SUM($DIRECT_COSTS) in the Control line. This is the equivalent of @SUM($A:$A$3..$A:$A$10). If you press ABS (F4) again, 1-2-3/G converts the formula back to @SUM(DIRECT_COSTS). Because of the ABS key's behavior with range names, you will find it easier to avoid using range names in your formulas whenever you want to enter anything other than a pure absolute or relative range reference.

Copying Cell References between Files

As mentioned, you can use 1-2-3/G's Copy command to copy information between open files. However, when you copy formulas from one file to another, the cell references in those formulas will refer to the destination file.

Imagine you have two open files in memory, SHEET1.WG1 and SHEET2.WG1. If you copy a formula that includes an absolute reference from SHEET1.WG1 to SHEET2.WG1, the absolute reference remains unchanged. However, it now refers to the destination file (SHEET2.WG1). For example, suppose in the file SHEET1.WG1, cell A1 contains the absolute cell reference +$A:$B$10. You copy this formula to cell C5 in the file SHEET2.WG1. Cell C5 now contains the same cell reference +$A:$B$10, but it references that cell in SHEET2.WG1, not SHEET1.WG1.

Copying formulas with relative and mixed cell references between files is a similar case. That is, after copying, the cell references in those formulas now refer to the destination file. Additionally, the cell references in those formulas are adjusted in the usual way to reflect the new position of the formula in the worksheet. For example, suppose you have the same two files referenced in the previous paragraph, SHEET1.WG1 and SHEET2.WG1, open on the desktop. In the file SHEET1.WG1, cell A1 contains the formula +A2. This formula is then copied to cell A4 in the SHEET2.WG1 file. Cell A4 in the SHEET2.WG1 file now contains the formula +A5, which references cell A5 in SHEET2.WG1, not SHEET1.WG1.

Note

> For more on copying data between files with the Copy command, see "Copying between Files" earlier in this chapter.

Copying Link Formulas

As you recall, when you use a formula to establish a link between worksheet files, you enter a file reference in double-angle brackets (<< >>) followed by a cell or range reference. For example, to use the value in cell A:A1 of the file named BUDGET in the current file, you place the formula +<<BUDGET>>A:A1 in a cell in the current file.

Suppose you then want to copy the link formula to another location within the same file or to another file. You can easily use the Copy command to accomplish this. However, there are some things to keep in mind:

- When you copy a link formula to another location (within the same file or in another file), 1-2-3/G does not adjust the file component of the formula; it only adjusts the cell reference. For example, suppose you have the formula +<<BUDGET>>A:A1 in cell A1 of the active file, SALES, and you copy this formula to cell A:B1 of a file named SAVE_BUD. The formula in SAVE_BUD reads +<<BUDGET>>A:B1.
- When you copy a link formula that contains a range name to another location (within the same file or in another file), 1-2-3/G does not adjust the range name. For example, suppose you copy the formula +<<BUDGET>>GROWTH from the active file, SALES, to another file in memory, SAVE_BUD. The formula will still read +<<BUDGET>>GROWTH in its location in SAVE_BUD.
- When you copy a formula that contains a relative range name to another worksheet file, 1-2-3/G converts the range name to an address and adjusts the address according to its new location. For example, suppose you have assigned the range name GROWTH to cell H1. You then place the formula +GROWTH in cell H8. If you copy this formula from cell H8 to cell I8 in another file, 1-2-3/G converts the formula to read +I1 in the target file.
- When you copy a formula that contains an absolute range name to another worksheet file, the range name continues to refer to the original file. For example, suppose you have assigned the range name GROWTH to cell H1 in a file called BUDGET. You then place the formula +$GROWTH in cell H8. If you copy this formula from cell H8 to cell I8 in another file, the formula reads +<<BUDGET.WG1>>$GROWTH in the target file.

USING THE CLIPBOARD TO CUT AND PASTE

1-2-3/G, like other Presentation Manager applications, lets you use the clipboard to cut and paste data. The *clipboard* is a special memory buffer that holds whatever was last cut or copied. You can think of the clipboard as an invisible worksheet area you use to store data until you need it. After cutting or copying data to the clipboard, you can then paste the data from the clipboard to as many places as you want.

You access the clipboard through the Edit menu, which is available from nearly every 1-2-3/G tool and utility. To cut and copy data to the clipboard, you use the Edit Cut and Edit Copy commands. To paste data from the clipboard, you use the Edit Paste command.

You can use the clipboard to share data between worksheet files, graph files, and other tools and utilities. You can also use the clipboard to share data with other Presentation Manager applications, such as SideKick or WordPerfect for Presentation Manager.

How the Clipboard Works

Figure 4–56 illustrates how the clipboard works. Suppose you are working in Sheet 1 (a worksheet file), and you cut or copy data in Sheet 1 to the clipboard. You can then paste the data in the clipboard to any of the following:

- Another location in Sheet 1.
- Another worksheet file, such as Worksheet 2.
- A graph file.
- Another Presentation Manager application.

Once you cut or copy data to the clipboard, it remains there until you cut or copy new data. In fact, data remains in the clipboard even when you leave 1-2-3/G, provided you keep the Presentation Manager Desktop open.

You can also use the clipboard to link worksheet files. When you copy data to the clipboard, 1-2-3/G also copies the location of the data (for example, a cell or range address). You can then use the Edit Link Paste Link command in another worksheet file to establish a link between that file and the source file from which you copied the data. See "Linking Files with the Edit Command" in Chapter 2 for a complete description.

Why would you use the clipboard to cut and paste instead of using other 1-2-3/G commands such as Move and Copy? Here are a few important reasons:

- Once you cut or copy data to the clipboard, you can then paste this data to multiple locations.
- After cutting or copying data to the clipboard, you can then perform other operations before you paste the data from the clipboard.
- You can cut and paste data between 1-2-3/G and other Presentation Manager applications.

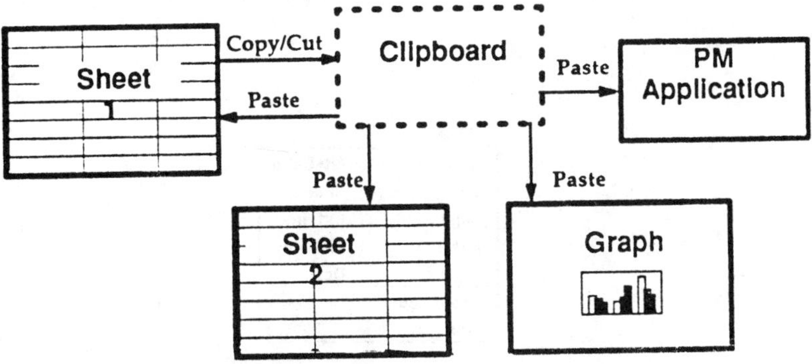

FIGURE 4–56 How the clipboard works

The Edit Menu

As mentioned, you use the Edit commands shown in Figure 4–57 to cut and paste data in 1-2-3/G. Here is a description of each command:

- **Undo** allows you to "take back" or undo your last action. If your last action cannot be undone, 1-2-3/G makes the Undo option unavailable (gray). The shortcut for this command is ALT-BACKSPACE. Edit Undo does not use the clipboard (see Chapter 1, "1-2-3/G Basics," for a complete description).
- **Cut** allows you to delete selected data and place it into the clipboard, replacing what was already in the clipboard. The shortcut for the Edit Cut command is SHIFT-DEL.
- **Copy** allows you to copy selected data to the clipboard. The original data remains unchanged. The shortcut for this command is CTRL-INS.
- **Paste** allows you to copy the data in the clipboard to an open worksheet file or tool on the desktop. You can paste the data in the clipboard to multiple locations. The shortcut for this command is SHIFT-INS.
- **Clear** erases selected data just like the Range Erase command. The Edit Clear command does not use the clipboard. The shortcut for this command is DEL. See "Erasing with Edit Clear" in this chapter for a complete description.
- **Paste Special** works like the Paste command, except that it allows you to paste only specific information from the clipboard. (The type of information you can paste is discussed in detail below.)
- **Link** creates, updates, deletes, or changes a link between a worksheet file and another tool on the desktop, or another Presentation Manager application. See Chapter 2, "Managing the Desktop," for a complete description of this command.

Cutting or Copying

The Edit Cut command "cuts" or deletes the current selection and places it in the clipboard. On the other hand, the Edit Copy command "copies" data to the

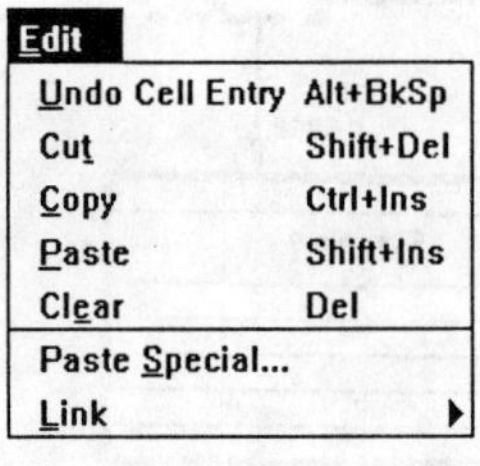

Edit	
Undo Cell Entry	Alt+BkSp
Cut	Shift+Del
Copy	Ctrl+Ins
Paste	Shift+Ins
Clear	Del
Paste Special...	
Link	▸

FIGURE 4–57 The Edit menu

clipboard, leaving the original data intact. Here are some highlights of the commands:

- Before you use Edit Cut or Edit Copy, you must select the data you want to apply the command to. You can select the data with the keyboard or the mouse.
- When you use Edit Cut or Edit Copy to move data to the clipboard, 1-2-3/G also moves the data's original formats, attributes, and other settings. Notes are moved to the clipboard as well.
- When you use Edit Cut, the cells from which you cut data retain their original formats, attributes, notes, and other settings.
- When you use the Edit Paste or Edit Paste Special command to paste the data you have cut or copied, cell references are adjusted like the Copy command. See "How Cell References Are Affected" below.
- If you cut or copy again, the original data in the clipboard is overwritten with the new data.

You can use Edit Cut and Edit Copy with a cell, a 2–D range, or a 3–D range. However, you **cannot** use these commands with any of the following:

- **A collection:** If you highlight a collection then select the Edit menu, 1-2-3/G makes the Cut and Copy options unavailable.
- **An entire column, row, worksheet:** If you select an entire worksheet by clicking on its Worksheet selector button (or by pressing ALT-SHIFT-HOME), 1-2-3/G makes the Edit Cut and Copy commands unavailable. The same is true if you select an entire column or row by clicking on the box surrounding the column letter or row number (or by pressing an ALT-SHIFT-arrow key sequence). Rather, you must specify the entire column, row, or worksheet as a range.

Suppose you have created the worksheet in Figure 4–58, and you want to cut the information in the range D1..D7 to the clipboard. Begin by highlighting the

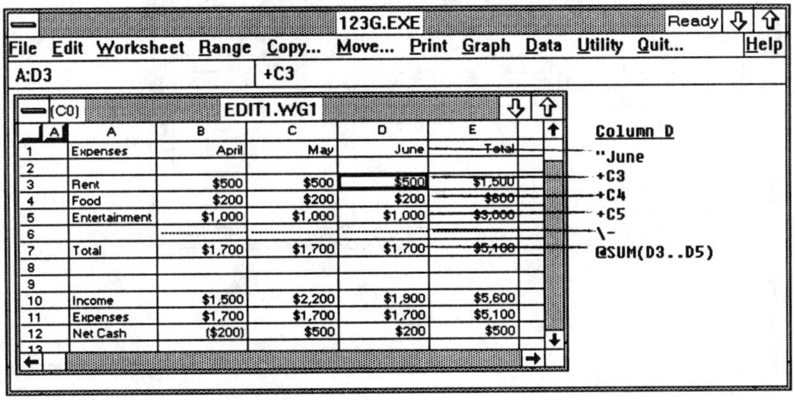

123G.EXE Ready

File Edit Worksheet Range Copy... Move... Print Graph Data Utility Quit... Help

A:D3 +C3

(C0) EDIT1.WG1

A	A	B	C	D	E
1	Expenses	April	May	June	Total
2					
3	Rent	$500	$500	$500	$1,500
4	Food	$200	$200	$200	$600
5	Entertainment	$1,000	$1,000	$1,000	$3,000
6					
7	Total	$1,700	$1,700	$1,700	$5,100
8					
9					
10	Income	$1,500	$2,200	$1,900	$5,600
11	Expenses	$1,700	$1,700	$1,700	$5,100
12	Net Cash	($200)	$500	$200	$500

Column D
"June
+C3
+C4
+C5
\-
@SUM(D3..D5)

FIGURE 4–58 A sample worksheet

range D1..D7 using the keyboard or the mouse. Next, select the Edit Cut command, or use the shortcut, SHIFT-DEL.

Figure 4–59 shows the result of the cut operation. The range D1..D7 is now blank, though all the cells in the range retain their formats, attributes, notes, and other settings. In fact, if you look closely at the upper-left corner of the worksheet window, you'll see "(CO)" indicating that cell D3 has retained its Currency, 0 formatting.

Rather than *cut* the information from the range D1..D7 and place in the clipboard, suppose you want to *copy* it to the clipboard instead. To do this, you would perform the same steps, but use Edit Copy (or its shortcut, CTRL-INS) in place of Edit Cut. When you have completed the command, the worksheet would continue to look like Figure 4–58, with all its original data intact.

After cutting or copying data to the clipboard, you can now perform any other operation you want on the worksheet file. The data in the clipboard remain intact as long as you do not cut or copy other data to the clipboard.

Pasting

After using Edit Cut or Edit Copy to cut or copy data to the clipboard, you can then use the Edit Paste command to copy the data in the clipboard to any of the following locations:

- The same worksheet.

123G.EXE (69.4) Ready

File Edit Worksheet Range Copy... Move... Print Graph Data Utility Quit... Help

A:D3

(C0) EDIT1.WG1

A	A	B	C	D	E	F
1	Expenses	April	May		Total	
2						
3	Rent	$500	$500		$1,000	
4	Food	$200	$200		$400	
5	Entertainment	$1,000	$1,000		$2,000	
6						
7	Total	$1,700	$1,700		$3,400	
8						
9						
10	Income	$1,500	$2,200	$1,900	$5,600	
11	Expenses	$1,700	$1,700	$0	$3,400	
12	Net Cash	($200)	$500	$1,900	$2,200	
13						
14						
15						
16						
17						
18						
19						
20						

FIGURE 4–59 After the Edit Cut command

- Another open worksheet file.
- An open Desktop tool.
- Another Presentation Manager application.

When you use Edit Paste to paste data from the clipboard, the current cell pointer location is used as the upper-left corner of your paste range, then the data are copied from the clipboard, keeping the data's original size and shape. Any existing information in the paste location is overwritten.

Returning to the example in Figures 4–58 and 4–59, suppose you want to paste the data in the clipboard to the same worksheet file, beginning in cell F1. Begin by highlighting cell F1. Next, select the Edit Paste command, or use the shortcut, SHIFT-INS. Figure 4–60 shows the result of this paste operation. The information previously in the range D1..D7 is now in the range F1..F7.

The information in the clipboard is still intact after the paste operation is complete. Therefore, if you highlight cell G1, then select the Edit Paste command again, the information in the clipboard is pasted to the range G1..G7. You can perform this paste operation as many times as you want. However, once you cut or copy new information to the clipboard, this original information is erased.

How Cell References Are Affected

As you review the previous example, notice in Figure 4–58 that cell D3 contains the formula +C3. Yet, after the cell's contents are cut and pasted to cell F3, the

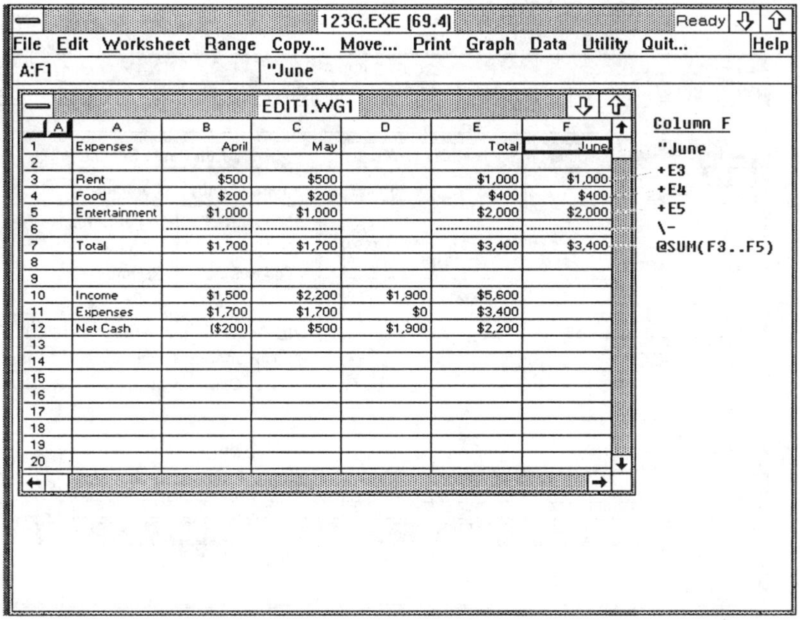

123G.EXE (69.4) Ready

File Edit Worksheet Range Copy... Move... Print Graph Data Utility Quit... Help

A:F1 "June

EDIT1.WG1

A	A	B	C	D	E	F
1	Expenses	April	May		Total	June
2						
3	Rent	$500	$500		$1,000	$1,000
4	Food	$200	$200		$400	$400
5	Entertainment	$1,000	$1,000		$2,000	$2,000
6						
7	Total	$1,700	$1,700		$3,400	$3,400
8						
9						
10	Income	$1,500	$2,200	$1,900	$5,600	
11	Expenses	$1,700	$1,700	$0	$3,400	
12	Net Cash	($200)	$500	$1,900	$2,200	
13						
14						
15						
16						
17						
18						
19						
20						

Column F
"June
+E3
+E4
+E5
\-
@SUM(F3..F5)

FIGURE 4–60 After pasting cut data

formula becomes +E3, as shown in Figure 4–60. The formula's relative address was adjusted to reflect its new location, just as in a copy operation. In fact, as you review all the pasted formulas in Figure 4–60, you'll notice that they have all been adjusted relative to their new location. The moral is: When you use Edit Cut followed by Edit Paste, cell references are adjusted as though you used the Copy command. (See "Copying" above for more information on how 1-2-3/G adjusts cell references.)

Pasting Using the Paste Special Command

When you use the Edit Paste command to paste data from the clipboard, 1-2-3/G applies not only the cell contents but also the notes, formats, attributes, and other settings of the cut or copied data. And, as you know, Edit Paste writes over any information in your paste range.

By using the Edit Paste Special command, however, you can gain more control over what elements are pasted from the clipboard to the paste range. When you select the Edit Paste Special command, a dialog box appears, as in Figure 4–61. Note that this is the same dialog box as the Copy Options dialog box shown previously in Figure 4–34.

You can choose any of the following options in the Edit Paste Special dialog box:

- **Type of entry:** Lets you choose the type of cells in the clipboard that are copied to your paste range—labels, numbers and/or formulas. 1-2-3/G normally copies all of these entries.

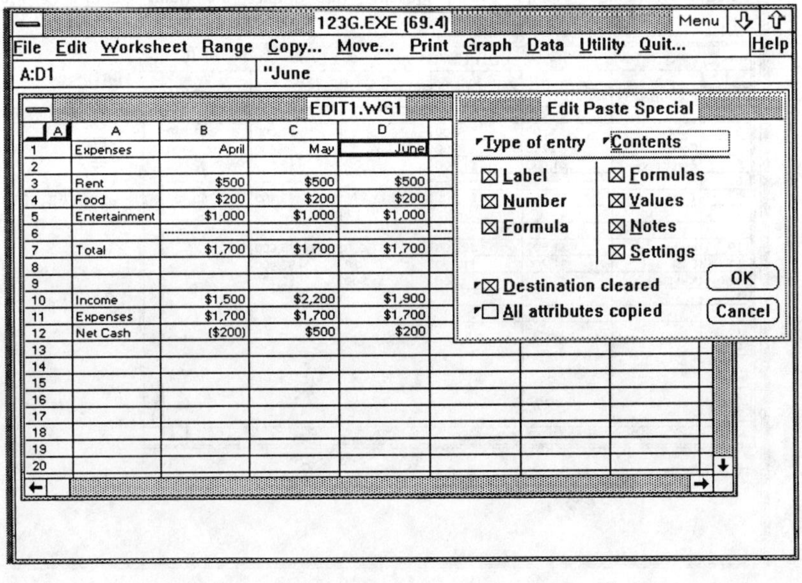

123G.EXE (69.4) Menu
File Edit Worksheet Range Copy... Move... Print Graph Data Utility Quit... Help
A:D1 "June

EDIT1.WG1

A	A	B	C	D
1	Expenses	April	May	June
2				
3	Rent	$500	$500	$500
4	Food	$200	$200	$200
5	Entertainment	$1,000	$1,000	$1,000
6				
7	Total	$1,700	$1,700	$1,700
8				
9				
10	Income	$1,500	$2,200	$1,900
11	Expenses	$1,700	$1,700	$1,700
12	Net Cash	($200)	$500	$200
13				
14				
15				
16				
17				
18				
19				
20				

Edit Paste Special
Type of entry: ☒ Label ☒ Number ☒ Formula
Contents: ☒ Formulas ☒ Values ☒ Notes ☒ Settings
☒ Destination cleared
☐ All attributes copied
OK Cancel

FIGURE 4–61 The Edit Paste Special dialog box

- **Contents:** Lets you choose the contents that the cells in your paste range receive— formulas, values, notes, and/or settings. For example, by turning off the Formulas option and leaving the Values option on, you can have 1-2-3/G paste values in place of formulas. As another example, by turning off the Notes option, you can prevent 1-2-3/G from copying to the paste range any notes you may have created for the original cells. The default setting is to paste all contents—formulas, values, notes, and settings.
- **Destination cleared:** When this option is selected (the default), all existing information in the paste range is erased prior to copying the clipboard data to the paste range. If you cancel this option, the Edit Paste Special command writes over only those cells in your paste range for which the corresponding cells in the clipboard contain information (data or settings). If cells in the clipboard are blank, the corresponding cells in your paste range are left untouched.
- **All attributes copied:** This option lets you control whether the attributes and settings associated with a column, row, worksheet, and/or worksheet file are copied to the paste range. For example, when this option is selected, and you copy and paste an entire column to a new location, the column width setting is also pasted. The default is not to copy any of these settings and attributes.

Each of these options is discussed in detail previously, under "The Copy Options Dialog Box."

When you select options in the Edit Paste Special dialog box, the information in the clipboard does not change. So you can specify different options for each Paste location.

After completing a Paste operation, the Edit Paste Special dialog box always reverts to the default settings shown in Figure 4–61. If you cancel the dialog box by pressing ESC, or by clicking on the cancel button, the dialog box also reverts to these default settings.

Cutting and Pasting between Tools

Thus far, all of the examples have shown how to cut and paste between worksheet files. But suppose you want to cut or copy data from a worksheet file and paste it to another 1-2-3/G tool, like the Note Utility. You can easily use the clipboard to accomplish this task.

For example, imagine you have the worksheet in Figure 4–62, and you want to cut the label from cell B14 and place it in the Note Utility. Begin by highlighting the cell as in Figure 4–62. Next, use the Edit Cut command to delete the label from the cell and place it in the clipboard. Next, activate the Note Utility by selecting the Utility Note command. To paste the label from the clipboard to the Note box, simply select Edit Paste. Figure 4–63 shows the results.

123G.EXE (69.4) Ready

File Edit Worksheet Range Copy... Move... Print Graph Data Utility Quit... Help

A:B14 'Income from April is low due to seasonal factors

EDIT1.WG1

A	A	B	C	D	E	F	G
1	Expenses	April	May	June	Total		
2							
3	Rent	$500	$500	$500	$1,500		
4	Food	$200	$200	$200	$600		
5	Entertainment	$1,000	$1,000	$1,000	$3,000		
6							
7	Total	$1,700	$1,700	$1,700	$5,100		
8							
9							
10	Income	$1,500	$2,200	$1,900	$5,600		
11	Expenses	$1,700	$1,700	$1,700	$5,100		
12	Net Cash	($200)	$500	$200	$500		
13							
14		Income from April is low due to seasonal factors					
15							
16							
17							
18							
19							
20							

FIGURE 4–62 **A worksheet with a note you want to place in the Note Utility**

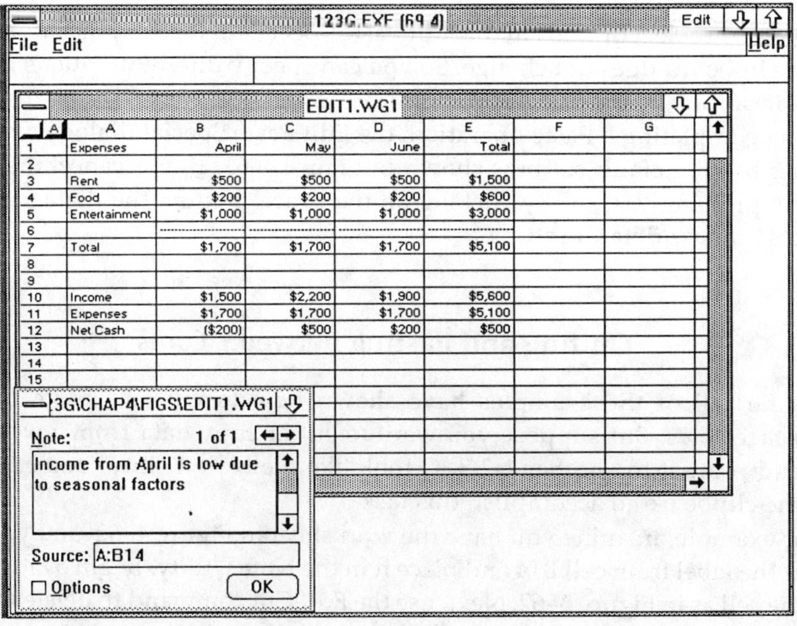

FIGURE 4–63 **After cutting the note from the worksheet and pasting it to the Note Utility**

Cutting and Pasting Between 1–2–3/G and Another PM Application

Besides using the clipboard to cut and paste data between different 1-2-3/G tools and utilities, you can also use it to share data between 1-2-3/G and other Presentation Manager programs. In fact, because all Presentation Manager programs share the same Edit commands, the steps for sharing data through the clipboard are identical to those described in the previous example.

In addition, when another Presentation Manager application supports Dynamic Data Exchange (DDE)—a protocol for sharing data between PM applications—you can use the Edit Link command to establish a "live" link between 1-2-3/G and that application. See Chapter 2, "Managing the Desktop," for a complete description.

Notes on Cutting and Pasting with the Clipboard

Keep in mind the following when you use 1-2-3/G's Edit Cut, Copy, Paste, and Paste Special commands:

- 1-2-3/G's Edit Paste command writes over any information in your paste range. Therefore, before you paste data, be sure that the new location does not include any information that you need.
- After you use the Edit Cut or Edit Copy command to cut or copy data to the clipboard, you cannot use the Undo feature to restore the previous clipboard data. However, you can restore data in a worksheet by undoing an Edit Clear, Edit Cut, Edit Paste, or Edit Paste Special command. Simply select Edit Undo (or press ALT-BACKSPACE) immediately after completing the command to activate 1-2-3/G's Undo feature and reverse the previous command.

COPYING FORMULAS AS VALUES: RANGE VALUE

By using 1-2-3/G's Range Value command, you can copy a selection and, in the process, convert the formulas within the selection to values and labels. Because this command copies only the current values of formulas, not the underlying formulas themselves, you can use it to take a "snapshot" of your data as of a particular point in time.

The process of using the Range Value command is identical to the Copy command. When you select Range Value, 1-2-3/G prompts you for a From range followed by a To range. When you complete the command, cells in the To range contain values and labels only and have the same formats, attributes, notes, and other settings as the cells in the From range.

Like the Copy command, you can use Range Value to copy a cell, range, collection, or even entire worksheets to another location in your file. You can also use Range Value to copy data between files.

Like many of the other commands in this chapter, the Range Value command now includes Confirm (✓) and Cancel (X) icons in the Control line. Click on the Cancel (X) icon at any time during a Range Value command to abort the operation. Click on the Confirm (✓) icon at the end of the Range Value command to complete the operation.

An Example

One of the most important applications for the Range Value command is in scenario generation. You can use Range Value to copy the results obtained in one scenario to another location in your file; the results in this new location are stored as values and labels only. After storing the data in another location, you can then return to the original location, run another scenario using different assumptions, and compare the results.

For example, suppose you have created the model in Figure 4–64 in which you are projecting first-year sales for a start-up company. You estimate first quarter sales as $100,000 and assume that sales will increase each quarter by 100% from the previous quarter, the assumption in A:B3. In addition, you estimate cost of goods sold (COGS) as 50% of the sales price, the assumption in cell A:B4. Finally, you estimate overhead expenses as $500,000 each quarter during the first six months, decreasing to $300,000 per quarter thereafter.

123G.EXE Ready

File Edit Worksheet Range Copy... Move... Print Graph Data Utility Quit... Help

A:D5 +D4*$B5

VALUE1.WG1

A	A	B	C	D	E	F	G	H
1			Q Ended	Q Ended	Q Ended	Q Ended	Year Ended	
2		Assumptions	31-Mar-90	30-Jun-90	30-Sep-90	31-Dec-90	31-Dec-90	
3		----------	----------	----------	----------	----------	----------	
4	Net Sales	100%	$100,000	$200,000	$400,000	$800,000	$1,500,000	
5	COGS	50%	$50,000	$100,000	$200,000	$400,000	$750,000	
6			----------	----------	----------	----------	----------	
7	Gross Profit		$50,000	$100,000	$200,000	$400,000	$750,000	
8	Overhead Expenses		$500,000	$500,000	$300,000	$300,000	$1,600,000	
9			----------	----------	----------	----------	----------	
10	Pre-Tax Net Profit		($450,000)	($400,000)	($100,000)	$100,000	($850,000)	

FIGURE 4–64 A sample worksheet to be used for scenario generation

Imagine that you want to run one scenario in worksheet A, copy the range A1..G10 to worksheet B using the Range Value command, run a second scenario in worksheet A, and compare the results. Perform the following steps:

1. Move the cell pointer to the upper-left corner of the range you want to copy, cell A:A1.
2. Select the Range Value command. The "From:" prompt contains the current selection in the form of a range, A:A1..A:A1.
3. Specify the range you want to convert to values, A:A1..A:G10. You can use any of the following methods:

   - Type **A:A1..A:G10**, or just **A1..G10**.
   - Highlight the range using the keyboard. Since the cell pointer is already anchored in cell A:A1, press → and ↓ until the range A:A1..A:G10 is highlighted.
   - Highlight the range using the mouse. Click on A:A1, and keeping the left button depressed, drag the pointer so the range A:A1..A:G10 is highlighted.

   The From range A:A1..A:G10 is now displayed in the Control line.
4. Press ENTER or click to the right of the "To:" prompt. (You cannot use the Confirm (✓) icon during this step.)
5. Specify a To range. Like other commands in this chapter, when you specify a To range, you need to provide only a single cell address. 1-2-3/G uses this cell as the upper-left corner of your To range, then moves the information in your From range, keeping its size and shape. If you specify a collection as your From range, 1-2-3/G maintains the relationship between the ranges that make up your collection in your To range.

   Use any of the following methods to specify the upper-left cell of your To range, B:A1:

   - Type **B:A1**.
   - Use the keyboard to move the cell pointer to B:A1. Since the cell pointer is now unanchored in A:A1, simply press CTRL-PGUP.
   - Use the mouse to click on B:A1.

   The To range B:A1 is now displayed in the Control line.
6. Press ENTER, or click on the Confirm (✓) icon in the Control line.

Figure 4–65 shows the results of the Range Value command. Although the worksheets A and B appear to be identical, you can tell that the cells in worksheet B contain no underlying formulas.

123G.EXE (69.4) Ready

File Edit Worksheet Range Copy... Move... Print Graph Data Utility Quit... Help

B:D5 100000

VALUE2.WG1

B	A	B	C	D	E	F	G
1			Q Ended	Q Ended	Q Ended	Q Ended	Year Ended
2		Assumptions	31-Mar-90	30-Jun-90	30-Sep-90	31-Dec-90	31-Dec-90
3							
4	Net Sales	100%	$100,000	$200,000	$400,000	$800,000	$1,500,000
5	COGS	50%	$50,000	$100,000	$200,000	$400,000	$750,000
6							
7	Gross Profit		$50,000	$100,000	$200,000	$400,000	$750,000
8	Overhead Expenses		$500,000	$500,000	$300,000	$300,000	$1,600,000
9							
10	Pre-Tax Net Profit		($450,000)	($400,000)	($100,000)	$100,000	($850,000)
11							

A	A	B	C	D	E	F	G	H
1			Q Ended	Q Ended	Q Ended	Q Ended	Year Ended	
2		Assumptions	31-Mar-90	30-Jun-90	30-Sep-90	31-Dec-90	31-Dec-90	
3								
4	Net Sales	100%	$100,000	$200,000	$400,000	$800,000	$1,500,000	
5	COGS	50%	$50,000	$100,000	$200,000	$400,000	$750,000	
6								
7	Gross Profit		$50,000	$100,000	$200,000	$400,000	$750,000	
8	Overhead Expenses		$500,000	$500,000	$300,000	$300,000	$1,600,000	
9								
10	Pre-Tax Net Profit		($450,000)	($400,000)	($100,000)	$100,000	($850,000)	
11								

FIGURE 4–65 Using the Range Value command to copy formulas as values

Because the formulas in worksheet A are still intact, you can now change the assumptions in worksheet A. For example, Figure 4–66 shows what happens when you change the value in cell A:B4 to 85% and the value in cell A:B5 to 30%. You can now easily compare the "frozen" values in worksheet B to the updated values in worksheet A.

Notes on Range Value

Keep in mind the following when you use the Range Value command:

- If recalculation is set to manual, be sure to press CALC (F9) before you begin the Range Value command. Otherwise, the values you copy with Range Value many not be current.
- Because literal values require less memory than formulas, you can use Range Value to decrease memory consumption in a large file. For example, many times you will use formulas to create repetitive or related information, such as dates. To convert formulas to values, use the Range Value command and specify the same To and From Range.

123G.EXE (69.4) Ready

File Edit Worksheet Range Copy... Move... Print Graph Data Utility Quit... Help

A:B5 0.3

(P0) VALUE3.WG1

B	A	B	C	D	E	F	G
1			Q Ended	Q Ended	Q Ended	Q Ended	Year Ended
2		Assumptions	31-Mar-90	30-Jun-90	30-Sep-90	31-Dec-90	31-Dec-90
3							
4	Net Sales	100%	$100,000	$200,000	$400,000	$800,000	$1,500,000
5	COGS	50%	$50,000	$100,000	$200,000	$400,000	$750,000
6							
7	Gross Profit		$50,000	$100,000	$200,000	$400,000	$750,000
8	Overhead Expenses		$500,000	$500,000	$300,000	$300,000	$1,600,000
9							
10	Pre-Tax Net Profit		($450,000)	($400,000)	($100,000)	$100,000	($850,000)

A	A	B	C	D	E	F	G	H
1			Q Ended	Q Ended	Q Ended	Q Ended	Year Ended	
2		Assumptions	31-Mar-90	30-Jun-90	30-Sep-90	31-Dec-90	31-Dec-90	
3								
4	Net Sales	85%	$100,000	$185,000	$342,250	$633,163	$1,260,413	
5	COGS	30%	$30,000	$55,500	$102,675	$189,949	$378,124	
6								
7	Gross Profit		$70,000	$129,500	$239,575	$443,214	$882,289	
8	Overhead Expenses		$500,000	$500,000	$300,000	$300,000	$1,600,000	
9								
10	Pre-Tax Net Profit		($430,000)	($370,500)	($60,425)	$143,214	($717,711)	

FIGURE 4–66 Comparing a new scenario in worksheet A with the "frozen" values in worksheet B

- If you want to convert a formula in a single cell to its underlying value, but you do not want to use the Range Value command, begin by moving the cell pointer to the cell. Next, press EDIT (F2), CALC (F9), then ENTER.
- Of course, if you erase information you need using the Range Value command, you can press ALT-BACKSPACE immediately after the Range Value command to activate 1-2-3/G's Undo feature and recover the information.

TRANSPOSING VALUES AND LABELS: RANGE TRANSPOSE

1-2-3/G's Range Transpose command lets you change the orientation of the current selection as you copy it to a new location. Like the Range Value command, Range Transpose converts formulas to their underlying values as it copies data to the new location. It also copies the same formats, attributes, notes, and other settings from the original selection to the new location.

In 1-2-3/G, you can use Range Transpose to transpose data in any of the following ways:

- From rows to columns (Rows/Columns).
- From columns to two or more worksheets (Columns/Worksheet).
- From one or more rows in one worksheet to two or more worksheets (Worksheet/Rows).

As in Release 3, you can use 1-2-3/G's Range Transpose command to transpose two- or three-dimensional ranges. You can even use Range Transpose to transpose ranges between two open files. However, you cannot use Range Transpose to transpose a collection.

Transposing a Two-Dimensional Range

When you select the Range Transpose command, 1-2-3/G displays the dialog box in Figure 4–67. As you can see, you must specify both a From and a To range. In addition, you must choose a transposition option: Rows/Columns, Columns/Worksheet, and Worksheet/Rows. The effect of using each of these options to transpose a 2-D range is discussed in the sections that follow.

Rows/Columns

You can easily transpose rows to columns for a 2–D range. For example, suppose you have the worksheet in Figure 4–67 in which cells A:A1, A:B1, and

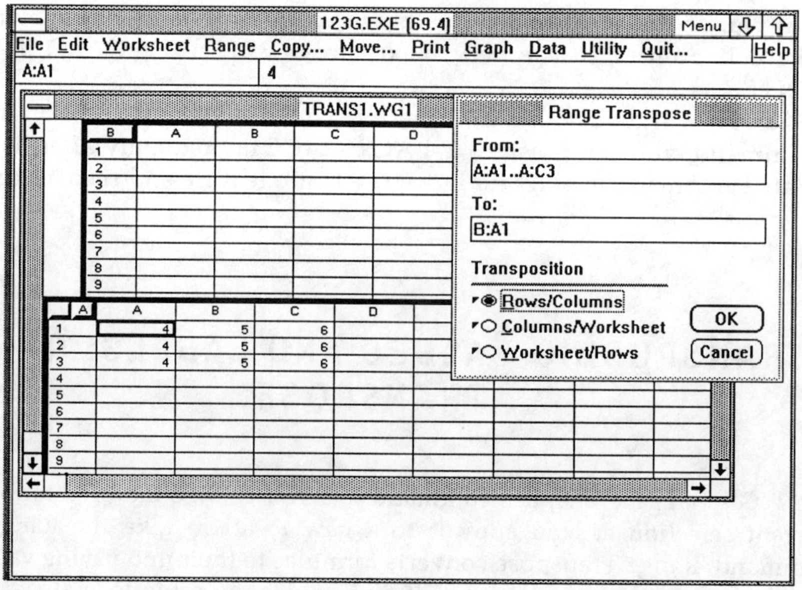

A	A	B	C	D
1	4	5	6	
2	4	5	6	
3	4	5	6	

FIGURE 4–67 Transposing a 2–D range with Range Transpose

A:C1 contain the values 4, 5, and 6, respectively. Cells A:A2 and A:A3 contain the formula +A:A1, cells B2 and B3 contain +A:B1, and cells C2 and C3 contain +A:C1. Imagine that you want to transpose the range A:A1..A:C3 to range B:A1..B:C3. Do the following:

1. Locate the cell pointer in the upper-left corner of the range you want to transpose, cell A:A1, and select the Range Transpose command. The Range Transpose dialog box appears, as in Figure 4-67. The "From:" prompt contains the current selection in the form of a range, A:A1..A:A1.

2. Select your From range. Specify the range you want to convert to values and labels, copy, and transpose, A:A1..A:C3. Use any of the following methods:

   - Type **A:A1..A:C3**, or just **A1..C3**.
   - Highlight the range using the keyboard. Since the cell pointer is already anchored in cell A:A1, press → and ↓ until the range A:A1..A:C3 is highlighted.
   - Highlight the range using the mouse. Click on cell A:A1 to anchor this cell at the beginning of your From range. Keeping the left button depressed, drag the pointer so the range A:A1..A:C3 is highlighted.

   The From range A:A1..A:C3 is now displayed in the Control line.

3. Press ENTER or TAB, or click on the To range box.

4. Select a To range. Like other commands in this chapter, when you specify a To range, you need to provide only a single cell address. 1-2-3/G uses this cell as the upper-left corner of your To range. Use any of the following methods to specify cell B:A1:

   - Type **B:A1**.
   - Use the keyboard to highlight the cell. After you specify your From range, the cell pointer is unanchored in A:A1. Simply press CTRL-PGUP to move to cell B:A1.
   - Use the mouse to highlight the cell. Simply click on cell B:A1.

   The To Range, B:A1, is now displayed in to the text box.
5. Press ENTER, or select the OK button, to accept the Rows/Columns option and complete the command.

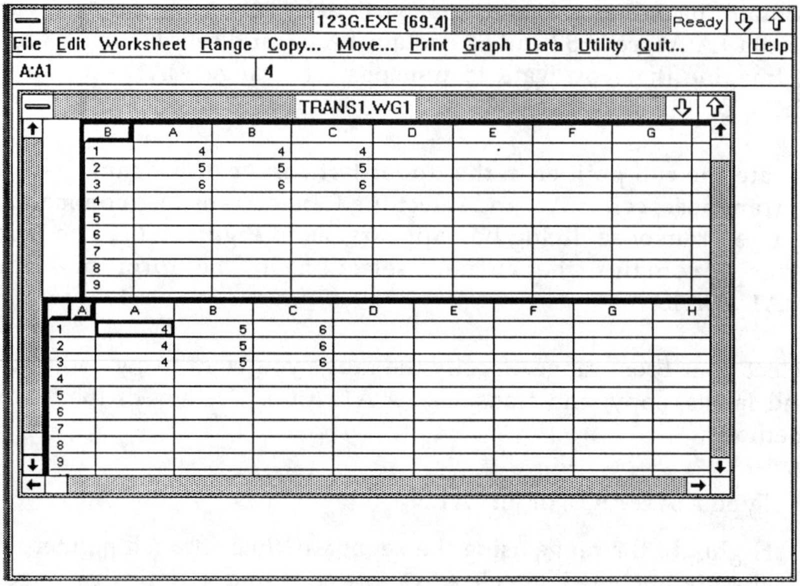

FIGURE 4–68 The results of the Rows/Columns option

The results of this Range Transpose operation are shown in Figure 4–68. As you can see, 1-2-3/G has copied the first column of the From range (A:A1..A:A3) to the first row in the To range (B:A1..B:C1), the second column of the From range (A:B1..A:B3) to the first row in the To range (B:A2..B:C2), and so on. The destination ranges, B:A1..B:C1, B:A2..B:C2 and so on, only include the current values of the formulas in the From range. The formulas themselves are not copied.

Columns/Worksheet

This option transposes each column in your From range to a column in a different worksheet. For example, Figure 4–69 shows the results when you start with the file in Figure 4–67, specify A:A1..A:C3 as your From range, B:A1 as your To range, and select the Columns/Worksheet option. As you can see, 1-2-3/G has copied the first column of the From range (A:A1..A:A3) to the first column in worksheet B (B:A1..B:A3), the second column of the From range (A:B1..A:B3) to the first column in worksheet C (C:A1..C:A3), and so on.

Worksheet/Rows

This option transposes each row in your From range to a row in a different worksheet. For example, suppose you start with the file in Figure 4–67, choose a From range of A:A1..A:C3, a To range of B:A1, and select the

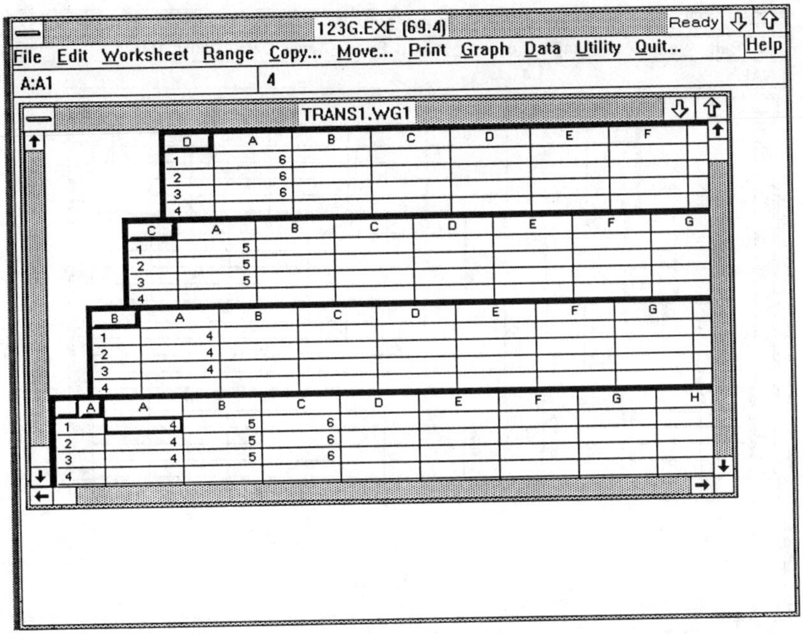

FIGURE 4–69 The results of the Columns/Worksheet option

Worksheet/Rows command. Figure 4–70 shows the results. In this case, 1-2-3/G has copied the first row of the From range (A:A1..A:C1) to the first row in worksheet B (B:A1..B:C1), the second row of the From range (A:A2..A:C2) to the first row in worksheet C (C:A1..C:C1), and so on.

Transposing a Three-Dimensional Range

As mentioned, you can also use the Range Transpose command to transpose a 3–D range. Just as with a 2–D range, the transposition options in the Range Transpose dialog box control the final orientation of the data. In all cases, however, when you specify a 3–D From range, the result is a 3–D range.

Rows/Columns

Figure 4–71 shows the results of using the Rows/Columns option when you specify a 3–D From range of A:A1..C:C3 and a To range of A:E1. Although Range Transpose is applied to three consecutive worksheets, the result is the same as using Range Transpose in a single worksheet. Each row in the From range is transposed to a column in the new location.

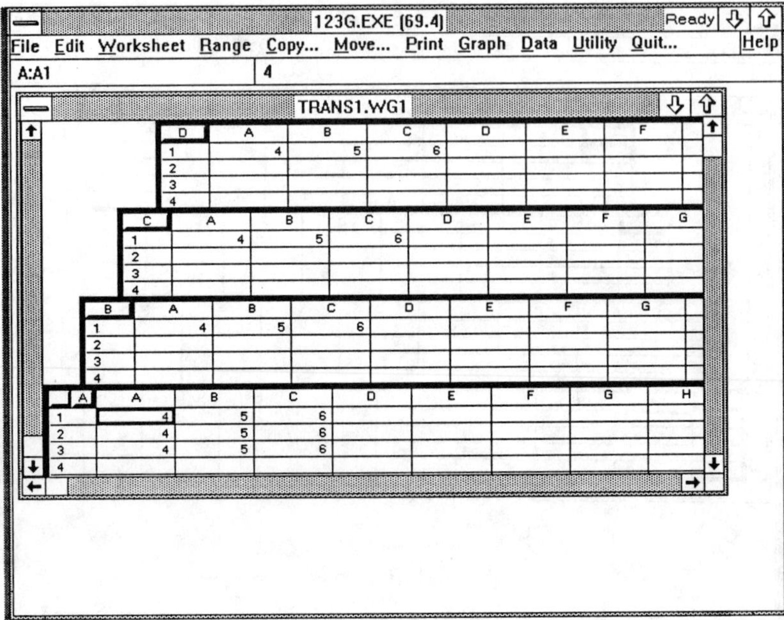

FIGURE 4–70 The results of the Worksheet/Rows option

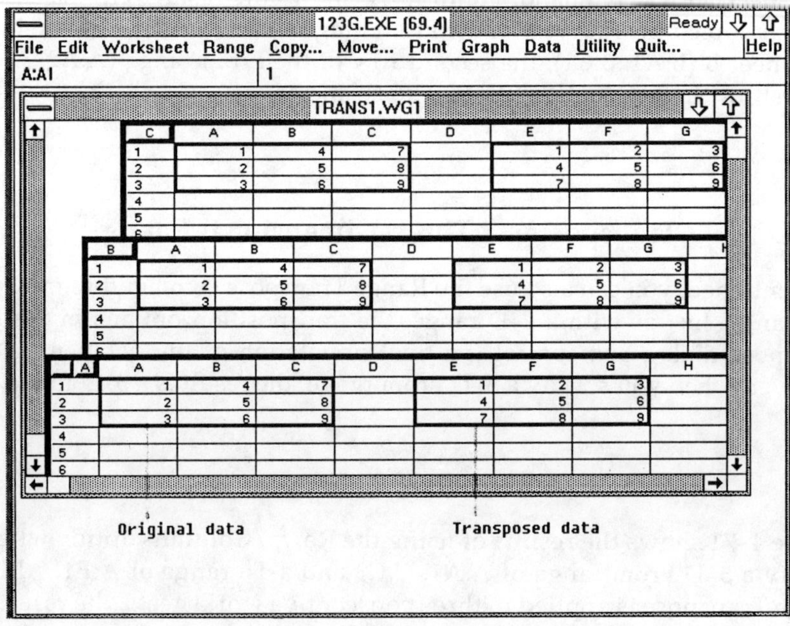

FIGURE 4–71 Transposing a 3-D range using Rows/Columns

Note

> You cannot use the mouse alone to specify a 3-D range for the Range Transpose command unless worksheets are grouped. Of course, you can use the mouse to specify a collection that encompasses the same cells as a 3-D range, but Range Transpose does not accept a collection. Instead, use the keyboard to specify a 3-D range.

Columns/Worksheet

Figure 4-72 shows a transposition of a 3-D range of data using the Columns/Worksheet option. Note that the first column of each worksheet in the From range is copied as a column to the first worksheet in the To range. The second column in each worksheet in the From range is copied as a column to the second worksheet in the To range, and so on.

Worksheet/Rows

Figure 4-73 shows the result of using the Worksheet/Rows option of the Range Transpose command. Note that the first row in each worksheet in the From range is copied as a row in the first worksheet of the To range. The second row in each worksheet in the From range is copied as a row to the second worksheet in the To range, and so on.

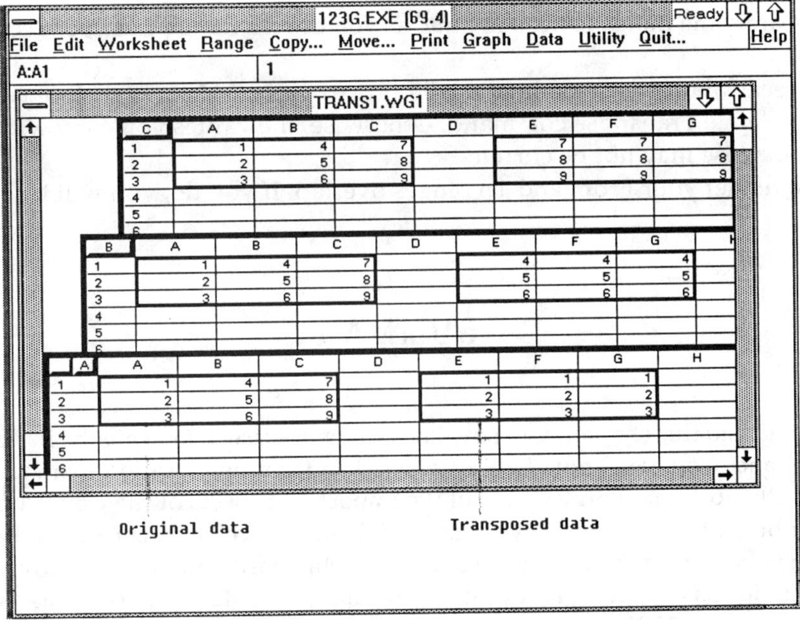

FIGURE 4-72 Transposing a 3-D range using Columns/Worksheet

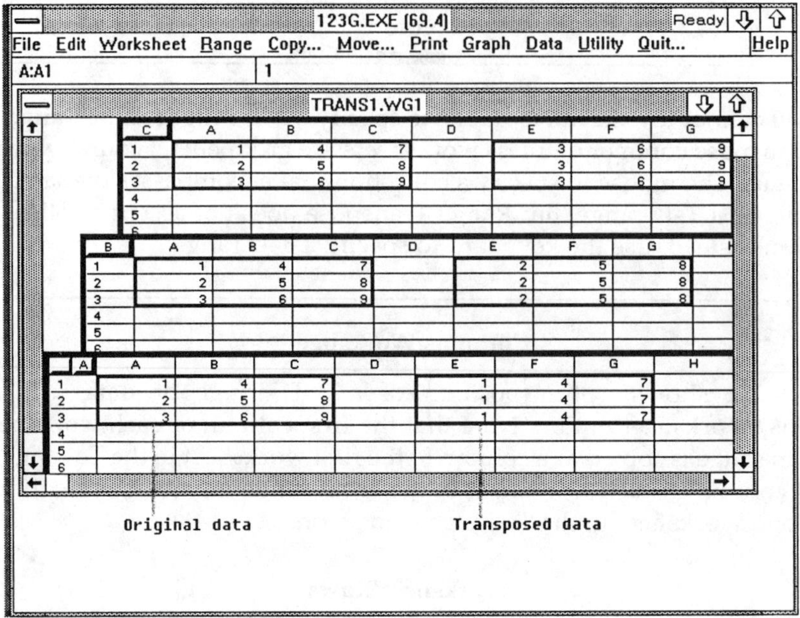

FIGURE 4–73 Transposing a 3-D range using Worksheet/Rows

Notes on Range Transpose

Here are some things to keep in mind as you use the Range Transpose command:

- If recalculation is set to manual, be sure to press CALC (F9) before you begin the Range Transpose command. Otherwise, the values you copy with Range Transpose may not be current.
- Do not let your From and To ranges overlap. If you do, you will lose data.

SUMMARY

Having read this chapter, you now know how to erase data using the Range Erase command. You also know how to move data from one location to another with Move. In addition, you learned all the important aspects of the Copy command, including the effects of relative, mixed, and absolute cell references. You have also learned how to cut and paste data using the clipboard. Finally, you learned about special forms of cutting and pasting, including how to copy formulas as values with the Range Value command, and how to transpose data with Range Transpose. You now have all the skills you need to effectively cut and paste data in 1-2-3/G.

CHAPTER

5

File Management

To manage your 1-2-3/G data files, you use the File command. The primary function of the File command is to create and open new and existing files on the desktop, and to save those files to disk. However, the File command is also used to perform other functions. For example, you can use it to erase a file on disk. You can also use it to combine the contents of a worksheet file on disk with a worksheet file in memory. Conversely, you can extract a selected range of data from a worksheet file in memory to a worksheet file on disk. In addition, you can use the File command to change directories, manage files on a network, import ASCII text files, and manage the 1-2-3/G desktop. With its broad range of functionality, a good working knowledge of how to use the File command can be an important part of getting the most out of 1-2-3/G.

The File command is available from all of 1-2-3/G's tools (Worksheet and Graph) as well as its utilities (Solver, Keystroke Editor, Screen Preview, and Note). This chapter approaches the File command from the standpoint of the Worksheet Tool menu, because it offers the most comprehensive set of options. In fact, some of the options discussed in this chapter (Xtract, Combine, and Import) do not apply to the Graph Tool, and are therefore not included in the Graph Tool menu. Further, in some utilities, various options on the File menu may appear grayed, meaning that you cannot select them from that particular utility.

The scope of the File command is too broad to cover in a single chapter. Therefore, at times, you will be referred to other chapters in this book for additional information. For example, the File Print command, when accessed from the Worksheet Tool menu, is used to print the contents of a worksheet file. Due to the many issues involved with printing a worksheet, this command is covered in Chapter 8, "Printing." The File Print command is also available from the Graph Tool menu for use in printing your graphs. Using the File Print command in this context is discussed in Chapter 7, "Graphs." In addition, the File Utility command is used to manage the 1-2-3/G desktop and is covered at length in Chapter 2, "Managing the Desktop." The File Admin command is used to manage 1-2-3/G files in a network environment. This command is covered in Chapter 12, "Networking 1-2-3/G." Finally, many of the user and default settings that affect the File Command are discussed in Appendix A, "Customizing 1-2-3/G."

What's New

Two new commands, File New and File Open, have been added to the File menu. These are required to accommodate 1-2-3/G's ability to support multiple files (windows) on the desktop. The File New command allows you to create a new worksheet or graph file in a separate window. The File Open command, on the other hand, allows you to open an existing file from disk in its own window. Both commands leave existing files (windows) open on the desktop. The File Retrieve command is now used to replace the file in the currently active window with another existing file from disk

When you create a new file in 1-2-3/G, you can specify the name of another existing file that will be used as a *template* for the new file. The data and settings from the template file are then used to create the new file. This handy feature can save you significant amounts of data entry and formatting time.

Like 1-2-3 Release 3, 1-2-3/G's File Save command allows you to save all the files in memory in a single operation and to back up files. When you select File Save with multiple files in memory, 1-2-3/G allows you to save all files at once, save file by file (accepting or rejecting files as you go), or to save only the currently active file. If a file already exits on disk, 1-2-3/G displays a Replace, Cancel, Backup menu. You are already familiar with Replace and Cancel. However, if you select Backup, 1-2-3/G first copies the original file to a default backup directory under the same name and then saves the updated file in memory in the original file's location on disk. Release 3 users will notice a subtle difference here. In Release 3, the file on disk is renamed with the same name and a .BAK extension, and the file from memory is then saved to disk.

The new File Print command allows you to print the contents of a graph or worksheet window. Using the File Print command to print worksheet files is covered in Chapter 8, "Printing." Using the File Print command to print graphs is covered in Chapter 7, "Graphs."

The File Admin command has been carried forward from 1-2-3 Release 3 to 1-2-3/G. This command is discussed at length in Chapter 12, "Networking 1-2-3/G." The File Admin command allows you to manage file reservations in a network environment. You can also use this command to update formula links between files and to change the source reference for formula links from one file to another. In addition, the File Admin command allows you to create tables of information about files that are open on the desktop as well as files stored on disk. This aspect of the File Admin command is discussed briefly in this chapter under "Getting Information About Files."

The new File Utility command allows you to manage the 1-2-3/G desktop. This command is discussed at length in Chapter 2, "Managing the Desktop." The File Utility command allows you to clear the desktop, copy the desktop, archive the desktop, and get information about the files that are currently open on the desktop.

The File Combine command has been slightly enhanced for 1-2-3/G. It now includes two new options, Multiply and Divide. As you may recall, the File Combine command allows you to combine the contents of a worksheet file on disk with a worksheet file in memory. The Add and Subtract options available from prior releases allow you to add or subtract values in the file on disk to or from the values in the active worksheet file. The new Multiply and Divide options simply extend this functionality by allowing you to multiply or divide the values in the active worksheet file by the values in the file on disk.

FILE BASICS

As you know, files contain data and are stored on disk. Each file is identified by its name and the path (drive and directory name) that describes its location on disk. This section begins with a brief overview of those components of the 1-2-3/G desktop that give you information about files that are currently in use. It then gives you some information about 1-2-3/G's file naming conventions. It also describes the types of files you may encounter while using 1-2-3/G.

The Desktop

Figure 5–1 shows an example of the 1-2-3/G desktop with a single window containing a worksheet file. A window is a frame through which you view a worksheet file. You can have up to 16 worksheet files open on the desktop, each in its own window. 1-2-3/G identifies the file contained in each window by showing its filename in the title bar at the top of the window. For example, in

Figure 5–1, the name of the worksheet file contained in the window is SALES.WG1.

The window containing the cell pointer is the *active* window. The commands that appear in the Menu bar apply to the active window. You can make another window the active window by clicking on its title bar. Or you can press NEXT WINDOW (CTRL-F6) to cycle through the windows that are currently open on the desktop. As yet another alternative, you can select Window from the Desktop Control Menu. 1-2-3/G displays a list of the windows that are open on the desktop; the name of the currently active window appears with a check mark. When you make a selection from this list, 1-2-3/G activates the window you specified.

1-2-3/G allows you to save the windows currently open on the desktop under a single desktop filename. When you save a desktop, 1-2-3/G creates a desktop file with a .DSK extension. Desktop files contain information about the names and disk locations of the files currently open on the desktop, the links between files, and the on-screen size, position, and status of each window. Once you create a desktop file, you can open that file at a later time and 1-2-3/G will restore the same set of files to the desktop as when you originally saved the desktop to disk. What's more, the window for each file will appear in the same position and have the same status as when you last saved the desktop. Thus, desktop files allow you to work with groups of related files as a single unit.

If you open a desktop file, the name of that file appears in the desktop title bar at the top of the 1-2-3/G window. For example, the name of the desktop in

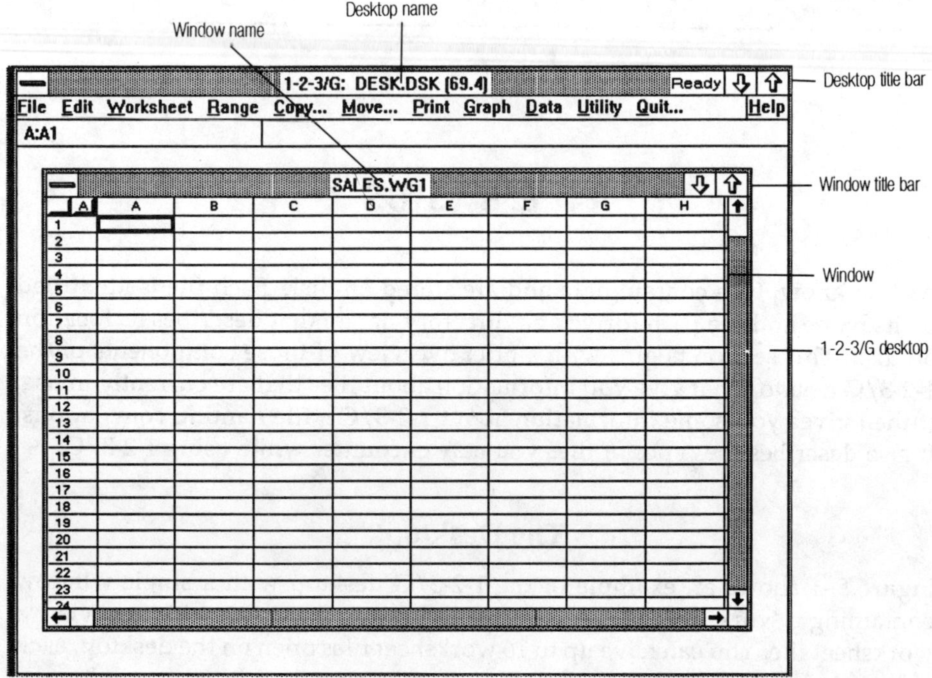

FIGURE 5–1 The 1-2-3/G desktop

Figure 5–1 is DESK.DSK. See "Saving Files" later in this chapter for details on how to actually save a desktop.

1-2-3/G also allows you to open more than one copy of a worksheet file, each in its own window. When multiple copies of a file are open on the desktop, each is referred to as a *view* of the file. When you change one view, other open views of the file are automatically updated to reflect the change. When you open a second view of a file, 1-2-3/G displays the name of the file in the window title bar followed by a number in parentheses—for example, SALES.WG1(2).

Opening multiple views of the same worksheet file allows you to more easily view divergent portions of the file. This can be especially handy when you are building a multiple-worksheet model with links between worksheets. For example, imagine you are working with a model that uses 10 consecutive worksheets. As you know, the maximum number of worksheets you can display in a single window with the Worksheet Window Perspective command is five. However, if you open two views of the file, you can see the first five worksheets in the first view and the second five worksheets in the second view. If the worksheets are linked, you can make a change in the first worksheet and watch as the other nine worksheets are updated.

Note

> For a complete discussion of how to manage the 1-2-3/G desktop, see Chapter 2, "Managing the Desktop."

Naming 1-2-3/G Files

1-2-3/G conforms to OS/2's file naming conventions. Like DOS, OS/2 Version 1.1 uses the File Allocation Table (FAT) system for storing and naming files. OS/2 1.2, on the other hand, allows you to choose from either the FAT system or the High Performance File System (HPFS).

Under the FAT system, filenames can be from one to eight characters in length. You can also follow the filename with an optional file extension that begins with a period (.) followed by up to three characters. For example, 1-2-3/G automatically assigns worksheet files an extension of .WG1.

Under the HPFS system, filenames can be from 1 to 254 characters in length. You can break the filename into as many individual parts as you want by separating each part of the name with a period (.).

It is recommended that you assign filenames that identify the contents of a file. For example, the filenames TAX90FED.WG1 and TAX90_ST.WG1 tell you that the first file contains data about 1990 federal taxes and the second file contains 1990 state tax information.

Other OS/2 file naming conventions are as follows:

- You can use any combination of letters, numbers, and underscores (_) when naming files. However, the characters ", /, \, [,], :, |, >, <, +, =, ;, the comma, *, ?, & (OS/2 1.2 only), and the period (OS/2 1.1 only) have special meanings either to OS/2 or 1-2-3/G and may not be used in filenames.
- You cannot use spaces in filenames.
- You can use any combination of upper-case or lower-case letters, since a filename is not case sensitive.

For example, the following filenames are acceptable under either the FAT or HPFS systems:

```
SALES_92.WG1    CASH-92.GPH    11_18_92.PRN    CLOSE!.DSK
```

Specifying Paths

The path identifies the location of a file on disk. It is followed by the file's name and its extension. The path consists of a drive letter, for example, C, followed by a colon (:) and the name of a directory containing the file. For example, to identify the file SALES.WG1 on the directory \123G\WORK located on drive C, you would specify C:\123G\WORK\SALES.WG1.

When you select a File command, 1-2-3/G displays a dialog box associated with that command. In most instances, the dialog box will contain a text box entitled "Filename," which allows you to specify the drive, path, and name of the file you want the current command to affect. By default, 1-2-3/G always displays the drive and path for the *current working directory* (usually C:\123/G\WORK) in the "Filename" text box. This is the directory in which 1-2-3/G searches for its data files. You can, of course, specify a different directory in the "Filename" text box, if you so desire.

If the active file is in the current working directory (the directory in which 1-2-3/G searches for its files), the worksheet window title bar displays only the

Note

> During the installation of 1-2-3/G, you specified a working directory for 1-2-3/G worksheets, graphs, and desktop files (probably \123G\WORK). You also specified a file template directory (probably \123G\TEMPLATE), a backup directory (probably \123G\BACKUP) for backup worksheet and graph files, and a directory for temporary files (probably \123G\TEMP). For a discussion of these directories, and methods to change these default directories, see "Changing Directories," later in this chapter. This is also discussed in Appendix A, "Customizing 1-2-3/G."

filename. For example, in Figure 5–1, since the file is located in the current directory, only the name of the file, SALES.WG1, appears in the title bar for the worksheet window. On the other hand, if the file is located outside the current working directory, 1-2-3/G displays the full path and filename in the worksheet window title bar. For example, suppose you have retrieved the file SALES.WG1 from the directory C:\MARKET, which is not the working directory. Then C:\MARKET\SALES.WG1 is displayed in the worksheet window title bar.

1-2-3/G's File Extensions

Although file extensions are optional in OS/2, 1-2-3/G always assigns a file extension to each file it creates. The extension assigned depends on the context. For example, if you use the File Save command to save a worksheet file, 1-2-3/G automatically adds a .WG1 extension to the name you provide. 1-2-3/G uses these extensions to locate and list specific file types for certain commands. You can use the file extensions assigned by 1-2-3/G as an indicator of the type of file you are dealing with. Here are some of the more common file extensions you'll encounter while using 1-2-3/G:

.WG1	Worksheet file, 1-2-3/G
.WK3	Worksheet file, 1-2-3 Release 3
.WK1	Worksheet file, 1-2-3 Releases 2, 2.01, and 2.2
.WKS	Worksheet file, 1-2-3 Release 1A
.WR1	Worksheet file, Lotus Symphony Version 1.1 and later
.GPH	Graph file, 1-2-3/G
.ENC	Encoded file, 1-2-3/G
.PRN	ASCII file, All 1-2-3 Releases
.DSK	Desktop file, 1-2-3/G

You can assign your own file extensions to 1-2-3/G files. When 1-2-3/G prompts you for a filename, simply enter the name of your choice, press period, and type an extension. However, if you use your own extensions, you may have trouble finding your files later. When 1-2-3/G lists files for commands, it only lists files whose extensions it automatically assigns and therefore easily recognizes. To list or select files with different extensions, you must make a special effort. In fact, the extra steps associated with locating your files may outweigh the benefit you gain by using your own file extensions.

SAVING FILES

When you enter data in a worksheet file, you are actually entering information into your PC's Random Access Memory (RAM). Your PC's RAM only stores the information temporarily. Therefore, if you turn your computer off, you lose the information. To save the data permanently, you must save the file containing the data to disk. To save a file to disk in 1-2-3/G, you use the File Save command. When you select the File Save command, 1-2-3/G displays the dialog box in Figure 5–2.

If only a single file is open on the desktop, 1-2-3/G displays the name of that file in the "File name" text box. For example, the file D:\CH5\SALES.WG1 appears in the "File name" text box in Figure 5–2. (See "Creating New Files" later for information on naming files.) In addition, the "Current File only" option button is selected.

To save the file under the name shown in the "File name" text box, select the OK command button, or press ENTER. The first time you save a new file, 1-2-3/G simply saves the file to disk and does not provide any confirmation. However, if the file already exists on disk, 1-2-3/G displays the Save Window menu box shown in Figure 5–3. The menu box contains three command buttons Cancel, Replace, and Backup—which perform the following functions:

- **Cancel:** Cancels the File Save command without saving the file. 1-2-3/G returns to READY mode.
- **Replace:** Replaces the file on disk with the currently active file.
- **Backup:** 1-2-3/G copies the original file on disk to the default backup directory, under the same name. It then saves the updated file in memory in the original file's location on disk.

Note

> You can use the Utility User Settings Preferences command to have 1-2-3/G automatically save or back up an existing file (without a confirmation) during the File Save command. See Appendix A, "Customizing 1-2-3/G," for more details.

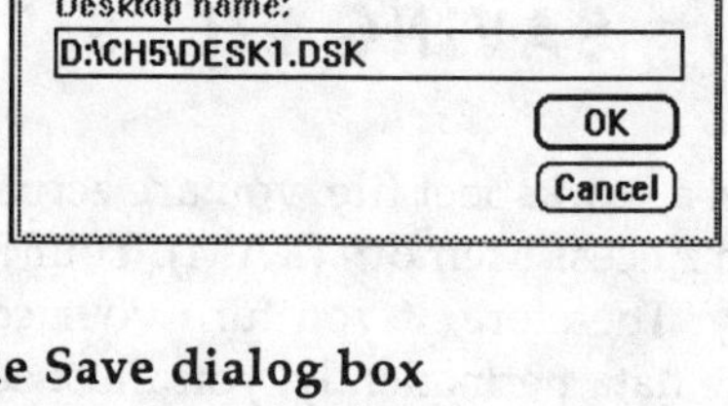

FIGURE 5–2 The File Save dialog box

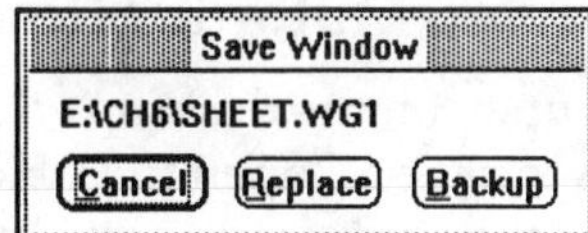

FIGURE 5–3 The Save Window menu box

Saving a File under a Different Name

You can also save a file in memory under a new name. For example, as you know, each time you start 1-2-3/G, it opens a new window containing a worksheet file and assigns that file a default name. For the first new worksheet file in the current directory, 1-2-3/G assigns the default name SHEET.WG1, for the second, SHEET1.WG1; and so on. 1-2-3/G uses this same file-naming strategy when you create a new file with the File New command (see "Creating Files" later). However, you do not have to save the file under the default name. Instead, you can provide a filename of your own that more closely describes the content of the file.

To save a single file under a different name, select the File Save command. 1-2-3/G displays the File Save dialog box shown in Figure 5–2 and automatically activates the "File name" text box. Type a new name and path for the file, or edit the current one, then select the OK command button, or press ENTER. 1-2-3/G saves the file under the name you specified.

To replace an existing file on disk whose name is different from the file in memory, select the File Save command. In the "File name" text box, type the name of the file on disk and press ENTER, or select the OK command button. As an alternative to typing the name of the file in the "File name" text box, you can press NAME (F3) to have 1-2-3/G show you a list of files in the current directory, as shown in Figure 5–4. Select the filename you want and press ENTER. 1-2-3/G displays the Save Window menu box shown earlier in Figure 5–3. Select Replace or Backup.

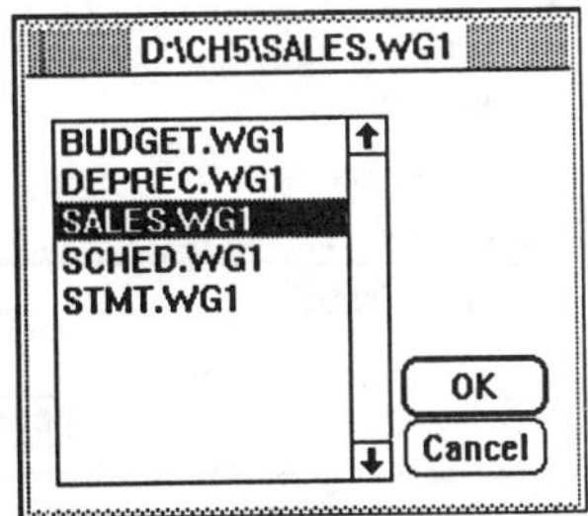

FIGURE 5–4 Pressing NAME (F3) during the File Save command

Saving Multiple Files

If there is more than one file open on the desktop when you select the File Save command, 1-2-3/G attempts to save all open files. However, you can choose to save all files, selected files, or the current file only. In addition, you can elect to save the files that are open on the desktop under a desktop filename. That way, you can recall those same files to the desktop at a later time as a single unit.

Saving All Files

If more than one file are open on the desktop when you select File Save, 1-2-3/G displays "ALL MODIFIED" in the "File name" text box as shown in Figure 5–5. In addition, the "All files" option button is selected and an X appears in the "Save Desktop" check box.

To save all files without saving the desktop as well, do either of the following:

- Remove the X from the "Save desktop" box by clicking on the check box. Select the OK command button, or press ENTER.
- Press TAB twice to move to the "Save Desktop" box and press the space bar. Select the OK command button, or press ENTER.

Whichever method you select, 1-2-3/G saves all new and existing files that have been modified to disk. The Save Window menu box is displayed for those existing files that have been changed. If an open file is not new or it has not been modified since you brought it into memory, 1-2-3/G does not save the file.

To save only the currently active file when multiple files are open on the desktop, simply press ESC. 1-2-3/G removes "ALL MODIFIED" from the "File name" text box and substitutes the path and name of the currently active file. The "Save desktop" box is no longer selected and the "Current file only" option

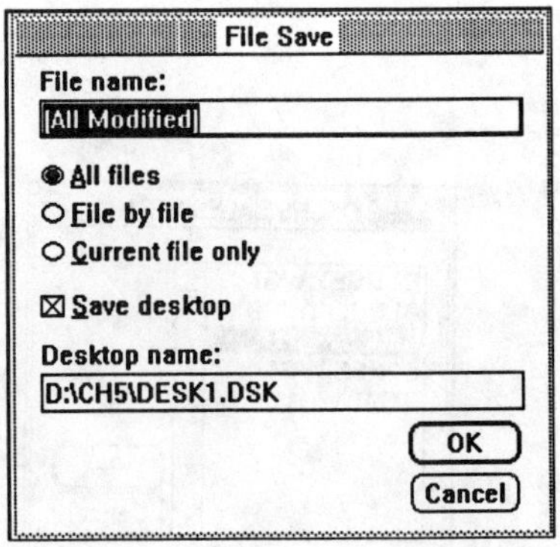

FIGURE 5–5 The File Save dialog box

button is selected instead of "All files." You can accept the name in the "File name" text box, or you can edit it, and complete the File Save command in the usual way. If the file already exists on disk, 1-2-3/G displays the Save Window menu box shown in Figure 5-3. Select Replace or Backup.

You can also save all open files that begin with a certain name. For example, imagine you have the files SALES.WG1 and SALES.GPH open on the desktop in addition to other files. To save only these two files, type **SALES** in the "File name" text box and select the "All files" option button. When you select the OK command button, or press ENTER, 1-2-3/G will save only those files named SALES, regardless of the extension.

Saving File by File

You can also save all the files on the desktop one at a time, accepting or rejecting files as you go. To do this, select the File Save command. 1-2-3/G displays the File Save dialog box with "ALL MODIFIED" in the "File name" text box. Select the "File by file" option button, then either select the OK command button or press ENTER. 1-2-3/G displays the second File Save dialog box shown in Figure 5–6. The name of the currently active file appears in the "File name" text box. This dialog box will be displayed for each open file on the desktop.

The three command buttons at the lower right of the dialog box in Figure 5–6 allow you to choose the fate of each open file. To save the current file, select the OK command button. 1-2-3/G saves the current file and advances to the next file. To avoid saving a file, Select the No command button. 1-2-3/G avoids saving the current file and advances to the next file. At any time you can stop the File Save command by selecting the Cancel command button. 1-2-3/G returns to READY mode, without saving further files.

Saving the Desktop

As mentioned, you can save the files currently open on the desktop to a desktop file with a .DSK extension. Desktop files do not contain any information from

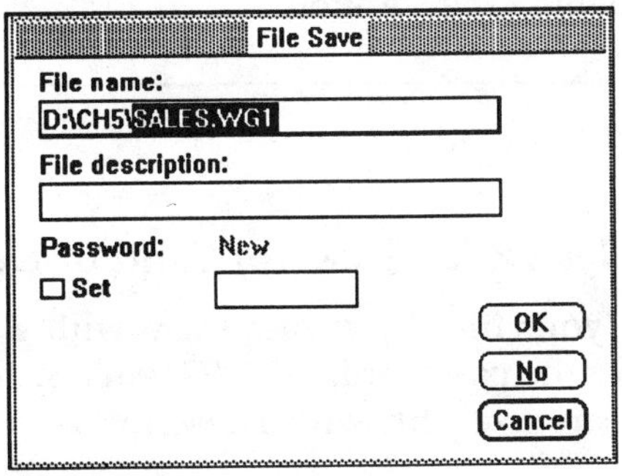

File Save
File name:
D:\CH5\SALES.WG1
File description:
Password: New
☐ Set
OK
No
Cancel

FIGURE 5–6 **The second File Save dialog box**

either worksheet or graph files. Instead, desktop files are "pointer" files that contain the path and names of files that are currently open in the desktop. In addition, desktop files contain information about the links between files and the relative size, position, and status of the windows on the desktop. Once you have saved the current desktop to a desktop file, you can reopen that desktop at a later time. When you do, all the files included in that desktop are recalled to the screen in a single operation. Thus, desktop files allow you to work with groups of related files as a single unit. In addition, you can include the same worksheet or graph file in more than one desktop, allowing you to easily share information among different desktops.

To save the current desktop, you need only select the "Save desktop" check box from the File Save dialog box. To do this, select the File Save command. 1-2-3/G displays the File Save dialog box as shown in Figure 5–5. If more than one file is open on the desktop, "ALL MODIFIED" appears in the "File name" text box and the "Save desktop" check box appears checked already. In addition, the "Desktop name" text box appears activated and displays a default desktop filename suggested by 1-2-3/G.

For the first desktop filename in the current directory, 1-2-3/G suggests a name of DESK.DSK; for the second, DESK1.DSK; for the third, DESK2.DSK; and so on. You can accept this filename, edit it, or type one of your own. When you select the OK command button, or press ENTER to complete the File Save command, 1-2-3/G saves the open files on the desktop. In addition, it creates a desktop file under the name you specified.

If you use the File Save command to save an existing desktop file, 1-2-3/G displays the Save Window menu box for each individual file. This includes worksheet and graph files as well as the desktop file.

Note

> For a description of how to open desktop files, see "Opening Existing Files," and "Replacing Existing Files," later in this chapter. For more information about how you can manage the 1-2-3/G desktop, see Chapter 2, "Managing the Desktop."

Saving Files with a Password and/or Description

You can also protect your files by saving them with a password. That way, unless someone knows the password, 1-2-3/G will not allow them to open the file. In addition, you can save a file with a description of up to 80 characters in length.

To save a file with a password, select the File Save command. 1-2-3/G displays the File Save dialog box. The "File name" text box is activated automatically. If there is only a single file open on the desktop, the name of that file is displayed in the "File name" text box. To save this file with a password, press END or use → to move the cursor to the end of the filename, press the space bar once, and type **p**. Next, select the OK command button or press ENTER. 1-2-3/G displays the second File Save dialog box shown in Figure 5–6. The "New" text box is activated automatically. In this text box, type a password of up to 15 characters. As you type, 1-2-3/G displays asterisks (*). To complete the password, press ENTER. The name of the "New" text box changes to "Verify." Type the password again, exactly as you typed it the first time. To complete verification and save the file with a password, press ENTER, or select the OK command button.

You can use any combination of letters and numbers in a password. You can even use Compose sequences to create characters not available on your keyboard (see Appendix B for more information on Compose sequences). However, passwords are case sensitive. Therefore, be sure to remember the exact sequence of upper- and lower-case characters you used in the password. If you cannot replicate the same sequence of characters in the future, 1-2-3/G will not allow you to open the file.

You can also save a file with a description of up to 80 characters in length. 1-2-3/G will then display that description for various commands. For example, in Chapter 2, the File Utility View Desktop command is discussed. This command allows you to get information about files that are included in the current desktop. When you select the name of a particular window during this command, 1-2-3/G will display information about the file in that window, including its filename and any description you may have assigned to the file.

To save a file with a description, select the File Save command. 1-2-3/G displays the File Save dialog box. Press END or → to move to the end of the filename, press the space bar once and type **d**. Next, press ENTER or select the OK command button. 1-2-3/G displays the second File Save dialog box shown in Figure 5–6. However, this time, the "File description" text box is activated. Type a description for the file of up to 80 characters in length and press ENTER or select the OK command button. 1-2-3/G saves the file with the description you specified.

Before you select OK or press ENTER to save a file with a description, you can also specify a password for the file. To do this, click on the "Set" check box in the "Password" section of the dialog box in Figure 5–6. 1-2-3/G places an X in the check box. Alternatively, you can press TAB to move to the "Set" check box and press the space bar to place the X in it. Whichever method you select, 1-2-3/G activates the "New" text box; you can then type and verify a password for the file.

To save a single file with a password when multiple files are open on the desktop, select the File Save command. 1-2-3/G displays the File Save dialog box with "ALL MODIFIED" in the "File name" text box. To save a specific file with a password, type the name of the file, press the space bar, type **p**, and press

ENTER. 1-2-3/G displays the second File Save dialog box shown in Figure 5-6. From there, you can assign the password of your choice.

To save more than one file with a password, select the "File by file" option button from the first File Save dialog box. Then, select the OK command button, or press ENTER. 1-2-3/G displays the second File Save dialog box shown in Figure 5-6. The "File name" text box is activated and shows the name of the first open file. You can specify both a description and a password for this file by using the methods described in the preceding paragraphs. To save the file, you can select the OK command button. 1-2-3/G advances to the next file. You can save this file with a password and/or description as well. Or, you can select the No command button to bypass saving the file and advance to the next open file.

Changing a Password or Description

To change or delete a password or description, make sure the file whose password or description you want to change is active. Then, select the File Save command. 1-2-3/G displays the File Save dialog box. Select the "File by file" option button, even though you may only have a single file in memory. 1-2-3/G displays a variation of the second File Save dialog box, as shown in Figure 5-7. The "File name" text box shows the name of the currently active file. If the file is password protected, the filename is followed by **[pp]**.

To change the description for the file, select the "File description" text box and edit the description in that box. To do this, either click on the "File description" or press TAB to move to it. Then, type a new description or edit the current one.

To change the password for the file, place an X in the "Change" check box either by clicking on it or by pressing TAB to move to it and pressing the space bar. 1-2-3/G activates the "Old" text box. Type the password you originally assigned to the file and press ENTER. After you type the password, the name of the "Old" text box changes to "New." Type the new password and press ENTER. The name of the text box changes to "Verify." Type the new password

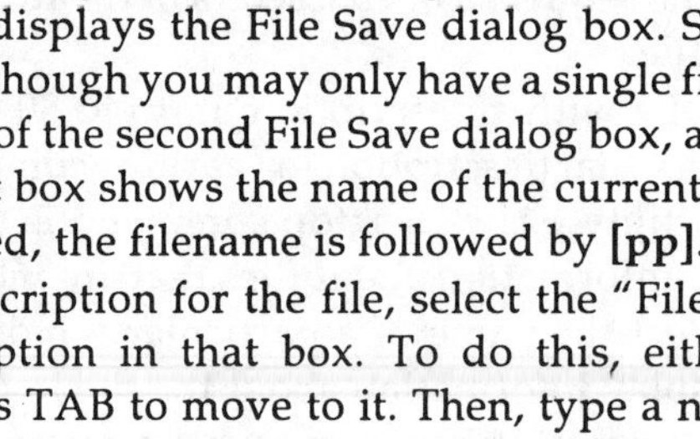

FIGURE 5-7 Changing a password with File Save

again and press ENTER, or select the OK command button. 1-2-3/G saves the file to disk with the new password.

To delete a password, simply delete the [pp] after the filename. Alternatively, select the "Clear" check box from the File Save dialog box in Figure 5–7. 1-2-3/G activates the "Old" text box. Type the old password and press ENTER, or click on the OK command button.

CREATING NEW FILES

To create a new worksheet or graph file, you use the File New command. When you select this command, 1-2-3/G displays the dialog box in Figure 5–8.

From the "Tool names" list box, select the type of new file you want to create. If you select the File New command from the Worksheet Tool menu, the default selection for the "Tool names" box is Worksheet. On the other hand, if you select the File New command from the Graph Tool menu, the default is Graph. The default name suggested by 1-2-3/G in the "Create window" text box changes, depending on your selection in the "Tool names" list box.

In the "Create window" text box, enter the name for the new file. Initially, however, 1-2-3/G suggests a default filename in this text box. For the first new worksheet file in a directory, 1-2-3/G suggests a default filename of SHEET.WG1. For the second new worksheet file, 1-2-3/G suggests a default filename of SHEET1.WG1, and so on. For the first new graph file in a directory, 1-2-3/G suggests a default filename of GRAPH.GPH. For the second new graph file, 1-2-3/G suggests a name of GRAPH1.GPH, and so on. You can accept this default filename, edit it, or type a new one of your own. If you specify a filename without an extension, 1-2-3/G automatically adds the appropriate file extension for you. If you are pressed for time, go ahead and accept the default filename; you can always change the name of the file when you later save it to disk.

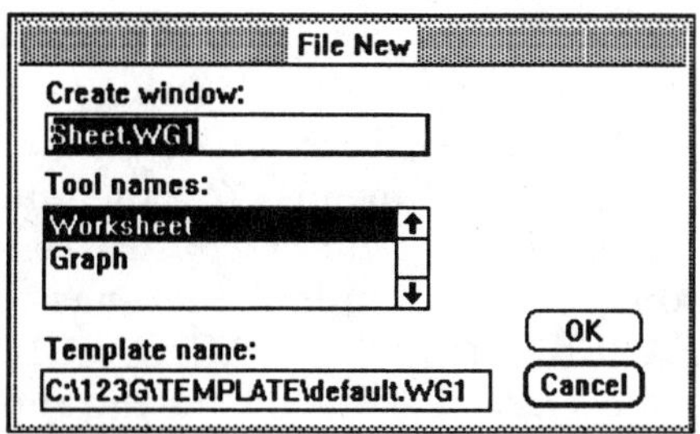

FIGURE 5–8 The File New dialog box

Note

> You can specify a file without an extension by adding a period . at the end of the filename.

To create the new file, select the OK command button, or press ENTER. 1-2-3/G creates the type of file you specified (worksheet or graph) under the name you specified. The new file is opened in its own window. That window then becomes the active window. Other windows currently open on the desktop remain open in the background.

Using Template Files

You can also create a new worksheet or graph file by using another existing file as a *template*. When you create the new file, it takes on the data and settings from the template file. If you have a series of settings that you use frequently, using a template file can save you time and effort. To specify another file as a template file, you use the "Template name" text box at the bottom of the File New dialog box shown in Figure 5–8.

Initially, the "Template name" text box shows the path to the default TEMPLATE directory. Unless you specify otherwise, 1-2-3/G automatically creates this directory when you install the product. This directory is a subdirectory of the directory that contains your 1-2-3/G program files. The name of this directory is usually C:\123G\TEMPLATE. To this directory, 1-2-3/G copies two sample files, DEFAULT.WG1 and DEFAULT.GPH. These are the default worksheet and graph template files. The names of these files appear in the "Template name" text box when you select the File New command. If you are creating a worksheet file, 1-2-3/G uses DEFAULT.WG1 as guide when creating the file. On the other hand, and if you are creating a graph file, 1-2-3/G uses DEFAULT.GPH as a guide. When you select OK to create the new file, it is created in the image of the appropriate DEFAULT file.

The default template files, DEFAULT.WG1 and DEFAULT.GPH, initially contain the settings you specified during the installation of 1-2-3/G. However, you can change these settings in one of two ways. The first way is to make a permanent change to 1-2-3/G's default settings. For example, imagine you select the User Settings Preferences, Directories, or International command from the Utility or Desktop Control menus. You then make a change to 1-2-3/G's default settings. To save the setting for future sessions, you select the Update command button. 1-2-3/G records the settings change in the current file as well as the DEFAULT.WG1 and DEFAULT.WG1 files, if appropriate. That way, when you create a new file, it will have the appropriate settings.

The second way to change the default settings in the DEFAULT.WG1 or DEFAULT.GPH files is to simply load either of the files into memory. Once the appropriate file is loaded, make your changes, and then save the file to the default TEMPLATE directory again.

Note

> If you delete the TEMPLATE directory, 1-2-3/G displays the path to the current directory in the "Template name" text box.

You can use any file you want as a template file. To do this, simply save the appropriate worksheet or graph files to the default TEMPLATE directory. When you use the File New command to create a new file, activate the "Template file" text box and either type the name of the file you want to use as a template or press NAME (F3) to select from a list of files in that directory. When you select OK to complete the File New command, 1-2-3/G will use the file you specified in the "Template file" as a template for the new file.

You can use any directory you want as a template directory. However, for 1-2-3/G to find that directory and display it in the "Template file" text box, you must use the User Settings Directories command. This command is available from either the Utility menu or the Desktop Control menu. When you select this command, 1-2-3/G displays a dialog box showing the default directories currently used by 1-2-3/G. From this dialog box, select "File template directory" and specify the path to the directory that contains your template files. To save the setting for the current session, select the OK command button. To save the setting for future 1-2-3/G sessions, select the Update command button. The next time you select the File New command, the path to this directory will be displayed in the "Template file" text box.

Note

> In early releases of 1-2-3/G, the User Setting Directories File template directory command doesn't always work as advertised. That is, when you change the template directory permanently, 1-2-3/G does not note the change. Instead, the File New "Template Name" text box appears blank. In this case, you must type the name of the new template directory in this text box. Check your copy of 1-2-3/G.

OPENING EXISTING FILES

To open an existing file on disk without affecting files displayed in other windows, use the File Open command. When you select this command, 1-2-3/G displays the dialog box in Figure 5–9.

> **Note**
>
> To replace the file in the currently active window with another existing file from disk, you use the File Retrieve command. See "Retrieving Existing Files" later in this Chapter.

Ultimately, the "File name" text box will contain the name of the file that you want to open. If you select the File Open command from the Worksheet Tool's menu, 1-2-3/G displays the path to the current directory follow by the wild-card *.W??. This causes 1-2-3/G to list all the worksheet files in the current directory in the list box below. (The files appear in alphabetical order by file extension.) The check boxes in the "File types" section show the types of files that can appear in the "File name" list box. To select a file to open, you can use any of the following techniques:

- Double-click on the filename in the "File name" list box.
- Click once on the filename and select the OK command button.
- Using the keyboard, press ↓ to highlight the name of the file and press ENTER.

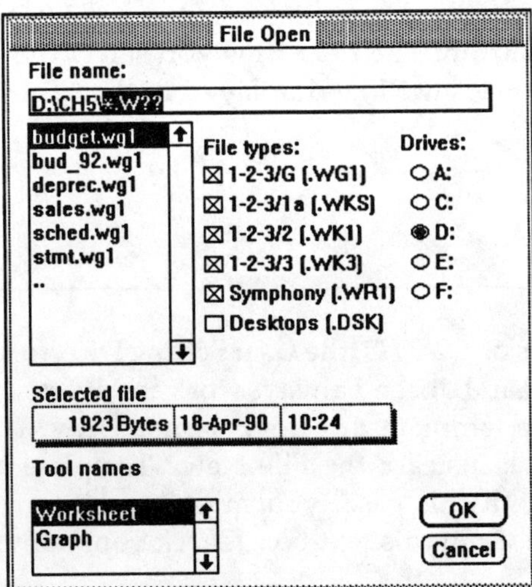

FIGURE 5–9 The File Open dialog box

• Type the name of the file in the "File name" text box and press ENTER.

Whichever method you choose, 1-2-3/G opens the file you selected and displays it in its own window. The new window then becomes the active window. Other windows that may already be open on the desktop are not affected.

You can use the various components of the File Open dialog box to modify the list of files displayed for your selection. For example, you can edit the drive and/or path in the "File name" text box and press ENTER. 1-2-3/G displays a list of files from the directory you specify. You can also use the option buttons in the "Drives" section to select another drive. 1-2-3/G remembers the last directory used on each drive. Further, you can select the two dots (..) in the "File name" list box. This causes 1-2-3/G to display files in the directory that is one level closer to the root directory on the directory tree. When you select a different drive or directory using any of these methods, the "File name" text box is automatically updated for the change.

You can use the "File types" check boxes to add or remove certain types of files from the "File name" list box. For example, notice in Figure 5–9 that the "Desktops (.DSK)" check box is not checked (this is the default). Therefore, the Desktop (.DSK) files in the current directory are not included in the adjacent "File name" list box. To have these files listed for your selection, simply click on the "Desktops (.DSK)" check box to place an X in that box. Alternatively, you can press TAB to move to the "File types" section followed by ↓ to select "Desktops (.DSK)" and press the space bar. To remove certain types of files from the list, simply remove the X from the appropriate check box by clicking on it or by moving to it and pressing the space bar.

You can also use the File Open dialog box to open an existing graph file. To do this, you use the "Tool Names" list box at the bottom of the File Open dialog box in Figure 5–9. For example, to open a graph file instead of the default worksheet file, select Graph from the "Tool names" list box. When you make this selection, the "File name" list and text boxes as well as the "File types" section are updated to reflect your choice. The File Open dialog box now appears as shown in Figure 5–10.

Note

You cannot open a graph file while Worksheet is selected in the "Tool names" list box. Conversely, you cannot open a worksheet file while Graph is selected in the "Tool names" list box. If you try either of these, 1-2-3/G will issue the "File type is unknown" error message. However, you can always open a desktop file, regardless of the selection in the "Tool names" list box.

Notice in Figure 5–10 that the wild-card file descriptor following the current directory listing in the "File name" text box has changed from *.W?? to *.GPH. This causes 1-2-3/G to list only graph files in the current directory in the "File names" list box. Further, only two option buttons are available in the "File types" section,

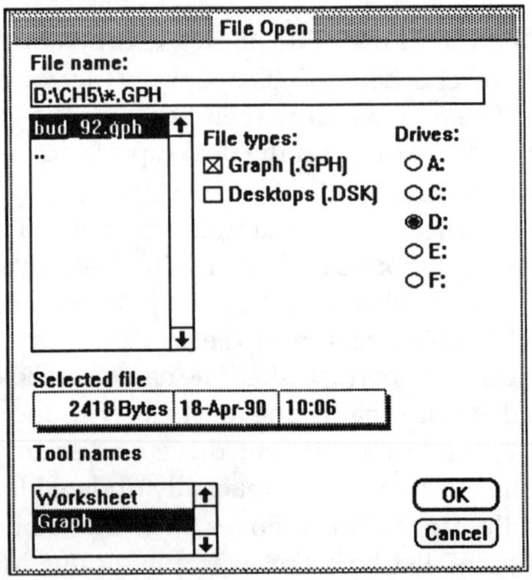

File Open
File name:
D:\CH5*.GPH
bud 92.gph
..
File types:
☒ Graph (.GPH)
☐ Desktops (.DSK)
Drives:
○ A:
○ C:
◉ D:
○ E:
○ F:
Selected file
2418 Bytes | 18-Apr-90 | 10:06
Tool names
Worksheet
Graph
OK
Cancel

FIGURE 5–10 **Selecting File Open from the Graph Tool menu.**

Graph (.GPH) and Desktop (.DSK). This is the same configuration that appears when you select the File Open command from the Graph Tool menu.

Tip: Opening a file or desktop at startup

> You can have 1-2-3/G automatically open a file or desktop when you start the program. To do this, you use the Utility User Settings Startup command. With this command you can instruct 1-2-3/G to open either a new file (.WG1 or .GPH), an existing file, or restore the state of the desktop as of the end of the last work session. See Appendix A, "Customizing 1-2-3/G," for more information on this command.

The following additional information may be of assistance to you when you are using the File Open command:

- If the file you are opening is password protected, 1-2-3/G will request the password when you attempt to open the file.
- If you are using 1-2-3/G on a network, 1-2-3/G may display a Yes/No message box that reads "Unable to obtain reservation," "Open Read Only?". This means that someone else is already using the file you are attempting to open, or that the directory that contains the file is read-only to you. If you select the Yes command button, 1-2-3/G opens the file, but it is read-only.

That is, you can view the file, but you cannot save it under the same name. However, you can save this file under a different filename. For more details about using 1-2-3/G on a network, see Chapter 12, "Networking 1-2-3/G."

- If you open a desktop file when another desktop file is already open, 1-2-3/G adds the windows from the new desktop file to those that are already open on the desktop. The name of the first desktop file, however, continues to be displayed in the desktop title bar at the top of your screen. If you save the desktop at this point, all the files from both desktops will be saved under the name of the first desktop.
- You can use the File Open command to open more than one copy of a file. Each copy is referred to as a view and is displayed in its own window. When you make a change to one view of the file, the other open views are automatically updated for the change.

REPLACING EXISTING FILES

Use the File Retrieve command to replace the file in the currently active window with another existing file from disk. This command closes the file in the currently active window and replaces it with the file from disk that you select. If you've made any changes to the currently active file since you loaded it into memory, however, 1-2-3/G prompts you to save those changes before closing the file. (To open an existing file in its own window, see "Opening Existing Files" in this chapter.)

In preparation for the File Retrieve command, activate the window whose file you want to replace, then select File Retrieve. When you select this command, 1-2-3/G displays the dialog box shown in Figure 5-11.

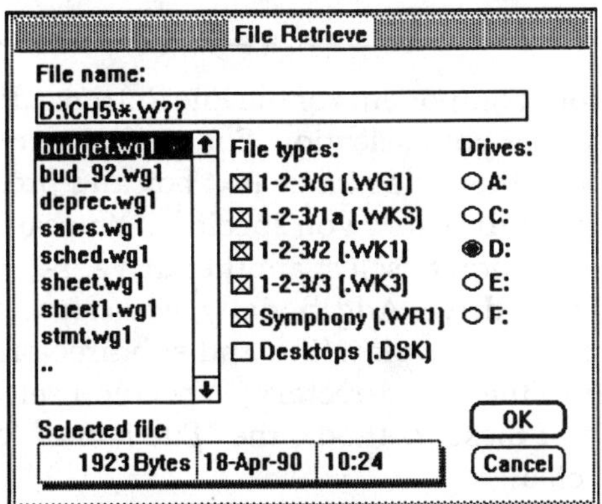

FIGURE 5-11 The File Retrieve dialog box

In the "File name" text box, 1-2-3/G displays the path to the current directory followed by a wild-card file extension of the same type as the active window (*.W?? or *.GPH). For example, in Figure 5–11, 1-2-3/G displays *.W??, because the File Retrieve command was selected from a worksheet window. This causes 1-2-3/G to list the names of worksheet files in the current directory in the list box below. (The filenames appear in alphabetical order by file extension.) The file types displayed in the list box are determined by the check boxes that appear in the "File types" section. To select a file to replace the currently active file, you can use any of the following methods:

- Double-click on the filename in the "File name" list box.
- Click once on the filename in the "File name" list box and select the OK command button.
- Using the keyboard, press ↓ to highlight the name of the file you want and press ENTER.
- Type the name of the file in the "File name" text box, and select the OK command button, or press ENTER.

Whichever method you choose, 1-2-3/G loads the file you selected, replacing the file in the currently active window. In the process, 1-2-3/G closes the old file. However, if you have made changes to the old file since you loaded it into memory, 1-2-3/G prompts you to save those changes prior to replacing the file.

Note

> If more than one view of the current file is open on the desktop when you select File Retrieve, 1-2-3/G displays an error message, indicating that more than one view of the file is open. Before you can replace the current file with another file from disk, you must close all but one view of the current file.

You can use the various components of the File Retrieve dialog box to modify the list of files displayed for your selection. For example, you can edit the drive and/or directory name in the "File name" text box and press ENTER. 1-2-3/G displays a list of files in the directory you specified. You can also use the option buttons in the "Drives" section to select another drive. 1-2-3/G remembers the last directory used on each drive. Additionally, you can select the two dots (..) in the "File name" list box to display files and subdirectories in the directory that is one level closer to the root directory. When you select a different drive or directory using any of these methods, the "File name" text box is automatically updated for the change.

You can use the "File types" check boxes to add or remove certain types of files from the "File name" list box. For example, notice in Figure 5–11 that the

"Desktops (.DSK) check box is not checked (this is the default). Therefore, Desktop (.DSK) files in the current directory are not included in the adjacent "File name" list box. To have these files listed for your selection, simply click on the "Desktops (.DSK)" check box to place an X in that box. Alternatively, you can press TAB to move to the "File types" section, followed by ↓ to select "Desktops (.DSK)," and press the space bar. To remove certain types of files from the list, simply remove the X from the appropriate check box by clicking on it or by moving to it and pressing the space bar.

If you select the File Retrieve command from a graph window, 1-2-3/G displays the File Retrieve dialog box as shown in Figure 5-12. Notice that the wild-card extension *.GPH now appears after the path to the current directory in the "File name" text box. This causes the names of graph files in the current directory to appear in the list box below. In addition, the "File types" section includes only two option buttons, "Graph (.GPH)" and "Desktop (.DSK)".

Note

Even when the current active file is a worksheet file, you can still use the File Retrieve command to retrieve a graph file. In the "File name" text box, enter the graph file including its .GPH extension. Or replace the *.W?? extension with *.GPH so that graph files are now displayed in the "File name" list box. Then select the appropriate file. You can use the same procedure to retrieve a worksheet file when the active window contains a graph file.

You may also find the following additional information to be of assistance when you are using the File Retrieve command:

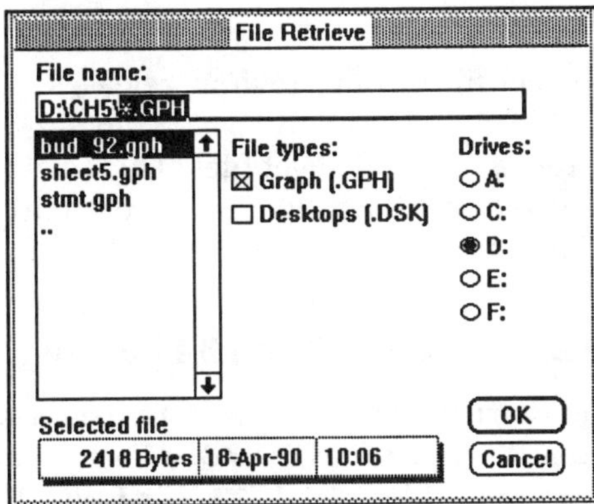

FIGURE 5-12 Selecting File Retrieve from the Graph Tool menu

- If you retrieve a desktop file while another desktop file is open, 1-2-3/G closes the first desktop before opening the second. If you've made any changes to the files in the first desktop, 1-2-3/G prompts you to save your changes prior to closing the files.
- If one or more of the individual files included in a desktop file are already open when you retrieve the desktop file, 1-2-3/G leaves those individual files on the desktop. If changes have been made to one or more of those files, though, 1-2-3/G prompts you to save the changes. When the desktop file is finally opened, the windows containing those files are resized and positioned just as they were when you last saved the desktop file.
- If you attempt to retrieve a password protected file, 1-2-3/G displays a Password dialog box, prompting you for the password. You have two chances to enter the correct password in the text box. Type the password and press ENTER or click on the OK button. 1-2-3/G then retrieves the file. If you type the password incorrectly, the text box is cleared and you can try again. If you type the wrong password a second time, however, 1-2-3/G displays the error message "Incorrect password." To retrieve the file, you must select the OK command button to clear the error message and try the File Retrieve command again.
- If you are running 1-2-3/G on a network, 1-2-3/G may display a Yes/No message box that says "Unable to obtain reservation," "Open Read Only?". This means that someone else is already using the file you are attempting to retrieve, or that the directory that contains the file is read-only to you. If you select the Yes command button, 1-2-3/G retrieves the file as read-only. That is, you can view the file, but you cannot save it under the same name. For more details about using 1-2-3/G on a network, see Chapter 12, "Networking 1-2-3/G."

SHARING FILES ACROSS LOTUS PRODUCTS

You can load worksheet files from previous releases of both 1-2-3 and Lotus Symphony inside 1-2-3/G. You can also save your 1-2-3/G worksheet files as 1-2-3 Release 2 and Release 3 worksheet files. This section discusses how to go about doing this. It also discusses some file compatibility issues you'll need to be aware of when you try.

Using 1-2-3 Releases 2 and 3 Files inside 1-2-3/G

You can use the File Retrieve or File Open commands to load 1-2-3 Release 2 files (.WK1) and 1-2-3 Release 3 files (.WK3) directly into 1-2-3/G. When you do, 1-2-3/G translates these files into 1-2-3/G's (.WG1) file format. However, 1-2-3/G continues to display the .WK1 or .WK3 file extension in the worksheet window title bar. Further, you can use 1-2-3/G's File Save command to save these files either in 1-2-3/G's file format (.WG1) or in their original format (.WK1 or .WK3). To do this, simply specify the appropriate file extension when you save the file. For example, to save a 1-2-3 Release 2 or 3 file in 1-2-3/G's file format, specify a .WG1 extension. To save in 1-2-3 Release 2's format, specify a .WK1 extension, and to save in 1-2-3 Release 3's format, specify a .WK3 extension.

There are a number of issues you should be aware of, though, when using 1-2-3 Release 2 and 3 files in 1-2-3/G. These are as follows:

- When you load a 1-2-3 Release 2 or 3 file into 1-2-3/G, it is translated into 1-2-3/G's file format. Conversely, when you save a 1-2-3/G file in 1-2-3 Release 2 or 3 format, 1-2-3/G must translate the file to the format you specify. This translation to and from different file formats can be a time-consuming process. Therefore, unless you intend to use the file in Release 2 or 3, save it in .WG1 format.
- 1-2-3 Release 2 uses the LICS character set (Lotus International Character Set) whereas 1-2-3/G uses the IBM-PC Multilingual code page 850 character set. Therefore, when you load a Release 2 file, some characters may not be properly displayed. To solve this problem, use 1-2-3/G's Worksheet Global Default Release 2 command to select either LICS or ASCII, depending on the character set used by the Release 2 file. Then try loading the file again.
- If the Release 2 or 3 file contains macros, you may have to use the Utility Macros Translate command to translate the macros into their 1-2-3/G equivalents. See Chapter 10, "Creating Macros," for information on how to use this command. To determine if translation is necessary, try running the macros in 1-2-3/G. If the macro is named with a single letter preceded by a backslash, for example \A, press CTRL followed by the appropriate letter. If the macro has a multiple-character name (Release 3 only) press RUN (ALT-F3) and select the name of the macro. If the macro runs just fine in 1-2-3 Release 2 or 3 but produces errors or will not run at all in 1-2-3/G, you probably will have to translate it.

Using 1-2-3/G Files in 1-2-3 Releases 2 and 3

As mentioned, you can save a 1-2-3/G worksheet file in 1-2-3 Release 2 or 3 format simply by specifying a .WK1 (Release 2) or .WK3 (Release 3) extension when you save the file. You can then load those files directly into the appropriate release of 1-2-3. However, 1-2-3/G includes features that previous releases do not. Therefore, these features, and possibly some data associated with them, will be lost when you save a 1-2-3/G (.WG1) file as a Release 3 or Release 2 file. What follows is a list of some things to watch out for.

- Release 3 supports multiple worksheet files, but Release 2 does not. Therefore, if you save a 1-2-3/G file in Release 2 (.WK1) format, make sure the data is stored all in one worksheet. If it is not, use the File New command to create a new worksheet file. When 1-2-3/G prompts you for a filename, specify a filename with a .WK1 extension. If formulas in the original.WG1 file refer to other worksheets, use the Range Value command to convert these formulas to their current values. Then, use the Copy command to copy the data from the multiple worksheets in the old .WG1 file to the single worksheet in the new .WK1 file. Finally, use the File Save command to save the single-worksheet .WK1 file to disk. For details on how to use the Range Value and Copy commands, see Chapter 4, "Cutting and Pasting Data."

- Most of 1-2-3/G's cell attributes are not available in 1-2-3 Release 3. However, when you save a 1-2-3/G file in Release 3 format (.WK3), 1-2-3/G saves cell attributes in an extended format record associated with the file. That way, if you reuse the file in 1-2-3/G, your cell attributes are restored intact. However, some attributes such as row heights, row hiding, and any attributes you've applied to an entire row, column, or worksheet that are not supported by Release 3 are not saved in the extended format record.
- When you save a .WG1 file to .WK1 (Release 2) format, 1-2-3/G does not save to an extended format record. Therefore, any 1-2-3/G–specific features are lost entirely. 1-2-3/G informs you of the potential for loss of data when you save the file.
- When you save a 1-2-3/G file in Release 3 (.WK3) format, graph settings and named print settings are saved. However, if you save a .WG1 file in .WK1 (Release 2) format, named print settings are not saved.
- The maximum length of a label in Release 2 (.WK1) is 240 characters. As you know, the maximum length of a label in 1-2-3/G is 512 characters. If you save a .WG1 file with labels in excess of 240 characters to Release 2 (.WK1) format, those labels are truncated at 240 characters.
- Release 2 does not support formulas in excess of 240 characters. If you save a 1-2-3/G file containing such formulas to a Release 2 (.WK1) file, the formulas are saved intact. However, the formulas will not function in the Release 2 file, unless you edit them down to 240 characters.
- If you save a 1-2-3/G file to Release 2 format (.WK1), and the file contains formula references to other files, 1-2-3/G converts the references to labels in the .WK1 file.
- If you save a 1-2-3/G file to Release 2 (.WK1) or Release 3 (.WK3) format, @ functions not supported by those releases are converted to labels.
- 1-2-3 Release 2 does not support undefined range names. Therefore, if you save a 1-2-3/G file containing undefined range names to Release 2 (.WK1) format, Release 2 displays ERR in place of those range names.
- As mentioned, 1-2-3 Release 2 use the LICS character set to store and display data. However, 1-2-3/G uses the IBM-PC Multilingual code page 850 character set. If you save a 1-2-3/G file to Release 2 format, and there is not a LICS equivalent for a code page 850 character, that character may be lost.

Using Lotus Symphony and 1-2-3 Release 1A Files in 1-2-3/G

You can use the File Retrieve or File Open command to load Lotus Symphony (.WR1) files (version 1.1 and later only) or 1-2-3 Release 1A (.WKS) files directly into 1-2-3/G. However, 1-2-3/G immediately renames these files with a .WG1 extension and converts them to 1-2-3/G's file format. (The original file on disk remains unaffected.) However, you cannot save Lotus Symphony or 1-2-3 Release 1A files in their original file formats. You can only save them as 1-2-3/G files (.WG1), 1-2-3 Release 3 files (.WK3), or 1-2-3 Release 2 files (.WK1).

If you need to use a .WR1 file in Symphony again after using it in 1-2-3/G, save it as a .WK1 file. Lotus Symphony is capable of loading .WK1 files. Keep in mind, however, that some of the features you may have added to the file in 1-2-3/G may be lost in Symphony.

CHANGING DIRECTORIES

When you select a File command, 1-2-3/G displays a list of filenames for your selection. These filenames are chosen from the *default* or *current working directory*. You can change this working directory in one of three ways. First, you can edit the directory shown in the "File name" text box for the File command you happen to be using. The second way is to use the File Directory command to change the current directory for the rest of your 1-2-3/G session. However, this is only a temporary solution. 1-2-3/G will once again use the default directory the next time you start the program. Finally, the third and most lasting way to change the directory used by 1-2-3/G is to use the User Settings Directories command. This command is available from either the Utility menu or the Desktop Control menu. It allows you to specify a default working directory and save that setting for future 1-2-3/G sessions.

Changing Directories during a Command

When you select a File command that reads files from disk, 1-2-3/G displays a dialog box that includes a text box entitled "File name." In this text box, 1-2-3/G lists the current default drive and directory followed by a file descriptor, *.W?? if the currently active file is a worksheet, and *.GPH if it is a graph. In most cases, 1-2-3/G also provides a list of files in the current directory for your selection. For example, Figure 5–13 shows the File Retrieve dialog box. In the "File name" list box 1-2-3/G lists the current drive and directory C:\123G\WORK\ followed by the file descriptor *.W??, causing 1-2-3/G to list all the worksheet files in this directory in the list box below. Suppose, however, that you want to see a list of files from a different directory. To do this, you have three alternatives.

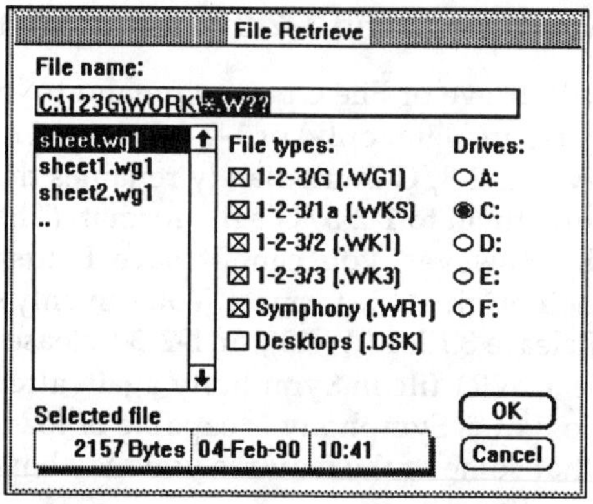

FIGURE 5–13 A typical File command dialog box

Pressing ESC

The first alternative for changing the current directory is to press the ESC key twice, once to clear the file descriptor (.W??) and again to clear the current directory. Then, simply type the new directory, including the drive name if needed, in the "File name" text box.

For example, imagine the current directory is C:\123G\WORK, and you want to retrieve a file from the directory C:\MARKET\SALES. To do this, select the File Retrieve command and press ESC twice, once to remove the file descriptor and again to clear the current drive and directory. Next type **C:\MARKET\SALES** (do not forget the last backslash) and press ENTER. 1-2-3/G automatically appends the *.W?? file descriptor for you and displays the files in the new directory in the list box for your selection.

Editing the Directory

The second option for changing the current directory during a File command is to edit the directory displayed in the "File name" text box. For example, imagine the "File name" text box currently contains C:\123G\WORK*.W??, causing 1-2-3/G to list the worksheet files in the C:\123G\WORK directory. To display the files in the directory C:\123G\SALES directory, press ← to move the cursor to the W in WORK. Press DEL four times, type **SALES**, and press ENTER. 1-2-3/G displays a list of worksheet files in the C:\123G\SALES directory for your selection.

Selecting the Two Dots (..)

You can also select the two dots (..) from the "File name" list box to display the files in the directory that is one level closer to the root directory. To select the two dots, either click on them or press ↓ to highlight them and press ENTER.

For example, imagine the File name list box currently contains C:\123G\WORK*W??, causing 1-2-3/G to list the worksheet files in the directory C:\123G\WORK. If you select the two dots, 1-2-3/G displays C:\123G*.W??, causing 1-2-3/G to display the worksheet files in the directory that is one level closer to the root directory.

Changing the Current Directory Temporarily

To change the current directory temporarily, you can use the File Directory command. When you select this command, 1-2-3/G displays the dialog box in Figure 5–14. In the "Directory name" text box, 1-2-3/G lists the drive and path for the current directory. The subdirectories for that directory appear in the list box below. To change the current directory, you can use any of the following techniques:

- Edit the contents of the "Directory name" text box.
- Press ESC to clear the contents of the "Directory name" text box and type a new drive and directory.
- Select a subdirectory from the "Directory name" list box below. To do this, select the name of the appropriate directory from the list box. 1-2-3/G places the name of the directory in the "Directory name" text box, and lists the subdirectories for that directory, if any, in the list box below.
- Select the two dots (..) from the "Directory name" list box. When you select the two dots, 1-2-3/G moves one level closer to the root directory and displays the names of directories and subdirectories at that level. You can then select the one you want.
- Select an option button from the Drives section of the dialog box. 1-2-3/G updates the "Directory name" text box, and shows the last directory used on

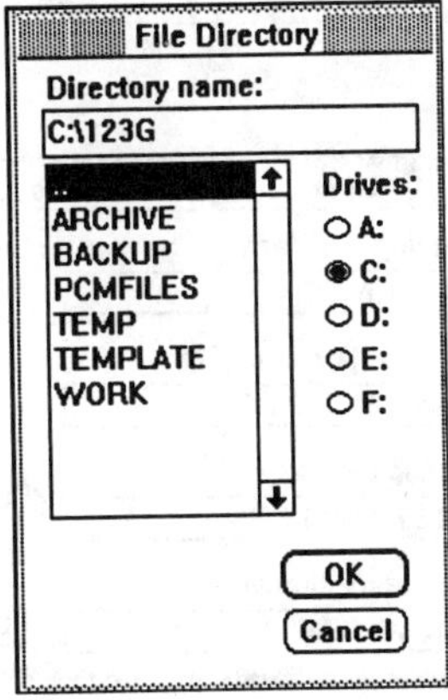

FIGURE 5–14 The File Directory dialog box

that drive. The subdirectories of that directory, if any, appear in the list box below.

To complete the File directory command, select the OK command button or press ENTER. 1-2-3/G removes the File Directory dialog box from the screen. The title bar of each open window is updated for the change. If the file in a given window has not been saved to the new directory, 1-2-3/G updates the title bar of the window to show the full path and filename for the file.

Changing the Current Directory Permanently

To change the current directory for the current 1-2-3/G session, as well as future sessions, you use the User Settings Directories command. This command is available from either the Utility menu or the Desktop Control menu. When you select this command, 1-2-3/G displays the dialog box in Figure 5–15. The text boxes in this dialog box show the default directories used by 1-2-3/G as follows:

- **Working directory:** The default directory in which 1-2-3/G stores and saves worksheet, graph, and desktop files. This is the directory 1-2-3/G uses for the File New, File Open, File Retrieve, and File Save commands. It is also the directory that is temporarily changed by the File Directory command. 1-2-3/G creates a default working directory when you install the program, usually C:\123G\WORK. To specify a new working directory, type the full drive and path name that describes the directory you want to use.
- **File template directory:** The default directory in which 1-2-3/G stores its template files. As you may recall from earlier in this chapter, you can use the File New command to create a new file by using an existing file as a template. The new file takes on the data and settings from the template file. When you select the File New command, 1-2-3/G searches this directory for the template file DEFAULT.WG1 or DEFAULT.GPH, depending on which tool is active. The path to this directory is displayed in the "Template name" text box of the

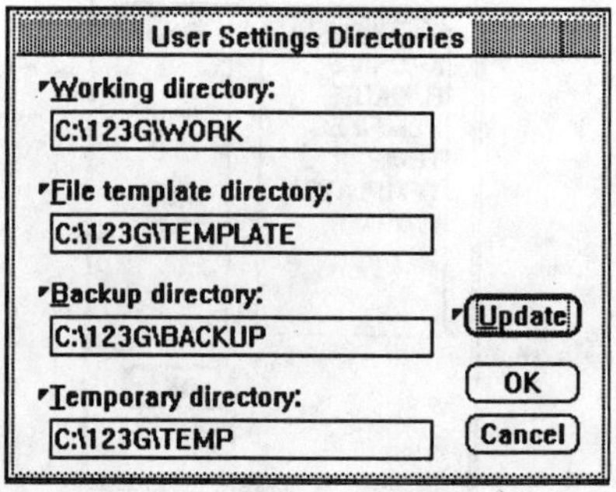

User Settings Directories
Working directory:
C:\123G\WORK
File template directory:
C:\123G\TEMPLATE
Backup directory:
C:\123G\BACKUP
Temporary directory:
C:\123G\TEMP
Update
OK
Cancel

FIGURE 5–15 The User Settings Directories dialog box

File New dialog box. When you install 1-2-3/G, a default template directory, usually named C:\123G\TEMPLATE, is created. To specify a new template directory, type the drive and path that describes the directory you want to use.

- **Backup directory:** The directory in which 1-2-3/G saves its backup files. When you use the File Save command to save an existing file, 1-2-3/G displays a Cancel, Replace, Backup menu. If you select Backup, 1-2-3/G copies the original file on disk to the default backup directory. It then saves the file from memory in the original file's disk location. When you install 1-2-3/G, a default backup directory, usually C:\123G\BACKUP, is created. To change the default backup directory used by 1-2-3/G, type the full drive and path for the directory you want to use.
- **Temporary:** The directory in which 1-2-3/G stores its temporary files. Temporary files are created by 1-2-3/G to support certain operations, such as printing or the undo feature. These files are deleted from this directory when you leave 1-2-3/G. When you install 1-2-3/G, a default temporary directory, usually C:\123G\TEMP, is created automatically. To change the directory 1-2-3/G uses to store its temporary files, type the full drive and path name for the directory you want to use.

You can complete the User Settings Directories command in one of two ways. If you select the Update command button, 1-2-3/G saves the new default directory settings and will use them for both the current work session and future 1-2-3/G sessions. On the other hand, if you press ENTER after specifying a new default directory, or you select the OK command button, 1-2-3/G will record the new default settings and use them for the current session only; the next time you start 1-2-3/G, it will revert to using the original default directories.

Note

Make sure you specify different default backup and working directories. If the two are the same, 1-2-3/G will not permit you to create backup files.

ERASING FILES ON DISK

To permanently erase files on disk, you use the File Erase command. This command lets you erase files created either by 1-2-3/G or by another software program. When you select the File Erase command, 1-2-3/G displays the dialog box in Figure 5–16.

Caution

You cannot undo the File Erase command. Therefore, exercise care with this command.

To select a file to erase, specify the name of that file in the "File name" text box. Initially, the "File name" text box contains the drive and path to the current directory followed by a file descriptor (*.W?? or *.GPH). The file descriptor used depends on whether you selected the File Erase command from a worksheet or a graph window. For example, in Figure 5–16, the File Erase command was entered from a worksheet window. Therefore, the *.W?? file descriptor is used and the worksheet files in the current directory appear in the list box below. To specify a specific file to erase, you can use any of the following techniques:

- Double-click on the filename in the "File name" list box.
- Click once on the filename in the "File name" list box and select the OK command button.
- Using the keyboard, press ↓ to highlight the name of the file and press ENTER.
- Type the name of the file in the "File name" text box, and select the OK command button, or press ENTER.

Whichever method you select, 1-2-3/G displays a File Erase confirmation dialog box. This dialog box prompts you whether you want to erase the file and contains both an OK and a Cancel command button. If you select OK, 1-2-3/G will erase the file you specified from disk. If you select Cancel, 1-2-3/G will cancel the File Erase command without erasing the file.

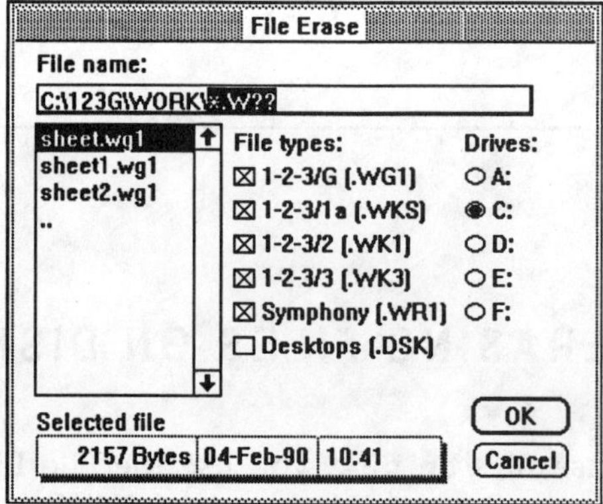

FIGURE 5–16 The File Erase dialog box

If you erase a worksheet or graph file that is currently open on the desktop, 1-2-3/G displays two dialog boxes after the File Erase dialog box. The first dialog box prompts you whether you want to erase the file on disk. The second prompts you whether you also want to close the window that contains that file. If you elect to close the window, and it is password protected, 1-2-3/G will request the password before closing the window.

Note

Do not confuse the File Erase command with either the Worksheet Erase or Worksheet Delete Sheet commands. Worksheet Erase clears a file from memory, but the associated file on disk is not affected. Worksheet Delete Sheet simply deletes one of the 256 worksheets in the currently active file.

You can use the various components of the File Erase dialog box to have 1-2-3/G display files in a directory other than the current directory for your selection. To do this, you can use any of the following techniques:

- Edit the drive or directory in the "File name" list box and press ENTER. 1-2-3/G displays the files from the directory you specified in the list box below.
- Use the check boxes in the file-type section to add or remove files from the adjacent list box.
- Select from the available option buttons in the "Drives" section of the dialog box. 1-2-3/G remembers the last directory used on each drive and will update the "File name" text box accordingly.
- Select the name of any directory from the "File name" list box. 1-2-3/G will update the "File name" text box to display the files in that directory in the list box
- Select the two dots (..) from the "File name" list box. 1-2-3/G will move one level closer to the root directory and display the files and directories at that level.

Note

Even when entering the File Erase command from a worksheet window, you can still erase a graph file. In the "File name" text box, enter the graph file including its .GPH extension. Or replace the *.W?? extension with *.GPH so that graph files are now displayed in the "File name" list box. Then select the appropriate file. You can use the same procedure to erase a worksheet file from a graph window.

GETTING INFORMATION ABOUT FILES

The File Admin command is covered in detail in Chapter 12, "Networking 1-2-3/G." However, the File Admin Table command bears a brief mention here as well, because it provides the most comprehensive source of information about your files.

You can use the File Admin Table command to get information about files that are currently open on the desktop as well as files that are located on disk. This command creates a table of information in the worksheet about either the desktop, the links in the currently active file, or about specific types of files on disk.

When you select the File Admin Table command, 1-2-3/G displays the dialog box in Figure 5–17. Each of the option buttons in this dialog box can be used to create a different type of table, as follows:

- **Active:** Creates a table of files currently open on the desktop.
- **Links (formulas):** Creates a table of files linked to the currently active file by formula reference.
- **Edit Links:** Creates a table of files linked to the currently active file by the Edit Link command.
- **Connected drives:** Creates a table showing the drive letters currently available on your system.
- **Desktop windows:** Creates a table of information about windows currently open on the Presentation Manager desktop, including the Presentation Manager screen itself.
- **Worksheet:** Creates a table of worksheet files located in the directory you specify. When you select this option button, 1-2-3/G activates the "File name" text box and shows the drive and path to the current directory. You can accept this directory, edit it, or type a new drive and/or directory.
- **Graph:** Creates a table of graph files located in the directory you specify. When you select this option button, 1-2-3/G activates the "File name" text

File Admin Table
File type
File name
Active
Worksheet
Links(formulas)
Graph
Edit links
Print
Connected drives
Other
Desktop windows
Range:
A:A1
OK
Cancel

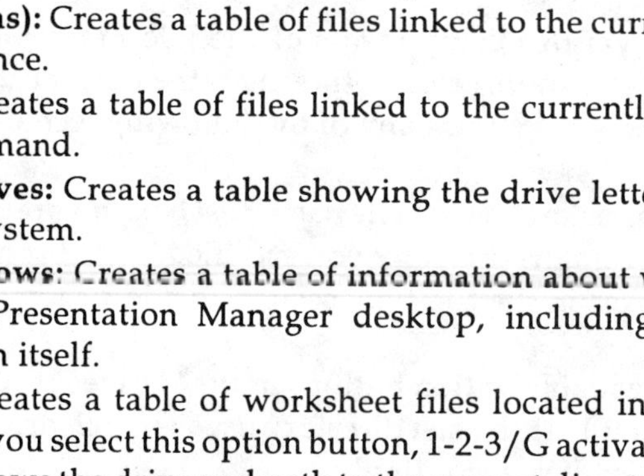

FIGURE 5–17 **The File Admin Table dialog box**

box and shows the drive and path to the current directory. You can accept this directory or provide a new one.

- **Print:** Creates a table of print (.PRN) files located in the directory you specify. When you select this option button, 1-2-3/G activates the "File name" text box and shows the drive and path to the current directory. You can accept this directory, edit it, or type a new drive and/or directory.
- **Other:** Creates a table of all files located in the directory you specify. When you select this option button, 1-2-3/G activates the "File name" text box and shows the drive and path to the current directory. You can accept this directory, edit it, or type a new drive and/or directory.

Once you select a specific type of table, 1-2-3/G activates the "Range" text box, prompting you for a location for the table. Specify a single address or range name that defines the upper-left corner of where you want the table to begin. To complete the File Admin Table command, select the OK command button, or press ENTER. 1-2-3/G writes the table into the worksheet starting at the location you specified in the "Range" text box. The table appears in columns of adjacent cells. 1-2-3/G uses as many cells as it needs to create the table you specified. All cells in the path of the table are overwritten with the new data.

Note

> For a more complete discussion of the File Admin Table command, as well as an example of each type of table, see Chapter 12, "Networking 1-2-3/G."

EXTRACTING DATA TO FILES ON DISK

To extract data from a worksheet file to a file on disk, you use the File Xtract command. This command allows you select data from a specific range, collection, or worksheet and copy that data to a new or existing file on disk. When 1-2-3/G copies the data, it also copies any range names, formats, and settings associated with the range containing the data. When you select the File Xtract command, 1-2-3/G displays the dialog box in Figure 5–18.

If you select the "Formulas" option button (the default), 1-2-3/G extracts all labels, values, and formulas from the range you select. On the other hand, if you select the "Values" option, 1-2-3/G still copies both the labels and values in the selected range, but formulas are copied as their current values, not as formulas.

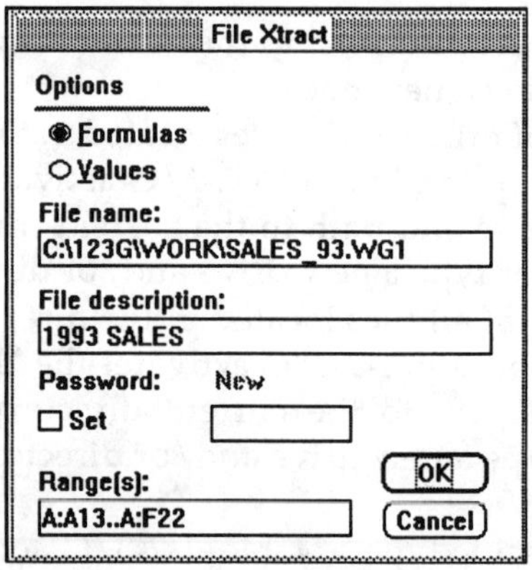

File Xtract

Options

◉ Formulas
○ Values

File name:
C:\123G\WORK\SALES_93.WG1

File description:
1993 SALES

Password: New
☐ Set

Range(s):
A:A13..A:F22

OK
Cancel

FIGURE 5–18 The File Xtract dialog box

To specify a file on disk to extract the data to, you use the "File name" text box. In this box, 1-2-3/G initially displays the drive and path to the current directory. This is followed by the name of the first available new worksheet file, using 1-2-3/G's file-naming scheme. For example, if the last worksheet file you allowed 1-2-3/G to create in the current directory was named SHEET2.WG1, 1-2-3/G displays SHEET3.WG1. You can accept this filename, edit it, type one of your own, or press NAME (F3) to have 1-2-3/G display a list of files for your selection.

Note

> Be aware that when you extract data to an existing file, 1-2-3/G overwrites all the data in the existing file with the extracted data.

You can also assign a description or set a password for the file on disk that you extract the data to. To assign a description, select the "File description" text box and type a file description of up to 80 characters. To specify a password, place an X in the "Password Set" check box. 1-2-3/G activates the "New" text box. Type a password of up to 15 characters. 1-2-3/G displays asterisks (*) as you type. You can type any combination of letters or numbers. However, passwords are case sensitive. To complete the password, press ENTER. The name of the "New" text box changes to "Verify." Type the password again, exactly as you typed it the first time, and press ENTER.

To specify a range of data to extract, you use the "Range(s)" text box. Initially, 1-2-3/G displays the current selection in this box. However, you can specify a range address (including a 3-D range), a range name, a collection, or a worksheet (for example A:).

To extract the current selection to the file shown in the "File name" text box, select the OK command button, or press ENTER. 1-2-3/G writes the selected range, along with its settings and range names, to the file on disk. The data is entered in the new file starting in cell A:A1. If you selected the name of any existing file, 1-2-3/G displays the Cancel, Replace, Backup menu. If you select Cancel, 1-2-3/G cancels the File Xtract command, without writing data to disk. If you select Replace, 1-2-3/G overwrites the file on disk with the extracted data. If you select Backup, 1-2-3/G copies the file on disk to the default backup directory, usually C:\123G\BACKUP, before saving the extracted data to the file on disk.

As mentioned, when you extract data to a file on disk, the range being extracted is entered into the worksheet file starting in cell A:A1. Any formulas are adjusted to reflect their new positions in the worksheet. For example, Figure 5–19 shows a sample worksheet that includes data on two years sales by a strategic business unit for a small chemical company. To extract the range A:A13..A:F22 from this file, begin by selecting that range. Next, select the File Xtract command. 1-2-3/G displays the File Xtract dialog box. In the "File name" text box, specify the filename SALES_93.WG1. To extract the data, select the OK command button. 1-2-3/G writes the data in the range A:A13..A:F22 to the SALES_93.WG1 file on disk. To see the SALES_93.WK1, select the File Retrieve command to load the file. When you load the file, it appears as shown in Figure

1-2-3/G [69.4] Ready

File Edit Worksheet Range Copy... Move... Print Graph Data Utility Quit... Help

A:A1 'ABC Chemical Company, Ltd.

SALES.WG1

A	A	B	C	D	E	F
1	ABC Chemical Company, Ltd.					
2	Sales by SBU - 1992					
3						
4		(Q1)	(Q2)	(Q3)	(Q4)	TOTAL
5	Colors	4,435,236	4,213,474	4,080,417	5,322,283	18,051,411
6	Copy Dye	8,870,472	8,426,948	8,160,834	10,644,566	36,102,821
7	Brighteners	5,322,283	5,056,169	4,896,501	6,386,740	21,661,693
8	Food Colors	7,096,378	6,741,559	6,528,667	8,515,653	28,882,257
9	Pharmacuticals	2,661,142	2,528,085	2,448,250	3,193,370	10,830,846
10						
11	Total	28,385,510	26,966,235	26,114,670	34,062,612	115,529,027
12						
13	Sales by SBU - 1993					
14						
15		(Q1)	(Q2)	(Q3)	(Q4)	TOTAL
16	Colors	4,523,941	4,297,744	4,162,025	5,428,729	18,412,439
17	Copy Dye	9,047,881	8,595,487	8,324,051	10,857,458	36,824,877
18	Brighteners	5,428,729	5,157,292	4,994,431	6,514,475	22,094,926
19	Food Colors	7,238,305	6,876,390	6,659,241	8,685,966	29,459,902
20	Pharmacuticals	2,714,364	2,578,646	2,497,215	3,257,237	11,047,463
21						
22	Total	28,953,221	27,505,560	26,636,963	34,743,865	117,839,608
23						

FIGURE 5–19 A sample worksheet file

5–20. Notice the positioning of the data in Figure 5–20. Although the data occupied the range A:A13.A:F22 in the original file, it now occupies the range A:A1..A:F10 in the new file.

When you use the File Xtract Formulas option, make sure you also extract any ranges referenced by the formulas extracted. Otherwise, you may get unexpected results. For example, imagine you have the formula +A:A100 in cell A:A10. Imagine further that you extract the range A:A10..A:F20 to a file on disk. When the formula arrives in the new file, it is located in cell A:A1. Further, the formula now reads +A:A90. A:A90 in the new file is blank. Therefore the formula returns 0.

If you extract a formula that refers to a named range, extract the entire named range as well. Otherwise, the extracted range name won't refer to the correct range in the new file.

If you extract formulas that refer to other files, consider using an absolute reference. For example, imagine you have the formula +<<C:SALES\MARKET.WG1>>A:A10 in cell A:A10 of the current file. Further, imagine you extract the range A:A10..A:F20 to a file on disk. When the formula arrives in the new file, it reads +<<C:SALES\MARKET.WG1>>A:A1 and will not return the correct results. However, if you use an absolute reference such as +<<C:SALES\MARKET.WG1>>$A:$A$1 to begin with, this problem is avoided. For more about using absolute references, see Chapter 4, "Cutting and Pasting Data."

Note

> You can extract data from any open worksheet file. This includes worksheet files from previous versions of 1-2-3, including 1-2-3 Release 1A, 2, and 3, as well as Lotus Symphony.

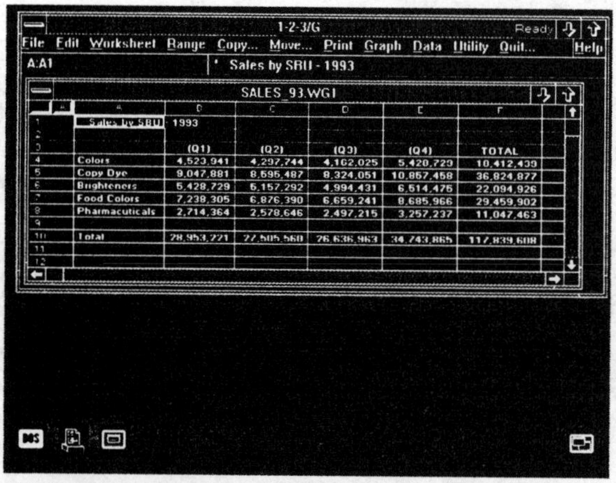

FIGURE 5–20 A new file created with File Xtract

COMBINING FILES

To combine one file with another, you use the File Combine command. This command allows you to combine the contents of a file on disk with the file in the active window. The combining starts at the location of the cell pointer. This command is often used to combine subsidiary financial statements into one consolidated corporate statement.

You can use the File Combine command to copy information from a worksheet file on disk to the active worksheet file. You can also use it to add numbers from a worksheet file on disk to numbers in the active worksheet file, or to subtract numbers in a worksheet file from numbers in the active worksheet file. Additionally, two new features of the File Combine command now allow you to multiply or divide the values in the active worksheet file by the values in another worksheet file on disk.

Caution

The File Combine command combines two files starting at the location of the cell pointer, working downward and to the right. Therefore, before you use File Combine, make sure you locate the cell pointer in the upper-left corner of where you want the combining process to begin. Otherwise, you may not get the results you want. Further, you may overwrite some important data. To minimize the effect of mistakes when using File Combine, save the current worksheet file before you use this command. That way, you can always recover your work. Additionally, you can also recover your work by using 1-2-3/G's Edit Undo command to reverse the effects of File Combine.

When you select the File Combine command, 1-2-3/G displays the dialog box in Figure 5-21. To begin, first select an option button from the "Function" section of the dialog box to specify the type of combining operation you want. The purpose of each one of these option buttons is explained below. Next, use the option buttons in the "Source" section to select whether you want the entire file from disk combined with the file in the active window, or just a selected range. If you select "Entire file" (the default), 1-2-3/G will combine the entire file from disk with the file in the active window. If you select "Named/ Specified range," 1-2-3/G activates the adjacent text box. Type the range address, collection, or range name that defines the range from the file on disk that you want combined with the active file. Press ENTER to confirm your selection. 1-2-3/G activates the "File name" text box.

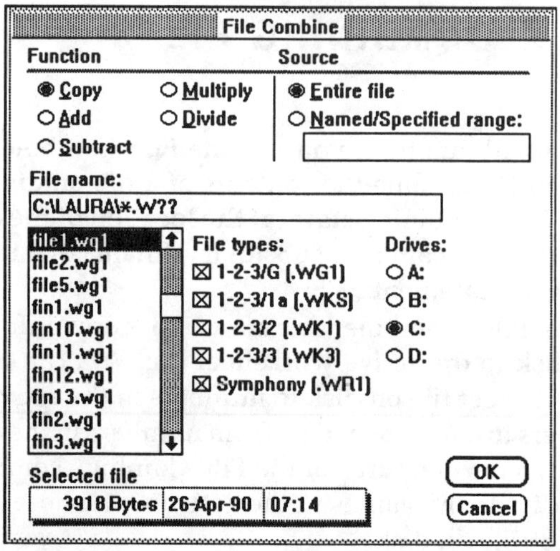

FIGURE 5–21 **The File Combine dialog box**

In the "File name" text box, specify the name of the file on disk that you want to combine with the current file. Initially, 1-2-3/G displays the drive and path to the current working directory followed the wild-card file descriptor *.W??, In Figure 5–21, this path is C:\LAURA. The list box below lists the worksheet files in this directory. Either type the name of the file on disk that you want to use, or select it from the list box below. To complete the File Combine command, select the OK command button, or press ENTER. Starting at the location of the cell pointer, 1-2-3/G combines either all or part of the contents of the file on disk with the file in the active window.

When you highlight the name of a file in the "File name" list box, 1-2-3/G shows the size of that file as well as the date and time it was last saved in the "Selected file" text box. For example, in Figure 5–21, when FILE1.WG1 is highlighted in the list box, the "Selected file" box indicates that this file contains 3918 bytes and was last saved on April 26, 1990 at 7:14 AM. This can be a useful feature when you are combining two large files with limited memory available.

The results of the combining operation depend on your selection in the "Function" section of the File Combine dialog box. Each of these function options has the following effect, starting at the location of the cell pointer:

- **Copy:** Copies all or part of the Source file (file on disk) to the file in the active window, starting at the location of the cell pointer. Any information in the active worksheet that is below and to the right of the cell pointer is *replaced* by the information from the source file. However, cells in the active worksheet file that are overlaid by blank cells in the file on disk are not affected. Furthermore, all relative, mixed, and absolute cell addresses in formulas copied from the file on disk are adjusted and now reference cells in the active worksheet file. See Chapter 4, "Cutting and Pasting Data," for a discussion of copying relative, mixed, and absolute cell references.

- **Add:** Adds the numbers, and the results of numeric formulas, in the file on disk to the corresponding cells in the active worksheet file. If a cell in the active file is blank, it takes on the value of the corresponding cell in the file on disk. If the cell in the active file contains a label or formula, the incoming value is ignored.
- **Subtract:** Subtracts numbers, and results of numeric formulas, in the file on disk from the corresponding cells in the active worksheet file. If a cell in the active worksheet is blank, and the corresponding cell in the source range contains a number or the result of a numeric formula, the incoming value is subtracted from zero. Cells in the active file containing labels or formulas are not affected.
- **Multiply:** Multiplies values in the active worksheet file by values in corresponding cells in the file on disk. Cells in the active file that are blank or contain labels or formulas are not affected.
- **Divide:** Divides values in the active worksheet file by values in corresponding cells in the file on disk. Cells in the active file that are blank or contain labels or formulas are not affected.

Note

As mentioned, the Add, Subtract, Multiply, and Divide options have no effect on cells in the active worksheet file if they contain numeric formulas. This can lead to incorrect consolidation values. For this reason, you should only use these options when ranges in the active file contain values, not numeric formulas.

You can use the various components of the File Combine dialog box to have 1-2-3/G display a list of files from directories other than the current directory. To do this, you can use any of the following techniques:

- Edit the drive or path in the "File name" text box.
- Select a subdirectory from the "File name" list box. 1-2-3/G displays the files in the directory you selected. The "File name" text box is updated to reflect your choice
- Select the parent directory, displayed as two dots (..). 1-2-3/G moves one level closer to the root directory and displays files and subdirectories at that level. The "File name" text box is updated accordingly.
- Select an option button from the "Drives" section (for example, A, B, C, or D shown in Figure 5–21). 1-2-3/G displays the last directory used on that drive in the "File name" text box. The files in that directory appear in the list box below.

You can also use the check boxes in the "File types" section of the File Combine dialog box to add or remove specific types of files from the list box. For example, to remove 1-2-3 Release 2 (.WK1) filenames from the list box, click on the "1-2-3/2 (.WK1)" check box. 1-2-3/G removes the X from the check box and .WK1 files no longer appear in the list box. Alternatively, you can press TAB to move the "File types" section, followed by ↓, to highlight the check box you want. Then, press the space bar to remove the X from the appropriate check box.

A File Combine Example

Suppose you want to create a consolidated income statement for the two subsidiaries shown in Figure 5-22. You want to combine the first quarter subsidiary statements from FILE1.WG1 and FILE2.WG1 into one consolidated statement, FILE5.WG1. (Keep in mind during this example that 1-2-3/G will be using the information from the files FILE1.WG1 and FILE2.WG1 on disk.) Notice that FILE5.WG1 has been set up to accommodate the information that will be combined from FILE1.WG1 and FILE2.WG1. FILE5 also contains corporate expenses such as G+A and Interest that are not included in the subsidiary statements.

To consolidate these statements, begin by combining the first-quarter numbers from the appropriate divisions into your master file, FILE5.WG1, using the following procedure:

123G.EXE: DESK7.DSK — Ready

File Edit Worksheet Range Copy... Move... Print Graph Data Utility Quit... Help

A:B2 150000

FILE5.WG1

A	A	B	C	D
1	CONSOLIDATED	Q End	Q End	Q E
2		03/31/90	06/30/90	09/3
3	Sales			
4	DM+L			
5	Manuf. Exp.			
6		------------	------------	-------
7	GP			
8	Mark. Exp.			
9		------------	------------	-------
10	Corporate Income	$0	$0	
11	G+A Exp	$100,000		
12	Interest Exp	$200,000		
13		------------	------------	-------
14	NI Before Tax	($300,000)	$0	
15				
16				
17				
18				
19				
20				
21				
22				
23				

FILE2.WG1

A	A	B	C	D
1	DIVISION 2	03/31/90	06/30/90	09/30/90
2	Sales	$500,000		
3	DM+L	$225,000		
4	Manuf. Exp.	$75,000		
5		------------		
6	GP	$200,000		
7	Mark. Exp.	$200,000		
8		------------		
9	Income	$0		
10				
11				

(C0) FILE1.WG1

A	A	B	C	D
1	DIVISION 1	03/31/90	06/30/90	09/30/90
2	Sales	$150,000		
3	DM+L	$30,000		
4	Manuf. Exp.	$22,500		
5		------------		
6	GP	$97,500		
7	Mark. Exp.	$22,500		
8		------------		
9	Income	$75,000		

FIGURE 5-22 **Setting up your master file (active worksheet file)**

1. Locate the cell pointer in the upper-left cell of where you want the incoming information to be combined, cell B3 in FILE5.WG1.
2. Select the File Combine command. 1-2-3/G displays the File Combine dialog box.
3. Select the "Copy" option button from the "Function" section.
4. Next, specify the range in your source file you want to combine, A:B2..A:B9 in FILE1. To do this, select the "Named/Specified range" option button from "Source: section and enter the range **A:B2..A:B9** in the adjacent text box. Press ENTER to confirm you selection. 1-2-3/G activates the "File name" text box.
5. Enter your source file, **FILE1.WG1**, in the "File name" text box.
6. Press ENTER or click on the OK command button to complete the File Combine command. 1-2-3/G copies the information from the range A:B2..A:B9 file on disk (FILE1.WG1) with the file in the active window (FILE5.WG1), starting in cell A:B3 of that file. Your screen now looks like Figure 5–23.
7. As a precaution, save the information in FILE5.WG1 by using the File Save command.

Next, add the information for Division 2 file, FILE2.WG1, to the Division 1 information now in FILE5.WG. To do this, perform the following steps:

1. Make sure the cell pointer is still located in cell A:B3 of FILE5.WG1.

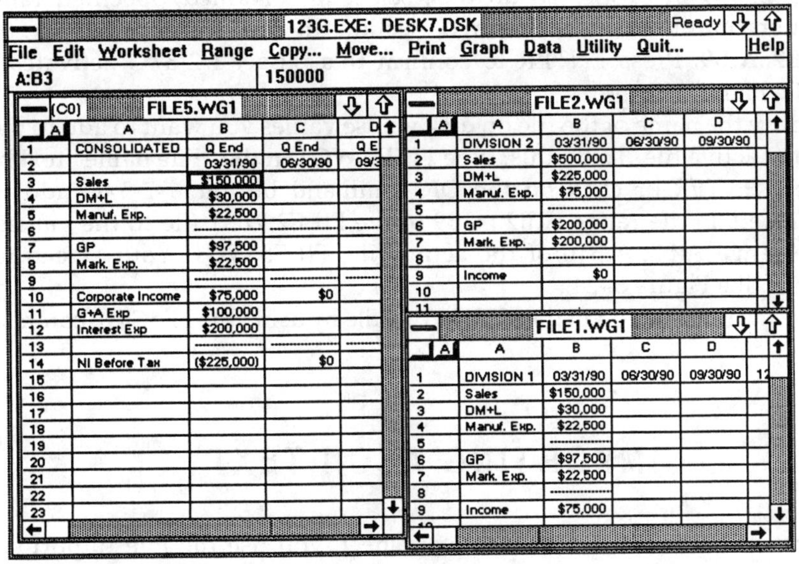

FIGURE 5–23 Using the File Combine Copy command

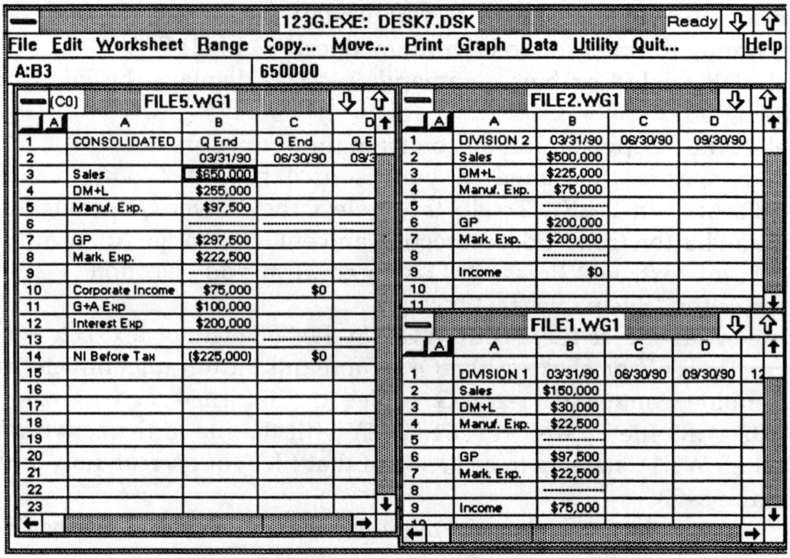

123G.EXE: DESK7.DSK — Ready

File Edit Worksheet Range Copy... Move... Print Graph Data Utility Quit... Help

A:B3 650000

(C0) FILE5.WG1

	A	B	C	D
1	CONSOLIDATED	Q End	Q End	Q E
2		03/31/90	06/30/90	09/3
3	Sales	$650,000		
4	DM+L	$255,000		
5	Manuf. Exp.	$97,500		
6		----------	----------	----------
7	GP	$297,500		
8	Mark. Exp.	$222,500		
9		----------	----------	----------
10	Corporate Income	$75,000	$0	
11	G+A Exp	$100,000		
12	Interest Exp	$200,000		
13		----------	----------	----------
14	NI Before Tax	($225,000)	$0	
15				
16				
17				
18				
19				
20				
21				
22				
23				

FILE2.WG1

	A	B	C	D
1	DIVISION 2	03/31/90	06/30/90	09/30/90
2	Sales	$500,000		
3	DM+L	$225,000		
4	Manuf. Exp.	$75,000		
5		----------		
6	GP	$200,000		
7	Mark. Exp.	$200,000		
8		----------		
9	Income	$0		
10				

FILE1.WG1

	A	B	C	D
1	DIVISION 1	03/31/90	06/30/90	09/30/90
2	Sales	$150,000		
3	DM+L	$30,000		
4	Manuf. Exp.	$22,500		
5		----------		
6	GP	$97,500		
7	Mark. Exp.	$22,500		
8		----------		
9	Income	$75,000		

FIGURE 5–24 Using the File Combine Add command

2. Select the File Combine command. 1-2-3/G displays the File Combine dialog box.
3. Select the "Add" option button from the "Function" section.
4. Specify the range in your source file you want to add to your consolidated file, B2..B9 in FILE2. To do this, select the "Named/Specified range" option button from the "Source" section. In the adjacent text box, type **A:B2..A:B9**. Press ENTER to confirm this range. 1-2-3/G activates the "File name" text box.
5. Specify the name of the file on disk whose values you want to add to those in the active file. To do this, type **FILE2.WG1** in the "File name" text box.
6. Press ENTER or click on the OK command button. 1-2-3/G adds the numbers in the range A:B2..A:B9 of the FILE2.WG1 file to the values in the range A:B3..A:B10 of the active file, FILE5.WG1. Your screen now looks like Figure 5–24.
7. Save the information in the FILE5.WG1 file by using the File Save command.

IMPORTING ASCII TEXT

To import ASCII text files into the worksheet, you use the File Import command. This command allows you to import the contents of ASCII files into the worksheet as either text or as labels and numbers in separate cells.

In terms of file formats, ASCII (American Standard Code for Information Interchange) files are often viewed as the lowest common denominator among IBM-PC and compatible software programs. Therefore, many software programs offer a facility for saving files in ASCII text format, allowing you to easily share data between different software programs. For example, the .PRN files you create with 1-2-3/G's Print File command are standard ASCII text files.

The File Import command offers two options, Text and Numbers. The Text option is used to import the contents of a standard ASCII text file into the worksheet as labels. The lines of text from the ASCII file are stored as labels in a column of consecutive cells, one label per cell. The Numbers option, on the other hand, imports either text strings and numbers or just numbers, leaving the text strings behind. However, instead of storing the incoming data as labels in a column of cells, the text strings and/or numbers are parsed into individual cells, a row of cells for each line in the ASCII file. For 1-2-3/G to know how to appropriately split up each line of ASCII text file into individual cells, each line of the file must be properly *delimited.*

Figure 5–25 shows an example of a standard ASCII text file. Figure 5–26, on the other hand, shows an ASCII text file that has been delimited. Notice that the text strings and numbers in each line of the ASCII file in Figure 5–26 are separated by commas. Notice further that the text strings are enclosed in quotes. The commas tell 1-2-3/G where to end one entry and start the next—that is, how to split up the line into individual cells. The quotes, on the other hand, indicate to 1-2-3/G that a particular entry is to be imported and stored as a label.

Note

> If 1-2-3/G encounters a CTRL-Z (end of file marker) anywhere in an ASCII file, it will stop importing data at that point, even though the end of the file may not have been reached.

```
SALES BY SBU    (Q1)     (Q2)     (Q3)     (Q4)    TOTAL
Colors          123123   116967   113273   147748   501111
Copy Dye        246246   233934   226546   295495  1002221
Brighteners     147748   140360   135928   177297   601333
Food Colors     196997   187147   181237   236396   801777
Pharmaceuticals  73874    70180    67964    88649   300666

Total           787987   748588   724948   945585  3207108
```

FIGURE 5–25 A standard ASCII text file

```
"SALES BY SBU","(Q1)","(Q2)","(Q3)","(Q4)","TOTAL"
"Colors",123123,116967,113273,147748,501111
"Copy Dye",246246,233934,226546,295495,1002221
"Brighteners",147748,140360,135928,177297,601333
"Food Colors",196997,187147,181237,236396,801777
"Pharmacuticals",73874,70180,67964,88649,300666

"Total",787987,748588,724948,945585,3207108
```

FIGURE 5–26 A delimited ASCII text file

Caution

When you use the File Import command to import the contents of an ASCII file into the worksheet, 1-2-3/G overwrites all cells that are in the path of the incoming data. Therefore make sure you have plenty of room below and to the right of the cell pointer before using File Import. If you do accidentally delete some important data, press ALT-BACKSPACE, or select Edit Undo, to undo the File Import Text command.

The Text Option

To import a standard (nondelimited) ASCII file into the worksheet, you use the File Import Text command. This command imports the contents of an ASCII text file into the worksheet as labels, starting at the location of the cell pointer. The lines of text from the ASCII file are stored as long labels in a column of cells, one label per cell. Each line of the ASCII text file must end with a carriage return/line feed and may not exceed 512 characters in length. In preparation for the File Import Text command, position the cell pointer in the first cell where you want the listing to begin.

When you select the File Import Text command, 1-2-3/G displays the dialog box in Figure 5–27. In the "File name" text box, 1-2-3/G displays the drive and path to the current working directory followed by the wild-card file descriptor *.*. This causes 1-2-3/G to list all the files in the current directory in the list box below. To select an ASCII file, you can use any of the following techniques:

- Double-click on the name of the file.
- Click once on the name of the file and Select the OK command button or press ENTER.
- Type the name of the file in the "File name" text box and press ENTER.

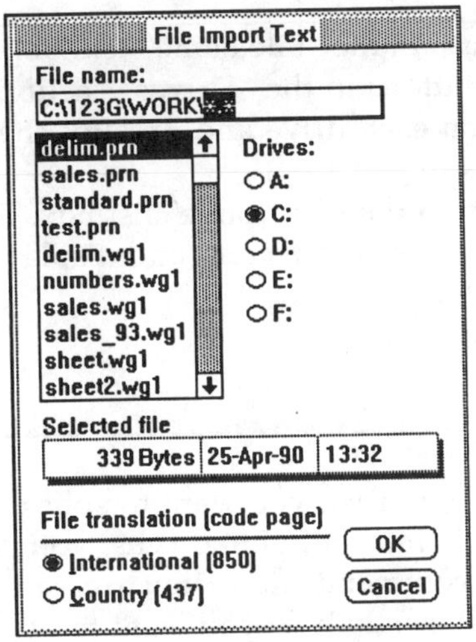

FIGURE 5–27 The File Import Text dialog box

• Press ↓ to highlight the name of the file and press ENTER.

Whichever method you select, 1-2-3/G imports the ASCII file into the worksheet, starting at the location of the cell pointer. As mentioned, the lines of text from the ASCII file are stored as long labels in a column of cells, one label per cell. If there is a blank line in the ASCII text file, 1-2-3/G leaves a blank cell in the column. For example, Figure 5–28 shows the standard ASCII text file shown earlier in Figure 5–25 after it has been imported into the worksheet. As you can see, each row in the worksheet contains a long label.

To display a list of files outside the current directory for the File Import Text command, you can use any of the following techniques:

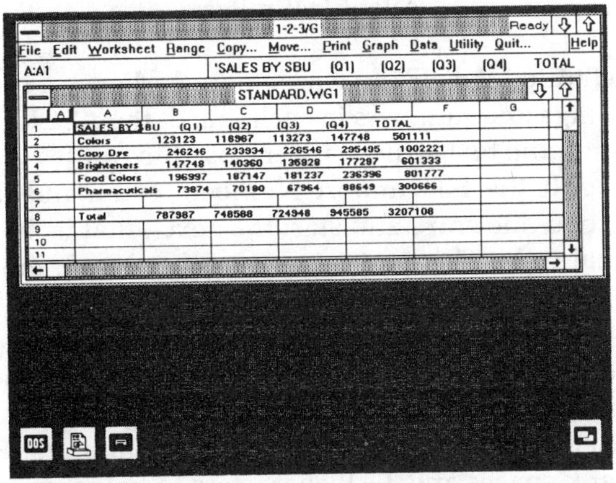

FIGURE 5–28 An ASCII text file imported with File Import Text

- Edit the drive and/or path in the "File name" text box and press ENTER.
- Select from the option buttons in the "Drives" section. 1-2-3/G remembers the last directory used on each drive and updates the "File name" list box accordingly.
- Select the two dots (..) from the "File name" list box. This causes 1-2-3/G to move one level closer to the root directory and display files, directories, and subdirectories at that level.

Note

> If, after using File Import Text, you want to split up the words and numbers in long labels into individual cells, you can use the Data Parse command. This command allows you to create a custom format line that tells 1-2-3/G exactly how you want to break up a range of long labels. For a complete discussion of this command, see Chapter 9, "Data Management."

The Numbers Option

The File Import Numbers command allows you to import numbers from a standard (nondelimited) ASCII text file, or both labels and numbers from a delimited ASCII file. Either way, 1-2-3/G places each incoming data item in a separate cell, one row of cells for each line in the ASCII file. However, before you use the File Import Numbers command, you need to know a little about how to use delimiter characters in ASCII files.

About Delimiters

A sample of a delimited ASCII file was shown earlier in Figure 5–26. In that figure, the text strings and numbers in each line of the ASCII file are separated by commas. Further, the text strings are enclosed in quotes. When you import this type of file with the File Import Numbers command, the commas tell 1-2-3/G where to end one entry and start the next—that is, how to split up the line into individual cells. The quotes, on the other hand, indicate to 1-2-3/G that a particular entry is to be imported and stored as a label.

In addition to using commas as delimiter symbols, you can also use ; (semicolon), or . (period), and to indicate a text string, you can use either ' (single quote), or " (double quote). If text strings, including a single letter or a set of letters, are not enclosed in quotes, they become delimiters. Further, 1-2-3/G also considers blank spaces and TAB characters to be delimiters. A TAB character, however, is also imported as a blank cell eight characters wide.

If the ASCII file you are importing includes numbers with commas as a thousands separator, take them out. Otherwise, 1-2-3/G will split the number wherever a comma occurs. You do not need to worry about decimal separators, however. 1-2-3/G honors the default decimal separator, usually the period (.). To specify a different default decimal separator, you use the User Settings International Decimal command. This command is available from either the Utility menu or the Desktop Control menu.

Using the File Import Numbers Command

When you select the File Import Numbers command, 1-2-3/G displays the dialog box in Figure 5–29. Notice that the structure of this dialog box is exactly the same as the File Import Text dialog box shown earlier in Figure 5–27. You use its components in exactly the same way.

For example, imagine you want to import just the numbers from the standard ASCII text file shown earlier in Figure 5–25. In this case, the text strings are not enclosed in quotes. Therefore, they will not be imported. However, the numbers in this file are separated by spaces, which serve as delimiters. When this file is imported into the worksheet, it will appear as shown in Figure 5–30. To import this file, move the cell pointer to cell A:A1 and select the File Import Numbers command. 1-2-3/G displays the dialog box in Figure 5–29. In the "File name" text box, specify the name of the ASCII file you want to import, or select it from the list box below. To complete the command, select the OK command button. 1-2-3/G imports just the numbers from the ASCII file, the text strings are left behind. Your worksheet looks like Figure 5–30.

If the ASCII file is fully delimited, you can import both labels and numbers into the worksheet. For example, imagine you want to import the fully

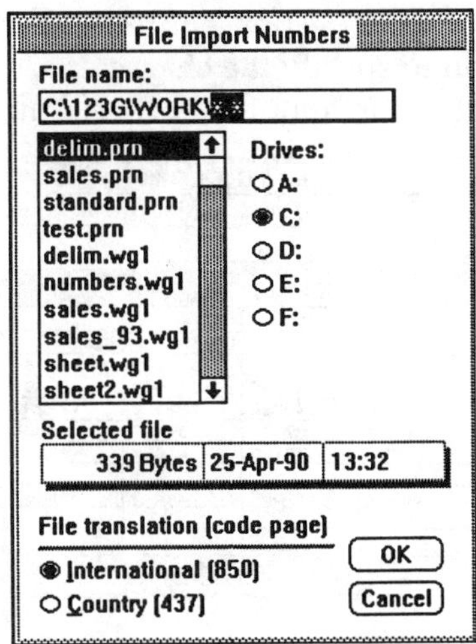

FIGURE 5–29 The File Import Numbers dialog box

1-2-3/G (69.4) Ready

File Edit Worksheet Range Copy... Move... Print Graph Data Utility Quit... Help

A:A1 1

NUMBERS.WG1

A	A	B	C	D	E	F	G
1	1	2	3	4			
2	123123	116967	113273	147748	501111		
3	246246	233934	226546	295495	1002221		
4	147748	140360	135928	177297	601333		
5	196997	187147	181237	236396	801777		
6	73874	70180	67964	88649	300666		
7							
8	787987	748588	724948	945585	3207108		
9							
10							

FIGURE 5-30 A standard ASCII text file imported with the File Import Numbers command

delimited ASCII text file shown earlier in Figure 5-26. In each line of this file, the labels are enclosed in quotes and both the labels and numbers are separated by commas. Therefore, when this file is imported into the worksheet, it will appear as shown in Figure 5-31. To import this file, select the File Import Numbers command. 1-2-3/G displays the File Import Numbers dialog box. In the "File name" text box, specify the name of the file or select it from the list box below. To complete the command, select the OK command button. 1-2-3/G imports the contents of the ASCII file as shown in Figure 5-31.

Changing the Code Page

Both the File Import Text and Number dialog boxes, shown in Figures 5-27 and 5-29, respectively, contain a section entitled "File Translation (code page)." This section allows you to specify the character set that was used to create the file you want to import. By default, 1-2-3/G uses the IBM-PC Multilingual code

1-2-3/G (69.4) Ready

File Edit Worksheet Range Copy... Move... Print Graph Data Utility Quit... Help

A:F1 'TOTAL

DELIM.WG1

A	A	B	C	D	E	F	G
1	SALES BY SBU	(Q1)	(Q2)	(Q3)	(Q4)	TOTAL	
2	Colors	123123	116967	113273	147748	501111	
3	Copy Dye	246246	233934	226546	295495	1002221	
4	Brighteners	147748	140360	135928	177297	601333	
5	Food Colors	196997	187147	181237	236396	801777	
6	Pharmaceuticals	73874	70180	67964	88649	300666	
7							
8	Total	787987	748588	724948	945585	3207108	
9							
10							

FIGURE 5-31 A delimited ASCII text file imported with the File Import Numbers command

page 850 character set. (A complete listing of this character set appears in Appendix B of this book.) However, many foreign countries use the IBM code page 437 character set. If the ASCII file you want to import is a code page 437 file, select the "Country (437)" option button from the "File Translation (code page)" section of the File Import Text or Numbers dialog box. When 1-2-3/G imports the file, it will translate the code page 437 characters into code page 850 characters. In most cases, there is an equivalent code page 850 character for each code page 437 character. If there is not an equivalent, 1-2-3/G will use the closest code page 850 character.

Note

To change the code page used by the File Import (and File Print) command, you use the User Settings International command (see Appendix A, "Customizing 1-2-3/G," for more information). Changing this setting does *not* change the 850 code page character set 1-2-3/G uses. To change the default character set used by 1-2-3/G, you must adjust your CONFIG.SYS file. See Appendix B in this book for more information on this.

SUMMARY

This chapter shows you how to use the File command to manage your files in 1-2-3/G. After a brief discussion about file basics, this chapter shows you how to use the File Save command to save your files to disk. Using the File Save command, you can save just the currently active file, or you can save all the files on the desktop in a single operation. This chapter also shows you how to save a file with password protection. That way, if someone does not know the password, 1-2-3/G will not allow them to open and use the file.

This chapter also shows how to use the File New command to create new worksheet and graph files. In addition, this chapter shows you how to use one file as a template for creating another file. The new file takes on the same data and settings as the template file.

The File Open and File Retrieve commands are also discussed in this chapter. The File Open command allows you to open a file on the desktop without affecting other open files. The File Retrieve command, on the other hand, replaces an open file with another existing file from disk.

The File Directory command is discussed in the chapter as well. This command allows you to specify a new working directory that 1-2-3/G uses to search for its data files.

This chapter also shows you how to use the File Erase command to erase files on disk. Although this command is designed to erase 1-2-3/G's data files, you can also use it to erase files created by other software programs.

The File Extract, Combine, and Import commands are also covered in this chapter. The File Extract command extracts the data in a selected range, collection, or worksheet to a worksheet file on disk. You can use File Combine to combine the contents of a worksheet file on disk with the worksheet file in memory. You can also combine the entire file from disk with the file in memory or you can specify that only a selected range be combined. Finally, 1-2-3/G's File Import command allows you to import ASCII files into the worksheet.

Functions

1-2-3/G includes *functions,* which are powerful tools that perform specialized calculations. Functions are essentially abbreviated formulas that are used to efficiently and easily perform a specific task. 1-2-3/G includes mathematical and statistical functions, which perform typical numeric calculations such as summing numbers. 1-2-3/G also provides functions that perform trigonometric, financial, date and time calculations, even logical analysis. In addition, 1-2-3/G also provides string functions, which manipulate labels, and special functions, which let you determine the position of the cell pointer, return operating system information, indirectly reference cells, and more.

Since functions are valuable time-saving tools for every 1-2-3/G user, this chapter serves as both a tool to learn how to use functions, and also as a convenient reference guide. As you can imagine, 1-2-3/G's functions are used in a wide range of disciplines, such as financial analysis, accounting, statistics, and trigonometry. Therefore, this chapter also serves as a refresher guide on these subjects.

What's New

1-2-3/G has expanded the number of functions it offers in every category except mathematical functions. Most of these functions, although new to Release 2 and 2.2 users, were first introduced in Release 3.

1-2-3/G also offers new commands that improve on familiar functions. For example, 1-2-3/G's @ROUND function rounds only a single value and changes both the displayed and stored value to the rounded value. However, the Range Attributes Precision command now allows you to format a range of numbers so that only a specified number of places after the decimal are used in calculations. These improved methods and alternative commands are discussed in TIPS and NOTES in this chapter.

In 1-2-3/G, some existing functions have been improved over previous releases. For example, functions such as @SUM and @AVG now automatically adjust a range argument even if you delete a cell that begins or ends the range. Any changes from previous releases are discussed under each function. (See Chapter 3 for more information.)

Function arguments can now include cell references from other 1-2-3/G worksheet files. Thus, you can link files through functions. For example, if two files are open, information in one file is automatically updated when pertinent information in the other file changes.

Finally, 1-2-3/G now provides a "point-and-shoot" feature originally introduced in Release 3 that allows you to choose a function from an on-screen list. You can now also access a description of each function, including its arguments, through the Help system. See "On-Line Help with Functions" in this chapter.

Tip: Pointing to function arguments

If, while entering a function, you point to a range and then press ENTER, 1-2-3/G now automatically includes the closing parenthesis. For example, suppose in cell A7, you want to enter the function @SUM(A1..A5). Type **@SUM(**, then point to the range A1..A5 using either the mouse or keyboard. This range is now highlighted and the Control line displays @SUM(A1..A5. Press **ENTER**, and 1-2-3/G completes the function by adding the ending parenthesis.

FUNCTION BASICS

1-2-3/G's functions all use the following *syntax*, or structure:

@FUNCTION(argument1,argument2,...,argumentn)

The @ symbol must *always* precede the name of a function. If you forget to use the @ symbol, 1-2-3/G assumes that you are typing a label, not a function. Do not leave any space between the @ symbol and the function name. You can type in the name of the function using any combination of upper-case and lower-case letters. Do not leave any space between the function name and its arguments. In 1-2-3/G the maximum length of a function plus its arguments has increased to 512 characters, the maximum length of cell entries in 1-2-3/G.

Tip: Pointing and shooting functions

1-2-3/G now provides a "point-and-shoot" method of specifying functions. For example, suppose you want to use the @SUM function. After you enter the @ symbol, press F3 (NAME). The @Functions dialog box shown in Figure 6–1 appears on your screen, listing all of 1-2-3/G's functions. Either use the keyboard or the mouse to scroll down and select the @SUM function you want. Then either press ENTER or click on the OK button in the @Functions dialog box. The selected function now appears in the Control line, followed by the beginning parenthesis for your @SUM argument. If the function does not use an argument, such as @PI, no beginning parenthesis is included.

A function operates on *arguments*. Arguments provide the information on which a function acts. *Always* enclose arguments in parentheses. Some functions use a single argument, while others require multiple arguments. Multiple arguments are separated by *argument separators*, usually a comma. Do not leave any space between multiple arguments, or between a beginning or ending parenthesis and an argument. If you enter your arguments incorrectly, 1-2-3/G disallows your entry.

The default argument separator in 1-2-3/G is a comma (,). You can also use a semicolon (;), the international argument separator, or a period (.). You can only use *one* of these argument separators at any time. Use the Desktop Control

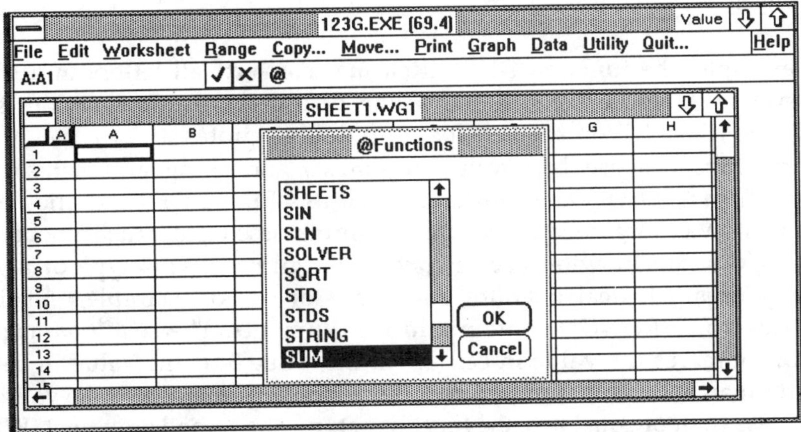

FIGURE 6–1 The @Functions dialog box

menu or the Utility option on 1-2-3/G's Main Menu to access the User Settings International Number Format Argument command and change the argument separator to a period or semicolon. See Appendix B, "Customizing 1-2-3/G," for more details.

Functions act on these different types of arguments:

- Values.
- Strings.
- Locations (cells, ranges, and/or collections).
- Conditions (logical formulas).
- Attributes (an item enclosed in double quotes ("")).

Value arguments can be any of the following:

- Literal numbers.
- Numeric formulas or functions that return values.
- Locations: cell or range addresses containing values or formulas that return values (including another function).

For example, the functions @SUM(A1..A3) and @SUM(COSTS), where the range name COSTS is assigned to the range A1..A3, would both return the sum of the values in cells A1, A2, and A3. For *most* functions, if any of these cells are blank or contain a label or label prefix, 1-2-3/G assigns a value of 0 to that cell.

Functions that accept *string* arguments use any of the following:

- Literal strings (letters, numbers and symbols enclosed in double quotation marks).
- String formulas or functions that return strings.
- Locations: cell or range addresses containing string formulas or literal strings.

For example, the function @UPPER(*string*) converts all letters in a string to upper-case. If you enter a literal string directly into this function, such as @UPPER("Peter"), you *must* enclose it in double quotes.

Some functions use both value arguments and string arguments, such as @RIGHT(*string,value*). Other functions, such as @PI and @ERR, do not even use arguments. Valid arguments for a function are discussed under each function below.

1-2-3/G's @IF function uses a *condition* argument. This type of argument usually uses a logical operator such as = or >. For example, the function @IF(A5>3,5,"WRONG") contains three arguments. The *condition* argument, A5>3, compares the value in cell A5 to the value 3. If the value in cell A5 is greater than 3, this function returns the second argument, 5. If the value in cell A5 is less than or equal to 3, the function returns the second argument, WRONG. Condition arguments are discussed in detail in "Logical Functions" in this chapter.

Some special functions require an *attribute* argument. For example, @CELLPOINTER(*attribute*) returns a value or label describing a specific attribute of a cell, such as its color or format. See "Special Functions" in this chapter.

You cannot preselect an argument for a function prior to selecting that function. Rather, you must specify the argument while entering the function.

On-Line Help with Functions

1-2-3/G now provides easier access to on-line help for functions. Simply press F1, then choose @Function Index from the main Help menu. If you select a particular function from the list, 1-2-3 then provides a description of that function, including its arguments.

You can also access information about a particular function when you use 1-2-3/G's "point-and-shoot" feature. When you build a formula, type @, then press NAME (F3). 1-2-3 provides you with a list of all functions. Select the proper function, then press HELP (F1). Once again 1-2-3/G provides a description of that particular function, including its arguments. If you have already entered the function name in the Control Line and want information about the arguments for that function, simply press HELP (F1). 1-2-3/G will take you to a help screen for that specific function. For more about using 1-2-3/G's Help system, see Chapter 1.

GENERAL MATHEMATICAL FUNCTIONS

1-2-3/G's mathematical functions, shown in Table 6–1, either manipulate or calculate values. 1-2-3/G has added no new mathematical functions.

TABLE 6–1 1-2-3/G's Mathematical Functions

Function	Returns
@ABS	Absolute (positive) value of a number
@ROUND	Rounded value of a number at a specified precision
@INT	Integer portion of a number
@MOD	Modulus (remainder) of a division operation
@SQRT	Square root of a positive number or 0
@RAND	Random value between 0 and 1

Most of these functions operate on a *value* argument, and all of these mathematical functions return *value results*.

Absolute Value: @ABS

The @ABS function calculates the positive or absolute value of a number. The form of this function is

@ABS (*x*)

where *x* is a literal number, a numeric formula, another function that returns a value, or a reference to a cell that contains one of these. You cannot apply @ABS to a range or collection of cells; instead the function must appear in each cell.

For example, the function @ABS(-2.3) returns 2.3, while @ABS(3.5) returns 3.5. The function @ABS("label") returns 0 because 1-2-3/G assigns a value of 0 to labels, label prefixes, and blank cells. If a cell returns the values NA or ERR, @ABS also returns NA or ERR.

Useful applications of this function include

- Forcing the result of a formula or function to be positive, using ABS(*x*), or *negative*, using –ABS(*x*).
- Calculating the square root of a negative number, using @SQRT(@ABS(–*x*)) Otherwise, @SQRT(–*x*) returns ERR.

Rounding a Value: @ROUND

The @ROUND function rounds a value to a specified number of decimal places, or *precision*. The form of this function is

@ROUND (*x*,*places*)

where x and places are either literal numbers, numeric formulas, other functions that return values, or references to cells that contain one of these. The @ROUND function assigns a 0 value if an argument is a blank cell, a cell containing spaces, a label, or a label prefix. If a cell evaluates to ERR or NA, the @ROUND function also returns this value. You cannot use @ROUND on a range or collection of cells, but must use this function in each cell.

The *x* argument is the value that you want to round. Use your *places* argument to specify where to round the value. Enter the number of places to the right or left of the decimal point where you want rounding to occur, up to 17 places. Any digit less than 5 is rounded down, while numbers equal to or greater than 5 are rounded up. For example, the @ROUND function returns the following values:

Function	Returns
@ROUND(456.789,2)	456.79
@ROUND(-456.789,2)	-457.79
@ROUND(456.789,-2)	500
@ROUND(-456.789,-2)	-500

As shown above, when the *places* argument is positive, @ROUND rounds to the *right* of the decimal place; when *places* is negative, the value is rounded to the *left* of the decimal point.

Note

You can use the Range Attributes Precision Limit Precision command to round values in a *range* of cells. However, this command rounds a value for calculations *only*. The cell still displays and stores the full decimal precision of the value. The advantage to using the Range Attributes Precision Limit Precision command, instead of @ROUND, is that you can apply the command to a range of cells. On the other hand, if you use @ROUND, you must apply it to each cell of the multiple-cell range. See Chapter 3 for more details on the Range Attributes Precision command.

Returning an Integer: @INT

The @INT function returns only the integer portion of a value without rounding that value. The form of this function is

```
@INT(x)
```

where x is a literal number, a numeric formula, another function that returns a value, or a reference to a cell that contains one of these. The @INT argument cannot be a range or collection of cells; you must use this function in each cell. This function returns a 0 value if an argument is a blank cell, a cell containing spaces, a label or a label prefix. If a cell evaluates to ERR or NA, @INT also returns this value.

The @INT function returns only the integer portion of a value without rounding that value. For example, @INT(456.79) returns the value 456. The value is *not* rounded. The value stored in this cell is now 456, not 456.79. Similarly, @INT(-456.79) returns the value -456.

Suppose you have the value 5.5 in cell A1. In cell A2, @INT(A1) displays the value 5. However, cell A2 still contains the value 5.5. However, if cell A3 contains +A2, cell A3 displays and stores the value 5.

Note

Use @INT(@NOW) to obtain the date number of the current date. The current time, which is the decimal portion of the date value, is truncated.

Tip: The difference between @ROUND, @INT, Range Format, and Range Attributes Precision

1-2-3/G offers two functions and two commands that can affect the way in which a value is displayed, and in which another cell containing a formula referencing this cell displays and stores its value:

Function/ Command	Current Cell	Cells Referencing Current Cell
@ROUND	Rounds value up or down.	Displays and stores rounded value only.
@INT	Returns integer portion of value.	Displays and stores integer only.
Range Format 0 places	Changes only displayed value.	Displays and stores full precision.
Range Attributes Precision Limit precision	Full precision displayed and stored.	Uses limited precision of current cell.

Let's examine the different results obtained by using @ROUND, @INT, Range Format with 0 decimal places, and Range Attributes Precision. Suppose you have the example in Figure 6–2. You need to calculate the number of production employees needed for your company's increased sales. As shown in cell B5, if 72,000 units need to be produced and each worker can produce 11,000 per month, then

6.545 workers are needed. If you could actually employ 6.545 people, the correct labor cost is $130,909 shown in cell D5.

Suppose your company has decided that until a full-time employee is needed, other employees will work overtime to meet the production quota. In cell B6, @INT(B5) returns the value 6, the correct number of employees. The @INT function truncates, or loses the integer portion of 6.55, and displays the value 6. If your employees work overtime without pay (assume they receive a year-end bonus), cell D6 contains the correct projected labor cost of $120,000. So cells referencing a cell containing @INT use the integer returned.

Now suppose your company decides that after an extra person is needed more than 50% of the time, it will immediately hire an additional person. In cell B7, @ROUND(B5,0) displays the correct value 7. Cell D7, which references cell B7, contains the correct projected labor cost of $140,000. So cells referencing a cell containing @ROUND use the rounded value.

Cell B8 contains the formula +B5. Since this cell is formatted for 0 decimal places, 6.545 is rounded up and the value 7 is displayed. But this cell still *contains* the value 6.545. So the labor cost in cell D8 of $130,909 is calculated as 6.545*$20,000. This is the same labor cost calculated in cell D5, when the calculated number of personnel is used.

Finally, cell B10 also contains the formula +B5. However, this cell is formatted using the Range Attributes Precision Limit Precision 2 command. Notice that value displayed in cell B10 is *not* formatted to

123G.EXE — Ready

File Edit Worksheet Range Copy... Move... Print Graph Data Utility Quit... Help

A:B5 +B1/B2

(F7) C:\LAURA\ROUND1.WG1

A	A	B	C	D	E	F
1	Units to be Produced	72,000				
2	Monthly Units Produced Per Person	11,000				
3						
4	Number Personnel Needed		Salary	Labor Cost		
5	+B1/B2	6.5454545	$20,000	$130,909		
6	Using @INT(B5)	6	$20,000	$120,000		
7	Using @ROUND(B5,0)	7	$20,000	$140,000		
8	+B5 Formatted (F0)	7	$20,000	$130,909		
9	Using Range Attributes Precision:					
10	Limit Precision 2 places	6.5454545	$20,000	$131,000		
11						

FIGURE 6–2 The difference between @ROUND, @INT, Range Format, and Range Attributes Precision

two decimal places. Rather, the calculated value is both displayed and stored in cell B10. However, the calculated labor cost in cell D10 is $131,000. This is the same value in cell D7, when the value in cell B7 is rounded to two places. So the Range Attributes Precision Limit Precision 2 command rounds the value in cell B10 for *calculations only*.

Returning the Remainder: @MOD

Use the @MOD function to calculate the remainder, or *modulus* of a division operation. For example the modulus of 5/2 is 1; 2 goes into 5 two times and leaves 1 remaining, the modulus. The form of this function is

@MOD (*numerator,denominator*)

where *numerator* is the value to be divided, and *denominator* is the value you divide your *numerator* by. Both arguments must evaluate to a value, so you can use a literal number, or a numeric formula, another function that equates to a value, or a reference to a cell containing one of these. If either of these arguments evaluate to NA or ERR, @MOD also returns this value. The @MOD function assigns a value of 0 to labels, label prefixes, blank cells, and cells that contain blank spaces. If your *denominator* is 0, @MOD returns ERR. The sign of the *denominator* determines the sign of the value returned. For example @MOD(-5,2) returns 1, but @MOD(5,-2) returns -1. Notice that @MOD(2,5) returns the numerator value 2 when the numerator is smaller than the denominator.

An Example

Suppose you produce the number of units in Figure 6–3. You want to calculate the number of unpalleted units left over each month. In cell B6, @MOD(B4,B5) calculates 30 remaining unpalleted units in April. Notice in cell E6, for the quarter ended June 30, 1990, @MOD(E4,E5) returns the modulus 0, since all of the units produced in that quarter fit on pallets.

Note

You can use the @MOD function to calculate the day of the week (see "Date and Time Arithmetic" in this chapter).

Calculating the Square Root: @SQRT

Use 1-2-3/G's @SQRT function to determine the square root of a nonnegative value. The form of this function is

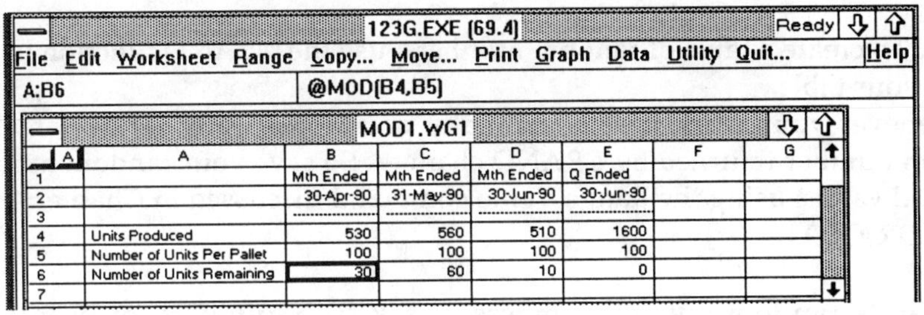

123G.EXE (69.4) Ready

File Edit Worksheet Range Copy... Move... Print Graph Data Utility Quit... Help

A:B6 @MOD(B4,B5)

MOD1.WG1

A	A	B	C	D	E	F	G
1		Mth Ended	Mth Ended	Mth Ended	Q Ended		
2		30-Apr-90	31-May-90	30-Jun-90	30-Jun-90		
3							
4	Units Produced	530	560	510	1600		
5	Number of Units Per Pallet	100	100	100	100		
6	Number of Units Remaining	30	60	10	0		
7							

FIGURE 6–3 Using the @MOD function

`@SQRT(x)`

where *x* can be 0 or any positive value entered as a literal number, cell reference, or a numeric formula or function that returns a positive value. If x is a negative number, @SQRT returns ERR. Instead, use @SQRT(@ABS(-x)) to calculate the square root of a negative value. @SQRT(0) returns 0. The @SQRT function evaluates to 0 if an argument is a blank cell, a cell containing spaces, a label or a label prefix. If a cell evaluates to ERR or NA, @SQRT also returns this value. You must use @SQRT in each cell in a range; you cannot use a range of cells as your @SQRT argument.

Using the @SQRT function is the same as raising a value to the 1/2 power using ^.5. For example, both @SQRT(9) and 9^.5 return the value 3.

Note

> Use 1-2-3/G's ^ operator to raise a value to different powers. For example, 2^3 cubes the value 2 and returns the value 8; 8^(1/3) takes the cube root of 8 and returns the value 2. However, 8^1/3 is evaluated as (8^1)/3 and returns the value 2.67 due to 1-2-3/G's order of precedence (see Chapter 1).

Generating Random Values: @RAND

Use the @RAND function to generate random numbers in your worksheet. Since this function uses no arguments, simply enter @RAND in a cell. The @RAND function generates a random number from 0 to 1, up to 18 decimal places. To create a table of random numbers, use the @RAND function in each cell in your table.

Whenever your worksheet is manually or automatically recalculated, the random number returned by @RAND changes. So save your random numbers as literal values using the Range Value command discussed in Chapter 4.

Use @RAND to:

- Generate random invoice numbers, check stub numbers, or orders in a *test of internal controls* (a test to verify the accuracy of internal accounting procedures).
- Generate random serial numbers to test for adherence to production specifications for quality control.
- Use @RAND*1000 to create a random number between 0 and 1,000.
- Create a random *integer* between 10,000 and 99,999. Use @INT(@RAND*100,000) to return an integer without rounding. Use @ROUND(@RAND*1,000,000) to round a value to 0 places.

STATISTICAL FUNCTIONS

1-2-3/G includes functions for statistical analysis. Some of these functions, such as @SUM and @AVG, are among the most commonly used 1-2-3/G functions. (See Chapter 9 for a discussion of equivalent database functions.) Table 6–2 shows 1-2-3/G's statistical functions, including three new functions—@VARS, @STDS, and @SUMPRODUCT—first introduced in Release 3.

All of 1-2-3/G's statistical functions operate on *values* and return *value results*.

TABLE 6–2 1-2-3/G's Statistical Functions

Function	Returns
@SUM	Sum of a list of values
@SUMPRODUCT	Sum of the products of equal-sized ranges of values
@COUNT	Number of nonblank cells in a list of values
@AVG	Average of nonblank cells in a list of values
@MIN	Minimum value in a list of values
@MAX	Maximum value in a list of values
@VAR	Population variance of a list of values
@STD	Population standard deviation of a list of values
@VARS	Sample variance of a list of values
@STDS	Sample standard deviation of a list of values

Summing Values: @SUM

@SUM is the most commonly used function in 1-2-3/G. This function adds a group of values. The form of this function is

```
@SUM(list)
```

A *list* argument consists of one or more *items*, each separated by an argument separator, which is usually a comma. Each item represents a single value or a group of values. Most often @SUM uses a *range* as an argument, such as @SUM(B1..B6). However, a *list* argument can include individual cell addresses, numbers, numeric formulas, other functions, ranges, or any combination of these. For example, @SUM(5,C6,B1..B6) includes a valid *list* argument. The three items in this *list* represent eight values. As another example, the function

```
@SUM(A:B1..C:D3,SALES,Z:F20,@SUM(D:D1..D:D5), <<SHEET2.WG1>>A:A5)
```

shows a valid *list* argument containing a variety of items. Notice that three-dimensional ranges and references to other worksheet files are now valid items in a *list* argument for 1-2-3/G's statistical functions.

If *list* includes a blank cell or a cell containing a label, 1-2-3/G assigns a value of 0 to that cell. If any cell in your argument evaluates to ERR or NA, @SUM returns that value.

An Example

Suppose you have the worksheet SUM1 in Figure 6–4. You want to sum the values in column A and record the result in cell A:A6. Simply use @SUM(A1..A4) to return the value 1,000 shown in cell A:A6. This is equivalent to @SUM(A1,A2,A3,A4) or +A1+A2+A3+A4. You can also sum across columns. For example, in cell A:E8 of the SUM1 file in Figure 6–4, the function @SUM(A8..D8) sums the values in row 8 and also returns 1,000.

Note to Release 2 Users

When you add or delete cells at the beginning or end of a range in a statistical function, 1-2-3/G now *automatically adjusts the range coordinates.* Suppose, in the example above, you delete row 1. In the process, the beginning range reference A1 is deleted. In previous editions, @SUM(A1..A4) would become @SUM(ERR) and return ERR. In 1-2-3/G, @SUM (A1..A4) becomes @SUM(A1..A3) (because row 1 is deleted the other rows move up to fill in the gap).

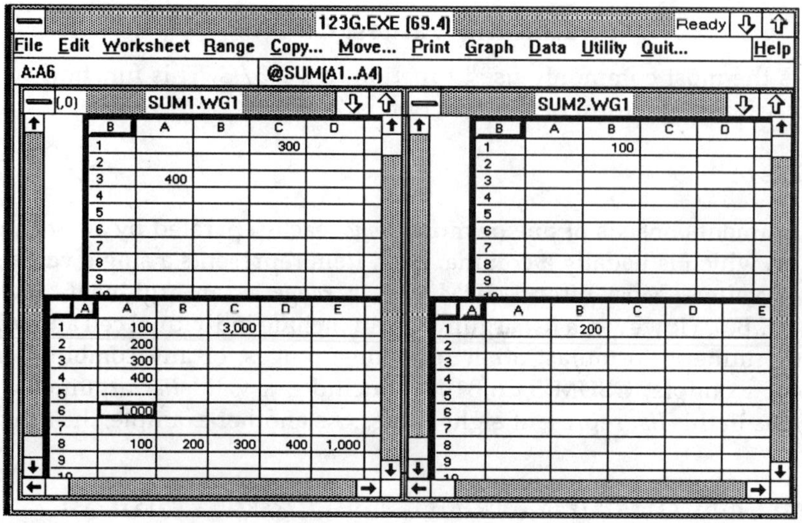

FIGURE 6–4 Using @SUM

As another example, cell A:C1 in SUM 1 (see Figure 6–4) contains the function **@SUM(A1..A4,A8..D8,B:C1,B:A3,<<SUM2.WG1>>A:B1..B:B1)** and returns the value 3,000. In SUM1, this *list* argument includes the two-dimensional ranges A:A1..A:A4 and A:A8..A:D8, and the single-cell addresses B:A3 and B:C1 in the SUM1.WG1 file. This *list* also includes the three-dimensional range A:B1..B:B1 in SUM2.WG1 file. Notice in this formula that you must include a file reference, <<SUM2.WG1>>, when you reference a range that is located outside the current worksheet file.

1-2-3/G returns the same result—3,000—if you arrange your arguments separately and then combine them, as in:

```
@@SUM(A1..A4)+@SUM(A8..D8)+B:C1+B:A3+@SUM(<<SUM2.WG1>>A:B1..B:B1)
```

Summing Products: @SUMPRODUCT

The @SUMPRODUCT function is a new statistical function offered in 1-2-3/G that saves worksheet space and memory. Use @SUMPRODUCT to return only the resulting sum of a series of multiplication formulas. The form of this function is

```
@SUMPRODUCT(list)
```

where *list* must be composed of equal sized, multiple-cell ranges. Each range is separated by an argument separator, which is usually a comma. If any cell in your argument evaluates to ERR or NA, @SUMPRODUCT returns this value. Furthermore, this function assigns a value of 0 to any labels, label prefixes, blank cells, or cells that contain spaces.

In your *list* argument, each range *must* contain the same number of cells, otherwise @SUMPRODUCT returns ERR. Additionally, @SUMPRODUCT returns ERR if you use single-cell range references, such as @SUMPRODUCT(A1,A2,A3). However, the function returns the correct result when you structure these single-cell range arguments as if they where multiple-cell ranges, for example

```
@SUMPRODUCT(A1..A1,B1..B1,C1..C1)
```

You can only use @SUMPRODUCT for equal-shaped *parallel* ranges. For example, @SUMPRODUCT(A1..A5,B1..F1) returns ERR because the range A1..A5 runs down a column, while B1..F1 runs across a row. Furthermore, @SUMPRODUCT(A1..B2,A3..D3) also returns ERR, because although these ranges are parallel and contain the same number of cells, they are not equal-shaped.

Suppose you have the investment portfolio in Figure 6–5, and you want to calculate your net sale proceeds after broker commissions. In cell E4, you could enter +B4*C4*C4, then copy this formula to cells E5 and E6. Finally, you could use @SUM(E4..E6) in cell E8 to arrive at the value $92,134.50. Or, you can now just use @SUMPRODUCT(B4..B6,C4..C6,D4..D6), as in cell F8, and arrive at the same result.

In the example above, @SUMPRODUCT multiplies across rows, since each range is one column wide. For example, in the formula @SUMPRODUCT(A1..A2,B1..B2), @SUMPRODUCT multiplies across rows and returns the result of the formula A1*B1+A2*B2. However, if each range spans more than one column, @SUMPRODUCT multiplies by columns. For example, when @SUMPRODUCT(A1..B2,C1..D2) uses ranges that run across columns, it multiplies across rows—A1*C1+A2*C2+B1*D1+B2*D2.

123G.EXE: DESK1.DSK (69.4) Ready

File Edit Worksheet Range Copy... Move... Print Graph Data Utility Quit... Help

A:F8 @SUMPRODUCT(B4..B6,C4..C6,D4..D6)

(C2) SUM3.WG1

A	A	B	C	D	E	F
1		Selling		Percentage		
2	Stock	Share Price	Number Shares	after Comisions	Net Cash	
3	============	============	============	============	============	
4	IBM	110	200	97.0%	$21,340.00	
5	Microsoft	104.5	500	98.0%	$51,205.00	
6	Adobe	58	350	96.5%	$19,589.50	
7					----------------	
8					$92,134.50	$92,134.50
9						

FIGURE 6–5 Using @SUMPRODUCT

123G.EXE: DESK1.DSK [69.4] Ready

File Edit Worksheet Range Copy... Move... Print Graph Data Utility Quit... Help

A:G8 @SUMPRODUCT(B4..C6,D4..E6)

(C2) SUM4.WG1

A	A	B	C	D	E	F	G
1		Units at	Units at			Inventory	
2	Product	Price 1	Price 2	Unit Price	Unit Price	Value	
3	==========	==========	==========	==========	==========	==========	
4	Product A	20,000	40,000	$1.00	$1.50	$80,000.00	
5	Product B	50,000	30,000	$2.00	$2.20	$166,000.00	
6	Product C	2,000	10,000	$5.50	$10.00	$111,000.00	
7						----------	
8						$357,000.00	$357,000.00
9							

FIGURE 6–6 Using @SUMPRODUCT

Suppose you want to calculate the inventory value of the products shown in Figure 6–6. In cell F4, you could use +B4*D4+C4*E4, then copy this formula to cells F5 and F6. Then you could use @SUM(F4..F6) in cell E8 to arrive at the inventory value of $357,000. You could also use @SUMPRODUCT (B4..B6,D4..D6)+@SUMPRODUCT(C4..C6,E4..E6) to arrive at this total. Or, as in cell G8, you can just use @SUMPRODUCT(B4..C6,D4..E6) to arrive at the same result. Notice that @SUMPRODUCT in this case multiplies the value in the first cell in the first range, cell B4, by the value in the first cell in the second range, cell D4. It also multiplies the information in cell C4 by the value in cell E4. So you can use multi-column ranges in your @SUMPRODUCT argument, as long as each range contains the same number of cells, is shaped in the same, and the ranges are parallel to one another.

Finding the Number of Values in a Range: @COUNT

1-2-3/G's @COUNT function counts the number of nonblank cells in an argument. The form of this function is

@COUNT (*list*)

where *list* is any combination of items and each item represents a single value or a group of values. Each item is separated by an argument separator, which is usually a comma. Most often *list* is a *range*. However, each item in your *list* argument can be individual cell addresses, numbers, numeric formulas, other functions, 2-D or 3-D ranges, or any combination of these, even in other worksheet files.

Understanding how 1-2-3/G's @COUNT works will help you understand how the @AVG function works, which you will use much more frequently. The @COUNT function returns the number of cells in a range that are *not* blank. It also counts (assigns a value of 1) to the following:

- a value, or a cell containing a value.
- a cell that evaluates to ERR or NA.
- a label or label-prefix, or cells containing these.
- an undefined range name.

Problems with @COUNT

The @COUNT function *sometimes* counts blank cells. For example, if cell B1 is blank, and your argument only includes one blank cell, as in the function @COUNT(B1), @COUNT returns 1. However, @COUNT(B1..B2) returns 0 when both cells B1 and B2 are blank. But @COUNT(B1,B2) when both cells B1 and B2 are blank returns 2, because this function is the same as @COUNT(B1)+@COUNT(B2). As you can imagine, this can create a significant problem when you include a single-cell item or a named collection that includes a single-cell item in your *list* argument.

An Example

It's easier to understand how @COUNT works by looking at an example. Suppose you want to analyze the values in Figure 6–7. @COUNT appears in row 6 of this figure and returns the following:

Cell	Function	Value	Reason
B6	@COUNT(B1..B3)	3	0 in cell B2 counted
C6	@COUNT(C1..C3)	3	label in cell C2 counted
D6	@COUNT(D1..D4)	4	label in cell D4 counted
E6	@COUNT(E1..E3)	2	blank cell E2 not counted
F6	@COUNT(F1,F2,F3)	3	blank cell F2 counted

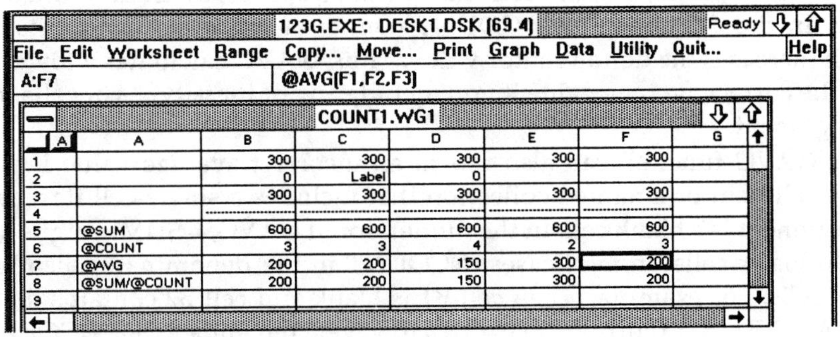

123G.EXE: DESK1.DSK [69.4] Ready

File Edit Worksheet Range Copy... Move... Print Graph Data Utility Quit... Help

A:F7 @AVG(F1,F2,F3)

COUNT1.WG1

A	A	B	C	D	E	F	G
1		300	300	300	300	300	
2		0	Label	0			
3		300	300	300	300	300	
4							
5	@SUM	600	600	600	600	600	
6	@COUNT	3	3	4	2	3	
7	@AVG	200	200	150	300	200	
8	@SUM/@COUNT	200	200	150	300	200	
9							

FIGURE 6–7 Using @COUNT and @AVG

Calculating an Average: @AVG

1-2-3/G's @AVG function calculates the average, or the *arithmetic mean* of a group of values. This is the sum of all values divided by the number of values. The form of this function is

```
@AVG(list)
```

where *list* is any combination of items and each item represents a single value or a group of values. Most often *list* is a range, such as @AVG(B1..B6). However, a *list* argument can include individual cell addresses, numbers, numeric formulas, other functions, 2–D and 3–D ranges or any combination of these, even in other worksheet files. For example, @AVG(5,C6,B1..B6) includes a valid *list* argument. If any cell in your argument evaluates to ERR or NA, @AVG returns ERR or NA.

Problems with @AVG

The @AVG function can return an incorrect average value when your argument includes any of the following:

- A label or label-prefix, a blank cell that contains spaces, or an undefined range name.
- A blank cell that is either a single-cell item or a single-cell item in a named collection.

To understand these inherent problems of the @AVG function, you should think of the way that @AVG(*list*) computes an average as @SUM(*list*)/ @COUNT (*list*). In the numerator, @SUM *includes* and assigns a 0 value to a label or label-prefix, a blank cell that contains spaces, or an undefined range name. In the denominator, @COUNT counts or *includes* them in its count, which increases the denominator value. Thus, @AVG calculates a lower value than the correct average value if you include any of these types of cells in your *list* argument.

The @AVG function can also return an incorrect average value if either a single-cell item or a named collection that includes a single-cell item in your *list* argument is a blank cell. In the numerator of @AVG, @SUM assigns a value of 0 to blank cells. In *most* cases, @COUNT in the denominator also ignores blank cells. For example, when cell B1 is blank and cell B2 contains the value 10, @AVG(B1..B2) returns 10 (10/1). However, remember that @COUNT(B1) returns 1 when a single-cell argument is a blank cell. So @AVG(B1,B2) calculates this function as @SUM(B1..B2)/(@COUNT(B1)+@COUNT(B2)), or (0+10)/2, and returns 5. So be careful when you use @AVG with a single-cell item or a named collection that includes a single-cell item.

An Example

Let's return to Figure 6–7. The @AVG function appears in row 7 of that figure and returns the following:

Cell	Function	Value	Reason
B7	@AVG(B1..B3)	200	0 in cell B2 counted
C7	@AVG(C1..C3)	200	label in cell C2 counted
D7	@AVG(D1..D4)	150	cells D2 and D4 counted
E7	@AVG(E1..E3)	300	blank cell E2 not counted
F7	@AVG(F1,F2,F3)	200	blank cell F2 counted

Notice that @SUM/@COUNT in row 8 returns the same values as @AVG.

Returning Minimum and Maximum Values: @MIN and @MAX

1-2-3/G's @MIN and @MAX functions return the minimum and maximum values in a group of values. The forms of these functions are

```
@MIN(list)
@MAX(list)
```

where *list* is any combination of items and each item represents a single value or a group of values. Most often *list* is a range, such as @MIN(B1..B6). However, a *list* argument can include individual cell addresses, numbers, numeric formulas, other functions, ranges, or any combination of these. Three-dimensional ranges and references to other worksheet files are now valid items in *list*.

Both @MIN and @MAX assign a value of 0 to labels, label prefixes, undefined range names, and blank cells containing spaces. However, both of these functions *ignore* blank cells. If any cell in *list* returns NA or ERR, both @MAX and @MIN also return this value.

Suppose you have the worksheet in Figure 6–8. You are projecting net cash flow for the first quarter in 1991 and 1992. You want to find the minimum and maximum monthly cash balances for 1991 and for 1992. In cell A:B6, @MIN(A:B4..A:D4) returns the 1991 minimum monthly cash balance of -$100,000. In cell A:B7, the function @MAX(A:B4..A:D4) returns the maximum 1991 monthly cash balance of -$20,000. Both functions *ignore* the blank cell A:C4.

For 1992, in cell B:B6, @MIN(B:B4..B:D4) returns the correct monthly cash balance, -$100,000. However, @MAX does not return the correct maximum monthly cash balance in 1992. In cell B:B7, the function @MAX(B:B4..B:D4) returns 0 because it evaluates the label in cell B:C4 as 0.

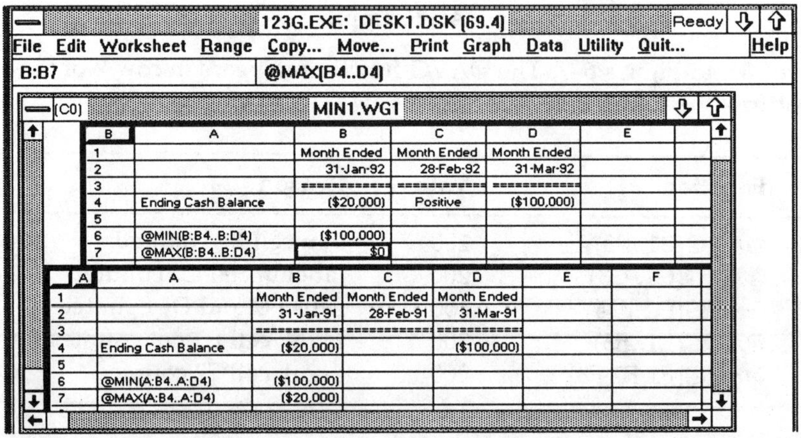

123G.EXE: DESK1.DSK (69.4) Ready

File Edit Worksheet Range Copy... Move... Print Graph Data Utility Quit... Help

B:B7 @MAX(B4..D4)

(C0) MIN1.WG1

B	A	B	C	D	E
1		Month Ended	Month Ended	Month Ended	
2		31-Jan-92	28-Feb-92	31-Mar-92	
3		===========	===========	===========	
4	Ending Cash Balance	($20,000)	Positive	($100,000)	
5					
6	@MIN(B:B4..B:D4)	($100,000)			
7	@MAX(B:B4..B:D4)	$0			

A	A	B	C	D	E	F
1		Month Ended	Month Ended	Month Ended		
2		31-Jan-91	28-Feb-91	31-Mar-91		
3		===========	===========	===========		
4	Ending Cash Balance	($20,000)		($100,000)		
5						
6	@MIN(A:B4..A:D4)	($100,000)				
7	@MAX(A:B4..A:D4)	($20,000)				

FIGURE 6–8 Using @MAX and @MIN

Tip: Using @MAX and @MIN to calculate an average after discarding the smallest and largest values

Suppose you want to discard the smallest and largest values in the range A1..A5 before you calculate the average value. In cell B1, you can use @MIN(A1..A5), to return the smallest value, and you can use @MAX(A1..A5) in cell B2 to return the largest value. You cannot use @AVG(A1..A5,-B1–B2) to find the average of the remaining values because it will count seven items and return an incorrect average. Rather, you can use @SUM(A1..A5,-B1,-B2)/(@COUNT(A1..A5)-2)

Advanced Statistical Functions: @VAR, @STD, @VARS, and @STDS

1-2-3/G provides advanced statistical functions to evaluate both a population and a sample of that population. A population is the entire group of values you want to analyze—for example, the age of each individual in the United States, or the average number of errors in a 1-2-3/G spreadsheet. However, you generally evaluate a *sample* of a population when it is uneconomical or impossible to gather information about the entire population. For samples that include thirty or more *random* selections from a population, statistical analysis has shown that such a sample can provide an accurate indication of the characteristics of the population.

An important statistic when evaluating a population is the mean (average value). You can calculate the mean for either the entire population or a sample from that population using the @AVG function.

Two other indicators, the *variance* and the *standard deviation,* measure the reliability of a calculated mean value. The *variance* measures the amount of variation of all values from the mean (average), while the *standard deviation* calculates the degree of dispersion about the mean. 1-2-3/G provides two advanced statistical functions, the *population variance* (@VAR) and the *population standard deviation* (@STD) for evaluating the reliability of a population mean. 1-2-3/G's *sample variance* (@VARS) and *sample standard deviation* (@STDS) are used to evaluate the reliability of a sample mean.

Population Statistics: @VAR and @STD

The *population variance* measures the amount of dispersion in an entire population. It calculates the amount of variation of all values from the mean (average). The equation for the population variance is

$$\text{Population Variance} = \frac{\Sigma(i - \text{avg})^2}{n} = \frac{\Sigma(i - \text{@AVG(list)})^2}{\text{@COUNT(list)}}$$

where *i* is the value of one item in the population and *n* is the number of values (items). You would manually calculate the variance by subtracting the average value of the population from each value, squaring each result, adding all these squared values, and finally dividing this total by *n*, the number of values in the population.

The variance indicates the reliability of the average value. If all values in the population are the same, each item then equals the average value, and the variance is 0. So the *lower* the variance, the less the individual values vary from the mean, and the more reliable the average value is.

The *standard deviation* is used more commonly than the variance because it returns a number that is easier to analyze. The standard deviation calculates the *degree* of dispersion within a population of values. That is, the standard deviation calculates the degree to which all values in the population deviate from the mean value (average). The equation for the population standard deviation is

$$\text{Population Standard Deviation} = \sqrt{\text{Population Variance}}$$

In a normally distributed population, approximately 68% of the items in this population fall within plus or minus one standard deviation of the mean (average). Approximately 95% fall within plus or minus two standard deviations of the mean. A low standard deviation indicates that all of the items in a population are closely clustered around the mean value.

1-2-3/G's population variance and standard deviation functions are much easier to use than these mathematical formulas. The forms of these functions are

```
@VAR(list)
@STD(list)
```

where *list* is any combination of items and each item represents a single value or a group of values. Most often *list* is a range, such as @VAR(B1..B6). However, a *list* argument can include individual cell addresses, numbers, numeric formulas, other functions, ranges, or any combination of these. Three-dimensional ranges and references to other worksheet files are now valid items in *list*. If any cell in your *list* argument evaluates to ERR or NA, either of these functions return this value.

Note

As shown in the equations above, you should think of the way that 1-2-3/G calculates the variance and standard deviation as functions of @AVG and @COUNT. So *all* advanced statistical functions have the same problems as the @AVG and @COUNT functions. In most cases, blank cells will not affect the results. However, to ensure correct results, make sure that your *list* does not include any blank cells containing spaces, labels, label prefixes, and undefined range names. (See "Problems with @COUNT" and "Problems with @AVG" for more details.)

Suppose you have the worksheet in Figure 6–9, and you want to analyze the ages compiled from a group of 30 people in the range B:A2..B:F6. First, let's assume that this group is the entire *population*. As shown in cell A:B3, @AVG(B:A2..B:F6) shows that, on average, the population is 51.17 years old. In cell A:B5, @STD(B:A2..B:F6) calculates that one population standard deviation is 22.41. Thus, approximately 68% of the population is between 28.76 and 73.57 years old. In cell A:B4, @VAR(B:A2..B:F6) shows that the population variance is 502.01, which is simply the population standard deviation squared, or $(22.41)^2$.

Sample Statistics: @VARS and @STDS

The *sample* variance calculates the amount of variation of all *sample* values from the *sample* mean value (average). The equation for the sample variance is

$$\text{Sample Variance} = \frac{\Sigma(s - \text{avg})^2}{(n - 1)} = \text{Population Variance} \times \frac{n}{(n - 1)}$$

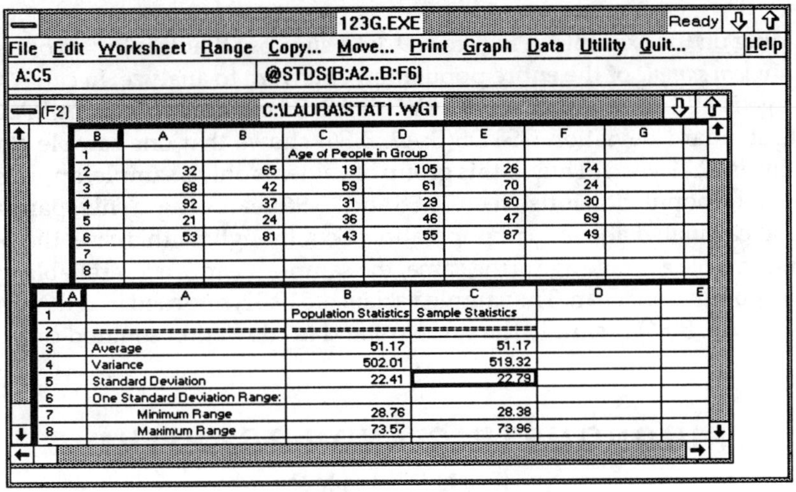

123G.EXE Ready

File Edit Worksheet Range Copy... Move... Print Graph Data Utility Quit... Help

A:C5 @STDS(B:A2..B:F6)

(F2) C:\LAURA\STAT1.WG1

B	A	B	C	D	E	F	G
1			Age of People in Group				
2	32	65	19	105	26	74	
3	68	42	59	61	70	24	
4	92	37	31	29	60	30	
5	21	24	36	46	47	69	
6	53	81	43	55	87	49	
7							
8							

A	A	B	C	D	E
1		Population Statistics	Sample Statistics		
2	==========================	===============	===============		
3	Average	51.17	51.17		
4	Variance	502.01	519.32		
5	Standard Deviation	22.41	22.79		
6	One Standard Deviation Range:				
7	Minimum Range	28.76	28.38		
8	Maximum Range	73.57	73.96		

FIGURE 6–9 Using advanced statistical functions

where s is the value of one item in the sample and n is the number of values (items). The average is calculated for the sample.

As shown in the formula above, the sample variance is equal to the population variance multiplied by $[n/(n - 1)]$, or the *degrees of freedom*. This formula yields a slightly larger variance than the population variance to compensate for sample errors.

The *sample* standard deviation calculates the degree to which the values in the *sample* deviate from the *sample* mean (average). The sample standard deviation is calculated as

$$\text{Sample Standard Deviation} = \sqrt{\text{Sample Variance}}$$

1-2-3/G's sample variance and standard deviation functions are much easier to use than their mathematical equivalents. The forms of these functions are

```
@VARS(list)
@STDS(list)
```

where *list* is any combination of items and each item represents a single value or a group of values. Most often *list* is a range. However, a *list* argument can include individual cell addresses, numbers, numeric formulas, other functions, 2-D or 3-D ranges, or any combination of these.

If any cell in your *list* argument evaluates to ERR or NA, either of these functions return this value. To ensure correct results, make sure that your argument does not include any undefined range names, blank cells, blank cells containing spaces, labels, or label prefixes.

Building on the example in Figure 6–9, let's suppose that this group of values is just a *random sample* of the entire population you want to analyze. In cell A:C3, the mean age is still calculated using @AVG(B:A2..B:F6). However, in cell A:C5, the sample standard deviation @STDS(B:A2..B:F6) shows that one sample standard deviation is 22.79 years. Thus, if this group of values is only a sample, approximately 68% of the population is between 28.38 and 73.96 years of age. This span is larger than that calculated above for a population. So although, in this case, the population and sample average age is the same, the sample mean is a *less* reliable number than the population mean. The sample variance, 519.32, returned in cell A:C4 using @VARS(B:A2..B:F6) is simply the sample standard deviation squared or $(22.79)^2$.

TRIGONOMETRIC AND LOGARITHMIC FUNCTIONS

1-2-3/G includes the same trigonometric and logarithmic functions as previous releases of 1-2-3. These functions are primarily used in engineering and other scientific applications. Table 6–3 shows 1-2-3/G's trigonometric and logarithmic functions.

Most of these functions operate on a *value* argument and all return *value results.*

Calculating Pi and Angle Conversions: @PI

Use the @PI function to calculate the value of pi to 17 decimal places. *Pi,* defined as the ratio of the circumference of a circle to the diameter, is equal to 3.14159265358979324. Since this function takes no argument, simply enter

TABLE 6–3 1-2-3/G's Trigonometric and Logarithmic Mathematical Functions

Function	Returns
@PI	Constant value pi 3.14159265358979324
@SIN	Sine of a value
@COS	Cosine of a value
@TAN	Tangent of a value
@ASIN	Arcsine of the sine of an angle
@ACOS	Arccosine of the cosine of an angle
@ATAN	Arctangent of the tangent of an angle
@ATAN2	Arctangent of the tangent of two values, *Y/X*
@EXP	Value of the constant *e* raised to a specified power
@LN	Natural logarithm in base *e*
@LOG	Base 10 logarithm

@PI in a cell. Because 1-2-3/G uses the entire 17-digit value, regardless of the format you use, using @PI retains accuracy in your calculations.

Figure 6–10 shows the relationship between the 360 degrees of a circle and pi (2 pi = 360 degrees). Calculate the circumference, *C*, of a circle, as *C* = @PI*D, where *D* is the diameter. Calculate the area, *A*, of a circle using *A* =@PI*R^2, where *R* is the radius.

Most of 1-2-3/G's other trigonometric functions use arguments expressed in radians. Use @PI to convert values expressed in degrees to radians before you use these functions. Or, with 1-2-3/G's inverse trigonometric functions, use @PI to convert values obtained in radians to degrees. Just use the following conversion factors:

Conversion	Conversion (Multiplication) Factor
Degrees to radians	@PI/180
Radians to degrees	180/@PI

For example, convert 180 degrees to radians using 180*(@PI/180), which returns 3.14159 radians (which is pi). Convert 1.5 pi (1.5*@PI radians) to degrees using 1.5*@PI*(180/@PI), which returns 270 degrees.

Other Trigonometric Conversions: @SIN, @COS, and @TAN

1-2-3/G's @SIN, @COS, and @TAN functions calculate the sine, cosine, and tangent of an angle. The forms of these functions are

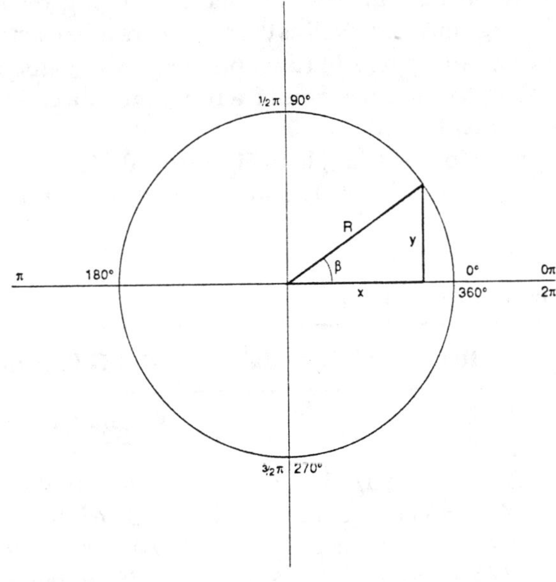

FIGURE 6–10 Trigonometric relationships

@SIN(*Angle b in radians*)
@COS(*Angle b in radians*)
@TAN(*Angle b in radians*)

Your argument must be a value expressed in radians. So you can enter your argument as a literal number, a numeric formula, another function that returns a value, or a reference to a cell that contains one of these. Convert an argument in degrees to radians by multiplying it by the conversion factor @PI/180 before you use one of these functions.

Table 6–4 shows these trigonometric functions for the triangle in Figure 6–10. This table also includes other trigonometric relationships, such as the secant and tangent, that can be calculated using 1-2-3/G's trig functions.

Suppose, in Figure 6–10, you know that the angle *b* is 30 degrees, and that X is 7 feet. What is *Y*? The tangent of *B* equals *Y*/*X*. So you can use @TAN to solve for *Y*. First convert *b*, 30 degrees, to radians using 30*@PI/180, which returns .534359. Now use @TAN(.534359), which returns the value .57735. You can also obtain this value all at once using @TAN(30*@PI/180). So Tan(*B*) = .57735 = *Y*/7. Solving for *Y* returns a value of 4.0414 feet.

Inverse Trigonometric Functions: @ASIN, @ACOS, @ATAN, @ATAN2

The @ASIN, @ACOS, @ATAN, and @ATAN2 functions calculate an angle's size using the sine, cosine, and tangent as their arguments. These functions are the inverse functions of 1-2-3/G's @SIN, @COS, and @TAN functions. Table 6–5 provides an overview of these inverse functions, including their minimum and maximum acceptable arguments, as well as the range of results each function returns.

The @ASIN, @ACOS and @ATAN functions require a value argument. This can be a literal number, a numeric formula, a function, or a cell reference. These functions all return a result in *radians*.

For example, suppose for the triangle in Figure 6–10, *X* is 5 and *R* is 10. Cosine *b* is then 5/10 (*X*/*R*) or .5 radians. The arccosine of *b*, or the angle *b*, can be

TABLE 6–4 Trigonometric Functions

Trig Function	Mathematical Formula	1-2-3/G Function
Sine *b*	*Y*/*R*	@SIN(*angle b in radians*)
Cosine *b*	*X*/*R*	@COS(*angle b in radians*)
Tangent *b*	*Y*/*X* = sine *b*/cosine *b*	@TAN(*angle b in radians*)
Cotangent *b*	*X*/*Y* = 1/tangent *b*	1/@TAN(*angle b in radians*)
Secant *b*	*R*/*X* = 1/cosine *b*	1/@COS(*angle b in radians*)
Cosecant *b*	*R*/*Y* = 1/sine *b*	1/@SIN(*angle b in radians*)

TABLE 6–5 Inverse Trigonometric Functions

Trig Function	1-2-3/G Function	Argument Min	Argument Max	Result Min	Result Max
Arcsine *b*	@ASIN(*sine b*)	-1	1	-pi/2	pi/2
Arccosine *b*	@ACOS(*cosine b*)	-1	1	0	pi
Arctangent *b*	@ATAN(*tangent b*)	none	none	-pi/2	pi/2
Arctangent *b*	@ATAN2(X,Y)	none*	none*	-pi	pi

*If Y = 0, @ATAN2 = 0. If X = 0 and Y = 0, @ATAN2 returns ERR.

calculated as @ACOS(.5), which returns 1.0472 *radians*. Multiply this value by 180/@PI to convert this value to 60 degrees. You can obtain this value all at once using the formula @ACOS(5/10)*(180/@PI).

The @ATAN2 function calculates the arctangent, or angle size, using the tangent *Y/X*. @ATAN2 uses two arguments, *X* and *Y*, which are the triangle sides shown in Figure 6–10. Both the *X* and *Y* arguments must evaluate to a value. @TAN2 returns an angle in *radians*. Notice that @ATAN2(1,0) returns 0 but @ATAN2(0,0) returns ERR.

An Example

Suppose you fly your own plane and you want to build your own runway in a cornfield you own. The maximum runway length can be 750 feet. Unluckily, a 75–foot barn is located at the end of the cornfield, which you want to clear by 50 feet. Under these conditions, your plane's maximum angle of climb is 15 degrees. Is this an acceptable runway for your plane? Using Figure 6–10, *X* is 750 and *Y* is 125 (barn and margin). Using @ATAN2(750,125) returns .165149 radians. Using .165149*180/@PI converts this value to 9.46 degrees. Since this is less than 15 degrees, your plane's maximum angle of climb for these parameters, you can build the planned runway and safely take off.

Exponential Function: @EXP

1-2-3/G provides three logarithmic functions: @EXP, @LN, and @LOG, which are all closely related. The @EXP function computes the value of e^x, or the constant value *e* (approximately 2.718282) raised to the power of x. The form of this function is

```
@EXP(x)
```

where *x* is any value between -709 and 709 entered as a literal number, or a numeric formula, function, or cell reference that returns a value.

For example, @EXP(1) = 2.7182818, while @EXP(@LN(1)) = 1, since the natural log is the inverse of the exponential function. For an x argument between -227 and 230, 1-2-3/G displays the results of @EXP. However, for values of x between -227 and -709, and between 230 and 709, 1-2-3/G can store but not display the results. @EXP is the inverse function of @LN discussed below.

Natural Logarithm: @LN

The @LN function computes the natural logarithm of a value in *base e*. The mathematical equation of the natural logarithm is $e^z = x$, where $z = \ln(x)$. The form of this function is

@LN (*x*)

where x is any value greater than 0. This can be a literal number, a numeric formula, a function, or a reference to a cell.

For example, @LN(5) returns 1.61, @LN(.0001) returns -9.21, but @LN(0) returns ERR. @LN(@EXP(1)) returns 1, since the natural log is the inverse of the exponential function.

Tip: Using @LN to determine a learning curve

Suppose you plot some x and y data points and they seem to represent an exponential curve of the general form $Y = Kx^n$ (a learning curve). You want to confirm that they do represent a learning curve, and if so, determine K and n. Use @LN to convert this exponential formula to a linear formula by taking the natural log of each side of the equation. This yields @LN(y)=@LN(K)+n@LN(x). Now, by performing a linear regression for your points @LN(y) and @LN(x), you can determine @LN(K), the y intercept, and n, the slope of the line. You can now use the exponential formula to determine new data points, since you have solved for K and n using @LN. See Chapter 9, "Data Management," for a discussion of linear regression.

Base 10 Logarithm: @LOG

1-2-3/G's @LOG function computes the common logarithm using base 10. The mathematical equation of the base 10 log is $10^z = x$, where $\log(x) = z$. Since this function uses base 10, log(10) = 1. The form of this function is

@LOG (*x*)

where x is any value greater than 0 entered as a literal number, or a numeric formula, function, or cell reference that returns a value.

For example, @LOG(5) returns .69897, @LOG(.05) returns -1.30103, but @LOG(0) returns ERR. @LOG(10) returns 1, since this function uses base 10.

LOGIC AND ERROR-TRAPPING FUNCTIONS

1-2-3/G includes logic and error-trapping functions you can use to evaluate or test conditions. By using these functions, you can add decision-making to your spreadsheet, database, or macro.

Table 6–6 shows 1-2-3/G's logical and error-trapping functions, including the @ISRANGE function first offered in Release 3, and two new functions, @ISEMPTY and @ISNAME.

Conditional Tests: @IF

One of the most powerful tools in 1-2-3/G is the @IF function. You can use @IF to create conditional or decision-making tests for almost any situation that has at least two possible outcomes. The form of this function is

@IF(*condition,true-result,false-result*)

TABLE 6–6 Logic and Error-Trapping Functions

Function	Returns
@IF	True argument if condition true, false argument otherwise
@TRUE	Value 1
@FALSE	Value 0
@ERR	Value ERR
@NA	Value NA
@ISERR	Value 1 if argument is value ERR, 0 otherwise
@ISNA	Value 1 if argument is value NA, 0 otherwise
@ISNUMBER	Value 1 if argument is a value, 0 otherwise
@ISSTRING	Value 1 if argument is a string, 0 otherwise
@ISEMPTY	Value 1 if argument is a blank cell, 0 otherwise
@ISRANGE	Value 1 if argument returns a defined range name, 0 otherwise
@ISNAME	Specified value if argument returns a range

The *condition* argument is the test that you want to evaluate. If the *condition* argument is true, @IF returns your *true-result* argument; if *condition* is false, @IF returns *false-result*.

The Condition Argument

Usually, the *condition* argument in the @IF function is a *conditional test,* which compares two items to each other using a *logical operator* such as = or >. Simple logical operators are listed in Table 6–7. Each item in this comparison can be a value or a string. As you know, you can enter a value using a literal number, or a cell reference, numeric formula, or function that returns a value. You can enter a string as a literal string, or a formula, function, or cell reference that returns a string. Remember to enclose a string in double quotes if you enter it directly into the @IF function.

When you use a logical operator in a *condition* argument, 1-2-3/G evaluates the test, then returns either true (value 1) or false (value 0). Logical operators create a condition that results in a distinct true or false condition. For example, the test 5 > 20 returns false (0) since 5 is not greater than 20. The conditional test B5="Noel" returns true (1) if cell B5 contains the string Noel and false (0) otherwise. Conditional tests that are functions or formulas, such as +B5/40*45 and @SUM(A:B5..D:Z20)100 are also valid condition arguments. A condition argument can now even reference information in other files. For example, in the file TEST1, <<TEST2.WG1>>A:C4=A:B5 is a valid conditional test.

True and False Arguments

In the @IF function, the *true result* and *false result* can be a string, a value, or another condition. If one of these arguments is another @IF function, it is known as *nesting* @IF functions, which is discussed in "Nesting @IF Functions" below.

For example, in the function @IF(B2=20,20, "ERROR"), the *condition* argument B2 = 20 says to compare the value in cell B2 and the value 20. If the value

TABLE 6–7 Simple Logical Operators

Operator	Operation
=	Equal to
<	Less than
>	Greater than
<=	Less than or equal to
>=	Greater than or equal to
<>	Not equal to

in cell B2 equals 20, this function returns 20, the *true-result*. Otherwise, it returns ERROR, the *false-result*.

Note

When you enter a literal string directly into the @IF function, be sure to enclose it in double quotes. Otherwise, @IF returns ERR.

Using @IF with Value Arguments

Suppose you have created the worksheet in Figure 6–11, which contains the number of *LeBlonds' 1-2-3/G Handbooks* printed at a time. For print runs of 10,000 books or less, the cost is $20 per book. However, for any runs greater than 10,000, the cost decreases to $15 per book. What is the cost of each print run? In cell C3, the function @IF(B3>10000,B3*15,B3*20) calculates the cost of printing books on April 15, 1990. The *condition* argument compares the number of books printed in cell B3—20,000—to 10,000. Since 20,000 is greater than 10,000, the @IF function returns the *true-result* argument B3*15, or $300,000. In cell C4, when the printing run of 10,000 in cell B4 is *not* greater than 10,000, this function returns the *false-result* argument B3*20, or $200,000.

Note

When cell A3 is blank, @IF(A3=0,1,0) returns the *true-result* value 1, since 1-2-3/G evaluates a blank cell as if it contains the value 0.

123G.EXE: DESK1.DSK [69.4] Ready

File Edit Worksheet Range Copy... Move... Print Graph Data Utility Quit... Help

A:C3 @IF(B3>10000,B3*15,B3*20)

(C0) LOGIC1.WG1

A	A	B	C	D	E	F
1	DATE	NUMBER PUBLISHED	TOTAL COST			
2	==============	==================	==============			
3	15-Apr-90	20,000	$300,000			
4	01-May-90	10,000	$200,000			
5	16-May-90	15,000	$225,000			
6	31-May-90	20,000	$300,000			
7	15-Jun-90	5,000	$100,000			
8	30-Jun-90	20,000	$300,000			
9		----------	----------			
10	Total	90,000	$1,425,000			

FIGURE 6–11 Using @IF with values

Using @IF with String Arguments

You can also use a string argument in an @IF function. 1-2-3/G evaluates a string in the *condition* argument, using the following rules:

- Spelling differences matter.
- Spacing differences matter, including extra leading or trailing spaces, or spaces between words and letters.
- Capitalization differences do not matter.
- Label prefixes do not matter.

Suppose you have created the inventory worksheet in Figure 6–12. You want to create a table that shows your purchase price for each type of car you carry. In cell E3, enter the formula **@IF($B3=E$1,$C3*$D3,"")**. The dollar signs create mixed references that freeze the column references of B3, C3, and D3, and the row reference E1 when you copy this function to the collection E4..E7,F3..G7. In cell E3, this @IF function tests the string in cell B3 for equality with the string in cell E1. If they are equal, it returns the value returned by C3*D3, or number of units * cost/unit. If the *condition* argument is false, it returns a null string ("").

As you can see in Figure 6–12, 1-2-3/G evaluates the capitalized headings in row 1 as equal to the strings in column B. However, since the string Hyundai in cell B6 includes leading spaces, it is not equal to the string HYUNDAI in cell F1. So the *false-result* argument, a null string, is returned in cell F6. Likewise, a null string is returned in cell F7 because the label in cell B7, Jaguar X KE, includes an extra space.

123G.EXE — Ready

File Edit Worksheet Range Copy... Move... Print Graph Data Utility Quit... Help

A:E3 @IF($B3=E$1,$C3*$D3,"")

(C0) C:\LAURA\LOGIC2.WG1

A	A	B	C	D	E	F	G	H
1	Date	Item	Number	Price/Unit	FERRARIS	HYUNDAI	JAGUAR XKE	
2	=========	=============	=======	==========	==========	==========	===========	
3	01/01/90	Ferraris	2	($150,000)	($300,000)			
4	01/31/90	Hyundai	10	($20,000)		($200,000)		
5	03/02/90	Jaguar XKE	3	($90,000)			($270,000)	
6	04/01/90	Hyundai	5	($5,000)				
7	05/01/90	Jaguar X KE	5	($90,000)				
8								
9								

FIGURE 6–12 Using @IF with strings and values

Note

If you do want to differentiate between upper and lower case, use the @EXACT function in the @IF function. For example, if cell A1 contains the label MARCIA, @IF(@EXACT(A1,"Marcia"),1,0) returns the false value 0. See "String Functions" in this chapter.

Note

1-2-3/G assigns a value of 0 to both strings and blank cells. For example, suppose cell A2 is blank. In cell A3, you enter the function @IF("LABEL"=A2,1,0). This formula evaluates the string "LABEL" as being equal to the value of the blank cell A2 and returns a *true-result* value of 1.

Tip: Using @IF to concatenate strings and blank cells

Suppose you have created the database of names in Figure 6–13. For sorting purposes, the first, middle, and last names have each been entered in separate cells. However, some people do not have middle names; for example, cell B3 is blank. In cell D3, you can *concatenate*, or add together, these strings using the formula

```
@IF (B3 ="",A3&" "&C3,A3&" ""&B3&" "&C3)
```

then copy this formula to cell D4.

The function in cell D3 tests cell B3. Since cell B3 is blank, this function returns the *true-result* argument and adds together only the first and last names in cells A3 and C3. However, cell B4 is not blank, so the function in cell D4 returns the *false-result* argument and concatenates the first, middle, and last names in cells A4, B4, and C4. Notice that the *true-result* and *false-result* arguments add a space between each string concatenated, such as the middle and last name.

TABLE 6-8 Compound Logical Operators

Compound Logical Operators	Operation
#AND#	And
#OR#	Or
#NOT#	Not

Compound Logical Operators

You can also use the compound logical operators, shown in Table 6–8, in an @IF function. Compound logical operators allow you to create complex tests by combining multiple conditions in one @IF function.

When you use the #AND# operator, your *condition* argument becomes a multicondition test. For example,

```
@IF(B2>100#AND#B3>20#AND#B4>15,"MET GOALS","BELOW GOALS")
```

is a *three* condition test. It returns the *true-result* argument MET GOALS if the value in cell B2 is greater than 100 *and* the value in cell B3 is greater than 20 *and* the value in cell B4 is greater than 15. If *any* of these conditions are false, this function returns the *false-result* argument BELOW GOALS.

When you use the #OR# operator, if *any condition* argument is true, the *true* argument is returned. For example,

```
@IF(B2>100#OR#B3>20#OR#B4>15,"MET GOALS","BELOW GOALS")
```

returns the *true-result* argument if *any of these conditions* are true. So if B2>100 *or* B3>20 *or* B4>15, then MET GOALS is returned. Only if *all* of these conditions are false does this function return the *false-result* argument BELOW GOALS.

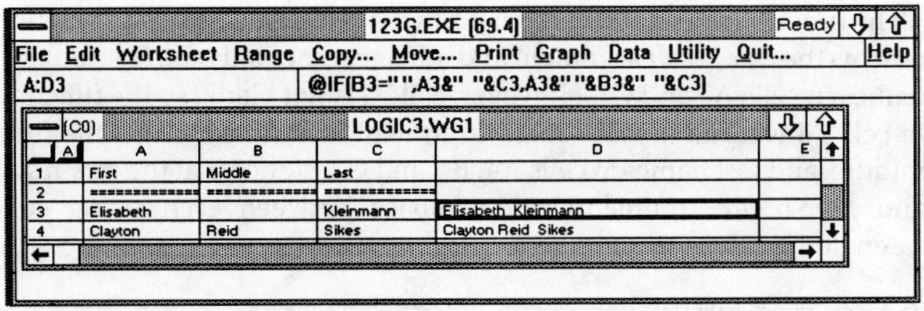

FIGURE 6–13 Using @IF to concatenate strings and blank cells

The #NOT# conditional operator negates your conditional test. In other words, #NOT# tells the @IF function to analyze the *opposite* of the *condition* argument. For example,

```
@IF(B2>100,"MET SALES","BELOW GOALS")
```

returns MET SALES if the value in cell B2 is greater than 100, and returns BELOW GOALS otherwise. However,

```
@IF(#NOT#B24>100,"MET SALES","BELOW GOALS")
```

returns MET SALES if the value in B2 is less than or equal to 100, and returns BELOW GOALS otherwise.

You can mix the #AND# and #OR# complex logical operators in condition arguments, provided you use parentheses to control the order of preference. For example, 1-2-3/G does not accept the following formula:

```
@IF(B2>100#AND#B3>20#OR#B4>15,"MET GOALS","BELOW GOALS")
```

However, by using parentheses to create separate and distinct conditions, 1-2-3/G correctly evaluates the conditions in the following formula:

```
@IF((B2>100#AND#B3>20)#OR#(B2>100#AND#B4>15),"MET GOALS",
"BELOW GOALS")
```

You can also use *nested* @IF functions to correctly model this logic.

Nesting @IF Functions

You can *nest* @IF functions by including another @IF function as your *true-result* and/or *false-result* arguments. Nesting @IF functions creates a hierarchy in your logic. By combining nested @IF functions and compound operators, you can create a function that performs very complex decision-making.

Use nested @IF functions when there are more than two solutions. In the previous example, for the *condition* to be true, if the value in cell B2 is greater than 100, then *either* the value in cell B3 must be greater than 20 *or* the value in cell B4 must be greater than 15. As shown in Figure 6–14, cell D2 contains the function

```
@IF(B2>100,@IF(B3>20#OR#B4>15,"MET GOALS","MET SALES
GOAL"),"BELOW GOALS")
```

1-2-3/G evaluates the first @IF function as follows:

Condition	Result	
B2>100	False	Returns *false-result* BELOW GOALS
B2>100	True	Evaluates *true-result* B3>#OR#B4>15

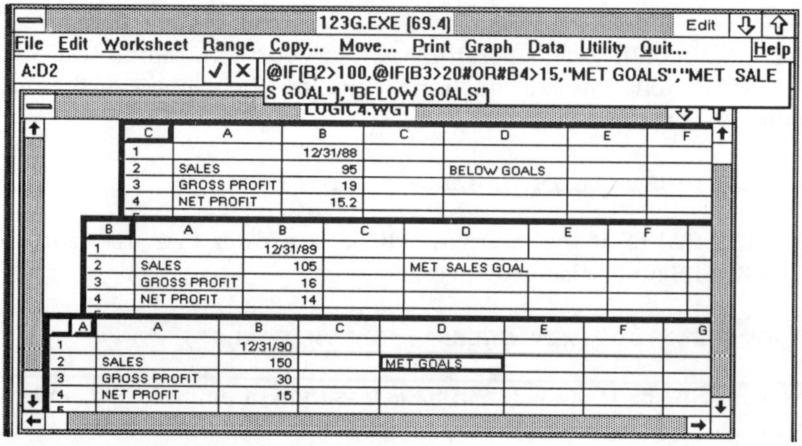

FIGURE 6–14 **Nesting @IF functions**

In cell C:B2 in Figure 6–14, the 1988 sales value of 95 is less than 100. Therefore the @IF function in cell C:D2 returns the false argument BELOW GOALS. But if the condition argument in the first @IF function is true, 1-2-3/G then evaluates the second @IF function as follows:

Condition	**Condition**	**Result**
B3>20 True	B4>15 True	Returns *true-result* MET GOALS
B3>20 True	B4>15 False	Returns *true-result* MET GOALS
B3>20 False	B4>15 True	Returns *true-result* MET GOALS
B3>20 False	B4>15 False	Returns *false-result* MET SALES GOAL

In cell A:B2 in Figure 6–14, the 1990 sales value of 150 is greater than 100. So 1-2-3/G *evaluates* the second @IF function, which is the *true-result* argument of the first @IF function. The value in cell A:B3, 30, is greater than 15, but the value in cell A:B4, 15, is *not* greater than 15. However, since only one of these conditions must be met, the *true-result* argument of the *second* @IF function, MET GOALS, is returned in cell A:D2.

Notice that in the second @IF function, if *neither* of the conditions is true, the *false-result*, MET SALES GOAL, is returned. This happens in cell B:D2. In cell B:B2, the 1989 sales value of 105 is greater than 100, so 1-2-3/G evaluates the first @IF function as true and then evaluates the second @IF function. However, neither the value in cell B:B3, 16, is greater than 20, nor is the value in cell B:B4, 14, greater than 15. So 1-2-3/G evaluates the second @IF function as false and returns the *false-result* argument of the *second* @IF function, MET SALES GOAL.

True and False Values: @TRUE and @FALSE

1-2-3/G's @TRUE function returns the *Boolean* true value 1. @FALSE returns the Boolean false value 0. These functions do not require arguments.

These functions are typically used as the *true-result* and *false-result* arguments in an @IF function or the @CHOOSE function (see "Lookup Functions" in this chapter), or in macros. For example, the function @IF(A6="Expenses",@TRUE,@FALSE) returns the value 1 if cell A6 contains the label Expenses, and the value 0 otherwise. The function @IF(A6="Expenses","TRUE","FALSE") returns the label TRUE if cell A6 contains the label Expenses, and the label FALSE otherwise.

Tip: Using Range Format User to convert @TRUE and @FALSE values to labels

Use the Range Format User command to convert values returned by @TRUE and @FALSE, or any values of 0 and 1 in a range, to the labels TRUE and FALSE. Suppose the cells in the range A1..A4 contain and display the following:

Cell	Contains	Displays	After Using Range Format User
A1	@TRUE	1	TRUE
A2	1	1	TRUE
A3	@FALSE	0	FALSE
A4	0	0	FALSE

Select the Range Format User command. In the User format box, specify the user format N"TRUE";N"FALSE";N"TRUE". In the Ranges box, specify the range A1..A4. The cells in this range now display the labels shown above, but the contents of these cells remain unchanged. See "Creating User Defined Formats" in Chapter 3 for more details.

Indicating an ERR Value: @ERR

Sometimes you may actually want to place the value ERR (error) in your spreadsheet. The @ERR function, which requires no argument, returns the special *value* ERR, not the label ERR.

Use @ERR with @IF to create error-trapping logic. For example, suppose you have created a worksheet file to balance your checkbook. You always want to keep a $500 cash balance in your checking account. If the ending balance is in cell D10, the function @IF(D10<500,@ERR,D10) returns ERR if the cash balance is below $500, and the balance in cell D10 otherwise.

Using @ERR can create a ripple effect throughout your spreadsheet, because the value ERR takes precedence over all other values. Suppose cell D7 contains +D6, while cell D6 contains +D5. If you enter @ERR in cell D5, cell D6, which directly references cell D5, and cell D7, which indirectly references cell D5 through cell D6, also return ERR. Use @ISERR discussed below to stop this ripple effect.

Flagging an Unknown Value: @NA

1-2-3/G's @NA function, which also requires no argument, returns the special *value* NA (not available). In a spreadsheet you can flag that you are missing a needed value by entering @NA in the appropriate cell. Or use @NA to easily determine which formulas in a worksheet file are dependent on a particular value.

Any cells and formulas that refer to a cell containing @NA, as well as cells and formulas indirectly depending on this cell, also return the value NA. Use @ISNA discussed below to stop this ripple effect. The only exception is when a dependent cell also contains the value ERR. Suppose cell D5 contains @NA. Cell D6 contains +D5 and returns NA. Cell D7 contains +D6+D8, but cell D8 contains ERR. Cell D7 returns ERR, not NA, because the value ERR takes precedence over all other values.

Testing for ERR and NA: @ISERR and @ISNA

Use 1-2-3/G's @ISERR and @ISNA functions to test for the special *values* ERR (error) and NA (not available) in a worksheet. The forms of these functions are

@ISERR (*x*)
@ISNA (*x*)

where *x* can be any value or string, or even a condition. You can enter *x* as a literal number or string, or a formula, function, or cell reference that returns a value or string.

These functions evaluate *x* and return the following:

Argument evaluates to	@ISERR returns	@ISNA returns
value NA	0	1
value ERR	1	0
other	0	0

The @ISNA function only returns the true value 1 for the *value* NA. It returns the false value 0 for the label NA. Similarly, @ISERR only returns the true value 1 for the value ERR, and returns the value 0 otherwise, including the label ERR.

Using @ISERR to Divide by Zero

One of the most common causes of the value ERR in a spreadsheet is division by 0. For example, suppose cell A1 contains the formula 100/A2. If cell A2 contains the value 0, cell A1 returns the value ERR. To overcome this problem without changing your other spreadsheet logic, use @IF(@ISERR(100/A2),0,100/A2) in cell A1. This formula returns the value 0 instead of ERR if cell A2 contains 0, and returns the value 100/A2 otherwise.

Blocking the Ripple Effect

Since the value ERR takes precedence over all other values, using the @ERR function can create a ripple effect throughout your spreadsheet. Returning to the previous example, suppose cell D7 contains +D6, D6 contains +D5 and cell D5 contains @ERR. You can use @ISERR to prevent cells D6 and D7 from also returning ERR. In cell D6, use @IF(@ISERR(D5),0,D5), which returns 0 instead of ERR. Otherwise, it returns the value in cell D5. Thus, ERR is not returned in any other cells that indirectly reference cell D5 through cell D6. If cell D5 returns the value NA, you can use @ISNA in the same manner as the @ISERR function above to stop the ripple effect of NA in your spreadsheet.

Testing the Contents of a Cell: @ISSTRING, @ISNUMBER, and @ISEMPTY

1-2-3/G's functions @ISSTRING, @ISNUMBER, and the new @ISEMPTY, test whether an argument is a string, a value, or a blank cell. The forms of these functions are

@ISSTRING(*x*)
@ISNUMBER(*x*)
@ISEMPTY(*x*)

where *x* can be any value or string, or even a condition. You can enter *x* as a literal number or string, or a formula, function, or cell reference that returns a value or string.

These functions evaluate *x* and return the following:

Argument evaluates to	@ISSTRING returns	@ISNUMBER returns	@ISEMPTY returns
Single value	0	1	0
Special values ERR or NA	0	1	0
Blank cell	0	0	1
Label, label prefix	1	0	0
Blank cell with spaces	1	0	0

@ISNUMBER only returns the Boolean true value 1 for a value. @ISSTRING only returns the Boolean true value 1 for a string. @ISEMPTY returns the true value 1 only when a cell is blank. For all other arguments, including blank cells containing spaces, @ISEMPTY returns the false value 0. If x is a range or collection (including those entered into one of these functions as a defined range name), these functions return the false value 0.

Note to Release 2 and 3 Users

In previous releases, @ISNUMBER returned the true value 1 when a cell was blank. It now returns the value 0 when its argument is a blank cell. @ISEMPTY now returns 1 when a cell is blank.

Use @ISNUMBER or @ISSTRING to prevent the incorrect *type* of information from being entered into a formula or cell location. Use @ISEMPTY in a macro to check that a cell is blank before information is entered into that cell. Or use @ISEMPTY with @IF to flag needed database information, such as missing zip codes.

For example, suppose you have entered the addresses in Figure 6-15 in a database. For sorting purposes, each portion of an address, the city, state, and zip code, has been entered in a different cell. You want to *concatenate* or add together the city, state, and zip code into one string. However, zip codes can be entered as either strings or values. Furthermore, if you are missing a zip code, you want to flag that you need this information. In cell D3, enter the following formula:

```
@IF(@ISSTRING(3C)=1,+A3&","&B3&""&C3,@IF(@ISEMPTY(C3)=1,"NEED
ZIPCODE",+A3&","&B3&""&@STRING(C3,0)))
```

This function says that if cell C3 contains a string (@ISSTRING returns 1), then concatenate the strings in cells A3, B3, and C3. If cell C3 is not a string, but cell C3 is empty (@ISEMPTY = 1), return the label NEED ZIP CODE. If cell C3 does not contain a string and is not empty (therefore, cell C3 must contain a value),

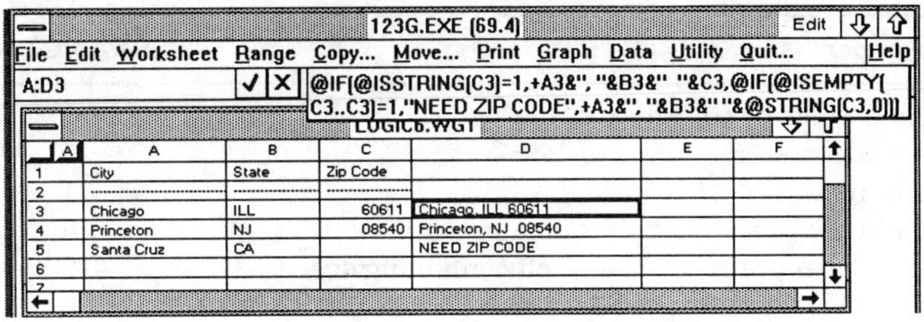

123G.EXE (69.4) Edit

File Edit Worksheet Range Copy... Move... Print Graph Data Utility Quit... Help

A:D3 @IF(@ISSTRING(C3)=1,+A3&", "&B3&" "&C3,@IF(@ISEMPTY(C3..C3)=1,"NEED ZIP CODE",+A3&", "&B3&" "&@STRING(C3,0)))

LOGIC6.WG1

A	A	B	C	D	E	F
1	City	State	Zip Code			
2	----------	----------	----------			
3	Chicago	ILL	60611	Chicago, ILL 60611		
4	Princeton	NJ	08540	Princeton, NJ 08540		
5	Santa Cruz	CA		NEED ZIP CODE		
6						
7						

FIGURE 6–15 Using @ISSTRING to concatenate strings and values, and @ISEMPTY to flag missing information

then concatenate the strings in cells A3, B3, and C3, after @STRING converts the value in cell C3 to a string. Notice that when the information in cells A3, B3, and C3 is concatenated, this formula adds a comma (,) and a space between the information in cells A3 and B3, as well as a space between the information in cells B3 and C3. See "String Functions" below for a discussion of @STRING.

Note

See @CELLPOINTER and @CELL under "Special Functions." These functions can also be used to determine whether a cell contains a string.

Testing for Range Names: @ISRANGE and @ISNAME

1-2-3/G includes two functions that test range names, @ISRANGE, first introduced in Release 3, and the new @ISNAME function.

The @ISRANGE function tests whether its argument is acceptable to a function that requires a range argument. The form of this function is

@ISRANGE(*x*)

where *x* is the address or name of a range or a collection. For the following arguments, @ISRANGE returns:

X Argument is	@ISRANGE returns
Defined range or collection name	1
Range address	1
Cell address	1
Cell address preceded by + starting a formula	0
A label, label prefix, or blank cell containing spaces	0
Undefined range or collection name	0
A value, including special values ERR and NA	0

Note

In early releases of 1-2-3/G, @ISRANGE returns 0 for a named collection, even though the documentation and help screen for this function says it returns 1. Check your copy of 1-2-3/G.

If you enter *x* as a single cell address, @ISRANGE converts it to a range. For example, if you enter **@ISRANGE(A5)** in a cell, 1-2-3/G changes this to @IS RANGE(A5..A5) and returns the value 1.

The function @ISRANGE(COSTS) returns the value 1 when COSTS is a defined range name and 0 otherwise. However, @ISRANGE("COSTS") always returns the value 0. Furthermore, when 5 is a defined range name, @ISRANGE(5) returns 0, but @ISRANGE($5) returns 1.

One of the most common uses for the @ISRANGE command is in conjunction with the @IF function to test for a named range before it is used in a formula or function that requires a defined range name. For example, the formula

```
@IF(@ISRANGE(COSTS=1,@AVG(COSTS),"NOT A RANGE NAME")
```

returns the average value of the numbers in the range COSTS, if COSTS is a defined range and @ISRANGE returns 1. Otherwise, this formula returns the label NOT A RANGE NAME.

The @ISRANGE function is also commonly combined with an {IF} macro command to test for the presence of a named range before it is used in a macro command. For example, the following macro uses @ISRANGE as an argument to the {IF} macro command to test for the presence of the range named OUTPUT:

```
\P        {IF @ISRANGE(OUTPUT)}/pprOUTPUT~gq{QUIT}
          {BRANCH SETRANGE}
```

```
SETRANGE  /rncOUTPUT~A1..I110~
          {BRANCH \P}
```

If the result of @ISRANGE is 1, indicating the range name OUTPUT is defined, the macro executes the commands to print the range to the printer. If the result of @ISRANGE is 0, the range name is not defined, and the macro skips to the next line where the {BRANCH} causes the macro to branch to a routine, SETRANGE, that defines the output range.

The new @ISNAME function, because it returns more detailed information, now provides a more flexible function than @ISRANGE for many applications. The @ISNAME function tests to see if an argument is a range name. The form of this function is

@ISNAME(*string*)

where *string* can be a literal string, formula or function that returns a string, or a single cell address or range name returning any of these, even from another worksheet file. For the following arguments, @ISNAME returns:

Argument evaluates to	@ISNAME Returns
A label not representing a range name	0
Defined range entered as a cell or range address	0
Undefined range name	1
Defined range name	2
Defined collection name	3
Range name for an external database table	4
Second range name for an external database table (an alias)	5
Value or blank cell	ERR

Note

In early releases of 1-2-3/G, @ISNAME returns 5 for a range name for an external database table even though the documentation and help screen for this function say it returns 4. Check your copy of 1-2-3/G.

If you enter a defined range name directly into this function, make sure that you enclose it in double quotes. For example, if INCOME is a defined range name, @ISNAME(INCOME) returns ERR, but @ISNAME("INCOME") returns 2. In addition, if 5 is a defined range name, @ISNAME("5") returns 2. @ISNAME returns the value 1 for an undefined range name in the current file (a range name not yet defined, or whose range coordinates have been undefined using Range Name Undefine).

Note

> Make sure you recalculate your worksheet before you use the result the @ISNAME function returns. If you change the status of a range or collection name, such as defining or deleting it, the result returned by @ISNAME is not always automatically updated until your worksheet is recalculated.

You cannot use @ISNAME to test for range names in other files because @ISNAME always returns 0, unless the range or collection name is also present in the current file. You can, however, use a cell from another file as an argument to @ISNAME. For example, suppose you have two worksheet files in memory, TAX.WG1 and BOOK.WG1. You place the formula @ISNAME(<<TAX.WG1>>A1) in a cell in the BOOK.WG1 file. If cell A1 of TAX.WG1 contains a string that represents the name of a range in BOOK.WG1, @ISNAME returns 1 (for an undefined range name) or 2 (for a defined range name).

LOOKUP FUNCTIONS

1-2-3/G provides the functions in Table 6–9 that "look up" or retrieve a specific item from a list or table. *Each* item in a list or table can be a string or a value.

1-2-3/G also includes a new lookup function, @COORD, which given the numeric coordinates of a cell address, returns the corresponding 1-2-3/G cell address, using either absolute, relative, or mixed addressing.

Selecting an Item from a List: @CHOOSE

1-2-3/G's @CHOOSE function returns a specified item from a list. Usually, you will only use the @CHOOSE function with a small list of items. The form of this function is

```
@CHOOSE(offset,list)
```

Your *list* argument is a group of items that you want the @CHOOSE function to select from. Enter *list* directly into the @CHOOSE function, separating each item in *list* by an argument separator (usually a comma). Each item in *list* can be a value

TABLE 6-9 1-2-3/G's Lookup Functions

Function	Returns
@CHOOSE	Specified item from a list
@INDEX	Specified item from an index table
@VLOOKUP	Specified item from a vertical lookup table
@HLOOKUP	Specified item from a horizontal lookup table
@COORD	Absolute, mixed, or relative cell address

or a string. You can use a literal number or string, or a formula, function, or a cell reference that returns a value or string. If an item in *list* refers to a blank cell, @CHOOSE returns the value 0. The @CHOOSE function returns ERR if you enter a literal string directly into *list* without enclosing it in double quotes.

The @CHOOSE function is usually used with a small *list* argument because you must enter each item in list directly into the @CHOOSE function. If you specify *list* as a range or collection, @CHOOSE returns ERR. To retrieve an item from a large group of items or from a range, use one of the other lookup functions discussed below.

The *offset* argument specifies the item in *list* @CHOOSE retrieves. *Item 1 in list has an offset value of 0*, the second item an offset value of 1, and so on. The last item in a list of *n* items has an offset value of *n* - 1. For example, in the three-item *list* argument, 5,B5, "Tom," the value 5 has an *offset* value of 0, the cell address B5 an *offset* of 1, and the label Tom an *offset* value of 2.

Your *offset* argument must be a value. This can be a literal number, a numeric formula, a function, or to a reference cell containing one of these. However, @CHOOSE returns ERR if *offset* is negative, or greater than *n* - 1 items.

Suppose, you want to use the @CHOOSE function to calculate 1989 federal taxes for different taxable incomes. To do this, you might set up the worksheet in Figure 6–16. The range A6..E9 of this worksheet contains a tax table for single persons. Column D of that range contains the different federal tax rates in the range D6..D8, and the label "Worksheet" in cell D9. To select the first value from this list, you might use the formula @CHOOSE(0,D6,D7,D8,D9). Because the *offset* value in this formulas is 0, 1-2-3/G chooses 15%, the first item in the list.

Now suppose you want to calculate the actual tax for an individual. To do this, you can use the @CHOOSE function in conjunction with the @IF function, as shown in Figure 6–16. The taxable income for the individual appears in cell B12. Beneath this cell in the range B16..B19 are a series of @IF functions that use the @CHOOSE function as an argument. (For your convenience, each of these formulas is shown as text in the cell immediately to the right.) For example, the formula

```
@IF(B12>A7#AND#B12<=B7,+C7+(B12-E7)*@CHOOSE(1,D6,D7,D8,D9),0)
```

1-2-3/G Ready

File Edit Worksheet Range Copy... Move... Print Graph Data Utility Quit... Help

A:B17 @IF(B12>A7#AND#B12<=B7,+C7+(B12-E7)*@CHOOSE(1,D6,

(,2) SHEET.WG1

A	A	B	C	D	E	F	G	H
1								
2	Tax Table - Single Persons							
3								
4		But not	Base	Tax	Amunt			
5	Over	over---	Tax	Rate	over---			
6	0	18500	0	15%	0			
7	18500	44900	2782.5	28%	18500			
8	44900	93130	10160.5	33%	44900			
9	93130			Worksheet				
10								
11	Taxable							
12	Income	22,000						
13								
14	Bracket	Tax	Formulas					
15								
16	Tax 15%	0.00	@IF(B12<=B6,@CHOOSE(0,D6,D7,D8)*B12,0)					
17	Tax 28%	3,762.50	@IF(B12>A7#AND#B12<=B7,+C7+(B12-E7)*@CHOOSE(1,D6,D7,D8),0)					
18	Tax 33%	0.00	@IF(B12>A8#AND#B12<=B8,+C8+(B12-E8)*@CHOOSE(2,D6,D7,D8),0)					
19	Worksheet	0.00	@IF(B12>A9,@CHOOSE(3,D6,D7,D8,D9),0)					
20								

FIGURE 6–16 Using the @CHOOSE function

appears in B17. The first part of this formula, @IF(B12>A7#AND#B12<=B7, evaluates the contents of cell B12 (taxable income). If taxable income is greater than cell A7 in the tax table, but less than or equal to cell B7, the first argument in the @IF function is used. Otherwise, the second argument, 0, is used. The first argument in the @IF function is +C7+(B12–E7)*@CHOOSE(1,D6,D7,D8,D9). The @CHOOSE function in this argument selects the appropriate tax rate from the table. Because the *offset* value is 1, 1-2-3/G selects the second item in the *list*, 28%. This percentage is multiplied by the difference between taxable income and the maximum amount for the 15% bracket. This is then added to the base tax (2782.50) for the 28% bracket. This returns the tax owed of $3,762.50.

Note

Normally, the formulas in the range B16..B19 of Figure 6–16 are combined into a single @IF function with multiple arguments. However, this results in a somewhat large, hard-to-read formula. Therefore, the formula is written over several cells in Figure 6–16. In addition, all references to cells in the tax table and taxable income cells are normally absolute references. That way, you can copy the formula around the worksheet and it will still reference the correct cells.

The formulas in the range B16..B19 of Figure 6–16 all use a similar strategy for calculating the tax due. However, the formula in cell B19 is of interest, because it returns a string instead of a value. This cell contains the formula @IF(B12>A9,@CHOOSE(3,D6,D7,D8,D9),0). Because the *offset* value is 3, 1-2-3/G returns the fourth item in the *list*. In this case that item is the label "Worksheet" in cell D9.

Selecting an Item from an Index Table: @INDEX

1-2-3/G's @INDEX function is a useful way to organize and retrieve data when there is a nonlinear relationship between data, such as in tax tables or in accelerated depreciation tables. Actually, 1-2-3/G's lookup functions were originally developed specifically for tax tables.

The @INDEX function selects a specified item from an *index table*. An index table is a continuous range where each cell contains a string or value. This can be a literal, a number, a string, a formula, a function, or a reference that contains one of these.

An index table cannot be a 2–D or 3–D collection. However, in 1-2-3/G an index table can be a three-dimensional range spanning more than one worksheet. @INDEX returns the item from the index table that corresponds to the "offset coordinates" you specify.

The form of this function is

@INDEX(*range,column-offset,row-offset,worksheet-offset*)

Range is an index table entered as a range address or a range name. If an item selected in *range* is a blank cell, @INDEX returns the value 0 for that cell.

The @INDEX function selects an item from the index table specified by your *range* argument using "offset coordinates": a *column-offset*, a *row-offset*, and, for three-dimensional index tables, a *worksheet-offset*. You can specify each *offset* argument as a value. This can be a literal number, or a numeric formula, function, or cell reference that returns a value.

An item in a two-dimensional table is described by two "offset coordinates": the *column-offset* and the *row-offset*. The *column-offset* argument specifies the column position of the item you want to retrieve. In your index table, *column 1 is offset 0*. Similarly, *row-offset* specifies the row position of the item in your index table you want to retrieve. In your index table, *row 1 is offset 0*.

The @INDEX function in 1-2-3/G now includes an *optional worksheet-offset* argument for a three-dimensional *range*. In your index table, *worksheet 1 is offset 0*. For example, suppose you have created a three-dimensional table in the range A:A1..B:A2. Using offset coordinates, cell A:A1 is represented by a *worksheet-offset* of 0, while cell B:A1 is represented by a *worksheet-offset* of 1. If you ignore the *worksheet-offset* argument, @INDEX assumes a *worksheet-offset* of 0, and *only* returns items from the first worksheet in the table.

The @INDEX function returns ERR if you specify any *offset* argument greater than *n* - 1 (for example, a *column-offset* of *n*, where *n* is the number of columns in *range*), or if you use a negative *offset* argument.

Suppose in Figure 6–17, you have created the three-dimensional index table A:A4..B:C6, which lists the full names of employees. In cell A:H4, the function @INDEX($A:A$4..B:C$6,E4,F4,G4) returns the string Peter. Notice that Peter is the first cell in the index table and is represented by offset coordinates of 0,0,0. This *range* argument includes mixed addressing (dollar signs) to keep this range constant when the @INDEX function is copied to the collection A:H5..A:H6,B:H4..B:H6. In cell B:H6, @INDEX($A:A$4..B:C$6,E6,F6,G6) retrieves the label Kramer, which is represented by the offset coordinates 2,2,1 in the index table. That is, this label is in column 3, row 3, worksheet 2 of the index table, or cell B:C6.

Selecting an Item from a Vertical Lookup Table: @VLOOKUP

The @VLOOKUP function selects and returns a specified item from a *vertical lookup table.* A vertical lookup table is a two-dimensional continuous range composed of at least two columns and two rows. It cannot be a collection. The left-most column is called the *index column.*

Each cell in the *index column* must contain a value. This can be a literal number, a formula, a function, or a reference to a cell containing one of these. On the other hand, each cell in the index column may also contain a string. This can be a literal string, a reference to a cell containing a string, a formula, or a function that returns a string. The cells in the other columns of a vertical lookup table may contain a mixture of either strings or values. Special considerations

123G.EXE — Ready

File Edit Worksheet Range Copy... Move... Print Graph Data Utility Quit... Help

A:H4 @INDEX($A:A$4..$B:C$6,E4,F4,G4)

C:\LAURA\LOOK2.WG1

B	A	B	C	D	E	F	G	H	I
1		INDEX			COLUMN	ROW	WORKSHEET		
2		TABLE			OFFSET	OFFSET	OFFSET	@INDEX	
3	=======	=======	=======		========	=======	============	==========	
4	Stanley	S.	Steamer		0	0	1	Stanley	
5	John	Edward	Cahill		1	1	1	Edward	
6	Barbara	Bender	Kramer		2	2	1	Kramer	

A	A	B	C	D	E	F	G	H	I
1		INDEX			COLUMN	ROW	WORKSHEET		
2		TABLE			OFFSET	OFFSET	OFFSET	@INDEX	
3	========	========	=======		========	========	============	==========	
4	Peter	Paul	Patrick		0	0	0	Peter	
5	Mary	Pat	Campbell		1	1	0	Pat	
6	Margaret		Martin		2	2	0	Martin	

FIGURE 6–17 Using the @INDEX function

concerning the use of values and strings in vertical lookup tables are discussed in the examples below.

The @VLOOKUP function searches the index column of the vertical lookup table to find the information (value or string) that you specify. Once that information is found, @VLOOKUP returns information from the same row in the vertical lookup table, and from the column you specify.

The form of this function is

```
@VLOOKUP(x,range,column-offset)
```

Your *x* argument is the information in the index column of the vertical lookup table that you want to search for. *X* can be any value or string, that is, a literal number or string, or a formula, function, or cell reference that returns a value or string.

Range is a vertical lookup table entered using a range address or a range name. Although the @VLOOKUP function accepts a three-dimensional *range*, it only returns information from the first worksheet in *range*.

Column-offset specifies the column position of the item you want to retrieve in the vertical lookup table. You must specify *column-offset* as a value.

The index column has an offset value of 0. The second column in your vertical lookup table has an offset value of 1. Your *column-offset* argument can be any *value* argument between 1 and *n* - 1, where *n* is the number of columns in *range*. If you use a *column-offset* of 0, @VLOOKUP returns the value or string in the index column specified by *x*. @VLOOKUP returns ERR when any *column-offset* argument is greater than *n* - 1 or is a negative value.

Using @VLOOKUP with Values

When you use values in the index column of a vertical lookup table, the @VLOOKUP function compares the value *x* with the values in the index column. Starting with the first cell in the index column, it evaluates each cell until it finds the value that is equal to or *closest to but not greater than x*. Once this value is found, @VLOOKUP does not continue to search through the index column. For example, suppose your index column contains the values 1, 3, 5, and 3, and *x* is 4. @VLOOKUP selects the first value it encounters that is closest to but not greater than 4, which is the *first* 3. (That is why you should never include duplicate values in your index column, and why the values in your index column must always be in ascending order.) This function then selects a value in the same *row* as the first value 3, according to the *column-offset* argument you specify. If the value 3 is in cell A3, and the *column-offset* is 2, @VLOOKUP returns the value in cell C3.

For example, suppose after a year's employment your company gives a year-end bonus that is a percentage of an employee's monthly salary. This percentage differs, depending upon the number of years an employee has been with the company. In Figure 6–18, you have created a vertical lookup table in the range A4..B8. This is a properly constructed vertical lookup table because the index column:

- is the leftmost column.
- contains values in ascending order.
- contains no duplicate values.
- includes the lowest employment years, 0.
- includes *critical values,* values for which the corresponding values in *column B change.*
- includes the highest value, 20 years, for which the highest value in column B (15%) applies.

Figure 6–18 also shows the different values @VLOOKUP returns for different arguments. Notice in cell F4 that @VLOOKUP(D4,A4..B9,E4), when *column-offset* is 1, returns that an employee receives a 4% bonus for five years of employment. This lookup function searches for the value 5 in the index column, beginning in cell A4. When it finds the value 5 in cell A6, it moves across row 6 one column, then retrieves the value 4% in cell B6.

Likewise, for seven years of employment, the function @VLOOKUP(D5,A4..B9,E5) in cell F5 also returns that an employee receives a 4% bonus. This @VLOOKUP function searches for the value closest to but not greater than 7 in the index column, and selects the value 5 in cell A6.

In cell F6, @VLOOKUP(D6,A4..B9,E6) returns that an employee with 25 years of employment (*x*) should receive a 15% bonus. This function @VLOOKUP finds the years of employment in the index column that is closest to but not greater than 25, selects 20 years in cell A9, then returns the corresponding value in column B.

Notice that the index column in Figure 6–18 includes the value 0, which represents less than one year of employment. So in cell F8, @VLOOKUP(D8,A4..B9,E8) returns that an employee with six-months, employment receives no bonus. If there

123G.EXE Ready
File Edit Worksheet Range Copy... Move... Print Graph Data Utility Quit... Help
A:F4 @VLOOKUP(D4,A4..B9,E4)
(P0) C:\LAURA\LOOK3.WG1

A	A	B	C	D	E	F	G
1	Years of	Percentage of				@VLOOKUP	
2	Employment	Monthly Salary		X	Column-Offset	Returns	
3	================	================		==========	============	============	
4	0	0%		5	1	4%	
5	1	2%		7	1	4%	
6	5	4%		25	1	15%	
7	10	7%		0.5	1	0%	
8	15	10%					
9	20	15%					

FIGURE 6–18 Using @VLOOKUP with Values

was no value less than 1 in the index column, @VLOOKUP(D8,A4..B9,E8) would return ERR .

Although in this example the vertical lookup table only includes two columns, you can easily add more columns to this table. For example, suppose managers receive a different bonus for the same number of years of employment. You could add a third column to your index table to include these percentages. Your vertical lookup table *range* would now be A4..C9. To retrieve these values from column C, simply use a *column-offset* argument of 2 in @VLOOKUP.

In Figure 6–18, if column B were to contain strings, @VLOOKUP would perform in the same manner, except that it would return labels from column B rather than values. However, when you use strings in the index column, special considerations must be taken into account.

Using @VLOOKUP with Strings

When you use strings in the index column of a vertical lookup table, @VLOOKUP requires an *exact match* between one of these strings and your *x* argument. For @VLOOKUP to consider these strings equal, they *must* have the

- Same capitalization.
- Same leading or trailing spaces.
- Same spacing between words.
- Same spelling.

For example, suppose in Figure 6–19 you have created the vertical lookup table in the range A4..C8. The index column lists the last names of employees. Columns B and C include the city and state of birth of each employee listed in column A.

In cell G4, @VLOOKUP(E4,A4..C8,F4) returns the city of birth in cell B4, Indianapolis, when *x* contains the label Watson, and *column-offset* is 1. The *x* argument and the label in cell A4 are an *exact* match. However, @VLOOKUP(E5,A4..C8,F5)

123G.EXE [69.4] Ready

File Edit Worksheet Range Copy... Move... Print Graph Data Utility Quit... Help

A:G4 @VLOOKUP(E4,A4..C8,F4)

(P0) LOOK4.WG1

A	A	B	C	D	E	F	G
1		City of	State of				@VLOOKUP
2	Name	Birth	Birth		X	Column-Offset	Returns
3	==========	==========	==========		=========	===========	===========
4	Watson	Indianapolis	Indiana		Watson	1	Indianapolis
5	Kinney	Richmond	Virginia		WATSON	1	ERR
6	Hugon	Paris	France		Zealer	2	California
7	Yawitz	St. Louis	Missouri		Zea ler	2	ERR
8	Zealer	Fresno	California				

FIGURE 6–19 Using @VLOOKUP with strings

returns ERR in cell G5, when the label WATSON in cell E5 (the *x* argument) does not exactly match any labels in the index column because it is in upper case.

Similarly, when the *x* argument Zealer and the label in cell A8 are an *exact* match, in cell G4 @VLOOKUP(E6,A4..C8,F6) returns the state of birth, California, from cell C8 since *column-offset* is 2. But in cell G8, @VLOOKUP(E8,A4..C8,F8) returns ERR because of the space in the middle of Zea ler in cell E8.

Selecting an Item from a Horizontal Lookup Table: @HLOOKUP

The @HLOOKUP function is similar to the @VLOOKUP functions in all respects except that @HLOOKUP selects and returns a specified item from a horizontal lookup table. A horizontal lookup table is also a two-dimensional range composed of at least two columns and two rows. But the @HLOOKUP function evaluates information you specify against the information in row 1, the index row. Starting with the left-most cell, it evaluates each cell along the index row until it finds the first value that is closest to but not greater than x. Based on the information it selects in the index row, @HLOOKUP then retrieves information from the same column, but in the row you specify.

The form of this function is

```
@HLOOKUP(x,range,row-offset)
```

X is the information you want to search for in the index row of the horizontal lookup table. *X* can be any value or string entered as a literal number or string, or a formula, function, or cell reference that returns a value or string.

Your *range* argument is a two-dimensional horizontal lookup table. Enter this argument using a range address or a range name. Although @HLOOKUP accepts a three-dimensional *range*, it only returns information from the first worksheet in *range*.

The *row-offset* argument specifies the row position of the item you want to retrieve in the vertical lookup table. You must specify *row-offset* as a value.

The index row has an offset value of 0. The second row in your horizontal lookup table has an offset value of 1. So your row-offset argument can be between 1 and *n* - 1, where n is the number of rows in range. If you use a row-offset of 0, @HLOOKUP returns the value or string in the index row specified by x. @HLOOKUP returns ERR when any row-offset argument is greater than *n* - 1, or is less than 0.

Using @HLOOKUP with Values and Strings

Suppose you have created the horizontal lookup table in the range B:C1..B:F3 in Figure 6–20. The index row, row 1, includes the last names of employees. The other rows in this horizontal lookup table include the first name of these employees and the number of children for whom the company pays health insurance.

Cell A:C3 contains the function @HLOOKUP(A3,B:C1..B:F3,B3). For the employee Hugon, this function returns the first name Sarah. @HLOOKUP starts in the left-most

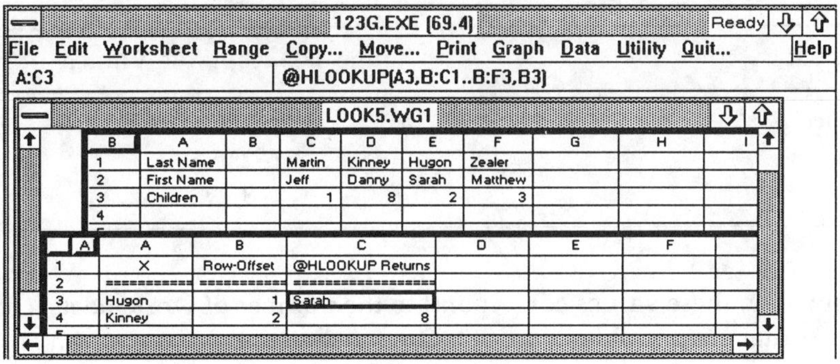

123G.EXE (69.4) Ready

File Edit Worksheet Range Copy... Move... Print Graph Data Utility Quit... Help

A:C3 @HLOOKUP(A3,B:C1..B:F3,B3)

LOOK5.WG1

B	A	B	C	D	E	F	G	H	I
1	Last Name		Martin	Kinney	Hugon	Zealer			
2	First Name		Jeff	Danny	Sarah	Matthew			
3	Children		1	8	2	3			
4									

A	A	B	C	D	E	F
1	X	Row-Offset	@HLOOKUP Returns			
2	==========	==========	================			
3	Hugon	1	Sarah			
4	Kinney	2	8			

FIGURE 6–20 Using @HLOOKUP

cell in the index row, cell B:C1, then compares *x* in cell A:A3 to each cell in this row until it finds an *exact* match in cell B:E1. It then uses the *row-offset* value 1 and returns the first name in cell B:E2. Similarly, in cell A:C4, @HLOOKUP(A4,B:C1..B:F3,B4) which uses a *row-offset* of 2 and returns the value 8. This indicates that employee Kinney has eight children enrolled in the company's insurance program.

Creating an Address from Offset Coordinates: @COORD

1-2-3/G's new @COORD function uses the numeric coordinates of a cell location in a worksheet file, then returns the corresponding cell address using the type of cell referencing you specify, absolute, relative, or mixed. The form of this function is

@COORD(*worksheet,column,row,absolute*)

where *worksheet, column,* and *row* are a cell's numeric coordinates. Each of these arguments must be a value entered as a literal number, or a formula, function, or cell reference that returns a value. You cannot use @COORD on a range of cells. Rather, you must apply this function to each cell in your range.

The @COORD arguments are *not* offset arguments. Rather, they represent the coordinates of an item in a 1-2-3/G worksheet file. For example, in @COORD(1,1,1), the argument coordinates (1,1,1) represent the cell in the first worksheet, row, and column, cell A:A1. The coordinates (26,3,2) represent the twenty-sixth worksheet, the third column and the second row a worksheet file, or cell Z:C2. These arguments accept the following values:

Argument	Range of Acceptable Values
Worksheet	1–256
Column	1–256
Row	1–8,192

As you know, these values correspond to the number of worksheets, columns, and rows that are possible in a 1-2-3/G worksheet file. If you use an argument outside of these acceptable ranges, @COORD returns ERR.

The *absolute* argument tells 1-2-3/G the type of mixed, relative, or absolute addressing you want the cell address to be. When you use the values below, @COORD returns the following type of address:

Absolute Argument	Formula	Cell Address	Worksheet	Column	Row
1	+$A:$A$1	Absolute	Fixed	Fixed	Fixed
2	+$A:A$1	Mixed	Fixed	Changes	Fixed
3	+$A:$A1	Mixed	Fixed	Fixed	Changes
4	+$A:A1	Mixed	Fixed	Changes	Changes
5	+A:$A$1	Mixed	Changes	Fixed	Fixed
6	+A:A$1	Mixed	Changes	Changes	Fixed
7	+A:$A1	Mixed	Changes	Fixed	Fixed
8	+A:A1	Relative	Changes	Changes	Changes

If you use a value other than 1 through 8 for your *absolute* argument, @COORD returns ERR. Notice that these *absolute* values correspond to the number of times you press ABS (F4) to create the same mixed, absolute, or relative cell address. For more information on mixed, absolute, and relative cell addressing, see "Copying Formulas" in Chapter 4.

Suppose you have the worksheet in Figure 6-21. In cell E4, @COORD (A4,B4,C4,D4) uses the worksheet coordinates (1,1,1) and the *absolute* argument 8. So this function returns the relative cell address A:A1. Notice that it does *not* return the contents of cell A:A1.

In cell E5, @COORD(A5,B5,C5,D5) uses the worksheet coordinates (5,20,300) and the *absolute* argument 8. So it returns the relative cell address E:T300. For these same coordinates, @COORD returns the absolute cell address $E:$T$300 when *absolute* is 1, and the mixed cell address $E:T300 when *absolute* is 4.

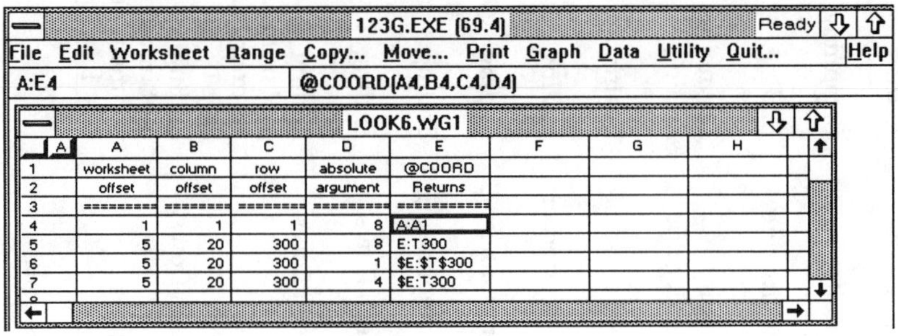

123G.EXE (69.4) Ready

File Edit Worksheet Range Copy... Move... Print Graph Data Utility Quit... Help

A:E4 @COORD(A4,B4,C4,D4)

LOOK6.WG1

A	A	B	C	D	E	F	G	H
1	worksheet	column	row	absolute	@COORD			
2	offset	offset	offset	argument	Returns			
3	=========	========	========	=========	===========			
4	1	1	1	8	A:A1			
5	5	20	300	8	E:T300			
6	5	20	300	1	$E:$T$300			
7	5	20	300	4	$E:T300			

FIGURE 6–21 Using @COORD

Note

Use @COORD with the @@ function to return the *contents* of the cell address returned by @COORD. In Figure 6–21, @@(@COORD(1,1,1,8)) returns the label "worksheet" in cell A:A1.

FINANCIAL FUNCTIONS

1-2-3/G's financial functions help you analyze financial opportunities and alternatives using the time value of money. The premise is that cash in hand today is worth more than cash received in the future, where this extra value is any interest you can earn between today and a future date. To analyze financial opportunities, you must convert any future cash values to a present value through discounting. These future cash flows are discounted by a rate of return (interest rate) that compensates you for the risk of the investment.

1-2-3/G's financial functions are powerful tools you can use in financial analysis. However, because of their complexity, they can easily be misused. So make sure that you thoroughly understand the underlying assumptions of a financial function before you use it to model an investment scenario. For easy reference, the important assumptions have been listed for each financial function.

1-2-3/G includes functions that analyze single investments, annuities, and unequal cash flows. Table 6–10 is a handy reference guide listing these functions, as well as their arguments, assumptions, and the results returned.

TABLE 6–10 1-2-3/G's Financial Functions

1-2-3/G Function	Calculates	Cash Flow Argument	Interest or Discount Rate AND Time Period	Payment Occurs in Period
@PV(p,i,n)	Present Value of an annuity	One annuity payment	Per Period of annuity	Beginning
@PV(p,i,n)*(1+i)	Present Value of an annuity due	One annuity due payment	Per Period of annuity due	Ending
@PMT(p,i,n)	Annuity payment per period	One annuity payment	Per period of annuity	Beginning
@PMT(p,i,n)(1+i)	Annuity due payment per period	One annuity due payment	Per Period of annuity due	Ending
@FV(p,i,n)	Future Value of an annuity	One annuity payment	Per Period of annuity	Beginning
@FV(p,i,n)*(1+i)	Future Value of an annuity due	One annuity due payment	Per Period of annuity due	Ending
@TERM(p,i,FV)	Payment periods for annuity to reach FV	One annuity payment	Calculated as per Period of annuity	Beginning
@TERM(p,i,FV/(1+i))	Payment periods for annuity due to reach FV	One annuity due payment	Calculated as per Period of annuity due	Ending
@CTERM(i,FV,PV)	Payment periods for initial investment to reach FV	Initial investment, enter as positive	Per period of compounding period calculated	Ending
@RATE(FV,PV,n)	Compound return on initial investment	Initial investment, enter as positive	Per Period of compounding period calculated	Ending
@NPV(i,cash flow range)	Net Present Value, no initial investment	Range of equal or unequal cash flows	Per period between flows	Ending
@NPV(i,cash flow range)–IO	Net Present Value, initial investment	Range of equal or unequal cash flows, excluding initial investment	Per period between flows	Ending, except initial investment on Day 1
@IRR(i guess, cash flow range)	Internal Rate of Return, initial investment	Range of equal or unequal cash flows, initial investment in first cell	Per period between flows, rate calculated	Ending, except initial investment on Day 1

p = payment per period
i = interest rate per period in decimal or percentage form
n = number of payments
IO = initial investment

Relevant Assumptions:

All payments of interest reinvested at interest or discount rate until end of investment period

Rate is constant over investment period

All periods must be equal

Rate determines time period

Period is largest interval that makes intervals equal

Tip: The *interest* or *discount rate* argument

All of 1-2-3/G's financial functions either use or solve for an *interest rate* or *discount rate*. The underlying assumptions of the *rate* are fundamental to understanding 1-2-3/G's financial functions.

In any cash flow analysis, there are three distinct variables—the cash flow, the interest rate, and the number of periods (number of payments)—and one implicit variable, the time period between cash flows. The *interest rate* determines the *equal* time period between cash flows that a financial function uses in its calculation. So if you use a yearly interest rate, 1-2-3/G assumes that the time period between cash flows is one year. If you use a monthly interest rate, then the time period between cash flows is one month. (A common convention is to use a monthly interest rate equal to the annual rate divided by 12.) Therefore, when you use one of 1-2-3/G's financial functions, remember:

- All time periods between cash flows are equal, and this time period is determined by the *interest rate* used.
- Use an interest rate corresponding to *one* time period between cash flows.

In addition, the following *interest rate* assumptions are made in all financial calculations:

- the *interest rate* is *constant* over the entire investment period.
- any cash received during the investment period is immediately reinvested at your *rate* until the end of the investment period.
- interest is compounded at the end of each *equal* time period.

Present Value of an Annuity and Annuity Due: @PV

1-2-3-/G's @PV function computes the *present value (PV)* of an *ordinary annuity,* assuming equal payments are made at the *end* of equal time periods. Thus, @PV calculates the value today of a future stream of cash flows discounted at some fixed *discount* (interest) rate. The present value is expressed mathematically as

$$\text{PV} = \text{payment per period} * \frac{1-(1+\text{interest rate})^{-n}}{\text{interest rate}}$$

where *n* is the number of payments made. The form of 1-2-3/G's easier-to-use @PV function is

```
@PV(payment,interest rate,number of payments)
```

The *payment* argument is the value of *one* of the equal annuity payments, while *interest rate* is the constant rate earned for *one* time period. The *number of payments* argument is the number of equal payments made. Each of these arguments must be a value entered as a literal number, or a formula, function, or cell reference that returns a value.

The @PV function assumes:

- All payments are equal and occur at the *end* of equal time periods.
- *Interest rate* is for *one* time period and is constant over the investment period.
- All payments received are immediately reinvested at your *interest rate* until all payments end.

Calculating the PV of an Annuity

Imagine that you need to evaluate two investment alternatives. The first option pays you $10,000 at the *end* of every six-month period for 10 years. You can invest these payments and earn 12 percent annually. What is the present value of this alternative? As shown in Figure 6–22, you use a $10,000 *payment* in cell B3, a 6% *semi-annual interest rate* in cell B4, and 20 *number of payments* in cell B5. In cell B6, @PV(B3,B4,B5) returns $114,699.

123G.EXE [69.4] Ready

File Edit Worksheet Range Copy... Move... Print Graph Data Utility Quit... Help

A:B6 @PV(+B3,B4,B5)

(C0) FIN1.WG1

A	A	B	C	D	E
1	Payment Occurs	End of Period		Beginning of Period	
2	Payment Interval	6 months		6 months	
3	Payment	$10,000		$10,000	
4	Interest Rate Per Period	6%		6%	
5	Number of Payments	20		20	
6	PRESENT VALUE OF ANNUITY	$114,699		$114,699	
7	Conversion Factor			1.06	
8	PRESENT VALUE OF ANNUITY DUE			$121,581	

FIGURE 6–22 Calculating PV of an Annuity and an Annuity Due

Note

> For an annuity with *unequal* payments, use the @NPV function.

Calculating the Present Value of an Annuity Due

Your second financial alternative is to receive the same payments shown in Figure 6–22, but at the *beginning* of each period. To calculate the value of this alternative, you must adjust the result of the @PV function using an *annuity due* as your *payment* argument. This is equivalent to moving all payments ahead one period. To do this, you use the following conversion:

```
(1+interest rate)*@PV(payment,interest rate,number of
payments)
```

Returning to Figure 6–22, in cell D8 the formula +D6*D7 multiplies the result of the @PV function of an annuity by the conversion factor 1.06. So the PV of an annuity due is $121,581, while the PV of the same annuity is $114,699. Obviously, you would rather have payments occur at the beginning of each period.

Annuity and Annuity Due Payment Per Period: @PMT

1-2-3/G's @PMT function calculates the fixed payment per period required to repay a principal amount, given a fixed interest rate and a specified number of payment periods. Typically, @PMT is used to calculate the fixed payment needed to repay a mortgage or loan. Since the principal amount is the present value, the *payment per period* can be expressed mathematically by rearranging the PV equation to

$$\text{Payment per period} = \text{principal amount} * \frac{\text{interest rate}}{1 - (1 + \text{interest rate})^{-n}}$$

where n is the number of payments made. The form of 1-2-3/G's function is

```
@PMT(principal,interest rate,number of payments)
```

Your *principal* is simply the amount of principal borrowed. The *number of payments* argument is the number of *equal* time periods over which payments are made until the *principal* is repaid. You can also think of it as the number of payments, as long as the time period between each payment is equal. Your *interest rate* is then the fixed rate for *one* payment period. So if payments occur monthly, use the annual rate divided by 12. Each of these arguments must be entered as a value. You can use a literal number, or a numeric formula, function, or cell reference that returns a value.

Remember, @PMT assumes:

- All payments are equal and occur at the *end* of equal time periods.
- The payment amount applied to principal and interest varies for each period.
- *Interest rate* is the rate for *one* time period, which is constant over the repayment period.

Calculating Fixed Payments at the End of Each Period

Suppose you are considering the various 12% fixed-rate $150,000 mortgage loan options available to you in Figure 6–23. You can get a 20–, 30–, or 40–year mortgage, which you pay at the end of every month. As shown in Figure 6–23, you can use @PMT to figure the monthly payments for each of these mortgages. In cell B8, @PMT(B1,B2,B7) returns a monthly payment of $1,652 for a 20–year mortgage. Since payments are made monthly, a 1% *monthly rate* in cell B2 and 240 *monthly payments* in cell B7 are used as the arguments. In cell C8, @PMT(B1,B2,C7) calculates that you would pay 360 payments of $1,543 if you choose the 30–year mortgage. Similarly, @PMT(B1,B2,D7) shows that it would take 480 $1,513 payments to pay off a $150,000 mortgage over 40 years.

Calculating Fixed Payments at the Beginning of Each Period

You can also use @PMT to calculate the fixed payment per period when each payment is made at the *beginning* of each time period. Just use the following conversion formula:

```
@PMT(principal,interest rate,number of payments)/
(1+interest rate)
```

123G.EXE (69.4) Ready

File Edit Worksheet Range Copy... Move... Print Graph Data Utility Quit... Help

A:B8 @PMT(B1,B2,B7)

(C0) FIN8.WG1

A	A	B	C	D	E	F	G
1	Loan Amount	$150,000					
2	Monthly Interest Rate	1.0%					
3	Beginning Loan Date	01-Jan-91					
4	================================	========	========	========			
5	Mortgage Term	20 year	30 year	40 year			
6	================================	========	========	========			
7	Monthly Payments	240	360	480			
8	@PMT returns Payment at END of Month	$1,652	$1,543	$1,513			
9	Conversion Rate	101%	101%	101%			
10	Monthly Payment at BEGINNING of Month	$1,635	$1,528	$1,498			
11							

FIGURE 6–23 Using @PMT to evaluate loans paid at the beginning and ending of periods

The @PMT function is *divided* by the conversion factor (1+*interest rate*). This is equivalent to paying all payments one period early, so one period of interest is not paid.

Now suppose you can also pay the different fixed-rate mortgage options in Figure 6–23 at the *beginning* of the month. To calculate the monthly payments of these mortgages, you still use the result of @PMT for payments made at the end of the month. Next, you divide the result of the @PMT function by the conversion factor (1+*interest rate*), or 1.01 in row 9 of Figure 6–23. The monthly payments made at the beginning of each month are calculated in row 10. In cell B10, +B8/B9 returns a payment of $1,635. As can be seen for all mortgages, smaller payments are required if paid at the beginning rather than at the end of each month.

Using @PMT to Create an Amortization Table

Suppose you are buying a home and will be incurring a $150,000, 30-year, 12% fixed-rate mortgage on January 1, 1991. What is your principal balance at the end of the first year? You can use the results of the @PMT function to create an amortization table and determine the balance.

First, you need to calculate your monthly payment using the @PMT function. As shown in Figure 6–24, in the file FIN6, the formula in cell B5, @PMT(B2,B3,B4), calculates that you will pay $1,543 a month for 30 years using a $150,000 *principal* argument, a 1% *monthly interest rate*, and 360 *number of payments*.

Now you can create an amortization table like the one in the file FIN7 in Figure 6–24. In column A, the payment dates have been entered using 1-2-3/G's @DATE function. The beginning balance in column B is simply the previous

123G.EXE (69.4) Ready

File Edit Worksheet Range Copy... Move... Print Graph Data Utility Quit... Help

A:D5 (+<<FIN6.WG1>>A:B$3*12/365)*B5*(A5-A4)

FIN6.WG1

A	A	B
1	Beginning Loan Date	01-Jan-91
2	Loan Amount	$150,000
3	Monthly Interest Rate	1.0%
4	Monthly Payments	360
5	Monthly Payment	$1,543
6		
7		
8		
9		
10		
11		
12		
13		
14		
15		
16		
17		

(C0) FIN7.WG1

A	A	B	C	D	E	F
1	Payment	Beginning	Monthly	Interest	Principal	Ending
2	Date	Balance	Payment	Paid	Paid	Balance
3	=========	========	=======	=======	========	========
4	31-Jan-91	$150,000	$1,543	$1,479	$63	$149,937
5	28-Feb-91	$149,937	$1,543	$1,380	$163	$149,774
6	31-Mar-91	$149,774	$1,543	$1,526	$16	$149,757
7	30-Apr-91	$149,757	$1,543	$1,477	$66	$149,692
8	31-May-91	$149,692	$1,543	$1,526	$17	$149,674
9	30-Jun-91	$149,674	$1,543	$1,476	$67	$149,608
10	31-Jul-91	$149,608	$1,543	$1,525	$18	$149,589
11	31-Aug-91	$149,589	$1,543	$1,525	$18	$149,571
12	30-Sep-91	$149,571	$1,543	$1,475	$68	$149,503
13	31-Oct-91	$149,503	$1,543	$1,524	$19	$149,484
14	30-Nov-91	$149,484	$1,543	$1,474	$69	$149,416
15	31-Dec-91	$149,416	$1,543	$1,523	$20	$149,395
16			----------	----------	----------	
17	Payments		$18,515	$17,911	$605	

FIGURE 6–24 Creating a loan amortization table using @PMT

month's ending balance in column F. The monthly payment in column C, $1,543 is the result returned by the @PMT function in FIN6, cell B5. In column D, interest paid is calculated as daily interest rate times the days in the month times the beginning principal balance.For example, in cell D5, the interest paid in February, 1991 is (<<FIN6.WG1>>A:B$3*12/365)*(A5–A4)*B5, or $1,380. This formula is copied to cells D6..D15. However, in cell D4, the interest paid in the first month, January 1991, is calculated using the formula (<<FIN6.WG1>>A:B$3*12/365)*(A4–<<FIN6.WG1>>A:B1)*B4. This formula uses the beginning loan date, January 1, 1991 in cell B1 in the File FIN6, to calculate the number of days interest has accrued.

The principal paid in column E is simply the monthly payment in column C less the interest paid in column D. Finally, in column F, the ending balance is the beginning balance in column B less the principal paid in column E.

As shown in row 17 of FIN7.WG1, in 1991 you make payments totaling $18,515, of which $17,911 is interest and $605 is principal. As shown in cell F15, on December 31, 1991, your principal balance is $149,395.

Note

You can also create an amortization schedule based on a 360-day year using 1-2-3/G's @D360 date function. See "Date and Time Arithmetic" in this chapter.

Note

For *adjustable*-rate mortgages, use the @PMT function to calculate the new fixed payment for each year that rates change, decreasing the *number of payments* by those already made, using the new beginning balance from your amortization table as your *principal* argument, and using the new monthly *interest rate.* In the example above, if your annual interest rate increased to 14% in year two, @PMT (149395,.14/12,(240–12)) would return the new fixed payment of $1,876.

Future Value of an Annuity and Annuity Due: @FV

1-2-3/G's @FV function returns the future value (FV) of an ordinary annuity, based on equal payments made at the end of equal time periods. Mathematically, the future value is computed as

$$FV = \text{payment per period} * \frac{1 - (1 + \text{interest rate})^{-n} - 1}{\text{interest rate}}$$

where *n* is the number of payments that will be made. The form of 1-2-3/G's @FV function is

@FV(*payment,interest rate,number of payments*)

The *payment* argument is the value of *one* of the equal payments of the annuity, while *interest rate* is a constant rate earned for each time period. Your *number of payments* argument is simply the number of equal payments that will be made. Each of these arguments can be entered as a literal number, or a numeric formula, function, or cell reference that returns a value.

The @FV function assumes:

- Future value is calculated on the *date of the last payment.*
- All payments are equal and occur at the *end* of equally spaced time periods.
- *Interest rate* is for *one* time period, and is constant over the investment period.
- All payments received are immediately reinvested at *interest rate* until the end of the investment period.

Calculating the FV of an Annuity

Once again, imagine that you have two investment alternatives. The first option is that your company allows you to automatically deduct $1,000 from each end-of-the month paycheck and deposit it in a savings account that returns 10% annually. What will be the future value of your savings account in one year? As shown in Figure 6–25, you use a $1,000 *payment* in cell B3, a *monthly interest rate* of .10/12, which is displayed as .8333% in cell B4, and 12 *number of payments* in cell B5. In cell B6, the function @FV(B3,B4,B5) returns the value $12,566.

123G.EXE Ready

File Edit Worksheet Range Copy... Move... Print Graph Data Utility Quit... Help

A:B6 @FV(+B3,B4,B5)

(C0) C:\LAURA\FIN2.WG1

A	A	B	C	D	E
1	Payment Occurs	End of Period		Beginning of Period	
2	Payment Interval	6 months		6 months	
3	Payment	$1,000		$1,000	
4	Interest Rate Per Period	0.8333%		0.8333%	
5	Number of Payments	12		12	
6	FUTURE VALUE OF ANNUITY	$12,566		$12,566	
7	Conversion Factor			1.0083	
8	FUTURE VALUE OF ANNUITY DUE			$12,670	
9					

FIGURE 6–25 Calculating FV of an annuity and an annuity due

Calculating the FV of an Annuity Due

Your second financial alternative is to make the same payments shown in Figure 6–25, but at the *beginning* of each period. To calculate the future value of this alternative, you must adjust the result of the @FV function using an *annuity due* as your *payment* argument. This is equivalent to moving all payments ahead one period. Just use the following conversion formula:

```
(1+interest rate)*@FV(payment,interest rate,number of
payments)
```

Returning to Figure 6–25, you can now calculate the FV of your second alternative, transferring $1,000 at the *beginning* of each month to a savings account that also earns 10% interest annually. In cell D8 in Figure 6–25, the formula +D6*D7 multiplies the result of the @FV function by the conversion factor 1.0083. So the FV of the annuity due is $12,670, while the FV of the annuity is $12,566. Once again, it is more advantageous for you to make payments at the beginning of each month.

Calculating the Term of an Annuity: @TERM

For an ordinary annuity that earns a fixed interest rate, 1-2-3/G's @TERM function calculates the number of time periods required to reach a specified future value. Mathematically, this can be expressed as

$$\text{Term} = \frac{\text{Ln}[1 + ((\text{FV} * \text{interest rate})/\text{payment})]}{\text{Ln}(1 + \text{interest rate})}$$

where Ln is the natural log. 1-2-3/G's much easier-to-use function is

```
@TERM(payment,interest rate,FV)
```

where your *payment* argument is the value of *one* of the equal payments of the annuity, and *interest rate* is a constant rate earned for *one* time period. Your *future value* argument is simply the desired value in the future you want to achieve through this investment strategy. Each of these arguments must be a value. You can use a literal number, or a numeric formula, function, or cell reference that returns a value.

The @TERM function returns a value that represents the number of compounding periods needed to reach your *future value*, where one period is the time period used in your *interest rate* argument. This function assumes:

- All payments are equal and occur at the *end* of equally spaced time periods.
- *Interest rate* is for *one* time period, which is constant over the investment period.

- Interest is compounded at the end of each period—monthly if a payment is made monthly, yearly if payments are made yearly.
- All payments received are immediately reinvested at your *interest rate* until the day the future value is achieved.
- The *term* returns a value in the *same units* as the time period used in your *interest rate* argument, which you may need to convert to years.

Calculating the Term for an Annuity

Suppose you want to save $100,000 for your retirement. You plan to save $1,000 per month, and you can earn a 12% annual return. How long will it take you to reach your objective? In Figure 6–26, you use a $1,000 monthly *payment* in cell B2, and a 1% monthly *interest rate* in cell B3. If you save $1,000 at the *end* of each month, in cell B7, @PMT(B2,B3,B4) calculates that it will take you 69.66 time periods, or months, to reach your $100,000 goal in cell B4. In cell B9, 69.66 periods is divided by 12 to convert this term to 5.81 years.

Calculating the Term for an Annuity Due

You can also use @TERM to calculate the number of periods required for an annuity due to reach a future value, when payments occur at the *beginning* of each period. This is equivalent to moving all payments ahead one period, so each payment in effect earns one more period of interest. Just use the following conversion formula:

```
@TERM(payment,interest rate,FV/(1+interest rate))
```

To calculate the term of an annuity due, you divide your *future value* argument by the conversion factor *1+interest rate.* In Figure 6–26, if you transfer $1,000 at the *beginning* of each month to a savings account, @PMT(E2,E3,E6) in cell E7 calculates that it will take 69.16 months, or 5.76 years to reach $100,000.

123G.EXE (69.4) Ready

File Edit Worksheet Range Copy... Move... Print Graph Data Utility Quit... Help

A:B7 @TERM(B2,B3,B4)

(F2) FIN9.WG1

A	A	B	C	D	E	F	G
1	Payment in Time Period	Beginning		Payment in Time Period	Ending		
2	Monthly Payment	$1,000		Monthly Payment	$1,000		
3	Monthly Interest Rate	1%		Monthly Interest Rate	1%		
4	Future Value Desired	$100,000		Future Value Desired	$100,000		
5				Conversion Rate	101%		
6				Converted Future Value	$99,010		
7	@TERM(B2,B3,B4)	69.66		@TERM(E2,E3,E6)	69.16		
8	Conversion	12.00		Conversion	12		
9	Number of years	5.81		Number of years	5.76		

FIGURE 6–26 Using @TERM for an annuity and annuity due

Tip: Using @TERM to calculate the number of remaining payments for different mortgage payments

You can use @TERM to calculate the number of payments needed to pay off a mortgage for a given monthly payment. The trick to using the @TERM function in this application is to use a *negative* monthly *payment* argument and a *positive* loan balance as your *future value* argument.

Suppose you have a 12% fixed-rate mortgage with an $100,000 outstanding balance. In Figure 6–27, @PMT(A6,B1,B2) in cell B6 returns the current mortgage term, 480 months or 40 years, when you make the monthly *payment* of -$1,009 and use a $100,000 loan balance as your *future value* argument. As shown in cell B7, if you increase your monthly payment to -$1,100 in cell A7, @PMT(A7,B1,B2) returns that you will pay off your mortgage in only 240.99 months, or 20.08 years. Figure 6–27 also shows how @TERM calculates other *terms* for increasing monthly mortgage payments.

Note

You can calculate the payment per period needed to reach a future value using the @TERM function and 1-2-3/G's Backsolver. See Chapter 13, "Backsolver and Solver," for an example.

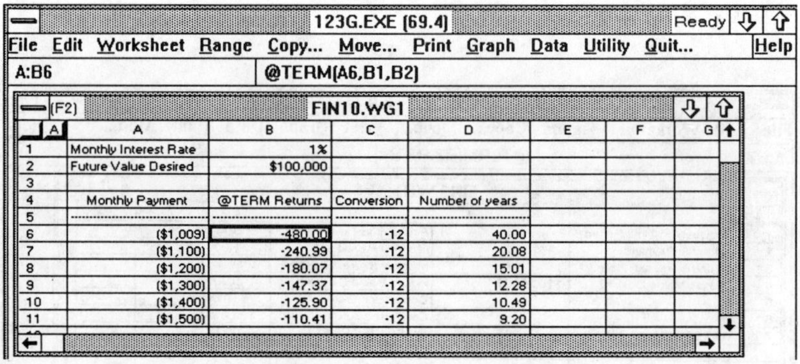

123G.EXE (69.4) — Ready

File Edit Worksheet Range Copy... Move... Print Graph Data Utility Quit... Help

A:B6 @TERM(A6,B1,B2)

(F2) FIN10.WG1

	A	B	C	D	E	F	G
1	Monthly Interest Rate	1%					
2	Future Value Desired	$100,000					
3							
4	Monthly Payment	@TERM Returns	Conversion	Number of years			
5							
6	($1,009)	-480.00	-12	40.00			
7	($1,100)	-240.99	-12	20.08			
8	($1,200)	-180.07	-12	15.01			
9	($1,300)	-147.37	-12	12.28			
10	($1,400)	-125.90	-12	10.49			
11	($1,500)	-110.41	-12	9.20			

FIGURE 6–27 Using @TERM to calculate the number of

Calculating the Term of an Investment: @CTERM

1-2-3/G provides the @CTERM function which computes the number of periods required for a *single investment* to reach a specified future value. This can be expressed mathematically as

Term of an Investment = Ln(FV/PV)/Ln(1+interest rate)

where Ln is the natural logarithm. 1-2-3/G's easier-to-use function is

@CTERM(*interest rate,FV,PV*)

Each of the arguments in @CTERM must evaluate to a value. You can use a literal number, or a numeric formula, function, or cell reference that returns a value.

Your *FV* argument is simply the desired value in the future you want to achieve. The *PV* is the initial investment made at the beginning of the investment period. Enter both of these arguments as positive values or both as negative values, even though one is a cash outflow and the other is a cash inflow. The *interest rate* is the interest rate per period of compounding. So if interest is compounded monthly, use a monthly *interest rate* argument. The @CTERM function returns a value that represents the number of compounding periods needed to reach your *future value,* where one period is the time period used in your *interest rate* argument.

Keep the following in mind when you use @CTERM:

- Only one investment is made, which occurs on the first day of the investment period.
- Enter both *PV* and *FV* using the same sign.
- Interest is earned at the *end* of each equal time period, and immediately reinvested at your *interest rate* until the day the future value is achieved.
- Use an *interest rate* for *one* time period over which interest is compounded, which is constant over the investment period.
- @CTERM returns a value in the *same units* as the time period used in your *interest rate* argument, which you may want to convert to years.

Suppose you can invest $50,000 in an instrument that pays 12% annually, compounded monthly. You also can invest this money in another financial instrument that pays a 12.25% annual interest, compounded semiannually. Which investment will reach your $100,000 goal sooner?

In Figure 6–28, you evaluate Alternative 1 in column B. In cell B8, the function @CTERM(B7,B3,B4) shows that 69.66 compounding periods are needed to grow your $50,000 *PV* in cell B3 to a $100,000 *FV* in cell B4, when you use a 1% monthly compounded *interest rate* in cell B7. The formula in cell B10, +B8/B9, divides 69.66 by 12 to convert these monthly periods to 5.81 years. However, in cell C8, @CTERM(C7,C3,C4) returns 11.66 compounding periods when you use a 6.125% semiannual *interest rate* in cell C7 to match the compounding period of this investment. In cell C10, the formula +C8/C9 divides 11.66 by 2 to convert these semiannual periods to 5.83 years. This analysis indicates that you should invest in Alternative 1, since it reaches your $100,000 goal sooner than Alternative 2.

Calculating the Interest Rate of an Investment: @RATE

1-2-3-/G's @RATE function calculates the *implied* periodic interest rate an *initial investment* earns to reach a specified future value. Mathematically, the compound implied rate is equal to

$$\text{Compound Interest Rate} = (FV/PV)^{1/n} - 1$$

where *n* is the number of time periods over which interest is compounded. The form of 1-2-3/G's function is

@RATE(*FV,PV,number of compounding periods*)

All of your arguments in the @RATE function must be entered as values, that is, a literal number, or a numeric formula, function, or cell reference that returns a value.

The *FV* argument is the value of the investment at the end of all compounding time periods. The *PV* is the single investment made at the beginning of the investment period. Enter both of these arguments as positive, or both as negative, even though *PV* is a cash outflow (investment), and *FV* an inflow. Your *number of compounding periods* argument is the number of *equal* periods for which interest is compounded. For example, if your investment returns a specified future value in 1.5 years, then the number of *equal* compounding

123G.EXE (69.4) Ready

File Edit Worksheet Range Copy... Move... Print Graph Data Utility Quit... Help

A:B8 @CTERM(B7,B3,B4)

(F2) FIN11.WG1

A	A	B	C	D	E
1		Alternative 1	Alternative 2		
2		----------	----------		
3	Investment	$50,000	$50,000		
4	Future Value Desired	$100,000	$100,000		
5	Annual Interest Rate	12.00%	12.25%		
6	Compounding Occurs	Monthly	Semi-Annually		
7	Interest Rate Per Compounding Period	1.00%	6.125%		
8	@CTERM returns	-69.66	-11.66		
9	Conversion Factor	12	2		
10	Number of years to reach FV	-5.81	-5.83		
11					

FIGURE 6–28 Using @CTERM to evaluate investments

periods is 3. The @RATE function returns the interest rate for *one* period of compounding.

Remember, when you use @RATE:

- Only one investment is made, which occurs on the first day of the investment period.
- Enter both *PV* and *FV* using the same sign.
- Interest is earned at the *end* of each equal time period, and immediately reinvested at your calculated @RATE value until the day the future value is achieved.
- @RATE returns an *interest rate* for *one* time period over which interest is compounded, which you may want to convert to an annual rate.

The @RATE function is commonly used to calculate implied compound interest rates of zero-coupon bonds, compound rates of returns of equity investments, and implied compound growth rates for sales, profits, and other financial indicators. For example, suppose you purchased 1,000 shares of two stocks on January 1, 1987, each for $10 a share. You sell Stock 1 for $40,000 on December 31, 1988. You sell Stock 2 on June 30, 1989 for $70,000. Which stock earned a greater annualized return?

As shown cell B8 of Figure 6–29 @RATE(B6,B4,B8) returns a 100% compounded return for Stock 1 when you use a $40,000 *FV* in cell B6, a $10,000 *PV* in cell B4, and 2 for the *number of compounding periods* in cell B8. The compounding period is one year. So, the annualized return realized by this investment is 100%. However, in cell C8, @RATE(C6,C4,C8) computes a 47.58% compounded return per period for Stock 2. Since this stock was held for 2.5 years, or 5 six-month periods, 5 is used for *number of compounding periods* in cell C8. Thus, the annualized return for Stock 2 is calculated as 95.15% in cell C11. So Stock 1 yields the greater annualized return.

Note

> To calculate the rate returned by an annuity or unequal cash flows, use the @IRR function discussed below.

Net Present Value: @NPV

The *Net Present Value* (NPV) is the value today of a stream of future cash flows discounted at some rate. Mathematically, NPV is equal to

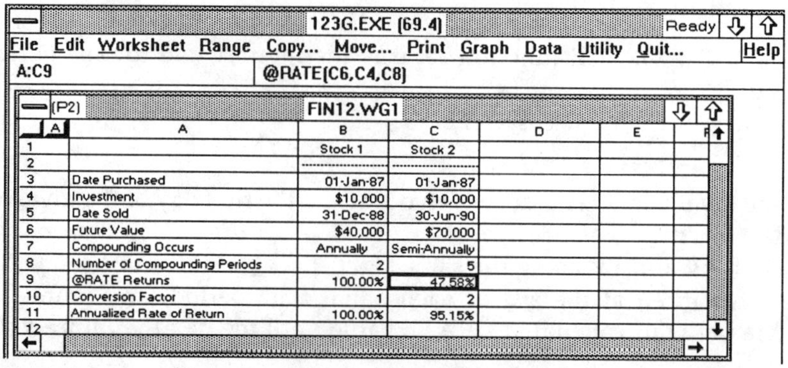

123G.EXE (69.4) Ready

File Edit Worksheet Range Copy... Move... Print Graph Data Utility Quit... Help

A:C9 @RATE(C6,C4,C8)

(P2) FIN12.WG1

	A	B	C	D	E
1		Stock 1	Stock 2		
2					
3	Date Purchased	01-Jan-87	01-Jan-87		
4	Investment	$10,000	$10,000		
5	Date Sold	31-Dec-88	30-Jun-90		
6	Future Value	$40,000	$70,000		
7	Compounding Occurs	Annually	Semi-Annually		
8	Number of Compounding Periods	2	5		
9	@RATE Returns	100.00%	47.58%		
10	Conversion Factor	1	2		
11	Annualized Rate of Return	100.00%	95.15%		

FIGURE 6–29 Using @RATE to find the implied return of two investments

$$NPV = \sum \frac{\text{Cash Inflows - Cash Outflows}}{(1 + \text{discount rate})^{-n}} - \text{Initial Investment}$$

where n is the number of time periods over which the cash flows occur. The NPV equation includes an initial investment on the first day of the investment period, and allows *unequal* cash flows, each occurring at the *end* of equal time periods. 1-2-3/G's form of this function is

@NPV(*discount rate,cash flow range*)

Your *cash flow range* argument is the stream of unequal or equal cash flows that, using the *discount rate*, are discounted back to the first day of the investment period. These cash flows are entered into a two- or three-dimensional *continuous* range, where each cell represents a payment date, all time periods between payments are *equal*, and these cash flows occur at the *end* of each equal time period. The first cell in this range represents the first cash flow at the *end* of the first period, *not* your initial investment. Enter each cash flow, except for any initial investment, in a separate cell in your range, cash inflows as positive, and cash outflows (investments) as negative. Include a cell in this range for each equal time period, even if no cash flow occurs.

Enter your *cash flow range* in the @NPV function as either a range address or a range name. You can now use a three-dimensional *range*, and even a range in another 1-2-3/G file, but you cannot use a collection, even if it is entered using a defined range name. Each cell in your *cash flow range* must contain a value—a literal number, or a numeric formula, function, or cell reference that returns a value. The @NPV function evaluates any blank cell or any cell containing a label as equal to a 0 cash flow for that period.

The *discount rate* is the return you require, given the risk of the investment being evaluated. Your *discount rate* argument conveys to 1-2-3/G the length of each time period between payments in your *cash flow range*. If you use a yearly discount rate, 1-2-3/G assumes that the time period between cash flows (each cell) is one year. So the discount rate must be consistent with the time periods used in your *cash flow range*. Enter your *discount rate* as a value in percentage or decimal form.

1-2-3/G's @NPV function differs from the NPV mathematical equation since it does *not* include an initial investment value. So you must subtract any initial investment from the @NPV result for your other cash flows.

When you use @NPV, remember:

- Any initial investment is *not* included in *cash flow range*, but is subtracted from the result of @NPV.
- Enter cash inflows as positive, investments as negative.
- Cash flows can be unequal, but all cash flows occur at the *end* of each time period.
- *All* time periods between these cash flows must be equal, and *each* time period must be represented by a cell in *cash flow range*, even when no cash flow occurs.
- Use a *discount rate* for *one* time period, which is constant over the investment period
- All cash inflows are immediately reinvested at the *discount rate* until the end of the investment period.

Evaluating the Result of @NPV

The *discount rate* used in the @NPV function is the rate you require to compensate for the risk of an investment. A negative NPV indicates that the investment should not be made. If the NPV is positive, then the investment should be made. In actuality, in a world of scarce funds, an investment that yields a positive NPV is usually evaluated and ranked against other positive Net Present Value projects.

An Example

Suppose you are asked to invest $200,000 in a company in two stages. The first $100,000 is needed on January 1, 1991 to finance a new product introduction, and the second $100,000 is needed on December 31, 1991 for the second phase of this product roll-out. In return, you will receive three payments of $100,000 every six months beginning on June 30, 1992, then $200,000 on December 30, 1994. You have analyzed the risk of this venture and decided that 18% is an appropriate annual discount rate. Should you make this investment?

You have created the worksheet in Figure 6–30 to analyze this opportunity. The *cash flow range*, C6..H6, which excludes your initial investment, uses six-month time periods. Notice that in the period ending June 30, 1992 no cash flow occurs. Since each time period is six months, you use the six-month *discount rate*, 9% in cell B10. In cell B12, @NPV(B10,C6..H6) returns $248,139. But in cell

B14, the NPV of the investment is $148,139, after you have subtracted the initial $100,000 investment from the value @NPV returns. Since $148,139 is a positive NPV, you should make the investment.

Note

> As shown in Figure 6–30, you *can* use the @NPV function when cash flows occur in *unequal* time periods. In this case, some cash flows occur annually, while others occur every six months. The range C6..H6 uses a time period, six months, that is the *lowest common denominator* for all time periods. Any time period when no cash flow occurs, such as in cell C6, is represented as 0 cash flow. The @NPV *discount rate* is a six-month rate to reflect the six-month time period between cash flows.

Internal Rate of Return: @IRR

1-2-3/G's @IRR function calculates the *internal rate of return (IRR)* of an investment. The IRR is the discount rate, in percentage form, for which the NPV mathematical equation is 0. That is, IRR is the discount rate when the present value of cash inflows equals the present value of cash outflows. Therefore, IRR can be expressed mathematically as

$$0 = \text{NPV} = \sum \frac{\text{Cash Inflows - Cash Outflows}}{(1 + \text{IRR})^{-n}} - \text{Initial Investment}$$

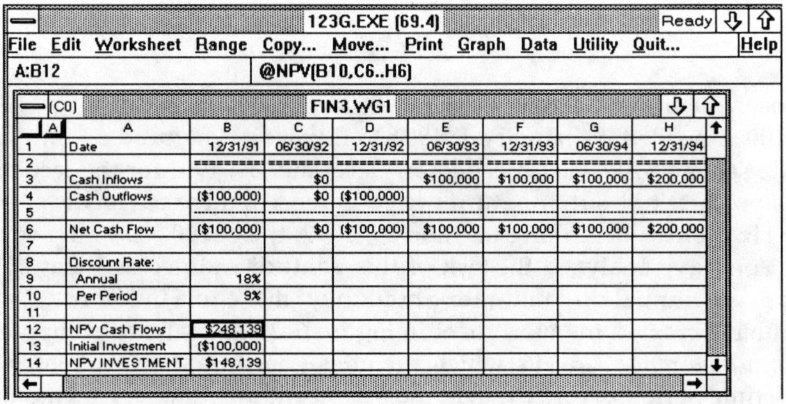

123G.EXE [69.4] Ready

File Edit Worksheet Range Copy... Move... Print Graph Data Utility Quit... Help

A:B12 @NPV(B10,C6..H6)

(C0) FIN3.WG1

	A	B	C	D	E	F	G	H
1	Date	12/31/91	06/30/92	12/31/92	06/30/93	12/31/93	06/30/94	12/31/94
2		=========	=========	=========	=========	=========	=========	=========
3	Cash Inflows		$0		$100,000	$100,000	$100,000	$200,000
4	Cash Outflows	($100,000)	$0	($100,000)				
5		---------	---------	---------	---------	---------	---------	---------
6	Net Cash Flow	($100,000)	$0	($100,000)	$100,000	$100,000	$100,000	$200,000
7								
8	Discount Rate:							
9	Annual	18%						
10	Per Period	9%						
11								
12	NPV Cash Flows	$248,139						
13	Initial Investment	($100,000)						
14	NPV INVESTMENT	$148,139						

FIGURE 6–30 Using @NPV with unequal cash flows

where *n* is the number of equal time periods over which the cash flows occur.

Traditionally, you would calculate an IRR by trial and error, entering guesses into the NPV mathematical equation, then manually calculating the NPV until you found the IRR for which the NPV equalled 0. 1-2-3/G's @IRR function performs this iterative process for you. The form of this function is

```
@IRR(rate of return guess,cash flow range)
```

Your *rate of return guess* is the value the @IRR function uses to calculate the actual IRR. Enter your *rate of return guess* as a value in percentage or decimal form. You can use a literal number, or a numeric formula, function, or cell reference that returns a value. In most cases, you should use a value between 0 and 1.

Your *cash flow range* argument is the stream of unequal or equal cash flows that the calculated IRR discounts back to the first day of the investment period. Enter these cash flows into a two- or three-dimensional *continuous* range. In your *cash flow range,* the first cell represents the first day of the investment period, while all other cells represent the *ending* day of a time period, where all time periods are *equal*. Enter cash inflows as positive values, and cash outflows (investments) as negative values. So, in the first cell, enter the initial investment as negative. In the second cell, enter the first cash flow at the *end* of the first period, then all other cash flows in this manner. Remember to include a cell in this range for each time period, even if no cash flow occurs.

Enter your *cash flow range* in the @IRR function as either a range address or a range name. You can now use a three-dimensional *range,* and even a range in another 1-2-3/G file, but you cannot use a collection, even if it is entered using a defined range name. Each cell in your *cash flow range* must evaluate to a value. The @IRR function evaluates any blank cell or any cell containing a label as equal to a 0 cash flow for that period.

The @IRR function uses your *rate of return guess,* and, in 30 or fewer iterations, tries to calculate an IRR value to within .0000001. If successful, this function returns the IRR value for *one* time period of your *cash flow range*; if unsuccessful, it returns ERR.

An Example

Suppose you are again evaluating the potential investment in Figure 6–30, but you want to calculate the IRR of this investment. Figure 6–31 shows how IRR is computed for these cash flows. The *cash flow range* in B6..H6, which includes your initial investment, uses six-month time periods. Notice that in the period ending June 30, 1992 no cash flow occurs. In cell B9, @IRR(B8,B6..H6) returns 27.67%. But this IRR value is for *one* six-month time period of your cash flow range. So the *annual* IRR for this investment is 55.34% in cell B12.

123G.EXE (69.4) Ready

File Edit Worksheet Range Copy... Move... Print Graph Data Utility Quit... Help

A:B9 @IRR(B8,B6..H6)

(P2) FIN4.WG1

A	A	B	C	D	E	F	G	H
1	Date	12/31/91	06/30/92	12/31/92	06/30/93	12/31/93	06/30/94	12/31/94
2		=========	=========	=========	=========	=========	=========	=========
3	Cash Inflows		$0		$100,000	$100,000	$100,000	$200,000
4	Cash Outflows	($100,000)	$0	($100,000)				
5		---------	---------	---------	---------	---------	---------	---------
6	Net Cash Flow	($100,000)	$0	($100,000)	$100,000	$100,000	$100,000	$200,000
7								
8	Discount Rate Guess	10.00%						
9	IRR returns	27.67%						
10		2						
11		---------						
12	Annual IRR	55.34%						

FIGURE 6–31 Calculating the IRR for a range of cash flows

Evaluating the Result of @IRR

The @IRR function returns a *rate of return* value. This value is usually compared to a "hurdle rate" or minimum return, to determine whether this investment should be made. Like the NPV discount rate, the required rate of return should be evaluated so that the risk of an investment is taken into account. In the example above, suppose you require an 18% annualized rate of return for an investment with this type of risk. Since this particular project has an IRR of 55.34%, you should certainly invest in this venture.

To use the @IRR function properly, you must be able to evaluate a result returned by @IRR and interpret whether it is a reasonable value for your *cash flow range.* In some cases, @IRR returns ERR or incorrect values for certain cash flow ranges.

When @IRR Returns Incorrect Values

The @IRR function returns *correct* IRR values for a "normal" stream of cash flows: one or more time periods of net cash outflows, followed by a series of cash inflows. As you know, if the @IRR function does not converge on a value within 30 iterations, it returns ERR. This occurs when

- Your rate of return guess is too far from the actual IRR value.
- Your *cash flow range* is not "normal."

The @IRR function may return a suspect IRR value instead of ERR for the following "nonnormal" cash flows that

- Include a $0 initial investment.
- Change sign more than once, such as when a later investment is required.
- Include relatively large outflows near the end of the investment period.
- Have an IRR value less than 0% or greater than 100%.

An Example When @IRR Returns an Incorrect Value

Let's examine a situation when @IRR returns suspect values. Suppose you are evaluating an investment that has the cash flows in Figure 6–32. An initial $100,000 investment is required, as well as a $600,000 investment later in the investment period; so this cash flow stream changes sign more than once. In addition, the cash outflows exceed expected inflows during the time period analyzed, so the rate of return is obviously negative. Depending on the IRR guess used in row 5, the @IRR function in row 6 returns 0, ERR, or -60.02%.

Use the @NPV function to confirm the correct IRR value. In row 7, the @NPV function uses the IRR value returned by @IRR in row 6 as the *discount rate* argument. As shown in cell D7, @NPV(D6,C3..G3)+B3 returns a NPV of 0 when IRR is -60.02%. (Remember, you should not include the initial investment in *cash flow range*. Rather, add the initial negative investment in cell B3 to the result the @NPV function returns.) So an IRR of -62% is the correct IRR of the correct cash flow range.

Remember, when you use @IRR:

- Enter cash inflows as positive, investments as negative.
- An initial investment is entered separately in the *first* cell of your *cash flow range*.
- Cash flows can be unequal, but *all* cash flows, except your initial investment, occur at the *end* of each time period.
- *All* time periods between these cash flows must be equal, and *each* time period must be represented by a cell in *cash flow range*, even when no cash flow occurs.
- All cash inflows are immediately reinvested at your *IRR* until the end of the investment period.

123G.EXE (69.4) Ready

File Edit Worksheet Range Copy... Move... Print Graph Data Utility Quit... Help

A:D7 @NPV(D6,C3..G3)+B3

(C0) FIN5.WG1

A	A	B	C	D	E	F	G	H
1	Date	12/31/91	12/31/92	12/31/93	12/31/94	12/31/95	12/31/96	
2		=========	=========	=========	=========	=========	=========	
3	Net Cash Flow	($100,000)	$100,000	$100,000	$200,000	($600,000)	$200,000	
4								
5	IRR Guess	0%	20%	40%	60%	80%	100%	
6	IRR returns	0.00%	ERR	-60.02%	-60.02%	ERR	-60.02%	
7	NPV using IRR value	($100,000)	ERR	$0				
8								

FIGURE 6–32 Cash Flows for which @IRR returns multiple values

- @IRR returns an IRR for *one* time period, which you may need to convert to an annual rate.
- The @IRR function returns suspect results for some *cash flow ranges,* so check the value @IRR returns by using it in the @NPV function to see if it returns an NPV of $0.

DEPRECIATION FUNCTIONS

1-2-3/G offers the four functions shown in Table 6–11 for calculating depreciation. If you have used a previous release of 1-2-3/G, you'll notice that 1-2-3/G now includes a new depreciation function, @VDB, which allows you to calculate depreciation using different MACRS (Modified Accelerated Cost Recovery System) depreciation methods. You can specify the rate of declining-balance depreciation, as well as whether you want to switch to a tax straight-line depreciation method when it exceeds the declining-balance depreciation expense.

Using Partial-Year Conventions

In many cases you will want to use a *partial-year convention* with 1-2-3/G's depreciation functions. The most commonly used, the *half-year convention,* assumes that all new assets are placed in service on July 1. The first year depreciation expense is one-half of a full year's depreciation. An asset is then depreciated over one more year than its classification, where the remaining one-half year depreciation is expensed in the last year. For example, a five-year asset is depreciated over six years. This is an important concept to understand when you use 1-2-3/G's depreciation functions to calculate tax depreciation.

Straight-Line Depreciation: @SLN

Use 1-2-3/G's @SLN function to calculate straight-line depreciation. This depreciation method, which allocates an equal portion of the cost of an asset over each period, computes depreciation for each period as

Depreciation/Period = (Cost – Salvage Value)/Periods of Useful Life

TABLE 6–11 1-2-3/G's Depreciation Functions

Function	Calculates
@SLN	Straight-line depreciation
@SYDS	Sum-of-the-years'-digits depreciation
@DDB	Double-declining-balance depreciation
@VDB	Variable-declining-balance depreciation, switching to tax straight-line.

The form of 1-2-3/G's function is

```
@SLN(cost,salvage value,life)
```

Your *cost* argument is the total of the purchase price and installation costs, including freight-in. The *salvage value* argument is the estimated asset value at the end of the depreciation period.

The *life* argument is the total number of *equal periods* over which an asset is depreciated. If you use a half-year convention, *life* is the number of six-month periods. For example, for a three-year asset, use 6 as *life* (6 six-month periods). The @SLN function calculates the depreciation expense for *one* time period of your *life* argument. So you must use a depreciation function for each period or year for which you expense depreciation.

Enter all of these arguments as values—a literal number, or a numeric formula, function, or cell reference that returns a value.

Using @SLN with the Half-Year Convention

Suppose you purchase and install an asset for $20,000 on June 30, 1990. This asset has a three-year life and an estimated $2,500 salvage value at the end of this period. You are computing tax depreciation (which uses a half-year convention), so in Figure 6–33 you expense depreciation over four years. You calculate depreciation in the first year using a $20,000 *cost* in cell B1, a $2,500 *salvage value* in cell B2, and 6 six-month periods as your *life* argument in cell B3. Since only a half-year's depreciation is expensed in the first year, 1990, and in the last year, 1994, a $2,917 depreciation expense for these periods is calculated using @SLN($B1,$B2,$B3). (Mixed addressing is used to keep these arguments constant when this function is copied across row 8.) In 1991 and 1992, a full-year's depreciation is returned by @SLN($B1,$B2,$B3)*2. Notice that the fully depreciated asset balance in cell E9 contains the estimated salvage value.

Tip: Using @SLN to calculate amortization

You can use the @SLN function to calculate amortization. Suppose you have incurred start-up costs, which are amortized monthly over 60 months. Simply use a *life* of 60, then multiply the results of your @SLN function for one month by the number of months amortization is expensed in each year.

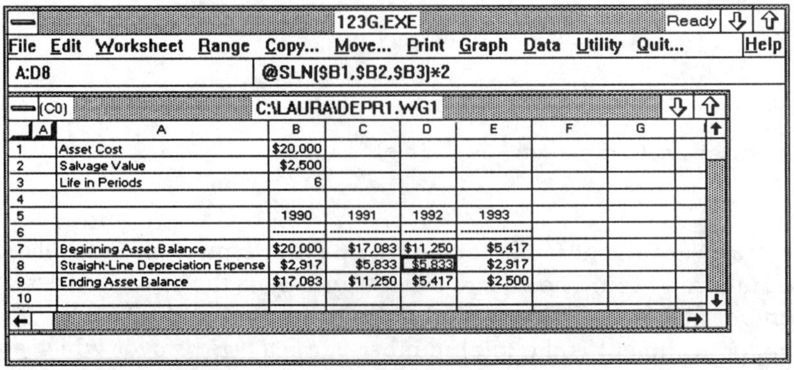

123G.EXE Ready

File Edit Worksheet Range Copy... Move... Print Graph Data Utility Quit... Help

A:D8 @SLN($B1,$B2,$B3)*2

(C0) C:\LAURA\DEPR1.WG1

A	A	B	C	D	E	F	G
1	Asset Cost	$20,000					
2	Salvage Value	$2,500					
3	Life in Periods	6					
4							
5		1990	1991	1992	1993		
6		----------	----------	----------	----------		
7	Beginning Asset Balance	$20,000	$17,083	$11,250	$5,417		
8	Straight-Line Depreciation Expense	$2,917	$5,833	$5,833	$2,917		
9	Ending Asset Balance	$17,083	$11,250	$5,417	$2,500		
10							

FIGURE 6–33 Using @SLN with a half-year convention

Note

Current tax laws allow you to switch to straight-line depreciation in the first tax year that it yields a larger expense than MACRS. However, this MACRS straight-line depreciation is *not* conventional straight-line depreciation. So you cannot easily use @SLN to figure straight-line depreciation after switching from MACRS. However, 1-2-3/G's @VDB function correctly figures MACRS straight-line depreciation expense after switching from a declining-balance method.

Sum-of-the-Years'-Digits Depreciation: @SYD

The *Sum-of-the-years'-digits* depreciation method allocates a larger depreciation expense in the earlier years of depreciation. The depreciation per period is calculated as

$$\text{SYD per period} = (\text{cost - salvage value}) * \frac{(n - p + 1)}{(n * (n + 1)/2)}$$

where *n* is the number of periods of useful life and *p* is the specific depreciation period for which depreciation is being calculated. The depreciation *rate* each period, $(n - p + 1)/(n * n + 1)/2)$, is equal to the Remaining years of useful life divided by the Sum of the years of useful life. For an asset with a two-year useful life, the denominator $(n * (n + 1)/2)$ is equal to $2 * (3/2)$ or 3 (1 + 2, or the sum-of-the years' digits). The numerator in the first year of depreciation, $(n - p + 1)$, is equal to $(2 - 1 + 1)$ or 2. Therefore, 2/3 or 66.67% of the original cost of the asset is depreciated in the first year.

1-2-3/G's form of this function is

@SYD(*cost,salvage value,life,depreciation period*)

Your *cost* argument is the total of the purchase price and installation costs, including freight-in. The *salvage value* argument is the estimated asset value at the end of the depreciation period.

Your *life* argument is the total number of *equal periods* over which an asset is depreciated. Remember, if you use a half-year convention, *life* is the number of six-month periods. @SYD calculates the depreciation expense for the time period you specify by your *depreciation period* argument. For example, if you use 6, @SYD calculates the depreciation for period 6.

Enter all of these arguments as values—a literal number, or a numeric formula, function, or cell reference that returns a value.

Suppose in Figure 6–34, you want to calculate SYD depreciation for a three-year asset purchased and installed for $20,000 on June 30, 1990, which has an estimated $2,500 salvage value. For each period of depreciation, you use a $20,000 *cost*, a $2,500 *salvage value* and a *life* of three years. The only argument which varies is the *depreciation period* shown in row 7. So in cell D9, @SYD($B1,$B2,$B3,D7) calculates a depreciation expense in year three of $2,917. (Mixed addressing is used to keep these arguments constant when this function is copied across row 9.) Once again, the fully-depreciated asset balance in cell E10 equals the estimated salvage value.

123G.EXE Ready
File Edit Worksheet Range Copy... Move... Print Graph Data Utility Quit... Help
A:D9 @SYD($B1,$B2,$B3,D7)
(C0) C:\LAURA\DEPR2.WG1

A	A	B	C	D	E	F	G
1	Asset Cost	$20,000					
2	Salvage Value	$2,500					
3	Life in Periods	3					
4							
5		1990	1991	1992			
6		----------	----------	----------			
7	Beginning Period	1	2	3			
8	Beginning Asset Balance	$20,000	$11,250	$5,417			
9	SYD Depreciation Expense	$8,750	$5,833	$2,917			
10	Ending Asset Balance	$11,250	$5,417	$2,500			

FIGURE 6–34 Calculating depreciation using @SYD

Double-Declining-Balance Depreciation: @DDB

The DDB (double declining balance) method also allocates a larger depreciation expense in the earlier years of an asset's life. The DDB depreciation per period is calculated as

DDB per period=(2/useful life in periods) * remaining book value

When you use the DDB method, the depreciation rate, 2 divided by the useful life in periods, remains constant. However, the *remaining book value varies* (original cost - accumulated depreciation), and decreases each period by the previous period's depreciation expense. For this reason, the DDB formula never fully depreciates an asset. For example, for a three-year asset, depreciation in the third year is calculated as (2/3) * remaining book value. So you *always* use a "plug" value in the final depreciation period to fully write off the depreciable portion of an asset. (The "plug" value is equal to the original cost less the accumulated depreciation for the previous years.)

1-2-3/G's form of this function is

```
@DDB(cost,salvage value,life,depreciation period)
```

Your *cost* argument is the total of the purchase price and installation costs, including freight-in. The *salvage value* argument is the estimated asset value at the end of the depreciation period.

Your *life* argument is the total number of *equal periods* over which an asset is depreciated. Remember, if you use a half-year convention, *life* is a six-month period.

The @DDB function calculates the depreciation expense for the time period you specify by your *depreciation period* argument. For example, for a three-year asset depreciated over three years, you would use 1 as your *depreciation period* argument for the first year, 2 in the second year, and 3 in the third year.

Enter each of these arguments as a value—a literal number, or a numeric formula, function, or cell reference that returns a value.

Calculating DDB Depreciation using the Half-Year Convention

Let's again return to the example of a three-year asset purchased and installed for $20,000 on June 30,1990, with a $2,500 salvage value. Your company uses the half-year convention and the DDB method of depreciation. You need to calculate the yearly depreciation expense for this asset.

As shown in Figure 6–35, you use 1-2-3/G's @DDB function to calculate the depreciation. For each period of depreciation, you use a $20,000 *cost* in cell B1, and a $2,500 *salvage value* in cell B2. Since you use the half-year convention, you will depreciate this asset over four years, six months in year 1 and six months in year 4. So you need to use a *life* argument of 6 six-month periods in cell B3. In Figure 6–34, for each year, use the following *depreciation period* arguments and @DDB function:

Year	Depreciation Period	@DDB Function
1990	1	@DDB(B1,B2,B3,1)
1991	2 and 3	@DDB(B1,B2,B3,2)+@DDB(B1,B2,B3,3)
1992	4 and 5	@DDB(B1,B2,B3,4)+@DDB(B1,B2,B3,5)
1993	6	@DDB(B1,B2,B3,6)

The only argument that varies is the *depreciation period* shown in row 5. So in cell D7, @DDB(B1,B2,B3,D5) calculates a $2,693 depreciation expense for *depreciation period* 3 in cell D5. In cell C7, @DDB(B1,B2,B3,D4) returns a $4,444 depreciation expense for period 2. In cell C13, +C7+D7 returns the sum of $4,444+$2,693, or a $7,407 depreciation expense for 1991. Notice that in cell G7, the @DDB function automatically calculates the $134 "plug" value in the last depreciation period.

Notice that in row 10, the *constant* depreciation rate per period is the depreciation expense in row 7 divided by the *remaining* book value in row 6. Row 14 shows this same depreciation rate for each *year* of depreciation. For example, in the first year, DDB depreciation is only a half-year expense. So cell B14 contains the formula +B10, and returns the DDB rate of 33.33%. However, the second year is a full year of depreciation. So cell C14 contains the formula +C10+D10, which calculates the DDB rate for the second year of depreciation as 66.67% of adjusted book value. Likewise, cell D14 contains the formula +E10+F10 and also returns a DDB rate of 66.67%. In the final year this is a "plug" rate of 100% to fully depreciate the asset.

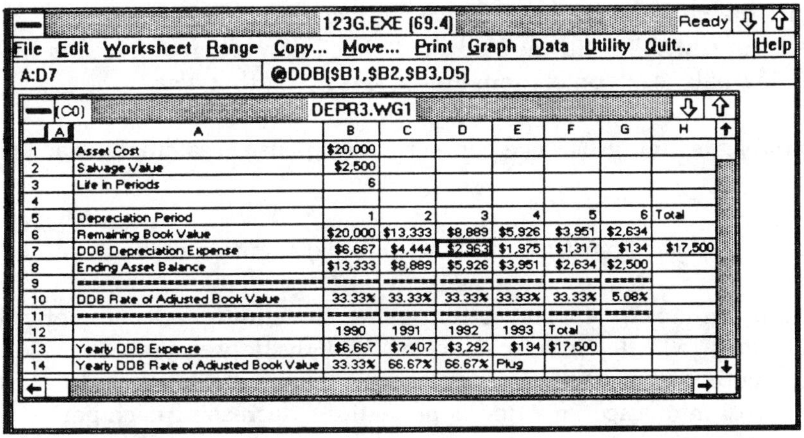

123G.EXE (69.4) Ready

File Edit Worksheet Range Copy... Move... Print Graph Data Utility Quit... Help

A:D7 @DDB($B1,$B2,$B3,D5)

(C0) DEPR3.WG1

A	A	B	C	D	E	F	G	H
1	Asset Cost	$20,000						
2	Salvage Value	$2,500						
3	Life in Periods	6						
4								
5	Depreciation Period	1	2	3	4	5	6	Total
6	Remaining Book Value	$20,000	$13,333	$8,889	$5,926	$3,951	$2,634	
7	DDB Depreciation Expense	$6,667	$4,444	$2,963	$1,975	$1,317	$134	$17,500
8	Ending Asset Balance	$13,333	$8,889	$5,926	$3,951	$2,634	$2,500	
9	================================	======	======	======	======	======	======	
10	DDB Rate of Adjusted Book Value	33.33%	33.33%	33.33%	33.33%	33.33%	5.08%	
11	================================	======	======	======	======	======	======	
12		1990	1991	1992	1993	Total		
13	Yearly DDB Expense	$6,667	$7,407	$3,292	$134	$17,500		
14	Yearly DDB Rate of Adjusted Book Value	33.33%	66.67%	66.67%	Plug			

FIGURE 6–35 Using @DDB with the half-year convention

Caution

> In most cases, for a $0 salvage value, or a salvage value less than 5% of *cost*, and for relatively small asset values, @DDB does *not* automatically calculate the DDB "plug" value in the final year. Instead, use 1-2-3/G's new @VDB function using a 200% declining balance. Or be sure to sum the depreciation expense to make sure @DDB fully calculates the correct depreciation.

Note

> MACRS assumes a half-year convention, $0 salvage value, and switches to straight-line depreciation when it exceeds declining-balance depreciation. @DDB has trouble calculating depreciation for a $0 salvage value and does not switch to straight line. So for 200% declining-balance MACRS depreciation, use @VDB instead of @DDB to calculate MACRS depreciation.

Declining-Balance Depreciation: @VDB

The @DDB function, which uses the double-declining-balance method of depreciation, is a specific case of 1-2-3/G's @VDB function. The @VDB function allows you to calculate MACRS depreciation for different asset classes. You can

- Specify the *rate* of declining-balance depreciation.
- Switch to a MACRS SL method of depreciation when it exceeds MACRS declining-balance depreciation, unless specified otherwise.

A variable declining-balance depreciation expense is calculated each period as

VDB per period = (*rate*/useful life in periods) * remaining book value

where *rate* is the rate of depreciation using a declining-balance method. For example, for a 150% declining-balance method, the depreciation *rate* is 1.5. Like the DDB method, this rate remains constant while the *remaining book value varies* (original cost minus accumulated depreciation), decreasing each period by the previous period's depreciation expense. Once again, any VDB method never fully depreciates an asset. For example, for a three-year asset and a 150% declining balance method, depreciation in the third year is calculated as (1.5/3)

* remaining book value. This method *always* uses a "plug" value in the final period to fully expense the depreciable portion of an asset.

1-2-3/G's form of this function is

```
@VDB(cost,salvage value,life,start-period,end-period,
[depreciation rate],[SL-switch])
```

Enter each of these arguments as a value—a literal number, or a numeric formula, function, or cell reference that returns a value.

The *cost* argument is the total of the purchase price and installation costs, including freight-in. The *salvage value* argument is the estimated asset value at the end of the depreciation period.

Time Period Arguments

To calculate MACRS depreciation, @VDB uses three arguments to specify the period for which depreciation is being calculated. In the @VDB function, *life* is the total number of depreciation periods in *years*, even if you use the half-year convention. For a *specific* depreciation period, *start-period* is the beginning of the depreciation period, while *end-period* is the end of this depreciation period. The @VDB function calculates the depreciation expense for *one* time period you specify by your *start-period* and *end-period* arguments. So these arguments are different for *each* depreciation period.

Note

> MACRS assumes a $0 salvage value. If you use the @VDB function with a salvage value greater than $0 and a life argument of years, you will calculate the incorrect depreciation per period. However, suppose you have a three-year asset. If you use a life of 6 six-month periods and the corresponding start-period and end-period arguments, @VDB will calculate the correct depreciation per period.

Optional Arguments

The @VDB function has two optional arguments, the *depreciation rate* and the *SL-switch* argument. Use your *depreciation rate* argument to specify the declining-balance method you want. Use any value greater than 0. For example, use 1.75 for a 175% declining-balance method. If you do not include this argument in the @VDB function, @VDB calculates 200% declining balance depreciation like the @DDB function. However, you must include a *depreciation rate* argument if you want to include a *SL-switch* argument.

The *SL-switch* argument tells 1-2-3/G whether you want to switch to straight-line depreciation once MACRS straight-line depreciation exceeds MACRS declining-balance depreciation. *SL-switch* must be either 0 or 1. If *SL-switch* is 0, @VDB switches to straight-line when appropriate; if it is 1, @VDB simply calculates the declining-balance method of depreciation you specify. If you do not specify this argument, 1-2-3/G assumes a default value of 0 and switches to straight-line when appropriate.

Using @VDB Without Switching to Straight-Line

Suppose you want to calculate the depreciation per year of a $20,000 asset with $0 salvage value. For current tax laws, this equipment is a five-year class asset that is depreciated using a 200% declining-balance method and the half-year convention. You do not want to switch to straight-line depreciation. In Figure 6–36 you use a $20,000 *cost* in cell B1, a $0 *salvage value* in cell B2, a *life* of five years in cell B4, a *depreciation-rate* of 2 in cell B3, a *SL-switch* of 1 in cell B7, and the appropriate *start-period* and *end-period* arguments in rows 5 and 6.

In cell B9, the MACRS depreciation for the first year is calculated as $4,000 using the formula @VDB($B1,$B2,$B4,B5,B6,$B3,$B7). (Mixed addressing is used to keep all arguments constant except *start-period* and *end-period*, when this function is copied across row 9.) As shown in cell B13, this is equivalent to the remaining book value of $20,000 times the DDB rate of 20% (.5*(2/5)). The 20% DDB rate is for a half-year, so all other years use 40%—except for the final year, which is a "plug" rate or 100% of the remaining book value.

In row 9, similar @VDB functions are used to calculate the MACRS depreciation in the remaining years. The values returned all correspond to the DDB expense calculated in row 13. Notice that @VDB correctly calculates the "plug" value in the final year of depreciation.

123G.EXE — Ready

File Edit Worksheet Range Copy... Move... Print Graph Data Utility Quit... Help

A:B9 — @VDB($B1,$B2,$B4,B5,B6,$B3,$B7)

(C0) C:\LAURA\DEPR5.WG1

A	A	B	C	D	E	F	G	H
1	Cost	$20,000						
2	Salvage Value	$0						
3	Depreciation Rate	2						
4	Life	5						
5	Start-Period	0.0	0.5	1.5	2.5	3.5	4.5	
6	End-Period	0.5	1.5	2.5	3.5	4.5	5.0	
7	SL-switch	1						
8		Year 1	Year 2	Year 3	Year 4	Year 5	Year 6	Total
9	DDB Depreciation Expense	$4,000	$6,400	$3,840	$2,304	$1,382	$2,074	$20,000
10	======================	=======	=======	=======	=======	=======	=======	==========
11	Remaining Balance	$20,000	$16,000	$9,600	$5,760	$3,456	$2,074	
12	DDB Depreciation Rate	20.00%	40.00%	40.00%	40.00%	40.00%	100.00%	
13	DDB Depreciation Expense	$4,000	$6,400	$3,840	$2,304	$1,382	$2,074	
14	New Balance	$16,000	$9,600	$5,760	$3,456	$2,074	$0	

FIGURE 6–36 Using @VDB and a *SL-switch* of 1

Calculating MACRS Declining-Balance and Straight-Line Depreciation

If you are planning to use @VDB to calculate depreciation for tax purposes this section will help you understand all the intricacies of using the function in this way. This section discusses

- The basics of MACRS depreciation.
- Using @VDB to calculate MACRS declining-balance and straight-line depreciation.

THE BASICS OF MACRS DEPRECIATION At the time this book was written, current tax laws allowed you to switch to a straight-line method of depreciation for the first tax year that this method yields a larger expense than MACRS declining-balance expense. Table 6–12, taken from 1989 IRS publications, shows the applicable declining-balance rate for each class of property, and the first year that the straight-line method yields an equal or greater deduction.

However, your MACRS deduction using straight-line depreciation is calculated differently than the @SLN function. MACRS straight-line depreciation is calculated using the *remaining book value* (original cost minus accumulated depreciation), which decreases each period by the previous period's depreciation expense. Furthermore, the straight-line rate per period is not constant, but *increases* each period as a percentage of the remaining book value.

Note

> MACRS is a relatively recent tax depreciation method. As a result the @VDB function may not be appropriate for assets placed in service before MACRS went into effect.

TABLE 6–12 Depreciation Periods when MACRS Straight Line Is More Advantageous Than Declining Balance

Class	Declining-balance rate	Year when SL more advantageous
3	66.67%	3
5	40.00%	4
7	28.57%	5
10	20.00%	7
15	10.00%	7
20	7.50%	9

USING @VDB TO CALCULATE MACRS DECLINING BALANCE AND STRAIGHT-LINE DEPRECIATION Now that you know the basics of MACRS depreciation, this section discusses how the @VDB function

- Calculates MACRS declining-balance depreciation.
- Evaluates MACRS declining-balance and straight-line depreciation.
- Switches to MACRS straight-line depreciation when it exceeds declining-balance depreciation.

Note

If you use @VDB to calculate tax depreciation, make sure you check your results against current tax publications.

Let's return to our example of a five-year, $20,000 asset. You want to calculate MACRS depreciation for this asset. Remember, MACRS assumes a $0 salvage value, a half-year convention, and switches to straight-line in year four. So in Figure 6–37 you calculate the MACRS depreciation in year one as @VDB(B1,B2,B4,B5,B6,B3,B8). This is the same formula used in the previous example, except that your SL-switch argument in cell B8 is 0. All other depreciation expenses in row 10 are calculated in a similar manner.

When *SL-switch* is 0, this @VDB function should return a MACRS straight-line depreciation when it exceeds the double-declining-balance depreciation. How does @VDB accomplish this? First, let's compute the tax straight-line deprecia-

123G.EXE Ready

File Edit Worksheet Range Copy... Move... Print Graph Data Utility Quit... Help

A:B10 @VDB($B1,$B2,$B4,B5,B6,$B3,$B8)

(C0) C:\LAURA\DEPR6.WG1

	A	B	C	D	E	F	G
1	Cost	$20,000					
2	Salvage Value	$0					
3	Depreciation Rate	2					
4	Life	5					
5	Start-Period	0.0	0.5	1.5	2.5	3.5	4.5
6	End-Period	0.5	1.5	2.5	3.5	4.5	5.0
7	==================	==========	==========	==========	==========	==========	==========
8	SL-switch	0					
9		Year 1	Year 2	Year 3	Year 4	Year 5	Year 6
10	Depreciation Expense	$4,000	$6,400	$3,840	$2,304	$2,304	$1,152
11	==================	==========	==========	==========	==========	==========	==========
12	MACRS % of COST	0.2	0.32	0.192	0.1152	0.1152	0.0576
13	MACRS Expense	$4,000	$6,400	$3,840	$2,304	$2,304	$1,152

FIGURE 6–37 Using @VDB to calculate MACRS depreciation

tion for this asset, then compare it to double-declining-balance depreciation. This is shown in Figure 6–38.

MACRS straight-line depreciation uses a rate for each period equal to

$$\text{Straight-Line Rate} = \frac{\text{Years of Depreciation in Period}}{\text{Years of Life Remaining at Beginning of Period}}$$

For example, for a five-year asset, the first year of MACRS straight-line depreciation rate is 10% (.5/5) as shown in cell B3, since a half-year convention is used. But the second year, the depreciation percentage is calculated as (1/4.5) or 22.22% in cell C3, since only .5 years of depreciation has been expensed in the previous year. Each year this rate increases as the number of years remaining decreases.

MACRS and @VDB calculate straight-line depreciation per period as

$$\text{SL Depreciation Per Period} = \text{Rate Per Period} * \text{Remaining Book Value}$$

where remaining book value is the asset value after *either* the declining-balance rate *or* the straight-line rate has been applied. MACRS depreciation, and the @VDB function, switches to straight-line in the period when it is greater than the declining-balance depreciation.

As shown in Figure 6–38, straight-line depreciation is calculated in row 8 as the straight-line rate in row 7 times the remaining book value in row 5. DDB depreciation is calculated in row 11 as the DDB rate in row 10 times the remaining book value in row 5. These DDB expenses are the same values

123G.EXE (69.4) Ready

File Edit Worksheet Range Copy... Move... Print Graph Data Utility Quit... Help

A:E13 @IF(E8>E11,E8,E11)

(C0) DEPR7.WG1

A	A	B	C	D	E	F	G
1	Numer of Years	0.5	1	1	1	1	0.5
2	Years Remaining	5	4.5	3.5	2.5	1.5	1
3	SL Depreciation Rate	10.00%	22.22%	28.57%	40.00%	66.67%	100.00%
4	=====================	=======	=======	=======	=======	=======	=======
5	Remaining Book Value	$20,000	$16,000	$9,600	$5,760	$3,456	$1,152
6	------------------------	-------	-------	-------	-------	-------	-------
7	SL Rate	10.00%	22.22%	28.57%	40.00%	66.67%	100.00%
8	SL Expense	$2,000	$3,556	$2,743	$2,304	$2,304	$1,152
9	------------------------	-------	-------	-------	-------	-------	-------
10	DDB Rate	20.00%	40.00%	40.00%	40.00%	40.00%	100.00%
11	DDB Expense	$4,000	$6,400	$3,840	$2,304	$1,382	$2,074
12	------------------------	-------	-------	-------	-------	-------	-------
13	MACRS DEPRECIATION	$4,000	$6,400	$3,840	$2,304	$2,304	$2,074
14	New Balance	$16,000	$9,600	$5,760	$3,456	$1,152	$0
15	=====================	=======	=======	=======	=======	=======	=======
16	COST	$20,000	$20,000	$20,000	$20,000	$20,000	$20,000
17	MACRS % of COST	0.2	0.32	0.192	0.1152	0.1152	0.0576
18	MACRS Expense	$4,000	$6,400	$3,840	$2,304	$2,304	$1,152

FIGURE 6–38 Computing MACRS straight-line and double-declining-balance depreciation

calculated in Figure 6–37, when *SL-switch* is 1. The larger of straight-line depreciation in row 8 and DDB depreciation in row 11 is returned in row 13 as MACRS depreciation, then subtracted from the remaining book value in row 5 to calculate the ending book value in row 14.

In row 13, MACRS depreciation is the DDB expense in row 11 until year 4. In year 4, the straight-line expense in cell E8 and the DDB expense in cell E11 are both $2,304. Thereafter, in years five and six, the straight-line expense is returned since it exceeds the DDB expense.

In row 18, the MACRS depreciation expense is computed as a check, using IRS 1989 MACRS rates for a five-year asset as a percentage of *cost*. Notice that these values are the same as those calculated in row 13. Obviously, using @VDB is a much easier method to use than performing the calculations in Figure 6–38.

STRING FUNCTIONS

1-2-3/G offers numerous functions that operate on strings. All of these functions have been included in previous releases. Some of the operations that you can perform with these functions are

- *Concatenating* (joining together) strings, or strings and values
- Editing strings and labels
- Converting values to strings and strings to values
- Testing for strings and values

Table 6–13 provides a complete list of 1-2-3/G's string functions, organized by functionality.

String Information Functions

1-2-3/G has two string information functions, @LENGTH and @FIND, which return information about a particular string. In many cases, you will *nest* these functions within one of the Text Editing functions shown in Table 6–13 to help you edit a *string* argument. These functions are also commonly used in macros to return information about cell contents.

Returning the Length of a String: @LENGTH

The @LENGTH function returns a *value* equal to the number of characters in a string. The form of this function is

@LENGTH(*string***)**

where *string* can be a literal string (letters, numbers and symbols enclosed in double quotes), or a string formula, function, or cell reference that returns a string. It can even be a string located in another worksheet file. If you do not enclose a

TABLE 6-13 1-2-3/G's String Functions

String Functions	Operation
Information	**Calculates**
@LENGTH	Number of characters in a string
@FIND	Starting position of a substring in a string
Text Editing Functions	**Performs**
@LOWER	Converts all characters to lower case
@UPPER	Converts all characters to upper case
@PROPER	Converts first character in each word to upper case; all others to lower case
@TRIM	Deletes leading and trailing spaces, and extra spaces between words
@REPLACE	Replaces *n* characters in a string with a new string, or adds a new string to the start or end of a string
@LEFT	Extracts *n* characters starting from the left of a string
@RIGHT	Extracts *n* characters starting from the right of a string
@MID	Extracts *n* characters in a string after start-point
@REPEAT	Repeats string *n* times
Conversion Functions	**Converts**
@STRING	Value to a string
@VALUE	String to a value
Test Functions	**Tests**
@EXACT	Two strings for equality
@N	The first cell in a range for a value
@S	The first cell in a range for a string
IBM Multilingual Character Functions	**Performs**
@CHAR	Converts IBM Multilingual Character code number to a character
@CODE	Converts character to IBM Multilingual Character code number

label directly entered into @LENGTH in double quotes, 1-2-3/G disallows the entry. If *string* is a value, a blank cell, or a range, @LENGTH returns ERR. However, @LENGTH evaluates a null *string* argument, "", as 0, and returns 0.

The @LENGTH function counts all characters within a string, including numbers, leading and trailing spaces, and spaces between words. For example, in cell B4 of Figure 6–39, @LENGTH(A4) returns the value 4, while in cell B5, @LENGTH(A5) returns the value 6. Since the string "Bora", in cells A4 and A5 appears the same, the string in cell A5 must then contain 2 trailing spaces.

In cell B6, @LENGTH(A4&A5) returns 10, when the strings in cells A4 and A5 are concatenated without adding a space in between. But in cell B7, @LENGTH(A7) returns 11, when the formula +A1&" "&A2 in cell A7 concatenates these strings and adds a space in between.

Typical applications of @LENGTH include:

- Determining the length of a string or substring within a string (see "Text Editing Functions" below).
- In a macro, testing entries requiring a specific length, such as zip codes.

Returning the Starting Point of a Substring: @FIND

The @FIND function returns the position of the first occurrence of a substring within a string after a specified start-point. The form of this function is

@FIND(*substring,string,start-point*)

Your *string* argument is a string you want to evaluate. The *string* argument can even be two strings concatenated, or joined together, because they return a single *string*. Your *substring* argument is the string you are searching for within *string*.

123G.EXE — Ready

File Edit Worksheet Range Copy... Move... Print Graph Data Utility Quit... Help

A:B6 @LENGTH(A4&A5)

C:\LAURA\STRING1.WG1

A	A	B	C	D	E	F	G	H
1		@LENGTH	Cell B			@FIND	Cell F	
2	String	Returns	Contains	Substring	Start	Returns	Contains	
3	----------	----------	----------	----------	------	----------	----------	
4	Bora	4	@LENGTH(A4)	Bora	0	0	@FIND(D4,A4,E4)	
5	Bora	6	@LENGTH(A5)	Bora	1	ERR	@FIND(D5,A5,E5)	
6		10	@LENGTH(A4&A5)					
7	Bora Bora	11	@LENGTH(A7)	Bora	3	5	@FIND(D7,A7,E7)	
8	Bora Bora			BORA	3	ERR	@FIND(D8,A8,E8)	

FIGURE 6–39 Using @LENGTH and @FIND

Both of these arguments must evaluate to a string—a literal string (letters, numbers, and symbols enclosed in double quotes), or a string formula, function, or cell reference that returns a string. If either argument is directly entered into the @FIND function, it must be enclosed in double quotes, or 1-2-3/G disallows the entry. If either argument is a value, a blank cell, or a range, @FIND returns ERR.

Your *substring* argument must be an *exact* match for @FIND to locate it within *string*. @FIND does *not* recognize the following as an exact match:

- Different spelling.
- Different capitalization.
- Different accent marks.
- Different spacing.

If it does not find an exact match for these or for any other reasons, @FIND returns ERR.

The *start-point* argument specifies the point in *string* where you want @FIND to begin searching. The *start-point* must be a value between 0 and *n* - 1, where *n* is the number of characters in *string*, including blank spaces. A *start-point* argument assumes an offset of 0. That is, in your string, the leftmost character, position 1, has a *start-point* of 0 (including blank spaces). So for a 0 *start-point,* @FIND begins searching at the first character. The last *string* character, *n*, has a *start-point* of *n* - 1. If *start-point* is negative or greater than *n* - 1, @FIND returns ERR. Since *start-point* must be a value, you can use a literal number, or a cell reference, numeric formula, or function that returns a value.

The @FIND function returns a value that represents the *first* occurrence of your *substring* beginning at *start-point*. Like the *start-point*, the @FIND function returns a value using an offset of 0. For example, in Figure 6–39 in cell F4, @FIND(D4,A4,E4) returns 0, when you search for the *substring* "Bora." Using a *start-point* of 0, @FIND begins searching at the first character. It finds the *substring* "Bora" in the first position of *string*, so @FIND returns the offset value 0. However, in cell F5, @FIND(D5,A5,E5) returns ERR when a *start-point* of 1 is used. Since @FIND starts searching at the *o* in the *string* "Bora" in cell A5, no match is found for the *substring* "Bora."

In cell F7, @FIND(D7,A7,E7) returns the offset value 5 when it searches for the *substring* "Bora" using a *start-point* of 3. This function begins searching at the leftmost *a*. The @FIND function finds the *second* occurrence of "Bora" which has an offset value of 5. However, when your *substring* is "BORA" in cell D8, @LENGTH(D8,A8,E8) returns ERR, because the strings have a different case.

Typically, you will use @FIND to

- Return offset locations (*start-point* arguments) of substrings for the @REPLACE, @MID, @LEFT, and @RIGHT functions.
- Return *number of character* arguments for the @REPLACE function.
- In a macro, to locate a particular sequence of characters.

Text Editing Functions

1-2-3/G provides nine functions that edit text in a worksheet. These functions are listed in Table 6-13 under Edit functions.

Changing Character Case: @LOWER, @UPPER, and @PROPER

1-2-3/G's @LOWER, @UPPER, and @PROPER functions alter the *case* or capitalization of a string. The forms of these functions, and the case change they return are as follows:

1-2-3/G Function	Converts string to
@LOWER(*string*)	Lower-case characters.
@UPPER(*string*)	Upper-case characters.
@PROPER(*string*)	Proper case: the first letter in *string*, and each letter after a space or nonalphabetic character are changed to upper case; all other characters are converted to lower case.

The *string* argument can be a literal string (letters, numbers, and symbols enclosed in double quotes) directly entered into one of these functions. You can also use a string formula or function that returns a string, or a cell reference that returns any of these. However, if *string* is a value, a blank cell, or a range, these functions return ERR.

You can concatenate strings in your *string* argument, since they evaluate to a single *string*. You cannot use @LOWER, @UPPER, or @PROPER on a range of cells, but must use one of these functions in each cell in a range.

As shown in Figure 6-40, the @UPPER, @LOWER, and @PROPER functions return different results for the same *string* argument in cell A3. In cell C3, @LOWER(A3) converts all letters to lower case, while in cell C4, @UPPER(A3) converts all letters to upper case. In cell C5, @PROPER(A3) converts to upper case:

- The leftmost character.
- Each letter after a blank space.
- Any letter after a nonalphabetic character (punctuation marks, values, and other nonletter characters such as + and $), even when no blank space separates them.

The @PROPER function changes capitalization correctly *only* when there is proper spacing between words in your *string*. So in cell C5, because of the incorrect placement of a blank space, @PROPER(A3) does not capitalize the first letter *b* in the third "bora," but does capitalize the second letter *o*. However, @PROPER correctly capitalizes the *B* in the fourth "Bora" since it directly follows a comma.

123G.EXE [69.4] Ready

File Edit Worksheet Range Copy... Move... Print Graph Data Utility Quit... Help

A:C9 @PROPER(A6&" "&A7)

STRING2.WG1

A	A	B	C	D
1	String	Function in Column C	Result	
2	==================	==================	=====================	
3	bora BORAb ora,BORA	@LOWER(A3)	bora borab ora,bora	
4		@UPPER(A3)	BORA BORAB ORA,BORA	
5		@PROPER(A3)	Bora Borab Ora,Bora	
6	BORA			
7	bora			
8		@PROPER(A6&A7)	Borabora	
9		@PROPER(A6&" "&A7)	Bora Bora	

FIGURE 6–40 Using @LOWER, @UPPER, and @PROPER

When the *string* argument is the result of concatenating two strings, the capitalization returned by @PROPER depends on the spacing between the concatenated strings. In cell C8, @PROPER(A6&A7) joins two strings without a space, so the *b* in cell A7 is not capitalized. However, in cell C9, @PROPER(A6&" "&A7) adds one space between the two strings, so both *B*'s are capitalized.

Typical applications of these functions include:

- Converting strings to one case.
- In a database, converting all labels to one case before using the Data Sort command, since capitalization can affect how this command sorts labels.

Trimming Extra Blank Spaces in a String: @TRIM

The @TRIM function deletes, or trims, unnecessary blank spaces in a string. The form of this function is

```
@TRIM(string)
```

where *string* is a literal string (letters, numbers, and symbols enclosed in double quotes) directly entered into the function, or a string formula, function, or cell reference that returns a string. However, if *string* is a value, a blank cell, or a range, @TRIM returns ERR.

You cannot use @TRIM on a range of cells. Rather, you must apply @TRIM to each cell separately. However, *string* can be multiple strings concatenated together that return a single *string*.

The @TRIM function deletes

- Any leading spaces at the beginning of *string*.
- Any trailing spaces at the end of *string*.

- Any consecutive blank spaces after a blank space within *string*.

However, @TRIM always leaves one space between concatenated strings.

In Figure 6–41, suppose you have the *string* "Peter Piper" in cell A4. In cell B4, @LENGTH(A4) informs us that this *string* is 11 characters long, including one blank space. But in cell B5, @LENGTH(A5) returns that the *string* in cell A5 is 20 characters, which includes three leading spaces at the beginning of the *string*, an extra space between "Peter" and "Piper," and five trailing spaces at the end of this *string*. In cell C5, @TRIM(A5) trims all but one space and returns a string 11 characters long, as the @LENGTH(C5) function in cell D5 shows. In cell B6, @LENGTH(A6) returns that the string in cell A6, "Picked 1,000 Peppers" has a length of 21. But @TRIM(A5) returns a string of 20 characters, because it trims the leading space from this *string*.

@TRIM always leaves one space between two concatenated strings, even if you specify an additional space in your *string* argument. For example, in Figure 6–40, cell A7 contains the formula +A5&A6, which has a length of 41 (20 characters from cell A5, 21 from cell A6). In cell C7, @TRIM(A7) returns a string with a length of 32, deleting all leading, trailing, and extra spaces between words. (This length of 32 is one greater than the combined lengths in cells D4 and D5, because @TRIM leaves a space between two strings when they are concatenated.) However, in cell C8, @TRIM(A5&" "&A6) also returns a string with a length of 32, even though an extra space has been included in the concatenation formula.

Common applications of the @TRIM function include:

- Editing labels in a spreadsheet.
- Trimming extra spaces when concatenating strings.
- In a macro, controlling the number of spaces in data entry.
- In a database, trimming spaces that can affect how the Data Sort command sorts entries.

123G.EXE — Ready

File Edit Worksheet Range Copy... Move... Print Graph Data Utility Quit... Help

A:C8 @TRIM(A5&" "&A6)

C:\LAURA\STRING3.WG1

A	A	B	C	D	E
1		@LENGTH	@TRIM	@LENGTH	
2	String	Returns	Returns		
3	================================	==========	============================	==========	
4	Peter Piper	11			
5	Peter Piper	20	Peter Piper	11	
6	Picked 1,000 Peppers	21	Picked 1,000 Peppers	20	
7	Peter Piper Picked 1,000 Peppers	41	Peter Piper Picked 1,000 Peppers	32	
8			Peter Piper Picked 1,000 Peppers	32	
9					

FIGURE 6–41 Using @TRIM

Extracting a Substring from a String: @LEFT, @RIGHT, @MID

1-2-3/G provides three functions that return a specified portion of a string while leaving your original *string* intact. The form of these functions are

```
@LEFT(string,number of characters)
@RIGHT(string,number of characters)
@MID(string,start-point,number of characters)
```

The *string* argument can be a literal string (letters, numbers, and symbols enclosed in double quotes), or a string formula, function, or cell reference that returns a string. If a literal string is directly entered into one of these functions, it must be enclosed in double quotes or 1-2-3/G disallows the entry. If *string* is a value, a blank cell, or a range, ERR is returned.

You cannot use any of these functions on a range of cells, but must apply a function to each cell separately. However, your *string* argument can be strings concatenated together since a single *string* is returned.

These functions use the following start-points:

Function	Start-Point
@LEFT	Leftmost edge of *string*
@RIGHT	Rightmost edge of *string*
@MID	*Start-point* argument you specify, beginning from the leftmost edge of *string*

The *start-point* argument for the @MID function must be between 0 and *n* - 1, where *n* is the number of characters in *string*, including blank spaces. The first character has a *start-point* of 0. The last character in *string*, *n*, has an offset of *n* - 1. If *start-point* is negative, @MID returns ERR. If *start-point* is greater than *n* - 1, @MID returns a null string ("").

Both the *start-point* and *number of characters* arguments must be values. So you can use a literal number, or a numeric formula, function, or cell reference that returns a value.

For all three functions, the *number of characters* argument represents the number of characters, including blank spaces that you want extracted from *string*. The @MID function returns the specified *number of characters* beginning at *start-point*. So *number of characters* can be between 1 and *n*, where *n* is the total length of your *string* argument. If you use a value outside of this range, these functions return the following:

Number of Characters	@LEFT,@RIGHT, @MID Return
Negative	ERR
0	null string ("")
Greater than *n*-1	@LEFT and @RIGHT return entire *string*, @MID returns the remaining portion of *string* after *start-point*.

Suppose you have the worksheet in Figure 6–42, in which you have entered the *string* "Peter Piper" down column A. (Notice that @LENGTH(A4) in cell B4 returns 11.) Here are the substrings of this *string* that the @LEFT and @RIGHT functions extract, given the same *number of characters* argument:

String	Number of Characters	@LEFT Returns	@RIGHT Returns
Peter Piper	1	Leftmost character "P"	Rightmost character "r"
Peter Piper	5	Five leftmost characters "Peter	Five rightmost "characters "Piper"
Peter Piper	12	Entire 11 character string "Peter Piper"	Entire 11 character string "Peter Piper"

As shown in column D, @LEFT(A4,C4) begins extracting from the leftmost edge of the *string* argument and returns the leftmost character "P" when *number of characters* is 1. In column E, using the same arguments, the @RIGHT(A4,C4) function begins extracting from the rightmost edge of *string*, and returns the rightmost character "r".

In Figure 6–42, the @MID function begins extracting at the leftmost edge of the *string* argument, beginning with the *start-point* you specify. When you use a *start-point* of 0, such as @MID(A4,F4,C4) in cell G4, the @MID function is the

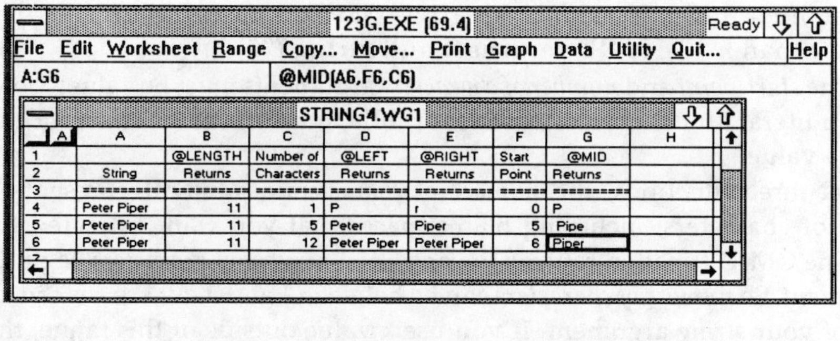

123G.EXE [69.4] Ready

File Edit Worksheet Range Copy... Move... Print Graph Data Utility Quit... Help

A:G6 @MID(A6,F6,C6)

STRING4.WG1

A	A	B	C	D	E	F	G	H
1		@LENGTH	Number of	@LEFT	@RIGHT	Start	@MID	
2	String	Returns	Characters	Returns	Returns	Point	Returns	
3	==========	=========	=========	=========	==========	======	==========	
4	Peter Piper	11	1	P	r	0	P	
5	Peter Piper	11	5	Peter	Piper	5	Pipe	
6	Peter Piper	11	12	Peter Piper	Peter Piper	6	Piper	

FIGURE 6–42 Using @LEFT, @RIGHT, and @MID

same as the @LEFT function. That is, it begins extracting at the first character (offset value of 0), and returns the leftmost character "P."

In cell G5, @MID(A5,F5,C5) returns the substring "Pipe." A *start-point* of 5 tells this function to begin extracting at the character that has an offset value of 5. So @MID extracts five characters from *string*, starting with the sixth character, which is a blank space. Likewise, in cell G6, @MID(A6,F6,C6) returns the substring "Piper" when the *start-point* is 6. This function begins extracting *at* the seventh character "P." Since the *number of characters* argument is 12, which is greater than the length of the *string* after the *start-point*, @MID returns the remaining string, "Piper."

You can use the @FIND(*substring,string,start-point*) function to determine the @MID function's *start-point* argument. In cell G5 of Figure 6–42, you want the @MID function to extract the leftmost characters starting with the blank space in the *string* in cell A5. Since this is a unique character in *string*, @FIND(" ",A5,0) returns an offset value of 5, which is the *start-point* used in cell F5. So in cell G5, you can use the function @MID(A5,@FIND(" ",A5,0),C6) to return the substring "Pipe." On the other hand, in cell G6, @MID(A6,F6,C6) uses a *start-point* of 6. It begins extracting beginning with the "P" in "Piper." This is not a unique character in *string*, but the blank space preceding it is. So you can use @FIND (" ",A6,0)+1 to return the *start-point* argument of 6, and in cell G6, @MID(A6,@FIND(" ",A6,0)+1,C6) to return the remaining string "Piper."

Common applications of the @LEFT, @RIGHT, and @MID functions include:

- Copying only part of a label to another cell.
- Extracting part of a label to use in a database or macro.
- Using @LEFT or @MID to truncate entries so that they are consistent (such as converting Expenses and Expense to a consistent entry Exp).

Replacing or Adding a String: @REPLACE

The @REPLACE function is a powerful text editing function you can use to:

- Replace a portion of a string with a new string.
- Replace an entire string with a new string.
- Add a new string at the beginning or end of an existing string.

The form of this function is

```
@REPLACE(string,start-point,number of characters,
new-string)
```

Both your *string* and *new-string* arguments can be any string entered as a literal string (letters, numbers, and symbols enclosed in double quotes), or a formula, function, or cell reference that returns a string. You cannot use @REPLACE on a range of cells. Rather, you must apply @REPLACE to each cell separately. The @REPLACE function returns ERR if either argument is a value or a multiple-cell range.

The @REPLACE function begins replacing at your *start-point* working from the leftmost edge of *string*. This argument must be between 0 and *n*, where *n* is the total length of your *string*. The first character (including blank spaces) has a *start-point* of 0. The last character in *string, n*, has an offset value of *n* - 1.

Both the *start-point* and *number of character* arguments must be a value entered as a literal number, or a numeric formula, function, or cell reference that returns a value.

Your *number of characters* argument specifies the total number of characters, including blank spaces and nonalphabetic characters, that you want replaced in *string*. This argument can be between 0 and *n*, the total length of your *string*. The @REPLACE function replaces the *number of characters* you specify beginning at your *start-point*. Table 6–14 shows the results you obtain by using the @REPLACE function with different *start-point* arguments.

Adding a New String at the Beginning or End of a String

Suppose you have the string "Peter P." in Figure 6–43. You can use the @REPLACE function to edit this string in a variety of ways. In Figure 6–43, column A contains the *string* argument "Peter P." Column B contains the length of each string in column A, calculated using the @LENGTH function. For example, cell B4 contains @LENGTH(A4) and returns a length of 8. Column C contains *start-point* arguments, column D *number of character* arguments, and column E *new-string* arguments. Column F contains @REPLACE functions and displays the results of using each of these arguments. Finally,

TABLE 6–14 Results of @REPLACE for Different *start-point* and *number of character* Arguments

Start-point	Number of characters	@REPLACE
Less than 0	Any	Returns ERR.
0	0	Adds *new-string* in front of *string*.
	n	Replaces *string* with *new-string*
	1 to *n* - 1	Replaces *number of characters* in *string* with *new-string*.
1 to *n* - 1	1 to *n* - 1	Replaces portion of *string* specified by *number of characters* argument, starting with *start-point*.
n	Any	Adds *new-string* to end of *string*.
Larger than *n*	Any	Treats *start-point* as equal to *n*.

Tip: Using @LENGTH and @FIND in the @REPLACE function

The @LENGTH and @FIND functions can make it considerably easier to calculate your *start-point* and *number of character* arguments in the @REPLACE function. Either of these functions can be directly entered into the @REPLACE function as the appropriate argument. Table 6–15 provides a convenient reference guide for using the @LENGTH and @FIND functions in different applications of the @REPLACE function.

TABLE 6–15 Using @FIND and @LENGTH to Determine *start-point* and *number of characters* Arguments for

@REPLACE New-String	@REPLACE Start-Point	@REPLACE Number of Characters
Added:		
In front of *string*	0	0
At end of *string*	@LENGTH(*string*)	0
Replaces:		
Entire *string*	0	@LENGTH(*string*)
At start of *string*	0	@FIND("C",*string*,0)
At end of *string*	@FIND("C",*string*,0)	@LENGTH(*string*)-*start-point*
In middle of *string*	@FIND("C",*string*,0)	@FIND("E",*string*,0)+ 1–start-*point*

where:

- "C" is a unique character in *string*, or the first occurrence of a nonunique character, which is the leftmost character being replaced.
- "E" is the last character in the portion of *string* to be replaced, and is either a unique character in *string*, or the first occurrence of a nonunique character.

123G.EXE (69.4) Ready

File Edit Worksheet Range Copy... Move... Print Graph Data Utility Quit... Help

A:F4 @REPLACE(A4,C4,D4,E4)

STRING5.WG1

A	A	B	C	D	E	F	G
1			Start	Number of			@REPLACE
2	String	@LENGTH	Point	Characters	New-String	@REPLACE	Performs
3	=======	==========	=====	=========	=========	==============	================================
4	Peter P.	8	0	0	Mr.	Mr.Peter P.	Adds new-string in front of string
5	Peter P.	8	8	0	Pumpkin	Peter P. Pumpkin	Adds new-string at end of string
6	Peter P.	8	0	8	Paul Jones	Paul Jones	Replaces string with new-string
7	Peter P.	8	0	5	Paul	Paul P.	Replaces beginning of string with new-st
8	Peter P.	8	6	2	Pumpkin	Peter Pumpkin	Replaces end of string with new-string
9	Peter P.	8	1	4	atrick	Patrick P.	Replaces middle of string with new-string

FIGURE 6–43 **Different applications of the @REPLACE function**

column G gives a description of the operation each @REPLACE function in column F performs.

In some cases, the @REPLACE function is equivalent to concatenating two strings. In cell F4, the @REPLACE function uses both a start-point and a number of characters arguments of 0. So this function adds the new-string "Mr." in front of the string argument without changing string. In cell F5, @REPLACE uses a start-point of 8, and a number of characters argument of 0. Since the length of string is 8, the last character has an offset value of 7 (n - 1). Therefore, the start-argument specifies to start after the end of your string and the number of characters argument says to replace no characters in string. As explained in cell H5, this function adds the new-string " Pumpkin" after string without changing string. Notice that a blank space is included at the beginning of new-string to separate the end of string and the beginning of new-string.

In cell F6, the @REPLACE function uses a *start-point* of 0 and a *number of characters* argument equal to the entire length of *string*, 8. The entire *string* is replaced with the *new-string* "Paul Jones."

When you want an argument in the @REPLACE function to equal the entire length of *string*, use @LENGTH(*string*) to determine this value. In Figure 6–43, @LENGTH(*string*) can be used to determine:

- The *start-point* argument in cell C5, when adding a *new-string* to the end of *string*, as in @REPLACE(A5,@LENGTH(A5),D5,E5).
- The *number of characters* argument in cell D6, when replacing the entire *string* with your *new-string*, as in @REPLACE(A6,C6,@LENGTH(A6),E6).

Replacing a Portion of a String with a New-String

You can also use the @REPLACE function to replace a portion of your *string* argument with a *new-string*. Returning to Figure 6–43, the @REPLACE function in cell F7 replaces only the beginning portion of string with the *new-string* "Paul" and returns the label "Paul P." Recall that when you want to start replacing at the first character of *string*, a *start-point* of 0 is used. To replace only the first name "Peter," which has a length of 5, your *number of characters* argument should also be 5.

To help determine the *number of characters* argument for @REPLACE, you can use the @FIND function. For example, in cell F7 of Figure 6–43, imagine you want to replace all characters *before* the blank space in *string*. Since the blank space is a unique character in *string*, @FIND(" ",A7,0) returns an offset value of 5. By using this @FIND function as your *number of characters* argument, @REPLACE replaces the first five characters in *string* with the *new-string* "Paul."

In cell F8, the @REPLACE function replaces only the end portion of *string*, "P.", with the *new-string* argument in cell E8, "Pumpkin." A *start-point* of 6 and a *number of characters* argument of 2 are used so that two characters, beginning with character 7 (which has an offset value of 6), are replaced after the blank space in *string*.

You can achieve the same results in cell F8 of Figure 6–43 by using both the @FIND and @LENGTH functions to determine the *start-point* and *number of characters* arguments. In this case, you want to replace all characters beginning with the second "P" in string, which is not a unique character in *string*. However, the blank cell directly preceding this character is unique. The function @FIND(" ",A8,0)+1 (cell C8) is used as the *start-point* argument, and returns an offset value of 6. Since you are replacing the remaining *string*, your *number of characters* argument in cell D8 is simply @LENGTH(A8)-C8, where cell C8 contains your *start-point*. So in cell F8 of Figure 6–43, you can use the function @REPLACE (A8,@FIND(" ",A8,0)+1,@LENGTH(A8)-C8,E8).

Finally, in cell F9, to replace the middle portion of *string*, "eter," with the *new-string* "atrick," you need to use a *start-point* of 1, so @REPLACE begins replacing beginning with the second character (which has an offset of 1), and a *number of characters* argument of 4, representing the length of the substring to be replaced, "eter." In cell C9, the *start-point* can be calculated as @FIND("e",A9,0), which returns 1, since "e" is the first occurrence of this letter in *string*. In cell D9 the *number of characters* argument is calculated as 4 using the function @FIND("r",A9,0)+1–C9, where C9 is your *start-point*. Using these arguments, in cell F9 the @REPLACE function replaces the four characters after the first "P" with the *new-string* in cell E9, and returns the label "Patrick P.".

Creating Repeating Labels: @REPEAT

1-2-3/G's @REPEAT function repeats a character pattern a specified number of times. This is a useful function when formatting worksheets and creating spreadsheet headings. The form of this function is

@REPEAT(*string*,*n*)

where *string* is a literal string (letters, numbers, and symbols enclosed in double quotes), or a cell reference, formula, or function that returns a string. Enter *n* as a value—a literal number, or a numeric formula, function, or cell reference that returns a value.

Your *string* argument can be any printable character or combination of characters, including numbers and symbols, entered as a *label*. If you enter *string* directly into the @REPEAT function, it must be enclosed in double quotes marks or 1-2-3/G disallows the entry. Your *n* argument specifies the number of times that you want *string* to be repeated in a cell.

The @REPEAT function duplicates your *string* *n* times in a cell. Like other string functions, @REPEAT must be used in each cell where you want this pattern to occur. It cannot be applied to a range of cells.

Figure 6–44 shows the labels different @REPEAT functions return given the *string* arguments in column A and the *n* arguments in column B. In cell C4, @REPEAT(A4,B4) repeats the *string* "+/" two times, as specified by *n* in cell B4. Notice that since you specified two repeats for a two-character string, @REPEAT returns a label four characters long. In cell C5, @REPEAT(A5,B5) repeats the string "Profit" five times. Finally, in cell C6, @REPEAT(A6,B6) repeats the string "5–" three times. This *string*, "5–," has been entered as a label in cell A6.

The @REPEAT function repeats your *string* *n* times regardless of the column width. So, the @REPEAT function is different from the repeating label prefix \ (backslash), which repeats a label the width of a cell. For example, if you enter

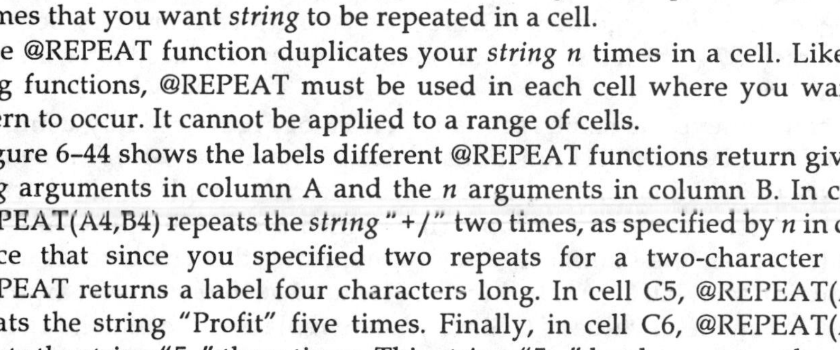

123G.EXE (69.4) Ready

File Edit Worksheet Range Copy... Move... Print Graph Data Utility Quit... Help

A:C4 @REPEAT(A4,B4)

STRING6.WG1

A	A	B	C	D	E
1			@REPEAT		
2	String	N	Returns		
3	==========	=====	==		
4	+/	2	+/+/		
5	Profit	5	ProfitProfitProfitProfitProfit		
6	5-	3	5-5-5-		

FIGURE 6–44 Using @REPEAT to create patterns

\+/ in cell C4 of Figure 6–44, the label +/ is repeated the entire length of this cell, which has a column width of 40.

Conversion Functions: @VALUE and @STRING

1-2-3/G includes two conversion functions: @VALUE and @STRING. The @VALUE function converts strings into values, while @STRING converts values into strings.

Converting a Value to a String: @STRING

The @STRING function converts a value to a string or label. The @STRING function is frequently used in database applications. It also is sometimes used in worksheets to create headings and labels. But the most powerful application of the @STRING function is in concatenating, or joining together, a value and a string into a single string.

The form of this function is

@STRING(*value,number of places*)

Your *value* argument is the number you want to convert to a label. 1-2-3/G disregards any formatting of the value, such as commas or dollar signs. Your *number of places* argument must be an integer between 0 and 15, which specifies the number of decimal places @STRING includes in the label it returns. If your *number of places* argument is negative or greater than 15, @STRING returns ERR. The @STRING function rounds your *value* argument to the *number of places* you specify, just like the @ROUND function.

Both of the @STRING function arguments must be entered as a value—a literal number, or a cell reference, formula, or function that returns a value.

The @STRING function returns a *label* that is the *value* argument rounded to the *number of places* specified. You cannot use @STRING on a range of cells. Rather, you must apply @STRING to each cell separately. If your *value* argument is actually a label or a blank cell, @STRING returns the value 0, not a label.

Figure 6–45 shows different results returned by the @STRING function for the *value* arguments in column A and the *number of places* arguments in column B. In cell C4, @STRING(A4,B4) adds two decimal places and returns the *label* 5.00. Likewise, @STRING(A5,B5) rounds the *value* $1,000.5 to 0 places, disregards all formatting ($ sign, comma, and period), and returns the label 1001. Finally, in cell C6, @STRING(A6,B6) returns the *value* 0 when cell A6 is blank.

Concatenating a Value and a Label

The most useful application of the @STRING function is to concatenate a value and a string into one label. Suppose in Figure 6–46, you want to combine the labels in column A with the values in column B to create one label in column C. In cell C3, +A3&" "&@STRING(B3,0) returns the label "Year Ended 1990."

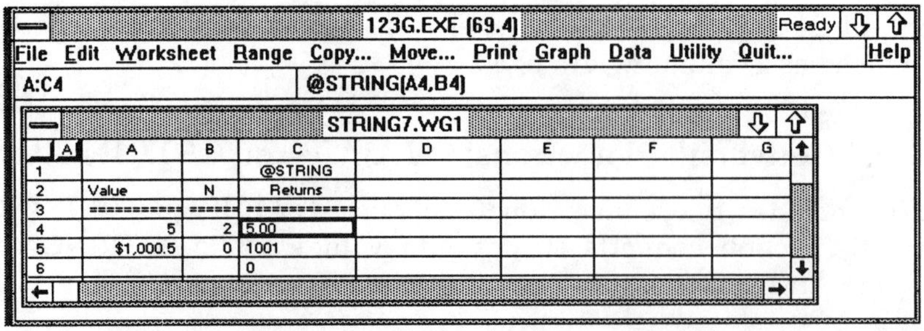

123G.EXE [69.4] Ready

File Edit Worksheet Range Copy... Move... Print Graph Data Utility Quit... Help

A:C4 @STRING(A4,B4)

STRING7.WG1

A	A	B	C	D	E	F	G
1			@STRING				
2	Value	N	Returns				
3	==========	======	============				
4	5	2	5.00				
5	$1,000.5	0	1001				
6			0				

FIGURE 6–45 Using @STRING to convert values to labels

Note

Use the Range Value command to replace the @STRING function with the literal string it returns. (See Chapter 4 for more details on RangeValue.)

Likewise, in cell C4, +A4&" "&@STRING(B4,0) returns the label "Illinois 60611." Both of these functions add a space between the label and value, and use a 0 *number of places* argument so that each value is displayed as an integer in the resulting label.

Converting a String to a Value: @VALUE

1-2-3/G's @VALUE function converts strings to values. The @VALUE function is often used to convert data from external sources, such as the Dow Jones News Retrieval Service, or CompuServe, that has been imported into the worksheet as labels. (See "Importing ASCII Files" in Chapter 5.)

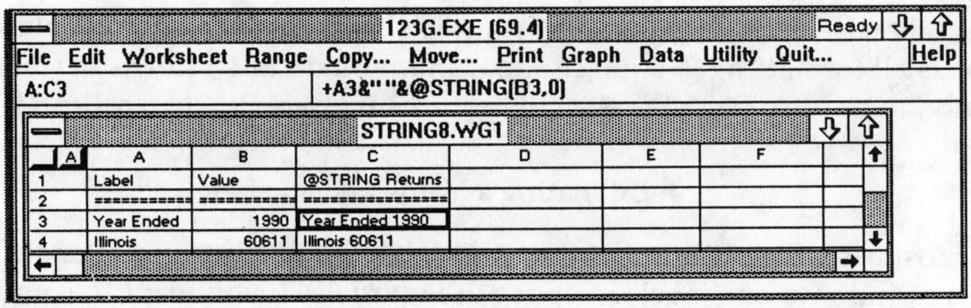

123G.EXE [69.4] Ready

File Edit Worksheet Range Copy... Move... Print Graph Data Utility Quit... Help

A:C3 +A3&" "&@STRING(B3,0)

STRING8.WG1

A	A	B	C	D	E	F
1	Label	Value	@STRING Returns			
2	==========	==========	===============			
3	Year Ended	1990	Year Ended 1990			
4	Illinois	60611	Illinois 60611			

FIGURE 6–46 Using @STRING to concatenate a value and a label

The form of this function is

@VALUE(*numeric string*)

where your *numeric string* argument must be a value expressed as a string. So you can use a literal string, numeric formula, or function that returns a *numeric string*, or a cell reference that contains any of these. This function evaluates a blank cell as 0, and returns ERR for a nonnumeric *string* argument.

The @VALUE function can convert a *numeric string* containing:

- A standard number (2.7).
- A number in scientific format (2E-1).
- A mixed number (3 1/3).
- A number using one of 1-2-3/G's standard formats ($20.5 or 2%).
- Any of the above that includes leading or trailing spaces (2.7).
- The address of a cell containing one of the above.

The @VALUE function *cannot* convert a *numeric string* when:

- The value and formatting are separated ($ 3.20).
- It includes nonnumeric characters (5 percent).
- It is composed of a formula or a function (@SUM(A3..A5)).
- It resembles a user-defined format.

Figure 6–47 shows different results returned by the @VALUE functions in row 2 for the *numeric string* arguments in row 1. The results are summarized as follows:

Numeric String	@VALUE	@VALUE Returns
100	Ignores two leading spaces	100
$100.00	Ignores $ sign and two decimal places	100
$ 100	Cannot evaluate $ sign separated from numeric label	ERR
99 4/5	Converts fraction to decimal	99.8
@SUM(A3..A7)	Cannot convert function	ERR
2*50	Cannot convert formula	ERR

You can use the values returned by the @VALUE function in formulas or functions. In Figure 6–47, @VALUE(G1) returns ERR, since cell G1 contains the label "2*50". However, in cell H1, @VALUE("2")*@VALUE("50") returns the value 100.

123G.EXE (69.4) Ready

File Edit Worksheet Range Copy... Move... Print Graph Data Utility Quit... Help

A:H2 @VALUE("2")*@VALUE("50")

STRING9.WG1

	A	B	C	D	E	F	G	H	I
1	Numeric String	100	$100.00	$ 100	99 4/5	@SUM(B1..F1)	2*50		
2	@VALUE Returns	100	100	ERR	99.8	ERR	ERR	100	

FIGURE 6–47 Using @VALUE

Note

> Use the Range Value command to convert a range of labels to values. (See Chapter 4 for more details on Range Value.)

Note

> Use the Data Parse command to convert a range of numeric strings to values. (See Chapter 9 for more details on Data Parse.)

Test Functions: @EXACT, @N, and @S

1-2-3/G provides three string functions you can use to test worksheet entries- @EXACT, @N, and @S. Typically, these functions are used in database applications.

Testing Two Strings for Equality: @EXACT

The @EXACT function performs a conditional test to see if two strings are *exactly* equal. (For more information on conditional testing, see the @IF function in this chapter.) The form of this function is

```
@EXACT(string1,string2)
```

where *string1* and *string2* are each strings entered as a literal string (letters, numbers, and symbols enclosed in double quotes), or a cell reference, string formula, or function that returns a string.

The @EXACT function evaluates the *string1* and *string2* arguments as being equal if they have the same capitalization, accents, punctuation, spacing between words, leading and trailing spaces, and length. @EXACT returns 1 (true) if the two strings are identical, and returns 0 (false) if they are not. However, if either *string1* or *string2* is a value or a blank cell, @EXACT returns ERR.

The @EXACT function performs a more rigorous equality test than the conditional test performed by the @IF function. For this reason, the @EXACT function is commonly used to

- Test existing database entries during query operations.
- In a macro, to test information as it is being entered into a database.
- Test a password for equality before running a macro.

Figure 6–48 compares the results returned by the @EXACT and the @IF functions for the same arguments in columns A and column B. For example, @EXACT(A3,B3) in cell C3, and @IF(A3=B3,1,0) in cell D3 both evaluate the *string1* and *string2* arguments in cells A3 and B3 as equal and return the true value 1. Furthermore, both of these functions return the false value 0 in row 4, when these arguments use different spacing (*string1* in cell A4 contains two leading spaces), and in row 5, when the arguments are spelled differently (*string2* in cell B5 contains an "e"). However, in cell C6, the @EXACT function returns the false value 0 when *string1* and *string2* use different capitalization (the "R" is capitalized in *string2*), but @IF returns the true value 1 for these arguments since it is not sensitive to case.

Tip: Why you should use @IF instead of @EXACT to evaluate null strings, blank cells, and cells containing spaces only

The @EXACT function returns ERR when both arguments evaluate to either a blank cell, a null string (""), or a cell containing spaces only. For example, suppose cell A8 is a blank cell, and cell B8 is either a blank cell, a null string, or a cell containing spaces only. The function @EXACT(A8,B8) returns ERR for these arguments. However, @IF(A8=B8,1,0) evaluates all of these cell contents as equal and returns 1.

Testing Ranges for Values and Strings: @N and @S

1-2-3/G provides two functions that test the first cell in a range for a value or string. The form of these functions are

@N(*range*)

@S(*range*)

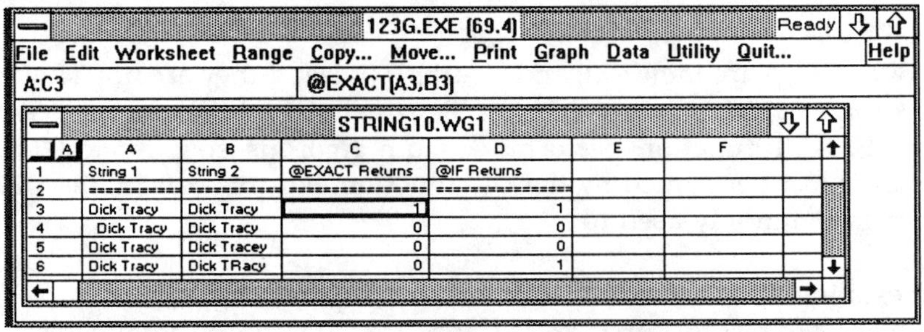

123G.EXE (69.4) Ready

File Edit Worksheet Range Copy... Move... Print Graph Data Utility Quit... Help

A:C3 @EXACT(A3,B3)

STRING10.WG1

A	A	B	C	D	E	F
1	String 1	String 2	@EXACT Returns	@IF Returns		
2	==========	==========	===============	===============		
3	Dick Tracy	Dick Tracy	1	1		
4	Dick Tracy	Dick Tracy	0	0		
5	Dick Tracy	Dick Tracey	0	0		
6	Dick Tracy	Dick TRacy	0	1		

FIGURE 6–48 @EXACT versus @IF

where your *range* argument can be a range name or address in the current worksheet file or another open file. 1-2-3/G disallows the entry if *range* is a collection address, and returns ERR if *range* is the name of a collection. If you enter a single cell address, 1-2-3/G converts this argument to a range address.

The @N and @S functions test only the upper leftmost cell in your *range*. The @N function tests for a value, while @S tests for a string. The @N and @S functions return the following:

Upper Leftmost Cell in Range Contains	@N returns	@S returns
Value	Value in cell	Null String ("")
String	0	Label in cell
Blank Cell	0	Null string ("")

Note

You can also use the @ISNUMBER and @ISSTRING logical functions to test for strings and values in a cell. See "Logic and Error-Trapping Functions" earlier in this chapter.

The most common application of these functions is testing user input during data entry. For example, you can use the following statements in a macro to ensure that zipcodes are entered as labels and not values:

```
{IF @S(B2)=""}{INDICATE "ENTER ZIP AS A LABEL"}
```

In these statements, if cell B2 does not contain a label, the function @S(B2) returns a null string (""), and the macro then displays the indicator ENTER ZIP AS A LABEL.

IBM Multilingual Character Set Functions: @CHAR and @CODE

A personal computer actually translates the numbers, letters, and symbols you enter from your keyboard into codes before it processes the information. Today, all computers use ASCII (American Standard Code for Information Interchange). This system uses 256 characters between 0 and 255 to represent each letter, number, and symbol.

Previous releases of 1-2-3 use LICS (Lotus International Character Set). For characters between 32 and 127, LICS and ASCII are identical. In addition, LICS characters from 0 to 32 are used for control codes, which are unprintable. Above character 132, LICS departs from ASCII for special and international characters.

1-2-3/G uses the IBM Multilingual Character set on code page 850, shown in Appendix B, "1-2-3/G Character Set," of this book. This character set is different than the LICS character set. In particular, the IBM Multilingual character set does not include many of the Greek letters and other common mathematical characters such as pi. Even if you change the Country selection using the Utility User Preferences command, 1-2-3/G still uses the character codes on code page 850.

1-2-3/G also provides a secondary character set that includes characters from 18 European countries, which corresponds to code page 437. Code page 437 differs from code page 850 for many character codes above code 154, and includes many of the commonly used mathematical symbols, including Greek letters. You can switch to this code page, or another country code page, by including certain interrelated statements in your CONFIG.SYS file. See Appendix B of this book for more details.

1-2-3/G provides two functions that work with the IBM Multilingual Character set—@CHAR and @CODE.

Note

> Release 2.2 provided the @CLEAN function, which is not included in 1-2-3/G.

Displaying IBM Multilingual Characters: @CHAR

The @CHAR function uses an IBM Multilingual Character Set code number and returns the character that code number represents. The form of this function is

@CHAR (*value*)

where you can enter your *value* argument as a literal number, or a cell reference, formula, or function that returns a value. This argument must be an integer between 0 and 255, representing the acceptable code numbers on code page 850 (see Appendix B). If *value* is not an integer, the @CHAR function uses only the integer portion without rounding the value. For any *value* outside of this range, or a string, @CHAR returns ERR.

For example, the function @CHAR(100) returns the lowercase *d*, and CHAR(171) returns ½. However, @CHAR(260) returns ERR because this value is not a valid IBM Multilingual Character.

Note

> Some monitors cannot display and some printers cannot print all IBM Multilingual Characters. When possible, 1-2-3/G then uses a fallback presentation that resembles the desired character. If no character approximates the desired character, nothing is displayed or printed.

Returning the IBM Multilingual Character Code: @CODE

The @CODE function returns the opposite of the @CHAR function. This function converts an IBM Multilingual Character Set character to its corresponding code number. The form of this function is

@CODE (*character*)

where your *character* argument must be entered as a label, even if the character is a number. Your *character* argument must be an IBM Multilingual Character Set character shown on code page 850. Otherwise, 1-2-3/G returns ERR. If you enter a label with more than one character, the @CODE function only operates on the first character in your *character* argument.

For example, the function @CODE("$") returns the number 36, which tells you that 1-2-3/G uses code number 36 for $. If cell A1 contains the label "Perpendicular," @CODE(A1) returns 80, for the first character, which is an upper-case P.

DATE AND TIME ARITHMETIC

One of the most powerful features of 1-2-3/G is its date and time functions. Date functions allow you to perform calculations using date-numbers and time functions allow you to perform calculations using time numbers. 1-2-3/G also offers the @NOW function, which returns both the date and time. This function is discussed in "Calculating with Combined Dates and Times" later in this chapter.

You can use these functions to calculate a particular date or time and to compute the difference between dates or times. You can use 1-2-3/G's date and time functions for accounts receivable and payable aging, scheduling, as well as calculating interest on loans and creating loan amortization tables.

Date Functions

1-2-3/G includes seven date functions shown in Table 6–16. The @D360 function was first introduced in Release 3. The @TODAY function, removed from Release 2, was reintroduced in Release 3.

Date Function Basics

Date functions either use or return a *date-number*. A date-number is an integer assigned by 1-2-3/G to a particular date. All of 1-2-3/G's date functions use a basic unit of 1 day, which is equal to the value 1. Furthermore, 1-2-3/G uses an arbitrary starting point of January 1, 1900. So January 1, 1900 has a date-number of 1, January 2, 1900, a date-number of 2, and so on. 1-2-3/G assigns date-numbers through December 31, 2099, which has a date-number of 73050.

TABLE 6–16 1-2-3/G's Date Functions

Date Function	Performs
@DATE	Returns a date-number given a day, month, and year.
@DATEVALUE	Converts a date string to a date-number.
@DAY	Returns the day of the month from a date-number.
@MONTH	Returns the number of the month from a date-number.
@YEAR	Returns the year from a date-number.
@D360	Calculates the number of days between two date-numbers using a 360–day year.
@TODAY	Calculates a date-number for the current date.

Entering a Date: @DATE

The @DATE function is the most commonly used date function in 1-2-3/G. You can use the @DATE function to

- Create date headings in your worksheet.
- Enter a date in your worksheet, which can then be used in calculations.

The form of this function is

@DATE (*year,month,day*)

where the *year, month,* and *day* arguments must each be a value—a literal number, or a cell reference, formula, or function that returns a value. If any of these arguments is not a value, @DATE returns ERR.

The @DATE function arguments must be within the following limits:

Argument	Minimum Value	Maximum Value
year	0 (year 1900)	199 (year 2099)
month	1 (January)	12 (December)
day	1	last day in a particular month

The @DATE function only uses the *integer* portion of a number. For example, if the *month* argument evaluates to either 5 or 5.6, @DATE uses the integer 5 as this argument. So the value 5.6 is not rounded, but is truncated, and only the integer portion 5 is used.

The @DATE function automatically detects nonexisting dates and disallows the entry. For example, 1-2-3/G disallows the entry if you try to enter a *day* of 31 when your *month* argument is 11 (November), since November only has 30 days. Furthermore, 1-2-3/G disallows the entry @DATE(91,2,29) because 1991 is not a leap year.

The @DATE function converts dates to a single date-number, or an integer between 1 and 73050 as discussed in "Date Function Basics" above. For example, @DATE returns the following date-numbers:

Date	@DATE Function	Date-number @DATE Returns
January 1, 1900	@DATE(00,1,1)	1
April 17, 1991	@DATE(91,4,17)	33345
February 29, 1992	@DATE(92,2,29)	33663
December 31, 200	1@DATE(101,12,31)	37256

You cannot easily interpret a date-number returned by the @DATE function unless it is date formatted. You can format a date-number in a variety of ways using the Range Format Date/Time command. (Formatting dates is discussed in detail in Chapter 3.)

USING @DATE AND THE DATA FILL COMMAND TO CREATE PAYMENT DATES You can now use the @DATE function with 1-2-3/G's improved Data Fill command to create consecutive dates that occur on a specific day of the month. For example, suppose you are buying a home and will be incurring a $150,000, 30-year, 12% fixed-rate mortgage on January 1, 1991. Payments are made at the end of each month. You want to create a loan amortization table for the first year of this loan.

You can create the sequential monthly payment dates in Figure 6–49, beginning on January 31, 1991 as follows:

1. Select the Data Fill command and specify your Fill range as A4..A15.
2. Specify the first payment date as your Start. For example, enter **@DATE(91,1,31)**. You can now also enter your Start value as **1/31/91**. (The next time you select the Data Fill command, this Start value is shown as the date-number 33269).
3. Specify a Step value of 1 and select the Month Series.
4. Specify a very large Stop value such as 999999. Figure 6–49 shows these selections in the Data Fill dialog box.
5. Select OK or press ENTER. 1-2-3/G uses your selections and creates a progressive series of date-numbers, each on the last day of a month.
6. Format your Fill range using the Range Format Date/Time D1 command (D1 format) so that the month, year, and day are displayed in each cell. Figure 6–50 shows the results.

Tip: Use Data Fill to fill a range with dates

When you are entering a range of dates, rather than use 1-2-3/G's date functions, use Data Fill instead. 1-2-3/G's Data Fill command provides many different ways to create sequential dates in a range or a collection. You can use this command to create dates that increase or decrease by year, quarter, month, week, or day. You can even create headings by weekdays, which is especially helpful for production scheduling. You can also use the Data Fill command to create custom date headings using the Linear Series option. The date headings created by the Data Fill command are date-numbers which can be used in calculations. See Chapter 9 for a complete discussion.

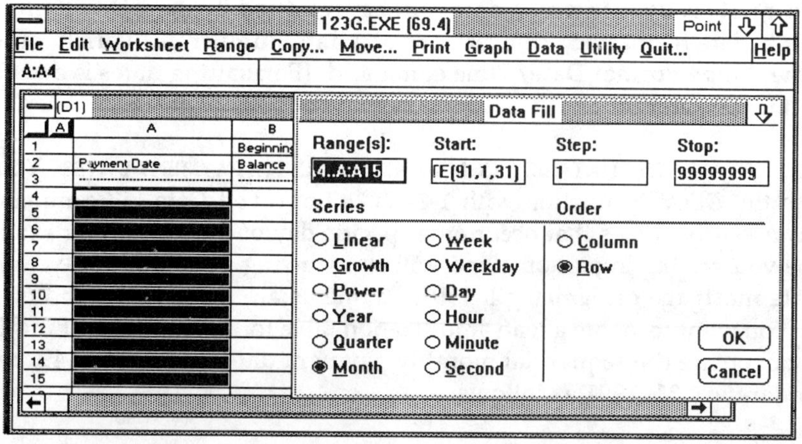

FIGURE 6–49 Specifying Data Fill selections

ADDING AND SUBTRACTING DATES TO CREATE A LOAN AMORTIZATION TABLE

One of the most common applications of the @DATE function is subtracting dates. When you subtract the results of two @DATE functions, the value returned represents the number of days between these dates.

For example, suppose you are buying a home and will be incurring a $150,000, 30-year, 12% fixed-rate mortgage on January 1, 1991. What is the principal balance at the end of the first year?

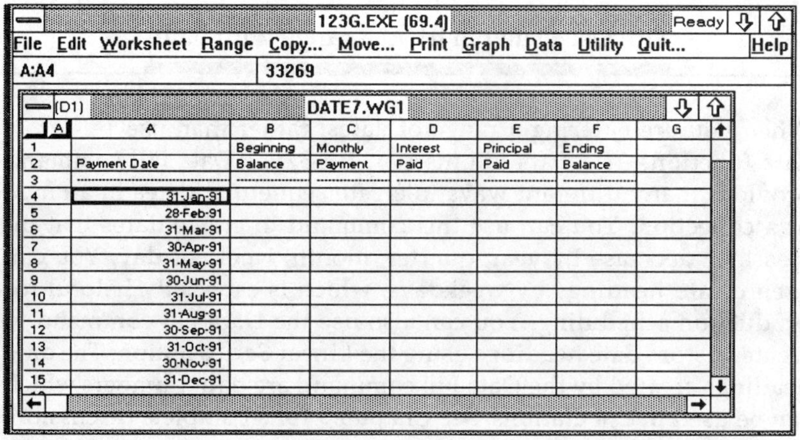

	A	B	C	D	E	F	G
1		Beginning	Monthly	Interest	Principal	Ending	
2	Payment Date	Balance	Payment	Paid	Paid	Balance	
4	31-Jan-91						
5	28-Feb-91						
6	31-Mar-91						
7	30-Apr-91						
8	31-May-91						
9	30-Jun-91						
10	31-Jul-91						
11	31-Aug-91						
12	30-Sep-91						
13	31-Oct-91						
14	30-Nov-91						
15	31-Dec-91						

FIGURE 6–50 Using the Data Fill command and @DATE to create monthly payment dates

You can use the @DATE function to create an amortization table like the one in Figure 6–51. The payment dates have been entered in column A using 1-2-3/G's @DATE function and the Data Fill Command, as discussed in the previous section.

The beginning balance in column B is simply the previous month's ending balance in column E. The monthly payment in column C, $1,543, is the result returned by the function, @PMT(150000,.12/12,30*12). (See "Present Value of an Annuity and Annuity Due: @PV" earlier in this chapter.) In column D, interest paid is calculated as

days between payments * principal balance * daily interest rate

For example, in cell D5, the interest paid in February 1991 is (A5–A4)*B5*(.12/365), or $1,380. This formula has been copied to the range E6..E15. However, in cell D4, the first interest payment is calculated as (A4–@DATE(91,1,1))*B4*(.12/365) since January 1, 1990 is the beginning loan date at which interest begins to accrue.

The principal paid in column E is simply the monthly payment in column C less the interest paid in column D. Finally, in column F, the ending balance is the beginning balance in column B less the principal paid in column E. As shown in cell F15, on December 31, 1991, your principal balance is $149,395.

Calculating the Number of Days between Two Dates Using a 360–day Year: @D360

1-2-3/G includes the @D360 function originally introduced in Release 3. This function calculates the number of days between two dates, assuming a 360–day year. Typical applications of the @D360 function include:

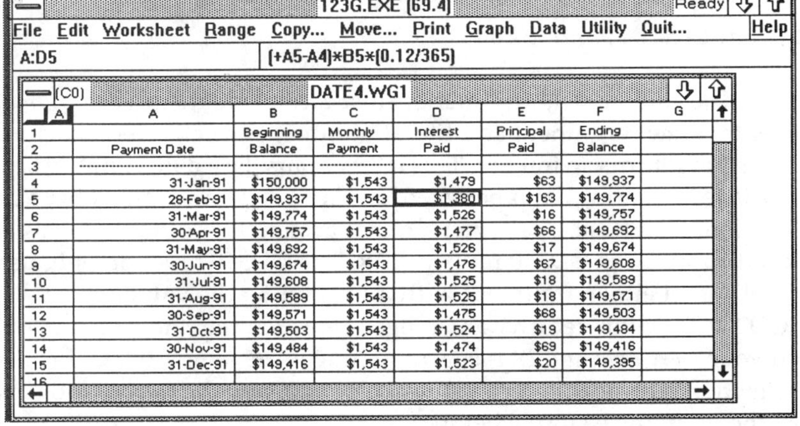

123G.EXE (69.4) Ready

File Edit Worksheet Range Copy... Move... Print Graph Data Utility Quit... Help

A:D5 (+A5-A4)*B5*(0.12/365)

(C0) DATE4.WG1

A	A	B	C	D	E	F	G
1		Beginning	Monthly	Interest	Principal	Ending	
2	Payment Date	Balance	Payment	Paid	Paid	Balance	
3	----------	----------	----------	----------	----------	----------	
4	31-Jan-91	$150,000	$1,543	$1,479	$63	$149,937	
5	28-Feb-91	$149,937	$1,543	$1,380	$163	$149,774	
6	31-Mar-91	$149,774	$1,543	$1,526	$16	$149,757	
7	30-Apr-91	$149,757	$1,543	$1,477	$66	$149,692	
8	31-May-91	$149,692	$1,543	$1,526	$17	$149,674	
9	30-Jun-91	$149,674	$1,543	$1,476	$67	$149,608	
10	31-Jul-91	$149,608	$1,543	$1,525	$18	$149,589	
11	31-Aug-91	$149,589	$1,543	$1,525	$18	$149,571	
12	30-Sep-91	$149,571	$1,543	$1,475	$68	$149,503	
13	31-Oct-91	$149,503	$1,543	$1,524	$19	$149,484	
14	30-Nov-91	$149,484	$1,543	$1,474	$69	$149,416	
15	31-Dec-91	$149,416	$1,543	$1,523	$20	$149,395	
16							

FIGURE 6–51 Using @DATE to create a loan amortization table

Tip: Using @DATE to determine the day of the week a date represents

You can use the @DATE function to determine the day of the week a date represents. For example, suppose you want to know what day of the week you where born on. Your birth date is June 6, 1956. The formula

```
@CHOOSE(@MOD(@DATE(56,6,6),7),"Saturday","Sunday",
Monday","Tuesday","Wednesday","Thursday","Friday")
```

returns the label "Wednesday" in the current cell.

In this formula, the @MOD function divides the date-number returned by @DATE(56,6,7) by 7 and returns the modulus 4. The @CHOOSE function then uses this value, 4, as the *offset* argument, and returns the fifth item in the *list* argument, "Wednesday." (Remember, the first item in the *list* argument, "Saturday," has an offset value of 0). Saturday is *always* used as the first item in *list*, since in 1-2-3/G, date-number 1 (January 1, 1900) fell on a Sunday. Therefore, the *list* argument in this function is designed so that Sunday, item 2, has an offset value of 1.

- Calculating accounts receivable and payables aging based on a 360–day year.
- Computing interest on loans and bonds when a 360–day year is applied.

The form of this function is

```
@D360(start-date,end-date)
```

The *start-date* and *end-date* arguments must each evaluate to a *date-number*. So you can enter either argument as a literal number, or a cell reference, formula, or function that returns an integer. This integer must be a date-number between 1 and 73050, representing dates between January 1, 1900 and December 31, 2099. (See "Date Function Basics," above.) If either argument is outside of this range, a blank cell, or a string, @D360 returns ERR. The @D360 function only uses the integer portion of either argument without rounding the value.

The @D360 function returns an integer representing the number of days between your *start-date* and *end-date*, assuming a 360–day year. Unluckily, the @D360 function returns different values, depending on the *start-date* or *end-date* used, as shown in the example below.

Figure 6–52 shows the results obtained by the @D360 function for different *start-date* and *end-date* arguments. Column A contains *start-date* arguments,

123G.EXE (69.4) Ready

File Edit Worksheet Range Copy... Move... Print Graph Data Utility Quit... Help

A:D11 @D360(A11,B11)

DATE3.WG1

A	A	B	C	D	E	F	G
1	Start-Date	End-Date	Difference	@D360 Returns			
2	====================	==========	==========	==============			
3	01-May-90	01-May-91	365	360			
4	01-May-91	01-May-90	-365	-360			
5	--------------------	----------	----------	--------------			
6	01-Jan-90	01-Feb-90	31	30			
7	01-Feb-90	01-Mar-90	28	30			
8	01-Mar-90	01-Apr-90	31	30			
9	--------------------	----------	----------	--------------			
10	31-Jan-90	28-Feb-90	28	28			
11	28-Feb-90	31-Mar-90	31	32			
12	30-Apr-90	31-May-90	31	30			

FIGURE 6–52 Using @D360 to calculate the number of days between two dates, assuming a 360–day year

while column B contains *end-date* arguments. Both arguments have been entered using the @DATE function, then formatted using the D1 date format. Column C contains the difference between the dates in column A and column B. For example, cell C3 contains +A3–B3. Finally, column D contains the results returned by the @D360 function for the *start-date* and *end-date* arguments in columns A and B. For example, cell D3 contains @D360(A4,B4).

In cell D3, the function @D360(A3,B4) calculates 360 days between the *start-date* May 1, 1991, and the *end-date* May 1, 1990. In cell C3, the actual number of days between these two dates is calculated as 365 days by the formula +B3–A3. However, in cell D4, the function @D360(A4,B4) returns the value -360 when the *start-date* is greater than the *end-date.*

In cells D6, D7, and D8, the @D360 function returns 30 days when a *start-date* and *end-date* both occur at the beginning of the month. For example, in cell D6, the @D360 function returns 30 days when the *start-date* is February 1, 1990, and the *end-date* is March 1, 1990. However, when a *start-date or* an *end-date* does not occur on the first day of a month, the @D360 function uses 30 days for each month, except February, which it evaluates as 28 days, and March, which it evaluates as 32 days. This can be seen in cells D10, D11, and D12 in Figure 6–52.

USING @D360 TO CREATE A LOAN AMORTIZATION TABLE You can use the @D360 function to create a loan amortization table, when interest is calculated using a 360–day year. Let's return to the example in Figure 6–51, where you will be incurring a $150,000, 30–year, 12% fixed-rate mortgage on January 1, 1991. What is the principal balance at the end of the first year, when interest is calculated using a 360–day year?

In Figure 6–53, the payment dates have been entered using the @DATE function and the Data Fill command as described above in "Using @DATE and the Data Fill Command to Create Payment Dates." The beginning balance, the

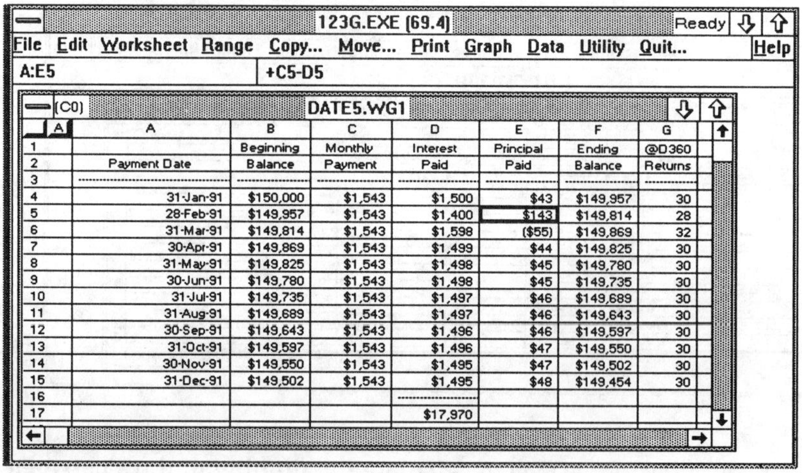

123G.EXE (69.4) Ready

File Edit Worksheet Range Copy... Move... Print Graph Data Utility Quit... Help

A:E5 +C5-D5

(C0) DATE5.WG1

A	A	B	C	D	E	F	G
1		Beginning	Monthly	Interest	Principal	Ending	@D360
2	Payment Date	Balance	Payment	Paid	Paid	Balance	Returns
3	------------	------------	------------	------------	------------	------------	------------
4	31-Jan-91	$150,000	$1,543	$1,500	$43	$149,957	30
5	28-Feb-91	$149,957	$1,543	$1,400	$143	$149,814	28
6	31-Mar-91	$149,814	$1,543	$1,598	($55)	$149,869	32
7	30-Apr-91	$149,869	$1,543	$1,499	$44	$149,825	30
8	31-May-91	$149,825	$1,543	$1,498	$45	$149,780	30
9	30-Jun-91	$149,780	$1,543	$1,498	$45	$149,735	30
10	31-Jul-91	$149,735	$1,543	$1,497	$46	$149,689	30
11	31-Aug-91	$149,689	$1,543	$1,497	$46	$149,643	30
12	30-Sep-91	$149,643	$1,543	$1,496	$46	$149,597	30
13	31-Oct-91	$149,597	$1,543	$1,496	$47	$149,550	30
14	30-Nov-91	$149,550	$1,543	$1,495	$47	$149,502	30
15	31-Dec-91	$149,502	$1,543	$1,495	$48	$149,454	30
16				------------			
17				$17,970			

FIGURE 6–53 Using @D360 in interest calculations

monthly payment, the principal paid, and the ending balance are all calculated in the same manner as Figure 6–51. However, in column D, interest paid is calculated as

days in the month of 360–day year * principal balance * daily interest rate of 360–day year

In cell D4, the first interest payment is calculated as @D360(@DATE (90,12,31),A4)*B4*(.12/360). By using one day before the beginning loan date of January 1, 1990, as shown in cell G5, @D360(@DATE(90,12,31),A4) returns 30 days. Notice that the daily interest rate is calculated as .12/360 for a 360–day year.

In cell D5, the interest paid in February, 1991 is calculated as @D360(A4,A5)* B5*(.12/360) or $1,400. The interest paid in each month is calculated in the same manner by copying this formula to the range D6..D15.

In column G, since payments occur at the end of each month, the @D360 function returns 28 days for February, 32 days for March, and 30 days for all the other months in the year. This 32–day month in March causes the negative amortization in cell E6. However, the total days used in these calculations are 360 days, or a 360–day year. As shown in cell F15, on December 31, 1991, your principal balance is $149,454.

Converting a Date String to a Date-number: @DATEVALUE

You can use the @DATEVALUE function to convert a date entered as a string to a date-number. By using @DATEVALUE you can

- Convert a date label, such as a heading, to a date-number used in calculations.
- Convert a date label imported from another file, such as a word processing file, to a date-number that can be used in calculations.

The form of this function is

```
@DATEVALUE(string)
```

where your *string* argument can be a literal string (letters, numbers, and symbols enclosed in double quotes), or a cell reference, string formula, or function that returns a string. The *string* argument must use one of the five 1-2-3/G date formats. The @DATEVALUE function returns the following values for each of these formats:

Date Format	Date Format	@DATEVALUE	@DATEVALUE Returns
DD-Mon-YY	D1	@DATEVALUE("31-Oct-92")	33908
DD-Mon	D2	@DATEVALUE("31-Oct")	33177
Mon-YY	D3	@DATEVALUE("Oct-92")	33878
MMo/DD/YY	D4	@DATEVALUE("10/31/92")	33908
MMo/DD	D5	@DATEVALUE("10/31")	33177
	None	@DATEVALUE("Oct 31, 1992")	ERR

For both of the date formats D1 and D4, which display the entire date for October 31, 1992, @DATEVALUE returns the corresponding date-number 33908. However, for the other date formats, 1-2-3/G provides any missing information. In the example above, when using a D3 format (Mon-YY), 1-2-3/G assumes the first day of the month, and returns a date-number, 33878, which corresponds to the date October 1, 1992. When using a D2 or D5 format, 1-2-3/G assumes the current year from your system clock. In the example above, for a *string* argument using the D2 or D5 format, @DATEVALUE returns the date-number 33177, which corresponds to the date October 31, 1990. Finally, when you use a format that is not one of these acceptable date formats, such as October 31, 1992, the @DATEVALUE function returns ERR. The @DATEVALUE function also returns ERR for any *strings* that represent dates before January 1, 1900 and after December 31, 2099.

Returning the Day, Month, or Year from a Date-number: @DAY, @MONTH, and @YEAR

1-2-3/G includes three functions you can use to extract the day, month, or year from a date-number: @DAY, @MONTH, and @YEAR. The form of these functions are

```
@DAY(date-number)
@MONTH(date-number)
@YEAR(date-number)
```

where your *date-number* argument can be a literal number, or a cell reference, formula, or function that returns an integer. Furthermore, *date-number* must be an integer between 1 and 73050, representing dates between January 1, 1900 and December 31, 2099. (See "Date Function Basics," above.) If your *date-number* argument is outside of this range, a blank cell, or a string, all of these functions return ERR. These functions only use the integer portion of *date-number* without rounding the value.

For a *date-number* argument, @YEAR returns the year, @MONTH returns the month, and @DAY returns the day this *date-number* represents. These functions return values that are equivalent to the corresponding arguments in the @DATE function. For example, the date-number 33839 is returned by the function @DATE(92,8,23). For this date-number, the @YEAR function returns the value 92, which is the same as the *year* argument in the @DATE function. So the results returned by these functions are *not* date-numbers, but values.

Tip: A shortcut to calculate the number of days, months, and years between two dates

You can use the @DAY, @MONTH, and @YEAR functions to calculate the number of days, months, and years between two dates. For example, suppose you want to determine the number of days, months, and years between January 20, 2005 and December 3, 1961.

In Figure 6–54, cell A3 displays the date 02–Jan-2005. This cell contains the formula @DATE(105,1,2), which is formatted using the D1 date format. This date corresponds to the date-number 38354 in cell B3, since cell B3 contains the formula +A3. Cell A4, which displays the date 03–Dec-61, contains the formula @DATE(61,12,3), which corresponds to the date-number 22618 in cell B4. The value 15,736, calculated in cell B6, is the difference between these dates. In other words, there are 15,736 days between these two dates. But how many days, months, and years does this represent?

In cell C6, @YEAR(B6) shows that there are 43 years between January 2, 2005 and December 3, 1961. In cell D4, the formula @MONTH(B6)-1 shows that there are 0 months between these dates. (You must *always* subtract 1 from the value @MONTH returns.) Finally, in cell E6, @DAY(B6) returns 30 days. So there are 43 years and 30 days between December 31, 1961 and January 2, 2005.

123G.EXE [69.4] Ready

File Edit Worksheet Range Copy... Move... Print Graph Data Utility Quit... Help

A:D6 @MONTH(B6)-1

DATE1.WG1

A	A	B	C	D	E	F	G
1	Date Format	Date Value	@YEAR	@MONTH -1	@DAY		
2	====================	==========	==========	===========	==========		
3	02-Jan-2005	38354					
4	03-Dec-61	22618					
5		----------------					
6		15736	43	0	30		
7							

FIGURE 6–54 Using @DAY, @MONTH, and @YEAR to calculate the number of days, months, and years between two dates

Note

Use the formula @YEAR(A1)+1900, when cell A1 contains a date-number, to return the year of the date. For example, when cell A1 contains @DATE(90,7,22), this formula returns 1990.

Tip: Using @MONTH to return the *name* of a month

You can use the @MONTH function with the @CHOOSE function to return the *name* of a month rather than the value assigned to a month. In Figure 6–55, column A contains three dates entered using the @DATE function, which are formatted using 1-2-3/G's D1 date format. In cell B1, the function

```
@@CHOOSE(@MONTH(A1)-1,"January","February","March",
"April","May","June","July","August","September",
"October","November","December")
```

returns the label "April". The @CHOOSE function assigns an offset value of 0 to the first label January in its *list* argument, an offset value of 1 to February, and an offset value of 11 to December. However, @MONTH returns a value of 1 for January and a value of 12 for December. So in cell B2, the function @MONTH(A2)-1 is used as the *offset* argument in the @CHOOSE function to return the correct label. In cell B2, this function returns the label "June" for the date 01–June-90 in cell A2, and the label "December" for the date 25–Dec-05 in cell A3.

Returning the Current Date: @TODAY

1-2-3/G includes the @TODAY function originally included in Release 1A. This function returns the current date as a date-number, using your system clock. This function requires no arguments. Use the @TODAY function:

- To date a worksheet.
- In date calculations.

The @TODAY function is updated every time your worksheet is manually or automatically recalculated. For example, if you enter @TODAY in cell A1 on January 2, 1990, it will return this date, in the date format you specify. If you open this file the next day, @TODAY returns the date January 3, 1990, in the date format specified.

Since the @TODAY function uses your system clock, make sure the operating system time and date are correct. If you want to modify the operating system time and date in midsession, you must do so through OS/2 or Presentation Manager.

Suppose an employee is vested in your company's pension program after a seven-year period. Figure 6–56 shows a list of employees in column A. Column B contains their hire dates entered using the @DATE function. You can use the @TODAY function to *automatically* create an updated list of employees vested, each time you open this file. For example, cell C3 contains the formula:

```
@IF(@TODAY-B3>(365*7),"Vested","Not Vested")
```

This formula calculates the number of days between today and an employee's hire date (@TODAY-B3), then compares it to the number of days in seven years (365*7). When this value is greater than seven years, as in cell B3, this function

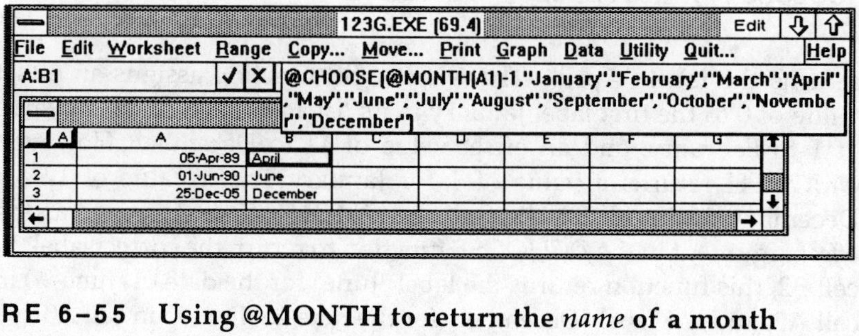

```
123G.EXE (69.4)
File Edit Worksheet Range Copy... Move... Print Graph Data Utility Quit... Help
A:B1  @CHOOSE(@MONTH(A1)-1,"January","February","March","April","May","June","July","August","September","October","November","December")

   A          B
1  05-Apr-89  April
2  01-Jun-90  June
3  25-Dec-05  December
```

FIGURE 6–55 **Using @MONTH to return the *name* of a month**

123G.EXE (69.4) Ready

File Edit Worksheet Range Copy... Move... Print Graph Data Utility Quit... Help

A:C3 @IF(@TODAY-B3>(7*365),"Vested","Not Vested")

(C0) DATE10.WG1

A	A	B	C	D	E	F	G	H
1	Employee	Hire Date	Pension Status					
2	=========	=========	============					
3	T. Reusche	18-May-72	Vested					
4	P. Anastas	02-Nov-85	Not Vested					
5								

FIGURE 6–56 Using @TODAY with @IF

returns the label "Vested"; otherwise it returns the label "Not Vested" as in cell C4.

Note

> Use the @NOW function to return a date/time-number representing both the current date and time.

Note

> You can freeze the date returned by @TODAY by using the Range Value command on the cell containing this formula.

Time Functions

1-2-3/G includes 5 time functions shown in Table 6–17. All of these functions are available in previous releases of 1-2-3.

Time Function Basics

All of 1-2-3/G's time functions either use or return a *time-number*, a decimal between 0 and 1 that represents a particular time of day. All of 1-2-3/G's time functions use a basic unit of 1 day, which is equal to the value 1. So times are expressed as decimal numbers between 0 and 1, where 1.0 equals 24 hours. A *time-number* returned by one of these functions represents the amount of time

TABLE 6-17 1-2-3/G's Time Functions

Time Function	Performs
@TIME	Returns a time-number for a given hour, minute, and second.
@TIMEVALUE	Converts a time string to a time-number.
@HOUR	Returns the hour of the day from a time-number.
@MINUTE	Returns the minutes from a time-number.
@SECOND	Returns the seconds from a time-number.

that has elapsed since midnight. So the value .5 is equal to 12 hours, or noon, since 12 hours have elapsed since midnight.

1-2-3/G's time values do not differentiate between days. Rather, 1-2-3/G's time values are cyclical, starting over at each midnight. For example, the time-number .5 represents noon for each day.

You will find the following values useful when using 1-2-3/G's time functions:

Time Unit	Decimal Value
1 day	1.0
1 hour	0.041666667
1 minute	0.000694444
1 second	0.000011474

Entering a Time: @TIME

The @TIME function is the most commonly used time function in 1-2-3/G. Like the @DATE function, you can use the @TIME function to:

- Create time headings in your worksheet.
- Enter a time in your worksheet, which is then used in calculations.

The form of this function is

@TIME(*hours,minutes,seconds*)

where the *hours, minutes,* and *seconds* arguments must each be a value—a literal number, or a cell reference, formula, or function that returns a value. If any of these arguments is not a value, @TIME returns ERR.

The @TIME function uses arguments based on military time (for example, 18:00:00 is 6 PM). So the arguments of the @TIME function must be integers within the following limits:

Argument	Minimum Value	Maximum Value
hours	0 (midnight)	23 (11 P.M.)
minutes	0	59
seconds	0	59

If an argument is outside of the appropriate range, @TIME returns ERR.

The @TIME function converts a time to a *time-number,* or decimal between 0 and 1. (See "Time Function Basics," above.) For example, @TIME returns the following time-numbers:

TIME	@TIME Function	Time-number @TIME Returns	Formatted Using D6
12:15:00 AM	@TIME(0,15,0)	0.0104166667	12:15:00 AM
12:00:01 PM	@TIME(12,00,01)	0.5000115474	12:00:01 PM
11:59:59 PM	@TIME(23,59,59)	0.9999884259	11:59:59 PM
12:05:00 PM Next Day	@TIME(24,05,00)	ERR	ERR

In the example above, the last function, @TIME(24,05,00), returns ERR because the *hours* argument, 24, is outside of the acceptable range.

You cannot easily interpret a time-number returned by the @TIME function unless it is time formatted. You can format a time-number using the Range Format Date/Time command. (Formatting time-numbers is discussed in detail in Chapter 3.) The time-numbers in the example above are formatted using the D6 time format.

Tip: Entering a time into a worksheet without using @TIME

You can now enter a time directly into a worksheet without using the @TIME function. Suppose you want to enter the time 11:30:00 AM in cell A1. Simply type 11:30:00 or 11:30 AM in this cell. 1-2-3/G automatically converts this time to the time-number .479167 in the Control line and enters this value in cell A1. Now, if you format this cell using the D6 time format, this time-number is displayed as 11:30:00 AM.

As you know, 1-2-3/G uses a military clock for times. So to enter the time 11:30:00 PM, type either 11:30:00 PM or 23:30:00 in a cell. 1-2-3/G converts this time to the time-number .97917. This time-number can now be used in calculations, or formatted and used as a heading in your worksheet.

You cannot use this method to enter a time in a formula. For example, 1-2-3/G disallows the entry 2:02 PM+20.

Tip: Using @TIME and the Data Fill command to create time headings

1-2-3/G's newly revised Data Fill command now provides many different ways to create sequential time-numbers in a range or a collection. You can use this command to create times that increase or decrease by hours, minutes, or seconds. You can even use the Data Fill command to create a custom set of time headings using Linear selection.

Suppose you want to create a production schedule worksheet where the headings for each column are the production hours in each day from 9:00 AM to 4:00 PM. You can use the @TIME function with the Data Fill command to create consecutive times in a range. The times returned are time-numbers that can be used in calculations.

To create sequential times in a range beginning at 9:00 AM, first select the Data Fill command. In Figure 6–57, specify your Fill range as B1..I1. Specify a Start value that is the first hour of production time as @TIME(9,0,0) or simply 09:00 AM. (The next time you select the Data Fill command, this Start is shown as the time-number .375.) Specify a Step value of 1 and the Hour Series option. Specify a very large Stop value of 999999. Finally, select OK or press ENTER. 1-2-3/G uses these selections and create a progressive series of time-numbers in the range B1..I1, increasing the time in each cell by one hour. Finally, you need to format this range using the Range Format Date/Time 7 command (D7 format) so that the hour and minutes are displayed in each cell. Figure 6–57 shows the results.

See Chapter 9 for more about the Data Fill command.

ADDING TIMES One of the most common applications of the @TIME function is adding two time-numbers returned by this function. Suppose you want to begin a production run at 9:00 that takes 4.5 hours. In Figure 6–57, cell B3, which is formatted with Range Format Date/Time 7, contains the formula +B1+@TIME(4,30,0). This formula calculates that the run will be finished at 1:30 PM. Notice that you must use the @TIME function when adding times. If you use the formula +B1+4.5, you would calculate the incorrect ending time of 4.875, or 9:00 PM.

Now suppose you want to begin production Run 2 at 1:00 PM, which takes 14 hours to complete. In cell F4, which is time formatted, the formula +F1+@TIME(14,0,0) returns 3:00 AM. However, this is 3:00 AM the next day.

SUBTRACTING TIMES When you subtract the results of two @TIME functions, the result returned is the time elapsed between these two times. For example, suppose in Figure 6–58, you want to have production Run 3 end at 3:00 PM. This run takes 3.5 hours to complete. In cell H5, the formula +H1–@TIME(3,30,0) calculates that you must start this production run at 11:30 AM. Once again, you must use the @TIME function when subtracting times. If you just used the formula +H1–3.5, returns the number–2.875 is returned, or the incorrect beginning time of 3:00 AM.

As you know, 1-2-3/G's time values are cyclical, starting over each midnight. Returning to Figure 6–58, suppose you want to finish production Run 4 at noon. This product takes 20 hours to complete. In cell E4, +E1–@TIME(20,0,0) returns a value of–.33333, which when time formatted, returns 4:00 PM in cell E5.

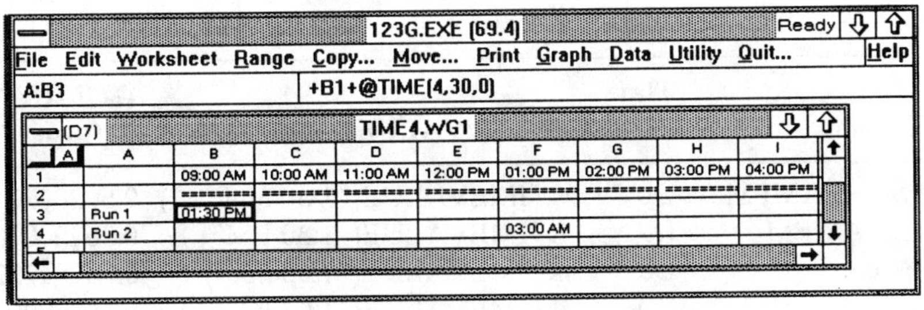

123G.EXE (69.4) Ready

File Edit Worksheet Range Copy... Move... Print Graph Data Utility Quit... Help

A:B3 +B1+@TIME(4,30,0)

(D7) TIME4.WG1

A	A	B	C	D	E	F	G	H	I
1		09:00 AM	10:00 AM	11:00 AM	12:00 PM	01:00 PM	02:00 PM	03:00 PM	04:00 PM
2		========	========	========	========	========	========	========	========
3	Run 1	01:30 PM							
4	Run 2					03:00 AM			

FIGURE 6–57 Adding Times

123G.EXE (69.4) Ready

File Edit Worksheet Range Copy... Move... Print Graph Data Utility Quit... Help

A:E4 +E1-@TIME(20,0,0)

(F5) TIME3.WG1

A	A	B	C	D	E	F	G	H	I
1		09:00 AM	10:00 AM	11:00 AM	12:00 PM	01:00 PM	02:00 PM	03:00 PM	04:00 PM
2		========	========	========	========	========	========	========	========
3	Run 3							11:30 AM	
4	Run 4				-0.33333				
5	Run 4				04:00 PM				

FIGURE 6–58 Subtracting times

However, this is 4:00 PM of the previous day. Therefore, you must begin this production run at 4:00 the day before it is to be finished.

Converting a String to a Time-Number: @TIMEVALUE

You can use the @TIMEVALUE function to convert a time label (a time entered as a string) to a time-number. You can use this function in your worksheet:

- To convert a time label, such as a heading, to a time-value used in calculations.
- To convert a time label imported from another file, such as a word processing file, to a time-value used in calculations.

The form of this function is

@TIMEVALUE(*string*)

where your *string* argument is a time label—a literal string (letters, numbers, and symbols enclosed in double quotes), or a cell reference, string formula, or function that returns a string.

The *string* argument must be in one of the four 1-2-3/G time formats. The @TIMEVALUE function returns the following time-numbers for each of these time formats:

Time Format	Time Format	@TIMEVALUE	@TIMEVALUE Returns
HH:MMi:SS AMPM	D6	@TIMEVALUE("1:30:30 PM")	0.562847222
HH:MMi AMPM	D7	@TIMEVALUE("1:30 PM")	0.562500000
HH:MMi:SS	D8	@TIMEVALUE("13:30:30")	0.562847222
HH:MMi	D9	@TIMEVALUE("13:30")	0.562500000
	D8	@TIMEVALUE("26:30:30")	ERR

In the preceding table, the @TIMEVALUE function returns the corresponding time-number .562847222 for the D6 and D8 time formats, which display the entire time in hours, minutes, and seconds. However, for the D7 and D9 time formats, 1-2-3/G assumes the missing seconds information is 0 and returns a time-number of .5625. The time-number returned by the @TIME function can be used in calculations.

The @TIMEVALUE function returns ERR for any *strings* that use unacceptable time formats, or use time values outside of the acceptable range for @TIME function arguments. So @TIMEVALUE("26:30:30") returns ERR because the hour component, 26, is an unacceptable value (see "Converting Times to Time-numbers: @TIME" above).

Returning the Hours, Minutes, or Seconds from a Time-Number: @HOUR, @MINUTE, and @SECOND

1-2-3/G includes three functions you can use to extract the hour, minute, or seconds from a time-number: @HOUR, @MINUTE, and @SECOND. The form of these functions are

```
@HOUR(time-number)
@MINUTE(time-number)
@SECOND(time-number)
```

where your *time-number* argument can be a literal number, numeric formula or function that returns a decimal value, or a cell reference that contains any of these. Furthermore, *time-number* must be a decimal value between 0 and 1, representing times between 12:00 midnight and 11:59:59 PM (see "Time Function Basics," above), otherwise these functions return ERR. If your *time-number* argument is a blank cell, or a string, all of these functions return 0.

Suppose you enter the function @TIME(23,5,0) in cell A3, which returns a time-number of .96180555, as in Figure 6–59. Cell B3, which is time formatted, contains the formula +A3. So this time-number represents 11:05:00 PM. In cell C3, @HOUR(A3) returns the value 23, which represents the number of hours in this time-number. Likewise, the function @MINUTE(A3) returns 5 minutes, while @SECOND(A3) returns 0 seconds for this time-number.

As you know, 1-2-3/G's time-numbers are cyclical, starting over again from 0 at each midnight. So when cell A4 contains the time-number 1.5, 1-2-3/G evaluates this as the time-number, .5, or 12 noon. Therefore, the function @HOUR(A4) returns 12 hours, while @MINUTE(A4) and @SECOND(A4) return 0.

The @HOUR, @MINUTE, and @SECOND functions return values that are equivalent to the corresponding arguments in the @TIME function. For example, the time-number .96180556 in cell A3 is returned by the function @TIME(23,5,0) shown in the Control line. For this time-number, the @HOUR argument returns the @TIME *hours* argument 23. So the results returned by the

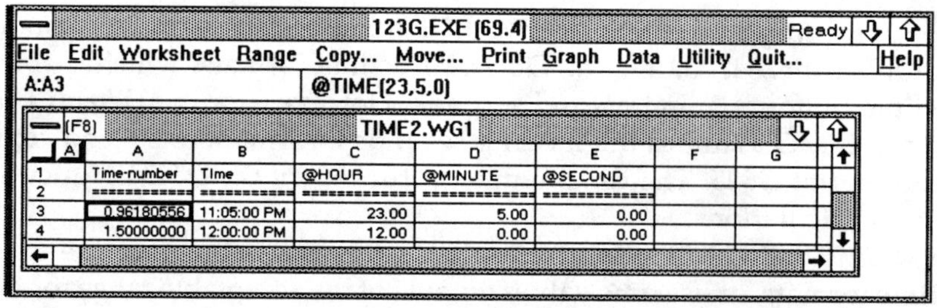

123G.EXE (69.4) Ready

File Edit Worksheet Range Copy... Move... Print Graph Data Utility Quit... Help

A:A3 @TIME(23,5,0)

(F8) TIME2.WG1

A	A	B	C	D	E	F	G
1	Time-number	Time	@HOUR	@MINUTE	@SECOND		
2	===========	==========	============	============	============		
3	0.96180556	11:05:00 PM	23.00	5.00	0.00		
4	1.50000000	12:00:00 PM	12.00	0.00	0.00		

FIGURE 6–59 **Using the @HOUR, @MINUTE, and @SECOND functions**

@HOUR, @MINUTE, and @SECOND functions are *not* time-numbers, but integers.

Combined Dates and Times

You can also use 1-2-3/G's date and time functions together to calculate combined date and time values. In addition, 1-2-3/G provides the @NOW function, which returns a combined date/time number.

Combined Dates and Times Basics

Combined date and time values use the same concepts as 1-2-3/G's date and time functions. A combined date/time-number is a single value, the integer portion representing a date-number, and the decimal portion representing a time-number on that date. (See "Date Function Basics" and "Time Function Basics" above for more details.) For instance, the number 3973.5833 represents 2:00 PM on April 12, 1990. You can create this combined date/time number using the formula

```
@DATE(90,4,12)+@TIME(14,2,0)
```

Suppose 32973.5833, the date/time-number returned by this formula, is in cell A1. As is the case with the @NOW function, you cannot format a single cell to display both the current date and time returned by this value. First, you must format cell A1 to display the date April 12, 1990. Then you need to enter the formula +A1 in cell A2 and format this cell to display the time 2:00 PM.

Calculating with Combined Dates and Times

Like John Madden, suppose you only travel by train. You need to be in Los Angeles on October 1, 1990 at 3:00 PM. A train trip from New York takes three days and seven hours, without delays. What is the latest train you can take out of New York?

First, specify your arrival time using the formula @DATE(90,10,1)+ @TIME(15,0,0). Next, specify your travel time as (3+@TIME(7,0,0)). So the formula

```
@DATE(90,10,1)+@TIME(15,0,0)-(3+@TIME(7,0,0))
```

returns the date/time value 33144.333. When this value is formatted as a date, it returns September 28, 1990; when it is formatted as a time, it returns 8:00 AM. Therefore, the latest train you can take is at 8:00 AM on September 28, 1990.

Returning the Current Date and Time: @NOW

The @NOW function, which requires no arguments, uses your system clock to return a combined date/time-number that represents the current date and time. The integer portion of the value returned is a date-number representing the current date, while the decimal portion is a time-number representing the current time.

Every time your worksheet is manually or automatically recalculated, the value returned by the @NOW function is automatically updated using your system clock. For example, suppose the operating system date is set to April 12, 1990 and the time is set to 2:02 PM. If you enter the @NOW function in cell A1, it returns the value 32975.5833. (If you need to modify the operating system time and date while in 1-2-3/G, you must do so using OS/2 or Presentation Manager.)

Note

> You can replace the @NOW function with the value it returns using the Range Value command. (See Chapter 4 for more details.)

Since the @NOW function returns a combined date/time-number, you cannot format a single cell to display both the current time and date. If you format cell A1 as a date, 1-2-3/G uses the integer portion of this value, 32975, as a date-number and returns the date April 2, 1990 in the date format you specify. If you time-format this cell, 1-2-3/G uses the decimal portion of this number, .5833, as a time-number, and returns the time 2:00 PM.

Note

> Use the TODAY function to return a date-number for the current date.

SPECIAL FUNCTIONS

1-2-3/G has several functions that do not fit into the other categories. These functions, listed in Table 6–18, include the following new functions: @SHEETS, @?, @??, @INFO, and @SOLVER.

Counting the Number of Columns, Rows, or Worksheets in a Range: @COLS, @ROWS, and @SHEETS

1-2-3/G includes three functions that return the number of columns, rows, and worksheets in a range. The form of these functions are:

@COLS(*range*)
@ROWS(*range*)
@SHEETS(*range*)

where your *range* argument must be a range name or address. Your range can be two- or three-dimensional. However, 1-2-3/G disallows your entry if your argument is a collection address, and returns ERR if it is a collection name.

TABLE 6–18 1-2-3/G's Special Functions

Special Function	Returns
@COLS	Number of columns in a range.
@ROWS	Number of rows in a range.
@SHEETS	Number of worksheets in a range.
@@	Value or string referenced by another cell.
@? and @??	Marks the place of an unknown add-in function you tried to import.
@CELL	Attribute of upper-left cell in a range.
@CELLPOINTER	Attribute of current cell.
@INFO	Operating system information for the current session.
@SOLVER	Solver information requested by one of the eight query arguments.

If you specify a three-dimensional *range* argument, the @COLS and @ROWS functions return the same number of columns or rows as for a two-dimensional argument. For example, both @COLS(A1) and @COLS(A:A1..B:A1) return 1, since 1-2-3/G evaluates column A in worksheets A and B as a single column. On the other hand, @SHEETS(A1) returns 1, while @SHEETS(A:A1..B:A1) returns 2, since @SHEETS counts the number of worksheets.

These functions are frequently used to determine the number of columns, rows, and worksheets in a named range. Another common application of these functions is in macros, where they are typically used to determine the number of columns, rows, or worksheets in a range, so other tasks can be performed that are based on the size of this range. For example, @SHEETS can be used in a macro to determine the number of sequential worksheets.

Indirectly Referencing Cells: @@

You can use 1-2-3/G's @@ function to indirectly reference a cell through another cell. The form of this function is

```
@@(location)
```

where your *location* argument must be a single cell reference expressed as a string. You can enter this argument as a range name or address, or as a formula that returns the address or name of a single cell expressed as a string. The @@ function returns ERR for an argument that is a collection or a multiple-cell range.

Suppose the cells in a worksheet contain the following:

	Scenario 1			Scenario 2	
Cell	**Contains**	**Returns**	**Cell**	**Contains**	**Returns**
A1	25	25	A1	25	25
B1	+A1	25	B1	'A1	A1
C1	@@(B1)	ERR	C1	@@(B1)	25

In both Scenario 1 and 2, cell A1 contains the value 25. In Scenario 1, cell B1 contains the formula +A1, and the function @@(B1) in cell C1 returns ERR. However, in Scenario 2, cell B1 contains the *string* A1, and @@(B1) in cell C1 returns the value 25. Since the *location* argument evaluates to a single cell address expressed as a string, A1, the @@ function returns the contents of the cell that is referenced by that cell's label contents, 25.

You can use the @@ function to build powerful conditional formulas. For example, suppose cell C10 contains the formula @@(B10), and cell B10 contains the formula @IF(A1="","B1","C1"). If cell A1 is empty (or has a 0 value), the formula in cell B10 returns the label "B1". Therefore, the @@(B10) formula in cell C10 returns the contents of cell B1. However, if cell A1 is not empty, the formula in cell B10 returns the label "C1" and the @@(B10) formula in cell C10 returns the contents of cell C1.

Marking an Unknown Add-in @Function: @? and @??

In previous releases of 1-2-3, you could use add-in @functions created using the Add-In Tool Kit, or use supplemental products that included add-in @functions. Unfortunately, when you import Release 2 and 3 files into 1-2-3/G, these add-in @functions are not recognized. Instead, 1-2-3/G replaces each add-in @function name with @? or @??. 1-2-3/G then evaluates the @? and @?? functions as the special value NA.

Determining an Attribute of a Cell: @CELL and @CELLPOINTER

1-2-3/G has two functions, @CELL and @CELLPOINTER, that return information about an attribute of a cell. The @CELLPOINTER function returns a value or label that describes an attribute of the current cellpointer location. The @CELL function returns a value or label that describes an attribute of the upper-left cell of a range. The forms of these functions are

@CELLPOINTER(*attribute*)
@CELL(*attribute,range*)

Your *attribute* argument can be one of the 58 different attributes shown in Table 6–19. Remember to enclose an attribute in double quotes if you enter it directly into the @CELL or @CELLPOINTER function. These functions return ERR for all arguments except those in Table 6–19.

As shown in Table 6–19, 1-2-3/G now includes *attribute* arguments for individual cell attributes set using the Range command, and *attribute* arguments for the worksheet file, set using the Worksheet Global commands. If a Range command has not been used on an individual cell, @CELL and @CELLPOINTER return the worksheet file attribute for a single-cell *attribute* argument.

@CELL's *range* argument can be either a range name or address. If you enter a single cell as *range*, 1-2-3/G converts it into a single-cell range address. 1-2-3/G disallows your entry if your *range* argument is a collection address, and returns ERR if it is a collection name.

Note

Since the results returned by @CELL and @CELLPOINTER are not always automatically recalculated, be sure to recalculate your worksheet to update the results returned by these functions.

For example, suppose you use the Range Format command on the range A1..B1 in Figure 6–60. All other cells are globally formatted. Column A contains *attribute* arguments. Column B displays the results returned by the @CELL function for these arguments. These @CELL functions evaluate the attributes of cell A1, the upper-left cell in the *range* argument A1..B2, regardless of the cellpointer location. For example, in cell B5, @CELL(A5,A1..B2) returns the center label prefix ^ when cell A5 contains the *attribute* argument "prefix." However, in cell B6, @CELL(A6,A1..B2) returns the global label prefix ' indicating left-alignment, since the "sprefix" *attribute* argument is used in cell A6. In cell B7, the @CELL function returns the path and filename C:\LAURA\SPEC2.WG1 for the *filename* attribute argument.

For the "address" *attribute,* @CELL(A8,A1..B2) in cell B8 of Figure 6–60 returns the 2–D absolute address of the first cell in the *range* argument, $A$1. (When the "coord" *attribute* is used, the 3–D absolute address $A:$A$1 is returned.) Likewise, the worksheet coordinates of the first cell, A1, in the range A1..B2, is 1,1,1 (column,row,sheet), so the @CELL function returns 1 for the "col" *attribute,* 1 for the "row" *attribute,* and 1 for the "sheet" *attribute,* as shown in the range A9..A11 of Figure 6–60.

123G.EXE — Ready

File Edit Worksheet Range Copy... Move... Print Graph Data Utility Quit... Help

A:A2 'label

(C0) C:\LAURA\SPEC2.WG1

A	A	B	C	D	E
1	label	$500			
2	label				
3	Attribute	@CELL	@CELLPOINTER		
4	==========	========================	========================		
5	prefix	^	'		
6	sprefix	'	'		
7	filename	C:\LAURA\SPEC2.WG1	C:\LAURA\SPEC2.WG1		
8	address	$A$1	$A$2		
9	col	1	1		
10	row	1	2		
11	sheet	1	1		
12					

FIGURE 6–60 Using @CELL and @CELLPOINTER

However, the results returned by @CELLPOINTER in the range C5..C11 of Figure 6–60 vary, depending on the cellpointer location, for the same set of *attribute* arguments (column A). For example, in Figure 6–60, the cellpointer is located in cell A2, so the @CELLPOINTER functions in column C return the specified attribute information for cell A2. The global label prefix ' is returned for both the single-cell and worksheet *attribute* arguments in column A (cells C2 and C3). Therefore, a nonglobal label prefix has not been specified for cell A2. However, if the cellpointer is located in cell A1, the @CELLPOINTER functions in column C return information for that cell, and would return the same information as the @CELL functions in column B. If the cellpointer is located in a blank cell, such as cell B2, @CELLPOINTER returns nothing for those particular attributes.

The function @CELLPOINTER(A8) returns the same path and filename as the @CELL function in cell B8. However, since @CELLPOINTER returns the specified attribute information for the current cellpointer location, cell A2, for the "address" *attribute*, @CELLPOINTER(A8) returns the 2-D absolute address of cell A2, $A$2. Likewise, @CELLPOINTER returns the worksheet coordinates of this cell, A:A2, and returns 1 for the "col" *attribute*, 2 for the "row" *attribute*, and 1 for the "sheet" *attribute*.

Typically, the @CELL function is used in a macro to check the attributes of a cell location before a certain type of entry is allowed. The @CELLPOINTER function is also commonly used in macros as well as in conditional @IF functions to check the contents of the current cellpointer location. For example, the following macro checks the contents of the current cellpointer location. If the cell is empty, this macro branches to the routine named FILL_IT. Otherwise, it branches to the routine named FORMAT_IT.

```
{IF @CELLPOINTER("contents")=""}{BRANCH FILL_IT}
{BRANCH FORMAT_IT}
```

TABLE 6-19 Attribute Arguments for @CELL and @CELLPOINTER

Attribute for Single Cell	Global Attribute for Worksheet File	Status
"zerosuppress"	"szerosuppress"	Global zero suppressions status: 1 if suppressed, 0 if not suppressed, or if a label is defined for zeros

(continued)

TABLE 6-19 Attribute Arguments for @CELL and @CELLPOINTER (Cont.)

Attribute for Single Cell	Global Attribute for Worksheet File	Status
"protect"	"sprotect"	Cell protection status: 1 protected, 0 otherwise
		Format
"format"	"sformat"	Cell format such as F2 (fixed, 2 places)
"parentheses"	"sparentheses"	Parentheses format, 1 formatted with parentheses, 0 otherwise.
		Alignment
"prefix"	"sprefix"	Label prefix, such as ^ for centered
"vprefix"	"svprefix"	Value alignment, such as * for left-aligned
		Border-line Pattern A—D for:
"bborder"	"sbborder"	Bottom border pattern
"lborder"	"slborder"	Left border pattern
"rborder"	"srborder"	Right border pattern
"tborder"	"stborder"	Top border pattern
		Background palette color A—P for:
"blcolor"	"sblcolor"	Label
"bvcolorneg"	"sbvcolorneg"	Negative value
"bvcolorpos"	"sbvcolorpos"	Positive value
		Foreground palette color A—P for:
"flcolor"	"sflcolor"	Label
"fvcolorneg"	"sfvcolorneg"	Negative value
"fvcolorpos"	"sfvcolorpos"	Positive value
		Font
"fontid"	"sfontid"	Font id as letter from A to T
"fontnamep"	"sfontnamep"	Printer font name
"fontnames"	"sfontnames"	Screen font name
"fontpointp"	"sfontpointp"	Printer font point size
"fontpoints"	"sfontpoints"	Screen font point size
"fontattrib"	"sfontattrib"	Font attribute: 4-digit string, 1 selected, 0 unselected, such

(continued)

TABLE 6–19 **Attribute Arguments for @CELL and @CELLPOINTER (Cont.)**

Attribute for Single Cell	Global Attribute for Worksheet File	Status
		as 0101 for bold unselected, italic selected, underline unselected, and strikeout selected
		Setting
"calprecision"	"scalprecision"	Calculating precision, NA for full precision, an integer from 0 to 15 if limited by Range Attributes Precision
"longlabel"	"slonglabel"	Long label setting, 0 for short label, 1 for long label
		Miscellaneous
"filename"		Cell filename, including path, such as C:\123G\WORK \SHEET1.WG1
"address"		2–D absolute address of cell, such as $A$1
"coord"		3–D absolute address of cell, such as $A:$A$1
"col"		Cell column number from 1 to 256
"row"		Cell row number from 1 to 8192
"sheet"		Cell worksheet number from 1 to 256
"contents"		Contents of cell, such as 2*B5
"type"		Type of data in cell: b for blank, l for label, v for value or formula
"width"		Column width of cell
"color"		Color status of a negative value in cell: 1 if in color, 0 otherwise

Returning Operating System Information: @INFO

1-2-3/G includes a new function, @INFO, which returns specified information about the operating system. The form of this function is

`@INFO(attribute)`

where your *attribute* argument must be one of the attributes listed in Table 6–20. Remember to enclose an attribute in double quotes if it is entered directly into the @INFO function. The @INFO function returns ERR for all arguments except those in Table 6–20.

Note

> Since OS/2 uses virtual memory, the values returned by @INFO for the "totmem" and "memavail" arguments are less accurate than the value returned by the "memused" argument. For this reason, when you want to keep track of the size of an application, use @INFO("memused").

TABLE 6–20 The @INFO *Attribute* Arguments

Attribute	@INFO Returns
"directory"	Current path
"system"	Name of the operating system
"osversion"	Current operating system version
"release"	Release number of 1-2-3/G
"numfile"	Current number of open files
"memavail"	Amount of available memory
"memused"	Amount of memory being used for data
"totmem"	Total available memory (current available and current used)
"origin"	Address of the first cell in a window that contains the cellpointer
"osreturncode"	Value returned by the most recent system command or {SYSTEM} macro command
"recalc"	The strings "automatic" or "manual" describing the current recalculation mode
"mode"	Current mode: 0–WAIT, 1–READY, 2–LABEL, 3–MENU, 4–VALUE, 5–POINT, 6–EDIT, 10–HELP, 99–all other modes

The @INFO function is most commonly used in macros. You can use it to:

- Provide 1-2-3/G status information to the user, such as a warning that memory is low.
- Act on 1-2-3/G status information, such as determining the current path and using it to save a file, or closing open windows if memory is low.

For example, the following statements in a macro use the @INFO function to determine if memory currently used is greater than 90% of total memory. If it is, the macro displays a MEMORY LOW indicator.

```
{IF @INFO("memused")>.9*@INFO("totmem")}{INDICATE "MEMORY LOW"}
```

Returning Information about Solver: @SOLVER

1-2-3/G includes a new function, @SOLVER, which returns information about the status of 1-2-3/G's new Solver Utility. (For more information about the Solver Utility, see Chapter 13.) The form of this function is

@SOLVER(*query-string*)

where your *query-string* argument must be one of the eight queries listed in Table 6–21. The @SOLVER function returns ERR for all arguments except those in Table 6–21. Remember to enclose a *query-string* in double quotes if entered directly into the @SOLVER function.

For a given *query-string* argument in Table 6–21, @SOLVER returns one of the values listed under @SOLVER Returns in the table. As you can see, there are several possible results for each *query-string*, depending on the progress of the Solver in solving the current problem.

The @SOLVER function is used primarily in macros that control the operation of the Solver. In fact, the example that follows shows you how you can use the value returned by the @SOLVER function to control the flow of a macro.

Note

Do not place the @SOLVER function in any of the worksheets that Solver uses to solve the current problem. The @SOLVER function is recalculated whenever 1-2-3/G recalculates the worksheet containing it. As soon as the Solver finishes solving a problem, the @SOLVER function is updated, causing the worksheet to recalculate. Solver will interpret this recalculation as a change to the problem and will discard the answers it found up to that point.

Example

The following example is an excerpt from a macro that runs the Solver. The macro is composed of two parts, a calling routine (\A) and a subroutine (CHECKIT). In the subroutine, the @SOLVER function is used with the "done" *query-string* argument to direct the operation of the macro.

```
\A           /usRESALE.WG1/sp{CHECKIT}
             {TOOLMENU}n

CHECKIT {IF @SOLVER("done")=1}/ao{RETURN}
        {WAIT @NOW+@TIME(0,0,3)}{BRANCH CHECKIT}
```

The first line of macro invokes the Solver by selecting the Utility Solver command and activating the RESALE.WG1 file (already in memory). In the same line, the Solve Problem command is selected from Solver's main menu to begin solving the problem previously defined in the RESALE.WG1 file. Finally, the CHECKIT subroutine is called.

In the first line of the CHECKIT subroutine, the @SOLVER function is used as the argument for the {IF} command. If @SOLVER("done") equals 1, meaning the solver is finished solving the problem, the Answer Optimal command is selected from Solver's main menu. This command displays the optimal answer in the worksheet. Control is then passed back to the second line of the calling routine (/A) and the Solver is minimized.

However, if the Solver is not done solving the problem, control is passed to the second line of the CHECKIT subroutine. This line pauses the macro for three seconds, before branching back to the first line of the CHECKIT subroutine. The first line of the CHECKIT subroutine once again checks the status of the Solver. Thus, a continuous loop is executed based on the value of the @SOLVER function. Only when the Solver is finished solving the problem, is the macro allowed to continue.

TABLE 6-21 **The @SOLVER Query-String Arguments**

Query-string Argument	Question asked by query-string	@SOLVER Returns	Meaning
"consistent"	All constraints satisfied by current answer?	1	True
		2	At least one constraint returned 0 (false)
"done"	Solver done?	1	Finished
		2	Still in process

TABLE 6-21 The @SOLVER Query-String Arguments (*Continued*)

Query-string Argument	Question asked by query-string	@SOLVER Returns	Meaning
		3	Solver active, but has not yet started
		ERR	Solver inactive
"moreanswers"	Can Solver find more answers?	1	All answers found
		2	More answers may exist if Solve Continue chosen, or Solve in answer window selected
"needguess"	Are guesses needed for Solver to find an answer?	1	No guesses needed
		2	Guesses needed
		ERR	Solver inactive, or no answer in worksheet
"numanswers"	Number of answers or attempts Solver Found?	Number	Number of answers or attempts found by Solver
		ERR	Solver inactive, or has not yet solved the problem
"optimal"	Status of optimal answer?	1	Optimal answer
		2	Best answer found
		3	Problem unbounded
		4	No answer found, or no optimization found
		ERR	Solver inactive

(continued)

TABLE 6-21 The @SOLVER Query-String Arguments (*Continued*)

Query-string Argument	Question asked by query-string	@SOLVER Returns	Meaning
"progress"	Progress made by Solver?	Number	Percent of solving completed
		ERR	Solver inactive, or has not begun solving
"result"	Solver's result?	1	Solver found at least 1 answer
		2	No answers found, but representative attempts available
		ERR	Solver inactive, or has not yet solved the problem

SUMMARY

In this chapter, you have seen that 1-2-3/G offers an expanded group of functions that offer you more power and flexibility than ever. For example, now 1-2-3/G's functions can be used between worksheet files, and in some cases, with three-dimensional ranges. As you have seen, 1-2-3/G's functions are one of the most indispensable tools for mathematical, financial, statistical, logical, string, date and time, and special calculations.

Graphs

One of the most appealing features of 1-2-3/G is its powerful graphics capability. For example, you can create nine different graph types in 1-2-3/G: area, bar, high-low-close-open (HLCO), line, overlapped-bar, pie, stacked-bar, 3–D bar, and XY. In addition, you can combine multiple graph types to create a style all your own, for example, a combination bar and line graph. 1-2-3/G also offers a variety of ways to enhance your graphs, including the ability to change fonts, colors, and line widths and to attach notes, arrows, and lines. In fact, 1-2-3/G's graphics so far outstrip its predecessors that the graphics are reason enough to use the program.

In many ways, 1-2-3/G's graphics capabilities are as powerful as those offered by the leading presentation graphics programs, such as Harvard Graphics and Lotus Freelance Plus. And although 1-2-3/G does not offer freehand drawing or the ability to load and use clip art (bitmaps), the graphs that 1-2-3/G creates are often more visually appealing.

In previous releases of 1-2-3, the only way to create a graph was by using the Graph commands on 1-2-3's main menu. In 1-2-3/G, however, you can create a graph using the Worksheet window's Graph commands or the Graph Tool. In general, you use the Graph commands to quickly create a graph from worksheet data, then use the Graph Tool commands to enhance the graph in a number of ways.

This chapter describes how to create graphs using both the Graph commands and Graph Tool. For the most part, the topics are covered in the order in which you are likely to use them. First, you will learn how to create a basic graph and save it for later sessions. You'll then learn all the different ways you can enhance a graph—for example, by changing its type or by adding legends, titles, and a variety of other objects. Finally, you'll learn how to print graphs, and to preview graphs before you print them.

What's New

If you have created graphs in a previous release of 1-2-3, you'll soon find that many of the familiar Graph commands are available, but that they are located in slightly different places on the Graph menu. For example, to set X labels in 1-2-3 Release 2.2, you use the /Graph X command. In 1-2-3/G, however, you use the Graph Add Ranges X command. But these traditional Graph commands just scratch the surface of 1-2-3/G graphics power. An entirely new set of commands are available from the Graph Tool window.

Like Release 3, 1-2-3/G offers three new graph types: area graphs, high-low-close-open (HLCO), and horizontal graphs. In addition, 1-2-3/G offers two entirely new graph types: overlapping bar graphs and 3–D bar graphs. Further, you can combine multiple graph types to create your own unique graph type. For example, you may start out with a bar graph, then change the graph type for an individual data series to a line.

Here are some other new features of 1-2-3/G's graphs:

- You can create a second *y*-axis and assign ranges to it.
- You can use the Graph window's Type Gallery command to select a graph type.
- You can select your own fonts, colors, and display patterns.
- Changing a graph object is easy in 1-2-3/G. To change an object, you simply highlight it in the graph (by clicking on it or by pressing TAB). You can then perform an action on the object, such as change its contents.
- You can add your own notations, including text, lines, and arrows.
- You can move and resize graph objects.
- You can have up to 23 data ranges in most graphs.
- As in Release 3, you can print directly from 1-2-3/G and place graphs and worksheet data on the same page.
- You can link data from different worksheets, even from different files.

These are just some of the major enhancements to 1-2-3's graphs. You'll find many others as you read through the chapter.

ELEMENTS OF A GRAPH

Whenever you create a graph in 1-2-3/G, it always appears within a Graph window, as shown in Figure 7–1. The bulk of the information for the graph appears within the *plot frame,* which is the rectangular border that surrounds the bars in Figure 7–1. On the left side of the plot frame is the *y-axis,* and at the bottom of the plot frame is the *x-axis.* The lower-left corner of the plot frame, where the *x*- and *y*-axes meet, is the *origin.* All graphs, except pie graphs, have *x*- and *y*-axes.

The y-axis always contains a numeric scale representing the range of values in your graph. 1-2-3/G automatically assigns this scale based on the values you are graphing. The tick marks along the y-axis represent units of measure, spaced at even intervals. Y-axis labels appear to the left of the y-axis tick marks and describe the y-axis scale. 1-2-3/G creates these labels automatically based on the y-axis scale, and you cannot edit them.

The *x*-axis, on the other hand, represents each item in a data series, often time periods, with each tick mark representing a week, month, or year, for example. The *x*-axis can also represent expense items, salespeople, regions, and the like. X *labels* usually appear along the *x*-axis of a graph with each label identifying an item in a data series. X labels are taken from (linked to) cells in a worksheet file.

The *x*-axis can also represent a numeric scale in the case of an XY graph. When the *x*-axis is used in this capacity, 1-2-3/G creates the X labels automatically, based on the *x*-axis scale.

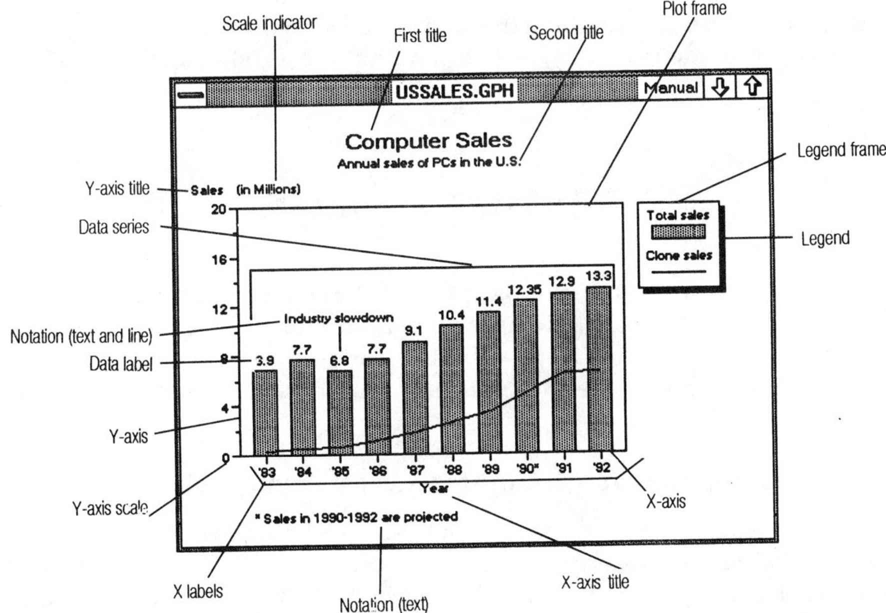

FIGURE 7–1 The elements of a graph window

When you select values to appear in a graph, they are represented as a *data series*. A data series is simply the graphic representation of a *data range*, a set of worksheet values. There are actually two data series in Figure 7–1—one appears as a group of bars and the other as a line. A data series can also be represented by an area, a group of pie slices, or a group of symbols.

Here are some other elements you are likely to find in a graph:

- **Data label:** A label placed near a data point indicating the actual value of that point (see "Adding Data Labels").
- **First title:** The main title of a graph. You can enter the first title manually, or you can link it to a cell in a worksheet file (see "Titles").
- **Second title:** The secondary title of a graph. You can enter the second title manually, or you can link it to a cell in a worksheet file.
- **Legend:** A set of legend labels and their accompanying patterns that acts as a key to the data series in a graph. The legend labels and patterns appear within a *legend frame*. Legend labels are often taken from (linked to) cells in a worksheet file (see "Legends").
- **Notation:** There are three types of notation in 1-2-3/G: text, lines, and arrows. You can add as many notations as you like to a graph (see "Annotating a Graph").
- **Scale indicator:** A description of the units used for the scale of a graph. You can have 1-2-3/G create the scale indicator automatically or you can assign it yourself manually (see "Controlling the Scale Indicator").
- ***x*-axis title:** The title describing the data assigned to the x-axis of a graph. You can assign the title manually, or you can link it to a cell in a worksheet file. (In an XY graph, the x-axis title describes the x-axis scale.)
- ***y*-axis title:** The title describing the data assigned to the *y*-axis of a graph. You can assign the title manually, or you can link it to a cell in a worksheet file.

CREATING A GRAPH

There are two ways to create a graph in 1-2-3/G. You can use the Graph commands in the Worksheet window's main menu, or you can use the Edit Link command from the Graph window's main menu. The sections that follow describe how to use these different methods for creating a graph.

Using the Graph Commands to Create a Graph

By far the easiest way to create a graph in 1-2-3/G is to use the Graph commands from the Worksheet window's main menu. You can create a graph *manually* by using Graph commands to assign different graph elements, such as data ranges, X labels, legends, and titles. In addition, you can have 1-2-3/G create a graph for you *automatically* by using Graph View or Graph Setup. In general, you use

Graph View when you want to accept all of 1-2-3/G's default settings for creating the graph—for example, the graph type and the way 1-2-3/G automatically interprets data ranges from a worksheet file. On the other hand, you use Graph Setup when you want to have more control over these settings.

Creating a Graph Manually—An Example

Although you can have 1-2-3/G automatically create a graph with Graph View or Graph Setup, before you do so, it first helps to understand how to manually create a graph using the Graph commands. That way, you can better control how 1-2-3/G interprets your data when you have it automatically create a graph.

The first part of manually creating a graph with the Graph command is setting data ranges. *Data ranges* are the actual worksheet ranges from which 1-2-3/G creates your graph. To manually set data ranges in 1-2-3/G, you use the Graph Add Ranges command.

For example, suppose you want to create a graph that compares the yearly sales of PCs versus "clones" using the data in the worksheet file in Figure 7–2. When you select Graph Add Ranges, your screen shows a dialog box, as in Figure 7–3. Enter your first data range by choosing A and selecting to the total sales range, B6..B15, in Figure 7–2. Next, enter the second data range by choosing B and selecting the clone sales range, C6..C15. Figure 7–3 shows how your data range settings should appear. Press ENTER or select OK to complete the command.

After setting the data ranges, you can take a look at the resulting graph by selecting Graph View. 1-2-3/G creates the line graph in Figure 7–4.

Even though this graph correctly depicts the relationship between the values you selected, it does not really tell you much. You can easily enhance the graph to tell a more complete story by changing its default titles and legends and by adding more enhancements to the graph, such as X labels.

From this point on, you can use the Graph Tool menu to enhance the graph. However, when you are first starting to work with 1-2-3/G's graphs, you may find it easier to enhance a graph by returning to the Worksheet window and using the Graph menu. After creating a graph, you can redisplay the Worksheet window's main menu by pressing NEXT WINDOW (CTRL-F6), or use the Window command from the Desktop control menu. Of course, you may want to reposition the Graph window so that it and the Worksheet window appear next to each other on the screen, making it easier for you to move back and forth between the two windows.

After returning to the Worksheet window, you can add some X labels to the graph by selecting the Graph Add Ranges command and choosing the X box (see Figure 7–3). Point to the labels in the range A6..A15, and select OK or press ENTER. When you later switch to the Graph Window with NEXT WINDOW

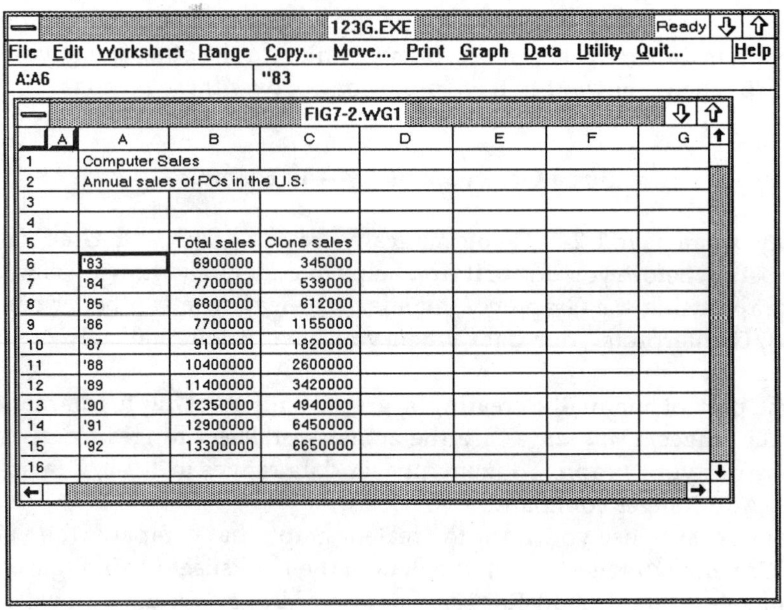

123G.EXE Ready

File Edit Worksheet Range Copy... Move... Print Graph Data Utility Quit... Help

A:A6 "83

FIG7-2.WG1

A	A	B	C	D	E	F	G
1	Computer Sales						
2	Annual sales of PCs in the U.S.						
3							
4							
5		Total sales	Clone sales				
6	'83	6900000	345000				
7	'84	7700000	539000				
8	'85	6800000	612000				
9	'86	7700000	1155000				
10	'87	9100000	1820000				
11	'88	10400000	2600000				
12	'89	11400000	3420000				
13	'90	12350000	4940000				
14	'91	12900000	6450000				
15	'92	13300000	6650000				
16							

FIGURE 7–2 Some sample data to be graphed

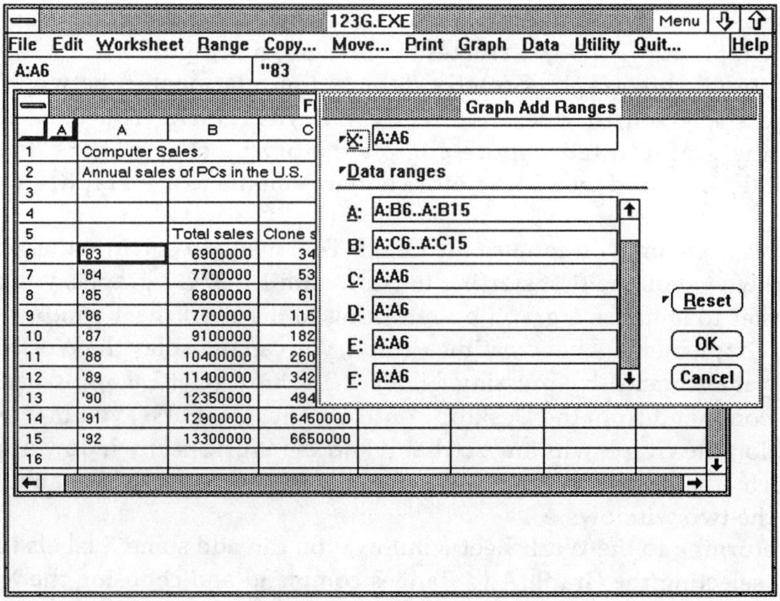

123G.EXE Menu

File Edit Worksheet Range Copy... Move... Print Graph Data Utility Quit... Help

A:A6 "83

Graph Add Ranges

X: A:A6

Data ranges

A: A:B6..A:B15

B: A:C6..A:C15

C: A:A6

D: A:A6

E: A:A6

F: A:A6

Reset

OK

Cancel

FIGURE 7–3 The Graph Add Ranges dialog box

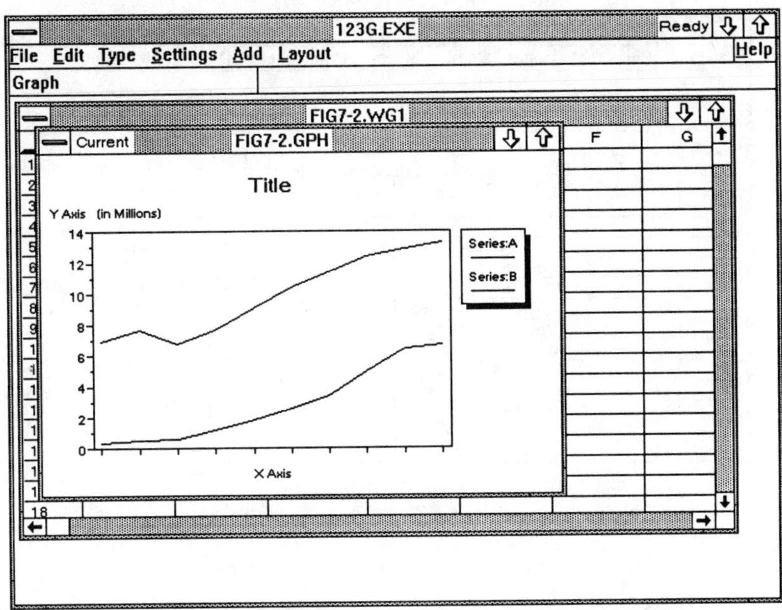

FIGURE 7–4 After selecting Graph View

(CTRL-F6), labels for each year will now appear under the corresponding tick marks.

To change the graph's default titles to more descriptive titles, select the Graph Options Titles command. 1-2-3/G then shows a dialog box, as in Figure 7–5. To clear the default titles (Title, X Axis, and Y Axis) from the dialog box, select the Reset option. Next, to set the first (or main) title for the graph, select the First option and type **\A1**. The backslash tells 1-2-3/G to take the contents of the cell that follows, in this case cell A1, Computer Sales, and apply it to the first title. (Without the backslash, 1-2-3/G would interpret this as a literal string. See "Titles" later for more information.) Likewise, to apply the contents of cell A2, Annual sales of PCs in the U.S., to the Second title for the graph, type **\A2**.

Next, to change the graph's default legend labels to more descriptive labels, select the Graph Options Legends command. 1-2-3/G displays a dialog box similar to the one in Figure 7–6. To clear the default legend labels (Series:A, Series:B, Series:C, and so on) from the dialog box, select the Reset option. Next, to apply the contents of cell B5, Total sales, to the legend for the A data range, select the A option and type **\B5**. Next, select the B option and type **\C5** to apply the contents of cell C5, Clone sales, to the legend for the B data range.

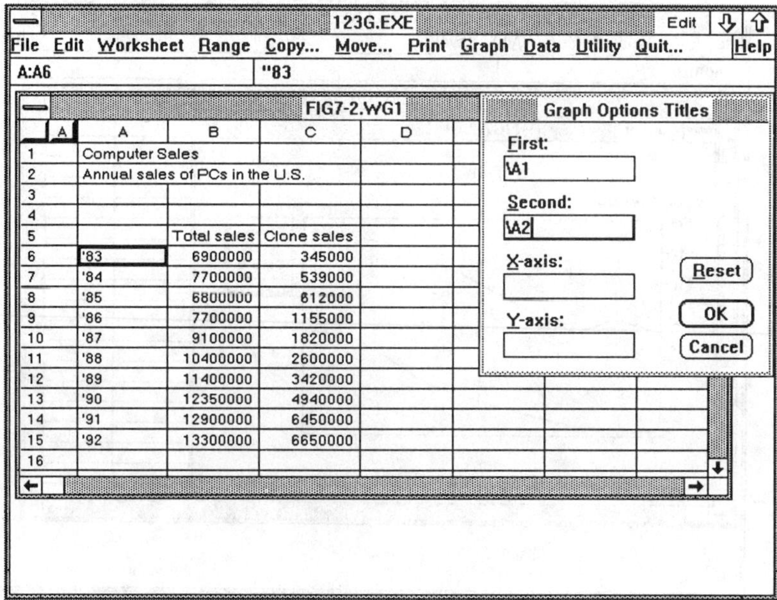

FIGURE 7–5 The Graph Options Titles dialog box

123G.EXE Edit

File Edit Worksheet Range Copy... Move... Print Graph Data Utility Quit... Help

A:A6 "83

Graph Options Legends

Data ranges

A: \B5

B: \C5

C:

D:

E:

F:

Range: A:A6

Reset

OK

Cancel

	A	B	C
1	Computer Sales		
2	Annual sales of PCs in the U.S.		
3			
4			
5		Total sales	Clone s
6	'83	6900000	34
7	'84	7700000	53
8	'85	6800000	61
9	'86	7700000	115
10	'87	9100000	182
11	'88	10400000	260
12	'89	11400000	342
13	'90	12350000	494
14	'91	12900000	6450000
15	'92	13300000	6650000
16			

FIGURE 7–6 The Graph Options Legends dialog box

After changing the graph's titles and legends and adding X labels to the graph, you can redisplay the updated Graph window by pressing NEXT WINDOW (CTRL-F6), or use the Window command from the Desktop control menu. Figure 7–7 shows the results.

Suppose you want to see how the graph in Figure 7–7 would look as a bar or area graph. Changing the graph type is simple, and you can experiment with different graph types without losing your current settings. To change the graph in Figure 7–7 from a line graph (the default) to a bar graph, perform either of the following:

- Choose Type from the Graph Tool menu and select Bar from the command options.
- Return to the worksheet window by pressing NEXT WINDOW (CTRL-F6), select the Graph Type command, choose the Bar option followed by OK, and press NEXT WINDOW again to redisplay the Graph window.

Once you have created a graph, if you make any changes to the values in the data ranges, 1-2-3/G automatically updates the graph to reflect the changes. Suppose, for example, that you receive updated information indicating that clone sales in 1990 are 5,500,000 units instead of 4,940,000. If you return to the

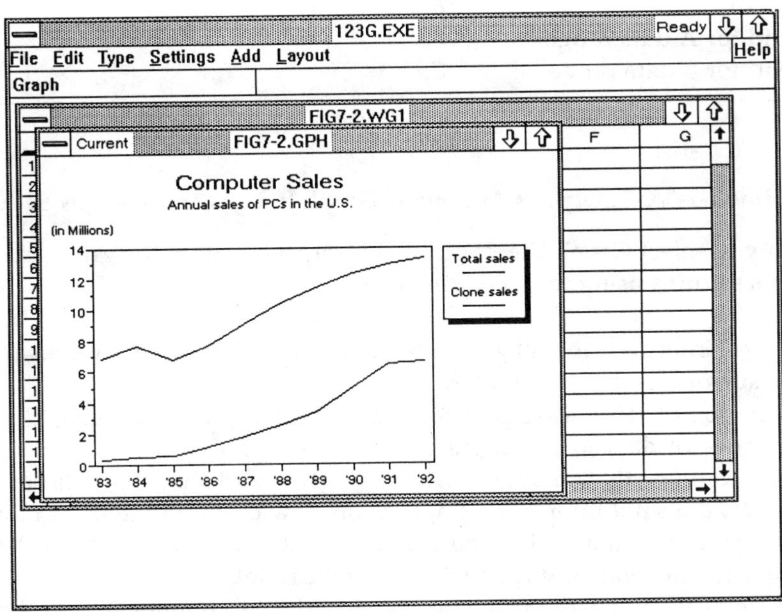

FIGURE 7–7 After adding X labels, titles, and legends

worksheet window and enter this new value in cell C13 of Figure 7–2, your graph will adjust automatically to reflect the change. To see the updated graph, press NEXT WINDOW (CTRL-F6).

Creating a Graph Automatically with Graph View

You can have 1-2-3/G automatically create a graph for you by selecting the single-worksheet range that encompasses all the data you want to graph (an *automatic graph range*) and choosing Graph View. Alternatively, you can locate the cell pointer anywhere within the range before selecting Graph View. If you use the second method, you must make sure that the automatic graph range is surrounded by the worksheet borders (column letters and row numbers) or by two consecutive blank columns and rows.

For example, suppose you want to have 1-2-3/G automatically create a graph of the data on PC sales in Figure 7–2. You can either highlight the range A5..C15, or locate the cell pointer anywhere within this range, and select Graph View. 1-2-3/G creates the line graph in Figure 7–8 using the following settings:

Graph Element	Setting
X label range	A6..A15
A data range	B6..B15
B data range	C6..C15
Legend for A data range	\B5
Legend for B data range	\C5

How 1-2-3/G Interprets Automatic Graph Ranges and Assigns Settings

When you select Graph View, 1-2-3/G interprets automatic graph ranges and assigns settings using the following rules:

- 1-2-3/G interprets the range you have selected or the single-worksheet range that surrounds the cell pointer.
- If you do not select a range before choosing Graph View, 1-2-3/G identifies the range of data to be graphed by searching for two blank rows and two blank columns that surround the data, or the worksheet boundaries. That is, 1-2-3/G does not interpret a single blank row or column to mean the end of a range. For example, in Figure 7–9A, A1..G7 is a range that 1-2-3/G can properly interpret, and A11..D13 is one it cannot.

Figure 7–9B shows the results of placing the cell pointer within the correct automatic graph range, A1..G7, and selecting Graph View. Here are the data ranges that 1-2-3/G automatically assigns

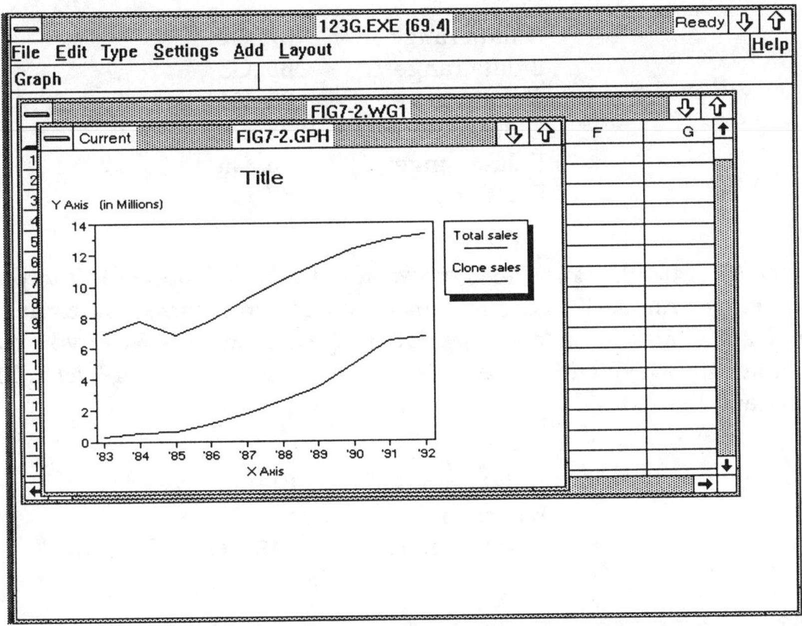

FIGURE 7–8 After using Graph View to create a line graph from the data in Figure 7–2

123G.EXE [69.4] Ready

File Edit Worksheet Range Copy... Move... Print Graph Data Utility Quit... Help

A:A1

FIG7-9.WG1

	A	B	C	D	E	F	G	H	I
1		APR	MAY	JUN	JUL	AUG	SEP		
2	Gears	11	13	16	29	30	30		
3	Bearings	7	9	10	18	23	41		
4	Wheels	15	16	20	24	28	41		
5	Spokes	12	18	23	34	52	72		
6	Tires	17	35	19	34	55	84		
7	Valves	9	11	14	16	20	36		
8									
9									
10	JUN PARTS SALES					JUL PARTS SALES			
11	Gears	16	Spokes	23		Gears	29	Spokes	34
12	Bearings	10	Tires	19		Bearings	18	Tires	34
13	Wheels	20	Valves	14		Wheels	24	Valves	16
14									
15									
16									

Correct automatic graph range (A1..G7)

Incorrect automatic graph range (A11..D13)

FIGURE 7–9A Correct and incorrect automatic graph ranges for creating a graph with Graph View

A data range:	B2..G2
B data range:	B3..G3
C data range:	B4..G4
D data range:	B5..G5
E data range:	B6..G6
F data range:	B7..G7

On the other hand, Figure 7–9C shows how 1-2-3/G's automatic interpretation of data ranges can easily go awry when you use an incorrect automatic graph range. 1-2-3/G makes the following data range assignments when you place the cell pointer anywhere within the incorrect automatic graph range, A11..D13, and select Graph View:

A data range:	B11..Ill
B data range:	B12..I12
C data range:	B13..I12

- 1-2-3/G creates as many data ranges as there are rows or columns of values in the range. You can have up to 23 data ranges in a graph, each identified by a letter A–W. For example, for the data in Figure 7–2, 1-2-3/G reads the range A5..C15 and assigns the first column of values, B6..B15, to the A data range and the second column of values, C6..C15, to the B data range. The values in the A data range are displayed by the upper line in Figure 7–3, and the values in the B data range are displayed by the lower line. 1-2-3/G uses the data ranges created with Graph View for all subsequent Graph commands.

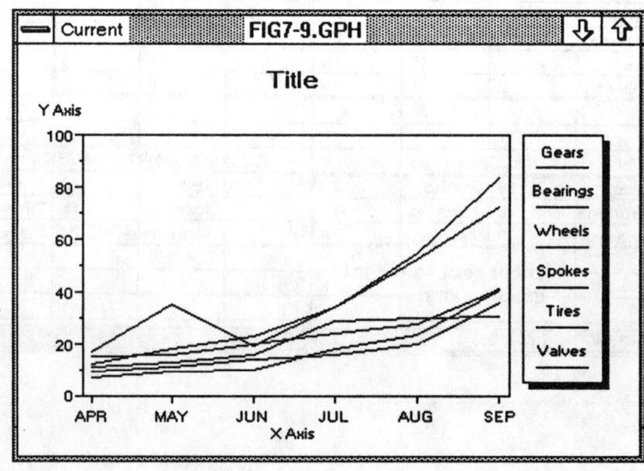

FIGURE 7–9B Results of Graph View with the correct automatic graph range

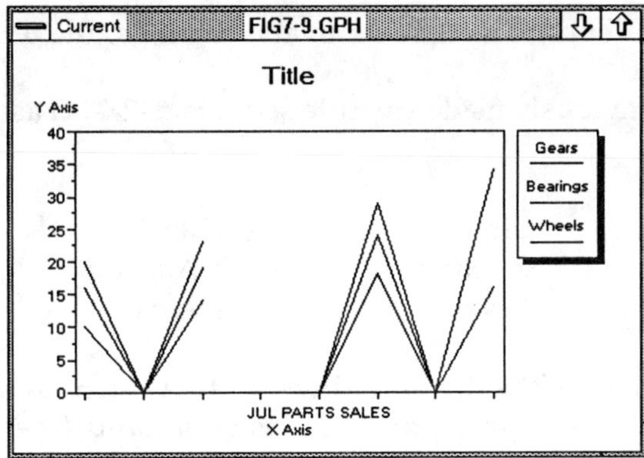

FIGURE 7–9C Results of Graph View with the incorrect automatic graph range

- If the range you have selected has more rows than columns (as is the case in Figure 7–2), 1-2-3/G interprets it in a columnwise fashion. In addition, if it finds labels in the first column of the range, they become X labels. If it finds labels in the first row of the range, they become legend labels.
- If the range you have selected has more columns than rows, or the same number of columns and rows (as is the case for the correct range at the top of Figure 7–9A), 1-2-3/G interprets it in a rowwise fashion. In addition, labels in the first column of the range become legend labels, and labels in the first row of the range become X labels.

Note

> If you want to override 1-2-3/G's rowwise or columnwise interpretation, use the Orientation option of the Graph Setup command instead of Graph View (see the next section).

Note

> When you select Graph View, if 1-2-3/G cannot find any legend labels, it automatically assigns the text Series:A, Series:B, and so on as the legends for the graph.

- 1-2-3/G uses the current Graph command settings, including the current graph type.
- If you haven't previously made any title settings, 1-2-3/G assigns these titles to the graph:

First:	Title
X-axis:	X Axis
Y-axis:	Y Axis

One way to change the title settings is to return to the Worksheet window and use the Graph Options Titles command (see "Titles" below for more detailed information). Another option is to select the title from the Graph window by clicking on it or by pressing TAB repeatedly until the title is highlighted, then type the new title in the Contents box on the right side of the Control line (see "Selecting and Changing Graph Objects" below).

Note

If you have previously specified data ranges for the current graph, 1-2-3/G uses the current settings rather than interpret new data ranges from the worksheet file. If you still want 1-2-3/G to interpret the data anyway, you have two options: (1) you can use the Graph Reset command to reset *all* the current graph settings; or (2) you can use the Graph Add Ranges Reset command to reset the data ranges for the current graph. See "Resetting Graph Settings" for more information.

Creating a Graph with Graph Setup

Another way to automatically create a graph from worksheet data is to use the Graph Setup command. The advantage of using Graph Setup over Graph View is that you gain more control over the type of graph that 1-2-3/G creates (by default, 1-2-3/G will only create a line graph) and how 1-2-3/G interprets settings from the worksheet file.

For example, suppose you want to create a bar graph from the data in Figure 7–2. When you select Graph Setup, 1-2-3/G displays the dialog box shown in Figure 7–10. To create a bar graph, simply select the Bar option from the list of seven graph types and select OK, or press ENTER. Figure 7–11 shows the results. (See "Graph Types" later for a description of the seven different graph

123G.EXE — Menu

File Edit Worksheet Range Copy... Move... Print Graph Data Utility Quit... Help

A:A6 "83

FIG7-

	A	B	C
1	Computer Sales		
2	Annual sales of PCs in the U.S.		
3			
4			
5		Total sales	Clone sale
6	'83	6900000	34500
7	'84	7700000	53900
8	'85	6800000	61200
9	'86	7700000	115500
10	'87	9100000	182000
11	'88	10400000	260000
12	'89	11400000	342000
13	'90	12350000	494000
14	'91	12900000	6450000
15	'92	13300000	6650000
16			

Graph Setup

Type: Line (selected), Bar, Pie, XY, Stacked bar, 3-D bar, Area

Orientation: Rowwise, Columnwise (selected)

[X] X labels from first column

[X] Legends from first row

Range(s): A:A5..A:C15

OK Cancel

FIGURE 7–10 The Graph Setup dialog box

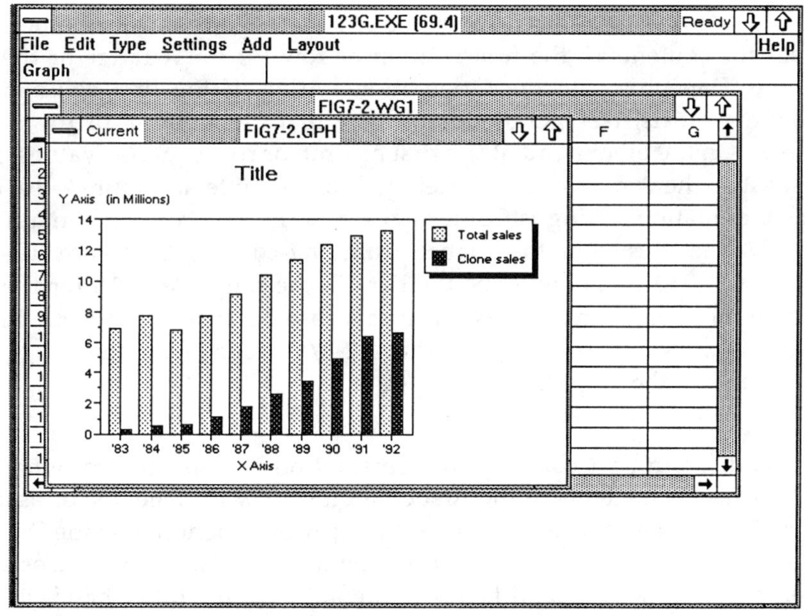

FIGURE 7–11 Results of the Graph Setup command

types available from the Graph Type and Graph Setup commands available from the Worksheet window and the nine different graph types available from the Graph window's Type command.)

Besides the graph type, here are some of the other settings you can control with the Graph Setup command:

- **Range(s)**: If you have not selected a range before choosing Graph Setup, 1-2-3/G automatically reads the data surrounding the cell pointer and displays the range in the Range(s) box. (It follows the same rules for interpreting ranges as for Graph View. See the previous section.) For example, in Figure 7–10 notice that 1-2-3/G has automatically determined that A:A5..A:C15 is the appropriate worksheet range to interpret. If you want 1-2-3/G to interpret another range, choose the Range(s) box and select the range you want.

- **Orientation**: Based on the shape of the range in the Range(s) text box, 1-2-3/G determines whether to graph the data by column or by row and sets the Orientation option to Columnwise or Rowwise accordingly. To override this setting, simply select the opposite option button. For example, in Figure 7–10, 1-2-3/G has automatically determined that Columnwise is the appropriate orientation setting because the graph range (A:A5..A:C15) has more rows that columns. If you prefer rowwise interpretation, simply select the Rowwise option button.

- **X labels from first column/row**: This option lets you control whether 1-2-3/G uses the contents of the first column or row for the X range or the A data range. Depending on the Orientation setting, if the first column or row contains labels, 1-2-3/G by default uses that first column or row for the X labels. On the other hand, if the first column or row contains values, 1-2-3/G uses it as the A data range by default. For example, in Figure 7–10, because the Orientation setting is Columnwise and the first column contains labels, 1-2-3/G has turned on the X labels from first-column option box. If you turn this box off, 1-2-3/G will use the data in the range A6..A15 for the A data range (not something you want in this case because the labels will have a value of zero and the data series that 1-2-3/G creates from this range will not be visible in the graph).

- **Legends from first column/row**: This option lets you control whether 1-2-3/G uses the contents of the first column or row for legends, or assigns the text Series A, Series B, and so on as the legends. Depending on the Orientation setting, if the first column or row contains labels, 1-2-3/G uses the first column or row as legend labels by default. On the other hand, if the first column or row contains values, 1-2-3/G assigns the text Series A, Series B, and so on to the legend labels. For example, in Figure 7–10, because the

Orientation is Columnwise and the first row (B5..C5) contains labels, 1-2-3/G uses the contents of that row as legend labels.

Using the Graph Tool to Create a Graph—An Example

As mentioned, the Graph commands in the Worksheet window's main menu are the easiest way to create a graph in 1-2-3/G. When you use a Graph command, such as Graph View or Graph Setup, 1-2-3/G creates links between source data in your worksheet file and graph objects in the Graph Tool window. These links are updated whenever you change the data in your worksheet file. That way, your graph always reflects the latest values in your worksheet file.

Rather than use Graph commands to create a graph, you can use the Edit Link Create command from the Graph Tool menu to create a graph. Although it is unlikely that you will want to create an entire graph this way (Graph View and Graph Setup are much easier), it is important to know how to use Edit Link Create so that you can add different objects to a graph and pull the data for those objects from worksheet files.

Here are the basic steps you need to perform to create a graph with the Graph Tool:

- Create a Graph Window with File New.
- Use Edit Link Create to link graph objects to source data in the worksheet file.

For example, suppose you want to use the Graph Tool to create a line graph of the data in A5..C15 of Figure 7–2. Perform the following steps:

1. With the file in Figure 7–2 open on the desktop, choose the File New command. 1-2-3/G displays a dialog box, as in Figure 7–12.
2. Select Graph from the Tool names list box, then select OK. 1-2-3/G displays the Graph window in Figure 7–13.
3. Select the Edit Link Create command from the Graph Tool menu. Figure 7–14 shows the dialog box that appears.
4. To specify the worksheet file and range to graph, choose the "Source file and item" text box. Use either of the following methods to specify the worksheet file and range:

    - Point to the range A5..C15 in the worksheet file.
    - Select the filename in the list box, and type the range address A5..C15 following the filename.

    Figure 7–14 shows how your screen should appear.

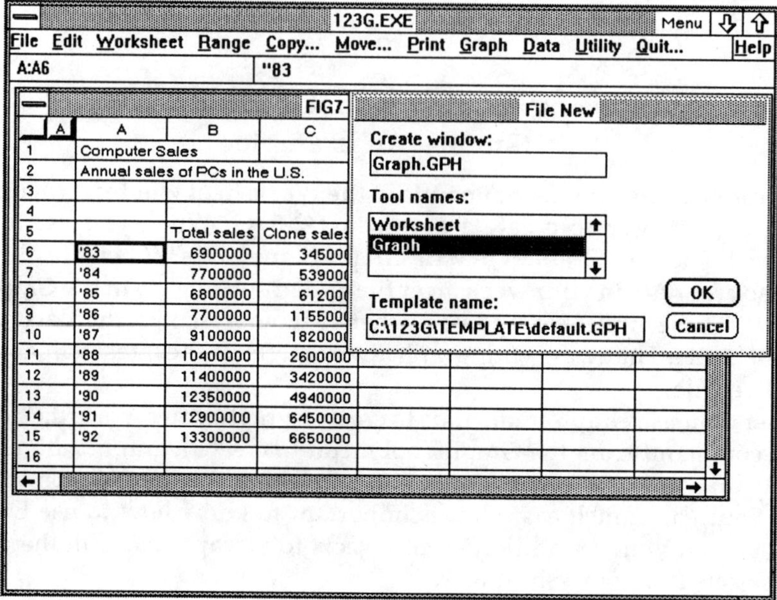

FIGURE 7–12 Creating a graph file with File New

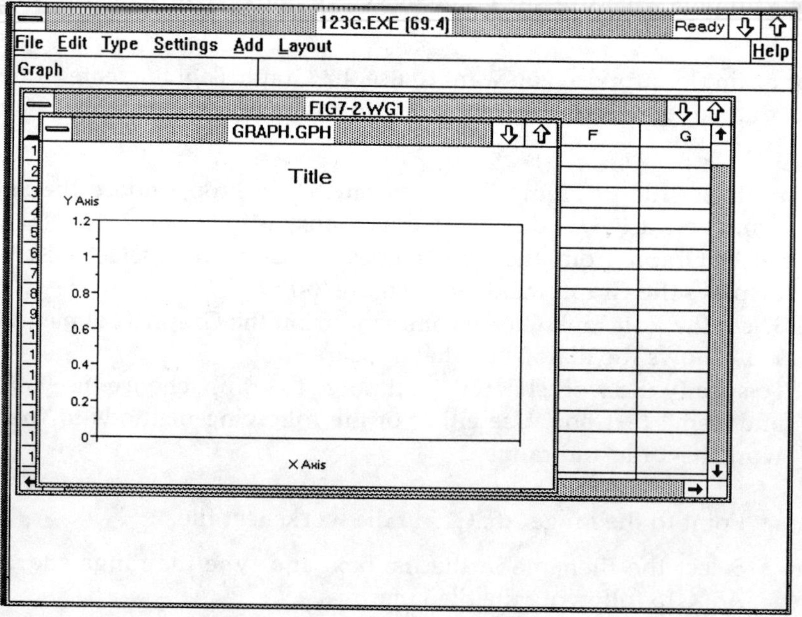

FIGURE 7–13 A new graph file

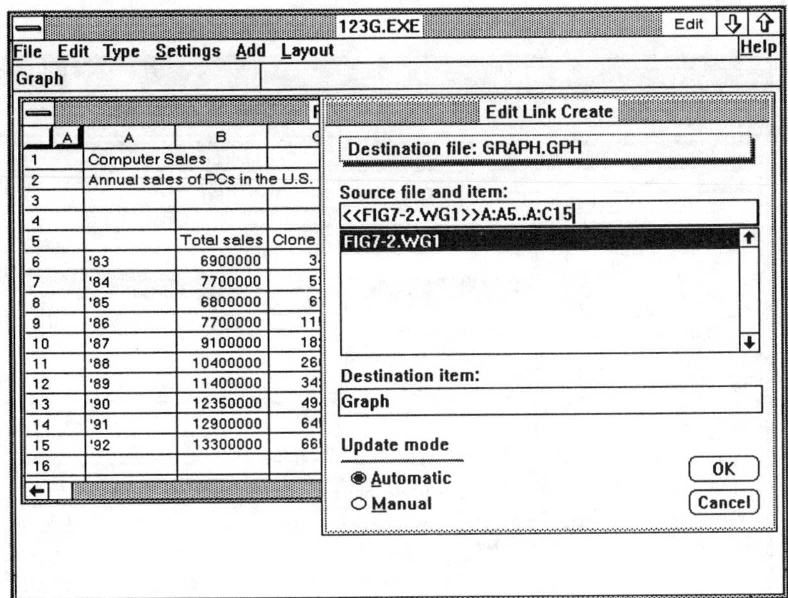

FIGURE 7–14 **The Edit Link Create dialog box**

Note

> Notice that you are specifying a single three-column range of worksheet data that encompasses all the data ranges, X labels, and legend labels for the graph. 1-2-3/G interprets this range using the rules outlined in "How 1-2-3/G Interprets Automatic Graph Ranges and Assigns Settings" above.

5. Select the "Destination item" text box and press NAME (F3) to see a complete list of available destinations. Examples of some destinations are the entire graph or particular objects, such as data series, X labels, legend labels, and titles. Figure 7–15 shows how your screen appears.

Note

> When you first select Edit Link Create, the name that appears within the "Destination item" text box corresponds to the currently selected graph element (see "Selecting and Changing Graph Elements" below for information on how to select a graph element).

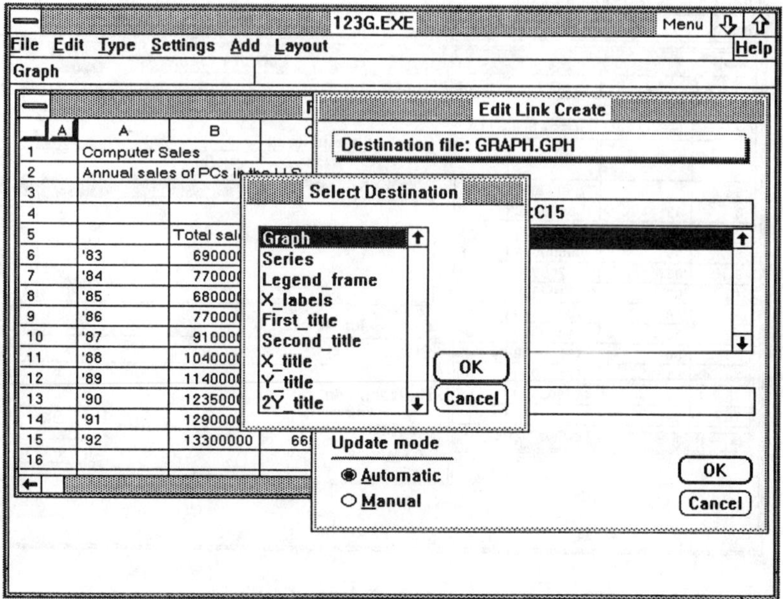

FIGURE 7–15 After selecting the "Destination item" text box and pressing NAME (F3)

6. Select the destination that you want to link the source data to. For this example, choose Graph from the list and select OK.
7. (optional) Choose an Update mode. Select Automatic (the default) if you want 1-2-3/G to update the link automatically when you change the values in the worksheet. Select Manual if you want the link to be updated only when you select the Edit Link Update command. (See "Updating Links" below for more on Edit Link Update.)
8. Select OK to complete the Edit Link Create command. Figure 7–16 shows the results.

Note

Besides Edit Link Create, another way to create a link between a graph object and data in a worksheet file is to use the Edit Link Paste Link command. This command lets you create a link using the clipboard and is actually far easier to use than the Edit Link Create command, once you know how (see "Pasting Links" near the end of the chapter).

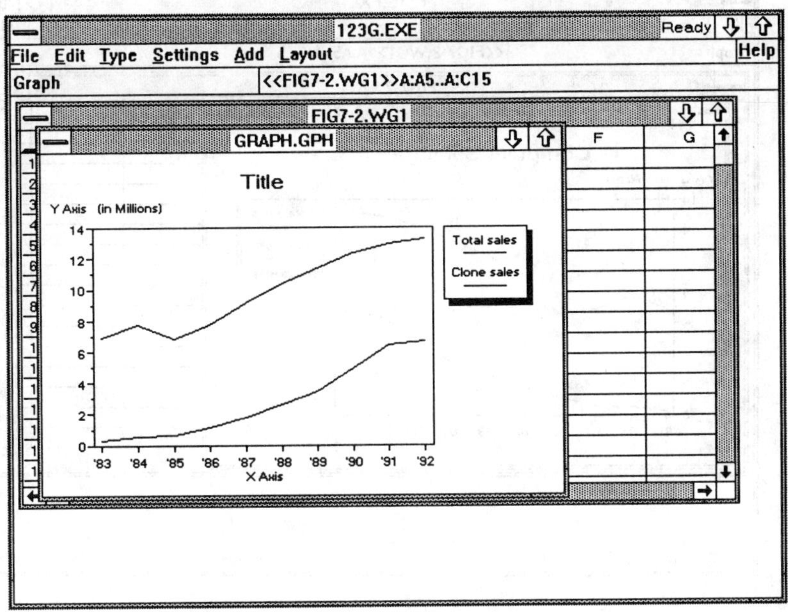

FIGURE 7–16 Results of Edit Link Create

Linking Individual Graph Objects with Edit Link Create

Although the previous example shows how to use the Edit Link Create command to link an entire range of graph data to a Graph window, you can also use it to link individual objects, such as data ranges, X labels, titles, and the like. For example, suppose you want to add a first title to the graph in Figure 7–16 and pull the data for the title from cell A1 of the worksheet file in Figure 7–2. Perform the following:

1. With the Graph Tool window in Figure 7–16 active on the desktop, select the Edit Link Create command (Figure 7–14).
2. Select the "Source file and item" text box and specify <<FIG7-2.WG1>>A:A1 as the worksheet file and range.
3. Select the "Destination item" text box and press NAME (F3) to see a complete list of available destinations.
4. Choose First_title from the list and select OK.
5. Select OK to complete the Edit Link Create command. Figure 7–17 shows the results.

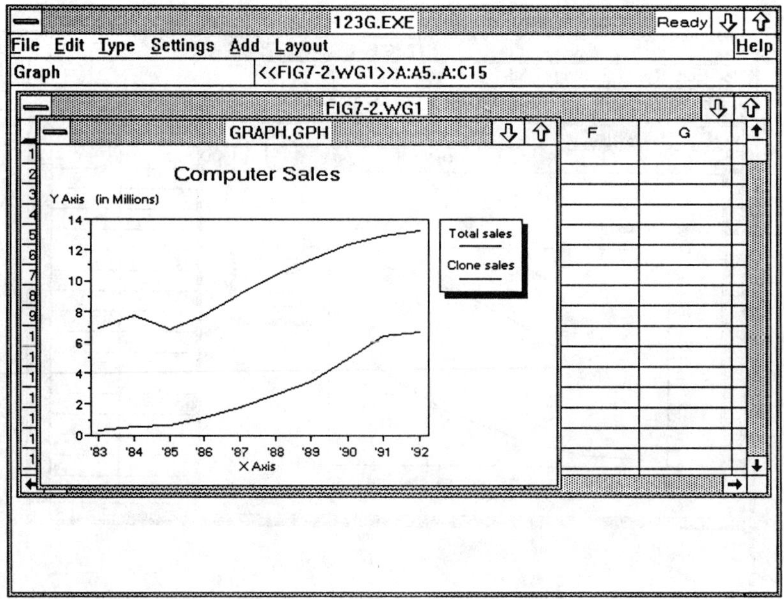

FIGURE 7–17 After adding a first title with the Edit Link Create command

From this point on, whenever you change the contents of cell A1 in the worksheet file, the first title in the graph will be automatically updated to reflect the change.

Error Messages from Edit Link Create

If you attempt to use the Edit Link Create command and you get an error message, the error is usually due to one of the following reasons:

- **The object is already linked:** If this is the case, either delete the link and try again or edit the link (see the next section).
- **The object does not support links:** You cannot create links to certain graph objects—for example, the *y*-axis scale.
- **A related object is already linked:** You cannot create links to certain graph objects when their descendant objects are already linked. For example, suppose you have created a link to a legend label. You then try to create a link to the legend frame (which would assign links to all the legend labels within the frame). 1-2-3/G issues an error message because the legend label is already linked.

Tip: Using undo with graphs

While the Graph Tool appears on the screen, you can undo the last command or action by selecting the Edit Undo command, or using its shortcut ALT-BACKSPACE. However, you can only undo the *last* command or action. (See "Undoing Actions—Edit Undo" for more on the Edit Undo command.)

Although you can undo the last command or action from the Graph Tool, you cannot undo Graph commands that you have executed from the Worksheet window. If you try, 1-2-3/G simply displays an error message indicating that you cannot undo a Graph command.

SAVING A GRAPH

There are three ways to save a graph in 1-2-3/G:

- If you create a graph using the Graph commands in the Worksheet window's main menu, you can save its settings as part of the worksheet file. In addition, by naming graph settings using the Graph Name command, you can save more than one set of graph settings per worksheet file. When you save named graph settings, 1-2-3/G also saves the links between the worksheet file and the graph.
- You can save the graph as a separate file with a .GPH extension. When you save a graph file, 1-2-3/G also saves the links between the graph file and the associated worksheet file.
- You can save the graph file as part of a desktop (.DSK) file. 1-2-3/G saves not only the links between the graph files and worksheet files but also the contents and position of the windows on the desktop. See Chapter 2, "Managing the Desktop," for more information.

Saving a Graph as Part of a Worksheet File

Suppose you have created a graph using the Worksheet window's Graph commands. When you save the worksheet file, besides saving all the current worksheet data, 1-2-3/G also saves *all* the current graph settings that you have made. In fact, it even saves the settings you have made from the Graph Tool, such as titles, legends, and annotations.

Because 1-2-3/G automatically saves the current graph settings when you save the worksheet file, you can easily create a graph from these settings the next time you load the worksheet file into memory. All you have to do is open the worksheet file and select Graph View. 1-2-3/G instantly displays the graph.

Naming Your Graph Settings

Each time you create a new graph with the Worksheet window's Graph commands, you are actually changing the settings of the current graph. You can preserve the current graph settings before you begin a new graph by giving those settings a name. You do this with the Graph Name Create command.

The name you select is attached to the current graph settings and is saved with your worksheet file when you save the worksheet file using File Save. Once you have named your graph, you can create a new graph without losing the current graph settings. You can then view or modify your named graphs at a later time with the Graph Name Use command, or the macro command {GRAPHON}.

Note

> Creating a graph name using Graph Name Create and saving the worksheet file with File Save does not save the associated graph (.GPH) file. You must save the graph file separately (see "Saving a Graph (.GPH) File").

Naming New Graph Settings

To name a graph for the first time, select the Graph Name command. Figure 7–18 shows the dialog box that 1-2-3/G displays. Select Create from the option buttons. Next, move to the "Graph name" text box and type in a name of up to 15 characters. Select OK to confirm your entry and return to Ready mode. The next time you use the Graph Name command, the graph name you created will appear within the Graph name list box.

Note

> If the current graph can be named and saved as part of a worksheet file, it will display the word "Current" in the Graph window title bar. In general, the word "Current" does not appear when you have closed a Worksheet window associated with a Graph window.

Here are some rules to keep in mind when you are naming your graphs:

- Avoid using graph names that include spaces, commas, semicolons, or the characters + *—/ & > < @ and #. If you use any of these characters, you will have difficulty using the graph name in a macro.

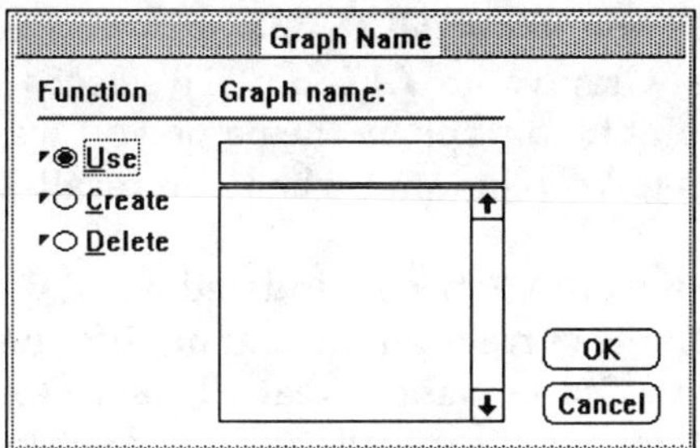

FIGURE 7–18 The Graph Name dialog box

- Avoid using a graph name that already exists. The current graph settings will replace the settings for that name.
- Avoid names that look like cell addresses, such as PI2 or GR15. Otherwise, you may have difficulty using the graph name in a macro.
- Do not use 1-2-3/G function names, macro command keywords, or 1-2-3/G key names (such as GRAPH) as graph names.

The process of naming a graph attaches a name to the type, data ranges, titles, legends, and other settings that you have chosen from the Graph menu. It does not create a graph file, however. See the previous section on "Creating a Graph" for information on creating a graph file.

Note

> Once you have named your current graph, you can prepare for a new graph by clearing all of the current settings with the Graph Reset command. See the section on "Resetting Graph Settings" in this chapter for more information.

Recalling Named Graph Settings

Once you have created a graph name, you can recall it using the Graph Name Use command. For example, imagine that you want to view a named graph after making changes to values in the graph's data ranges. To do this, you make the named graph settings current with the Graph Name Use command. In addition to making the named graph current, 1-2-3/G displays the named graph in the current Graph window.

When you select Graph Name, all the names you have assigned to graph settings appear in the "Graph name" list box. To select a name, choose the Use option button then point to, or type in, the name you want and select OK.

Here are two things to keep in mind when you recall named graph settings:

- Named settings are not automatically updated when you change them. If you make a named graph the current graph, and modify the settings, you need to save them again with Graph Name Create. Be sure to save your worksheet file with File Save if you want to recall the named settings in a future session.
- Recalling a graph with the Graph Name Use command resets the current graph to the incoming settings. If you don't want to lose your current graph, give it a name with Graph Name Create before you make another graph current.

Tip: The practical differences between saving a .GPH File and saving Named Graph Settings

Because you can name graph settings and save them in a worksheet file, you may wonder why you would ever want to save a graph (.GPH) file. After all, you can always recreate a graph by loading a worksheet file, choosing the named graph settings you want, and selecting Graph View.

Here are two cases where saving a graph file is beneficial:

- When you create a graph manually using the Graph Tool (see "Using the Graph Tool to Create a Graph—An Example"), 1-2-3/G does not automatically save the graph settings you have made with the current worksheet file. Rather those settings are stored in the graph file. Therefore, if you want to save the graph settings you've made, you must save the graph file using File Save.
- Suppose you have created a graph file using data in one worksheet file. You then decide that you want to use this graph file with the data in another worksheet file. By saving the graph file, you can later apply its settings to another worksheet file by moving the graph file's links from its original source worksheet to a new source worksheet (see "Moving Links" later).

Deleting Graph Names

You can delete named graph settings in your worksheet file with the Graph Name Delete command. Once you use the command, however, you cannot retrieve your settings with Graph Name Use or with the macro command {GRAPHON}. Because you cannot use Undo to recover deleted graph names (or any other Graph commands for that matter), use this command with caution.

Saving a Graph (.GPH) File

To save a graph in a separate .GPH file, you use the File Save command. After selecting this command, enter the name you want to use for the active file in the File name text box. Next, select the "Current file only" option button to save only the active graph file. Select OK to complete the command and have 1-2-3/G save the graph file. (See Chapter 5, "File Management," for more on saving files.)

Saving a Graph File as Part of the Desktop

To save a graph file as part of the current desktop, select the File Save command. Next, turn on the "Save desktop" check box, if it isn't on already. Select OK to complete the command. 1-2-3/G saves the links between the graph file(s) and the worksheet file(s) in the current Desktop (.DSK) file. See Chapter 2, "Managing the Desktop," for more details.

CLOSING A GRAPH WINDOW

When you have completed your work with a Graph window, you can close the Graph window in the same way you would close a Worksheet window. Select Close from the Window Control menu, or use the shortcut CTRL-F4. If 1-2-3/G displays a message asking you whether you want to save the window before closing, select OK to save the file or No to close the window without saving the file.

Note

> If you do not save the graph file before closing the window, the data in the graph file will be lost.

GRAPH TYPES

Using the Worksheet window's Graph Setup or Graph Type command, you can choose from seven graph types: line, bar, pie, XY, stacked bar, 3-D bar, and area. On the other hand, by using the Graph window's Type command, you can choose from nine different graph types: the seven that appear for Graph Setup and Graph Type plus high-low-close-open (HLCO) and overlapped-bar.

This section describes how to change the graph type using the Worksheet window's Graph menu and the Graph Tool's Type menu. In addition, each graph type is described here with examples showing how you can use them.

Selecting a Type from the Worksheet Window

From the Worksheet window, the simplest way to change the graph type is to select the Graph Type command. Figure 7-19 shows the dialog box that appears. To choose one of the seven graph types, simply turn on the option button associated with that type. After you select a type, your choice remains in effect for the rest of the session, or until you change it.

As mentioned, you can also select from the same set of seven graph types by using the Graph Setup dialog box. In general, you select a graph type with Graph Setup as part of having 1-2-3/G automatically create a graph (see "Creating a Graph with Graph Setup" above). As with the Graph Type command, the graph type you choose with Graph Setup remains in effect throughout the rest of the session, or until you change it.

Selecting a Type from the Graph Tool

Another way to change the graph type is by using the Graph Tool's Type menu. Here are the advantages of using the Type menu:

- You can access 1-2-3/G's graph gallery to select from a variety of preformatted graphs.
- You can directly select from nine different graph types and use these types to change some or all of the data series in a graph.

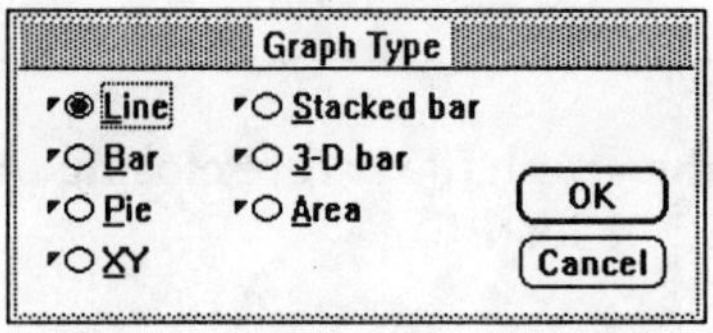

Graph Type

Line | Stacked bar
Bar | 3-D bar
Pie | Area
XY

OK
Cancel

FIGURE 7-19 The Graph Type dialog box

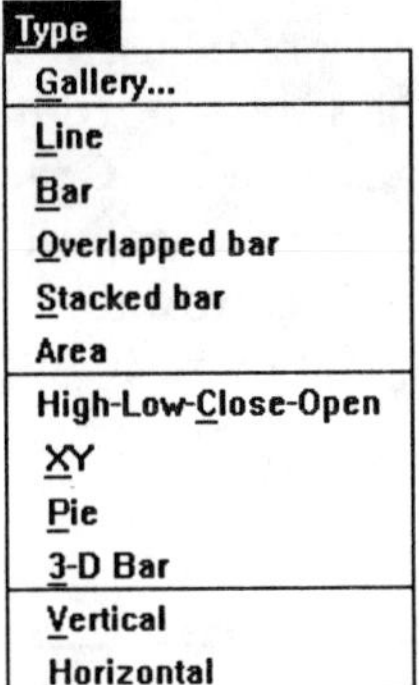

FIGURE 7–20 The Graph Tool's Type menu

- You can control the orientation (vertical/horizontal positioning) of a graph. Figure 7–20 shows the options in the Type menu.

The Graph Gallery

Rather than build a graph using different graph commands and options, you can select from a gallery of preformatted styles by using the Graph Tool's Type Gallery command. When you select this command, 1-2-3/G displays a dialog box like the one in Figure 7–21. Notice that the dialog box includes all nine graph types. When you choose a type, 1-2-3/G instantly displays a gallery of icons associated with that type. Figure 7–21 shows the styles available for line graphs.

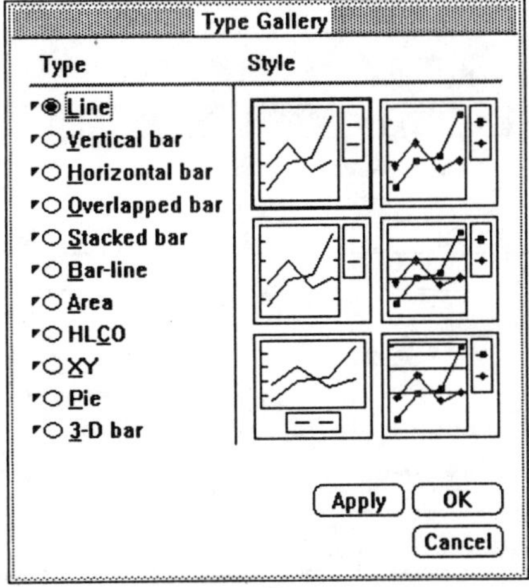

FIGURE 7–21 The Type Gallery dialog box

To select a style, simply click on an icon. 1-2-3/G signals that you have selected the icon by displaying a dark border surrounding the icon. To see the effect your selection will have on the Graph window, choose the Apply option. You can select and apply as many different styles as you like to the Graph window, and 1-2-3/G will continue to display the dialog box on the screen. Once you arrive at the style you want, select OK to return to Ready mode.

Note

> By double-clicking on a gallery icon, you can simultaneously select a style and return to Ready mode.

Line Graph

Line graphs plot one point for each value in a data range, and represent each data range as a series of points connected by lines, as shown in Figure 7–22. They are generally used to show differences between data ranges and how those differences change over time. As with most other graph types, you can assign up to 23 data ranges for line graphs (see "Data Ranges" later).

For example, the line graph in Figure 7–22 plots the total monthly sales from the worksheet in Figure 7–23 over a three-month period. Here are the range settings for the graph:

X range	B5..D5
A range	B6..D6
B range	B7..D7
C range	B8..D8

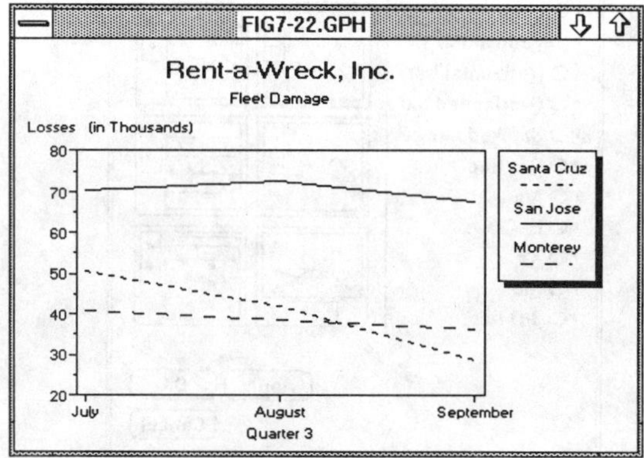

FIGURE 7–22 A line graph with three data ranges

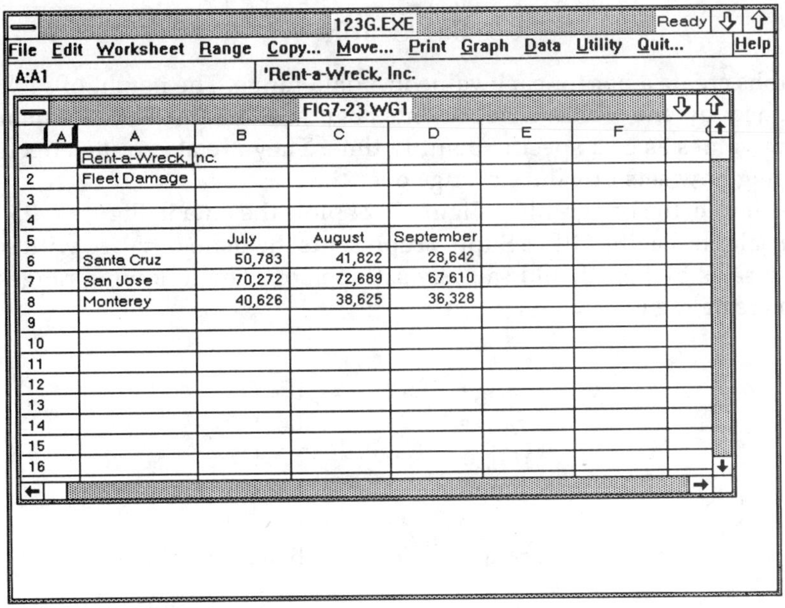

123G.EXE							Ready
File Edit Worksheet Range Copy... Move... Print Graph Data Utility Quit...							Help
A:A1	'Rent-a-Wreck, Inc.						

FIG7-23.WG1

A	A	B	C	D	E	F
1	Rent-a-Wreck, Inc.					
2	Fleet Damage					
3						
4						
5		July	August	September		
6	Santa Cruz	50,783	41,822	28,642		
7	San Jose	70,272	72,689	67,610		
8	Monterey	40,626	38,625	36,328		
9						
10						
11						
12						
13						
14						
15						
16						

FIGURE 7–23 **Data for the line graph in FIGURE 7–22**

In fact, these settings are assigned automatically if you create the graph using Graph Setup or Graph View. The graph titles have been added manually, however (see "Titles" later).

1-2-3/G offers several options for line formats. You can choose to omit the markers marking each data point (not present in Figure 7–22) or the connecting lines, or display the graph with the 1-2-3/G default of lines only (see "Changing the Line Format for Line Series").

Note

A line graph can sometimes be misleading because of the *y*-axis scaling. 1-2-3/G uses a different method for selecting the *y*-axis origin in line graphs than in bar graphs. A bar graph's *y*-axis origin is always zero. In a line graph, however, 1-2-3/G selects a value several points lower than the lowest data point in the graph and uses that value as the y-axis origin, as shown in Figure 7–22. Therefore, the resulting difference between data points can be accentuated by a line graph. You can correct this by manually scaling the *y*-axis (refer to the section on "Manually Scaling Axes" later in this chapter).

Bar Graph

Bar graphs create a bar for each value in a data range. The height of each bar is determined by the value it represents. Bar graphs are used frequently to compare values as of a specific point in time. They are also quite effective for comparing how sets of values change over time.

For example, the bar graph in Figure 7–24 plots the data in Figure 7–25. Third quarter sales of Pacific Office Supply represents the main data set, with subsets showing sales by month and sales by salesperson. The following ranges were used to create the graph:

X range	B5..D5
A range	B6..D6
B range	B7..D7
C range	B8..D8
D range	B9..D9
E range	B10..D10

Bar graphs are very similar to line graphs because they measure numeric relationships in the same way. The choice is really a visual one, determined by which type best depicts what you are trying to say.

Overlapped Bar Graph

An overlapped bar graph is identical to a standard bar graph except that the bars that form a set overlap one another. In general, you use an overlapped bar graph in favor of a standard bar graph when you want to emphasize the first data series—the one that appears in front.

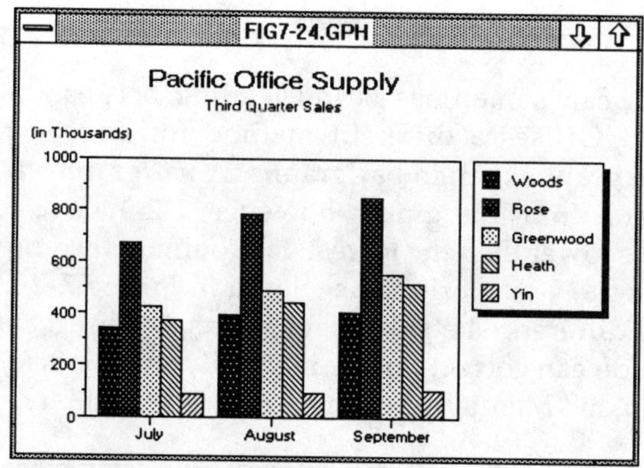

FIGURE 7–24 A sample bar graph

123G.EXE — Ready

File Edit Worksheet Range Copy... Move... Print Graph Data Utility Quit... Help

A:A1 'Pacific Office Supply

FIG7-25.WG1

A	A	B	C	D	E	F
1	Pacific Office Supply					
2	Third Quarter Sales					
3						
4						
5		July	August	September		
6	Woods	345,333	397,874	408,804		
7	Rose	674,718	786,531	851,559		
8	Greenwood	427,823	490,946	554,987		
9	Heath	372,182	445,025	521,269		
10	Yin	92,255	93,263	107,981		
11						
12						
13						
14						
15						
16						

FIGURE 7–25 Data for the bar graph in FIGURE 7–24

Note to Release 2 Users

In Release 2, the leftmost and rightmost bars are positioned adjacent to the left and right edges of the plot frame. The resulting graph has a rather squeezed look to it. In 1-2-3/G, however, additional space is provided between the leftmost and rightmost bars improving the overall look of the graph.

For example, Figure 7–26 shows an overlapped bar graph using the data in Figure 7–25. The same data ranges were used to create this graph as for the standard bar graph described in the previous section. Notice the special emphasis given to the data for Woods.

Stacked Bar Graph

In a stacked bar graph, each set of data is stacked vertically on top of the other, rather than side-by-side as in a standard bar graph. Figure 7–27 shows the data

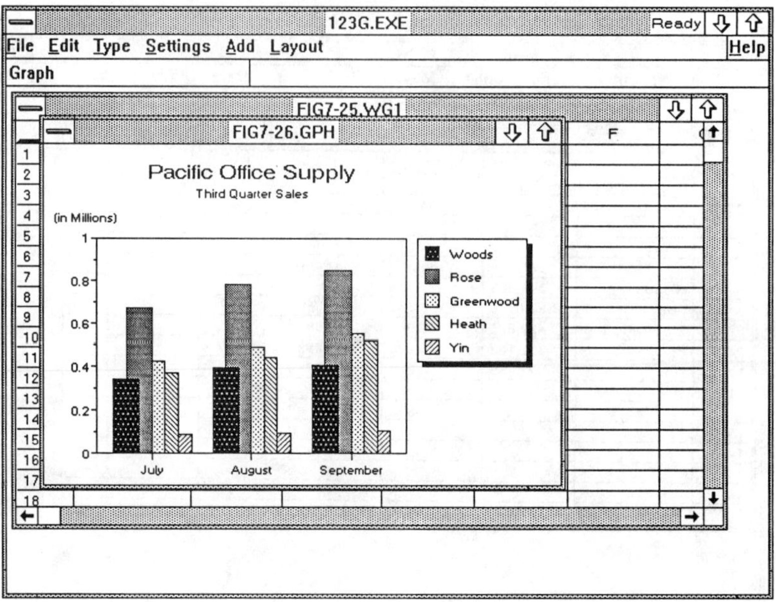

FIGURE 7–26 An overlapped bar graph

in Figure 7-25 in stacked bar format. The advantage of this type of graph over other bar graphs is that it emphasizes the total of the values and each part's contribution to it. Notice that the stacked bar graph shows total sales, while the previous bar graphs show only individual sales.

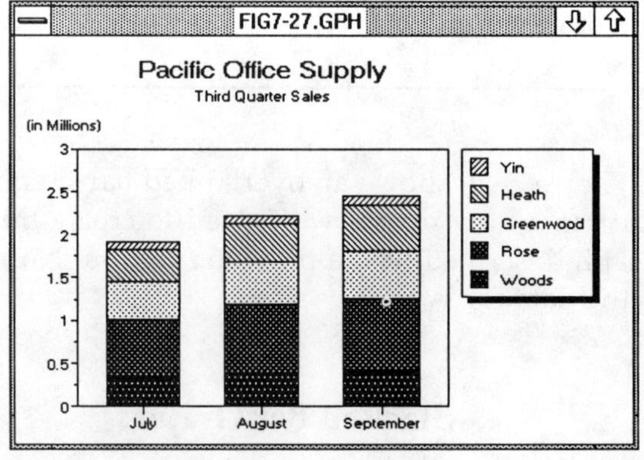

FIGURE 7–27 A stacked bar graph

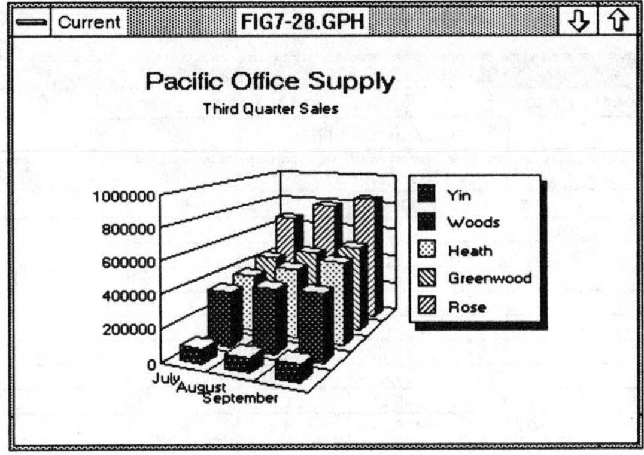

FIGURE 7-28 A 3-D bar graph

When you use more than one data range in a stacked bar graph, each bar is divided vertically into sections representing the values in each data range. The A range value is at the bottom of the bar, with the B range above it, the C range above the B range, and so on.

3-D Bar Graph

A 3-D bar graph plots bars in three-dimensional space. For example, Figure 7-28 shows a 3-D bar graph of the data in Figure 7-29. The following ranges were used to create the graph:

X range	B5..D5
A range	B6..D6
B range	B7..D7
C range	B8..D8
D range	B9..D9
E range	B10..D10

Notice that the data in Figure 7-29 is the same as in Figure 7-25 except that it has been sorted in ascending order. By sorting it in this way, you make sure that all the bars are visible when you plot the graph. Of course, there will be many cases where your data does not sort this conveniently, and the 3-D graph format is not appropriate. In addition, you will find that this type of graph works best when you use only a small amount of data.

Area Graph

Area graphs stack your data series one on top of another and fill the area between series with colors and/or patterns. Area graphs are similar to stacked

	A	B	C	D	E	F
1	Pacific Office Supply					
2	Third Quarter Sales					
3						
4						
5		July	August	September		
6	Yin	92,255	93,263	107,981		
7	Woods	345,333	397,874	408,804		
8	Heath	372,182	445,025	521,269		
9	Greenwood	427,823	490,946	554,987		
10	Rose	674,718	786,531	851,559		
11						
12						
13						
14						
15						
16						

FIGURE 7–29 Data used to produce the graph in FIGURE 7–28

bar graphs in that they emphasize the overall trend of your data over time. However, area graphs do a better job than stacked bar graphs of emphasizing a connection between time periods.

In general, you use area graphs only when you are graphing more than one data range. If you are graphing only a single data range, you are probably better off using a line graph.

The area graph in Figure 7–30 shows the sales of two divisions of a company over a one-year period (the data for the graph appears in Figure 7–31). A graph of this type makes apparent how much each division contributes to sales; it also helps show the trend in company-wide sales. You use the following ranges to create the graph:

X range	A6..A17
A range	B6..D17
B range	C6..C17

In fact, these are the same ranges that are assigned automatically when you create the graph with Graph Setup or Graph View.

Notice that when you create an area graph, 1-2-3/G stacks your data just as though you were creating a stacked bar graph.

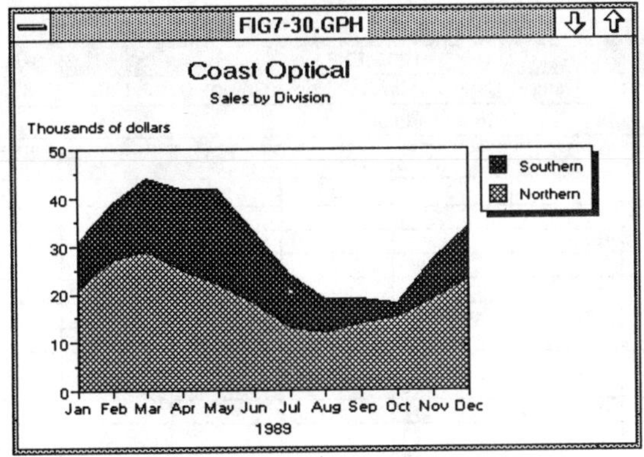

FIGURE 7–30 An area graph

Note

> If you want to fill the area between data ranges using colors and/or patterns, but you do not want 1-2-3/G to stack your data, you can change the graph type for each data series. See "Combining Graph Types—Mixed Graphs" below for more details.

High-Low-Close-Open (HLCO) Graph

Like Release 3, 1-2-3/G offers a high-low-close-open (HLCO) graph for charting stock market data. HLCO graphs use vertical lines to connect each set of high and low data points, and tick marks along each line to signify the closing and opening values. The following list shows the important graph settings for an HLCO graph and what 1-2-3/G uses each setting for:

- **X range:** The *x*-axis labels, normally time values in an HLCO graph.
- **A range:** The set of *high* values. Each high value is used as the top of a vertical line.
- **B range:** The set of low values. Each low value is used as the bottom of a vertical line.
- **C range:** The set of *closing* values. Each closing value appears as a right tick mark on a vertical line.
- **D range:** The set of *opening* values. The opening value appears as a left tick mark on a vertical line.

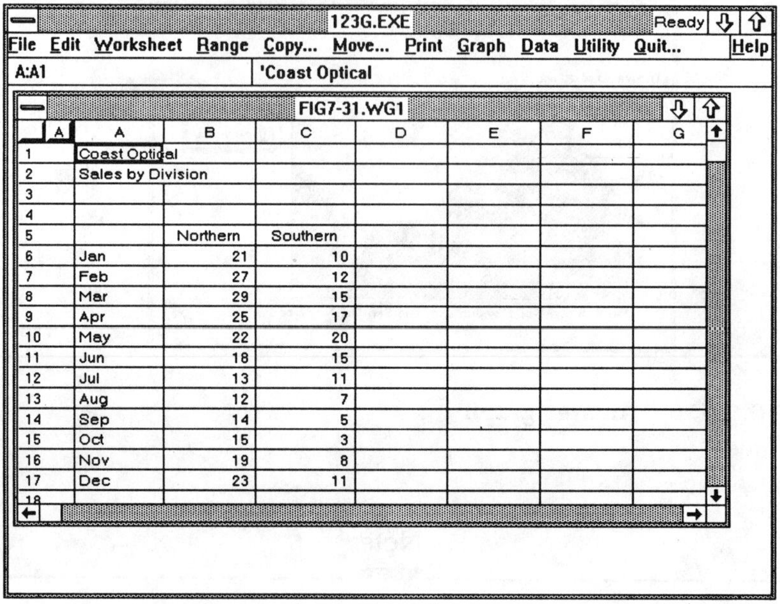

123G.EXE Ready

File Edit Worksheet Range Copy... Move... Print Graph Data Utility Quit... Help

A:A1 'Coast Optical

FIG7-31.WG1

A	A	B	C	D	E	F	G
1	Coast Optical						
2	Sales by Division						
3							
4							
5		Northern	Southern				
6	Jan	21	10				
7	Feb	27	12				
8	Mar	29	15				
9	Apr	25	17				
10	May	22	20				
11	Jun	18	15				
12	Jul	13	11				
13	Aug	12	7				
14	Sep	14	5				
15	Oct	15	3				
16	Nov	19	8				
17	Dec	23	11				
18							

FIGURE 7-31 **The data for the graph in FIGURE 7-30**

- **E range:** The set of bars that appear behind the high-low-close-open lines. (The E data range is automatically assigned to a second *y*-axis.)
- **F through W range:** Each range is plotted as a line against the *y*-axis.

Note

> You can use nearly any combination of data ranges in an HLCO graph. For example, you can include an A, B, and F range. At a minimum, you must include the A and B ranges.

A Simple HLCO Example

Figure 7-32 shows a simple HLCO graph plotted from the data in Figure 7-33. The following ranges were used to produce the graph:

X range	A6..A15
A range	B6..B15
B range	C6..C15

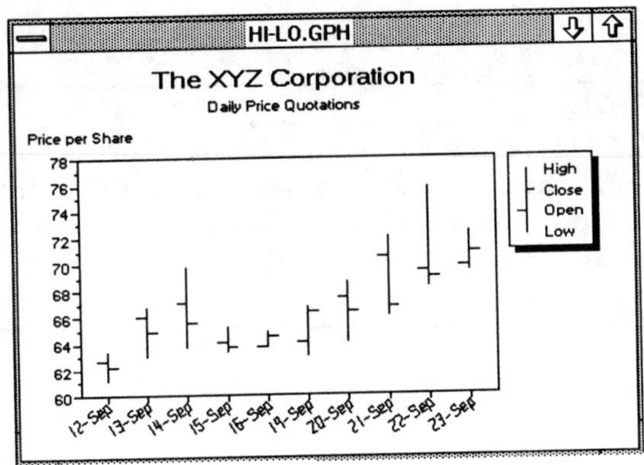

FIGURE 7–32 A simple HLCO graph

C range	D6..D15
D range	E6..E15

Figure 7–33 shows a good technique to use when creating a HLCO graph. The data is organized in parallel columns in the order of the graph name: high, low, close, and open. By organizing your data in this way, you will avoid confusing the data ranges for a HLCO graph.

123G.EXE Ready

File Edit Worksheet Range Copy... Move... Print Graph Data Utility Quit... Help

A:A1 'The XYX Corporation

FIG7-33.WG1

A	A	B	C	D	E	F	G
1	The XYX Corporation						
2	Daily Price Quotations						
3							
4							
5		High	Low	Close	Open		
6	12-Sep	63.375	61.125	62.250	62.625		
7	13-Sep	66.750	63.000	64.875	66.000		
8	14-Sep	69.750	63.750	65.625	67.125		
9	15-Sep	65.250	63.375	63.750	64.125		
10	16-Sep	64.875	63.750	64.500	63.750		
11	19-Sep	66.750	63.000	66.375	64.125		
12	20-Sep	68.625	64.125	66.375	67.500		
13	21-Sep	72.000	66.000	66.750	70.500		
14	22-Sep	75.750	68.250	69.000	69.375		
15	23-Sep	72.375	69.375	70.875	69.750		
16							
17							
18							
19							

FIGURE 7–33 The data for the HLCO graph in FIGURE 7–32

Note

> Because the HLCO type is not offered from the Worksheet window's Graph commands, the easiest way to create an HLCO graph is to use another graph type from the Graph menu (for example, line) then change the type in the Graph Tool window.

A More Complicated HLCO Example

Figure 7–34 shows a slightly more complicated version of an HLCO graph. This example uses the E and F graph ranges to display an underlying bar graph and a connecting line. In this example, the underlying bar graph shows the volume, and the connecting line shows the average selling price for each day. The data for the graph appears in Figure 7–35.

To produce the graph in Figure 7–34, you assign the same data ranges as for the simple HLCO example above. You also assign the following ranges:

E range	F7..F16
F range	G7..G16

Notice that the graph has a second *y*-axis. In fact, whenever you designate an E range for an HLCO graph, 1-2-3/G automatically assigns it to a second *y*-axis, and the A–D and F–W ranges are automatically assigned to the first *y*-axis. (For more on this topic, see "Adding a Second *Y*-Axis," later.)

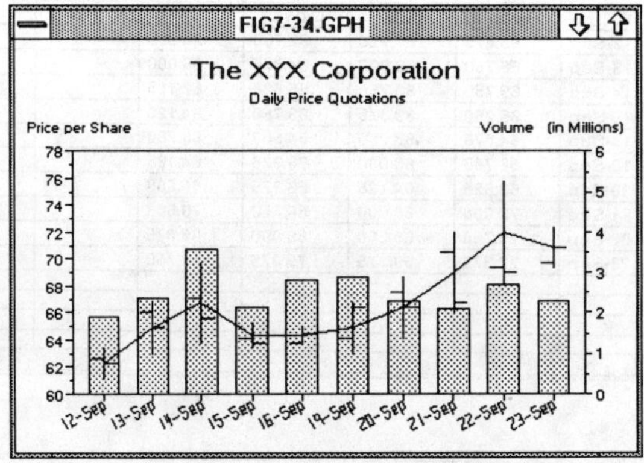

FIGURE 7–34 A more complicated HLCO graph

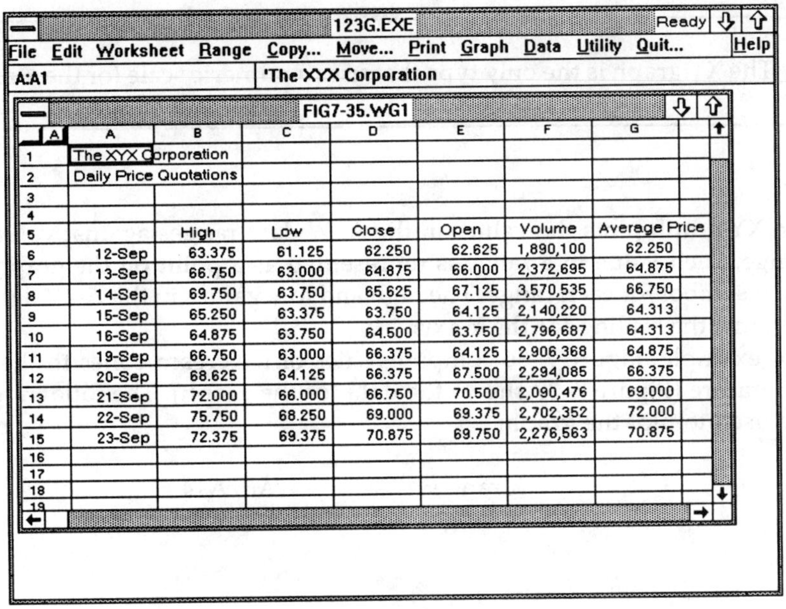

123G.EXE — Ready

File Edit Worksheet Range Copy... Move... Print Graph Data Utility Quit... Help

A:A1 'The XYX Corporation

FIG7-35.WG1

A	A	B	C	D	E	F	G
1	The XYX Corporation						
2	Daily Price Quotations						
3							
4							
5		High	Low	Close	Open	Volume	Average Price
6	12-Sep	63.375	61.125	62.250	62.625	1,890,100	62.250
7	13-Sep	66.750	63.000	64.875	66.000	2,372,695	64.875
8	14-Sep	69.750	63.750	65.625	67.125	3,570,535	66.750
9	15-Sep	65.250	63.375	63.750	64.125	2,140,220	64.313
10	16-Sep	64.875	63.750	64.500	63.750	2,796,687	64.313
11	19-Sep	66.750	63.000	66.375	64.125	2,906,368	64.875
12	20-Sep	68.625	64.125	66.375	67.500	2,294,085	66.375
13	21-Sep	72.000	66.000	66.750	70.500	2,090,476	69.000
14	22-Sep	75.750	68.250	69.000	69.375	2,702,352	72.000
15	23-Sep	72.375	69.375	70.875	69.750	2,276,563	70.875
16							
17							
18							
19							

FIGURE 7–35 The data for the HLCO graph in FIGURE 7–34

Tip: Controlling how 1-2-3/G displays *x*-axis labels

Notice in Figure 7–34 that 1-2-3/G displays the *x*-axis labels on an angle to prevent them from overlapping one another. You can also stagger *x*-axis labels or have them appear vertically. To control the position of *x*-axis labels, you use the Graph Tool's Settings Position Axis Labels X command (see "Repositioning Axes and Their Elements" below for more on this command).

XY Graph

An XY graph, sometimes called a *scatter plot* or *scatter diagram,* plots one set of values against the values in another set. XY graphs are often used to predict or analyze trends, or depict the frequency of an event. For example, you can use an XY graph to plot the relationship between the number of sales calls made and number of orders received, the rate of absenteeism and the days of the year, or the number of ice cream cones sold and the outside temperature.

Note

> The XY graph is the only type that uses a numeric scale for the *x*-axis.

An XY graph plots the values in the A–W data ranges against values in the X range. Each value in a range is represented as a point on the graph, with a special symbol for each range. The high and low values in the A–W data ranges determine the scaling for the Y axis.

For example, Figure 7–36 compares sales of ice cream cones to the outside temperature (Figure 7–37 shows the data for the graph). The following ranges were used to plot the graph:

X range	A6..A14
A range	B6..B14

Note

> If you try to create the graph in Figure 7–36, you may encounter the following problems:
>
> - When you first create the graph, 1-2-3/G shows connecting lines between the data points. To show markers only, as in Figure 7–36, select the Type Gallery command and choose Style A from the six XY graph styles.
> - If you use Graph View or Graph Setup to create the graph, 1-2-3/G makes some invalid assumptions about your automatic graph range. That is, it makes the following incorrect data range assignments:
>
> | | |
> |---|---|
> | A range | A6..A14 |
> | B range | B6..B14 |
>
> To create the graph in Figure 7–36, you must set the data ranges manually using the Graph Add Ranges command (see the proper settings above). In fact, whenever you create an XY graph with Graph Setup or Graph View, you should always double check your data range settings.

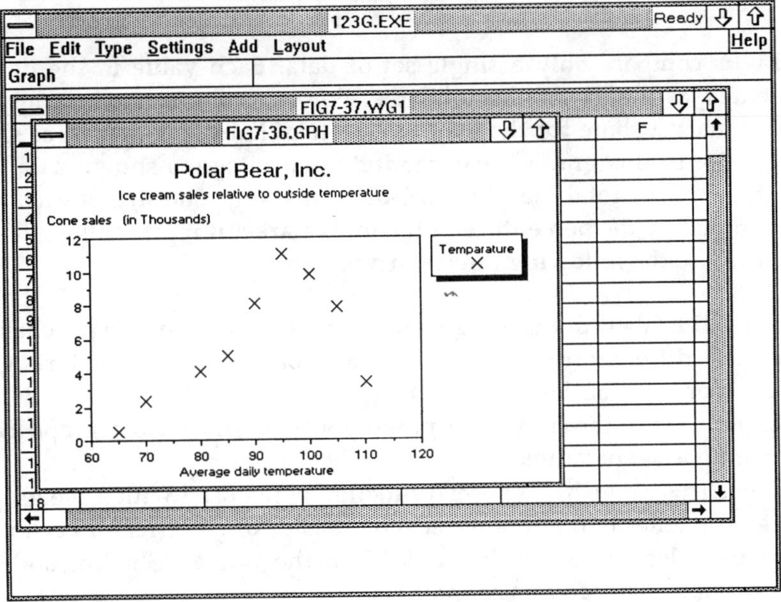

FIGURE 7-36 An XY graph

123G.EXE Ready

File Edit Worksheet Range Copy... Move... Print Graph Data Utility Quit... Help

A:A1 'Polar Bear, Inc.

FIG7-37.WG1

A	A	B	C	D	E	F
1	Polar Bear, Inc.					
2	Ice cream sales relative to outside temperature					
3						
4						
5	Temparature	Sales				
6	65	505				
7	70	2342				
8	80	4096				
9	85	4989				
10	90	8101				
11	95	11041				
12	100	9825				
13	105	7867				
14	110	3431				
15						
16						

FIGURE 7-37 The data used to create the graph in FIGURE 7-36

Pie Graph

Pie graphs compare only a single set of data. Each value in the data set is represented as a slice of the total pie. For example, suppose you want to compare market share for the major vendors of hard disk drives, as shown in Figure 7–38. In this graph, each vendor's percentage is shown as a slice (or percentage) of the total pie (the hard-drive market). The size of each pie slice is determined by the percentage of the total market it represents.

You can use the following ranges in a pie graph:

- **X range:** The labels in this range appear in the legend for the pie chart. (Note that this is different from previous releases of 1-2-3 where the X range labels appear alongside of the pie slices.)
- **A range:** This is the only data range you use, since a pie graph can only compare one set of values.
- **B range:** This range has a special function when used with a pie graph. The values you enter in the B range set colors and/or patterns for each pie slice, and cause selected slices to "explode" from the pie (see "Shading and Exploding Pie Slices" later in this chapter.)
- **C range:** 1-2-3/G uses the data in this range to determine whether percent labels appear next to pie slices.

See "Enhancing Pie Graphs" for a complete description of how to use the B and C data ranges to enhance a pie graph.

Here are the ranges that were used to construct the pie graph in Figure 7–38 (the data for the graph appears in Figure 7–39):

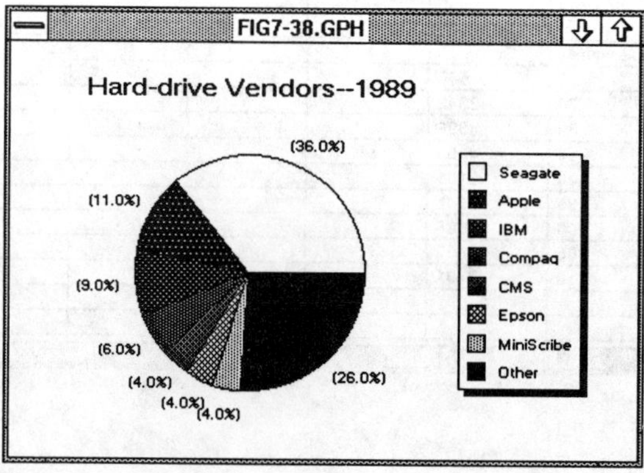

FIGURE 7–38 A pie graph

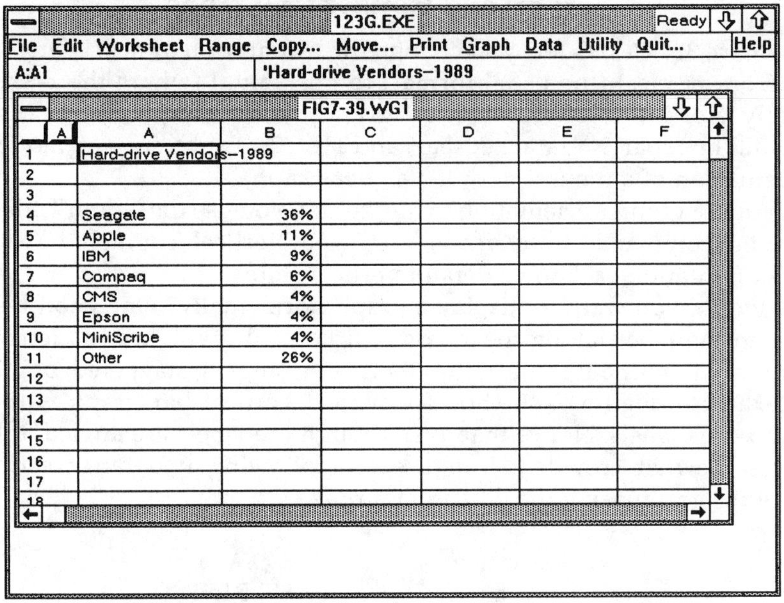

123G.EXE — Ready

File Edit Worksheet Range Copy... Move... Print Graph Data Utility Quit... Help

A:A1 'Hard-drive Vendors–1989

FIG7-39.WG1

A	A	B	C	D	E	F
1	Hard-drive Vendors–1989					
2						
3						
4	Seagate	36%				
5	Apple	11%				
6	IBM	9%				
7	Compaq	6%				
8	CMS	4%				
9	Epson	4%				
10	MiniScribe	4%				
11	Other	26%				
12						
13						
14						
15						
16						
17						

FIGURE 7–39 The data for the graph in FIGURE 7–38

X range	A4..A11
A range	B4..B11

In fact, these are the data ranges that 1-2-3/G assigns automatically when you create the graph using Graph Setup or Graph View.

Note

When you create a pie graph, your data does not have to be in percentage form, as in Figure 7–39. 1-2-3/G will divide up the pie properly even if the data consists of conventional numbers, such as sales or expense figures.

Vertical and Horizontal Graphs

Like Release 3, 1-2-3/G lets you change the orientation of nearly any type of graph from vertical (the usual format) to horizontal (where the *x*-axis runs vertically along the left side of the graph). For example, you can create horizontal line, bar, XY, stacked-bar, and HLCO graphs. You cannot change the orientation of a pie graph or a 3-D bar graph.

To change a graph's orientation to horizontal, you use the Graph Tool's Type Horizontal command. Conversely, the Type Vertical command resets the graph's orientation back to its default vertical state.

Why would you want to display a graph horizontally? One good reason is that when the labels along the *x*-axis of a vertical graph are too long or too numerous to fit without some of the labels being angled, staggered, or jumbled.

For example, Figure 7–40 shows a typical vertical bar graph with many lengthy x-axis labels. Notice that even though the labels are angled, they still appear somewhat crowded. You use the following two range settings to produce the graph using the data in Figure 7–41:

X range	A7..A15
A range	B7..B15

Note

In general, you should only use a horizontal graph when you are graphing a single point in time. If you want the graph to compare values over time, you are better off using a vertical graph.

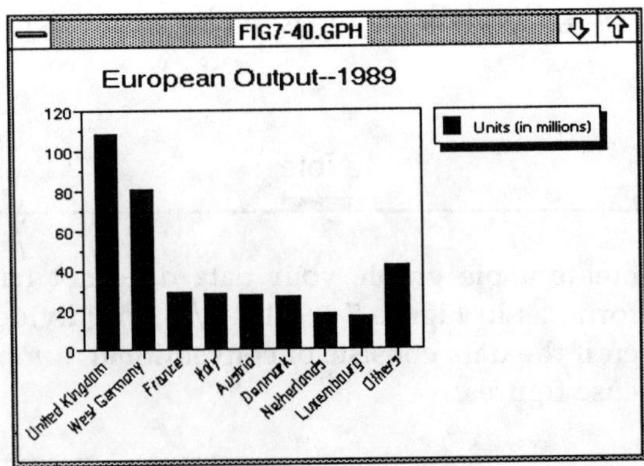

FIGURE 7–40 A typical vertical bar graph with lengthy x-axis labels

Figure 7–42 shows the same bar graph rotated horizontally using the Type Horizontal command. Notice that with the increased room for labels, the graph becomes much more readable.

Combining Graph Types

In 1-2-3/G you can easily combine graph types in a single graph (for example, a line and a bar graph). Combining graph types is useful when you want to contrast related sets of data.

To combine two graph types in a single graph, you simply select a data series in the Graph window and assign the graph type you want to it. For example, Figure 7–43 shows a standard bar graph using the data in Figure 7–44. This graph displays XYZ Corporation's earnings (by quarter) and dividends paid to stockholders graphed as bars. You create this bar graph in the usual way (for example, by using Graph Setup), assigning the following data ranges:

X range	A9..A20
A range	B9..B20
B range	C9..C20

123G.EXE — Ready

File Edit Worksheet Range Copy... Move... Print Graph Data Utility Quit... Help

A:A4 'Country

FIG7-41.WG1

A	A	B	C	D	E	F
1	European Output–1989					
2						
3						
4	Country	Units (in millions)				
5	United Kingdom	109				
6	West Germany	80.6				
7	France	28.6				
8	Italy	28				
9	Austria	27				
10	Denmark	26.6				
11	Netherlands	18.4				
12	Luxembourg	16.6				
13	Others	41.8				
14						
15						
16						
17						
18						

FIGURE 7–41 The data for the bar graphs in FIGURE 7–40 and FIGURE 7–42

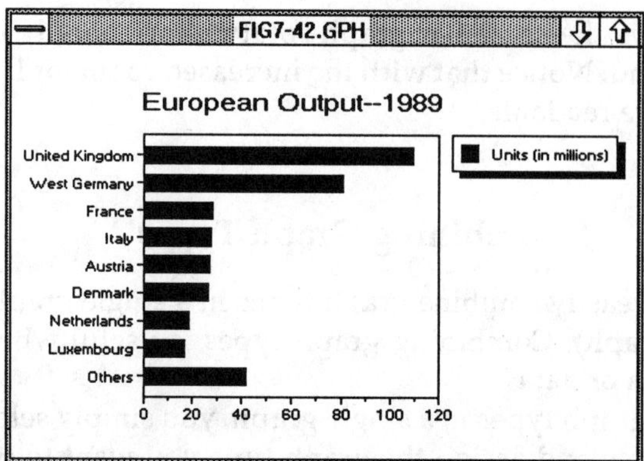

FIGURE 7–42 A horizontal bar graph with more room for x-axis labels

Suppose you want to change the data series showing dividends paid to stockholders so that it appears as a line. You can select this data series by clicking on it (see "Selecting Objects" below for more details). Next, you select the Type command, and when 1-2-3/G shows the Type dialog box, you select Line. After 1-2-3/G redraws the graph, you can unselect the data range by clicking in a blank area outside the plot frame. Figure 7–45 shows the resulting graph. Notice how combining the two graph types does a better job of emphasizing the relationship between earnings and dividends.

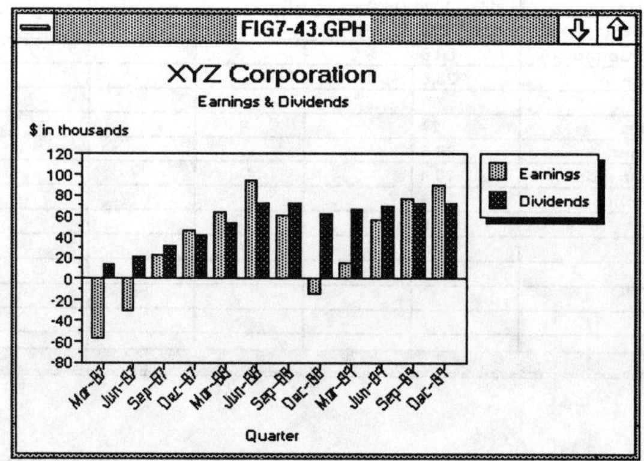

FIGURE 7–43 A standard bar graph

123G.EXE Ready

File Edit Worksheet Range Copy... Move... Print Graph Data Utility Quit... Help

A:A1 'XYZ Corporation

FIG7-44.WG1

A	A	B	C	D	E	F	G
1	XYZ Corporation						
2	Earnings & Dividends						
3							
4							
5	Quarter	Earnings	Dividends				
6	Mar-87	-57	13.5				
7	Jun-87	-30	21				
8	Sep-87	22.5	31.5				
9	Dec-87	45	42				
10	Mar-88	63	52.5				
11	Jun-88	94.5	72				
12	Sep-88	60	72				
13	Dec-88	-15	61.5				
14	Mar-89	15	66				
15	Jun-89	55.5	69				
16	Sep-89	76.5	72				
17	Dec-89	90	72				
18							

FIGURE 7–44 The data for graphs in FIGURE 7–43 and FIGURE 7–45

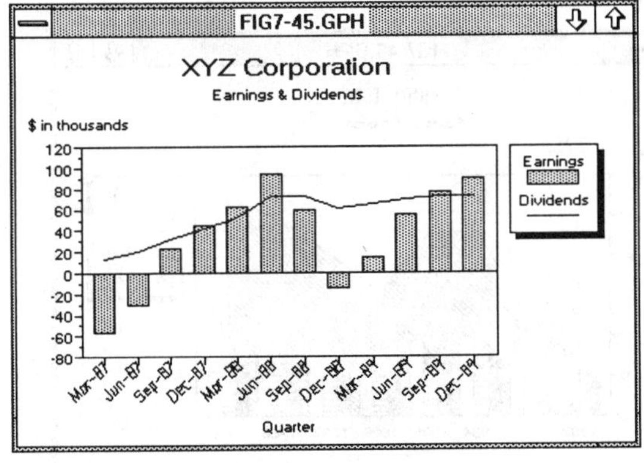

FIGURE 7–45 A combined bar and line graph

Note

You cannot combine pie, 3–D bar, XY, and HLCO graphs with other graph types. In fact, when you select the Type command to change the type for a data series, 1-2-3/G shows only those types that you can combine with the current graph type; the others are grayed.

Combining two graph types in a single graph is also useful for showing the overall trend of component sets of data. For example, Figure 7–46 shows a mixed graph of the Pacific Tile sales data in Figure 4–47. This graph displays each division's sales as bars and total sales as an area (total sales is found by adding the sales volume for each division). Combining graph types in this way makes it easy to compare the sales of one division with another, while the area displaying total sales gives a quick assessment of the overall sales trend.

To produce the graph in Figure 7–46, you set the following data ranges using the data in Figure 7–47:

X range	A9..A16
A range	B9..B16
B range	C9..C16
C range	D9..D16
D range	E9..E16

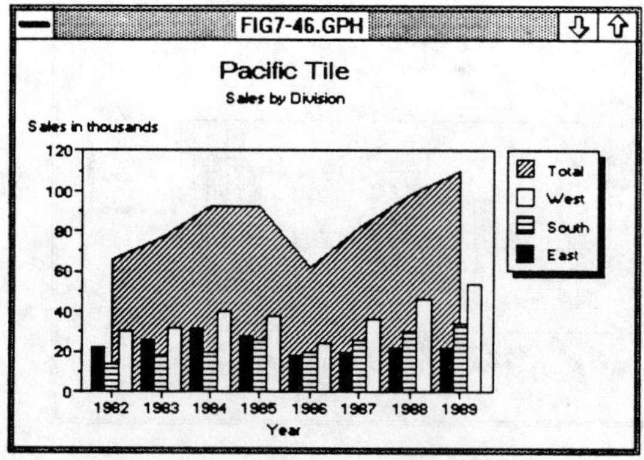

FIGURE 7–46 A combined bar and area graph

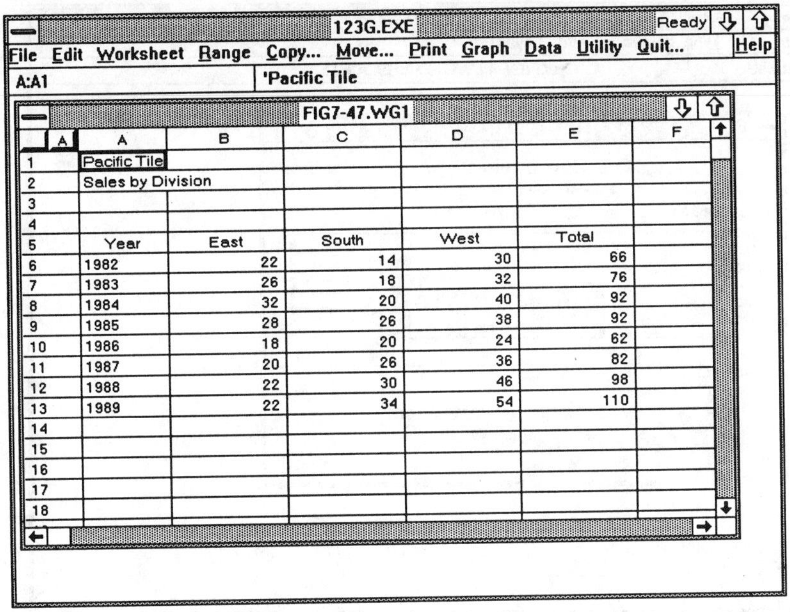

123G.EXE — Ready

File Edit Worksheet Range Copy... Move... Print Graph Data Utility Quit... Help

A:A1 'Pacific Tile

FIG7-47.WG1

A	A	B	C	D	E	F
1	Pacific Tile					
2	Sales by Division					
3						
4						
5	Year	East	South	West	Total	
6	1982	22	14	30	66	
7	1983	26	18	32	76	
8	1984	32	20	40	92	
9	1985	28	26	38	92	
10	1986	18	20	24	62	
11	1987	20	26	36	82	
12	1988	22	30	46	98	
13	1989	22	34	54	110	
14						
15						
16						
17						
18						

FIGURE 7–47 The data for the graph in FIGURE 7–46

You then click on the total sales data series and select the Type Area command. After 1-2-3/G redraws the graph, you can unselect the data series by clicking in a blank area outside the plot frame.

SELECTING AND CHANGING GRAPH OBJECTS

One of the biggest advantages of 1-2-3/G's graphics over previous releases is the ease with which you can select graph objects and change their contents. This section describes how to select objects using the keyboard and the mouse. It also describes how to edit the contents of an object, including objects that are linked to worksheet files.

Selecting Objects

Many Graph Tool commands require that you select a graph object before using the command. To select an object in a Graph window, you can use the mouse or the keyboard.

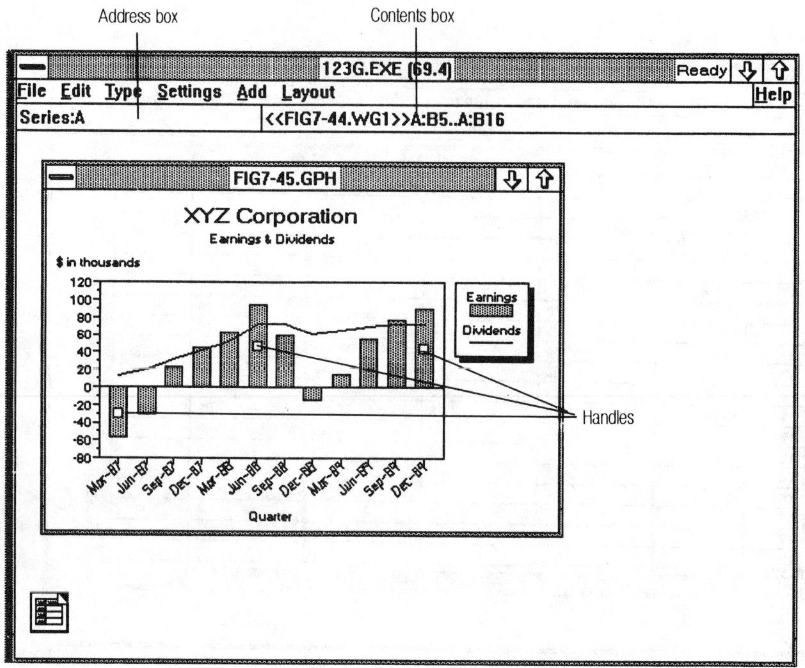

FIGURE 7–48 1-2-3/G places handles on the object you select, in this case, the A data series

To select an object using the mouse, you simply click on it. 1-2-3/G places *handles* on the edges of the object and displays the name of the object in the *address box* (the box that appears on the left side of the Control line). Handles appear as small white boxes around axes and data series. They appear as small black boxes around all other objects. For example, Figure 7–48 shows the handles that appear when you click on the A data series.

Tip: Double-clicking on graph objects.

If you double-click on an axis, axis labels, a data series, the legend frame, or the plot frame, 1-2-3/G displays a Settings dialog box associated with the object. For example, suppose you double-click on the A data series in Figure 7–48. 1-2-3/G displays the Settings Series Options dialog box, as in Figure 7–49. (This is the same dialog box that 1-2-3/G displays when you select the A data series and then choose the Settings Series Option command.)

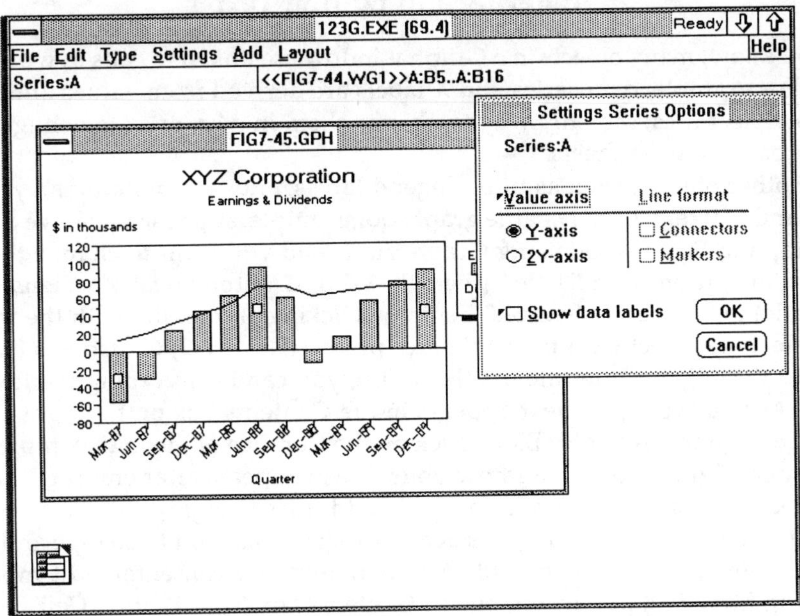

FIGURE 7–49 **The Settings dialog box that appears after double-clicking on the A data series**

Note

> When you first activate a Graph window, no handles appear in the graph window. When no handles appear, it means that the entire graph is selected.

To select an object using the keyboard, simply press TAB (or SHIFT-TAB). As you press TAB, 1-2-3/G moves the handles from one object to the next, eventually returning to where you started from.

Note

> To select a graph object from within a macro, you use the Edit Select Object command. See "Working with the Graph Tool's Edit Commands" later for more on this command.

Entering and Editing Text

As you know, many objects in a Graph window are linked to cells in worksheet files. For example, data series and X labels are derived from values and labels in worksheet files; the only way to change them in a graph is to change them in their source worksheets.

For other objects, such as titles, legend labels, and text (notations), you can enter and edit text directly in the graph. For example, suppose you have created the graph in Figure 7–50 using Graph View, and you want to change the first title of the graph from "Title" (the title 1-2-3/G automatically assigns to the first title) to "Power by Source." Begin by clicking on the title with the mouse. (To select the object with the keyboard, press TAB.) 1-2-3/G displays handles around the edges of the title. At this point, you can begin typing the text you want. As you type, your text appears in the Contents box on the right side of the Control line. Press ENTER or click on the Confirm (✓) icon to complete the text entry. Figure 7–51 shows how your screen appears after entering the new title. (See "Titles" later for other ways to add titles to a graph.)

To edit text in a graph, simply select the object you want to change and enter the new text in place of the old. Alternatively, you can enter Edit mode by pressing EDIT (F2) or clicking on the Contents box (see "Editing Cell Entries" in Chapter 1 for a description of Edit mode).

Tip: Editing text in a graph by double-clicking

Just as for worksheet entries, the quickest way to edit text in a graph is to double-click on the object you want to edit. 1-2-3/G immediately places you in Edit mode and locates the cursor at the end of the text entry in the Contents box.

Editing Links

When a graph object is linked to a worksheet file (or another PM application), the address of the link appears in the Contents box. For example, in Figure 7–52 the Contents box shows <<POWER.WG1>>A:A6..A:A10, indicating that the X labels are linked to the range A:A6..A:A10 in the source file POWER.WG1.

You can change a link by specifying a new reference in the Contents box; this new reference can even be a new source file. For example, suppose you want to change the link for the X labels in Figure 7–52 to the range B:A6..B:A10. You can edit the link using the following steps:

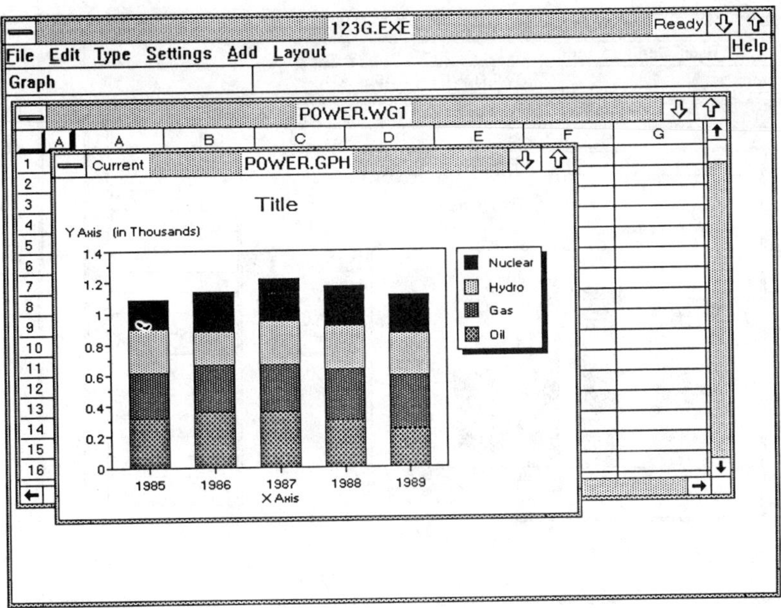

FIGURE 7–50 After creating a graph with Graph View

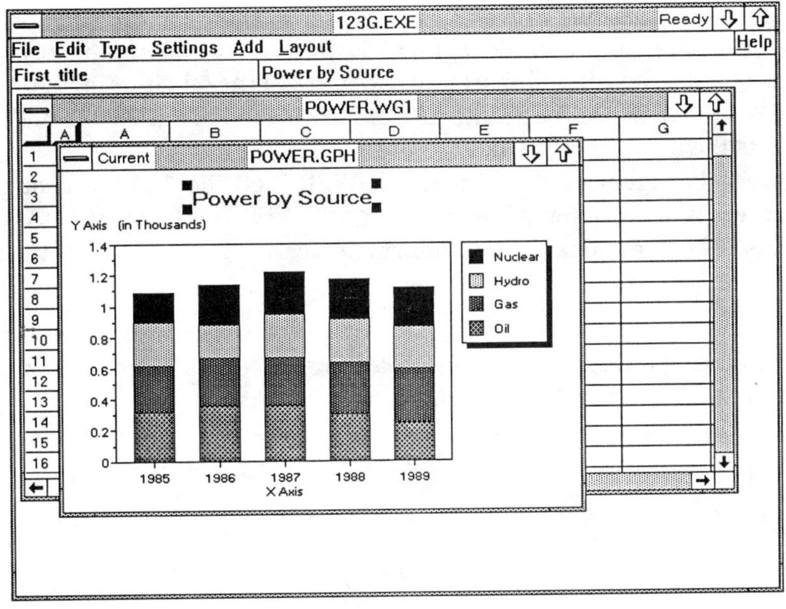

FIGURE 7–51 Entering a new title

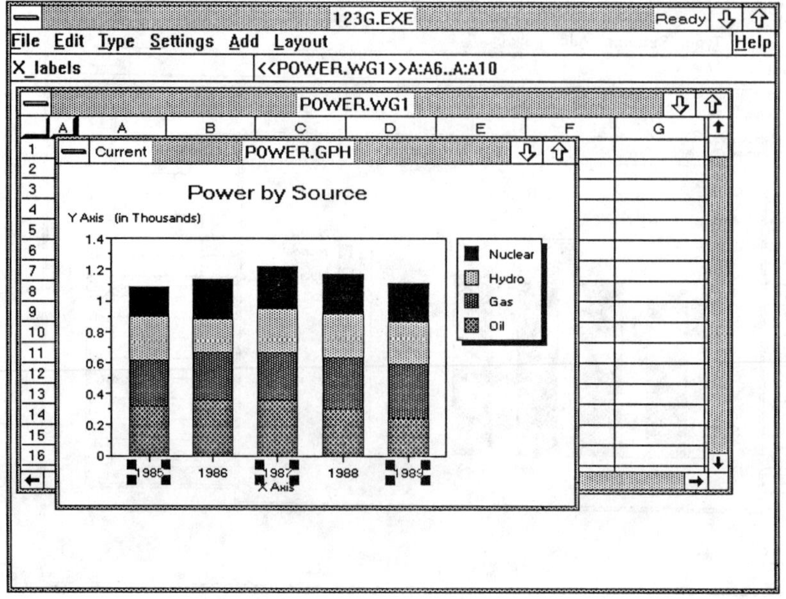

FIGURE 7–52 **X labels are linked to the range A:A6..A:A10 in the file POWER.WG1**

1. With the source file, POWER.WG1, open on the desktop, click on the X labels in the Graph window (press TAB if you are using the keyboard). 1-2-3/G displays handles around the edges of the labels as in Figure 7–52.
2. Click anywhere in the Contents box, or press EDIT (F2). 1-2-3/G highlights the address in the box.
3. Select the range B:A6..B:A10 in the POWER.WG1 file. 1-2-3/G changes the address in the Contents box to read <<POWER.WG1>>B:A6..B:A10.
4. Press ENTER or click on the Confirm (✓) icon. 1-2-3/G updates the graph to reflect the change.

Besides editing links, you can also *create* links for the following graph objects by entering the source in the Contents box:

- Data series
- Data labels
- Titles
- X labels
- Legend frame
- Legend labels

Note

> Noticeably absent from this list of graph objects for which you can edit and create links are titles and legend labels. You cannot create links for titles and legend labels in the Control line; you must use the Edit Link Create command instead. You can, however, edit existing links for these objects.

For more information on editing links, see "Working with the Graph Tool's Edit Commands," later.

MANIPULATING GRAPH OBJECTS

In previous releases of 1-2-3, once you added an object to a graph, you were stuck with the way 1-2-3 chose to display it. For example, if you added a title to a graph, 1-2-3/G controlled where the title appeared on the graph, and you could not change its position.

In 1-2-3/G, however, you can move most objects within a Graph window. You can also change the size of many objects by grabbing a handle and dragging it to a new location. You can also move links from one source to another.

Moving a Graph Object

To move a graph object in 1-2-3/G, you can use the mouse or keyboard. The objects you can move are

- Axis titles
- Legend frame
- Notation (text, lines, and arrows)
- Pie slices
- Plot frame
- Titles

For example, suppose you have the graph in Figure 7-53, and you want to move the legend frame to a new position in the Graph window. To move the frame using the mouse, perform the following:

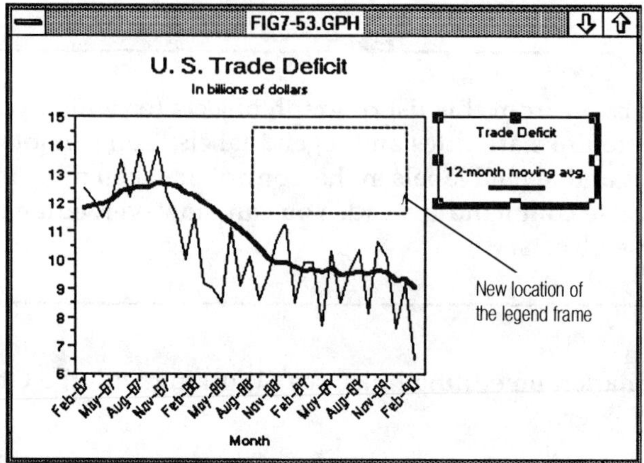

FIGURE 7–53 Preparing to move the legend frame

1. Click on the legend frame to select it.
2. Keeping the mouse button depressed, drag the legend frame to the new location.
3. Release the mouse button.

Figure 7–54 shows the results.

As you begin to move the legend frame, a dotted box appears around the frame. Then, when you have completed the move, the legend frame appears in the new location.

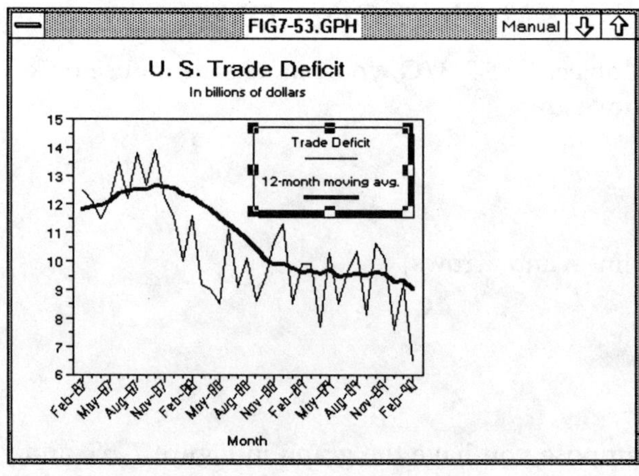

FIGURE 7–54 After moving the legend frame to a new location

To move the legend frame with the keyboard, perform these steps:

1. Press TAB (or SHIFT-TAB) to select the legend frame.
2. Press the arrow keys to move the dotted box to a new location on the screen.
3. Press ENTER to complete the move.

Note

You can also move the legend frame using the Settings Position Legend command (see "Repositioning Legends" later).

Tip: Returning a graph to its original composition

Suppose you move or change the size of a graph object, then decide that you want to return the graph to the way it was before you made the change. To return a graph to its original composition, you use the Layout Auto Compose command.

Here's the rationale: 1-2-3/G has two graph modes—Auto Compose mode and Manual mode. Before you move or size a graph object manually, your graph is in *Auto Compose mode.* In this mode, the Graph Tool automatically chooses the layout for the graph. As it places objects in the window, it adjusts the graph to avoid overlapping graph objects and to keep spacing even.

When you move a graph object or change its size, the composition mode shifts to *Manual mode.* In this mode, graph objects can overlap and spacing can be uneven. You can tell the Graph Tool is in Manual mode when a Manual status indicator appears in the title bar, as in Figure 7–54. Notice that in this figure, the legend frame overlaps the plot frame, a condition that does not normally occur in Auto Compose mode.

By selecting the Layout Auto Compose command, you return the Graph Tool to Auto Compose mode. 1-2-3/G redraws the graph and removes the Manual indicator from the title bar.

Be aware that when you select the Layout Auto Compose command, 1-2-3/G eliminates all the changes you have made to a graph by moving and resizing graph objects.

Changing the Size of a Graph Object

Suppose you have created the graph in Figure 7–54 in which the legend frame overlaps the plot frame. As a result of moving the legend frame, the graph looks slightly out of balance in the Graph window. You can easily change the size of the plot frame to restore some balance to the graph.

To size the plot frame using the mouse, perform the following steps:

1. Select the plot frame by clicking on it. 1-2-3/G displays handles around the edge of the plot frame, as in Figure 7–55.
2. Drag one handle to a new position.
3. Release the mouse button.

As you begin to change the size of the plot frame, a dotted box appears around the edge of the plot frame. After completing the resizing operation, the dotted box disappears from view and the plot frame appears in its place.

To size the plot frame using the keyboard, perform these steps:

1. Press TAB (or SHIFT-TAB) to select the plot frame.
2. Press . (period) to select a handle on the plot frame. By pressing period repeatedly, you can move from one handle to the next in clockwise fashion. A bold cross marks the handle that is currently selected.
3. Use the arrow keys to move the handle to a new location.
4. Press ENTER to complete the operation.

Figure 7–56 shows the results of dragging the right edge of the plot frame to a new location.

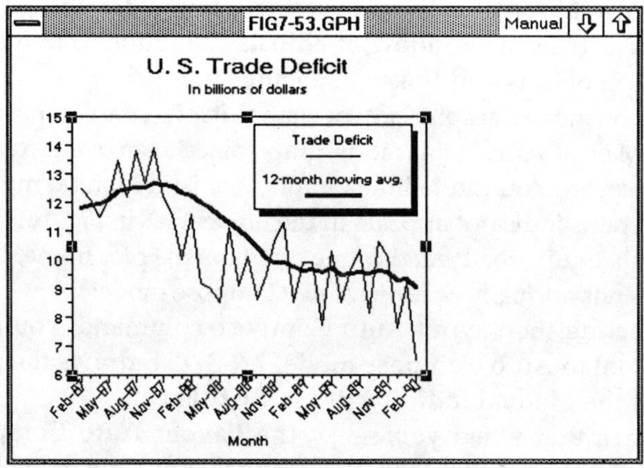

FIGURE 7–55 Preparing to resize the plot frame

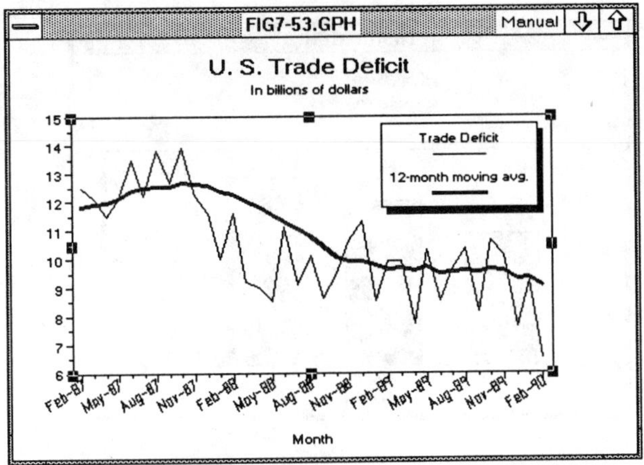

FIGURE 7–56 After resizing the plot frame

Note

> Besides the plot frame, the only other objects you can size in a graph are line and arrow notations.

Moving Links

Suppose you have created the graph in Figure 7–57 that shows projected sales for the Hardware division of a company. You then decide that you want to create a similar graph for the Automotive division. If the worksheets that contain the data have the same layout, you can easily create a new graph by moving the links from the source file containing the Hardware division data to the source file containing the Automotive division data.

For example, to move graph links from HARDWARE.WG1 file to the AUTO.WG1 file, use the Edit Link Move command as follows:

1. With the files HARDWARE.WG1, AUTO.WG1, and DIVISION.GPH open on the desktop, activate the Graph window that contains the DIVISION.GPH file.
2. Choose Edit Link Move. Figure 7–58 shows the dialog box that appears.
3. Select the currently linked worksheet file—HARDWARE.WG1—in the "Current source" list box.

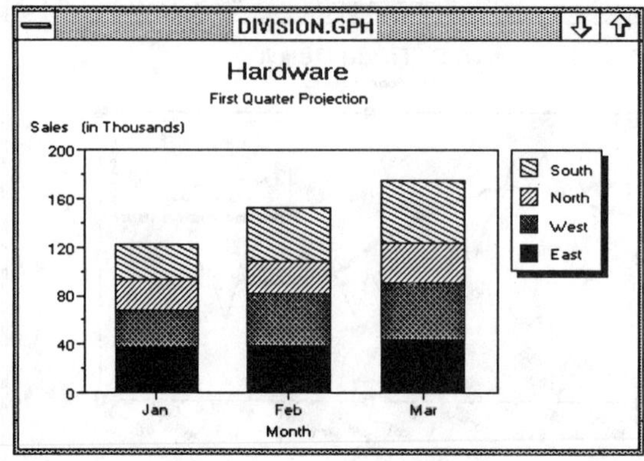

FIGURE 7–57 A sample graph

Note

Moving graph links from one source file to another works best when both worksheet files have the same layout. When you move links from one source file to another, 1-2-3/G changes the filename portion of each link reference (the portion between the double-angle brackets << >>) but keeps the cell address or range reference the same—for example, from <<HARDWARE.WG1>>A1 to <<AUTO.WG1>>A1. Therefore, unless the data in the new source file is located in exactly the same cell locations, the links will not reference the proper data.

Edit Link Move
Destination file: DIVISION.GPH
Current source:
HARDWARE.WG1
HARDWARE.WG1
New source:
AUTO.WG1
AUTO.WG1
HARDWARE.WG1
Action
Move links
Delete links
Cancel

FIGURE 7–58 The Edit Link Move dialog box

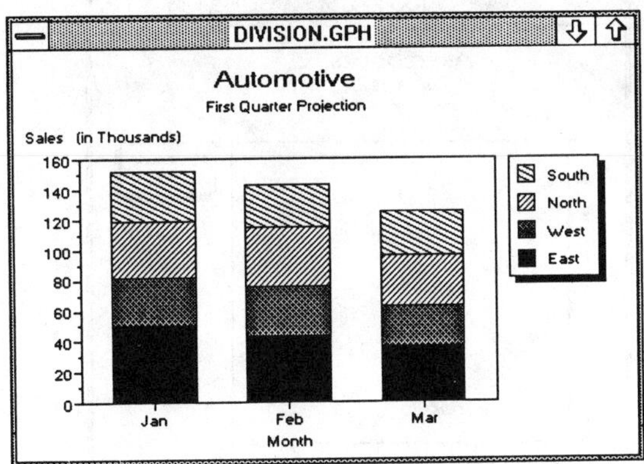

FIGURE 7–59 Results of moving the links to a new source file

4. In the "New source" text box, select the name of the worksheet file you wish to move the links to—AUTO.WG1.
5. Select Move links.

Figure 7–59 shows the results of moving links to the new source file, AUTO.WG1

ENHANCING A GRAPH

This section describes the many ways you can enhance your graphs in 1-2-3/G. To enhance your graphs, you can use the Worksheet window's Graph command or the Graph Tool. As you will soon see, however, the Graph Tool offers far more options.

Titles

As in previous releases, 1-2-3/G lets you add up to four titles to a graph—two at the top (the first and second titles), one below the *x*-axis (the *x*-axis title), and one to the left of the *y*-axis (the *y*-axis title). Figure 7–60 shows an XY graph with all four titles set up.

The first and second titles are the graph titles located at the top of the graph in Figure 7–60, "Aftershocks" and "April 18, 1990." The x-axis and y-axis titles usually describe something about the values measured along each axis. For example, the y-axis title in Figure 7–60 explains that the values

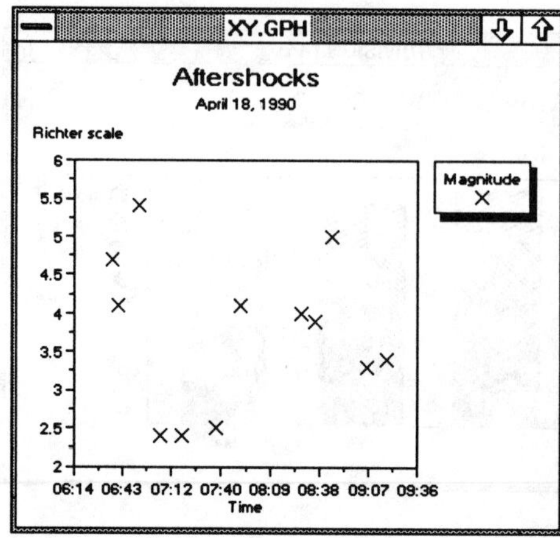

FIGURE 7–60 An XY graph with all graph titles assigned

along the y-axis are "Richter scale" values, and the values along the x-axis are "Time" values.

As you know, when you create a graph automatically using Graph View or Graph Setup, 1-2-3/G automatically assigns the following text to this:

First:	Title
X-axis:	X Axis
Y-axis:	Y Axis

You can change the title text from either the Worksheet window or the Graph Tool.

Assigning a Title from the Worksheet Window

To assign titles from the Worksheet window, select the Graph Options Titles command. Figure 7–61 shows the dialog box that appears. Next, select the title option you want and use one of the following methods to enter it:

- Type in the text for the title. You can enter up to 512 characters, but be aware that 1-2-3/G will truncate characters that don't fit within the Graph window or on the printed page.
- Type \ followed by a cell address or range name of the cell containing the text you want to use as a title, for example, **\A1**.

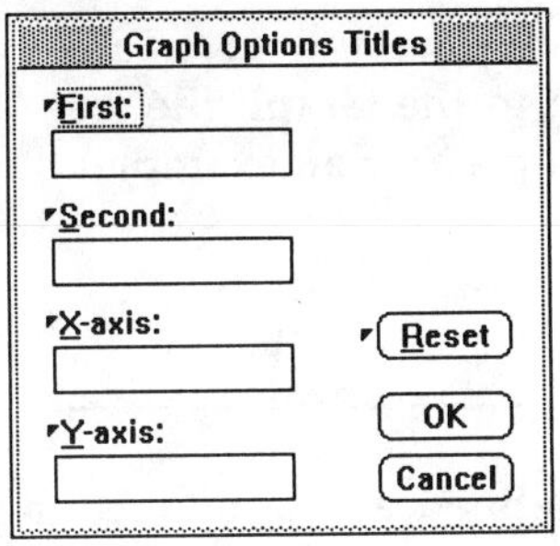

Graph Options Titles
First:
Second:
X-axis:
Y-axis:
Reset
OK
Cancel

FIGURE 7–61 **The Graph Options Titles dialog box**

The advantage of the second method is that you can change your graph title simply by changing the contents of the cell where it is located.

Note

If you use the backslash method for assigning graph titles, be aware that 1-2-3/G treats cell addresses (and range names) in a graph title as absolute. Therefore, If you move your label to another cell, or change its location in the spreadsheet by inserting or deleting rows or columns, the cell address in your graph title setting does not adjust. You will lose your graph title, or end up with the wrong label as your title.

Note

You can clear all the graph titles in the current graph by selecting the Reset option from the Graph Options Titles dialog box.

Changing a Title from the Graph Tool

To change a title from the Graph window, start by clicking on the title or by pressing TAB (or SHIFT-TAB) repeatedly until the title is highlighted (see "Selecting Objects" above). Next, perform one of the following:

- Type the new title in the Contents box on the right side of the Control line (see "Entering and Editing Text" earlier in this chapter).

- Use the Edit Link Create command to create a link between a cell in a worksheet file and a title in the Graph file (see "Using the Graph Tool to Create a Graph—An Example" for an example).

Note

> If you have already defined a title by creating a link, you cannot change the title by replacing it with literal text. Rather, you must first delete the link, then enter the new text.

Adding a Title from the Graph Tool

Occasionally, you may want to add a title to a graph. For example, suppose you have created a graph with Graph View or Graph Setup. 1-2-3/G does not automatically create a second title for the graph. To add a Second title, select the Add Title command followed by the Second option. Table 7–1 shows the options that appear in the cascade menu for the Add Title command, where 1-2-3/G locates them in the Graph window, and the text that automatically 1-2-3/G assigns to the title.

For example, when you select the Second option, 1-2-3/G inserts the text "Second Title" at the top of the graph, below the First title. To change the text that 1-2-3/G displays for this title, you must edit the title (see the previous section).

Here are some notes to keep in mind as you work with graph titles from the Graph Tool:

- If your graph already has a title, its corresponding option in the Add Title command will appear grayed.

Table 7–1 The Add Title Menu Options

Option	Location	Automatic Text
First	Top center	Title
Second	Top center (below first title)	Second Title
X-axis	Bottom center	X Axis
Y-axis	Top left	Y Axis
2Y-axis	Top right (above second *y*-axis)	2Y Axis

- You can delete a title from a graph by clicking on it and pressing DEL (the shortcut for Edit Clear). If you change your mind and want to recover the title, press ALT-BACKSPACE immediately. (See "Deleting Graph Objects" below for more information.)
- You can choose different fonts for your graph titles (see "Changing Text Fonts and Text Styles" later in this chapter).

Data Ranges and X Labels

As you know, when you select the Graph View or Graph Setup command, 1-2-3/G automatically assigns data ranges and the X range (for X labels or pie slice labels). Suppose, however, that you want to add an additional range to your graph. You can add ranges from the Worksheet window or the Graph Tool.

Adding Data Ranges and X Labels from the Worksheet Window

To add a data range or X range from the Worksheet window, select the Graph Add Ranges command. Figure 7–62 shows the dialog box that appears. You can specify up to 23 data ranges (A through W) and an X range (the range that contains X labels or pie slice labels). See "Creating a Graph Manually—An Example" for a detailed discussion.

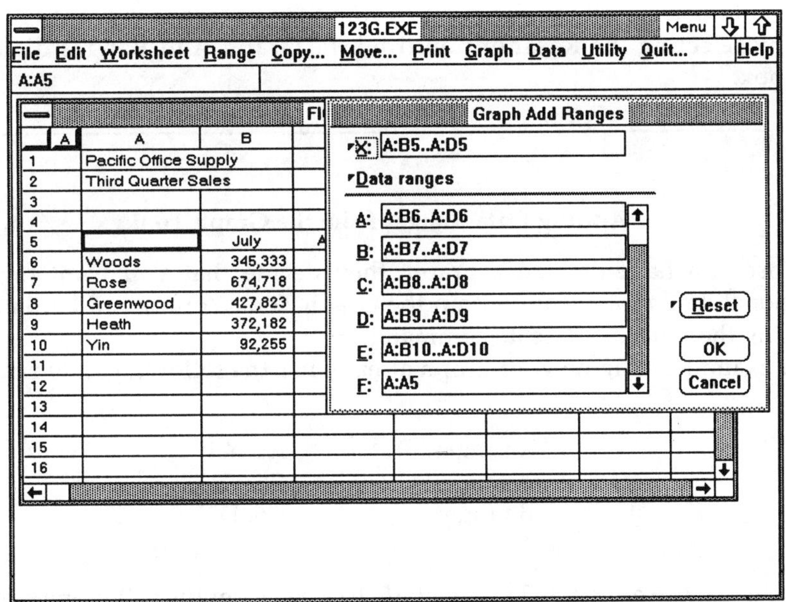

FIGURE 7–62 The Graph Add Ranges dialog box

Here are some things to keep in mind when you enter ranges:

- You can use data ranges from different worksheet files, as long as those files are open on the desktop. You cannot use collections, however.
- All data ranges should have the same number of cells.
- If you choose a data range that is more than a single column, row, or worksheet, 1-2-3/G interprets the data in a columnwise fashion within each worksheet. For example, if you select A:B1..B:C2 as a data range, 1-2-3/G uses the data in the order A:B1, A:B2, A:C1, A:C2, A:C3, B:B1, B:B2, B:C1, B:C2, and B:C3.

Note

> If you need to assign more data ranges than appear in the Graph Add Ranges dialog box, use the scroll bar to scroll down to additional range options.

Note

> You can clear all the data ranges and X range for the current graph by selecting the Reset option from the Graph Add Ranges dialog box.

Adding Data Ranges from the Graph Tool

Suppose you have created a graph, then decide that you want to add an additional data range from within the Graph Tool. You can add a data range by using the Edit Link Create command.

For example, imagine your graph already has the following data ranges:

X range:	A6..A17
A range:	C6..C17
B range:	D6..D17

and you want to assign a C range of E6..E17. Perform the following steps:

1. Select Edit Link Create.

2. To specify the worksheet file and range to graph, choose the "Source file and item" text box and point to the range E6..E17 in your chosen worksheet file.
3. Select the "Destination item" text box and press NAME (F3) to see a complete list of available destinations.
4. Choose "Series" from the list then select OK to complete the command.

Note

> The items that appear within the destination list include only those graph objects that have not yet been assigned links.

When you select "Series" as the destination, 1-2-3/G creates a link between your chosen worksheet file and the first available data series. In the current example, because the A series (Series:A) and B series (Series:B) are already linked, 1-2-3/G creates a link to the C series (Series:C). Note that if you want to create a link directly to a specific series, enter the object name directly in the "Destination item" text box, for example, **Series:C.**

See "Using the Graph Tool to Create a Graph—An Example" for a more detailed discussion of options in the Edit Link Create dialog box.

Adding X Labels from the Graph Tool

Suppose you have created a graph without any X labels, as in Figure 7-63. You then enter a range of labels in a worksheet file that you want to use as X labels in your graph. To add X labels from the Graph Tool, you use the

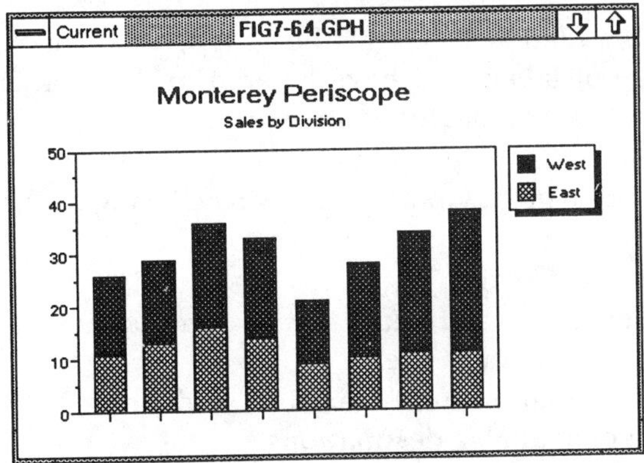

FIGURE 7-63 A graph without any X labels

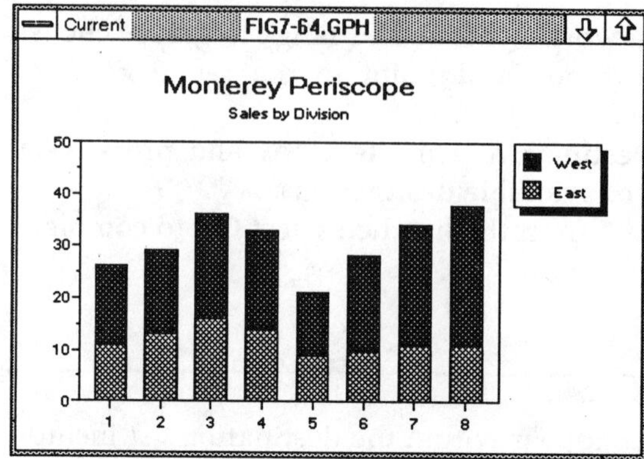

FIGURE 7–64 The Add X Labels command places integers along the x-axis

Add X Labels command. When you select this command, 1-2-3/G automatically assigns numbers from 1 to the maximum number of data points in the data series and places these numbers below the tick marks on the x-axis, as in Figure7–64.

Note

> If your graph already has X Labels, the Add X Labels command will appear grayed.

After you have added X labels to the graph, you can then create a link between the range of labels you have entered in the worksheet file and the current graph file. Perform the following steps:

1. Select the X labels in the Graph window by clicking on them or by pressing TAB.
2. Choose Edit Link Create.
3. Select the "Source file and item" text box and point to the range of labels in your chosen worksheet file.
4. Select the "Destination item" text box and press NAME (F3) to see a complete list of available destinations.
5. Choose "X_labels" from the list then select OK to complete the command.

Figure 7–65 shows some sample results.

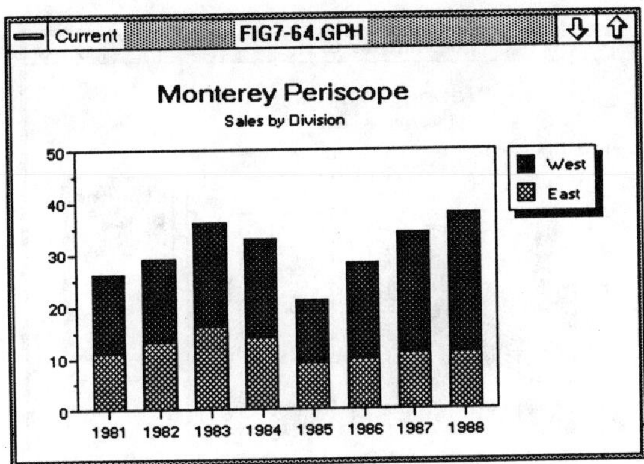

FIGURE 7–65 **After linking labels from a worksheet file to the current graph file**

Note

> The items that appear within the destination list include only those graph objects that have not yet been assigned links.

Legends

As you know, each data range in a bar graph has its own color or hatch pattern. Adding a legend to your bar graph identifies each data range with a legend label, as shown in Figure 7–66. In a line graph, legend labels are used to identify each symbol (or marker) assigned to a data range.

When you use Graph View or Graph Setup to create a graph, 1-2-3/G creates a legend for you automatically (see "How 1-2-3/G Interprets Automatic Graph Ranges and Assigns Settings," earlier). Nevertheless, the labels assigned to the legend may be incorrect, in which case you will need to know how to change the legend settings. In addition, if you have created a graph manually, you will need to know how to add a legend. This section shows you how to add or change legends from the Worksheet window or the Graph Tool.

Assigning Legend Labels from the Worksheet Window

To assign legend labels from the Worksheet window, select the Graph Options Legends command. Figure 7–67 shows the dialog box that appears. You can define your legend labels one data range at a time with

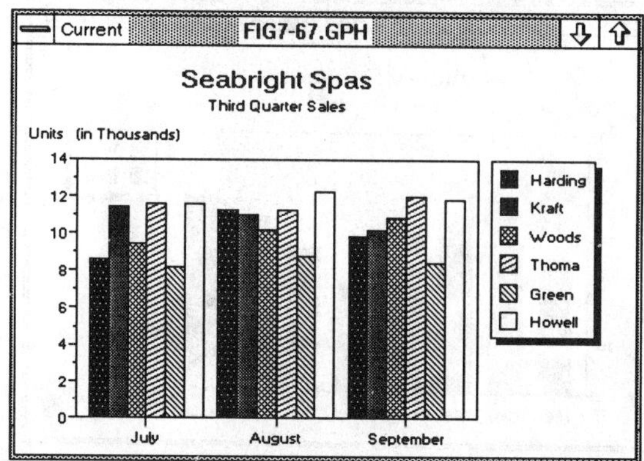

FIGURE 7-66 A bar graph with data ranges A through F and matching legend labels

with options A–W, or use the Range option to define all the legend labels in one step.

If you choose to define the legend for each data range individually, choose the letter of the data range and use either of the following methods to enter the legend:

- Type in the legend text. You can enter up to 512 characters, but be aware that the longer your legend label, the less room 1-2-3/G will have for the plot frame.
- Type \ followed by a cell address or range name of the cell containing the text you want to use as the legend label. For example, in Figure 7-68, because cell A6 contains the legend for the A range, you would type **\A6**.

The advantage of the second method is that you can change your graph title simply by changing the contents of the cell where it is located.

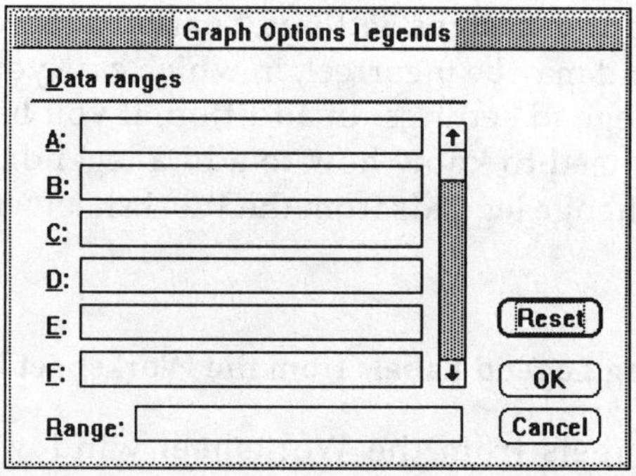

Graph Options Legends

Data ranges

A:
B:
C:
D:
E:
F:
Range:

Reset
OK
Cancel

FIGURE 7-67 The Graph Options Legends dialog box

Note

If you need to assign more legend labels than appear in the Graph Options Legends dialog box, use the scroll bar to scroll down to additional options.

You can also define your legends in one step. To do this, you must have the legend labels in a contiguous range of cells. In the example in Figure 7–68, the group of labels located in the range A6..A11 can be used to define the legends for data ranges A through F. Use the Range option in the Graph Options Legends command, and point to or type in the range containing the legends.

Tip: Using string formulas to create titles, legends, and data labels

You can use string formulas to combine worksheet labels and values in titles, legends, and data labels. These formulas are easy to construct, once you learn a few simple rules, and they allow you to add a lot more information to your graphs. Since you probably have both the labels and values you need already entered in your worksheet, your string formulas can be constructed using cell references rather than actual data.

Suppose you have the label Department in cell B12 of your worksheet, and the value 12 in cell C14. You can build a string formula using the cell addresses as follows:

```
+B12&" "&@STRING(C14,0)
```

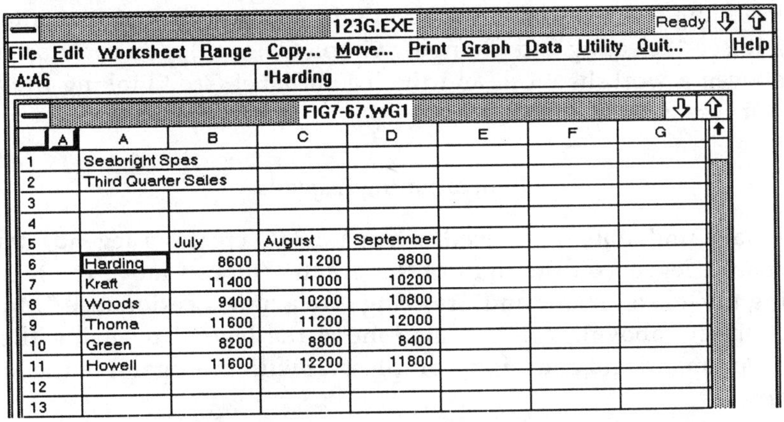

123G.EXE Ready

File Edit Worksheet Range Copy... Move... Print Graph Data Utility Quit... Help

A:A6 'Harding

FIG7-67.WG1

A	A	B	C	D	E	F	G
1	Seabright Spas						
2	Third Quarter Sales						
3							
4							
5		July	August	September			
6	Harding	8600	11200	9800			
7	Kraft	11400	11000	10200			
8	Woods	9400	10200	10800			
9	Thoma	11600	11200	12000			
10	Green	8200	8800	8400			
11	Howell	11600	12200	11800			
12							
13							

FIGURE 7–68 **Sample worksheet used to create legends**

and place it in a cell. You can then reference the cell address of this formula when defining a legend. The result of this string formula is the same as typing the legend manually, but you now have a formula that is automatically updated if you make changes to the data in cells B12 and C14. For more information on string formulas, refer to Chapter 1, "1-2-3/G Basics," and Chapter 6, "Functions."

Adding a Legend Frame or Legend Label from the Graph Tool

There are two kinds of legend objects that you can add to a graph in the Graph window: a legend frame and a legend label. To add a legend frame to a graph, you use the Add Legend Frame command. 1-2-3/G places a legend frame on the right-hand side of the graph and assigns it the default legend labels Series:A, Series:B, and so on. (To change these default legend labels, you can type in new text or create a link between the label and a worksheet file. See "Selecting and Changing Graph Objects" above for more information.)

Suppose, on the other hand, you want to add only a single legend label to a graph. To do so, you use the Add Legend Label command. When you select this command, 1-2-3/G displays a dialog box similar to the one in Figure 7–69. Letters are grayed if they match a data series that does not appear in the graph, or the data series has already been assigned a legend label. For example, in Figure 7–69, A through F are available, but G through W are not. To add a legend label corresponding to the F data series, for example, you would select F. 1-2-3/G creates a default legend label, in this case Series:F. (When you add a legend label, if a legend frame is not already present in the graph, 1-2-3/G creates one.)

After adding a legend label to the graph, you can change its contents by editing it (see "Selecting and Changing Graph Objects"). You can also create a link between a worksheet cell and the legend label (see "Linking Individual Graph Objects with Edit Link Create).

Repositioning Legends

As you have undoubtedly noticed, when 1-2-3/G creates a legend, it always positions the legend on the right of the graph. You can move the legend by selecting the legend frame and dragging it to a new location (see "Moving a Graph Object" above). You can also move the legend by using the Type Gallery command and choosing a graph style with the legend in the location you want.

Another more precise way to reposition the legend is to use the Settings Position Legend command from the Graph Tool. For example, suppose you

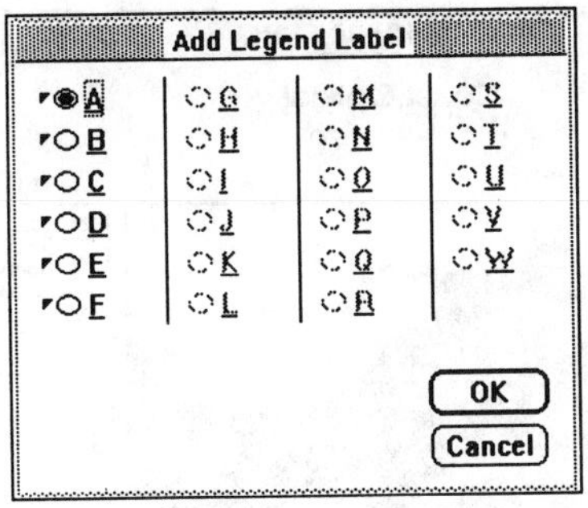

Add Legend Label

A B C D E F G H I J K L M N O P Q R S T U V W

OK

Cancel

FIGURE 7–69 **The Add Legend Label dialog box**

have the graph in Figure 7–70 (the data for this graph appears in Figure 7–31), and you want to move the legend to the bottom of the graph. Begin by selecting the Settings Position Legend command. 1-2-3/G displays the dialog box in Figure 7–71. Select the Bottom option to position the plot frame at the bottom of the graph with the legend labels side-by-side. In addition, suppose you want to move the legend inside the plot frame. Select the Inside option. Figure 7–72 shows the results of these settings.

Deleting Legends

You can use any of the following methods to delete legends and legend labels:

- To delete legend labels individually from the Worksheet window, begin by selecting the Graph Options Legend command. Next, select the letter associated with the legend label; 1-2-3/G highlights the contents of the box. Press DEL to clear the legend definition and select OK, or press ENTER. When you redisplay the graph, the legend label for that data range is gone.
- To delete all legend labels at once from the Worksheet window, select the Graph Options Legends command and choose the Reset option. 1-2-3/G removes the entire legend from the graph, including the legend frame.
- To delete legend labels individually from the Graph window, select the individual legend label within the legend frame by clicking on it (or pressing TAB) and pressing DEL.
- To delete the entire legend from the Graph window, select the legend frame by clicking on it (or pressing TAB) and press DEL.

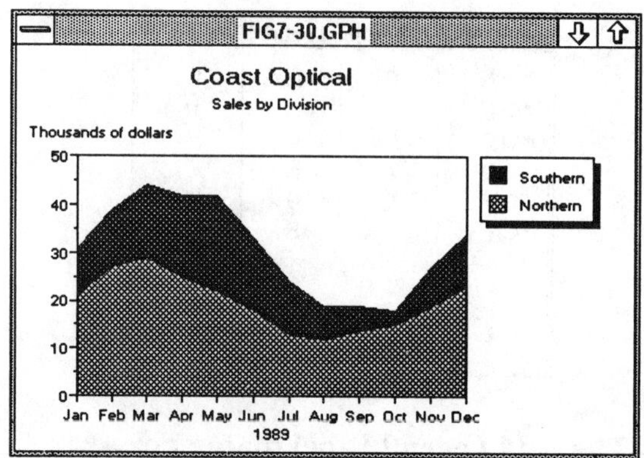

FIGURE 7–70 **A sample graph whose legend you want to move**

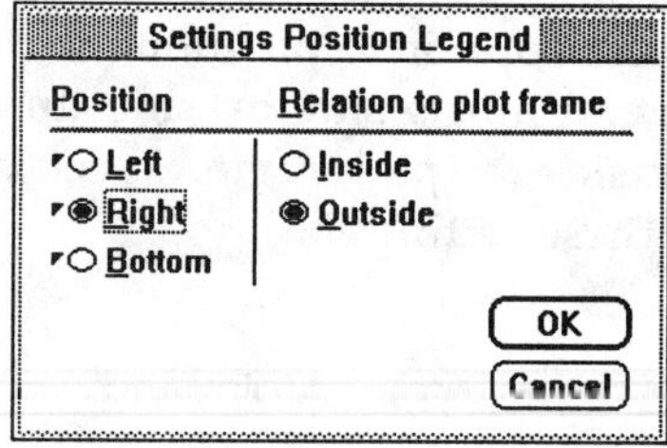

FIGURE 7–71 **The Settings Position Legend dialog box**

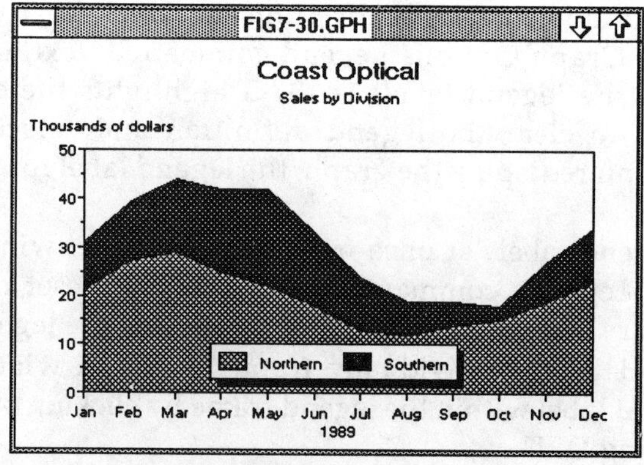

FIGURE 7–72 **After moving the legend to the bottom of the graph, inside the plot frame**

Note

If you delete an entire legend using DEL from the Graph Tool, 1-2-3/G still retains the links to the worksheet. Therefore, if you later add a legend to the graph (using Add Legend Frame), 1-2-3/G displays the original legend that you previously deleted, including any links. To get around this problem, you can delete each legend label's link before deleting the entire legend from the graph (see "Deleting Links" later). That way, when you later add a legend to the graph, it will not have any residual links.

Changing Fonts

To change the font of any graph object that includes text or numbers, you use the Settings Font command from the Graph window. For example, suppose you have the graph in Figure 7–73, and you want to change the font of the second title (1952–1987) to match the first title. Perform the following steps:

1. Select the second title by clicking on it or by pressing TAB (or SHIFT-TAB).
2. Choose Settings Font. 1-2-3/G displays the dialog box in Figure 7–74.
3. Choose the font you want from the Fonts list box, in this case, Helvetica 14.
4. Select OK.

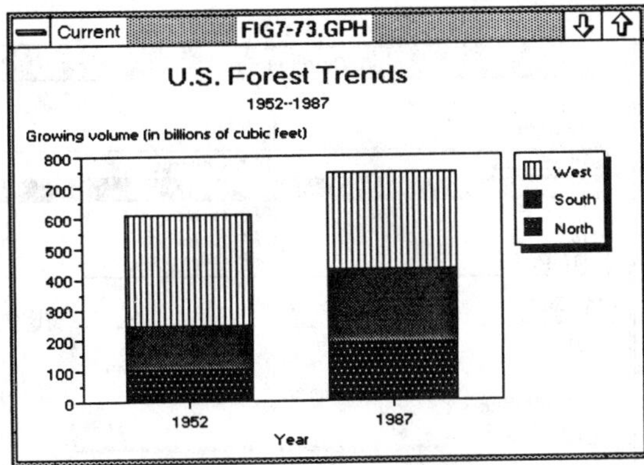

FIGURE 7–73 Before changing the font for the second title

Note

This dialog box is nearly identical to the one that appears when you select the Range Attributes Font command in the Worksheet window. In fact, the only difference between the two is that Settings Font dialog box does not have a Range(s) box. See Chapter 3, "Formatting the Worksheet," for a more complete discussion of how to change fonts.

Figure 7–75 shows the result of the change. As you review the results, notice also that the x-axis and y-axis titles are in italic type. In addition, the legend labels appear in bold. Keep in mind that you can use Settings Font to change the font and attributes of *any* graph object that contains text or numbers.

Changing Text Color and Justification

Besides changing the font, you can also change the color and justification (positioning) of selected text from the Graph window. Lotus refers to the color and justification settings as the *text style,* and you use the Settings Text Style command to change these settings.

Note

You can only change the justification for the first title, second title, and annotation text.

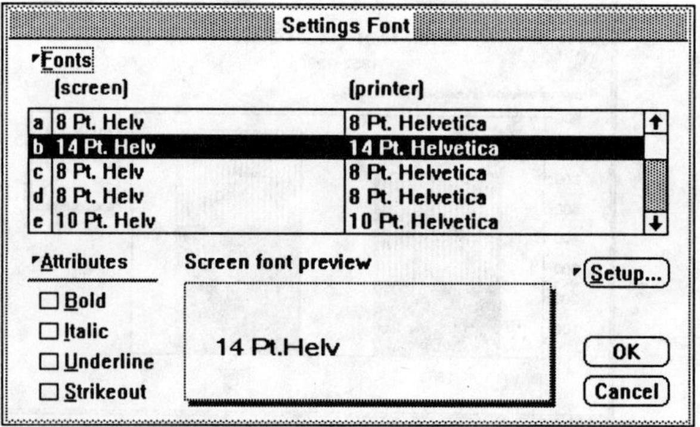

FIGURE 7–74 The Settings Font dialog box

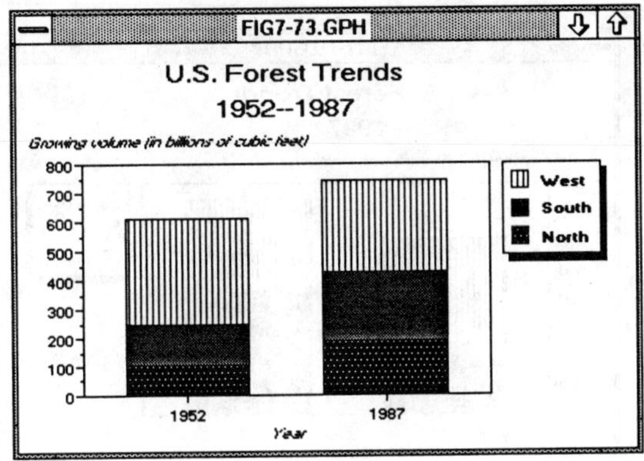

FIGURE 7–75 **Results of changing the font for the second title**

For example, suppose you have the graph in Figure 7-75, and you want to left-justify the second title in relation to the first title. In addition, suppose you want to display the second title in red. Perform the following steps:

1. Select the second title by clicking on it or pressing TAB.
2. Choose the Settings Text Style command. Figure 7-76 shows the dialog box that appears.
3. Select the appropriate Color option, in this case "e" for red. (Although you cannot see colors in Figure 7-76, 1-2-3/G actually displays 16 different colors for the Color options.)
4. Select Left for left justification.
5. Select OK.

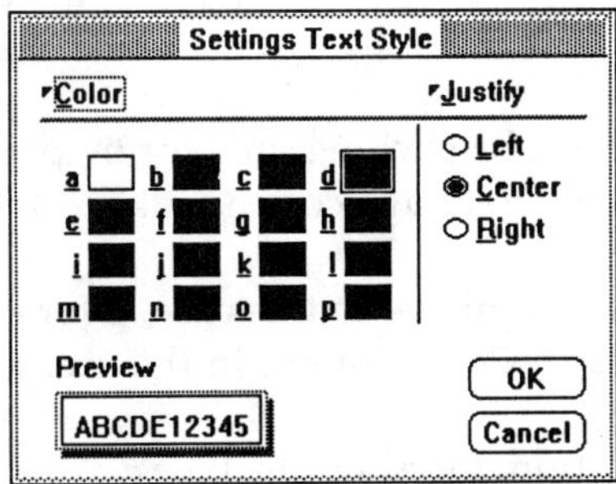

FIGURE 7–76 **The Settings Text Style dialog box**

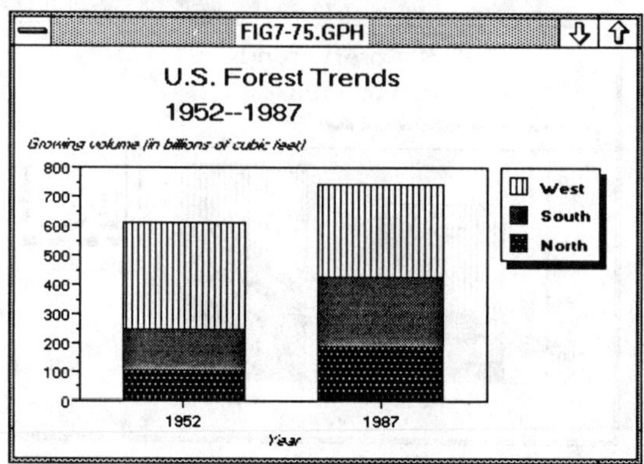

FIGURE 7–77 After left-justifying the second title

Figure 7–77 shows the results of left-justifying the second title, though, it does not show the change in the title's color.

Changing Line and Edge Styles

For all graph objects, you can change the style, width, and color of lines and edges from the Graph window. For example, you can change the width of the plot frame line or the legend frame line. You can also change the width of the border surrounding a series of bars in a bar graph. Lotus refers to the color and the pattern of a selected object or the border around a selected object as the *line/edge style*. You can change the line/edge style of *any* object, except the entire graph.

For example, suppose you want to make the line for the plot frame thicker. Perform these steps:

1. Select the plot frame by clicking on it, or by pressing TAB.
2. Select the Settings Line/Edge command. 1-2-3/G displays the dialog box in Figure 7–78.
3. Choose a Line style option—in this case, g for an uninterrupted line.
4. (Optional) Choose a Color option. In this example, d (black, the default) will do.
5. Select a Width option, for example, b or c.
6. Select OK.

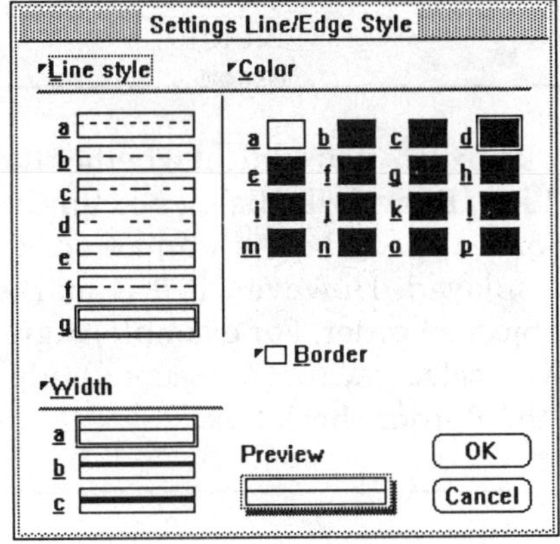

FIGURE 7–78 The Settings Line/Edge dialog box

Figure 7–79 shows the thicker plot frame line.

Note

> When you select b or c for the Width option, 1-2-3/G automatically chooses a Line style of g and grays the other options.

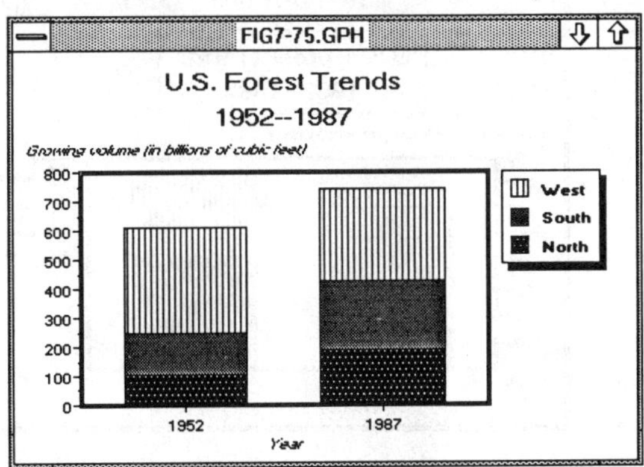

FIGURE 7–79 After changing the width of the plot frame line

Note

The Border check box lets you control whether the settings you make in the Settings Line/Edge Style dialog box apply to the border of an object. If the Border check box is unmarked, the selected object's border is not displayed. However, if it is marked, the settings are applied to the object's border. For example, Figure 7–80 shows what happens when you select the first (or second) title, choose a Line style of g, and mark the Border check box.

Changing Colors and Patterns

1-2-3/G lets you change the colors and patterns of areas within a graph from the Graph Tool. The objects for which you can change the area color or pattern are the graph background, titles, axis labels, scale indicators, text, bar series, area series, pie slices, legend frame, and plot frame. To change the appearance of an area in a graph, you use the Settings Area Style command.

Note

If you want to change the color of lines (such as the lines in a line graph or line notations), use the Settings Line/Edge Style command (see the previous section).

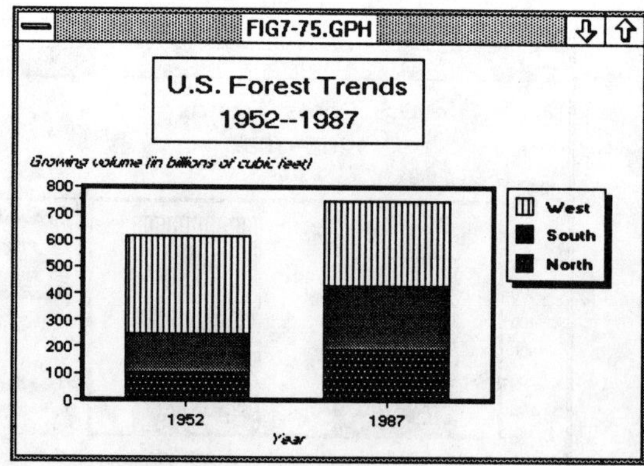

FIGURE 7–80 Results of selecting the first (or second) title and marking the Border check box

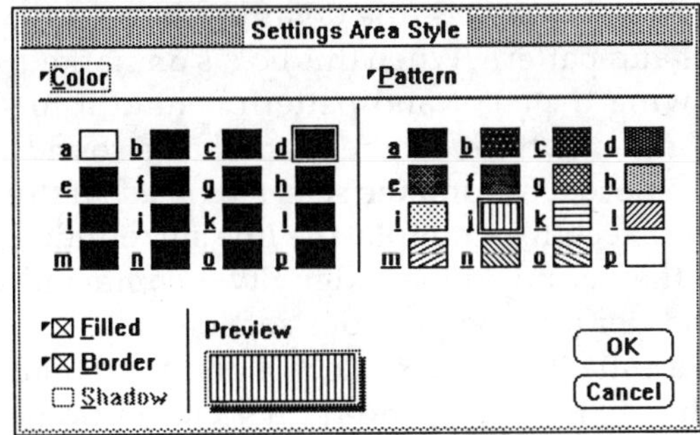

FIGURE 7–81 The Settings Area Style dialog box

For example, suppose you have the graph in Figure 7–80, and you want to change the color or pattern for the West bar series. Perform the following steps:

1. Select the bar series by clicking on it, or pressing TAB (or SHIFT-TAB).
2. Select the Settings Area Style command. 1-2-3/G displays the dialog box in Figure 7–81.
3. Select the color and/or pattern for the series, for example, color d (black) and pattern p (no pattern).
4. Select OK.

Figure 7–82 shows the results.

Here is an explanation of the check boxes available in the Settings Area Style dialog box:

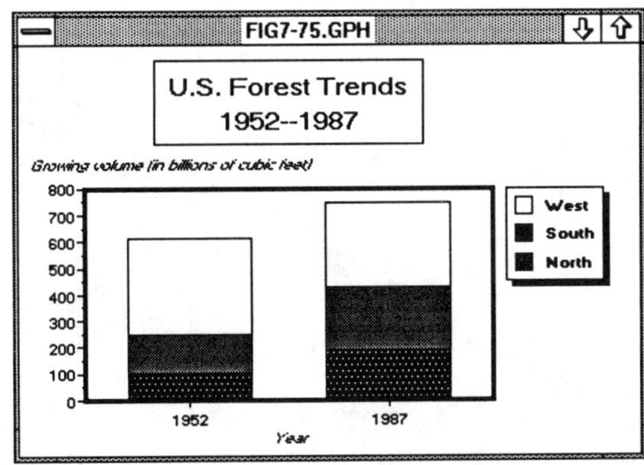

FIGURE 7–82 After changing the pattern for the West bar series

- **Filled:** When this box is marked (the default), the selected object appears in your chosen color and pattern. When this box is unmarked, the object appears transparent, allowing the color and pattern behind it to show through (for example, the color and pattern for the graph background).
- **Border:** Displays a border around the selected object. If this box is unmarked, the border for the object (for example, the line surrounding a bar series) does not appear. Use the Settings Line/Edge Style command to change the appearance of the border (see the previous section).
- **Shadow**: Displays a shadow for the selected object, similar to the shadow that appears automatically for the legend frame. This option appears grayed for all objects except the first and second graph titles and the legend frame.

Annotating a Graph

Annotating your graphs is particularly easy in 1-2-3/G. There are three types of annotation: text, lines, and arrows. To add annotation to a graph, you use the Add Notation command from the Graph Tool.

Adding Text Notation

Suppose you have the graph in Figure 7–83, and you want to add some text explaining the reason for the dip in sales in 1985. Perform the following steps:

1. Select the Add Notation Text command. 1-2-3/G displays "Text Note" in the upper-right corner of the graph, as in Figure 7–84.
2. Enter the text annotation, for example, **Industry slowdown**, and press ENTER. 1-2-3/G displays the new text in place of the old.

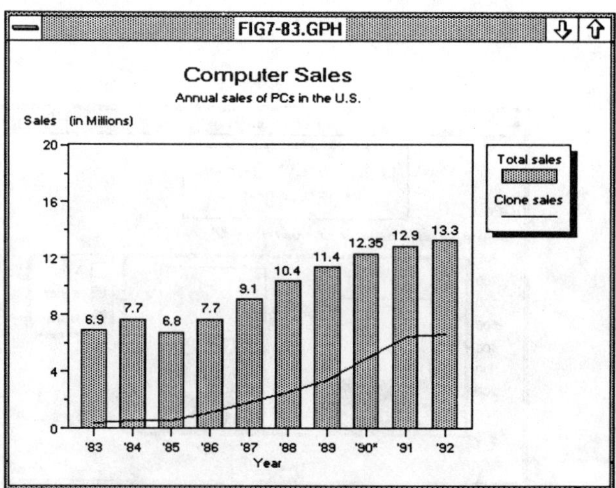

FIGURE 7–83 A graph prior to adding annotation

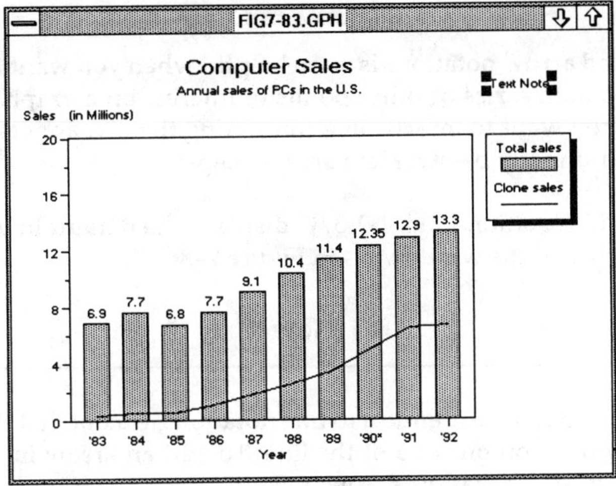

FIGURE 7–84 **Preliminary note that appears after selecting the Add Notation Text command**

3. While the text annotation is still the selected object, move it to the location you desire, as in Figure 7-85. If you are using the mouse, drag the text annotation to the new location. If you are using the keyboard, press the appropriate arrow keys, then press ENTER.

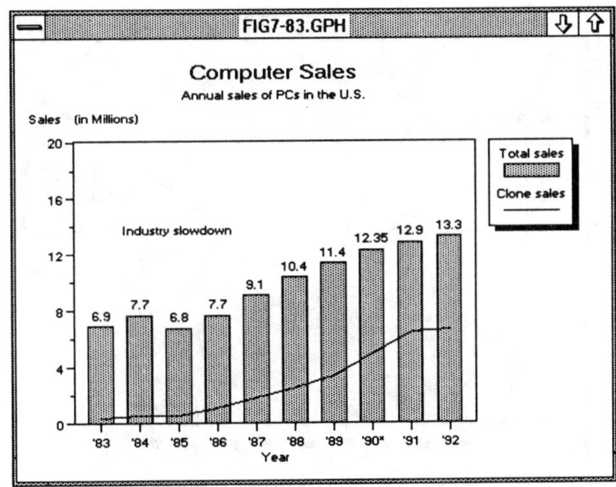

FIGURE 7–85 **After moving the text annotation to the desired location**

Adding Lines and Arrows

Adding line and arrow notations is often helpful when you want to connect text annotations to data series or other points of interest on a graph. For example, imagine that you want to insert a line connecting the text annotation in Figure 7–85 to the bar directly below. Here are the steps:

1. Select Add Notation Line. 1-2-3/G displays the default line in the upper-right corner of the window, as in Figure 7–86.

Note

> Arrow notations are identical to line notations, except that they have an arrow head on one end of the line. To add an arrow instead of a line, select Add Notation Arrow in Step 1.

2. While the line is still selected, move the entire line, or one end of the line, using the mouse or the keyboard (see "Moving a Graph Object" and "Changing the Size of a Graph Object," above).

Figure 7–87 shows the results after you have positioned the line to the desired location.

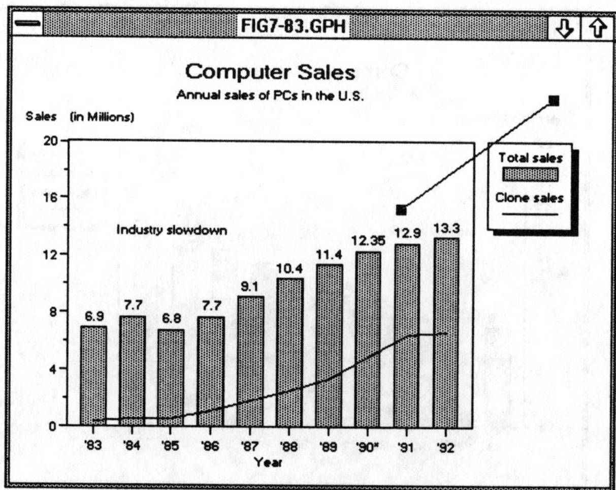

FIGURE 7–86 The default line that appears when you select Add Notation Line

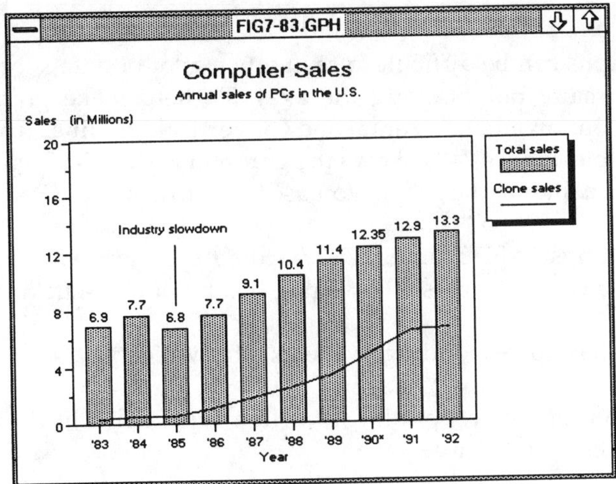

FIGURE 7–87 After positioning the line notation

Note

> You can delete an annotation (text, line, or arrow) by selecting it and pressing DEL, or by choosing the Edit Clear command.

Changing Arrow Heads

You can add or change arrow heads for an existing line or arrow annotation by using the Settings Arrow Heads command. For example, suppose you want to add an arrow head to the line annotation in Figure 7–87. Select the line, then choose the Settings Arrow Heads command. 1-2-3/G displays the dialog box in Figure 7–88. (You can also access this dialog box by double-clicking on a line or arrow annotation.) You can then choose the button corresponding to the arrow head(s) you want and select OK.

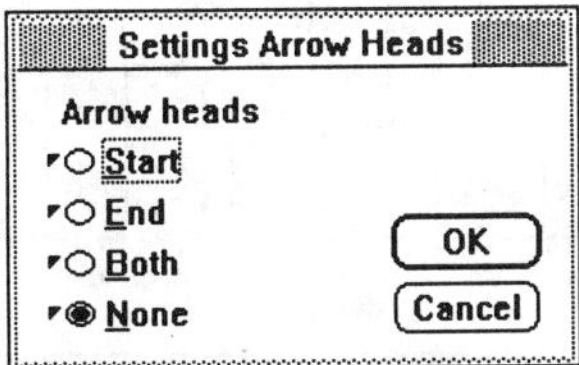

FIGURE 7–88 The Settings Arrow Heads dialog box

Adding Grid Lines

Sometimes graphs can be difficult to read when a lot of data is being graphed and there are many points along the axes. To help make graphs easier to comprehend, you can add horizontal and/or vertical grid lines from the Graph Tool. For example, Figure 7–89 shows the graph in Figure 7–87 with y-axis grid lines. To add grid lines to the graph, you use the Settings Grid/Frame command as follows:

1. Select Settings Grid/Frame. 1-2-3/G displays the dialog box in Figure 7–90. (You can also access this dialog box by double-clicking on the plot frame.)
2. Mark the box corresponding to the axis for which you want grid lines to appear, in this case the Y-axis box.
3. Select a button corresponding to a line type: solid lines (the default), dotted lines, or gray lines.
4. Select OK.

Note

If you want to remove grid lines, select the Settings Grid/Frame command and unmark the X-axis, Y-axis, or 2Y-axis check box.

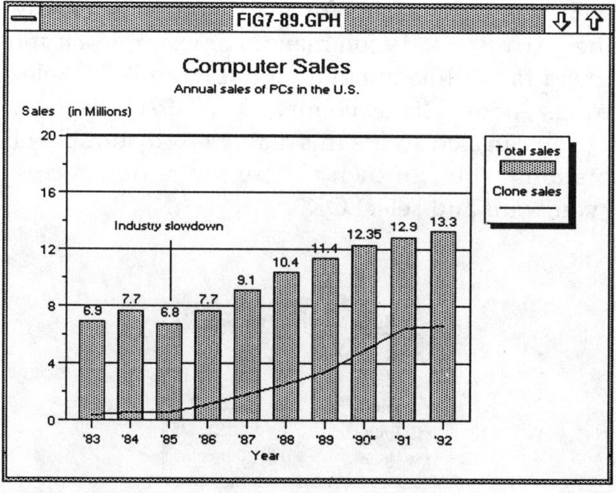

FIGURE 7–89 A graph with y-axis grid lines

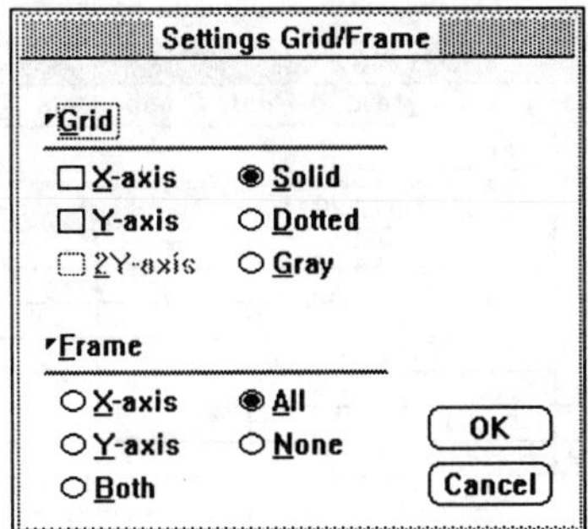

FIGURE 7–90 **The Settings Grid/Frame dialog box**

Tip: When to use grid lines

As a general rule, you should use grid lines sparingly. Whereas bar and stacked bar graphs are sometimes easier to read with horizontal grid lines, vertical grid lines usually detract from these graph types. On the other hand, line graphs and especially XY graphs can often benefit from both vertical and horizontal grid lines. For some ideas of when grid lines can help a graph's appearance, check the graph icons in the Graph Tool's Type Gallery command.

Changing the Appearance of the Plot Frame

You can also use the Settings Grid/Frame command to change the appearance of the plot frame in a 1-2-3/G graph, including the axis lines. Here is an explanation of the Frame options that appear in the Settings Grid/Frame dialog box in Figure 7–90:

- **X-axis:** Displays the *x*-axis only (all other border lines are removed from the plot frame).
- **Y-Axis:** Displays the *y*-axis only (all other border lines are removed from the plot frame).
- **Both:** Displays lines for both the *x*-axis and *y*-axis, but not the other border lines.
- **All:** Displays all four border lines (this is the default).
- **None:** Displays no border lines.

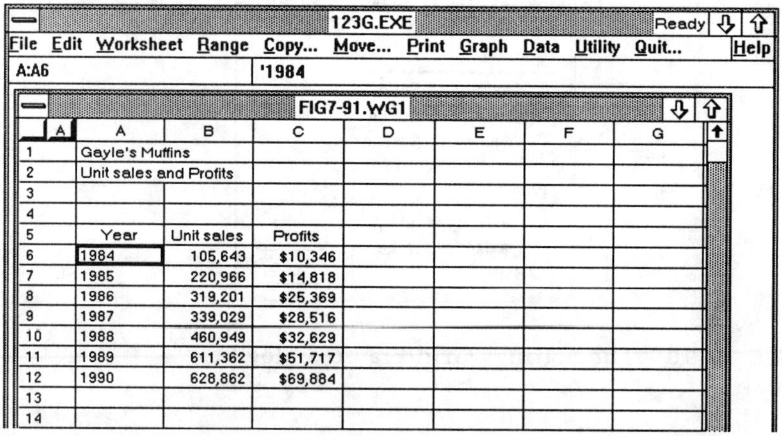

123G.EXE — Ready

File Edit Worksheet Range Copy... Move... Print Graph Data Utility Quit... Help

A:A6 '1984

FIG7-91.WG1

A	A	B	C	D	E	F	G
1	Gayle's Muffins						
2	Unit sales and Profits						
3							
4							
5	Year	Unit sales	Profits				
6	1984	105,643	$10,346				
7	1985	220,966	$14,818				
8	1986	319,201	$25,369				
9	1987	339,029	$28,516				
10	1988	460,949	$32,629				
11	1989	611,362	$51,717				
12	1990	628,862	$69,884				
13							
14							

FIGURE 7–91 Related data of different orders of magnitude

Adding a Second Y-Axis

In Release 2, one of the most noticeable shortcomings of 1-2-3's graphics was its inability to graph related sets of data that are of different orders of magnitude. For example, suppose you want to graph the data in Figure 7–91. The unit sales numbers are in hundred thousands, and the profit numbers are in ten thousands. If you graph the data as a line graph, you can hardly see the fluctuations in the profit line.

In 1-2-3/G, however, you can set up two *y*-axes for the same graph. For example, you can plot sales (in units) on the left *y*-axis and profits (in dollars) on the right *y*-axis. Even though their scales differ markedly, it is easy to compare sales and profits on the same graph. Figure 7–92 shows an example. The graph has the following range settings:

X range	A6..A12
A range	B6..B12
B range	C6..C12

Assigning Data Ranges to the Second Y-Axis

To create a graph with a second *y*-axis, you begin by creating a graph in the usual way, for example, with Graph View or Graph Setup. You can then assign one or more data series to the second y-axis using the Settings Series Option command.

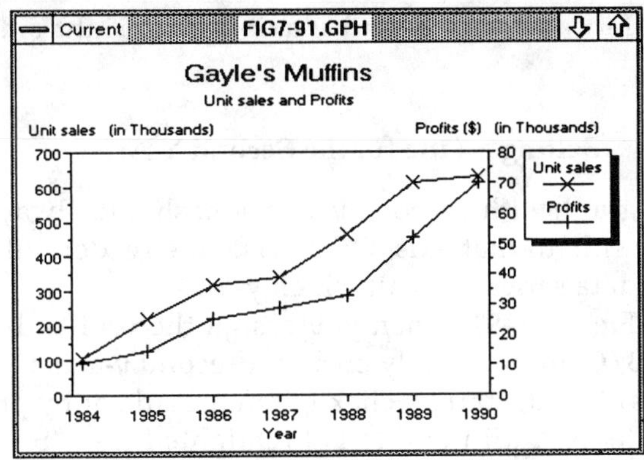

FIGURE 7–92 A second *y*-axis

For example, suppose you have created a standard line graph of the data in Figure 7-91. To assign the profits data range to a second *y*-axis, perform the following steps:

1. Select the data series you want to assign to the second *y*-axis, in this case the profit series (Series:B).
2. Choose the Settings Series Options Command. 1-2-3/G displays the dialog box in Figure 7-93. (You can also access this dialog box by double-clicking on the data series.)
3. Select 2Y-axis from the Value axis buttons.
4. Select OK.

The graph then appears as in Figure 7-92. By default, the sales data series remains assigned to the first *y*-axis. Notice that 1-2-3/G always assigns the

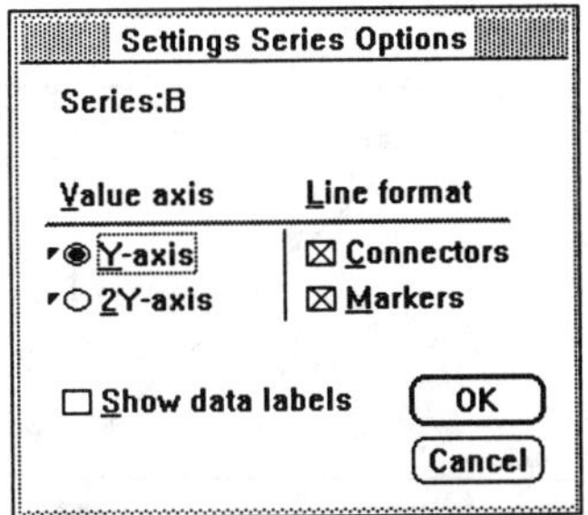

FIGURE 7–93 The Settings Series Options dialog box

first y-axis to the left and the second y-axis to the right side of a vertical graph.

Setting a Title for the Second Y-Axis

When you create a graph with a second y-axis, you should always take the extra step of assigning a title to that axis. Otherwise, the reader will not be able to distinguish which data series go with which y-axis.

For example, in Figure 7–92, when you assign the profits data series to the second y-axis, 1-2-3/G automatically creates a second y-axis title of "2Y Axis." To change this default text, start by clicking on the title or by pressing TAB (or SHIFT-TAB) repeatedly until the title is highlighted (see "Selecting Objects" above). Next, perform one of the following:

- Type the new title in the Contents box on the right side of the Control line (see "Entering and Editing Text" earlier in this chapter).
- Use the Edit Link Create command to create a link between a cell in a worksheet file and the second y-axis title in the Graph file. When you use this command, make sure to choose 2Y_title from the list of available objects in the Destination item box (see "Using the Graph Tool to Create a Graph—An Example" for more information).

Adding Data Labels

Occasionally, you may create a graph in 1-2-3/G and find that it is difficult to discern the actual amount of the values being graphed. One way around this problem is to add data labels. Data labels are actual numbers that appear next to data points within a graph, as shown in Figure 7–94.

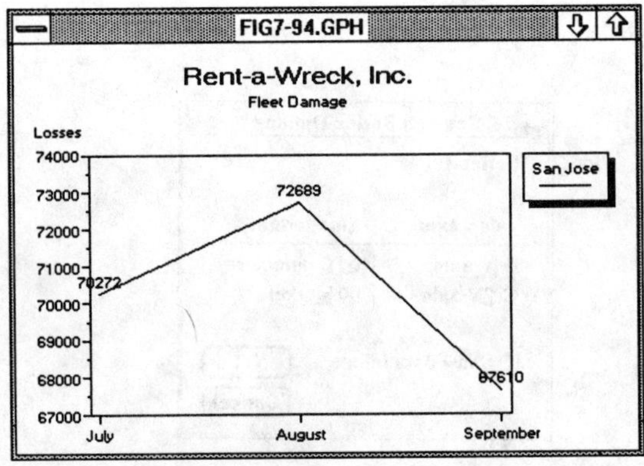

FIGURE 7–94 A line graph with data labels

Note

> You cannot show data labels in XY, HLCO, pie, or 3–D bar graphs.

To add data labels to the graph in Figure 7–94, you would perform the following steps:

1. Select the data series for which you want to display data labels, in this case the only data series in the graph (Series:A).
2. Choose Settings Series Options. 1-2-3/G displays a dialog box similar to the one in Figure 7–93. (You can also double-click on a data series to display the dialog box.)

Note

> To assign data labels to all the data series at once, use the Settings Series Options command without first choosing a data series.

3. Mark the Show data labels check box.

Note

> The Show data labels check box has three states: grayed (this happens only when you are applying the command to all data ranges), marked, and unmarked (blank). When the check box is grayed, 1-2-3/G does not change the data labels setting, but leaves it as it is. When the check box is marked, 1-2-3/G displays data labels, and when it is unmarked, 1-2-3/G does not display data labels.

4. Select OK.

Changing the Location of Data Labels

When you first add data labels to a graph, the initial position of the data labels depends on the type of graph you have created. For example, in a line graph, the data labels always appear above each data point. In a bar or stacked bar graph, data labels appear above each bar if the values are positive. But if the values are negative, the data labels appear below the bars.

Suppose, however, that you want to change the position of the data labels within the graph. For example, imagine that you want to reposition the data labels in Figure 7–94 so that they appear to the right of the data points. You can use the Settings Data Labels command to change the position of the data labels, as follows:

1. Select the data labels whose position you want to change.

Note

> To change the position of all the data labels in the graph at once, use the Settings Data Labels command without first selecting a set of data labels.

2. Choose Settings Data Labels. 1-2-3/G displays the dialog box in Figure 7–95. (You can also activate the dialog box by double-clicking on a set of data labels.)

Note

> You cannot access the Settings Data Labels command unless you have already added data labels to the graph.

3. Turn on the button corresponding to the position you want for the data labels—in this case, the Right button.
4. Select OK.

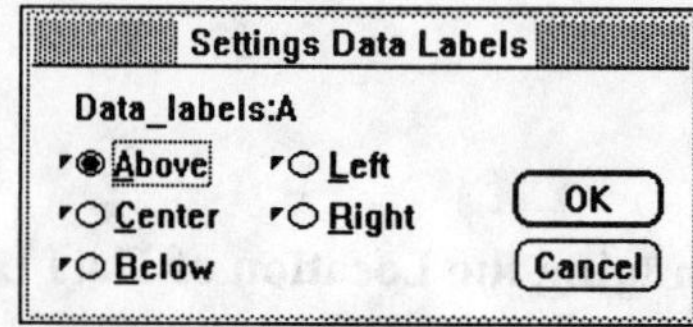

FIGURE 7–95 **The Settings Data Labels dialog box**

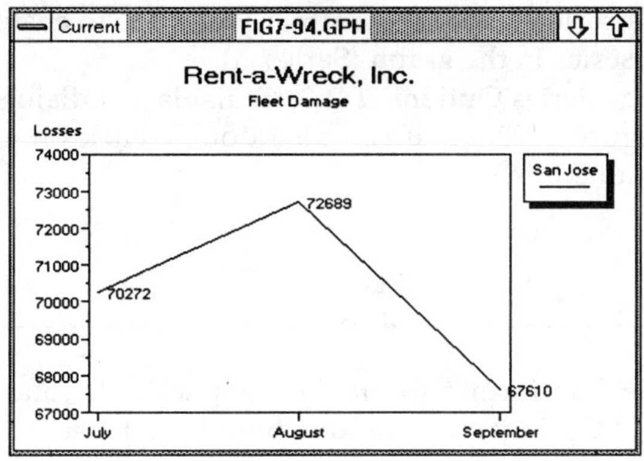

FIGURE 7–96 After positioning the data labels to the right of the data points

Figure 7–96 shows the results.

Note

> For bar or stacked bar graphs, 1-2-3/G restricts the placement of the data labels to above or below the bars. Therefore, selecting the Left or Right button has the same effect as selecting the Below or Above button, respectively.

Changing the Line Format for Line Series

As you know, when you create a line graph using Graph View or Graph Setup, 1-2-3/G plots a point for each value in a data range and connects the points with lines. By using the Settings Series Options command, you can change the line format to show special markers at each data point, markers only without any connecting lines, or neither connecting lines nor markers.

For example, suppose you have the graph in Figure 7–97, and you want to change the line format so that markers appear at each data point without any connecting lines. Perform the following steps:

1. Select the data series whose line format you want to change, in this case the only data series in the graph (Series:A).
2. Choose Settings Series Options. 1-2-3/G displays a dialog box similar to the one in Figure 7–93. (You can also double-click on a data series to display the dialog box.)

Note

> To change the line format to all the data series at once, use the Settings Series Options command without first choosing a data series.

3. Mark the Markers check box.

Note

> The Markers check box has three states: grayed (this happens only when you are applying the command to all data ranges), marked, and unmarked (blank). When the check box is grayed, 1-2-3/G does not change the markers setting, but leaves it as it is. When the check box is marked, 1-2-3/G displays markers, and when it is unmarked, 1-2-3/G displays no markers.

4. Unmark the Connectors check box.

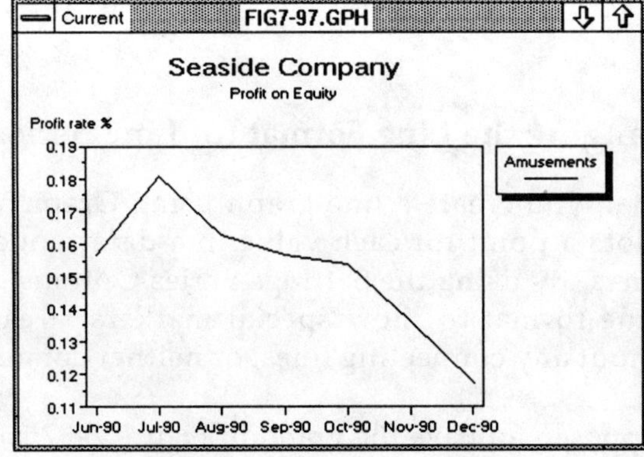

FIGURE 9–97 A typical line graph with connecting lines but no markers

Note

The Connectors check box also has three states: grayed, marked, and unmarked (blank). When the check box is grayed, 1-2-3/G does not change the markers setting, but leaves it as it is. When the check box is marked, 1-2-3/G displays markers, and when it is unmarked, 1-2-3/G displays no markers.

5. Select OK.

Figure 7–98 shows the results of the new line format settings.

Note

If you unmark both the Connectors and Markers boxes, and turn on the Show data labels box, 1-2-3/G shows data labels only, as in Figure 7–99. However, if you use this line format, you must make sure that your graph has only a single data series. If your graph has multiple data series, you will not be able to tell which data points go with which data series.

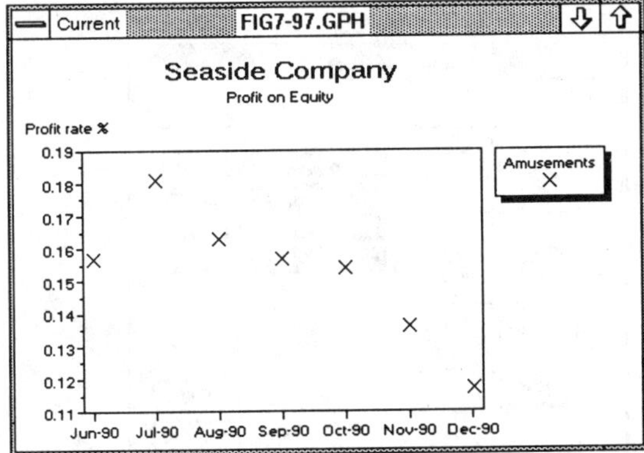

FIGURE 7–98 A line graph with markers but no connectors

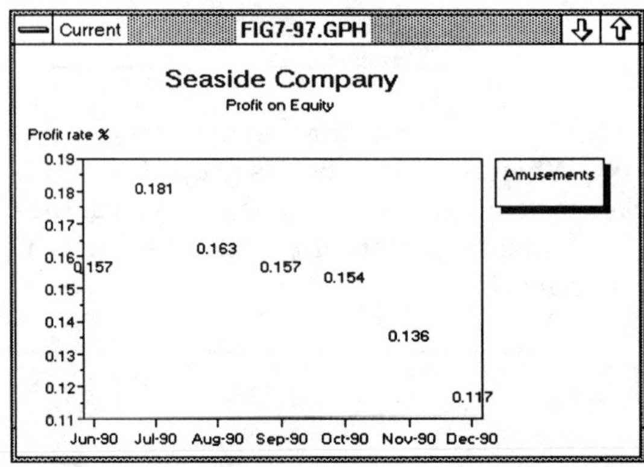

FIGURE 7–99 **A line graph that shows data labels only**

Changing the Marker Style

If you have added markers to a line graph or XY graph, you can change the color and style of those selected markers with the Settings Marker Style command. For example, suppose you have the graph in Figure 7–98, and you want to change the standard markers for the A data series from Xs to diamonds. Perform the following steps:

1. Select the data series whose markers you want to change, in this case the only data series in the graph (Series:A).
2. Choose Settings Marker Style. 1-2-3/G displays the dialog box in Figure 7–100.
3. Choose a Marker option, in this case g (for diamonds). 1-2-3/G instantly shows the result of your choice in the Preview box.

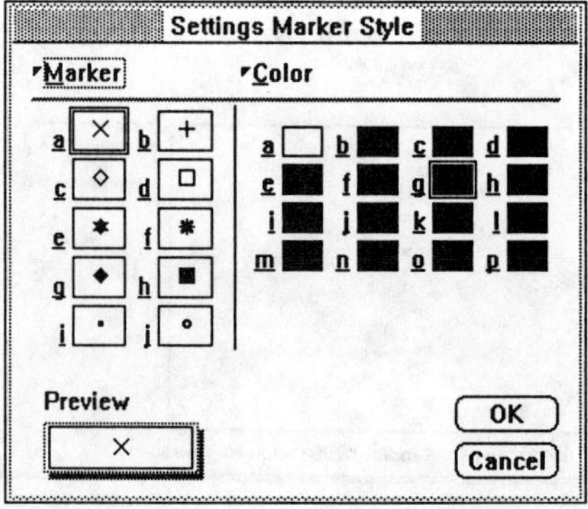

FIGURE 7–100 **The Settings Marker Style dialog box**

4. If you want to change the color of the markers, choose a Color option.
5. Select OK.

Figure 7–101 shows the results of changing the marker style.

Note

> Before you can change the marker style, you must make sure to add markers to the data series. If the series doesn't contain markers (or if no series are selected), the Marker Style option will appear grayed in the Settings menu.

Changing Number Formats

When 1-2-3/G displays numbers in a graph (such as axis labels, data labels, and pie labels), it shows them in General format. If you want to change the format of the numbers (for example, from General to Currency, 2 decimal places), you can use the Settings Number Format command. Of course, changing a number's format in a graph does not change the way 1-2-3/G stores the number in the worksheet.

When you select the Number Format command, 1-2-3/G displays the following options in a cascade menu:

- **X Labels:** Lets you format all the numbers along the *x*-axis.
- **Y Labels:** Lets you format all the numbers along the *y*-axis.
- **2Y Labels:** Lets you format all the numbers along the second *y*-axis, if one is present.

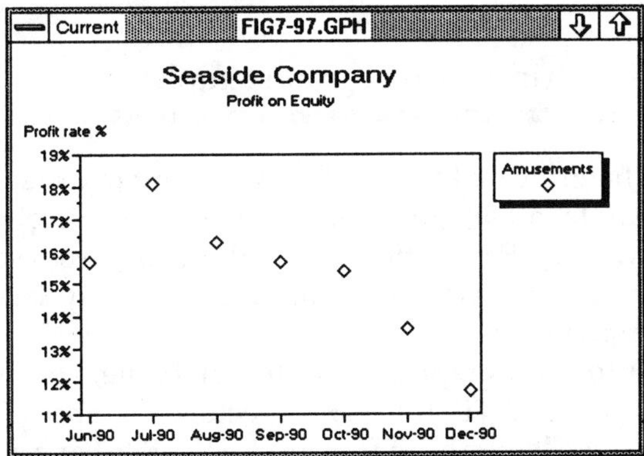

FIGURE 7–101 **After changing the marker style to diamonds**

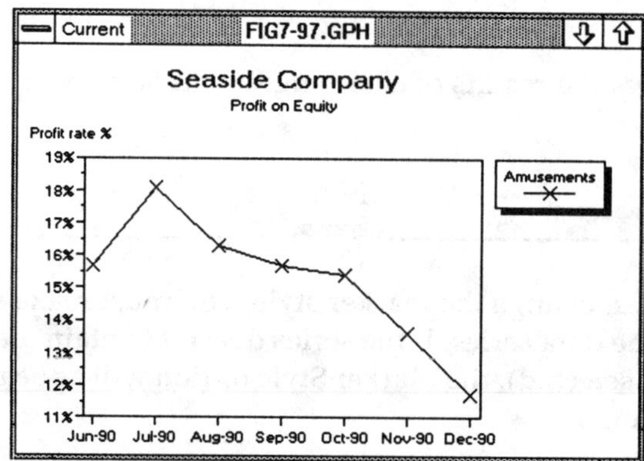

FIGURE 7–102 After changing the *y*-axis labels to Percent format

- **Data Labels:** Lets you format the data labels for a selected data series, or all the data labels in the graph, if data labels are in use.
- **Pie Labels:** Lets you format the numbers in a pie graph.
- **All:** Lets you format all the numbers in the graph window, including numbers along the axes, the data labels, and pie labels.

Once you select an option from the menu, 1-2-3/G displays a dialog box that is nearly identical to the Worksheet window's Range Format dialog box. See Chapter 3, "Formatting the Worksheet," for a complete discussion of how to use the dialog box.

For example, suppose you have a variation of the graph in Figure 7–98, and you want to change the format of the y-axis labels from General format to Percent, zero decimal places. Figure 7–102 shows the results of the Settings Marker Style Y Labels command.

Tip: Creating graph templates

Suppose you have created a graph that you want to use several times over, for example, a bar graph showing accounts receivable aging that you use weekly. Rather than create the graph from scratch each time, you can store the Graph file and then call it up later, in effect creating a template file.

If you want to use a graph file as a template file, you should save it in the C:\WORK\TEMPLATE directory, a special directory designed specifically for this purpose. Use the File Save command in the usual way, but specify C:\WORK\TEMPLATE as the target directory for the file.

Any graph file you create can serve as a template file. For example, suppose you have a Graph file named AR90.GPH that you have saved in the C:\WORK\TEMPLATE directory. To use this file as a template file, perform the following steps:

1. Select File New.
2. Select Graph from the Tool names list box.
3. Enter the path and name of the template file in the Template name text box, for example, enter:
   C:\WORK\TEMPLATE\AR90.GPH
4. Select OK.

When you load the file into memory, it is still linked to the original source worksheet file. To change all the links at once to a new source worksheet file, use the Edit Link Move command (see "Moving Links" above for a complete description). See Chapter 5, "File Management," for more on how to use template files.

Controlling the X-Axis Skip Factor

If you have several X labels in your graph, or the X labels are rather long, 1-2-3/G does its best to prevent them from crowding one another. It usually solves the crowding problem in one of the following ways:

- By using a skip factor (for example, a skip factor of 2 means that every other X label appears).
- By angling the X labels.
- By staggering the X labels between two rows.
- By displaying X labels vertically beneath the *x*-axis instead of horizontally.

In some cases, 1-2-3/G uses a combination of these methods to prevent the X labels from crowding one another. Nevertheless, you may not like the results.

For example, the HLCO graph in Figure 7–103 displays dates for the X labels. To prevent crowding, 1-2-3/G displays every other label (a skip factor of 2) and angles the labels on their sides. Although the results are acceptable, you may feel that you can improve the readability of the graph by increasing the X label skip factor to 5, a number that is better suited to stock market data where a week's worth of pricing data has five entries.

To change the X label skip factor, you use the Settings Scale X command. Figure 7–104 shows the dialog box that appears. To set the skip factor to 5, select the Manual button and enter **5** in the text box. When you select OK to complete the command, 1-2-3/G displays the graph in Figure 7–105.

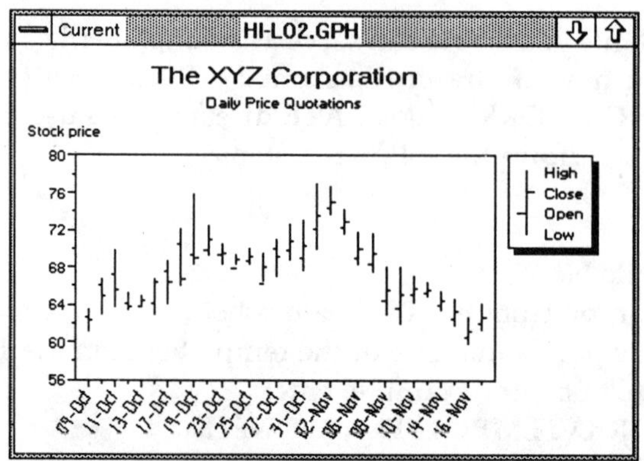

FIGURE 7–103 1-2-3/G prevents X label crowding by using a skip factor and angling the labels

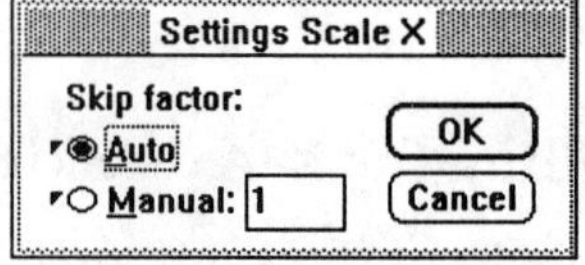

FIGURE 7–104 The Settings Scale X dialog box

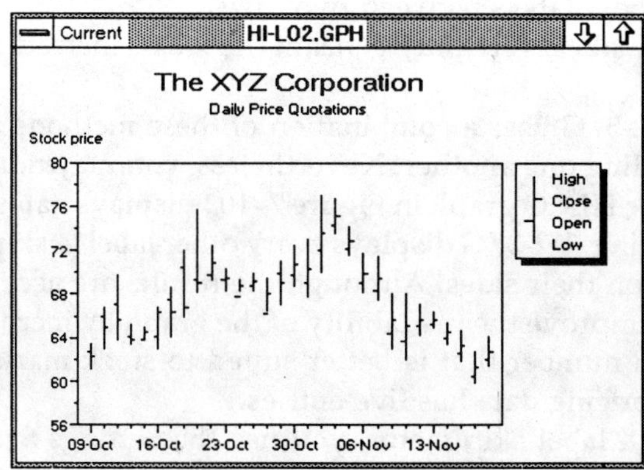

FIGURE 7–105 After manually setting the X label skip factor

Note

> If you want to control whether 1-2-3/G staggers, angles, or displays your X labels vertically, use the Settings Position Axis Labels command (see "Repositioning Axes and Their Elements," below).

Changing the Appearance of Numeric Axes

Although 1-2-3/G's automatic scaling capabilities are usually sufficient, sometimes the way it scales numeric axes can distort the relationships between graph values. If the upper and lower limits of the *x*-axis (in the case of XY graphs), *y*-axis, or 2*y*-axis scales are not set appropriately, the graph may not tell the real story.

To change the scaling of a graph axis, you use the Settings Scale command. You can also use this command to control the appearance of tick marks, remove the scale indicator, or change the type of scale (for example, from standard linear scaling to percent or logarithmic scaling).

Changing the X, Y, and 2Y Scales

Before you attempt to manually scale your graph, you must first understand how 1-2-3/G performs its automatic scaling. In the case of a line graph, for example, the lower and upper limits of the Y axis are determined by the lowest and highest values in the graph data ranges. 1-2-3/G sets the lower limit a point or two below the lowest data value, and the upper limit several points higher than the highest data value. This affects the placement of the lines or data points, and may distort the proportions of the graph. If this is the case, you will want to adjust your y-axis scale manually with the Settings Scale command.

When you select Settings Scale, 1-2-3/G presents a cascade menu with the following options:

- **X:** Lets you control the scaling of the X axis for XY graphs. If the graph is not an XY graph, 1-2-3/G only lets you change the skip factor for X labels (see "Controlling the X-Axis Skip Factor" above).
- **Y:** Lets you control the scaling of the *y*-axis.
- **2Y:** Lets you control the scaling of the second (2Y) *y*-axis; if your graph does not have a second *y*-axis, this option is grayed.

For example, suppose you have the graph in Figure 7–106, which presents a line graph of first quarter sales for The Sail Shop. At first glance, it appears that

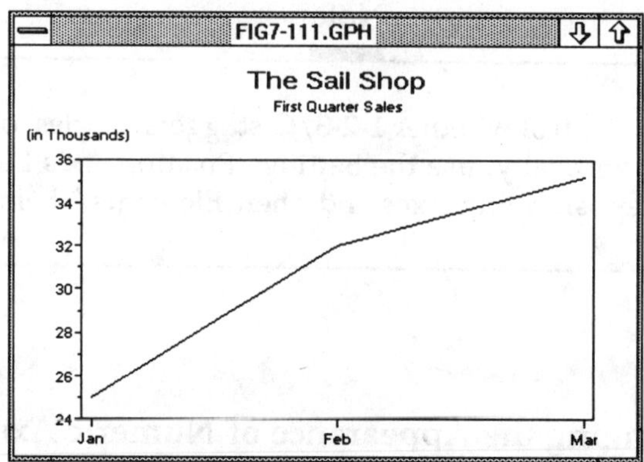

FIGURE 7–106 A line graph with automatic scaling

sales are soaring. But a closer look reveals that, although sales did go up, they did not have the meteoric rise the graph portrays. Setting the *y*-axis scale manually gives a much truer picture of what really happened.

To change the *y*-axis scaling, begin by selecting the Settings Scale Y command. 1-2-3/G presents the dialog box in Figure 7–107. (In the case of an XY graph, 1-2-3/G displays identical dialog boxes for the Settings Scale X and Y commands.) To present a more realistic, albeit less exciting, picture of first quarter sales, suppose you want to set an upper limit for the scale of $40,000 and a lower limit of $20,000.

To set the upper limit, choose the Manual button for the Upper limit option and enter **40000** in the text box. Repeat the process for the Lower limit option but enter **20000** in the text box. Select OK to complete the command. Figure

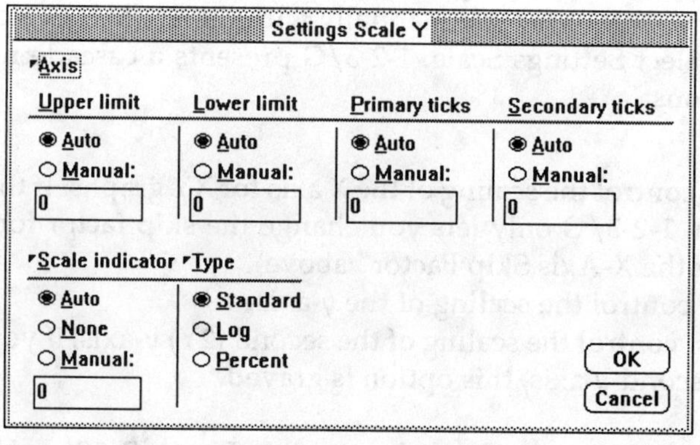

FIGURE 7–107 The Settings Scale Y dialog box

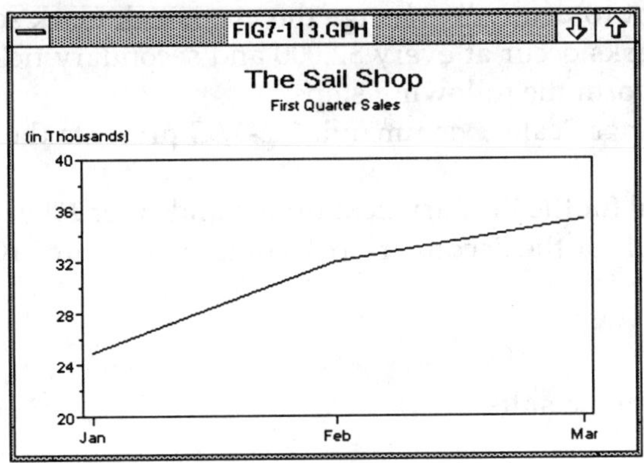

FIGURE 7–108 After scaling the y-axis manually

7–108 shows the results. Notice that the line has flattened out quite a bit, but it still shows that sales are going up significantly.

After manually adjusting the scale on your graph, you may decide that it looked better with the 1-2-3/G default scaling. To return to automatic scaling, use the Settings Scale command again. Next, select the menu option corresponding to the scale you want to change—X, Y, or 2Y—then select the Auto buttons for both the Upper and Lower limit options.

Note

If the value you enter for the upper limit is lower than some of the values in your data ranges, 1-2-3/G does not include those values in the graph display. The same is true for the lower limit. For example, say that the lowest number in your data range is 50, and you select 100 as the lower limit of your *y*-axis scale. The value 50 is not included in your graph because 1-2-3/G cannot fit it into the manual scale you selected. In most cases, you will want to include all values in your graph and should take special care to set the scale limits accordingly. However, using the scale limits to exclude values can be handy when you want to focus in on a range of values, or leave out missing values.

Changing the Appearance of Tick Marks

When 1-2-3/G draws a graph, it determines the distance between primary (longer) tick marks automatically. The same is true for secondary (shorter) tick marks. For example, in Figure 7–108, the primary tick marks along the *y*-axis occur at $4,000 intervals, and the secondary tick marks occur at $2,000 intervals.

Suppose you want to manually change the *y*-axis tick mark settings so that the primary tick marks occur at every $2,000 and secondary tick marks occur at every $1,000. Perform the following steps:

1. Select the Settings Scale Y command. 1-2-3/G presents the dialog box in Figure 7–107.
2. Choose Manual for the Primary ticks option and enter **2000** in the text box.
3. Choose Manual for the Secondary ticks option and enter **1000** in the text box.
4. Select OK.

Figure 7–109 shows the results.

Controlling the Scale Indicator

The scale indicator that appears at the top of the *y*-axis in Figure 7–109 is automatically set by 1-2-3/G. It indicates the order of magnitude of the data being graphed. If the highest value is over one thousand, as is the case in Figure 7–109, the indicator reads "(in Thousands)." If the highest value is over one million, the indicator states "(in Millions)."

Here are a few of the most common situations that may cause you to want to change (or remove) the scale indicator:

- You may not like the way 1-2-3/G has scaled your data. For example, 1-2-3/G may have scaled the data in millions, and you want it scaled in thousands. To get around this problem, you can manually change the scale indicator to use a different scaling factor.
- Sometimes you may enter data in a worksheet in abbreviated fashion. That is, you may enter millions as thousands (for example, 1,575,000 as 1,575) to

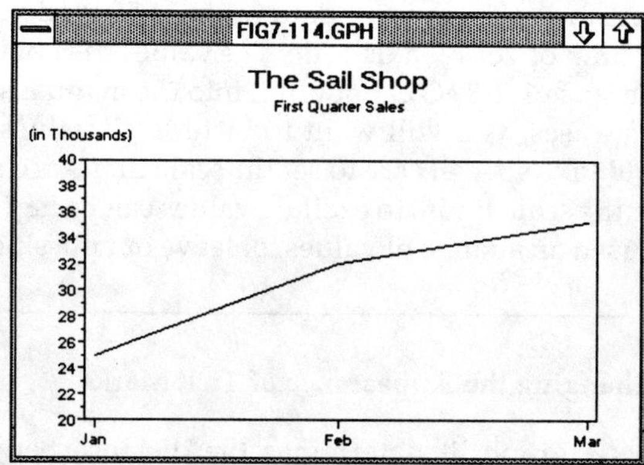

FIGURE 7–109 After changing the primary and secondary tick marks for the *y*-axis

make the entries easier to work with. Because 1-2-3/G does not know your intent, it interprets the values as thousands, and the scale indicator reads "(in Thousands)." In this case, you may want to suppress the scale indicator and enter your own scaling information in the axis title.

- You may enter a *y*-axis title that includes the same information as the scale indicator, making the indicator redundant. For example, suppose you have entered the *y*-axis title, "Sales in Thousands of Dollars," and the indicator also states "(in Thousands)." In this case, you'll want to suppress the indicator to avoid duplication.

Suppose you want to manually change the scale indicator for the *y*-axis and have 1-2-3/G use a different scaling factor. Select the Settings Scale Y command and choose the Manual button for the Scale indicator option (Figure 7–107). Next, enter the exponent for the power of 10 you want. For example, if you want the indicator to read "(in Thousands)," enter 3. Similarly, if you want it to read "(in Millions)," enter 6.

Note

> Make sure you enter an exponent that is a multiple of 3—for example, 12, 9, 6, 3, 0, -3, -6, or -9. If you use a number that is not a multiple of 3, 1-2-3/G uses a "(Times 1eX)" format for the scale indicator. For example, the number 5 produces the scale indicator "(Times 1e5)."

On the other hand, suppose you want to suppress the *y*-axis scale indicator altogether. Select the Settings Scale Y command and choose the None button for the Scale indicator option (shown in Figure 7–107). When you select OK to complete the command, you will see that the scale indicator is no longer part of the display. If you have omitted the scale indicator, you may want to enter text describing the scale in the *y*-axis title.

Changing the Scale Type

By default 1-2-3/G uses standard linear scaling to scale numeric axes. You can, however, change 1-2-3/G's method of scaling to percent or logarithmic scaling.

PERCENT SCALING In percent scaling, 1-2-3/G changes the Y or 2Y scale from actual values to a percent scale. The *y*-axis displays a minimum of 0% and a maximum of 100%. You can use percent scaling for any graph, but you will soon

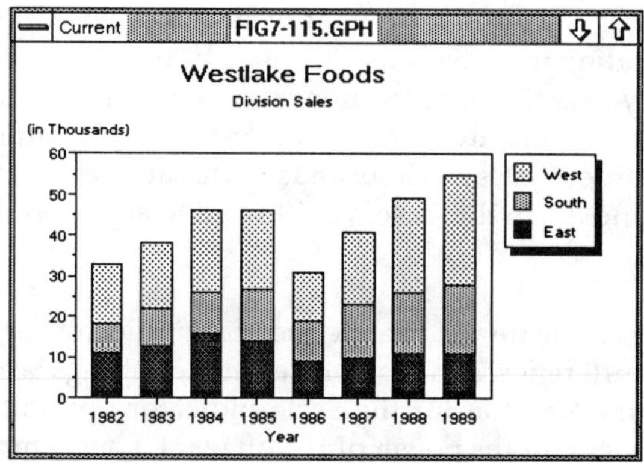

FIGURE 7–110 A standard stacked-bar graph

discover that it is only effective for stacked graphs, in particular for stacked-bar and area graphs.

For example, Figure 7–110 shows a stacked-bar graph. To convert the *y*-axis scale to a percent scale, you use the Settings Scale Y command and choose Percent for the Type option (see Figure 7–107). When you select OK to complete the command, you see the graph in Figure 7–111. Notice that the actual sales figures are lost in the graph, but you can more easily see each division's contribution to the total sales of the company in each year, as well as how that contribution is changing over time.

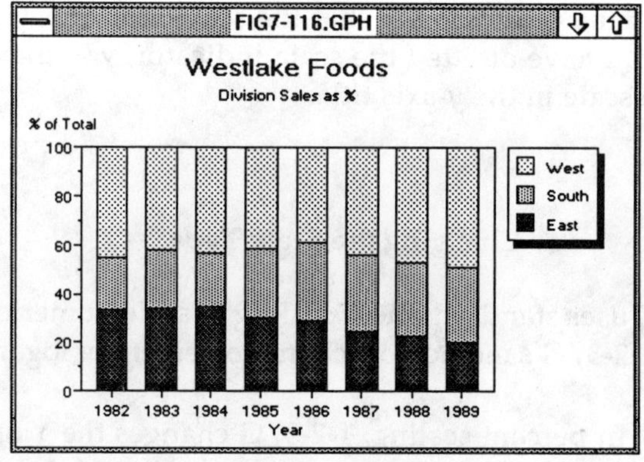

FIGURE 7–111 After changing the *y*-axis to percent scaling

Note

> You cannot change the X axis, even a numeric X axis, to percent scaling.

LOGARITHMIC SCALING Like Release 3, 1-2-3/G lets you use logarithmic scaling in your graphs. You can set logarithmic scaling for any numeric axis (*x*-axis, *y*-axis, or second *y*-axis).

The advantage of logarithmic scaling is that you can compare widely diverging values on the same graph. For example, suppose you created the bar graph in Figure 7–112 from the data in Figure 7–113. Notice that some of the data points are rather large while others are relatively small. In fact, several of the bars that 1-2-3/G creates from the smaller numbers cannot even be seen.

Figure 7–114 shows the same graph when you format the *y*-axis for logarithmic scaling using the Settings Scale Y command and choose Log for the Type option (see Figure 7–107). Notice that 1-2-3/G places evenly spaced tick marks along the *y*-axis; however, the numbers that are assigned to the marks increase exponentially.

To reset the scaling back to standard linear scaling, you use the Settings Scale Y command and choose Standard for the Type option.

Repositioning Axes and Their Elements

1-2-3/G offers several options for repositioning axes and their related objects. For example, you can change the position of entire axes, axis titles, axis labels, and tick marks.

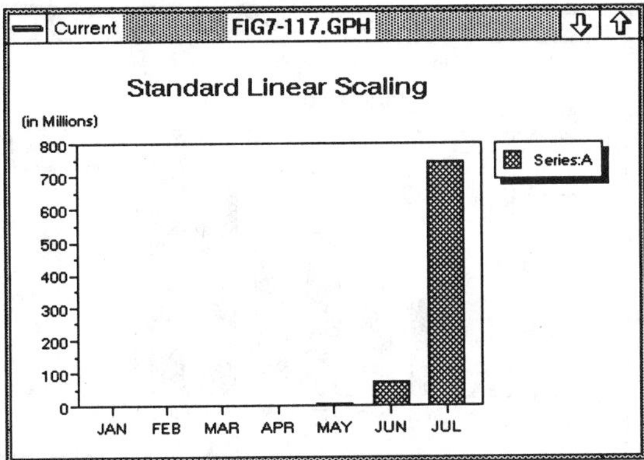

FIGURE 7–112 **Standard linear scaling**

123G.EXE — Ready

File Edit Worksheet Range Copy... Move... Print Graph Data Utility Quit... Help

A:A1 'Standard Linear Scaling

FIG7-117.WG1

A	A	B	C	D	E	F	G
1	Standard Linear Scaling						
2							
3							
4	JAN	54					
5	FEB	7,420					
6	MAR	74,200					
7	APR	742,000					
8	MAY	7,420,000					
9	JUN	74,200,000					
10	JUL	742,000,000					
11							

FIGURE 7–113 Data for the graph in FIGURE 7–112

Entire Axis

In 1-2-3/G you can easily change the position of the *y*-axis or the second *y*-axis. For example, suppose you have created a standard vertical graph, like the one in Figure 7–114, and you want to change the position of the *y*-axis from the left side of the plot frame (the default) to the right side. To change the position of the *y*-axis, you use the Settings Position Y-Axis command. 1-2-3/G displays the dialog box in Figure 7–115. Select the Right option followed by OK. Figure 7–116 shows the results.

Here are some things to keep in mind if you want to change the position of an axis:

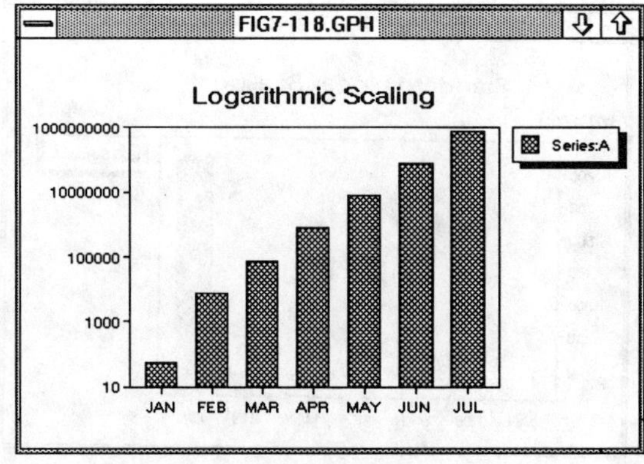

FIGURE 7–114 Logarithmic scaling

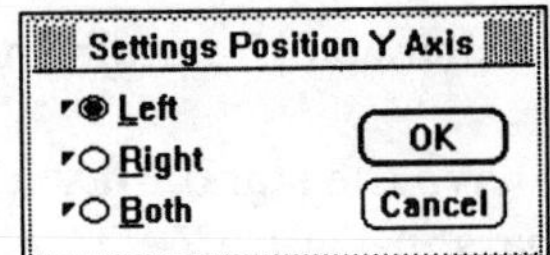

FIGURE 7–115 **The Settings Position Y Axis dialog box**

- Selecting Both from the Settings Position Y-Axis dialog box causes the *y*-axis to appear on the right and left sides of the plot frame.
- If your graph is oriented horizontally, 1-2-3/G automatically changes the Left and Right options to Upper and Lower in the Settings Position Y-Axis dialog box.
- If your graph already contains a second *y*-axis, or you have assigned all the data series to the second *y*-axis, the Y-Axis option appears grayed in the Settings Position menu.
- If your graph contains a second *y*-axis, you can change its position with the Settings Position 2Y-Axis command. (1-2-3/G displays the same dialog box as in Figure 7–115.) However, if you have plotted data against the *y*-axis, the 2Y-Axis option appears grayed.
- You cannot change the position of the *x*-axis.

Axis Titles

If the orientation of an axis is vertical, you can change the orientation of its axis title with the Settings Position Title command. In addition, you can use this

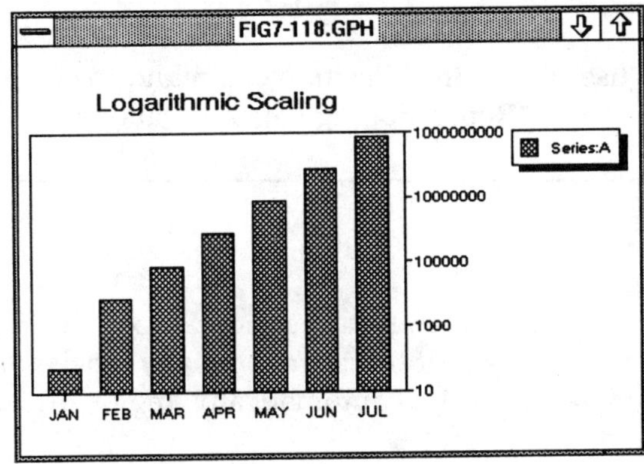

FIGURE 7–116 **After changing the position of the *y*-axis to the right side of the graph**

command to change the placement of the scale indicator (if one is present), relative to the axis title.

For example, suppose you have the standard vertical graph in Figure 7–117 (the data for this graph appears in Figure 7–23), and you want to change the *y*-axis title to a vertical orientation as well. Select the Settings Position Title Y command. 1-2-3/G displays the dialog box in Figure 7–118. Choose the Vertical button from the Orientation options. When you select OK, you get the effect shown in Figure 7–119.

Note

> Although you can change the orientation of the axis title for any axis (the *x*-axis, *y*-axis, or second *y*-axis), the axis must be oriented vertically. If it is oriented horizontally, its option appears grayed in the Settings Position Title cascade menu.

You can also use the Settings Position Title command to change the orientation of the scale indicator in relation to the axis title. For example, if you select the Below button from the Scale Indicator options (Figure 7–118), 1-2-3/G displays the scale indicator below the axis title. On the other hand, choosing the Appended button causes 1-2-3/G to display the scale indicator in the usual fashion, that is, appended to the end of the axis title.

Note

> You can also use the Settings Position command to change the position of legends. See "Repositioning Legends" above.

Axis Labels

When 1-2-3/G places labels along the horizontal axis, it displays them in a side-by-side fashion. However, if there are too many labels for them to appear horizontally side-by-side, 1-2-3/G automatically angles the labels to fit along the axis.

Besides angling labels, 1-2-3/G can also display them in a staggered or a vertical position. To change the way 1-2-3/G positions the labels along the horizontal axis, use the Settings Position Axis Labels command.

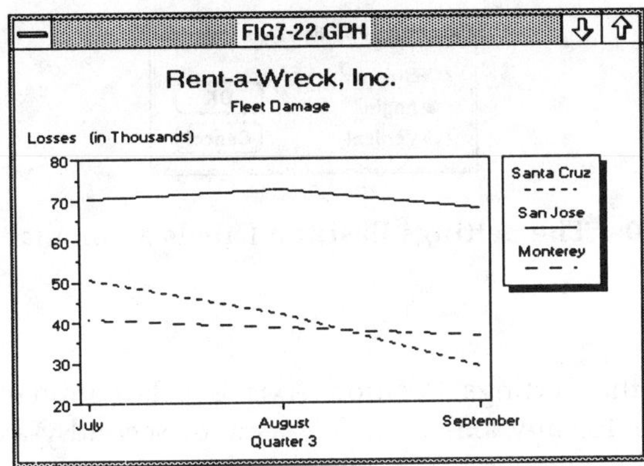

FIGURE 7–117 Standard placement of a vertical axis title

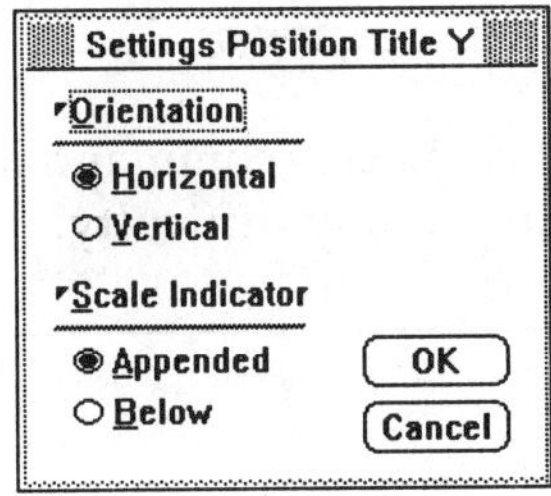

FIGURE 7–118 The Settings Position Title Y dialog box

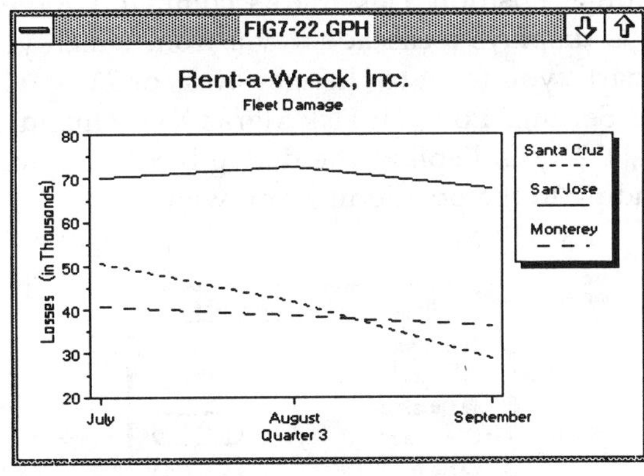

FIGURE 7–119 After changing the vertical axis title to a vertical orientation

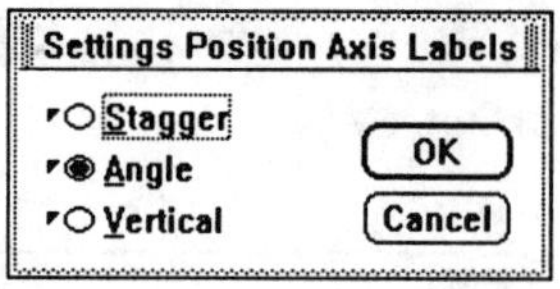

Settings Position Axis Labels
Stagger
Angle
Vertical
OK
Cancel

FIGURE 7–120 **The Settings Position Labels X command**

You can use the Settings Position Axis Labels command to change the position of labels for any axis (x-axis, y-axis, or second y-axis), provided the axis is horizontal. However, when an axis is vertical, the option for that axis (X, Y, or 2Y) appears grayed in the Settings Position Axis Labels cascade menu. All the Settings Position Axis Labels options display the dialog box in Figure 7–120.

Note

> The Settings Position Axis Labels command has no effect if the labels will fit side-by-side without any difficulty.

Tick Marks

In its default state, 1-2-3/G displays tick marks along the outside edge of the plot frame. However, you can specify more precisely where tick marks appear by using the Settings Position Tick Marks command. When you select this command, 1-2-3/G displays a cascade menu from which you can choose the axis whose tick marks you want to change—X, Y, or 2Y.

If you select the Settings Position Tick Marks X command and your graph is not an XY graph, 1-2-3/G displays the dialog box in Figure 7–121. Choose a button corresponding to the positioning you want.

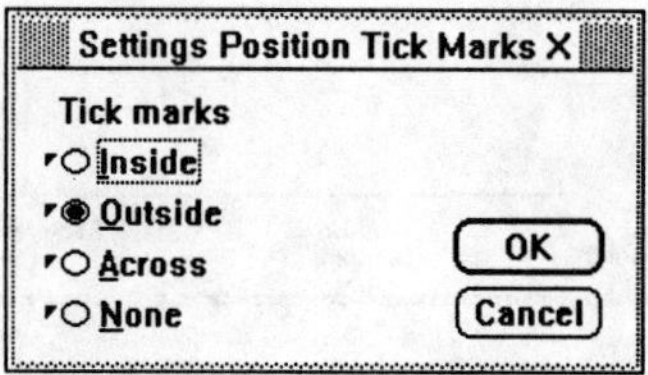

FIGURE 7–121 **The Settings Position Tick Marks X dialog box when the current graph is not an XY graph**

Button	Effect
Inside	Tick marks appear inside the plot frame.
Outside	Tick marks appear outside the plot frame.
Across	Tick marks cross the axis.
None	No tick marks appear.

On the other hand, suppose your graph is an XY graph, 1-2-3/G displays the dialog box in Figure 7–122 when you select the Settings Position Tick Marks X command. In fact, this is the same dialog box that appears when you choose the Settings Position Tick Marks Y or 2Y command (if these options are available). Notice that this dialog box lets you change the position of both the primary and secondary (shorter) tick marks.

Enhancing Pie Graphs

1-2-3/G lets you enhance pie graphs in several ways. For example, you can change the colors and patterns of pie slices. You can also control whether pie slices are exploded (slightly separated from the rest of the pie). You can also specify whether the pie labels in a pie graph display percentage signs.

Changing Colors and Patterns

The easiest way to change the color and pattern of a pie slice in a pie graph is to do so manually. You select the pie slice you want to change, then use the Settings Area Style command (see "Colors and Patterns" for a complete discussion).

However, to maintain compatibility with previous releases of 1-2-3, you can also assign colors or hatch patterns to a pie graph by entering special values in the B data range (the second row or column of data for a pie graph). The B data range you create must be the same size as the A data range. You

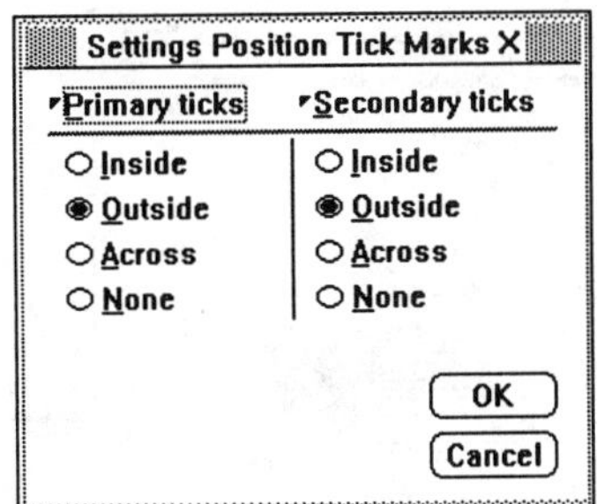

FIGURE 7–122 The Settings Position Tick Marks dialog box for all other graph types

then enter values from 1 to 16 in each cell of the range. 1-2-3/G uses the values in the B data range to control the colors of pie slices (if you are using a color monitor) or set the patterns for pie slices (if you are using a black-and-white monitor).

Note

The values 1 to 16 that you can enter in the B data range correspond exactly to the Color options (a through p) that are available in the Settings Area Style command's dialog box. For example, a value of 1 in the B data range produces a white pie slice (the same color as the a option in the Settings Area Style dialog box).

For example, suppose you have the pie graph in Figure 7–123, and you want to change the colors of the pie slices. Figure 7–124 shows some sample worksheet data you could use (the B data range is C5..C8). If you are using a color monitor, the colors produced by the sample B-range values are

Value	Color produced
5	red
6	green
7	blue
8	aqua

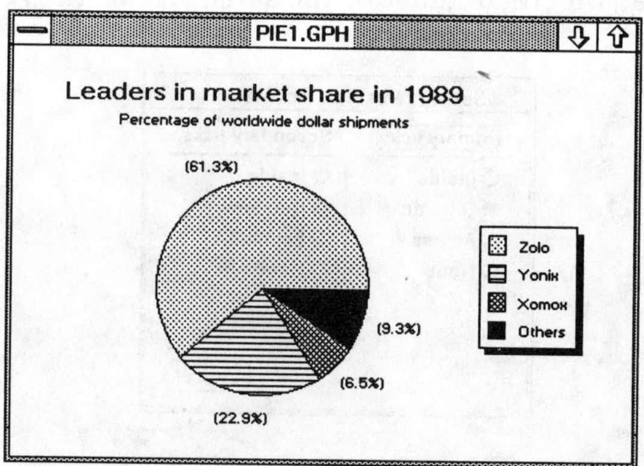

FIGURE 7–123 A typical pie graph

To make sure that 1-2-3/G uses your B-range values, use the Settings Pie Choices command and select the B-range button from the Colors options (Figure 7–125) followed by OK. 1-2-3/G instantly uses the special values from your B data range to control the colors and/or patterns for your pie graph. (This step may not be necessary if you created the graph automatically using Graph View or Graph Setup; 1-2-3/G will have already made this setting.)

Note

> Suppose you are using a color monitor, and you have set colors and patterns manually using the Settings Area Style command. You then use a B data range to set colors for the pie slices. 1-2-3/G keeps the patterns you set manually using the Settings Area Style command but uses the colors from the B data range.

Exploding Pie Slices

If you want to emphasize a pie slice in your pie graph, you can explode it (pull it out from the pie). The easiest way to explode a pie slice is to simply move the pie slice manually using the keyboard or the mouse (see "Moving a Graph Object" above for more details). For example, Figure 7–126 shows an exploded pie slice.

As in previous releases of 1-2-3, you can also explode a pie slice by adding 100 to the B-range value that corresponds to the pie slice you want to explode. For example, suppose you want to produce the same exploding pie slice that

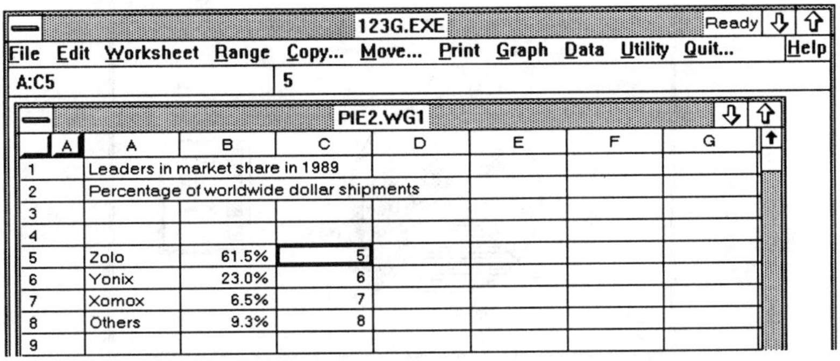

123G.EXE — Ready

File Edit Worksheet Range Copy... Move... Print Graph Data Utility Quit... Help

A:C5 5

PIE2.WG1

A	A	B	C	D	E	F	G
1	Leaders in market share in 1989						
2	Percentage of worldwide dollar shipments						
3							
4							
5	Zolo	61.5%	5				
6	Yonix	23.0%	6				
7	Xomox	6.5%	7				
8	Others	9.3%	8				
9							

FIGURE 7–124 A worksheet containing B data range values

Settings Pie Choices

Color: B-range / Manual
Explosion: B-range / Manual
Percent labels: C-range / None / All
Show values
OK
Cancel

FIGURE 7–125 The Settings Pie Choices dialog box

appears in Figure 7–126 but use a B-data range to do it. You would use the same B-range values shown in Figure 7–124, but enter 107 in place of 7 in cell C7.

Again, to make sure that 1-2-3/G recognizes your B-range values, use the Settings Pie Choices command and select the B-range button from the Explosion options (Figure 7–125).

Showing Percent Labels

Yet another way you can control the appearance of pie graphs is to display (or remove) percent labels. For example, Figure 7–126 shows percent labels next to each pie slice. To determine whether 1-2-3/G displays percent labels, you use the Settings Pie Choices command (Figure 7–125) and select a Percent labels option as follows:

- **C-range:** If you select this option, 1-2-3/G uses the values in the C data range (the third row or column of data for a pie graph) to control the display of individual percent labels. The C range must have the same number of entries

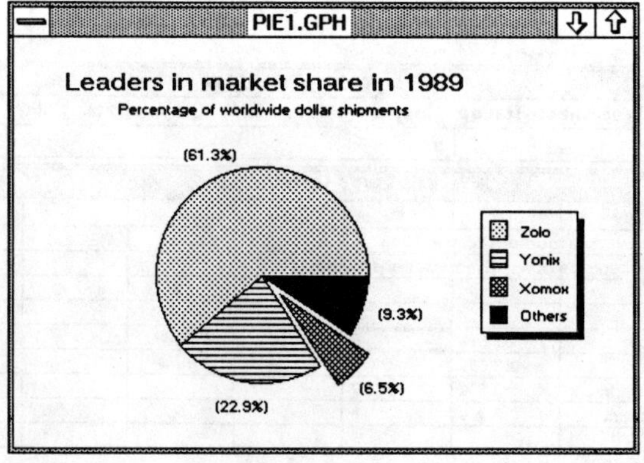

FIGURE 7–126 An exploding pie slice

as the A range. Enter 0 in the C-range cells corresponding to the slices for which you do not want to display percent labels, and enter 1 in those cells for which you do want to display percent labels.

- **None:** Select this option if you do not want any percent labels.
- **All:** Select this option to display percent labels for all slices.

Showing Values Next to Pie Slices

If you like, you can have 1-2-3/G display data values next to the pie slices in a pie graph. Select the Settings Pie Choices command (Figure 7–125), and choose the Show values option. Figure 7–127 shows the effect.

RESETTING GRAPH SETTINGS

Suppose you have completed work on a graph and saved your settings. You now want to begin creating a new graph. To prepare for the new graph, you should begin by clearing all of the current settings with the Worksheet window's Graph Reset command.

However, if you want to retain some of the existing settings for your new graph, you can use any of the following Graph commands to clear specific settings:

- **Graph Add Ranges Reset:** Resets all the current data range and X range settings.
- **Graph Options Titles Reset:** Clears all the current graph title settings.
- **Graph Options Legends Reset:** Clears all the current legend label settings.

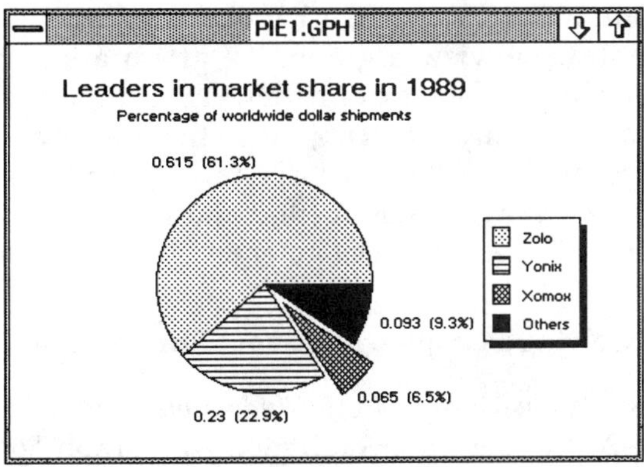

FIGURE 7–127 Showing values next to pie slices

All those settings that you do not clear with one of these commands remain in effect and are used with the new graph.

PRINTING GRAPHS

In Release 2, before you can print a graph, you must save the graph to a .PIC file with the Graph Save command. Next, you must exit 1-2-3, start the PrintGraph program, and load the .PIC file into PrintGraph—a long and tedious process. Printing your graphs is much easier in 1-2-3/G because you print them directly from the Graph Tool using the File Print Print Graph command.

This section describes how to use the File Print Print Graph command to print your graphs. It also discusses how to preview your graphs before you print them.

Previewing a Graph

Before you print a graph, it is helpful to preview it. That way, you can avoid wasting paper and time if the settings are not exactly the way you want them.

There are two ways to preview a graph in 1-2-3/G. You can use Layout Printer View or File Print Print Graph. Using Layout Printer View is appropriate if you want to see how your graph will appear on the printed page, but you may still want to move or resize graph objects. The disadvantage of Layout Printer View is that it shows only the graph; you cannot see other data that may appear on the final printed page, such as worksheet data, headers, footers, and the like.

On the other hand, File Print Print Graph is a better option when you want to see how your graph will appear with other data on the page. When you use File Print Print Graph to preview a graph, the graph appears in a separate preview window. The disadvantage of previewing a graph in this way is that you cannot change or move any graph objects in the preview window.

Previewing a graph with File Print Print Graph is a necessary prelude to printing a graph and worksheet data together and is discussed in "Printing a Graph and a Worksheet Together," in Chapter 8.

Previewing a Graph with Layout Printer View

Figure 7–128 shows a typical graph in a *Window view mode* (the data for this graph is in Figure 7–25). This is the default mode for Graph Tool and is useful for creating and enhancing graphs. The problem with Window view mode is that it does not always give a reliable indication of how your graph will appear when printed.

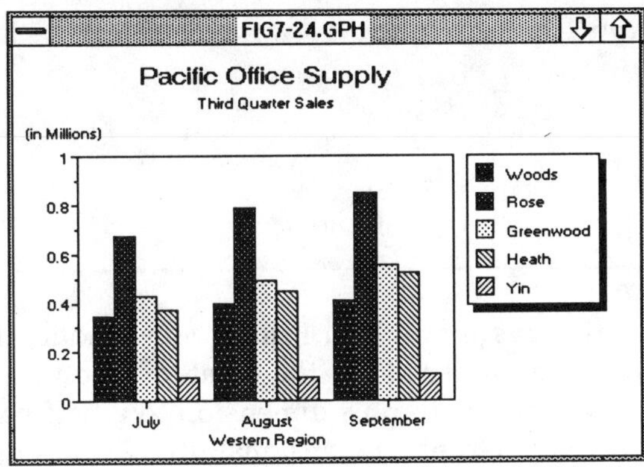

FIGURE 7–128 Window view mode

To see how your graph will appear on the printed page, use the Layout Printer View command. When you select this command, 1-2-3/G switches to *Printer view mode,* and changes the fonts from Screen fonts to Printer fonts (see Chapter 3, "Formatting the Worksheet," for a description of Screen and Printer fonts). Figure 7–129 shows an example of Printer view mode. Notice that 1-2-3/G displays a Preview indicator in the title bar when the window is in Printer view mode.

When you switch to Printer view mode, you can still use all the same commands and options that are available in Window view mode. For example, you can move and resize graph objects, change titles, add legends, and the like. However, because graph text appears very small in Printer view mode, you may not be able to see the effect of your text-related changes.

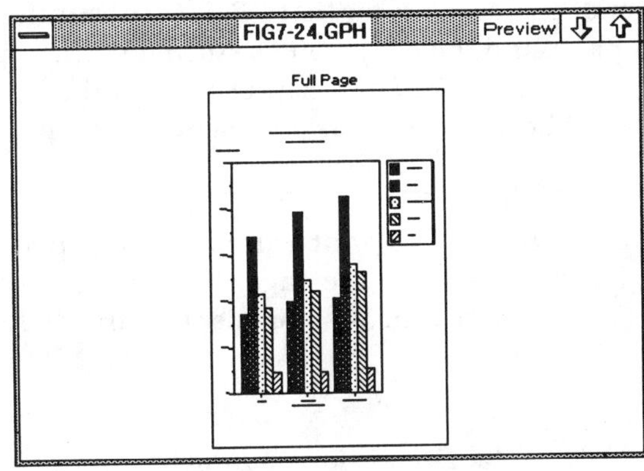

FIGURE 7–129 Printer view mode

To return the Graph Tool to Window view mode, select the Layout Window View command.

Note

> When 1-2-3/G displays a graph in Printer view mode, it uses the dimensions you've established for the printed graph size. For example, if you have set the graph's dimension to a half-page in size (using File Print Print Graph Dimensions), the graph appears in a half-page in Printer view mode.

Sizing and Positioning a Graph on the Printed Page

In preparation for printing a graph, you may want to change its size and position on the printed page. In its default state, 1-2-3/G prints your graph using a full page and centers the graph within the page margins. Using the File Print Print Graph command, you can change these settings to print a graph of any size you want and position it anywhere on the page.

Note

> To change other print options (such as the margins, headers and footers, number of copies, patterns that 1-2-3/G substitutes for colors on the printed page, and the like), you use the File Print Options and File Print Colors commands. See Chapter 8, "Printing," for a complete discussion of how to use these commands to set print options.

For example, suppose you want to print a graph on the top half of a new page and center the graph horizontally on the page. To make these settings, choose the File Print Print Graph command. 1-2-3/G displays the dialog box in Figure 7–130.

The Dimensions Buttons

Here is a description of the Dimensions buttons you can choose from:

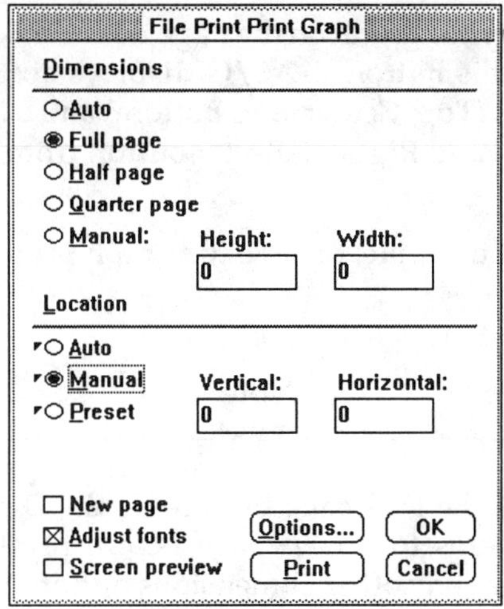

FIGURE 7–130 The File Print Print Graph dialog box

- **Auto:** Fits the graph within the blank portion of the page. Using this option lets the Graph Tool use the entire page (if it is available), or fit the graph below (or to the right) of other data on the page.
- **Full page:** Fits the graph within a new page.
- **Half page**: Fits the graph within a half page.
- **Quarter page:** Fits the graph within a quarter page.
- **Manual:** Lets you enter the exact dimensions for the printed graph in the Height and Width text boxes. (Use inches or millimeters, depending on the Measurement option for the User Settings International command.)

In the current example, to change the graph dimensions from a full page (the default) to half a page, select the Half page button.

The Location Buttons

To change the location of the graph, use one of the following Location buttons:

- **Auto:** Automatically positions the graph as close to the top of the page and as near the left margin as possible.
- **Manual**: Lets you control the exact position of the graph. When you click on this button, 1-2-3/G displays Vertical and Horizontal text boxes, as shown in Figure 7–130. Enter the distance from the top margin to the top of the graph in the Vertical text box. Enter the distance from the left margin to the left edge of the graph in the Horizontal text box.

- **Preset**: Lets you justify the graph on the page both vertically and horizontally. When you click on this button, 1-2-3/G displays six new buttons: a list of three Vertical buttons (Top, Center, and Bottom) and a list of three Horizontal buttons (Left, Center, and Right). Select a button from each list.

Building on the current example, to have the graph print at the top of the page, select the Auto button.

Note

When you choose the Full page button for the Dimensions option, 1-2-3/G always skips to a new page before printing your graph. However, if you use any other Dimensions option, 1-2-3/G will print the graph on the current page, provided there is enough room. If you want to always skip to the top of a new page when you print your graph, turn on the New page check box in the File Print Print Graph dialog box.

Note

In its default state, 1-2-3/G always scales fonts in proportion to the Dimension option you've chosen. However, if you want 1-2-3/G to always use the Screen fonts, regardless of the Dimension option you choose, turn off the Adjust fonts check box in the File Print Print Graph dialog box.

Checking the Size and Position by Previewing

After you have set the size and position for your graph, you will want to preview your graph before you print it. Mark the Screen preview check box in the File Print Print Graph dialog box, then select Print. By previewing your graph in this way, you can check to see whether you have chosen some incorrect settings. For example, you may find that 1-2-3/G prints only part of the graph on the page, indicating that you have set the Manual location settings too high. (See Chapter 8 for more on using the Preview utility.)

Printing a Graph

After you have sized and positioned your graph for printing, and previewed the graph to check your settings, you are ready to print your graph to a printer or an encoded file on disk. The steps for printing a graph are identical to those for printing a worksheet. See Chapter 8 for a complete discussion of printing. That chapter also describes how to print a graph and a worksheet on the same page.

WORKING WITH THE GRAPH TOOL'S EDIT COMMANDS

In previous chapters, you learned how to use the Edit commands to cut, copy, and paste data between worksheet files. In the Graph Tool, however, you can use the Edit commands to cut, copy, and paste graph objects. You can also use them to create and change links between graph files and worksheet files.

This section describes how to use the Edit commands to

- Delete graph objects (Edit Clear)
- Cut and paste graph objects (Edit Cut, Edit Copy, and Edit Paste, and Edit Paste Special)
- Work with links (Edit Link)
- Select graph objects (Edit Select Object)
- Undo actions (Edit Undo)

Deleting Graph Objects

The easiest way to remove a graph object is to select it, then choose Edit Clear (or DEL). For example, suppose you want to remove the *x*-axis title from a graph. Simply click on the title, and select Edit Clear or press DEL.

When you delete an object using Edit Clear, besides clearing the selected graph object, 1-2-3/G also deletes the link between the worksheet file and the graph file, if one exists. If you want to recover a graph object that you have cleared, and restore its link (if one existed), choose Edit Undo immediately (or press ALT-BACKSPACE, the shortcut for Edit Undo).

Cutting and Pasting Graph Objects

You can also use the Edit commands to cut objects from one graph file and paste them to another using the clipboard. You can even cut and paste an entire graph.

To copy a graph object to the clipboard, you use Edit Copy (CTRL-INS). To remove a graph object and place it in the clipboard, you use Edit Cut (SHIFT-DEL). Once a graph object is in the clipboard, you use Edit Paste (SHIFT-INS) to place the contents of the clipboard into the active graph.

For example, imagine that you want to copy the first title from one graph file and place it in another. Perform the following steps:

1. Select the first title in the source graph.
2. Choose Edit Copy (or CTRL-INS) to place the graph title in the clipboard.
3. Activate the Graph window containing the target graph.
4. Select the first graph title in the target graph.
5. Choose Edit Paste (or SHIFT-INS) to copy the contents of the clipboard to the active graph file.

The target graph instantly displays the text for the new graph title.

Note

When you use the clipboard to copy a graph object from one graph file to another, 1-2-3/G does not copy any worksheet links.

How 1-2-3/G Uses the Clipboard

When you use Edit Cut or Edit Copy to cut or copy a graph object to the clipboard, 1-2-3/G places the graph object in the clipboard in text format. In addition, when you use Edit Paste to paste the object to a graph file or to a worksheet file, 1-2-3/G reads the text format from the clipboard and uses it in the graph file.

If you cut or copy the *entire* graph, 1-2-3/G places it in the clipboard in three formats: text, metafile, and bitmap. Because 1-2-3/G can read the text format from the clipboard, you can use the Edit Paste command to copy the entire graph from the clipboard to a worksheet or graph file. Other programs can read the entire graph from the clipboard in metafile or bitmap format. Examples of applications that can read bitmap and metafile formats from the clipboard are screen capture programs, graphics programs, and some word processors.

The Results of Pasting Data in a Graph

The results of pasting data into a graph depend on the graph object you've selected before using Edit Paste. Table 7–2 summarizes the results. As you review the table, keep in mind that the source of the data can be a graph file, another 1-2-3/G tool (such as a worksheet file or the keystroke editor), or even another PM application.

TABLE 7-2 Results of Pasting Data in a Graph

Graph Object Selected	Results
Data series	Replaces the selected data series using the data in the clipboard as numbers.
Title	Replaces the selected title using the data in the clipboard as a label.
Legend label	Replaces the selected legend label using the data in the clipboard as a label.
Legend frame	Replaces all the legend labels using the data in the clipboard as labels.
Data labels	Replaces all the data labels using the data in the clipboard as labels.
X labels	Replaces all the X labels using the data in the clipboard as labels.
Text notation	Replaces the selected text notation using the data in the clipboard as a label.
Graph	Separates the clipboard data into X labels, data series, and legend labels and replaces only these items in the graph.

Note

You cannot paste arrow or line notations from the clipboard because 1-2-3/G cannot store these items in the clipboard.

Notes on Pasting Data

Here are some things to keep in mind as you use the Edit Paste command to paste clipboard contents to a graph file:

- Regardless of the origin of the data, when you use the Edit Paste command to paste data from the clipboard to a graph, 1-2-3/G pastes text only. If you want to paste a link from a worksheet file, use the Edit Link Paste Command instead (see "Pasting Links" below).
- You can use the Edit Paste command to paste an automatic graph range to a graph file. Recall that an automatic graph range is a single-worksheet range that encompasses all the data you want to graph. (See "How 1-2-3/G Interprets Automatic Graph Ranges and Assigns Settings" above for a complete description of an automatic graph range.) Before you can paste an automatic graph range, you must copy it to the clipboard using the Edit Copy command.

- If you want to control the way that 1-2-3/G interprets an automatic graph range when you paste it from the clipboard to a graph file, you can use the Edit Paste Special command. This command lets you control whether 1-2-3/G interprets the data in columnwise or rowwise fashion. It also lets you control whether X labels are taken from the first row (or column) and whether legend labels are taken from the first column (or row).

Working with Links

As you know, when you create a graph with Graph View or Graph Setup, 1-2-3/G automatically creates a series of links between source data in your worksheet file and graph objects in the Graph window. Suppose, however, that you want to create or edit individual links. In this case, you will want to use the Edit Link command from the Graph Tool menu. Besides creating and editing links, you can also Edit Link, to move, delete, and update links.

How Graph File Links Work

When you use the Edit Link command in a graph file, the graph file is known as the *destination* of the data provided by other files. The file that provides the data is known as the *source.* The source file can be a 1-2-3/G worksheet file or a file from any other application that supports DDE (Dynamic Data Exchange).

DDE is a special message protocol that 1-2-3/G and other PM application programs use to communicate with one another. For example, suppose you have linked the data in a PM application file (the source) to a 1-2-3/G graph file (the destination). You then change the data in the source file. The PM application program sends DDE messages to 1-2-3/G to update information in the destination (graph) file. 1-2-3/G reads these messages and immediately updates the graph file. (See Chapter 2, "Managing the Desktop," for more on DDE.)

Note

> The way you link to 1-2-3/G from another PM application depends entirely on that application. Therefore, you should see the documentation for that application if you want to create a link to 1-2-3/G.

Creating Links

As you recall, to create a link between the active graph file and a source file, you use the Edit Link Create command. The source file can be a 1-2-3/G worksheet file or a file from another PM application that supports DDE. See "Using the Graph Tool to Create a Graph—An Example" for a description of the Edit Link Create dialog box and an example of how to use the command to create a link between a worksheet file and a graph file.

Editing Links

The easiest way to edit a link when you want to specify a new reference or a new source file is to modify the link directly in the contents box (see "Selecting and Changing Graph Objects" above for more details). However, you can also use the Edit Link Edit command to change a link. In fact, this command is the only way that you can change the update mode for the link (for example, from manual to automatic) without having to first delete the link and then recreate it from scratch.

When you select the Edit Link Edit command, 1-2-3/G displays the dialog box in Figure 7-131. The dialog box options are described as follows:

- **Destination file:** Specifies the name of the active graph file (you cannot change the contents of this box).
- **Destination item:** Displays a list of currently linked graph objects from which you can choose. When you first access the dialog box, the currently selected object appears in the text box.
- **Source and file item:** Displays the source file for the currently selected object in double-angle brackets, followed by the location of the data within the source file. You can accept the source, edit the source, or enter an entirely new source. To see a list of available source files, press NAME (F3). Lotus application filenames appear in upper case in the list box and other PM application filenames appear in lower case.

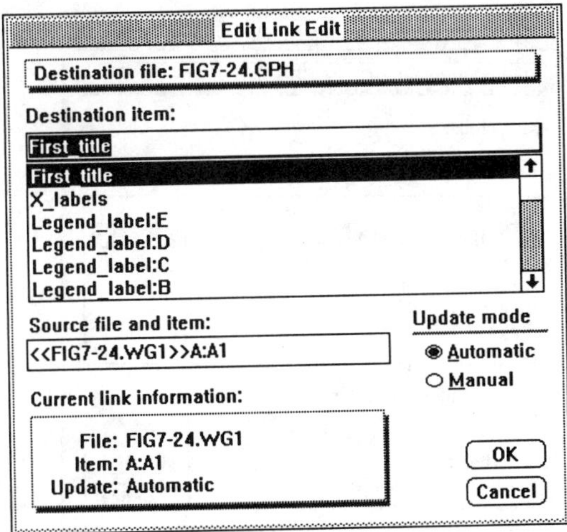

FIGURE 7-131 The Edit Link Edit dialog box

- **Update mode:** Lets you determine how the link will be updated. If you select the Automatic button, the graph will be updated whenever the source changes. If you select Manual, the graph will be updated only when you select the Edit Link Update command (see "Updating Links," below).
- **Current link information:** Displays the file (source), item (range), and update method for the current link.

Deleting Links

Suppose you want to freeze the contents of a graph object so that it does not change. To do so, you can use the Edit Link Delete command to delete the link between the graph object and the source file. You can also use this command to delete all the links to the active graph file.

Note

> Deleting a link does not mean deleting the graph object but freezing it so it will not change.

Figure 7-132 shows the dialog box that appears when you select the Edit Link Delete command. The options are described as follows:

- **Destination file:** Specifies the name of the active graph file (you cannot change the contents of this box).

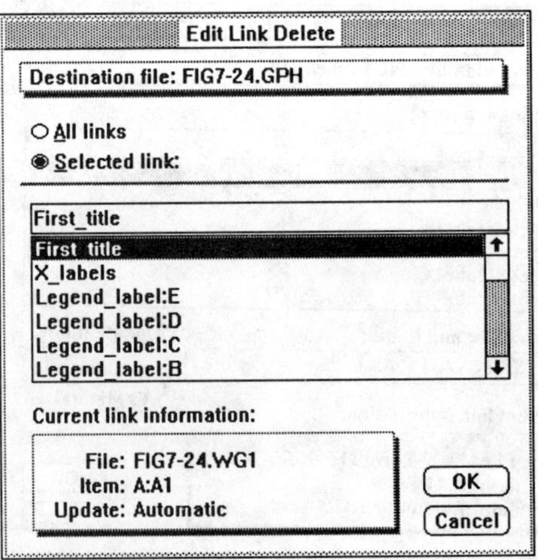

FIGURE 7-132 The Edit Link Delete dialog box

- **All links:** Choosing this option deletes all the links to the active graph file. All links is the default if you have not selected an object before accessing the command.
- **Selected link:** Select this option if you want to delete links for individual graph objects. If you have selected an object before choosing the command, the text box shows the currently selected object. You can accept this choice or select another from the list.
- **Current link information:** Displays the file (source), item (range), and update method for the current link.

Moving Links

Suppose you have created a graph file using the data in one worksheet file. You then decide that you want to use the graph file with another worksheet file altogether. If the two worksheet files have an identical layout, you can easily move all the links in the active graph file to another source file. The command you use to move all graph links at once is Edit Link Move. See "Manipulating Graph Objects" above for a complete description of how to use the Edit Link Move command to move links.

Pasting Links

When you use the Edit Copy command to copy worksheet data (not graph data) to the clipboard, 1-2-3/G also copies a link reference to the clipboard as well. Therefore, you can use Edit Link Paste Link to paste the link reference to a graph object.

For example, suppose you have the graph in Figure 7–133, and you want to replace the first graph title with a label from the SALES.WG1 file. Perform the following steps:

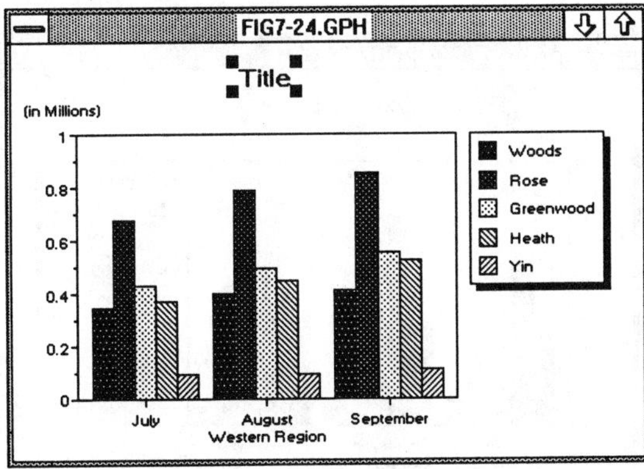

FIGURE 7–133 A graph whose default first title you want to replace with a worksheet label

1. Select the first title in the graph file.
2. Return to the Worksheet window (use CTRL-F6) and select the cell that contains the label you want to use in the graph.
3. Select Edit Copy. 1-2-3/G places a copy of the label in the clipboard along with a link reference.
4. Return to the Graph window and select Edit Link Paste Link.

1-2-3/G copies the link reference from the clipboard to the first title, as shown in Figure 7–134.

Note

> 1-2-3/G only copies a link reference to the clipboard when you use Edit Copy. It does not copy a link reference when you use Edit Cut.

Updating Links

If you have created manual links to the active graph file (using Edit Link Create or Edit Link Edit) and you want to update those links, use the Edit Link Update command. The dialog box in Figure 7–135 will appear. This step is unnecessary if you have used only automatic links in your graph; 1-2-3/G updates your graphs automatically whenever the source data changes.

Selecting Graph Objects

The easiest way to select a graph object is to click on it, or press TAB (or SHIFT-TAB). However, you can also select an object using the Edit Select Object

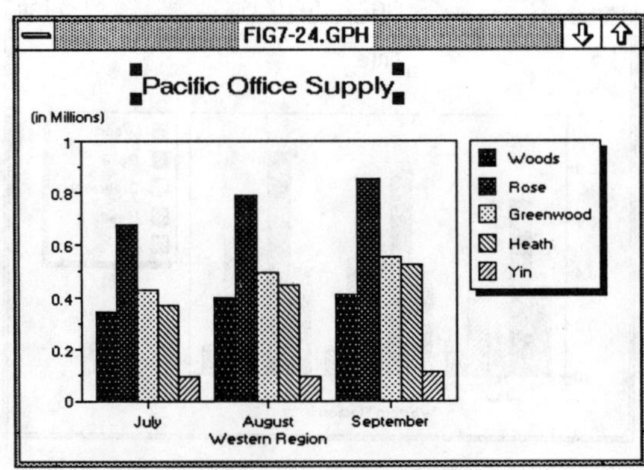

FIGURE 7–134 After pasting a link reference to the first graph title

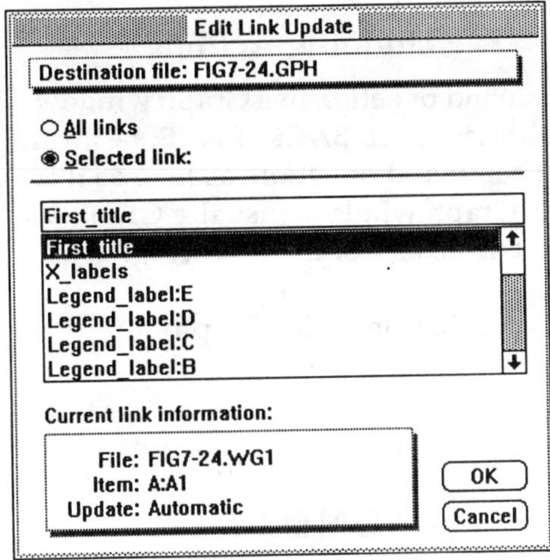

FIGURE 7–135 The Edit Link Update dialog box

command. As mentioned, this command is most often used to select an object from within a macro. However, Edit Select Object is also helpful for selecting objects that are hard to pinpoint with the mouse or the keyboard, such as data series that are so small they are nearly indistinguishable from the *x*-axis, or bars that appear hidden by other bars in a 3-D bar graph.

When you choose the Edit Select Object command, 1-2-3/G presents the following options in a cascade menu:

Edit Select Option	Selects
Series	A data series. If selected, 1-2-3/G will present you with the Edit Select Series dialog to choose a particular series.
Legend	The legend frame or one of the labels in the legend.
Title	The first or second graph title or an axis title
Axis	An axis scale, scale indicator, or label along an axis.
Data Labels	A group of data labels.
Plot Frame	The plot frame.
Pie	The entire pie graph, a slice of a pie graph, or the data labels in the pie graph.
Notation	A notation.
Graph	The entire graph.

Undoing Actions

To reverse the last command or action in a Graph window, select the Edit Undo command, or use its shortcut ALT-BACKSPACE. Be aware, however, that you can only undo the *last* command or action, as long as it is not the command or action that created the Graph window (usually Graph View or Graph Setup). In addition, you cannot undo any of the following:

- File commands (except File Print Print Graph).
- Edit Link.
- Edit Select Object.

SUMMARY

As you've seen in this chapter, 1-2-3/G offers an impressive assortment of graphics features. Besides letting you create nine different graph types, you can also create many variations of the standard graph types by changing the type for individual data series. You can also add many enhancements to your graphs (such as titles, fonts, colors, and annotations), as well as resize and move graph objects. With all the ways to control a graph's appearance, you can be reasonably certain that 1-2-3/G has the power to create virtually any graph you need.

Printing

1-2-3/G provides two commands for printing worksheet data, the Print command and the File Print command. The File Print command is new to 1-2-3/G. It offers all the functionality of the Print command, plus more. Both the Print and File Print commands are covered in this chapter.

Note

> The Print and File Print commands covered in this chapter are discussed in the context of printing worksheet data. To print the contents of a graph window, you must use the File Print command available from the Graph tool menu. See Chapter 7, "Graphs," for information on how to print your graphs.

What's New

> You can now print your work in 1-2-3/G by using either the Print command or the File Print command. Inclusion of the File Print command was necessary to conform to both the Systems Application Architecture (SAA) and Common User Access (CUA) standards for Presentation Manager.
>
> If you're an experienced 1-2-3 user, you may prefer to use the Print command initially, because of its similarity to previous release of 1-2-3. Be aware, though, that some of the options previously available on the Print menu for 1-2-3 Releases 2 and 3 have either been eliminated, changed, or moved to the new File Print menu in 1-2-3/G. This will undoubtedly cause problems when you read files from Release 2 and 3 into 1-2-3/G and attempt to use the printing macros in those files.

1-2-3/G offers a useful new utility called the Preview utility. This utility allows you to preview the precise layout of your output in a WYSIWYG (what you see is what you get) fashion, before you print it. Initially, Preview shows you each of the individual pages in your output in miniature. To preview a specific page, you can move to that page and zoom in on it (increase its displayed size). Thus, you can see exactly what data is on which page and how it will appear when printed. If you discover a problem, you can return to the worksheet and fix it, rather than waiting through an extensive print cycle.

1-2-3/G also allows you to print to an encoded file. When you print to an encoded file, 1-2-3/G sends not only characters but also printer control codes, text formatting, and any graphics that would normally be sent your printer. You can print an encoded file directly from the OS/2 system prompt, without having to use 1-2-3/G. That way, you can print the data either at a later time or on another computer.

1-2-3/G lets you name the current print settings and reuse them. This long-overdue feature partially eliminates the need for building multiple print macros to recreate settings.

1-2-3/G also supports printing in the background. That is, you can continue to work in 1-2-3/G while your data is printing. You may recall that this is not possible in 1-2-3 Release 2.

Like 1-2-3 Release 3, 1-2-3/G allows you to print a worksheet with a frame of column letters and row numbers. Thus, you can identify the location of the data in the worksheet from your printed output.

Headers and footers are essentially the same. However, the new ## (double pound) sign allows you to print page numbers in headers or footers starting on a specific page. In addition, the new tilde symbol allows you include multiple lines in a header or footer.

1-2-3/G also allows you to choose the number of copies you want to print. This eliminates the need to reenter the Print command multiple times to print the same range of data.

You can also choose starting and stopping points for multiple-page documents. For example, if you have a 10-page document, you can start printing on page 5 and stop printing on page 7.

In 1-2-3/G, you can use the Range Attributes Color command to assign different colors to the background of cells. If you have a color printer, 1-2-3/G will print that color. However, if you do not have a color printer, 1-2-3/G will print a black and white pattern that is assigned to that color. What's more, by using the new File Print Color Map command, you can choose which patterns are assigned to what colors. For example, imagine you've used the Range Attributes Color command to assign a red background to a range of cells containing a table. You can then assign a densely dotted pattern (causing a light gray appearance) to the color red. When the table is printed on your black and white printer, it appears with black characters on a light gray background.

PRINTING, FUNDAMENTALS

Figure 8–1 shows a sample worksheet with some data in the range A:A1..A:F24. To print this range of data, you can use either the Print Printer command or File Print Print Worksheet command. Whichever one of these commands you select, 1-2-3/G displays the same dialog box. An example of the Print Printer dialog box appears in Figure 8–2.

In its simplest from, printing is a three-step process. First, you must specify the range you want to print in the Range(s) text box. Next, select the Go command button to send the data to the print queue. Finally, select the Quit command button to begin printing. For example, to print the range of data in Figure 8–1, specify the range A:A1..A:F24 (or its range name) in the Range(s) text box. Then, select the Go command button. Finally, select the Quit command button. 1-2-3/G sends the data to your printer and returns you to the current worksheet.

As mentioned, when you select the Go command button, 1-2-3/G sends the data in the print range to the print queue. The print queue is an area of your computer's memory that is used to store information temporarily. Only when you select the Quit command button to return to the worksheet is the data sent to your printer.

The print queue is capable of storing more than one print job. Therefore, you can specify several different ranges to print in the Range(s) text box, selecting the Go command button after each one. When you select Quit to return to the worksheet, 1-2-3/G sends each range you specified to your printer in the order in which you selected them. To leave blank lines between print ranges, or to print each range on a separate page, select the Line or Page command buttons before selecting Go for each print range.

You can also specify a collection in the Range(s) text box. When you do, 1-2-3/G sends each range of the collection to the print queue in the order in which you selected them.

1-2-3/G remembers your previous print range. That is, if you've used the Print Printer or File Print Print Worksheet command previously in the current session, 1-2-3/G shows you that same range in the Range(s) text box the next time you select the command. You can accept this selection, edit, or make a new selection.

The example in this section demonstrates printing in its most basic form. Before you select the Go command button, however, to send the data to the

123/G [69.4] Ready

File Edit Worksheet Range Copy... Move... Print Graph Data Utility Quit... Help

A:A1 'Expenses:

FIG8-1.WG1

A	A	B	C	D	E	F	G
1	Expenses:						
2	Description	Acct.	Jan-92	Feb-92	Mar-92	QTR 1	
3	Insurance	801	437	437	437	1,310	
4	Legal/Acctg.	802	5,000	0	1,500	6,500	
5	Salaries	803	10,385	10,385	11,539	32,308	
6	P/R Tax	804	114	114	127	355	
7	Supplies	805	350	250	450	1,050	
8	Rent	806	1,800	1,800	1,800	5,400	
9	Phone	807	270	270	270	810	
10	Miscellaneous	808	450	450	450	1,350	
11	Travel	809	1,900	0	1,900	3,800	
12	Maintenance	810	200	200	200	600	
13	Mailing	811	225	225	225	675	
14	Printing	812	850	0	0	850	
15	Equipment	813	1,550	0	2,345	3,895	
16	Benefits	814	439	439	439	1,317	
17	Bank Charges	815	30	30	30	90	
18	Interest	816	292	292	292	875	
19	Property Tax	817	0	0	0	0	
20	Income Tax	818	3,750	0	0	3,750	
21	Amortization	819	161	161	161	483	
22	Depreciation	820	1,292	1,292	1,292	3,875	
23							
24		Total	29,494	16,344	23,456	69,294	
25							

FIGURE 8–1 Some sample worksheet data for printing

print queue, you can specify the following additional attributes for a given print job:

- **Display options:** You can control the printing of worksheet grid lines and cell borders and you can also have the column letters and row numbers in the worksheet frame printed with your output.

Print Printer

Range(s): A:A1..A:F24

Display options

☐ Side frame ☒ Colors and shading

☐ Top frame ☒ Borders and grids

Headings

Rows:

Columns:

Format output

◉ As displayed

○ Formulas

☐ Screen preview

Go | Line | Page | Options... | Quit | Cancel

FIGURE 8–2 1-2-3/G displays the same dialog box whether you select Print Printer or File Print Print Worksheet

- **Headings:** You can specify rows or columns of data that will print along the top and left edges of each page.
- **Headers and Footers:** You can specify a header and/or footer that will print with each page.
- **Margins:** You can specify different settings for the top, bottom, left, and right margins.
- **Number of Copies:** You can choose the number of copies of each page.
- **Print Density:** You can choose a draft quality setting, as a opposed to a near letter quality setting, for a print job.
- **Named settings:** You can give the current print settings a name, so that you can quickly recall them for use at a later time.

The balance of this chapter shows you how to specify each of these attributes for a given print job. However, before doing so, the next three sections explain more about basic printing skills. For example, you'll learn about how 1-2-3/G breaks up a large report onto separate pages. You'll also learn about how 1-2-3/G prints in the background and about printing to files.

Note

Consider using 1-2-3/G's new Preview utility to preview a print job before sending it to your printer. That way, you can see exactly what your print job will look like before it is printed. See "Using the Preview Utility" later in this chapter for more details on this.

PRINTING A LARGE RANGE

When you print a large range (a range that is wider or longer than a single page), 1-2-3/G breaks up that range into individual pages. 1-2-3/G determines the amount of data that will fit on each page by using the current top, bottom, left, and right margin settings. The margin settings determine the amount of white space between the edges of the paper and your document.

1-2-3/G measures margins in inches (or millimeters, depending on the Utility User Settings International Measurement setting). The default setting for the top, bottom, left, and right margins is 1 inch, measured from the edge of the paper to the edge of your document. See "Changing the Margins" later in this chapter for information on how to change 1-2-3/G's default margin settings.

1-2-3/G prints the data in the print range in sets of columns, working from left to right. It will complete printing the data in the first set of columns before moving on to the next set of columns, and so on. The number of columns that will fit across each page is determined by the left and right margin settings. The number of rows of data that will fit on each page is determined by the top and bottom margin settings.

Figure 8–3 shows a sample worksheet that encompasses the range A:A1..A:N58. Figure 8–4 shows that same worksheet printed with 1-2-3/G's default margin settings. Notice that the upper-left portion of the worksheet is printed on page 1, the lower-left portion on page 2, the upper-right portion on page 3, and the lower-right portion on page 4. In this example, 1-2-3/G prints the first seven columns and 42 rows of the print range on page 1. It completes printing the data in the first seven columns on page 2 before starting with the next set of seven columns, which are printed on pages 3 and 4.

In addition to the margin settings, there are other factors that determine the amount of data that will fit on each page. Among the most prevalent of these is the size of the fonts you select for printing. As you may recall from Chapter 3, you can use the Range Attributes Font or Worksheet Global Attributes Font commands to specify various type styles and sizes (fonts) for printing a given range or worksheet. The larger the font you select, the taller and wider each character appears when printed. The width has an impact on the number of characters that will fit between the left and right margins. The height affects the number of lines that will fit between the top and bottom margins.

Column widths and row heights also have an impact on the amount of data that will fit within the current margins. If you use the Worksheet Column command to increase the width of columns, fewer columns will fit between the right and left margins. Further, if you use the Worksheet Row command to increase row heights, fewer rows will fit between the top and bottom margins.

Finally, even headers and footers have a bearing on the amount of data that will fit on each page. Headers and footers contain one or more lines of descriptive text that appear at the top and/or bottom of each printed page. For example, a typical header or footer might include the name of the report, your company name, and a page number. When you include a header or footer in a document, 1-2-3/G allocates additional space between the top and bottom margins. For more about including headers and footers in your documents, see "Headers and Footers" later in this chapter.

Because of the multiplicity of factors that influence the amount of data that can fit on a page, about the only way you can get an accurate picture of what data will be printed on which page is to use 1-2-3/G's new Preview utility. Initially, this utility shows you each page of your printed output in miniature. However, you can zoom in on a given page (increase the displayed size) to see what data is on that page and how it will appear when printed.

PRINTING, IN THE BACKGROUND

1-2-3/G sends each print job to a print queue before it goes to your printer. After information is released to the print queue, you can continue to work in 1-2-3/G. Thus, printing takes place in the background, without interrupting your 1-2-3/G work session.

The print queue is an area of memory that is used to hold information temporarily. The print queue is capable of holding more than one print job. Each print job is processed (sent to your printer) in the order in which it is sent to the print queue. After all print jobs have been completed, the print queue is empty.

To see what is going on with your 1-2-3/G documents that are printing in the background, you can use the File Print Status command. When you select this command, 1-2-3/G displays the dialog box in Figure 8–5.

At the top of the File Print Status dialog box, 1-2-3/G displays the status and destination of the current print job (the print job in progress). If nothing is printing, 1-2-3/G displays the message "No job in progress" in place of the status and destination information. Immediately above the command buttons at the bottom of the dialog box, 1-2-3/G displays information about other print jobs that are waiting in the print queue. If no print jobs are waiting, 1-2-3/G displays the message "No Jobs in Print Queue," as shown in Figure 8–5.

The command buttons at the bottom of the File Print Status dialog box give you a certain measure of control over your 1-2-3/G documents in the print queue. Each one of these command buttons performs the following function:

- **Delete Current:** Stops the current print job and deletes it from the print queue. This command button also resets the page count to 1 and starts the next print job at the top of a new page.
- **Delete All:** Stops the current print job and deletes all remaining print jobs that are waiting to be printed.
- **Complete:** Disables background printing. The File Print Status dialog box remains on your screen until the current print job as well as any print jobs waiting in the queue have been completed. Selecting this command button also disables the Suspend/Resume command button explained next. After printing is completed, the File Print Status dialog box disappears from your screen. You can use this command in a macro to stop further use of 1-2-3/G until printing is completed.
- **Suspend/Resume:** If a print job is underway, this command button says Suspend. When you select Suspend, 1-2-3/G stops the current print job and changes the name of the command button to Resume. If you select Resume, 1-2-3/G starts printing again and changes the name of this command button back to Suspend.

A:	A	B	C	D	E	F	G	H	I	J	K	L	M	N
1	Projected Cash Flow—ABC Company													
2														
3	Date	Jan–92	Feb–92	Mar–92	Apr–92	May–92	Jun–92	Jul–92	Aug–92	Sep–92	Oct–92	Nov–92	Dec–92	Total
4														
5	Cash	28,737	24,716	29,630	29,533	19,939	26,473	29,273	26,288	33,442	39,256	35,115	45,335	
6														
7	Income													
8	Profit Center 1	8,000	7,840	7,683	7,530	8,282	9,111	8,282	8,452	9,297	9,018	9,288	9,567	102,350
9	Profit Center 2	8,400	8,232	8,067	7,906	8,697	9,566	8,697	8,874	9,762	9,469	9,753	10,045	107,467
10	Profit Center 3	8,820	8,644	8,471	8,301	9,131	10,045	9,131	9,318	10,250	9,942	10,240	10,548	112,841
11	Profit Center 4	9,261	9,076	8,894	8,716	9,588	10,547	9,588	9,784	10,762	10,439	10,752	11,075	118,483
12	Profit Center 5	9,724	9,530	9,339	9,152	10,067	11,074	10,067	10,273	11,300	10,961	11,290	11,629	124,407
13	Profit Center 6	10,210	10,006	9,806	9,610	10,571	11,628	10,571	10,787	11,865	11,509	11,854	12,210	130,627
14	Profit Center 7	10,721	10,506	10,296	10,090	11,099	12,209	11,099	11,326	12,458	12,085	12,447	12,821	137,158
15														
16	Total Income	65,136	63,833	62,557	61,306	67,436	74,180	67,436	68,812	75,694	73,423	75,625	77,894	833,332
17														
18	Cost of Goods:													
19	Profit Center 1	2,800	2,744	2,689	2,635	2,899	3,189	2,899	2,958	3,254	3,156	3,251	3,348	35,822
20	Profit Center 2	2,940	2,881	2,824	2,767	3,044	3,348	3,044	3,106	3,417	3,314	3,413	3,516	37,614
21	Profit Center 3	3,087	3,025	2,965	2,905	3,196	3,516	3,196	3,261	3,587	3,480	3,584	3,692	39,494
22	Profit Center 4	3,241	3,177	3,113	3,051	3,356	3,691	3,356	3,424	3,767	3,654	3,763	3,876	41,469
23	Profit Center 5	3,403	3,335	3,269	3,203	3,524	3,876	3,524	3,596	3,955	3,836	3,951	4,070	43,542
24	Profit Center 6	3,574	3,502	3,432	3,363	3,700	4,070	3,700	3,775	4,153	4,028	4,149	4,274	45,719
25	Profit Center 7	3,752	3,677	3,604	3,532	3,885	4,273	3,885	3,964	4,360	4,230	4,357	4,487	48,005
26	Direct Labor	13,027	12,767	12,511	12,261	13,487	14,836	13,487	13,762	15,139	14,685	15,125	15,579	166,666
27														
28	Total COGS	35,825	35,108	34,406	33,718	37,090	40,799	37,090	37,847	41,631	40,383	41,594	42,842	458,333

FIGURE 8–3 A large worksheet

29														
30	Expenses:													
31	Insurance	437	437	437	437	437	437	437	437	437	437	437	437	5,241
32	Legal/Acctg.	5,000	0	1,500	5,000	0	1,500	5,000	0	1,500	5,000	0	1,500	26,000
33	Salaries	10,385	10,385	11,539	10,385	10,385	13,846	10,385	10,385	11,539	10,385	10,385	13,846	133,847
34	P/R Tax	114	114	127	114	114	152	114	114	127	114	114	152	1,472
35	Supplies	350	250	450	350	250	450	350	250	450	350	250	450	4,200
36	Rent	1,800	1,800	1,800	1,800	1,800	1,800	1,800	1,800	1,800	1,800	1,800	1,800	21,600
37	Phone	360	360	360	360	360	360	360	360	360	360	360	360	4,320
38	Miscellaneous	450	450	450	450	450	450	450	450	450	450	450	450	5,400
39	Travel	1,900	2,500	1,900	1,900	2,500	1,900	1,900	2,500	1,900	1,900	2,500	1,900	25,200
40	Lodging	475	625	475	475	625	475	475	625	475	475	625	475	6,300
41	Meals	95	125	95	95	125	95	95	125	95	95	125	95	1,260
42	Maintenance	400	400	400	400	400	400	400	400	400	400	400	400	4,800
43	Mailing	325	325	325	325	325	325	325	325	325	325	325	325	3,900
44	Printing	850	950	1,050	850	950	1,050	850	950	1,050	850	950	1,050	11,400
45	Equipment	1,550	0	2,250	1,550	0	2,250	1,550	0	2,250	1,550	0	2,250	15,200
46	Equipment Rental	550	550	550	550	550	550	550	550	550	550	550	550	6,600
47	Benefits	2,439	2,439	2,439	2,439	2,439	2,439	2,439	2,439	2,439	2,439	2,439	2,439	29,268
48	Bank Charges	30	30	30	30	30	30	30	30	30	30	30	30	360
49	Interest Expense	292	292	292	292	292	292	292	292	292	292	292	292	3,500
50	Property Tax	0	0	0	3,850	0	0	0	0	0	3,850	0	0	7,700
51	Income Tax	3,750	0	0	3,750	0	0	3,750	0	0	3,750	0	0	15,000
52	Consulting	1,300	1,300	1,300	1,300	1,300	1,300	1,300	1,300	1,300	1,300	1,300	1,300	15,600
53	Utilities	161	161	161	161	161	161	161	161	161	161	161	161	1,934
54	Trade Journals	319	319	319	319	319	319	319	319	319	319	319	319	3,828
55														
56	Total Expense	33,331	23,811	28,248	37,181	23,811	30,581	33,331	23,811	28,248	37,181	23,811	30,581	353,930
57														
58	Cash Flow	(4,020)	4,914	(98)	(9,594)	6,535	2,800	(2,985)	7,154	5,814	(4,141)	10,220	4,471	21,069

FIGURE 8–3 A large worksheet (*continued*)

A:	A	B	C	D	E	F	G	H
1	Projected Cash Flow—ABC Company							
2								
3	Date	Jan-92	Feb-92	Mar-92	Apr-92	May-92	Jun-92	Jul-92
4								
5	Cash	28,737	24,716	29,630	29,533	19,939	26,473	29,273
6								
7	Income							
8	Profit Center 1	8,000	7,840	7,683	7,530	8,282	9,111	8,282
9	Profit Center 2	8,400	8,232	8,067	7,906	8,697	9,566	8,697
10	Profit Center 3	8,820	8,644	8,471	8,301	9,131	10,045	9,131
11	Profit Center 4	9,261	9,076	8,894	8,716	9,588	10,547	9,588
12	Profit Center 5	9,724	9,530	9,339	9,152	10,067	11,074	10,067
13	Profit Center 6	10,210	10,006	9,806	9,610	10,571	11,628	10,571
14	Profit Center 7	10,721	10,506	10,296	10,090	11,099	12,209	11,099
15								
16	Total Income	65,136	63,833	62,557	61,306	67,436	74,180	67,436
17								
18	Cost of Goods:							
19	Profit Center 1	2,800	2,744	2,689	2,635	2,899	3,189	2,899
20	Profit Center 2	2,940	2,881	2,824	2,767	3,044	3,348	3,044
21	Profit Center 3	3,087	3,025	2,965	2,905	3,196	3,516	3,196
22	Profit Center 4	3,241	3,177	3,113	3,051	3,356	3,691	3,356
23	Profit Center 5	3,403	3,335	3,269	3,203	3,524	3,876	3,524
24	Profit Center 6	3,574	3,502	3,432	3,363	3,700	4,070	3,700
25	Profit Center 7	3,752	3,677	3,604	3,532	3,885	4,273	3,885
26	Direct Labor	13,027	12,767	12,511	12,261	13,487	14,836	13,487
27								
28	Total COGS	35,825	35,108	34,406	33,718	37,090	40,799	37,090
29								
30	Expenses:							
31	Insurance	437	437	437	437	437	437	437
32	Legal/Acctg.	5,000	0	1,500	5,000	0	1,500	5,000
33	Salaries	10,385	10,385	11,539	10,385	10,385	13,846	10,385
34	P/R Tax	114	114	127	114	114	152	114
35	Supplies	350	250	450	350	250	450	350
36	Rent	1,800	1,800	1,800	1,800	1,800	1,800	1,800
37	Phone	360	360	360	360	360	360	360
38	Miscellaneous	450	450	450	450	450	450	450
39	Travel	1,900	2,500	1,900	1,900	2,500	1,900	1,900
40	Lodging	475	625	475	475	625	475	475
41	Meals	95	125	95	95	125	95	95
42	Maintenance	400	400	400	400	400	400	400
43	Mailing	325	325	325	325	325	325	325
44	Printing	850	950	1,050	850	950	1,050	850

Page 1

A:	I	J	K	L	M	N
1						
2						
3	Aug-92	Sep-92	Oct-92	Nov-92	Dec-92	Total
4						
5	26,288	33,442	39,256	35,115	45,335	
6						
7						
8	8,452	9,297	9,018	9,288	9,567	102,350
9	8,874	9,762	9,469	9,753	10,045	107,467
10	9,318	10,250	9,942	10,240	10,548	112,841
11	9,784	10,762	10,439	10,752	11,075	118,483
12	10,273	11,300	10,961	11,290	11,629	124,407
13	10,787	11,865	11,509	11,854	12,210	130,627
14	11,326	12,458	12,085	12,447	12,821	137,158
15						
16	68,812	75,694	73,423	75,625	77,894	833,332
17						
18						
19	2,958	3,254	3,156	3,251	3,348	35,822
20	3,106	3,417	3,314	3,413	3,516	37,614
21	3,261	3,587	3,480	3,584	3,692	39,494
22	3,424	3,767	3,654	3,763	3,876	41,469
23	3,596	3,955	3,836	3,951	4,070	43,542
24	3,775	4,153	4,028	4,149	4,274	45,719
25	3,964	4,360	4,230	4,357	4,487	48,005
26	13,762	15,139	14,685	15,125	15,579	166,666
27						
28	37,847	41,631	40,383	41,594	42,842	458,333
29						
30						
31	437	437	437	437	437	5,241
32	0	1,500	5,000	0	1,500	26,000
33	10,385	11,539	10,385	10,385	13,846	133,847
34	114	127	114	114	152	1,472
35	250	450	350	250	450	4,200
36	1,800	1,800	1,800	1,800	1,800	21,600
37	360	360	360	360	360	4,320
38	450	450	450	450	450	5,400
39	2,500	1,900	1,900	2,500	1,900	25,200
40	625	475	475	625	475	6,300
41	125	95	95	125	95	1,260
42	400	400	400	400	400	4,800
43	325	325	325	325	325	3,900
44	950	1,050	850	950	1,050	11,400

Page 3

FIGURE 8–4 The same worksheet as in FIGURE 8–3 after printing

A:	A	B	C	D	E	F	G	H
45	Equipment	1,550	0	2,250	1,550	0	2,250	1,550
46	Equipment Rental	550	550	550	550	550	550	550
47	Benefits	2,439	2,439	2,439	2,439	2,439	2,439	2,439
48	Bank Charges	30	30	30	30	30	30	30
49	Interest Expense	292	292	292	292	292	292	292
50	Property Tax	0	0	0	3,850	0	0	0
51	Income Tax	3,750	0	0	3,750	0	0	3,750
52	Consulting	1,300	1,300	1,300	1,300	1,300	1,300	1,300
53	Utilities	161	161	161	161	161	161	161
54	Trade Journals	319	319	319	319	319	319	319
55								
56	Total Expense	33,331	23,811	28,248	37,181	23,811	30,581	33,331
57								
58	Cash Flow	(4,020)	4,914	(98)	(9,594)	6,535	2,800	(2,985)

Page 2

A:	I	J	K	L	M	N
45	0	2,250	1,550	0	2,250	15,200
46	550	550	550	550	550	6,600
47	2,439	2,439	2,439	2,439	2,439	29,268
48	30	30	30	30	30	360
49	292	292	292	292	292	3,500
50	0	0	3,850	0	0	7,700
51	0	0	3,750	0	0	15,000
52	1,300	1,300	1,300	1,300	1,300	15,600
53	161	161	161	161	161	1,934
54	319	319	319	319	319	3,828
55						
56	23,811	28,248	37,181	23,811	30,581	353,930
57						
58	7,154	5,814	(4,141)	10,220	4,471	21,069

Page 4

FIGURE 8–4 The same worksheet as in FIGURE 8–3 after printing (*continued*)

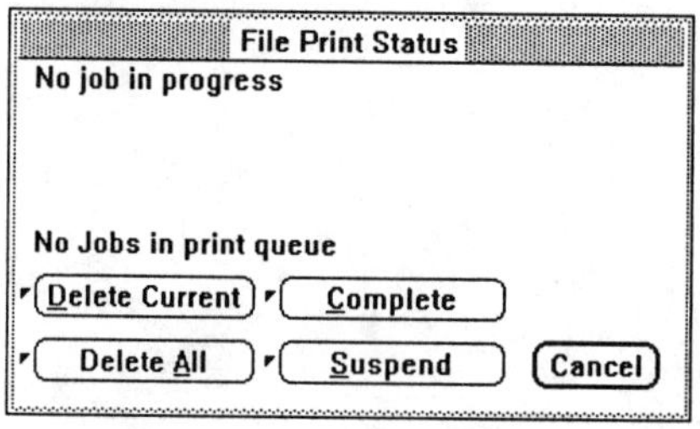

File Print Status

No job in progress

No Jobs in print queue

Delete Current | Complete

Delete All | Suspend | Cancel

FIGURE 8–5 The File Print Status dialog box

Note

> Printing to a File is not considered a background operation. Therefore, further use of 1-2-3/G is suspended until printing is completed.

PRINTING, TO A FILE

1-2-3/G also allows you to send printed output to a file on disk. You can select from two different types of files, an ASCII text file or an encoded file. Encoded files contain all the same information that would normally be sent to your printer. For example, in addition to data, encoded files contain printer control codes, text formats, and graphics. Encoded files can be used to print the same output at a later time or on another computer. You can print an encoded file from the OS/2 system prompt, without having to activate 1-2-3/G.

ASCII files, on the other hand, contain only lines of data, each line ending with a line-feed carriage return character. ASCII files can be imported directly into many popular software programs or back into 1-2-3/G with the File Import command.

Printing to an Encoded File

To create an encoded file, you can use either the Print Encoded command or the File Print command. The procedure for creating an encoded file depends on which of these commands you select.

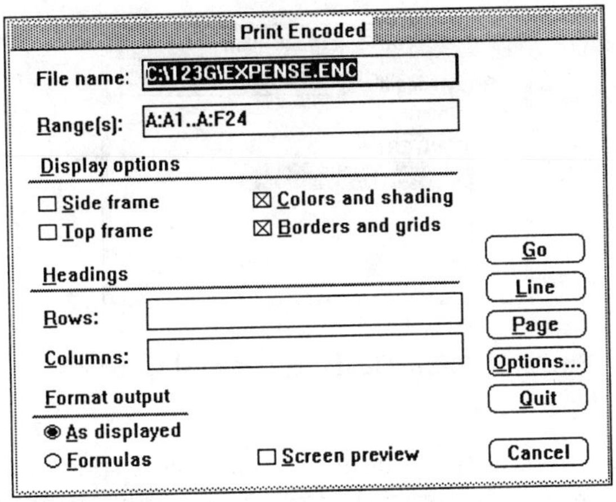

FIGURE 8–6 The Print Encoded dialog box

If you select the Print Encoded command, 1-2-3/G displays the dialog box in Figure 8–6. This dialog box is exactly like the Print Printer or File Print Print Worksheet dialog box in all respects save one. That difference is the File name text box at the top of the Print Encoded dialog box. This text box allows you specify the name of the file you want to print to. Otherwise, you use the dialog box exactly as though you were sending the output to your printer.

Encoded files have an .ENC extension. It is not necessary to specify this file extension, however, since 1-2-3/G provides it automatically. For example, imagine you want to print a range from the current worksheet to a file named EXPENSE.ENC in your C:\123G directory. To do this, select Print Encoded. 1-2-3/G displays the Print Encoded dialog box. Select File name and type the file name C:\123G\EXPENSE. Press ENTER to confirm your entry. Next, use the Range(s) text box to specify the range you want to print. Then, specify any additional settings you need. When you're ready, select the Go command button to queue the print job. Finally, select Quit to begin printing. 1-2-3/G creates the EXPENSE.ENC file.

As an alternative to using the Print Encoded command to create an encoded file, you can use the File Print menu. However, using this method involves selecting two commands. First, select the File Print Destination command to display the dialog in Figure 8–7. Select the "Encoded file" option button from this dialog box and type the name of the encoded file you want to create. To complete the command, select the OK command button.

To create the encoded file, select the File Print Print Worksheet command. 1-2-3/G displays the File Print Print Worksheet dialog box. Specify the range you want to print to the file in the Range(s) text box. Then, specify any additional settings you may require. When you're ready, select the Go command button. Then select the Quit command button to begin printing. 1-2-3/G

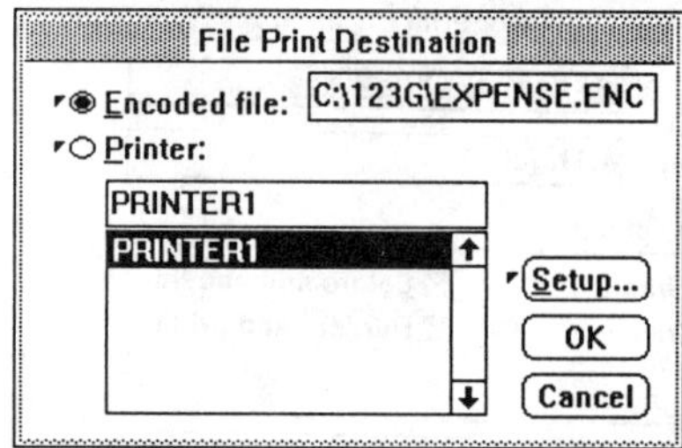

FIGURE 8–7 The File Print Destination dialog box

creates the .ENC encoded file under the name you specified in the File Print Destination dialog box. To return to printing to your printer again, select the File Print Destination command and select the Printer option button. Select the OK command button to complete the command.

Once you specify an encoded (.ENC) file as the default destination with the File Print Destination command, that file remains the default destination for the current 1-2-3/G session, unless you change it. For example, if you subsequently select the Print Print Encoded or File Print Destination commands, 1-2-3/G will show the name of the .ENC file you specified earlier. Moreover, the output from the File Print Print Worksheet command is also routed to that file. Therefore, unless you want to overwrite the .ENC file, make sure you use the File Print Destination command again and select the Printer option button. This will restore 1-2-3/G to sending your printed output to your printer.

Note

The File Print Destination dialog box also allows you to select a different printer. It does this by giving you access to Presentation Manager's printer control dialog boxes from within 1-2-3/G. See "Changing Printers" toward the end of this chapter for more on how to select a different printer.

Caution

As mentioned, when you create an encoded file, printer specific control codes are sent to that file. Therefore, the encoded file can only be printed on the type of printer that is listed as the current printer in the File Print Destination dialog box.

You can print an encoded file directly from the OS/2 system prompt by using the COPY command. To do this, select the OS/2 full screen or windowed command prompt from the Start Programs window (OS/2 1.1) or the Group-Main window (OS/2 1.2). Presentation Manager displays the OS/2 system prompt. From there, use the COPY command followed by the appropriate filename and printer port. For example, to print the encoded file MYFILE.ENC to the first parallel port, use the command COPY MYFILE.ENC/b LPT1. Notice the /b (binary file) switch here. This switch is simply a precaution. It assures that the entire file will be copied based on its physical size. Without this switch, OS/2 will stop copying if it encounters an end-of-file marker (CTRL-Z). Normally, this character is located at the physical end of the file. However, it can be located almost anywhere in a file that contains 1-2-3/G graphics.

Printing to ASCII Text File

To print to an ASCII text file, there is only one available command, Print File. When you select this command, 1-2-3/G displays the dialog box in Figure 8–8. Despite the similarity between this dialog box and the other Print and File Print dialog boxes, most of its options appear grayed (nonselectable). In fact, you can only send raw data to ASCII text files. Text enhancements such as headers, footers, and margins are ignored. Each row of data from the worksheet is stored as a line of text in the ASCII file.

To create an ASCII text file, select Print File. 1-2-3/G displays the dialog box in Figure 8–8. Select "File name" and type the name for the ASCII file in the adjacent text box. Confirm your entry by pressing ENTER. You do not need to specify an extension for the file. 1-2-3/G will automatically provide a .PRN file extension for you. To select a range to print to the file, select the Range(s) text box and specify a range address or range name from the current file. When you're ready, select the Go command button to queue the print job. To begin printing, select the Quit command button. 1-2-3/G creates the ASCII text file under the name you specified with a .PRN file extension.

Tip: For Release 2 and 3 Users

As you may recall, in prior versions of 1-2-3, it is necessary to set the top, bottom, and left margins to zero, and the right margin to 240, when printing to an ASCII file. This is not necessary in 1-2-3/G. It is done for you automatically. If you want to print with margins, you must print to an encoded file.

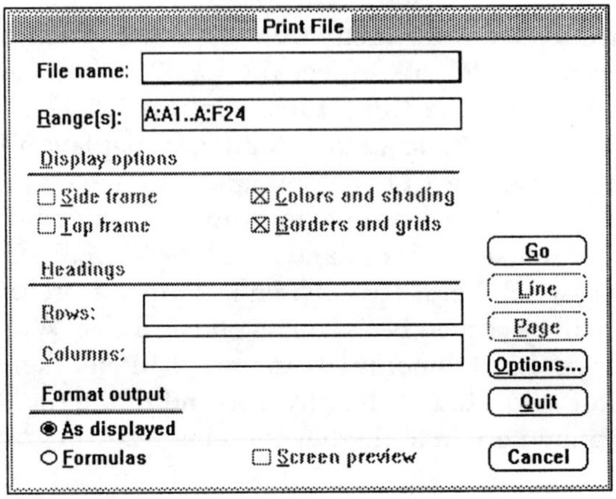

FIGURE 8–8 The Print File dialog box

CONTROLLING THE PAPER IN THE PRINTER

1-2-3/G allows you to advance the paper in your printer by a single line or an entire page. To advance the paper by a single line, select the Line command button from the Print Printer or File Print Print Worksheet dialog box, shown once again in Figure 8-9. To advance the paper by an entire page, use the Page command button.

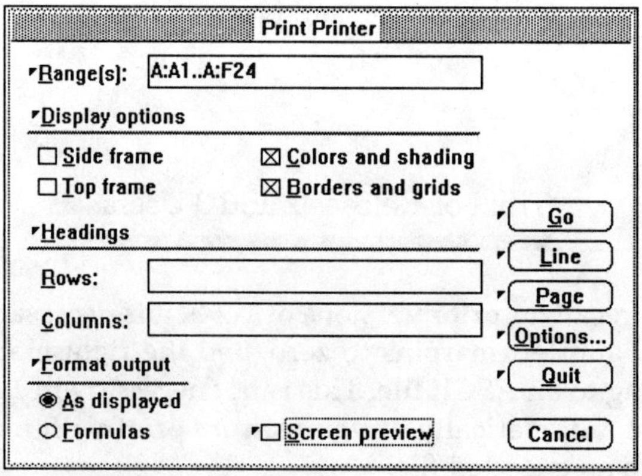

FIGURE 8–9 Select Line or Page to advance the paper in the printer

The Line command button allows you to include blank lines between consecutive print ranges. For example, imagine you want to print several different ranges from the current worksheet, leaving three blank lines between each of them. To do this, specify the first range in the Range(s) text box and select the Go command button to send it to the queue. Then, select the Line command button three times. Repeat this sequence of events for the remaining ranges you want to print. When you select the Quit command button to send the data to your printer, the ranges are printed with three blank lines between them.

To advance the paper in your printer by a full page, select the Page command button from the dialog box shown in Figure 8–9. When you select Page, 1-2-3/G advances the paper in your printer by a single page. Select this command button before selecting Go to have individual ranges printed on separate pages.

1-2-3/G maintains an internal page counter. It does this by keeping track of the amount of data printed on each page. When the amount of data consumes the available space between the top and bottom margins (set with Options Margins from either the Print Printer or File Print Print Worksheet dialog boxes), 1-2-3/G begins a new page. Therefore, when you select the Page command button to advance the printer by a single page, 1-2-3/G advances the paper only as needed to get to the top of the next page.

CONTROLLING DISPLAY OPTIONS

In 1-2-3/G, you can select various display options for your printout. For example, worksheet grid lines and cell borders are printed automatically. However, you can turn these off, so that they do not print. Additionally, cell background colors are printed automatically, provided you have a color printer. If you have a black and white printer, 1-2-3/G prints a shaded pattern for cell background colors. However, you can also turn both of these off. Finally, if you want, you can print a worksheet with the column letters and/or the row numbers displayed. That way, you can identify the location of the data in your worksheet from your printout.

To control the display of these attributes, you use the check boxes in the "Display options" section of the Print Printer or File Print Print Worksheet dialog box. For example, as you can see in Figure 8–9, the "Display options" section contains the following check boxes: "Side frame," "Top frame," "Colors and shading," and "Borders and grids."

Borders and Grids

The "Borders and grids" check box controls the printing of cell borders and grid lines. As you may recall, you can use the Range Attributes Border command to create borders that surround the edges of cells. Further, unlike previous versions of 1-2-3, 1-2-3/G displays grid lines in the worksheet to separate one cell from another. Both of these display attributes are printed automatically when you print a selected range from a worksheet. However, if you remove the X from the "Borders and grids" check box, 1-2-3/G will not include cell borders or grid lines in your printout. To remove the X, either click your mouse on the check box, or press D to select "Display options." Press ↓ to move to "Borders and grids" and press the SPACEBAR to remove the X.

Note

> Your worksheet will print a little faster if you suppress the display of cell borders and grid lines. Keep this in mind if print time is an issue.

If you want to suppress the printing of grid lines but not cell borders, you can use the Worksheet Global Screen Attributes Settings command and remove the X from the "Grid lines" check box. This will suppress the display of grid lines but cell borders are not affected.

Colors and Shading

To suppress the printing of background colors and shading, remove the X from the "Colors and shading" check box. Imagine you use the Range Attributes Color or Worksheet Global Attributes Color command to assign a color to the one or more cells in the worksheet. When you print the range that contains these cells, 1-2-3/G attempts to print the colors you've selected. If you do not have a color printer but your printer supports graphics, 1-2-3/G will print a black and white shading pattern associated with that particular color. To determine the shade pattern that is associated with each displayed color, select the File Print Color Map command. This command shows you what patterns are currently associated with each displayed color and allows you to assign different patterns to each color. See the next section, entitled "Assigning Patterns to Colors," for more on the File Print Color Map command. For more on the Range Attributes Color and Worksheet Global Attributes Color commands, see Chapter 3, "Formatting Worksheets."

Side and Top Frames

As mentioned, you can print a range from a worksheet with the top frame (column letters) and/or side frame (row numbers) displayed. That way, you can identify the location of the printed data within your worksheet. To print the top frame, place an X in the "Top frame" check box in Figure 8–9. To print

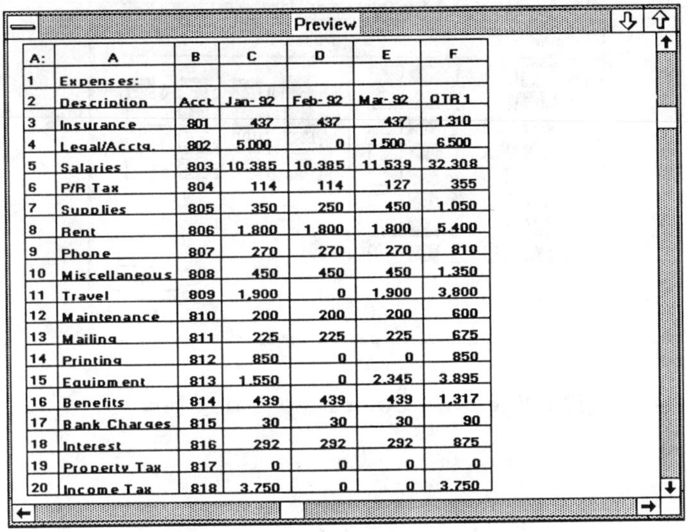

Preview

A:	A	B	C	D	E	F
1	Expenses:					
2	Description	Acct	Jan-92	Feb-92	Mar-92	QTR 1
3	Insurance	801	437	437	437	1,310
4	Legal/Acctg.	802	5,000	0	1,500	6,500
5	Salaries	803	10,385	10,385	11,539	32,308
6	P/R Tax	804	114	114	127	355
7	Supplies	805	350	250	450	1,050
8	Rent	806	1,800	1,800	1,800	5,400
9	Phone	807	270	270	270	810
10	Miscellaneous	808	450	450	450	1,350
11	Travel	809	1,900	0	1,900	3,800
12	Maintenance	810	200	200	200	600
13	Mailing	811	225	225	225	675
14	Printing	812	850	0	0	850
15	Equipment	813	1,550	0	2,345	3,895
16	Benefits	814	439	439	439	1,317
17	Bank Charges	815	30	30	30	90
18	Interest	816	292	292	292	875
19	Property Tax	817	0	0	0	0
20	Income Tax	818	3,750	0	0	3,750

FIGURE 8–10 A sample printout with the worksheet frame displayed

the side frame as well, place an X in the "Side frame" check box. Figure 8–10 shows a sample range printed to the Preview utility window with both the top and side frames displayed.

Printing a range with the side and top frames displayed is a good way to document your worksheet for archival purposes. It may also be of use if you're training others how to use 1-2-3/G.

ASSIGNING PATTERNS TO COLORS

As mentioned, you can assign background colors to cells with the Range Attributes Color or Worksheet Global Attributes Color commands. When you print the contents of those cells, 1-2-3/G will print the background color as well, provided, of course, that you have a color printer. If not, 1-2-3/G will print a black and white shaded pattern that is assigned to that color.

The File Print Color Map command shows you black and white shading patterns that are associated with each displayed color. This command also allows you to change the pattern associated with a particular color. When you select the File Print Color Map command, 1-2-3/G displays the dialog box in Figure 8–11.

Each of the colors available in 1-2-3/G appears in blocks on the left side of the File Print Color Map dialog box. Each color block is assigned a letter (a

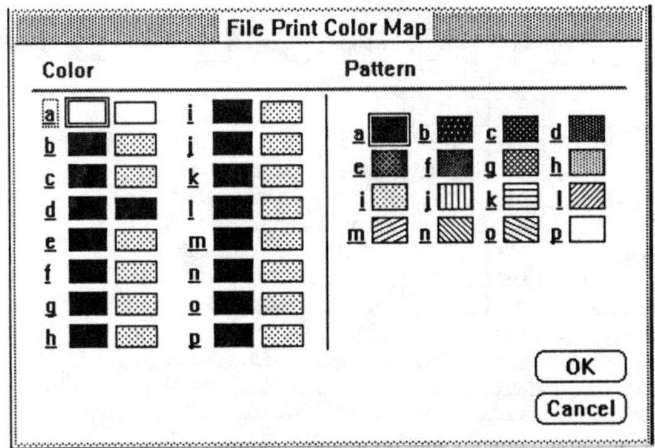

FIGURE 8–11 The File Print Color Map dialog box

> **Note**
>
> As mentioned, you can suppress the printing of colors or shading patterns. To do this, remove the X from the "Colors and shading" check box located in the "Display options" section of either the Print Printer or File Print Print Worksheet dialog boxes.

through p). Adjacent to each color block is a second block that shows the pattern assigned to that color. 1-2-3/G's available shading patterns appear on the right side of the File Print Color Map dialog box.

To change the pattern associated with a particular color block, begin by selecting that color block from the left side of the dialog box. To do this, either click your mouse on the color block or press its letter. To assign a pattern to that color, select the pattern you want from the right side of the dialog box. To do this, either click on the block that contains the pattern you want or press its letter. To complete the command, select the OK command button or press ENTER.

PRINTING COLUMN AND ROW HEADINGS

Many worksheet models have labels in the top row and leftmost column that identify the contents of each column and row. However, when you select a range to print that is far removed from these labels, your column and row titles are lost. To solve this problem, however, you can specify rows of data that will print along the top edge of each page. You can also specify columns of data that will print along the left edge of each page. When the final output is printed, 1-2-3/G will print the appropriate column and row titles for the columns and rows that are included in the print range. Using this technique, you can create a single-page or multiple-page printout that will have the appropriate column and row titles, regardless of the print range you select.

Note for Release 2 and 3 Users

In previous releases of 1-2-3, column and row headings are referred to as borders. In those releases, you select borders for printing with the Print Printer Options Borders command.

To select rows and/or columns of data that will print along the top and/or left edges of each page, you use the Headings section of the Print Printer or File Print Print Worksheet dialog box. For example, Figure 8–12 shows the File Print Print Worksheet dialog box with the row and column heading ranges already filled in. These row and column heading ranges apply to the highlighted range in the worksheet in Figure 8–13. When this range is printed, it will appear as in Figure 8–14.

To specify one or more rows of data that will print along the top edge of each page, select Headings. Then select Rows and specify the range that includes a

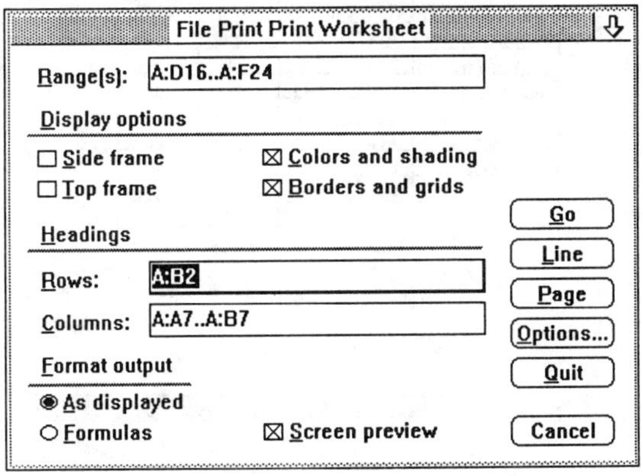

File Print Print Worksheet

Range(s): A:D16..A:F24

Display options

☐ Side frame ☒ Colors and shading

☐ Top frame ☒ Borders and grids

Headings

Rows: A:B2

Columns: A:A7..A:B7

Format output

◉ As displayed

○ Formulas ☒ Screen preview

Go | Line | Page | Options... | Quit | Cancel

FIGURE 8–12 The File Print Print Worksheet dialog box

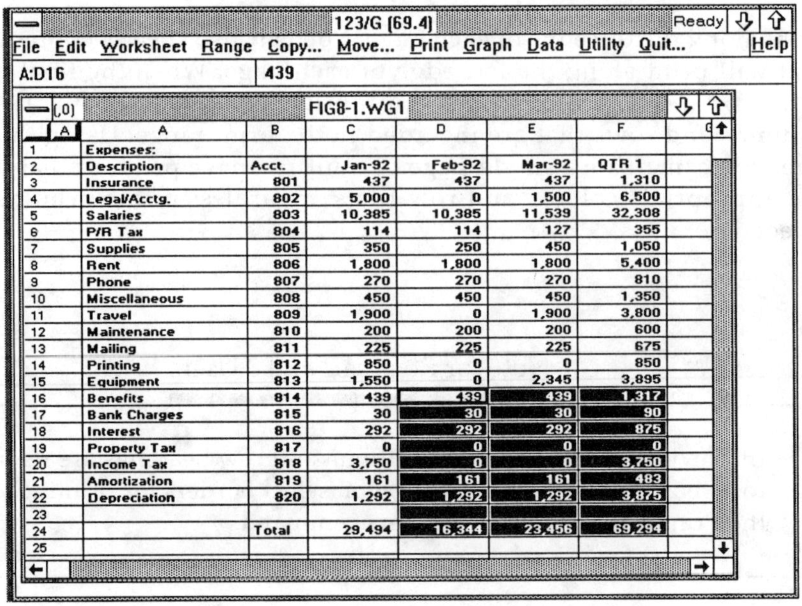

123/G [69.4] Ready

File Edit Worksheet Range Copy... Move... Print Graph Data Utility Quit... Help

A:D16 439

FIG8-1.WG1

A	A	B	C	D	E	F
1	Expenses:					
2	Description	Acct.	Jan-92	Feb-92	Mar-92	QTR 1
3	Insurance	801	437	437	437	1,310
4	Legal/Acctg.	802	5,000	0	1,500	6,500
5	Salaries	803	10,385	10,385	11,539	32,308
6	P/R Tax	804	114	114	127	355
7	Supplies	805	350	250	450	1,050
8	Rent	806	1,800	1,800	1,800	5,400
9	Phone	807	270	270	270	810
10	Miscellaneous	808	450	450	450	1,350
11	Travel	809	1,900	0	1,900	3,800
12	Maintenance	810	200	200	200	600
13	Mailing	811	225	225	225	675
14	Printing	812	850	0	0	850
15	Equipment	813	1,550	0	2,345	3,895
16	Benefits	814	439	439	439	1,317
17	Bank Charges	815	30	30	30	90
18	Interest	816	292	292	292	875
19	Property Tax	817	0	0	0	0
20	Income Tax	818	3,750	0	0	3,750
21	Amortization	819	161	161	161	483
22	Depreciation	820	1,292	1,292	1,292	3,875
23						
24		Total	29,494	16,344	23,456	69,294
25						

FIGURE 8–13 A range highlighted for printing

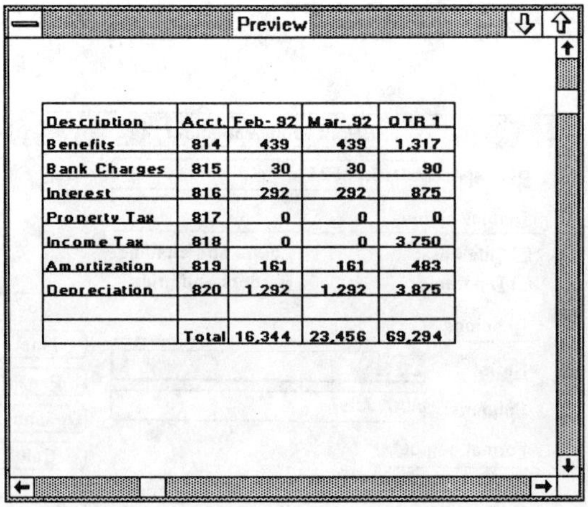

Preview

Description	Acct.	Feb-92	Mar-92	QTR 1
Benefits	814	439	439	1,317
Bank Charges	815	30	30	90
Interest	816	292	292	875
Property Tax	817	0	0	0
Income Tax	818	0	0	3,750
Amortization	819	161	161	483
Depreciation	820	1,292	1,292	3,875
	Total	16,344	23,456	69,294

FIGURE 8–14 The range in FIGURE 8–13 printed with column and row headings

single cell from each of the rows you want to use. For example, to print the row of dates (row 2) in Figure 8–13 along the top of each page, select any cell from row 2, for example cell A:B2. If you specify more than one row here, make sure they are adjacent rows. You cannot specify a collection in this text box.

To specify one or more columns of data that will print along the left edge of each page, select Headings and select Columns. In the adjacent text box, specify a range that includes a single cell from each of the columns you want to use. For example, to specify the columns of descriptions and account numbers in Figure 8–13 (columns A and B), specify the range A:A7..A:B7. Once again, the columns must be adjacent to one another. You cannot specify a collection here.

Note

Make sure the print range you select does not overlap the columns and/or rows you've selected as heading ranges. If there is an overlap, 1-2-3/G will print your column and row headings twice.

PRINTING, CELL FORMULAS

Normally, 1-2-3/G will print your data as it appears on your screen. However, you can also create a listing that shows you the contents and formatting of each cell. An example of such a listing appears in Figure 8–15, displayed in the Preview utility window. A listing like the one in Figure 8–15 can be useful for documenting an important worksheet.

To create a cell contents listing, begin by specifying the range you want to print in the Range(s) test box. Then, select the Formulas option button from the "Format output" section of the Print Printer or File Print Print Worksheet dialog box. Next, select the Go command button to queue the print job followed by the Quit command button to begin printing. 1-2-3/G creates a printout similar to the one in Figure 8–15.

The listing in Figure 8–15 shows the contents of each cell in the highlighted range A:D16..A:F24 of Figure 8–13. Each line in a cell contents listing can potentially include four items: the cell address; the formatting for the cell; the width of the cell; and finally the contents of the cell, in that order. The listing is presented row by row and only nonblank cells are listed. If the width or formatting for a cell matches the current global settings, no reference is made to the format or width of the cell. For example, the first entry in the listing in Figure 8–15 reads A:D16 (,0) 439. This identifies cell A:D16, formatted as Comma with 0 displayed decimal places, containing the number 439. No

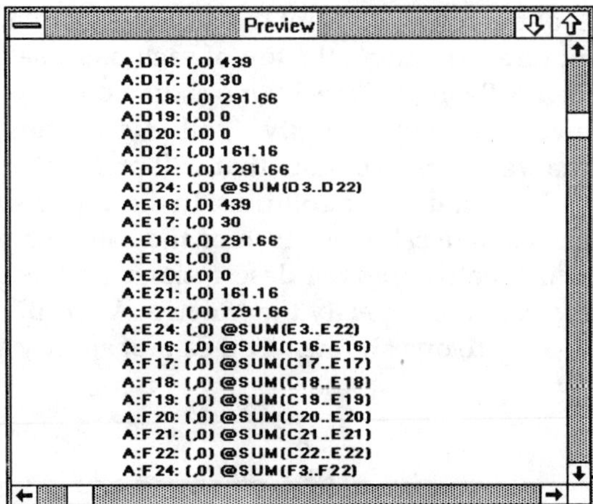

FIGURE 8–15 **A cell contents listing**

reference is made to the width of the cell, because the width of the column containing the cell matches the current global setting for the worksheet.

SPECIFYING ADDITIONAL PRINTING OPTIONS

As mentioned, before you send your printed output either to your printer or to file, you can specify various options that affect the print job as a whole. For example, you might want to specify a header or a footer that will print with each page or the number of copies of the document you want. To specify these options, you use the Options dialog box shown in Figure 8–16. This dialog box allows you to specify the following attributes for the current print job:

- Headers and footers.
- Number of copies.
- Print density (draft versus final.)
- Top, bottom, left, and right margins.
- A starting and stopping page for a multiple-page print job.
- A name for the current print settings. This allows you to quickly recall the current print settings at a later time.

To access the Options dialog box in Figure 8–16, you can use any one of the following five commands:

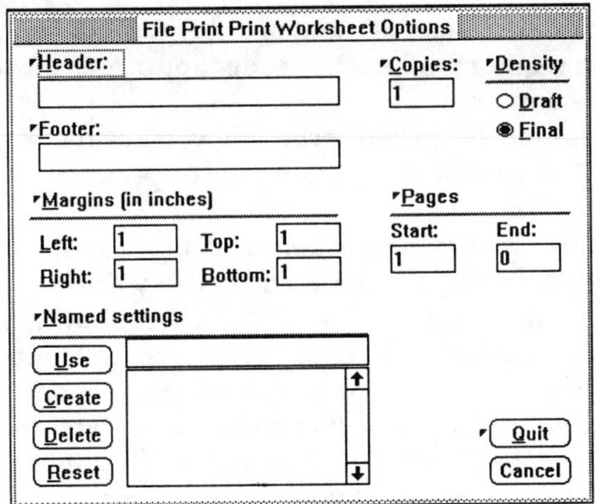

FIGURE 8–16 The Options dialog box

- Print Printer and select the Options command button.
- Print File and select the Options command button.
- Print Encoded and select the Options command button.
- File Print Print Worksheet and select the Options command button.
- File Print Options.

The Options dialog box shown in Figure 8–16 is always the same, regardless of how you access it. However, when you make a selection in the Options dialog box, that selection applies to all the Print and File Print commands. For example, imagine you select the File Print Options command to display the options dialog box. Next, you specify several print settings and select the Quit command to accept those settings and exit the dialog box. Then, you select the Print Printer command or the File Print Print Worksheet command and select the Options command button. 1-2-3/G displays the Options dialog with those exact same settings. However, those settings now apply to the Print Printer or File Print Print Worksheet command, depending on which one you are using.

The sections that follow show you how to use the various components of the Options dialog box to specify settings for the current print job. After you specify one or more settings, you can exit the Options dialog box and save those settings by selecting the Quit command button. To exit without saving any settings, select the Cancel command button.

Headers and Footers

Headers and footers are descriptive lines of text that appear at the top and/or bottom of each page. For example, a typical header or footer might include a page number, the name of the report, and possibly the date on which the report was printed. As you might imagine, the header appears at the top of each page and the footer at the bottom.

To specify a header for the current print job, you use the Header text box in the Options dialog box shown in Figure 8–16. To specify a footer, you use the Footer text box.

The conventions for specifying headers and footers are exactly the same. Therefore, the two will be discussed interchangeably throughout this section.

The maximum length of a header or footer is 512 characters, and you can include up to three entries in a header or footer. The first entry is left-aligned, the second is centered, and the third is right-aligned. Separate each of these entries with a split vertical bar (|). (On some computers this character may appear as a solid bar.) If a header or footer has only a single entry, that entry will appear left-aligned. However, if you precede that entry with a single split vertical bar, it will appear centered, and if you precede it with two split vertical bars, it will appear right-aligned.

To have sequential page numbers printed in a header or footer, you use the number sign (#). To print today's date, you use the at sign (@). You can precede either of these with text to identify them, for example Page # or Printed @. The date format used is Date 4 (mm/dd/yy), unless you specify otherwise with the User Settings International Date format command.

For example, imagine you are printing a budget analysis report. You might use the following as a header or footer:

```
Printed @|Budget Analysis|Page #
```

This causes the text string "Printed" followed by today's date to be left-aligned. The string "Budget Analysis" is centered, and the string "Page" followed by the current page number is right-aligned.

To begin printing with a specific page number, you can use the number sign twice (##) followed by the page number you want to begin with. For example, the entry **||Page ##10** will cause the string starting with "Page" to appear right-aligned and page numbering to start at 10.

Exact page numbers can also be defined in a header or footer. For example, the entry **||Page 10** will cause the entry "Page 10" to be right-aligned on the page.

To include more than one line in a header or footer, separate each line with a tilde (~). For example, you might use the following entry for a header or footer:

```
Budget Analysis||Page #~Confidential
```

This causes the string "Budget Analysis" to appear left-aligned and the string "Page" followed by the current page number appears right-aligned. In the second line of this header or footer, the string "Confidential" appears left-aligned.

You can also use the contents of a cell in a header of footer. To do this, use a \ (backslash) followed by a cell address or range name. For example, to use the contents of cell A100, type **\A100**. You must type the entry; you cannot type a backslash and point to it.

The backslash method allows you to include a date, other than the current system date, in a header or footer. It also allows you to display that date in a different format. For example, imagine you have the function @DATE(92,1,10) in cell A:E1. Imagine further that you have formatted that cell as Date 1 (DD-Mon-YY) using the Range Format Date 1 command. To display this date in a header or footer, you would use the entry \A:E1. When your report is printed, 1-2-3/G displays the date 10–Jan-92 as a left-aligned label.

If you use the backslash method to specify the contents of a cell as header or footer text, it must be the first entry in the footer. Additionally, you cannot specify a second backslash cell reference in a header or footer. However, you can precede the entry with one or two split vertical bars to control its alignment.

Note

If you use the backslash (\) cell address method of specifying header or footer text, 1-2-3/G does not update the Header or Footer text boxes when you move the data in the cell to another location. Therefore, your header or footer text is lost. For example, if you use Move, Edit Cut, Worksheet Insert, or Worksheet Delete to move the header or footer text, 1-2-3/G continues to refer to the cell you referenced in the Header or Footer text box.

Changing the Number of Copies

To change the number of copies printed by 1-2-3/G, you use the Copies text box in the Options dialog box, shown earlier in Figure 8–16. The default number of copies is one. However, you can specify as many copies as you want by changing the number in the Copies text box. The number of copies 1-2-3/G actually prints, however, is dependent on Presentation Manager's setting for the number of copies. The number that appears in the Copies text box is multiplied by the Presentation Manager setting. Therefore, if the Presentation Manager setting is two copies, and you specify four copies in the Copies text box, 1-2-3/G will print eight copies.

Changing Print Density

Some printers offer both a draft and a letter quality, or near letter quality, setting. The draft text is of poorer quality, but printing takes less time. If your printer offers both a draft and letter quality, or near letter quality, setting (and the printer driver you are using supports that feature) 1-2-3/G allows you to take advantage of it.

To select a draft printing mode, you use the Density section of the Options dialog box shown in Figure 8–16. This section has two option buttons, Draft and Final. The Final option button is the default. When this option button is selected, 1-2-3/G prints all data, grid lines, cell borders, multiple fonts, and so on in the highest quality print your printer has to offer. However, if you select the Draft option button, 1-2-3/G prints only raw data using your printer's lowest quality text. The result is a poorer quality printout, but it is printed faster.

Printing Part of a Report

1-2-3/G also allows you to select specific pages on which to start and stop printing. To specify starting and stopping pages, you use the Pages section of the Options dialog box in Figure 8–16. In the Start text box, specify the page number on which you want to start printing. In the End text box, specify the number of the last page, on which you want to end printing. To print from the starting page all the way to the end of a report, specify a 0 in the End text box. For example, imagine you only want to print pages 7 through 10 of a 10 page report. To do this, specify the number 7 in the Start text box and 0 or 10 in the End text box.

Changing the Margins

Margin settings determine the amount of white space between the edges of the paper and your document. 1-2-3/G allows you to specify a setting for the top, bottom, left, and right margins.

1-2-3/G measures margins in inches (or millimeters, depending on the Utility User Settings International Measurement setting). The default setting for the top, bottom, left, and right margins is 1 inch. Margins are measured from the edge of the page to the edge of your document.

To change the margin settings, you use the Margins section of the Options dialog box in Figure 8–16. To change a specific margin, select the text box that corresponds to that margin and type a new value for the margin. For example, to change the left margin to 1–1/2 inches (meaning 1–1/2 inches from the left side of the paper), select Left and type the number 1.5 in the adjacent text box. Press ENTER to confirm your entry. You can specify a number with up to three places after the decimal.

1-2-3/G uses the margin settings you specify to position your output on the printed page. Margin settings also affect the amount of data that will fit on a page, and therefore, where 1-2-3/G ends one page and begins the next one. See "Printing a Large Report," earlier in this chapter for a discussion of how 1-2-3/G uses the current margin settings to break up a large print range into multiple pages.

Note

To see the impact that the current margin settings will have on your printed document, use the Preview utility covered later in this chapter. This utility allows you to view each of your pages before printing them.

Named Settings

1-2-3/G allows you to save the current print settings under a name. Thus, you can create several different sets of named print settings for the current worksheet file and quickly recall a given set whenever you need it. To create named settings, you use the "Named settings" section of the Options dialog box shown earlier in Figure 8–16. This section allows you to assign a name to the current print settings, use existing named settings, and delete named settings.

To assign a name to the current print settings, select the Create command button. 1-2-3/G activates the "Named settings" text box. Type the name you want to use for the settings and press ENTER. 1-2-3/G assigns the name you specified to the current print settings and places that name in the list box below.

To reuse an existing set of named settings, select the Use command button. 1-2-3/G activates the "Named settings" text box. Either type the name of the settings you want to use or select the name from the list box below. 1-2-3/G replaces the current print settings with named settings. If you have not as yet assigned a name to the current print settings, they are lost.

To delete a specific set of named settings, select the Delete command button. 1-2-3/G activates the "Named settings" text box. Either type the name you want to delete or select it from the list box below. Press ENTER to complete your selection. 1-2-3/G deletes the named settings you specified.

Note

If a particular named setting is highlighted in the list box, 1-2-3/G will delete it when you select Delete. Therefore, it is a good practice to select the Use command button first to select a set of named settings before you select Delete.

To delete all the current named settings, select the Reset command button. 1-2-3/G deletes all the named settings in the Named settings list box and reverts to using the most recent print settings.

About Headers, Footers, and Margins in Previous Releases

As you know, 1-2-3/G measures the top, bottom left and right margins in inches (or millimeters) from the edge of the paper. This is a significant departure from previous release of 1-2-3. For example, in 1-2-3 Releases 2 and 3, the top and bottom margins are measured in standard lines (about 6 lines per vertical inch). On the other hand, the left and right margins are measured in characters (about 10 characters per horizontal inch).

Due to this character-based measurement system in previous releases, it is very easy to establish hard and fast rules as to the number of lines that will fit on a page. For example, the default number of lines per page in Release 2 or 3 is 66 lines. The default top and bottom margins consume two lines each. In addition, three lines are reserved at the top and bottom of each page for headers and footers. Therefore, a total of 10 lines are consumed by margins, headers, and footers. This leaves room for 56 lines of text in the body of the document.

It is also easy in Releases 2 and 3 to predict the number of characters that will fit on each line. For example, the default left margin is four characters and the default right margin is 76 characters. Both are measured in standard characters (about 10 per inch) from the left edge of the page. Therefore, the default right margin setting of 76 characters, less the default left margin setting of four characters, allows you to print 72 characters on each line. Thus, if you are printing a worksheet range that is eight columns wide at nine characters per column, you can fit all eight columns across the page.

However, in 1-2-3/G, things are not quite so straightforward. In 1-2-3/G you can specify different type styles and sizes (fonts) for the text in the body of a document. In addition, you can specify multiple-line headers and footers. Therefore, the number of characters across the page and the number of lines down are constantly subject to change. Under these circumstances, it becomes necessary to measure the top, bottom, left, and right margins in inches rather than characters. Further, it can be very difficult to predict the amount of data that will fit on each page. In fact, about the only way that you can get an accurate indication of the amount of data that will fit on each page with the current settings is to use the Preview utility covered in the next section.

1-2-3/G does, however, account for the character-based measurement system in previous releases. For example, when you open a 1-2-3 Release 2 (.WK1) or Release 3 (.WK3) file in 1-2-3/G window, 1-2-3/G converts the right margin setting for that file to inches (assuming 10 characters per inch). If the right print margin is less than 80 characters in the orginal file, 1-2-3/G assumes a page size that is 8.5 inches across. On the other hand, if the right margin setting is greater than 80 characters, 1-2-3/G assumes a page size of 14 inches across.

Conversely, when you save a file in .WK1 (Release 2) or .WK3 (Release 3) format, 1-2-3/G converts inches to characters. If the right margin is less than 8 inches, 1-2-3/G assumes a page size that is 8.5 inches across when saving the file. On the other hand, if the right margin is greater than 8 inches, 1-2-3/G assumes a page size that is 14 inches across when saving the file.

USING THE PREVIEW UTILITY

To preview a print job before you print it, use the Preview utility. This utility has its own menu and occupies its own window. Initially, the Preview utility shows you the pages of your output in miniature. To preview a specific page, you can zoom in on it (increase its displayed size). If you discover a problem, you can return to the worksheet and fix it. Otherwise, you can send the data directly from the Preview utility window to your printer or to a file.

To activate the Preview utility, select the Screen preview check box from either the Print Printer, Print Encoded, or the File Print Print Worksheet dialog boxes. Then, select Go followed by Quit. 1-2-3/G displays the Preview window overtop of the current worksheet. Figure 8–17 shows an example of what the Preview window looks like.

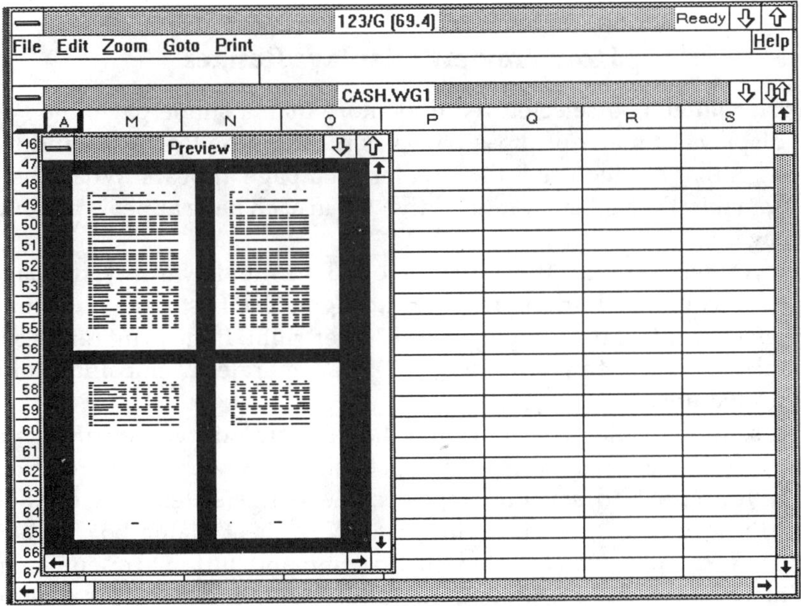

FIGURE 8–17 The Preview utility window

As mentioned, the Preview utility has its own menu. This menu allows you to perform the following:

- Zoom in (increase the displayed size) on pages in the Preview window (Zoom).
- Move around the Preview window (Goto).
- Remove a range from the Preview window (Edit).
- Print the contents of the Preview window (Print).
- Create new files and open existing files in separate windows, change the current directory, and manage the desktop (File).

The layout of the Preview utility screen is relatively straightforward. The Preview menu appears in the menu bar at the top of you screen. To the right of this menu, 1-2-3/G displays a Help box that gives you access to context-sensitive help for the Preview utility. To access help, press HELP (F1) or click on the Help text box.

Immediately below the menu bar is the control line. On the left side of the control line, 1-2-3/G shows both the current page and the total number of pages in the print job. As you move from page to page in the Preview window, 1-2-3/G updates this listing. That way, you know where you are at all times. On the right side of the Control line, 1-2-3/G shows the current print range. However, if you send more than one print range to the Preview utility (you selected Go for several different print ranges before selecting Quit), 1-2-3/G only shows you the first print range in the control line.

How Preview Displays Ranges

If the print range you selected requires more than a single page, the Preview utility displays as many of those pages as it can in the Preview window. The more pages that are required, the smaller each page appears. When the pages become smaller than a 1-inch square, the text in each page appears as a blurred, gray image.

When you send a multiple-page print job to the Preview utility, the pages are arranged in columns working from left to right. The first page appears in the upper-left corner and the last page in the lower-right. If the print range consists of a single column with many rows, 1-2-3/G separates each column of pages with a dotted line.

If you send multiple print ranges to the Preview utility, they are displayed one right after the other in the order in which they were sent. For example, imagine you specified several ranges in the Range(s) text box of the Print Printer, Print Encoded, or File Print Print Worksheet dialog box. In between specifying each range, you selected the Go command button to queue each print job. When you select the Quit command to send them to the preview utility, they are displayed in the Preview window similar to the arrangement in Figure 8–18.

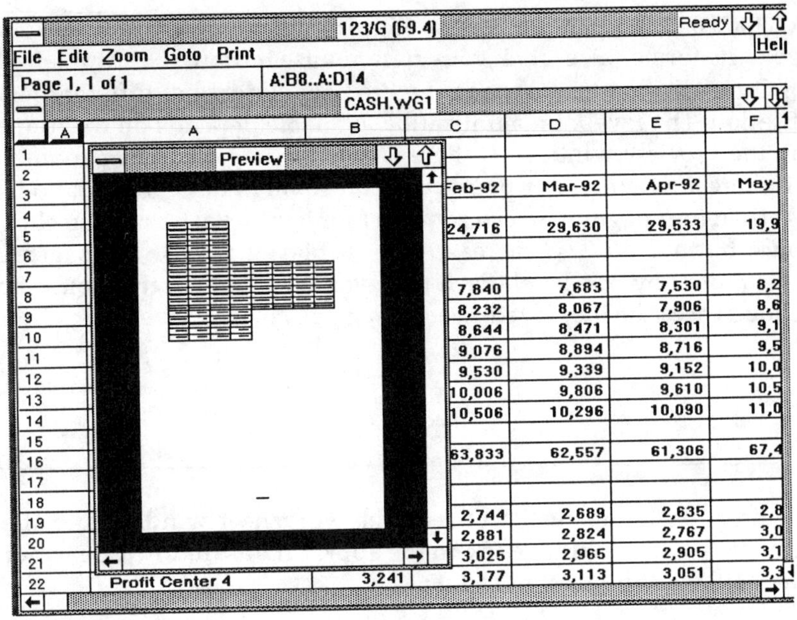

FIGURE 8–18 The Preview window after printing multiple ranges

Notice that there is no separation between the print ranges in Figure 8–18. To separate consecutive ranges when printing, you can select the Line or Page command buttons before you select the Go command button to queue each range. When you select Line, 1-2-3/G advances the printer by a single line, resulting in a blank line at the end of the current print range. When you select page, 1-2-3/G ends the current page, causing the next print range to begin on a new page.

Moving Around the Preview Window

You can move around the preview window by using your mouse or your keyboard. Both methods are discussed in the sections that follow.

With the Mouse

To move around the Preview window with your mouse, use the scroll bars at the right and bottom edges of the Preview window. To preview a specific page, move the mouse pointer to any page in the Preview window. When you do this, the shape of the mouse pointer is transformed to the shape of a magnifying glass. The page you've selected is also identified on the left side of the Control Line. To zoom in on that specific page, click your left mouse button. 1-2-3/G increases the displayed size of the page. To move around within that page, use the scroll bars on the right and bottom edges of the Preview window. To return the page to its former size, click your right mouse button.

1-2-3/G can display the pages in the Preview window at different levels of magnification. The level of magnification available depends on the number of pages in the Preview window. If there is a single page, you can zoom in two levels. If there are two to four pages, you can zoom in three levels, and if there are more than four pages, you can zoom in four levels. Each time you click your left mouse button, 1-2-3/G increases the displayed size of the pages in the preview window by one level. Each time you click your right mouse button, 1-2-3/G decreases the displayed size of the pages by one level.

Note

To move back and forth between the worksheet window and the Preview window, either click on the appropriate window title bar or press NEXT WINDOW (CTRL-F6).

With Keyboard

To move around the Preview window by using your keyboard, you must use a combination of the Zoom and Goto commands in conjunction with the arrow keys. To begin, select the Zoom command. 1-2-3/G displays the following menu:

- **Farthest:** Reduces the size of the pages in the window to the smallest size.
- **Out**: Reduces the size of the pages in the window to the next smallest size and centers the view in the middle of the Preview window.
- **Page:** Displays the pages in the window at about the size of one full page and centers the view in the middle of the Preview window.
- **In:** Increases the size of pages in the window to the next largest size and centers the view in the middle of the Preview window.
- **Closest**: Increases the size of the pages in the window to the largest size available and centers the view in the middle of the Preview window. The data in each page is displayed at about the same size as it is displayed in the worksheet.

Select from the Page, In, or Closest options to increase the page size to the level you want. If you're not sure at first, select "In" several times to increase the page size one level at a time. When you're ready to Preview a specific page, select the Goto command. 1-2-3/G displays the following menu:

- **Home**: Moves to the first page (upper left).
- **Up**: Up one page.
- **Down**: Down one page.
- **Left:** Left one page.
- **Right:** Right one page.
- **End**: Moves to the last page (lower right).

Use these Goto command options to focus the view of the Preview window on the page(s) you want. To move around within a specific page, use the arrow keys.

Once you have increased the displayed size of the pages in the Preview window you can press HOME to move to the first page or END to move to the last page. You can also press PGDN to move down one page or PGUP to move up one page. In addition, you can use the use the ↑, ↓, →, and ← keys to gradually move from one page to the next.

Printing from Preview

If you like what you see in the Preview window, you can send the data to your printer or to an encoded file. To do this, select the Print command from the Preview menu. This command has one option, Printer. When you select this option, 1-2-3/G sends the range(s) in the Preview window to the OS/2 print queue. Where it gets sent from there depends on how you accessed the Preview utility. For example, if you accessed the Preview utility from the Print Printer or File Print Print Worksheet dialog box, the data is sent to your printer. On the other hand, if you accessed the Preview Utility from the Print Encoded dialog box, or you selected File Print Destination Encoded and then selected File Print Print Worksheet, the data is sent to an encoded file.

Correcting Errors

There are two methods you can use to correct any errors you discover while previewing pages in the Preview window. Both methods involve removing the affected print range from the Preview window. You can then return to the worksheet, correct the error, and reprint the data to the Preview window.

The most obvious method of clearing a range from the Preview window is to close the Preview window (removing all ranges), return to the worksheet, and start all over again. To do this, press CTRL-F4 or click on the Window Control box (or press ALT-HYPHEN) and select Close from the menu that appears. 1-2-3/G closes the Preview window and you are automatically returned to the worksheet. You can now make the necessary changes and preview the corrected print range again.

Alternatively, you can use the undo feature to remove the last print range sent to the Preview window, but leave the preview window open. To remove the last print range sent to the Preview window, select the Edit command from the Preview menu. This command has a single option, Undo. When you select

Undo, 1-2-3/G removes the last print range sent to the Preview window. Pressing ALT-BACKSPACE has the same effect. If the range you removed is the only range in the Preview window, the window goes blank (gray), but the Preview window remains open.

Once you have removed a print range from the Preview window, you can return to the worksheet, correct any errors, and reprint the range. To return to the worksheet, click on the title bar of the worksheet window, or press NEXT WINDOW (CTRL-F6). Once you are back in the worksheet window, you can correct any errors you may have discovered while in Preview. To reprint the range, select Print Printer or File Print Print Worksheet.

Using Preview's File Command

Consistent with the Design of 1-2-3/G, the Preview utility gives you access to the File menu. You can use this menu to select the File New, File Open, File Directory, File Print, and File Utility commands. The File New and File Open commands allow you to create new files or open existing files in other windows. The File Print command allows you to access the File Print Status command. As you may recall from earlier in this chapter, this command allows you to view the status of current and pending 1-2-3/G print jobs. You can use this command to stop the current print job, suspend it temporarily, or delete pending print jobs. Finally, the File Utility command allows you to manage the 1-2-3/G desktop.

Printing a Graph and a Worksheet Together

In much the same way that you can send print ranges from a worksheet window to the Preview utility, you can also send the contents of a graph window to the Preview utility. In this way, you can print a graph and a worksheet together on the same page.

Figure 8–19 shows a sample worksheet containing sales data by quarter over a period of five years. Figure 8–20 shows a graph created from the data in Figure 8–19. Finally, Figure 8–21 shows the graph and the worksheet appearing on the same page in the Preview window. When you select Preview's Print Printer command to print this document, the graph and the worksheet will appear on the same page.

To set up the Preview window as shown in Figure 8–21, begin by creating the worksheet in Figure 8–19. When you're ready, use the Graph command to create the graph in Figure 8–20. For information on how to use the Graph command and the Graph Tool to create a graph, see Chapter 7, "Graphs." Once the graph is created, select File Print Print Graph from the Graph tool menu. 1-2-3/G displays the File Print Print Graph dialog box. From this dialog box, select the "Half page" option, so that the graph only occupies half a page when printed. Then, select the "Screen preview" check box, so that the print job is sent to the Preview window. Finally, select the Print command button to begin

123G.EXE (69.4) Ready

File Edit Worksheet Range Copy... Move... Print Graph Data Utility Quit... Help

A:A1

GDATA.WG1

A	A	B	C	D	E	F	G
1			Sales By Quarter				
2			In Millions				
3	Year	Quarter 1	Quarter 2	Quarter 3	Quarter 4	Total	
4	1991	25	22	24	29	100	
5	1992	28	24	26	32	110	
6	1993	30	27	29	35	121	
7	1994	33	29	32	39	133	
8	1995	37	32	35	42	146	
9							
10							

FIGURE 8–19 A sample worksheet

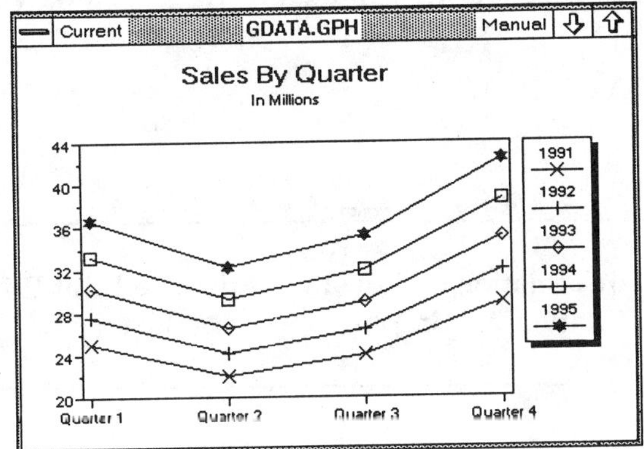

FIGURE 8–20 A graph created by using the data in FIGURE 8–19

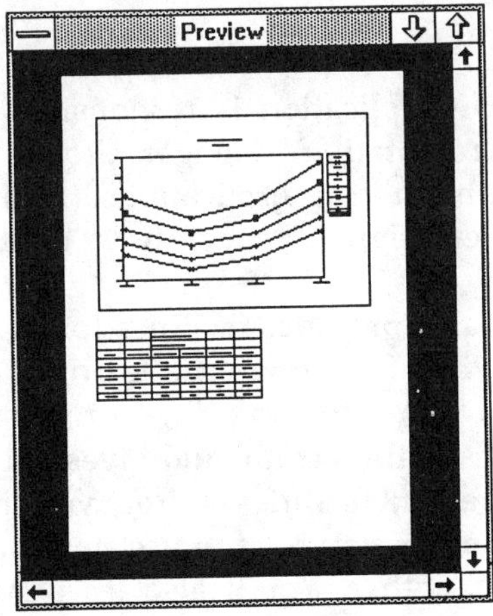

FIGURE 8–21 A worksheet range and a graph in the Preview window

printing. 1-2-3/G sends the contents of the graph window to the Preview window.

To send the data in the worksheet window in Figure 8–19 to the Preview window as well, click on the title bar for the worksheet or press NEXT WINDOW (CTRL-F6) to move to it. 1-2-3/G activates the worksheet window and displays the Worksheet Tool menu. Select File Print Print Worksheet. In the Range(s) text box, specify the range that contains the worksheet data (A:A1..A:F8). Select the "Screen preview" check box to send the data to the Preview window. Then select the Line command button several times to leave blank lines between the worksheet range and the graph. Finally, select Go followed by Quit. 1-2-3/G sends the worksheet range to the Preview window as shown in Figure 8–21.

To print the graph and the worksheet together, select Print Printer from the Preview menu. 1-2-3/G sends the contents of the Preview window to your printer.

Note

For additional information on how to use the File Print Print Graph command, see Chapter 7, "Graphs."

PRINTER CONTROL

Unlike DOS, where each application is responsible for providing its own printer drivers, OS/2 Presentation Manager allows you to install a single printer driver for use with multiple applications. (Printer drivers are software programs that tell Presentation Manager how to interact with a specific printer.)

Presentation Manager also provides facilities for managing printer drivers. For example, you can switch from one printer driver to another and activate specific features offered by a particular printer driver.

1-2-3/G's File Print Destination command gives you access to Presentation Manager's printer management facilities without your having to leave 1-2-3/G. The sections that follow show you how to use this command to change from one installed printer to another. You'll also learn how to activate specific printing features offered by a sample printer driver that drives a Hewlett Packard LaserJet printer.

Printing with different fonts is also related to the printer driver you happen to be using. That is, a given printer driver may offer fonts in addition to those that are initially available through Presentation Manager. To take advantage of those fonts, however, you must install them in 1-2-3/G. A brief discussion of printing with different fonts appears toward the end of this section.

Changing Printers

To select a different printer you use the File Print Destination command. When you select this command, 1-2-3/G displays the dialog box in Figure 8–22. In the list box 1-2-3/G shows the names of the printers that you've installed for Presentation Manager. The name of the printer currently in use is highlighted. To select a different printer, click on the name of that printer or highlight it, and select the OK command button or press ENTER. 1-2-3/G returns you to the worksheet and will now use the printer you specified both for printing and for creating encoded files.

For a printer to be listed in the File Print Destination list box, you must install a driver for that printer by using Presentation Manager, not 1-2-3/G. For information on how to install a printer driver, refer to the documentation that came with your copy of Presentation Manager.

Specifying Printing Properties

Once you've installed a printer for Presentation Manager, you can use the File Print Destination command to activate specific printing properties supported by that printer. For example, if your printer supports properties such as landscape (sideways) printing or manual feed, you can turn these properties on or off.

The File Print Destination dialog box does not in itself allow you to control the printing properties of a particular printer. Instead, it gives you access to the Presentation Manager dialog boxes that control the operation of installed printers. To access these Presentation Manager dialog boxes, first select the name of the printer whose operation you want to control from the File Print Destination list box (Figure 8–22) then select the Setup command button.

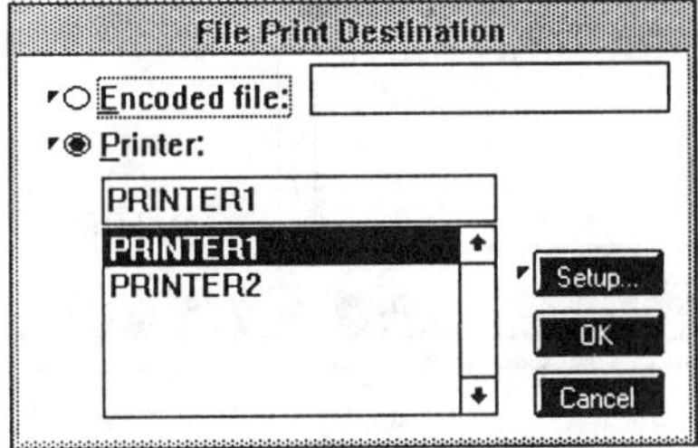

FIGURE 8–22 The File Print Destination dialog box.

When you select the Setup command button, 1-2-3/G shows you the Presentation Manager dialog boxes that correspond to the specific printer you selected. The content of the dialog boxes displayed may vary depending on the printer you selected. However, you can use these dialog boxes to activate specific features for the selected printer.

Figure 8–23 shows a sample Presentation Manager dialog box that was accessed by selecting File Print Destination Setup. This Printer Properties dialog box corresponds to an HP (Hewlett Packard) LaserJet Classic printer driver capable of running the HP Series II printer. This printer offers numerous features, including the ability to print in landscape mode (sideways) and to accept pages that are fed manually.

To specify landscape printing or manual feed for the LaserJet Printer, select the Jobs command button from the dialog box in Figure 8–23. Presentation Manager displays the dialog box in Figure 8–24. To specify landscape (sideways) printing, select the Landscape option button from the Orientation section of the dialog box in Figure 8–24. To specify manual feed, select the Manual option button from the "Paper feed" section. To save these settings, select the OK command button. Presentation Manager returns you to the dialog box in Figure 8–23. Select the OK command button from this dialog box. Presentation Manager returns you to 1-2-3/G's File Print Destination dialog box. Select the OK command button from this dialog box to return to the worksheet.

The File Print Destination Setup command simply gives you access to Presentation Manager's Printer Properties, Job Properties, and Options dialog boxes. These dialog boxes allow you to activate specific printing properties for a particular installed printer. As mentioned, the options available in these dialog boxes may vary according to the specific printer driver you've installed. Therefore, the dialog boxes in Figures 8–23 and 8–24 are shown solely as examples

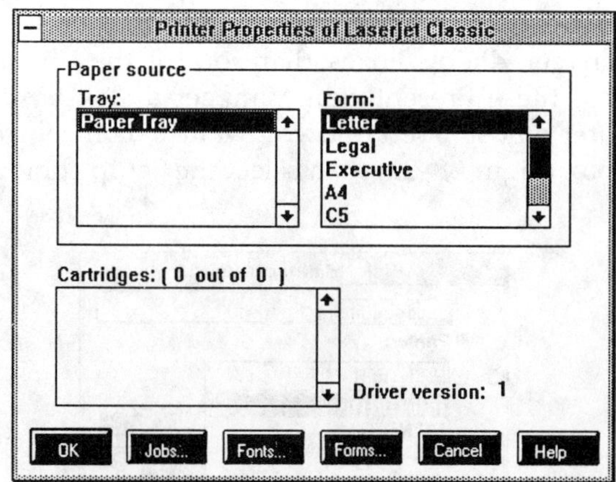

FIGURE 8–23 The Printer Properties dialog box for the HP LaserJet printer driver

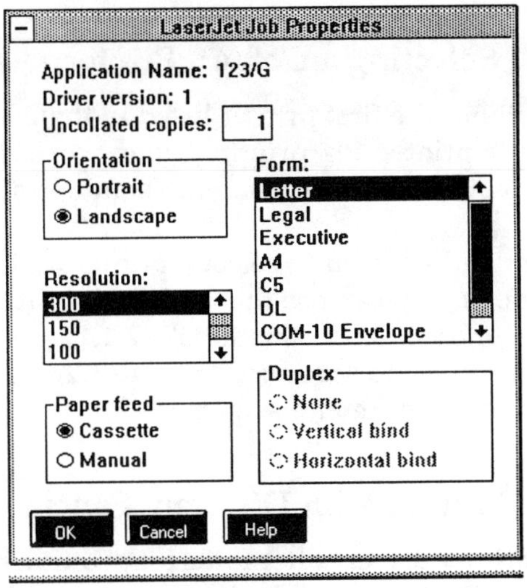

LaserJet Job Properties

Application Name: 123/G
Driver version: 1
Uncollated copies: 1

Orientation
Portrait
Landscape

Form:
Letter
Legal
Executive
A4
C5
DL
COM-10 Envelope

Resolution:
300
150
100

Duplex
None
Vertical bind
Horizontal bind

Paper feed
Cassette
Manual

OK Cancel Help

FIGURE 8–24 **The Jobs dialog box for the HP LaserJet printer driver**

of how you might select specific printing properties for a particular installed printer.

Be aware that when you make a printer settings change with File Print Destination Setup, Presentation Manager records that change as the default setting for that printer. In fact, if you leave 1-2-3/G (or Presentation Manager) and restart it again, Presentation Manager will use those same settings to print your work. Therefore, unless you intend to use those settings permanently, make sure you use the File Print Destination Setup command a second time to change those settings back to the way they were.

Note

Do not use the File Print Destination Setup command in a macro. This command takes you back to Presentation Manager temporarily and your macro will simply stop executing at that point. Instead, use the {SYSTEM} command. This command allows you to exit 1-2-3/G temporarily and run an OS/2 program or batch file. For example, if you're running OS/2 Version 1.2, the macro command {SYSTEM PMSPOOL} exits 1-2-3/G temporarily and runs the PMSPOOL.EXE file. This file displays the Print Manager on your screen. You can then use the Print Manager's menus to change the settings for a particular installed printer. When you close the Print Manager window, you are returned to 1-2-3/G.

Selecting a Default Printer

Normally, 1-2-3/G will use the first printer listed in the File Print Destination List box as the default printer for printing your work. However, through Presentation Manager you can select a different default printer that will be used by 1-2-3/G.

Presentation Manager allows you to select a printer that will be used as the default by all applications. You can use this built-in feature to specify a printer driver that 1-2-3/G supports. To do this in OS/2 1.1, use the Control Panel, Setup, Printer Defaults command sequence. In OS/2 1.2, use the Print Manager, Setup, Application Defaults command sequence.

Printing with Different Fonts

As mentioned, some printer drivers offer fonts for printing in addition to those made available through Presentation Manager. To print with these fonts from 1-2-3/G, however, you must install them in 1-2-3/G. For example, when you install IBM OS/2 Presentation Manager Version 1.2, four type styles are automatically installed for you—Helvetica, Times Roman, Courier, and System Proportional. System Proportional aside, all of these type styles come in varying point sizes and all of them can be used to display and print your data. However, if your printer driver offers additional fonts, you must set up 1-2-3/G to recognize them.

As you may recall from Chapter 3, you can select a font for printing a given worksheet by using the Worksheet Global Attributes Font command. Further, you can select a font for printing a given range by using the Range Attributes Font command. Formatting worksheets and ranges with these commands is discussed in detail in Chapter 3, "Formatting Worksheets." However, a brief review of how to choose printer fonts with these commands follows.

The Worksheet Global Attributes Font and Range Attributes font commands display essentially the same dialog boxes. Therefore, the two commands will be discussed almost interchangeably throughout this section.

When you select the Worksheet Global Attributes Font command, 1-2-3/G displays the dialog box in Figure 8–25. 1-2-3/G shows you essentially the same dialog box when you select the Range Attributes Font command. In this dialog box, the Fonts list box contains 20 slots (a-t), each containing a screen font and a printer font. The screen font appears on the left and the printer font appears on the right. When you select a font from a given slot for formatting a worksheet or range, 1-2-3/G will display your data on screen using the screen font and will print your data using the printer font.

To change the printer fonts displayed in the Fonts list box in Figure 8–25, you select the Setup command button. When you select this button, 1-2-3/G shows you the dialog box in Figure 8–26. The Fonts list box appears again in this dialog box, showing you the same screen and printer fonts as in the previous dialog box. To select a different printer font for a given slot, first select the slot (a–t) that you want to change. Then select the Printer button from the Device section.

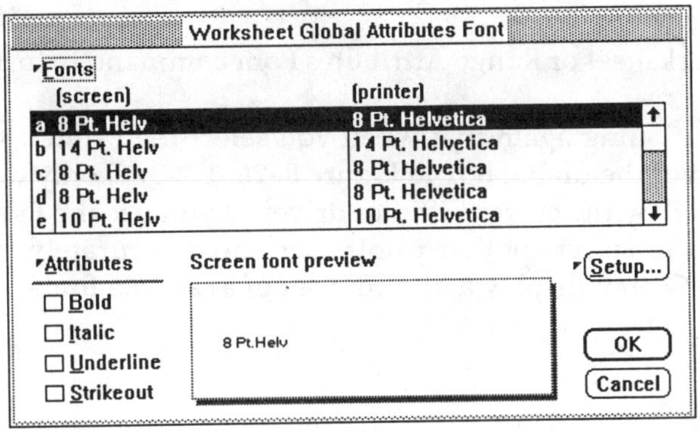

Worksheet Global Attributes Font

Fonts

	[screen]	[printer]
a	8 Pt. Helv	8 Pt. Helvetica
b	14 Pt. Helv	14 Pt. Helvetica
c	8 Pt. Helv	8 Pt. Helvetica
d	8 Pt. Helv	8 Pt. Helvetica
e	10 Pt. Helv	10 Pt. Helvetica

Attributes: Bold, Italic, Underline, Strikeout

Screen font preview: 8 Pt.Helv

Setup... OK Cancel

FIGURE 8–25 The Worksheet Global Attributes Font dialog box

1-2-3/G displays the font types that are supported by the current printer driver in the "Font type" list box. When you select a font type from this list box, 1-2-3/G displays the point sizes available for that font in the "Point size" list box. Select the point size you want from this list box. To complete the change, select the Change command button followed by the OK command button. 1-2-3/G substitutes the printer font you selected on the right side (the printer side) of the appropriate slot and returns you to the previous dialog box. You can then complete the Worksheet Global Attributes Font command to format

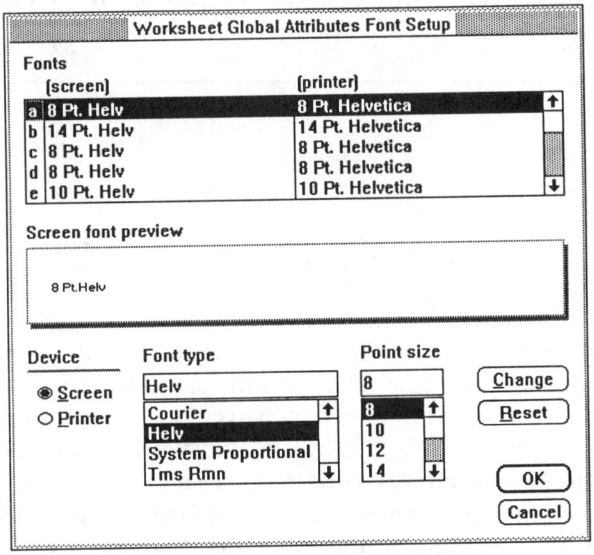

Worksheet Global Attributes Font Setup

Fonts

	[screen]	[printer]
a	8 Pt. Helv	8 Pt. Helvetica
b	14 Pt. Helv	14 Pt. Helvetica
c	8 Pt. Helv	8 Pt. Helvetica
d	8 Pt. Helv	8 Pt. Helvetica
e	10 Pt. Helv	10 Pt. Helvetica

Screen font preview: 8 Pt.Helv

Device: Screen, Printer

Font type: Helv — Courier, Helv, System Proportional, Tms Rmn

Point size: 8 — 8, 10, 12, 14

Change Reset OK Cancel

FIGURE 8–26 The Worksheet Global Attributes Font Setup dialog box

the current worksheet or Range Attributes Font command to format the current selection.

It bears mentioning again that when you select the Printer button from the Device section of the dialog box in Figure 8–26, 1-2-3/G only displays the font types supported by the current printer driver. If you use the File Print Destination command to select another printer (or, more accurately, another printer driver), 1-2-3/G may display a different set of available fonts.

Note

> The printer fonts with which you format a range or worksheet can have an impact on print time. Many printers, such as the HP LaserJet, have resident fonts. Resident fonts are either burned into the printer's memory or are provided by a cartridge that plugs into the printer. When you print a 1-2-3/G range that is formatted with a printer font that is not a resident font, the current printer driver must either create a bitmap of the characters included in the range or send the appropriate instructions to the printer to "build" the characters. This can be a time-consuming process. For this reason, printing with resident fonts is generally faster than printing with nonresident fonts that are made available either through Presentation Manager or through a particular printer driver. Therefore, if print speed is an issue, consider formatting the print range in a font that is resident to your printer.

USING PAGE BREAKS

As an alternative to having 1-2-3/G choose where to end one page and start the next, you can insert a page break symbol into the worksheet. A page break symbol is simply a split vertical bar followed by two colons, |::. (On some computers the split vertical bar may be displayed as a solid vertical bar.) When 1-2-3/G encounters a page break symbol, it ends the current page and starts a new one.

To insert a page break symbol, you can use the Worksheet Page Break command or you can insert the page break manually. If you select the Worksheet Page Break command, 1-2-3/G inserts a new row into the worksheet above the location of the cell pointer and places a page break symbol in the cell that is immediately above the current cell. 1-2-3/G updates all range name definitions and cell references in formulas to accommodate the new row.

If you select a multiple-cell range prior to using Worksheet Page Break, 1-2-3/G only inserts a partial row into the worksheet. Thus, the position of data outside the selected range remains unaffected.

To avoid inserting a new row into the worksheet, simply move the cell pointer to where you want the page break symbol, type **|::**, and press ENTER. 1-2-3/G places a page break symbol in the worksheet in the cell that contains the cell pointer.

Page break symbols must be located in the first column of the print range. Otherwise, 1-2-3/G will interpret the page break symbol as a label and print it. In addition, be aware that any data located in the same row as the page break symbol will not be printed.

Figure 8–27 shows a page break symbol in cell A:A29. This page break was inserted manually, so as to avoid inserting a new row. When this page break symbol is encountered in a print range, 1-2-3/G will end the current page at row 29 and start a new page.

When you enter a page break symbol in a row, that page break applies to the entire row. This may cause more than one page break to occur in a given print job. For example, as you may recall from earlier in this chapter, 1-2-3/G prints your work in sets of columns. It will complete printing all the rows in the first set of columns before moving on to the next set of columns. If the row containing the page break symbol occurs in both the first and any subsequent sets of columns, 1-2-3/G initiates a page break whenever that row is encountered.

123/G (69.4) Ready

File Edit Worksheet Range Copy... Move... Print Graph Data Utility Quit... Help

A:A29 |::

CASH.WG1

A	A	B	C	D	E	F
19	Profit Center 1	2,800	2,744	2,689	2,635	2,8
20	Profit Center 2	2,940	2,881	2,824	2,767	3,0
21	Profit Center 3	3,087	3,025	2,965	2,905	3,1
22	Profit Center 4	3,241	3,177	3,113	3,051	3,3
23	Profit Center 5	3,403	3,335	3,269	3,203	3,5
24	Profit Center 6	3,574	3,502	3,432	3,363	3,7
25	Profit Center 7	3,752	3,677	3,604	3,532	3,8
26	Direct Labor	13,027	12,767	12,511	12,261	13,4
27						
28	Total COGS	35,825	35,108	34,406	33,718	37,0
29	::					
30	Expenses:					
31	Insurance	437	437	437	437	4
32	Legal/Acctg.	5,000	0	1,500	5,000	
33	Salaries	10,385	10,385	11,539	10,385	10,3
34	P/R Tax	114	114	127	114	1
35	Supplies	350	250	450	350	2
36	Rent	1,800	1,800	1,800	1,800	1,8
37	Phone	360	360	360	360	3
38	Miscellaneous	450	450	450	450	4
39	Travel	1,900	2,500	1,900	1,900	2,5
40	Lodging	475	625	475	475	6

FIGURE 8–27 A worksheet with a page break symbol

Hiding Data from Printing

If there is data in the print range that you do not want printed, you can hide the data. To hide the data, you can hide the column or row that contains it, or you can format a rectangular range as hidden. Whichever method you choose, the hidden data will not be displayed in your final printout.

To hide columns of data, you can use the Worksheet Column command and select the Hide option button. 1-2-3/G hides the columns in the current selection and shifts the rest of the columns in the worksheet to the left. To hide rows of data, you can use the Worksheet Row command and select the Hide option button. 1-2-3/G hides the rows in the current selection and shifts the remaining rows in the worksheet upward. Finally, to hide a rectangular range of data, you can use the Range Format Hidden command. This command causes the data in the current selection to disappear from view. The position of the data in the remainder of the worksheet is not affected.

Regardless of the method you select for hiding data, the formulas in the hidden range continue to perform their respective calculations. However, the hidden range does not print. For more on the Worksheet Column, Worksheet Row, and Range Format commands, see Chapter 3, "Formatting Worksheets."

SUMMARY

This chapter covers printing in 1-2-3/G. It begins with printing basics, showing you how to select a range to print and how to send that range of data to your printer. This chapter also discusses printing a large range (a range that requires more than a single page) and shows you how 1-2-3/G uses the current margin settings to break up a large range into individual pages.

This chapter also discusses 1-2-3/G's ability to print in the background. In 1-2-3/G, each print job you generate is sent to a print queue. The print queue is an area of your computer's memory that is used to store information temporarily. Because of this queue, you can keep on working in 1-2-3/G while your data is printing. However, if you want to stop a particular print job, this chapter shows you how to use the File Print Status command to manage the print jobs in the print queue.

This chapter also shows you how to print to files. For example, it shows you how to print to an encoded file. Encoded files contain all the same data and printer control codes that would normally be sent to your printer. You can print an encoded file either at a later time or on another computer, without having to use 1-2-3/G. On the other hand, this chapter also shows you how to print to an ASCII file so that you can use your 1-2-3/G data with other software programs.

In this chapter, you also learn how to control the paper in the printer. That is, you learn how to advance the print head by a line or a page to leave blank spaces between print ranges.

This chapter also shows you how to print a worksheet range with and without enhancements. For example, you can print a range with and without cell borders, background shading, and the worksheet grid. You can also print a range with the row numbers and column letters in the worksheet frame displayed.

In addition to printing display enhancements, this chapter shows you how to specify additional printing options. For example, it teaches you how to print with headers and footers, control the number of copies, change the print density, or print only part of a report. Further, it shows you how to print a range using columns or rows of data as headings for the columns and rows that are included in the print range. In addition, it shows you how to change the default margins to affect the positioning of data on the page. Finally, it shows you how to save the current print settings under a name, so that you can reuse them at a later time.

This chapter also discusses 1-2-3/G's new Preview utility. This utility allows you to preview your work before it is printed. That way, you can correct any errors in the worksheet before the data is printed. In addition, you can use this utility to print a worksheet and a graph on the same page.

This chapter also discusses how you can control the printer from within 1-2-3/G. For example, you learn how to change from one installed printer to another. You also learn how to specify different printing properties, such as landscape mode or manual feed, for the current print job. You also learn how to select a default printer and how to print with different fonts.

Data Management

To access 1-2-3/G's data management facilities, you use the Data command. This command allows you to create, manipulate, and analyze data that is located either in your worksheet or in database files created by software products other than 1-2-3/G.

The Data command has two primary applications. On the one hand, you can use it to query and manipulate information stored in database tables. (As you'll soon see, database tables provide a structured environment for the storage and retrieval of information.) On the other hand, the Data command is used to create new data, to analyze existing data, or to arrange existing data in a more meaningful way. The following is a preview of the Data commands that will be discussed in this chapter:

- **Data Query:** Locates and manipulates data in 1-2-3/G database tables or in external database tables.
- **Data External:** Connects an external database table to 1-2-3/G, allowing you to exchange information between that table and your worksheet.
- **Data Sort:** Sorts columns of data in your worksheets in a specified order.
- **Data Fill:** Quickly fills a range with sequential numbers, dates, or times.
- **Data Parse:** Parses words and numbers in long labels into separate cells.
- **Data Table:** Allows you to perform "what-if" analysis by substituting sets of values into one or more formulas. The results of each substitution are recorded in a table.
- **Data Distribution:** Allows you to count the values in range of your worksheet that fall within a given interval.
- **Data Matrix:** Solves problems using linear equations.
- **Data Regression:** Performs regression analysis, allowing you to predict future trends for a data set.

What's New

A number of useful new features have been added to 1-2-3/G that enhance its data management capabilities. For example, a Series option has been added to the Data Fill command that allows you to fill a range with date values advancing by year, quarter, month, week, or weekday. You can also use the Series option to advance time values by hours, minutes, and seconds

The Data Sort command has been enhanced to allow you to sort a data set using more than two fields. This command now includes an Extra option that allows you to specify up to 253 additional fields on which to sort a database.

A new command, Data External, has been added that allows you to connect 1-2-3/G to a database table created by another software program. For example, you can connect to a database table created by dBASE III PLUS. Once 1-2-3/G is connected to the external table, you can use the Data Query commands to copy records from the external database to a 1-2-3/G worksheet. Conversely, you can add records from your 1-2-3/G worksheet to the external database table.

The Data Table command has been enhanced to allow you to use more than two variables to build data tables. In fact, two new commands have been added, Data Table 3 and Data Table Labeled. Data Table 3 allows you to build a three-dimensional data table that evaluates three variables in a formula. On the other hand, the Data Table Labeled command allows you to build a three-dimensional data table that evaluates a virtually unlimited number of variables in an unlimited number of formulas.

The Data Query command has been enhanced to allow you to modify existing records in a database table. The new Modify Extract option allows you to extract records based on given criteria. You can then modify these records as needed. When you're done, you can use the Modify Replace option to put those records back where they came from.

You can also specify multiple input ranges (database tables) for the Data Query commands and the database @functions. Thus, you can locate and extract selected data from two or more database tables at the same time.

1-2-3/G also allows you to create computed columns in the output range for the Data Query command. This is done by using formulas in the first row of the criteria range instead of field names. Using computed columns, you can, for example, multiply the contents of one field by another for those records that are copied to the output range.

DATABASE BASICS

In 1-2-3/G, a database is a collection of one or more database tables. Each database table contains related information organized into columns and rows. For example, Figure 9-1 shows a small section taken from an employee database table. This table will be used throughout this chapter to demonstrate 1-2-3/G's data management capabilities. For here on, this table will be referred to as the EMPBASE table.

Each row in the database table constitutes a *record*. A record contains all the necessary information about a particular item in the database table. For example, in Figure 9-1 the first record in the database is located in the range A2..F2. It describes employee number 1239, named Suzanne Piper, hired 02/01/92, earning $30,000, and working in the Accounting department.

Each column in a database table constitutes a *field*. A field contains a particular type of information for each record. For example, in Figure 9-1, the first field is located in column A; it contains employee identification numbers for each record. The second field, located in column B, contains the first name of each employee, and so on. Each field in a database table must contain a single data type. That is, it must contain either all labels, all numbers, all date values, and so on. That way, each field represents a uniform block of information.

1-2-3/G (69.4) Ready

File Edit Worksheet Range Copy... Move... Print Graph Data Utility Quit... Help

A:A1 ^ID

EMPBASE.WG1

A	A	B	C	D	E	F
1	ID	FIRSTNAME	LASTNAME	DOH	SALARY	DEPT
2	1239	Suzanne	Piper	02/01/92	30,000	ACCTG
3	1201	John	Haenszel	07/31/89	45,000	ADMIN
4	1265	Jean	Stevenson	08/15/90	27,000	SALES
5	1295	Jim	Taylor	12/10/90	33,000	QC
6	1258	Robin	Lang	06/07/91	24,000	MANU
7	1217	David	Carlson	09/19/90	55,000	ADMIN
8	1246	Jeff	Martin	10/31/91	22,000	PURCH
9	1263	Cynthia	Rhodes	04/01/90	32,000	SALES
10	1234	Henry	Bullock	01/14/92	38,000	MARKET
11	1278	Keith	Davis	04/12/92	34,000	MANU
12	1256	Ron	Woods	07/18/92	37,000	ENGR
13						
14						
15						
16						

FIGURE 9–1 The employee database table

At the top of each field is a *field name*. The field name is a label that identifies the contents of each field. For example, the name of the first field in the database table in Figure 9-1 is ID. The second field is named FIRSTNAME, the third LASTNAME, and so on.

Field names must be at the top of the column of data to which they correspond, and there can be no blank cells between the field names and the first row of data. In addition, field names must be labels. You cannot use a number or formula as a field name, unless you precede it with a label prefix (', ", or ^). What's more, each field name in a database table must be unique. As you'll soon see, field names are used to search a database table for specific information. If two field names are the same, 1-2-3/G will not know which field to search and will issue an error message.

Each database table must be confined to a single worksheet. Therefore, the size of a database table is limited by the size of your worksheet. As you know, each worksheet has 8,192 rows and 256 columns. Therefore, the maximum number of records you can have in a database table is 8,191 (8,192 less one row for the field names), and the maximum number of fields you can have in the table is 256.

CREATING A DATABASE TABLE

This section shows you how to set up a 1-2-3/G database table. It begins with a brief overview of database design considerations. It then shows you how to enter records in a database table, format its appearance, and edit selected records.

Designing a Database

Each database table you create should be geared to a specific purpose, that is, a particular report or function. Therefore, before creating a database table, consider how you will actually use the information in the table.

For example, consider the case of an employee database. Most likely, you will need information for paychecks, mailings, benefits, and so on. However, rather than try to suit all of these needs with a single huge database, it is to your advantage to break up the information into smaller database tables. Each table would contain fields of related information. For example, you may have one database table containing strictly payroll data, another containing addresses, and yet another containing benefits information. That way, you will not be forced to view unrelated information when paging through the records or fields in a database.

As you design your database, consider including a field in each table that uniquely identifies each record. In database parlance, this is referred to as a *key* field. For example, building on the employee database example, you can give each employee a unique number. That way, if two employees have the same name, you will still be able to accurately locate the record for a particular employee.

You can also use a key field to match records across two or more database tables. For example, imagine once again that you have an employee database composed of three tables, one for payroll, one for addresses, and one for benefits. Each table contains a key field containing a unique number that identifies each employee's record. Using this field, you can search all three database tables at the same time and locate specific information from each table for a given employee.

If you elect to use one large database table instead of a series of smaller ones, you can group the fields you use most frequently at the beginning of the table. Grouping related information in adjacent fields will cut down on your having to scroll to the right or left when viewing the database.

Entering Data

To enter data in a database, begin by locating the cell pointer in the upper-left corner of where you want the database to begin. In the first row of the table, type in the field names in adjacent cells. For example, the field names in Figure 9–1 appear in the range A:A1..A:F1. To add the first record to the database table, move the cell pointer to the first cell in the first row immediately below the field names (Cell A:A2 in Figure 9–1). Next, type in the information for each field in the first record in adjacent cells, moving from left to right. When you complete the first record, move on to the second one, and so on, until you complete entering the initial set of records.

You can enter virtually anything you like in a database field, including numbers, text, @functions, or formulas. For example, to enter a date you might use the @DATE function. Or, to calculate the contents of a given field in a record, you might use a formula that refers to other cells in that same record or to cells outside the database table. If you use formulas or @functions with cell references, however, keep the following two rules of thumb in mind:

- If the formula refers to data in the same record, use a relative reference.
- If the formula refers to data located outside the database, use an absolute reference.

You'll find these two rules of thumb to be important when you later sort the database table (See "Sorting a Database" later in this chapter). When you sort a database table, 1-2-3/G rearranges its records based on the contents of one or more of its fields. Thus, your formulas may be moved to new cell locations. Accordingly, 1-2-3/G adjusts the cell references for those formulas to reflect their new locations relative to cell A1. If the formula refers to data in the same record, the referenced data will move along with the record, and your formula will continue to return a valid result. However, if the formula refers to cells outside the database table, it may no longer refer to the appropriate range of cells. To solve this problem, use an absolute reference in the formula. That way, you can rest assured that the formula will always reference the correct range.

Tip: Adding records with commands and macros

You can add records to an existing database table by using the Data Query Modify Insert command. This command allows you to copy records from a selected range and append them to the end of a database. See "Adding Records" later in this chapter under "Using the Data Query Commands" for more details on this. You can also use the {FORM} and {APPENDBELOW} macro commands to create a custom form for entering data records and appending those records to a database table. See Chapter 11, "The Macro Programming Language," for more on these macro commands.

Formatting the Database

Once you've entered the initial set of records for a database table, you may want to format its appearance. For example, the database in Figure 9–1 has been formatted in the following way:

- The Range Label Labels Center command was used to center the field name labels in the range A:A1..A:F1.
- The Worksheet Column command was used to set the width of column A to seven characters, column B to 10 characters, Column C to 11 characters, and column D to 10 characters.
- The Range Format Date 4 command was used to display the date values in column D in Date 4 format.
- The Range Format , (Comma) 0 command was used to display the values in column E in Comma format with 0 places displayed after the decimal.

Editing Records

You edit the cells in a 1-2-3/G database table in the same way you edit the cells in any other area of the worksheet. For example, to edit the contents of a given cell, move the cell pointer to that cell and press EDIT (F2), or double-click your mouse, to place its contents in the Control Line. Then, edit the entry as necessary. When you're ready, press ENTER to confirm your changes.

To insert a record into the middle of a database, use the Worksheet Insert Row command to create a blank row where you want the new record to appear. Complete the job by typing in the information for each field in the new record.

Note

As an alternative to using the Worksheet Insert Row command to insert a record into a database, you can add the record to the end of the database and use the Data Sort command to sort it into position. See "Sorting a Database" in the next section for more details.

To delete records from a database table, you can use the Worksheet Delete Row Partial command. To do this, highlight the row of adjacent cells containing the record you want to delete. Then, select the Worksheet Delete Row Partial command and press ENTER. 1-2-3/G deletes the part of the row you selected. The records located below this row are shifted upward to close up the space.

Note

As an alternative to using Worksheet Delete Row to delete a database record, you can use the Data Query Delete command. For information on how to use this command, see "Deleting Records" later in this chapter under "Using the Data Query Commands." The advantage to using the Data Query Delete command is that you can establish criteria for the command. Only those records that meet your criteria are deleted from the database. Thus, instead of paging through the database looking for the records you want to delete, you can let 1-2-3/G do the work.

To add a new field to the database, you can use the Worksheet Insert Column command. To do this, locate the cell pointer one column to the right of where you want the new field inserted. Then, select the Worksheet Insert Column command and press ENTER. 1-2-3/G inserts a new column to the left of the cell pointer. To finish the job, enter a new field name in the cell that is adjacent to the other field names in the database. Beneath that field name, enter the new data for each record in the database table.

SORTING A DATABASE

You can sort the records in a database table by using the Data Sort command. This command allows you to rearrange records in a database table based on the contents of one or more of its fields. For example, you might want to sort the records in the EMPBASE table shown earlier in Figure 9-1 by last name. That way, you can easily scan records in the table and quickly find the record for a particular employee.

Data Sort Basics

When you select the Data Sort command, 1-2-3/G displays the dialog box in Figure 9-2. This dialog box allows you to select the range of database records you want to sort as well as one or more fields on which you want to sort those records. It also allows you to specify the order of the sort. You can choose from either descending or ascending.

Note

> Although this section discusses the Data Sort command in the context of sorting a database, you can also use the Data Sort command to sort adjacent columns of data in any 1-2-3/G worksheet.

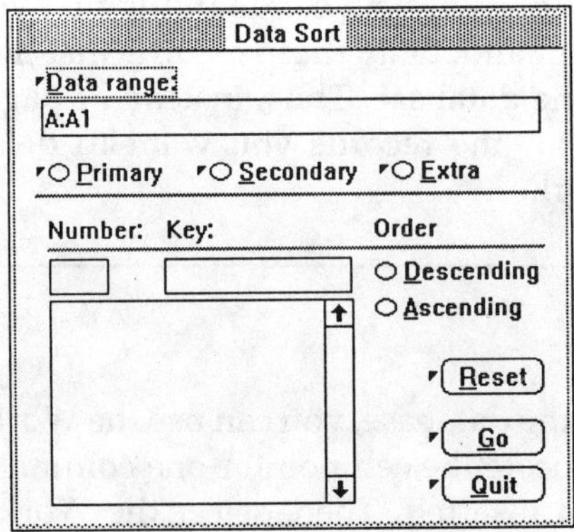

FIGURE 9-2 **The Data Sort dialog box**

Use the "Data range" text box at the top of the Data Sort dialog box to specify the range of records you want to sort. You can specify a range that includes all the records in a database table, or just some of them. When you specify a range to sort, however, make sure that it does **not** include the field names at the top of the database table. Otherwise, when the sort is completed, those field names may end up in the body of the database, thereby obscuring its structure. For example, to sort all the records in the EMPBASE table shown again in Figure 9-3, you would specify the range A:A2..A:F12.

You can select the range of records you want to sort either before or during the Data Sort command. If you select the range before, the "Data range" text box displays this range when you select the Data Sort command.

Note

When selecting a sort range, make sure you select all the fields that are included in each record you want to sort. Otherwise, when you later sort the database, 1-2-3/G will only sort those fields included in the sort range, leaving the remaining fields unsorted. The result is a mismatching of fields from record to record. If this happens, press ALT-BACKSPACE immediately to use the undo feature to reverse the Data Sort command. Provided the undo feature is not disabled (you used the Worksheet Global Default Set undo Disable command), 1-2-3/G will restore the database to its former order.

Once you've selected a range to sort, you're ready to select one or more fields on which you want to sort the database table. 1-2-3/G allows you to select up to 255 fields on which to sort a database table. In addition, you can select a sort order (ascending versus descending) for each field. To select the fields on which to sort the database, you use the Primary, Secondary, and Extra option buttons in conjunction with the Number and Key text boxes from the Data Sort dialog box in Figure 9-2. To select a sort order for a given field, you use the Descending or Ascending options from the Order section of the Data Sort dialog box. The use of each of these option buttons and text boxes will be explained in the sections that follow in the context of examples. Briefly, however, the function of each of these option buttons and text boxes is as follows:

- **Primary:** Specifies the field that receives the first order of precedence in the sort. After selecting this option button, select the Key text box and specify a single cell from the column that contains the field you want to use as the primary sort field.
- **Secondary:** Specifies the field that receives the second order of precedence in the sort. After selecting this option button, select the Key text box and specify

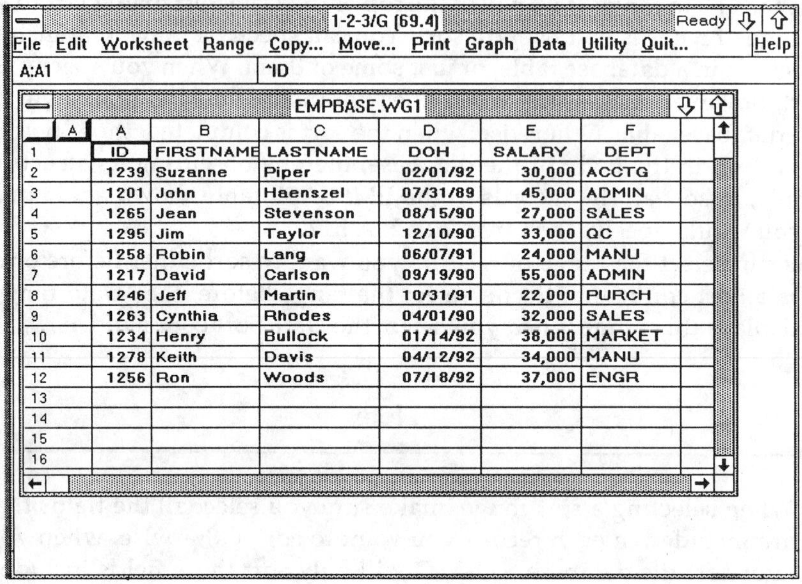

1-2-3/G [69.4] Ready

File Edit Worksheet Range Copy... Move... Print Graph Data Utility Quit... Help

A:A1 ^ID

EMPBASE.WG1

A	A	B	C	D	E	F
1	ID	FIRSTNAME	LASTNAME	DOH	SALARY	DEPT
2	1239	Suzanne	Piper	02/01/92	30,000	ACCTG
3	1201	John	Haenszel	07/31/89	45,000	ADMIN
4	1265	Jean	Stevenson	08/15/90	27,000	SALES
5	1295	Jim	Taylor	12/10/90	33,000	QC
6	1258	Robin	Lang	06/07/91	24,000	MANU
7	1217	David	Carlson	09/19/90	55,000	ADMIN
8	1246	Jeff	Martin	10/31/91	22,000	PURCH
9	1263	Cynthia	Rhodes	04/01/90	32,000	SALES
10	1234	Henry	Bullock	01/14/92	38,000	MARKET
11	1278	Keith	Davis	04/12/92	34,000	MANU
12	1256	Ron	Woods	07/18/92	37,000	ENGR
13						
14						
15						
16						

FIGURE 9–3 **The employee database table (EMPBASE.WG1)**

a single cell from the column that contains the field you want to use as the secondary sort field.

- **Extra:** Allows you to specify additional sort fields beyond the primary and secondary sort fields—up to 253 of them. After selecting this option button, use the Key text box to select a single cell from the column that contains the field you want to use. To select a second extra sort field, select the Extra option again and use the Key text box to specify a single cell from the column that contains that field. Every time you select a new extra field, the number in the Number text box will be incremented by one, indicating the extra field's order of precedence in the sort.
- **Key:** Allows you to specify a single cell address or range name that defines the field (column) you want to use as a primary, secondary, or extra sort field.
- **Number:** Allows you to specify a number for an extra sort field. The number you specify determines the order of precedence the extra field receives during the sort.
- **Order:** Allows you to specify either a descending or ascending sort order for a Primary, Secondary, or Extra sort field. The Descending option button (the default) sorts the contents of a field alphabetically from Z to A and numerically from highest to lowest. The Ascending option button sorts a field from A to Z alphabetically and from lowest to highest numerically.
- **Reset:** Cancels the current ranges you've set for the Data Sort command.
- **Go:** Performs the sort.

Sorting on a Single Field

This section shows you how to sort the EMPBASE table shown in Figure 9–3 in ascending order using a single field. The field used to perform the sort will be the LASTNAME field (column C of Figure 9–3). As you might imagine, this field contains the last names of employees included in the EMPBASE table. When the sort is completed, the records in the EMPBASE table will be arranged in order by last name, as in Figure 9–4.

To sort the records in EMPBASE table, begin by selecting the sort range A:A2..A:F12. To do this, click your mouse button on cell A:A2 and hold it down. Then drag to highlight the range A:A2..A:F12 and release. Alternatively, you can move the cell pointer to cell A:A2 and press CTRL-. (CTRL-PERIOD) to anchor it. Then, highlight the range A:A2..A:F12.

When you're ready, select the Data Sort command. 1-2-3/G displays the Data Sort dialog box. Your sort range appears in the "Data range" text box. To select a primary sort field, click on the Primary option button, or press TAB to move this option button and press ENTER. Then, click on the Key text box, or press TAB to activate the Key text box. 1-2-3/G enters Point mode. Specify a single-cell range from column C (the LASTNAME field) of the EMPBASE table. Confirm your selection by pressing ENTER.

When you specify a primary sort field, 1-2-3/G records your selection in the list box below. For example, if you selected cell A:C1 in the Key text box as a primary sort field, 1-2-3/G displays **P.(D)A:C1** in the list box below. Breaking this listing down, the P stands for Primary, the (D) means a descending sort order, and A:C1 is the cell address you selected.

123/G (69.4) Ready

File Edit Worksheet Range Copy... Move... Print Graph Data Utility Quit... Help

A:A1 ^ID

FIG9-4.WG1

A	A	B	C	D	E	F
1	ID	FIRSTNAME	LASTNAME	DOH	SALARY	DEPT
2	1234	Henry	Bullock	01/14/92	38,000	MARKET
3	1217	David	Carlson	09/19/90	55,000	ADMIN
4	1278	Keith	Davis	04/12/92	34,000	MANU
5	1201	John	Haenszel	07/31/89	45,000	ADMIN
6	1258	Robin	Lang	06/07/91	24,000	MANU
7	1246	Jeff	Martin	10/31/91	22,000	PURCH
8	1239	Suzanne	Piper	02/01/92	30,000	ACCTG
9	1263	Cynthia	Rhodes	04/01/90	32,000	SALES
10	1265	Jean	Stevenson	08/15/90	27,000	SALES
11	1295	Jim	Taylor	12/10/90	33,000	QC
12	1256	Ron	Woods	07/18/92	37,000	ENGR
13						
14						
15						
16						

FIGURE 9–4 The EMPBASE table sorted on the LASTNAME field

To specify an ascending order for the sort, click on the Ascending option button in the Order section of the Data Sort dialog box. Alternatively, press TAB to move to this Order section and press ↓ to move to Ascending and press ENTER. Whichever method you choose, 1-2-3/G updates the Key list box to read P.(A)A:A1. As you might imagine, the (A) stands for a ascending sort order.

To complete the Data Sort command, select the Go command button. 1-2-3/G sorts the records in the EMPBASE table using the contents of the last name field as a guide. The records now appear in ascending order by last name, as shown in Figure 9–4.

Note

1-2-3/G remembers ranges you've set for the Data Sort command. That is, if you've previously specified ranges for the Data Sort command during the current session, 1-2-3/G shows you those same ranges the next time you select the command. To cancel the current Data Sort ranges, select the Reset command button.

Sorting on Two Fields

In this section, you'll sort the EMPBASE table in ascending order by department and by last names within each department. To do this, you'll select both a primary and secondary sort field for the Data Sort command. The primary field will be the DEPT field (column F of Figure 9–4) and the secondary field will be LASTNAME (column C of Figure 9–4). When the sort is completed, your screen should look like Figure 9–5.

In preparation for the Data Sort command, select the range A:A2..A:F12. When you're ready, select the Data Sort command. 1-2-3/G displays the Data Sort dialog box with the range A:A2..A:F12 already displayed in the "Data range" text box.

To specify a primary sort field, select the Primary option button. Next, click on the Key text box or press TAB to move to it. Specify the address or range name of any cell in the DEPT field (column F of Figure 9–4). To specify an ascending order for this field, select the Ascending option button from the Order section of the Data Sort dialog box. 1-2-3/G records your choice in the list box below.

To specify a secondary sort field, select the Secondary option button. Next, click on the Key text box or press TAB to move to it. Specify the address or range name a single cell from the LASTNAME field (column C of Figure 9–4). To specify an ascending order for this field, select the Ascending option button from the Order section of the Data Sort dialog box. 1-2-3/G records your selection in the list box. For example, if you specified cell A:C1 in the Key text box, 1-2-3/G records **S.(A)A:C1** in the list box below. The S in the listing stands for secondary. The (A) stands for ascending order, and A:C1 is the cell you selected.

To complete the Data Sort command, select Go from the Data Sort dialog box. 1-2-3/G sorts the EMPBASE table by department and by last names within those departments. Your screen now looks like Figure 9-5.

Sorting on More than Two Fields

As mentioned, 1-2-3/G allows you to specify up to 255 fields on which to sort a database. To specify additional fields beyond the primary and secondary fields, you use the Extra option button in the Data Sort dialog box.

The following example shows you how to use the Extra option button to sort the EMPBASE table in Figure 9-5 in ascending order using three fields. It will be sorted first by department, then by date of hire within each department, and finally by salary. When the sort is complete, the EMPBASE table will appear as in Figure 9-6.

In this example, the DEPT field (column F of Figure 9-5) will be the primary sort field. The DOH field (column D of Figure 9-5) will be the secondary sort field, and the SALARY field (column E) will be the third sort field. To set up this sort of configuration, perform the following steps:

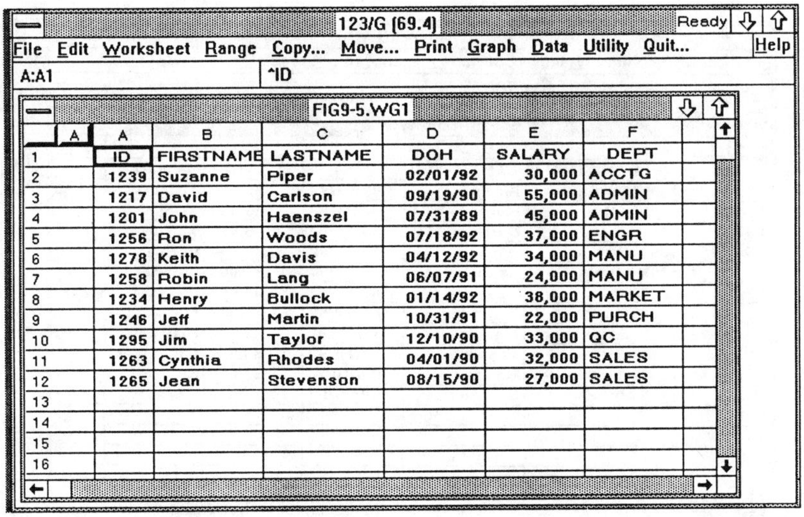

123/G (69.4) Ready

File Edit Worksheet Range Copy... Move... Print Graph Data Utility Quit... Help

A:A1 ^ID

FIG9-5.WG1

A	A	B	C	D	E	F
1	ID	FIRSTNAME	LASTNAME	DOH	SALARY	DEPT
2	1239	Suzanne	Piper	02/01/92	30,000	ACCTG
3	1217	David	Carlson	09/19/90	55,000	ADMIN
4	1201	John	Haenszel	07/31/89	45,000	ADMIN
5	1256	Ron	Woods	07/18/92	37,000	ENGR
6	1278	Keith	Davis	04/12/92	34,000	MANU
7	1258	Robin	Lang	06/07/91	24,000	MANU
8	1234	Henry	Bullock	01/14/92	38,000	MARKET
9	1246	Jeff	Martin	10/31/91	22,000	PURCH
10	1295	Jim	Taylor	12/10/90	33,000	QC
11	1263	Cynthia	Rhodes	04/01/90	32,000	SALES
12	1265	Jean	Stevenson	08/15/90	27,000	SALES
13						
14						
15						
16						

FIGURE 9-5 The EMPBASE table sorted by department and last name

1. In preparation for the Data Sort command, select the data range A:A2..A:F12. When you're ready select the Data Sort command. 1-2-3/G displays the Data Sort dialog box with this range already displayed in the "Data range" text box.
2. Select the Primary option button. Next, click on the Key text box or press TAB to move to it. In this text box, specify the address or range name of any cell in the DEPT field (column F) of the EMPBASE table. Specify an ascending order for this field by selecting the Ascending option button from the Order section of the Data Sort dialog box. 1-2-3/G records your selection in the list box below.
3. Select the Secondary option button. Next, click on the Key text box or press TAB to move to it. In this text box, specify the address or range name of any cell in the DOH (Date of Hire) field (column D) of the EMPBASE table. Specify an ascending order for this field by selecting the Ascending option button from the Order section of the Data Sort dialog box. 1-2-3/G records your selection in the list box below.
4. Select the Extra option button. Next, click on the Key text box or press TAB to move to it. Notice that the number **1** is displayed in the Number text box. This indicates that the sort field you are about to select will be the first extra sort field. In the Key box, specify the address or range name of any cell in the SALARY field (column E) of the EMPBASE table. Specify an ascending order for this field by selecting the Ascending option button from the Order section of the Data Sort dialog box. 1-2-3/G records your selection in the list box below.
5. To perform the sort, select the Go command button from the Data Sort dialog box. 1-2-3/G sorts the EMPBASE table as shown in Figure 9–6.

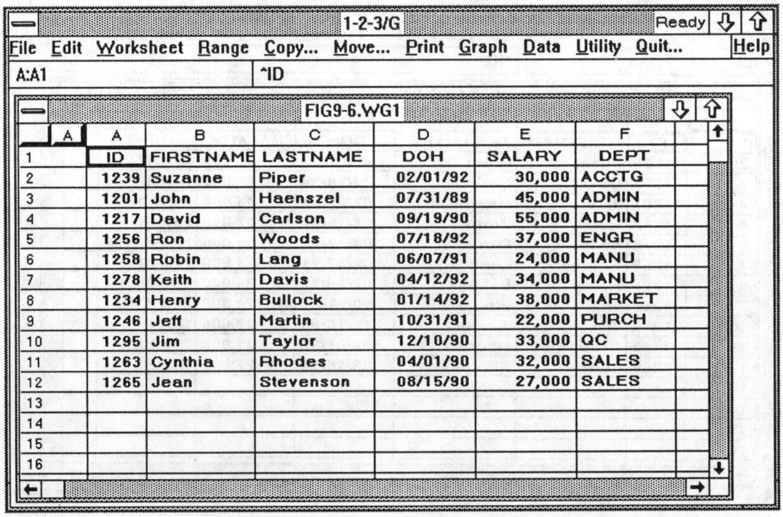

1-2-3/G Ready

File Edit Worksheet Range Copy... Move... Print Graph Data Utility Quit... Help

A:A1 ^ID

FIG9-6.WG1

A	A	B	C	D	E	F
1	ID	FIRSTNAME	LASTNAME	DOH	SALARY	DEPT
2	1239	Suzanne	Piper	02/01/92	30,000	ACCTG
3	1201	John	Haenszel	07/31/89	45,000	ADMIN
4	1217	David	Carlson	09/19/90	55,000	ADMIN
5	1256	Ron	Woods	07/18/92	37,000	ENGR
6	1258	Robin	Lang	06/07/91	24,000	MANU
7	1278	Keith	Davis	04/12/92	34,000	MANU
8	1234	Henry	Bullock	01/14/92	38,000	MARKET
9	1246	Jeff	Martin	10/31/91	22,000	PURCH
10	1295	Jim	Taylor	12/10/90	33,000	QC
11	1263	Cynthia	Rhodes	04/01/90	32,000	SALES
12	1265	Jean	Stevenson	08/15/90	27,000	SALES
13						
14						
15						
16						

FIGURE 9–6 The EMPBASE table sorted on three fields

In the preceding example, the Extra option button was used to specify a single extra sort field. However, as mentioned, you can use the Extra option button to specify up to 253 extra sort fields. Each time you select the Extra option button, 1-2-3/G increases the number that appears in the Number text box. And, each extra sort field you select is recorded in the list box below. For example, if you selected cell A:E1 in step 4 of the previous example, 1-2-3/G records **1.(A)A:E1** in the list box. The 1 indicates this is the first extra sort field, the (A) stands for ascending order, and A:E1 is the address of the cell you selected.

Editing Sort Ranges

As you've probably noticed by now, 1-2-3/G remembers the ranges you've set for the "Data Sort" command. In fact, 1-2-3/G shows you those same ranges each time you enter the command. However, you can easily change the current range settings for the Data Sort command. For example, to change the range specification in the "Data range" text box, simply click on the box, or press TAB, to activate it. Then, use the usual techniques to select a new range address or range name.

To change a primary or secondary sort field specification, select the Data Sort command, and then select from either the Primary or Secondary option buttons. 1-2-3/G activates the Key text box. In addition, the highlight in the list box below is moved to the sort field listing you selected. At this point, you can specify a new range address or range name in the Key text box. You can also choose from the Ascending or Descending option buttons to change the order of the sort for that field. To confirm your selection, press ENTER. 1-2-3/G updates the contents of the list box.

To change an extra sort field, select the Extra option button from the Data Sort dialog box. 1-2-3/G activates the Number text box. Type in the number that corresponds to the extra field that you want to change. 1-2-3/G activates the Key text box and moves the highlight in the list box below to the extra field listing you specified. At this point you can use the Key text box or the Ascending or Descending option buttons to modify the range specification and sort order for the selected extra sort field. To confirm your changes, press ENTER.

You can also click your mouse on any existing listing in the list box that is located below the Number and Key text boxes. When you select a listing, 1-2-3/G updates the various sections of the Data Sort dialog box to reflect the selections for that listing. You can change any of the settings for the listing. When you make a change, 1-2-3/G updates the listing accordingly.

To reset all ranges for the Data Sort command, select the Reset command button from the Data Sort dialog box. 1-2-3/G deletes all data range and sort field settings from the Data Sort dialog box.

Choosing a New Sort Sequence

You can change the sort sequence used by 1-2-3/G. To do this, you use the User Settings International command. The command is available from either the Utility menu or the Desktop Control menu. When you select this command, 1-2-3/G displays a rather extensive settings sheet. In the top-right corner of this settings sheet, there is a section entitled "Sort options." In this section are three option buttons, "ASCII," "Numbers Last," and "Numbers First." Select the sort option you want. To save the setting for future 1-2-3/G sessions, select the Update command button, located at the lower-left of the settings sheet. To return to the current worksheet, select the OK command button.

The Numbers First sequence is the default sort order for 1-2-3/G. Assuming an ascending sort order, the Numbers First sequence sorts your data in the following order:

1. Blank cells.
2. Labels containing numbers from smallest to highest.
3. Labels composed of all letters from A to Z. Capitalization is ignored.
4. Labels with pure nonalphanumeric symbols.
5. Numbers.

The Numbers Last sort sequence is similar to Numbers First. However, labels composed of all letters are sorted before labels containing numbers. In particular, the Numbers Last sequence sorts your data in the following way:

1. Blank cells.
2. Labels composed of all letters from A to Z. Capitalization is ignored.
3. Labels containing numbers from smallest to highest.
4. Labels with pure nonalphanumeric symbols.
5. Numbers.

The ASCII sort sequence sorts your data on the basis of each character's ASCII value. Because of this, upper-case letters are sorted before lower-case letters. The ASCII sequence sorts data in the following order:

1. Blank cells.
2. All labels, using their ASCII values. Capitalization is honored.
3. Numbers.

Tip: For Release 2 and 3 Users

1-2-3/G does not ignore hyphens (-) and apostrophes (') embedded in labels when sorting with the Numbers First and Numbers Last sort sequences. Labels containing these characters are sorted before labels without embedded hyphens and apostrophes. However, in Releases 2 and 3 of 1-2-3, embedded hyphens and apostrophes are ignored.

QUERYING A DATABASE

To query a database table, you use the Data Query command. This command allows you to perform the following operations with a database table:

- Locate records that meet specific criteria (Data Query Find).
- Copy all records that meet specific criteria to a new location (Data Query Extract).
- Copy only unique records that meet specific criteria to a new location (Data Query Unique).
- Delete records that meet specific criteria (Data Query Delete).
- Modify records that meet specific criteria (Data Query Modify).
- Append records to a database table (Data Query Modify Insert).

Data Query Basics

When you select the Data Query command, 1-2-3/G displays the dialog box in Figure 9–7. At the top of this dialog box are three rather important text boxes: Input, Criteria, and Output. These text boxes allow you to specify the input, criteria, and output ranges used by the Data Query command.

The input range is the range address or range name that contains the database table you want to search. The criteria range is a range address or range name that contains the selection criteria that will be used to locate specific records in the database table. All Data Query commands require both an input range and a criteria range specification. The output range, on the other hand, is a range address or range name location to which records from the database table will be copied. Specifying an output range is only necessary when you use one of the Extract options to extract (copy) records from the database table. The records extracted are chosen based on the selection criteria in the criteria range.

In case this all seems a bit confusing, the sections that follow discuss the use of the input, criteria, and output ranges in more detail. In addition, a short

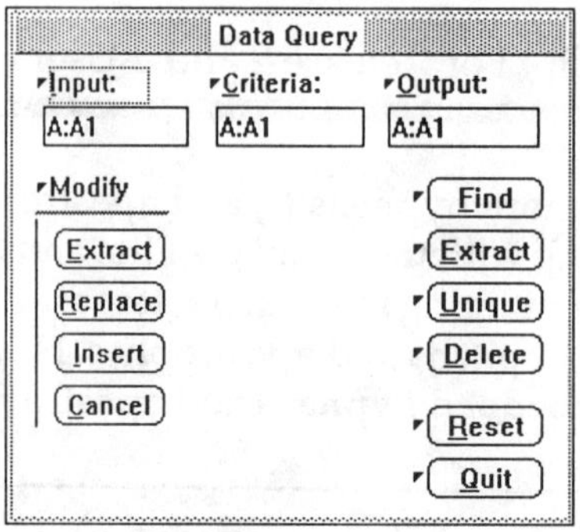

Data Query

Input: A:A1 | Criteria: A:A1 | Output: A:A1

Modify: Extract, Replace, Insert, Cancel

Find, Extract, Unique, Delete, Reset, Quit

FIGURE 9–7 The Data Query dialog box

example follows that shows you how to extract records that meet specific criteria from the EMPBASE database table shown again in Figure 9-8.

Input Range

The input range is a range name or address that defines the database table you want to search. This range includes the records you want to search as well as

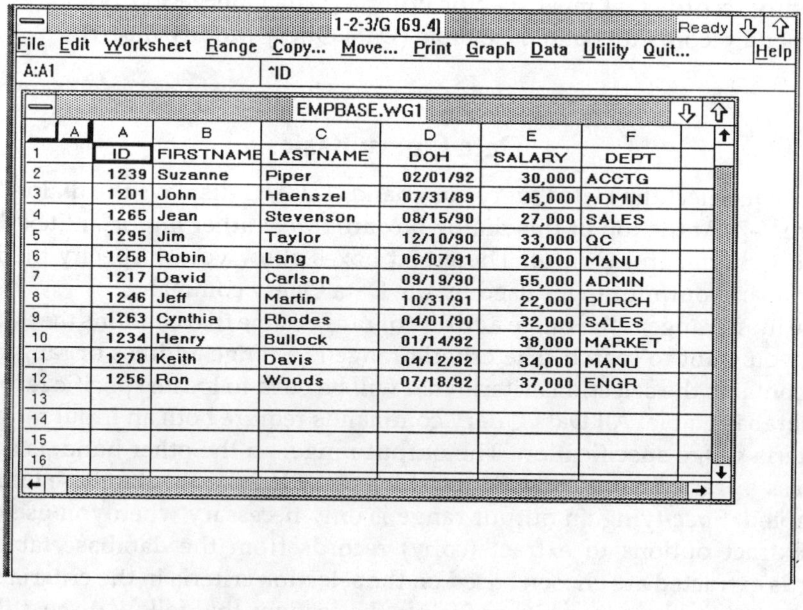

1-2-3/G (69.4) Ready

File Edit Worksheet Range Copy... Move... Print Graph Data Utility Quit... Help

A:A1 ^ID

EMPBASE.WG1

A	A	B	C	D	E	F
1	ID	FIRSTNAME	LASTNAME	DOH	SALARY	DEPT
2	1239	Suzanne	Piper	02/01/92	30,000	ACCTG
3	1201	John	Haenszel	07/31/89	45,000	ADMIN
4	1265	Jean	Stevenson	08/15/90	27,000	SALES
5	1295	Jim	Taylor	12/10/90	33,000	QC
6	1258	Robin	Lang	06/07/91	24,000	MANU
7	1217	David	Carlson	09/19/90	55,000	ADMIN
8	1246	Jeff	Martin	10/31/91	22,000	PURCH
9	1263	Cynthia	Rhodes	04/01/90	32,000	SALES
10	1234	Henry	Bullock	01/14/92	38,000	MARKET
11	1278	Keith	Davis	04/12/92	34,000	MANU
12	1256	Ron	Woods	07/18/92	37,000	ENGR
13						
14						
15						
16						

FIGURE 9–8 The EMPBASE table

the *field names* at the top of the database table. As you'll soon see, 1-2-3/G uses these field names to locate specific records in the database table. For example, to specify the EMPBASE table in Figure 9–8 as an input range for the Data Query command, you would use the input range specification A:A1..A:F12, or its corresponding range name, in the Input text box of the Data Query dialog box.

The input range can be located in a worksheet in the current file, another open file, or in a file on disk. To specify an input range in another open file, or in file on disk, you use a file reference enclosed in double angle brackets << >> followed by a range address or a range name from that file. For example, to use the range A:A1..A:H100 from a file named SALES.WG1 located in a directory called MARKET as an input range, you would specify the following in the Input text box:

```
<<C:\MARKET\SALES.WG1>>A:A1..A:H100
```

You can also specify multiple input ranges for the Data Query command. That way, 1-2-3/G will search multiple database tables at the same time to find the information you want. To specify multiple input ranges in the Input text box, include the range address or range name of each table separated by commas, for example A:A1..A:F12,B:A1..B:F12. For more on using Multiple input ranges with the Data Query command, see "Querying Multiple Database Tables" later in this chapter.

You can also use an external database table as an input range for the Data Query command. External database tables are created by software programs other that 1-2-3/G, such as dBASE III PLUS. To do this however, you must first connect to the external table and assign it a 1-2-3/G range name by using the Data External command. This command lets you activate a manufacturer-specific Datalens driver that allows 1-2-3/G to access the external table. For more on using external database tables, see "Querying External Database Tables" later in this chapter.

Tip: For Release 2 and 3 Users

1-2-3/G and 1-2-3 Release 3 do not allow you to have repeating field names in the input range for a Data Query command. In other words, if the field names in the database table are not unique, an error message results. 1-2-3 Release 2, however, does allow you to use the same field name more than once in a database table. Because of this, you may get unexpected results when you attempt to extract records from the database table, because Release 2 may or may not be using the correct field.

Criteria Range

The criteria range is a range address or range name that contains the selection criteria that will be used to locate records in the input range (database table). You must have entered your selection criteria in this range before you select the Data Query command. Once the selection criteria is entered into the worksheet, you can select the Data Query command and specify the range address or range name that contains your selection criteria in the Criteria text box.

The criteria range can be located in any open worksheet file and must contain at least two vertically adjacent cells. However, as you'll soon see, the criteria range can be multiple columns wide and multiple rows deep. In the top row of the criteria range are field names that exactly match those in the input range. In one or more rows immediately beneath these field names are labels, values, or formulas that define search conditions for each field name. For example, the contents of the criteria range used to search the EMPBASE table in Figure 9–8 might appear as follows:

```
SALARY
'>35000
```

This tells 1-2-3/G to search the SALARY field of the EMPBASE table to find all those records with a value greater than $35,000 in the SALARY field.

The selection criteria just shown are relatively simple by comparison. You can, of course, specify more complex criteria for selecting records from a 1-2-3/G database table. In fact, an entire section, "Defining Criteria," appears later in this chapter, devoted to the topic.

If you leave the criteria range blank, 1-2-3/G automatically selects all the records in the input range. For example, if the criteria range contains only field names with nothing beneath those field names, 1-2-3/G selects all records in the input range when you execute a Data Query command. You can, however, leave blank rows in the criteria range. If at least one row contains a valid search argument, 1-2-3/G will honor that search argument and ignore any blank rows. However, if there are no valid search arguments, and you leave a row blank, 1-2-3/G will select all the records in the input range.

Output Range

Defining an output range is only necessary when you want to extract (copy) selected records from the input range to another location. The output range defines the location to which those records are copied. Like the input and criteria ranges, you must prepare the output range before selecting the Data Query command. Once the output range is prepared, you can select the Data Query command and specify the location of the output range in the Output text box.

At a minimum, the output range must contain a single row. However, you can also specify a multiple-row output range. The top row of the output range contains one or more field names that exactly match those in the input range. When data is copied from the input range, it appears in the rows immediately below this first row of field names.

If you specify a single-row output range, 1-2-3/G erases all cells beneath the first row of field names and the bottom of the worksheet when the data is copied from the input range. Therefore, if you specify a single-row output range, make sure you do not have any important data located beneath the first row of field names and the bottom of the worksheet. On the other hand, if you specify a multiple-row output range, 1-2-3/G only uses the number of rows you specified when data is copied from the input range. If 1-2-3/G finds more records in the input range than there are rows in the output range, 1-2-3/G copies as many records as there are available rows in the output range and then issues an error message.

You can change the order of field names in the output range. Regardless of the order of field names in the input range, 1-2-3/G uses the order of field names in the output range as a guide when copying data from the input range to the output range.

You do not have to use all the field names from the input range in the output range. Instead, you can use only the field names you need. When 1-2-3/G copies data to the output range, it will do so only for those field names that are included in the output range.

Tip: For Release 2 and 3 Users

1-2-3/G and Release 3 do not allow identical input and output ranges. Release 2, on the other hand, does allow you to specify the same range as both an input and an output range.

Extracting Records: An Example

The following example shows you how to use the Data Query command to copy selected records from the EMPBASE table to an output range. Only records with a value greater than $35,000 in the SALARY field of the EMPBASE table will be copied. When the data query is completed, your screen should look like Figure 9–9. To execute the data query in Figure 9–9, perform the following steps:

1. Make sure EMPBASE table shown in Figure 9–9 is present on your screen.
2. Move the cell pointer to cell A:E1 (the cell containing the SALARY field name) and select the Copy command. Press ENTER to select cell A:E1 as

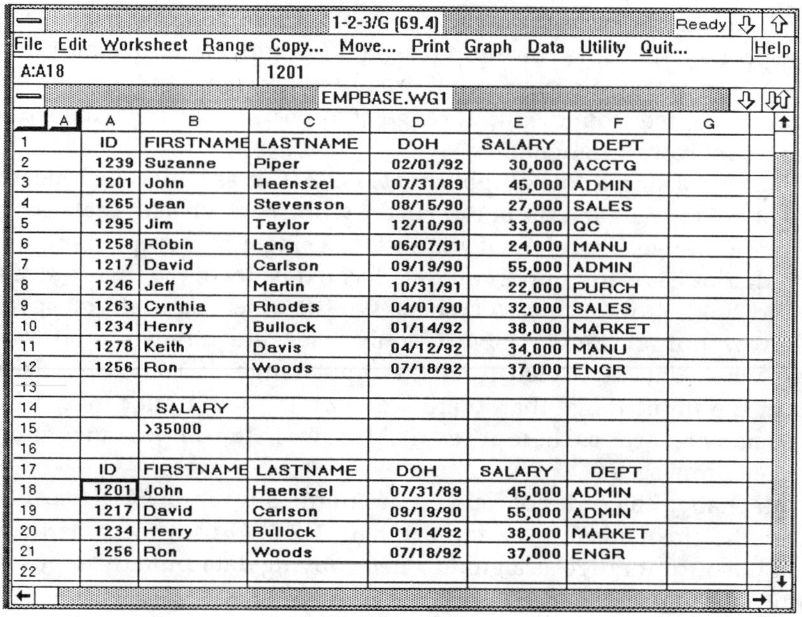

1-2-3/G [69.4] Ready

File Edit Worksheet Range Copy... Move... Print Graph Data Utility Quit... Help

A:A18 1201

EMPBASE.WG1

A	A	B	C	D	E	F	G
1	ID	FIRSTNAME	LASTNAME	DOH	SALARY	DEPT	
2	1239	Suzanne	Piper	02/01/92	30,000	ACCTG	
3	1201	John	Haenszel	07/31/89	45,000	ADMIN	
4	1265	Jean	Stevenson	08/15/90	27,000	SALES	
5	1295	Jim	Taylor	12/10/90	33,000	QC	
6	1258	Robin	Lang	06/07/91	24,000	MANU	
7	1217	David	Carlson	09/19/90	55,000	ADMIN	
8	1246	Jeff	Martin	10/31/91	22,000	PURCH	
9	1263	Cynthia	Rhodes	04/01/90	32,000	SALES	
10	1234	Henry	Bullock	01/14/92	38,000	MARKET	
11	1278	Keith	Davis	04/12/92	34,000	MANU	
12	1256	Ron	Woods	07/18/92	37,000	ENGR	
13							
14		SALARY					
15		>35000					
16							
17	ID	FIRSTNAME	LASTNAME	DOH	SALARY	DEPT	
18	1201	John	Haenszel	07/31/89	45,000	ADMIN	
19	1217	David	Carlson	09/19/90	55,000	ADMIN	
20	1234	Henry	Bullock	01/14/92	38,000	MARKET	
21	1256	Ron	Woods	07/18/92	37,000	ENGR	
22							

FIGURE 9–9 Records extracted with Data Query Extract

the From. range. 1-2-3/G prompts you for a To. range. Move the cell pointer to cell A:B14 and press ENTER. 1-2-3/G copies the label SALARY from cell A:E1 to A:B14.

3. Press HOME to move the cell pointer to cell A:A1 and select the Copy command again. 1-2-3/G prompts you for a From. range. Press END-→ to highlight all the field names in the first row of the EMPBASE table and press ENTER. 1-2-3/G prompts you for a To. range. Move the cell pointer to cell A:A17 and press ENTER. 1-2-3/G copies the field names in row 1 to row 17.
4. Move the cell pointer to cell A:B15 (beneath the SALARY field name) and enter the label **'>35000**.
5. Select the Data Query command. 1-2-3/G displays the Data Query dialog box.
6. In the Input text box, specify the range A:A1..A:F12. Notice that this range includes all the records in the EMPBASE table as well as its field names.
7. In the Criteria text box, specify the range A:B14..A:B15. Notice that this range includes both the field name, SALARY, as well as the search argument '>35000. Thus, 1-2-3/G will search for records with a value greater than $35,000 in the SALARY field of the EMPBASE table.
8. In the Output text box, specify the range A:A17..A:F17. Notice that this single-row output range includes all the field names from the EMPBASE

table and that they appear in the same order. Therefore, all the fields from the appropriate records will be copied and the order of the fields will be the same as the EMPBASE table.

9. Select the Extract command button located on the right side of the Data Query dialog box. 1-2-3/G copies those records in the input range that match the criteria in the criteria range to the output range. Your screen should look like Figure 9–9.
10. Select the Quit command button to leave the Data Query dialog box and return to the current worksheet.

1-2-3/G remembers the ranges you've set for the Data Query command. It shows those same ranges in the Data Query dialog box the next time you enter the command. To change an individual input, criteria, or output range specification, select the appropriate text box and specify a new range address or range name. Alternatively, you can cancel all Data Query ranges by selecting the Reset command button from the Data Query dialog box.

Note

You can press QUERY (F7) to repeat the most recent Data Query command. For example, imagine you've just completed using the Data Query Extract command. You can modify the criteria range and press QUERY (F7). 1-2-3/G copies a new set of records to the output range using your revised selection criteria.

Defining Criteria

This section discusses the various types of selection criteria that you can define in the criteria range. As mentioned, 1-2-3/G uses the selection criteria you specify in the criteria range to select records for the Data Query commands. You prepare the criteria range in advance and then use the Data Query Criteria command to point to the range that contains those criteria.

At a minimum, each criteria you specify is composed of two elements—a field name from the input range and a search argument. A field name appears in the first row of the criteria range and determines which field in the input range (database table) will be searched. The search argument, on the other hand, appears beneath the field name to which it corresponds and states a condition that must be met for a record to be selected. When you execute a Data Query command, 1-2-3/G scans the fields in the input range (database table) referenced by the field names in the criteria range. Only those records that meet the search argument beneath this field name are selected.

You can have more than one field name in the criteria range—up to 32 of them. That way, you can search multiple fields in a database table at the same time. When you use multiple field names, however, you must locate each of them in adjacent cells in a single row. See "Defining Multiple Criteria" later for more details on this.

You can use various types of search arguments in the criteria range. For example, you can specify labels or values that exactly match an entry in a given field. When 1-2-3/G finds that label or value, it selects the record that contains it. You can also use comparison formulas as search arguments in the criteria range. Comparison formulas are useful for selecting groups of records. For example, you can create a formula that causes 1-2-3/G to select a record only when the value in a given field exceeds 35,000. The sections that follow show you how to create each of these search argument types and use them with the Data Query Extract command to select records from the EMPBASE table.

Using Label Criteria

Figure 9-10 shows an example of how you might use label criteria to search a database table. In this case, the criteria range is A:B14..A:B15. A single field, DEPT, appears in the first row of this criteria range. Notice that this field name

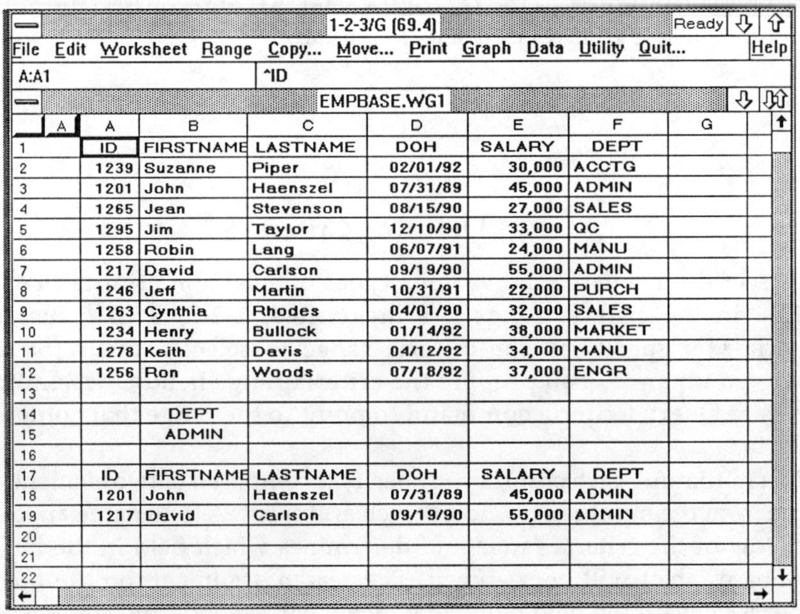

1-2-3/G [69.4] Ready

File Edit Worksheet Range Copy... Move... Print Graph Data Utility Quit... Help

A:A1 ^ID

EMPBASE.WG1

A	A	B	C	D	E	F	G
1	ID	FIRSTNAME	LASTNAME	DOH	SALARY	DEPT	
2	1239	Suzanne	Piper	02/01/92	30,000	ACCTG	
3	1201	John	Haenszel	07/31/89	45,000	ADMIN	
4	1265	Jean	Stevenson	08/15/90	27,000	SALES	
5	1295	Jim	Taylor	12/10/90	33,000	QC	
6	1258	Robin	Lang	06/07/91	24,000	MANU	
7	1217	David	Carlson	09/19/90	55,000	ADMIN	
8	1246	Jeff	Martin	10/31/91	22,000	PURCH	
9	1263	Cynthia	Rhodes	04/01/90	32,000	SALES	
10	1234	Henry	Bullock	01/14/92	38,000	MARKET	
11	1278	Keith	Davis	04/12/92	34,000	MANU	
12	1256	Ron	Woods	07/18/92	37,000	ENGR	
13							
14		DEPT					
15		ADMIN					
16							
17	ID	FIRSTNAME	LASTNAME	DOH	SALARY	DEPT	
18	1201	John	Haenszel	07/31/89	45,000	ADMIN	
19	1217	David	Carlson	09/19/90	55,000	ADMIN	
20							
21							
22							

FIGURE 9-10 Using label criteria to select records

matches the DEPT field name in the EMPBASE table. The DEPT field contains the name of the department in which each employee works. In the second row of the criteria range, A:B15, the label ADMIN appears. When this data query is performed, 1-2-3/G will search the DEPT field in the EMPBASE table and select those records that contain the label ADMIN in the DEPT field.

The results of using this criteria with the Data Query Extract command are shown beneath the output range A:A17..A:F17. Notice that only two records have been selected, indicating that there are two records in the EMPBASE table that contain the label ADMIN in the DEPT field.

To perform this data query yourself, begin by setting up the criteria and output ranges as you see them in Figure 9–10. When you're ready, select the Data Query command. 1-2-3/G displays the Data Query dialog box. In the Input text box, specify the range A:A1..A:F12, which includes all the records in the EMPBASE table and its field names. In the Criteria text box, specify the range A:B14..A:B15, which includes the DEPT field name as well as the search argument ADMIN. In the Output text box, specify the range A:A17..A:F17, which includes the row of field names in row 17. Finally, select the Extract command button. 1-2-3/G copies the selected records from the EMPBASE table to the output range. To return to the worksheet, select the Quit command button.

Normally, 1-2-3/G is not case sensitive when searching database fields for labels. For instance, in the previous example, the label search argument ADMIN will locate records with ADMIN, Admin, or admin in the DEPT field. If case sensitivity in label searches is important to you, there are two things you can do. First, you can use the @EXACT function in your criteria range search argument. For example, to find records with the label Admin, but not ADMIN or admin, in the previous example, you can use the formula @EXACT(+F2,"Admin"). See Chapter 6, "Functions," for more details on the @EXACT function.

Alternatively, you can select the ASCII sort sequence. To do this, select the User Settings International Sort options ASCII command from either the Utility or Desktop Control menu. With this sort sequence, 1-2-3/G interprets labels on the basis of each letter's ASCII value. Because each upper-case letter has a different ASCII value than its lower-case counterpart, 1-2-3/G honors capitalization when scanning labels.

Using Wildcards

You can use wild-card characters in place of letters in label search arguments. Wild-card characters serve as place holders for one or more letters in a label and serve to represent any letter. 1-2-3/G offers the following wild-card characters:

? Takes the place of any single letter.
* Takes the place of all letters to the end of a label.

Imagine you want to search the EMPBASE table for Jean Stevenson's record, but you can't remember the last name is spelled Stevenson or Stevensen. To find this record, you can use the label search argument Stevens?n beneath the field name LASTNAME. When this data query is executed, 1-2-3/G will select records with either Stevenson or Stevensen in the LASTNAME field.

Figure 9–11 shows an example of how you might use the * wild-card character in a label search argument in the criteria range. Once again, the criteria range is A:B14..A:B15. In the top row of this range is the label DEPT, representing the DEPT field in the EMPBASE table. Beneath this field name, the label a* appears. When this data query is processed, 1-2-3/G selects all records whose labels in the DEPT field begin with the letter a or A. The results of this data query are shown in the output range A:F17..A:G20.

As with OS/2 or DOS, you cannot use the * wild-card character to represent any group of letters. For example, you cannot use the search argument b*ger to find the labels Berger or Burger. Unfortunately, once 1-2-3/G encounters the * wild-card character, it ignores all other characters to the end of the label.

Negating Labels

You can also precede a label search argument with a ~ (tilde) to exclude records with that label from being selected. For example, imagine you want to select all

1-2-3/G [69.4] Ready

File Edit Worksheet Range Copy... Move... Print Graph Data Utility Quit... Help

A:A1 ^ID

EMPBASE.WG1

A	A	B	C	D	E	F	G
1	ID	FIRSTNAME	LASTNAME	DOH	SALARY	DEPT	
2	1239	Suzanne	Piper	02/01/92	30,000	ACCTG	
3	1201	John	Haenszel	07/31/89	45,000	ADMIN	
4	1265	Jean	Stevenson	08/15/90	27,000	SALES	
5	1295	Jim	Taylor	12/10/90	33,000	QC	
6	1258	Robin	Lang	06/07/91	24,000	MANU	
7	1217	David	Carlson	09/19/90	55,000	ADMIN	
8	1246	Jeff	Martin	10/31/91	22,000	PURCH	
9	1263	Cynthia	Rhodes	04/01/90	32,000	SALES	
10	1234	Henry	Bullock	01/14/92	38,000	MARKET	
11	1278	Keith	Davis	04/12/92	34,000	MANU	
12	1256	Ron	Woods	07/18/92	37,000	ENGR	
13							
14		DEPT					
15		a*					
16							
17	ID	FIRSTNAME	LASTNAME	DOH	SALARY	DEPT	
18	1239	Suzanne	Piper	02/01/92	30,000	ACCTG	
19	1201	John	Haenszel	07/31/89	45,000	ADMIN	
20	1217	David	Carlson	09/19/90	55,000	ADMIN	
21							
22							

FIGURE 9–11 Using wild-card characters to select records

records from the EMPBASE table, except those with Bullock in the LASTNAME field. To do this, you can specify the following criteria:

```
LASTNAME
~Bullock
```

You can also combine this negation symbol with a wild-card character. For example, to select all records from the EMPBASE table except those that begin with the letter B in the LASTNAME field, you can specify the following criteria:

```
LASTNAME
~b*
```

Value Criteria

1-2-3/G also allows you to use values as search arguments to select records from database table. For example, Figure 9–12 shows a data query that uses a value as a search argument in the Criteria range. In Figure 9–12, the criteria range is A:B14..A:B15. In the top row of this criteria range the label SALARY appears, representing the SALARY field in the EMPBASE table. As you might imagine, the SALARY field contains the annual salary earned by each employee

1-2-3/G [69.4] Ready

File Edit Worksheet Range Copy... Move... Print Graph Data Utility Quit... Help

A:B14 ^SALARY

EMPBASE.WG1

A	A	B	C	D	E	F	G
1	ID	FIRSTNAME	LASTNAME	DOH	SALARY	DEPT	
2	1239	Suzanne	Piper	02/01/92	30,000	ACCTG	
3	1201	John	Haenszel	07/31/89	45,000	ADMIN	
4	1265	Jean	Stevenson	08/15/90	27,000	SALES	
5	1295	Jim	Taylor	12/10/90	33,000	QC	
6	1258	Robin	Lang	06/07/91	24,000	MANU	
7	1217	David	Carlson	09/19/90	55,000	ADMIN	
8	1246	Jeff	Martin	10/31/91	22,000	PURCH	
9	1263	Cynthia	Rhodes	04/01/90	32,000	SALES	
10	1234	Henry	Bullock	01/14/92	38,000	MARKET	
11	1278	Keith	Davis	04/12/92	34,000	MANU	
12	1256	Ron	Woods	07/18/92	37,000	ENGR	
13							
14		SALARY					
15		37000					
16							
17	ID	FIRSTNAME	LASTNAME	DOH	SALARY	DEPT	
18	1256	Ron	Woods	07/18/92	37,000	ENGR	
19							
20							
21							
22							

FIGURE 9–12 Using value criteria to select records

in the EMPBASE table. In the second row of the criteria range, cell A:B15, the value 37000 appears. When this data query is processed, 1-2-3/G will select only those records with 37,000 in the SALARY field.

The results of using these criteria with the Data Query Extract command are shown in the output range A:A17..A:F18 of Figure 9–12. Notice that only a single record has been selected, indicating that only one record in the EMPBASE table has the value 37,000 in the SALARY field.

You can also use date or time values to search for records. For example, using the EMPBASE table again, imagine you want to locate the records of all employees hired on 02/01/92. To do this, enter the following criteria in the criteria range A:B14..A:B15 of Figure 9–12:

```
DOH
@DATE(92,2,1)
```

The DOH field name refers to DOH (Date of Hire) field in the EMPBASE table. The @DATE(92,2,1) function beneath this field name causes 1-2-3/G to calculate the date value for 02/01/90, which is 33635. However, if you attempt to use a Data Query command at this point, 1-2-3/G will issue an error message. To perform the data query, you must first transform the @DATE function to its current value by using the Range Value command. The Range Value command will in effect remove the @DATE function and replace it with the value for the function. To do this, move the cell pointer to cell A:B15 and select Range Value. Press ENTER twice to confirm cell A:B15 as both the From. and To. for the Range Value command. You can now perform the data query.

Comparison Formulas

You can also use comparison formulas in the criteria range. Comparison formulas allow you to select records when the value in a given field falls within a certain range. For example, using the EMPBASE table, you might want to select the records of those employees whose salary exceeds $35,000.

Comparison formulas contain three basic components as follows:

- A reference to the first data cell in a field of the input range.
- An operator.
- A value for comparison.

Figure 9–13 shows the comparison formula +E2>35000 beneath the field name SALARY in the criteria range A:B14..A:B15. Breaking this formula down, the +E2 is a reference to the first data cell in the SALARY field of the EMPBASE table (A:A1..A:F12). The > symbol is a logical operator meaning greater than. Finally, the 35000 is the value used for comparison. When 1-2-3/G processes this data query, it reviews each value in the SALARY field of the EMPBASE table. Those records with values in excess of $35,000 in this field are selected.

1-2-3/G [69.4] Ready

File Edit Worksheet Range Copy... Move... Print Graph Data Utility Quit... Help

A:B15 +E2>35000

(T) AND.WG1

A	A	B	C	D	E	F
1	ID	FIRSTNAME	LASTNAME	DOH	SALARY	DEPT
2	1239	Suzanne	Piper	02/01/92	30,000	ACCTG
3	1201	John	Haenszel	07/31/89	45,000	ADMIN
4	1265	Jean	Stevenson	08/15/90	27,000	SALES
5	1295	Jim	Taylor	12/10/90	33,000	QC
6	1258	Robin	Lang	06/07/91	24,000	MANU
7	1217	David	Carlson	09/19/90	55,000	ADMIN
8	1246	Jeff	Martin	10/31/91	22,000	PURCH
9	1263	Cynthia	Rhodes	04/01/90	32,000	SALES
10	1234	Henry	Bullock	01/14/92	38,000	MARKET
11	1278	Keith	Davis	04/12/92	34,000	MANU
12	1256	Ron	Woods	07/18/92	37,000	ENGR
13						
14		SALARY				
15		+E2>35000				
16						
17	ID	FIRSTNAME	LASTNAME	DOH	SALARY	DEPT
18	1201	John	Haenszel	07/31/89	45,000	ADMIN
19	1217	David	Carlson	09/19/90	55,000	ADMIN
20	1234	Henry	Bullock	01/14/92	38,000	MARKET
21	1256	Ron	Woods	07/18/92	37,000	ENGR
22						

FIGURE 9–13 **A comparison formula in the criteria range**

Note

You must enter criteria-range comparison formulas as formulas, not as labels.

The results of the data query in Figure 9–13 are shown in the output range A:A1..A:F21. Notice that four records have been selected, indicating that four employees included in the EMPBASE table earn in excess of $35,000.

The greater than (>) logical operator shown in the previous example is only one of the available operators that you can use in a comparison formula. Table 9–1 shows a complete list of the logical operators you can use in a comparison formula.

The comparison formula in cell A:B15 of Figure 9–13 has been formatted with the Range Format Text command, so that you can see it. Normally, when you enter a comparison formula, 1-2-3/G displays a 0 or 1 in the cell. Comparison formulas perform a logical test. The test is either true (1) or false (0). For example, when you first enter the formula +E2>35000 in cell A:B15 of Figure

TABLE 9–1 1-2-3/G's Logical Operators

Operator	Description
=	Equals
< >	Not equal
<	Less than
>	Greater than
<=	Less than or equal to
>=	Greater than or equal to
#NOT#	Logical NOT
#AND#	Logical AND
#OR#	Logical OR

9–13, 1-2-3/G displays 0, because the contents of cell A:E2 (30,000) when compared to the value 35,000 returns false.

Because comparison formulas include a reference to the first data cell of a field in the input range, you can locate them under any field name in the criteria range. For example, imagine in Figure 9–13 that there are several field names in the first row of the criteria range (row 14). You can locate the formula +E2>35000 under any field name and 1-2-3/G will still process the data query correctly.

You can leave out the input-range reference in a comparison formula. For example, instead of using the formula +E2>35000 in cell A:B15 of Figure 9–13, you can enter the label '>35000. However, this label search argument must appear under the field name to which it corresponds, in this case SALARY. Otherwise, the data query may return unexpected results.

You can also use a label as a comparison value in a comparison formula. However, make sure you enclose the label in quotes. Otherwise, 1-2-3/G will issue an error message. For example, imagine you want to extract the records of employees in the EMPBASE table whose last names are between L and Z. To do this, you can use the formula +C2>"K*" in cell A:B15 of Figure 9–13. The +C2 in this formula references the LASTNAME field in the EMPBASE table. Because of this field reference, you do not need to use the LASTNAME field name in cell A:B14 of Figure 9–13. Once again, the logical operator > is used to specify a greater than test. Finally, the letter K appears followed by the * wild-card character. When this data query is processed, 1-2-3/G will select the records of those employees whose last names start with a letter that comes after the letter K.

If you do not use an input-range reference in a comparison formula, you do not have to enclose labels in quotes. For example, building on the example in the previous paragraph, you can use the following criteria in the range A:B14..A:B15 of Figure 9–13:

```
LASTNAME
'>M*
```

In this case, the LASTNAME field name refers to the LASTNAME field in the input range (EMPBASE table). When 1-2-3/G encounters an operator as the first character in the label '>M* below, it automatically substitutes the input-range reference for you.

Tip: Name the first data cell in each field

> Use the Range Name Labels Down command to name the first data cell in each field of the input range (database table). That way, you can substitute range names in place of cell address in your comparison formulas, making them appear more intelligible. For example, to name the first data cell of each field in the EMPBASE table, move the cell pointer to cell A:A1 and enter the Range Name Labels Down command. Press END-→ to highlight the row of field names (A:A1..A:F1) and press ENTER to complete the command. 1-2-3/G names the cells in row 2 (A:A2..A:F2) by using the labels in row 1. Once these cells are named, you can use those names in your comparison formulas. For example, instead of the formula +E2>35000 in cell A:B15 of Figure 9–13, you can use the formula +SALARY>35000.

Defining Multiple Criteria

The data query examples thus far in this chapter all use a single criterion to select records from a database table. However, 1-2-3/G also allows you to define multiple criteria to select records. For example, using the EMPBASE table, imagine you want to select the records of those employees who were hired after 01/01/91 and who make more than $30,000. That is, for a record to be selected, both the first *and* second conditions must be true. Or, imagine you want to see the records of those employees who work either in Sales or in Manufacturing. In this case, either one *or* the other condition must be true for the record to be selected.

As mentioned, you can include more than one field name in the first row of the criteria range, up to 32 of them. The field names must appear in adjacent cells. Beneath each field name, you can define a different search argument.

Thus, you can specify multiple criteria for the selection of records from a database table.

The "AND" Query

When search arguments appear in the same row of the criteria range, there is an implied "AND" relationship between them. That is, the conditions defined by all the search arguments in that row must be met for a record to be selected from the input range.

Figure 9–14 shows an example of two field names in the criteria range with a search argument beneath each one. The first field name, DOH, appears in cell A:B14. Beneath this field name the comparison formula +D2>@DATE(91,1,1) instructs 1-2-3/G to select records with a date value after 01/01/91 in the DOH (Date of Hire) field of the EMPBASE table. The second field name, SALARY, appears in cell A:C14 of Figure 9–14. Beneath this field name, the label '>30000 instructs 1-2-3/G to select all records with a value greater than $30,000 in the SALARY field of the EMPBASE table. Since both search arguments appear in the same row of the criteria range, both must be met for a record to be selected from the EMPBASE table.

1-2-3/G Ready

File Edit Worksheet Range Copy... Move... Print Graph Data Utility Quit... Help

A:B15 +D2>+@DATE(91,1,1)

D:\CH9\FIG9-14.WG1

A	A	B	C	D	E	F
1	ID	FIRSTNAME	LASTNAME	DOH	SALARY	DEPT
2	1239	Suzanne	Piper	02/01/92	30,000	ACCTG
3	1201	John	Haenszel	07/31/89	45,000	ADMIN
4	1265	Jean	Stevenson	08/15/90	27,000	SALES
5	1295	Jim	Taylor	12/10/90	33,000	QC
6	1258	Robin	Lang	06/07/91	24,000	MANU
7	1217	David	Carlson	09/19/90	55,000	ADMIN
8	1246	Jeff	Martin	10/31/91	22,000	PURCH
9	1263	Cynthia	Rhodes	04/01/90	32,000	SALES
10	1234	Henry	Bullock	01/14/92	38,000	MARKET
11	1278	Keith	Davis	04/12/92	34,000	MANU
12	1256	Ron	Woods	07/18/92	37,000	ENGR
13						
14		DOH	SALARY			
15		1	>30000			
16						
17	ID	FIRSTNAME	LASTNAME	DOH	SALARY	DEPT
18	1234	Henry	Bullock	01/14/92	38,000	MARKET
19	1278	Keith	Davis	04/12/92	34,000	MANU
20	1256	Ron	Woods	07/18/92	37,000	ENGR

FIGURE 9–14 Multiple search arguments in the same row

To process this data query, begin by setting up the criteria and output ranges as they appear in Figure 9–14. When you're ready, select the Data Query command. 1-2-3/G displays the Data Query dialog box. In the Input text box, specify the range A:A1..A:F12 which includes the EMPBASE table. In the Criteria text box, specify the range A:B14..A:C15, which includes both field names and their search arguments. In the Output text box, specify the single-row output range A:A17..A:F17, which includes the field names in row 17. Finally, select the Extract command button. 1-2-3/G extracts those records from the EMPBASE table with a date value after 01/01/91 in the DOH field and a value greater that $30,000 in the SALARY field.

The "OR" Query

You can also have more than one row of search arguments in the criteria range. When search arguments appear in different rows of the criteria range, there is an implied "OR" relationship between them. That is, 1-2-3/G selects records when either one *or* the other condition is true. For example, Figure 9–15 shows a single field name in the criteria range with two search arguments in different rows beneath it. The field name, DEPT, appears in cell A:B14. Beneath this field name, the label SALES appears in cell A:B15 and the label MANU appears in cell A:B16. When this data query is processed, 1-2-3/G will select those records from the EMPBASE table with either the label SALES or the label MANU in the DEPT field.

To process this data query, begin by setting up the criteria and output ranges as they appear in Figure 9–15. When you're ready, select the Data Query command. In the input text box, specify the range of the EMPBASE table, A:A1..A:A12. In the Criteria text box, specify the range A:B14..A:B16, which includes the DEPT field name and both labels beneath it. In the Output text box, specify the range A:A18..A:F18, which includes the field names in row 18.

1-2-3/G [69.4] Ready

File Edit Worksheet Range Copy... Move... Print Graph Data Utility Quit... Help

A:B14 ^DEPT

EMPBASE.WG1

A	A	B	C	D	E	F
13						
14		DEPT				
15		SALES				
16		MANU				
17						
18	ID	FIRSTNAME	LASTNAME	DOH	SALARY	DEPT
19	1265	Jean	Stevenson	08/15/90	27,000	SALES
20	1258	Robin	Lang	06/07/91	24,000	MANU
21	1263	Cynthia	Rhodes	04/01/90	32,000	SALES
22	1278	Keith	Davis	04/12/92	34,000	MANU
23						

FIGURE 9–15 Multiple search arguments in different rows

Finally, select the Extract command button. 1-2-3/G extracts those records that contain the label SALES or the label MANU in the DEPT field of the EMPBASE table. Your screen should look like Figure 9–15.

Combining "AND" and "OR" Queries

You can also combine "AND" and "OR" relationships in the criteria range. For example, Figure 9–16 shows three field names in the criteria range A:B14..A:D16 with multiple search arguments located in the two rows beneath each field name. The field names in the top row of the criteria range are DOH, SALARY, and DEPT. Beneath the DOH and SALARY field names, the same search arguments appear in both rows. However, in the two rows beneath the DEPT field name, the search arguments differ. 1-2-3/G will select records from the EMPBASE table, either when all the arguments in the first row are true or when all the arguments in the second row are true.

The criteria range in Figure 9–16 breaks down as follows. Beneath the DOH field name (cell A:B14), the argument +D2>@DATE(91,1,1) appears in rows 15 and 16. This causes 1-2-3/G to select records when the DOH field in the EMPBASE table contains a date value after 01/01/91. Beneath the SALARY field name (cell A:C14), the argument '>30000 appears in rows 15 and 16, causing 1-2-3/G to select records with a value greater than $30,000 in the SALARY field of the EMPBASE table. Finally, beneath the DEPT field name (cell A:D14), different labels appear in row 15 versus row 16. Row 15 contains the label SALES and row 16 contains the label MANU. When this data query is processed, 1-2-3/G will select records with either the label SALES or the label MANU in the DEPT field. However, for a record to be selected from the EMPBASE table, it must also contain a value

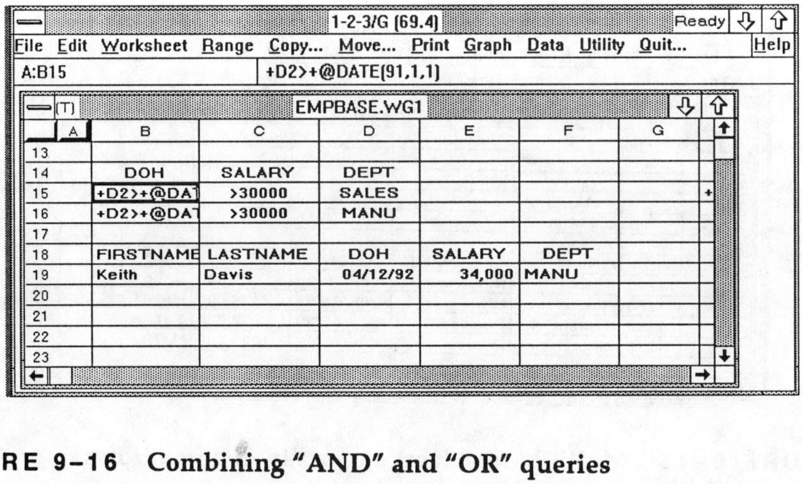

1-2-3/G (69.4) Ready

File Edit Worksheet Range Copy... Move... Print Graph Data Utility Quit... Help

A:B15 +D2>+@DATE(91,1,1)

(T) EMPBASE.WG1

	A	B	C	D	E	F	G
13							
14		DOH	SALARY	DEPT			
15		+D2>+@DA1	>30000	SALES			
16		+D2>+@DA1	>30000	MANU			
17							
18		FIRSTNAME	LASTNAME	DOH	SALARY	DEPT	
19		Keith	Davis	04/12/92	34,000	MANU	
20							
21							
22							
23							

FIGURE 9–16 Combining "AND" and "OR" queries

greater than $30,000 in the SALARY field and a date value after 01/01/91 in the DOH field.

The #AND#, #OR#, and #NOT# Logical Operators

You can also use the #AND#, #OR#, and #NOT# logical operators to combine search arguments in the criteria range. When you use the #AND# operator to combine two search arguments, both arguments must be met for a record to be selected. When you use the #OR# logical operator to combine search arguments, 1-2-3/G will select a record when either one or the other argument is met. Finally, the #NOT# operator allows you to exclude a search argument. That is, all records will be selected except those that meet the search argument.

Figure 9–17 shows an example of how you might use the #AND# operator in the criteria range to query the EMPBASE table. The criteria range in Figure 9–17 is A:B14..A:B15. In the first row of this range, the field name DOH appears, which corresponds to the DOH (Date of Hire) field in the EMPBASE table. In the second row of this range, the following search argument appears:

```
+D2>=@DATE(91,1,1)#AND#D2<=@DATE(91,12,31)
```

The first half of the search argument, before the #AND# operator, selects all records from the EMPBASE table with date value greater than or equal to 01/01/91. The second part of this search argument, after the #AND# operator, selects all records with a date value in the DOH field that is less than or equal to 12/31/91. However, the #AND# in effect joins the two conditions and both must be met before a record is selected. Therefore, when this data query is processed, 1-2-3/G will select the records of those employees hired between

1-2-3/G [69.4] Ready

File Edit Worksheet Range Copy... Move... Print Graph Data Utility Quit... Help

A:B15 +D2>=@DATE(91,1,1)#AND#D2<=@DATE(91,12,31)

(T) EMPBASE.WG1

A	A	B	C	D	E	F
13						
14		DOH				
15		+D2>=@DA				
16						
17						
18	ID	FIRSTNAME	LASTNAME	DOH	SALARY	DEPT
19	1258	Robin	Lang	06/07/91	24,000	MANU
20	1246	Jeff	Martin	10/31/91	22,000	PURCH
21						
22						
23						

FIGURE 9–17 The #AND# logical operator

01/01/91 and 12/31/91. The results of this data query are shown in the output range A:A18..A:F20 of Figure 9–17.

Figure 9–18 shows an example of how you might use the #OR# operator in the criteria range to query the EMPBASE table. The criteria range in Figure 9–18 is A:B14..A:B15. The first row of this range contains the field name DEPT, corresponding to the DEPT field in the EMPBASE table. Beneath this field name appears the search argument +F2="SALES"#OR#F2="MANU". The first half of this search argument, before the #OR# operator, selects all records with the label SALES in the DEPT field. The second half, after the #OR# argument, selects all records with the label MANU in the DEPT field. However, the #OR# operator joins the two conditions such that a record will be selected when either one or the other condition is true. The results of this data query are shown in the output range A:A18..A:F22 of Figure 9–18.

The #NOT# logical operator allows you to select all records except those that meet a specific condition. For example, imagine you want to select all records from the EMPBASE table except those with the label MANU in the DEPT field. To do this, you can use the search argument #NOT#F2="MANU" in the cell A:B15 of the criteria range A:B14..A:B15 of Figure 9–18. When this data query is processed, 1-2-3/G will select all the records in the EMPBASE table except those with the label MANU in the DEPT field.

Using the Data Query Commands

In the preceding sections of this chapter, the Data Query Extract command was used to demonstrate how you can copy selected records from a database table to an output range. However, the Data Query Extract command is but one of the Data Query commands offered by 1-2-3/G. In fact, you can use the following additional Data Query commands to manage database tables:

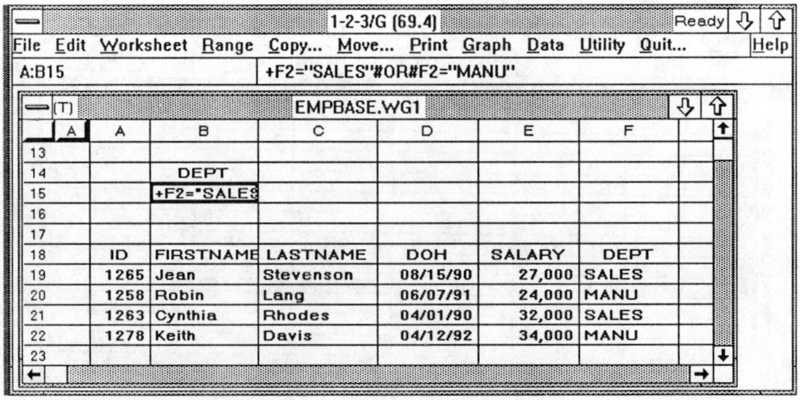

1-2-3/G [69.4] Ready

File Edit Worksheet Range Copy... Move... Print Graph Data Utility Quit... Help

A:B15 +F2="SALES"#OR#F2="MANU"

(T) EMPBASE.WG1

A	A	B	C	D	E	F
13						
14		DEPT				
15		+F2="SALES				
16						
17						
18	ID	FIRSTNAME	LASTNAME	DOH	SALARY	DEPT
19	1265	Jean	Stevenson	08/15/90	27,000	SALES
20	1258	Robin	Lang	06/07/91	24,000	MANU
21	1263	Cynthia	Rhodes	04/01/90	32,000	SALES
22	1278	Keith	Davis	04/12/92	34,000	MANU
23						

FIGURE 9–18 The #OR# logical operator

- **Data Query Find:** Finds selected records in the input range that match the criteria in the criteria range.
- **Data Query Unique:** Copies only unique records from the input range to the output range.
- **Data Query Delete:** Deletes selected records in the input range that match the criteria in the criteria range.
- **Data Query Modify:** Allows you to copy selected records to an output range, modify them, and then put them back where they came from. This command also allows you to append records from an output range to the end of a database.

Each of these commands is covered in more detail in the sections that follow.

Locating Records

To locate specific records, you can use the Data Query Find command. This command allows you to locate records in the input range (database table) that match the criteria in the criteria range. When a matching record is found, 1-2-3/G highlights that record. The Data Query Find command is useful when you want to find and edit specific records or when you want to test the criteria in the criteria range prior to deleting or extracting records.

The Data Query Find command requires that you specify an input range and a criteria range. However, because the Data Query Find command is only used to located specific records, an output range specification is not required.

Figure 9–19 shows an example of a record from the EMPBASE table that has been located and highlighted by using the Data Query Find command. Notice that all the fields in the record are highlighted. The input range specification for this data query is A:A1..A:F12, which includes all the records from the EMPBASE table and its field names. The criteria range is A:B14..A:B15, which includes the field name DEPT with the label SALES beneath it. Thus, when this data query is executed, 1-2-3/G will locate all records in the EMPBASE table that have the label SALES in the DEPT field.

To execute the data query in Figure 9–19, select the Data Query command. 1-2-3/G displays the Data Query dialog box. Use the Input and Criteria text boxes to specify the input and criteria ranges described in the previous paragraph. As mentioned, an output range is not required. Finally, select the Find command button. 1-2-3/G locates and highlights the first record in the EMPBASE table that has the label SALES in the DEPT field. In addition a FIND indicator is displayed in the title bar of the worksheet window. Your screen should look similar to Figure 9–19.

If no matching records are found during the Data Query Find command, 1-2-3/G beeps and returns you to the Data Query dialog box. However, once a record has been successfully located, you can perform any of the following:

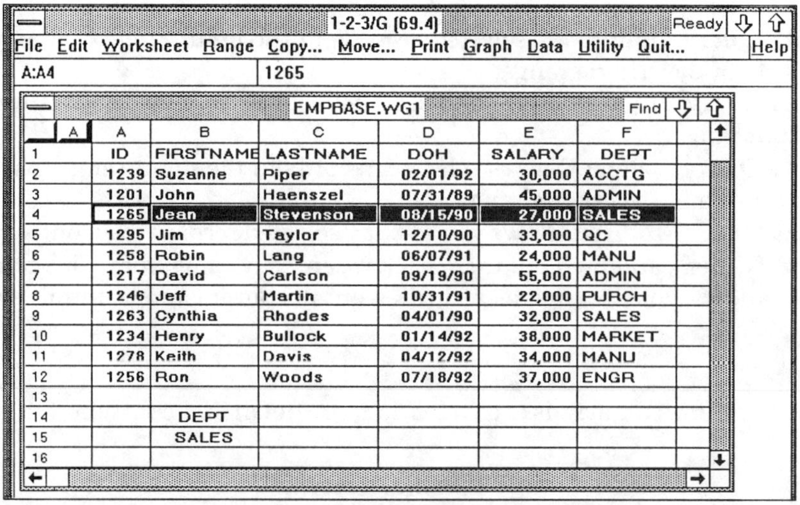

	A	B	C	D	E	F
1	ID	FIRSTNAME	LASTNAME	DOH	SALARY	DEPT
2	1239	Suzanne	Piper	02/01/92	30,000	ACCTG
3	1201	John	Haenszel	07/31/89	45,000	ADMIN
4	1265	Jean	Stevenson	08/15/90	27,000	SALES
5	1295	Jim	Taylor	12/10/90	33,000	QC
6	1258	Robin	Lang	06/07/91	24,000	MANU
7	1217	David	Carlson	09/19/90	55,000	ADMIN
8	1246	Jeff	Martin	10/31/91	22,000	PURCH
9	1263	Cynthia	Rhodes	04/01/90	32,000	SALES
10	1234	Henry	Bullock	01/14/92	38,000	MARKET
11	1278	Keith	Davis	04/12/92	34,000	MANU
12	1256	Ron	Woods	07/18/92	37,000	ENGR
13						
14		DEPT				
15		SALES				
16						

FIGURE 9–19 A record located with Data Query Find

- Press → or ← to move among the fields in a highlighted record.
- Press EDIT (F2) to edit the contents of any field.
- Press ↓ to see the next record in the input range that meets the criteria in the criteria range. Conversely, you can press ↑ to see the previous record.
- Press HOME to move to the first record in the input range that matches your selection criteria. Conversely, you can press END to move to the last record.
- Press ENTER or ESC to return to the Data Query dialog box.
- Press QUERY (F7) to end the Data Query Find command and return to the worksheet. 1-2-3/G leaves the cell pointer on the last record found.

Note

In 1-2-3/G, hidden columns and rows are temporarily redisplayed when you select the Data Query Find command. That way, you can see all the data located by Data Query Find. This is a change from 1-2-3 Releases 2 and 3, in which data in hidden columns is not displayed during the Data Query Find command.

Extracting Only Unique Records

To extract only unique records from a database table, you use the Data Query Unique command. For example, imagine you are working with a customer mailing-list database table. Imagine further that the names and addresses of some customers are listed twice. To create a new database table that includes a single record for each customer, you can use the Data Query Unique command to extract a single copy of each unique record to an output range.

Much like the Data Query Extract command, the Data Query Unique command requires that you specify an input range, a criteria range, and an output range.

The uniqueness of records is determined by the field names that are included in the output range for the Data Query Unique command. That is, two records are only considered to be duplicates when both records have the same contents in each field included in the output range. For example, the only field in the EMPBASE table in which information is repeated is the DEPT field. Otherwise, the information in the remaining fields varies from record to record. Therefore, there are no duplicate records in the EMPBASE table. However, Figure 9–20 shows what happens when you use the DEPT field as the only field in the output range with the Data Query Unique command. Notice that only a single

1-2-3/G [69.4] Ready

File Edit Worksheet Range Copy... Move... Print Graph Data Utility Quit... Help

A:B17 ^DEPT

EMPBASE.WG1

A	A	B	C	D	E	F
4	1265	Jean	Stevenson	08/15/90	27,000	SALES
5	1295	Jim	Taylor	12/10/90	33,000	QC
6	1258	Robin	Lang	06/07/91	24,000	MANU
7	1217	David	Carlson	09/19/90	55,000	ADMIN
8	1246	Jeff	Martin	10/31/91	22,000	PURCH
9	1263	Cynthia	Rhodes	04/01/90	32,000	SALES
10	1234	Henry	Bullock	01/14/92	38,000	MARKET
11	1278	Keith	Davis	04/12/92	34,000	MANU
12	1256	Ron	Woods	07/18/92	37,000	ENGR
13						
14		DEPT				
15						
16						
17		DEPT				
18		ACCTG				
19		ADMIN				
20		ENGR				
21		MANU				
22		MARKET				
23		PURCH				
24		QC				
25		SALES				

FIGURE 9–20 **Data Query Unique copies only unique records to the output range**

copy of each department name is copied to the output range. This is because the contents of the DEPT alone were used as the basis for determining if there were duplicate records in the EMPBASE table.

To perform the data query in Figure 9–20 yourself, start by setting up the criteria and output ranges as they appear in Figure 9–20. For example, to set up the criteria range, enter the field name DEPT in cell A:B14. Leave cell A:B15, beneath this field name blank. That way, 1-2-3/G will automatically select all the records in the input range. For the output range, enter the field name DEPT in cell A:B17. To execute the data query, select the Data Query command to display the Data Query dialog box. In the Input text box, specify the range A:A1..A:F12, which includes the EMPBASE table. In the Criteria text box specify the range A:B14..A:B15. In the Output text box, specify the range A:B17. Finally, select the Unique command button. 1-2-3/G searches the DEPT field of the EMPBASE table and extracts only the unique department names from each record in the table.

When you use Data Query Unique to copy unique records to an output range, 1-2-3/G sorts those records in ascending order. For example, notice in the output range (A:B17..A:B25) in Figure 9–20, 1-2-3/G displays the department names in alphabetical order. If you copy more that one field in each record to the output range, 1-2-3/G uses the first field included in the output range to sort the records.

Deleting Records

To delete records that meet specific criteria, you use the Data Query Delete command. When you execute this command, 1-2-3/G deletes the records in the input range that match the criteria in the criteria range. The input range is then compressed to close up the space previously occupied by the deleted records. Because no records are extracted by Data Query, you need only specify an input and criteria range for this command.

Note

> If you accidentally delete the wrong records with Data Query Delete, you can press ALT-BACKSPACE to use the undo feature to reclaim the lost data. Alternatively, you can use the Data Query Find command first to make sure your criteria selects the correct records to begin with.

Imagine that an employee has left the company and you want to delete his or her record from the EMPBASE table. To do this, you might set up the data query shown in Figure 9–21. In the criteria range (A:A14..A:A15) of Figure 9–21 a single field name, ID, appears with the number 1234 beneath it. The ID field name corresponds to the ID (employee identification number) field in the EMPBASE table. The number beneath this field name belongs to Henry Bullock (row 10) in the EMPBASE table. To delete this record, select the Data Query command to display the Data Query dialog box. In the Input text box, specify the range A:A1..A:F12. which includes the EMPBASE table. In the Criteria text box, specify the range A:A14..A:A15. Then, select the Delete command button. 1-2-3/G displays a message box with Delete and Cancel command buttons. If you select the Delete command button, 1-2-3/G deletes the record for Henry Bullock from the EMPBASE table and closes up the space previously occupied by the record. The size of input range for the Data Query command is now reduced to A:A1..A:F11. If you select the Cancel command button from the message box, the record is not deleted.

Modifying Records

To modify records that meet specific criteria, you can use the Data Query Modify command. The Extract option for this command allows you to copy

1-2-3/G [69.4] Ready

File Edit Worksheet Range Copy... Move... Print Graph Data Utility Quit... Help

A:A15 1234

EMPBASE.WG1

A	A	B	C	D	E	F
1	ID	FIRSTNAME	LASTNAME	DOH	SALARY	DEPT
2	1239	Suzanne	Piper	02/01/92	30,000	ACCTG
3	1201	John	Haenszel	07/31/89	45,000	ADMIN
4	1265	Jean	Stevenson	08/15/90	27,000	SALES
5	1295	Jim	Taylor	12/10/90	33,000	QC
6	1258	Robin	Lang	06/07/91	24,000	MANU
7	1217	David	Carlson	09/19/90	55,000	ADMIN
8	1246	Jeff	Martin	10/31/91	22,000	PURCH
9	1263	Cynthia	Rhodes	04/01/90	32,000	SALES
10	1234	Henry	Bullock	01/14/92	38,000	MARKET
11	1278	Keith	Davis	04/12/92	34,000	MANU
12	1256	Ron	Woods	07/18/92	37,000	ENGR
13						
14	ID					
15	1234					
16						
17						
18						
19						
20						
21						
22						

FIGURE 9–21 Preparing the criteria range for the Data Query Delete command

records that meet specific criteria to an output range. When you extract records with this option, 1-2-3/G remembers where it got the records. Once the records are copied to the output range, you can edit the contents of fields in those records as you like. Once editing is complete, you can use the Replace option of the Data Query Modify command to put those records back in their original positions in the input range.

Imagine an employee included in the EMPBASE table has been moved to a new department and has been given a raise. You need to modify the record for that employee. Figure 9–22 shows a record extracted from the EMPBASE table with Data Query Modify Extract. The record extracted belongs to Henry Bullock (row 10) of the EMPBASE table. Figure 9–23 shows that same record after it has been modified and returned to the EMPBASE table with Data Query Modify Replace. Notice that the record has been returned to its original position (row 10) in the EMPBASE table.

Note

In order for the Data Query Modify Replace command to function correctly, you must use it immediately after Data Query Modify Extract command. If you perform any Data Query or Data External commands after using Data Query Modify Extract, 1-2-3/G will issue an error message when you attempt to use Data Query Modify Replace.

Note

When you use Data Query Modify Extract to extract fields with formulas to an output range, 1-2-3/G extracts only the current values of those formulas. The same thing happens when you return records with formulas to the input range with Data Query Modify Replace; the underlying formulas are lost and are replaced by their current values.

To extract, modify, and return a record, as shown in Figures 9–22 and 9–23, begin by setting up your criteria and output ranges. In Figure 9–22, the criteria range A:A14..A:A15 contains the field name ID with the number 1234 beneath it. Thus, when this data query is executed, 1-2-3/G will search the ID field of

1-2-3/G [69.4] Ready

File Edit Worksheet Range Copy... Move... Print Graph Data Utility Quit... Help

A:A1 ^ID

EMPBASE.WG1

A	A	B	C	D	E	F
1	ID	FIRSTNAME	LASTNAME	DOH	SALARY	DEPT
2	1239	Suzanne	Piper	02/01/92	30,000	ACCTG
3	1201	John	Haenszel	07/31/89	45,000	ADMIN
4	1265	Jean	Stevenson	08/15/90	27,000	SALES
5	1295	Jim	Taylor	12/10/90	33,000	QC
6	1258	Robin	Lang	06/07/91	24,000	MANU
7	1217	David	Carlson	09/19/90	55,000	ADMIN
8	1246	Jeff	Martin	10/31/91	22,000	PURCH
9	1263	Cynthia	Rhodes	04/01/90	32,000	SALES
10	1234	Henry	Bullock	01/14/92	38,000	MARKET
11	1278	Keith	Davis	04/12/92	34,000	MANU
12	1256	Ron	Woods	07/18/92	37,000	ENGR
13						
14	ID					
15	1234					
16						
17	ID	FIRSTNAME	LASTNAME	DOH	SALARY	DEPT
18	1234	Henry	Bullock	01/14/92	38,000	MARKET
19						
20						
21						
22						

FIGURE 9–22 A record extracted with Data Query Modify Extract

1-2-3/G [69.4] Ready

File Edit Worksheet Range Copy... Move... Print Graph Data Utility Quit... Help

A:E18 @ROUND(38000*1.2,2)

(,0) EMPBASE.WG1

A	A	B	C	D	E	F
1	ID	FIRSTNAME	LASTNAME	DOH	SALARY	DEPT
2	1239	Suzanne	Piper	02/01/92	30,000	ACCTG
3	1201	John	Haenszel	07/31/89	45,000	ADMIN
4	1265	Jean	Stevenson	08/15/90	27,000	SALES
5	1295	Jim	Taylor	12/10/90	33,000	QC
6	1258	Robin	Lang	06/07/91	24,000	MANU
7	1217	David	Carlson	09/19/90	55,000	ADMIN
8	1246	Jeff	Martin	10/31/91	22,000	PURCH
9	1263	Cynthia	Rhodes	04/01/90	32,000	SALES
10	1234	Henry	Bullock	01/14/92	45,600	ADMIN
11	1278	Keith	Davis	04/12/92	34,000	MANU
12	1256	Ron	Woods	07/18/92	37,000	ENGR
13						
14	ID					
15	1234					
16						
17	ID	FIRSTNAME	LASTNAME	DOH	SALARY	DEPT
18	1234	Henry	Bullock	01/14/92	45,600	ADMIN
19						
20						
21						
22						

FIGURE 9–23 Data Query Modify Replace returns a modified record to the input range

the EMPBASE table and select that record with the number 1234 in the ID field. The output range in Figure 9–22 is A:A17..A:F17, which contains copies of all the field names from the EMPBASE table.

To extract the records for modification, select the Data Query command. 1-2-3/G displays the Data Query dialog box. In the Input text box, specify the range A:A1..A:F12. In the Criteria text box, specify the range, A:A14..A:A15. In the Output text box, specify the range A:A17..A:F17. Then, select the Extract option from the Modify section (left side) of the Data Query dialog box. 1-2-3/G extracts the record for employee ID 1234 to the output range. Select the Quit command button to return to the worksheet. You can now modify the record as you like. For example, Figure 9–23 shows the same record after the SALARY and DEPT fields have been modified.

To return the record to the EMPBASE table, select the Data Query command again. This time, select the Replace option from the Modify section (left side) of the Data Query dialog box. 1-2-3/G returns the modified record to its original position in the EMPBASE table. As you can see in Figure 9–23, row 10, the row the record originally came from, has been updated for the change. Select the Quit command button from the Data Query dialog box to return to the worksheet.

Adding Records

You can use the Data Query Modify Insert command to add records to the end of database table. This command copies records from the output range and adds them to the end of the input range. The input range is then expanded to accommodate the additional records. For this command, you need only specify an input range and an output range. A criteria range is not necessary.

For example, imagine you want to add a record to the end of the EMPBASE table. To do this, you can use the record shown in the output range A:A17..A:F18 of Figure 9–23 as a template. That is, beneath each field name you can type in the appropriate data. When you're ready, select the Data Query command. 1-2-3/G displays the Data Query dialog box. In the Input text box, specify the range A:A1..A:F12, which includes the EMPBASE table and its field names. In the Output text box, specify the range A:A17..A:F18, which includes the first row of field names and the record you want to add. Finally, select the Insert option button from the Modify section (left side) of the Data Query dialog box. 1-2-3/G copies the record from the output range and appends it to the end of the input range.

Creating Computed Columns in the Output Range

Computed columns allow you to perform calculations in the output range using information extracted from a database table. To create computed columns in the output range, you use formulas in the first row of the output range instead of field names. For example, imagine you want to evaluate the impact of giving every employee in the EMPBASE table a 10% raise next year. To do this, you can use formulas in the output range, as shown in Figure 9–24.

The output range in Figure 9–24 starts in row 17. This output was generated by using the Data Query Extract command with the criteria in the range A:B14..A:B15. (This criteria selects all the records from the EMPBASE table.) The first three cells of this output range (A:A17..A:C17) contain field names from the EMPBASE table. However, cells A:D17 and A:E17 contain formulas that create computed data in the output range. For example, cell A:D17 contains the formula +SALARY*1.1. The output in the column beneath this formula is computed by multiplying the data from the SALARY field of the EMPBASE table by 1.1 for those records that have been selected. Additionally, cell A:E17 contains the formula +SALARY*1.1–SALARY. The output beneath this formula is computed by multiplying the data in the SALARY field by 1.1 and then subtracting the contents of the SALARY field for those records that have been selected.

Note

The cells containing the formulas in the range A:D17..A:E18 of Figure 9–24 have been formatted with the Range Format Text command, so that you can see them. Otherwise, 1-2-3/G displays ERR in the cell when you enter the formulas.

1-2-3/G (69.4) Ready

File Edit Worksheet Range Copy... Move... Print Graph Data Utility Quit... Help

A:E17 +SALARY*1.1-SALARY

EMPBASE.WG1

A	A	B	C	D	E	F
14		SALARY				
15		>0				
16						
17	ID	LASTNAME	SALARY	+SALARY*1.1	+SALARY*	
18	1239	Piper	30,000	33000	3000	
19	1201	Haenszel	45,000	49500	4500	
20	1265	Stevenson	27,000	29700	2700	
21	1295	Taylor	33,000	36300	3300	
22	1258	Lang	24,000	26400	2400	
23	1217	Carlson	55,000	60500	5500	
24	1246	Martin	22,000	24200	2200	
25	1263	Rhodes	32,000	35200	3200	
26	1234	Bullock	38,000	41800	3800	
27	1278	Davis	34,000	37400	3400	
28	1256	Woods	37,000	40700	3700	
29						

FIGURE 9–24 Computed columns in the output range

The previous example shows a single field name used in computed column formula. However, you can also use more than one field name reference in a computed column formula. For example, imagine you are working with a sales database table that includes fields for unit price, units sold, and sales tax. You can create a computed column that multiplies units sold by unit price and adds the sales tax.

Aggregate Columns in the Output Range

You can use selected @functions in place of field names in the output range to create aggregate columns. Aggregate columns are used to compute values for a group of related records. For example, imagine you want to calculate the total and average salaries paid to each department included in the EMPBASE table. To do this, you can set up the data query shown in Figure 9-25.

Note

The output in Figure 9-25 was generated by using the Data Query Extract command with the criterion shown in the range A:B14..A:B15. This criterion has the effect of selecting all records from the EMPBASE table.

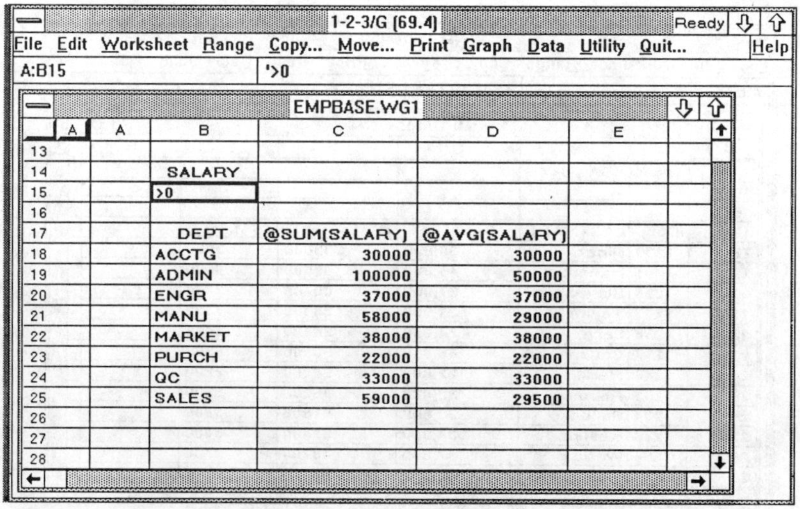

1-2-3/G (69.4) Ready

File Edit Worksheet Range Copy... Move... Print Graph Data Utility Quit... Help

A:B15 '>0

EMPBASE.WG1

A	A	B	C	D	E
13					
14		SALARY			
15		>0			
16					
17		DEPT	@SUM(SALARY)	@AVG(SALARY)	
18		ACCTG	30000	30000	
19		ADMIN	100000	50000	
20		ENGR	37000	37000	
21		MANU	58000	29000	
22		MARKET	38000	38000	
23		PURCH	22000	22000	
24		QC	33000	33000	
25		SALES	59000	29500	
26					
27					
28					

FIGURE 9–25 Aggregate columns in the output range

The output range in Figure 9–25 starts in row 17. The aggregate columns in this output range are columns D and E. The data in these aggregate columns is computed by using the formulas that appear in cells A:C17 and A:D17, formatted with Range Format Text. The values computed by these aggregate-column formulas are based on the field names that appear in the top row of the output range. As you can see in Figure 9–25, only the DEPT field name appears in cell A:B17. This field name has the effect of grouping the selected records based on the contents of the DEPT field of EMPBASE table. As you know, the DEPT field of the EMPBASE table contains the names of departments in which each employee works.

The values in the aggregate columns are computed as follows. Cell A:C17 contains the formula @SUM(SALARY). This formula sums the values in the SALARY field of the EMPBASE table for each group of selected records. Cell A:D17, on the other hand, contains the formula @AVG(SALARY), which calculates an average of the SALARY field for each group of selected records. As mentioned, the grouping of the records selected is determined by the DEPT field name that appears in cell A:B17.

1-2-3/G allows you to use the following @functions to create aggregate columns in the output range:

@AVG	Takes an average for a group of values.
@SUM	Sums a group of values.
@COUNT	Provides a count of the number of values in a group.
@MIN	Returns the smallest value in a group.
@MAX	Returns the highest value in a group.

For more about these @functions, see Chapter 6, "Functions."

Querying Multiple Database Tables

1-2-3/G allows you to query multiple database tables at the same time. However, before you can query multiple tables, you must join the tables by using the contents of a key field that is common to all the tables. Finally, to query the tables, you must specify the range address or name of each table as multiple input ranges for the Data Query command. In this fashion, 1-2-3/G allows you to set up a semi-relational database system in which you can search for related records in two or more database tables at the same time.

You may recall that earlier in this chapter, it was recommended that when you design a database table, you include a key field. A key field allows you to uniquely identify each record in a database table. For example, in the EMPBASE table, the key field is the ID field. This field contains a unique number for each employee in the EMPBASE table. This number can be used to match records in the EMPBASE table to records in other tables. For example, Figure 9–26 shows a companion table, ADDRESS (worksheet C), to the EMPBASE table (now in

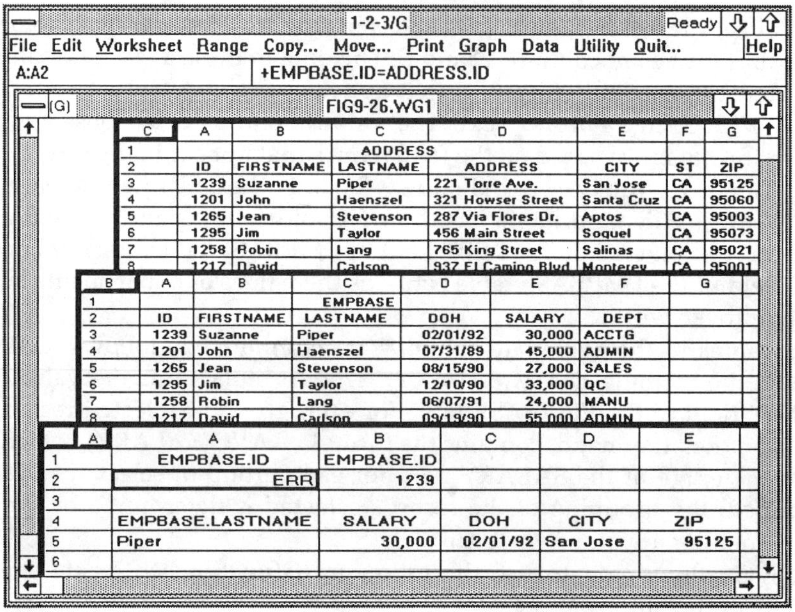

1-2-3/G — Ready

File Edit Worksheet Range Copy... Move... Print Graph Data Utility Quit... Help

A:A2 +EMPBASE.ID=ADDRESS.ID

(G) FIG9-26.WG1

C	A	B	C	D	E	F	G
1			ADDRESS				
2	ID	FIRSTNAME	LASTNAME	ADDRESS	CITY	ST	ZIP
3	1239	Suzanne	Piper	221 Torre Ave.	San Jose	CA	95125
4	1201	John	Haenszel	321 Howser Street	Santa Cruz	CA	95060
5	1265	Jean	Stevenson	287 Via Flores Dr.	Aptos	CA	95003
6	1295	Jim	Taylor	456 Main Street	Soquel	CA	95073
7	1258	Robin	Lang	765 King Street	Salinas	CA	95021
8	1217	David	Carlson	937 El Camino Blvd	Monterey	CA	95001

B	A	B	C	D	E	F	G
1			EMPBASE				
2	ID	FIRSTNAME	LASTNAME	DOH	SALARY	DEPT	
3	1239	Suzanne	Piper	02/01/92	30,000	ACCTG	
4	1201	John	Haenszel	07/31/89	45,000	ADMIN	
5	1265	Jean	Stevenson	08/15/90	27,000	SALES	
6	1295	Jim	Taylor	12/10/90	33,000	QC	
7	1258	Robin	Lang	06/07/91	24,000	MANU	
8	1217	David	Carlson	09/19/90	55,000	ADMIN	

A	A	B	C	D	E
1	EMPBASE.ID	EMPBASE.ID			
2	ERR	1239			
3					
4	EMPBASE.LASTNAME	SALARY	DOH	CITY	ZIP
5	Piper	30,000	02/01/92	San Jose	95125
6					

FIGURE 9–26 Joining tables using a common field

worksheet B). The ADDRESS database table has a key field, also named ID (column A), that corresponds to the ID field in the EMPBASE table (column A). Both fields use the same unique number to identify the record that belongs to each employee. Thus, the ID field can be used to match the record for an employee in the EMPBASE table to his or her associated record in the ADDRESS table.

To join two tables, you must create a special formula, called a *join formula,* in the criteria range. Join formulas allow you to match a record in one table to an associated record in another table. This is done by equating the contents of a key field in one table to the contents of a key field in another table. The two fields must contain the same type of data (label or value) and should contain the same information. For example, you can create a join formula that equates the contents of the ID fields in the EMPBASE and ADDRESS tables shown in Figure 9-26. See the next section entitled "Joining Tables" for more on how to create join formulas in the criteria range.

As mentioned, to query two database tables at the same time, you must specify the range addresses or names of each table as multiple input ranges for the Data Query command. To do this, select the Data Query command to display the Data Query dialog box. In the Input text box, specify the range addresses or range names of the tables you want to search, separated by commas.

Note

> You cannot specify multiple input ranges for the Data Query Delete command or the Data Query Modify commands.

Joining Tables

As mentioned, to query two tables at the same time, you must join the database tables. To do this, you must create a join formula in the criteria range. Join formulas equate the contents of a field in one table to a field in another table. That way, you can match a record in one table to an associated record in another table. Join formulas take the following form:

```
+field1=field2
```

where *field1* is a field name from the first table and *field2* is a field name from the second table.

If field name you want to use is the same in both tables, you must use the Range Name Create command to assign each table a range name. That range name is then used in the join formula to identify the field for that table. In this case, the join formula takes the following form:

```
+range1.field1=range2.field2
```

where *range1* is the range name for the first table and *range2* is the range name for the second table. For example, imagine you want to link the EMPBASE and ADDRESS tables shown in worksheets B and C of Figure 9–26 on the ID field. To do this, use the Range Name Create command to assign the name EMPBASE to the range B:A2..B:F13 in worksheet B. Then, use the same command to assign the name ADDRESS to the range C:A2..C:G13 in worksheet C. Finally, enter the following join formula in cell A:A2 of the criteria range A:A1.A:B2 of worksheet A:

```
+EMPBASE.ID=ADDRESS.ID
```

When you enter a join formula, 1-2-3/G will display ERR in the cell. For example, in Figure 9–26, the join formula just described appears in cell A:A2, and 1-2-3/G displays ERR in that cell. This has no bearing on the success or failure of your data query. If the ERR bothers you, use the Range Format Text command to format the display of the formula as text.

In the previous example, the key fields in both tables have the same name. Therefore, it is necessary to use a range name to correctly identify the field in each table. However, if the two field names are unique, the use of range names are not required. For example, to join two tables using the unique field names PART and INV_NO, you can use the following formula:

```
+PART=INV_NO
```

The same basic naming principles apply when setting up your criteria and output ranges for a multiple-table query. That is, if the field names are unique to both tables, you do not need to precede the field name with a range name. However, if the same field name occurs in both tables, you must precede it with a range name. For example, you may have noticed that a field entitled LASTNAME appears in both the EMPBASE and ADDRESS tables in Figure 9–26. To refer to the LASTNAME field in the EMPBASE table, you would use the field name EMPBASE.LASTNAME. Conversely, to refer to the LASTNAME field in the ADDRESS table, you would use the field name ADDRESS.LASTNAME. If you do not use this convention, you may get the error message "Field reference is ambiguous" when you eventually execute the data query.

To join more than two tables for a data query, you must use two join formulas. You can locate these formulas in vertically adjacent cells in the criteria range. Alternatively, you can create a compound join formula by using the #AND# operator between two or more join formula; for example:

```
+range1.field1=range2.field2#AND#range2,field2=range3.field3
```

Querying Multiple Tables: An Example

This section shows you how to set up the data query in Figure 9–26. Throughout this section, it is assumed that the EMPBASE table is located in worksheet B and the ADDRESS table is located in worksheet C of the active file, as shown in Figure 9–26.

The EMPBASE and ADDRESS tables have matching field names. Therefore, to be able to freely use these field names in your data query, you must assign a range name to both tables. Do this by using the Range Name Create command to assign the name EMPBASE to the range B:A2..B:F13 and the name ADDRESS to the range C:A2..C:G13.

The next step is to set up your criteria range. In this example, the criteria range appears in worksheet A in the range A:A1..A:B2. In cell A:A1 of this range, the field name EMPBASE.ID appears. The same field name appears in cell A:B1. In both cases, this field name refers to the ID field in the EMPBASE table. The EMPBASE range name is necessary here because both the EMPBASE and ADDRESS tables contain an ID field name. Beneath the field name in cell A:A1, the join formula +EMPBASE.ID=ADDRESS.ID appears in cell A:A2. This formula equates the ID field in the EMPBASE table to the ID field in the

ADDRESS table. Finally, in cell A:B2, the number 1239 appears. When this data query is processed, 1-2-3/G will equate the ID field in the EMPBASE and ADDRESS tables and locate the record in each table that has the employee number 1239 in the ID field.

Once the criteria range is set up, you're ready to set up an output range. For example, in Figure 9–26, the output range begins in row 4 of worksheet A. Notice the first field name in cell A:A4 reads EMPBASE.LASTNAME. Once again, the LASTNAME field appears in both the EMPBASE and ADDRESS tables. Therefore, it is necessary to precede the field name in this case with a range name. However, the remaining field names in the output range, SALARY, DOH, CITY, and ZIP, are unique to either the EMPBASE or the ADDRESS tables. Therefore, you need not precede these field names with a table range name. Notice that the first two field names, SALARY and DOH, come from the EMPBASE table, and the second two field names, CITY and ZIP, come from the ADDRESS table.

To execute the data query, select the Data Query command to display the Data Query dialog box. In the Input text box, type the range names of the two tables with a comma between them, for example, **EMPBASE,ADDRESS**. Alternatively, press NAME (F3) to display the range names in the current file, and select the range names from that list. In the Criteria text box, specify the range A:A1..A:B2. In the Output text box, specify the range A:A4..A:E4. Finally, select the Extract command button. 1-2-3/G locates the record with the number 1239 in the ID field of both the EMPBASE and ADDRESS tables. It then refers to the field names included in the output range to determine which fields to copy from which record to the output range. As you can see, data in the output range belongs to employee Piper (EMPBASE table), earning $30,000 (EMPBASE table), hired 2/01/92 (EMPBASE table), living in San Jose (ADDRESS table), zip code 95125 (ADDRESS table).

Imagine in the previous example that you did not know the ID number (1239) for employee Piper. Instead, you only know the last name. Since the two tables (EMPBASE and ADDRESS) are joined on a common field (ID), 1-2-3/G matches the record for an employee in the EMPBASE table with the record for that same employee in the ADDRESS table. Therefore, you only need to know some unique fact about an employee that is included in either table to search for information about that employee. For example, if you happen to know that the last name Piper is unique in both tables, you can change the selection criteria in the range A:A1..A:B2 of Figure 9–26 and get the same results for the data query. That is, instead of using EMPBASE.ID as a field name in cell A:B1, you can use either EMPBASE.LASTNAME or ADDRESS.LASTNAME. Below either of these field names, place the label Piper. When you execute the data query, 1-2-3/G locates the record for Suzanne Piper in both the EMPBASE and ADDRESS tables. The information from both of these records that is referenced by the field names in the output range is then copied to the output range, just as it appears in Figure 9–26.

USING THE DATABASE @FUNCTIONS

1-2-3/G offers a number of @functions that are useful for analyzing information contained in database tables. Like all 1-2-3/G @functions, the database @functions take specific input arguments and return a particular result based on those arguments. The database @functions are covered here, rather than in Chapter 6, "Functions," because of their close relationship to database management.

Syntax and Usage

All the database @functions begin with the symbol @ followed by the letter D, for example @DSUM. The syntax for all the database @functions, except @DQUERY, is as follows:

@Dfunction(:input field,*criteria*)

Each component of this syntax has the following meaning:

- *@Dfunction* is the name of the @function you want to use. You can choose from @DAVG, @DCOUNT, @DGET, @DMAX, @DMIN, @DSUM, @DSTD, @DSTDS, @DVAR, or @DVARS. You can either type in this name or you can type @ and then press NAME (F3). 1-2-3/G displays the @Functions dialog box. Select the name of the @function you want, for example DSUM, and press ENTER. 1-2-3/G adds the function name to the @ in the Control Line and displays @DSUM(. You can then add the remaining arguments for the database @function.
- *input* is the range name or address of the database table you want to query. Thus, defining an input range argument here performs exactly the same function as defining an input range for the Data Query command. You can specify a single input range or multiple input ranges separated by commas.
- *field* is the field in the input range you want to search. You can only specify a single *field* argument for a database @function. This *field* argument can be an *offset value,* an actual field name enclosed in quotes, or a reference to a cell that contains one of these. To use an offset value, specify the number of the field you want to search. The first field in the database table is automatically assigned the value 0, the second field is 1, the third field 2, and so on. To use a field name, enclose the name of the field you want to search in quotes. For example, to specify a field named SALARY in the input range, type **"SALARY"**.
- *criteria* is the range that contains the criteria that will be used to select records from the input range. You use exactly the same conventions to specify criteria for the database @functions as you do for the Data Query command. See "Defining Criteria" earlier in this chapter for more details on how to define selection criteria.

Figure 9–27 shows an example of a database @function in cell A:E19. The formula reads @DAVG(A1..F12,"SALARY",B14..B15). (For your convenience, this same function is shown as text starting in cell A:B19.) The @DAVG function computes an average of the values in a field of the input range, for those records that have been selected. The input range argument in this case is A1..F12, which includes the EMPBASE table and its field names. The field argument "SALARY" refers to the SALARY field in the EMPBASE table. The equivalent offset value in this case would be 4, because the SALARY field is the fifth field in the EMPBASE table. Finally, the criteria range argument is B14..B15. This range includes the field name SALARY with the label >30000 beneath it. Thus, only records that contain a value in excess of $30,000 in the SALARY field of the EMPBASE table are selected for use with the database @function.

One nice feature of the database @functions is that they are recalculated whenever the data to which they refer changes. That way, you can change the selection criteria in the criteria range and watch as the database @function is automatically updated.

You can also use the database @functions to query external database tables (database table created by software products other than 1-2-3/G). See "Querying External Database Tables" later in this chapter for more on how to work with external database tables.

1-2-3/G (69.4) Ready

File Edit Worksheet Range Copy... Move... Print Graph Data Utility Quit... Help

A:E19 @DAVG(A1..F12,"SALARY",B14..B15)

(,0) EMBASE.WG1

A	A	B	C	D	E	F	G	H
1	ID	FIRSTNAME	LASTNAME	DOH	SALARY	DEPT		
2	1239	Suzanne	Piper	02/01/92	30,000	ACCTG		
3	1201	John	Haenszel	07/31/89	45,000	ADMIN		
4	1265	Jean	Stevenson	08/15/90	27,000	SALES		
5	1295	Jim	Taylor	12/10/90	33,000	QC		
6	1258	Robin	Lang	06/07/91	24,000	MANU		
7	1217	David	Carlson	09/19/90	55,000	ADMIN		
8	1246	Jeff	Martin	10/31/91	22,000	PURCH		
9	1263	Cynthia	Rhodes	04/01/90	32,000	SALES		
10	1234	Henry	Bullock	01/14/92	38,000	MARKET		
11	1278	Keith	Davis	04/12/92	34,000	MANU		
12	1256	Ron	Woods	07/18/92	37,000	ENGR		
13								
14		SALARY						
15		>30000						
16								
17		@DFUNCTION			RESULT			
18								
19		@DAVG(A1..F12,"SALARY",B14..B15)			39,143			
20								
21		@DCOUNT(A1..F12,"SALARY",B14..B15)			7			
22								
23		@DMAX(A1..F12,"SALARY",B14..B15)			55,000			
24								
25		@DMIN(A1..F12,"SALARY",B14..B15)			32,000			
26								
27		@DSUM(A1..F12,"SALARY",B14..B15)			274,000			
28								

FIGURE 9–27 Examples of database @functions

Tip: For Release 2 and 3 Users

> Both 1-2-3/G and 1-2-3 Release 3 require that the actual field name in the input range that is referenced by the database @function be a label. If the field name in the input range is not a label, the @function evaluates to ERR. Release 2, however, does not require that the field name in the input range be a label. In addition, with 1-2-3/G and Release 3, if two field names in the input range are the same, the database @function will evaluate to ERR. However, Release 2 does not test for duplicate field names in the input range, and therefore, the @function does not evaluate to ERR.

You can specify multiple input ranges for the database @functions. When 1-2-3/G reads the arguments for database @functions, it does so from right to left. The first argument encountered is the criteria range, the second is interpreted as the field argument, and any remaining arguments are input ranges.

When you specify multiple input ranges for a database @function, you must use a join formula in the criteria range to join the two tables on a common field. Moreover, you must use a field name reference in the database @function, or a reference to a cell that contains a field name instead of an offset value.

Further, if the tables you're querying contain the same field names, you must precede the field name in the database @function with a range name for a specific table, for example EMPBASE.SALARY. Therefore, the database @function might look something like @DAVG(EMPBASE,ADDRESS,EMPBASE.SALARY,CRIT_RANGE), where EMPBASE and ADDRESS are the range names of two database tables, EMPBASE.SALARY references the SALARY field in the EMPBASE table, and CRIT_RANGE is a range name that refers to a criteria range containing a join formula that joins the EMPBASE and ADDRESS tables. See "Querying Multiple Database Tables" earlier in this chapter for more details on how to set up a data query that uses multiple input ranges.

Finally, although 1-2-3/G tolerates only a single *field* argument in a database @function that contains multiple input ranges, you can make that *field* argument a reference to a cell that contains a field name. When you change the field name in that cell, either manually or with a macro, 1-2-3/G stuffs the new field name into the database @function. That way, by modifying a single cell, you can quickly search a different field in a different table, without having to directly edit the database @function.

Applying the Database @Functions

This section provides a brief description of how you might apply each of the database @functions. Unless stated otherwise, each @function discussed in the following section will use the same *input*, *field*, and *criteria* arguments as the example just discussed in cell A:E19 of Figure 9–27. As you may recall, the argument specifications for this @function are as follows:

- *input* argument: A1..F12. This range includes the EMPBASE table and its field names.
- *field* argument: "SALARY" refers to the SALARY field in the EMPBASE table. The equivalent offset value in this case would be 4, because the SALARY field is the fifth field in the EMPBASE table.
- *criteria* argument: B14..B15. This range includes the field name SALARY with the label >30000 beneath it. Thus, only records that contain a value in excess of $30,000 in the SALARY field of the EMPBASE table will be selected for use with the database @function. Seven records from the EMPBASE table fall within this category.

The @DAVG Function

The @DAVG function takes an average of the values in a field of the input range for those records that meet the criteria in the criteria range. Figure 9–27 shows an example of the @DAVG function in cell A:E19. This function adds the contents of the SALARY field for seven records selected from the EMPBASE table. That sum is then divided by the number of records selected, seven, to compute the average salary for those records.

The @DCOUNT Function

The @DCOUNT function counts the nonblank cells in a field of the input range for those records that meet the criteria in the criteria range. Figure 9–27 shows an example of the @DCOUNT function in cell A:E21. Notice that this cell contains the number 7. Thus, seven records in the EMPBASE table meet the criteria in the range B:14..B:15 of figure 9–27. Therefore, seven employees in the EMPBASE table earn in excess of $30,000.

Note

Keep in mind that the @DCOUNT only counts nonblank cells (cells that are not empty). Therefore, if one or more cells in the field referenced by the *field* argument for the @DCOUNT function are blank, you may not get an accurate count. For example, imagine the criteria range B:14..B:15 in Figure 9–27 contained the field name DEPT with the label ADMIN beneath it. Thus, 1-2-3/G will select only those records in the EMPBASE table with the label ADMIN in the DEPT field. If the SALARY field for one of these records is blank, 1-2-3/G will not count that record.

The @DGET Function

The @DGET function gets a single value or label from a field of the input range the record that meets the criteria in the criteria range. Figure 9–28 shows an example of this function in cell A:B17. As you can see in the Control Line of Figure 9–28, the input argument for this @function is A1..F12, which includes the EMPBASE table and its field names. The field argument is "SALARY", which refers to the SALARY field in the EMPBASE table. Finally, the criteria range argument is B14..B15. This range includes the field name LASTNAME with the label Piper beneath it. Thus, only the record with Piper in the LASTNAME field will be selected.

The @DGET is only useful when you want to get a single value or label from a database table. In fact, if more than one record meets the criteria in the criteria range, the @DGET function returns ERR. Use this function when you want to get a single value or label for a macro or a formula.

The @DMAX and @DMIN Functions

The @DMAX function returns the highest value in a field of the input range for those records that meet the criteria in the criteria range. Conversely, the @DMIN function returns the lowest value. An example of the @DMAX function appears in cell A:E23 of Figure 9–27. It returns the value 55000. An example of the @DMIN function appears in cell A:E25 of Figure 9–27 and returns the value 32000. Thus, of the seven records that meet the criteria in the range B14..B15 of

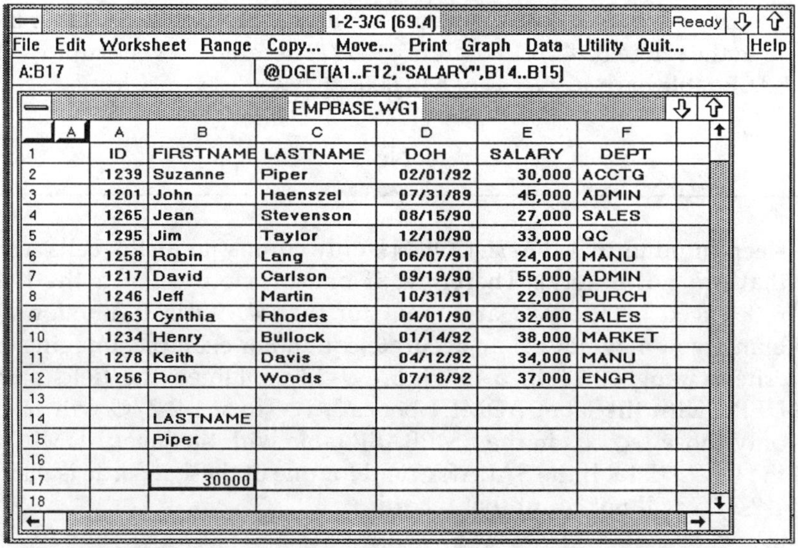

1-2-3/G (69.4) Ready

File Edit Worksheet Range Copy... Move... Print Graph Data Utility Quit... Help

A:B17 @DGET(A1..F12,"SALARY",B14..B15)

EMPBASE.WG1

A	A	B	C	D	E	F
1	ID	FIRSTNAME	LASTNAME	DOH	SALARY	DEPT
2	1239	Suzanne	Piper	02/01/92	30,000	ACCTG
3	1201	John	Haenszel	07/31/89	45,000	ADMIN
4	1265	Jean	Stevenson	08/15/90	27,000	SALES
5	1295	Jim	Taylor	12/10/90	33,000	QC
6	1258	Robin	Lang	06/07/91	24,000	MANU
7	1217	David	Carlson	09/19/90	55,000	ADMIN
8	1246	Jeff	Martin	10/31/91	22,000	PURCH
9	1263	Cynthia	Rhodes	04/01/90	32,000	SALES
10	1234	Henry	Bullock	01/14/92	38,000	MARKET
11	1278	Keith	Davis	04/12/92	34,000	MANU
12	1256	Ron	Woods	07/18/92	37,000	ENGR
13						
14		LASTNAME				
15		Piper				
16						
17		30000				
18						

FIGURE 9–28 The @DGET function

Figure 9–27, the highest value in the SALARY field is $55,000 and the lowest is $32,000.

The @DQUERY Function

The @DQUERY function is used exclusively to query external database tables. This function gives you access to a product-specific function or command in an external database and returns the result of that function to a 1-2-3/G criteria range. See "Using @DQUERY" later in the chapter under "Querying External Database Tables" for more information on this @function.

The @DSUM Function

The @DSUM function sums the values in a field of the input range for those records that meet the criteria in the criteria range. This particular function is among the most frequently used of the database @functions. An example of the @DSUM function appears in cell A:E27 of Figure 9–27. Notice that this function returns a value of 274,000. Thus, the sum of the values in the SALARY field for the seven records selected from the EMPBASE table is $274,000.

The @DSTD and @DVAR Functions

The @DSTD function calculates the standard deviation for a population of values taken from a field of a database table. The standard deviation is a measure of the degree to which a series of values varies from the mean (average). The closer the value of the standard deviation is to zero, the more reliable is the mean value. For example, Figure 9–29 shows a table of test scores for 20 students. To determine the standard deviation for all the students' test scores in this table, you can use the @DSTD function as shown in cell A:E22 of Figure 9–29. The formula in cell A:E22 is also shown as a label in cell A:A22, to make it easier to read and understand.

The values used by the @DSTD function come from a field of the input range for those records that meet the criteria in the criteria range. For example, the formula in call A:E20 of Figure 9–29 reads @DSTD(A1..D20,"TOTAL",F1..F2). Thus, the *input* range for this function is A:A1..A:D20, which includes the table of test scores and its field names. The *field* argument is "TOTAL", which refers to the TOTAL field (column D) in the table of test scores. Finally, the *criteria* range argument is F1..F2. This range contains a single field name with the label >0 beneath it. Therefore, 1-2-3/G will select all the records in the table of test scores.

The value for the @DSTD function in cell A:E22 is 199. This means that, as a general rule of thumb, the tests scores will fall within 199 points of the mean (one standard deviation) 68% of the time, and 95% of time the test scores will fall within two standard deviations or 298 points of the mean. To determine the mean, you can use the @DAVG function with the same *input, field,* and *criteria* arguments.

123/G [69.4] Ready

File Edit Worksheet Range Copy... Move... Print Graph Data Utility Quit... Help

A:E22 @DSTD(A1..D20,"TOTAL",F1..F2)

(F0) TEST.WG1

A	A	B	C	D	E	F	G	H
1	STUDENT	MATH	VERBAL	TOTAL		TOTAL		
2	23451	401	435	836		>0		
3	23488	546	698	1244				
4	23525	678	707	1385				
5	23562	414	448	862				
6	23599	559	711	1270				
7	23636	691	720	1411				
8	23673	456	579	1035				
9	23710	557	691	1248				
10	23747	445	525	970				
11	23784	664	679	1343				
12	23821	711	456	1167				
13	23858	323	446	769				
14	23895	589	723	1312				
15	23932	463	543	1006				
16	23969	433	588	1021				
17	24006	567	607	1174				
18	24043	578	658	1236				
19	24080	679	692	1371				
20	24117	645	768	1413				
21								
22	@DSTD(A1..D20,"TOTAL",F1..F2)				199			
23								
24	@DVAR(A1..D20,"TOTAL",F1..F2)				39633			
25								
26	@DSTDS(A1..D20,"TOTAL",F1..F2)				205			
27								
28	@DVARS(A1..D20,"TOTAL",F1..F2)				41835			

FIGURE 9–29 The @DSTD, @DVAR, @DSTDS, and @DVARS functions

The @DSTD function uses the population method of calculating the standard deviation for a list (population) of values. This method assumes that the values selected from the database table represent the entire population, instead of a sample. If the values do not represent the entire population, this method may not be reliable due to possible errors in collecting the data. Further, the population method is most reliable when the population is rather large. In fact, when the population is less than 30 values, the result of the @DSTD function may be called into question. In these cases, you're better off using the @DSTDS function covered in the next section. The equation used by the @DSTD function to calculate the standard deviation is as follows:

$$\text{Standard Deviation} = \sqrt{\frac{\Sigma(V_i - \text{avg})^2}{n}}$$

where V_i = the ith value
avg = the average of the values
n = the number of values

EQUATION 9-1 The @DSTD function for calculating standard deviation

Note

> The standard deviation is the square root of the variance for all selected values from the mean.

The @DVAR function is used to calculate the population variance for a series of values. The variance is a calculation of the average squared deviation from the mean and is the square of the standard deviation. The variance is the traditional method for measuring the variability of a data set.

The values used by @DVAR are taken from a specific field of a database table. For a value to be selected for use, it must meet the criteria in the criteria range. Figure 9–29 shows an example of the @DVAR function in cell A:E24. The value calculated is 39,633. Notice that this function uses the same *input, field,* and *criteria* arguments as the @DSTD function in cell A:E22. Therefore, this variance is related to the standard deviation calculation in cell A:E22. In fact, if you take the square root of 39633, you get 199.

Once again, the @DVAR function uses the population method for calculating the variance for a list (population) of values. This method assumes that the values selected from the database table represent the entire population, instead of only a sample. If the values do not represent the entire population, this method may not be reliable, due to possible errors in collecting the data. As mentioned, the population method is most reliable when the population is large. When the population is less than 30 values, the result of the @DVAR function may be questionable. In these cases, try using the @DVARS function covered in the next section. The equation used by the @DVAR function to calculate the variance is as follows:

$$\text{Variance} = \frac{\Sigma(V_i - \text{avg})^2}{n}$$

where V_i = the ith value
avg = the average of the values
n = the number of values

EQUATION 9-2 The @DVARS function for calculating variance

The @DSTDS and @DVARS Functions

You can use the @DSTDS function to calculate the sample standard deviation for a list of values from a database table. The values used are taken from a specific field of a database table. For a value to be selected for use, it must meet the criteria in the criteria range. Figure 9–29 shows an example of the @DSTDS function in cell A:E26.

The @DSTDS function works exactly the same way as the @DSTD function. However, it uses the sample method, as opposed to the population method, to calculate the standard deviation. The sample method is more reliable when the values in a list represent only a sample of the available values, instead of the entire population, or when the number of values is small (less than 30). In general the sample method results in a standard deviation that is slightly larger than the population method. This tends to compensate for any errors in the sampling process. For example, as you can see in Figure 9–29 the value in cell A:E26, calculated with @DSTDS, is slightly higher than the value in cell A:E22, calculated with @DSTD, for the same set of data. The @DSTDS function uses the formula in Equation 9–3 to calculate the standard deviation:

$$\text{Standard Deviation} = \sqrt{\frac{\Sigma(V_i - \text{avg})^2}{n - 1}}$$

where V_i = the ith value
avg = the average of the values
n = the number of values

EQUATION 9-3 The @DSTDS function for calculating standard deviation (sample method)

The @DVARS function calculates the sample variance for a series of values in a field of a database table. For a value to be selected for use, it must meet the criteria in the criteria range. Figure 9–29 shows an example of the @DSTDS function in cell A:E28.

The @DVARS function works exactly the same way as the @DVAR function. However, as you might imagine, it uses the sample method, instead of the population method, to calculate the variance. As mentioned, the sample method is more reliable when the values in a list represent only a sample of the available values, instead of the entire population, or when the number of values is small (less than 30). Once again, the sample method results in a variance that is slightly larger than the population method. This tends to compensate for any errors in the sampling process. For example, as you can see in Figure 9–29 the value in cell A:E28, calculated with @DVARS, is slightly higher than the value in cell A:E24, calculated with @DVAR, for the same set of data. The @DVARS function uses the following formula to calculate the variance:

$$\text{Variance} = \frac{\Sigma(V_i - \text{avg})^2}{n-1}$$

where V_i = the ith value
avg = the average of the values
n = the number of values

EQUATION 9-4 The @DVARS function for calculating variance (sample method)

QUERYING EXTERNAL DATABASE TABLES

To work with data in external tables, you use the Data External command. External database tables are tables created by software products other than 1-2-3/G—for example, dBASE III PLUS. The Data External command allows you not only to use information from external tables inside 1-2-3/G, but also to add records to external tables and to create new external tables.

To use an existing external database table, or to create a new one, 1-2-3/G must have access to a special driver called a Datalens driver. Datalens drivers tell 1-2-3/G how to interact with a specific type of database table.

Datalens drivers are usually created by independent software developers and manufacturers, not by Lotus. Therefore, you may need to get the Datalens driver from the company that manufactures and distributes your particular database product. When you get the Datalens driver, it should come with instructions on how to install it on your hard disk.

To give you an idea of how Datalens drivers work, Lotus has included a sample driver with 1-2-3/G. This driver allows you to work with dBASE III or DBASE III PLUS database (.DBF) files. This driver is automatically copied onto your 1-2-3/G program directory when you install the product. In addition, 1-2-3/G provides three external tables, EMPFILE.DBF, ADDFILE.DBF, and DEPFILE.DBF for you to practice with. This sample driver and the EMPFILE.DBF table will be used in the sections that follow to show you how to work with data in external database tables.

As mentioned, to work with data in external tables, you use the Data External command. This command allows you to perform the following:

- Activate a Datalens driver and connect 1-2-3/G to one or more external tables (Data External Use).
- Disconnect an external table from 1-2-3/G (Data External Reset).

- Create a list of external tables or a list of fields in an external table in your worksheet (Data External List).
- Delete an external table (Data External Delete).
- Pass a command to an external database, refresh the worksheet for any changes that may have occurred in an external table, or choose a new character set for an external table (Data External Other).

Connecting to an External Table

Before you can use information in an external database table, you must connect that table to 1-2-3/G. To do this, you use the Data External Use command. Once a particular table is connected to 1-2-3/G, you can use the Data Query commands or the database @functions to access information in that table. When you select the Data External Use command, 1-2-3/G displays the dialog box in Figure 9-30.

Note

For the Data External Use command to work, 1-2-3/G must be able to find the files that make up the Sample driver. These files are located on your 1-2-3/G program directory. Therefore, make this directory the current directory by using the File Directory command. Or, if you plan to use the Sample driver regularly, you can include the path to your 1-2-3/G program directory in the PATH statement in your CONFIG.SYS file.

At the top of the Data External Use dialog box is a text box initially entitled, "Connection (Drivers)." Ultimately this text box will contain a *table name* that describes the table you want to connect to 1-2-3/G. You can use the list box below to build a table name, or you can type the table name into the "Connec-

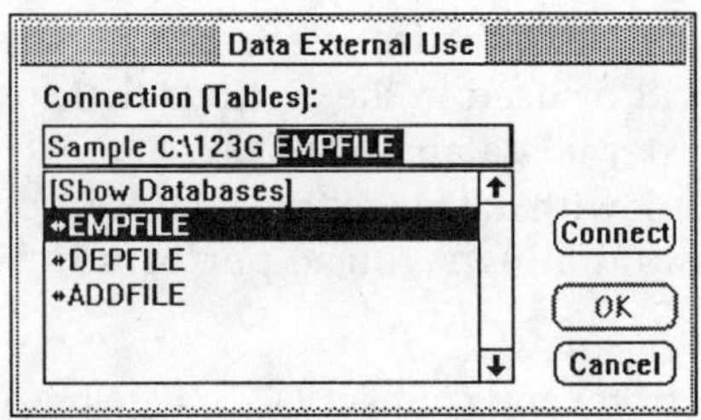

FIGURE 9–30 The Data External Use dialog box

tion (Drivers)" text box. A table name consists of three elements: a Datalens driver name, a database name or disk location, and the name of the table you want to use. A single space must appear between each element. For example, to connect the EMPFILE.DBF table to 1-2-3/G, type the following table name in the Connection Drivers text box:

```
SAMPLE C:\123G EMPFILE
```

To connect the EMPFILE table to 1-2-3/G, select the Connect command button. 1-2-3/G prompts you for a range name for the table. It does this by changing the title of the "Connection (Drivers)" text box to "Connection (Range Name)" and displays a default range name that matches the filename for the table, in this case EMPFILE. As you'll soon see, you refer to the table in commands and formulas by using this range name.

To confirm the default range name, select the Connect command button again. To complete the Data External Use command, select the OK command button. The EMPFILE table is now connected to 1-2-3/G and you can refer to it be using the EMPFILE range name.

If you don't want to use the default range name for an external table, you can provide one of your own. To do this, simply type the range name when prompted by 1-2-3/G. However, the range name cannot match an existing range name. Select the Connect command button or press ENTER to confirm the range name and complete the Data External Use command by selecting the OK command button. 1-2-3/G connects the table you selected and assigns it the range name you specified.

Rather than type the table name in the "Connection (Drivers)" text box, you can use your mouse or your keyboard to select the components that make up the table name from the list box below. However, before you attempt this, be aware that 1-2-3/G will search the current directory for the SAMPLE driver and its associated tables. As mentioned, these files are stored on your 1-2-3/G program directory. If this directory is not the current directory, take a moment to use the File Directory command to specify the 1-2-3/G program directory as the current directory.

Once your 1-2-3/G program directory is the current directory, select the Data External Use command. When you select this command, 1-2-3/G displays the name Sample in the "Connection (Drivers)" text box as well as in the list box below. To confirm this name, press ENTER, double-click on it, or select the Connect command button. 1-2-3/G changes the name of the Connection text box to "Connection (Databases)," and displays **(Show Drivers)** in the list box below followed by the names of external databases, for example C:\123G. Double-click on the name of the database you want, or highlight it and press ENTER, or select the Connect command button. 1-2-3/G adds the selected database name to the table name in the Connection text box.

Once the driver and database names are selected, 1-2-3/G changes the name of the Connection text box to "Connection (Tables)" and displays a list of available tables. Double-click on the table name you want, or highlight it and press ENTER, or select the Connect command button. 1-2-3/G adds the name of the table to the table name above and changes the name of the Connection text box to "Connection (Range Name)." At this point 1-2-3/G displays a default range name that matches the filename for the table. You can confirm this range name, and complete the Data External Use command, by selecting the Connect command button followed by the OK command button.

Note

> If an external table is already connected to 1-2-3/G, a double arrow appears next to the name of table in the list box when you select the Data External Use command.

Note

> As mentioned, to use the list box method to define a table name, the directory that contains the SAMPLE driver must be the current directory. However, you can have 1-2-3/G list the names of associated tables in different directories by modifying your LOTUS.BCF file. See "Modifying the LOTUS.BCF File" later in this chapter for details on how to do this.

As mentioned, you use the range name you assign to an external table to refer to it in commands and formulas. Further, you can connect to the same table several times and assign it a different range name each time. That way, you can refer to the same table by using different range names (aliases). If a table is already connected, 1-2-3/G displays ???? as its default range name. To assign the table a new range name, change ???? to a unique range name of your choosing.

Listing External Tables and Fields

The Data External List command allows you to create a list of fields in an external table in your worksheet. It also allows you to create a list of tables associated with a particular Datalens driver.

Before you use the Data External List command to create a list of fields for a particular table, that table must already be connected to 1-2-3/G. To connect a table to 1-2-3/G, you use the Data External Use command, as described in the previous section. However, if all you need is a list of tables associated with a particular Datalens driver, it is not necessary to connect those tables in advance.

When you select the Data External List command, 1-2-3/G displays the dialog box in Figure 9–31. The Choice section of this dialog box provides two option buttons, Tables and Fields. Select the Tables option button to create a list of tables associated with a particular Datalens driver. Select the Fields option button to create a list of fields from a particular table.

To create a list of tables associated with a database product, 1-2-3/G requires that you provide a Datalens driver name followed by a space and the name of the database. This information must appear in the "Connection (Drivers)" text box. Once this information is provided, 1-2-3/G prompts you to select a location for the table.

To begin, make sure the Tables option button is selected. When it is, 1-2-3/G displays the names of available Datalens drivers located in the current directory in the list box to the right. For example, in Figure 9–31 the SAMPLE driver appears in the list box. To select this driver, double-click on its name in the list box or highlight it and select the Connect command button. 1-2-3/G adds the name to the "Connection (Drivers)" text box.

Once you select a Datalens driver, 1-2-3/G displays the names of databases in the current directory that are associated with the driver you selected. For example, if you selected the SAMPLE driver, 1-2-3/G displays C:\123G in the list box. To select this database name, double-click on it or highlight it and select the Connect command button. At this point, 1-2-3/G moves the highlight to the "Output Range" text box, thereby prompting you for a location for the table. Specify a single-cell range where you want the upper-left corner of the table to begin. When you're ready, select the OK command button. 1-2-3/G writes a three column table into the worksheet starting in the cell you specified in the Output range text box. This list contains the names of tables associated with

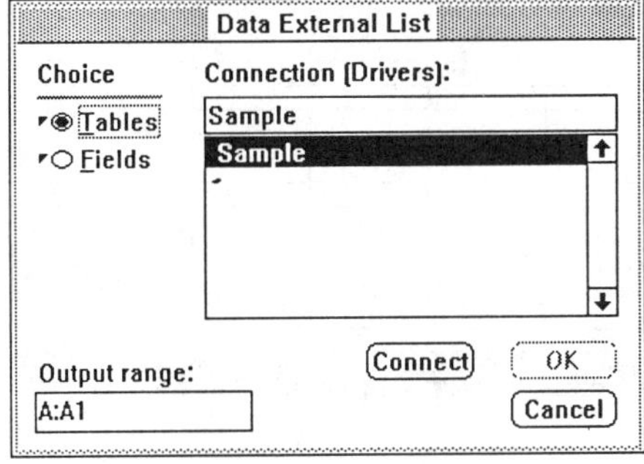

FIGURE 9–31 The Data External List dialog box

the database you selected. For example, Figure 9–32 shows a list of table names associated with the SAMPLE driver starting in cell A:A1.

The first column of the table listing (A:A1..A:C3 in Figure 9–32) shows the names of three tables, EMPFILE, DEPFILE, and ADDFILE. These names represent the EMPFILE.DBF, DEPFILE.DBF, and ADDFILE.DBF sample files that come with your copy of 1-2-3/G. The remaining two columns in the table are reserved for table descriptions and other information that are not required by either the SAMPLE driver or by dBASE III.

To create a list of fields in an external table, select the Fields option button from the Choice section of the Data External List dialog box. When you make this selection, 1-2-3/G changes the name of the list box to the right from "Connection (Drivers)" to Table. In the list box, 1-2-3/G shows the names of tables that are already connected to 1-2-3/G. To select a table name, double-click on it, or highlight it and press ENTER. 1-2-3/G places the name of that table in the text box above and moves the highlight to the "Output range" text box. In this text box, specify a single cell range where you want the upper-left corner of the table to begin. When you're ready, select the OK command button. 1-2-3/G writes a six-column table into the worksheet starting at the cell you specified in the "Output range" text box. For example, Figure 9–32 shows a fields listing for the EMPFILE.DBF table starting in cell A:A7.

Each column in the fields listing in the range A:A7..A:F12 of Figure 9–32 gives you information about content and structure of the fields in the EMPFILE.DBF file. The contents of each of these columns, and what they mean, will be discussed in more detail later in this chapter under "About Table Definitions." Collectively, however, the fields listing in Figure 9–32 represents a *table definition* for the EMPFILE file. As you'll soon see, you can use this table definition

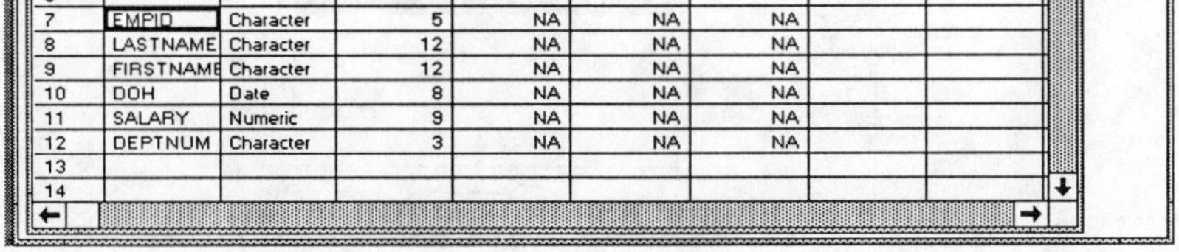

1-2-3/G [69.4] Ready

File Edit Worksheet Range Copy... Move... Print Graph Data Utility Quit... Help

A:A7 'EMPID

D:\CH9\SHEET3.WG1

A	A	B	C	D	E	F	G	H
1	EMPFILE	NA	NA					
2	DEPFILE	NA	NA					
3	ADDFILE	NA	NA					
4								
5								
6								
7	EMPID	Character	5	NA	NA	NA		
8	LASTNAME	Character	12	NA	NA	NA		
9	FIRSTNAME	Character	12	NA	NA	NA		
10	DOH	Date	8	NA	NA	NA		
11	SALARY	Numeric	9	NA	NA	NA		
12	DEPTNUM	Character	3	NA	NA	NA		
13								
14								

FIGURE 9–32 The Data External List command can create either a list of tables associated with a Datalens driver or a list of fields in an external table

as a reference when you copy records from the EMPFILE table into a 1-2-3/G worksheet. You can also use it as a model for creating a new external database table. However, before you begin using this table definition to create new external tables, it is helpful to know a little more about dBASE database tables in general and about the SAMPLE driver in particular.

About the Sample Driver

As mentioned, the SAMPLE driver can be used to add to and create database tables that are compatible with dBASE III and dBASE III PLUS. You can also use the SAMPLE driver to manage data in tables that are compatible with dBASE IV. However, the dBASE IV files cannot contain fields that contain any new data types that are specific to dBASE IV, specifically the Type F (floating) numeric data type. You cannot use the SAMPLE driver with dBASE II files.

The SAMPLE driver is only for use with dBASE database (.DBF) files. You cannot use it to modify other types of dBASE files, for example, index files (.NDX or .MDX), form files (.FRM), label files (.LBL), or memo files (.DBT).

The SAMPLE driver is aptly named. That is, it is only intended to give you a sampling of the power of the Datalens technology. It is not a fully functional driver. Nonetheless, the SAMPLE driver does allow you to perform the following:

- Create a new dBASE III .DBF database file by using the Data External Create command.
- Append records to the end of an existing dBASE database table by using Data Query Modify Insert, Data Query Extract, and Data Query Unique. The records you want to append can be located in a 1-2-3/G worksheet or in another dBASE database table.
- Copy records from a dBASE database table into a 1-2-3/G worksheet by using the Data Query Extract or Data Query Unique commands.

On the other hand, the SAMPLE driver has the following limitations:

- You cannot delete records in a dBASE database table using Data Query Delete.
- You cannot modify existing records in a dBASE database table by using Data Query Modify Replace.
- You cannot delete an existing dBASE database table using the Data External Delete.
- You cannot send commands to dBASE using either Data External Other Command or @DQUERY.

The sections that follow discuss all the commands available from the Data External menu. Obviously, some of the techniques and commands discussed will not be applicable to the SAMPLE driver. However, as more database developers embrace the Datalens technology and develop fully functional drivers for 1-2-3/G, these commands and techniques will come into use.

Note

The SAMPLE driver does not update any existing indexes for a dBASE database table. Therefore, if you use the Data Query Modify Insert, Data Query Extract, or Data Query Unique commands to append records to a database table, your indexes for that table will be outdated. To update the indexes, it is recommended that you use the REINDEX command from within dBASE to rebuild the affected indexes.

About Table Definitions

As mentioned, table definitions describe the structure of a database. For example, the table definition for the EMPFILE.DBF sample file shown earlier in Figure 9–32 is shown again in the range A:A1..A:F12 of Figure 9–33. As you may recall, this table definition was created by using the Data External List Fields command.

1-2-3/G uses a standard table definition format for all Datalens drivers. Each row in a table definition describes a field in an external table. Therefore, there is one row for each field in the table. Each table definition you create contains six columns, each column describes an attribute for a specific database table field. Some Datalens drivers will use all six columns. However, many drivers, like the SAMPLE driver, only need some of the fields in the table definition to adequately describe a database field.

The following is a description of each of the columns shown in the table definition in Figure 9–33. The discussion is biased toward the columns used by the SAMPLE driver, and therefore, dBASE III.

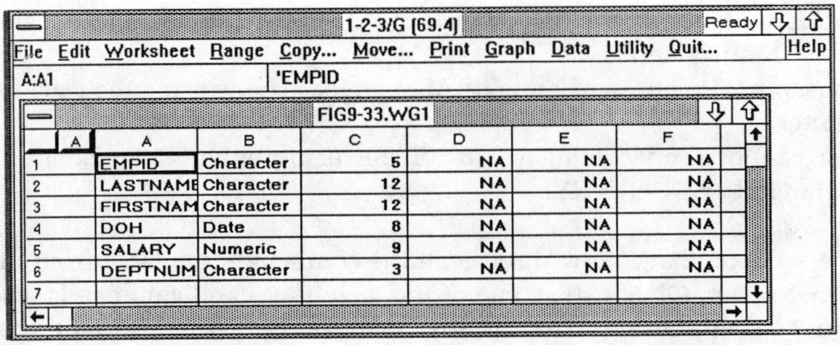

1-2-3/G [69.4] Ready

File Edit Worksheet Range Copy... Move... Print Graph Data Utility Quit... Help

A:A1 'EMPID

FIG9-33.WG1

A	A	B	C	D	E	F
1	EMPID	Character	5	NA	NA	NA
2	LASTNAME	Character	12	NA	NA	NA
3	FIRSTNAM	Character	12	NA	NA	NA
4	DOH	Date	8	NA	NA	NA
5	SALARY	Numeric	9	NA	NA	NA
6	DEPTNUM	Character	3	NA	NA	NA
7						

FIGURE 9–33 The table definition for the EMPFILE.DBF external database table

Column 1: Field name The first column in a table definition shows the name of the field. For example, the first field in the table definition in Figure 9–33 is EMPID. The format of field names is often restricted by the Datalens driver you are using. For example, the SAMPLE driver imposes the naming conventions of dBASE III. That is, a field name can only be a maximum of 10 characters in length, including underscores, and must begin with a letter. In addition, dBASE III supports a maximum of 128 total fields.

Column 2: Data type The second column describes the type of data in the field. This is analogous to 1-2-3/G's classifications of data as labels or values. The data types available may vary from one Datalens driver to the next, depending on the database product supported by that driver. The SAMPLE driver supports the following data types from dBASE III:

- **Character:** Character fields contain text strings. The contents of these fields appear as labels in 1-2-3/G. The maximum width of a character field in dBASE III is 254 characters.
- **Numeric:** Numeric fields contain numbers. The maximum width of a numeric field in dBASE III is 19 characters, including the decimal.
- **Date:** Date fields contain dates. The contents of these fields are translated into date values in 1-2-3/G. Date fields are always eight-characters wide in dBASE III. Therefore, if you create an external table with a date field, it will automatically have an eight-character width.
- **Logical:** Logical fields are a single character wide and contain a "true" (T,t,Y or y) or "false" (F, f, N, or n) value. In 1-2-3/G, true values are assigned the value 1 and false values are assigned the number 0. Logical fields are useful in situations where there are only two possibilities, for example SALARY=TRUE and HOURLY=FALSE. When you create a dBASE table with a logical field, that field is automatically one character wide.
- **Memo:** The SAMPLE driver does not support dBASE III memo fields. Memo fields reference a file with a .DBT extension that contains short messages for each record in the database. When you copy records from a dBASE table that contains memo fields into the worksheet, the worksheet column that would ultimately contain the memo field is left blank. Additionally, you cannot create a dBASE III table that contains a memo field from within 1-2-3/G. You can, however, append records to a table that already contains a memo field, but the new records are given blank memo fields.

Column 3: Field width The third column (column C) of the table definition in Figure 9–33 contains the width in characters for each field. As mentioned, character fields can have a width of up to 254 characters. Numeric fields can be up to 19 characters wide, including the decimal point. When creating a dBASE III table from within 1-2-3/G, you can specify the number of places to appear after the decimal. To do this, provide a number that represents the number of places in front followed by a comma and the number of places to appear after the decimal. For example, the entry 6,2 will result in a nine-character width with six places in front of the decimal and two after. It is not necessary to specify a width for date or logical fields when creating a dBASE III table from within 1-2-3/G. Date fields are automatically given a width of nine characters and logical fields are automatically given a width of one character.

Column 4: Column labels The fourth column in a table definition is used to provide an alternate name for a field. The column is not needed by dBASE III and, therefore, is not used by the SAMPLE driver. 1-2-3/G displays NA in this field.

Column 5: Field Description The fifth column in a table definition is used to provide a brief description for a field. The column is not needed by dBASE III and, therefore, is not used by the SAMPLE driver. 1-2-3/G displays NA in this field.

Column 6: Field Creation String The fifth column in a table definition is used to provide a field creation string. The column is not needed by the dBASE III and, therefore, is not used by the SAMPLE driver. 1-2-3/G displays NA in this field.

Copying Records from an External Table

As mentioned, once you have connected an external table to 1-2-3/G, you can use the Data Query commands, as well as the database @functions, to query that table. As you may recall, you connect 1-2-3/G to an external table by using the Data External Use command. During this command, the external table is assigned a 1-2-3/G range name. From then on, you can use the range name you assigned to refer to the external table.

Figure 9-34 shows an example of how you can use the Data Query Extract command to copy the records from the EMPFILE external table into the worksheet. To recreate the data query in Figure 9-34 yourself, perform the following steps:

1. Starting with a fresh worksheet, select the Data External Use command. Use the techniques described earlier in this chapter under "Connecting to an External Table" to connect the EMPFILE sample file to 1-2-3/G and assign it the default range name of EMPFILE. Remember to use the File Directory command to make your 1-2-3/G program directory the current directory. That way, 1-2-3/G will be able to find both the SAMPLE driver and the EMPFILE table.
2. With the cell pointer in cell A:A1, use the Data External List Fields command to create a table definition for the EMPFILE table, starting in cell A:A1. The use of this command is described earlier in this chapter under "Listing External Tables and Fields."
3. Select the Range Transpose command. For a From range, specify the range A:A1..A:A6. For a To range, specify A:A11. 1-2-3/G copies the

1-2-3/G [69.4] Ready

File Edit Worksheet Range Copy... Move... Print Graph Data Utility Quit... Help

A:A1 'EMPID

D:\CH9\FIG9-34.WG1

A	A	B	C	D	E	F
1	EMPID	Character	5	NA	NA	NA
2	LASTNAME	Character	12	NA	NA	NA
3	FIRSTNAM	Character	12	NA	NA	NA
4	DOH	Date	8	NA	NA	NA
5	SALARY	Numeric	9	NA	NA	NA
6	DEPTNUM	Character	3	NA	NA	NA
7						
8	EMPID					
9						
10						
11	EMPID	LASTNAME	FIRSTNAME	DOH	SALARY	DEPTNUM
12	10001	Grey	John	12/31/86	45000	043
13	10002	Needleman	Peter	08/07/84	33000	043
14	10003	Langly	Jason	04/02/87	80000	017
15	10004	Louden	Tammy	09/08/86	25000	017
16	10005	Louden	Pete	05/04/87	33000	010
17	10006	Tomlin	Marsha	09/19/83	68000	009
18	10007	Yeager	Shane	09/02/88	100000	009
19	10008	Harris	Andy	01/03/88	78000	025
20	10009	Patton	Tim	07/04/87	50000	025
21	10010	Bates	Joseph	04/08/85	10000	010
22	10011	Lainê	Françoise	01/11/86	38000	043

FIGURE 9–34 Records from the EMPFILE.DBF external table are copied into the worksheet with Data Query Extract

field names from the table definition at the top Figure 9–34 and transposes them to a row arrangement in row 11, where they will serve as the top row of the output range.

4. Select the Copy command. For a From Range, specify cell A:A1. For a To range, select cell A:A8. 1-2-3/G copies the EMPID field name to cell A:A8. The range A:A8..A:A9 will then serve as the criteria range.
5. Select the Data Query command. 1-2-3/G displays the Data Query dialog box.
6. In the Input text box, type **EMPFILE**. Alternatively, you can press NAME (F3) and select the EMPFILE range name.
7. In the Criteria text box, specify the range A:A8..A:A9. This includes the EMPID field name and blank cell beneath it. As you may recall, if you leave the row below the field names in the criteria range blank, 1-2-3/G will select all the records in the input range.
8. In the Output text box, specify the single-row output range A:A11..A:F11. This includes the row of field names in row 11.
9. Select the Extract command button. 1-2-3/G copies the records from the EMPFILE external table into the worksheet.
10. Select the Quit command button from the Data Query dialog box to return to the worksheet in READY mode.

Tip: Joining external tables

You can use a join formula in the criteria range to relate one external table to another. You can then specify the range names of the two external tables as multiple input ranges for the Data Query command. See "Querying Multiple Database Tables" earlier in this chapter for more details on how to query multiple database tables.

Appending Records to an External Table

You can also append records to an existing external table. The records you append can be located in a worksheet or in another external table. To append records to an external table, you can use either the Data Query Extract, Data Query Unique, or Data Query Modify Insert commands.

Note

To append records to an external table, the data types within the fields of those records must match the fields in the external table. Otherwise, 1-2-3/G will issue an error message when you attempt to append the records. Further, the width of the fields in the records you're appending should be less than or equal to the width of fields in the external table. If the field widths for the records you're appending are too wide, the contents of some entries may be truncated.

Imagine you want to append some records currently located in your worksheet to the end of the EMPFILE external table. To do this, select the Data Query command. 1-2-3/G displays the Data Query dialog box. In the Input text box, specify the range that contains the records located in the worksheet that you want to append. In the Criteria text box, specify the range in the worksheet that contains criteria that will select the records you want to append. Finally, in the Output text box, specify the range name for the external table, in this case EMPFILE. When you're ready, select the Unique or Extract command button. 1-2-3/G appends the records from the input range in the worksheet to the end of the EMPFILE table.

You can also append records from one external table to another with Data Query Extract or Unique commands. To do this, specify in the Input text box the range name of the external table that you want to append the records from. In the Criteria text box, specify the range that contains the criteria that will be used to select records from the input range (database table). In the Output text box, specify the range name of the external table you want to append the records to.

For the Data Query Modify Insert command, you swap the input and output ranges when appending records. That is, if you're appending records from the worksheet, your input range is the range name for the external table and your output range contains the records in the worksheet that you want to append. A criteria range is not required. If you're appending records from another table, your input range is the table you want to append to and your output range is the table you want to append from. Once again, the criteria range is not used. In both cases, since the criteria range is not used, all the records from the output range are appended to the input range.

Caution

If you press QUERY (F7) to repeat a Data Query Extract, Data Query Unique, or Data Query Modify Insert command that references an external table, 1-2-3/G appends all the records in the output range to the external table. This can present a problem in that you cannot delete the records from within 1-2-3/G. As mentioned, the Sample driver does not support the Data Query Delete command.

Using Database @Functions with External Tables

You can also use the database @functions with external databases. To do this, the external table must already be connected to 1-2-3/G with the Data External Use command. As an *input* range argument for the database @function, use the 1-2-3/G range name for the external table. For the *field* argument, you must use a field name from the external table enclosed in quotes (" "), as opposed to an offset value. For the *criteria* range argument, specify a range in the worksheet that contains the appropriate field names and search arguments to select the records you want from the external table. For more on how to use the database @functions, see "Using the Database @Functions" earlier in this chapter.

Note

> When you use a database @function to query an external table, the database @function is recalculated each time the worksheet is changed in any way. If the external table is large, this can become a time-consuming affair.

Using @DQUERY

The @DQUERY function allows you to access a product-specific function in an external database program. The result of that function can then be used in a 1-2-3/G criteria range to select records from an external table associated with the database. The syntax for the @DQUERY function is:

@DQUERY(*function*[,*extension-arguments*])

where *function* is the name of the external database function you want to use enclosed in quotes and *extension-arguments* is a list of one or more arguments for the function separated by commas.

Note

> The @DQUERY function is not supported by the SAMPLE driver.

You can only use @DQUERY in a 1-2-3/G criteria range to select records from a specific external table. Additionally, the @DQUERY function does not support multiple input ranges.

Imagine you are working with an external database program that supports the function SOUNDSLIKE(*character string*). This function returns the contents of a field in the record that is closest to *character string*. You want to use this function in a 1-2-3/G criteria range to search a character field called LASTNAME in an external table. To do this, you might use the following formula in a 1-2-3/G criteria range:

```
+LASTNAME=@DQUERY(SOUNDSLIKE("Adams")
```

Note

> You can also use the Data External Other Command command to pass a command to an external database in its own command format. See "Using the Data External Other Command" later in this chapter for more details on this.

Creating a New External Table

To create a new external table, you use the Data External Create command. This command allows you to create a new table by using either another database table as a model or by using a table definition. When you select the Data External Create command, 1-2-3/G displays the dialog box in Figure 9-35.

When you create a new table with Data External Create, the new table is empty (has no records). However, once the new table is created, you can add records to that table by using either the Data Query Extract, Data Query Unique, or Data Query Modify Insert commands.

Using an Existing Table as a Model

Imagine you want to create a new external table by using the EMPBASE table in Figure 9-36 as a model. To do this, perform the following steps:

1. Select the Data External Create command. 1-2-3/G displays the dialog box in Figure 9-35.
2. In the Connection text box, specify a name for the new table preceded by appropriate driver and database name. For example, to create a new table called NEW, type **SAMPLE C:\123G NEW** and press ENTER. Alterna-

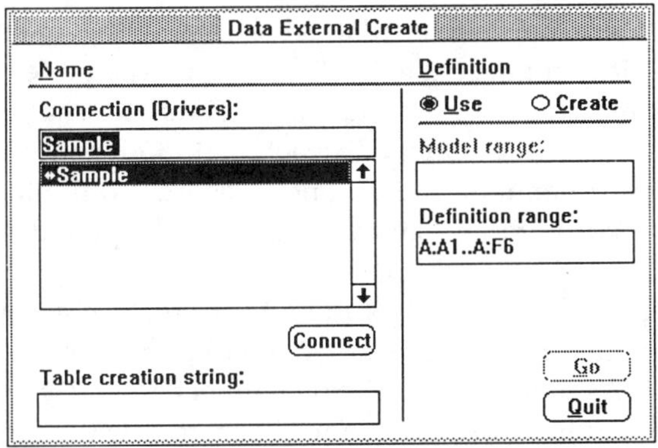

FIGURE 9-35 The Data External Create dialog box

tively, you can double-click on SAMPLE driver name in the Connection list box. 1-2-3/G lists the names of databases (C:\123G) in the current directory. Double-click on C:\123G in the Connection list box. Then, type **NEW** and select the Connect command button.

3. After you specify a name for the new table, 1-2-3/G prompts you for a range name for the table. It does this by displaying the default range name NEW in the Connection text box. You can accept this range name by pressing ENTER or you can edit the name and press ENTER. 1-2-3/G moves the cursor to the "Table creation string" text box.
4. Press ENTER to leave the "Table creation string" text box and move to the Definition section of the Data External Create dialog box. Although some Datalens drivers require that you specify a table creation string, the SAMPLE driver does not.
5. Select the Create option button. 1-2-3/G moves the cursor to the "Model range" text box.
6. In the "Model range" text box, specify a range address or range name that includes the first row of field names in the EMPBASE table and the first record (A:A1..A:F2). Press ENTER to move to the "Definition range" text box.
7. In the "Definition range" text box, specify a single-cell range in a blank area of the worksheet. For example, in Figure 9–36 the cell selected is A:B14..A:B14. (If you specify a single-cell address here, for example A:B14, 1-2-3/G will issue an error message when you later select the Go command button to create the new table.)
8. Select the Go command button. 1-2-3/G creates a six-column table definition that starts in the cell you specified in the "Definition range" text box (A:B14...A:G19 in Figure 9–36). The table definition created matches that of the existing table you specified in the Model range text box. This table definition is then used to create the new external table under the name you specified.

When you create a new table, that table is empty (contains no records). However, that table is connected to 1-2-3/G and you can refer to it by using the 1-2-3/G range name you assigned during the Data External Create command. Thus, you can use the Data Query Extract, Data Query Unique, or the Data Query Modify Insert command to add new records to the table. For more on how to append records to an external table, see "Appending Records to an External Table" earlier in this chapter.

To use another external table as a model for creating a new external table, you must connect the model table to 1-2-3/G before using the Data External Create command. As you may recall, you connect an external table to 1-2-3/G by using the Data External Use command. Then, follow the same steps outlined in the previous example. However, in step 6, specify the range name of the external table in the "Model range" text box.

123/G [69.4] Ready

File Edit Worksheet Range Copy... Move... Print Graph Data Utility Quit... Help

A:B14 'ID

D:\CH9\EMPBASE.WG1

A	A	B	C	D	E	F	G
1	ID	FIRSTNAME	LASTNAME	DOH	SALARY	DEPT	
2	1239	Suzanne	Piper	02/01/92	30,000	ACCTG	
3	1201	John	Haenszel	07/31/89	45,000	ADMIN	
4	1265	Jean	Stevenson	08/15/90	27,000	SALES	
5	1295	Jim	Taylor	12/10/90	33,000	QC	
6	1258	Robin	Lang	06/07/91	24,000	MANU	
7	1217	David	Carlson	09/19/90	55,000	ADMIN	
8	1246	Jeff	Martin	10/31/91	22,000	PURCH	
9	1263	Cynthia	Rhodes	04/01/90	32,000	SALES	
10	1234	Henry	Bullock	01/14/92	38,000	MARKET	
11	1278	Keith	Davis	04/12/92	34,000	MANU	
12	1256	Ron	Woods	07/18/92	37,000	ENGR	
13							
14		ID	Numeric	4	NA	NA	NA
15		FIRSTNAME	Character	7	NA	NA	NA
16		LASTNAME	Character	5	NA	NA	NA
17		DOH	Date	8	NA	NA	NA
18		SALARY	Numeric	5	NA	NA	NA
19		DEPT	Character	5	NA	NA	NA
20							
21							
22							
23							

FIGURE 9–36 The EMPBASE.WG1 table and its table definition

Using a Table Definition

You can also create a new table by using a table definition. As you may recall, you can use the Data External List Fields command to create a table definition for an existing table. You can then modify that table definition to suit your needs. Alternatively, you can type the table definition into the worksheet manually. For more about table definitions, see "About Table Definitions" earlier in this chapter.

Once the table definition is created, select the Data External Create command and follow the steps outlined in the previous example. However, in step 5 select the Use option button instead of the Create option button, and skip step 6 altogether. In step 7, specify in the "Definition range" text box the range that contains the table definition you've already created. Then, select the Go command button. 1-2-3/G creates the new external table by using the table definition you specified in the "Definition range" text box.

Deleting an External Table

To delete an external table, you use the Data External Delete command. As mentioned, this command is not supported by the SAMPLE driver. However, when you select this command, 1-2-3/G displays the dialog box in Figure 9–37.

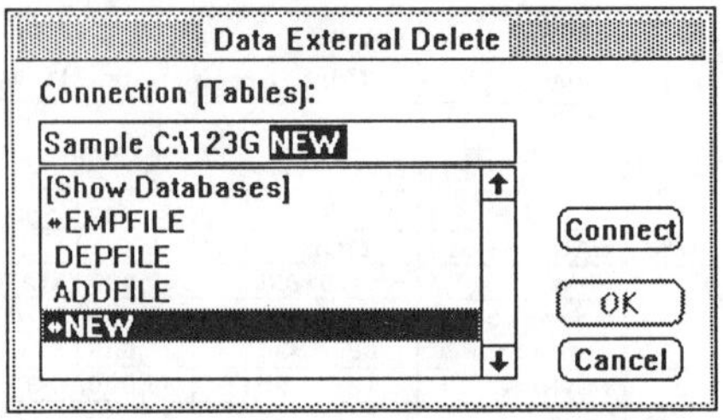

Data External Delete

Connection [Tables]:

Sample C:\123G NEW

[Show Databases]
*EMPFILE
DEPFILE
ADDFILE
*NEW

Connect

OK

Cancel

FIGURE 9–37 The Data External Delete dialog box

To specify a table to delete, specify the name of that table in the Connection text box preceded by the appropriate Datalens driver and database names. For example, to delete the NEW table, type **SAMPLE C:\123G NEW** and select the Connect command button. 1-2-3/G displays a Yes/No confirmation box. Select from Yes or No. 1-2-3/G returns you to the Data External Delete dialog box. At that point you can select additional tables to delete. To remove the Data External Delete dialog box from the screen, select the OK command button.

Using the Data External Other Command

The Data External Other command offers three options, Refresh, Command, and Translate. The Refresh option allows you to specify a time interval for the update of the worksheet. The Command option allows you to pass a command string to an external database, (This option is not supported by the SAMPLE driver.) Finally, the Translate option allows you to specify a new character set to use for an external table.

The Data External Refresh command is useful when you're working on a local area network (LAN). This command allows you to specify a time interval in seconds for the update of external table references in the worksheet. Database @functions are recalculated and the most recent Data Query or Data Table commands are reexecuted. That way, you can be sure you are using the most recent information.

When you select the Data External Other Refresh command, 1-2-3/G displays the dialog box in Figure 9–38. This dialog box contains three option buttons, Automatic, Manual, and Interval. To have the worksheet updated automatically, select Automatic. Then select Interval and specify the number of seconds you want between updates. Select Manual (the default) to turn off automatic update. To return to the worksheet, select the OK command button.

Use the Data External Other Command to pass a command string to an external database program. (As mentioned, the SAMPLE driver does not support this command.) Before you use this command, make sure you have con-

Data External Other Refresh
Automatic
Manual
Interval:
1 seconds
OK
Cancel

FIGURE 9-38 The Data External Refresh dialog box

nected the external database table to 1-2-3/G by using the Data External Use command.

When you select Data External Other Command, 1-2-3/G displays the dialog box in Figure 9-39. In the Connection text box specify the name of the database that you want to send the command to. Precede the database name with the appropriate Datalens driver name. In the "Command string" text box type the command you want to send to the database program using the appropriate syntax for that database. You can use commands that interact with the database but that do not require any specific output. To send the command, select the OK command button.

The Data External Other Translate command allows you to select a character set that will be used by a Datalens driver. (Character sets are used to display and store data.) The character set you specify is used whenever data is copied to or from an external table. The SAMPLE driver uses IBM's code Page 850 (multilingual PC) character set, as does 1-2-3/G. If the Datalens driver you're using expects a different character set, you must specify that character set for the Datalens driver to work properly. To determine which character set is used by your particular Datalens driver, consult the documentation that came with the driver.

When you select the Data External Other Translate command, 1-2-3/G displays the dialog box in Figure 9-40. In the Connection text box, specify the name

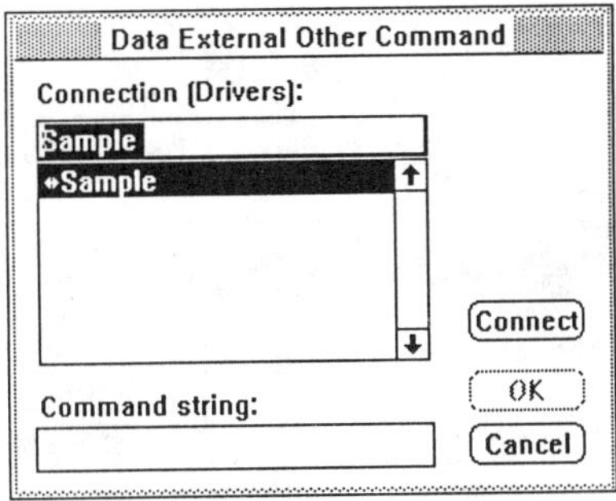

FIGURE 9-39 The Data External Other Command dialog box

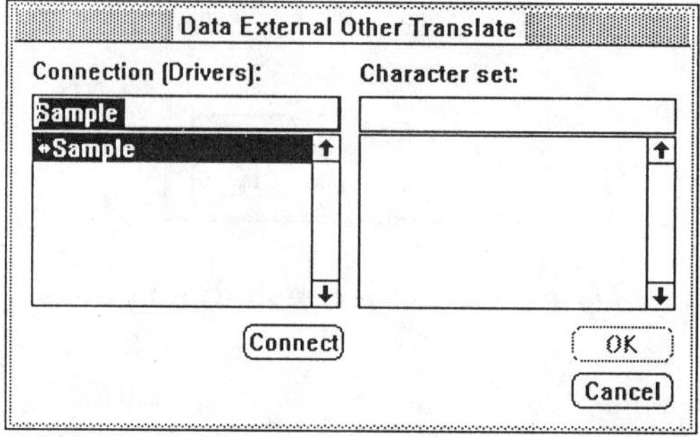

FIGURE 9–40 The Data External Other Translate dialog box

of the Datalens driver followed by the name (directory) of the database supported by that driver. For example, to use a different character set with a dBASE III table located in the directory C:\FOREIGN, type **SAMPLE C:\FOREIGN** in the Connection text box. When you're ready, select the Connect command button. 1-2-3/G displays the available character sets in the "Character set" list box. Select the Character set you want to use from the "Character set" list box and complete the command by selecting the OK command button.

Disconnecting an External Table

To disconnect one or more external tables, you use the Data External Reset command. When you select this command, 1-2-3/G displays the dialog box in Figure 9-41. The "Connected tables" list box shows a list of range names for tables that are currently connected to the current worksheet file. To disconnect all tables for the current worksheet file, select the All command button. To disconnect a specific table, select the range name for that table and then select the Reset command button. To return to the worksheet, select the OK command button.

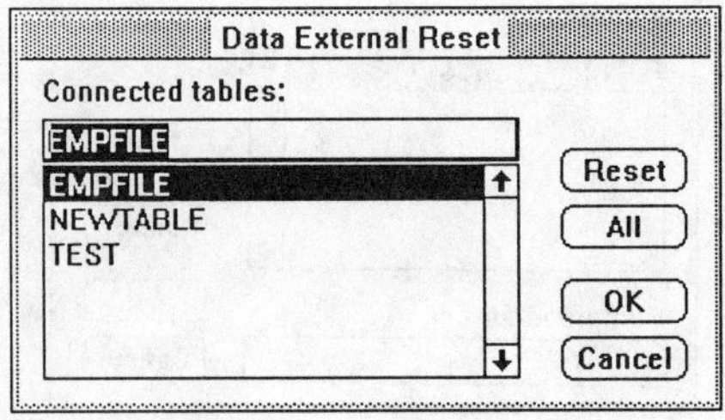

FIGURE 9–41 The Data External Reset dialog box

It is always a good idea to disconnect an external table after you are finished using it. However, be aware that disconnecting an external table may have the following effects:

- Database @functions that refer to the table display ERR. However, when you reconnect the table with Data External Use, those @functions will once again calculate correctly.
- Data Query and Data Table commands that refer to the external table result in an error message. Once again, you can solve this problem by reconnecting the appropriate external table with Data External Use.
- If the disconnected table is the last table associated with a database, 1-2-3/G disconnects the database. If that database is the last database associated with a particular Datalens driver, 1-2-3/G also disconnects the driver.

Modifying the LOTUS.BCF File

The LOTUS.BCF file instructs 1-2-3/G which directories to list when you select a Data External command. By default, 1-2-3/G only searches the current directory when you select a Data External command. To have 1-2-3/G search for tables in other directories, you must include the path to those directories in your LOTUS.BCF file.

The LOTUS.BCF file is automatically copied onto your 1-2-3/G program directory when you install 1-2-3/G.

The LOTUS.BCF file is an ASCII file. Therefore, you can modify its contents by using any editor that reads and saves files in ASCII format, like the OS/2 System Editor.

Initially, the LOTUS.BCF file contains the following listing:

```
DN="Sample" DL="LTSDBASE"
DD="Lotus sample dBASE III Datalens Driver Version 1.0";
```

Although it doesn't look like it, this is a single statement composed of three elements, DN, DL, and DD. Each of these elements has the following meaning:

DN: Shows the name of the Datalens driver as it appears on your screen when you select a Data External command. The driver name must appear in quotes. In this case, DN="Sample" causes 1-2-3/G to display Sample.

DL: Informs 1-2-3/G of the filename of a particular Datalens driver. In this case, 1-2-3/G will look for a filename that begins with LTSDBASE.

DD: Shows a description for the Datalens driver. This element of the statement is optional.

Each statement you include in the LOTUS.BCF file *must* end with a semicolon (;). As you can see from the above listing, the statement can take up more than one line.

To have 1-2-3/G list additional directories for a Data External command, you must add a statement for each directory that begins with DB. In addition, you must include a DN statement that references the SAMPLE driver. The word Sample must be typed exactly as it appears in the first DN statement in the file. You can also include an optional DD statement to describe the directory. Thus, each new statement will take the following form:

```
DB="path" DN="Sample" DD="description";
```

For example, imagine you have a directory, C:\DBASE, that contains your dBASE III files. To have 1-2-3/G list this directory each time you select a Data External command, you can add the following statement to your LOTUS.BCF file:

```
DB="C:\DBASE" DN="Sample" DD="dBASE files";
```

FILLING A RANGE WITH VALUES

You can use the Data Fill command to fill a range of adjacent cells with sequential numbers, dates, times, or percentages. For example, imagine you are creating a cash flow model that tracks cash and expenses by month for the current year. You can use the Data Fill command to quickly fill a row or column of adjacent cells with date values that progress by month.

When you select the Data Fill command 1-2-3/G displays the dialog box in Figure 9–42. In the Range(s) text box, specify the range address or range name of the range of adjacent cells you want to fill. You can also specify a collection here, if you so desire. In the Start text box, specify a value you want 1-2-3/G to use as the first value when filling the range. In the Step text box, specify a number by which you want to increment the value in each cell. In the Stop text

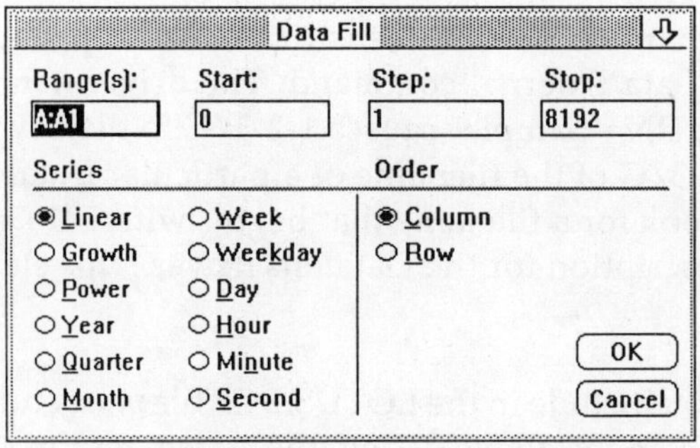

FIGURE 9–42 The Data Fill dialog box

box, specify a value you want 1-2-3/G to use as the last value when filling the range.

When you select OK command button to execute the Data Fill command, 1-2-3/G fills the range you specified in the Range(s) text box. The start value appears in the first cell of the range. The value in each cell thereafter is incremented by the step value. The data fill continues until either the stop value is reached or the range is full.

You can use any of the following to specify a start, step, or stop value:

- A number.
- A reference to a cell.
- A Range name that refers to a cell.
- A formula that evaluates to a number.
- A percentage, such as 10%.
- The @DATE, @TIME, or @NOW functions.
- A date or time entered in one of 1-2-3/G's acceptable date or time formats, for example 01/01/92.

Figure 9–43 shows a series of sequential numbers in the range A:A2..A:A20. To fill this range yourself, begin by moving the cell pointer to cell A:A2 and select the Data Fill command. 1-2-3/G displays the Data Fill dialog box. In the Range(s) text box, specify the range A:A2..A:A20. In the Start text box, type the number **1** and press ENTER. The number 1 already appears as a step value in Step text box. Press ENTER to accept this value.

123/G [69.4] Ready

File Edit Worksheet Range Copy... Move... Print Graph Data Utility Quit... Help

A:A1 'Numbers

FIG9-43.WG1

A	A	B	C	D	E	F	G
1	Numbers		Dates		Times		Percents
2	1		Jan-92		08:00 AM		10.00%
3	2		Feb-92		09:00 AM		20.00%
4	3		Mar-92		10:00 AM		30.00%
5	4		Apr-92		11:00 AM		40.00%
6	5		May-92		12:00 PM		50.00%
7	6		Jun-92		01:00 PM		60.00%
8	7		Jul-92		02:00 PM		70.00%
9	8		Aug-92		03:00 PM		80.00%
10	9		Sep-92		04:00 PM		90.00%
11	10		Oct-92		05:00 PM		100.00%
12	11		Nov-92		06:00 PM		110.00%
13	12		Dec-92		07:00 PM		120.00%
14	13		Jan-93		08:00 PM		130.00%
15	14		Feb-93		09:00 PM		140.00%
16	15		Mar-93		10:00 PM		150.00%
17	16		Apr-93		11:00 PM		160.00%
18	17		May-93		12:00 AM		170.00%
19	18		Jun-93		01:00 AM		180.00%
20	19		Jul-93		02:00 AM		190.00%

FIGURE 9–43 Example ranges filled with numbers, dates, and times

Further, the number 8192 already appears as a stop value in the Stop text box, more than adequate to fill the small range you've specified. Press ENTER to accept this value.

To execute the Data Fill command, select the OK command button, or press ENTER. 1-2-3/G fills the range A:A2..A:A20 with sequential numbers. The start value, 1, appears in cell A:A2. The cells in the balance of the fill range are filled by adding the step value to the previous value. The data fill is stopped when the selected range is full, long before the stop value is reached.

Note

> 1-2-3/G remembers the fill range, as well as the start, step, and stop values for the Data Fill command. If you've used the command previously in the current session, 1-2-3/G shows you the same fill range and values the next time you select the command.

The Series section of the Data Fill dialog box allows you to change the way the step value is used. For example, the first three option buttons, Linear, Growth, and Power, perform the following:

- Linear: Adds the step value to previous value (the default).
- Growth: Multiplies the previous value by the step value.
- Power: Uses the step value as an exponent for the previous value.

The balance of the options in the Series section are used when filling a range with dates or times.

The Order section of the Data Fill dialog box allows you to change the column versus row orientation for the Data Fill command. Ordinarily, the Data Fill command fills a range a column at a time. For example, imagine you specify a rectangular fill range that includes three columns. When the Data Fill command is executed, 1-2-3/G fills the first column, then the second, and finally the third. However, if you select the Row option button from the Order section, 1-2-3/G fills the first row, then the second row, and so on.

You can also specify a three-dimensional range for the Data Fill command. When you do, 1-2-3/G performs the data fill a worksheet at a time. When the range in the first worksheet is full, 1-2-3/G moves onto the second worksheet, and so on, until either the range you specified is full or the stop value is reached.

As mentioned, you can also fill a range with dates or times. For example, imagine you want to fill a range with dates values that advance by month, starting with January of 1992. Such a range appears in column C of Figure 9–43. To do this, move the cell pointer to the beginning of the range you want to fill (cell A:C2 in Figure 9–43) and select Data Fill. 1-2-3/G displays the Data Fill dialog box.

In the Range(s) text box, specify the range you want to fill (A:C2..A:C20) and press ENTER. In the Start text box, type **@DATE(92,1,1)** and press ENTER. Accept the value of 1 in the Step text box by pressing ENTER. In the Stop text box, use the @DATE function again to specify the date you want to use to stop the data fill. Press ENTER to confirm your entry. (Alternatively, you can type 999999 for a stop value, or another arbitrarily high number that 1-2-3/G cannot possibly reach.) From the Series section, select the Month option button. To complete the Data Fill command, select the OK command button, or press ENTER. 1-2-3/G fills the range with date values that advance by month. To make these values appear as dates, use the Range Format Date/Time command to format the filled range using the date format of your choice.

Note

Instead of using the @DATE function to enter a start or stop value in the previous example, you can enter a date in one of 1-2-3/G's acceptable date formats, for example 01/01/92. See Chapter 3, "Formatting Worksheets," for more on 1-2-3/G's acceptable date formats.

As mentioned, the Series section of the Data Fill dialog box allows you to change the way a step value is used. In addition to the Linear, Growth, and Power options covered earlier, 1-2-3/G offers the following options for controlling step values for dates and times:

- **Year:** Advances date values by year.
- **Quarter:** Advances date values by 90 days.
- **Month:** Advances date values by months.
- **Week:** Advances date values by seven days.
- **Weekday:** Advances date values by weekdays (Monday–Friday)
- **Day**: Advances Date values by days.
- **Hour:** Advances time values by hours.
- **Minute:** Advances time values by minutes.
- **Second:** Advances time values by seconds.

Tip: For Release 3 Users

The coding system for date and time step values has been carried forward from Release 3. That is, as a short cut to selecting the Month option from the Series section of the Data Fill dialog box, you can type 1m in the Step text box. That way, 1-2-3/G will advance date values by one month.

CREATING DATA TABLES

To create Data tables, you use the Data Table command. This command allows you to perform "what-if" analysis by evaluating one or more sets of numbers in one or more formulas. The result of using each set of numbers with each formula is recorded in a table of adjacent cells.

1-2-3/G allows you to create various types of data tables. The type of data table you choose depends on how many variables you have in the formula(s) you're evaluating. Variables are the parts of a formula that you want to change. For example, the @PMT(principal,interest,term) function discussed in Chapter 6 is used to calculate loan payments. This function takes three arguments—principal, interest, and term—and therefore has three potential variables. To test this formula you can use any of the following commands:

- **Data Table 1:** Evaluates the effect of changing one variable in one or more formulas. For example, you might evaluate the effect of varying rates of principal on loan payments with a fixed interest rate and term.
- **Date Table 2:** Evaluates the effect of changing two variables in a single formula. For example, you might evaluate the effect on your loan payment of varying both the principal and the interest rate for a fixed term.
- **Data Table 3:** Evaluates the effect of changing three variables in a single formula. For example, you might evaluate the effect that various amounts of principal, various rates of interest, and various terms have on your loan payment.

In addition to Data Table 1, 2, and 3, 1-2-3/G includes the Data Table Labeled command. This command allows you to evaluate a virtually unlimited number of variables in an unlimited number of formulas.

The Data Table 1 Command

The Data Table 1 command allows you to substitute a series of test values into one or more formulas. The result of using each test value is recorded in a table beneath the appropriate formula. Figure 9–44 shows a data table in the range B4..C18 that was created with the Data Table 1 command. It shows the effect of substituting various values as the *principal* argument for the @PMT(*principal,interest,term*) function. The result is a table showing monthly loan payments for various levels of principal investment. You might use a data table like this to determine how much you can afford to pay for a new home.

Before you can use the Data Table 1 command, you must set up the framework for the range that will contain the data table. To begin, enter the values you want to test in a column of cells. For example, in Figure 9–44, numbers ranging from 100,000 to 230,000 appear in the range A:B5..A:B18. This column of values will define the leftmost boundary of the table. Along the top row of the table, enter one or more formulas that will use the test values. For example, Figure 9–44 shows a formula in cell A:C4. Although only a single formula is shown, you can enter as many formulas as you like along the top row of the table. Make sure, however, that you leave the cell at the top of the leftmost column of test values blank.

The @function in cell A:C4 reads @PMT(B1,0.105/12,30*12). It has been formatted with the Range Format Text command so that you can see it. Other-

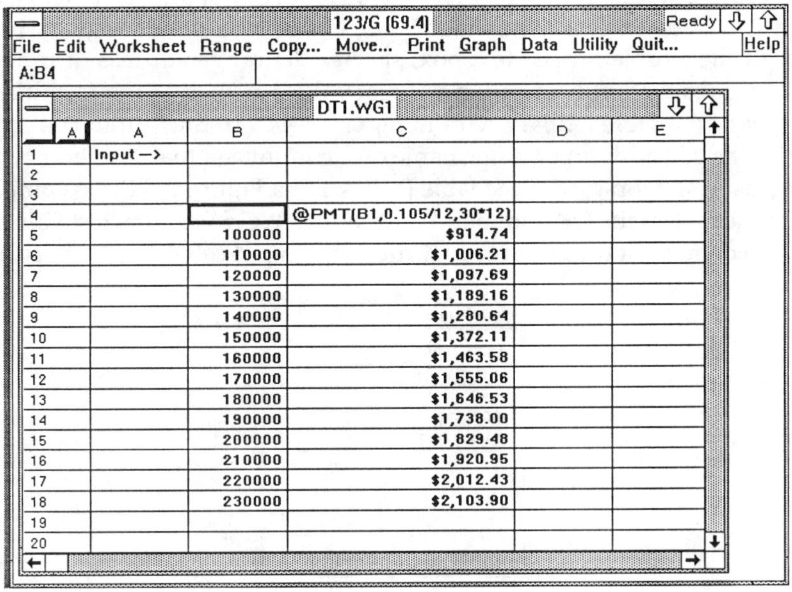

123/G (69.4) Ready

File Edit Worksheet Range Copy... Move... Print Graph Data Utility Quit... Help

A:B4

DT1.WG1

A	A	B	C	D	E
1	Input –>				
2					
3					
4			@PMT(B1,0.105/12,30*12)		
5		100000	$914.74		
6		110000	$1,006.21		
7		120000	$1,097.69		
8		130000	$1,189.16		
9		140000	$1,280.64		
10		150000	$1,372.11		
11		160000	$1,463.58		
12		170000	$1,555.06		
13		180000	$1,646.53		
14		190000	$1,738.00		
15		200000	$1,829.48		
16		210000	$1,920.95		
17		220000	$2,012.43		
18		230000	$2,103.90		
19					
20					

FIGURE 9–44 A data table created with Data Table 1

wise, 1-2-3/G will display 0 in the cell. The first argument in the function, B1, is the *principal* argument for the @PMT function. The B1 is a reference to cell A:B1. This cell will be the *input* cell for the Data Table 1 command. When you execute the Data Table 1 command, 1-2-3/G will feed each test value in the leftmost column of the data table into this input cell, and thereby into the formula in cell A:C4. The result of using each test value will be recorded in a column of cells beneath the formula in the cell A:C4. Each result is placed in the row that is adjacent to its test value.

Note

The remaining arguments in the @PMT function in cell A:C4 of figure 9–44 have no relevance to the Data Table 1 command. However, the second argument, 0.105/12, is the *interest* argument for the @PMT function. This reflects a 10.5% interest divided by 12 months. The third argument, 30*12, is the *term* argument for the @PMT function. It reflects a 30-year term multiplied by 12 months in each of the years.

Once the framework of the data table is prepared, you're ready to use the Data Table 1 command to calculate the output results for the table. When you select the Data Table 1 command. 1-2-3/G displays the dialog box in Figure 9–45. In the "Table range" text box, specify the range address or range name that includes the leftmost column of test values as well as the formulas in the top row of the table (A:B4..A:C18 in Figure 9–44). In the "Input cell" text box, specify the cell address or range name of the input cell that is referenced by the formulas in the top row of the table (cell A:B1 in Figure 9–44). To complete the command, select the OK command button. 1-2-3/G routes the test values in the leftmost column of the table range through the input cell and into the formula(s)

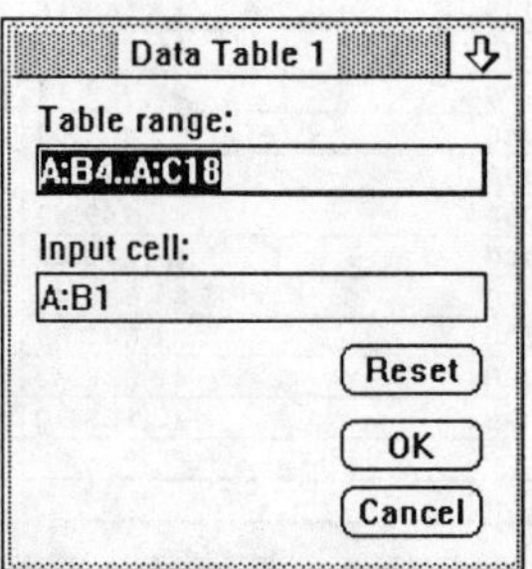

FIGURE 9–45 **The Data Table 1 dialog box**

in the top row of the table. The result of using each test value is recorded beneath the appropriate formula in the same row as the test value that generated the result.

To quickly repeat the most recent Data Table command, press TABLE (F8). 1-2-3/G will repeat the most recent Data Table command using the ranges you've previously established.

Note

1-2-3/G remembers the ranges you've set for the Data Table 1 command. That is, if you've established ranges for the command previously during the current session, 1-2-3/G shows you those same ranges the next time you enter the command. To cancel the existing ranges for the Data Table 1 command, select the Reset command button from the Data Query dialog box.

Using Data Table 1 with a Database @Function

Figure 9–46 shows an example of how you can use a database @function with the Data Table 1 command to build a data table. The data table in the range A:B14..A:C22 uses the @DSUM function to query the EMPBASE table and calculate the total salary paid to the employees in each department.

Note

This section assumes you are familiar with the use of the database @functions. If you're not, take a moment to read the section entitled "Using the Database @Functions" earlier in this chapter.

To create the data table in Figure 9–46 yourself, begin by setting up the framework for the table. To do this, enter the name for each department from the DEPT field of the EMPBASE table in the leftmost column of the table range (A:B15..A:B22). In the top row of the table range (cell A:C14), enter the formula: @DSUM(EMPBASE,"SALARY",E14..E15), where EMPBASE is the range name that refers to the EMPBASE table, "SALARY" refers to the SALARY field in that table, and E14..E15 is the criteria range for the database @function. To set up

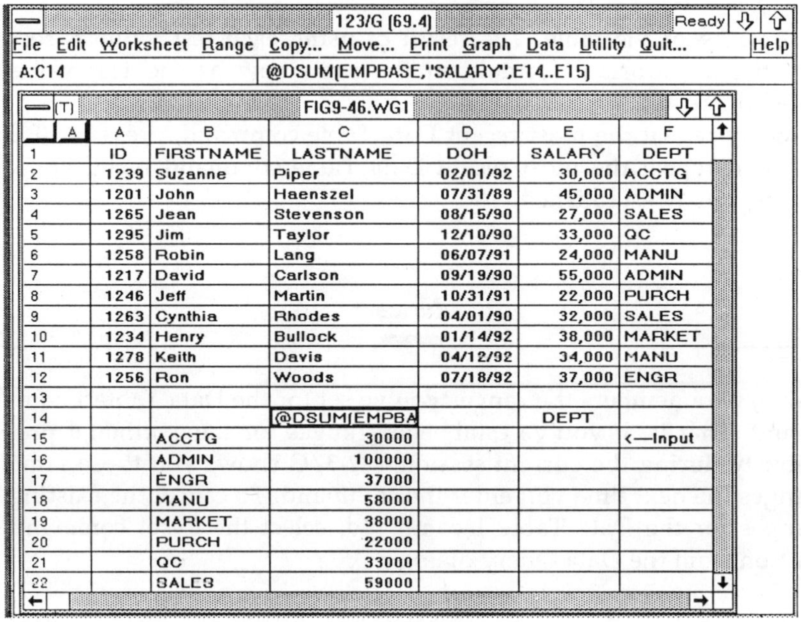

123/G (69.4) Ready

File Edit Worksheet Range Copy... Move... Print Graph Data Utility Quit... Help

A:C14 @DSUM(EMPBASE,"SALARY",E14..E15)

(T) FIG9-46.WG1

A	A	B	C	D	E	F
1	ID	FIRSTNAME	LASTNAME	DOH	SALARY	DEPT
2	1239	Suzanne	Piper	02/01/92	30,000	ACCTG
3	1201	John	Haenszel	07/31/89	45,000	ADMIN
4	1265	Jean	Stevenson	08/15/90	27,000	SALES
5	1295	Jim	Taylor	12/10/90	33,000	QC
6	1258	Robin	Lang	06/07/91	24,000	MANU
7	1217	David	Carlson	09/19/90	55,000	ADMIN
8	1246	Jeff	Martin	10/31/91	22,000	PURCH
9	1263	Cynthia	Rhodes	04/01/90	32,000	SALES
10	1234	Henry	Bullock	01/14/92	38,000	MARKET
11	1278	Keith	Davis	04/12/92	34,000	MANU
12	1256	Ron	Woods	07/18/92	37,000	ENGR
13						
14			@DSUM(EMPBA		DEPT	
15		ACCTG	30000			<—Input
16		ADMIN	100000			
17		ENGR	37000			
18		MANU	58000			
19		MARKET	38000			
20		PURCH	22000			
21		QC	33000			
22		SALES	59000			

FIGURE 9–46 Using Data Table with the @DSUM function

the criteria range for the @function, move the cell pointer to cell A:E14 and enter the field name DEPT, referring to the DEPT field in the EMPBASE table. Do not enter a search argument below this field name. Instead, cell A:E15 will be used as the input cell for the Data Table 1 command.

When you're ready, select the Data Table 1 command. 1-2-3/G displays the Data Table 1 dialog box shown in Figure 9–45. In the "Table range" text box, specify the range that includes the leftmost column of department names as well as the @DSUM function at the top of the table (A:B14..A:C22). In the "Input cell" text box, specify the single-cell range A:E15 beneath the DEPT field name in the criteria range A:E14..A:E15 for the database @function. To complete the command, select the OK command button. 1-2-3/G fills in the data table.

To fill in the data table in Figure 9–46, 1-2-3/G routes the department names from the leftmost column of the table range into the criteria range for the @DSUM function. The results of using each name with the @DSUM function is recorded in the table range. For example, for the first iteration of the Data Table 1 command, the field name ADMIN is substituted into the criteria range A:E14..A:E15. Therefore, 1-2-3/G will sum the SALARY field for those records that contain the label ADMIN in the DEPT field of the EMPBASE table. This result is placed in the first row of the data table in the cell that is adjacent to the ADMIN department name. This process continues until all department names from the leftmost column have been substituted and the data table is completed.

The Data Table 2 Command

Use the Data Table 2 command when you want to evaluate the effect of changing two variables in a single formula. For example, building on the @PMT example shown earlier, imagine you want to calculate monthly loan payments using varying levels of both principal *and* interest. To do this, you can use the Data Table 2 command to create the data table shown in Figure 9–47.

Similar to Data Table 1, you must set up the framework for the data table prior to using the Data Table 2 command. To begin, decide on a location for the table. Then, in the leftmost column of that range, enter the first set of test values. In the leftmost column (A:B5..A:B19) of the table in Figure 9–47, various principal investment values ranging from $100,000 to $230,000 are shown. These values are formatted with the Range Format Currency 0 command, to make them appear more attractive.

In the top row of the table range, enter the second set of test values. For example, in Figure 9–47, various interest rates ranging from 10.5% to 11.5% appear in the range A:C4..A:F4. These values have been formatted with the Range Format Percent 2 command, to make them appear as percentages.

123/G (69.4) Ready

File Edit Worksheet Range Copy... Move... Print Graph Data Utility Quit... Help

A:B5 @PMT(B1,B2/12,B3)

(T) DT2.WG1

A	A	B	C	D	E	F
1	Input 1->					
2	Input 2->					
3	Term	360				
4						
5		@PMT(B1	10.00%	10.50%	11.00%	11.50%
6		$100,000	877.57	914.74	952.32	990.29
7		$110,000	965.33	1,006.21	1,047.56	1,089.32
8		$120,000	1,053.09	1,097.69	1,142.79	1,188.35
9		$130,000	1,140.84	1,189.16	1,238.02	1,287.38
10		$140,000	1,228.60	1,280.64	1,333.25	1,386.41
11		$150,000	1,316.36	1,372.11	1,428.49	1,485.44
12		$160,000	1,404.11	1,463.58	1,523.72	1,584.47
13		$170,000	1,491.87	1,555.06	1,618.95	1,683.50
14		$180,000	1,579.63	1,646.53	1,714.18	1,782.52
15		$190,000	1,667.39	1,738.00	1,809.41	1,881.55
16		$200,000	1,755.14	1,829.48	1,904.65	1,980.58
17		$210,000	1,842.90	1,920.95	1,999.88	2,079.61
18		$220,000	1,930.66	2,012.43	2,095.11	2,178.64
19		$230,000	2,018.41	2,103.90	2,190.34	2,277.67
20						
21						
22						

FIGURE 9–47 A data table created with Data Table 2

At the intersection of the first column and the top row (cell A:B5 in Figure 9–47), enter the formula that will be used to evaluate the first and second set of test values. As you're building this formula, make sure you reference two cells located outside the table range. These will be your first and second input cells for the Data Table 2 command. For example, the formula in cell A:B5 of Figure 9–47 reads @PMT(B1,B2/12,B3). In this formula, the reference B1 is the *principal* argument for the @PMT function and it refers to cell A:B1. Through this first input cell, 1-2-3/G will route the test values in the leftmost column of the table range. The second reference in the @PMT formula, B2/12, is the *interest* argument and it refers to cell A:B2. Through this second input cell, 1-2-3/G will route the test values in the top row of the table range. The third reference, B3 is the *term* argument for the @function and it refers to cell A:B3. This cell contains the static value 360, meaning 360 months.

When you're ready, select the Data Table 2 command. 1-2-3/G displays the dialog box in Figure 9–48. In the "Table range" text box, specify the range address or range name that includes leftmost column and the top row of test values as well as the formula at the intersection of these (A:B5..A:F19 in Figure 9–47). In the "Input cell 1" text box, specify the range address or range name of the first input cell (A:B1). In the "Input cell 2" text box, specify the range address or range name of the second input cell (A:B2). To complete the Data Table 2 command, select the OK command button. 1-2-3/G fills in the data table.

When you execute the Data Table 2 command, 1-2-3/G routes the values in the leftmost column of the table range through input cell 1. The test values in the top row of the table range are routed through input cell 2. The result of each iteration of the Data Table 2 command is recorded at the intersection of the appropriate column and row. For example, for the first iteration of the Data Table 2 command in Figure 9–47, 1-2-3/G uses the value $100,000 from cell A:B6. This value is routed through cell A:B1. At the same time, the value 10% from cell A:C5 is routed through cell A:B2. At this point, the @PMT formula in cell A:B5 reads @PMT(100000,.1/12,360). The result of this formula is 877.57,

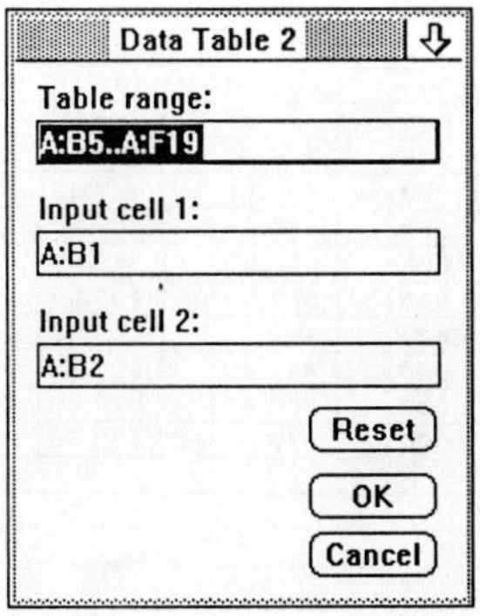

Data Table 2
Table range:
A:B5..A:F19
Input cell 1:
A:B1
Input cell 2:
A:B2
Reset
OK
Cancel

FIGURE 9–48 The Data Table 2 dialog box

and that result is placed in cell A:C6 at the intersection of the two test values. The process continues until all the test values have been used and the data table is full.

Using Data Table 2 with a Database @Function

You can also use the Data Table 2 command with the database @functions to query a database table. The results of the query are recorded in a data table. For example, Figure 9–49 shows a data table in the range A:B15..A:E18 that was created with Data Table 2 command. This data table shows air travel expenses broken down both by month and by employee. The information used to create the data table is taken from the expense report database table at the top of Figure 9–49. This expense report database table shows travel expenses by category for a group of salespersons.

Unlike the Data Table 1 command discussed earlier in this chapter, the Data Table 2 command allows you to substitute two test values at a time into the criteria range for the database @function. Thus, you can build a data table by using two search criteria to search a database table, instead of only one.

To create the data table in Figure 9–49, begin by setting up the table range. In the leftmost column of that table range, enter the names of sales persons from the EMPLOYEE field of the expense report table. For example, the names Sharrock, Morris, and Marvuglio appear in the range A:B16..A:B18 of Figure

123/G (69.4) Ready

File Edit Worksheet Range Copy... Move... Print Graph Data Utility Quit... Help

A:B15 @DSUM(EXPENSE,"AIR",B12..C13)

(T) EXPENSE.WG1

A	A	B	C	D	E	F	G
1	ID	EMPLOYEE	DATE	AIR	CAR	HOTEL	MEALS
2	0178	Sharrock	Jan-92	872.00	78.48	218.00	95.92
3	0199	Morris	Jan-92	1,267.00	114.03	316.75	139.37
4	0129	Marvuglio	Jan-92	440.00	39.60	110.00	48.40
5	0178	Sharrock	Feb-92	997.00	89.73	249.25	109.67
6	0199	Morris	Feb-92	2,075.00	186.75	518.75	228.25
7	0129	Marvuglio	Feb-92	620.00	55.80	155.00	68.20
8	0178	Sharrock	Mar-92	665.00	59.85	166.25	73.15
9	0199	Morris	Mar-92	1,570.00	141.30	392.50	172.70
10	0129	Marvuglio	Mar-92	320.00	28.80	80.00	35.20
11							
12		EMPLOYEE	DATE				
13							
14							
15		@DSUM(EXI	Jan-92	Feb-92	Mar-92		
16		Sharrock	872.00	997.00	665.00		
17		Morris	1,267.00	2,075.00	1,570.00		
18		Marvuglio	440.00	620.00	320.00		
19							
20							
21							
22							

FIGURE 9–49 Using Data Table 2 with the @DSUM function

9–49. Along the top row of the table, enter the appropriate date values from the DATE field of the expense report table. For example, the dates Jan-92, Feb-92, and Mar-92 appear in the range A:C15..A:E15. At the intersection of the left-most column and the topmost row (A:B15), enter the formula @DSUM(EXPENSE,"AIR",B12..C13), where EXPENSE is the range name for the expense report table, "AIR" refers to the AIR field in the expense report table, and B12..C13 is the criteria range for the database @function.

Once the table frame is prepared, you can set up the criteria range for the @DSUM function. In cell A:B12 enter the label EMPLOYEE, which refers to the EMPLOYEE field in the expense report table. In cell A:C12 enter the label DATE, which refers to the DATE field in the expense report table. Be sure to leave the cells beneath both of these labels blank. These will be your input cells for the Data Table 2 command.

When you're ready, select the Data Table 2 command. 1-2-3/G displays the Data Table 2 dialog box. In the "Table range" text box, specify the range A:B15..A:E18. This range includes the leftmost column of test values, the top row of test values, and the @DSUM formula. In the "Input cell 1" text box, specify the single-cell range A:B13 beneath the EMPLOYEE field name in the criteria range for the @DSUM function. In the "Input cell 2" text box, specify the single-cell range A:C13, beneath the DATE field name in the criteria range for the @DSUM function. To execute the Data Table 2 command, select the OK command button. 1-2-3/G fills in the data table.

The Data Table 3 Command

The Data Table 3 command allows you to evaluate the effect of changing three variables at a time in a formula. This command is also capable of producing a three-dimensional data table that extends backward through multiple worksheets.

As you might imagine, the Data Table 3 command supports three input cells. Input cell 1 accepts the input of test values from the leftmost column of the table range. Input cell 2 accepts the input of test values from the top row of the table range. Input cell 3 accepts input of a single test value from the cell that is located at the intersection of the leftmost column and the top row of the table range. Therefore, to have more than one test value for input cell 3, the table range must be three-dimensional (occupy more than one worksheet).

Unlike the Data Table 1 and 2 commands, the formula for the Data Table 3 command is not included in the table range. Instead, the formula is located in a cell outside the table range called the Formula cell.

Imagine you want to use the @PMT function to calculate monthly loan payments for various rates of principal and interest over a term of 15, 20, and 30 years. To do this, you can use the Data Table 3 command to create the three-dimensional data table in Figure 9–50. To create this data table, perform the following steps:

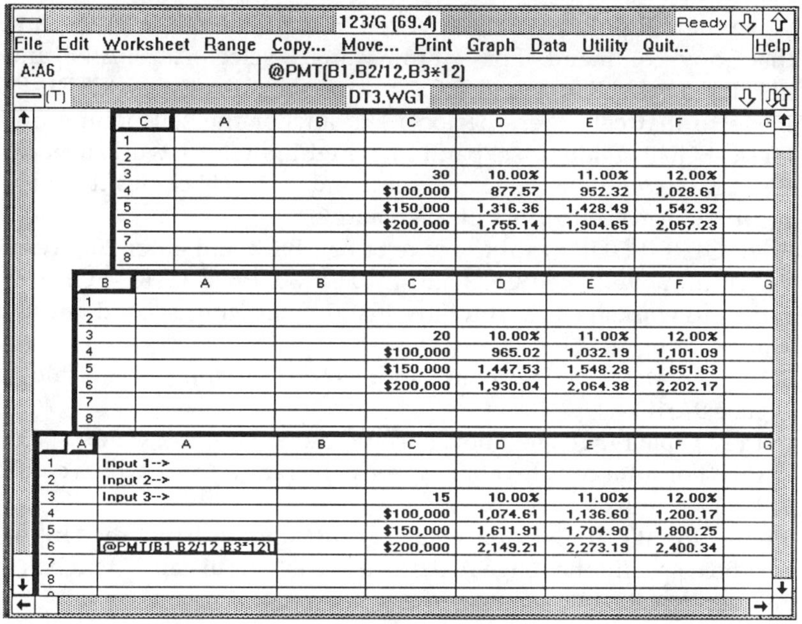

123/G (69.4) Ready

File Edit Worksheet Range Copy... Move... Print Graph Data Utility Quit... Help

A:A6 @PMT(B1,B2/12,B3*12)

(T) DT3.WG1

C	A	B	C	D	E	F	G
1							
2							
3			30	10.00%	11.00%	12.00%	
4			$100,000	877.57	952.32	1,028.61	
5			$150,000	1,316.36	1,428.49	1,542.92	
6			$200,000	1,755.14	1,904.65	2,057.23	
7							
8							

B	A	B	C	D	E	F	G
1							
2							
3			20	10.00%	11.00%	12.00%	
4			$100,000	965.02	1,032.19	1,101.09	
5			$150,000	1,447.53	1,548.28	1,651.63	
6			$200,000	1,930.04	2,064.38	2,202.17	
7							
8							

A	A	B	C	D	E	F	G
1	Input 1-->						
2	Input 2-->						
3	Input 3-->		15	10.00%	11.00%	12.00%	
4			$100,000	1,074.61	1,136.60	1,200.17	
5			$150,000	1,611.91	1,704.90	1,800.25	
6	@PMT(B1,B2/12,B3*12)		$200,000	2,149.21	2,273.19	2,400.34	
7							
8							

FIGURE 9–50 **A three-dimensional data table created with Data Table 3**

1. Enter a series of principal values in a column of the current worksheet. In Figure 9–50, a series of principal values appears in the range A:C4..A:C6 formatted with the Range Format Currency 0 command. These values will be routed through input cell 1 as the *principal* argument for the @PMT function. Make sure you leave a blank cell at the top of this column. You'll fill in this cell in step 2.
2. Move the cell pointer to the top of the column of principal values (cell A:C3) and enter the number *15*. This value will be routed through input cell 3 as the *term* argument for the @PMT function.
3. Move the cell pointer one cell to the right and enter a series of interest rates working from left to right. For example, a series of interest rates ranging from 10.00% to 12.00% appear in the range A:D3..A:F3 of Figure 9–50. These values are formatted with the Range Format Percent 2 command. These test values will be routed through input cell 2 as the *interest* argument for the @PMT function.
4. Move the cell pointer to a cell outside the table range (A:A6) in Figure 9–50, and enter the formula **@PMT(B1,B2/12,B3*12)**. The cell containing this formula will be the Formula cell for the Data Table 3 command. The B1 in this formula is a reference to cell A:B1, which will be input cell 1 for the Data Table 3 command. The B2 is a reference to cell A:B2, which will be input cell 2. Finally, the B3 is a reference to cell A:B3, which will be the input cell 3.

5. Move the cell pointer to the first cell in the table range (A:C3) and select the Copy command. For a From range, select A:C3..A:F6 and press ENTER. Then, click on cell B:C3 in worksheet B, or press CTRL-PGUP to move to that cell. Press period (.) to anchor the cell pointer and press CTRL-PGUP again to expand the highlight into worksheet C. Press ENTER to complete the Copy command. 1-2-3/G copies the table frame in worksheet A into worksheets B and C.
6. Press CTRL-PGUP again to move to cell B:C3 and enter **20**. Press CTRL-PGUP to move to cell C:C3 and ENTER **30**. Press CTRL-PGDN twice to return to worksheet A. You have just defined your second and third test values for input cell 3.
7. Select the Data Table 3 command. 1-2-3/G displays the dialog box in Figure 9–51.
8. In the "Table range" text box, specify the range A:C3..C:F6.
9. In the "Formula cell" text box, specify the range A:A6, which contains the @PMT formula.
10. In the "Input cell 1" text box, specify the range A:B1. In the "Input cell 2" text box, specify the range A:B2; and in the "Input cell 3" text box, specify the range A:B3.
11. To complete the Data Table 3 command, select the OK command button. 1-2-3/G fills in the data tables in worksheets A, B, and C.

The data table in worksheet A of Figure 9–50 shows monthly loan payments for principal values of $100,000, $150,0000, and $200,00 at interest rates of 10%, 11%, and 12% over a term of 15 years. The data tables in worksheet B and C

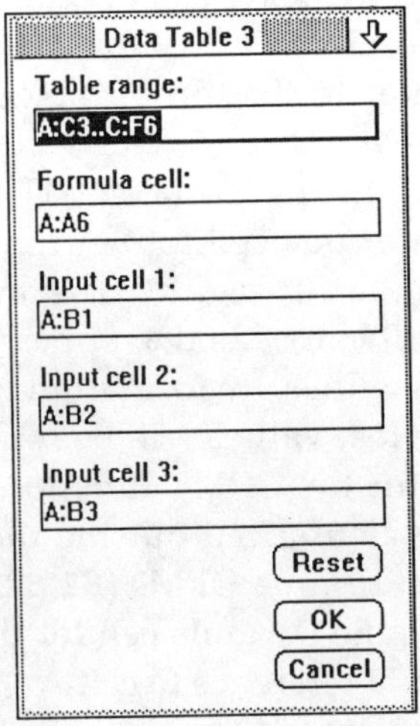

Data Table 3
Table range:
A:C3..C:F6
Formula cell:
A:A6
Input cell 1:
A:B1
Input cell 2:
A:B2
Input cell 3:
A:B3
Reset
OK
Cancel

FIGURE 9–51 The Data Table 3 dialog box

show monthly payments for the same principal values and interest rates over a term of 20 years and 30 years, respectively.

Using Data Table 3 with a Database @Function

You can also use a database @function with the Data Table 3 command to query a database table. For example, Figure 9–52 shows an example client service database table. This database table shows services provided to clients for a small computer consulting company. The example that follows will show you how to use the Data Table 3 command in conjunction with the @DSUM function to query this client service database table and create the three-dimensional data table shown in Figure 9–53. This data table shows each category of service broken down by client and month.

To create the data table in Figure 9–53, begin by creating the client service database table shown in Figure 9–52 in worksheet A. Next, press CTRL-PGUP to move to worksheet B. Then, start building the framework for the first table in the table range. In cell B:A2, enter the label **Hardware**. This comes from the SERVICE field of the client service table. In the column beneath this cell (B:A3..B:A5), enter the names of each client from the CLIENT field of the client service database table. Finally, in the top row of the table (B:B2..B:D2), enter the dates from the DATE field of the client service table.

When you're ready, use the Copy command to copy the table frame in worksheet B back to worksheets C and D, as shown in Figure 9–53. Once this is done, press CTRL-PGUP to move to worksheet C and enter the label **Software** in cell C:A2. Press CTRL-PGUP again to move to worksheet D and enter the label **Training** in cell D:A2. Then, press CTRL-PGDN twice to return to worksheet B.

Now that the framework for each table in the table range is prepared, you're ready to create the @DSUM formula and its criteria range. To create the formula, move the cell pointer to cell B:E2 and enter **@DSUM(A:A1..A:D10,"AMOUNT",A7..C8)**, where A:A1..A:D10 is the range that contains the

123/G [69.4] Ready

File Edit Worksheet Range Copy... Move... Print Graph Data Utility Quit... Help

A:A1 'CLIENT

FIG9-52.WG1

A	A	B	C	D	E	F	G
1	CLIENT	SERVICE	DATE	AMOUNT			
2	ABC Corp.	Hardware	Jan-92	$8,770			
3	Aptos Title	Software	Jan-92	$345			
4	Allied,Inc	Training	Feb-92	$450			
5	Aptos Title	Hardware	Mar-92	$7,650			
6	ABC Corp.	Software	Jan-92	$789			
7	Aptos Title	Training	Feb-92	$670			
8	Allied,Inc	Hardware	Feb-92	$9,870			
9	ABC Corp.	Software	Mar-92	$650			
10							

FIGURE 9–52 The client service database table

	A	B	C	D	E	F	G
1							
2	Training	Jan-92	Feb-92	Mar-92			
3	ABC Corp.	0	0	0			
4	Aptos Title	0	670	0			
5	Allied,Inc	0	450	0			
6							
7							
8							

	A	B	C	D	E	F	G
1							
2	Software	Jan-92	Feb-92	Mar-92			
3	ABC Corp.	789	0	650			
4	Aptos Title	345	0	0			
5	Allied,Inc	0	0	0			
6							
7							
8							

	A	B	C	D	E
1					
2	Hardware	Jan-92	Feb-92	Mar-92	@DSUM(A:A1..A:D9,"AMOUNT",A7..C8)
3	ABC Corp.	8770	0	0	
4	Aptos Title	0	0	7650	
5	Allied,Inc	0	9870	0	
6					
7	CLIENT	DATE	SERVICE		
8					

FIGURE 9–53 Using Data Table 3 with the @DSUM function

client service table, "AMOUNT" refers to the AMOUNT field in that table, and A7..C8 refers to the criteria range you're about to create. (This same formula appears in cell B:E2 of Figure 9–53, formatted with Range Format Text command.) To create the criteria range for this formula, move the cell pointer to cell B:A7 and enter the field name CLIENT, corresponding to the CLIENT field name in the client service table. Do the same for the DATE and SERVICE field names in cells B:B7 and B:C7, respectively.

To fill in the table range, select the Data Table 3 command, 1-2-3/G displays the Data Table 3 dialog box. In the "Table range" text box, specify the range B:A2..D:D5, which includes the table frames in worksheets B, C, and D. In the Formula cell text box, specify the single-cell range B:E2, which includes the @DSUM formula. In the "Input cell 1" text box, specify the single-cell range B:A8, beneath the CLIENT field name. In the "Input cell 2" text box, specify the single-cell range B:B8, beneath the DATE field name. Finally, in the "Input cell 3" text box, specify the single-cell range B:C8, beneath the SERVICE field name. When you're ready, select the OK command button. 1-2-3/G fills in the table range. The data table in worksheet B contains revenue from hardware sales, broken down by client and month. Worksheets C and D contain similar information for revenue generated from software sales and training.

The Data Table Labeled Command

The Data Table Labeled command allows you to evaluate a virtually unlimited number of variables in an unlimited number of formulas. This command is not for the faint hearted, however. At first, this command will seem unnecessarily complex, until you get the hang of it. Despite this complexity, the Data Table Labeled command does offer some unique advantages. For example, as mentioned, you're no longer limited to a specific number of variables that can be evaluated by a formula. In addition, your row and column input values do not have to be adjacent to the table of output results. Thus, you can use information that already exists in your worksheet to create the data table.

Figure 9–54 shows an example of a data table created with the Data Table Labeled command. This data table was created by substituting various test values into the same @PMT(*principal,interest,term*) function used in previous Data Table command examples. However, in this example a fourth variable, down payment, will be added.

When you select the Data Table Labeled command, 1-2-3/G displays the dialog box in Figure 9–55. Before proceeding to create the example in Figure 9–54, let's take a moment to discuss the components of the dialog box in Figure 9–55 and what each of them means.

You use the "Formula range" text box to specify the range that includes the formulas you want to evaluate as well as labels that identify those formulas.

1-2-3/G Ready
File Edit Worksheet Range Copy... Move... Print Graph Data Utility Quit... Help
A:A7 @PMT(B1-B4,B2/12,B3*12)
DTL.WG1

C	A	B	C	D	E	F	G
1				30			
2					10%	11%	12%
3							
4			25,000$	100,000$	658.18	714.24	771.46
5				150,000$	1,096.96	1,190.40	1,285.77
6				200,000$	1,535.75	1,666.57	1,800.07
7							

B	A	B	C	D	E	F	G
1				20			
2					10%	11%	12%
3							
4			25,000$	100,000$	723.77	774.14	825.81
5				150,000$	1,206.28	1,290.24	1,376.36
6				200,000$	1,688.79	1,806.33	1,926.90
7							

A	A	B	C	D	E	F	G
1	PriNcipal			15	----------	Formula	----------
2	Interest				10%	11%	12%
3	Term						
4	Down Pmt.		25,000$	100,000$	805.95	852.45	900.13
5				150,000$	1,343.26	1,420.75	1,500.21
6	Formula			200,000$	1,880.56	1,989.04	2,100.29
7	ERR						

FIGURE 9–54 A 3-D data table created with Data Table Labeled

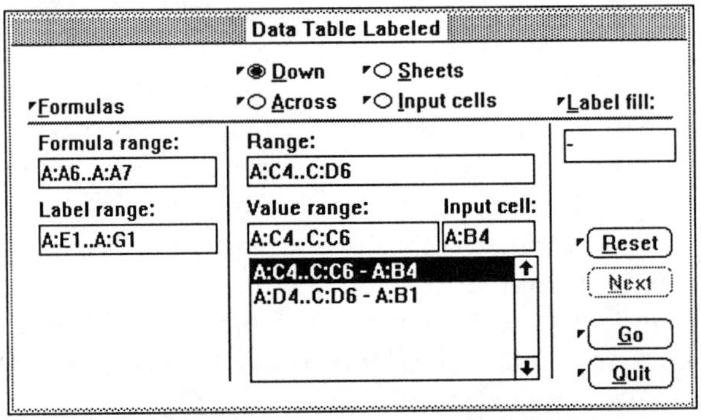

FIGURE 9–55 **The Data Table Labeled dialog box**

For example, in Figure 9–54, the label "Formula" appears in cell A:A6. Beneath this label, in cell A:A7, the formula @PMT(B1–B4,B2/12,B3*12) appears. As you'll soon see, the label in cell A:A6 identifies the formula in cell A:A7. You can use any label you want to identify a formula. However, the label must be positioned immediately above the formula.

You can include as many formulas as you want in the Formula range. However, each formula must have a label that identifies it. All the labels must be in adjacent cells in the first row of the formula range and all the formulas must be in the second row of the formula range, each beneath the appropriate label.

The "Label range" text box allows you to specify the range that contains your formula labels. Formula labels tell 1-2-3/G which formulas you want to use and where. The label range usually spans the columns that will ultimately contain the data table. For example, in Figure 9–54, the Label range is A:E1..A:G1. This range contains the label '—————Formula———————. During the Data Table Labeled command, this label will tell 1-2-3/G that you want to use the formula beneath the label "Formula" in cell A:A8 in the columns spanned by this label. The hyphens (-) on either side of the word *Formula* tell 1-2-3/G that you want to use this formula in more than one column—in this case, columns E, F, and G. These hyphens are called *label-fill* characters and are used to extend the use of a formula across more than one column.

The Down option button allows you to specify the range(s) of input values that are arranged in columns. For example, in Figure 9–54 a range of input values resides in column D (D4..D6) of worksheets A, B, and C. (You'll see how this range is used in a moment.) When you select the Down option, 1-2-3/G immediately activates the Range text box. In this text box, you can specify the range that contains one or more columns of input values. After you specify a range, 1-2-3/G immediately places that range in the "Value range" text box and activates the "Input cell" text box. In the "Input cell" text box, you can specify a single-cell range that will be used as the input cell for that range of test values.

The input cell you specify must be referenced by the formula in the Formula range.

You can also specify a range for the Down option that includes more than one column. If you do, 1-2-3/G will prompt you for a separate input cell for each individual column of test values. This is how 1-2-3/G breaks the three variable limit imposed by the Data Table 3 command. For example, in Figure 9–54, the Down range will be A:C4..A:D6, which includes two columns, C and D. Notice that column C contains a single value, $25,000 (the down payment). When a single test value appears in an input range followed by blank cells, 1-2-3/G uses that value until another value is encountered. So, for each iteration of the Data Table Labeled command in this example, 1-2-3/G will use the value $25,000 as the down payment value. You'll see how this works in a moment.

If you specify a range in the Range text box that includes more than one column of input values, 1-2-3/G shows the range specification for each individual column in the list box below. For example, Figure 9–55 shows two entries in the list box for the Down option. Once the individual column ranges are displayed in the list box, you can use the "Value range" text box, in conjunction with the Input cell text box, to select an input cell for each individual column of values.

The Across option button allows you to specify ranges of test values that are arranged in rows. For example, in Figure 9–54 ranges of input values appear in row 2 (E2..G2) of worksheets A, B, and C. As soon as you select the Across option, 1-2-3/G activates the Range text box, which allows you to specify the range that includes your row(s) of input values. Immediately after you specify a range, 1-2-3/G activates the "Input cell" text box to allow you to specify an input cell for those values.

Similar to the Down option, you can specify more than one row for the Across option. If you do, 1-2-3/G will prompt you for a separate input cell for each row of test values.

The Sheets option button allows you to specify a three-dimensional range of input values. Like the Data Table 3 command, the Data Table Labeled command allows you to create a three-dimensional data table in consecutive worksheets, as shown in Figure 9–54. The three-dimensional range of input values in Figure 9–54 is A:D1..C:D1.

The "Input cells" option button allows you to review all the input ranges you've set as well as the input cells for each of those ranges. When you select this option, 1-2-3/G displays the ranges you've selected and their input cells in the list box. Each list takes the form input range-input cell. For example, in Figure 9–55, 1-2-3/G displays A:C4..C:C6–A:B4 as the first listing in the list box. A:C4..C:C6 in the input range and A:B4 is the input cell. Once you start the review of your input ranges, you cannot stop until the review is completed. However, during the review, you can make any changes you want.

The "Label fill" text box shows the default label-fill character. If you want to use a new label-fill character, specify that character in this box.

The example that follows gives you a step-by-step procedure for creating the data table in Figure 9–54 using the Data Table Labeled command. As mentioned, this example evaluates the same @PMT(*principal,interest,term*) function used in previous Data Table command examples. However, in this example, a fourth input cell will be used to account for the down payment on the loan. Starting with a fresh worksheet, perform the following steps:

1. This step is optional. Enter the labels Principal, Interest, Term, and Down Pmt. in cells A:A1, A:A2, A:A3, and A:A4, respectively. These labels will help to remind you where each of your input cells are located.
2. Move the cell pointer to cell A:A6 and enter the label "Formula." Later on, this label will be used to identify the formula you're about to enter. If you want, you can use another more descriptive label, such as "Payments."
3. In cell A:A7, enter the formula @PMT(B1–B4,B2/12,B3*12), where B1 is a reference cell A:B1 (Principal), B4 is a reference to cell A:B4 (Down Pmt.), B2 is a reference to cell A:B2 (Interest), and B3 is a reference to cell A:B3 (Term). If you were to use the Range Name Labels Right command to name the cells in the column B using the labels on column A, you could enter this formula as @PMT(PRINCIPAL-DOWN PMT.,INTEREST,TERM). When you enter the formula, 1-2-3/G displays ERR in the cell. This is normal. Disregard it for now.
4. Move the cell pointer to cell A:C4 and enter the value 25,000. This value appears in cell A:C4 of Figure 9–54, formatted with the Range Format Currency 0 command. This value will be used as the down-payment value for each iteration of the Data Table Labeled command. Its input cell will be A:B4.
5. Move the cell pointer to cell A:D4 and enter the values 100,000, 150,000, and 200,000 in three adjacent cells in column D. These values appear in the range A:D4..A:D6 of Figure 9–54, formatted with the Range Format Currency 0 command. These values will be used as the principal test values. The input cell for these values will be A:B1.
6. Move the cell pointer to cell A:D1 and enter the number 15. This will be the term argument for the @PMT function and its input cell will be A:B3.
7. Move the cell pointer to cell A:E2 and enter the values .1, .11, and .12 in a row of adjacent cells. These values appear in the range A:E2..A:G2 of Figure 9–54, formatted with the Range Format Percent 0 command. These values will be used as the interest test values. The input cell for these values will be A:B2.
8. Move the cell pointer to cell A:C1 and select the Copy command. Copy the range A:C1..A:G6 straight back into worksheets B and C. Then press CTRL-PGUP to move to worksheet B and enter the value 20 in cell B:C4. Press CTRL-PGUP to move to worksheet C and enter the value 30 in cell C:C4. Press CTRL-PGDN twice to return to worksheet A.

9. Move the cell pointer to cell A:E1 and enter the following formula label: '——————Formula————————. Make sure this label spans columns E, F, and G. This label identifies the formula that you want to use to create the table. Notice that the name *Formula* in the label exactly matches the label above of the @PMT formula in cell A:A7. The label-fill characters on either side extend the use of the @PMT formula over columns E, F, and G. If, in step 2, you decided to use another label to identify the formula, make sure you use the same label in this step. Also, you do not need to copy this formula label back to worksheet B and C. If you're building a three-dimensional data table with Data Table Labeled, you need only specify a formula label in the first worksheet.
10. Select the Data Table Labeled command. 1-2-3/G displays the Data Table Labeled dialog box shown in Figure 9–55. Put your mouse aside for the balance of this procedure.
11. Press ENTER to select the "Formula range" text box. In this text box, specify the range A:A6..A:A7, which includes the formula in cell A:A6 and its label. Press ENTER to confirm your selection. 1-2-3/G activates the "Label range" text box.
12. In the "Label range" text box, specify the range A:E1..A:G1, which includes the label in cell A:E1 at the top of the table. Press ENTER to confirm your selection.
13. Press D to select the Down option button. 1-2-3/G activates the Range text box. Specify the range A:C4..C:D6, which includes the down-payment value in cell C4 as well as the principal values in column D of worksheets A, B, and C. Press ENTER to confirm your selection. 1-2-3/G activates the "Value range" text box, and displays the two three-dimensional input ranges you have selected in the list box below.
14. Press ENTER to confirm the first input range A:C4..C:C6, which includes the down-payment value of $25,000 in worksheets A, B, and C. 1-2-3/G activates the "Input cell" text box, prompting you to specify an input cell for that range. Specify cell A:B4 and press ENTER. 1-2-3/G once again activates the "Value range" text box and displays the second input range you selected, A:D4..C:D6, which includes the principal values in worksheets A, B, and C. Press ENTER to have 1-2-3/G activate the "Input cell" text box, prompting you for an input cell for this range. Specify cell A:B1 as an input cell and press ENTER.
15. Press A to select the Across option button. 1-2-3/G activates the Range text box. Specify the range A:E2..C:G2 in this text box, which includes the interest test values in worksheets A, B, and C. Press ENTER twice, once to confirm your entry and again to have 1-2-3/G activate the "Input cell" text box. In this text box, specify the range A:B2 and press ENTER.
16. Press S to select the Sheets option button. 1-2-3/G activates the Range text box. Specify the range A:D1..C:D1 in this text box, which includes the term test values in worksheets A, B, and C. Press ENTER twice, once to confirm

your entry and again to have 1-2-3/G activate the "Input cell" text box. In this text box, specify the range A:B3 and press ENTER.

17. Press G to select the Go command button, 1-2-3/G fills in the data table. Your screen should look like Figure 9–54.

Note

If you use the Down, Across, or Sheets option buttons to specify an input range that includes multiple columns, rows, or worksheets, 1-2-3/G displays your selections in the list box below and activates the Next command button. By selecting this command button, you can move from one selection to the next, specifying input cells.

Notice in Figure 9–54 that there is a blank row between the row of interest rates (A:E2..A:G2) and the table of output results. You can place labels in this row to identify the contents of each column, without interfering with the Data Table Labeled command.

You can also leave a blank column, row, or worksheet in a data table you create with Data Table Labeled. To do this, simply leave a blank cell in your column, row, or sheet input ranges.

1-2-3/G locates the table of output results for the Data Table Labeled command at the intersection of your column and row input variables. Therefore, if you want, you can locate the table of output results far away from your column and row input ranges. For example, imagine you have a row of input values in the range A:G1..A:N1. Imagine further that you have a column of input values in the range A:A10..A:A15. With this configuration, 1-2-3/G will locate the table of output results in the range A:G10..A:N15.

Note

You can also use the Data Table Labeled command with a database @function to query a database table. To do this, use the same procedure just described. However, in the Formula range specify the database @function of your choice. Also, make sure you set up a criteria range for that function that includes field names from the database table. The cells beneath these field names will be your input cells for the Data Table Labeled command. Finally, when you set up the table frame for each data table, use data from the appropriate fields in the database table.

PARSING LABELS INTO CELLS

You can use the Data Parse command to parse the words and numbers contained in long labels into individual cells. After parsing, the words and numbers that make up the long labels are stored in individual cells as labels and values. That way, you can use the data in formulas and commands, just as you would any other data in your 1-2-3/G worksheet.

The Data Parse command is most often used after the File Import Text command. This command imports the contents of an ASCII text file into the worksheet. The lines of text are stored in a column of consecutive cells as long labels, one label per cell. For example, Figure 9–56 shows a series of long labels, starting in column A, that were imported into the worksheet. For more about the File Import Text command, see Chapter 5, "File Management."

When you select the Data Parse command, 1-2-3/G displays the dialog box in Figure 9–57. The sequence of events for parsing a range of long labels is as follows:

1. Use the Create command button to create a format line and insert it into the worksheet. Format lines contain special symbols that tell 1-2-3/G how to break up the words and numbers in the long labels into individual cells.
2. Use the Edit option to edit the format line, if necessary.
3. Specify an *input column* range—the column that contains the labels you want to parse and the format line—in the "Input column" text box.
4. Specify an output range in the "Output range" text box. This is usually a single-cell range that marks the upper-left corner of the location where you want the parsed data copied to.
5. Select the Go command button to have 1-2-3/G copy the parsed labels to individual cells in the output range using the format line as a guide.

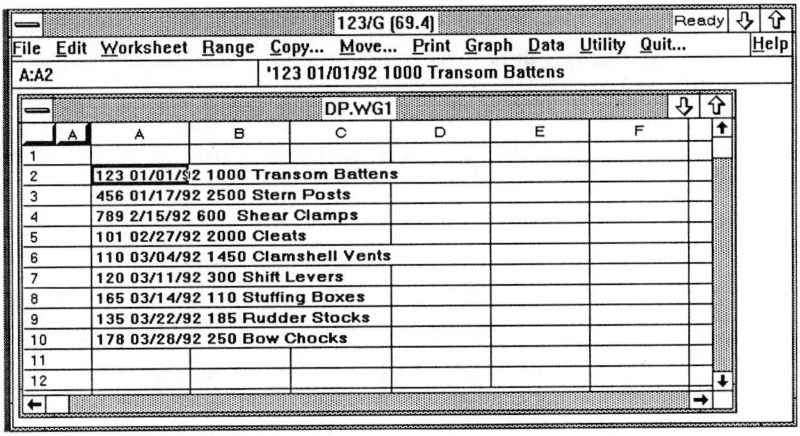

123/G (69.4) Ready

File Edit Worksheet Range Copy... Move... Print Graph Data Utility Quit... Help

A:A2 '123 01/01/92 1000 Transom Battens

DP.WG1

A	A	B	C	D	E	F
1						
2	123 01/01/92 1000 Transom Battens					
3	456 01/17/92 2500 Stern Posts					
4	789 2/15/92 600 Shear Clamps					
5	101 02/27/92 2000 Cleats					
6	110 03/04/92 1450 Clamshell Vents					
7	120 03/11/92 300 Shift Levers					
8	165 03/14/92 110 Stuffing Boxes					
9	135 03/22/92 185 Rudder Stocks					
10	178 03/28/92 250 Bow Chocks					
11						
12						

FIGURE 9–56 Long labels stored in a column of cells

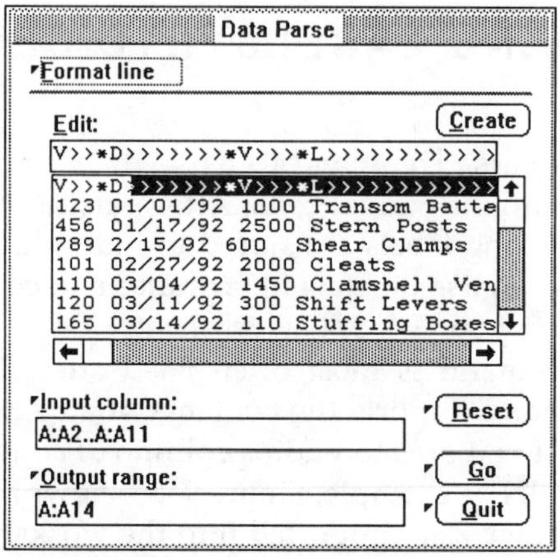

```
Data Parse
Format line
Edit:                                        Create
V>>*D>>>>>>>*V>>>*L>>>>>>>>>>>>>
V>>*D>>>>>>>*V>>>*L>>>>>>>>>>>>>
123 01/01/92 1000 Transom Batte
456 01/17/92 2500 Stern Posts
789 2/15/92 600  Shear Clamps
101 02/27/92 2000 Cleats
110 03/04/92 1450 Clamshell Ven
120 03/11/92 300 Shift Levers
165 03/14/92 110 Stuffing Boxes
Input column:                                Reset
A:A2..A:A11
Output range:                                Go
A:A14                                        Quit
```

FIGURE 9–57 The Data Parse dialog box

Format Lines Basics

Before attempting to parse the long labels in Figure 9–56 into individual cells, you'll need to understand some format line basics. As mentioned, format lines contain special symbols that tell 1-2-3/G how to break up the words and numbers in long labels into individual cells. There are four basic categories of format symbols as follows:

L Label
V Value
D Date
T Time

When 1-2-3/G encounters what is perceived to be a label, value, date, or time, it places one of these symbols in the format line. After that symbol, 1-2-3/G uses continuation characters, >, for as long as the label, value, date, or time lasts. When 1-2-3/G encounters a blank space, it assumes that the word or number to the left and to the right belong in separate cells. Blank spaces are symbolized by an asterisk (*). For example, imagine you have the label "By 12/31/92 sales will total $10,000,000" in the worksheet. 1-2-3/G will create the following format line for this label:

```
L>*D>>>>>>>*L>>>>*L>>>*L>>>>*V>>>>>>>>>>
By 12/31/92 sales will total $10,000,000
```

If you want 1-2-3/G to skip a particular entry when parsing a long label, you can use the S symbol. This symbol causes 1-2-3/G to ignore the word or number beneath it. Because 1-2-3/G assumes that all words and numbers in a long label are to be parsed, it does not automatically insert an S symbol when you create a format line. Instead, you must manually insert the S symbol, and any continuation characters required, by editing the format line.

When you use the Data Parse command to create a format line, 1-2-3/G creates a "best-guess" format line. That is, the format line may not produce the results you want. To solve this problem, you must edit the format line. The example that follows shows you how to edit a format line.

Parsing Long Labels: An Example

In this section the Data Parse command will be used to parse the long labels in Figure 9–56 into individual cells, as shown at the bottom of Figure 9–58. During the example, each component of the Data Parse dialog box will be used.

In this example, it will be necessary to edit the format line created by 1-2-3/G. As mentioned, when 1-2-3/G encounters a blank space in a long label, it assumes you want the entry to the left and the right placed in separate cells. However, most of the long labels in Figure 9–56 contain two-word descriptions that should appear in a single cell. Therefore, in the example that follows, a space symbol (*) and a label symbol (L) will be removed from the format line created by 1-2-3/G, and replaced with two continuation characters (>>).

123/G (69.4) Ready

File Edit Worksheet Range Copy... Move... Print Graph Data Utility Quit... Help

A:A2 |V>>*D>>>>>>>>*V>>>*L>>>>>>>>>>>>>>>

DP.WG1

A	A	B	C	D	E	F	G
1							
2	V>>*D>>>>>>>*V>>>*L>>>>>>>>>>>>>>>						
3	123 01/01/92 1000 Transom Battens						
4	456 01/17/92 2500 Stern Posts						
5	789 2/15/92 600 Shear Clamps						
6	101 02/27/92 2000 Cleats						
7	110 03/04/92 1450 Clamshell Vents						
8	120 03/11/92 300 Shift Levers						
9	165 03/14/92 110 Stuffing Boxes						
10	135 03/22/92 185 Rudder Stocks						
11	178 03/28/92 250 Bow Chocks						
12							
13							
14	123	33604	1000	Transom Battens			
15	456	33620	2500	Stern Posts			
16	789	33649	600	Shear Clamps			
17	101	33661	2000	Cleats			
18	110	33667	1450	Clamshell Vents			
19	120	33674	300	Shift Levers			
20	165	33677	110	Stuffing Boxes			
21	135	33685	185	Rudder Stocks			
22	178	33691	250	Bow Chocks			

FIGURE 9–58 Parsing long labels into individual cells

In preparation for the Data Parse command, locate the cell pointer on the cell that contains the first label in the input column (cell A:A2 in Figure 9–56). When you're ready, perform the following steps:

1. Select Data Parse. 1-2-3/G displays the dialog box in Figure 9–57.
2. Select the Create command button. 1-2-3/G analyzes the label in cell A:A2 and creates a best-guess format line. That format line is placed in the Edit text box. At the same time, a new row 2 is inserted into the worksheet, and the same format line is placed in cell A:A2 of that new row. The long labels beneath the new format line are pushed downward to accommodate the new row.
3. Select Edit. 1-2-3/G activates the Edit text box. Press END to move the cursor to the last character in the format line. Then press ← to move the cursor to the first asterisk (*) you encounter. Press DEL twice to remove both the asterisk (*) and the label symbol (L) that follows it. Type > (greater than) twice to replace these characters with continuation characters. Press ENTER to confirm your change.
4. In the Input column text box, specify the range A:A2..A:A11, which includes the format line and the long labels in column A.
5. In the Output range text box, specify a single-cell range that marks the upper-left corner of the location where you want the parsed data copied to (cell A:A14 in Figure 9–56).
6. Select the Go command button. 1-2-3/G copies the long labels in the range A:A3..A:A11 to the output range and parses the data into individual cells. Your screen should look like Figure 9–58.

Tips on Data Parse

When 1-2-3/G creates a format line, it does so by using the first long label in the input-column range as a model. If this label is not representative of the other labels in the column, 1-2-3/G may not parse the data for all the labels correctly. Therefore, you may have to edit the format line and parse the data several times before you get the precise configuration you want.

If you make a mistake when editing a format line, and you don't want your changes recorded in the worksheet, press CTRL-BREAK. This cancels the edit and returns you to the worksheet in READY mode, without editing the format line.

Format lines are essentially nonprinting labels. When 1-2-3/G creates a format line, it is preceded with a split vertical bar (|) label prefix. This prefix causes the format line to be displayed, but not printed. In fact, you can create your own format lines directly from the keyboard, provided you use the split vertical bar to begin them. In some cases, you may prefer this method, to avoid having a new row inserted into the worksheet by the Data Parse command.

In some instances, you may want to use more than one format line. For example, imagine you are working with a column of labels that is 100 cells deep

(A:A1..A:A100). The first 50 labels are somewhat uniform and can be properly parsed with a single format line. The format of the second set of 50 labels, however, is noticeably different from the first 50. In this case, you can use the Data Parse command twice, once for the first 50 labels and again for the second 50.

Theoretically, the maximum number of long labels you can parse with Data Parse is 8,192. However, as you've probably noticed, 1-2-3/G displays your long labels from the input-column range in the list box of the Data Parse dialog box. 1-2-3/G will only parse the number of long labels that can fit in this list box. The maximum capacity of this list box is 64,000 characters. Therefore, if each of your labels is 64 characters long, the maximum number of labels you can parse is 1,000.

Note

In the preceding example, the long labels in the input-column range appear in consecutive cells. However, if the input-column range contains a blank row, 1-2-3/G will ignore that row when copying the parsed data to the output range.

CALCULATING A FREQUENCY DISTRIBUTION

To calculate a frequency distribution for a range of values, you use the Data Distribution command. A frequency distribution tells you how many values in a range fall within a specific interval. For example, imagine you're working with aptitude test scores for a class of students. The lowest possible grade on the test is 0 and the highest is 800. You need a quick count on how many test scores are between 0 and 500, 501 and 600, 601 and 700, and 701 and 800. To do this, you can use the Data Distribution command to set up the worksheet in Figure 9–59.

The Data Distribution command requests two ranges, a *values* range and a *bin* range. You must set up both of these ranges before you execute the Data Distribution command. The values range contains the list of values you want to test. This list can be in an open worksheet file or in a worksheet file on disk. The bin range contains the intervals that you want to use to perform the test. For example, in Figure 9–59 the values range is A:A2..A:A23. This range contains the list of numeric test scores.

On the other hand, the bin range is A:E2..A:E4. This range contains the numbers 500, 600, and 700. When 1-2-3/G calculates the data distribution, the

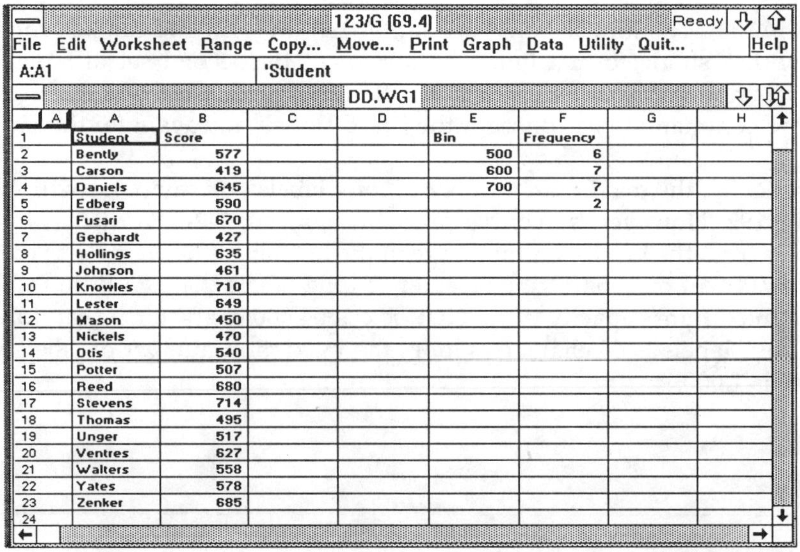

123/G (69.4) Ready

File Edit Worksheet Range Copy... Move... Print Graph Data Utility Quit... Help

A:A1 'Student

DD.WG1

A	A	B	C	D	E	F	G	H
1	Student	Score			Bin	Frequency		
2	Bently	577			500	6		
3	Carson	419			600	7		
4	Daniels	645			700	7		
5	Edberg	590				2		
6	Fusari	670						
7	Gephardt	427						
8	Hollings	635						
9	Johnson	461						
10	Knowles	710						
11	Lester	649						
12	Mason	450						
13	Nickels	470						
14	Otis	540						
15	Potter	507						
16	Reed	680						
17	Stevens	714						
18	Thomas	495						
19	Unger	517						
20	Ventres	627						
21	Walters	558						
22	Yates	578						
23	Zenker	685						
24								

FIGURE 9–59 **Using Data Distribution to calculate a frequency distribution**

count for each interval is recorded in the column immediately to the right of the bin range in the cell that is adjacent to each interval.

Each count value represents the number of values in the values range that is less than or equal to the adjacent bin value, but greater than the previous bin value. For example, in Figure 9–59, six test scores are greater than 0 but less than 500, seven scores are less than 600 but greater than 500, and so on. In addition, 1-2-3/G always displays an extra number at the end of the count results. This represents the number of values in the values range that are higher than the last value in the bin range. As you can see in Figure 9–59, two test scores are higher than 700, the last value in the bin range.

To execute the Data Distribution command, begin by entering the data for the value and bin ranges. In either case you can use numbers or formulas that evaluate to numbers. The numbers in the values range can be arranged in a column, as in Figure 9–59, or in a rectangular block of adjacent cells. However, the numbers in the bin range must be arranged in a column of adjacent cells. Further, the numbers must be arranged in ascending order (lowest to highest). When you're ready, select the Data Distribution command. 1-2-3/G prompts you for a values range. Highlight the range that includes the list of values you want to count and press ENTER. 1-2-3/G prompts you for a bin range. Highlight the range that contains your bin intervals. 1-2-3/G records the results for the data distribution in the column to the right of the bin range.

The Data Distribution command is only useful for counting numbers that fall within a given interval. It does not count cells with labels or blank cells. In addition, if any cells in the values range contain NA, these are counted in the lowest bin interval. Further, if any cells in the values range contain ERR, these are counted with the values that are higher than the last bin value.

Note

> You cannot specify a collection as the values range for the Data Distribution command.

USING DATA MATRIX

The Data Matrix command allows you to invert and multiply matrices to solve linear equations with multiple variables. This command has two options—Invert, which allows you to create the inverse of a matrix, and Multiply, which allows you to multiply one matrix by another. The two are used together to solve multiple equations containing multiple variables.

Note

> The sections that follow assume you are familiar with the principles of matrix algebra. Therefore, the primary emphasis will be placed on how to use the Data Matrix Multiply and Invert commands.

About Matrices

A matrix is a rectangular table of values. For example, Figure 9-60 shows a matrix of values in the range A:A2..A:B3. In the sections that follow, the size of a matrix will be expressed in the following form: *rows* x *columns*, where *rows* is the number of rows in the matrix and *columns* is the number of columns. For example, the matrix in Figure 9-60 is a 2x2 matrix. The maximum matrix size supported by the Data Matrix Invert command is an 80x80 matrix and the maximum matrix size supported by Data Matrix Multiply is a 256x256 matrix.

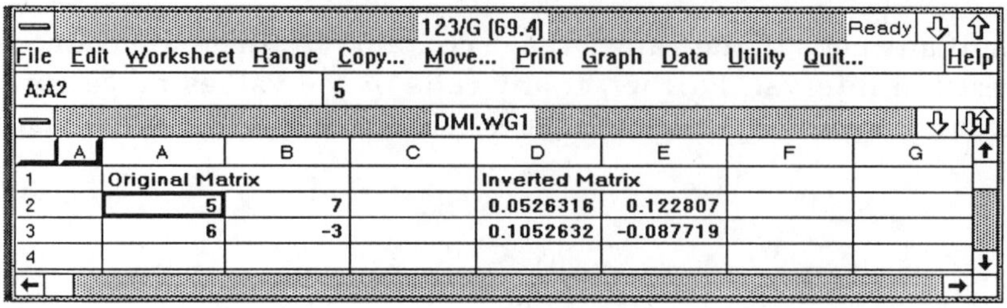

	A	B	C	D	E	F	G
1	Original Matrix			Inverted Matrix			
2	5	7		0.0526316	0.122807		
3	6	-3		0.1052632	-0.087719		
4							

FIGURE 9–60 Before and after the Data Matrix Invert command

Inverting Matrices

To solve a system of linear equations with Data Matrix, begin by entering the coefficients for the equations into the worksheet as a matrix of values. Enter the constants in a separate matrix. Then, create the inverse of the matrix of coefficients by using the Data Matrix Invert command.

The Data Matrix command will only invert square matrices. That is, the number of columns in the matrix must equal the number of rows. If the number of columns does not equal the number of rows, 1-2-3/G will issue an error message when you attempt to invert the matrix.

Some square matrices do not have an inverse. If a matrix does not have an inverse, 1-2-3/G will issue an error message when you attempt to invert it.

When you select the Data Matrix invert command, 1-2-3/G prompts you in the Control Line for a From range. Specify the range address or range names of the range that contains the matrix you want to invert (A:A2..A:B3 in Figure 9–60) and press ENTER. 1-2-3/G prompts you for a To range. Specify a single-cell address or range name that defines the upper-left corner of where you want the inverted matrix to begin (A:D2 in Figure 9–60). 1-2-3/G creates the inverse of the original matrix and displays the results in the To range as a matrix of values.

Multiplying Matrices

The Data Matrix multiply command is used to multiply the values in the columns of one matrix by the values in the rows of a second matrix. The results of this multiplication are recorded in a third matrix of solution results. Thus, after you have created the inverse of a matrix of coefficients with Data Matrix Invert, you can use the Data Matrix Multiply to multiply that inverse matrix by a second matrix of constants for the equations. The resulting matrix of solution results contains the solution values for the variables in your equations.

For the Data Matrix Multiply command to work, the number of columns in the first matrix must equal the number of rows in the second matrix. For example, Figure 9–61 shows two matrices that are compatible for the Data Matrix Multiply command. The first matrix in the range A:A2..A:D5 is a 4x4

123/G (69.4) Ready

File Edit Worksheet Range Copy... Move... Print Graph Data Utility Quit... Help

A:A1 'First Matrix

DMM.WG1

A	A	B	C	D	E	F	G
1	First Matrix						
2	1	5	9	13			
3	2	6	10	14			
4	3	7	11	15			
5	4	8	12	16			
6							
7	Second Matrix						
8	1						
9	2						
10	3						
11	4						
12							
13	Solution Matrix						
14	90	<—=1*1+5*2+9*3+13*4					
15	100						
16	110						
17	120						
18							
19							
20							

FIGURE 9–61 Using Data Matrix Multiply to multiply two matrices

matrix (it contains four rows and four columns). The second matrix, in the range A:A8..A:A11, is a 4x1 matrix (four rows and one column). Therefore, these two matrices are compatible because the number of columns in the first matrix matches the number of rows in the second matrix.

When you select the Data Matrix Multiply command, 1-2-3/G displays the dialog box in Figure 9–62. In the "First matrix" text box, specify the range name or address of the first matrix (A:A2..A:D5 in Figure 9–61). In the Second matrix text box, specify the range name or address of the second matrix (A:A8..A:A11). In the "Output matrix" text box, specify the single-cell range where you want the matrix of solution results to begin (A:A14). To complete the command, select the OK command button, or press ENTER. 1-2-3/G multiplies the values

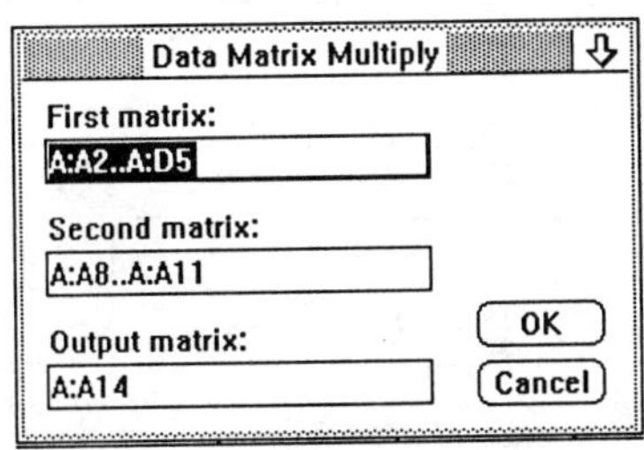

FIGURE 9–62 The Data Matrix Multiply dialog box

in the columns of the first matrix by the values in the rows of the second matrix. The results are recorded in a third matrix of values, starting in the cell you specified in the "Output matrix" text box. This third matrix has the same number of rows as the first matrix and the same number of columns as the second matrix.

You can also use the Data Matrix command to multiply two three-dimensional matrices. However, the matrix ranges in each worksheet are treated separately.

Note

When you use Data Matrix Multiply to multiply a column of entries by a single cell, the maximum number of entries allowed in the column is 6553.

Solving Equations: An Example

This section shows you how to simultaneously solve for X and Y in two equations by using the Data Matrix command. The two equations appear as labels in the range A:B2..A:B3 of Figure 9–63.

To begin, enter the coefficients (5, 7, 6, and -3) for the equations into the worksheet as a matrix of values. These values appear in the range A:B5..A:C6 of Figure 9–63. Next, enter the constants for the equations (50 and 5) in a second matrix. These values appear in the range A:E5..A:E6.

123/G [69.4] Ready

File Edit Worksheet Range Copy... Move... Print Graph Data Utility Quit... Help

A:A1

DMSOLV.WG1

A	A	B	C	D	E	F
1		Equations				
2		5x+7y=50				
3		6x-3y=5				
4						
5		5	7		50	
6		6	-3		5	
7						
8						
9		Inverted Matrix			Solution range (results)	
10		0.0526316	0.122807		X=	3.245614
11		0.1052632	-0.087719		Y=	4.8245614
12						

FIGURE 9–63 Solving equations with Data Matrix

When you're ready, select the Data Matrix Invert command. 1-2-3/G prompts you for a From range. Highlight the range that contains the matrix of coefficients (A:B5..A:C6) and press ENTER. 1-2-3/G prompts you for a To range. Specify cell A:B10 and press ENTER. 1-2-3/G creates a matrix that is the inverse of the coefficients starting in cell A:B10.

Select the Data Matrix Multiply command. 1-2-3/G displays the Data Matrix Multiply dialog box. In the "First matrix" text box, specify the matrix that contains the inverse of the coefficients (A:B10..A:C11). In the "Second matrix" text box, specify the range that contains the matrix of constants (A:E5..A:E6). In the "Output matrix" text box, specify a single-cell range where you want the matrix of solution results to begin (A:F10). To complete the command, select the OK command button or press ENTER. 1-2-3/G creates a third matrix of solution results. This matrix contains the solution values for the X and Y equations shown in the range A:B2..A:B3 of Figure 9–63.

REGRESSION ANALYSIS

Regression analysis can be used to predict trends for a set of data, based on events that have occurred in the past. To perform regression analysis with 1-2-3/G, you use the Data Regression command.

A regression analysis creates statistics that describe the degree to which two or more sets of data are related. If a relationship is found to exist, you can use the regression statistics to create a regression formula that will predict a future trend for one of the data sets. For example, imagine you want to determine the number of homes that will sell in a geographic area in the upcoming month. You're reasonably sure that home sales are tied to mortgage loan rates. To determine if such a relationship exists, you can perform regression analysis using historical data for both home sales and mortgage rates from previous months. If a statistical relationship exists, you can use that relationship, in conjunction with your best-guess estimate of next month's mortgage rates, to predict the number of homes that will sell in the up-coming month.

Data Regression Basics

Each set of data used in a regression analysis is referred to as a *variable*. The data set whose future trend you want to predict is called the *dependent* variable. The other data sets that will be used as the basis for that prediction are called the *independent* variables. For example, Figure 9–64 shows a table of variables in the range A:B2..A:D13. Each column in this table contains a different data set (variable). The last column in the table, labeled Houses, shows the number of homes sold over the last 12 months. This is the dependent variable (the variable whose future trend you want to predict). The second column (column B) in the table, labeled Rates, shows the average rate for 30-year fixed mortgages during

123/G (69.4) Ready

File Edit Worksheet Range Copy... Move... Print Graph Data Utility Quit... Help

A:D26 +D23*G18+E17

(,0) DR.WG1

A	A	B	C	D	E	F	G	H
1	Month	Rates	Points	Houses				
2	1	9.50%	2	11,750				
3	2	10.00%	2	11,163				
4	3	10.50%	1.75	10,604				
5	4	10.75%	1.5	10,074				
6	5	10.50%	1.5	10,276				
7	6	10.25%	1.5	10,481				
8	7	10.00%	1.75	11,005				
9	8	9.75%	2	11,225				
10	9	10.00%	1.75	11,001				
11	10	10.25%	1.5	10,781				
12	11	10.50%	1.5	10,565				
13	12	10.75%	1.5	10,354				
14								
15								
16			Regression Output:					
17		Constant			22622.081		Rate	
18		Std Err of Y Est			150.90204		10.50%	
19		R Squared			0.9083617			
20		No. of Observations			12			
21		Degrees of Freedom			10			
22								
23		X Coefficient(s)		-115833.8				
24		Std Err of Coef.		11634.413				
25								
26		House Sales =		10,460				
27								
28								

FIGURE 9–64 **Using Data Regression to perform regression analysis**

each of the last 12 months. Because the values in this data set will be used to predict the future trend of the dependent variable (Houses), this data set will be the independent variable for the regression.

1-2-3/G allows you to perform simple regression and multiple regression. To differentiate between the two, simple regression is when you use a single independent variable; multiple regression is when you use more than one independent variable. For example, building on the home sales analogy in Figure 9–64, a simple regression can be performed by using a single independent variable (mortgage rates) to predict home sales (the dependent variable). However, an example of multiple regression would be if you used more than one independent variable (for example, mortgage rates and points on the loan) to predict home sales (the dependent variable).

Independent variables are denoted by the letter X. The dependent variable is denoted by the letter Y. 1-2-3/G allows you to use up to 16 independent variables (X) to predict a value for the dependent variable Y. If there is more than one independent variable, each X variable is assigned a number. For example, the first independent variable is X1, the second X2, and so on.

The Data Regression command creates a table of output results that contain the statistics for the regression analysis. An example of a table of output results is shown in the range A:B:16..A:E24 of Figure 9–64. This table, created entirely by 1-2-3/G, contains the following information:

- **Constant:** Identifies the location where the best-fit regression line crosses the Y axis (*y*-axis intercept) when the data points for the regression variables are graphed.
- **Standard error of Y Estimate:** Standard error for estimated Y values.
- R^2: Expresses as a value between 0 and 1 the degree to which the independent and dependent variables are related. The closer this value is to 1, the stronger the relationship is, and the more reliable are the results of the regression.
- **Number of Observations:** The number of values in the independent Observations (X) and dependent (Y) variable ranges.
- **Degrees of Freedom:** Shows the number of observations (rows in the X range) minus the number of independent variables (columns in the X range) minus 1.
- **Slope of X Coefficient:** This is the amount by which the dependent variable increases you increase the independent variable by one unit. 1-2-3/G creates an X coefficient for each independent variable.
- **Standard error of the X Coefficients:** This is the standard error for each X coefficient. This value should be less than one-half of the X coefficient for there to be a relationship between the independent and dependent variables.

Once the regression results are available, you can use a regression formula to predict a future value for Y, the dependent variable, for given values of X, the independent variable. In simple regression, this formula takes the form:

```
Y=Coeff. of X1*X1+Constant
```

The formula is expanded for multiple regression as follows:

```
Y=Coeff. of X1*X1+Coeff. of X2*X2+...Coeff. of
Xn*Xn+Constant
```

The sections that follow show examples of how to use these formulas in simple and multiple regression.

Simple Regression: An Example

This section shows you how to use the Data Regression command to perform simple regression using the data in Figure 9–64. Toward the end of the example, you'll enter a regression formula that predicts home sales (the dependent Y variable) for a given mortgage rate (the independent X variable).

To begin, start by entering the data for your X and Y variables in adjacent columns. Make sure you have an equal number of independent and dependent variable values, and that they correspond to the same time period. For example, Figure 9–64 shows a range of data set up for the Data Regression command. In column B, mortgage rates (Rates) appear in a column of adjacent cells, one entry for each month. The home sales for the same time period appear in column D (Houses), one entry for each month. (The data in column C will be used in the multiple regression example later in this chapter.)

When you're ready, select the Data Regression command. 1-2-3/G displays the dialog box in Figure 9–65. In the "X-range text" box, specify the range that contains the monthly mortgage rates (A:B2..A:B13). In the "Y-range" text box, specify the range that contains the monthly house sales (A:D2..A:D13). In the "Output range" text box, specify a single-cell range where you want the table of output results to begin (cell A:B16). To complete the Data Regression command, select the OK command button. 1-2-3/G creates the table of regression output results starting in cell A:B16.

Note

Notice that the Intercept section of the Data Regression dialog box was not used in the previous example. The option buttons in this section determine whether 1-2-3/G automatically computes the Y-axis intercept (the default), or whether zero is used as the intercept. To select zero as the intercept, select the Zero option button.

Now that the table of output results is available, you're ready to predict the future—that is, the number of homes that may sell next month. To do this, you'll use a simple regression formula in the form Y=Coeff of X1*X1+Constant, where Y is the calculated value for the dependent variable you are solving for, Coeff.

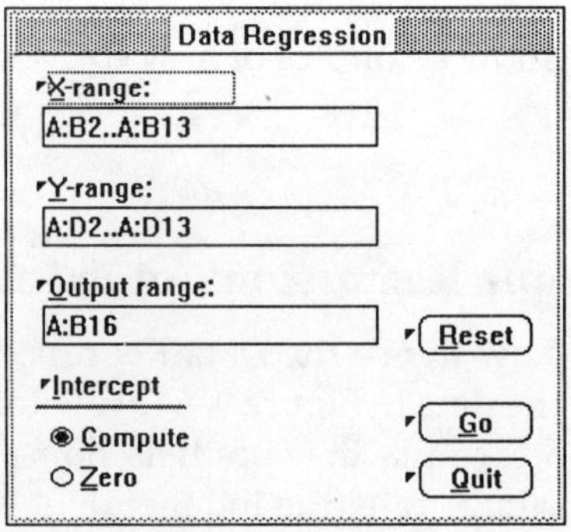

Data Regression
X-range:
A:B2..A:B13
Y-range:
A:D2..A:D13
Output range:
A:B16
Reset
Intercept
Compute
Zero
Go
Quit

FIGURE 9–65 The Data Regression dialog box

of X1 refers to the X Coefficient(s) value in the regression table (A:D23), X1 is your best estimate of the mortgage loan rate for next month (A:G18), and Constant refers to the Constant value in the regression table (A:17). Therefore, in any cell of your choosing (cell A:D26 in Figure 9–64), enter the formula **+D23*G18+E17.**

The result of this regression formula is 10,460, meaning that approximately 10,460 houses may sell next month. To determine how much credibility you can place in this estimate, take a look at the R^2 value in the regression table. The value for R^2 is approximately .908, very close to 1. This indicates that 91% of the time mortgage loan rates have a direct impact on the number of homes sold in the area. For additional interpretation of the remaining values in the regression table, it is recommended you consult a standard text on statistical analysis.

Graphing Regression Results

You can also graph the results of the Data Regression command. To do this, you perform the following:

1. Use the Data Regression command to create a table of regression results.
2. Use the Data Sort command to sort the X (independent) and Y (dependent) values in ascending order, using the column of X values as the Primary key.
3. Use regression formulas to calculate new values of the Y (dependent) variable for each value of the X (independent) variable.
4. Use the Graph command to create an XY graph. For graph range X, use the X (independent variable) values. For graph range A, use the original Y (dependent variable) values; and for graph range B, use the newly calculated Y (dependent variable) values.

In case this all seems a bit complicated to you, the following example should clear up any questions you may have.

Figure 9–66 shows the same regression variables and output results as in Figure 9–64. However, the X and Y variable ranges have been sorted in ascending order using the X variable range as the Primary key. In addition, a new column (column E), labeled CALC-Y, has been added to the table of variables. This column contains calculated values of Y (the dependent variable) for each value of X (the independent variable).

To set up the worksheet in Figure 9–66, use the Data Regression command to create a table of regression results. To do this, follow the steps outlined in the previous section.

Once the regression results are available, select the Data Sort command. 1-2-3/G displays the Data Sort dialog box. In the "Data range" text box, specify the range A:A2..A:D13, which includes columns of X and Y variables in Figure 9–66. Next, select the "Primary" option button. Then, select the Key text box and specify the single-cell range A:B2. This tells 1-2-3/G to use the mortgage

123/G [69.4] Ready

File Edit Worksheet Range Copy... Move... Print Graph Data Utility Quit... Help

A:E2 +$D$23*B2+$E$17

(,0) DSGRAPH.WG1

A	A	B	C	D	E
1	Month	Rates	Points	Houses	CALC-Y
2	1	9.50%	2	11,750	11,618
3	2	9.75%	2	11,225	11,328
4	3	10.00%	2	11,005	11,039
5	4	10.00%	1.5	11,001	11,039
6	5	10.00%	2	11,163	11,039
7	6	10.25%	1.5	10,781	10,749
8	7	10.25%	1.5	10,481	10,749
9	8	10.50%	1.5	10,276	10,460
10	9	10.50%	1.5	10,604	10,460
11	10	10.50%	1.5	10,565	10,460
12	11	10.75%	1.5	10,074	10,170
13	12	10.75%	1.5	10,354	10,170
14					
15					
16			Regression Output:		
17		Constant			22622.081
18		Std Err of Y Est			150.90204
19		R Squared			0.9083617
20		No. of Observations			12
21		Degrees of Freedom			10
22					
23		X Coefficient(s)		-115833.8	
24		Std Err of Coef.		11634.413	
25					
26					
27					
28					

FIGURE 9–66 Preparing regression variables for graphing

rate (Rates) column to perform the sort. Finally, select the Ascending option button to specify an ascending sort. To complete the command, select the OK command button or press ENTER. 1-2-3/G sorts the table of variables as shown in Figure 9–66.

Once the table is sorted, move the cell pointer to cell A:E2 and enter the following formula: +$D$23*B2+$E$17. This simple regression formula breaks down as follows. $D$23 is an absolute reference to the X Coefficient(s) value in the regression table. B2 is a reference to first value in the X variable range (the independent variable), and $E$17 is an absolute reference to the Constant value in the regression results table. When you're ready, select the Copy command. For the From range, specify cell A:E2, which contains the simple-regression formula. For a To range, specify A:E3..A:E13. Press ENTER to complete the command. 1-2-3/G copies the formula down column E, creating a calculated value of Y, the dependent variable, for each value of X, the independent variable.

Select the Graph command and select the Type option. 1-2-3/G displays the Graph Type dialog box. Select the XY option button and select OK. Next, select the Graph Add Ranges command. 1-2-3/G displays the Graph Add Ranges dialog box. In the X: text box, specify the range A:B2..A:B13, which includes the range of X variables. In the A: text box, specify the range A:D2..A:D13, which includes the original Y variables. In the B: text box, specify the range

A:E2..A:E13, which includes the newly calculated values for Y. To complete the command, select the OK command button, or press ENTER.

Select the Graph command again and select View from the menu that appears. 1-2-3/G displays a graph window similar to the one in Figure 9-67. Further, the Graph menu replaces the Worksheet menu at the top of your screen. Unlike Figure 9-67, however, there are lines depicting graph ranges A and B. (The graph range A line is straight and the graph range B line is jagged.) To make the graph appear as in Figure 9-67, you must remove the connecting lines for graph range B (the jagged line) and display its markers. To do this, click your mouse anywhere on the graph range B line, or press TAB until it is selected. Then, select the Settings Series Options... command. 1-2-3/G displays the Settings Series dialog box. Select "Line format" and remove the X from the Connectors check box and place an X in the Markers check box. To complete the command, select the OK command button. The body of your graph should now look similar to Figure 9-67. To complete the graph, add titles and axis labels, as shown in Figure 9-67.

Note

> For more about how to create graphs, see Chapter 7, "Graphs."

Multiple Regression: An Example

As mentioned, 1-2-3/G allows you to use up to 16 independent variables (X) with the Data Regression command to calculate the value for the dependent variable (Y). Thus, rather than use 30-year fixed mortgage rates as the only basis

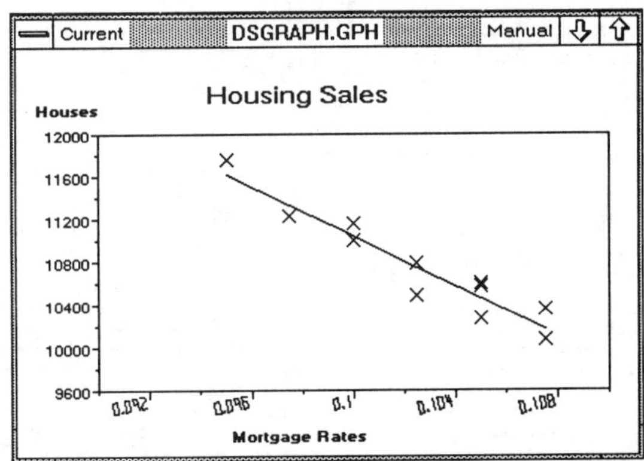

FIGURE 9–67 Plotting a "best-fit" regression line

for predicting home sales, you might want to use points (the financing charge) as a second independent variable.

To perform multiple regression, simply expand your X-range specification for the Data Regression command to include adjacent columns of independent variables. When the tables of regression results are generated, 1-2-3/G will calculate an X coefficient for each set of independent variables. You can then use each of these coefficients in a multiple regression formula that takes the form:

```
Y=Coeff. of X1*X1+Coeff. of X2*X2+...Coeff. of Xn*Xn+Constant
```

Figure 9–68 shows the same mortgage rate/home sales example shown in previous Data Regression examples. However, notice that regression results table contains two X coefficients instead of one, as in the previous example. The first X coefficient (A:D23) applies to the mortgage rate (Rates) independent variable and the second (A:E24) applies to the points (Points) independent variable.

To create the regression results in Figure 9–68, select the Data Regression command. 1-2-3/G displays the Data Regression dialog box. In the "X-range" text box, specify the range A:B2..A:C13, which includes both the mortgage rates

123/G (69.4) Ready

File Edit Worksheet Range Copy... Move... Print Graph Data Utility Quit... Help

A:D26 +D23*G18+E23*G21+E17

(,0) DRM.WG1

A	A	B	C	D	E	F	G	H
1	Month	Rates	Points	Houses				
2	1	9.50%	2	11,750				
3	2	10.00%	2	11,163				
4	3	10.50%	1.75	10,604				
5	4	10.75%	1.5	10,074				
6	5	10.50%	1.5	10,276				
7	6	10.25%	1.5	10,481				
8	7	10.00%	1.75	11,005				
9	8	9.75%	2	11,225				
10	9	10.00%	1.75	11,001				
11	10	10.25%	1.5	10,781				
12	11	10.50%	1.5	10,565				
13	12	10.75%	1.5	10,354				
14								
15								
16			Regression Output:					
17		Constant			19023.819		Rate	
18		Std Err of Y Est			139.00903		10.50%	
19		R Squared			0.9300133			
20		No. of Observations			12		Points	
21		Degrees of Freedom			9		1.5	
22								
23		X Coefficient(s)		-90015.88	567.29157			
24		Std Err of Coef.		18821.911	339.97531			
25								
26		House Sales =		10,423				
27								
28								

FIGURE 9–68 Multiple Regression analysis

and points values. In the "Y-range" text box, specify the range A:D2..A:D13, which includes historical home sales by month. In the "Output range" text box, specify the single cell range A:B16. To complete the command, select the Go command button, or press ENTER. 1-2-3/G creates the regression results table beginning in cell A:B16.

To generate an estimate of home sales for next month, begin by providing your own estimates of next month's mortgage rates and point values. For example, in Figure 9–68 the value 10.5% appears in cell A:G18, as an estimated mortgage rate, and the value 1.5 appears in cell A:G21 as an estimated point rate. In cell A:B26, enter the regression formula **+D23*G18+E23*G21+E17**. This formula multiplies the X coefficient for mortgage rates (D23) by the estimate for next month's mortgage rates (G18). It also multiplies the X coefficient for points (E23) by the estimate for next month's points (G21). These two values are then added to Constant value from the regression results table (E17).

The result of the formula in cell A:D26 is 10,423, indicating that with a 10.5% mortgage rate and a point rate of 1.5, approximately 10,423 may sell in the upcoming month. To determine the reliability of this estimate, refer to the R^2 value in cell A:E19 of the regression results table. This cell contains a value of .93, very close to one. This indicates that 93% of the time mortgage rates and point rates have an impact on the number of homes sold in the area.

SUMMARY

This chapter familiarizes you with 1-2-3/G's data management commands. It begins with an overview of how to design and create a 1-2-3/G database table. Once the database table is created, this chapter shows you how to use the Data Sort command to sort the records in the database table using the contents of one more fields.

In addition to sorting records in a database, this chapter shows you how to use the Data Query command to query a database table. Particular emphasis is placed on showing you different forms of criteria that you can use to search for the records you want. In addition, the various Data Query commands are covered in detail to provide you with the tools you need to effectively manage records in a database table. Finally, this chapter shows you how to use the Data Query command to query multiple database tables at the same time.

This chapter also discusses the database @functions. These handy functions allow you to quickly calculate various statistics for the values in a selected field of a database table.

This chapter also shows you how to use the Data External command to connect 1-2-3/G to an external table (database tables created by software packages other than 1-2-3/G). Once an external table is connected, you can access its records almost as though they were located in a 1-2-3/G worksheet.

This chapter also familiarizes you with Data commands that allow you to manipulate data. For example, it shows you how to use the Data Fill command to quickly fill a range with sequential numbers, dates, or times. It also discusses the Data Parse command, which allows you to parse the words and numbers in long labels into individual cells.

This chapter also covers Data commands that help you to analyze data. For example, it shows you how to use the Data Table command to perform "what-if" analysis by substituting multiple values into one or more formulas and recording the results in a data table. In addition, this chapter covers the Data Distribution command, which allows you to calculate a frequency distribution for a range of values. The Data Matrix command is also covered here. This command allows you to invert and multiply matrices to solve for variables in linear equations. Finally, this chapter covers the Data Regression command. This command allows you to predict future trends for a data set, based on events that have occurred in the past.

Creating Macros

Macros allow you to automate the operation of 1-2-3/G. The uses for macros are pretty much limited by your imagination.

In its most basic form, a macro is simply a series of labels entered in consecutive cells in a column of the worksheet. The characters in each label provide instructions to 1-2-3/G. For example, the instructions might tell 1-2-3/G to move the cell pointer, make a cell entry, or select a command. Once these label instructions are entered, you can assign a name to the first cell of the macro—for example, \Q. To run the macro, simply press CTRL-Q. 1-2-3/G will sequentially execute the instructions you've specified, just as if you typed them from your keyboard. In this context, macros can be used as a means to perform repetitive tasks. For example, you might create a macro that prints a series of different reports for a given worksheet file.

Macros can also be more than simply an alternative to entering commands and keystrokes from your keyboard. 1-2-3/G's macro facility includes a comprehensive macro programming language. This language includes a rich assortment of commands that give it the power of a higher level language such as BASIC or Pascal, but it works entirely within 1-2-3/G. For example, the language includes commands that let you get user input, control the order in which macro instructions are executed, and many more sophisticated processes. By using this programming language, you can create custom applications that perform sophisticated data management tasks. For example, you might create an application that allows another user to enter data in a custom form and then add that data to a 1-2-3/G database. The entire process takes place under the control of your macro.

This chapter gives you the basics you'll need to create simple macros. For example, you'll learn how to enter a macro in the worksheet and run it. You'll also learn how to use 1-2-3/G's new Keystroke Editor to automate the creation of simple macros. Programming with macros, however, is deferred to the next chapter.

What's New

If you are an experienced macro programmer, the first thing you'll probably notice is that invoking macros is slightly different in 1-2-3/G. For example, in previous releases of 1-2-3, most of your macros are probably named with a backslash (\) followed by a single letter, for example **\A**. To invoke these macros, you press ALT followed by the letter, for example ALT-A. However, in 1-2-3/G the ALT key has been replaced by the CTRL key. Therefore, you now activate that same macro by pressing CTRL-A.

Like 1-2-3 Release 3, you can assign conventional range names to macros in 1-2-3/G. Thus, you are no longer limited to single-letter macro names. To run a macro with a conventional range name, press RUN (ALT-F3). When you press RUN, 1-2-3/G shows you a dialog box that lists the range names in the current file as well as the names of other open worksheet files. To run a macro located in the current worksheet file, select the range name for that macro. To run a macro stored in another open worksheet file and have it execute in the current worksheet file, select the name of an open worksheet file from the list box. 1-2-3/G then shows you the range names for that file. When you select a macro name from this list 1-2-3/G runs that macro as though it were located in the current worksheet file.

1-2-3/G also includes the Keystroke Editor. This utility captures every keystroke you make in 1-2-3/G and translates it into macro instructions. To activate the Keystroke Editor, you use the Utility Macros Keystroke Editor command. When you select this command, 1-2-3/G opens the Keystroke Editor window and shows you the keystrokes you've entered recently. You can then use the Edit Copy and Edit Paste commands to copy all or part of those keystroke instructions to the worksheet for use as a macro. Or, you can have the Keystroke Editor play back selected keystrokes before you copy them into the worksheet. That way, you can test the macro before you create it.

You can also use your 1-2-3 Release 2 and 3 macros inside 1-2-3/G. However, due to 1-2-3/G's diverse feature set, your 1-2-3 Release 2 and 3 macros may not function in 1-2-3/G the way they should. To help solve this problem, 1-2-3/G includes a macro translator program. This program lets you translate your 1-2-3 Release 2 and 3 macros for use in 1-2-3/G.

1-2-3/G also includes a number of new macro programming commands that allow you to manage files in 1-2-3/G's window-based environment. For a discussion of these commands, see Chapter 11, "The Macro Programming Language."

CREATING A MACRO: AN EXAMPLE

The easiest way to help you understand what a macro is, and how it works, is to show you how to create a simple macro and then run it. Therefore, in this section, you'll learn how to create and run the macro in Figure 10-1. This macro enters a series of descriptive labels in a row of cells in the worksheet. The labels entered by the macro are Quarter 1, Quarter 2, Quarter 3, and Quarter 4. You might use this macro, or one like it, to save you time in entering labels that you use frequently.

As mentioned, a macro is a series of labels stored in a column of consecutive cells in the worksheet. To create a macro, you must first enter the labels that describe to 1-2-3/G what you want the macro to do. Once the labels are entered, you must give the macro a name. Once the macro is named, it's ready to run.

Entering the Macro

The first step for creating a macro is to choose its location in the worksheet. Basically, you can locate a macro anywhere you want. However, macros are normally placed in an out-of-the-way location in the worksheet (see "Where to Locate Macros" later in this chapter for more details). Once you've chosen a spot for the macro, you're ready to begin entering it. In the example that follows, the macro will be entered beginning in cell A:B1.

To enter the macro in the worksheet, move the cell pointer to cell A:B1 and enter the following labels. Do not be concerned about what these labels actually do. This will be discussed later. Enter the labels just as you would any other label in 1-2-3/G (making sure, of course, that you enter them exactly as they appear here).

Figure 10-1 shows what your screen should look like when you're finished entering the labels.

1-2-3/G [69.4] Ready

File Edit Worksheet Range Copy... Move... Print Graph Data Utility Quit... Help

A:A7

QUARTER.WG1

A	A	B	C	D	E	F
1		Quarter 1 {RIGHT}				
2		Quarter 2 {RIGHT}				
3		Quarter 3 {RIGHT}				
4		Quarter 4~				
5						

FIGURE 10-1 A sample macro that enters labels in a row of cells

Cell	Entry
A:B1	Quarter 1{RIGHT}
A:B2	Quarter 2{RIGHT}
A:B3	Quarter 3{RIGHT}
A:B4	Quarter 4~

Naming the Macro

Once you've entered the labels for the macro, you're ready to give it a name. To name a macro, you use the Range Name Create command to assign a range name to the first cell of the macro. You can then use that name to invoke the macro.

The range name you assign depends on how you want to invoke the macro (see "Naming Macros" later). However, for now, assume you want to invoke the macro by using a CTRL-letter sequence, for example CTRL-Q. That way, you can invoke the macro by holding down the CTRL key and pressing **Q**. To use this method, you must assign a range name that begins with a backslash (\) followed by a single letter that will be used to invoke the macro, for example \Q.

To name the macro, move the cell pointer to cell A:B1 and select the Range Name Create command. 1-2-3/G displays the Range Name Create dialog box. In the "Range name" text box, type **\Q** and press ENTER. 1-2-3/G activates the "Range(s)" text box. Confirm the current selection (A:B1..A:B1) by pressing ENTER or by selecting the OK command button. That macro now has a name and is ready to run.

Invoking the Macro

Before you invoke the macro, move the cell pointer to cell A:B7, away from the macro itself. This particular macro writes labels into the worksheet, starting at the location of the cell pointer. If you leave the cell pointer in its current position, it will overwrite the first cell of your new macro.

To invoke the macro, press CTRL-Q. 1-2-3/G begins searching the current worksheet file for the \Q range name. When it finds that range name, it starts executing the macro, starting at the location of the cell pointer. In this case, 1-2-3/G places the quarters for the year (Quarter 1, Quarter 2, and so on) in a row of four adjacent cells (A:B7..A:E7), as shown in Figure 10–2. If 1-2-3/G cannot find the \Q range name when you press CTRL-Q, it simply beeps and does nothing.

How the Macro Works

The macro is Figure 10–2 works like this. When you press CTRL-Q and 1-2-3/G locates the \Q range name in the current file, it begins executing the macro

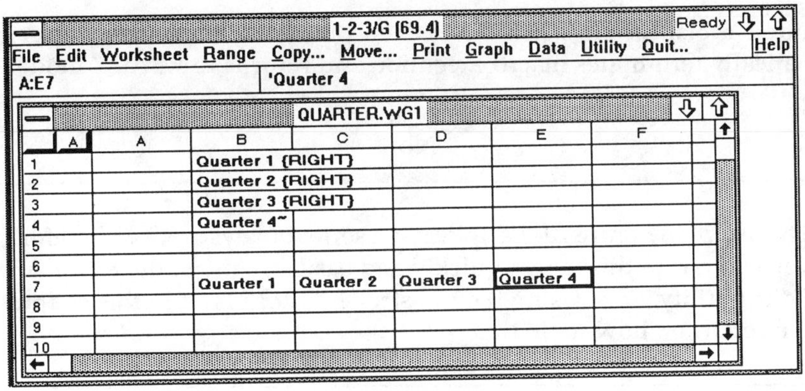

1-2-3/G [69.4] Ready

File Edit Worksheet Range Copy... Move... Print Graph Data Utility Quit... Help

A:E7 'Quarter 4

QUARTER.WG1

A	A	B	C	D	E	F
1		Quarter 1 {RIGHT}				
2		Quarter 2 {RIGHT}				
3		Quarter 3 {RIGHT}				
4		Quarter 4~				
5						
6						
7		Quarter 1	Quarter 2	Quarter 3	Quarter 4	
8						
9						
10						

FIGURE 10–2 The macro enters labels in a row of cells

instructions in the upper-left cell of that range (cell A:B1 in this case). Starting with the label in that cell, 1-2-3/G begins interpreting the characters in that label, one at a time. Each character is acted on as if you entered it from your keyboard. For example, when 1-2-3/G encounters the *Q* in "Quarter 1," it acts as though you typed that character. The same is true for the *u*, *a*, *r*, and the rest of the characters in the text string "Quarter 1."

When 1-2-3/G encounters a left curly brace ({) in a label, it knows that a special macro keystroke instruction is about to follow. (A left curly brace can also mean that a programming command such as {IF} or {FOR} is about to follow.) In this case, when 1-2-3/G encounters {RIGHT} in the label in cell A:B1 of Figure 10–2, it acts as though you pressed the → key. The cell pointer is moved one cell to the right. This also has the effect of completing the entry "Quarter 1." If you started the macro in cell A:B7, the label "Quarter 1" now appears in that cell and the cell pointer is located on cell A:C7.

When 1-2-3/G reaches the end of a label in a macro, it automatically moves down one cell and begins interpreting and executing the characters in the next label. For example, in the case of the macro in Figure 10–2, 1-2-3/G moves to cell A:B2, which contains a label similar to cell A:B1. 1-2-3/G executes the instructions in this label in the same way. That is, it enters the character string "Quarter 2" in cell A:C7 and moves the cell pointer one cell to the right. This same process is performed for the label in cell A:B3. However, you'll notice that the label in cell A:B4 of the macro ends with a ~ (tilde) instead of {RIGHT}. In macros, the tilde is the equivalent of pressing the ENTER key. Therefore, 1-2-3/G places the label "Quarter 4" in the current cell (A:E7) and leaves the cell pointer in that location.

After completing the last line of the macro in Figure 10–2, 1-2-3/G moves down one cell to look for further macro instructions. However, 1-2-3/G instead encounters a blank cell. When 1-2-3/G encounters a blank cell in a macro, it automatically terminates macro execution and returns to READY mode.

Note

The macro in Figure 10–1 duplicates a series of keystrokes. Therefore, you can create this macro quickly and easily by using the Keystroke Editor utility. See "Using the Keystroke Editor" later in this chapter for details on how to do this.

MACRO BASICS

If you followed along in the early part of this chapter, you have just created your first simple macro. You now have a sense of how macros work. However, to get the most out of your macros, you'll need to learn some more basic macro skills. For example, you'll need a thorough understanding of macro syntax and macro keystroke instructions. You'll also need to know more about naming, running, and documenting macros. These fundamental topics are discussed in the sections that follow.

Syntax

In their simplest form, macros are made up of a series of instructions that exactly replicate 1-2-3/G keystroke sequences. These keystroke instructions are stored as labels in consecutive cells in a column of the worksheet. The sections that follow show you the various types of keystroke instructions you can use in a macro.

Keystroke Instructions

Macro keystroke instructions represent keys on your keyboard. They cause 1-2-3/G to respond as though you had actually pressed a specific key. There are two types of macro keystroke instructions:

- **Single-character keys:** Letters that represent characters on your keyboard such as /, r, f, c, or 2.
- **Keynames:** Names within curly braces ({ }) that represent cell pointer movement keys, function keys, and so on, for example {UP}, {DOWN}, {GOTO}, and {NAME}.

Single-character keys represent keys in the typewriter portion of your keyboard. You can string these keys together to have 1-2-3/G perform commands. For example, imagine you want to create a macro that formats a single cell in Currency 2 format. To do this, type ' (a label prefix) to make the entry a label. Then type / (slash), which activates 1-2-3/G's main menu. You can follow this with *r* to select the Range command from that menu. You can then use *f* to select the Format option, followed by *c* to select the Currency format and 2 to select the number of decimal places. As you know from the previous example, the ~ (tilde) symbol represents the ENTER key. This character should appear twice, once to confirm the number of decimal places and again to complete the Range Format Currency 2 command. When you enter this macro in the worksheet, it will appear in a single cell as follows:

```
'/rfc2~~
```

Note

> See "Using Menu Commands in Macros" later in this chapter for additional examples of macros that use menu commands.

The rest of the keys on your keyboard are represented by macro keynames enclosed in curly braces ({ }). For example, in the sample macro at the beginning of this chapter the {RIGHT} macro keyname was used to move the cell pointer one cell to the right. Other keynames are available for 1-2-3/G's arrow keys, its function keys, certain editing keys, and other keys. Table 10–1 shows a list of the macro keynames available in 1-2-3/G.

For example, imagine you want to create a macro that sums a column of cells above the location of the cell pointer. To do this, you might create the following macro:

```
'@SUM({END}{UP}.{END}{UP})~
```

As you know, the @SUM function sums a range of values. To start the function, the first part of the macro, @SUM, begins forming the formula in the current cell. The first set of keynames, {END}{UP}, replicates the END UP key sequence, which places 1-2-3/G in POINT mode and moves the cell pointer to the first filled cell above the location of the cell pointer. The period (.) anchors the cell pointer for the @SUM function, causing 1-2-3/G to begin highlighting a range. The {END} and {UP} keynames appear a second time, causing the cell pointer to jump upward to the last filled cell in a range of consecutively filled cells. The closed parenthesis ")" finishes the @SUM function, and the tilde (the equivalent of the ENTER key) enters the finished @SUM function in the current cell.

TABLE 10-1 1-2-3/G's Macro Keynames

Category	1-2-3/G Key	Macro Keyname
Pointer movement	→	{RIGHT} or {R}
	←	{LEFT} or {L}
	↑	{UP} or {U}
	↓	{DOWN} or {D}
	CTRL-→ or TAB	{BIGRIGHT}
	CTRL-← or SHIFT-TAB	{BIGLEFT} or {BACKTAB}
	HOME	{HOME}
	END	{END}
	PGUP	{PGUP}
	PGDN	{PGDN}
	CTRL-PGDN	{PREVSHEET} or{PS}
	CTRL-PGUP	{NEXTSHEET} or {NS}
	CTRL-HOME	{FIRSTCELL} or {FS}
	END CTRL-HOME	{LASTCELL} or {LS}
	TAB	{TAB}
Function Keys	HELP (F1)	{HELP}
	EDIT (F2)	{EDIT}
	NAME (F3)	{NAME}
	ABS (F4)	{ABS}
	GOTO (F5)	{GOTO}
	WINDOW (F6)	{WINDOW}
	QUERY (F7)	{QUERY}
	TABLE (F8)	{TABLE}
	CALC (F9)	{CALC}
	F1–F12 Keys	{F*n*} where n is 1–12
	TRACE (SHIFT-F2)	{TRACE}
	OPTIONS (SHIFT-F3)	{OPTIONS}
	BOUND (SHIFT-F4)	{BOUND}
	HIDE (SHIFT-F6)	{HIDE}
	GROUP (SHIFT-F7)	{GROUP}
	DETACH (SHIFT-F8)	{DETACH}
	STEP (ALT-F2)	{STEP}
	RUN (ALT-F3)	{RUN}
Editing Keys	EDIT (F2)	{EDIT}
	BACKSPACE	{BACKSPACE} or {BS}
	DEL	{DELETE}
	INS	{INSERT} or {INS}

(continued)

TABLE 10–1 1-2-3/G's Macro Keynames (*cont.*)

Category	1-2-3/G Key	Macro Keyname
Other Keys	ALT	{ALT}
	CTRL	{CTRL}
	CTRL-. (period)	{ANCHOR}
	CTRL-BREAK	{BREAK}
	CTRL-SPACEBAR	{SELECT}
	Desktop Control menu (ALT-SPACEBAR)	{DESKMENU}
	ENTER	~
	ESC	{ESCAPE} or {ESC}
	SHIFT	{SHIFT}
	Window Control menu (ALT-HYPHEN)	{TOOLMENU}
	/, <, F10	/, {F10} or {MENU}
	~ (tilde)	{~}
	{ (open brace)	{{}
	} (closed brace)	{}}

Note

> You cannot replicate mouse pointer selections in macros, only keyboard selections.

Selecting Keynames with NAME (F3)

1-2-3/G offers a convenience feature for selecting macro keynames. If you type a left curly brace and then press NAME (F3), 1-2-3/G displays all macro keynames and macro programming commands in a list box, as shown in Figure 10–3. To select a keyname or command, click on it and select the OK command button, or highlight it and press ENTER. 1-2-3/G adds the keyname or command to your macro. Using this feature can help you to avoid one of the most common macro errors, the misspelling of keynames or commands.

Keys that do not have Macro Keynames

Certain keys on your keyboard do not have macro equivalents. Therefore, you cannot invoke these keys from within a macro. A list of these keys follows:

- CAPS LOCK
- NUM LOCK

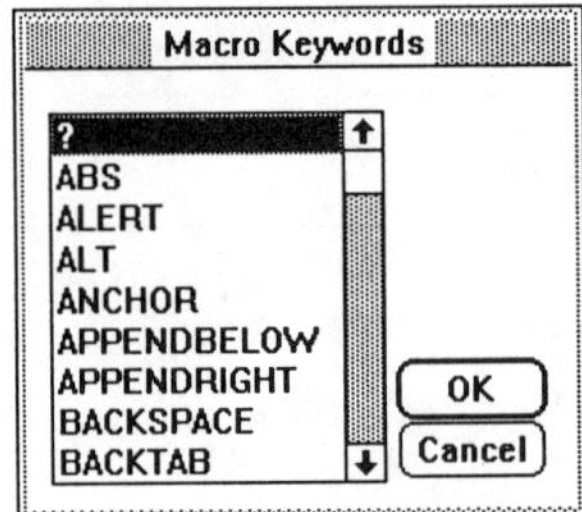

FIGURE 10–3 Typing { and pressing NAME (F3)

- SCROLL LOCK
- PRINT SCREEN

In addition, certain keys do not have direct macro keyname equivalents, because you can accomplish the same thing through other means. Some examples follow:

Key	Macro Equivalent
COMPOSE (ALT-F1)	{ALT}{F1}
UNDO (ALT-BACKSPACE)	{ALT}{BS}
NEXT WINDOW (CTRL-F6)	{CTRL}{F6}
CLOSE WINDOW (ALT-F4)	{ALT}{F4}

Alternate Keynames

In Table 10–1, you'll notice that 1-2-3/G offers some alternative forms for certain keynames. For example, the macro keyname for the → key can be {RIGHT} or {R}. An excerpt from Table 10–1 showing you a list of these keys appears in Table 10–2. You'll notice that, in most cases, the alternative is an abbreviation for the original keyname. In practice, experienced macro programmers use the abbreviated forms of the keynames because they are easier to type. In addition, the Keystroke Editor uses the abbreviated form when recording your keystrokes. See "Using the Keystroke Editor" later in this chapter for more about the Keystroke Editor.

Repeating Pointer Movement Instructions

One of the more common operations you must handle in macros is moving the cell pointer. For example, imagine you want to move the cell pointer down three cells. To do this, you might include the following line in your macro:

```
{DOWN}{DOWN}{DOWN}
```

TABLE 10-2 Keyname Alternatives

1-2-3/G Key	Keyname	Alternative
→	{RIGHT}	{R}
←	{LEFT}	{L}
↑	{UP}	{U}
↓	{DOWN}	{D}
CTRL-PGDN	{PREVSHEET}	{PS}
CTRL-PGUP	{NEXTSHEET}	{NS}
CTRL-HOME	{FIRST CELL}	{FS}
END CTRL-HOME	{LASTCELL}	{LS}
BACKSPACE	{BACKSPACE}	{BS}
INS	{INSERT}	{INS}
ESC	{ESCAPE}	{ESC}

However, 1-2-3/G allows you to use a shorthand convention for repeating cell pointer movements. That is, instead of repeating the keyname multiple times, you can follow the keyname with a value indicating the number of times you want the operation repeated. For example, rather than repeating the {DOWN} keyname three times, you can use the following line in your macro:

```
{DOWN 3}
```

For this to work, a space must appear between the value and the macro instruction. Further, both must be enclosed within curly braces.

Capitalization

Basically, capitalization doesn't really matter in macros. You can use both upper- and lower-case letters. 1-2-3/G doesn't know the difference. For example, /RFC2range1~~ will work every bit as well as /rfc2RANGE1~~. However, to make your macros more readable and help your organization, there are a few standard conventions you should consider, as follows:

- Use uppercase for instructions in braces, for example {HOME}.
- Range names should be capitalized, for example SALES.
- Keystrokes should be in lowercase, for example /rfc2~~.

These conventions are by no means mandatory. However, they will make your macros easier to read, both by you and by someone else. These conventions will also make debugging your macros easier, because you'll be able to tell at a glance the difference between macro instructions, range names, and other keystrokes.

Breaking Up Macro Instructions

You can place as many macro instructions in a cell as you like, provided, of course, that the total number of characters does not exceed 512 (the maximum length of a label in 1-2-3/G). However, when you break up macro instruction segments into multiple cells, the macro tends to be more readable. For example, the first line of the macro shown earlier in Figure 10–2 reads 'Quarter 1{RIGHT}, causing 1-2-3/G to enter the label "Quarter 1" in the current cell and move right one cell. Similar instructions appear in the remaining labels (A:B2..A:B4) that make up the balance of the macro. Figure 10–4, on the other hand, shows the same macro rewritten in a two-line configuration. When you execute this macro, it will have the same effect.

Notice, that the entry "Quarter 3" in Figure 10–4 is split onto two lines. This will not have any adverse effect on the operation of the macro, since 1-2-3/G processes the keystrokes one at a time when moving from one line to the next. You *cannot*, however, split up a macro instruction that is enclosed in curly braces. These must appear all on one line. Otherwise, 1-2-3/G will not be able to recognize the instruction and will issue an error message.

In general, you can split up your macro any way you like. However, you do sacrifice readability when you jam multiple macro instructions onto a single line. For example, it is a bit easier to read the macro in Figure 10–2 than it is to read the macro in Figure 10–4.

Label Prefixes

All macro instruction labels must begin with a label prefix ('). However, 1-2-3/G ignores the first label prefix in a label when processing macro instructions. It uses the second character following the label prefix to determine the type of entry that will be placed in the cell.

For example, in the macro in Figure 10–2, the first macro instruction label in cell A:B1 reads 'Quarter 1{RIGHT}. When 1-2-3/G processes this label, the first character it encounters after the label prefix is the letter "Q". Because this entry starts with a letter, 1-2-3/G determines that the entry in the current cell will be

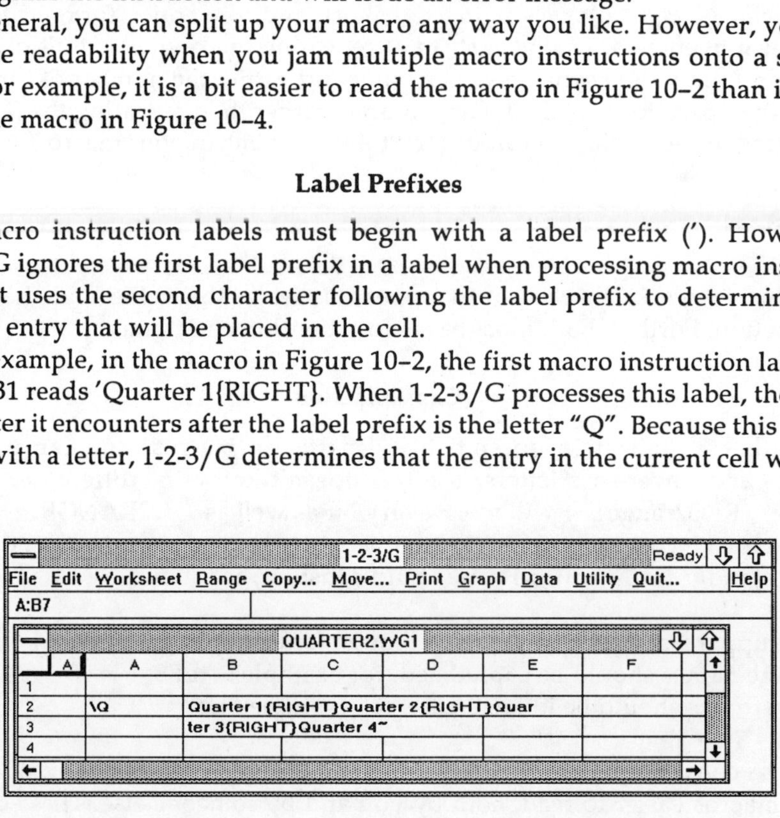

1-2-3/G Ready
File Edit Worksheet Range Copy... Move... Print Graph Data Utility Quit... Help
A:B7
QUARTER2.WG1

A	A	B	C	D	E	F
1						
2	\Q	Quarter 1{RIGHT}Quarter 2{RIGHT}Quar				
3		ter 3{RIGHT}Quarter 4~				
4						

FIGURE 10–4 The macro in Figure 10–2 written as two lines

a label, just as if you were typing the entry from the keyboard. Accordingly, 1-2-3/G provides the default label prefix (usually ') for the entry.

However, imagine you want to modify the macro in Figure 10–2 so that the labels "Quarter 1", "Quarter 2", and so on appear centered when placed in each cell. To do this, you can provide your own label prefix, for example, '^Quarter 1. That way, the macro will appear as shown in the range A:B1..A:B4 of Figure 10–5. When you run this macro, 1-2-3/G ignores the first label prefix in each cell, but not the second, and centers the labels created by the macro. The output for the macro will then appear as shown in the range A:B7..A:E7 of Figure 10–5.

On the other hand, suppose that instead of placing the labels "Quarter 1", "Quarter 2", "Quarter 3," and so on, you want to use the numeric label entries 3/92, 6/92, 9/92, and 12/92. To have these entries placed in the worksheet as labels, you must provide a second label prefix, for example ''6/92. When 1-2-3/G processes the entry, it will ignore the first label prefix but not the second, and will place the entry in the current cell as a label.

Imagine now that you want 1-2-3/G to make a numeric entry from within a macro. To do this, place only a single label prefix (') in front of the entry when building the macro. For example, imagine that you want 1-2-3/G to place the numbers 1990, 1991, 1992, and 1993 in separate cells in the worksheet. To do this, include the entries '1990, '1991, '1992, and '1993. 1-2-3/G will accept these entries as labels in the body of your macro. However, when you run the macro, 1-2-3/G will ignore the first label prefix and encounter the number *1*. At that point, 1-2-3/G determines that the entry will be a value, just as if you were typing the entry from the keyboard.

Where to Locate Macros

Macros are stored in the worksheet as labels. Therefore, you can easily edit them, just as you would any other label. You can also move or copy them to new positions in the current worksheet or in another worksheet. However, if

1-2-3/G (69.4) Ready

File Edit Worksheet Range Copy... Move... Print Graph Data Utility Quit... Help

A:A1

QUARTER.WG1

A	A	B	C	D	E
1		^Quarter 1 {RIGHT}			
2		^Quarter 2 {RIGHT}			
3		^Quarter 3 {RIGHT}			
4		^Quarter 4~			
5					
6					
7		Quarter 1	Quarter 2	Quarter 3	Quarter 4
8					
9					
10					

FIGURE 10–5 Adding label prefixes to a macro

your macros are located in the same worksheet as the data ranges they affect, you can easily damage a macro with a careless command. For example, the following commands are notorious for damaging macros:

- **Worksheet Insert Row:** You might insert a row into the middle of a macro, causing it to end prematurely.
- **Worksheet Delete Row:** You might delete an important instruction from a macro, causing an error. Or the deleted row might cause two macros to become joined, so that one executes immediately after the other.
- **Range Erase:** You might erase the macro.
- **Worksheet Delete Column:** You might delete the column containing the macro.
- **File Retrieve:** If you replace the file in the active window, without first using File Save to save the worksheet containing the macro, you lose the macro.

Virtually all of these problems can be solved with a simple Edit Undo (ALT-BACKSPACE) command. However, to use Edit Undo in a timely manner, you must be aware that there is a problem. Often, damaged macros are not discovered until long after it's too late to do anything about it. To avoid damage to your macros, there are a number of techniques you can use:

- Do not locate you macros in the same worksheet as the data ranges they affect. For example, if your macros will be performing their magic in worksheet A, locate the macros in worksheet B. 1-2-3/G will still be able to find the range names that define the first cell of your macros and will run them as though they were located in the current worksheet.
- If you have macros that you intend to run regularly in various worksheet files, consider placing those macros in a macro library. 1-2-3/G allows you to create a worksheet file composed entirely of macros. As long as that worksheet file is open on the desktop, you can run its macros from any active worksheet file. The macros will perform as though they were located in the current worksheet file. See "Running Macros" later in this section and "Building a Macro Library" later in this chapter for more details on this.
- If you must place a macro in the same worksheet as the data ranges it affects, place the macro well below and to the right of the active area of the worksheet. This will place the macro out of sight and possibly avoid damage from careless commands. As added insurance, however, you may want to use the Worksheet Global Protection Enable command to enable global protection for the worksheet. Then, use the Range Unprotect command to unprotect those data ranges that are either used by the macro or by you.

Naming Macros

To name a macro, place the cell pointer on the first cell of the macro and select Range Name Create. 1-2-3/G displays the Range Name Create dialog box. In the "Range Name" text box, type the range name you want to use to run the macro, for example **\Q**, and press ENTER. 1-2-3/G activates the "Range(s)" text box. Press ENTER again to confirm the current selection. 1-2-3/G assigns the range name to the first cell of the macro. (The \Q range name is shorthand for CTRL-Q, which is the actual key sequence you would use to start the macro.)

There are two types of range names you can assign to a macro, a backslash (\) range name or a conventional range name of up to 15 characters in length. The type of range name you select depends on how you want to start the macro.

The backslash (\) method for naming macros is the traditional method used to name macros since the first release of 1-2-3. It involves a backslash followed by a letter (A through Z), for example \Q, or a number (1 through 9), for example \1. To start the \Q macro, for example, simply hold down the CTRL key and type the letter Q. 1-2-3/G searches for the \Q range name and runs the macro. The advantage to this method is its simplicity and ease of use. The disadvantage is that you are limited to 35 macros per worksheet file (\A–\Z and \1–\9), plus one additional range name \0 (backslash zero) for an auto-executing macro (see "Auto-Executing Macros" later in this chapter for more details on this).

On the other hand, if you assign a conventional range name to the first cell of a macro, you can have a virtually unlimited number of macros in a worksheet file. Further, you can assign a range name that briefly describes what the macro does. However, if you decide to assign a conventional range name to a macro, you must run that macro by using RUN (ALT-F3). See "Running a Macro with RUN (ALT-F3)" in the next section for details on how to use RUN.

For example, instead of naming the current macro \Q, imagine you wanted to assign it a range name of QUARTER. To do this, move the cell pointer to the first cell of the macro and select Range Name Create. 1-2-3/G displays the Range Name Create dialog box. In the "Range Name" type **quarter** and press ENTER twice, once to confirm the new range name and again to confirm the current selection.

Here are some things to keep in mind when assigning conventional range names to macros.

- Range names can be up to 15 characters and you can use any combination of letters or numbers. However, avoid using spaces, commas, semicolons, and periods.
- Take care not to use range names that are the same as cell addresses, @functions, macro programming commands, or macro keynames.
- Consider using a special character at the beginning of range names, for example \, to distinguish them from other range names. That way, when you select Range Name Create or RUN (ALT-F3), 1-2-3/G will list your macro range names, both backslash and conventional, as a group.

Using the Range Name Labels Right Command

One of the more common methods used to name macros is to place the range name for the macro in the cell immediately to the left of the macro's first cell. Then, name the macro by using the Range Name Labels Right command. By placing the name of the macro in the worksheet in this way, you have a constant visual reminder of the range name assigned to the macro.

For example, imagine you want to use the Range Name Labels Right command to assign the range name \Q to the macro shown earlier in Figure 10–5. To do this, place the label '\Q in cell A:A1, as shown in Figure 10–4. (Do not forget the label prefix, or 1-2-3/G will repeat the letter Q across cell A:A1.) Leaving the cell pointer in cell A:A1, select the Range Name Labels command. 1-2-3/G displays the Range Name Labels dialog box. By default, the "Right" option button is preselected. Press ENTER twice, once to accept the "Right" option button selection and again to accept the current range selection in the "Range(s)" text box. 1-2-3/G uses the label in cell A:A1 to name the cell immediately to the right. In this case, that cell is A:B1, the first cell of the macro. The macro now has both a name and a label that visually identifies the name you assigned it. You can now run the macro by typing CTRL-Q.

Note

> You can use the CTRL-letter sequence to run a macro that is contained in a macro library file, and its effects will take place in the current file. For example, imagine in the previous example that the \Q range name was located in an open file called MACROLIB.WG1, rather than the currently active file. When you press CTRL-Q in the current file, 1-2-3/G will locate the \Q range name in the MACROLIB.WG1 file. When it finds that range name, 1-2-3/G will execute the \Q macro as though it were located in the currently active file. For more on sharing macros across files, see "Building a Macro Library" later in this chapter.

Running Macros

1-2-3/G offers two methods you can use to run your macros. The method you choose depends on the range name you assigned to the macro.

Running a Macro with CTRL

If you assigned a backslash (\) range name, for example \Q, to a macro, you can run that macro by holding down the CTRL key and pressing the letter following the backslash. For example, if you assigned the range name \Q, press CTRL-Q to run the macro. When you press CTRL-Q, 1-2-3/G locates the \Q range name and runs the macro. To indicate that a macro is running, 1-2-3/G displays a CMD indicator in the desktop title bar.

Running a Macro with RUN (ALT-F3)

Whether you assign a backslash range name or a conventional range name to a macro, you can run that macro with RUN (ALT-F3). When you press RUN, 1-2-3/G displays the dialog box in Figure 10–6. In the list box, 1-2-3/G displays the range names in the current file, along with the names of other worksheet files that are open on the desktop. The file names appear in double-angle brackets << >>.

To run a macro located in the currently active file, specify its range name in the "Range Name" text box. You can either type the range name, or you can select it from the list box below. To confirm your selection, press ENTER, or select the OK command button. Whichever method you select, 1-2-3/G runs the macro you specified. To indicate that a macro is running, 1-2-3/G displays a CMD indicator in the desktop title bar.

To run a macro that is located in another open worksheet file, but to have its effects take place in the current file, select the name of that file from the list box. For example, imagine you want to run one of the macros in the file MACROLIB.WG1 file that appears in the list box in Figure 10–6. To do this, select **<<MACROLIB.WG1>>** from the list box. Either double-click on its name or highlight it and press ENTER. 1-2-3/G displays the range names from MACROLIB.WG1 file in the list box, as shown in Figure 10–7. When you select a macro range, 1-2-3/G runs the macro located in the MACROLIB.WG1 file, but its effects are seen in the currently active file. For more on sharing macros across worksheet files, see "Building a Macro Library File" later in this chapter.

You can also use RUN (ALT-F3) to "test fly" a macro that does not as yet have a range name. To do this, simply press RUN, 1-2-3/G displays the RUN dialog box. Press ESC, if necessary, to clear any range name that may appear in the "Range Name" text box. 1-2-3/G displays the current cell pointer location in the box and enters POINT mode. Use the arrow keys, or your mouse, to move

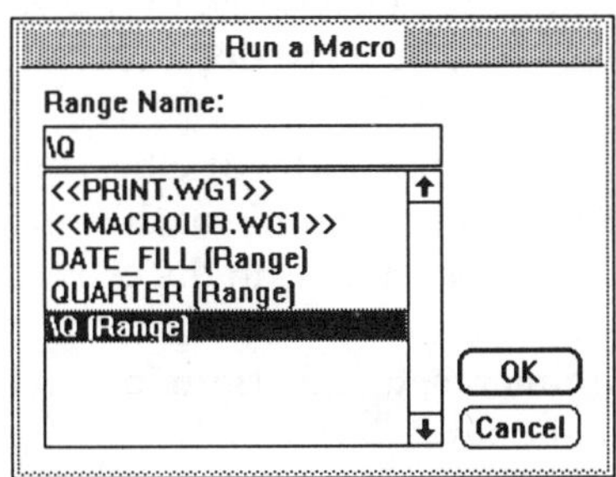

FIGURE 10–6 The Run dialog box

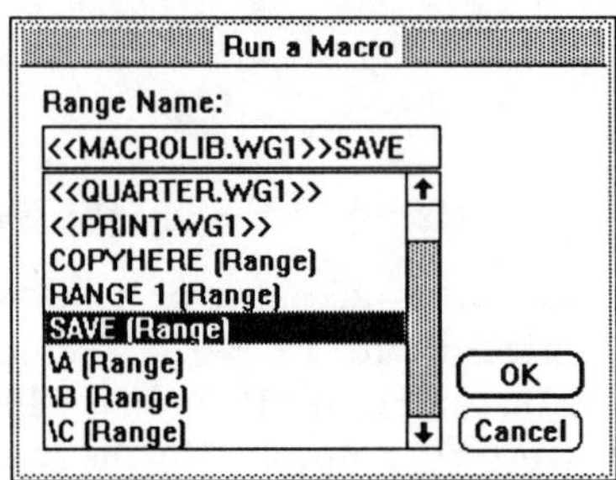

FIGURE 10–7 The range names in the MACROLIB.WG1 worksheet file

the cell pointer to the first cell in an unnamed macro and press ENTER. 1-2-3/G executes the macro.

The Effect of Macros on the Cell Pointer

When you run a macro, its effects take place starting at the location of the cell pointer. Once the macro starts running, 1-2-3/G reads the instructions in the first label of the macro one character at a time. When it finishes the instructions in the first label, it reads the label one cell below and starts executing the instructions for that label. However, the location of the cell pointer does not change. In fact, the location of the cell pointer is not at all affected by 1-2-3/G's current position in a macro. The cell pointer will only move if your macro instructions tell it to do so.

Documenting Macros

As your macros grow in size and complexity, it can become difficult to remember exactly what each line does, especially if you put the macro aside for a while. To deal with this problem, experienced macro programmers document their macros. That way, when it comes time to revise the macro, you, or someone else, can quickly determine what each line in the macro does.

There are three things you can do to document a macro:

- Place the name of the macro in the worksheet immediately to the left of its first cell. Figure 10–8 shows an example of this. In addition, if you name other cells in the macro, place those names in the cell that is immediately to the left of the named cell.
- Place descriptive comments to the right of each macro label that briefly indicate what the label does.
- If the macro instruction requires more than a brief comment, use the Note utility to attach one or more notes to the cell. To access this utility, you use the Utility Note command. See Chapter 1, "1-2-3/G Basics," for a complete description of how to use the Note utility.

Figure 10–8 shows an example of a documented macro. The macro's name /P appears in cell AA1. The labels that make up the macro appear in column AB, and the descriptive comments for each line appear in column AC.

Stopping a Macro

To stop a macro, you can press CTRL-BREAK. When you do, 1-2-3/G stops executing the macro and displays an error message box. Inside the box is the message "The Break key was pressed." Below this message 1-2-3/G shows the macro command that was being executed when CTRL-BREAK was pressed and its cell address. There is also an OK and a Help command button. Select OK to return to the worksheet in READY mode.

Note

You can prevent a user from stopping your macro with CTRL-BREAK. To do this, you use the {BREAKOFF} macro programming command covered in Chapter 11.

Saving Macros

Once you've finished creating a macro you can save it by using the File Save command to save the worksheet file that contains it. To use that macro again in another session, you must use the File Retrieve or File Open command to open the worksheet file containing the macro.

In addition, you may want to save the worksheet file before trying a new macro. That way, you are guaranteed of having a backup copy in case the macro does something unexpected to the worksheet. If something unexpected does happen, you can use the Edit Undo command, or ALT-BACKSPACE, to undo the effects of a macro. However, 1-2-3/G treats a macro as a single event for purposes of undo, and undoes the effects of the entire macro. See "Undoing a Macro" later in this chapter for more details.

Using Menu Commands in Macros

Thus far, most of the macro examples in this chapter have used simple keystroke instructions to enter data in the worksheet and move the cell pointer. However, you can also access 1-2-3/G's menu commands from a macro. This section provides some examples of macros that use menu commands.

A Command Macro Example

Suppose you are creating a model that will require numerous dates to be displayed in the worksheet. As you know, you can create a date in the worksheet by using the @DATE function. However, when you enter the @DATE function in a cell,

1-2-3/G [69.4] Ready

File Edit Worksheet Range Copy... Move... Print Graph Data Utility Quit... Help

A:AA1 '\P

PRINT.WG1

A	AA	AB	AC
1	\P	/fpps{DEL}	File Print Worksheet-Clear Screen preview box
2		r{D}{U}{BS}{?}~	Request a range from the user
3		oh{CE}@||Page #~q	Specify a Date/Page header
4		sgq	Send output to Preview utility
5			
6			

FIGURE 10–8 A documented macro

1-2-3/G displays a date value. To have this value displayed as a date, you must use the Range Format Date/Time command. To automate the formatting of dates, you might create the macro in Figure 10–9.

The macro in Figure 10–9 activates 1-2-3/G's main menu and selects the Range Format Date/Time 3 command (/rfd3). This command displays the Range Format dialog box, selects Date/Time as the cell format, and chooses Date 3 as the type of date format. At that point the "Range(s)" text box is activated, prompting you for a range to format. If you press ↓ on your keyboard at that point, 1-2-3/G reduces the size of the dialog box so that it appears as shown in Figure 10–10. The macro in Figure 10–9 replicates this keystroke by using the {D} or {DOWN} macro keyname. This is followed by the {U} or {UP} macro keyname to return the cell pointer to its original position. At that point you can highlight a range and press ENTER. 1-2-3/G will format the range you select in Date 3 format.

To create the macro in Figure 10–9, perform the following steps:

1. With the cell pointer in cell A:B1 type **'/rfd3{D}{U}**. (Remember to type the label prefix (') or 1-2-3/G will start executing the Range Format command.)

1-2-3/G Ready

File Edit Worksheet Range Copy... Move... Print Graph Data Utility Quit... Help

A:A1 '\D

SHEET5.WG1

A	A	B	C	D	E	F	G
1	\D	/rfd3{D}{U}					
2							
3							

FIGURE 10–9 A Range Format Date macro

	A	B	C	D	E	F
1	\D	/rfd3{D}{U}				
2						
3						
4						
5		32874	32904	32934	32964	32994
6						
7						
8						
9						
10						

FIGURE 10–10 Running the macro in Figure 10–9

2. Move the cell pointer to cell A:A1 and enter **'\D**. Once again, remember to type the label prefix or 1-2-3/G will repeat the letter D across the cell.
3. With the cell pointer in cell A:A1, select the Range Name Labels Right command and press ENTER or select OK. 1-2-3/G names cell A:B1 with the \D range name.

To execute the macro, move the cell pointer to the first date value in your model and select CTRL-D.

Note

> When the first character in a macro instructions is / (slash), \ (backslash), a number, or one of the numeric symbols +,-,@, ., (, #, or $, you must type a label prefix (', ^, or |) before typing the first character in the label.

Another Command Macro Example

Figure 10–11 shows an example of a generic print macro in the range A:AB1..A:AB4. This macro selects the File Print command and specifies a header that will appear at the top of each page. It then prompts the user for a range to print. After the user selects a range to print, the printed output is sent to the Preview utility for review.

Each line in the macro in Figure 10–11 performs a specific aspect of the printing operation. The function of each line is as follows:

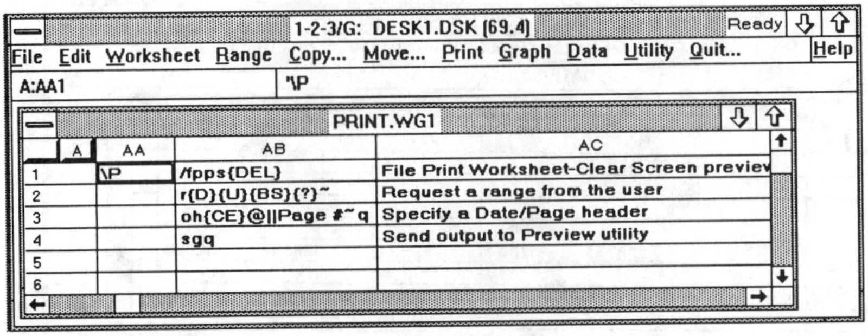

1-2-3/G: DESK1.DSK [69.4] Ready

File Edit Worksheet Range Copy... Move... Print Graph Data Utility Quit... Help

A:AA1 '\P

PRINT.WG1

A	AA	AB	AC
1	\P	/fpps{DEL}	File Print Worksheet-Clear Screen previe
2		r{D}{U}{BS}{?}~	Request a range from the user
3		oh{CE}@||Page #~q	Specify a Date/Page header
4		sgq	Send output to Preview utility
5			
6			

FIGURE 10–11 A sample print macro

- **/fpps{DEL}:** This line uses the / (slash) key to activate 1-2-3/G's main menu and select the File Print Print Worksheet command. Once the File Print Print Worksheet dialog box is displayed, the **s** in this line selects the "Screen preview" check box from the dialog box. The **{DEL}** represents the DEL key on your keyboard and has the effect of clearing the contents of the "Screen preview" check box, thereby turning "Screen preview" off. This is necessary, because the "Screen preview" check box may or may not be selected for that worksheet when you start the macro. As you'll soon see, the last line of the macro selects "Screen preview" again, to assure that the output is set to the Preview utility.
- **r{D}{U}{BS}{?}~:** The r in this line selects the "Range(s)" text box from the File Print Print Worksheet dialog box. The {D} keyname is the equivalent of pressing the ↓ key and causes the entire dialog box to be reduced to display only the "Range(s)" text box. The {U} keyname is the equivalent of the ↑ key and returns the cell pointer to its original position. The {BS} keyname is the equivalent of the BACKSPACE key. When pressed, this key frees (unanchors) the cell pointer, allowing you to move it freely around the worksheet and select the print range of your choice. The {?} command is a macro programming command that is discussed in the next chapter. This command pauses macro execution temporarily and awaits input from the user. This allows you to select a range to print. You can use either the keyboard or the mouse to select a range. However, you must press ENTER to confirm the range, When you do, the ~ (tilde) places the range you've selected in the "Range(s)" text box.
- **oh{CE}@||Page #~q:** The **o** in this line selects the "Options" command button from the File Print Print Worksheet dialog box. This causes the Options dialog box to be displayed. The **h** in turn selects the "Header" text box. The **{CE}** is a macro programming command that is discussed in the next chapter. This command clears any entry that may already be in the "Header" text box. Next the header text **@||Page #** is entered in the text box. This causes the current date to be left-aligned and the current page

number to be right-aligned at the top of each page. The ~ (tilde) key, which is the equivalent of the ENTER key, places the entry in the "Header" text box. Finally, the **q** selects the Quit command button from the Options dialog box to return to the File Print Print Worksheet dialog box.

- **sgq:** The **s** in this line selects "Screen preview" from the File Print Print Worksheet dialog box. (As you may recall, this selection was "blanked" in the first line of the macro.) This assures that the output will be set to the Preview utility. The **g** selects the Go command button to queue the print job. Finally, the **q** selects the Quit command button to exit the File Print Print Worksheet dialog box and begin printing. The macro is then ended and the Preview utility displays the printed range.

Tip: Using {DEL} to clear a check box

The use of the {DEL} keyname in the first line of the macro in Figure 10–11 to "blank" the current selection in a check box is somewhat unique. (The {CE} command will not work here.) To the authors' knowledge, this is not documented anywhere but here.

Selecting Commands by Using Their First Letters

When you create macros that use menu commands, make sure your instructions select those commands by using their first letters, rather than arrow-key equivalents such as {RIGHT} or {LEFT}. For example, /rfd3~ is preferable to /{RIGHT 3}~{DOWN 2}~~{UP 7}~~. Although, both are functionally equivalent, /rfd3~ is easier to read, understand, and debug. What's more, if your 1-2-3/G macros depend on the precise position of commands in a menu, you are bound to run into compatibility problems later on if Lotus should happen to add any options to the menu, something they have been known to do in the past.

Using Range Names Instead of Cell Addresses

Whenever possible, use range names in your macros instead of cell addresses. That way, if the data in the worksheet moves, your macros will remain up to date.

For example, imagine you have the label /fpprA:A1..A:F20~gq in a macro. The instructions in this label select the File Print Print Worksheet command, specify the range A:A1..A:F20 as a print range, and send the data to your printer. However, imagine you use either the Move or Edit Cut command to move the data in the range A:A1..A:F20 to another location in the worksheet. Your macro is now outdated. Or, imagine you use the Worksheet Insert or Worksheet Delete command to add or delete rows or columns included in the range A:A1..A:F20. Once again, the cell addresses in your macro remain static and are not updated for the change.

On the other hand, 1-2-3/G automatically updates range names when you change the position of data in the worksheet. For example, imagine you assign the name PRINT1 to the range A:A1..A:F20 and use that range name in your macro. If you use either the Move or Edit Cut commands to move that entire range, 1-2-3/G moves the PRINT1 range name along with it. Your macro remains up to date.

Further, if you insert or delete rows or columns in the middle of a named range, 1-2-3/G automatically adjusts the size of the named range accordingly. Therefore, if you insert or delete a row or column included in the PRINT1 range, your macro is automatically updated for the change in the size of the range.

When you use range names in your macros instead of cell addresses, your macros are dynamic. If the position of the data in the worksheet changes, your macros will continue to reference the correct data ranges.

Undoing a Macro

Suppose you run a macro and then decide that you don't like what just happened to your worksheet. You can undo the effect of the macro by selecting the Edit Undo command (or by pressing ALT-BACKSPACE).

When you select Edit Undo after a macro, 1-2-3/G undoes the entire macro. Although a macro may contain numerous commands, 1-2-3/G logs the execution of that macro as a single event and undoes the entire event. Further, if you press ALT-BACKSPACE (the shortcut for Edit Undo) during a macro, 1-2-3/G will undo the effects of the macro up to the point that you pressed ALT-BACKSPACE. For more about using the undo feature, see Chapter 1, "1-2-3/G Basics."

There are some commands that 1-2-3/G cannot undo. If you undo a macro containing one or more of these commands, 1-2-3/G displays an error message informing you that some commands in the macro were not undone.

Note

> If you include the Edit Undo command in a macro, 1-2-3/G will display the Edit menu, but it will not execute the command. Further, if you include the ALT-BACKSPACE key sequence in a macro, 1-2-3/G will ignore it.

AUTO-EXECUTING MACROS

An *auto-executing macro* is one that starts automatically when you open the worksheet file that contains it. To create an auto-executing macro, simply name the macro \0 (backslash zero) and save the worksheet file. The next time you use File Retrieve or File Open to open that worksheet file, 1-2-3/G will automatically execute the macro.

Auto-executing macros are especially useful when you want to create a custom application for use by others. For example, you might create an auto-executing macro that presents the user with a dialog box containing named command buttons. When a specific command button is selected, the macro branches to a subroutine that helps the user to perform a specific task. For more about creating dialog boxes and branching with macros, see Chapter 11, "The Macro Programming Language."

Auto-executing macros may also be useful in worksheet files that you use often. For example, imagine that you want to open a specific macro library file whenever a particular worksheet file is loaded. To do this, you might set up the auto-executing macro in Figure 10–12. The first line of the macro in cell A:B1 selects the File Open command. This causes 1-2-3/G to display the File Open dialog box. The {CE} clear entry command is then used to clear the contents of the "File name" text box. This is followed by the name of the macro library file (MACROLIB.WG1). Next, two tildes (~~) appear, one to confirm the filename and another to complete the File Open command. The macro library file is then opened on the desktop in a separate window, which by default becomes the active window.

To reactivate the original window—the window containing the auto-executing macro—the {WACTIVATE} command appears in the second line of the macro (cell A:B2). (You'll learn more about this command in Chapter 11.) This command allows you to activate a window by its name. Thus, you can activate

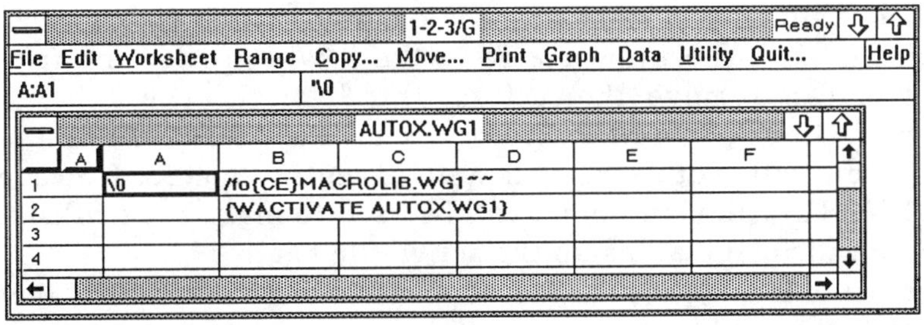

1-2-3/G Ready
File Edit Worksheet Range Copy... Move... Print Graph Data Utility Quit... Help
A:A1 '\0
AUTOX.WG1

A	A	B	C	D	E	F
1	\0	/fo{CE}MACROLIB.WG1~~				
2		{WACTIVATE AUTOX.WG1}				
3						
4						

FIGURE 10–12 A sample auto-executing macro

a specific window, regardless of how many other windows you may already have open on the desktop. By reactivating the file containing the original auto-execute macro, you can then continue your work session in that file.

Once you save an auto-executing macro in a worksheet file, 1-2-3/G executes that macro whenever you load the file. However, occasionally, you may need to turn off auto-executing macros for all worksheet files. To do this, you use the Worksheet Global Default Autoexec command. When you select this command, 1-2-3/G displays the Worksheet Global Default dialog box with the "Autoexec" section activated. This section contains two check boxes, "Native" and "Other." If you remove the X from the "Native" check box, 1-2-3/G will no longer run auto-executing macros in 1-2-3/G files. If you remove the X from the "Other" dialog, 1-2-3/G will no longer run auto-execute macros in 1-2-3 Release 2 and 3 files that you load into 1-2-3/G.

To exit the Worksheet Global Default dialog box, you have two choices. If you select the OK command button, 1-2-3/G will honor your selection for the current work session only. The next time you start 1-2-3/G, however, it will again run all auto-executing macros. On the other hand, if you select the "Update" command button to exit the dialog box, 1-2-3/G will save the setting for future work sessions.

Suppose you want to run an auto-executing file after you have already retrieved its file. To do this, press CTRL-0. 1-2-3/G executes the macro in the usual way. This is a subtle enhancement from previous releases of 1-2-3 (Releases 2.2 and 3 only) in which you must use RUN (ALT-F3) to rerun auto-executing macros.

If you use the File Open command in a macro to open a file that contains an auto-executing macro, the auto-executing macro in the newly opened file takes over. Although control will eventually return to the original macro once the auto-executing macro has finished running, the original macro will now operate in the newly opened worksheet file. To have the macro operate in the original window again, you must immediately follow the File Open command with the {WACTIVATE} command to reactivate the original window. If you want to prevent the auto-executing macro in the newly opened file from running, you can remove the X from the "Native" check box in the Worksheet Global Default dialog box. That way, 1-2-3/G will open the new file, but will not execute its auto-executing macro. However, the {WACTIVATE} command must still be used to make the worksheet file containing the original macro the active file again.

You can also include an auto-executing macro in a macro library file. When you open the macro library file, 1-2-3/G runs the auto-executing macro in the usual way. However, 1-2-3/G does not run the macro library's auto-executing macro when you load another worksheet file that does not have its own auto-executing macro.

Note

> If you run a macro in the currently active file that uses the File Retrieve command to replace the currently active file, the macro ends when the new file is opened.

If you want to get fancy, you can include an auto-executing macro in a start-up worksheet file. To specify a start-up worksheet file, you use the User Settings Startup command, available from either the Utility menu or the Desktop Control menu. (This command is covered in detail in Appendix A, "Customizing 1-2-3/G.") This command allows you to specify an existing worksheet file that 1-2-3/G will automatically load each time you start the program.

DEBUGGING A MACRO

Even the most experienced macro programmers make errors in their macros, causing them to perform unexpectedly. Often the error is not immediately apparent, and you must *debug* the macro. Debugging is simply a process of locating errors and removing or correcting them.

1-2-3/G offers two facilities for helping you to debug your macros, Step and Trace. You can access these facilities by using the Utility Macros Debug command. You can also press STEP (ALT-F2) and/or TRACE (SHIFT-F2) to access these debugging features. However, as you use these facilities to debug your macros, it may be helpful for you to know what some of the more common macro errors are, so that you know what to look for.

Often macro errors are the result of something simple. For example, you may have misspelled a macro programming command or keyname. Or, you may have omitted a tilde (~). For example, you used /cRANGE1RANGE2~ instead of /cRANGE1~RANGE2~. To correct such a problem, simply move the cell pointer to the cell that contains the errant label. Next, press EDIT (F2) to place the label in the Control Line. Finally, edit the label as you would any other label in 1-2-3/G and press ENTER. Other things to watch out for when debugging your macros are as follows:

- You may have used the wrong slash character. For example, you used a backslash (\) instead of a slash (/) to activate a menu or a slash (/) instead of a backslash (\) to name a macro.

- You may have used parentheses to enclose a command or keyname instead of curly braces, or you may have omitted a curly brace.
- If your macro uses range names, you may have used a range name that is undefined. Or, you may have assigned a range name that matches a macro keyname or command, for example {CLOSE} or {BREAK}.
- You may have forgotten a command menu letter or used the wrong letter.
- You may have omitted a space between a macro keyword, or a macro keyname, and its argument. For example, instead of {DOWN 3}, you used {DOWN3}.

In addition, 1-2-3/G often displays an error message box when an error occurs in a macro. This message box contains the label instruction that was being executed when the error occurred as well as its location (cell address). Take a moment to note the cell address and instruction. Then, select the OK command button to clear the error message box. Next, go to the cell referenced in the error message and edit the macro instruction. Then try running the macro again.

Using STEP Mode

STEP mode allows you to run a macro one instruction at a time. This handy debugging tool allows you to watch a macro as it is executing, up to the point where an error actually occurs. To turn STEP mode on, you can select the Utility Macros Debug command. When you select this command, 1-2-3/G displays the dialog box in Figure 10–13. Select the "Single Step" check box and select OK or press ENTER to exit the dialog box. From that point on, 1-2-3/G will execute macros one step at a time. To move from one instruction to the next, press any key. To indicate that STEP mode is on, 1-2-3/G displays a STEP indicator in the title bar of the desktop window when a macro is not active. On the other hand, when a macro is running, 1-2-3/G displays an SST indicator in the title bar of the desktop window. To turn STEP mode off, select Utility Macros Debug and remove the X from the "Single step" check box.

As an alternative to using the File Utility Debug command to turn on STEP mode, you can press STEP (ALT-F2). When you select this key sequence, the STEP indicator appears in the desktop title bar. To turn STEP mode off, press STEP (ALT-F2) a second time.

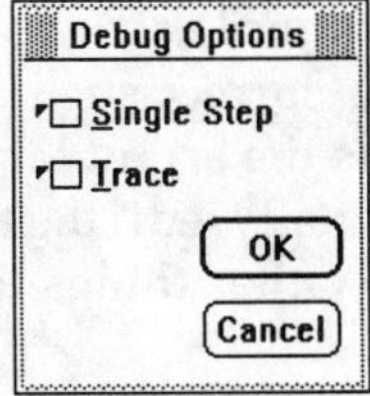

FIGURE 10–13 The Debug dialog box

Note

You can also turn on TRACE mode from the File Utility Debug dialog box at the same time as you turn on STEP mode. TRACE mode opens a window that displays the macro line that is about to be executed. If an error occurs, the source of the error is identified in the Trace window. See the next section for more details on Trace.

For example, imagine you are having trouble with the macro in Figure 10–14. This macro uses the Data Fill command to fill a row of 12 consecutive cells with the date values ranging from January 92 to December 92. It then uses the Range Format Date/Time command to format the date values in Date 3 format. However, this macro has an error in it. Although it's hard to tell from the figure, the first line of the macro (cellA:B1) reads /df{BS}.{R 11)~. The second to last character in the command line is a closed parenthesis, instead of a closed curly brace, as it should be.

To debug the macro in Figure 10–14 macro, turn STEP mode on and start the macro (press CTRL-F). To execute the first command (/), press any key. 1-2-3/G activates the main menu. When you press another key, the Data command is selected. Pressing another key selects the Fill option. The Data Fill dialog box is now displayed and the "Ranges" text box is activated. Pressing yet another key executes the {BS} key name. The color of the highlight in the "Range(s)" text box changes from black to gray, indicating 1-2-3/G has unanchored the cell pointer. Everything looks pretty good so far. However, when you press another key, 1-2-3/G displays an error message box indicating a syntax error is present. You now know that the macro instructions up through /df{BS}. are working just fine. However, when 1-2-3/G hits {R 11), an error results. At this point, you can see that a parenthesis exists where a curly brace belongs.

When you find an error with STEP mode, you do not need to turn STEP mode off to correct the problem. Instead, press CTRL-BREAK to terminate the macro. Then make your correction and start the macro again.

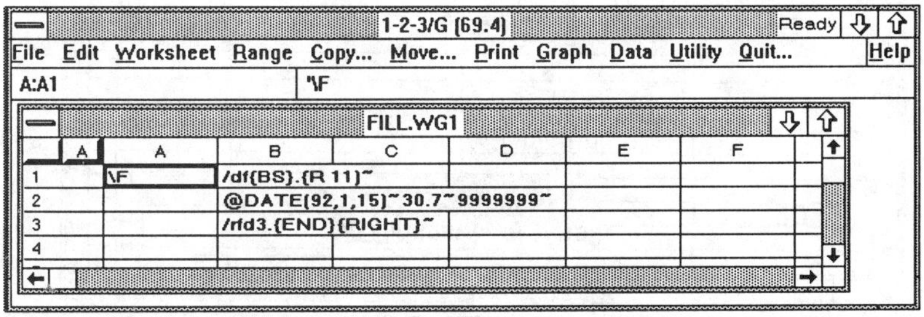

FIGURE 10–14 **A macro with an error in the first line**

Note

When you write a new macro, it is recommended that you run it through STEP mode one time. This simple procedure may show you errors of which you are not aware.

Using TRACE Mode

When you activate TRACE mode, 1-2-3/G displays a small window entitled Macro Trace. If you then start a macro, the Trace window shows the command line that is about to be executed and its location in the worksheet. If an error occurs while the macro is running, the errant instruction is highlighted in the Trace window. Figure 10–15 shows an example of what the Trace window looks like.

To activate TRACE mode, select the Utility Macros Debug command. 1-2-3/G displays the dialog box in Figure 10–13. Select the "Trace" check box followed by OK. 1-2-3/G displays the Trace window on the desktop. If you start a macro at this point, 1-2-3/G will show each line in the Trace window as it executes. To turn TRACE mode off, select Utility Macros Debug and remove the X from the "Trace" check box.

As an alternative to the Utility Macros Debug command, you can use TRACE (SHIFT-F2) to activate TRACE mode. To turn off TRACE mode, select TRACE (SHIFT-F2) a second time.

The Trace window is divided into two sections. The left side of the window shows the cell address of the macro command line that is currently executing. The right side shows the command line itself. If an error occurs while the command line is executing, 1-2-3/G highlights the errant instruction. For example, in Figure 10–15 the instruction {R 11) has been highlighted. At a glance you can see that a closed parenthesis exists where a closed curly brace belongs.

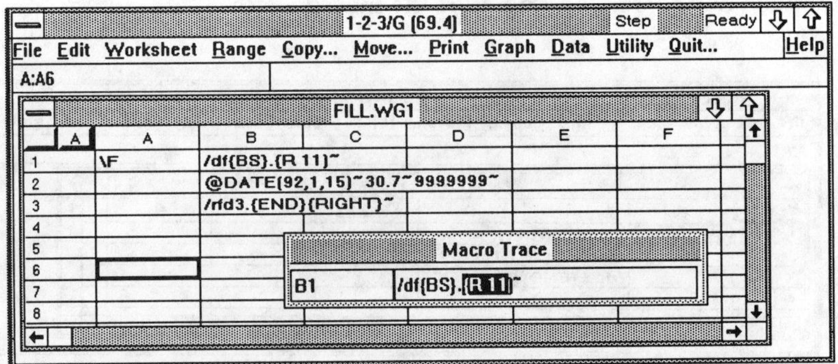

FIGURE 10–15 The Trace window highlights an error

To correct this problem, press CTRL-BREAK to terminate the macro and edit the label accordingly.

Tips on Debugging

You may find the following tips to be useful when debugging your macros:

- Use STEP mode and TRACE mode at the same time when debugging a macro. Otherwise, the commands in the Trace window may flash by so fast that you can't see what is going on.
- You can turn STEP mode on while a macro is executing. However, to do this, the macro must be halted while it is awaiting user input. Some examples of commands that halt macro execution to solicit user input include {?}, {GETLABEL}, {MENUBRACH}, or {MENUCALL}. See Chapter 11 for more on these commands.
- You can press STEP (ALT-F2) to turn STEP mode off while a macro is executing. When you press a key, 1-2-3/G will execute the rest of the macro at normal speed.
- You can also put "breaks points" in your macros to test specific sections of code. To create a break point, place a blank cell at the point where you want the macro to stop. Then start the macro. 1-2-3/G will execute the macro up to the point where the blank cell occurs. To test the next section of the macro, select RUN (ALT-F3). 1-2-3/G displays the Run dialog box. Press ESC to enter POINT mode and move the cell pointer to the first cell in the next section of the macro. When you're ready, press ENTER. 1-2-3/G executes the next section of the macro.
- You can also use RUN (ALT-F3) to start running a macro at a specific line. To do this, press RUN (ALT-F3) to have 1-2-3/G display the Run dialog box. Next, press ESC to enter POINT mode and move the cell pointer to the cell where you want macro execution to begin. Finally, press ENTER to have 1-2-3/G begin executing the macro, starting at the cell you specified.

BUILDING A MACRO LIBRARY

Suppose you have a series of macros that you use regularly. However, they are presently scattered throughout various worksheet files. Using those macros involves either loading the appropriate worksheet file and using RUN (ALT-F3), or copying the macros to the file you happen to be using at the time.

As an alternative to storing your commonly used macros in different worksheet files, you can store them in a single *macro library* file. Macro library files provide a convenient way of centrally storing your commonly used macros, saving you both disk space and time in searching worksheet files for the right macro. When you run a macro from a macro library, it executes as though it were located in the current file.

To create a macro library file, select the File New command. When 1-2-3/G displays the File New dialog box, specify the name MACROLIB.WG1 in the "File name" text box. Complete the command in the usual way. (As you'll see in a moment, the MACROLIB.WG1 filename is important.) Once the new MACROLIB.WG1 worksheet file is created, you can begin consolidating your commonly used macros from various sources, including other worksheet files or the Keystroke Editor. To do this, simply use the Copy command or the Edit Copy and Edit Paste commands to copy the macros to the new file. Make sure, however, to leave a blank cell between each of the macros in the worksheet file. Otherwise, you may get unexpected results. Figure 10-16 shows an example of some keyboard macros stored in a macro library file.

When you copy macros into a macro library file, make sure you remember to use the Range Name Create or Range Name Labels Right command to assign range names to those macros. As you assign each range name, make sure it is unique both to the macros in the macro library file and to the macros in other worksheet files you might be using when macro library is open. Otherwise, you may end up running the wrong macro.

Macro Library Conventions

The conventions for creating macros libraries are as follows:

- The macro library file must be named MACROLIB.WG1. However, you can have as many macro library files as you want, each located in a separate

1-2-3/G: DESK1.DSK (69.4) Ready

File Edit Worksheet Range Copy... Move... Print Graph Data Utility Quit... Help

A:A1 '\B

MACROLIB.WG1

A	A	B	C	D
1	\B	/wgaffa{TAB} ~	Bold - Slot a font	
2				
3	\D	@TODAY~/rfd4~	Date 4 stamp	
4				
5	\E	{EDIT}{HOME}'~	Label Maker	
6				
7	\A	@SUM({END}{UP}.{END}{UP})~	Add column above	
8				
9	\C	/rfc2~{BS}.{?}~	Currency 2 format	
10				
11	COPYHERE	/c{BS}{?}~~	Copy to current cell	
12				
13	\R	/rllc{D}{ESC}{?}~	Center Labels	
14				
15	SAVE	/fs{ESC 2}{?}~	Save single file	
16				
17	\F	/df{BS}.{R 11}~	Months in row--Date 3	
18		@DATE(92,1,15)~30.7~9999999~		
19		/rfd3.{END}{RIGHT}~		
20				
21	\P	/fpps{DEL}	Print to Preview	
22		r{D}{U}{BS}{?}~		
23		oh{CE}@||Page #~q		
24		sgq		
25				

FIGURE 10–16 A sample macro library

directory, but only one macro library file can be open on the desktop at any one time.

- To run a macro stored in a macro library, the MACROLIB.WG1 file must be open on the desktop.
- The range names in the macro library must be unique among the files in memory. If the same range name is assigned to a macro both in the current worksheet file and in the macro library, 1-2-3/G will run the macro in the worksheet.

Running Macros in a Macro Library

What does a macro library get you? That is, why store your macros in a filename MACROLIB.WG1, rather than a worksheet file with another name? The main reason is the ease with which you can run or call a macro.

You can run a CTRL-*letter* macro, for example \A, that is stored in a macro library file from any other open worksheet file. When you press CTRL-A, 1-2-3/G executes the \A macro in the macro library as though it were located in the current file. However, if the file containing your macros were named something other than MACROLIB.WG1, 1-2-3/G will not be able to find the \A range name.

To run a macro with a conventional range name that is stored in a macro library, select RUN (ALT-F3). When 1-2-3/G displays the RUN dialog box, select <<MACROLIB.WG1>>. 1-2-3/G shows you a list of range names in the macro library file. Select the range name that defines the macro you want. 1-2-3/G runs the macro as though it were located in the current file.

You can also store subroutines in macro libraries and use them more easily. For example, instead of specifying the full file and range name in a macro, such as <<FINANCE.WG1>>DEPREC, to call a macro subroutine in a file other than the active one, you need only specify DEPREC, provided the subroutine is located in MACROLIB.WG1. You can use this convention with many of the advanced macro commands discussed in the next chapter. For example, with the *{subroutine}* command, instead of typing out {<<FINANCE.WG1>>DEPREC}, simply {DEPREC} will suffice. You can also have your macro look for ranges in a macro library for other programming commands such as {BRANCH}, {DISPATCH}, {FOR}, {ONERROR}, {MENUBRANCH}, and {MENUCALL}.

Note

If a macro in a macro library includes a specific range name, that range name must exist in the file in which you run the macro. Otherwise, an error message will result.

Storing Data in Macro Library Files

You may also want to store tables of data for specific macros in a macro library file. For example, imagine you have a set of tax tables that you intend to use across more than one worksheet file. You can store those tables in a macro library with a macro that queries them. That way, you can call that macro from any open worksheet file, and use the data in the tables in that file. This can save you time in copying the tables and the macro from one worksheet to the next, and it can also save you disk space.

Organizing a Macro Library

A macro library file contains 256 worksheets, like any other 1-2-3/G worksheet file. You can use these separate worksheets to help organize your macro library. For example, you might put your keyboard macros in worksheet A, your database macros in worksheet B, and so on. This will help you to maintain an orderly macro library and allow you to quickly find a given macro when you need to.

USING THE KEYSTROKE EDITOR

The Keystroke Editor captures every keystroke you make in 1-2-3/G, regardless of which tool you happen to be using. Those keystrokes are then translated into 1-2-3/G macro commands. At any time, you can open the Keystroke Editor window and look at the keystrokes captured thus far. If you want, you can then copy those keystroke commands to the worksheet for use as a macro. You can also have Keystroke Editor "playback" selected keystrokes, so that you can see the results. If changes are required, you can edit the keystrokes in the Keystroke Editor window before copying them to the worksheet.

Note

> The Keystroke Editor only captures keystrokes. It does not capture mouse actions.

The Keystroke Editor is a 1-2-3/G utility. Therefore, it operates in its own window and has its own menu. To access the Keystroke Editor, you use the Utility Macros Keystroke Editor command from the Worksheet Tool menu. You can also select Keystroke Editor from the Desktop Control menu. Whichever method you select, 1-2-3/G displays the window and menu shown in Figure 10–17.

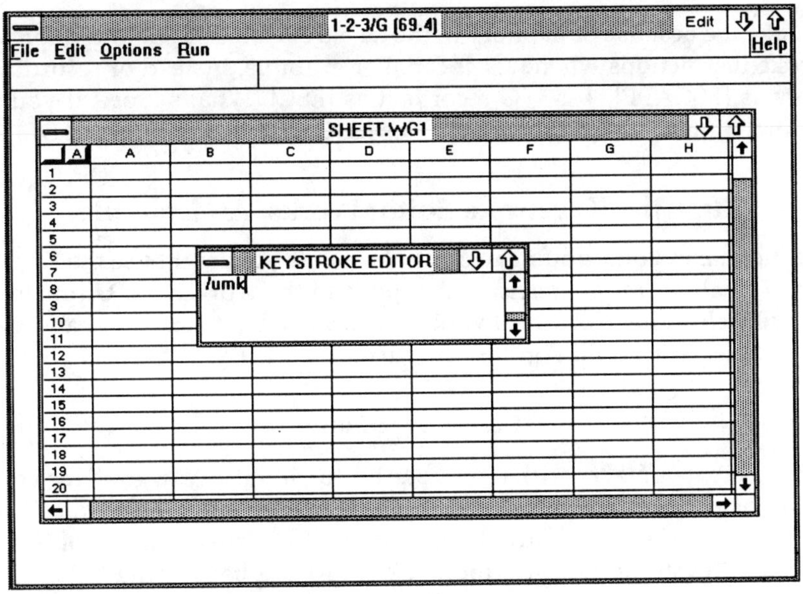

FIGURE 10–17 The Keystroke Editor window

How 1-2-3/G Stores Keystrokes

1-2-3/G captures all your keystrokes, whether the Keystroke Editor window is displayed or not. However, to control the amount of memory used for capturing keystrokes, 1-2-3/G sends those keystrokes to a memory buffer. This buffer holds about 16,384 bytes. Figuring about one character per byte, this memory buffer should be capable of holding around 16,000 characters. When the memory in the buffer is full, 1-2-3/G drops off the oldest characters in order to accommodate the most recent ones.

If the Keystroke Editor window is not active, this dropping and adding of characters occurs one character at a time. However, if the Keystroke Editor window is displayed, the oldest 128-byte block is dropped, making room for a new block of 128 characters.

Keystroke Translation

The Keystroke Editor translates every keystroke you make into an acceptable macro instruction. For example, the File Print Print Worksheet command becomes /fpp. When you press DEL, 1-2-3/G records {DEL}, and so on. However, when recording the function keys, 1-2-3/G does not use the names of the function keys. For example, NAME (F3) is captured as {F3}, not {NAME}, as you might expect.

To make the best use of memory in the keystroke buffer, 1-2-3/G abbreviates keystroke instructions whenever it can. For example, instead of recording the ESC key as {ESCAPE}, 1-2-3/G records it as {ESC}. What's more, if you press {ESC} three times, 1-2-3/G records this as {ESC 3}, instead of {ESC}{ESC}{ESC}.

How the Keystroke Editor Works: An Example

This section takes you through an example of how you might use the Keystroke Editor to create a simple macro and copy it to the worksheet. Ultimately the macro will select the Worksheet Global Attributes Font command and specify a 10-Point Helvetica Bold Font for the current worksheet.

Clearing the Buffer

Before you create a macro with Keystroke Editor, it's always a good idea to clear the keystroke buffer. That way, you will be starting with a clean slate. To clear the keystroke buffer, select the Utility Macro Keystroke Editor command to display the Keystroke Editor window. If you have been using 1-2-3/G for a while, the window should appear full of characters. When you're ready, select the Edit Clear All command from the Keystroke Editor menu. 1-2-3/G clears the keystrokes from the keystroke buffer, without giving you a warning message. The Keystroke Editor window now appears empty. To return to the worksheet, click your mouse on its title bar or press CTRL-F6 to move to it. If you press CTRL-F6, 1-2-3/G records {CTRL}{F6} in the Keystroke Editor window. Don't worry about this for now. You'll learn how to edit out undesirable keystrokes in a moment.

Note

> When you return to the worksheet, the Keystroke Editor window drops into the background. However, it remains open.

Capturing the Keystrokes

Once you've returned to the worksheet, you are ready to begin recording the keystrokes that will make up your macro. To begin, press **/** to activate 1-2-3/G main menu. Then type **wgaf**, for Worksheet Global Attributes Font. 1-2-3/G displays the Worksheet Global Attributes Font dialog box. Next, type **f** to select "Fonts." 1-2-3/G activates the "Fonts" section of the dialog box. Then type **e** to select font slot e. (Using the default Presentation Manager font set, slot e contains a 14-Point Helvetica font. You can press a letter for another font, if you so desire.) Having selected the font, press TAB to move to the Attributes section. Once there, type **b** to select the "Bold" check box. To complete the command, press ENTER.

If you typed the keystrokes in the previous paragraph, the Keystroke Editor should have recorded /wgaffe{TAB}b~. To see if this happened, activate the Keystroke Editor window. To do this you can click on the title bar for the window, press CTRL-F6 to move to it, or select the Utility Macros Keystroke Editor command. However, if you press any keys to activate the Keystroke Editor window, those keystrokes will be recorded in the window. Once again, don't worry about this. You can always edit them out.

When you activate the Keystroke Editor window, it contains the keystrokes /wgaffe{TAB}b~ as shown in Figure 10-18. However, if you look closely at Figure 10-18, it seems a mistake has been made. Instead of /wgaffe{TAB}b~ it reads /wgafffe{TAB}b~ (there is an extra f). No problem—the next section shows you how to fix this.

Editing Keystrokes

Editing keystrokes in the Keystroke Editor window is really rather simple. For example, to remove the extra f in Figure 10-18, make sure the Keystroke Editor is the active window. Then press ← to move the cursor to the first f and press DEL. 1-2-3/G deletes the character and closes up the space it occupied. If you have any other characters of your own that need deleting, please do so now. If you accidentally delete too many characters, don't worry about it. Simply use the arrow keys to move the cursor to the spot where the missing letter should be and type the appropriate letter(s).

Note

> To access Keystroke Editor's main menu with your keyboard, select ALT or MENU (F10). If you use the slash key (/), Keystroke Editor will ignore it and record it as a keystroke in the Keystroke Editor window.

If you have many characters to delete, you can use the Edit Clear command from Keystroke Editor's main menu. In preparation for this command, however, first highlight the characters you want to delete. To do this with your mouse, move the mouse pointer into the Keystroke Editor window. The shape of the mouse pointer changes to an I. Click and hold the left mouse button on the first character you want to delete and drag the mouse pointer to the right. As you drag, 1-2-3/G highlights the

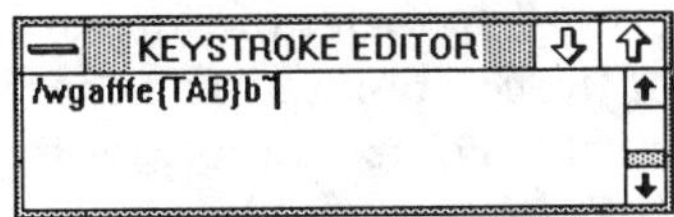

FIGURE 10-18 Captured keystrokes in the Keystroke Editor window

characters. Once the characters are highlighted, release the mouse button. To highlight characters with your keyboard, hold down the SHIFT key and use the arrow keys to expand the highlight. When you're ready, select Edit Clear or press DEL. The characters you highlighted are now permanently deleted from the keystroke buffer.

Playing Back the Keystrokes

Once you have the appropriate keystrokes recorded in the Keystroke Editor window, you can test those keystrokes by "playing" them back. This allows you to watch the 1-2-3/G desktop as the keystrokes are performed a second time.

You can play back all the keystrokes in the Keystroke Editor window, or just a selected group. If you do not select a group of keystrokes to play back, 1-2-3/G will play back all the keystrokes in the Keystroke Editor window. To play back a selected group of keystrokes, however, you must highlight those keystrokes. To do this, click and drag you mouse, or hold down the SHIFT key and use the arrow keys to expand the highlight.

When you're ready, select the Run Go command from Keystroke Editor main menu. 1-2-3/G deactivates the Keystroke Editor and plays back the keystrokes you selected. You can watch as the keystrokes are performed.

When the playback is completed, you can reactivate the Keystroke Editor window and make any required changes. You'll notice when you return to the Keystroke Editor window that no additional characters have been added as the result of playing the keystrokes back. If the existing keystrokes have the desired effect, you can copy them to the worksheet for use as a macro. Otherwise, you can edit the keystrokes and play them back again.

Copying the Keystrokes to the Worksheet

To copy the keystrokes in the Keystroke Editor window to the worksheet, you use the Edit Copy command followed by the Edit Paste command. You can copy all of the keystrokes in the Keystroke Editor window, or just a selected group. To copy selected group of characters, you must highlight those characters. To do this, click and drag you mouse or hold down the SHIFT key and use the arrow keys to expand the highlight. When you're ready, select the Edit Copy command from Keystroke Editor's menu. 1-2-3/G copies the characters you selected to the Clipboard.

To copy the keystroke characters from the Clipboard to the worksheet, activate the worksheet by clicking on its title bar or press CTRL-F6 to move to it. Then, move the cell pointer to where you want the new macro to begin. When you're ready, select the Edit Paste command from the menu for the worksheet window. 1-2-3/G copies the characters from the clipboard to the worksheet, starting at the location of the cell pointer. The characters are copied as labels in a column of consecutive cells. For example, Figure 10–19 shows what happens when you select the Edit Paste command with the cell pointer in cell A:B1.

Notice in Figure 10–19 that 1-2-3/G breaks up the characters copied from the Keystroke Editor into consecutive labels in a column of cells. 1-2-3/G breaks

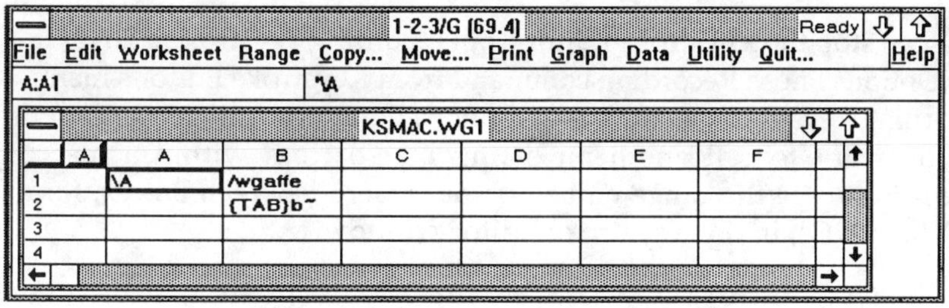

FIGURE 10–19 Keystrokes copied to the worksheet as a macro

the characters into lines based on the width of the cells in the current column. If you widen the column, 1-2-3/G will fit more characters on each line.

Naming and Running the Macro

Once the keystroke characters have been copied from the Keystroke Editor window to the worksheet as labels, you can name the new macro and run it just as you would any other macro in 1-2-3/G. For example, using Figure 10–19 as a model, move the cell pointer to cell A:A1 and type **\A**. Leave the cell pointer in cell A:A1 and use the Range Name Labels Right command to name the first cell of the macro (A:B1). To run the macro, press CTRL-A.

Tips on Using the Keystroke Editor

This section contains a number of tips you may find useful when using the Keystroke Editor to record macros.

- Consider typing the first letters of commands, rather than using the arrow keys to select commands. That way, your macro will appear more readable and be easier to debug when it is displayed in the Keystroke Editor window.
- You can also copy characters from the worksheet to the Keystroke Editor. To do this, select the Edit Copy command while in the worksheet and use the Edit Paste command in the Keystroke Editor window.
- You can have the Keystroke Editor minimized to an icon when keystrokes are played back. To do this, select the Options Minimize on Run command from the Keystroke Editor menu.
- You can debug the keystrokes in the Keystroke Editor window before copying them to the worksheet. To do this, select the Options Debug command from the Keystroke Editor menu. When you select this command, 1-2-3/G displays the same Debug Options dialog box that appears when you select the Utility Macros Debug command from the Worksheet Tool menu. See "Debugging a Macro" earlier in this chapter for details on how to debug macros.

- You can stop the Keystroke Editor from recording keystrokes. To do this, select the Options Pause Recording command from Keystroke Editor's menu. To start recording keystrokes again, select Options Pause Recording a second time.
- If you want to call another existing macro from within a macro you're recording, type the range name for that macro between braces, for example {MYMACRO}, in the Keystroke Editor window.

TRANSLATING MACROS

Lotus has made every effort to maintain keystroke compatibility between 1-2-3/G and prior releases of 1-2-3. Therefore, many of the macros you've created in prior releases will work in 1-2-3/G without modification. However, to offer the diverse feature set available in 1-2-3/G, as well as conform to the Presentation Manager–style interface, perfect keystroke compatibility with prior releases was simply not possible. Therefore, Lotus has included a Translate program with 1-2-3/G that translates macros from 1-2-3 Releases 2, 2.01, 2.2, and 3 for use with 1-2-3/G.

Not all of your Release 2 or Release 3 macros will require translation. To determine if translation is required, use the File Open or File Retrieve command to load the Release 2 (.WK1) or Release 3 (.WK3) worksheet file containing the macros into 1-2-3/G. Then try the macros. If the macros work the way they are supposed to, they do not need translating. However, if one or more of the macros causes an error or simply will not run, translation probably is required.

There are two ways you can access the Translate program. On the one hand, you can select the Utility Macros Translate command from the Worksheet Tool menu. When you select this command, 1-2-3/G displays the dialog box in Figure 10–20. On the other hand, you can run the Translate program directly from the OS/2 system prompt. Both methods are discussed in this section.

Note

> There are a number of commands in 1-2-3 Releases 2 and 3 that 1-2-3/G's Translate program simply cannot translate. There are also a few types of macros that 1-2-3/G may have difficulty translating. Most of these problems are related to the File, Print, and Graph menus in 1-2-3 Releases 2 and 3. For a listing of commands that cannot be translated as well as certain types of macros that may cause difficulty in translation, see "Translate Problems" at the end of this section.

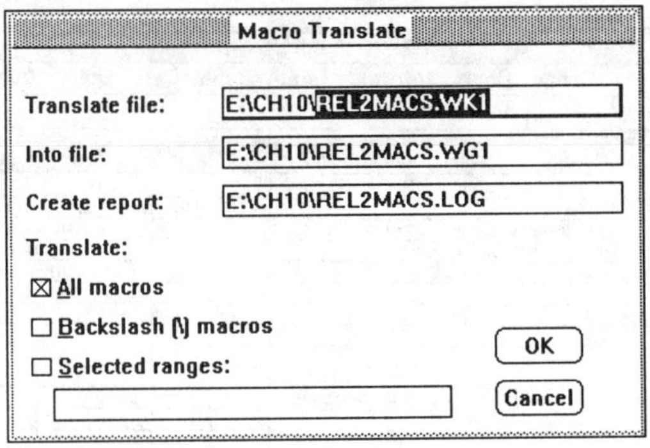

Macro Translate

Translate file: E:\CH10\REL2MACS.WK1

Into file: E:\CH10\REL2MACS.WG1

Create report: E:\CH10\REL2MACS.LOG

Translate:

☒ All macros

☐ Backslash (\) macros

☐ Selected ranges:

OK

Cancel

FIGURE 10–20 **The Translate dialog box**

The Translate program does not change your original 1-2-3 Release 2 (.WK1) or Release 3 (.WK3) file. Instead, it creates a new 1-2-3/G worksheet file (.WG1) in the current directory or the directory you specify. This new file contains the translated macros as well as any data from the Release 2 or 3 file. To see the effects the Translate program had on your macros, you must open the new 1-2-3/G worksheet file in a window and look at it.

Using the Utility Macros Translate Command

In preparation for the Utility Macros Translate command, load the 1-2-3 Release 2 (.WK1) or Release 3 (.WK3) worksheet file containing the macros you want translated into 1-2-3/G. You can use either the File Retrieve or File Open command to do this. For example, Figure 10–21 shows a Release 2 (.WK1) file already open on the desktop. After translation, the macros in this file will appear as shown in Figure 10–22.

Note

You do not need to load the Release 2 or Release 3 file to translate its macros with Utility Macros Translate. However, if you do, it makes the command go more smoothly. In addition, after translation, you can load the new 1-2-3/G file and compare the two side by side.

Once the Release 2 or 3 file is open on the desktop, activate it, and select Utility Macros Translate. 1-2-3/G displays the dialog box in Figure 10–20. In the "Translate file" text box, 1-2-3/G lists the path and name of the currently active worksheet file, provided it has a .WK1 or .WK3 extension. For example, in Figure 10–20, 1-2-3/G lists the filename REL2MACS.WK1. You can accept

1-2-3/G [69.4] Ready

File Edit Worksheet Range Copy... Move... Print Graph Data Utility Quit... Help

A:A1 '\A

REL2MACS.WK1

A	A	B	C	D	E	F	G	H	I
1	\A	/riCUSTFORM~					ADD	/rtINPUT~NEXT_DBR~	
2		{GETLABEL "Add to database (Y/N): ",YESNO}						{GOTO}NEXT_DBR~	
3		{IF YESNO="y"}{BRANCH ADD}						/rndNEXT_DBR~	
4		{BRANCH \A}						{DOWN}/rncNEXT_DBR~~	
5								{BRANCH \A}	
6	\C	/rlc{END}{R}~							
7									
8	\M	/ppomr240~qq							
9									
10	\X	/XLReturn to READY Mode (Y/N)? ~ANSWER~							
11		/XIANSWER="y"~/XGEND~							
12		/XGSTART~							
13									
14	\G	/gtb							
15		xRANGEX~aRANGEA~bRANGEB~							
16		otf{ESC}Three Year Plan~qvq							
17									
18									
19									
20									

FIGURE 10–21 A sample 1-2-3 Release 2 file with macros

this filename, or you can type the name of another .WK1 or .WK3 file on disk. If the file is stored outside the current directory, though, make sure to include the full drive and path to that directory in front of the filename.

In the "Into file" text box, 1-2-3/G displays the name of the new .WG1 file that will eventually contain the translated macros. By default, 1-2-3/G uses the

1-2-3/G [69.4] Ready

File Edit Worksheet Range Copy... Move... Print Graph Data Utility Quit... Help

A:A1 '\A

REL2MACS.WG1

A	A	B	C	D	E	F	G	H	I
1	\A	/riCUSTFORM~					ADD	/rtINPUT~NEXT_DBR~	
2		{GETLABEL "Add to database (Y/N): ",YESNO}						{GOTO}{esc}NEXT_DBR~	
3		{IF YESNO="y"}{BRANCH ADD}						/rndNEXT_DBR~	
4		{BRANCH \A}						{DOWN}/rncNEXT_DBR~~	
5								{BRANCH \A}	
6	\C	/rllc{END}{R}~							
7									
8	\M	/ppoqq							
9									
10	\X	{getlabel "Return to READY Mode (Y/N)? ";ANSWER}							
11		{if ANSWER="y"}{branch END}							
12		{branch START}							
13									
14	\G	/gtb/g							
15		axRANGEX~/gadaRANGEA~/gadbRANGEB~/g							
16		otf{home}{shift}{end}{del}Three Year Plan~/gv{?}{ctrl}{f4}n							
17									
18									
19									
20									

FIGURE 10–22 The macros in Figure 10–21 after translation

path and filename in the "Translate file" text box with a .WG1 extension. For example, in Figure 10–20, 1-2-3/G shows the name REL2MACS.WG1. You can accept this filename, or you can type a new one of your own. If you want the new .WG1 file stored in a directory outside the current directory, be sure to include the path and name of the directory in front of the filename.

Note

> You can also specify a .WK1 or a .WK3 file name here in the "Into file" text box.

In the "Create Report" text box, 1-2-3/G lists the name of an ASCII text file that will be used to record any errors that take place during translation. By default, 1-2-3/G uses the name of the file in the "Translate file" text box followed by a .LOG extension. For example, in Figure 10–20, 1-2-3/G lists the name REL2MACS.LOG. You can accept the default filename or provide one of your own. If you want the file stored outside the current directory, though, be sure to include the appropriate drive and path in front of the filename. After translation is complete, you can load this file into a word processor, or use the File Import command to view any errors that may have taken place during the translation.

The check boxes in the "Translate section" of the Translate dialog box allow you to select which macros you want translated. If you select "All macros" (the default), 1-2-3/G will translate all the macros in the Release 2 or 3 file. If you select "Backslash (\) macros", only those macros whose names begin with a backslash followed by a letter, for example **\A**, will be translated. If you select the "Selected ranges" check box, 1-2-3/G activates the adjacent text box. Type the range names of the macros you want translated, separating each of them with a comma. You must type the range names. You cannot point to them or press NAME (F3) to see a list of them.

Note

> When you translate a .WK1 or .WK3 file to a .WG1 file, 1-2-3/G assigns a temporary file format to the new .WG1 file. Therefore, you must open the temporary .WG1 file and use the File Save command to save the file in .WG1 format.

To complete the Utility Macros Translate command, select OK, or press ENTER. 1-2-3/G begins translating the macros in the REL2MACS.WK1 file. It also translates any subroutines called by those macros. It then creates a new file, REL2MACS.WG1 in this case, that contains the translated macros along with any data from the original file (REL2MACS.WK1). Any errors that occurred during the translation are recorded in the log file (REL2MACS.LOG). To see the effects of the translation, select the File Open command to load the new 1-2-3/G file (REL2MACS.WG1) from disk.

Examining and Testing the Changes

After you translate the macros in a Release 2 or 3 file to a new .WG1 file, load the new .WG1 file and examine the changes that occurred. Also, test each of the macros by running them. Sometimes the Translate program may not produce the results you expect. In addition, you may want to use the File Import Text command to import the .LOG file into the worksheet, to see if 1-2-3/G recorded any errors during translation.

As mentioned, Figures 10–21 and 10–22 show a before and after view of translating the macros in the REL2MACS.WK1 (Release 2) worksheet file. (Figure 10–22 shows the REL2MACS.WG1 1-2-3/G worksheet file.) Let's take a moment to look at some of the changes that took place.

In some cases the translation changes are rather subtle and do not materially affect the macro. For example, the first macro in Figure 10–21 (starting in cell A:B1) is a data entry macro. This macro used the Range Input command to display a custom form for data entry. When the user presses ESC to complete data entry, the macro poses the question "Add to database (Y/N)" in the Control Line. If the user types "y" and presses ENTER, the ADD subroutine (cell A:H1) is processed. This subroutine copies the new data to the database. If the user types anything else, the macro is repeated and the data entry form is again displayed. As you can see in Figure 10–22, this macro and its subroutine made it through translation completely intact. In fact, there is only one minor change in cell A:H2 of Figure 10–22. 1-2-3/G has added an {ESC} in between {GOTO} and the range name NEXT_DBR, to accommodate 1-2-3/G's new Range Goto dialog box.

The second macro in Figure 10–21, starting in cell A:B6, has also been slightly changed. This macro uses Release 2's Range Label Center command to center some labels in rows of consecutive cells. However, as you can see in Figure 10–22, it was necessary to slightly alter this macro. In 1-2-3/G, you must select the Range Label command and then select from "Labels," "Values," or "Cell display." Therefore, 1-2-3/G has added an extra *l* to the macro, to select "Labels" from the Range Label dialog box. Otherwise, the rest of the macro remains the same.

In some cases, the translation is not entirely successful. For example, in Figure 10–21, the third macro (starting in cell A:B8) uses Release 2's Print Printer Options Margins Right command to specify a right margin setting of 240 characters. However, in 1-2-3/G print margins are measured in inches (or millimeters), not characters. Therefore, is was necessary to materially alter this macro.

As you can see in Figure 10–22, the macro has been altered to select Print Printer Options Quit Quit. Therefore, this macro will display the Print Printer dialog box and select the "Options" command button. This causes 1-2-3/G to display the Options dialog box. The macro then selects the Quit command button twice, once from the Options dialog box and again from the Print Printer dialog box. This returns 1-2-3/G to READY mode. Therefore, the macro performs absolutely no function whatsoever, and will require a complete rewrite.

As mentioned, there are certain commands that 1-2-3/G cannot translate. Many of the Options selections from Release 2's Print Printer command are included in this category. See "Translate Problems" later in this section for more details on this.

The fourth macro in Figure 10–21, starting in cell A:B10, is an excerpt from a bigger macro. It uses /X macro commands to get a response from the user. Although the /X commands are supported in Release 2, 2.01, 2.2, and 3, they are a relic from Release 1A and are not supported in 1-2-3/G. However, each of these commands has an equivalent. For example, the /XL command is equivalent to the {GETLABEL} command. As you can see in Figure 10–22, 1-2-3/G engineers this translation nicely. In addition, the /XI command is equivalent to {IF}, and the /XG command is equivalent to {BRANCH}. These commands are also successfully translated.

The last macro in Figure 10–21, starting in cell A:B14, is a graph macro. This macro defines three graph ranges as well as a title for the graph and displays it on screen. As mentioned, 1-2-3/G often has difficulty translating macros that use the Graph command. However, in this case, 1-2-3/G completes the translation successfully. As you can see, though, it was necessary to substantially modify the macro to make it work in 1-2-3/G.

As a final precaution, let's take a look at the REL2MACS.LOG file to see what errors 1-2-3/G recorded during translation. To do this, move the cell pointer to a blank range in the worksheet and select File Import Text. 1-2-3/G displays the File Import Text dialog box. In the "File name" text box, type REL2MACS.LOG or select it from the list box below. Press ENTER or select OK to complete the command. 1-2-3/G imports the contents of the file into the worksheet, starting at the location of the cell pointer. The file contains the single entry **(A:B8) Print Printer Options Margins not supported in 1-2-3/G, omitted**. This coincides with the failure to effectively translate the print macro in cell A:B8.

Running Translate from the OS/2 or DOS System Prompt

You can also run the Translate program directly from the DOS or OS/2 system prompt. In fact, running Translate in this way provides you with a few more reporting options than running Translate from within 1-2-3/G. For example, you can have the contents of the error log file sent to the screen as 1-2-3/G is translating the file. You can also have 1-2-3/G create a detailed report that gives you information about the translation on a cell-by-cell basis.

The program that actually does the translating is 123GXMAC.EXE. You can run this program from either the DOS or OS/2 system prompt. The 123GXMAC.EXE program accepts up to six arguments, two of which are mandatory. The mandatory arguments are the type of worksheet file (Release 2 or 3) you are translating and the file names you want to translate from and to. The other four types of arguments are optional. These arguments allow you to specify various display, report, translation, and international options. Each of these argument types is explained in more detail below.

To use the 123GXMAC.EXE program, type **123gxmax** followed by a space at the OS/2 or DOS system prompt. Follow this with a display argument and an international argument. Then, follow these with the rest of the arguments you want to use in any order. Separate each argument with a space. The format of your command line entry should be as follows (the optional arguments are displayed in square braces []):

```
123GXMAC [display-option] [international-option]
worksheet-types macro-files [report-options]
[translation options]
```

Table 10-3 shows a description of what each of these arguments means.

The following command line example translates the 1-2-3 Release 2.01 file REL2MACS.WK1 to REL2MACS.WG1. All macros are translated and a report of errors is sent to your screen as they occur.

```
123GXMAC -do -m123r201 -iREL2MACS.WK1 -oREL2MACS.WG1
```

This next example translates the 1-2-3 Release 2.2 file SALEMAC.WK1 file to SALEMAC.WG1. However, it also sends a report to the file PROB.LOG of both original cell contents and translated cell contents for those cells used in the translation.

```
123GXMAC -m123r22 -iSALEMAC.WK1 -oSALEMAC.WG1 -LBVPROB.LOG
```

Finally, this next command line example translates the 1-2-3 Release 2.01 file PROD.WK1 to PROD.WG1, but only one conventional range name (SCHED) is translated. In addition, all backslash (\) macros are translated.

```
123GXMAC -m123r201 -iPROD.WK1 -oPROD.WG1 -rSCHED -k
```

Translate Problems

You cannot use the Translate program to translate files from 1-2-3 Release 1A (.WKS) or Symphony (.WR1) files. However, if you have access to a copy of 1-2-3 Release 2, 2.01, or 2.2, you can load those files into that product and save them as .WK1 files. Once they are saved in .WK1 format, you can translate them.

TABLE 10-3 Table of 123GXMAC.EXE Argument Descriptions

Argument	Description
display-option	Use this optional argument to send a report to your screen during the translation. To have 1-2-3/G report only the errors found during the translation, type **-de**. To have the entire translation shown on your screen, type **-do**. To turn off the screen display, type **-ds**.
internat'l-option	This optional argument lets you specify a default argument separator. Type **-a** followed by a ; (semicolon), . (period), or , (comma). The comma is the default and need not be specified.
worksheet-types	This mandatory argument shows the release of 1-2-3 used to create the file you want to translate. Type **-m** followed by 123R201 (Release 2.01), 123R22 (Release 2.2), or 123R30 (Release 3).
macro-files	This mandatory argument has two parts, the name of the file you want to translate from and the name of the file you want to translate to. Type **-i** followed by the full path and name of the Release 2 or 3 you want to translate. Leave a space, and type **-o** followed by the full path and name of the .WG1, .WK1, or .WK3 file you want to translate to.
report-option	This optional argument lets you record reports on the translation in a text file. Type **-LEN** to create a report of errors. Or, type **-L** followed immediately by one of these arguments: **B** shows the original cell contents and the translated contents, **S** shows only the original cell contents, **X** shows only the translated contents. To this, add: **V** shows only cells used in translation, or **A** shows all strings or labels. For example, -LBV shows a report of both original and translated cell contents, but only for those cells used in the translation. Immediately after the report-option, specify the name of the text file that will store the data, for example -LENPROBLEMS.LOG.
translation-option	This optional argument specifies one or more options for translation. To specify that only specific macros be translated, type **-r** followed by the appropriate range names, separating each of them by commas. To translate just backslash macros, for example \A, type **-k**. If you do not use a translation option argument, 1-2-3/G translates all the macros in the source file.

You cannot translate a file that has been password protected. To translate the file, you must remove the password protection. See Chapter 5, "File Management," for information on how to remove password protection from a worksheet file.

You cannot translate macros that activate or use add-in products. Add-ins are not supported in 1-2-3/G.

1-2-3/G has difficulty translating certain types of macros. A list of these follows:

- In Chapter 11, you'll learn about self-modifying macros. Self-modifying macros are capable of changing their own code. This is usually done by copying values or code to specific cells in the macro, so that it can change to meet the needs of a given situation. Before translating this type of macro, make sure that cells in the macro that will be changed contain either a value or acceptable macro code. In addition, make sure that the modifying instruction itself does not require translation.
- 1-2-3/G has difficulty translating macros that begin in a mode other than READY mode. For example, if the macro begins in MENU mode, 1-2-3/G may not translate it correctly.
- If the macro you're translating uses /File Xtract to extract data to something other than a .WG1 file, correct this before you translate the file. Otherwise the macro will not work in 1-2-3/G.
- In 1-2-3 Release 3, the commands {LASTFILE} and {NEXTFILE} allow you to navigate between files. However, commands that allow you to navigate between files are not supported in 1-2-3/G.

As mentioned, there are a number of commands that 1-2-3/G's Translate program does not support. In some cases, 1-2-3/G may replace the command with a comment, for example {—}, in the translated file. A list of nonsupported commands follows:

- /File—Erase and List.
- /Graph Group.
- /Graph Name Reset.
- /Graph Options—Format, Grid, Scale, Color, B&W, and Data Labels.
- /Graph Reset—A-F, Options, Ranges, and X.
- /Graph Type—Mixed and Features.
- /Print Printer—Align and Clear.
- /Print Printer Options—Margins, Setup, and Page-Length.
- /Print Printer Options Other—Formatted and Unformatted.
- /Worksheet Global Default—Printer, Status, and Update. The Other option is supported for international only.

SUMMARY

This chapter gives you the basic skills you need to begin creating macros. It gets you ready to make the most of the next chapter, "The Macro Programming Language."

The chapter begins with a discussion of macro basics. For example, you learned about the various types of keystroke instructions that you can include in a macro. You also learned how to name a macro and how to run it using either a CTRL-key sequence or RUN (ALT-F3). You also learned how to terminate macro execution and how to save macros for future use.

Using menu commands in macros was also covered in this chapter. Several examples are given that show you how to write a macro that access 1-2-3/G's menus. For example, you can now write a macro that formats or prints a worksheet range.

This chapter also shows you how to write an auto-executing macro. An auto-executing macro is a macro that is run automatically whenever you open the worksheet file containing it.

Debugging your macros was also covered in this chapter. Specifically, you learned how to use STEP and TRACE mode to locate and correct errors in your macros.

This chapter also shows you how to build a macro library. Macro libraries allow you to share your more commonly used macros across various worksheet files.

This chapter also shows how to use the Keystroke Editor utility to build a macro. This handy utility captures all the keystrokes you make in 1-2-3/G and translates them into macro instructions. You can then copy those keystroke instructions to the worksheet for use as a macro.

Finally, this chapter shows you how you can use 1-2-3/G's Translate program to translate your 1-2-3 Release 2 and 3 macros for use in 1-2-3/G. The Translate program may save you time and effort in updating your existing macros for use in 1-2-3/G.

The Macro Programming Language

In the previous chapter, you learned how to create simple 1-2-3/G macros. For the most part, the commands used in the chapter were representations of keystrokes. Although macros of this type can be quite useful, they can only take you so far in automating your work.

In this chapter, you will learn how to use 1-2-3/G's more advanced macro commands, those used for programming 1-2-3/G. With these commands you can perform any of the following:

- Get user input.
- Manipulate data in cells.
- End and suspend macro execution.
- Perform conditional processing.
- Branch.
- Call subroutines.
- Trap errors.
- Create data entry forms.
- Create custom dialog boxes.
- Change the effect of CTRL-BREAK.
- Control the screen.
- Control windows.
- Control recalculation.
- Access OS/2.
- Read and write ASCII files.

Table 11–1 shows 1-2-3/G's macro programming commands organized according to these different categories.

Each of these categories is discussed in detail in this chapter. In addition, near the end of the chapter, you'll find a section on using formulas in macro commands and how to create your own self-modifying macros.

What's New

As you might expect, 1-2-3/G incorporates many of 1-2-3 Release 3's macro commands. For example, the Release 3 commands for working with forms—{FORM}, {APPENDBELOW}, and {APPENDRIGHT}—are all available in 1-2-3/G. In addition, the {CE} or {CLEARENTRY} command is available for clearing the information that 1-2-3/G automatically displays following a Control line prompt or in a text box (for example, the filename information that automatically appears when you select File Retrieve). All of these commands are welcome additions to the power of 1-2-3/G.

In addition, 1-2-3/G has new programming commands:

- {WAITDIALOG} You can use this command to temporarily suspend a macro in order to respond to a dialog box. Without it, your macro would not be able to pause for input.
- {ALERT} Displays a given message in the first line of a dialog box and presents command buttons for you to select from.
- {TONE} Gives you more control over the frequency and duration of the bell than the {BELL} command.
- {WACTIVATE}, {WMOVE}, and {WSIZE} These new commands let you activate, move, and size windows on the 1-2-3/G desktop.

Besides these new commands, 1-2-3/G also incorporates many subtle changes to existing commands. For example, the {GETLABEL} and {GETNUMBER} commands now display dialog boxes. In addition, the {SYSTEM CMD} command lets you exit to the operating system temporarily in the same way as the /System command does in previous releases of 1-2-3.

Finally, if you have used the {MENUBRANCH} and {MENUCALL} commands to create your own custom menus in previous releases of 1-2-3, you know how useful these commands can be. In 1-2-3/G, however, your custom menus appear within dialog boxes. In fact, Lotus has shifted the emphasis of these commands from creating custom menus to creating custom dialog boxes. This is somewhat disappointing, especially if you expect to create your own custom menus that work like 1-2-3/G's command menu; there are no macro commands for doing this in 1-2-3/G. It is also disappointing from the standpoint that these commands represent the limit of 1-2-3/G's ability to create custom dialog boxes—while you can place items within a dialog box, you cannot create your own radio buttons or check boxes. Nevertheless, you can still use {MENUBRANCH} and {MENUCALL} to perform some powerful operations in 1-2-3/G (see "Creating Custom Dialog Boxes").

TABLE 11-1 Macro Programming Commands

Getting User Input

Command	Description
{?}	Suspends a macro for input until you press ENTER.
{ALERT *message, [type], [icon]*}	Displays *message* in the first line of a dialog box and presents command buttons for you to select from.
{CE} or {CLEARENTRY}	Clears the information that automatically appears in the Control line or text box—for example, the filename information that appears for File Retrieve.
{GET *location*}	Suspends macro execution until a key is pressed; stores the keypress in *location* as a label.
{GETLABEL *prompt,location*}	Displays *prompt* in a dialog box, waits for input, and stores the input as a string in *location.*
{GETNUMBER *prompt,location*}	Displays *prompt* in a dialog box, waits for input, and stores the input as a number in *location.*
{LOOK *location*}	Places the first keystroke you made during the noninteractive portion of a macro as a label in *location.*

Manipulating Data in Cells

Command	Description
{BLANK *location*}	Erases the contents of *location.*
{CONTENTS *target-location, source-location, [width], [cell-format]*}	Copies *source-location* to *target-location* as a label.
{LET *location,entry*}	Enters *entry* (a value or string) in *location.*
{PUT *location, column-offset row-offset,entry*}	Places a number or label in *location.*

(continued)

Stopping and Suspending Macros (*cont.*)

Command	Description
{QUIT}	Ends macro processing.
{WAIT *time-number*}	Suspends macro execution until the specified time number has elapsed.
{WAITDIALOG}	Temporarily suspends macro execution allowing you to respond to a 1-2-3/G dialog box.

Conditional Processing

Command	Description
{FOR *counter,start-number, stop-number, subroutine*}	Performs *subroutine* while *start-number* + *counter* is less than *stop-number*; each pass increases *counter* by *step-number*.
{FORBREAK}	Ends the current {FOR} loop.
{IF *condition*}	Evaluates whether *condition* is true or false. If true, executes the next command on the same line. If false, skips to the next line.

Branching

Command	Description
{BRANCH *location*}	Transfers macro control to *location*.
{DISPATCH *location*}	Performs an indirect branch to the cell whose name or address is in *location*.

Subroutines

Command	Description
{*subroutine [argument1], [argument2],..., [argumentn]*}	Performs a subroutine call, optionally passing arguments to it.
{DEFINE *location1*, location2, ...,*locationn*}	Specifies cells that will be used to store arguments to be passed to a subroutine.
{RESTART}	Clears the subroutine stack; 1-2-3/G then acts as though the next instruction is the beginning of a new macro.
{RETURN}	Used in subroutines to return macro control to the next macro instruction following the {*subroutine*} call.

Error Trapping

Command	Description
{ONERROR *branch-location,* *[message-location]*}	Branches to the macro instructions at *branch-location* when an error occurs.

Working with Data Entry Forms

Command	Description
{APPENDBELOW *target-location,* *source-location*}	Copies the data in *source-location* to the bottom of *target-location.*
{APPENDRIGHT *target-location,}* *source-location*	Copies the data in *source-location* to the right of *target-location.*
{FORM *input-location,* *[call-table],[include-list],* *[exclude-list]*	Suspends macro execution allowing you to enter input in a specified range.

Custom Dialog Boxes

Command	Description
{MENUBRANCH *location*}	Creates a dialog box with the items in *location,* waits for you to select an item from the dialog box, and branches to the instructions for that item.
{MENUCALL *location*}	Creates a dialog box with the items in *location,* waits for you to select an item from the dialog box, and performs a subroutine call to the instructions at *location.*

Changing the Effect of CTRL-BREAK

Command	Description
{BREAK}	Same as pressing CTRL-BREAK in a menu or a dialog box.
{BREAKOFF}	Disables {BREAK} and CTRL-BREAK during a macro.
{BREAKON}	Reinstates use of {BREAK} and CTRL-BREAK during a macro.

(continued)

Sounding Tones (*cont.*)

Command	Description
{BEEP *tone-number*}	Sounds a tone.
{TONE *frequency, duration*}	Sounds a tone of a specified frequency for a specified duration.

Controlling the Screen

Command	Description
{FRAMEOFF}	Turns off the display of the worksheet frame.
{FRAMEON}	Turns the display of the worksheet frame back on.
{GRAPHOFF}	Cancels a {GRAPHON} command.
{GRAPHON *[named-graph], [nodisplay]*}	Displays the current graph or a named graph.
{INDICATE *string*}	Changes the mode indicator to *string*.
{PANELOFF}	Prevents updating of the control panel.
{PANELON}	Reinstates updating of the control panel.
{WINDOWSOFF}	Prevents redrawing of the worksheet area of the screen.
{WINDOWSON}	Reinstates redrawing of the worksheet area of the screen.

Controlling Windows

Command	Description
{WACTIVATE *[windowname]*}	Makes the last active worksheet window, or the window specified by *windowname*, the active window.
{WMOVE *x,y, [windowname]*}	Moves the active window, or the window specified by *windowname*, *x* inches to the right and *y* inches above the lower-left corner of the 1-2-3/G desktop.
{WSIZE *x,y, [windowname]*}	Sizes the active window, or the window specified by *windowname*, *x* inches across and *y* inches high.

Controlling Recalculation

Command	Description
{RECALC *location,*	Recalculates the values in *location* in row-by-row

(continued)

Controlling Recalculation (*cont.*)

[condition], [iterations*]*}	fashion using the specified number of iterations.
{RECALCCOL location, *[condition],[iterations]*}	Recalculates the values in *location* in column by column fashion using the specified number of iterations or until *condition* is met.

Accessing OS/2

Command	Description
{SYSTEM *command*}	Temporarily exits 1-2-3/G and executes the specified OS/2 command.

Reading and Writing ASCII Files

Command	Description
{CLOSE}	Closes an open ASCII text file.
{FILESIZE *location*}	Enters the size (in bytes) of the open ASCII text file in *location*.
{GETPOS *location*}	Determines the position of the file pointer in the open text file; stores position in *location*.
{OPEN *file-name, access-type*}	Opens an ASCII file for processing.
{READ *byte-count, location*}	Reads the open ASCII file beginning at the current file pointer location, copies the specified number of bytes to *location*, and advances the file pointer by *byte-count*.
{READLN *location*}	Reads the open ASCII file beginning at the current file pointer location, places the remainder of the current line in *location*.
{SETPOS *offset-number*}	Positions the file pointer in the open ASCII file to *offset-number* byte positions from the start of the file.
{WRITE *string*}	Writes *string* to the open ASCII text file, beginning at the current file pointer location.
{WRITELN *string*}	Writes *string* followed by carriage return/linefeed to the open ASCII text file, beginning at the current file pointer location.

MACRO COMMAND SYNTAX

In the previous chapter, you learned several rules of macro command syntax. For example, you learned that every macro instruction must appear within curly braces, such as {DOWN}, and that you cannot split a macro instruction onto more than one line.

The same basic rules apply for all of 1-2-3/G's macro programming commands. However, macro programming commands that accept arguments, as is the case with most of 1-2-3/G's programming commands, have some additional syntax rules that are illustrated in Figure 11–1.

The first part of a macro instruction is the *keyword,* which names the action the macro instruction is to perform. The keyword is preceded by a left curly brace ({) and followed by a space.

Arguments provide the information necessary to execute the macro command and are separated by (you guessed it) argument separators, usually commas. (You can also use semicolons to separate arguments.) Arguments can be numbers, strings, cell addresses, range references, range names, or conditions (the result of logical formulas). The last argument is always followed by a right curly brace (}).

Some arguments are optional, in which case they appear in brackets ([ ]), for example, {WACTIVATE *[windowname]*}. This means that you can use {WACTIVATE} without an argument.

When arguments appear in italics without brackets, you *must* include them in the argument list. For example, {GETLABEL *prompt,location*} means that you must provide a *prompt* and a *location* argument.

Occasionally, you may want to omit an optional argument but include another optional argument that follows in the argument list. For example, the general format for the {ALERT} command is {ALERT *message,[type],[icon]*}. If you want to omit the *[type]* argument, you would use this syntax: {ALERT *message,,[icon]*}.

GETTING USER INPUT

1-2-3/G has several commands to help you get user input—{?}, {GET}, {GETLABEL}, {GETNUMBER}, {LOOK}, {ALERT}, and {CE}. You can use these commands to pause a macro and request numbers and labels, menu selections, responses to prompts and command buttons, and the like.

The {?} Command

As you learned in the previous chapter, the {?} (pause) command lets you pause a macro until the user presses ENTER. While the macro is suspended, the user

FIGURE 11–1 Macro command syntax

can type any number of keystrokes. These keystrokes might move the cell pointer or command menu pointer, complete part of a command, or enter data that the macro will then process.

For example, the \N macro in Figure 11–2 shows how you might use the {?} command to solicit a response from the user. This macro accesses the Note utility and places a table of cell and range notes in the worksheet starting at a cell location you provide. The macro begins by issuing the Utility Note Options Table command. Then, while 1-2-3/G is displaying the prompt "Enter:," the {?} command pauses the macro for you to enter a starting location for the table. When you press ENTER, as you often do to confirm a cell address or range name, 1-2-3/G interprets the key as an instruction to continue the macro, not as a confirmation response. Therefore, you must include a ~ (tilde) following the {?} in the macro. This instruction causes 1-2-3/G to accept your input. Without the tilde, the macro will not run as expected.

Note

There is one problem with the {?} command that is new to 1-2-3/G. Rather than pressing ENTER, suppose you complete a dialog box entry by clicking on the OK button. The {?} command remains in effect and may cause some problems farther down in your macro. In addition, if the {?} command is the last command in the macro, a CMD indicator remains in the worksheet window, signifying that the macro has not actually ended but is pausing for input. If you try to run another macro, 1-2-3/G will ignore your request; before you can invoke another macro, you must press ENTER until the CMD indicator is cleared. In general, if you want to pause a macro in a dialog box, use the {WAITDIALOG} command instead of {?}.

Keep in mind that you can use the {?} (pause) command to pause a macro at almost any point to get a response. For example, suppose you want to create a

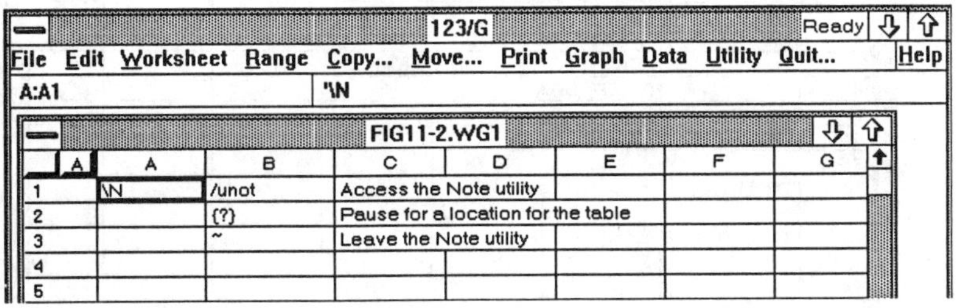

123/G Ready

File Edit Worksheet Range Copy... Move... Print Graph Data Utility Quit... Help

A:A1 '\N

FIG11-2.WG1

A	A	B	C	D	E	F	G
1	\N	/unot	Access the Note utility				
2		{?}	Pause for a location for the table				
3		~	Leave the Note utility				
4							
5							

FIGURE 11–2 The {?} Command

macro that jumps to a cell after pausing for you to provide a cell address or range name. Here is some sample code that you might use:

```
{GOTO}{?}~
```

This macro presses GOTO (F5), which, as you know, causes 1-2-3/G to display the Range Goto dialog box. You can then select a range name from the list, or enter a range name or cell address in the Range(s) text box. When you press ENTER, 1-2-3/G moves the cell pointer to the upper-left cell in the range. As with the previous example, a ~ (tilde) follows the {?} command because without it, you would have to press ENTER twice.

The {GET} Command

The {GET} command pauses a macro until you press a key. The syntax of the command is

{GET *location*}

When you press a key, 1-2-3/G stores your keystroke in *location* as a label. For example, if you press *y*, 1-2-3/G stores it as 'y. However, when you press any of the keys in Table 10–1 of Chapter 10, 1-2-3/G stores it in macro-instruction format. For example, if you press END, 1-2-3/G stores it as '{END}.

You can specify a cell address or a range name for *location*. If you specify a range, 1-2-3/G stores your keystroke in the upper-left cell of the range.

The {GET} command is used most frequently to get a single-letter response. For example, the first line of the macro in Figure 11–3 displays the prompt

123G.EXE (69.4) — Ready

File Edit Worksheet Range Copy... Move... Print Graph Data Utility Quit... Help

A:B2 '{GET KEYPRESS}

FIG11-3.WG1

A	A	B	C	D	E	F	G
1	\P	Choose F(ile) or P(rinter)?					
2		{GET KEYPRESS}					
3		{ESC}					
4		{IF KEYPRESS="f"}{BRANCH TO_FILE}					
5		{IF KEYPRESS="p"}{BRANCH TO_PRINTER}					
6		{BEEP}{BRANCH \P}					
7							
8	KEYPRESS	{FC}					
9							
10	TO_FILE	/pf{CE}{?}~gq					
11							
12	TO_PRINTER	/ppgq					
13							
14							

FIGURE 11–3 The {GET} command

"Choose F(ile) or P(rinter)?" in the Control line, prompting you to type F or P. The {GET KEYPRESS} command in the second line then pauses the macro and waits for you to press a key. It then records the key you press in the range KEYPRESS (cell B8). The next line in the macro, {ESC}, erases the prompt from the Control line. The {IF} statement in the next line then tests the label in the KEYPRESS range. If it is equal to 'f or 'F (you pressed *f* or *F*), the macro then executes the {BRANCH TO_FILE} command, which causes the macro to branch to the cell named TO_FILE (cell B10). As you can see, the instructions in this cell issue the Print File command, pause the macro for you to enter a filename (after clearing the File name box; see {CE} below), then issue the Go and Quit commands.

If you pressed a key other than *f* or *F*, the macro executes the second {IF} command in cell B5, which tests whether the label in KEYPRESS is equal to 'p or 'P (you pressed *p* or *P*). If it is equal to either one, the macro executes the {BRANCH TO_PRINTER} command, which causes the macro to branch to TO_PRINTER (cell B12). The code in this cell issues the Print Printer Go and Quit commands. However, if you pressed any key besides *f*, *F*, *p*, or *P*, the macro beeps and branches back to \P (the start of the macro, cell B1) and executes the macro again.

Note

In certain instances, you may want the user to respond to a prompt with an END key sequence, such as END →, END CTRL-PGUP, END CTRL-PGDN, and the like. When this is the case, you should use two {GET} commands together—for example, {GET KEY1}{GET KEY2}. The first {GET} command stores the END keystroke, and the second one stores the keystroke that follows (for example, {R} for →).

The {GETLABEL} Command

The {GETLABEL} command lets you get string input using a dialog box. The syntax of the command is

```
{GETLABEL prompt,location}
```

When 1-2-3/G executes this command, it displays a dialog box as in Figure 11-4. The first argument, *prompt*, is any text string of up to 88 characters in length to be used as a prompt. You can also use a range name or the address of a cell that contains the prompt string. You can even use a text formula to produce the prompt (see Chapter 1).

Once you type a response and press ENTER, or click on the OK button, 1-2-3/G stores your response in *location* as a left-aligned label. If you press ENTER or click on the OK button before typing anything, 1-2-3/G stores the default label prefix (usually ') in *location*. Like the other commands in this section,

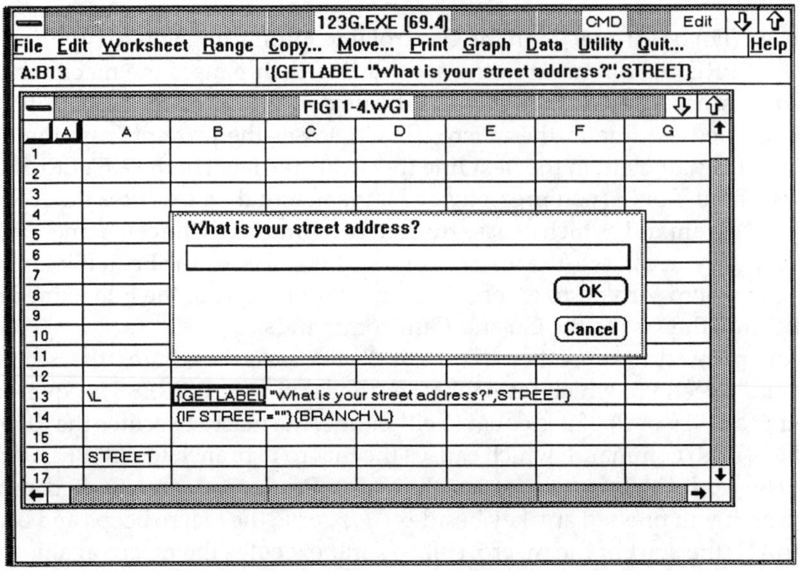

FIGURE 11–4 The {GETLABEL} command

you can supply a range name or cell address for *location*. If you specify a multicell range, 1-2-3/G will store your response in the upper-left cell of the range.

Figure 11–4 shows a macro that uses the {GETLABEL} command to get a street address and the dialog box that the macro produces. (The macro code begins in cell B13.) As you can see, the {GETLABEL} command in the first line of the macro places the prompt "What is your street address?" at the top of the dialog box. After you type a street address and press ENTER, or click on the OK button, 1-2-3/G stores your response in the range STREET (cell B16) as a label. The {IF} command in cell B14 then tests the label in STREET to see if it is equal to null (""), meaning that you pressed ENTER immediately. If it is equal to null, control transfers to the start of the macro so that you can try entering the street address again.

By using {GETLABEL} in this way, you can get not only standard text strings, but also alphanumeric strings that begin with numbers (such as "1234 Newport Ave.") without any concern that 1-2-3/G may reject them.

The {GETNUMBER} Command

The {GETNUMBER} command is similar to {GETLABEL} except that you use it to get numeric input. The syntax of the command is

{GETNUMBER *prompt,location*}

See {GETLABEL} for an explanation of the arguments.

The response you enter to a {GETNUMBER} command can be a number, a numeric formula (for example, @PI*3^2), or a reference to a cell containing a number or numeric formula. If you press ENTER, or click on the OK button, before typing a response, 1-2-3/G places ERR in *location*. In addition, if you enter a string, a string formula, or a reference to a string, 1-2-3/G also enters ERR in *location*.

Figure 11-5 shows the dialog box produced by the {GETNUMBER} command in cell B13. As you can see, the {GETNUMBER} command places the prompt "What is the invoice amount?" at the top of the dialog box. After you type a number and press ENTER, or click on the OK button, 1-2-3/G stores your response in the range INV_AMT (cell B16) as a number. For example, if you type **129.95** as a response, 1-2-3/G places that value in cell B16. Likewise, if cell A3 contains the number 129.95, and you type **A3** in response to the dialog box, 1-2-3/G also records 129.95 (the value in cell A3) in cell B16.

After you type a response, the {IF} command in cell B14 then tests the value in INV_AMT to see if it is equal to ERR, meaning you either typed a label in response to the prompt or pressed ENTER immediately without typing a response. If the cell contains ERR, the macro beeps and control transfers to the start of the macro (cell B13) to have you enter an invoice amount again.

The {LOOK} Command

The {LOOK} command checks the contents of the typeahead buffer for keystrokes and places the first keystroke in the buffer in a cell. The syntax of the command is

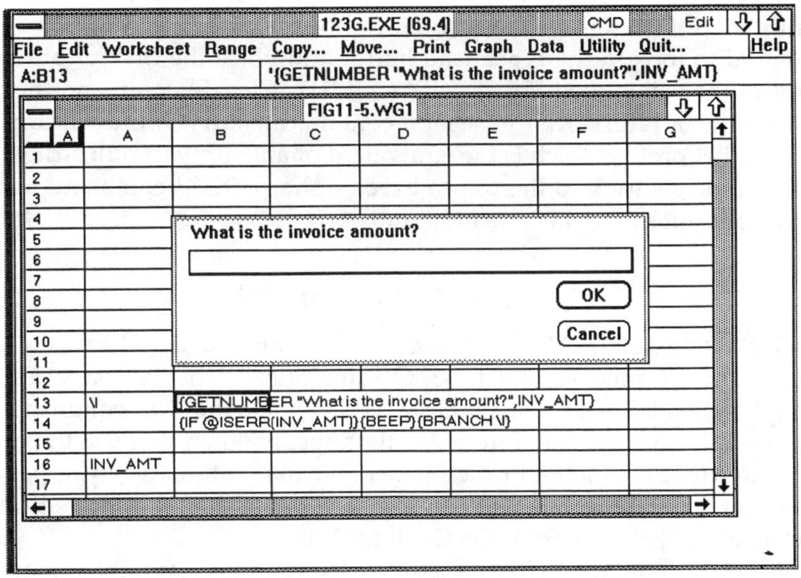

FIGURE 11-5 The {GETNUMBER} command

123G.EXE (69.4) Ready

File Edit Worksheet Range Copy... Move... Print Graph Data Utility Quit... Help

A:B1 '{LOOK FIRST_KEY}

FIG11-6.WG1

A	A	B	C	D	E	F	G
1	\K	{LOOK FIRST_KEY}					
2		{IF FIRST_KEY=""}{BRANCH \K}					
3							
4	FIRST_KEY	{RIGHT}					
5							
6							

FIGURE 11-6 **The {LOOK} command**

```
{LOOK location}
```

where *location* is the address or name of a cell in which you want to store a representation of the keystroke. If the typeahead buffer contains no keystrokes, 1-2-3/G stores the default label prefix (usually ') in *location*. If you specify a multicell range for *location*, 1-2-3/G stores the keystroke in the upper-left cell of the range.

The *typeahead buffer* is a section of memory where 1-2-3/G stores the keystrokes you type during the noninteractive part of a macro—that is, the part when the macro is not pausing for user input. 1-2-3/G then uses the keystrokes in the buffer in the next interactive macro command (for example, the next {?}, {GET}, {GETLABEL}, {ALERT}, or {MENUCALL} command).

One of the most common uses for the {LOOK} command is to break out of an infinite loop. For example, Figure 11-6 shows a macro that uses the {LOOK} command to look in the typeahead buffer and place the first keystroke in the buffer in the cell named FIRST_KEY (cell B4). The {IF} command then checks the contents of FIRST_KEY to see if it contains an entry. If the cell contains the default label prefix, which is the equivalent of an empty or null string (""), the macro branches back to the top to execute the {LOOK} command again. The macro continues in an infinite loop until you press a key.

The {CE} Command

Like 1-2-3 Release 3, 1-2-3/G offers the {CE} command, or {CLEARENTRY}, for clearing the information that 1-2-3/G automatically displays at a Control line prompt or in a text box. For example, you can use the {CE} command to clear the path information that automatically appears when you use the File Open or File Retrieve command or the range entry that automatically appears when you select Range Format. You can also use {CE} when you are editing a cell entry to clear the entry from the Contents box.

The {CE} command eliminates a difficulty you may have encountered when creating macros for Release 2: that of clearing a prompt when you are not sure whether the prompt has a previous entry or what the previous entry looks like. For example, consider the case where you want your macro to enter a print footer, but you're not sure whether a footer has already been entered. You might enter the following commands in a Release 2 macro:

```
/ppof*{ESC}Unaudited Financial Statements~qgq
```

This macro chooses the Print Printer Options Footer command and places an asterisk (*) in the footer line. If the prompt is empty, the asterisk serves as a temporary entry. Otherwise, the asterisk is added to the end of the existing entry in the prompt line. By adding this single character to the prompt line, you ensure that the {ESC} command that follows has an entry to clear (without some kind of entry, the {ESC} command would cause the macro to exit from the Print Printer Options Footer command prematurely). After clearing the entry, the macro enters the new footer, "Unaudited Financial Statements."

In 1-2-3/G, the {CE} command eliminates the need for this workaround. For example, you can use the following code to insert the footer from the previous example:

```
/ppof{CE}Unaudited Financial Statements~qgq
```

As mentioned, the {CE} command is particularly helpful for clearing the path information that automatically appears when you use the File Open or File Retrieve command. For example, the following macro code accesses the File Open dialog box, erases the default path information that automatically appears in the File name box, enters a new filename (YEAREND.WG1), and opens the file.

```
/fo{CE}YEAREND~
```

The {ALERT} Command

{ALERT} is a new 1-2-3/G macro command that lets you create a simple dialog box complete with command buttons. The syntax for the command is

{ALERT ***message, [type], [icon]*****}**

where *message* is the prompt that you want the macro to place at the top of the dialog box. You can use a text string, or the address or name of a cell containing a text string, for *message*. You cannot, however, use the address or name of a multicell range.

The *type* argument is an optional argument that lets you specify the type of command buttons that appear within the dialog box. You can enter 1, 2, or 3 for the *type* argument; a range name or cell address containing 1, 2, or 3; or a formula that evaluates to 1, 2, or 3. Here are the effects:

- **1** Causes 1-2-3/G to display a single OK command button. After you select the OK button, the macro continues execution with the next command in the cell below the {ALERT} command.
- **2** Causes 1-2-3/G to display OK and Cancel buttons. If you select OK, the macro continues execution with the next command in the cell below the {ALERT} command. If you select Cancel, the macro continues with the next command in the same cell as the {ALERT} command.
- **3** Causes 1-2-3/G to display Yes and No command buttons. If you select Yes, the macro continues execution with the next command in the cell below the {ALERT} command. If you select No, the macro continues with the next command in the same cell as the {ALERT} command.

The *icon* argument is an optional argument that lets you control the type of icon that 1-2-3/G displays in front of *message* in the dialog box. You can enter 1, 2, 3, or 4 for *icon*; a range name or cell address containing 1, 2, 3, or 4; or a formula that evaluates to 1, 2, 3, or 4. Here are the effects:

- **1** Displays a stop sign in OS/2 Version 1.2 (or a hand in OS/2 Version 1.1).
- **2** Displays an exclamation point.
- **3** Displays a question mark.
- **4** Displays an I icon in OS/2 Version 1.2 (or an asterisk in OS/2 Version 1.1).

Figure 11–7 shows a macro that uses the {ALERT} command and the dialog box that the command produces. Notice that a value of 3 for the *type* argument produces Yes and No command buttons, and a value of 3 for the *icon* argument produces a question-mark icon.

If you select the Yes command button in response to the dialog box, 1-2-3/G executes the commands in cell B2, which set the background of the worksheet frame to white. On the other hand, if you select the No command button, 1-2-3/G executes the {QUIT} command directly following the {ALERT} command, which ends the macro.

MANIPULATING DATA IN CELLS

1-2-3/G has four commands that let you manipulate data in cells—{BLANK}, {CONTENTS}, {LET}, and {PUT}. By using these commands, you can perform operations similar to the Range Erase, Range Value, and Copy commands. However, they are much quicker and in many ways more powerful.

The {BLANK} Command

The {BLANK} command lets you erase a cell or range of cells while keeping the cell formatting. In other words, the effects of the {BLANK} command are similar

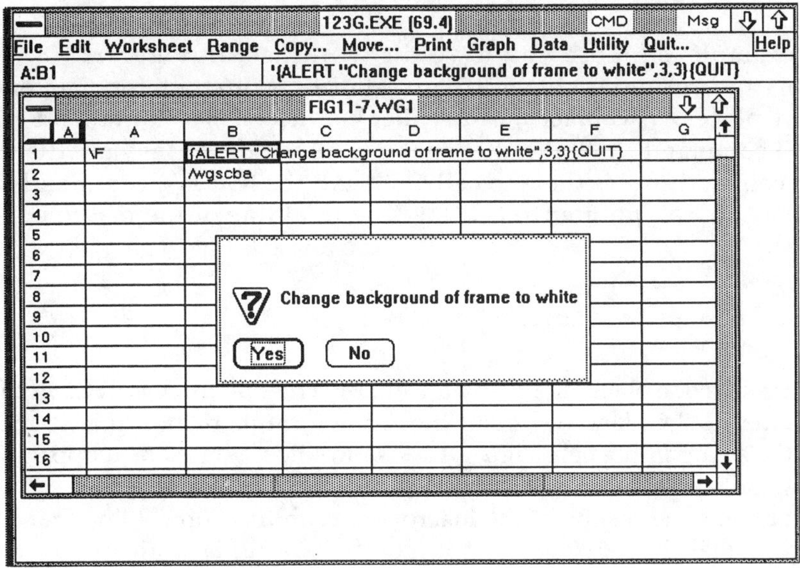

FIGURE 11–7 The {ALERT} command

to the Range Erase command without accessing the Range Erase dialog box. The syntax of the command is

```
{BLANK location}
```

where *location* is a cell or range.

For example, the command {BLANK B:D3..B:D5} erases the contents of cells B:D3, B:D4, and B:D5. Likewise, {BLANK ENTRY_FORM} erases the contents of the cells in the range named ENTRY_FORM.

The {CONTENTS} Command

The {CONTENTS} command copies a value or label in one cell to another cell as a label. The label that 1-2-3/G creates in the target cell resembles the contents of the original cell as they appear on the screen, including any cell formatting. This command is used most frequently when a worksheet contains a value that you would like to express as a label so that you can include it in a string formula. The syntax of the command is

```
{CONTENTS target-location,source-location,[width],[cell-format]}
```

where both *source-location* and *target-location* can be a cell or a range. If you specify a range, 1-2-3/G uses only the upper-left cell in the range.

For example, suppose you have the worksheet in Figure 11-8, which contains the formula 129.95*0.7 in cell B1, formatted for Currency, 2 decimal places. The macro, which begins in cell B4, contains a {CONTENTS} command that takes the contents of cell B1, as they are displayed in that cell, and copies them to cell C1. Next, the {GOTO} command in cell B5 moves the cell pointer to cell D1. The final line of the macro contains the label

```
'+"The sale price is"&C1{CALC}~
```

This macro code places the string formula **+"The sale price is"&C1** in cell D1, presses the {CALC} key to convert the string formula to an actual string, and enters the string in the cell. Figure 11-9 shows how your screen appears after running the macro.

As you view the results of the macro, notice in the Control line that cell C1 contains the label '   **$90.97**. This is a nine-character label that replicates the contents of cell B1 as they are displayed on the screen, including three blank spaces preceding the dollar sign ($).

Suppose you want to limit the number of blank spaces that precede the dollar sign in the label. To do so, you can use the optional *width* argument, which lets you control the width of the label that the {CONTENTS} command produces. The *width* argument can be a value, or a cell or range name that contains a value, between 0 and 512. For example, by placing the statement **{CONTENTS C1,B1,7}** in the first cell of the macro, 1-2-3/G displays the seven-character label ' **$90.97** in cell C1 and, thus, the label **'The sale price is $90.97** in cell D1 when you run the macro. Notice that there is only one space preceding the $, whereas in Figure 11-9 there are three spaces.

By including the optional *cell-format* argument as the last argument in the {CONTENTS} command, you can have 1-2-3/G format the label's contents to look like a numeric cell entry in the specified format. The *cell-format* argument

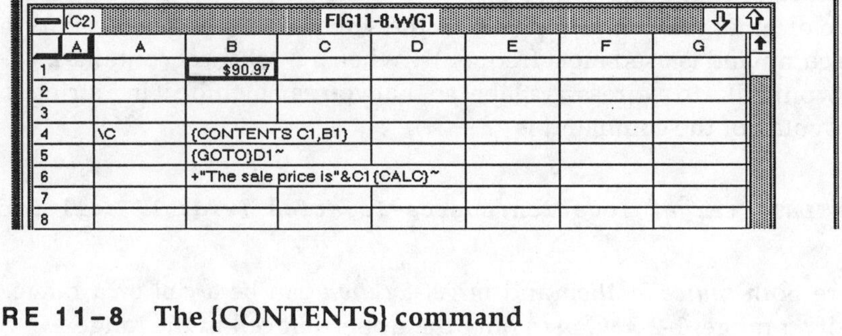

123G.EXE (69.4) Ready

File Edit Worksheet Range Copy... Move... Print Graph Data Utility Quit... Help

A:B1 129.95*0.7

(C2) FIG11-8.WG1

A	A	B	C	D	E	F	G
1		$90.97					
2							
3							
4	\C	{CONTENTS C1,B1}					
5		{GOTO}D1~					
6		+"The sale price is"&C1{CALC}~					
7							
8							

FIGURE 11-8 The {CONTENTS} command

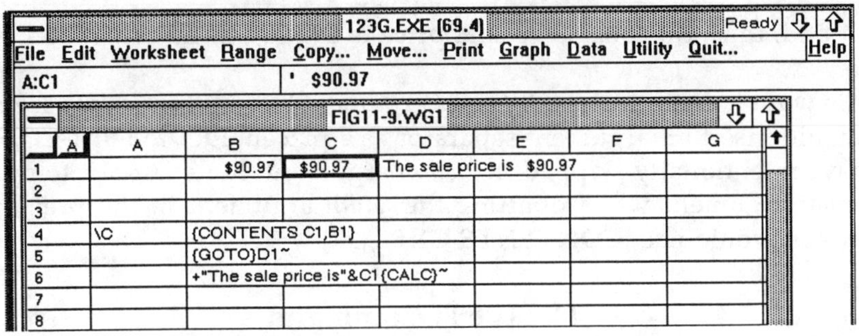

123G.EXE (69.4) Ready

File Edit Worksheet Range Copy... Move... Print Graph Data Utility Quit... Help

A:C1 ' $90.97

FIG11-9.WG1

A	A	B	C	D	E	F	G
1		$90.97	$90.97	The sale price is $90.97			
2							
3							
4	\C	{CONTENTS C1,B1}					
5		{GOTO}D1~					
6		+"The sale price is"&C1{CALC}~					
7							
8							

FIGURE 11-9 Results of the {CONTENTS} command

must be one of the code numbers from Table 11-2 (see Chapter 3 for an explanation of the available cell formats).

Continuing with the previous example, suppose you want the label the {CONTENTS} command produces to appear in Currency format with 0 decimal places (code 32). You could use the statement **{CONTENTS C1,B1,4,32}** in the first line of the macro. 1-2-3/G then displays the four-character label **' $91** in

TABLE 11-2 **Cell Formats for Use with the {CONTENTS} Command**

Code Number	Resulting Cell Format
0 to15	Fixed, 0 to 15 decimal places
16 to 31	Scientific, 0 to 15 decimal places
32 to 47	Currency, 0 to 15 decimal places
48 to 63	Percent, 0 to 15 decimal places
64 to 79	Comma, 0 to 15 decimal places
112	+/-
113	General
114	1 (DD-Mon-YY)
115	2 (DD-Mon)
116	3 (Mon-YY)
117	Text
118	Hidden
119	6 (HH:MMi:SS AM/PM)
120	7 (HH:MMi AM/PM)
121	4 (Long International Date)
122	5 (Short International Date)
123	8 (Long International Time)
124	9 (Short International Time)
127	Worksheet global cell format (set with the Worksheet Global Format command)

cell C1 and, thus, the label **'The sale price is $91** in cell D1 when you run the macro.

If you want to include the *cell-format* argument but omit the *width* argument, you should insert an argument separator as a placeholder to tell 1-2-3/G that you have intentionally skipped the *width* argument. For example, to specify a *cell-format* argument while omitting the *width* argument in the previous example, you would use **{CONTENTS C1,B1,,32}**.

The {LET} Command

Use the {LET} command when you want a macro to enter a value or label into a cell but you do not want to disturb the current cell-pointer location. The syntax of the command is

```
{LET location,entry}
```

where *location* can be either a cell or a range. As with the other commands in this section, if you specify a range, 1-2-3/G will use the upper-left cell of the range.

The *entry* argument can be a number, literal string, formula, or a reference to a cell that contains any of these. Note that if you use a formula for *entry*, 1-2-3/G will evaluate the formula and place the result in *location*—you cannot use {LET} to enter a formula in *location*.

Note

> {LET} does not force recalculation. If you want 1-2-3/G to recalculate, place a ~ (tilde) after the {LET} command.

123G.EXE Ready
File Edit Worksheet Range Copy... Move... Print Graph Data Utility Quit... Help
A:B1 '{LET NET_SALARY,SALARY-(FED+STATE+LOCAL+FICA)}~
FIG11-10.WG1

A	A	B	C	D	E	F	G
1	\L	{LET NET_SALARY,SALARY-(FED+STATE+LOCAL+FICA)}~					
2							
3	SALARY	$3,333.33					
4	FED	$766.67					
5	STATE	$200.00					
6	LOCAL	$30.00					
7	FICA	$255.00					
8	NET_SALARY	$2,081.66					
9							
10							

FIGURE 11-10 The {LET} Command

For example, suppose you want to create a macro that calculates net salaries after subtracting out withholding. You could use the simple macro in Figure 11–10 to accomplish this. When you execute this macro, the {LET} command stores the result of the formula SALARY-(FED+STATE+LOCAL+FICA) in the range NET_SALARY (cell B8). A ~ (tilde) is included at the end of the {LET} statement to have 1-2-3/G recalculate the worksheet.

The :string and :value Suffixes

You can use a :string or :value suffix (or their abbreviations :s and :v) to control how 1-2-3/G treats the *entry* argument of a {LET} command. If you place a :string suffix following the *entry* argument, 1-2-3/G treats the argument as a literal string and enters it in the worksheet as is. However, if you place a :value suffix following the *entry* argument, 1-2-3/G evaluates the argument first before entering it in the worksheet.

For example, if cell B1 contains the value 2 and cell B2 contains the value 4, when 1-2-3/G evaluates the command **{LET B3,B1+B2:v}~**, it places the value 6 in cell B3. However, when 1-2-3/G evaluates the command **{LET B3,B1+B2:s}~**, it places the label 'B1+B2 in cell B3. See "The {DEFINE} Command" for more on these suffixes.

The {PUT} Command

The {PUT} command is similar to the {LET} command in that it enters a value or label into a cell. However, {PUT} is different from {LET} because it enters the value or label into a range based on row and column offsets. The syntax of the command is

```
{PUT location,column-offset,row-offset,entry}
```

{PUT} enters a number or label in a cell within *location*, which can be a 2–D range of any size.

The *column-offset* and *row-offset* arguments are handled in a fashion similar to the offsets you use for the @VLOOKUP and @HLOOKUP functions (see Chapter 6). The first column of the range is offset 0, the second column is offset 1, and so on. The same is true for rows where the first row is offset 0, the second row is offset 1, and the like. For example, if the cell you wish to address is in the fourth column and fifth row of *location*, the *column-offset* and *row-offset* arguments are 3 and 4.

Note

> You must make sure that your *column-offset* and *row-offset* arguments do not reference a cell outside *location*. If they do, your macro will be interrupted with an error.

The *entry* argument can be a number, a literal string, a formula, or a reference to a cell that contains any of these. Note that if *entry* is a formula, 1-2-3/G places the current value of the formula in *location*, not the formula itself.

Note

> If *entry* is a string formula that begins with double quotes, be sure to include a + (plus) sign at the start of the string formula. Without it, 1-2-3/G will probably have trouble evaluating the formula and will therefore place ERR in *location*.

For example, suppose you have assigned the name TAX_TABLE to the range A1..C4. The command **{PUT TAX_TABLE,1,2,.3}** places the value .3 in cell B3.

As another example, suppose cell C1 contains the value 40 and C2 contains the value 20. The command **{PUT TAX_TABLE,0,3,C1*C2}** places the current value of the formula, 800, in cell A4.

As still another example, imagine that you have assigned the name MARITAL_STATUS to cell H2, and you have placed the label 'Married in that cell. The command **{PUT TAX_TABLE,2,3,+MARITAL_STATUS&" filing separately"}** places the current value of the string formula, 'Married filing separately, in cell C4.

STOPPING AND SUSPENDING MACROS

In the previous chapter, you learned that a macro ends when it encounters a blank cell. You can also end a macro by using the {QUIT} command. Suppose, however, that you want to stop a macro only temporarily. 1-2-3/G offers the {WAIT} command, which lets you suspend a macro for a specified amount of time. In addition, 1-2-3/G offers the new {WAITDIALOG} command, which suspends a macro while you respond to a dialog box.

The {QUIT} Command

The {QUIT} command terminates a macro immediately. You can use {QUIT} anywhere within a macro, either in the main macro routine or in a subroutine. If 1-2-3/G encounters {QUIT} in a subroutine, it terminates not only the subroutine but also the macro that called the subroutine.

{QUIT} is often used in combination with {IF} to end a macro when a certain value is reached, as in the following:

```
{IF ACCOUNTS<=1000}{BRANCH CONSOLIDATE}
{QUIT}
```

In this example, if the value in the cell named ACCOUNTS is less than or equal to 1000, the macro branches to the routine named CONSOLIDATE. However, when the value is greater than 1000, the macro terminates.

The {WAIT} Command

The {WAIT} command suspends a macro until a specified time. The syntax of the command is

```
{WAIT time-number}
```

where *time-number* represents a future point in time and can be a number, numeric formula, or a reference to a cell that contains one of these. Note that *time-number* must be expressed as a valid 1-2-3/G date and time serial number (see Chapter 1 for an explanation of 1-2-3/G's special date and time numbering system).

When {WAIT} suspends a macro, 1-2-3/G displays a red Wait indicator at the top of the screen. The indicator remains until the time defined by *time-number* has elapsed. 1-2-3/G then removes the indicator and proceeds with the commands following {WAIT}.

To interrupt a {WAIT} command, press CTRL-BREAK (1-2-3/G ignores all other keystrokes). 1-2-3/G immediately stops the macro and issues an error message. However, if a {BREAKOFF} command is in effect (which disables CTRL-BREAK), there is no way to stop the macro during the {WAIT} command. You can, of course, switch to another application program while the macro is running and wait out the {WAIT} command. Barring this, however, the only way to stop the {WAIT} command is to restart your computer.

In the example below, 1-2-3/G waits for five seconds, then beeps to alert you that the waiting period has elapsed.

```
{WAIT @NOW+@TIME(0,0,5)}
{BEEP}
```

The {WAITDIALOG} Command

The {WAITDIALOG} command pauses a macro and allows you to make entries in a dialog box. When you have completed your work in the dialog box, the next macro command executed depends on the way you exit the dialog box, as follows:

- If you select the OK button, the macro continues with the commands in the cell below the {WAITDIALOG} command.

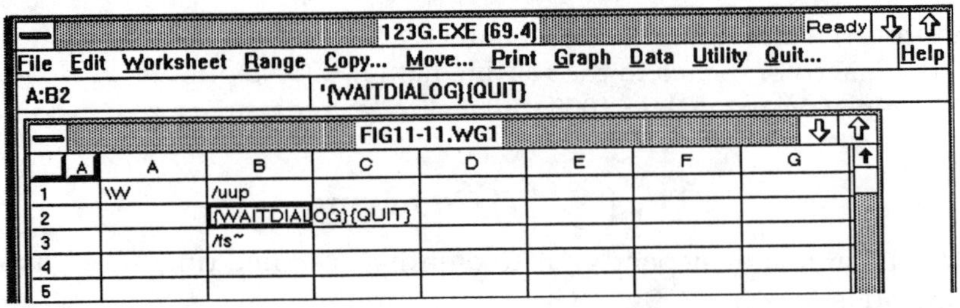

123G.EXE [69.4] Ready

File Edit Worksheet Range Copy... Move... Print Graph Data Utility Quit... Help

A:B2 '{WAITDIALOG}{QUIT}

FIG11-11.WG1

A	A	B	C	D	E	F	G
1	\W	/uup					
2		{WAITDIALOG}{QUIT}					
3		/fs~					
4							
5							

FIGURE 11–11 The {WAITDIALOG} command

- If you select the Cancel button, the macro continues with the commands in the same cell as the {WAITDIALOG} command.
- If you press CTRL-BREAK while in the dialog box, and {BREAKOFF} is not in effect, 1-2-3/G cancels the dialog box and ends the macro immediately.

As you might expect, if by selecting a dialog box option you access another dialog box, you can complete all your work in both dialog boxes before exiting the {WAITDIALOG} command.

For example, the macro in Figure 11–11 accesses the Utility User Settings Preferences dialog box then pauses, allowing you to choose one of the options in the dialog box that controls how 1-2-3/G saves files (for example, whether it writes over the existing file without confirmation or backs up your file). If you then select the OK button, the macro executes the File Save command in the cell below the {WAITDIALOG} command; this command saves the current file using the new setting you chose in the User Settings Preferences dialog box. However, if you select the Cancel button, the macro executes the {QUIT} command following the {WAITDIALOG} command, ending the macro.

CONDITIONAL PROCESSING

1-2-3/G has three macro commands for performing conditional processing—{IF}, {FOR}, and {FORBREAK}. These commands provide the raw ingredients you'll need to have your macros make decisions, act on them, and perform repetitive loops.

The {IF} Command

The {IF} command lets you make a decision when there are two alternative outcomes. The syntax of the command is

```
{IF condition}
```

where *condition* is a logical expression—an expression that compares two values or strings using a logical operator, such as = or < (see Chapter 1), and returns a true (1) or false (0) result. If *condition* results in any value other than 0, 1-2-3/G evaluates it as true, and the macro continues executing commands in the same cell immediately following the {IF}. If *condition* results in 0, 1-2-3/G interprets it as false, and the macro continues executing commands in the cell immediately below the {IF}; all instructions in the same cell as the {IF} are ignored. Besides 0, other values that 1-2-3/G interprets as false are logical false, a blank cell, text, ERR, and NA. Although *condition* is usually a logical expression, you can actually use any formula, number, literal string, or cell reference.

For example, suppose you want a macro to branch to different routines based on the result of a logical formula. The following {IF} command tests the value of a cell named ONORDER. If its value is greater than or equal to 500, the macro branches to a routine named CUMULATIVE. If the value is less than 500, the macro branches to a routine named GETNEXT.

```
{IF ONORDER>=500}{BRANCH CUMULATIVE}
{BRANCH GETNEXT}
```

As another example, suppose you want to create a macro that saves the active file in either of two ways based on its current name. If the filename begins with "SHEET," that is, you relied on 1-2-3/G to automatically assign the filename, you want the macro to issue the File Save command and prompt you for a new filename. However, if you have already assigned your own name to the file, you want to issue the File Save command and save the file without any interruption. Figure 11–12 shows a macro that accomplishes this task.

In this example, the {IF} command branches based on the value of the following logical expression:

```
@FIND("SHEET",@CELLPOINTER("filename"),0)
```

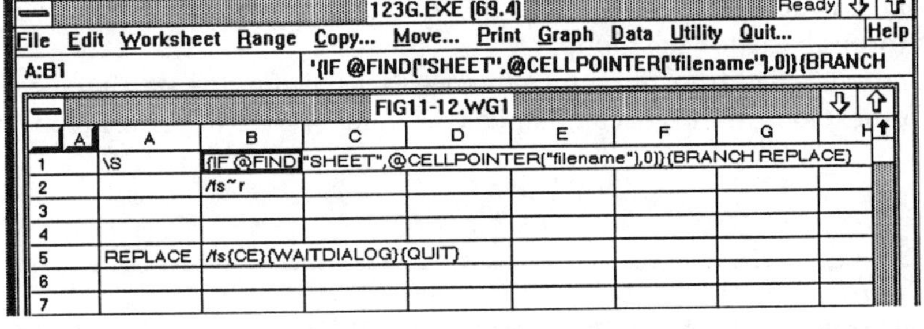

FIGURE 11–12 The {IF} command

In this expression, the function @CELLPOINTER("filename") returns the filename, including the path, of the current cell. The @FIND function then returns the position within the filename where the search string "SHEET" begins. For example, if the filename is "C:\123G\WORK\SHEET4.WG1," 1-2-3/G returns the offset number 13 (the first character is offset 0). However, if the filename does not contain "SHEET," the function returns ERR.

If the logical expression returns a positive number, the macro executes the {BRANCH} instruction immediately following the {IF}, which causes the macro to branch to the cell named REPLACE (cell B5). The instructions in REPLACE issue the File Save command, clear the existing filename from the File name box, and pause the macro to allow you to enter a new filename.

Now suppose you have already assigned a name to the file, and the name does not contain the pattern "SHEET." In this case, the logical formula evaluates to ERR, which 1-2-3/G interprets as false. The macro then executes the instructions in the cell below the {IF}. These instructions issue the File Save command, accept the file name that appears in the File Save dialog box, and replace the file on disk with the current file.

The {FOR} Command

The {FOR} command lets you build *iterative* (repetitive) loops in a macro. The syntax of the command is

```
{FOR counter,start-number,stop-number,step-number, subroutine}
```

where the arguments are defined as follows:

- *counter* is a cell in the worksheet where 1-2-3/G initially places the value in *start-number*. 1-2-3/G then updates *counter* each time the command completes a loop.
- *start-number* is the number to which *counter* is initially set when the command begins.
- *stop-number* tells 1-2-3/G when to stop the looping process. When *counter* exceeds *stop-number*, 1-2-3/G knows to stop.
- *step-number* defines the increment by which *counter* is increased following a pass through the for-next loop.
- *subroutine* is an address or range reference that specifies the starting location of the for-next loop, the set of commands you want 1-2-3/G to perform repeatedly.

Note

> Once *subroutine* starts, the commands within it cannot modify the *start-number*, *stop-number*, or *step-number* arguments.

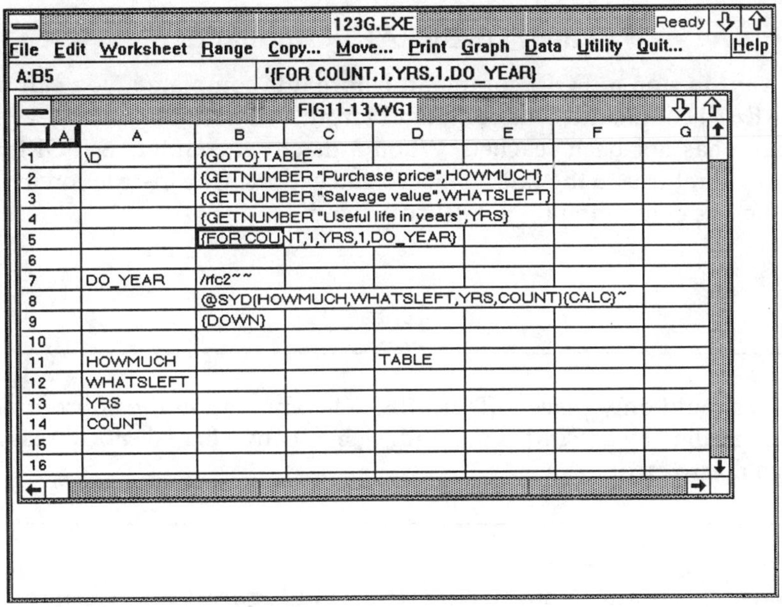

123G.EXE Ready

File Edit Worksheet Range Copy... Move... Print Graph Data Utility Quit... Help

A:B5 '{FOR COUNT,1,YRS,1,DO_YEAR}

FIG11-13.WG1

A	A	B	C	D	E	F	G
1	\D	{GOTO}TABLE~					
2		{GETNUMBER "Purchase price",HOWMUCH}					
3		{GETNUMBER "Salvage value",WHATSLEFT}					
4		{GETNUMBER "Useful life in years",YRS}					
5		{FOR COUNT,1,YRS,1,DO_YEAR}					
6							
7	DO_YEAR	/rfc2~~					
8		@SYD(HOWMUCH,WHATSLEFT,YRS,COUNT){CALC}~					
9		{DOWN}					
10							
11	HOWMUCH			TABLE			
12	WHATSLEFT						
13	YRS						
14	COUNT						
15							
16							

FIGURE 11–13 The {FOR} command

Suppose you want to create a macro that builds a sum-of-the-years-depreciation table. Figure 11–13 shows such a macro. The macro begins by moving the cell pointer to TABLE (cell E11). It then prompts you for the purchase price of the asset and stores your response in HOWMUCH (cell B11). Next, the macro prompts you for the salvage value and places your response in WHATSLEFT (cell B12). It then prompts you for the useful life in years and saves the value in YRS (cell B13). The macro then executes the {FOR} command in cell B5. This command sets up the counter argument as COUNT (cell B14). The start-number argument is 1, the stop-number argument is a reference to the YRS range (cell B13), and the *step-number* is 1. The subroutine argument is a reference to the cell named DO_YEAR (cell B7).

Here's a sample of the table that the macro produces when you choose a purchase price of $10,000, a salvage value of $1,000, and a useful life of 10 years:

E11: $1,636.36
E12: $1,472.73
E13: $1,309.09
E14: $1,145.45
E15: $981.82
E16: $818.18
E17: $654.55
E18: $490.91
E19: $327.27
E20: $163.64

The {FORBREAK} Command

If you want to stop a {FOR} command before it is completed, you can use the {FORBREAK} command. This command terminates a for-next loop, even if the stop value has not been reached. When a macro encounters a {FORBREAK} command, it returns to the calling macro and executes the instruction in the cell below the one containing the {FOR} command.

Note

> You should only place a {FORBREAK} command in the subroutine being called by a {FOR} command. Using it anywhere else will result in a macro error.

Suppose you want to modify the macro in Figure 11-13 so that it stops executing if the @SYD function returns an error—which occurs, for example, when you enter an invalid number for the cost, salvage value, or useful life. You can insert a {FORBREAK} command in the macro as in Figure 11-14.

123G.EXE — Ready

File Edit Worksheet Range Copy... Move... Print Graph Data Utility Quit... Help

A:B9 '{IF @CELLPOINTER("contents")="ERR"}{ESC 2}{FORBREAK}

FIG11-14.WG1

A	A	B	C	D	E	F	G
1	\D	{GOTO}TABLE~					
2		{GETNUMBER "Purchase price",HOWMUCH}					
3		{GETNUMBER "Salvage value",WHATSLEFT}					
4		{GETNUMBER "Useful life in years",YRS}					
5		{FOR COUNT,1,YRS,1,DO_YEAR}					
6							
7	DO_YEAR	/rfc2~~					
8		@SYD(HOWMUCH,WHATSLEFT,YRS,COUNT){CALC}~					
9		{IF @CELLPOINTER("contents")="ERR"}{ESC 2}{FORBREAK}					
10		{DOWN}					
11							
12	HOWMUCH			TABLE			
13	WHATSLEFT						
14	YRS						
15	COUNT						
16							

FIGURE 11-14 The {FORBREAK} command

BRANCHING

As you know, 1-2-3/G executes macro commands one after the other, moving from one cell of commands to the next until it encounters a blank cell or a {QUIT} command. You can, however, redirect the flow of macro control to a new cell location by branching. 1-2-3/G offers two commands for branching—{BRANCH} and {DISPATCH}.

The {BRANCH} Command

{BRANCH} transfers macro control to a different location and does not return. The syntax of the command is

```
{BRANCH location}
```

where *location* is the cell that contains the commands you want the macro to execute next. You can specify a cell address, a range reference, or a range name for *location*.

{BRANCH} is usually combined with {IF}, to perform "if-then-else" processing, as in this sequence:

```
{IF CASH>0}{BRANCH SPEND_IT}
{BRANCH BROKE}
```

In this case, 1-2-3/G tests the value in the cell named CASH. If the value is greater than 0, 1-2-3/G executes the {BRANCH} command following the {IF}, which transfers macro control to the cell named SPEND_IT. However, if the value in CASH is less than or equal to zero, 1-2-3/G executes the {BRANCH} command in the cell below the {IF}, which transfers control to the cell named BROKE.

Suppose you have created a worksheet file that contains two income statements, one for 1989 (stored in B:A1..B:H10) and the other for 1990 (stored in C:A1..C:H10). You now want to create a macro that will prompt you for which statement to print, and then print the appropriate statement based on your response. Figure 11–15 shows such a macro.

In this example, the {GETNUMBER} command at the start of the macro displays a dialog box with the prompt **Print 1989 or 1990 results (89 or 90)?**. When you enter a response, 1-2-3/G stores it in YEAR (cell B7). Next, the macro executes the first {IF} command, which tests the number in YEAR and, if it is equal to 89, transfers control to the cell named PRINT_89 (cell B9). If it is not equal to 89, the macro executes the second {IF}, which transfers control to the cell named PRINT_90 (cell B11) if the number in YEAR is equal to 90.

If you fail to enter either 89 or 90 in response to the {GETNUMBER} prompt, the macro executes the {ALERT} command, which displays a dialog box that contains OK and Cancel buttons. If you select Cancel, the macro executes the {QUIT} command following the {ALERT} command, which stops the macro. However, if you select OK, the macro branches back to the start so that you can try again. (See Figure 11–3 for another example of the {BRANCH} command.)

Note

> Do not confuse {BRANCH} and {GOTO}. {GOTO} moves the cell pointer to a new location, but {BRANCH} does not. {BRANCH} transfers macro control to a new location.

The {DISPATCH} Command

The {DISPATCH} command is similar to the {BRANCH} command, except that you use it for *indirect branching*, where you use the contents of one cell to point to another cell. The syntax of the command is

```
{DISPATCH location}
```

where *location* is a single cell containing the address or name of another cell.

The {DISPATCH} command causes 1-2-3/G to transfer control to the cell whose name or address appears in *location*. For example, suppose the cell named DEST contains the label 'PRINT_89. If 1-2-3/G encounters the command {DISPATCH DEST} in a macro, it does not branch to DEST. Rather, it looks in

123G.EXE — Ready

File Edit Worksheet Range Copy... Move... Print Graph Data Utility Quit... Help

A:B5 '{BRANCH \B}

FIG11-15.WG1

A	A	B	C	D	E	F	G
1	\B	{GETNUMBER "Print 1989 or 1990 results (89 or 90)?",YEAR}					
2		{IF YEAR=89}{BRANCH PRINT_89}					
3		{IF YEAR=90}{BRANCH PRINT_90}					
4		{ALERT "Invalid entry, enter 89 or 90",2,2}{QUIT}					
5		{BRANCH \B}					
6							
7	YEAR	90					
8							
9	PRINT_89	/pprB:A1..B:H10~gpq					
10							
11	PRINT_90	/pprC:A1..C:H10~gpq					
12							
13							

FIGURE 11–15 The {BRANCH} command

123G.EXE Ready

File Edit Worksheet Range Copy... Move... Print Graph Data Utility Quit... Help

A:B7 +"PRINT_"&@STRING(YEAR,0)

FIG11-16.WG1

A	A	B	C	D	E	F	G
1	\B	{GETNUMBER "Print 1989 or 1990 results (89 or 90)?",YEAR}					
2		{IF YEAR=89#OR#YEAR=90}{DISPATCH DEST}					
3		{ALERT "Invalid entry, enter 89 or 90",2,2}{QUIT}					
4		{BRANCH \B}					
5							
6	YEAR	90					
7	DEST	PRINT_90					
8							
9	PRINT_89	/pprB:A1..B:H10~gpq					
10							
11	PRINT_90	/pprC:A1..C:H10~gpq					
12							
13							

FIGURE 11–16 The {DISPATCH} command

DEST and uses its contents as the location to branch to, which in this case means that it branches to the cell named PRINT_89.

Figure 11–16 shows how you might modify the macro in Figure 11–15 to use the {DISPATCH} command. After the {GETNUMBER} command stores 89 or 90 to YEAR (cell B6), the formula in DEST (cell B7) evaluates to either PRINT_89 or PRINT_90. Therefore, when 1-2-3/G encounters the {DISPATCH} command, it performs an indirect branch to the contents of DEST. That is, 1-2-3/G looks in DEST then branches to the routine whose name resides in DEST, either PRINT_89 or PRINT_90.

SUBROUTINES

Although the {BRANCH} and {DISPATCH} commands let you change the flow of control to another macro, they do not return to the original macro. You can, of course, place another {BRANCH} or {DISPATCH} command at the end of the called macro to return control back to the original calling macro. But you run into difficulty when you want to reuse the called routine more than once. You find that you must modify the {BRANCH} or {DISPATCH} command at the end of the called routine in order to return control back to different points in the original calling macro.

To get around this problem, you can have the macro call a subroutine. When a macro calls a subroutine, 1-2-3/G transfers control to the first cell of the subroutine. Then, when it completes processing the commands in the subroutine, it returns control back to the calling macro.

The simplest way to call a subroutine is

{subroutine}

where *subroutine* is the range name (or address) for the subroutine's starting cell. The range name can actually refer to the entire subroutine, in which case 1-2-3/G begins executing commands at the upper-left cell of the range. But you are better off having the range name refer to the starting cell, in case you add or delete cells in the subroutine.

For example, the subroutine call {PRINT_IT} tells 1-2-3/G to execute the commands starting in the cell named PRINT_IT. Likewise, the subroutine call {ZA1} tells 1-2-3/G to execute the commands starting in cell ZA1.

When a macro calls a subroutine, 1-2-3/G begins at the first cell in the subroutine and executes the commands in the usual way, moving from one command to the next in sequential fashion. When 1-2-3/G encounters a blank cell or a {RETURN} command, it returns control back to the calling macro to the instruction following the {*subroutine*} command.

Subroutines are most useful when you want to reuse a block of code repeatedly. For example, suppose you have created the simple model at the top of Figure 11–17 to calculate the payment on a mortgage. You now want to create a macro to print the results of the model several times in a row, each time using a different interest rate.

The macro in Figure 11–17 uses a subroutine to print the payment model repeatedly. The macro begins by issuing the Print Printer Range command to set the print range to A1..B4. It then issues a {LET} command to place a value

123G.EXE (69.4) Ready

File Edit Worksheet Range Copy... Move... Print Graph Data Utility Quit... Help

A:B4 @PMT(PRINCIPAL,INTEREST/12,TERM*12)

(C2) FIG11-17.WG1

A	A	B	C	D	E	F	G
1	Principal	$268,000					
2	Interest	10%					
3	Term	40					
4	Payment	$2,275.71					
5							
6	\S	/pprA1..B4~q					
7		{LET INTEREST,.09}{PRINT_ONE}					
8		{LET INTEREST,.10}{PRINT_ONE}					
9		{LET INTEREST,.11}{PRINT_ONE}					
10		{LET INTEREST,.12}{PRINT_ONE}					
11		{LET INTEREST,.13}{PRINT_ONE}					
12							
13	PRINT_ONE	/ppgpq					
14							
15							
16							

FIGURE 11–17 The {subroutine} command

of .09 in the cell named INTEREST (B2). The next command, {PRINT_ONE}, makes a call to the PRINT_ONE subroutine, which transfers control to the cell named PRINT_ONE (cell B13) and begins executing the instructions in that cell. These instructions tell 1-2-3/G to issue the Print Printer command then select the Go, Page, and Quit options. When 1-2-3/G encounters the blank cell in B14, it transfers control back to the command following the subroutine call, in this case, to the {LET} command in cell B8.

Tip: Place commonly used subroutines in a macro library

> Consider placing your most commonly used subroutines in a macro library. That way, you can call them from within any macro (see Chapter 10).

The {RETURN} Command

When 1-2-3/G encounters a blank cell at the end of a subroutine, it transfers control back to the calling routine and executes the next command following the {*subroutine*} command. The {RETURN} command has the identical effect as a blank cell.

The {RETURN} command is most often used when a subroutine includes conditional processing. For example, suppose you want to modify the macro in Figure 11–17 so that it prompts you each time before printing the simple payment model at the top of the worksheet. Figure 11–18 shows how you might do this. In this case, the subroutine executes the {GETLABEL} command that, for the first pass through the subroutine, displays a dialog box with the prompt **Print for 0.09? (Y/N)** and stores your response in the cell named INPUT (B17). In the second line of the subroutine, the {IF} command tests the label in INPUT. If it is equal to "N," 1-2-3/G executes the {RETURN} command, which transfers control back to the main routine to the instruction following the {PRINT_ONE} subroutine call. Otherwise, the macro executes the printing instructions in cell B15.

Passing Arguments to Subroutines

Thus far, all the subroutine calls you have seen have been of the simple form, {*subroutine*}. However, when you pass arguments to a subroutine, the syntax is

```
{subroutine [argument1],[argument2],...,[argumentN]}
```

By passing arguments, you can have the subroutine act on a particular set of information. Arguments can be numbers, labels, formulas, or cell references. When you pass arguments, you must include a {DEFINE} macro command in the subroutine you are calling.

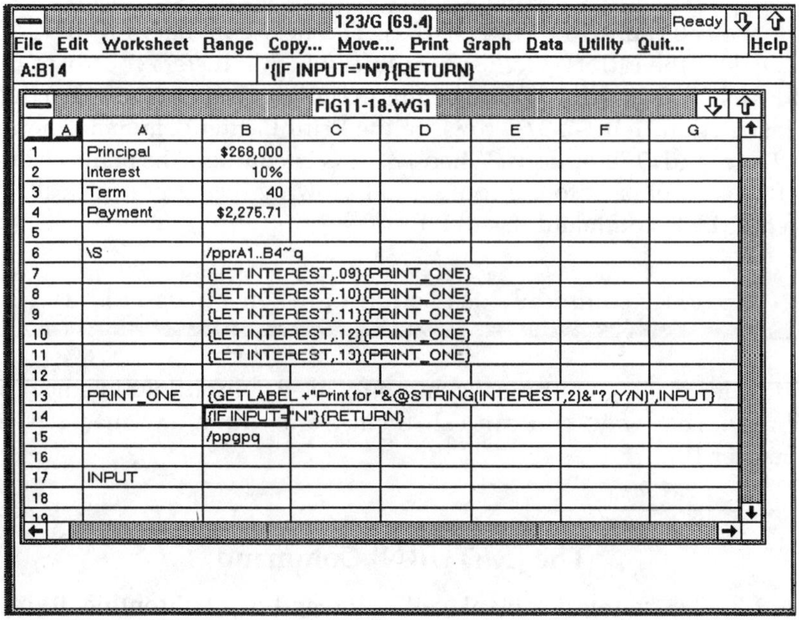

123/G (69.4) Ready

File Edit Worksheet Range Copy... Move... Print Graph Data Utility Quit... Help

A:B14 '{IF INPUT="N"}{RETURN}

FIG11-18.WG1

A	A	B	C	D	E	F	G
1	Principal	$268,000					
2	Interest	10%					
3	Term	40					
4	Payment	$2,275.71					
5							
6	\S	/pprA1..B4~q					
7		{LET INTEREST,.09}{PRINT_ONE}					
8		{LET INTEREST,.10}{PRINT_ONE}					
9		{LET INTEREST,.11}{PRINT_ONE}					
10		{LET INTEREST,.12}{PRINT_ONE}					
11		{LET INTEREST,.13}{PRINT_ONE}					
12							
13	PRINT_ONE	{GETLABEL +"Print for "&@STRING(INTEREST,2)&"? (Y/N)",INPUT}					
14		{IF INPUT="N"}{RETURN}					
15		/ppgpq					
16							
17	INPUT						
18							

FIGURE 11-18 The {RETURN} command

The {DEFINE} Command

The {DEFINE} command stores the arguments that are used in a subroutine. The syntax of the command is

{DEFINE *location1,location2,...,locationn*}

where each *location* argument specifies the storage location—a cell or range reference—for each argument used in a {*subroutine*} command.

When you pass arguments to a subroutine, the {DEFINE} command is usually the first command in the subroutine. However, you can actually place the {DEFINE} command anywhere within the subroutine, provided it appears before the commands that use the arguments that are passed.

As mentioned, the purpose of the {DEFINE} command is to store arguments so that a subroutine can use them. Before 1-2-3/G can do this, however, it must know what type of data you are passing, whether it is a value or a label, so that it can store it properly.

To tell 1-2-3/G the type of data you are passing, you can include a suffix after each *location* argument in a {DEFINE} command. The choices are *:string* (or :s) for string and *:value* (or :v) for value. Omitting the suffix is equivalent to using a :string suffix. A :string suffix (or no suffix) causes 1-2-3/G to store the argument as a label even if the argument looks like a number, formula, cell address, or range reference.

A :value suffix, on the other hand, causes 1-2-3/G to evaluate the argument before storing it. Of course, if the argument is a literal number, 1-2-3/G stores it as is. However, if the argument is a formula, 1-2-3/G evaluates it then stores the result as either a number (in the case of a numeric formula) or a label (in the case of a string formula). Finally, if the argument is a cell address or range name, 1-2-3/G looks in the referenced cell and stores its contents as a label or number.

An Example

Figure 11–19 shows a macro that positions the cell pointer to OUT (cell B15) then makes a subroutine call that passes four arguments. The {DEFINE} command at the beginning of the PUT_ROW subroutine stores the label Buy in the cell named FIRST (B10), the number 100 in SECOND (cell B11), the label "shares" in THIRD (cell B12), and the result of the formula @TODAY+1 in FOURTH (cell B13). The {LET} commands then enter the contents of these ranges in four consecutive cells—B15, C15, D15, and E15—as shown in Figure 11–19.

Note that 1-2-3/G treats label arguments the same regardless of whether you enclose them in quotes. For example, in Figure 11–19, the first argument (Buy) is not enclosed in quotes while the third argument ("shares") is.

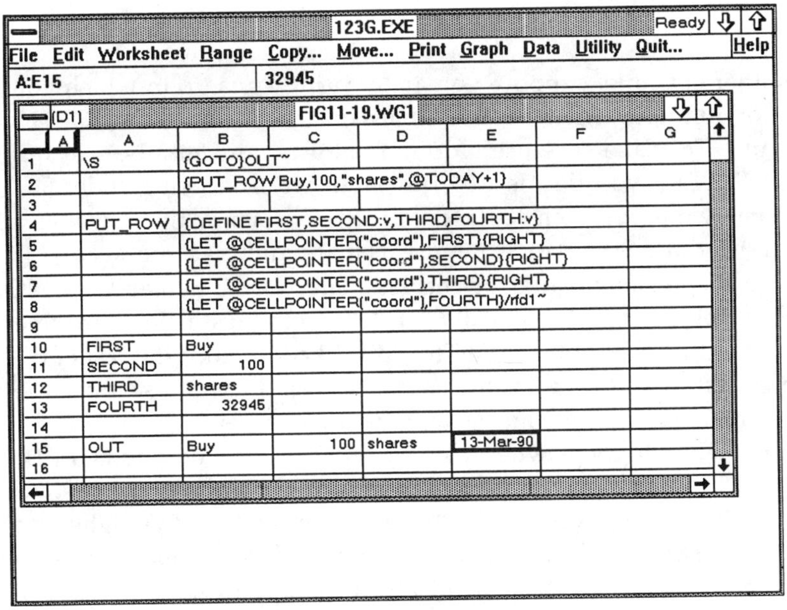

123G.EXE Ready

File Edit Worksheet Range Copy... Move... Print Graph Data Utility Quit... Help

A:E15 32945

(D1) FIG11-19.WG1

A	A	B	C	D	E	F	G
1	\S	{GOTO}OUT~					
2		{PUT_ROW Buy,100,"shares",@TODAY+1}					
3							
4	PUT_ROW	{DEFINE FIRST,SECOND:v,THIRD,FOURTH:v}					
5		{LET @CELLPOINTER("coord"),FIRST}{RIGHT}					
6		{LET @CELLPOINTER("coord"),SECOND}{RIGHT}					
7		{LET @CELLPOINTER("coord"),THIRD}{RIGHT}					
8		{LET @CELLPOINTER("coord"),FOURTH}/rfd1~					
9							
10	FIRST	Buy					
11	SECOND	100					
12	THIRD	shares					
13	FOURTH	32945					
14							
15	OUT	Buy	100	shares	13-Mar-90		
16							

FIGURE 11–19 The {DEFINE} command

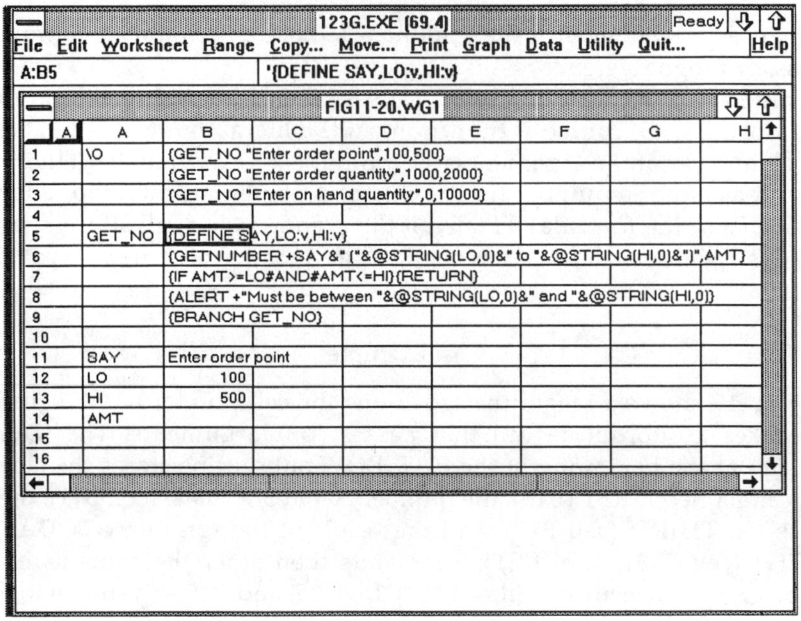

123G.EXE (69.4) Ready

File Edit Worksheet Range Copy... Move... Print Graph Data Utility Quit... Help

A:B5 '{DEFINE SAY,LO:v,HI:v}

FIG11-20.WG1

A	A	B
1	\O	{GET_NO "Enter order point",100,500}
2		{GET_NO "Enter order quantity",1000,2000}
3		{GET_NO "Enter on hand quantity",0,10000}
4		
5	GET_NO	{DEFINE SAY,LO:v,HI:v}
6		{GETNUMBER +SAY&" ("&@STRING(LO,0)&" to "&@STRING(HI,0)&")",AMT}
7		{IF AMT>=LO#AND#AMT<=HI}{RETURN}
8		{ALERT +"Must be between "&@STRING(LO,0)&" and "&@STRING(HI,0)}
9		{BRANCH GET_NO}
10		
11	SAY	Enter order point
12	LO	100
13	HI	500
14	AMT	
15		
16		

FIGURE 11–20 An error-checking subroutine

Another Example

As another example, suppose you are creating a macro in which you prompt users for numeric input several times in a row using the {GETNUMBER} command. To make sure users do not enter invalid numbers in response to {GETNUMBER}, you decide to write some error-checking code. Rather than create new code for each {GETNUMBER} command, though, you decide to write a subroutine that you can reuse as many times as you need.

Figure 11–20 shows an error-checking subroutine named GET_NO, which begins in cell B5. When you call GET_NO, you pass it three arguments—the first part of the prompt for a {GETNUMBER} command (the rest of the prompt is derived later), the lowest value you will accept in response to the {GETNUMBER} command, and the highest value you will accept.

Here is what happens when you execute the \O macro in cell B1. The first call to GET_NO passes the string "Enter order point" as the first part of the prompt, 100 as the lowest acceptable value, and 500 as the highest acceptable value. The {DEFINE SAY,LO:v,HI:v} command then stores the passed arguments. Because the first argument of the {DEFINE} command, SAY, has no suffix, 1-2-3/G stores the data as a label in the SAY range (cell B11). For the LO and HI arguments, the :v suffix causes 1-2-3/G to store the passed data as values in the ranges LO and HI (cells B12 and B13).

Enter order point (100 to 500)

OK

Cancel

FIGURE 11–21 The dialog box produced by the {GETNUMBER} command in Figure 11–20

After 1-2-3/G stores the passed data, it executes the {GETNUMBER} command in cell B6. Figure 11–21 shows the dialog box that the command produces. The prompt for the {GETNUMBER} dialog box is created with the following string formula:

```
+SAY&" ("&@STRING(LO,0)&" to "&@STRING(HI,0)&")"
```

After you enter a response to the dialog box and select OK, 1-2-3/G stores your response in AMT (cell B14). The {IF} command in cell B7 then tests the value in AMT. If it is greater than or equal to the lowest acceptable value and less than or equal to the highest acceptable value, the macro executes the {RETURN} command to return control back to the calling routine.

However, if your response is not within the acceptable bounds, 1-2-3/G executes the {ALERT} command in cell B8, which displays the dialog box in Figure 11–22. The prompt for the dialog box is produced by the following string formula:

```
+"Must be between "&@STRING(LO,0)&" and "&@STRING(HI,0)
```

When you select OK, the {BRANCH GET_NO} command transfers control back to cell B5 and executes the subroutine again.

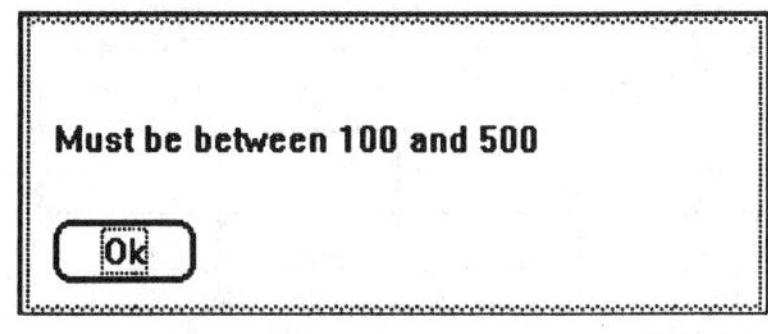

FIGURE 11–22 The error dialog box produced by the {ALERT} command in Figure 11–20

Note

> Do not use the {BRANCH} command to leave a subroutine. If you do, 1-2-3/G may not be able to return to the calling routine. As Figure 11–21 shows, however, you can use the {BRANCH} command to branch to different points within a subroutine.

The {RESTART} Command

When 1-2-3/G encounters a {*subroutine*} command in a subroutine, it immediately starts executing the new subroutine. Then, when the second subroutine ends, 1-2-3/G retraces its steps back to the first subroutine to the instruction following the initial subroutine call. When the first subroutine ends, 1-2-3/G then returns control to the calling macro. When one subroutine calls another, it is known as *nesting* subroutines or creating a *subroutine stack.*

If you do not want 1-2-3/G to retrace its steps back to previous subroutines, you can use the {RESTART} command. This command clears the subroutine stack. In other words, it causes the macro to end when the current subroutine ends. (Of course, if the current subroutine transfers control to another location, the macro does not end.)

For example, suppose you have created the macro in Figure 11–23 for entering orders. The main routine, MAIN, begins with an {ALERT} command, which

123G.EXE Ready

File Edit Worksheet Range Copy... Move... Print Graph Data Utility Quit... Help

A:B16 '{RESTART}{BRANCH NEXT_RTN}

FIG11-23.WG1

A	A	B	C	D	E	F	G
1	MAIN	{ALERT "Add another record",2,3}{QUIT}					
2		{GET_CUST#}					
3		{BRANCH MAIN}					
4	NEXT_RTN	{GOTO}TOTAL~					
5		...					
6							
7	GET_CUST#	{GETNUMBER "Enter the customer number",CUST#}					
8		{IF @ISERR(CUST#)}{BEEP}{BRANCH GET_CUST#}					
9		{GET_AMT}					
10		{RETURN}					
11							
12	GET_AMT	{GETNUMBER "Enter invoice amount (0 to quit)",AMOUNT}					
13		{IF @ISERR(AMOUNT)}{BEEP}{BRANCH GET_AMT}					
14		{IF AMOUNT}{LET TOTAL,TOTAL+AMOUNT}{RETURN}					
15		{ALERT +"The invoice total for today is $"&@STRING(TOTAL,2)}					
16		{RESTART}{BRANCH NEXT_RTN}					
17							
18	CUST#						
19	AMOUNT						
20	TOTAL						

FIGURE 11–23 The {RESTART} command

displays a dialog box that asks you whether you want to add another record to the order entry database. If you select OK, the macro calls the GET_CUST# subroutine, which begins in cell B7. This subroutine begins by prompting you for a customer number. If you enter an invalid customer number, such as a string, the macro beeps and branches back to the start of the subroutine to prompt you again. If your response is a number, the macro calls the GET_AMT subroutine that begins in cell B12. This subroutine prompts you for the invoice amount. If the invoice amount you enter is a number other than zero, the macro adds the amount to the total for the day and then returns to the GET_CUST# subroutine. However, if the invoice amount you enter is zero, meaning you wish to quit, the macro executes the {RESTART} command to clear the subroutine stack and then branches back to the main routine to execute additional commands.

Note that if you did not include the {RESTART} command to clear the subroutine stack but let the macro branch to the main routine anyway, you would get some unexpected results the next time 1-2-3/G completed a subroutine and attempted to retrace its steps through the subroutine stack. You can see the effect by removing the {RESTART} command from B16 and replacing the ellipses (...) in cell B5 with a {RETURN} command. When you execute the modified macro and enter **0** for the invoice amount (0 to quit), 1-2-3/G retraces it steps back through the subroutine stack and eventually reenters the loop in the main routine.

Note

> You can use the {RESTART} command within a *call-table* to cancel a {FORM} command. See "Working with Data Entry Forms" later for an example.

ERROR TRAPPING: THE {ONERROR} COMMAND

When an error occurs during a macro, 1-2-3/G normally displays an error message dialog box then terminates the macro. By using the {ONERROR} command, however, you can provide your own error handling and keep the macro running.

The {ONERROR} command lets you trap errors and branch to recovery routines during a macro. The syntax of the command is

```
{ONERROR branch-location, [message-location]}
```

where *branch-location* is a cell address or range name to which the macro can branch when a 1-2-3/G error occurs. By including the optional *message-location* argument, also a cell address or range name, you can gain access to the error message that 1-2-3/G normally displays in the error message dialog box; 1-2-3/G records the error message as a label in the specified location.

In the example in Figure 11–24, the macro begins with an {ONERROR} command that tells 1-2-3/G to branch to the range TROUBLE_SAVING (cell B7) if a 1-2-3/G error occurs and to store the error message in ERROR_MSG (cell B10). Next, the {GETLABEL} command prompts you for a filename, then saves the name in FILENAME (cell B4) as a label. It then tries to save the current file using that name. If you should enter an invalid name (for example, \SAMPLE), the macro places the error message in ERROR_MSG (cell B10) then branches to the error-handling routine that begins in TROUBLE_SAVING (cell B7). This routine causes 1-2-3/G to beep, display a dialog box that contains the prompt "Invalid character in filename," and branch back to the start of the \F macro.

Note

When 1-2-3/G encounters an {ONERROR} command, it does not immediately branch to *branch-location*. Rather, it waits until an error takes place before branching.

Although the macro in Figure 11–24 shows only one {ONERROR} command, you can actually place multiple {ONERROR} commands within a macro. In fact, you should place them at any point where there is a possibility of a 1-2-3/G error. However, if you use multiple {ONERROR} commands within a macro, you should

123G.EXE [69.4] Ready

File Edit Worksheet Range Copy... Move... Print Graph Data Utility Quit... Help

A:B1 '{ONERROR TROUBLE_SAVING,ERROR_MSG}

FIG11-24.WG1

A	A	B	C	D	E	F
1	\F	{ONERROR TROUBLE_SAVING,ERROR_MSG}				
2		{GETLABEL "Enter filename to save",FILENAME}				
3		/fs				
4	FILENAME		<—Filename from {GETLABEL} stored here			
5		~				
6						
7	TROUBLE_SAVING	{BEEP}{ALERT "Invalid character in filename"}				
8		{BRANCH \F}				
9						
10	ERROR_MSG					
11						
12						

FIGURE 11–24 The {ONERROR} command

have each one branch to a different routine. Note that an {ONERROR} command remains in effect only while the macro is running, and only until an error occurs.

Here are some things to keep in mind as you use {ONERROR}:

- {ONERROR} does not trap macro syntax errors. When 1-2-3/G encounters a syntax error, it displays an error message dialog box and terminates the macro.
- When you press CTRL-BREAK to stop a macro, 1-2-3/G issues an error and branches to the *branch-location* specified by the last {ONERROR} command. To prevent this from happening, you can use the {BREAKOFF} command to disable CTRL-BREAK.
- {ONERROR} clears the subroutine stack. Therefore, be sure to place a {BRANCH} command at the end of your error routine. Otherwise, you may leave the user in limbo.

WORKING WITH DATA ENTRY FORMS

Like Release 3, 1-2-3/G has three special commands for working with data-entry forms—{FORM}, {APPENDBELOW}, and {APPENDRIGHT}. Like the Range Input command, the {FORM} command lets you limit data entry to a specified data range. However, the {FORM} command gives you much greater control over user entries than the Range Input command allows. After entering data in a form, you can then use the {APPENDBELOW} and {APPENDRIGHT} commands to copy the data to the bottom or right of a database and automatically extend the database range in the process.

The {FORM} Command

The {FORM} command suspends macro execution to allow you to enter input in a specified range. As mentioned, {FORM} is similar to Range Input but offers additional options, such as the ability to assign special action keys and to allow (or disallow) certain keys during input. The syntax of this command is

```
{FORM input-location,[call-table],[include-list],[exclude-list]}
```

where *input-location* is the range that you have set up for user input, as in the data-entry form that appears in Figure 11–25. Like the Range Input command the *input-location* argument must include cells that have been unprotected using the Range Unprotect command. For example, in Figure 11–25, the *input-location* is A:A1..A:F18, and the range A:C3..A:C9 consists of unprotected cells. During the {FORM} command, you can input data only in the unprotected cells in

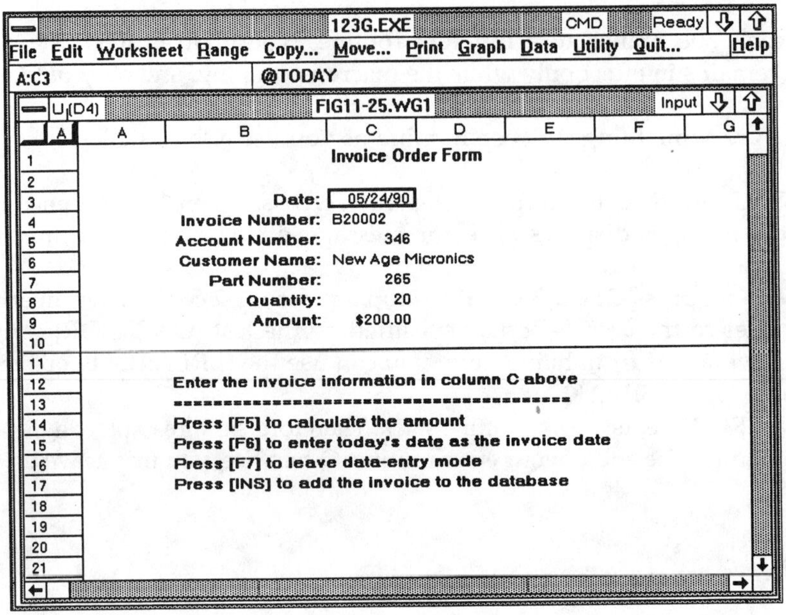

123G.EXE CMD Ready
File Edit Worksheet Range Copy... Move... Print Graph Data Utility Quit... Help
A:C3 @TODAY
U (D4) FIG11-25.WG1 Input

Invoice Order Form

Date: 05/24/90
Invoice Number: B20002
Account Number: 346
Customer Name: New Age Micronics
Part Number: 265
Quantity: 20
Amount: $200.00

Enter the invoice information in column C above
======================================
Press [F5] to calculate the amount
Press [F6] to enter today's date as the invoice date
Press [F7] to leave data-entry mode
Press [INS] to add the invoice to the database

FIGURE 11–25 A sample data-entry form for the {FORM} command

input-location, and pointer movement is restricted to those cells. The *input-location* can be any size you want, and can even be a 3–D range.

The optional *call-table* argument is a two-column range that includes a list of keys in the first column and macro commands (or formulas) that you assign each key in the adjacent column. During the {FORM} command, these keys perform the commands you assign them and revert to their original actions when the {FORM} command ends. You can assign actions to *any* keyboard key, including any typewriter keys and any macro keynames. (For a list of macro keynames, see Table 10–1 in Chapter 10.)

A sample *call-table* appears in Figure 11–26 in the ACTION_ KEYS range, A:J3..A:K6. (Table 11–3 shows all the ranges used in the example macro.) Notice that the *call-table* assigns macro instructions or formulas to the macro keynames {GOTO}, {WINDOW}, {QUERY}, and {INS} (F5, F6, F7, and INS).

Like the Range Input command, you end the {FORM} command by pressing ESC or ENTER. When you press either key, here is what happens:

- 1-2-3/G continues the macro by executing the next command following {FORM}.
- The cell pointer remains where it was when you pressed ENTER or ESC.

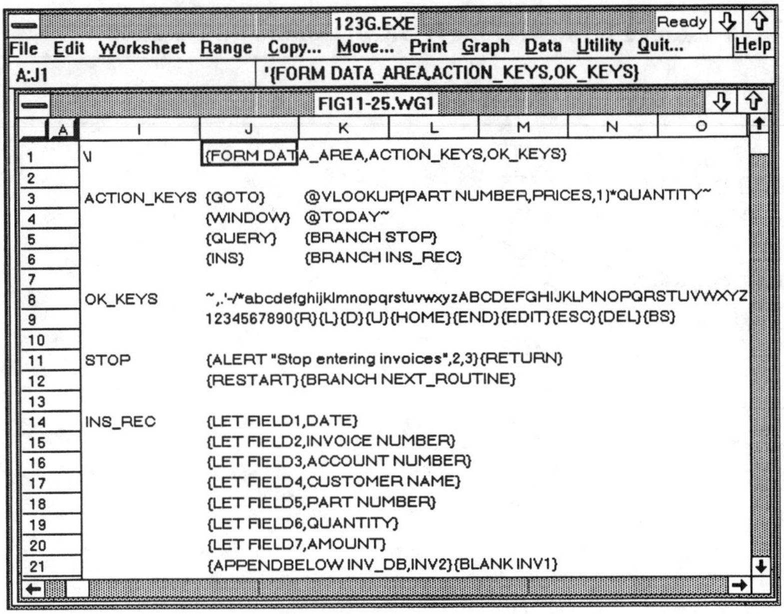

```
123G.EXE                                                   Ready
File  Edit  Worksheet  Range  Copy...  Move...  Print  Graph  Data  Utility  Quit...   Help
A:J1          '{FORM DATA_AREA,ACTION_KEYS,OK_KEYS}
FIG11-25.WG1
   A    I              J           K        L        M        N        O
1       \I             {FORM DATA_AREA,ACTION_KEYS,OK_KEYS}
2
3       ACTION_KEYS    {GOTO}      @VLOOKUP(PART NUMBER,PRICES,1)*QUANTITY~
4                      {WINDOW}    @TODAY~
5                      {QUERY}     {BRANCH STOP}
6                      {INS}       {BRANCH INS_REC}
7
8       OK_KEYS        ~,.'-/*abcdefghijklmnopqrstuvwxyzABCDEFGHIJKLMNOPQRSTUVWXYZ
9                      1234567890{R}{L}{D}{U}{HOME}{END}{EDIT}{ESC}{DEL}{BS}
10
11      STOP           {ALERT "Stop entering invoices",2,3}{RETURN}
12                     {RESTART}{BRANCH NEXT_ROUTINE}
13
14      INS_REC        {LET FIELD1,DATE}
15                     {LET FIELD2,INVOICE NUMBER}
16                     {LET FIELD3,ACCOUNT NUMBER}
17                     {LET FIELD4,CUSTOMER NAME}
18                     {LET FIELD5,PART NUMBER}
19                     {LET FIELD6,QUANTITY}
20                     {LET FIELD7,AMOUNT}
21                     {APPENDBELOW INV_DB,INV2}{BLANK INV1}
```

FIGURE 11–26 The {FORM} command and its associated options

- All the keys in the *call-table* resume their default 1-2-3/G actions.

Note

> You can locate a *call-table* anywhere within your worksheet file, or even in another worksheet file. If you select another worksheet file as the location for your *call-table*, be sure to use the full address (filename, worksheet letter, and range name or address) for the *call-table* argument.

The optional *include-list* argument is a range containing allowable keystrokes. Any keys omitted from this list are ignored during the {FORM} command. Like the *call-table* range, the *include-list* range can include any keyboard key. In Figure 11–26, the *include-list* argument is OK_KEYS; the name assigned to A:J8..A:J9. Notice that because the {FORM} command is case sensitive, the range includes a full set of lower-case and upper-case letters. Likewise, when you place a letter key in the *call-table* or *exclude-list*, make sure to include both lower and upper case, for example, a and A.

TABLE 11-3 Range Names for the {FORM} Command Example

Range Name	Address
\I	A:J1
ACCOUNT NUMBER	A:C5
ACTION_KEYS	A:J3..A:K6
AMOUNT	A:C9
CUSTOMER NAME	A:C6
DATA_AREA	A:A1..A:F18
DATE	A:C3
FIELD1	C:A2
FIELD2	C:B2
FIELD3	C:C2
FIELD4	C:D2
FIELD5	C:E2
FIELD6	C:F2
FIELD7	C:G2
INS_REC	A:J14
INV1	A:C3..A:C9
INV2	C:A2..C:G2
INVOICE NUMBER	A:C4
INV_DB	C:A7..C:G12
OK_KEYS	A:J8..A:J9
PART NUMBER	A:C7
PRICES	B:A3..B:B15
QUANTITY	A:C8
STOP	A:J11

Note

If you use an *include-list*, be sure to include ~ (tilde) and {ESC} in your list or you will not be able to use ENTER or ESC to exit the {FORM} command.

The optional *exclude-list* argument is a range containing a list of keystrokes to ignore during user input. Any keys omitted from this list are allowed during the {FORM} command. This argument, like the other optional arguments, can include any keyboard key. Here's a typical *exclude-list*:

```
BAD_KEYS      {HELP}{RUN}
```

This *exclude-list* prevents you from using the HELP (F1) and RUN (ALT-F3) keys during the {FORM} command.

Note

> If you use an *include-list* and you want to be able to use the SPACE-BAR when entering data in your form, make sure to include a blank space in the list of allowable keys. In fact, the label in cell A:J9 of Figure 11–26 includes a blank space following {BS}, although you cannot see it.

Note

> 1-2-3/G accepts only one list argument. Therefore, if you specify an *include-list*, you should not specify an *exclude-list*, and vice versa. In fact, if you specify both an *include-list* and an *exclude-list*, 1-2-3/G will use only the *include-list*.

If you wish to include an optional argument in the {FORM} command but omit preceding optional arguments, make sure you include an argument separator (usually a comma) for each missing argument. For example, here is some sample syntax for the {FORM} command in Figure 11–26 when you want to use an *exclude-list* named BAD_KEYS and omit the *include-list*:

```
{FORM DATA_AREA,ACTION_KEYS,,BAD_KEYS}
```

If you do not include any optional arguments for the {FORM} command, 1-2-3/G behaves exactly as it does during the Range Input command (see Chapter 3 for information on Range Input).

How the Example Macro Works

Here's how the {FORM} command in Figure 11–26 works. The *input-location* is DATA_AREA, A:A1..A:F18. The unprotected range within DATA_AREA is A:C3..A:C9 and is assigned the name INV1. As Figure 11–25 shows, rows 14 through 17 provide information about special keys you can use during data entry.

When 1-2-3/G encounters the {FORM} command, it moves the cell pointer to the first unprotected cell in DATA_AREA, which in this case is cell A:C3. From this point on, you can only move the cell pointer within the INV1 range. You can press any key included in the OK_KEYS range, A:J8..A:J9.

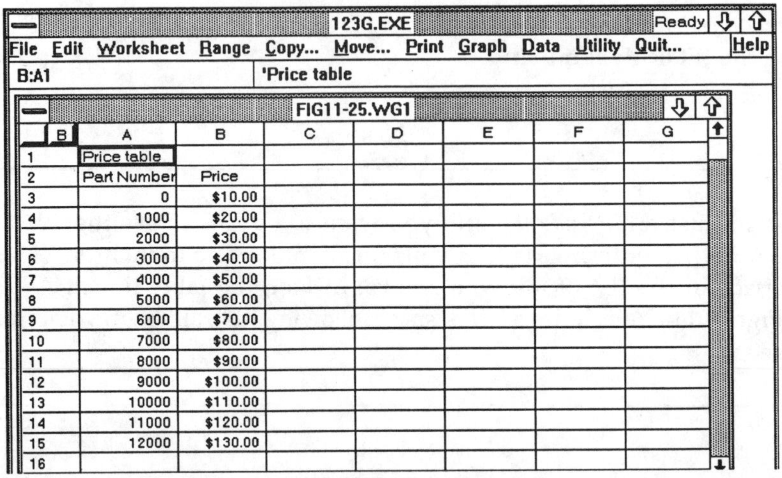

B	A	B	C	D	E	F	G
1	Price table						
2	Part Number	Price					
3	0	$10.00					
4	1000	$20.00					
5	2000	$30.00					
6	3000	$40.00					
7	4000	$50.00					
8	5000	$60.00					
9	6000	$70.00					
10	7000	$80.00					
11	8000	$90.00					
12	9000	$100.00					
13	10000	$110.00					
14	11000	$120.00					
15	12000	$130.00					
16							

FIGURE 11–27 The PRICES vertical lookup table, B:A3..B:B15

In addition, you can use any key in the *call-table* to assist in the data-entry process. These keys are assigned in the ACTION_ KEYS range, A:J3..A:K6. Here are the descriptions of the actions assigned to the key names:

• {GOTO} This key is intended for entering the invoice amount in cell C:C9. When you press F5, the macro performs a vertical lookup on a prices table (the range PRICES, B:A3..B:B15, in Figure 11–27), given the part number (the number you entered in cell A:C7). The macro then multiplies the price by the quantity in cell A:C8 (QUANTITY), places the result in the current cell, and returns to the {FORM} command.

• {WINDOW} This key is intended for entering the date in cell A:C3. When you press F6, the macro inserts @TODAY in the current cell and returns to the {FORM} command.

• {QUERY} When you press F7, the macro branches to STOP (cell A:J11) and displays a dialog box asking whether you want to stop entering invoices. If you select OK, the macro executes the {RESTART} command to clear the subroutine stack then branches to NEXT_ROUTINE (a routine not shown in the macro). If you select Cancel, the macro executes the {RETURN} command, which causes the macro to return to the {FORM} command.

• {INS} When you press INS, the macro branches to the INS_REC routine. The purpose of this routine is to add a record to the end of the invoice database, INV_DB. The series of {LET} commands move the data in the vertical range INV1 (A:C3..A:C9) to the horizontal range INV2 (C:A2..C:G2), one cell at a time beginning with DATE (A:C3). (The INV2 range is shown in Figure 11–28.) The final line of the routine uses the {APPENDBELOW} command to add a record to the end of the invoice database, INV_DB, automatically expanding the range in the process (see the next section for more on {APPENDBELOW}). The macro then blanks the input area, INV1, and returns to the {FORM} command.

Notes on the {FORM} Command

Here are some things to keep in mind when you use the {FORM} command in a macro:

- Despite the fact that the previous example uses an *include-list*, you are more likely to use an *exclude-list* than an *include-list*. The simple reason is that the list of keystrokes you want to disallow is usually far shorter than the list you want to accept. For example, suppose ABS (F4) and NAME (F5) are the only keys you want to disallow during data entry for the {FORM} command in Figure 11–26. You might enter the following EXCLUDE_KEYS range in place of the OK_KEYS range in Figure 11–26:

  ```
  EXCLUDE_KEYS      {ABS}{NAME}
  ```

  You would then use the following command in place of the existing {FORM} command in cell A:J1:

  ```
  {FORM DATA_AREA,ACTION_KEYS,,EXCLUDE_KEYS}
  ```

- Like the Range Input command, you cannot use any menu commands while the {FORM} command is in effect. This means, for example, that you cannot use the {MENU}, /, or {ALT} command in a *call-table* to access the menu, even if you put these keys in the optional *include-list*. Therefore, you cannot use menu commands (for example, /rt for Range Transpose) in the second column of a *call-table*.
- Besides ESC and ENTER, another way to leave the {FORM} command is by pressing CTRL-BREAK. Therefore, you cannot place the {BREAK} command in the *exclude-list*. If you do, 1-2-3/G will simply ignore it and allow CTRL-BREAK anyway. If you want to disallow CTRL-BREAK, place a {BREAKOFF} command before the {FORM} command.

The {APPENDBELOW} and {APPENDRIGHT} Commands

The {APPENDBELOW} and {APPENDRIGHT} commands let you copy data from one range (the source range) to the bottom or right of another range (the target range), automatically extending the address of the target range to include the appended data. The syntax of these commands is

```
{APPENDBELOW target-location,source-location}
```

```
{APPENDRIGHT target-location,source-location}
```

where *source-location* and *target-location* are both range names. The range name definition for target-location expands to include the appended data.

By combining the {APPENDBELOW} or {APPENDRIGHT} command with the {FORM} or Range Input command, you can take data from a data-entry form and copy it to a database. For example, the previous section shows how to use {APPENDBELOW} with the data-entry form in Figure 11–25. Here's another way to use {APPENDBELOW} with the same form. The following code appends the data you enter in the form to the bottom of the invoice database:

```
{FORM DATA_AREA}
/rtINV1~INV2~{APPENDBELOW INV_DB,INV2}
```

When 1-2-3/G encounters these commands, the {FORM} command pauses the macro, allowing you to enter invoice information in the unprotected range named INV1 (A:C3..A:C9) in the entry form named DATA_AREA (A:A1..A:F18). The macro then uses the Range Transpose command to transpose the data from its vertical orientation in the INV1 range to a horizontal orientation in the INV2

123/G Ready
File Edit Worksheet Range Copy... Move... Print Graph Data Utility Quit... Help
C:A13 33017
(D4) FIG11-25.WG1

C	A	B	C	D	E	F	G
1	FIELD1	FIELD2	FIELD3	FIELD4	FIELD5	FIELD6	FIELD7
2	05/24/90	B20002	346	New Age Micronic	265	20	$200.00
3							
4							
5							
6				Invoice Database			
7	DATE	INV_NO	ACCT_NO	CUST_NO	PART_NO	QUANTITY	AMOUNT
8	05/23/90	B19997	456	Cabrillo Tire Sales	920	3	$30.00
9	05/23/90	B19998	126	Pelligrini and Asso	170	5	$50.00
10	05/23/90	B19999	672	Shores Estates	803	12	$120.00
11	05/24/90	B20000	374	Groff Technical	196	9	$90.00
12	05/24/90	B20001	591	Ocean Auto Sales	842	100	$1,000.00
13	05/24/90	B20002	346	New Age Micronic	265	20	$200.00
14							
15							
16							
17							
18							
19							
20							
21							
22							
23							

FIGURE 11–28 Results of the {APPENDBELOW} command

range (C:A2..C:G2). Next, the macro appends the data in INV2 to the invoice database table, INV_DB, and expands INV_DB to include the new record (from C:A7..C:G12 to C:A7..C:G13), as shown in Figure 11–28.

{APPENDBELOW} and {APPENDRIGHT} cannot execute if either of the following conditions exist:

- When the number of rows (for {APPENDBELOW}) or the number of columns (for {APPENDRIGHT}) in the *source-location* is greater than the number of rows or columns available below or to the right of the *target-location*.
- When appending data would overwrite data below or to the right of the *target-location*.

Tip: Transposing data before using {APPENDBELOW} or {APPENDRIGHT}

One disadvantage of the {APPENDBELOW} and {APPENDRIGHT} commands is that they are incapable of changing the orientation of your data when they copy it to a database. This is not a problem if your data-entry form and database have the same orientation (for example, they are both oriented horizontally). But suppose, they are oriented differently.

For example, suppose you have the vertical input range INV1 (A:C3..A:C9 in Figure 11–25), and you want to use the {APPENDBELOW} command to copy the data in INV1 to the bottom of the INV_DB database (C:A7..C:G12 in Figure 11–28) in a horizontal format. If you use the following commands:

```
{FORM DATA_AREA}
{APPENDBELOW INV_DB,INV1}
```

1-2-3/G copies the data in INV1 to the end of the INV_DB database, all in the first column. It does not transpose the data to match INV_DB's horizontal format.

To get around this problem, you need to transpose the data to an intermediate range whose orientation matches your database. You can then use {APPENDBELOW} or {APPENDRIGHT} without any difficulty. Consider using Range Transpose (or a series of {LET} commands) to transpose the data to the proper orientation.

CREATING CUSTOM DIALOG BOXES

If you have worked with a previous release of 1-2-3, you know that one of the most appealing features of its macro facility was the ability to create your own custom menus. These menus worked just like 1-2-3's command menu, complete with command highlight and command descriptions.

In 1-2-3/G, however, the macro facility does not allow you to create custom menus that work like 1-2-3/G's command menu. Rather, you can create your own custom dialog boxes. In fact, Lotus has shifted the entire emphasis away from creating custom menus toward creating custom dialog boxes.

{MENUBRANCH} and {MENUCALL} are the commands you use to create custom dialog boxes. These commands are variations of the {BRANCH} and {*subroutine*} commands, allowing you to branch to dialog box instructions or call them as subroutines.

Whether you use {MENUCALL} or {MENUBRANCH} to create a dialog box depends on what you want to happen after an item in the dialog box is chosen and the commands associated with it are executed. For example, if you want your macro to return to the original calling routine and execute the commands following the command that creates the dialog box, you use the {MENUCALL} command. However, if you do not want your macro to return to the original calling routine, you can use {MENUBRANCH} instead.

The {MENUBRANCH} Command

The {MENUBRANCH} command creates a custom dialog box, waits for you to select an item, and branches to the macro commands associated with that item. It does not return to the calling routine. The syntax of the command is

{MENUBRANCH *location*}

where *location* refers to the upper-left cell in the range that contains the dialog box items, descriptions, and associated commands.

For example, Figure 11–29 shows a {MENUBRANCH} command in cell B19 and the dialog box the command creates. The *location* argument for the {MENU-BRANCH} command is MAIN, the name assigned to cell B21. Notice that this cell contains the label 'Add, which is the first item in the dialog box that the {MENUBRANCH} command creates.

If you select Add from the dialog box, the macro executes the {ADD} command, which makes a call to the ADD subroutine. When the ADD subroutine is completed, the macro ends because of the blank cell in B25; control never returns to the routine that contains the {MENUBRANCH} command.

However, if you select Cancel from the dialog box (or press ESC), the {MENUBRANCH} command is aborted and control returns to the instruction following the {MENUBRANCH} command in the original calling routine. For

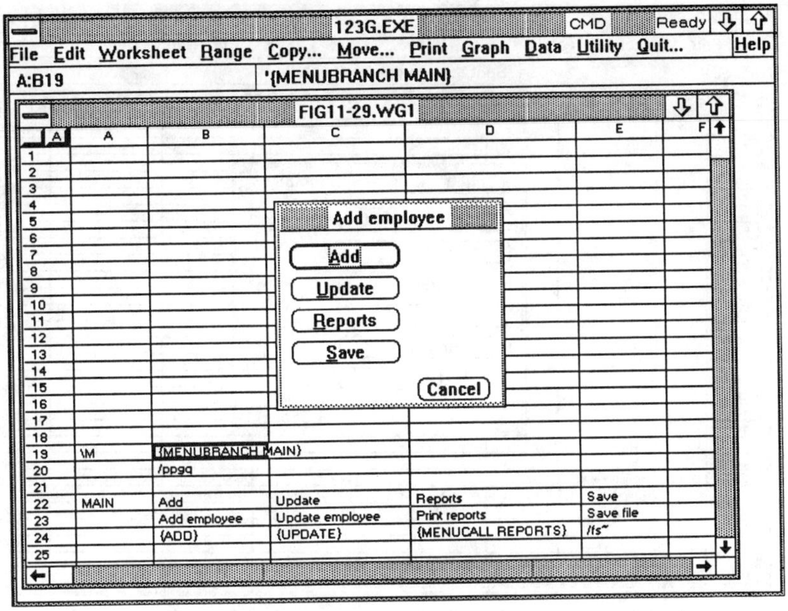

FIGURE 11–29 The {MENUBRANCH} command

example, if you select Cancel for the dialog box in Figure 11–29, the macro executes the printing instructions /ppgq in cell B20.

The {MENUCALL} Command

{MENUCALL} differs from {MENUBRANCH} in that it performs a subroutine call to the instructions associated with a dialog box item. The syntax for {MENUCALL} is identical to that of {MENUBRANCH}

{MENUCALL *location*}

{MENUCALL} displays the dialog box referenced by *location*, and waits for you to select an item. Once the instructions associated with the selected item are completed, macro control returns to the instruction immediately following the {MENUCALL} command in the calling routine, and the macro continues execution from that point.

For example, suppose you replace the {MENUBRANCH} command in cell B19 of Figure 11–29 with a {MENUCALL} command, and execute the macro. If you select Add, the macro executes the ADD subroutine then returns to the command following the {MENUCALL} command. Therefore, the macro always executes the printing instructions in cell B20,

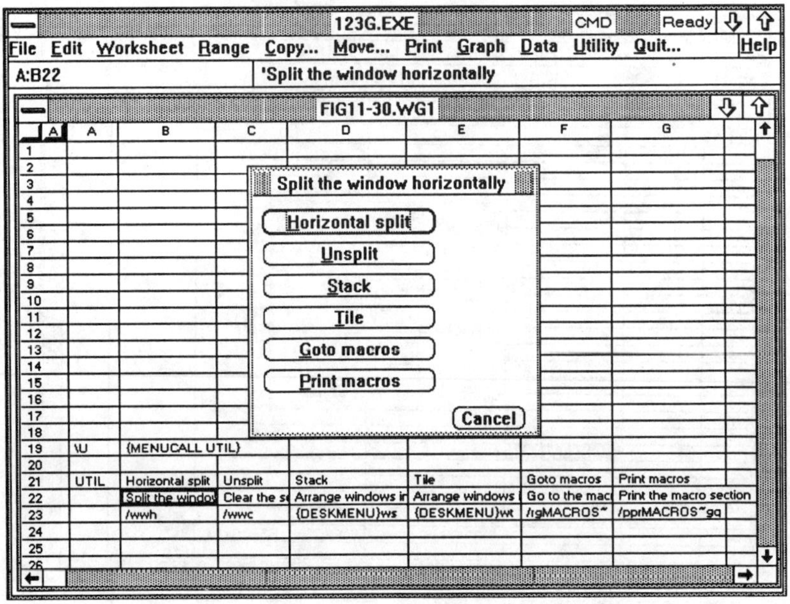

FIGURE 11–30 A sample utility dialog box

regardless of the item you select in the dialog box (even if you select Cancel or press ESC).

Creating a Custom Dialog Box

To create a custom dialog box, you need to create two sets of instructions. The first set includes either a {MENUBRANCH} or {MENUCALL} command. The second set includes the actual dialog box instructions themselves. This section describes how to enter these instructions and where to place them. After reading this section, you will get a chance to apply the concepts to create the custom dialog box in Figure 11–30.

To activate a dialog box, you need a macro routine that includes a {MENUBRANCH} or {MENUCALL} command. If all you want the macro to do is to activate the dialog box, place a {MENUBRANCH} or {MENUCALL} command in a cell by itself. (Make sure to assign a range name to the upper-left cell of the routine so that you can activate it later as a macro.)

As you enter the {MENUBRANCH} or {MENUCALL} command, you will need to decide on the location argument for the command. Typically, you will use a range name for the argument, although you can also use a cell address. For example, to create a simple routine whose only function is to activate the dialog box that begins in the cell named STARTUP, place the command {MENUBRANCH STARTUP} in a blank cell.

Next, you need to choose a location for the dialog box instructions. These instructions include dialog box item names, command descriptions, and associated commands, all in separate cells. Be sure to choose a location that has plenty of room. Here is the general format for the instructions to create a dialog box:

\M	{MENUBRANCH MENU_NAME}		
MENU_NAME	Item name 1	Item name 2	Item name 3
	Description 1	Description 2	Description 3
	Command set 1	Command set 2	Command set 3

Enter the dialog box item names in consecutive cells in the first row of the dialog box commands, as shown above and in row 22 of Figure 11–29. Be sure to leave a blank cell to the right of your last item; 1-2-3/G interprets a blank cell as the end of your item list. Here are some other guidelines for entering dialog box items:

- You can include up to eight items in your dialog box.
- You can enter items as labels, numbers, or string formulas.
- Dialog box items can be up to 128 characters long. Be aware, however, that if you make them wider than approximately 70 characters, the dialog box will extend beyond the edge of the screen. In general, you should keep your dialog box items relatively short and plan to use command descriptions to further explain each item as it is selected.
- Begin each dialog box item with a different letter or number. This lets you select from your dialog box by pressing the first character of the item. Suppose, for example, that you use Split and Stack as two items in your dialog box. If you press **S** when this dialog box is displayed, 1-2-3/G selects the first item that starts with the character S, in this case, Split. You can still select Stack, however, by clicking on it, or by highlighting it and pressing ENTER.

Next, enter a command description for each dialog box item in the cell directly below the item, as in row 23 of Figure 11–29. Here are some guidelines for entering the command descriptions:

- Command descriptions can be labels, numbers, or formulas.
- Although command descriptions can be up to 256 characters long, if you make them longer than approximately 70 characters, the dialog box will extend beyond the edge of the screen.
- As you enter your descriptions, do not be concerned if they look like they are overlapping one another. As long as you place each description in a separate cell, 1-2-3/G will have no trouble interpreting your descriptions, even though they may appear to overlap.

After entering the item names and descriptions for the dialog box, the next step is to enter the macro instructions that go with each item. Enter these instructions immediately below the description for that item (for example, row 24 of Figure 11–29). You can enter any commands you like. Be aware, however, that if you are using a {MENUBRANCH} command to activate the dialog box, the macro will branch to these instructions. If you are using a {MENUCALL} routine, the macro will call these instructions as a subroutine.

As the final step, you need to assign a name to the cell containing the first dialog box item (for example, MAIN or STARTUP). This name must be the same as the name you used for the *location* argument in the {MENUCALL} or {MENUBRANCH} command that activates your dialog box.

A Sample Dialog Box

Each item in the sample dialog box in Figure 11–30 performs a simple 1-2-3/G function, such as splitting or clearing a window, stacking or tiling windows, or printing the macro range. Use the following steps to create this macro dialog box:

1. Begin by selecting cell A19 and enter the label **'\U** in the cell. Next, use the Range Name Labels Right command to assign the name to cell B19. Next, in B19 enter **{MENUCALL UTIL}**.
2. Enter the label **UTIL** in cell A21. Next, use the Range Name Labels Right command to assign the name UTIL to cell B21.
3. With the cell pointer in cell B21, enter the following dialog box items and descriptions, each in its own separate cell. Use Figure 11–30 as a guide.

Item	Description
Horizontal split	Split the window horizontally
Unsplit	Clear the second window pane
Stack	Arrange windows in a stack
Tile	Arrange windows in tiles
Goto macros	Go to the macro section
Print macros	Print the macro section

4. Enter the macro instruction associated with each dialog box item in the third row of the dialog box (row 23), as shown in Figure 11–30.

Now you are ready to try your dialog box macro. Since you named the macro \U, press CTRL-U and the dialog box displays as in Figure 11–30, waiting for you to select an item.

Exiting from Macro Dialog Boxes

To exit from a macro dialog box, select Cancel or press ESC. 1-2-3/G returns control to the instruction immediately following the {MENUBRANCH} or {MENUCALL} command. Once you select a dialog box item, however, the only way you can stop the macro is with CTRL-BREAK. If you press CTRL-BREAK while your macro dialog box is displayed, you exit the dialog box and cancel the macro.

CHANGING THE EFFECT OF CTRL-BREAK: {BREAKOFF} AND {BREAKON}

As you know, you can stop a macro at any time by pressing CTRL-BREAK. But suppose you are developing a model, and you are concerned that if a user presses CTRL-BREAK, it might adversely affect your macro, or the user might see some sensitive data. To prevent this from happening, you can place a {BREAKOFF} command at the beginning of a critical operation in your macro to disable CTRL-BREAK, and then use the {BREAKON} command to reenable CTRL-BREAK once the commands have executed. The syntax of these commands is

```
{BREAKOFF}
```

```
{BREAKON}
```

Because {BREAKOFF} disables CTRL-BREAK while a macro is running, you should include it only after you have thoroughly tested your macro. Otherwise, if an error occurs that causes the macro to go into an infinite loop, here are the only ways you can stop the macro:

- In OS/2 1.1, press CTRL-ESC to activate the Task Manager. After a few minutes (sometimes less, sometimes more), the Task Manager will display a window indicating that 1-2-3/G is not responding. Select Enter to have the Task Manager cancel 1-2-3/G.
- In OS/2 1.2, press CTRL-ESC to activate the Task List. Next, highlight 1-2-3/G in the list and select End task to cancel 1-2-3/G. In some cases (if 1-2-3/G is awaiting input when canceled), this method will not work, and OS/2 will produce the same message as OS/2 1.1.
- Reboot your computer.

Any way you choose, the data you have entered since the last time the worksheet file was saved will be lost.

{BREAKON} undoes a {BREAKOFF} command, restoring the use of CTRL-BREAK in a macro. If you do not include a {BREAKON} command in your macro, 1-2-3/G automatically restores the use of CTRL-BREAK when the macro ends.

In the following example, {BREAKOFF} disables CTRL-BREAK prior to running the ACCTSREC subroutine. The macro then uses {BREAKON} to restore CTRL-BREAK following the completion of the subroutine.

```
...
{BREAKOFF}
{ACCTSREC}
{BREAKON}
```

The {BREAK} Command

The {BREAK} command produces the same effect as pressing CTRL-BREAK while you are in the middle of a 1-2-3/G operation, such as when you are responding to a 1-2-3/G command—it returns you to READY mode. Of course, if 1-2-3/G is already in READY mode when the macro encounters a {BREAK} command, the command has no effect. Note that {BREAK} does not stop a macro. {BREAK} has no connection whatsoever to the {BREAKOFF} and {BREAKON} commands.

For example, suppose you have the macro in Figure 11–31 that issues the File Save command then uses a {GETLABEL} command to pause the macro and

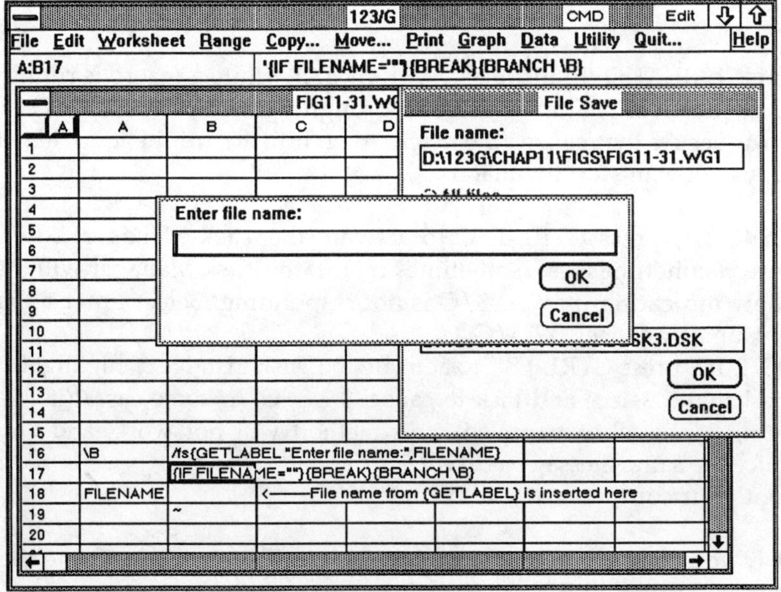

FIGURE 11–31 The {BREAK} command

request a filename. When you type a name and press ENTER, the {GETLABEL} command stores your response in FILENAME (cell B18). The macro then uses the contents of the range in response to the File Save command's File name prompt. However, if you do not type a filename but immediately press ENTER in response to the {GETLABEL} command, the macro executes the {BREAK} command following the {IF}. This command cancels the File Save command and returns 1-2-3/G to READY mode. The macro then branches back to the top and executes again.

Tip: Using {BREAK} to make sure a macro always runs

By placing {BREAK} at the beginning of a macro, you can ensure that the macro will run even if the user is entering data or in the middle of a 1-2-3/G command. Because the {BREAK} command always returns 1-2-3/G to READY mode, you can always be sure that the macro commands that follow will begin executing in the correct context.

SOUNDING TONES

1-2-3/G has two commands for accessing your computer's sound capabilities—{BELL} and {TONE}. The {BELL} command is a carryover from previous releases and lets you sound a short beep in one of four different tones. By contrast, the new {TONE} command lets you generate any sound your computer is capable of producing.

The {BEEP} Command

The {BEEP} command sounds your computer's bell. It is mostly used to draw the user's attention—for example, to alert a user that an error has occurred or a process is complete, to signal the beginning of an interactive command, and the like. The syntax of the command is

```
{BEEP [tone-number]}
```

where the optional *tone-number* argument controls the tone of the bell. There are four available tones, corresponding to the numbers 1–4. If you use a value outside this range, 1-2-3/G divides the number by four and uses the remainder as the value for the tone number. For example, {BEEP 10} is equivalent to {BEEP

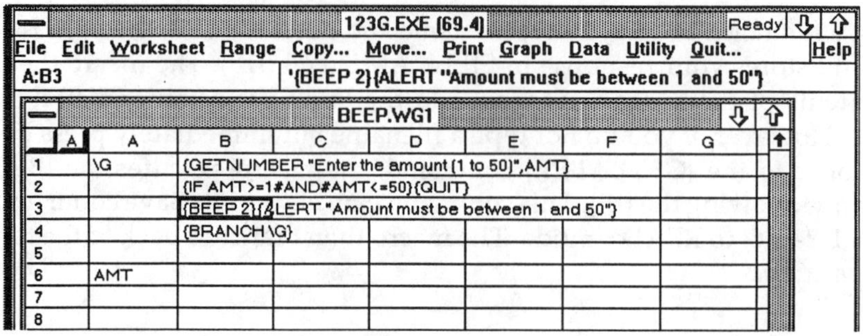

123G.EXE (69.4) Ready

File Edit Worksheet Range Copy... Move... Print Graph Data Utility Quit... Help

A:B3 '{BEEP 2}{ALERT "Amount must be between 1 and 50"}

BEEP.WG1

A	A	B	C	D	E	F	G
1	\G	{GETNUMBER "Enter the amount (1 to 50)",AMT}					
2		{IF AMT>=1#AND#AMT<=50}{QUIT}					
3		{BEEP 2}{ALERT "Amount must be between 1 and 50"}					
4		{BRANCH \G}					
5							
6	AMT						
7							
8							

FIGURE 11–32 The {BEEP} command

2} (if there is no remainder, 1-2-3/G uses tone 4). If you omit the *tone-number* argument, 1-2-3/G assumes a tone equivalent to {BEEP 1}.

Note

> If you have turned off your computer's sound using Presentation Manager's Control Panel, {BEEP} has no effect.

One of the most useful applications of {BEEP} is to signal an error. For example, the macro in Figure 11–32 prompts you for a number between 1 and 50. If you enter a number within the acceptable range, the macro quits. Otherwise, it sounds the bell then displays a dialog box telling you the cause of the error.

The {TONE} Command

The {TONE} command lets you sound a tone of a given frequency and duration. The syntax of the command is

{TONE *frequency,duration*}

where *frequency* is the pitch of the tone in cycles per seconds (hertz) and is a value or the address or name of a cell that contains a value. The *duration* argument is the amount of time the tone sounds in milliseconds. It too must be a value, or the address or name of a cell that contains a value.

The advantage of {TONE} over {BEEP} is that it lets you tailor the tone your macro produces to the given situation. For example, in the macro in Figure 11–33, the first {TONE} command sounds a brief, low tone to indicate that you must respond to the dialog box that the {GETNUMBER} command produces. If you

A	A	B	C	D	E	F	G
1	\G	{TONE 300,200}					
2	AGAIN	{GETNUMBER "Enter sales quantity",SALES}					
3		{IF @ISERR(SALES)}{BRANCH ERROR}					
4		{LET SALES,SALES*PRICE}					
5							
6	ERROR	{TONE 500,500}{BRANCH AGAIN}					
7							
8	SALES						
9	PRICE	20					
10							
11							

FIGURE 11–33 The {TONE} command

make an invalid entry, such as entering a label instead of a number, the macro branches to the ERROR routine, which issues a slightly higher pitch of longer duration, then branches to AGAIN to give you another try at the dialog box.

CONTROLLING THE SCREEN

1-2-3/G offers several commands for controlling the appearance of the screen during a macro. You can use these commands to place your own message in the mode indicator, turn off the frame surrounding worksheets, turn off the menu display, and freeze the window display.

The {INDICATE} Command

The {INDICATE} command lets you replace the contents of the mode indicator box on the right side of the Desktop Title bar with a given string, or make the mode indicator box appear blank. The syntax of the command is

{INDICATE [*string*]}

where *string* can be a label, cell reference, or string formula. The maximum length of *string* is approximately 75 characters (the maximum of characters that will fit in the Desktop Title bar). If *string* is too long, it is truncated. The highlighted mode indicator box expands and contracts to fit the length of the string in your argument.

For example, suppose cell A3 contains the label 'Enter invoice. The command {INDICATE A3} sets the mode indicator to Enter invoice, as shown in Figure 11–34. As another example, {INDICATE SWITCH_MODE} uses the contents of the SWITCH_MODE range as the *string* argument.

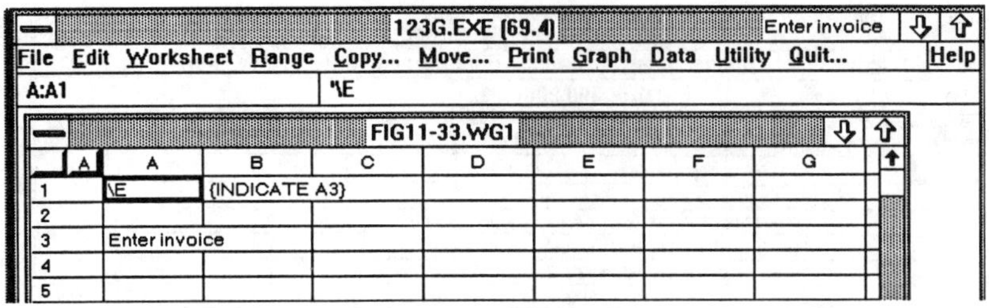

FIGURE 11–34 The {INDICATE} command

If you include an empty string as the *string* argument, as in {INDICATE ""}, the mode indicator box appears blank.

Unlike other macro commands for controlling the screen, the effect of {INDICATE} remains after your macro has ended. For example, if your macro issues the command {INDICATE "Daily balance"} and then does not reset the mode indicator, the indicator continues to display Daily balance after the macro has finished. You can reset the mode indicator in either of two ways: execute {INDICATE} without a *string* argument or leave 1-2-3/G.

The {FRAMEOFF} and {FRAMEON} Commands

The {FRAMEOFF} command turns off the display of 1-2-3/G's worksheet frame (column letters and row numbers) and grid lines. The frame and grid lines remain turned off until the macro encounters a {FRAMEON} command or the macro ends. The syntax of these commands is

```
{FRAMEOFF}
```

```
{FRAMEON}
```

For example, Figure 11–35 shows a 1-2-3/G worksheet window following a {FRAMEOFF} command. Notice that by eliminating the worksheet frame and grid lines during the data-entry process, you can help reduce the user's distraction, letting him or her focus on the data-entry area. To display the data-entry form in Figure 11–35, you would use commands similar to these:

```
{FRAMEOFF}
{FORM DATA_AREA,ACTION_KEYS,OK_KEYS}
{FRAMEON}
```

These commands turn off the worksheet frame and grid lines, display a data-entry form, and redisplay the frame and grid lines when the data-entry process is completed.

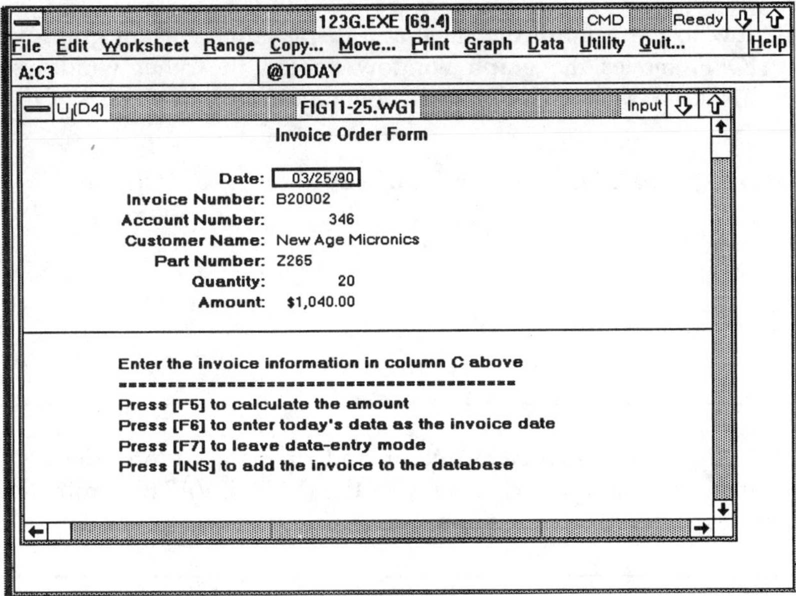

FIGURE 11–35 The effect of the {FRAMEOFF} command

Note

If your macro encounters a {WINDOWSOFF} command before the {FRAMEOFF} command, the results of {FRAMEOFF} will not display until a {WINDOWSON} command is issued. ({WINDOWSOFF} suppresses redrawing of the screen and is reversed by the {WINDOWSON} command.)

Note to Release 2 and 3 users

In previous releases of 1-2-3, the {BORDERSOFF} and {BORDERSON} commands work identically to the {FRAMEOFF} and {FRAMEON} commands. However, they are not available in 1-2-3/G. Use the {FRAMEOFF} and {FRAMEON} commands instead.

The {GRAPHON} and {GRAPHOFF} Commands

{GRAPHON} opens a Graph window and displays a graph in that window using the current graph settings. If a Graph window is already open, {GRAPHON} brings the window to the front of the stack and displays the current graph within it. {GRAPHOFF} moves the graph window behind the other windows on the 1-2-3/G Desktop. The syntax of these commands is

```
{GRAPHON [named-graph],[nodisplay]}
```

```
{GRAPHOFF}
```

Note

> Although the {GRAPHON} command opens a Graph window, it does not activate the window. Use the {WACTIVATE} command if you want to activate the window.

With no arguments, {GRAPHON} displays the Graph window until a {GRAPHOFF}, {?}, {GETNUMBER}, {GETLABEL}, {MENUBRANCH}, {MENUCALL}, or {INDICATE} command is encountered or the macro ends. At this point, 1-2-3/G moves the graph window behind the other windows on the Desktop.

The optional *named-graph* argument makes the named graph you specify the current graph. The name you supply for *named-graph* must be the name you assign to the graph settings using the Graph Name command, not the name of the graph file that contains the graph (see Chapter 7, "Graphs," for more on Graph Name).

When you use the optional nodisplay argument, *named-graph* is made the current graph but the Graph window is not displayed. For example, the command {GRAPHON SALES90,nodisplay} makes the graph SALES90 the current graph but does not open a Graph window. 1-2-3/G uses the SALES90 settings the next time it draws a graph.

The {GRAPHON} and {GRAPHOFF} commands let you create a graph slide show that displays one graph after another at intervals you choose. For example, the following macro displays a series of three graphs, each for three seconds, until you press a key. When you press a key, the macro executes the {GRAPHOFF} command, which places the Graph window behind the other windows on the desktop. If you do not press a key, however, the macro branches back to the top and executes again.

```
\G      {GRAPHON BARSALES}
        {WAIT @NOW+@TIME(0,0,3)}
        {GRAPHON 3DBARSALES}
        {WAIT @NOW+@TIME(0,0,3)}
        {GRAPHON LINESALES}
        {WAIT @NOW+@TIME(0,0,3)}
        {LOOK KEYMASHED}
```

```
{IF KEYMASHED=""}{BRANCH \G}
{GRAPHOFF}
```

The {PANELOFF} and {PANELON} Commands

{PANELOFF} freezes the Control line, title bar, and menu bar during macro execution. These areas of the screen are restored to their normal state when the macro encounters a {PANELON} command, or the macro ends. The syntax of these commands is

```
{PANELOFF}
{PANELON}
```

Note to Release 2 and 3 Users

In Release 2.2 and Release 3, to have 1-2-3 clear the control panel before freezing it, you must include a *clear* argument with the {PANELOFF} command, as in {PANELOFF clear}. In 1-2-3/G, however, the {PANELOFF} command automatically clears the Control line, making the clear argument unnecessary.

Tip: Using {PANELOFF} and {FRAMEOFF} together to clear the screen

Use the {PANELOFF} command before issuing the {FRAMEOFF} command to clear and freeze the title bar, menu bar, and Control line, leaving only the data within your worksheet file visible on the screen. For example, the following macro shows how you can use the {PANELOFF} and {FRAMEOFF} commands to change the look of the 1-2-3/G screen, as shown in Figure 11–36. (The {FRAMEOFF} command turns off the display of the worksheet frame and grid lines, and {FRAMEON} turns then back on.) Compare this figure to Figure 11–35 to see the effect of the {PANELOFF} command.

```
{PANELOFF}{FRAMEOFF}
{FORM DATA_AREA,ACTION_KEYS,OK_KEYS}
{PANELON}{FRAMEON}
```

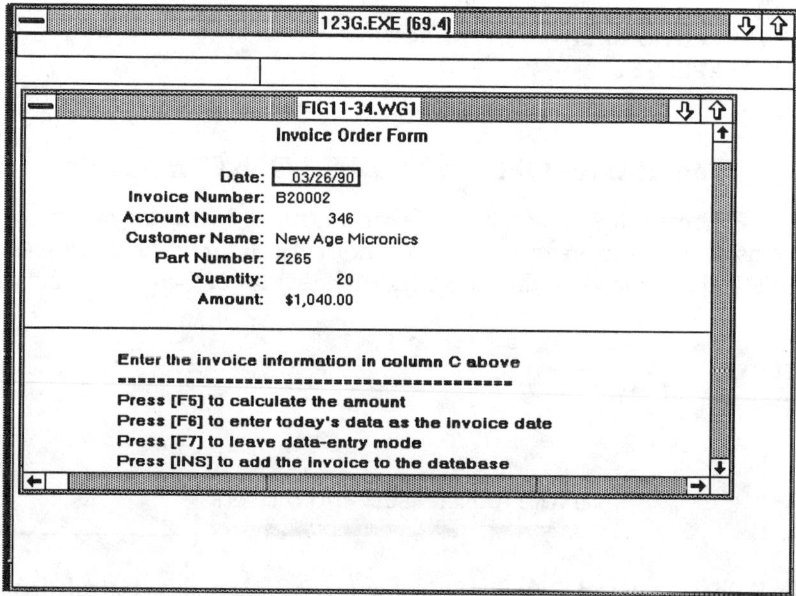

FIGURE 11–36 The effect of the {PANELOFF} and {FRAMEOFF} commands

After your macro executes a {PANELOFF} command, prompts and menus that would normally appear in the Control line, such as those from the Copy and Range Erase commands, do not display.

Note

> In 1-2-3/G, the {INDICATE} command has the same effect as the {PANELOFF} command. That is, besides placing a new indicator in the Control line, {INDICATE} also unfreezes the Control line, the menu bar, and the title bar.

The {WINDOWSOFF} and {WINDOWSON} Commands

Suppose you have written a macro that causes 1-2-3/G to redraw the screen repeatedly as it processes commands, producing a kind of flashing effect. You can eliminate the flashing by using the {WINDOWSOFF} command, which prohibits 1-2-3/G from redrawing the screen. The {WINDOWSOFF} also speeds up your macro because 1-2-3/G does not have to pause to redraw the screen while the macro is executing. The {WINDOWSOFF} command remains in effect until the macro encounters a {WINDOWSON} command, or the macro ends. The syntax of these commands is

```
{WINDOWSOFF}
{WINDOWSON}
```

The {WINDOWSOFF} command affects only the noninteractive parts of a macro. In other words, if the user needs to see a dialog box or message box in order to respond to the macro (for example, the dialog box that appears when you select the Range Format command), 1-2-3/G displays the box despite the {WINDOWSOFF} command.

In the following macro, the {WINDOWSOFF} command suppresses updating of the screen. Next, a data query operation extracts data to an output range, sorts the data in the output range in ascending order using the first field as the primary key, and then prints the output range. Finally, the {WINDOWSON} command cancels the {WINDOWSOFF}, and 1-2-3/G resumes normal worksheet display.

```
\W     {WINDOWSOFF}
       /dqeq{GOTO}OUTPUT~{DOWN}
       /dsd{BS}.{END}{RIGHT}{END}{DOWN}~p~ag
       /ppr{BS}.{END}{RIGHT}{END}{DOWN}~gq
       {WINDOWSON}
```

If you remove the {WINDOWSOFF} command from this macro, 1-2-3/G updates the screen repeatedly as it processes each command, slowing down macro execution, as well as providing a distracting "light show" for anyone watching.

CONTROLLING WINDOWS

1-2-3/G has three new macro commands for controlling windows—{WACTIVATE}, {WMOVE}, and {WSIZE}. Using these commands, you can perform any operation on windows that you would normally perform in READY mode using the mouse or the keyboard. For example, you can activate a window, rearrange windows on the desktop, or resize a window to something more to your liking.

The {WACTIVATE} Command

The {WACTIVATE} command makes the last active worksheet window, or the window you specify, the active window. The syntax of the command is

```
{WACTIVATE [windowname]}
```

where *windowname* is the name of an open window on the 1-2-3/G Desktop.

Although the *windowname* argument is optional, you are likely to find that you use it every time you use {WACTIVATE} to activate a particular window. For example, the following excerpt from a macro activates the Worksheet window named SALES90.WG1 and prints worksheet A of that file to the Preview utility window:

```
...
{WACTIVATE SALES90.WG1}
/fpprA:~sgq
...
```

Once you activate a window, the menu associated with that window becomes active. For example, when you access a Graph window, the menu for the Graph tool becomes the active menu. In the following excerpt from a macro the Graph window named YEAR_END.GPH is activated, the graph type is set to stacked bar, and *x*-axis grid lines are displayed.

```
...
{WACTIVATE YEAR_END.GPH}
/ts
/sggx~
...
```

Note

> You can use the {GRAPHON} command to open and optionally display a Graph window. However, {GRAPHON} does not activate the window.

The {WMOVE} Command

The {WMOVE} command lets you move the active window, or the window you specify, to a given position on the 1-2-3/G desktop. The syntax of the command is

```
{WMOVE x,y,[windowname]}
```

where *x* is the number of inches to the right and *y* is the number of inches above the lower-left corner of the 1-2-3/G desktop. Note that by using a large value for *x* or *y*, you can easily move the window either partially or completely out of view.

If you want to move a particular window, use the optional *windowname* argument, which can be the name of any open window on the desktop. If you use {WMOVE} without *windowname*, 1-2-3/G moves the active window.

For example, the following excerpt from a macro saves the name of the current window in cell A1. It then activates the Graph window named SALES90.GPH and moves it 1.5 inches to the right and 1 inch above the lower-left corner of the 1-2-3/G desktop. Next, the macro pauses for five seconds to display the graph. It then reactivates the original window, placing it at the front of the stack.

```
...
{LET A1,@CELLPOINTER("filename")}
{WACTIVATE SALES90.GPH}
{WMOVE 1.5,1,SALES90.GPH}
{WAIT @NOW+@TIME(0,0,5)}
{WACTIVATE A1}
...
```

Note that if you do not activate a window before moving it with {WMOVE}, the window retains its position in the stack, and you may not be able to see it behind the other windows. Therefore, in the previous example, the {WACTIVATE} command is used to bring the SALES90.GPH into view at the front of the stack before moving it with {WMOVE}.

Note

> If you want to specify *x* and *y* in millimeters rather than inches, use the Utility User Settings International dialog box to change the unit of measure to millimeters.

The {WSIZE} Command

The {WSIZE} command lets you set the active window, or a window you specify, to a particular width and height. The syntax of the command is

```
{WSIZE x,y,[windowname]}
```

where x is the width of the window from the left border to the right border, and y is the height of the window from the bottom border to the top border, both in inches. If you use a large value for x or y, you can easily move part of the window out of view.

If you want to size a particular window, use the optional *windowname* argument, which can be the name of any open window on the desktop. If you use {WSIZE} without *windowname*, 1-2-3/G sizes the active window.

For example, suppose you have opened a file on the desktop, then resized and moved it using the mouse or the keyboard. You then decide that you want to return the window to its original size and position. The following macro resizes the window to its approximate original size and position:

```
\R      {WSIZE 8.54,4.71}
        {WMOVE .0625,1.33}
```

Note

If you want to specify x and y in millimeters rather than inches, use the Utility User Settings International dialog box to change the unit of measure to millimeters.

CONTROLLING RECALCULATION: THE {RECALC} AND {RECALCCOL} COMMANDS

Suppose you have a macro that is located in a very large worksheet file with many complex formulas and dependencies. Rather than have the entire file recalculate when you change the contents of a cell, you can specify manual recalculation (using the Worksheet Global Manual Recalc Manual command) and then have your macro recalculate only specific areas of the worksheet as needed.

The {RECALC} and {RECALCCOL} commands allow you to specify a range within the worksheet file to be recalculated. {RECALC} recalculates the specified range row-by-row, and {RECALCCOL} recalculates it column-by-column. Both commands use the same syntax and accept the same arguments as follows:

```
{RECALC location,[condition],[iterations]}
```

```
{RECALCCOL location,[condition],[iterations]}
```

where *location* refers to a range address or named range in your worksheet file that you want to recalculate.

The optional *condition* argument is usually a logical expression or a reference to a cell that contains a logical expression. However, you can also use a number, formula, string, or cell reference for *condition.* Whichever you use, 1-2-3/G evaluates *condition* as true as long as it does not equal 0. When *condition* equals 0, however, 1-2-3/G evaluates it as false. Blank cells, strings, ERR, and NA equal 0 when used with *condition.*

Note

> If *condition* references a cell that contains a formula that must be recalculated for each iteration of a {RECALC} or {RECALCCOL} command, make sure to place the formula within *location.*

The optional iterations argument is the number of recalculations that you want to take place. The iterations argument can be a number, a formula that evaluates to a number, or a reference to a cell with a number or formula. This argument overrides the Worksheet Global Manual Recalc Iterations setting.

Quite often you will use the *condition* and *iterations* arguments together. In this case, the *iterations* argument specifies the maximum number of recalculations that you want to take place. The recalculations occur until either the *condition* argument is met or the number of iterations expires.

For example, the following command recalculates the cells in the range PROJECT in a column-by-column fashion until the value in the cell named INVEST is greater than or equal to 20,000 or the number of recalculations equals 10.

```
{RECALCCOL PROJECT,INVEST>=20000,10}
```

With either {RECALC} or {RECALCCOL}, only cells within location are recalculated. If the formulas within that range refer to cells located outside the range, those cells are not updated.

Because {RECALC} recalculates *location* in a row-by-row fashion, you should use it to recalculate formulas that are below and to the left of the cells on which those formulas depend. On the other hand, {RECALCCOL} recalculates *location* in a column-by-column fashion. Therefore, you should use it to recalculate formulas that are located above and to the right of the cells on which those formulas depend. If neither of these conditions are met, you will need to use the {CALC} command to recalculate your entire worksheet file.

In actual practice, because of 1-2-3/G's minimal and background recalculation, there are very few cases where you will need to use {RECALC} or {RECALCCOL} to recalculate a range independently of the rest of the worksheet file. In fact, you are likely to find a need for these commands only when you have a large model with many complex formulas and dependencies, and the worksheets in the model are set for manual recalculation.

The macro in Figure 11-37 shows an example of how you might use the {RECALC} command. This macro begins by using the {GETNUMBER} command to prompt you for sales and cost of goods sold (COGS) figures. Next, the macro recalculates the INCOME range (B1..B4) using the {RECALC} command. Finally, the macro displays the gross profit in an {ALERT} box.

In this example, you could have easily used the {CALC} command in place of {RECALC} to recalculate the entire worksheet. However, if you imagine that this worksheet is part of a much larger model with many worksheets and dependent formulas, you can see that {RECALC} is preferable because you do not have to wait for the rest of the file to be recalculated before using the results of the gross profit formula.

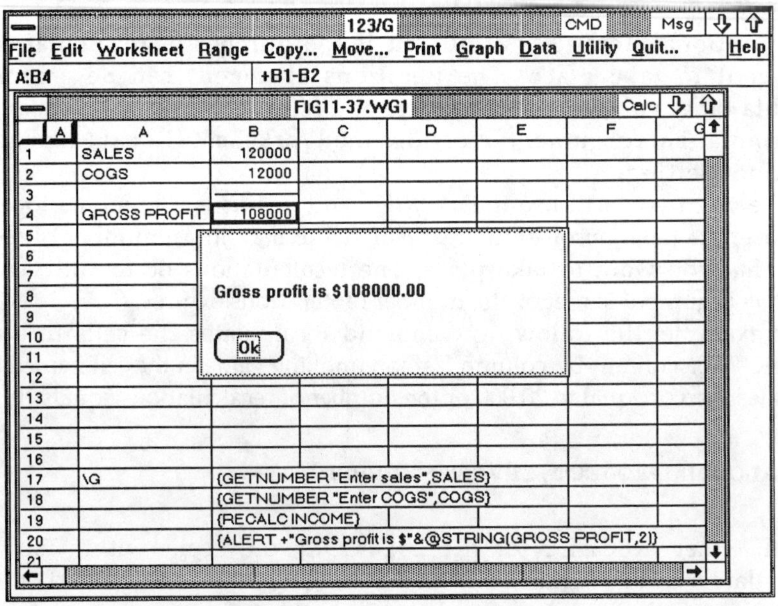

FIGURE 11-37 The {RECALC} command

ACCESSING OS/2: THE {SYSTEM} COMMAND

The {SYSTEM} command suspends macro execution and passes a command to OS/2. When OS/2 has completed the command, it returns control to 1-2-3/G, and the macro resumes at the next instruction. The syntax of the command is

{SYSTEM *command*}

where *command* is an OS/2 command, or batch file, of up to 128 characters in length. Even though *command* is a string argument, you do not have to enclose it in double quotes unless it contains a space. For example, {SYSTEM DIR} and {SYSTEM "COPY TEMP.PRN A:\"} are valid commands, but {SYSTEM COPY TEMP.PRN A:\} is not.

For example, the command {SYSTEM "FORMAT A:"} exits the 1-2-3/G session temporarily, displays an OS/2 windowed command prompt on the screen, and executes the FORMAT A: command to format the disk in drive A. When the FORMAT command is completed, the 1-2-3/G session resumes, and the macro continues executing any instructions that follow the {SYSTEM} command.

Another way to use the {SYSTEM} command is to substitute the name of a batch file for *command*. As you probably know, a batch file contains a list of OS/2 commands that are executed one right after another. By using a batch filename with the {SYSTEM} command, you can have OS/2 execute a series of commands with a single {SYSTEM} command (consult your operating system manual for information on how to create batch files).

Suppose you have created a batch file called ARCHIVE.BAT that includes commands for formatting a new floppy disk and copying files to it. The macro command to execute ARCHIVE.BAT would be {SYSTEM ARCHIVE.BAT}. The commands in ARCHIVE.BAT are executed one at a time by OS/2, and the 1-2-3/G session resumes when all commands listed in ARCHIVE.BAT file are completed.

Here are some tips for making the most of the {SYSTEM} command:

- If you want your macro to return you to the OS/2 windowed command prompt and allow you to work in that environment interactively, place {SYSTEM CMD} in your macro. (If you have used a previous release of 1-2-3, {SYSTEM CMD} is the equivalent of using the /System command.) This command suspends the 1-2-3/G session and returns to the operating system, where you can issue commands from the keyboard. You can then return to 1-2-3/G any time by typing **EXIT** and pressing ENTER at the OS/2 prompt.
- If you are writing a macro whose instructions will vary depending on the version of OS/2 the user is running, you can use @INFO("osversion") to determine the operating system version. For example, if you are using

OS/2 Version 1.1 on your system, @INFO("osversion") returns the label 'OS/2 Version 10.10. Likewise, if you are using OS/2 Version 1.2, the same function returns the label 'OS/2 Version 10.20 (see Chapter 5, "Functions," for more).
- Some OS/2 commands return an error code when they encounter a problem. If you want to read the error code in 1-2-3/G, use @INFO("osreturncode") following the {SYSTEM} command (see Chapter 5).

READING AND WRITING ASCII FILES

As you know, you can use the File Import command to read ASCII files from disk into the current worksheet file and the Print File command to write a range from the current worksheet file to an ASCII file on disk. Typically, you use these commands to read and write large chunks of data to and from disk.

But suppose that you want to work with smaller segments of an ASCII file. For example, consider the case where you want to read specific lines of information from an ASCII file, rather than the entire file. Alternatively, suppose you want to append information to the end of an existing file, without overwriting the rest of the file.

1-2-3/G has several little-used though very powerful commands for working with ASCII files—{OPEN}, {CLOSE}, {WRITE}, {WRITELN}, {READ}, {READLN}, {SETPOS}, {GETPOS}, and {FILESIZE}. The {OPEN} command allows you to open or create an ASCII file. Once the file is open, you can use the {WRITE} or {WRITELN} commands to write information from your 1-2-3/G worksheet file to the ASCII file. Conversely, you can use the {READ} or {READLN} commands to read information from the ASCII text file into your worksheet file. Once you've finished working with the ASCII file, you can use the {CLOSE} command to close it.

To read or write information starting at a specific position in an ASCII file, you can use the {SETPOS} command. This command allows you to set the position of the file pointer within an ASCII text file before reading from or writing to that file. The {GETPOS} and {FILESIZE} commands compliment the {SETPOS} command. {GETPOS} allows you to determine the current position of the file pointer, and the {FILESIZE} command allows you to determine the number of bytes (size) in the file.

The sections that follow explain the use of each of these commands in more detail. After explaining how to use each command, two examples are shown. The first example shows you how to write data to an ASCII text file. The second example shows you how to read specific data from an ASCII text file.

Opening a File

Before you can manipulate any data in an ASCII file, you must first open the file using the {OPEN} command. You can use this command to open either an existing ASCII file or to create an entirely new ASCII file. The {OPEN} command takes the form:

```
{OPEN filename,access-type}
```

where the *filename* is the name of the ASCII file, including its extension, that you want to open or create. You can provide a filename, or you can use a range address or range name that contains the full filename. If the file is located outside the current directory, you must enclose the filename in quotes, for example, "C:\ACCOUNTS\CLIENTS.PRN".

The *access type* argument is a letter that represents one of four modes you can use to access an ASCII text file. The access mode you use depends on what you want to do with the file. 1-2-3/G offers the following four access modes for the {OPEN} command:

- **W** (write): Creates a new file using the name you specify and places the file pointer at the beginning of that file. If a file with the same name already exists, 1-2-3/G overwrites it; all of the file contents will be lost. With this option you can both write to and read from the file that is created.
- **M** (modify): Opens an existing file and positions the file pointer at the beginning of the file. With this option you can both read from and write to the opened file. However, unlike the W (write) option, the M (modify) option can only be used to open an existing ASCII file, not create a new one.
- **R** (read): Opens an existing ASCII file and places the file pointer at the beginning of that file. However, you can only read from the file. You cannot write to it.
- **A** (append): Opens an existing ASCII file and places the file pointer at the end of the file. The file is write only. That is, you cannot read information from the file; you can only write to it. Use this option when you want to add information to the end of an existing ASCII file.

Only one ASCII file can be open at a time. If 1-2-3/G detects an open ASCII text file when the {OPEN} command is encountered, it will close the first text file before opening the second one.

If 1-2-3/G is successful in opening the specified text file, it passes macro control to the next cell of the macro. However, if the {OPEN} command fails to open the file, 1-2-3/G processes the instructions in the same cell as the {OPEN} command.

Closing a File

Once you open an ASCII file, it will remain open until you close it in one of three ways. The first way to close an open file is to use the {CLOSE} command. This command closes the currently open ASCII file and saves any changes you may have made to the file. The second way to close an open file is to include a second {OPEN} command in your macro. As mentioned, if 1-2-3/G detects an open ASCII file when it encounters an {OPEN) command, it will close the first file before opening the second. The third method of closing an ASCII file is to use the Quit command to leave 1-2-3/G. When you leave 1-2-3/G, any open ASCII file is automatically closed.

Because only one ASCII file can be open at a time, {CLOSE} requires no arguments. However, using {CLOSE} with an argument does not produce an error message. In fact, you may find that using a filename argument with {CLOSE} is helpful for documenting your macros. For example, {CLOSE "CLIENTS.PRN"} has the same effect as {CLOSE} (both simply close the currently open ASCII text file), but the former is more descriptive.

1-2-3/G will not execute any instructions that follow the {CLOSE} command in the same cell. Therefore, always use the {CLOSE} command on its own separate line.

In general, it's a good practice to close text files when you are finished using them. However, if you do not close a file, the file is closed for you automatically when you leave the 1-2-3/G desktop.

Writing to a File

When you open an ASCII text file with either the W (write), M (modify), or A (append) option, you can write information from your worksheet file directly to that file. 1-2-3/G offers two commands that you can use to write to a file—{WRITE} and {WRITELN}.

The {WRITE} Command

The {WRITE} command allows you to begin writing to the currently open ASCII file starting at the location of the file pointer. The {WRITE} command takes the form

{WRITE *string*}

where *string* is a literal string, a string formula, or a reference to a cell that contains a label or string formula. You cannot use numbers or formulas that evaluate to numbers. After 1-2-3/G finishes writing to the file, the file pointer is advanced one character beyond the last character written.

Note

{WRITE} only works if a text file is opened with the W (write), A (append), or M (modify) option of the {OPEN} command. The R (Read) option does not allow write access.

Tip: Using {WRITE} and {WRITELN} with the results of numeric formulas

To use {WRITE} or {WRITELN} to write a number or the results of a numeric formula to a text file, you can use the @STRING function to convert the number to a string. For example, here's a typical command:

```
{WRITE @STRING(SALES,2)}
```

1-2-3/G evaluates the @STRING function, then writes the results to the open ASCII file.

When one {WRITE} command follows another, the second command picks up where the first one left off. For example, to write the character string NonprofitCorporation to an open text file, you can use the following macro:

```
{WRITE "Nonprofit"}
{WRITE "Corporation"}
```

Note

If you use {WRITE} or {WRITELN} with a null string (""), 1-2-3/G produces the error message "String argument is invalid." In fact, you are most likely to encounter this message when you attempt to use {WRITE} or {WRITELN} to write the contents of an empty cell (for example, {WRITELN A:A1} when cell A:A1 is blank).

The {WRITELN} Command

The {WRITELN} command performs the same function as the {WRITE} command, with one exception. The {WRITELN} command automatically adds a carriage return/line feed to the end of each line of text. Otherwise, the syntax and usage for the command is identical. The {WRITELN} command takes the form:

{WRITELN *string*}

where *string* can be a literal string, a string formula, or a reference to a cell that contains a string or a string formula. You cannot use numbers or numeric formulas. However, you can use the @STRING function to convert values to strings—for example, {WRITELN @STRING(SALES,2)}. After 1-2-3/G finishes writing to the file, the file pointer is advanced one character beyond the last character written.

To be accessible to {WRITELN}, a text file must have been opened with the W (write), M (modify), or A (append) access argument.

Reading from a File

1-2-3/G offers two commands that allow you to read from an ASCII text file, {READ} and {READLN}. Both commands allow you to read a text string of up to 512 characters from an ASCII text file and store it in a cell of your choosing as a left-aligned label. The {READ} command allows you to choose a specified number of characters to be copied from a file. The {READLN} command, on the other hand, reads characters from a file until a carriage return/line feed combination is encountered. To read from a file with either command, you must have opened the file with either the W (write), M (modify), or R (read) option.

The {READ} Command

The {READ} command allows you to copy a specified number of characters from an open ASCII text file to a 1-2-3/G worksheet cell. The read operation begins at the current location of the file pointer. The {READ} command takes the form:

{READ *count,location*}

where *count* represents the number of characters you want to read and *location* is the cell in which you want the characters stored. 1-2-3/G starts reading at the current file pointer position. When the {READ} command is completed, the file pointer is advanced one character beyond the last character read.

The *count* argument must be a number between 0 and 512. You can also use a formula, function, or a reference to a cell that contains one of these. The *location* argument can be either a cell address or a range name. If you use a range name that contains multiple cells, only the upper-left corner cell is used.

The {READ} command is most useful when you are reading from an ASCII file with entries of equal length. If the length of each line varies, you may want to use the {READLN} command.

The {READLN} Command

The function of the {READLN} command is very similar to the {READ} command. However, instead of reading a specified number of characters from an ASCII file, the {READLN} command reads characters until a carriage return/line feed combination is encountered. The {READLN} command takes the form:

{READLN *location*}

where *location* is a cell address or range name. The {READLN} command starts reading at the current file pointer position and continues reading until a carriage return/line feed combination is encountered. The characters read are copied to the cell specified by *location*. The file pointer is then advanced to the next line in the file. However, if 512 characters are read before a carriage return/line feed is encountered, the read operation is cut off.

The {READLN} command can be of enormous benefit when the lines of text in an ASCII file are of variable length. Unlike the {READ} command where you must provide a specific number of characters to be read, the {READLN} command allows you to use the end of the current line as the determining factor in reading characters from an ASCII file.

Moving the File Pointer

When you use either the W (write), M (modify), or R (read) option of the {OPEN} command to open an ASCII file, the file pointer is automatically positioned at the beginning of the newly opened file. On the other hand, when you use the A (append) option of the {OPEN} command to open a file, the file pointer is positioned at the end of the file. After reading data from or writing data to an ASCII file, the file pointer is positioned one character beyond where you finished reading or writing.

To read data from or write data to a location in the middle of an ASCII file, you must reposition the file pointer to that location. To do this, you use the {SETPOS} command. To augment this command, you can use the {GETPOS} and {FILESIZE} commands. The {GETPOS} command tells you the current position of the file pointer, and the {FILESIZE} command tells you the overall size of the ASCII file in bytes.

The {SETPOS} Command

The size of an ASCII file is measured in bytes (characters). Each character is given a number. The first character is given the number 0, the second the number 1, the third the number 2, and so on to the end of the file. The {SETPOS} command allows you to use this numbering system to position the file pointer in preparation for reading or writing to a specific position in an ASCII file. The {SETPOS} command takes the form:

```
{SETPOS offset-number}
```

where *offset-number* is the number of the byte position within the ASCII file. The *offset-number* argument can be a number, a numeric formula, a function, or a reference to a cell that contains one of these. If you specify a number that exceeds the number of the last byte in the file, 1-2-3/G positions the file pointer one character beyond the last character in the file. Once the {SETPOS} command is executed, 1-2-3/G passes control to the next line of the macro. Instructions following the {SETPOS} command in the same cell are not executed.

As you might imagine, you must use the {OPEN} command to open an ASCII text file before you use the {SETPOS} command. If the text file is not open, 1-2-3/G will ignore the {SETPOS} command and continue to process the next instruction in the same cell as the {SETPOS} command.

The {GETPOS} Command

Use the {GETPOS} command to determine the current position of the file pointer in an open ASCII text file. The {GETPOS} command takes the form:

```
{GETPOS location}
```

where *location* is a cell address or range name. To this cell address or range name, 1-2-3/G copies a number that represents the character position of the file pointer in the currently open file, where 0 is the first position (character) in the file, 1 is the second position, 2 is the third position, and so on.

The {FILESIZE} Command

The {FILESIZE} command returns the total number of bytes in the currently open ASCII text file and stores the number in a cell of your choosing. The {FILESIZE} command takes the form:

```
{FILESIZE location)
```

where *location* is a range address or range name in the worksheet file in which the total byte count of the currently open ASCII will be stored.

Command Processing

If 1-2-3/G is successful in executing an {OPEN}, {WRITE}, {WRITELN}, {READ}, {READLN}, {SETPOS}, {GETPOS}, or {FILESIZE} command, it will pass control to the next cell of the macro. However, if the command is not successful, 1-2-3/G will process the instructions in the same cell that follow the command.

Examples

Figure 11–38 shows a simple macro that writes long labels in the range A1..A4 to the PAYROLL.PRN text file. Each label in the range is 29 characters long (a characteristic that will become most relevent when you later read from the PAYROLL.PRN file).

The macro begins in cell B6 by positioning the cell pointer to cell A:A1. Next, the command

```
{OPEN "PAYROLL.PRN",w}{BRANCH OPEN_ERR}
```

123G.EXE Ready

File Edit Worksheet Range Copy... Move... Print Graph Data Utility Quit... Help

A:A1 'Evan Sikes 24000

FIG11-38.WG1

A	A	B	C	D	E	F	G
1	Evan	Sikes	24000				
2	Drew	Gibson	22000				
3	Clive	Cleveland	21000				
4	John	Dunne	35000				
5							
6	\W	{HOME}					
7		{OPEN "PAYROLL.PRN",w}{BRANCH OPEN_ERR}					
8		{FOR COUNTER,1,4,1,WRITE_REC}					
9		{CLOSE}					
10							
11	COUNTER	5					
12							
13	WRITE_REC	{WRITELN @CELLPOINTER("contents")}					
14		{DOWN}					
15							
16	OPEN_ERR	{ALERT "Unable to open file"}					
17							
18							

FIGURE 11–38 **A macro that writes an ASCII text file**

opens the PAYROLL.PRN text file using the W (write) option. Therefore, each time the macro is used the PAYROLL.PRN file is overwritten. The {BRANCH OPEN_ERR} command is also included just in case the {OPEN} command is not successful in opening the file.

Next, the {FOR} command in cell B8 executes the WRITE_REC subroutine four times. WRITE_REC starts in cell B13 and uses the {WRITELN} command to write data from the worksheet file to the currently open ASCII text file. The *string* argument for the {WRITELN} command is @CELLPOINTER("contents"), which simply returns the current contents of the cell containing the cell pointer. Thus, this command will write the contents of the current cell to the current open ASCII file. The next command in the subroutine is {DOWN}, which moves the cell pointer down one cell each time the subroutine is executed. Finally, after the subroutine has been executed four times, control returns to the cell following the {FOR} command, cell B9, in the calling program. Cell B9 contains the {CLOSE} command, which closes the currently open ASCII file.

The next example, shown in Figure 11–39, reads data from the PAYROLL.PRN file created in the previous example. However, this macro includes the {SETPOS} command which lets you position the file pointer in an ASCII text file before reading or writing data.

The macro begins in cell B1 with the command

```
{OPEN "PAYROLL.PRN",r}{BRANCH OPEN_ERR}
```

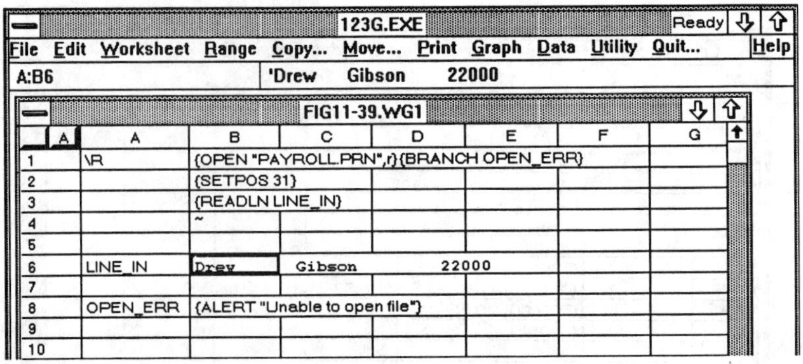

123G.EXE — Ready

File Edit Worksheet Range Copy... Move... Print Graph Data Utility Quit... Help

A:B6 'Drew Gibson 22000

FIG11-39.WG1

A	A	B	C	D	E	F	G
1	\R	{OPEN "PAYROLL.PRN",r}{BRANCH OPEN_ERR}					
2		{SETPOS 31}					
3		{READLN LINE_IN}					
4		~					
5							
6	LINE_IN	Drew Gibson 22000					
7							
8	OPEN_ERR	{ALERT "Unable to open file"}					
9							
10							

FIGURE 11–39 Using {SETPOS} to write to an ASCII text file

This command opens the existing PAYROLL.PRN file using the R (read) option. Thus, the file is read-only to 1-2-3/G. In the next line of the macro, {SETPOS 31} sets the file pointer to character 32 in the PAYROLL.PRN file. (Recall from earlier in this chapter that the first character in a file is given the number 0, the second 1, and so on. Thus, an *offset-number* argument of 31 for the {SETPOS} command actually means character 32 in the currently open file.) Also, notice in Figure 11–38 that the length of each record written to PAYROLL.PRN is 31 characters (29 characters for each label plus a carriage return followed by a linefeed). Therefore, you can control the current line position of the file pointer by using the {SETPOS} command to specify file pointer positions in 31-character increments. By specifying an offset value of 31, the file pointer is moved to the beginning of the second line in the PAYROLL.PRN file.

Once the PAYROLL.PRN file is opened, and the file pointer properly positioned, the {READLN} command reads data from the PAYROLL.PRN file and stores the data in LINE_IN (cell B6). As you can see, the label

```
'Drew       Gibson        22000
```

resides in the cell already. This label has been read from the second line of the PAYROLL.PRN file and copied into the worksheet file.

Notice that the last line in the macro contains a tilde (~). This command removes the CALC indicator from the Control line. Another alternative is to use {CALC} at the end of the macro, or simply press CALC (F9).

USING FORMULAS IN MACRO COMMANDS

As in most recent releases of 1-2-3, Lotus has increased the power of 1-2-3/G's macro language by allowing you to use @functions and formulas as arguments in macro commands. For example, rather than using a range address or range name as the *location* argument for the {BLANK} command, such as {BLANK A:C10}, you can include an @function, as follows:

```
{BLANK @CELLPOINTER("coord")}
```

The formula @CELLPOINTER("coord") returns the full address (worksheet letter, column letter, and row number) of the current cell, and provides the *location* argument needed for the {BLANK} command.

You can also substitute other types of formulas for string and numeric arguments, as long as each formula evaluates to the proper data type needed by the command. For example, suppose you want to prompt the user for his or her name using the {GETLABEL} command. You then want to incorporate the name, converted to proper case, in the prompt for a second {GETLABEL} command. You could use the following commands:

```
{GETLABEL "Please enter your name",A1}{GETLABEL +"Hello, "&@PROPER(A1)&". Please enter your SS#",A2}
```

If the user types the name BURT in response to the first {GETLABEL} prompt, the second prompt for the social security number looks like Figure 11-40.

As the first line of the macro shows, the {GETLABEL} command requires a string for its prompt argument. The prompt argument you've supplied in the second {GETLABEL} command is a formula that evaluates to a string, a perfectly acceptable alternative to a literal string.

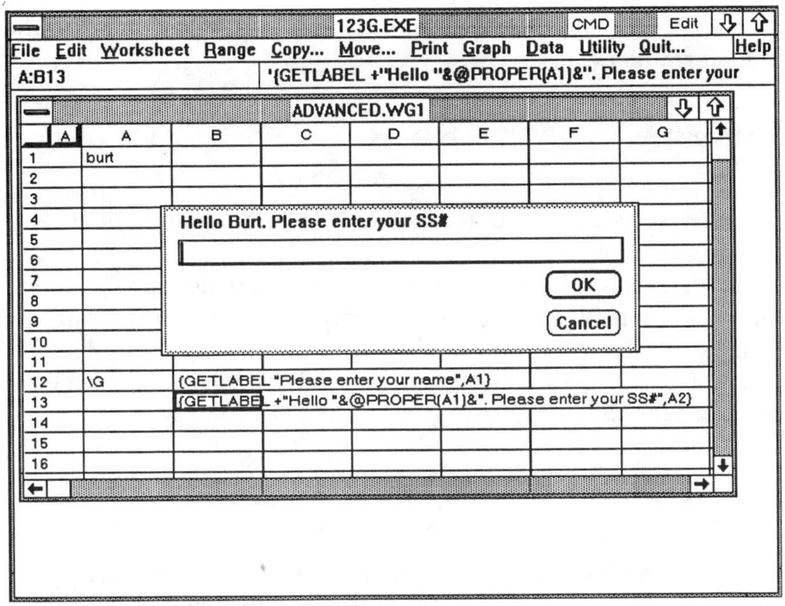

FIGURE 11-40 Using a formula to build the prompt for the {GETLABEL} command

SELF-MODIFYING MACROS

As you become more expert in programming macros, you will find yourself searching for ways to make your macros more flexible, that is, to have them work under a variety of circumstances. One of the most popular ways to increase the flexibility of macros is to make them self-modifying.

A *self-modifying macro* is one whose instructions change as certain conditions on the desktop or in a worksheet file change. For example, suppose you want to create a macro that determines the number of open windows, and if that number is 1, maximizes the current window on the desktop (enlarges it to fill the entire desktop). However, if the number of files is 2 or greater, you want the macro to tile the windows on the desktop. You can place the following formula in a cell in your macro:

```
@IF(@INFO("numfile")>1,"{DESKMENU}wt","{TOOLMENU}x")
```

@INFO("numfile") returns the current number of open files. If that number is greater than 1, the formula evaluates to

```
{DESKTOP}wt
```

causing the macro to access the Desktop Control menu and issue the Window Tile command. However, if the current number of open files is less than or equal to 1, the formula evaluates to

```
{TOOLMENU}x
```

which causes the macro to access the Window Control menu and issue the Maximize command.

As another example, suppose you want to create a macro that updates a summary section of a worksheet by copying the values from a column of monthly sales. Rather than tell 1-2-3/G which month to update, though, you would prefer to let your macro decide which month based on the current date. You can use the following string formula in your macro:

```
+"/cMONTH"&@STRING(@MONTH(@TODAY),0)&"~SUMMARY~"
```

@MONTH(@TODAY) determines the number of the current month from the current date and inserts it into the macro, combining it with the other macro instructions. For example, if the current month is March, the resulting macro commands look like this:

```
/cMONTH3~SUMMARY~
```

These instructions cause the macro to copy the sales data from the range named MONTH3 to the summary section.

SUMMARY

In this chapter you learned how to get user input and manipulate data in cells using 1-2-3/G's macro programming language. You also learned how to perform conditional processing, branching, and subroutine calls. In addition, you now know how to use macro commands to trap errors, create custom dialog boxes, control the screen and windows, and work with ASCII files. Finally, you learned two advanced macro techniques, including how to use formulas in macro commands and how to create self-modifying macros. By now you can fully appreciate the exceptional power of 1-2-3/G macros.

CHAPTER 12

Networking 1-2-3/G

The Standard (single-user) Edition of 1-2-3/G is not directly networkable. That is, you cannot share a single copy of the product among multiple users on a network. However, the Standard Edition of 1-2-3/G does include commands and features that allow you to run it from a workstation and effectively manage data files that are stored in shared directories on the network. A built-in file reservation and file-locking system virtually eliminates the possibility of two users overwriting each other's data. Further, 1-2-3/G's File Admin command provides facilities that allow you to protect, manage, and get information about 1-2-3/G data files that are stored on shared network directories.

To share a single copy of 1-2-3/G across a network, you must purchase the Server Edition of 1-2-3/G. In addition, you must purchase the appropriate number of Node Editions (licenses) required to adequately service the users on your network. The Server and Node Editions of 1-2-3/G are discussed only briefly in this chapter.

What's New

The Standard Edition of 1-2-3/G uses essentially the same file-sharing strategy as the Standard Editions of 1-2-3 Releases 2.2 and 3. However, the File Admin command has been slightly enhanced for 1-2-3/G.

Specifically, the File Admin Table command now offers options that allow you to get information about other open worksheet files and about the windows that are currently open on the desktop. In addition, you can get information about the drives to which 1-2-3/G has access, and you can get information about files linked to the current file both by formula and by the Edit Link command.

The File Admin command also includes a new Move-Links option. This option allows you to change the source-file reference for formula links from one file to another.

FILE-SHARING FUNDAMENTALS

One of the main concerns of operating in a network environment is file security. In an environment where two or more users have access to the same data files, there must be a mechanism that prevents those users from destroying each other's work. For example, imagine you load a worksheet file into 1-2-3/G and begin adding data to that file. At the same time, another user opens that same file and begins making changes. At this point, both users are working at cross purposes. If you save your copy of the file first, your changes will be overwritten when the other user saves his or her copy of the file.

Some of the responsibility for file sharing falls on your network software and your network administrator. Most network software packages allow your network administrator to assign special file-access privileges to specified directories and/or users on the network. For example, a given directory may have read/write/create privileges. That is, you can read an existing file from this directory, write the changes you make back to the original file, and you can also create new files in the directory. Some directories may not have all of these privileges, however. For example, a directory might be read-only. That is, you can view the files it contains, but you cannot change them or add new ones. In addition, not all users may have access to full privileges. For example, selected users may have read-only access to a given directory. That is, they can view the contents of the files in the directory, but they are denied write and create privileges.

Some of the responsibility for file sharing also falls on your applications software. In a read/write/create/deny-none environment where multiple users have full access privileges to shared files, your applications software must have a way of protecting the integrity of existing files. That is, you don't want two users working on the same file at the same time and destroying each other's work in the bargain. Instead, you want only one user at a time to have access to a given file. However, as soon as that user is finished with that file, it must be immediately available to other users. Most network applications do offer such a protection system, but it can be somewhat difficult to understand and to use.

HOW 1-2-3/G HANDLES FILE SHARING

Unlike some network applications, 1-2-3/G's file-sharing system is relatively straightforward. A built-in reservation system allows only one user at a time to make changes to a given worksheet file. Generally speaking, when you load a worksheet file into memory, you get the *reservation* for that file. This reservation is your guarantee that you can make changes to the file and save it under the same name.

Until you release the reservation, other users cannot make changes to the file and save it under the same name. They can load the file, view it, and even print its contents, but they cannot modify it and save it under the same name. When you release the reservation for the file, however, other users can immediately load that file and get its reservation. They can then add their changes to yours.

AN EXAMPLE NETWORK SESSION

Unless you specify otherwise, you get the reservation for a file automatically when you load the file into memory—unless, of course, someone else is already using the file. For example, suppose you use the File Retrieve command to load a worksheet file from a read/write/deny-none network directory. Imagine further that no one else is using that file. Under these circumstances, the file is opened in the current window and you have the reservation for that file. Because you have the reservation for that file, you can modify it and save it to disk under the same name.

Now, however, suppose someone else on the network, say Norm from Marketing, tries to open that same file while you are using it. When Norm attempts to open the file, 1-2-3/G displays the File Reservation Error message box in Figure 12–1 on his screen. This message box contains a Yes and a No command button. If Norm selects Yes, 1-2-3/G allows him to load the file without a reservation as a read-only file. That is, he can look at the file and change its contents, but he cannot save it under the same name. If Norm selects the No command button, 1-2-3/G cancels the file-load operation and returns to READY mode.

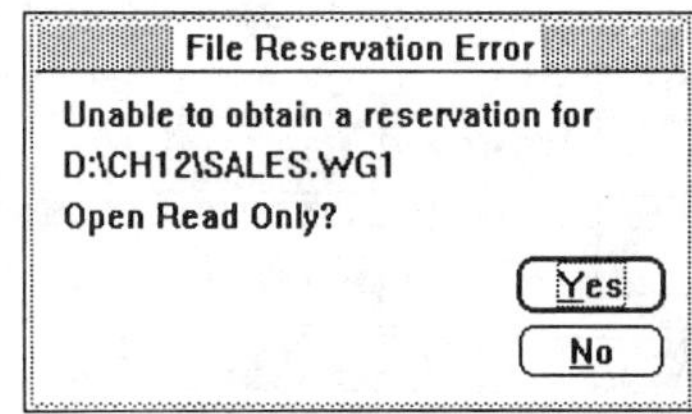

FIGURE 12–1 The File Reservation Error Message box

Suppose that Norm elects to open the file anyway, as read-only. To indicate that the file is read-only to Norm, 1-2-3/G displays an RO indicator on the right side of the worksheet window title bar, as shown in Figure 12–2.

If Norm attempts to use the File Save command to save the file under the same name, the error message box in Figure 12–3 appears on his screen. His only option is to select the OK command button from this message box to return to the worksheet in READY mode.

Now suppose you are finished using the file. You use the File Save command to save your changes to the file followed by the File Retrieve command to replace it with another file. This operation in effect clears the original file from your computer's memory. When you clear a file from memory, the reservation for that file is automatically released. Norm can now load that file into his computer's memory and automatically get the reservation for it. Because he has the reservation for the file, the RO indicator is not displayed in the worksheet window's title bar. Norm can now add his changes to yours and save the file under the same name.

The forgoing is but one of many possible file-sharing scenarios that you might encounter on a network. However, it gives you a feel for how 1-2-3/G's file-reservation scheme works in its default state. Note that you can change the default. That is, you can change the reservation setting. Instead of a user getting the reservation for a file automatically, you can force him or her to explicitly get the reservation for a file each time the file is used. To do this, you use the File Admin Reservation command. See "Managing File Reservations" later in this chapter for more details on this.

	A	B	C	D	E	F
1						
2			ABC Chemical, Inc			
3			Sales By Strategic Business Unit			
4						
5	SBU No.	Description	1992	1993	1994	1995
6	001	Inks	$10,000,000	$11,000,000	$12,100,000	$13,310,000
7	002	Paints	$8,000,000	$8,800,000	$9,680,000	$10,648,000
8	003	Platics	$3,000,000	$3,300,000	$3,630,000	$3,993,000
9	004	Varnishes	$900,000	$990,000	$1,089,000	$1,197,900
10	005	Brighteners	$20,000,000	$22,000,000	$24,200,000	$26,620,000
11	006	Copy Dye	$24,000,000	$26,400,000	$29,040,000	$31,944,000
12	007	Food Color	$16,000,000	$17,600,000	$19,360,000	$21,296,000
13	008	Insecticides	$12,000,000	$13,200,000	$14,520,000	$15,972,000
14	009	Agri-Chemicals	$480,000	$528,000	$580,800	$638,880
15	010	Pharmacutical	$26,400,000	$29,040,000	$31,944,000	$35,138,400
16	011	Acids	$1,200,000	$1,320,000	$1,452,000	$1,597,200
17	012	Intermediates	$6,600,000	$7,260,000	$7,986,000	$8,784,600
18						
19	Total		$128,580,000	$141,438,000	$155,581,800	$171,139,980
20						

FIGURE 12–2 A file opened as read-only in 1-2-3/G

FIGURE 12–3 Saving a file without a reservation causes an error message

Note

The File Admin command also allows you to protect selected settings in a file and to get information about 1-2-3/G files both in memory and on disk. You may find these two features to be useful both on and off the network. See "File Security" and "Getting Information about Files" later in this chapter for more information on these two topics.

SHARING 1-2-3/G PROGRAM FILES

If you are planning to use 1-2-3/G on a network, it may be of assistance for you to know a little about the Lotus network strategy for 1-2-3/G. Like Releases 2.2 and 3, 1-2-3/G comes in three different editions: Standard Edition, Server Edition, and Node Edition. The role of each of these editions is as follows:

- The Standard Edition of 1-2-3/G is a single-user version. This is the edition that most users own. You cannot share this product across multiple workstations. However, the file-reservation and file-locking features discussed in this chapter are built into the product. Therefore, you can run it from a workstation and successfully share worksheet files stored in network directories. Thus, the Standard Edition is a single-user, single-license, product for standalone use.
- The Server Edition is the true "network" edition of 1-2-3/G. This edition allows multiple users to share the same copy of 1-2-3/G. Once again, the file-reservation and file-locking system is built into the product, allowing you to safely share worksheet files in common network directories. The Server edition comes with the 1-2-3/G program disks, 1-2-3/G documentation, a LAN Administrators Guide, a Count utility, a NewUser utility, and a *single-user* license. The Count and NewUser utilities allow the network administrator to set the number of licenses for the system and add new users.

However, as mentioned, the Server Edition comes with only a single-user license for the network administrator. You must purchase a sufficient number of Node Editions (licenses) to cover the number of users you estimate will be concurrently using 1-2-3/G at any given time.

- The Node Edition is essentially a license to add another 1-2-3/G user to the network. The Node Edition comes with documentation only. In general, you should purchase a Node edition for each potential 1-2-3/G user on your system. However, the key here is concurrent usage. For example, imagine you have 12 people on the network who could potentially use 1-2-3/G. However, you estimate that 99% of the time only 10 of those users will be concurrently using 1-2-3/G. Therefore, you purchase only 10 Node Editions. If all 10 are in use, the eleventh person will be denied use of 1-2-3/G. Hopefully, that eleventh user will not be the president of the company trying out the network for the first time.

MANAGING FILE RESERVATIONS

As demonstrated above under "An Example Network Session," 1-2-3/G has a built-in file-reservation system. This simple yet effective system can help you to protect your data files in shared network directories. The file-reservation system will allow you to open a file and save it under the same name, unless you have the reservation for the file. When you open a file, you get its reservation automatically, provided no one else is using the file. While you have the reservation for that file, other users on the network cannot open the same file, make changes to it, and save it under the same name, unless you release the file's reservation.

Rather than relying solely on 1-2-3/G's automatic file-reservation system, you can control file reservations manually. To do this, you use the File Admin Reservation command. This command allows you to both get and release file reservations. You can also use this command to specify the reservation setting for the current worksheet file as automatic or manual. If the setting is automatic (the default), the user gets the reservation for a file automatically whenever it is opened on the desktop, provided of course that no one else is using the file. On the other hand, if the setting is manual, the user is forced to manually request the reservation each time the file is opened.

When you select the File Admin Reservation command, 1-2-3/G displays the dialog box in Figure 12–4. As you might imagine, the Get option button is used to get the reservation for a file and the Release option button is used to release the reservation. These options are discussed in more detail in the next section. To complete the File Admin Reservation command, select the OK command button or press ENTER.

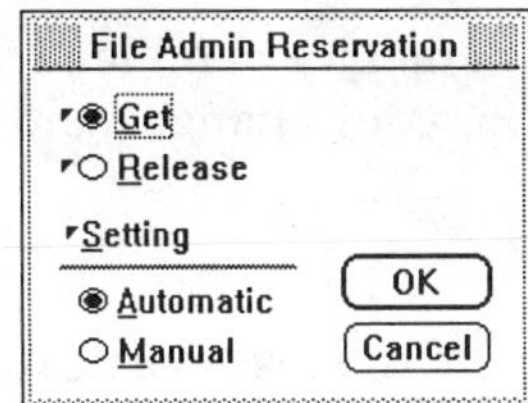

FIGURE 12–4 **The File Admin Reservation dialog box**

Getting and Releasing Reservations

Use the Get option button to get the reservation for a file that you have already opened. For example, imagine you use the File Open command to open a worksheet file that is currently in use by another workstation. The RO (read-only) indicator is now displayed in the title bar of the worksheet window. However, without saving the file, the other user releases the reservation for the file, thereby making it available for you. At that point, you can use the File Admin Reservation Get command to get the reservation for the file. When you select the OK command button or press ENTER to complete the command, 1-2-3/G removes the RO indicator from your screen, indicating that you have the reservation for the file. You can now make changes to the file and save it under the same name.

To release the reservation for a file, select the Release option button from the File Admin Reservation dialog box. This releases the reservation for the file and causes the RO (read-only) indicator to appear in the title bar of the worksheet window. Use this option when you only want to view a file but you do not want to modify it and save the changes. That way, the reservation remains available for other users who do want to modify and save the file.

You cannot get the reservation for a file if someone else has changed the file since you opened it. For example, imagine you retrieve a file into memory. Imagine further that you use the File Admin Reservation Release command to release the reservation for the file. Shortly thereafter, someone else loads the same file into memory, getting the reservation automatically. That user modifies the file, saves it to disk, and clears it from memory. In the meantime, you discover a problem in the file and you decide to modify it and save the changes.

To get the reservation for the file, you use the File Admin Reservation Get command. However, when you select the OK command button to confirm the command, 1-2-3/G displays the error message "File on disk is different from the file in the window." 1-2-3/G has detected that the file on disk has changed and will not allow you to save your changes on top of that file. When you select OK to clear the error message, the RO indicator remains on your screen. If you still want to save your changes, you can do one of two things. First, you can save your copy of the file under a different filename. Alternatively, you can clear your copy of the file from memory and load the modified copy of the file from disk. You can then make your changes and save them under the same filename.

Changing the Reservation Setting

You can change the reservation setting for a file from automatic (the default) to manual. If the setting is automatic, the reservation for the file is automatically available when the file is loaded into memory, provided, of course, that no one else has the reservation. If you specify a manual setting, the file's reservation is only available when you use the File Admin Reservation Get command. Otherwise, the RO (read-only) indicator appears in the worksheet window title bar.

To change the reservation setting for the current file, select the File Admin Reservation command. 1-2-3/G displays the dialog box in Figure 12–4. Select Setting and choose from either the Automatic or Manual option buttons. To complete the command, select the OK command button, or press ENTER. To save the setting, use the File Save command to save the file to disk.

FILE SECURITY

The File Admin Seal command allows you to protect (seal) a worksheet file from changes to selected format settings. It also allows you to protect the current reservation setting. The settings you protect are sealed with a password. To disable the seal, the user must know the password. When you select the File Admin Seal command, 1-2-3/G displays the dialog box in Figure 12–5.

If you select the "File seal" option button, the following commands appear grayed (nonselectable) for the current worksheet file when a user attempts to select them:

- File Admin Reservation Setting Automatic and Manual.
- Graph Name Create and Delete.

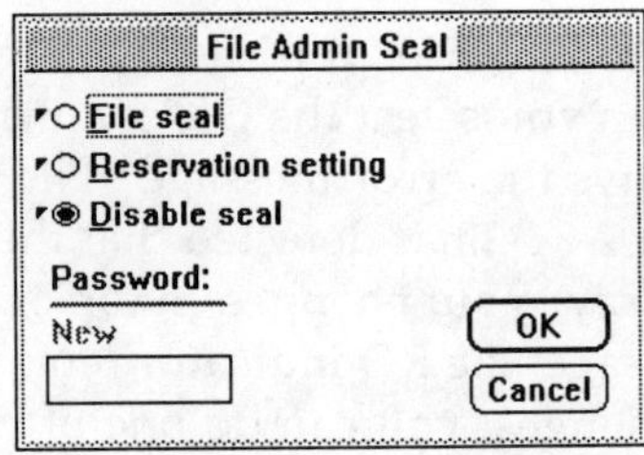

FIGURE 12–5 The File Admin Seal dialog box

- Range Attributes Border, Color, Font, and Precision; Range Format; Range Label; Range Name Create, Delete, Labels, Reset Undefine; Range Zero Suppress.
- Worksheet Column; Worksheet Row; Worksheet Hide; Worksheet Global (all commands except Worksheet Global Default).

When you select the "File seal" option button, 1-2-3/G activates the New text box, prompting you for a password. Type the password of your choice. As you type, 1-2-3/G displays asterisks in place of the characters. To complete the password, press ENTER. When you press ENTER, the name of the text box changes to Verify. Type the same password again, and press ENTER.

If you select the "Reservation setting" option button, only the current reservation setting (Automatic versus Manual) is sealed. When you select this option, 1-2-3/G activates the New text box, and you must type and verify a password, as just described. When you select OK to complete the File Admin Seal command, 1-2-3/G seals the current reservation setting for the file (set with the File Admin Reservation Setting command). If the current reservation setting is Automatic, you will get the reservation for the file automatically when you open it, provided no one else is using the file. On the other hand, if the setting is Manual, you must open the file and then use the File Admin Reservation Get command to get its reservation.

To disable the seal for a file, Select the File Admin Seal command, and select the "Disable seal" option button. 1-2-3/G activates the Old text box (formerly entitled New) and you must type the exact same password that was originally used to seal the file. If you are unable to provide the password, 1-2-3/G issues an error message.

If a password does not exist when you select the "File seal" or "Reservation setting" option buttons, the name of the Password text box is "New." If a password exists already, the name of the Password text box is "Old." To change the password, you must type the old password, followed by the new password, and then verify the new password.

Passwords can be 15 characters in length and are case sensitive. Therefore, make sure you remember the exact sequence of upper- and lower-case letters you used. You cannot disable the seal for a file unless you enter the password exactly.

The File Admin Seal command only seals the format settings for the current file. To protect the data in the file as well, you can use the Worksheet Global Protection Enable command. This command protects the worksheet from changes to existing data. To unprotect selected ranges for data entry, you can use the Range Unprotect command. Both of these commands are discussed in detail in Chapter 3 under "Protecting Your Worksheets."

In addition to protecting the data in the worksheet, you can save the file that contains that worksheet with a password. Unless a user knows the password, 1-2-3/G will not open the file.

Note

> You cannot seal a file and then save in 1-2-3 Release 2, (.WK1) format. If you try, 1-2-3/G will issue an error message when you attempt to save the file.

To save a file with a password, select the File Save command. When 1-2-3/G displays the File Save dialog box, type the name for the file followed by a space and the letter **p**. Press ENTER to confirm the filename. 1-2-3/G displays a second File Save dialog box and prompts you for a password for the file. Type a password of up to 15 characters. 1-2-3/G displays asterisks (*) as you type. To confirm the password, press ENTER. 1-2-3/G asks you to verify the password. Type the same password again and press ENTER. 1-2-3/G saves the file with the password you specified. See Saving Files in Chapter 5, "File Management," for more about saving files with a password.

GETTING INFORMATION ABOUT FILES

The File Admin Table command allows you to create a table of information about files that are open on the desktop as well as files stored on disk. This command can be useful in both single-user and network environments. When you select the File Admin Table command, 1-2-3/G displays the dialog box in Figure 12-6.

As you might imagine, each of the option buttons in the "File type" section of the dialog box in Figure 12-6 allows you to create a different type of table. Each of the available table types are described in the sections immediately following this one.

The option buttons in the left-hand column of the "File type" section in Figure 12-6 are used to create tables of information about files that are open on the desktop. When you select one of these option buttons, 1-2-3/G activates the "Range" text box, prompting you for a location for the table. Specify a single-

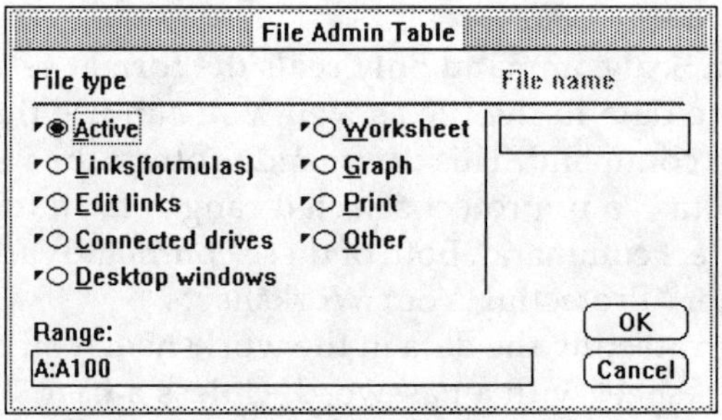

File Admin Table
File type
File name
Active
Links(formulas)
Edit links
Connected drives
Desktop windows
Worksheet
Graph
Print
Other
Range:
A:A100
OK
Cancel

FIGURE 12–6 The File Admin Table dialog box

cell address or range name that marks the upper-left corner of where you want the table to begin. Select the OK command button, or press ENTER, to have 1-2-3/G create the table.

Caution

> The File Admin Table command creates a table of information in a worksheet file. All the cells that are in the path of the table are overwritten with the new data. The table includes as many columns and rows as are required to generate the specific type of table you requested. If you inadvertently overwrite data with the File Admin Table command, select Edit Undo, or press ALT-BACKSPACE, to reclaim the lost information.

The option buttons in the right-hand column of the "File type" section in Figure 12–6 allow you to create tables of information about files on disk. When you select one of these option buttons, 1-2-3/G activates the "File name" text box, prompting you for a directory path and name. Initially, 1-2-3/G lists the path and name of the current directory in the "File name" box. You can press ENTER to accept this directory name or type a directory name of your own and press ENTER. When you press ENTER, 1-2-3/G activates the "Range" text box, prompting you for a location for the table. Specify a single-cell address or range name that marks the upper-left corner of where you want the table to begin. Select the OK command button, or press ENTER, to create the table.

As mentioned, the option buttons in "File type" section of the File Admin Table dialog box allow you to create various types of tables. The sections that follow describe each type of table.

The "Active" Option

The "Active" option button creates a table of information about worksheet files that are currently open on the desktop. The table includes the following information in adjacent columns for each open file: filename, date created, time created, size in bytes, number of worksheets containing data, modification status, and reservation status. Figure 12–7 shows an example table of information about open worksheet files.

Notice that 1-2-3/G displays either 1 or 0 in the modification status column (column F) and reservation status column (column G) of the table in Figure 12–7. If a 1 is displayed in the modification status column, it means the file has been modified since it was opened. Otherwise 1-2-3/G displays a 0 in this column. If a 1 is displayed in the reservation status column, it means you currently have the reservation for that file. If you do not have the reservation, 1-2-3/G displays a 0.

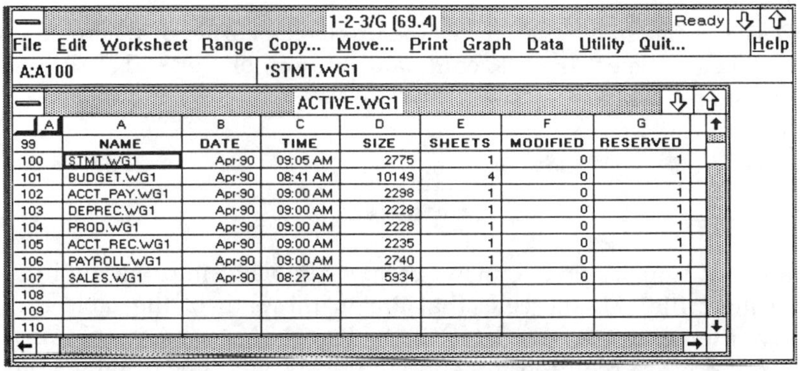

1-2-3/G [69.4] Ready

File Edit Worksheet Range Copy... Move... Print Graph Data Utility Quit... Help

A:A100 'STMT.WG1

ACTIVE.WG1

A	A	B	C	D	E	F	G
99	NAME	DATE	TIME	SIZE	SHEETS	MODIFIED	RESERVED
100	STMT.WG1	Apr-90	09:05 AM	2775	1	0	1
101	BUDGET.WG1	Apr-90	08:41 AM	10149	4	0	1
102	ACCT_PAY.WG1	Apr-90	09:00 AM	2298	1	0	1
103	DEPREC.WG1	Apr-90	09:00 AM	2228	1	0	1
104	PROD.WG1	Apr-90	09:00 AM	2228	1	0	1
105	ACCT_REC.WG1	Apr-90	09:00 AM	2235	1	0	1
106	PAYROLL.WG1	Apr-90	09:00 AM	2740	1	0	1
107	SALES.WG1	Apr-90	08:27 AM	5934	1	0	1
108							
109							
110							

FIGURE 12–7 **A table of open worksheet files**

Figure 12–7 is slightly misleading. First of all, the titles in the range A:A99..A:G99 do not appear when you generate the table. These were added later. In addition, the dates and times in columns B and C appear as date and time values when you create the table. To make these values appear as dates and/or times, you must use the Range Format Date/Time command. Finally, the file names in column A of the table were not displayed completely when the table was originally created. It was necessary to widen column A to fully display these labels. You'll find that similar format changes are necessary to display the information in most of the tables generated by the File Admin Table command.

The "Links(formula)" Option

The "Links(formula)" option button allows you to create a table of information about formula links in the current worksheet file. Formula links allow you to use information from other files in the current file (see Chapter 2). Before using this option, make sure the file containing the formula links is active. When you create the table, 1-2-3/G lists the following information for each link in the current file in adjacent columns: source filename, date created, time created, and size in bytes. Figure 12–8 shows an example of a "Links(formula)" table.

The "Edit Links" Option

The "Edit links" option button allows you to create a table of information about links in the current worksheet file that were created with the Edit Link Create command. Figure 12–9 shows an example "Edit links" table.

In preparation for using this option, make sure the file containing the links is the active file. When you create the table, 1-2-3/G list the following information in adjacent columns for each link in the current file:

1-2-3/G [69.4] Ready

File Edit Worksheet Range Copy... Move... Print Graph Data Utility Quit... Help

A:A100 'ACCT_PAY.WG1

LINKFORM.WG1

A	A	B	C	D	E	F	G	H
99	NAME	DATE	TIME	SIZE				
100	ACCT_PAY.WG1	Apr-90	09:00 AM	2298				
101	ACCT_REC.WG1	Apr-90	09:00 AM	2235				
102	DEPREC.WG1	Apr-90	09:00 AM	2228				
103	PAYROLL.WG1	Apr-90	09:00 AM	2740				
104	PROD.WG1	Apr-90	09:00 AM	2228				
105	SALES.WG1	Apr-90	08:27 AM	5934				
106								
107								
108								
109								
110								

FIGURE 12–8 **A table of worksheet files linked by formula to the current file**

- The range (destination) in the current file that contains the link (column A in Figure 12–9).
- The file and range (source) to which the formula link refers (column B in Figure 12–9).
- Whether the link is updated automatically or manually (column C of Figure 12–9).

The "Connected drives" Option

The "Connected drives" option creates a two-column table showing physical and logical drives on your computer. The letter for the drive, for example C:\, is listed in the first column and the label <DRIVE> appears in the second

1-2-3/G [69.4] Ready

File Edit Worksheet Range Copy... Move... Print Graph Data Utility Quit... Help

A:A101 'A:D10

EDLINK.WG1

A	A	B	C	D	E	F
100	DESTINATION	SOURCE	LINK TYPE			
101	A:D10	<<ACCT_PAY.WG1>>A:A17	Automatic			
102	A:D7	<<DEPREC.WG1>>A:A6	Automatic			
103	A:D7	<<PROD.WG1>>A:A2	Automatic			
104	A:D5	<<ACCT_REC.WG1>>A:A11	Automatic			
105	A:D3	<<ACCT_REC.WG1>>A:D16	Automatic			
106	A:D1	<<SALES.WG1>>A:D19	Automatic			
107	A:D10	<<ACCT_PAY.WG1>>A:A17	Automatic			
108	A:D7	<<DEPREC.WG1>>A:A6	Automatic			
109	A:D7	<<PROD.WG1>>A:A2	Automatic			
110	A:D5	<<ACCT_REC.WG1>>A:A11	Automatic			
111	A:D3	<<ACCT_REC.WG1>>A:D16	Automatic			
112	A:D1	<<SALES.WG1>>A:D19	Automatic			
113						
114						

FIGURE 12–9 **A table of links created with the Edit Link command**

1-2-3/G [69.4] Ready

File Edit Worksheet Range Copy... Move... Print Graph Data Utility Quit... Help

A:A100 'A:\

DRIVES.WG1

A	A	B	C	D	E	F	G	H
99								
100	A:\	<DRIVE>						
101	C:\	<DRIVE>						
102	D:\	<DRIVE>						
103	E:\	<DRIVE>						
104	F:\	<DRIVE>						
105								
106								

FIGURE 12–10 **A table of available drives**

column for each drive listed. Figure 12–10 shows a sample "Connected drives" table.

The "Desktop Windows" Option

The "Desktop windows" option button creates a table of information about the windows currently open on the desktop. This includes both the 1-2-3/G window as well as the Presentation Manager window. Figure 12–11 shows a sample "Desktop Windows" table.

For each open window, 1-2-3/G displays the following information in adjacent columns: window name, horizontal window location, vertical window location, the width of the window, the height of the window, minimization status, maximization status, window type, and reservation status. The locations and sizes of the windows (columns B, C, D,and E of Figure 12–11) are measured in inches or millimeters, depending on the Utility User Settings International Measurement setting. 1-2-3/G shows a 1 in the minimization and maximization status columns (columns F and G) if the window is minimized or maximized. Otherwise a zero is displayed in these columns. In the window-type column (column H), 1-2-3/G displays either Worksheet, Graph, Solver, Desktop (meaning 1-2-3/G's desktop), or Screen (meaning Presentation Manager's screen). In the Reservation column (column I), 1-2-3/G displays either Reservation (meaning you have the reservation), No Reservation, or N/A (not applicable).

The Worksheet, Graph, Print, and Other Options

The "Worksheet," "Graph," "Print," and "Other" option buttons allow you to create a table of information about specific types of files on disk. When you select one of these option buttons from the File Admin Table dialog box, 1-2-3/G activates the "File name" text box. This text box allows you to specify the path and name of the directory that will be used as the source of the table information. Depending on the option button you select, the following information will be displayed in the table:

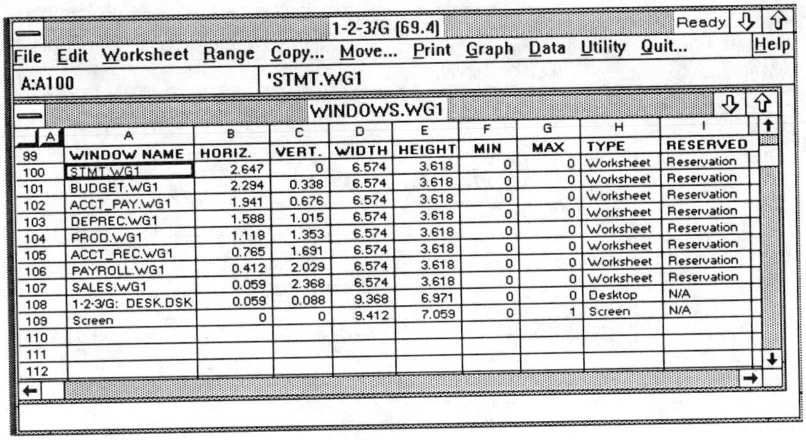

1-2-3/G [69.4] Ready

File Edit Worksheet Range Copy... Move... Print Graph Data Utility Quit... Help

A:A100 'STMT.WG1

WINDOWS.WG1

A	A	B	C	D	E	F	G	H	I
99	WINDOW NAME	HORIZ.	VERT.	WIDTH	HEIGHT	MIN	MAX	TYPE	RESERVED
100	STMT.WG1	2.647	0	6.574	3.618	0	0	Worksheet	Reservation
101	BUDGET.WG1	2.294	0.338	6.574	3.618	0	0	Worksheet	Reservation
102	ACCT_PAY.WG1	1.941	0.676	6.574	3.618	0	0	Worksheet	Reservation
103	DEPREC.WG1	1.588	1.015	6.574	3.618	0	0	Worksheet	Reservation
104	PROD.WG1	1.118	1.353	6.574	3.618	0	0	Worksheet	Reservation
105	ACCT_REC.WG1	0.765	1.691	6.574	3.618	0	0	Worksheet	Reservation
106	PAYROLL.WG1	0.412	2.029	6.574	3.618	0	0	Worksheet	Reservation
107	SALES.WG1	0.059	2.368	6.574	3.618	0	0	Worksheet	Reservation
108	1-2-3/G: DESK.DSK	0.059	0.088	9.368	6.971	0	0	Desktop	N/A
109	Screen	0	0	9.412	7.059	0	1	Screen	N/A
110									
111									
112									

FIGURE 12–11 A table of information about open desktop windows

- **Worksheet:** When you select this option button, 1-2-3/G displays the name of the current directory followed by the wild-card reference *.W*, for example C:\123G\WORK*.W*, in the "File name" text box. This will cause all files in the current directory whose file extensions begin with "W" to be listed in the table. (This will include worksheet files for all releases of 1-2-3, but may include others as well.) You can edit the path, directory name, and extension in the "File name" text box, if you so desire. When you create the table, 1-2-3/G lists the following information in adjacent columns for each file: filename, date created, time created, and file size in bytes. Figure 12–12 shows a sample "Worksheet" table that lists 1-2-3/G worksheet files in the current directory.
- **Graph:** When you select this option button, 1-2-3/G creates a table of graph (.GPH) files in the directory you specify in the "File name" text box. The table includes the same information as the "Worksheet" table in Figure 12–12.
- **Print:** When you select this option button, 1-2-3/G creates a table of print (.PRN) files in the directory you specify in the "File name" text box. The table includes the same information as the "Worksheet" table in Figure 12–12.
- **Other:** When you select this option button, 1-2-3/G creates a table of all files in the directory you specify in the "File name" text box, regardless of extension. The table includes the same information as the "Worksheet" table in Figure 12–12.

UPDATING LINKS TO OTHER FILES

The File Admin Links Refresh command allows you to manually update *formula* links in the current worksheet file. Formula links allow you to use information

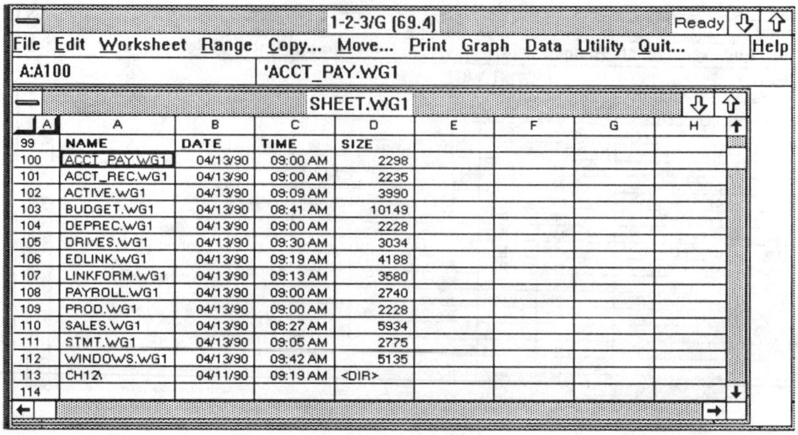

1-2-3/G [69.4] Ready

File Edit Worksheet Range Copy... Move... Print Graph Data Utility Quit... Help

A:A100 'ACCT_PAY.WG1

SHEET.WG1

A	A	B	C	D	E	F	G	H
99	NAME	DATE	TIME	SIZE				
100	ACCT_PAY.WG1	04/13/90	09:00 AM	2298				
101	ACCT_REC.WG1	04/13/90	09:00 AM	2235				
102	ACTIVE.WG1	04/13/90	09:09 AM	3990				
103	BUDGET.WG1	04/13/90	08:41 AM	10149				
104	DEPREC.WG1	04/13/90	09:00 AM	2228				
105	DRIVES.WG1	04/13/90	09:30 AM	3034				
106	EDLINK.WG1	04/13/90	09:19 AM	4188				
107	LINKFORM.WG1	04/13/90	09:13 AM	3580				
108	PAYROLL.WG1	04/13/90	09:00 AM	2740				
109	PROD.WG1	04/13/90	09:00 AM	2228				
110	SALES.WG1	04/13/90	08:27 AM	5934				
111	STMT.WG1	04/13/90	09:05 AM	2775				
112	WINDOWS.WG1	04/13/90	09:42 AM	5135				
113	CH12\	04/11/90	09:19 AM	<DIR>				
114								

FIGURE 12–12 **A table of worksheet files in the current directory**

from other files in the current file (see Chapter 2). When you open a file containing formula links, those links are automatically updated for any changes to files on disk to which the links refer. However, once the file is open, formula links are not updated for changes to files on disk. To update the links while the file is open, you must use File Admin Links Refresh. When you select this command, 1-2-3/G recalculates the formulas in the current file that refer to other open worksheet files as well as to worksheet files on disk. (Links you've created with the Edit Link command must be updated with the Edit Link Update command discussed in Chapter 2.) Thus, the File Admin Links Refresh command is needed in a network environment where files may be modified by other users without your knowledge. Using this command periodically gives you a reasonable assurance that you are using the most up-to-date information available.

MOVING FORMULA LINKS TO ANOTHER FILE

You can change the file to which the formula links in the current file refer. To do this, you use the File Admin Move-Links command. (To change the source-file reference for links created with the Edit Link command, you use the Edit Link Move command discussed in Chapter 2.)

When you select the File Admin Move-Links command, 1-2-3/G displays the dialog box in Figure 12–13. At the top of this dialog box, 1-2-3/G displays the name of the currently active worksheet in the "Destination" text box. You cannot modify the contents of this box. In the "Current source" list box, 1-2-3/G lists the files, both open and on disk, that are referenced by formulas in the current worksheet file. In the "New source" list box, 1-2-3/G lists the names of files, both open and on disk, in the current directory.

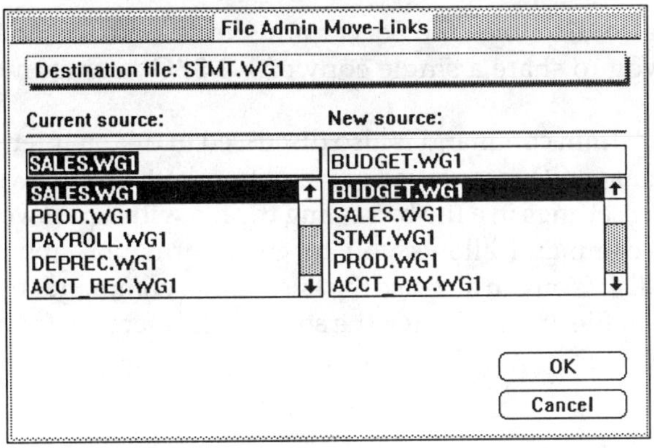

FIGURE 12–13 The File Admin Move-Links dialog box

To change the file to which link formulas in the current file refer, specify the name of the old file in the "Current source" text box and the name of the new file in the "New source" text box. For example, in Figure 12–13, the "New source" text box indicates that one or more of the formulas in the current file (STMT.WG1) refers to the file SALES.WG1. To change this reference to the file BUDGET.WG1 in the current directory, specify the name of that file in the "New source" text box. For example, in Figure 12–13, the filename BUDGET.WG1 appears in the "New source" text box. When you select the OK command button, or press ENTER, to complete the File Admin Move-Links command, 1-2-3/G changes the <<SALES.WG1>> file reference in the affected formulas to <<BUDGET.WG1>>. The range reference that follows the file reference remains the same. Therefore, the same ranges that were originally referenced in the file SALES.WG1 are now referenced in the file BUDGET.WG1.

Note

For a complete discussion of how to link worksheet files by using formulas, see Chapter 2, "Managing the Desktop."

SUMMARY

This chapter provides information about using 1-2-3/G on a network. Much of the discussion centers around 1-2-3/G's built-in file-locking and file-reservation system. This simple system allows multiple users to access data files on shared-network directories without destroying each other's work.

This chapter also discusses the Server and Node Editions of 1-2-3/G. These versions allow you to share a single copy of 1-2-3/G among multiple users on a network.

1-2-3/G's File Admin command is also discussed in this chapter. This command allows you to manage file reservations on a network. It also allows you to protect certain formatting settings in a file by sealing the file with a password. In addition, the File Admin command allows you to get information about files, both in memory and on disk. You can also use the File Admin command to update formula links in the current file and to change the source-file reference for link formulas in the current file.

The Backsolver and Solver

The Backsolver and Solver allow you to solve what-if problems in the worksheet. The Backsolver is useful when you already have a particular goal in mind and you want to see what it will take to reach that goal. The Solver, on the other hand, is useful when you're not sure what the best solution to a problem is. Instead, you want to see multiple solutions to the problem, based on constraints that you supply, of course, and choose the one solution that best fits the situation.

Note

Both the Backsolver and Solver are new for 1-2-3/G.

THE BACKSOLVER

The Backsolver is aptly named because it solves a problem by working backward from a goal you specify. It allows you to make a formula equal to a specific value by changing the value in one of the cells referenced by that formula.

Before you use the Backsolver, you must set up the problem you want to solve in the worksheet. Once the problem is set up, you can activate the Backsolver and solve the problem.

To activate the Backsolver, you use the Utility Backsolver command. When you select this command, 1-2-3/G displays the dialog box in Figure 13–1.

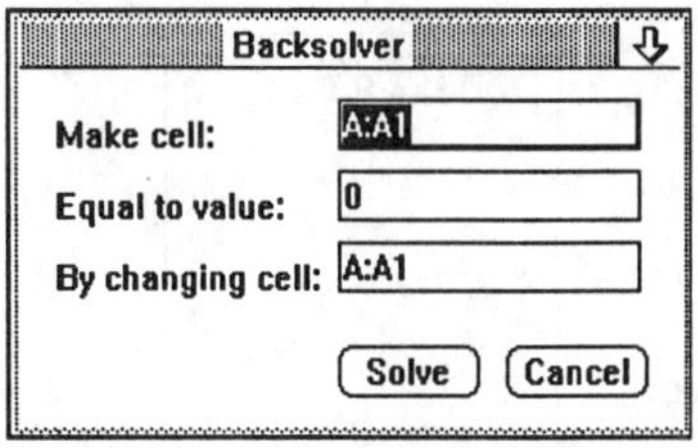

Backsolver	
Make cell:	A:A1
Equal to value:	0
By changing cell:	A:A1
	Solve Cancel

FIGURE 13–1 The Backsolver dialog box

The well-named text boxes in the Backsolver dialog box make using Backsolver almost effortless. In the "Make cell" text box, you specify the cell address or range name that contains the formula you want to solve. In the "Equal to value" text box, you specify the value you want that formula to eventually have. In the "By changing cell" text box, you specify a cell address or range name of a cell that is directly or indirectly referenced by the formula in the "Make cell" text box. To complete the command, select the Solve command button. 1-2-3/G begins substituting numbers into the cell you specified in the "By changing cell" text box. It keeps doing this until the formula in the cell you specified in the "Make cell" text box equals the value you specified in the "Equal to value" text box.

The results of using the Backsolver are recorded in the worksheet in the ranges you specified in the "Make cell" and "By changing cell" text boxes. If the cell you specified in the "By changing cell" text box contains a formula, Backsolver replaces that formula with the new value when it completes solving the problem. To revert the worksheet back to the way it was before you used Backsolver, select Edit Undo or press ALT-BACKSPACE.

Backsolver only solves one problem at a time. When it finishes solving the problem, the Backsolver dialog box disappears from your screen. To solve another problem, you must use the Utility Backsolver command again.

Solving a Sample Problem with Backsolver

Imagine your family has recently been blessed with a child. With any luck, 18 years hence that child will go away to college. By that time, you estimate that you must have amassed at least $100,000 to put that child through school. In addition, you are reasonably sure you can get a consistent 8% return from a money market fund investment. The only thing you don't know is how much money you need to put away each month to reach the $100,000 goal. To solve this problem, you can set up the worksheet in Figure 13–2.

In Figure 13–2, the @TERM function is used in conjunction with Backsolver to solve the problem referenced in the previous paragraph. The @TERM function calculates the number of equal payments required for an investment to

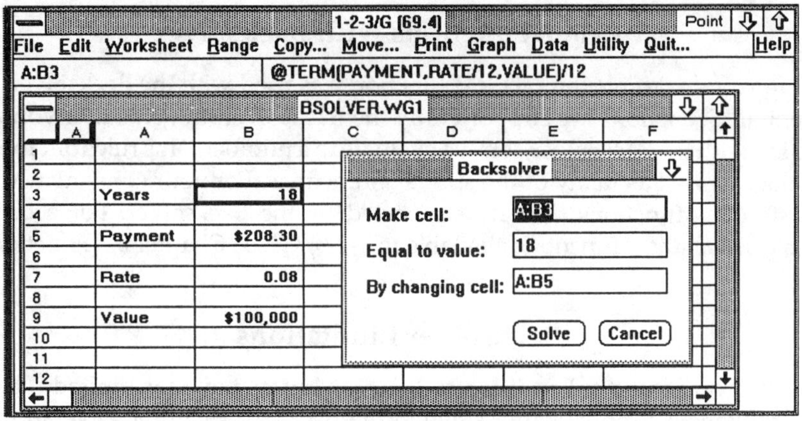

	A	B
1		
2		
3	Years	18
4		
5	Payment	$208.30
6		
7	Rate	0.08
8		
9	Value	$100,000

FIGURE 13–2 **The Backsolver used with @TERM**

reach a specific future value at a periodic interest rate. The @TERM function takes the form @TERM(*payments,interest,future-value*) and it appears in cell A:B3 of Figure 13–2 as follows:

```
@TERM(PAYMENT,RATE/12,VALUE)/12
```

where the PAYMENT range name refers to cell A:B5, the RATE range name refers to cell A:B7, and the VALUE range name refers to cell A:B9. The *interest* argument (defined by the range name RATE) is divided by 12, to evaluate to a monthly interest rate. The @TERM function itself is divided by 12, for the term of the investment to be expressed in years rather than total number of payments.

Once the problem is defined in the worksheet, as shown in Figure 13–2, you can use the Backsolver to solve for the monthly payment. To do this, select the Utility Backsolver command. 1-2-3/G displays the Backsolver dialog box. In the "Make cell" text box, specify the range A:B3, which contains the @TERM function. In the "Equal to value" text box, type the number 18, meaning 18 years. In the "By changing cell" text box, specify the range A:B5. This cell contains the payment value. It is this cell that 1-2-3/G will change until the @TERM function equals 18 years.

To solve the problem, select the Solve command button. 1-2-3/G begins substituting numbers into cell A:B5 until the @TERM function in cell A:B3 equals 18. When the problem is solved, the Backsolver dialog box disappears from your screen. The results are shown in cells A:B3 and A:B5. Cell A:B5, the formula cell, now equals 18 and cell A:B5, the payment cell, now contains the value $208.30. This indicates that you must salt away $208.30 each month for 18 years to have the $100,000 you need.

Using @Functions with Backsolver

In the previous example the @TERM function was used with the Backsolver. However, not all @functions are supported by the Backsolver. In general, if you use an @function with the Backsolver, it must evaluate to a number. This rules out the string @functions as well as many of the special @functions. For your convenience, Table 13–1 lists the @functions that are supported by the Backsolver. For a complete discussion of all the @functions available in 1-2-3/G, see Chapter 6, "Functions."

Backsolver Limitations

The Backsolver is a useful addition to 1-2-3/G, but its power is limited. There are some problems it simply cannot solve. If the Backsolver cannot solve a problem, 1-2-3/G displays a message indicating that either the problem cannot be solved or that Backsolver cannot solve it, and you must use the Solver to get the answer you need. The Backsolver also has the following additional limitations:

- Backsolver only tolerates a single reference in the "Make cell" text box. Therefore, you can only use Backsolver to evaluate a single formula.
- Backsolver only tolerates a single cell reference in the "By changing cell" text box. Therefore, you can only evaluate changing a single variable in one formula.
- To make use of Backsolver, you must already have a goal in mind.

TABLE 13–1 @Functions supported by Backsolver

@ABS	@INDEX	@ROWS
@COS	@INT	@SHEETS
@ASIN	@IRR	@SIN
@ATAN	@ISNUMBER	@SLN
@ATAN2	@LN	@SQRT
@AVG	@LOG	@STD
@CHOOSE	@MAX	@STDS
@COLS	@MIN	@SUM
@COS	@MOD	@SUMPRODUCT
@COUNT	@NOW	@SYD
@DDB	@PI	@TODAY
@EXP	@PMT	@VAR
@FALSE	@PV	@VARS
@FV	@RATE	@VDB
@HLOOKUP	@RAND	@VLOOKUP
@IF	@ROUND	

- The Backsolver doesn't have the muscle needed to handle multiple layers of dependencies. In fact, if the formula you are evaluating with Backsolver in the "Make cell" text box does not directly reference the cell you specified in the "By changing cell" text box, it is unlikely the Backsolver will be able to solve the problem.

The Solver utility addresses these weaknesses.

THE SOLVER UTILITY

Like Backsolver, the Solver utility can help you to solve what-if problems in the worksheet. However, unlike Backsolver, the Solver can provide more than one answer to a problem. Working within specific limits that you define, the Solver explores various possibilities when solving a problem, to find as many different answers as it can. It then allows you to look at each of those answers in the worksheet. It also defines for you what it perceives to be the best or optimal answer to the problem. Use the Solver utility when you're not sure what the best answer to a problem is or when you want to look at several possible solutions before choosing the one that best fits the situation.

Before you use the Solver, you must define the problem in the worksheet. The problem must include both *adjustable cells* and *constraint cells.* Adjustable cells are cells that the Solver is allowed to change in order to solve the problem. Constraint cells define limits within which the Solver must work when adjusting values in the adjustable cells.

In addition to the adjustable and constraint cells, Solver allows you to define an *optimal cell* for a problem. The optimal cell usually summarizes the problem in a meaningful way. When you define an optimal cell, Solver will attempt to minimize or maximize the value in that cell. For example, you may wish to maximize total profit or minimize total costs.

When you solve the problem, Solver plugs values into the adjustable cells and uses existing formulas in the worksheet to find as many answers to the problem as it can. Each answer must be within the limits defined by the constraint cells. Once the problem is solved, you can then have each of the answers displayed in the worksheet, one at a time. You can also create various reports that show not only what answers Solver found but also how they were calculated.

On the surface, the Solver appears to be just another linear programming package, but it's not. The Solver is capable of solving both linear and nonlinear problems. In addition, most linear programming packages can only provide a single answer (the optimal answer). The Solver, on the other hand, is capable of finding the optimal answer as well as other answers that meet the constraints you define.

The Solver uses a combination of two methods to solve problems. At first, Solver will attempt to solve problems symbolically (algebraically) using an extensive set of rules. If the symbolic method is not feasible, however, Solver will attempt to solve the problem numerically. The numeric method is essentially trial and error. Solver starts substituting numbers into the adjustable cells in the problem until its values gradually converge on an answer that meets the constraints you've defined. Although you do not need to know or specify the method (algebraic versus numeric) that Solver is using to solve a problem, you should know that the numeric method of solving a problem can be more time consuming.

You can continue to work in 1-2-3/G while Solver is solving a problem. Therefore, if Solver is working on a large or particularly complex problem that requires a long time to solve, you can return to 1-2-3/G and keep working. Solver will continue solving the problem in the background.

There are some problems the Solver cannot solve. In some cases, there just is not an answer to a given problem that falls within the constraints you've defined. In addition, the size and complexity of a given problem may cause Solver to exceed the limits of the random access memory (RAM) as well as the virtual memory (disk space) available on your computer. Solver analyzes a problem before providing answers for it. If Solver anticipates that providing answers will exceed available memory, it will not solve the problem.

The steps for solving a problem with Solver are as follows:

- Define the problem in the worksheet.
- Set up the constraints you want Solver to use when solving the problem.
- Activate the Solver and define the problem for it.
- Solve the problem.
- Review the answers that Solver provides and save the ones you want to keep.
- (Optional) Create reports that analyze the answers Solver found

Each of these steps are defined in detail in the sections that follow.

Defining the Problem

Before you're ready to use Solver, you must define the problem you want to solve in the worksheet. For example, Figure 13–3 shows a sample problem setup in the range A:A1..A:E7. This fictional data might be used by a small computer equipment reseller to analyze sales.

The problem in Figure 13–3 shows potential quantities (A:B2..A:B5) to be sold of computers, monitors, printers, and add-on boards. Based on the quantity of each item sold, the model shows sales dollars (A:C2..A:C2), cost (A:D2..A:D5), and gross profit (A:E2..A:E5) for each item. The values in the sales and cost columns (A:C2..A:D5) are derived from multiplying the quantity sold of each item by the appropriate retail and wholesale value in the pricing table in the range A:E11..A:G15. Thus, the whole model is driven by the quantity values in

1-2-3/G [69.4] Ready

File Edit Worksheet Range Copy... Move... Print Graph Data Utility Quit... Help

A:E7 @SUM(E2..E5)

(,0) RESALE.WG1

A	A	B	C	D	E	F	G
1		Quantity	Sales	Cost	Profit		
2	Computers	100	500,000	350,000	150,000		
3	Monitors	120	54,000	24,000	30,000		
4	Printers	60	150,000	132,000	18,000		
5	Boards	75	37,500	11,250	26,250		
6							
7	Total	355	741,500	517,250	224,250		
8							
9							
10						Pricing Table	
11		Min	Max			Wholesale	Retail
12	Computers	+B2>=150	+B2<=300		Computers	3,500	5,000
13	Monitors	+B3>=170	+B3<=320		Monitors	200	450
14	Printers	+B4>=60	+B4<=120		Printers	2,200	2,500
15	Boards	+B5>=75	+B5<=150		Boards	150	500
16	Profit	+E7<450000					
17							
18							
19							
20							

FIGURE 13–3 A sample problem set up in the worksheet

the range A:B2..A:B5. When you adjust one or more of the values in this range, the data in the rest of the problem changes to reflect the new values.

When you set up a model for the Solver, make sure it includes a range of one or more cells on which the rest of the values in the problem depend. When you later activate the Solver, you can select these cells as the *adjustable cells* for the problem (the range of one or more cells that Solver is allowed to change). As Solver changes the values in these cells, the rest of the cells in the worksheet are updated for the change. For example, in the problem in Figure 13–3, the adjustable cells will be A:B2..A:B5.

To define limits on how much the Solver can adjust the values of the adjustable cells, you must define constraints (limits) that the Solver can use. The constraints for the problem in Figure 13–3 appear in the range A:B12..A:C16. Defining constraints for a problem is covered in detail in the next section.

In addition to the adjustable cells, you can also include an *optimal cell* in a problem. The use of an optimal cell is entirely optional. However, an optimal cell summarizes the problem in a meaningful way and can be used to determine the ultimate goal in solving the problem. For example, in Figure 13–3, the optimal cell is A:E7. This cell summarizes gross profit for the problem. When you later solve this problem, the Solver will attempt to maximize the value in this cell. However, you can also have the solver minimize the value in the optimal cell. For example, instead of solving for maximum profit, you may want to solve for minimum cost.

Defining Constraints

The Solver requires that you define constraints (boundaries) for the adjustable cells in a model as well as for the optimal cell, if you decide to use one.

Constraints are simply logical formulas. As you may recall from Chapter 1, logical formulas have one of two answers: 1 (true) or 0 (false). Logical formulas use the following operators:

> Greater than
< Less than
= Equal to
>= Greater than or equal to
<= Less than or equal to
<> Not equal (not supported by Solver)

For example, the logical formula +B2>=150 appears in cell A:B12 of Figure 13-3. This defines a lower limit for the adjustment of cell A:B2. Solver may not adjust this cell below a value of 150 but may adjust it higher. Normally this formula would evaluate to 1 (True), because the value in cell A:B2 is already 150 or greater. However, in Figure 13-3, the Range Format Text command has been used in cell A:B2 to make the formula appear as text.

Tip: Formatting the display of constraint cells

Instead of having logical formulas in constraint cells return a 1 (true) or 0 (false), you can format these cells to display TRUE or FALSE. To do this, you use the Range Format User command to specify a user-defined format for the range that contains the logical formulas. First, select the range you want to format. Then, select the Range Format User command and press ENTER to select an undefined format slot. 1-2-3/G prompts you for a format string by activating the "User format" text box. Type **n"TRUE";n"FALSE";n"TRUE"** and press ENTER. This format string causes cells with a value greater that 0 to display TRUE, cells with a value of 0 to display FALSE, and cells with a value less than 0 to display TRUE. To complete the Range Format command, select the OK command button, or press ENTER. 1-2-3/G formats the range you specified. For more on specifying user-defined formats, see Chapter 3, "Formatting Worksheets."

The Solver does not support the use of the #AND#, #NOT#, and #OR# logical operators. These operators allow you to specify multiple conditions in logical formulas. Instead, Solver allows you to use multiple logical formulas (constraints) for a given cell. For example, notice in Figure 13-3, the Formula +B2<=300 appears in cell A:C12. This formula defines an upper limit of 300 for the adjustment of cell A:B2. This formula, in conjunction with the formula in cell A:B12, defines a constraint for cell A:B2 such that its value must be greater than or equal to 150 and less than or equal to 300. The formulas in the range A:B13..A:C15 define similar constraints for other adjustable cells in the problem (A:B3, A:B4, and A:B5).

If you decide to use an optimal cell, Solver requires that you also specify a constraint for that cell. For example, the formula +E7<450000 appears in cell A:B16 of Figure 13–3. This defines the upper limit of total gross profit as $450,000. This constraint also has an impact on the other adjustable cells in the range A:B2..A:B5 of Figure 13–3. The Solver may not adjust these cells such that the value in cell A:E7 exceeds $450,000. If you do not specify a constraint for the optimal cell, Solver may issue an "Optimal cell is unbounded" error message when you attempt to solve the problem.

Constraint cells *must* depend on the adjustable cells in some way. If a constraint cell does not depend directly or indirectly on an adjustable cell, 1-2-3/G will issue an error message when you attempt to solve the problem.

Activating the Solver

Once you've defined the problem and its constraints in the worksheet, you're ready to use the Solver. To activate the Solver, you use the Utility Solver command. When you select this command, 1-2-3/G displays the Solver Definition window shown in Figure 13–4. In addition, the Worksheet Tool menu is replaced by the Solver menu in the Control Line at the top of your screen.

The Solver Definition window allows you to specify both the adjustable and constraint cells that will be used to solve the problem you've set up in the worksheet. It also allows you to specify an optimal cell. When you select the Solve command button or the Solve command from Solver's main menu, Solver

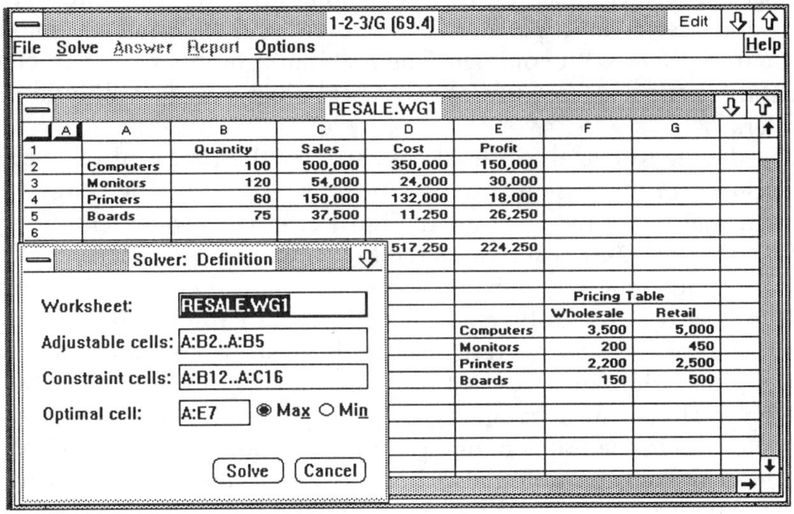

FIGURE 13–4 The Solver Definition window

analyzes the problem and starts searching for possible answers to the problem. When the Solver is finished solving a problem, you can have the answers it found displayed in the worksheet one at a time.

When the Solver Definition window in Figure 13–4 is initially displayed, the name of the current worksheet file appears in the "Worksheet" text box. You can edit this to specify another open worksheet file, if you so desire.

To specify the adjustable cells—the cells in the current model that Solver is allowed to change—select "Adjustable cells." 1-2-3/G activates the adjacent text box. Specify the range address or name that contains the adjustable cells in the current problem. For example, if you are solving the problem in Figure 13–3, specify the range A:B2..A:B5.

Adjustable cells must contain numbers. Solver will not adjust formulas. Additionally, if you specify a multiple cell range in the "Adjustable cells" text box that contains protected cells, blank cells, or cells with formulas, Solver ignores them. However, if you specify a single-cell range that is blank, but is referenced by other cells that are part of the problem, Solver places a number in the blank cell when you solve the problem.

To specify the constraint cells for the current problem, select "Constraint cells." Solver activates the adjacent text box. Specify the range address or name that contains your constraint cells (A:B12..A:C16 in Figure 13–3).

There are also some conventions that you should be aware of for the constraint-cells range. For example, notice that the constraint-cells range in Figure 13–3 (A:B12..A:C16) contains a blank cell (A:C16). If Solver encounters blank cells, cells with labels, or cells that contain nonlogical formulas in the constraint-cells range, it ignores them.

The range you specify in either the "Adjustable cells" or "Constraint cells" text boxes can be a range address, range name, collection, column, row, or worksheet. These can also be from the same or different open worksheet files. If you specify multiple entries in either text box, however, make sure you separate them with commas. The maximum number of characters the "Adjustable cells" or "Constraint cells" text boxes can accommodate is 512 characters.

If you decide to use an optimal cell, specify the range address or name of that cell in the "Optimal cell" text box. For example, the range address of the optimal cell in the problem in Figure 13–3 is A:E7. When you specify an optimal cell, 1-2-3/G activates the Max and Min option buttons. Select Max (the default) for now to have Solver maximize the value in the optimal cell. If you select Min, Solver will minimize the value in the optimal cell. An example of how you might utilize this feature appears later in this chapter in a section entitled "A Production Example."

The optimal cell must be a single cell, and it must be either one of the adjustable cells in the problem or a cell that depends directly or indirectly on one or more of the adjustable cells. The optimal cell can be located in any open worksheet file.

Note

When you save the current worksheet file, 1-2-3/G also saves the information from the Solver Definition window. That way, when you load the worksheet file at a later time and activate the Solver, the same ranges are displayed in the "Adjustable cells," "Constraint cells," and "Optimal Cells" text boxes.

Solving the Problem

To begin solving the problem currently defined in the Solver Definition window, select the Solve command button from that window. Alternatively, you can select the Solve command from the Solver's main menu and select Problem from the pulldown menu that appears. (To activate the menu, click on any option or press /, ALT, or F10.) You can also press SOLVE (F9) to begin solving. Whichever method you choose, Solver analyzes the problem you've defined for it and starts searching for available answers.

To inform you of its progress, Solver displays the Solver Progress dialog box in Figure 13-5. At the top of this dialog box, Solver displays messages that describe the current process that is underway. The Elapsed time and % Complete sections provide further information about the progress of the Solver. As the Solver accumulates additional answers, the length of the shaded bar in the middle of the Solver Progress dialog box grows in size.

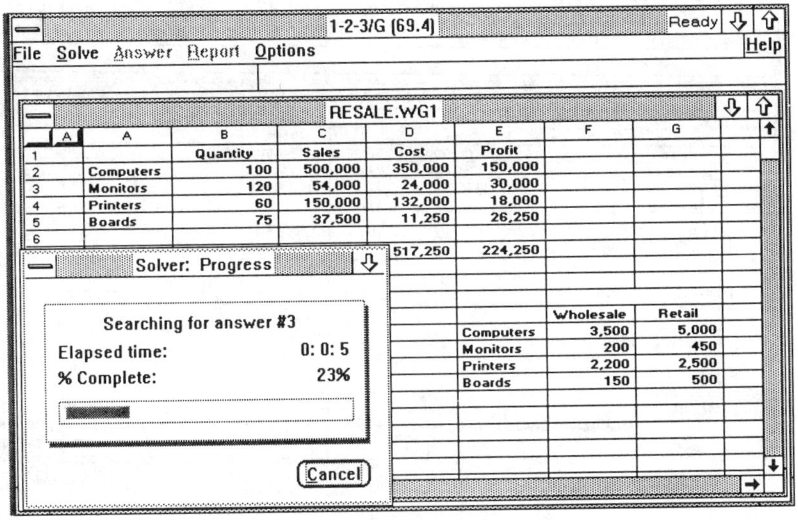

FIGURE 13–5 The Solver Progress window

When Solver has finished solving the current problem, it displays the Solver Answers window in Figure 13-6. You can use this window to review each of the answers the Solver has found. See "Reviewing and Saving Answers" in the next section for more details on this.

While the Solver is searching for answers, you can continue your work in 1-2-3/G and the Solver will keep working in the background. However, if you change the contents of the worksheet files that Solver needs to solve the current problem, Solver will display an error message and discard any answers it may have found. Solver then redisplays the Solver Definition window so that you can solve the problem again.

You can stop the Solver at any time and view the answers it has found thus far. To stop the Solver from finding further answers, you can select the Cancel command button from the Solver Progress dialog box. Alternatively, you can select Solve from the Solver's main menu and select Stop from the menu that appears. Whichever method you choose, Solver stops finding answers and displays the Answer window. You can then review the answers found thus far.

Reviewing and Saving Answers

When Solver finishes Solving a problem, it displays the Solver Answer window shown in Figure 13-6. This window tells you how many answers Solver has found and allows you to display each of them in the worksheet, one at a time.

If you specified an optimal cell in the Solver Definition window, the first answer displayed is the optimal answer or the best answer Solver could find, given the current constraints. To see the first answer, select the Answer com-

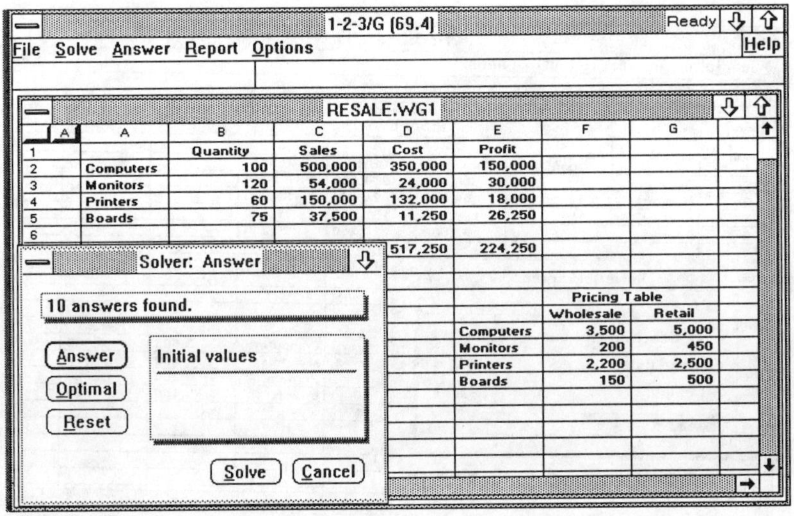

FIGURE 13-6 **The Solver Answer window**

mand button. Solver displays the first answer in the worksheet. The adjustable cells show the values Solver used to calculate the answer. The rest of the formulas in the worksheet that depend on those cells are updated to reflect the new values.

For example, Figure 13–7 shows the first, or optimal, answer to the problem originally shown in Figure 13–3. As you may recall, the adjustable cells in this problem are in the range A:B2..A:B5 and the constraint cells are in the range A:B12..A:C16. This answer indicates that the $450,000 gross profit can be derived from selling 188 computers, 320 monitors, 120 printers, and 150 add-on boards. Notice that all of these values are within the constraints in the range A:B12..A:C16.

To see additional answers, select the Answer command button. 1-2-3/G displays the next answer each time you select the Answer command button. Once you cycle through the available answers, Solver comes back to the first (optimal) answer. You can also display the optimal or best answer at any time by selecting the Optimal command button from the Answer window.

To cycle through the available answers by using your keyboard, you can use the Answer command from Solvers main menu. When you select this command, Solver displays the following options:

- **Optimal:** Displays the optimal answer.
- **Next**: Displays the next available answer.

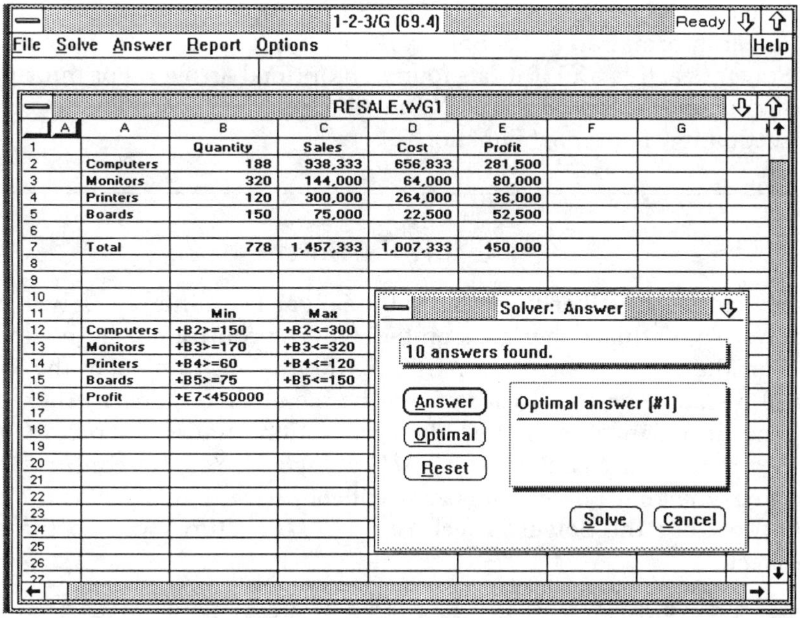

1-2-3/G [69.4] Ready

File Solve Answer Report Options Help

RESALE.WG1

A	A	B	C	D	E
1		Quantity	Sales	Cost	Profit
2	Computers	188	938,333	656,833	281,500
3	Monitors	320	144,000	64,000	80,000
4	Printers	120	300,000	264,000	36,000
5	Boards	150	75,000	22,500	52,500
6					
7	Total	778	1,457,333	1,007,333	450,000
11		Min	Max		
12	Computers	+B2>=150	+B2<=300		
13	Monitors	+B3>=170	+B3<=320		
14	Printers	+B4>=60	+B4<=120		
15	Boards	+B5>=75	+B5<=150		
16	Profit	+E7<450000			

Solver: Answer

10 answers found.

Answer | Optimal | Reset

Optimal answer (#1)

Solve | Cancel

FIGURE 13–7 Solver displays the optimal answer in the worksheet

- **First**: Displays the first answer.
- **Previous**: Displays the previous answer.
- **Last:** Displays the last answer.
- **Reset:** Displays the original values in the worksheet.

1-2-3/G retains a record of the values that were initially displayed in the worksheet before the Solver calculated its answers. To redisplay those values again, either select the Reset command button from the Solver Answer window or use the Answer Reset command from Solver's main menu.

To save an answer to a separate worksheet file, first use the Answer command button from the Solver Answer window or the Answer command to display that answer in the worksheet. Next, click on the title bar of the worksheet file or press NEXT WINDOW (CTRL-F6) to activate the worksheet file that contains the answer. Once you're back in the worksheet, the Worksheet Tool menu is again displayed at the top of your screen. From that menu, select the File Save command to save the file under a new name. To return to the Solver Answer window, click on it or press NEXT WINDOW (CTRL-F6) to activate it. The Solver menu is once again displayed in the Control Line at the top of your screen. You can then continue reviewing answers or close the Solver.

Tip: Getting information about solver from within a macro

You can use 1-2-3/G's new @SOLVER function from within a macro to get information about Solver. For example, you can determine if Solver is active and if it has found an optimal answer. For information about the new @SOLVER function, see the "Special Functions" section in Chapter 6, "Functions."

Closing the Solver

You can close the Solver from either the Solver Definition or Solver Answer windows. To do this, either click on the window control box in the upper-left corner of the window or press ALT—(ALT-MINUS) to display the Window Control menu. Then select Close from the menu that appears. Alternatively, you can select Cancel from the Solver Definition window or press CTRL-F4. Whichever method you choose, 1-2-3/G displays a Yes/No confirmation box informing you that Solver's answers will be discarded when you close the utility. To close the Solver, select Yes. 1-2-3/G returns you to the current worksheet.

If you want to restore the original values to the worksheet before closing the Solver, select Reset from the Solver Answer window or use the Reset option on the Answer menu. If you want to replace the original values in the worksheet with one of Solver's answers, make that answer current by using the Answer command button from the Answer window or by using Solver's Answer command. Then, close the Solver. 1-2-3/G replaces the original values in the worksheet with the answer you selected.

If you accidentally close the Solver without resetting the worksheet to display its initial values, you can still get those values back. To do this, select the Edit Undo command (or press ALT-BACKSPACE). This will activate the undo feature, allowing you to reclaim the lost data. However, you must select Edit Undo one time for each answer you displayed in the worksheet while Solver was active. For example, if you displayed three answers while Solver was active, you must select Edit Undo three times.

Getting More Answers

Initially, the Solver is set to find 10 answers. Therefore, it will stop solving when those 10 answers are found, provided, of course, that 10 are available. However, the Solver may also be able to find additional answers to the current problem. To determine if more answers are available, take a look at the Solve command button at the bottom of the Answer window shown in Figure 13–7. If the button appears grayed (nonselectable), no more answers are available. However, if the Solve command button appears active (black), more answers are available.

To view additional answers, select the Solve command button. Alternatively, you can select the Solve command from the main Solver menu and select Continue from the pulldown menu that appears. Whichever method you choose, Solver begins searching for the next 10 answers to add to the first 10.

As mentioned earlier in this chapter, you can stop the Solver from looking for further answers at any time. To do this, you can select Cancel from the Solver Progress dialog box or you can use the Solver Stop command available from the main Solver menu. When you use either of these methods to stop the Solver, the Solver Answer window is displayed and you can review the answers found thus far. To continue solving for further answers at that point, you can either select the Solve command button or use the Solve Continue command.

You can also change the number of answers the Solver looks for. To do this, you use the Options Number Answers command. When you select this com-

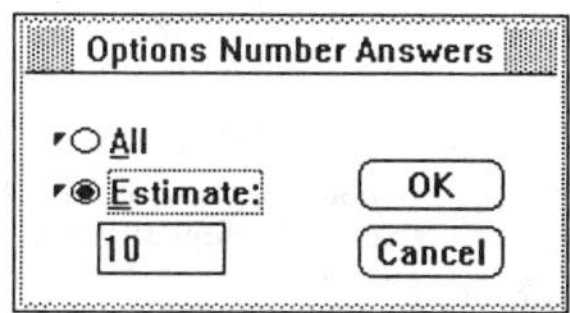

FIGURE 13–8 Use Options Number Answers to change the number of answers the Solver looks for.

mand, Solver displays the dialog box in Figure 13–8. To find as many answers as possible, select the All option button. To select a specific number of target answers, select the Estimate option button and type a number from 1 to 999 in the adjacent text box. To complete the command, select the OK command button or press ENTER.

When you specify a value in the Estimate text box, it is only an estimate. The Solver may or may not be able to find the number of answers you requested. However, Solver will stop looking for answers when it reaches the number you specified. Further, if you solve for an additional set of answers, Solver uses the value in the Estimate text box when searching for the second set of answers.

The Options Number Answers command applies only to the current worksheet file. If you activate the Solver from another worksheet file, the default number of answers will once again be 10.

Changing the Problem

If you make a change to the worksheet that contains the current problem while Solver is active, Solver discards any answers it may have found. For example, imagine you've just completed solving for a set of answers under a given set of constraints. However, you now wish to evaluate the same problem under a new set of constraints. Without closing the Solver, you activate the worksheet containing the problem and make a change that causes the worksheet to recalculate. When you return to the Solver, the message box in Figure 13–9 appears, informing you that the problem may have changed and that it will be necessary to solve the problem again. When you select OK from this message box, 1-2-3/G returns you to the Solver Definition window.

To solve the problem again, modify the cell addresses in the Solver Definition window if necessary, and select Solve. Solver generates a new set of answers to the revised problem.

The Solver Functions Keys

There are a number of function keys whose functions are different when Solver is active. Most of these function keys are simply alternatives to using the Solver

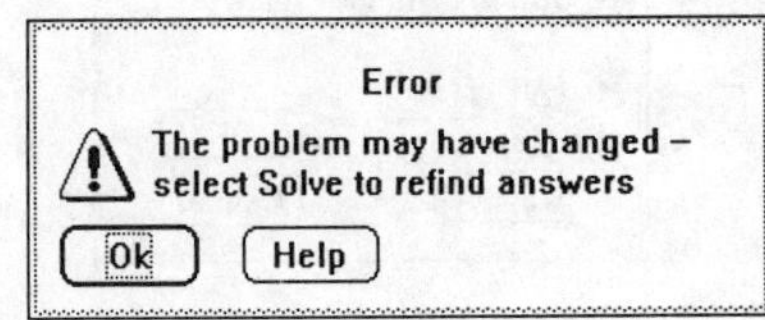

FIGURE 13–9 Changing the problem while Solver is active causes an error message

menus and may help to make your Solver session more productive. These function keys are as follows:

Key	Name	Function
F6	WINDOW	Toggles back and forth between Solver's Definition and Answer windows.
F7	FIRST	Displays the first answer.
F8	NEXT	Displays the next answer.
F9	SOLVE	Solves a problem.
F10	MENU	Activates the Solver menu.
SHIFT-F6	WORKSHEET	Activates the worksheet file named in the Definition window.
SHIFT-F7	LAST	Displays the last answer.
SHIFT-F8	PREVIOUS	Displays the previous answer.
SHIFT-F9	RESET	Restores the original data to the worksheet.

The Best Answer

When Solver is not sure whether it has the "optimal" answer (the answer that results in the highest or lowest value in the optimal cell), it displays the "best" answer. The best answer is the answer that is the closest mathematical match to the constraints you've specified. However, a better answer may exist. To indicate that the "best" answer, as opposed to the "optimal" answer, has been found, Solver displays "Best answer found" in the Answer window, as shown in Figure 13-10, when you display the first answer in the worksheet.

When you specify an optimal cell in the Solver Definition window, the Solver will attempt to optimize the value in that cell when solving a problem. At the same time, it will attempt to satisfy all the constraints you've specified. How-

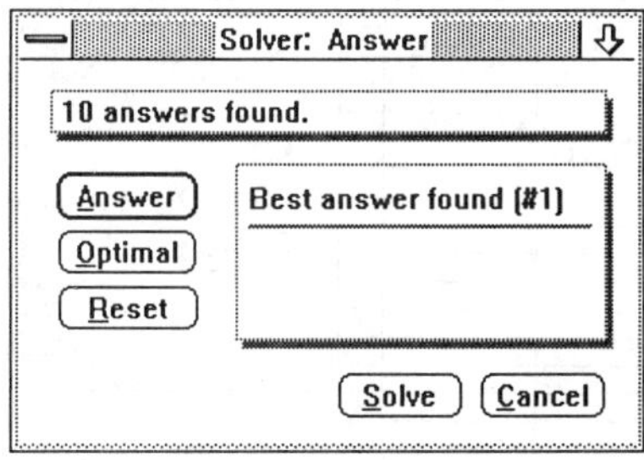

FIGURE 13–10 **Solver indicates it has found the "best" answer, as opposed to the "optimal" answer**

ever, in some cases, all the constraints are satisfied, but the Solver is not mathematically sure that it has found the optimal answer. In this case, it displays what it perceives to be the "best" mathematical answer, given the structure of the problem and the current constraints. This may, or may not, be the optimal answer. To solve for further, possibly better, answers, you can select the Solve Continue command.

The "best" answer may occur for a variety of reasons. One possibility is the improper use of @functions in the problem. The Solver only supports selected @functions and they can only be used in certain ways. See "Using @Functions with Solver" toward the end of this chapter for more details on this. Another possibility may be that the constraints are incorrectly set up for the current problem. There is a possibility that you can solve for the optimal answer by returning to the worksheet and changing one or more of the logical formulas in the constraint cells.

Attempts

At times, Solver will not be able to solve a problem and meet all the constraints you've specified. When this is the case, Solver will report in the Answer window the number of representative *attempts* it made to solve the problem. Attempts occur when the Solver cannot calculate an answer that results in all of the logical formulas in the constraint cells returning a value of 1 (true).

When no answers are available, the Solver Answer window appears as in Figure 13-11. The message "No answers found" appears at the top of the

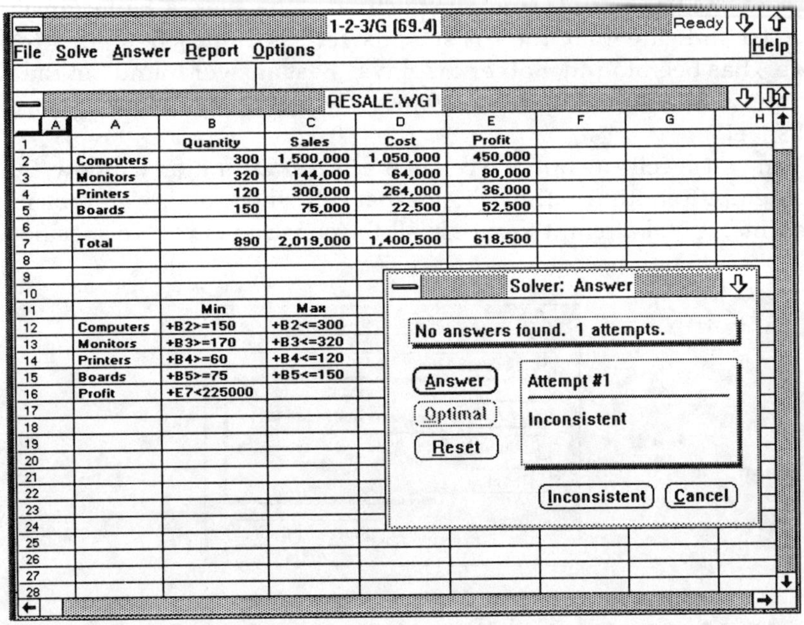

FIGURE 13-11 **An attempt is displayed in the worksheet**

window followed by the number of representative attempts the Solver made. When you select the Answer command button or the Answer First command, Solver displays the attempt in the worksheet. In addition, it displays the messages "Attempt 1" with "Inconsistent" beneath it in the Answer window. Further, the name of the Solve command button at the bottom of the Answer window changes to Inconsistent.

If you select the Inconsistent command button, Solver displays the Solver Report window in Figure 13–12. You can use this window to get an indication of what constraints (logical formulas) were not satisfied and why. At the top of the Report window in Figure 13–12, the address and range name of the first cell that contains an inconsistent constraint is displayed. If the cell does not have a range name, Solver displays the closest row and column labels. For example, in Figure 13–12, the first constraint that was not satisfied is located in cell A:B16. Beneath this, Solve displays the logical formula in that cell as it was originally written. It also displays the modification it estimates is required to make that logical formula return a 1 (true) for the current problem. For example, the Report window in Figure 13–12 indicates the logical formula in cell A:B16 is +E7<225000. This constraint would be satisfied if it were written as +E7<225000+393500 or +E7<618500. To see additional unsatisfied constraints, if any, select the Next command button.

Attempts usually occur when your constraints are inconsistent. That is, one or more constraint formulas will not allow the other constraint formulas to return a value of 1 (true). For example, notice in Figure 13–11, the logical formula in cell A:B16 has been changed to +E7<225000. (This formula was originally written as +E7<+450000 in Figure 13–3.) Cell A:E7 contains the total for gross profits and is the optimal cell for the problem. The adjustable cells for the problem are in the range A:B2..A:B5 and contain the quantity sold for each item. The constraints on these adjustable cells are in the range A:B12..A:C15. The minimum values for each adjustable cell are specified by the logical formulas in the range A:B12..A:B15. Even if all the adjustable cells in the range A:B2..A:B5 are set to their minimum values, as defined by the constraints, the total gross profit in cell A:E7 would still be $311,750. Therefore, setting a constraint on cell A:E7 such that its value must be less than $225,000 is inconsistent with the other constraint cells and makes solving the problem impossible.

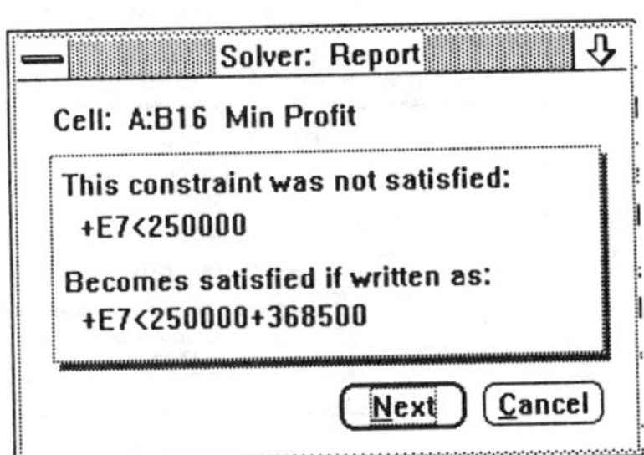

FIGURE 13–12 **A current-cell report of inconsistent constraints**

Guesses

When the Solver needs more information to solve a problem, it will ask you for guesses. Occasionally, a problem is too complicated or does not contain enough information for Solver to calculate an answer. When this happens, Solver displays the "No answers found" message in the Answer window followed by the number of attempts it made to solve the problem. When you select the Answer command button, or you use the Answer Optimal command, Solver displays the messages "Attempt 1," "Inconsistent," "Requires guesses" in the Answer window, as shown in Figure 13–13.

When Solver prompts you for a guess, it is asking you to provide a value for one or more of the adjustable cells in the current problem. To make a guess, select the Guess command button at the bottom of the Answer window or select the Solve Guesses command. Whichever method you choose, Solver displays the Solver Guess window in Figure 13–14.

The cell address at the top of the Solver Guess window identifies the adjustable cell for which Solver requires additional information. Below this, Solver displays the guess it formulated in its most recent attempt. In addition, the current value of the cell is displayed. To enter a new guess for the cell, enter a value in the "New guess" text box. To Solve the problem again using the new guess value, select the Solve command button. Solver attempts to solve the problem by using your new guess value.

When you provide a new guess value for an adjustable cell, you are providing Solver with additional information that may allow it to solve the problem. It is to your advantage to give your guesses some thought. The closer your guess is to the value that should ultimately be in the adjustable cell, the better chance Solver has of solving the problem.

In some cases Solver may require a new guess for more than one adjustable cell. If such is the case, the Next command button at the bottom of the Solver Guess window allows you to advance to the next adjustable cell in the problem and provide a guess for that cell.

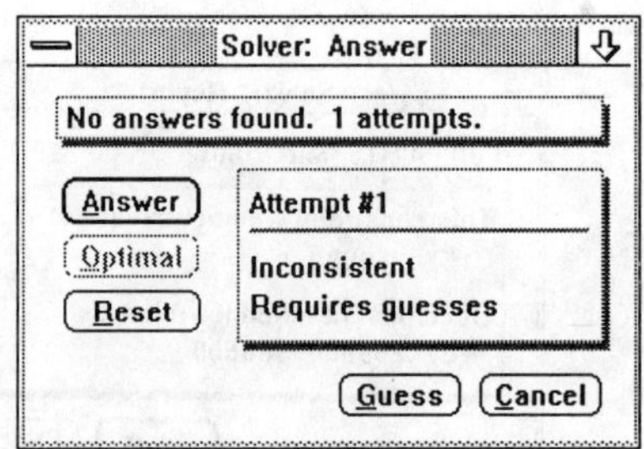

FIGURE 13–13 **The Solver request guesses when it needs additional information**

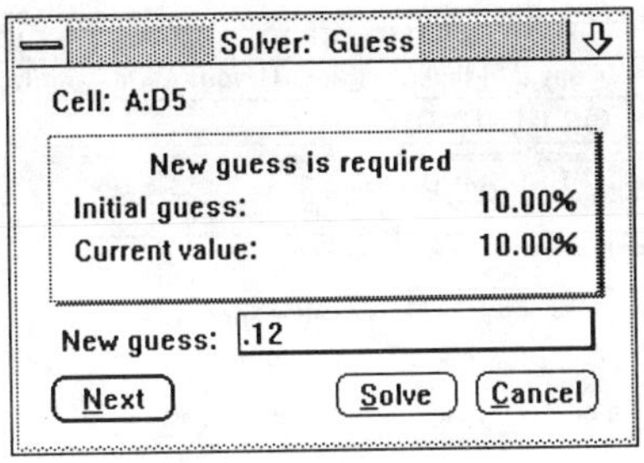

Solver: Guess	
Cell: A:D5	
New guess is required	
Initial guess:	10.00%
Current value:	10.00%
New guess:	.12
Next	Solve Cancel

FIGURE 13–14 The Solver Guess window

Roundoff Errors

One of the more common error messages you may encounter with the Solver is the "Roundoff error" message. This message is displayed in the Answer window when you attempt to view an answer in the worksheet. This error message results when there is a discrepancy between the Solver's calculations and the worksheet's calculations. This can happen when one or more of the logical formulas in the constraint cells return false (0) for five decimal places of precision. This may be caused by a percentage used in a constraint, for example +COST<=SALES*.3. Other sources of rounding errors might be square and other roots as well as exponentiation. In addition, the "Rounding error" message may result when you use the Range Attributes Precision command to limit the decimal precision of a cell or when you protect a worksheet so that the adjustable cells in a problem cannot be changed.

The "Roundoff error" message may appear for answers as well as attempts. If it appears for an answer, the answer is probably still valid, but a rounding error caused one or more of the constraint cells to evaluate to 0 (false). If the "Roundoff error" message appears for an attempt, the Solver has not been able to find a valid answer. To determine what constraint cells are affected by rounding errors, you can use the Report Inconsistent Constraints command to have Solver show you a list constraint cells that are inconsistent. See "Generating Reports" later in this chapter for more information on creating a report of inconsistent constraints.

A Production Example

Thus far, a rather simple sales/product-mix problem has been used to acquaint you with how the Solver works. However, the Solver is equipped to solve more difficult problems as well. For example, Figure 13–15 shows a manufacturing problem that involves three products: Product 1, Product 2, and Product 3. All three products have different cost and sales prices and require varying amounts of machine and labor hours to produce. The goal in solving this problem is to determine the appropriate amount of each product to produce that will result

1-2-3/G [69.4] Ready

File Edit Worksheet Range Copy... Move... Print Graph Data Utility Quit... Help

A:F12 @SUM(B12..D12)

(C0) PRODMOD.WG1

A	A	B	C	D	E	F
1		Product 1	Product 2	Product 3		Totals
2						
3	Units	10,000	10,000	10,000		
4						
5	Selling Price	$22	$20	$24		
6	Cost	$6	$5	$7		
7	Labor Hours	0.5	0.55	0.57		
8	Machine Hrs.	0.25	0.3	0.35		
9						
10	Revenue	$220,000	$200,000	$240,000		$660,000
11	Cost	$60,000	$50,000	$70,000		$180,000
12	Gross Profit	$160,000	$150,000	$170,000		$480,000
13						
14	Labor Hours	5,000	5,500	5,700		16,200
15	Machine Hrs.	2,500	3,000	3,500		9,000
16						
17	Forecast:					
18	Minimum	8,000	9,600	11,520		
19	Maximum	9,600	11,500	13,800		
20						
21	Constraints	Minimum	Maximum			
22	Product 1	+B3>=B18	+B3<=B19			
23	Product 2	+C3>=C18	+C3<=C19			
24	Product 3	+D3>=D18	+D3<=D19			
25	Labor	+F14<=18000				
26	Machine	+F15<=10000				
27						

FIGURE 13–15 A sample production problem

in the highest overall level of gross profit (cell A:F12). However, as is the case with most manufacturing problems, there are limits on the amount of labor and machine hours available. In addition, the model must produce to a sales forecast that meets the needs of the customer as opposed to the factory.

The model in Figure 13–15 breaks down as follows. The units to produce for each of the three products are shown in the range A:B3..A:D3. The selling price of each product is shown in the range A:B5..A:D5, and the unit cost for each product in the range A:B6..A:D6. These values are multiplied by the units to be produced of each product in row 3 to generate the total revenue and cost figures in rows 10 and 11. The unit labor hours required by each product are shown in the range A:B7..A:D7, and the unit machine hours are shown in the range A:B8..A:D8. These values are in turn multiplied by the unit production of each product in row 3 to calculate the total labor and machine hours consumed by each product in rows 14 and 15. Finally, the sales forecast for each product is shown in the range A:B18..A:D19. Two figures are shown for each product, the minimum and the maximum. Actual sales for each product should fall somewhere in between these two figures.

The adjustable cells in the problem in Figure 13–15 will be A:B3..A:D3 (the units to be produced of each product). Changing the values in these cells has the effect of changing the pertinent values in the rest of the problem. To define limits on how much the Solver can change the values in these cells, constraints are shown in the range A:B22..A:C26. For example, the formula +B3>=B18 in cell A:B22 stipulates that the value in cell A:B3 must be greater than or equal to the minimum sales forecast for Product 1. Conversely, the formula +B3<=B19 in cell A:C22 stipulates that the value in cell A:B3 must also be less than or equal to the maximum forecast for Product 1. The logical formulas in the range cell A:B23..A:B24 place similar constraints on the unit production of Products 2 and 3. Finally, the formula +F14<=18000 in cell A:B25 restricts the use of total labor hours to 18,000 or less, and the formula +F15<=10000 in cell A:B26 restricts the use of total machine hours to 10,000 or less.

To solve this problem, select the Utility Solver command. 1-2-3/G displays the Solver Definition window. In the "Adjustable cells" text box, specify the range A:B3..A:D3. In the "Constraint cells" text box, specify the range A:B22..A:C26. In the "Optimal cell" text box, specify the range A:F12, which contains the total gross profit figure for the problem. When you activate the "Optimal cell" text box, the Max option button is already selected. Accept this default for now. To solve the problem, select the Solve command button, or use the Solve Problem command. Solver analyzes the problem and solves it, finding 10 answers. It then displays the Answer window. To see the first or optimal answer displayed in the worksheet, select the Answer command button or use the Answer Optimal command. Solver displays the answer in Figure 13-16 in the worksheet.

The optimal answer found by Solver in Figure 13-16 tells you that you can glean the maximum profit by producing to maximum forecast for Products 1 and 2. However, Product 3 is only slightly above minimum forecast. The

1-2-3/G (69.4) Ready

File Edit Worksheet Range Copy... Move... Print Graph Data Utility Quit... Help

A:F12 @SUM(B12..D12)

(C0) PRODMOD.WG1

A	A	B	C	D	E	F	G
1		Product 1	Product 2	Product 3		Totals	
2							
3	Units	9,600	11,500	11,857			
4							
5	Selling Price	$22	$20	$24			
6	Cost	$6	$5	$7			
7	Labor Hours	0.5	0.55	0.57			
8	Machine Hrs.	0.25	0.3	0.35			
9							
10	Revenue	$211,200	$230,000	$284,571		$725,771	
11	Cost	$57,600	$57,500	$83,000		$198,100	
12	Gross Profit	$153,600	$172,500	$201,571		$527,671	
13							
14	Labor Hours	4,800	6,325	6,759		17,884	
15	Machine Hrs.	2,400	3,450	4,150		10,000	
16							
17	Forecast:						
18	Minimum	8,000	9,600	11,520			
19	Maximum	9,600	11,500	13,800			
20							
21	Constraints	Minimum	Maximum				
22	Product 1	+B3>=B18	+B3<=B19				
23	Product 2	+C3>=C18	+C3<=C19				
24	Product 3	+D3>=D18	+D3<=D19				
25	Labor	+F14<=18000					
26	Machine	+F15<=10000					
27							
28							

FIGURE 13-16 The optimal answer to the problem in Figure 13-15

primary constraint in force here is total machine hours available. Notice in cell A:F15 that the total machine hours consumed are exactly 10,000. This is within the constraint specified by the formula +F15<=10000 in cell A:C26.

You can also solve this problem to see the number of each units to produce that will result in the minimum cost. To do this, press WINDOW (F6) to return to the Solver definition window. Select "Optimal cell" and change the reference A:F12 to A:F11 (the total cost cell). Then select the Min option button, so that Solver will minimize the value in the optimal cell. To solve the problem, select the Solve command button or the Solve Problem command. Solver solves the problem and displays the Answer window. Select the Answer command button, or the Answer Optimal command, to display the optimal answer in the worksheet. Solver displays the answer in Figure 13-17. This answer indicates that you can minimize total costs by producing to the minimum forecast.

Generating Reports

The Solver allows you to generate various types of reports that show you not only what answers it found but also how they were found. To generate reports, you use the Report command from Solver's main menu. This command is only available after Solver has solved (or failed to solve) a problem and the Answer window is displayed. This Report command allows you to create seven different types of reports, as follows:

1-2-3/G (69.4) Ready

File Edit Worksheet Range Copy... Move... Print Graph Data Utility Quit... Help

A:F11 @SUM(B11..D11)

(C0) PRODMOD.WG1

A	A	B	C	D	E	F
1		Product 1	Product 2	Product 3		Totals
2						
3	Units	8,000	9,600	11,520		
4						
5	Selling Price	$22	$20	$24		
6	Cost	$6	$5	$7		
7	Labor Hours	0.5	0.55	0.57		
8	Machine Hrs.	0.25	0.3	0.35		
9						
10	Revenue	$176,000	$192,000	$276,480		$644,480
11	Cost	$48,000	$48,000	$80,640		$176,640
12	Gross Profit	$128,000	$144,000	$195,840		$467,840
13						
14	Labor Hours	4,000	5,280	6,566		15,846
15	Machine Hrs.	2,000	2,880	4,032		8,912
16						
17	Forecast:					
18	Minimum	8,000	9,600	11,520		
19	Maximum	9,600	11,500	13,800		
20						
21	Constraints	Minimum	Maximum			
22	Product 1	+B3>=B18	+B3<=B19			
23	Product 2	+C3>=C18	+C3<=C19			
24	Product 3	+D3>=D18	+D3<=D19			
25	Labor	+F14<=18000				
26	Machine	+F15<=10000				
27						

FIGURE 13-17 Minimizing the optimal cell to solve for least cost

- **Answer Table**: Shows the answers or attempts Solver found.
- **How Solved**: Shows how Solver found an answer or attempt.
- **What-If Limits**: Shows how much you can change the values in the adjustable cells in the current answer and still satisfy all the constraints.
- **Differences**: Allows you to compare one answer to another.
- **Inconsistent Constraints**: If the Solver could not solve a problem and there are inconsistent constraints present, this report helps define what those inconsistent constraints are.
- **Unused Constraints:** Shows the constraint cells that were not used to solve the current problem.
- **Cells Used**: Shows the cells used to solve the current problem.

Each of these reports is discussed in more detail in the sections that follow.

Five of the seven report types can be created in two forms, a *current cell* report or a *table* report. Current cell reports are displayed in a window and provide information about specific cells in a problem. The cells to which the report applies are highlighted in the worksheet, and a Next command button is provided that allows you to move from one cell to the next. Table reports, on the other hand, summarize the problem as a whole and are displayed in worksheet files. When you create a table report, Solver prompts you for the name of a new worksheet file in which to display the report. Once you provide a name, Solver opens a new worksheet window and displays the report in that window. That way, you can save the report for your reference or graph the results it contains.

The Answer Table Report

An answer table report shows you the values for each of the answers the Solver found for the current problem. It is stored in a separate worksheet file. If Solver was unable to solve the current problem, the answer table shows the values for each of the attempts the Solver made.

To create an answer table report, you use the Report Answer Table command available from Solver's main menu. When you select this command, 1-2-3/G prompts you for the name of the worksheet file that will contain the table. It does this by displaying the dialog box in Figure 13–18. For the first answer-table file, Solver suggests a default file name of ANSWER.WG1. For each subsequent answer-table file you create in the current directory, Solver adds a digit to the end of the filename, for example ANSWER1.WG1. You can accept the default filename, edit it, or type a new filename. To create the table of answers, select the OK command button, or press ENTER. Solver creates a new worksheet file under the name you specified and displays the table of answers in that file.

Figure 13–19 shows a sample worksheet file created with the Report Answer Table command. It contains the answer table report for the production problem shown earlier in Figure 13–15. You'll notice that the worksheet frame (the column letters and row numbers) and the grid lines are not displayed. It is as

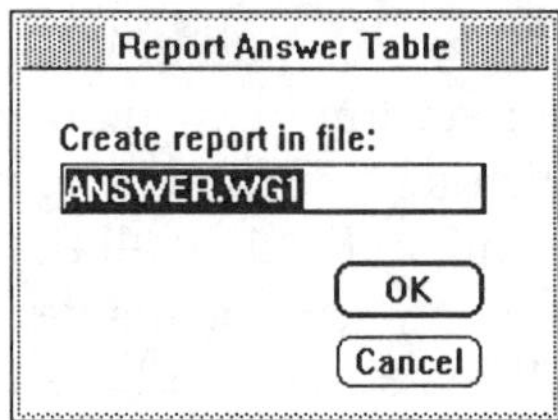

FIGURE 13–18 The Report Answer Table dialog box

though Solver selected the Worksheet Global Screen Attributes command and removed the X's from the "Grid lines," "Row frames," and "Column frames" check boxes. Additionally, the values for the table are enclosed in boxes, almost as though the Range Attributes Border command were used.

The answer table report in Figure 13–19 is divided into three sections. The first section shows the values for the optimal cell for each answer the Solver found. If you did not specify an optimal cell, this section does not appear in the report. The second section shows the values for the adjustable cells for each answer. The third section shows the values for each of the cells that Solver used to solve the problem.

Each section of the answer table report is divided into columns with headings to identify the contents of each column. The first heading in each section is Cell,

1-2-3/G [69.4] Ready

File Edit Worksheet Range Copy... Move... Print Graph Data Utility Quit... Help

A:A1 'Solver: Report Answer Table

ANSWER.WG1

Solver: Report Answer Table
Worksheet: PRODMOD.WG1
Solved: 04/06/90 13:45

Optimal cell

Cell	Name	Lowest value	Highest value	Answers Optimal (#1)	2	3	4
A:F12	Totals Gross Profit	$467,840	$527,671	$527,671	$526,956	$525,160	$521,94

Adjustable cells

Cell	Name	Lowest value	Highest value	Answers Optimal (#1)	2	3	4
A:B3	Product 1 Units	8,000	9,600	9,600	9,600	9,160	9,60
A:C3	Product 2 Units	9,600	11,500	11,500	9,831	9,600	11,50
A:D3	Product 3 Units	11,520	13,800	11,857	13,288	13,800	11,52

Cells used to solve problem

Cell	Name	Lowest value	Highest value	Answers Optimal (#1)	2	3	4
A:B10	Product 1 Revenue	$176,000	$211,200	$211,200	$211,200	$201,520	$211,20
A:B11	Product 1 Cost	$48,000	$57,600	$57,600	$57,600	$54,960	$57,60
A:B12	Product 1 Gross Profit	$128,000	$153,600	$153,600	$153,600	$146,560	$153,60
A:B14	Product 1 Labor Hours	4,000	4,800	4,800	4,800	4,580	4,80
A:B15	Product 1 Machine Hrs.	2,000	2,400	2,400	2,400	2,290	2,40
A:C10	Product 2 Revenue	$192,000	$230,000	$230,000	$196,613	$192,000	$230,00
A:C11	Product 2 Cost	$48,000	$57,500	$57,500	$49,153	$48,000	$57,50
A:C12	Product 2 Gross Profit	$144,000	$172,500	$172,500	$147,460	$144,000	$172,50
A:C14	Product 2 Labor Hours	5,280	6,325	6,325	5,407	5,280	6,32
A:C15	Product 2 Machine Hrs.	2,880	3,450	3,450	2,949	2,880	3,45
A:D10	Product 3 Revenue	$276,480	$331,200	$284,571	$318,912	$331,200	$276,48
A:D11	Product 3 Cost	$80,640	$96,600	$83,000	$93,016	$96,600	$80,64
A:D12	Product 3 Gross Profit	$195,840	$234,600	$201,571	$225,896	$234,600	$195,84

FIGURE 13–19 The answer table report is displayed in a worksheet file

which identifies the cell address of the cell. The next heading is Name, which identifies the cell's range name. If the cell does not have a range name, Solver uses the closest column and row labels. The next two headings, Lowest value and Highest value, show the lowest and highest value Solver found for the answers in each category. Finally, the values for each answer or attempt Solver found are displayed. If an optimal answer was found, it is displayed as the first answer followed by all the other answers. To see all the data you may have to use the mouse or keyboard to scroll downward or to the right.

The values displayed in the worksheet in Figure 13–19 are live numbers, not labels. Therefore, you can use them as you would any other numbers in a 1-2-3/G worksheet. For example, Figure 13–20 shows a graph based on the values in the highest and lowest columns in the Adjustable cells section of the answer table in Figure 13–19. To create this graph, highlight the range A:C10..A:E13 in Figure 13–19 and select Graph View. 1-2-3/G opens a graph window and displays the data in the form of a line graph. In addition, the Graph Tool menu appears in the Control Line at the top of your screen. From this menu, select Type Gallery. 1-2-3/G displays the Type Gallery dialog box. Select the "3–D bar" option button and select any type of 3–D bar graph you want from the Style section. To complete the command, select the OK command button. 1-2-3/G displays a graph similar to Figure 13–20. For more on how to create graphs in 1-2-3/G, see Chapter 7, "Graphs."

The How-Solved Report

The how-solved report shows you how Solver found the answer or attempt that is currently displayed in the worksheet. This report is displayed in a separate worksheet file that Solver creates.

Generally speaking, the how-solved report is one of the more comprehensive and useful reports offered by the Solver. It shows information about the optimal cell's value, the values for adjustable cells, binding constraints, and inconsistent

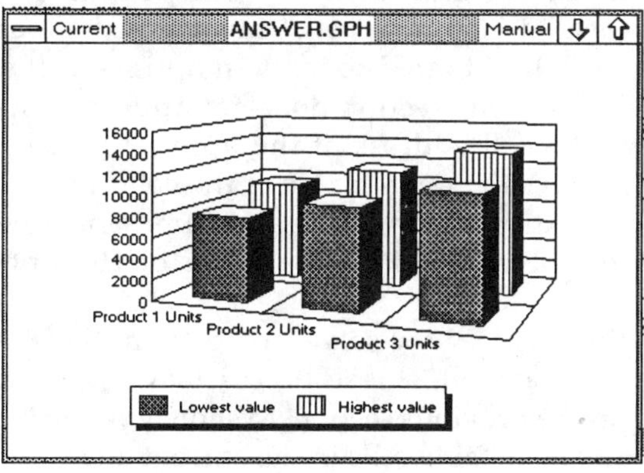

FIGURE 13–20 A graph depicts the highest and lowest values found for the adjustable cells in the answer table report

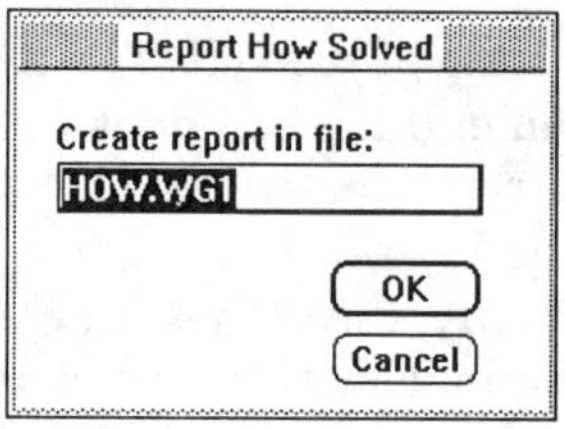

Report How Solved

Create report in file:

HOW.WG1

OK

Cancel

FIGURE 13–21 **The Report How Solved dialog box**

constraints. In short, it helps you to understand how the answers (or attempts) to a problem were determined.

To create a how-solved report, you use the Report How Solved command. First, however, you must solve the current problem. When the Answer window is displayed, use the Answer command button or the Answer command to display a particular answer in the worksheet. When you're ready, select the Report How Solved command. Solver displays the dialog box in Figure 13–21, prompting you for a name for the new worksheet file in which the how-solved report will be displayed. Initially, Solver suggests a filename of HOW.WG1. You can accept the name, edit it, or type a new one. To create the how-solved report for the current answer, select the OK command button, or press ENTER. Solver creates a new worksheet file under the name you specified and displays the report in that file. Your screen appears similar to Figure 13–22.

Due to the length of the how-solved report, the first part of it appears in Figure 13–22 and the second part in Figure 13–23. This particular how-solved report displays the values and formulas that were used to generate the first, or optimal, answer to the production problem shown earlier in Figure 13–15.

The how-solved report is broken down into four sections. The first two appear in Figure 13–22 and the second two in Figure 13–23. The first section in Figure 13–22, entitled "Optimal cell," identifies the location, name, and value of the optimal cell, if there is one. If an optimal cell was not specified for the current problem, this section does not appear. Beneath the heading Cell, Solver shows the cell address of the optimal cell. Beneath the Name heading, Solver displays the range name of the cell. If the cell does not have a range name, Solver displays the closest column and row labels. Beneath the heading Value, Solver displays the value of the optimal cell for the current answer.

The second section of the how-solved report, entitled "Adjustable cells," appears in Figure 13–22 as well. This section displays the same Cell, Name, and Value headings as in the previous section, to show you the location, name, and values for each of the adjustable cells in the current answer.

The third section of the how-solved report, entitled "Binding constraints," appears in Figure 13–23. This section identifies the constraints (logical for-

1-2-3/G [69.4] Ready

File Edit Worksheet Range Copy... Move... Print Graph Data Utility Quit... Help

A:A1 'Solver: Report How Solved

HOW.WG1

Solver: Report How Solved
Worksheet: PRODMOD.WG1
Solved: 04/06/90 15:54

Optimal answer (#1)

Answer #1 is one of 10 which satisfies all of the constraints.

This answer maximizes the value of cell A:F12 (Totals Gross Profit).

For this answer, the optimal cell attained the following value:

Optimal Cell

Cell	Name	Value
A:F12	Totals Gross Profit	$527,671

For this answer, Solver changed the values in the following adjustable cells:

Adjustable cells

Cell	Name	Value
A:B3	Product 1 Units	9,600
A:C3	Product 2 Units	11,500
A:D3	Product 3 Units	11,857

FIGURE 13–22 The how-solved report (partial)

mulas) that were binding on the current answer. Beneath the headings Cell, Name, and Formula, Solver lists the cell addresses, cell names, and logical formulas that had a direct bearing on the current answer or attempt.

The fourth and final section of the how-solved report is entitled "Unused constraints;" it appears in Figure 13–23. This section identifies the constraint

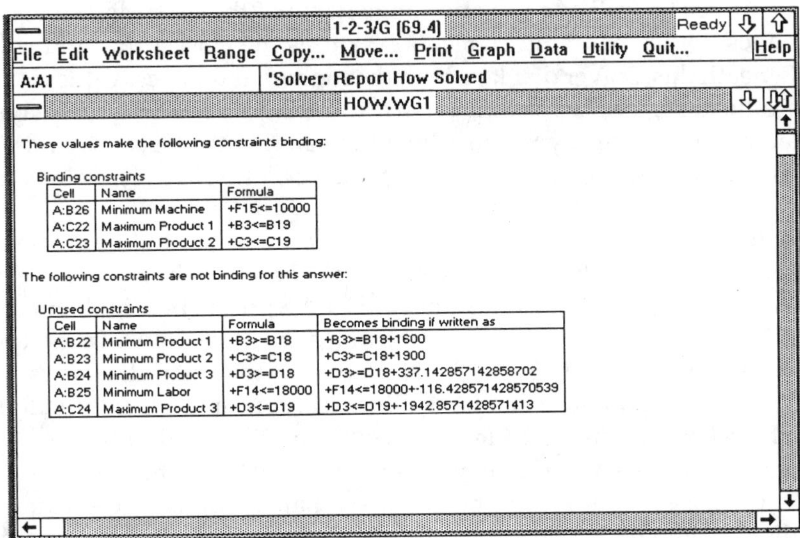
1-2-3/G [69.4] Ready

File Edit Worksheet Range Copy... Move... Print Graph Data Utility Quit... Help

A:A1 'Solver: Report How Solved

HOW.WG1

These values make the following constraints binding:

Binding constraints

Cell	Name	Formula
A:B26	Minimum Machine	+F15<=10000
A:C22	Maximum Product 1	+B3<=B19
A:C23	Maximum Product 2	+C3<=C19

The following constraints are not binding for this answer:

Unused constraints

Cell	Name	Formula	Becomes binding if written as
A:B22	Minimum Product 1	+B3>=B18	+B3>=B18+1600
A:B23	Minimum Product 2	+C3>=C18	+C3>=C18+1900
A:B24	Minimum Product 3	+D3>=D18	+D3>=D18+337.142857142858702
A:B25	Minimum Labor	+F14<=18000	+F14<=18000+-116.428571428570539
A:C24	Maximum Product 3	+D3<=D19	+D3<=D19+-1942.8571428571413

FIGURE 13–23 The how-solved report (continued)

cells in the current problem that were not binding on the current answer. Beneath the headings Cell, Name, and Formula, Solver lists the cell addresses, cell names, and logical formulas that were not involved in constraining the current answer or attempt. In addition, beneath the heading "Becomes binding if written as," Solver shows you the adjustment required to each logical formula that would make it binding on the current answer.

The What-If Limits Report

The what-if limits report tells you how much you can change the values in an adjustable cell for the current answer and still satisfy all the constraints. This report can be useful if you want to change an answer. This report option has both a current-cell report and a summary-table report available.

To create the what-if limits report, select the Report What-If Limits command from Solver's main menu. When you select this command, Solver displays a two-option menu with Current Cell and Table. To display the report in a current cell window, select Current Cell. To display the report in the form of a summary table displayed in a new worksheet file, select Table.

In preparation for the Report What-If Limits command, first use the Solver to solve the current problem. When the Answer window is displayed, use the Answer command button or the Answer command to display the answer you want to evaluate in the worksheet. When you're ready, select the Report What-If Limits command and then select from either Current Cell or Table.

If you selected Report What-If Limits Current Cell, Solver displays the current cell window in Figure 13–24. It also highlights the adjustable cells for the current problem in the worksheet. At the top of the window in Figure 13–24, Solver identifies the cell address and range name of the first adjustable cell. If the cell does not have a range name, Solver uses the closest row and column labels. Beneath this, Solver displays both the highest and lowest values it found for this adjustable cell across all answers. Below this, Solver displays the estimated range by which you can adjust the value for this particular cell and still satisfy all constraints for the current answer, provided the values in the other adjustable cells remain the same.

To see the what-if limits for the next adjustable cell, select the Next command button. For example, in Figure 13–24, the Next command button was selected twice to advance to the third adjustable cell in the production problem shown earlier in Figure 13–15. As you can see, the range of values Solver found for this cell across all answers is 11,520 to 13,800. However, to satisfy all constraints on this cell for the current answer—have all logical formulas return a value of 1 (true)—the range of adjustment must be between 11,520 and 11,857.

To create a summary table of what-if limits that will be displayed in a separate worksheet file, select the Report What-If Limits Table command. Solver displays the dialog box in Figure 13–25. Use this dialog box to provide a name for the new worksheet file in which the report will be displayed. Initially, Solver suggests a name of LIMITS.WG1. You can accept this name,

1-2-3/G (69.4) Ready

File Solve Answer Report Options Help

PRODMOD.WG1

	A	B	C	D	E	F	G
1		Product 1	Product 2	Product 3		Totals	
2							
3	Units	9,600	11,500	11,857			
4							
5	Selling Price	$22	$20	$24			
6	Cost	$6	$5	$7			
7	Labor Hours	0.5	0.55	0.57			
8	Machine Hrs.	0.25	0.3	0.35			
9							
10	Revenue	$211,200	$230,000	$284,571		$725,771	
11	Cost	$57,600	$57,500	$83,000		$198,100	
12	Gross Profit	$153,600	$172,500	$201,571		$527,671	
				6,759		17,884	
				4,150		10,000	
				11,520			
				13,800			

Solver: Report

Cell: A:D3 Product 3 Units

Lowest and highest values found:
11,520 to 13,800

What-if limits for answer #1:
11,520 to 11,857

Next Cancel

FIGURE 13–24 The what-if limits report is displayed for a single cell

edit it, or type a new one of your own. To create the table of what-if limits, select the OK command button, or press ENTER. Solver creates a new worksheet window and displays the report of what-if limits in that window, as shown in Figure 13–26.

The what-if limits table in Figure 13–26 shows that the current problem has three adjustable cells. (This report is tied to the first or optimal answer to the production problem shown earlier in Figure 13–15.) The cell address for each adjustable cell appears in the first column of the table beneath the heading Cell. In the second column of the table, beneath the heading Name, the range names for the adjustable cells are displayed. If the adjustable cells do not have range names, Solver uses the closest column and row labels. The third and fourth columns of the table show the lowest and highest values Solver found for each

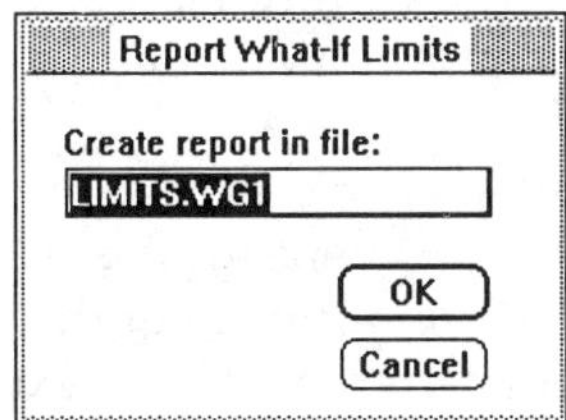

FIGURE 13–25 The Report What-If Limits Table dialog box

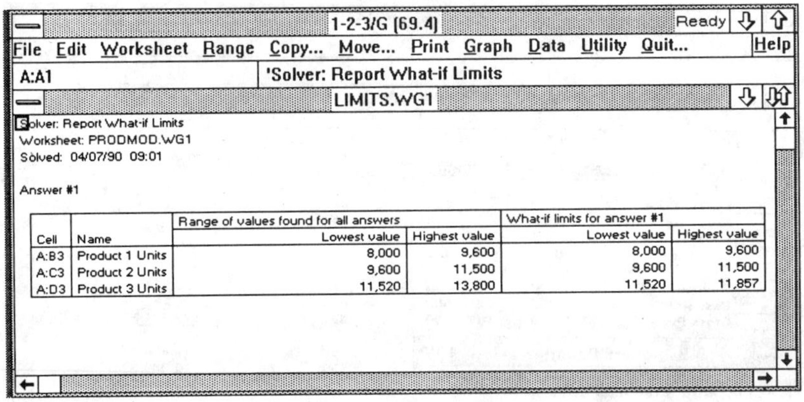

1-2-3/G [69.4] Ready
File Edit Worksheet Range Copy... Move... Print Graph Data Utility Quit... Help
A:A1 'Solver: Report What-if Limits
LIMITS.WG1

Solver: Report What-if Limits
Worksheet: PRODMOD.WG1
Solved: 04/07/90 09:01

Answer #1

Cell	Name	Range of values found for all answers		What-if limits for answer #1	
		Lowest value	Highest value	Lowest value	Highest value
A:B3	Product 1 Units	8,000	9,600	8,000	9,600
A:C3	Product 2 Units	9,600	11,500	9,600	11,500
A:D3	Product 3 Units	11,520	13,800	11,520	11,857

FIGURE 13–26 The table of what-if limits is displayed in a worksheet file.

adjustable cell across all answers. The fifth and sixth columns show the what-if limits for each adjustable cell for the current answer only. The values in these columns show the estimated range by which you can adjust the value for a particular adjustable cell and still satisfy all constraints. This is provided, of course, that the values in the other adjustable cells remain the same.

The Differences Report

The differences report allows you to compare one answer (or attempt) with another. It does this by showing you the values in the cells used by the first answer versus the values for those same cells in the second answer. The numeric and percentage difference between the cells are also shown. You can either look at all the cells used by both answers or you can limit the report to only those cells whose values differ by an amount you specify.

To create the differences report, you use the Report Differences command from Solver's main menu. However, in preparation for this command, first use the Solver to solve the current problem. When the Answer window is displayed, select the Report Differences command. Solver displays a two-option menu with Current Cell and Table. Select the Current Cell option to view the difference between individual cells, one by one. Select Table to see a summary table of differences displayed in a separate worksheet file.

If you select Report Differences Current Cell, Solver displays the dialog box in Figure 13–27. The two text boxes beneath the "Compare answers" heading allow you to specify the respective numbers of the two answers (or attempts) you want to compare. The "For differences >=" text box allows you to specify an amount by which the cells in the two answers must differ in order to be included in the report. If you accept the default of 0, Solver will show a difference report on all the cells in both answers where a difference occurs. To

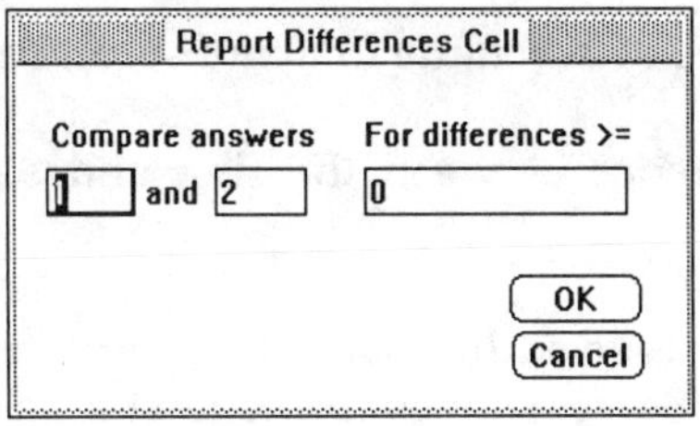

Report Differences Cell

Compare answers For differences >=

1 and 2 0

OK

Cancel

FIGURE 13–27 The Report Differences Current Cell dialog box

begin viewing difference reports on a cell-by-cell basis, select the OK command button. Solver replaces the Answer window with the current-cell report window in Figure 13-28. In addition, the cells that will be included in the report are highlighted in the worksheet.

At the top of the window in Figure 13-28, Solver identifies the cell address and range name of the cell on which it is currently reporting. If the cell does not have a range name, Solver uses the closest row and column label. Beneath this, Solver provides the following information:

- The value for the current cell for the first answer.
- The value for the current cell for the second answer.

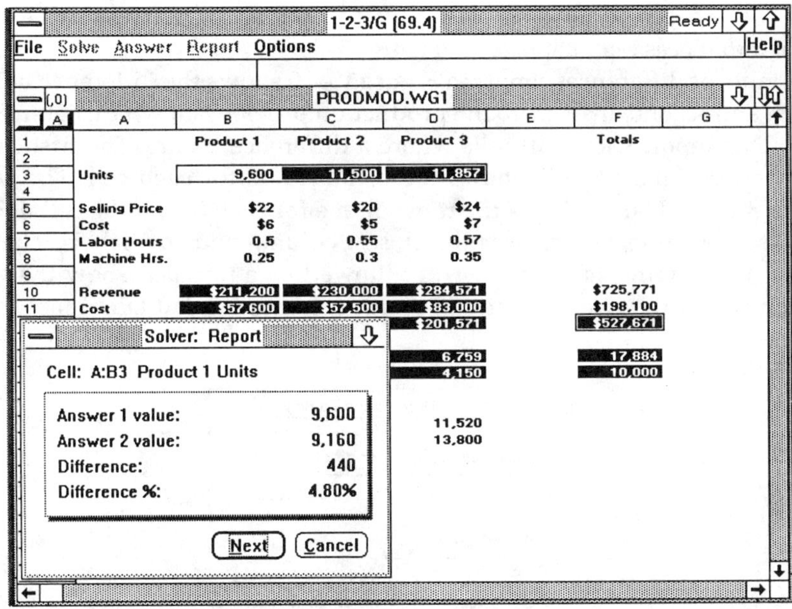

FIGURE 13–28 The differences report is displayed for a single cell

- The numeric difference between the first and second answer for this specific cell.
- The percentage difference between the first and second answer for this specific cell.

To see difference reports on additional cells in the current problem, select the Next command button. Solver moves to the next selected cell in the current problem and displays a difference report for that cell. The order of reporting is column by column. Solver reports on all selected cells in the first column of the problem before moving on to the next column, and so on.

To create a summary table of differences between one answer (or attempt) and another, select the Report Differences Table command. When you select this command, Solver displays the dialog box in Figure 13–29.

The text boxes beneath the "Compare answers" heading allow you to specify the respective numbers of the answers you want to compare. Therefore, enter the respective numbers for the two answers in these text boxes. The "For differences >=" text box allows you to specify a value by which the cells in the two answers must differ in order to be included in the report. If you accept the default value of 0, Solver will report on all cells used by both the first and second answers where a difference occurs. Finally, the "Create report in file" text box allows you to specify the name of a new worksheet file in which the report will be displayed. Initially, Solver suggests a default name of DIFFS.WG1 for the file. You can accept this name, edit it, or type a new one of your own. To create the table of differences report, select the OK command button, or press ENTER. Solver opens a new worksheet window under the name you specified and displays the differences report in that window. A sample table of differences report appears in Figure 13–30.

The table of differences report in Figure 13–30 shows the difference between the first and second answers to the production problem shown earlier in Figure 13–15. This report shows all cells where a difference occurs. The first column of the report, labeled Cell, shows the cell address for each cell. The second column labeled Name, shows the range name for each cell. If the cell does not have a range name, Solver uses the closest column and row labels. The third and fourth columns, labeled Answer followed by a number, show the values for each cell in the two answers. The fifth column, labeled Difference, shows

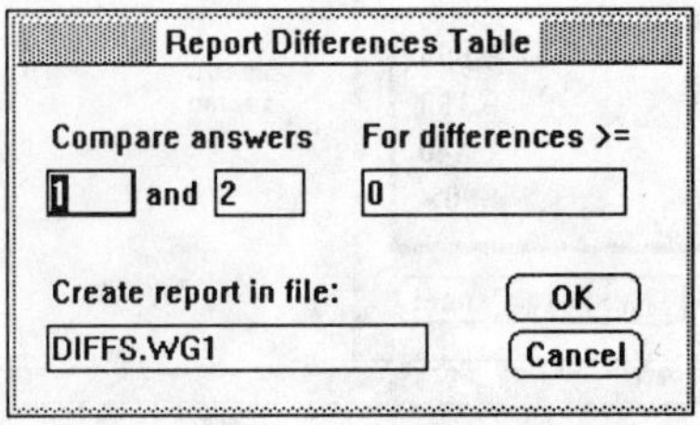

Report Differences Table

Compare answers For differences >=

1 and 2 0

Create report in file: OK

DIFFS.WG1 Cancel

FIGURE 13–29 The Report Differences Table dialog box

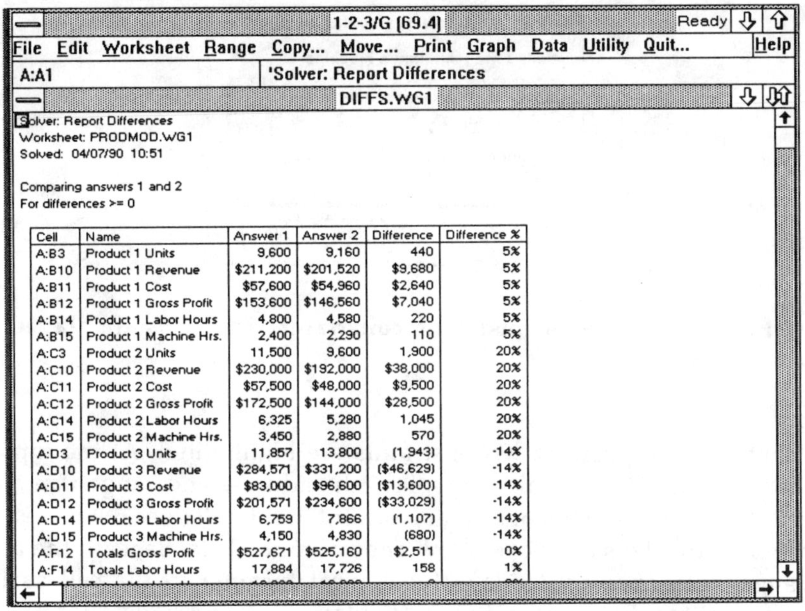

1-2-3/G [69.4] Ready

File Edit Worksheet Range Copy... Move... Print Graph Data Utility Quit... Help

A:A1 'Solver: Report Differences

DIFFS.WG1

Solver: Report Differences
Worksheet: PRODMOD.WG1
Solved: 04/07/90 10:51

Comparing answers 1 and 2
For differences >= 0

Cell	Name	Answer 1	Answer 2	Difference	Difference %
A:B3	Product 1 Units	9,600	9,160	440	5%
A:B10	Product 1 Revenue	$211,200	$201,520	$9,680	5%
A:B11	Product 1 Cost	$57,600	$54,960	$2,640	5%
A:B12	Product 1 Gross Profit	$153,600	$146,560	$7,040	5%
A:B14	Product 1 Labor Hours	4,800	4,580	220	5%
A:B15	Product 1 Machine Hrs.	2,400	2,290	110	5%
A:C3	Product 2 Units	11,500	9,600	1,900	20%
A:C10	Product 2 Revenue	$230,000	$192,000	$38,000	20%
A:C11	Product 2 Cost	$57,500	$48,000	$9,500	20%
A:C12	Product 2 Gross Profit	$172,500	$144,000	$28,500	20%
A:C14	Product 2 Labor Hours	6,325	5,280	1,045	20%
A:C15	Product 2 Machine Hrs.	3,450	2,880	570	20%
A:D3	Product 3 Units	11,857	13,800	(1,943)	-14%
A:D10	Product 3 Revenue	$284,571	$331,200	($46,629)	-14%
A:D11	Product 3 Cost	$83,000	$96,600	($13,600)	-14%
A:D12	Product 3 Gross Profit	$201,571	$234,600	($33,029)	-14%
A:D14	Product 3 Labor Hours	6,759	7,866	(1,107)	-14%
A:D15	Product 3 Machine Hrs.	4,150	4,830	(680)	-14%
A:F12	Totals Gross Profit	$527,671	$525,160	$2,511	0%
A:F14	Totals Labor Hours	17,884	17,726	158	1%

FIGURE 13–30 The table of differences report is displayed in a worksheet file

the numeric difference between the two answers for each cell; and the sixth column, labeled Difference %, shows the percentage difference.

The Inconsistent Constraints Report

The inconsistent constraints may help you understand why Solver was unable to solve a problem. When Solver cannot solve a problem, it calculates one or more representative attempts instead of answers. When you view the first of these attempts in the worksheet, Solver displays the message "Inconsistent" in the Answer window. This means that one or more of the logical formulas in the constraint cells returned 0 (false) instead of 1 (true). The inconsistent constraints report shows you not only which logical formulas were not satisfied, but also how you can change those logical formulas so that they will become satisfied.

Once an attempt is displayed in the worksheet, you can create an inconsistent constraints report. To do this, select the Report Inconsistent Constraints command from Solver's main menu. When you select this command, Solver displays a menu with two options, Current Cell or Table. Select Current cell to view an inconsistent constraints report on a cell-by-cell basis. Select Table to view a summary report of inconsistent constraints displayed in a separate worksheet file.

If you select Report Inconsistent Constraints Current Cell, Solver displays the current-cell report window in Figure 13–31. In addition, the cells in the work-

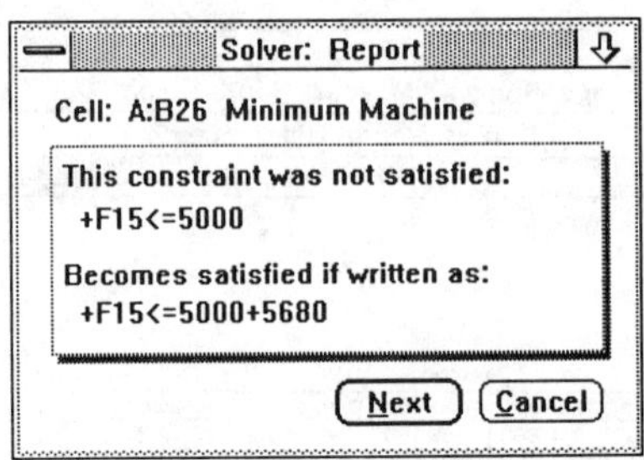

FIGURE 13–31 The inconsistent constraints report is displayed for a single cell

sheet that contain inconsistent constraints are highlighted. At the top of the window in Figure 13–31, Solver displays the address and range name of the first cell that contains an inconsistent restraint. If the cell does not have a range name, Solver displays the closest row and column labels. Beneath the address and range name, Solver displays the logical formula in the cell as it was originally written. Below that, Solver displays the same logical formula with the modifications it estimates are required to make the formula return a 1 (true). To see a report on the next cell that contains an inconsistent constraint, if any, select the Next command button.

Note

> You can access the same current-cell report shown in Figure 13–31 by selecting the Inconsistent command button from the bottom of the Answer window. This command button becomes available when you select the Answer command button, or when you use the Answer command, to display an attempt in the worksheet.

When you select Report Inconsistent Constraints Table command, Solver displays the dialog box in Figure 13–32. This dialog prompts you for the name of a new worksheet file in which the inconsistent constraints table will be displayed. Initially, Solver suggests the name of INCONS.WG1 for the new file. You can accept this name or provide one of your own. To create the report, select the OK command button, or press ENTER. Solver opens a new worksheet window under the name you specified and displays the table of inconsistent constraints for the current problem in that window. Your screen looks similar to Figure 13–33.

The inconsistent constraints table is composed of four columns. The first column, labeled Cell, shows the cell address of cells in the current problem with inconsistent restraints. The second column, labeled Name, shows the range

Inconsistent Constraints

Create report in file:

INCONS.WG1

OK

Cancel

FIGURE 13–32 The Report Inconsistent Constraints Table dialog box

name for those cells. If a cell does not have a range name, Solver uses the closest column and row labels. The third column, labeled "This constraint was not satisfied," shows the logical formula in each cell as it was originally written. The fourth column, labeled "Becomes satisfied if written as," shows the modification that Solver estimates is required to each logical formula, to make it return a 1 (true) for the current problem.

The Unused Constraints Report

The unused constraints report shows you a list of constraints the Solver did not use to find a given answer (or attempt). Inclusion of a constraint in this report does not always mean that the constraint is unnecessary for solving the problem as a whole. It simply means that the listed constraints were not binding on the current answer. The unused constraints report also shows you how to modify unused constraints to make them binding on the current answer. Therefore, you can use this report to show you how you can tighten existing constraints, to make them more realistic. It can also help you to identify unnecessary or superfluous constraints.

To create a report of unused constraints, you use the Report Unused Constraints command. In preparation for this command, however, first use the

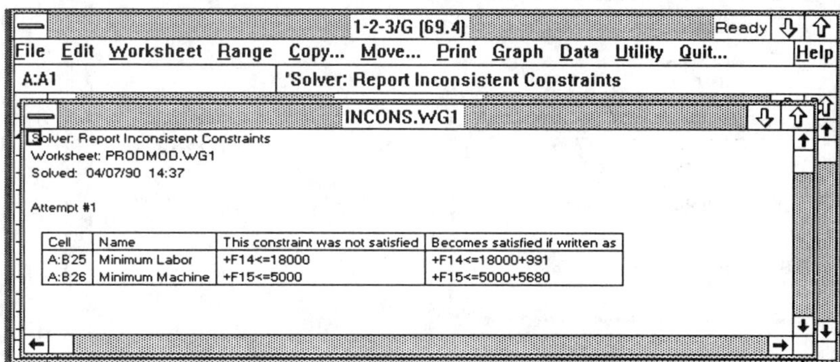

Cell	Name	This constraint was not satisfied	Becomes satisfied if written as
A:B25	Minimum Labor	+F14<=18000	+F14<=18000+991
A:B26	Minimum Machine	+F15<=5000	+F15<=5000+5680

FIGURE 13–33 The summary table of inconsistent constraints is displayed in a worksheet file

Solver both to solve the current problem and to display a particular answer (or attempt) in the worksheet. When you're ready, select the Report Unused Constraints command. Solver displays a menu with two options, Current Cell and Table. Select Current Cell to see a report on unused constraints, one cell at a time. Select Table to see a summary table of unused constraints displayed in a separate worksheet file.

If you select Report Unused Constraints Current Cell, Solver highlights the unused constraints in the worksheet and displays the first one in the window shown in Figure 13-34. At the top of the window, Solver displays the cell address and range name of the cell. If the cell does not have a range name, Solver uses the closest row and column labels. Beneath the current address and range name, Solver displays the constraint (logical formula) as it was originally written. Beneath this, Solver shows the modification it estimates is required to make the constraint binding on the current answer. To see the next unused constraint, select the Next command button.

To see a summary table of unused constraints displayed in a separate worksheet file, select Report Unused Constraints Table. Solver prompts you for a name for the file by displaying the dialog box shown in Figure 13-35. Initially, Solver suggest a name of UNUSED.WG1. You can accept this name, edit it, or type one of your own. To create the table of unused constraints, select the OK command button, or press ENTER. Solver opens a new worksheet file under the name you specified and displays the table in that file, similar to Figure 13-36.

The unused Constraints table is composed of four columns. The first column,

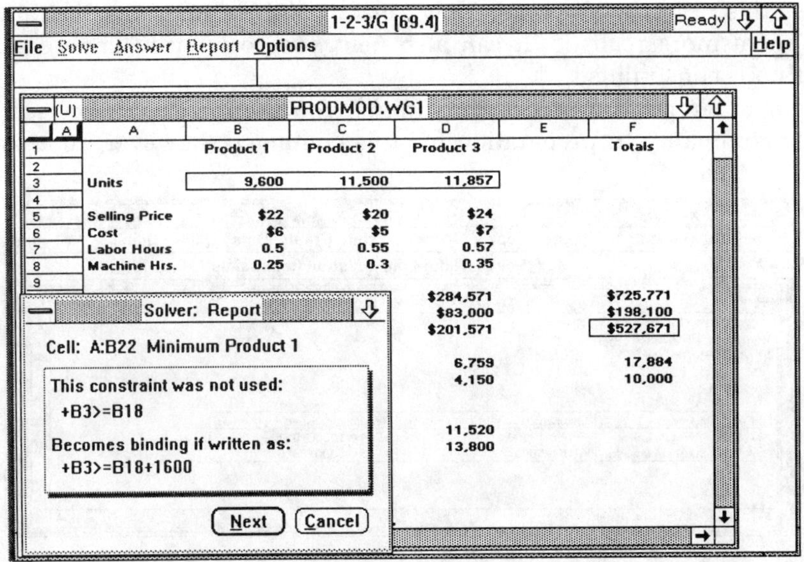

FIGURE 13-34 A report of unused constraints is displayed for a single cell.

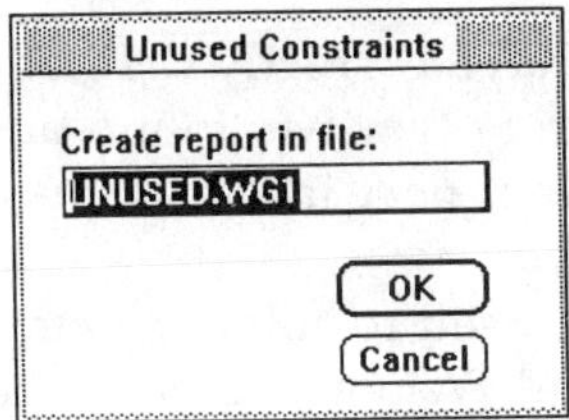

FIGURE 13-35 The Report Unused Constraints Table dialog box

abeled Cell, shows the address of the cell containing the unused constraint. The second column, labeled Name, shows the range name for the cell. If the cell does not have a range name, Solver shows the closest column and row labels. The third column of the table, labeled "This constraint was not used," shows the logical formula currently in each cell. Finally, the fourth column, labeled "Becomes binding if written as," shows you the modification Solver estimates is required to each logical formula that will make it binding on the current answer.

The Cells Used Report

The cells-used report identifies the adjustable, constraint, and optimal cells that were used to solve the current problem. This report may be of assistance in

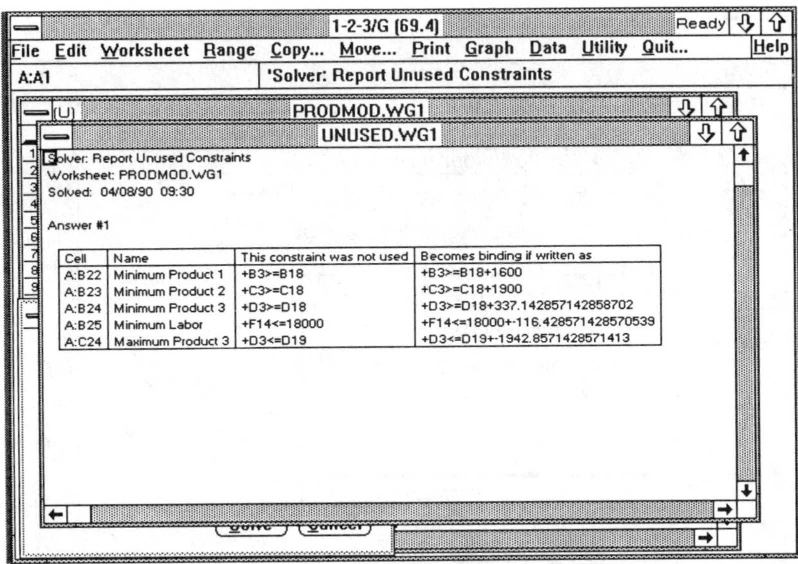

FIGURE 13-36 The unused constraints report is displayed in a worksheet file

showing you whether you have correctly defined a problem for the Solver. The report is available once Solver has found an answer (or attempt) to a problem. You can view this report in either the current-cell or summary-table format.

To create a report of cells used to solve the current problem, you use the Report Cells Used command. When you select this command, Solver displays a menu with two options, Current Cell and Table. Select Current Cell to view a report window for individual cells, one by one. To see a summary table of cells used that is displayed in a separate worksheet file, select the Table option.

If you select Report Cells Used Current Cell, Solver highlights the adjustable, constraint, and optimal cells in the current problem. It also replaces the Answer window with the current-cell report window shown in Figure 13–37. At the top of this window, Solver displays the address and range name, if any, of the first highlighted cell. If the cell does not have a range name, Solver displays the closest column and row labels. Beneath the address and name of the current cell, Solver displays a brief message that describes the role of the current cell in the problem. To see the next highlighted cell, select the Next command button.

To see a summary table of the adjustable, constraint, and optimal cells used in the current problem, select the Report Cells Used Table command. When you select this command, Solver prompts you for the name of a new worksheet file in which to display the table. To do this, it displays the dialog box shown in Figure 13-38 and, initially, suggests the name of CELLS.WG1 as a name for the new file. You can accept this name, edit it, or type a new one of your own. To

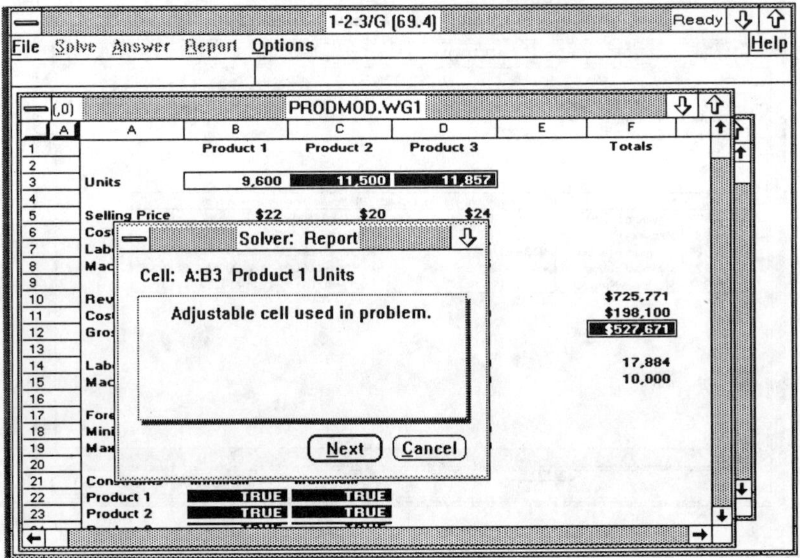

FIGURE 13–37 The cells-used report is displayed for a single cell

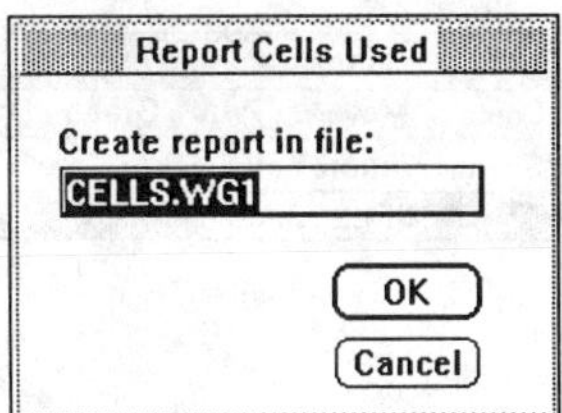

FIGURE 13–38 **The Report Cells Used Table dialog box**

create the table of cells used, select the OK command button, or press ENTER. Solver opens a new worksheet window under the name you specified and displays the table of cells used in that window. Your screen should look similar to Figure 13–39.

Note

If you activate the worksheet containing the problem without first closing the Solver, the cells-used report window in Figure 13–37 remains active. If you move the cell pointer to highlight an adjustable, constraint, or optimal cell, the report window displays messages that identify these cells. Further, if you move the cell pointer to a cell in the worksheet that was used to solve the problem, Solver displays the message "Formula used to solve the problem." However, if you move to a cell that Solver did not use to solve the problem, Solver displays the message "No information about this cell." (You can see the worksheet window and the report window at the same time if you tile the windows on the desktop).

The cells-used table is broken down into three sections, Optimal cell, Adjustable cells, and Constraint cells. If you did not specify an optimal cell for the current problem, the Optimal cell section is omitted. Each section shows the address and range name of the cell(s) included in that particular category. If a cell does not have a range name, Solver uses the closest row and column label, as shown in Figure 13–39.

Using @Functions with Solver

The Solver is capable of solving problems that contain selected @functions. However, there are certain rules you must observe when you use @functions in a problem. Otherwise, Solver may not be able find an optimal answer to the problem. These rules are as follows:

- Only selected @Functions are supported by Solver. Table 13–2 shows a list of them.

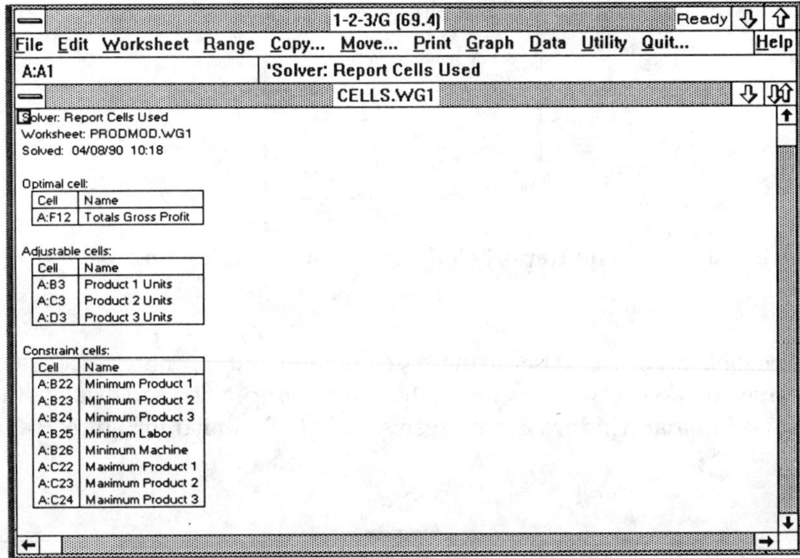

FIGURE 13–39 **The report of cells used is displayed in a worksheet file**

- The values for the arguments for the @function must not depend directly or indirectly on the value of an adjustable cell.
- The logical formulas in the constraint cells must not refer directly or indirectly to the cell that contains the @function.

In practice, you may find these rules to be somewhat restrictive. Generally speaking, when you use an @function in a problem, it is highly likely the value of its arguments will depend on the value in an adjustable cell. For example, Figure 13–40 shows the same production problem shown previously in Figure 13–15. As you may recall, the optimal cell in this problem is A:F12 (total gross profit) and the goal is to maximize the value in this cell. Further, the adjustable cells for this problem are in the range A:B3..A:D3 (units to produce). However, the problem has now been enhanced to include @IF functions in range A:B6..A:D6 (the unit cost cells). The format of the @IF function is:

```
@IF(condition,x,y)
```

where if *condition* is true, the function returns *x* and if *condition* is false, the function returns *y*. For example, cell A:D6 contains the function @IF(F14>=17000,7*1.1,7). With this formula, if the value in cell A:F14 (total labor hours) is greater than or equal to 17,000, the function returns $7.70 for a unit cost for Product 3. On the other hand, if the value in cell A:F14 is less than 17,000, the function returns a unit cost of $7.00 even.

TABLE 13-2 @Functions supported by Solver and Backsolver

@ABS	@INDEX	@ROWS
@COS	@INT	@SHEETS
@ASIN	@IRR	@SIN
@ATAN	@ISNUMBER	@SLN
@ATAN2	@LN	@SQRT
@AVG	@LOG	@STD
@CHOOSE	@MAX	@STDS
@COLS	@MIN	@SUM
@COS	@MOD	@SUMPRODUCT
@COUNT	@NOW	@SYD
@DDB	@PI	@TODAY
@EXP	@PMT	@VAR
@FALSE	@PV	@VARS
@FV	@RATE	@VDB
@HLOOKUP	@RAND	@VLOOKUP
@IF	@ROUND	

The Solver cannot find an optimal answer to the problem in Figure 13–40, because the values for the first argument in the @IF functions in the range A:B6..A:D6 are dependent on the values in the problem's adjustable cells. As the units of production in the adjustable cells (A:B3..A:D3) increase, so do the total labor hours in cell A:F14. Therefore, since the value in cell A:F14 is dependent on the value in the adjustable cells, so are the *condition* arguments for the @IF functions in the range A:B6..A:D6.

Despite the fact that Solver cannot find an optimal answer to the problem in Figure 13–40, it is capable of finding a "best" answer. That "best" answer is displayed in Figure 13–40. As you may recall, the Solver displays the "Best answer found" message in the Answer window when it is not mathematically sure whether it has found the optimal answer to the problem. To determine if this answer is usable as the optimal answer, you must rely on your own judgment. Alternatively, you can use the Solve Continue command to solve for further, possibly better, answers.

There are other problems associated with the use of @functions in problems. Some of these are as follows:

- Adding or multiplying @functions together makes a problem difficult to solve.
- Using large ranges with @HLOOKUP or @VLOOKUP or the statistical @functions makes a problem difficult to solve.
- Using @CHOOSE, @HLOOKUP, @IF, @INDEX, @INT, @MOD, @ROUND, or @VLOOKUP makes a problem difficult to solve.

1-2-3/G (69.4) Ready

File Solve Answer Report Options Help

PRODMOD2.WG1

A	A	B	C	D	E	F	G
1		Product 1	Product 2	Product 3		Totals	
2							
3	Units	9,600	11,500	11,857			
4							
5	Selling Price	$22	$20	$24			
6	Cost	$6.60	$5.50	$7.70	<===@IF(F14>=17000,7*1.1,7)		
7	Labor Hours	0.5	0.55	0.57			
8	Machine Hrs.	0.25	0.3	0.35			
9							
10	Revenue	$211,200	$230,000	$284,571		$725,771	
11	Cost	$63,360	$63,250	$91,300		$217,910	
12	Gross Profit	$147,840	$166,750	$193,271		$507,861	
13							
14	Labor Hours	4,800	6,325	6,759		17,884	
15	Machine Hrs.	2,400	3,450	4,150		10,000	
16							
17	Forecast:						
18	Minimum	8,000	9,600				
19	Maximum	9,600	11,500				
20							
21	Constraints	Minimum	Maximum				
22	Product 1	TRUE	TRUE				
23	Product 2	TRUE	TRUE				
24	Product 3	TRUE	TRUE				
25	Labor	TRUE					
26	Machine	TRUE					
27							
28							

Solver: Answer

10 answers found.

Answer

Optimal

Reset

Best answer found (#1)

Solve

Cancel

FIGURE 13–40 Solver is not able to find an optimal answer to the problem because @functions are used improperly

- Nesting @functions, especially @IF, makes a problem difficult to solve. Therefore, instead of nesting @functions, write the @function across several cells.
- Avoid using @functions in the current worksheet file that will cause a recalculation whenever Solver makes a change to a worksheet in that file. The Solver will interpret the recalculation as a change to the worksheet and will discard any answers it may have found. These @functions include @@, @CELL, @CELLPOINTER, @INFO, @ISNAME, @ISRANGE, @NOW, @RAND, @SOLVER, @TODAY, and any @D function (database @function) that refers to an external database table.

SUMMARY

This chapter shows you how to use Backsolver and Solver to solve what-if problems in the worksheet.

The Backsolver solves a problem by working backward from a goal you specify. It allows you to make a formula equal to a specific value by changing the value in one of the cells referenced by that formula. Therefore, the Backsolver is useful when you already have a specific goal in mind and you want to see what it will take to reach that goal. This chapter shows you how to activate the Backsolver and apply it to a given problem.

The Solver, on the other hand, is useful when you're not sure what the best answer to a problem is. Working within parameters that you define, the Solver is capable of exploring various possibilities to find multiple answers to a given problem. From among those answers, Solver can select the one answer that is the best mathematical solution to the problem. This chapter shows you how to set up a problem in the worksheet and use the Solver to solve that problem.

Once you have solved a problem, Solver allows you to create various types of reports. These reports can show you what answers were found, how those answers were found, how one answer compares to another, and how much you can change an answer and still remain within the constraints you've defined for the problem. This chapter shows you how to create each type of report as well as how you can use a report to help you solve a problem or to interpret the answers Solver found.

Customizing 1-2-3/G

This appendix describes how you can customize the operation of 1-2-3/G to suit your specific needs. The discussion in this appendix will focus on the following three areas:

- Changing the selections you made while installing 1-2-3/G.
- Changing default settings with the Worksheet Global Default command.
- Changing user settings with the User Settings command. This command is available from either the Desktop Control menu or the Utility menu.

CHANGING INSTALL.EXE SELECTIONS

When you installed 1-2-3/G, you ran the INSTALL.EXE program. This program was responsible for creating various directories on your hard disk and then copying the 1-2-3/G program files to those directories. After the program files are copied, INSTALL.EXE prompts you to specify various settings both for 1-2-3/G and for your system.

As part of the installation process, the INSTALL.EXE file is copied to the same directory in which your 1-2-3/G program files are stored (usually C:\123G). Therefore, you can modify many of the selections you made when you installed 1-2-3/G by simply running the INSTALL.EXE program again. To run the INSTALL.EXE program, perform the following steps:

1. From the Start Programs window (OS/2 1.1) or the Group-Main window (OS/2 1.2), select the OS/2 full-screen command prompt. The OS/2 command prompt is displayed.

2. Change to the directory containing your 1-2-3/G program files (usually C:\123G). If the 1-2-3/G program directory is on another drive, type the letter of the drive that contains the 1-2-3/G program directory, followed by a colon, for example **D:** and press ENTER. After the correct drive prompt is displayed, type **CD 123G** and press ENTER.
3. Type **INSTALL** and press ENTER. (If you are using a monochrome monitor, type **INSTALL MONO** and press ENTER.) The INSTALL.EXE program is started.
4. The first 1-2-3/G INSTALL.EXE program screen is now displayed. Press ENTER to exit this screen.
5. A second 1-2-3/G INSTALL.EXE program screen now appears that prompts you with the question: "Is this a first-time installation on your system?". Type **N** (No) in response to this prompt. If you type Y, you will be prompted to completely reinstall 1-2-3/G.

After you complete step 5, INSTALL.EXE will take you through a series of screens that allow you to modify the following settings for 1-2-3/G and for your system:

- **Directories:** 1-2-3/G uses four directories in addition to the program directory. The first of these is a working directory used to store data files (usually C:\123G\WORK). The second is a backup directory (usually C:\123G\BACKUP) used to store backup copies of your data files. The third is a template directory (usually C:\123G\TEMPLATE) containing files that are used as templates (models) for creating new files. The fourth and final directory is a temporary directory (usually C:\123G\TEMP) used to temporarily store files 1-2-3/G creates during its operation.

  INSTALL.EXE allows you to specify a new working, backup, template, or temporary directory, if you so desire. However, you can do the same thing from within 1-2-3/G by using the Utility User Settings Directories command. This command is discussed briefly later in this appendix under "The User Settings Directories Command" and in detail in Chapter 5, "File Management," under "Changing the Current Directory Permanently."
- **Country driver:** The character set and date, time, number, and currency formats vary from country to country. In deference to this, 1-2-3/G provides various drivers that allow it to display characters and formats for specific countries. INSTALL.EXE offers a variety of country drivers from which you can select.
- **Keyboard speed:** INSTALL.EXE allows you to modify the keyboard speed—how fast your system reacts to repeated keystrokes such as repeated arrow keys. See "Setting the Keyboard Speed" later in this section for more details on this.
- **CONFIG.SYS:** INSTALL.EXE will modify your system configuration file (CONFIG.SYS) to allow your system to effectively run 1-2-3/G. See "Modify-

ing CONFIG.SYS" later in this section for details on the changes made by 1-2-3/G.

- **Printer drivers:** You must install a printer driver for OS/2 in order to print your worksheets and graphs from within 1-2-3/G. When you ran INSTALL.EXE the first time, a series of Lotus-supplied printer driver files were copied from your 1-2-3/G program disks to your hard disk in compressed form. You can use INSTALL.EXE to install one or more of these drivers for use in OS/2. See "Adding Printer Drivers" later in this section for additional detail.
- **1-2-3/G's Title:** INSTALL.EXE—also prompts you whether you want the 1-2-3/G title in the Start Programs window (OS/2 1.1) or the Group-Main window (OS/2 1.2). If you have already installed this title, there is no need to do it again. However, if you want the title displayed, INSTALL.EXE will do this for you. For additional details on this, see "Displaying the 1-2-3/G Title" later in this section.
- **Fonts:** If you installed 1-2-3/G in OS/2 1.1, INSTALL.EXE prompted you to install various Helvetica, Courier, and Times Roman fonts. In OS/2 1.2, these fonts are already resident and installed. Therefore, the next time you run the INSTALL.EXE, font installation is not presented as an option. However, you can still install fonts for use with OS/2. See "Adding Fonts" later in this section for details on how to do this.

Note

> If you modified your system configuration file (CONFIG.SYS) by using the INSTALL.EXE program, you must restart your computer to take advantage of the changes.

Note

> If you upgrade from OS/2 Version 1.1 to OS/2 Version 1.2, make sure to run the INSTALL.EXE program again. Otherwise, 1-2-3/G will not run on the system.

Setting the Keyboard Speed

The keyboard speed determines the speed of worksheet navigation—how fast your system reacts to repeated keystrokes, such as depressed arrow keys. As mentioned, you can select a keyboard speed by using the INSTALL.EXE program. During INSTALL you are prompted with the question "Do you want to set the keyboard speed to Fast?". If you press ENTER to accept "Y" (the default fast speed), INSTALL.EXE inserts the line

```
C:\123G\SPEED.EXE Fast
```

into your OS/2 STARTUP.CMD file, located in the root directory. OS/2 reads this file each time you start your computer. (If a STARTUP.CMD file does not exist, it is created.) This command line in the STARTUP.CMD file runs the SPEED.EXE program in your 1-2-3/G program directory. This causes increased responsiveness to your keyboard and can speed up worksheet navigation.

Note

> The keyboard speed you choose with INSTALL.EXE becomes the keyboard speed for all programs you run in OS/2, including 1-2-3/G. If you want to delete the SPEED statement from the STARTUP.CMD file you can use a text editor capable of reading and writing ASCII files, such as the OS/2 system editor. That way, the next time you start your computer, all OS/2 applications (including 1-2-3/G) will respond at normal keyboard speed.

Note

> If you specify a fast keyboard speed when you run INSTALL.EXE the first time, a keyboard speed option is not included the next time you run INSTALL.EXE.

Rather than using the INSTALL.EXE program to place the speed statement in your STARTUP.CMD file, thereby affecting all the programs you run in OS/2, you can change your keyboard speed manually. To do this, you can run the SPEED.EXE program located in your 1-2-3/G program directory. That way, you can control the keyboard speed, based on your needs. To run the SPEED.EXE program, perform the following steps:

1. From the OS/2 full-screen command prompt, make the directory containing your 1-2-3/G program files current. To do this, type **cd 123G**, or the name of the directory that contains the 1-2-3/G program files. Press ENTER.
2. Once you're in the 1-2-3/G directory, type **speed f** to set keyboard speed to fast, or **speed m** to set keyboard speed to medium. Press ENTER.

The speed you set using this method is in effect for 1-2-3/G and all other OS/2 files until you reboot or turn off your computer. The system then returns to the default keyboard speed you entered during 1-2-3/G installation.

Tip: Put an EXIT in the STARTUP.CMD file

If you use the INSTALL.EXE program to place the SPEED statement in STARTUP.CMD file, OS/2 runs this file in a command-prompt window when you first start your computer. After OS/2 is up and running, the command-prompt window remains on your screen, causing an unsightly appearance. However, if you follow the SPEED statement with a line containing the string EXIT, OS/2 will close the command-prompt window and display only Presentation Manager.

Modifying CONFIG.SYS

The CONFIG.SYS file is one of the system configuration files run by OS/2 when you start your computer. This file contains various statements that set operating parameters for OS/2. 1-2-3/G requires three entries to be included in this file.

When you run the INSTALL.EXE program, you are prompted whether you want the CONFIG.SYS file updated. If you select "Y" (yes), CONFIG.SYS is updated for you. When INSTALL.EXE modifies your CONFIG.SYS file, it also makes a backup copy of your original file, called CONFIG.000. If a backup filename has already been made, INSTALL creates the backup file CONFIG.001 and so on.

Alternatively, you can update the CONFIG.SYS file yourself. To update this file yourself, you'll need a text editor capable of editing ASCII files, such as the OS/2 system editor. Load the CONFIG.SYS file into this editor. (The CONFIG.SYS file is located in the root directory, usually C:\.) On some systems, the file may be named CONFIG.OS2. However, make sure you have the right file. The file that has a PROTSHELL statement at the beginning, such as protshell=C:\os2\pmshell.exe, is the CONFIG file you want to modify. Once you have the correct file loaded, add or change the following statements:

Statement	Parameters
Threads	The value in the THREADS statement must be 64 or greater. For example, THREADS=128 is recommended.
IOPL	For certain printer drivers to work, the IOPL=YES statement must included in the CONFIG file.
Libpath	The LIBPATH statement must contain the drive letter and directory name for the 1-2-3/G program files. Usually this is C:\123G. However, in most cases other directories are also listed in this statement.

Modifying the PATH Statement for Data External Commands

If you want to use 1-2-3/G's Data External commands to query external database tables, you may want to modify the PATH statement in your CONFIG.SYS file to reference your 1-2-3/G program directory. That way, 1-2-3/G will be able to find the Sample driver, which allows you to connect external database tables to 1-2-3/G. Otherwise, whenever you want to use the Data External command, you'll have to use the File Directory or Utility User Settings Directories command to make your 1-2-3/G program directory the current directory.

To modify the PATH statement in your CONFIG.SYS file, simply load the file into an editor that is capable of reading and writing ASCII files (such as the OS/2 system editor). You'll find the CONFIG.SYS file located in the root directory, usually C:\, of your system. In that file, you'll find a SET PATH= statement. Add the 1-2-3/G program directory to the end of this statement.

The CONFIG.SYS file is not the only OS/2 configuration file that can be used to set the path for the current OS/2 session. In fact, you can include a PATH statement in any one of the following files:

- the CONFIG.SYS file (or CONFIG.OS2 on some systems).
- the STARTUP.CMD file.
- the OS2INT.CMD file.

You can also reset the path for the current session by entering a path statement at the OS/2 system prompt. With all of these options open to you, make sure you are consistent with your path statements. For example, if you have conflicting path statements in different files, the last path statement used will determine the default path for the current OS/2 session.

Note

You can easily determine if the 1-2-3/G program file is in your PATH statement. To do this, type **PATH** at the OS/2 system prompt. OS/2 will then display the current PATH statement, for example PATH= C:\OS2;C:\OS2\SYSTEM.

Displaying the 1-2-3/G Title

During the INSTALL.EXE program you are prompted whether you want the 1-2-3/G title added to the Presentation Manager window. If you accept this selection, INSTALL.EXE adds the 1-2-3/G title to the Start Programs window in OS/2 1.1 or to the Group-Main window in OS/2 1.2. This allows you to start 1-2-3/G directly from one of these windows. Otherwise, you'll have to type **123g** at the OS/2 system prompt.

If you decide not to use INSTALL.EXE to add the 1-2-3/G title to a Presentation Manager window, you can always do it at a later time. To do this, you can either run INSTALL.EXE a second time, or you can use Presentation Manager's facilities to add the title. If you decide to use Presentation Manager, the procedure varies, depending on the version you are using (Version 1.1 or Version 1.2). The procedures for installing the 1-2-3/G title in both versions follow.

OS/2 1.1: Adding the 1-2-3/G Title to the Start Programs Window

Use the following procedure to include the 1-2-3/G title in the Start Programs window of OS/2 1.1:

1. Open the Start Programs window, if it isn't open already. Use the Task Manager to do this.
2. In the Start Programs window, select Group from the Start Programs menu bar, then select Main Group from the pulldown menu.
3. The Main Group programs are now displayed in the Start Programs window. Select Program from the menu bar, then choose Add from the pulldown menu. The Add Program dialog box is now displayed.
4. Enter the following information:

   - In the "Program title" text box, type **1-2-3/G**, or any name you choose up to 60 characters.
   - Press TAB, or click on the "Path and filename" text box. Type the drive and path to your 1-2-3/G program directory followed by the program name, for example **C:\123G\123G.EXE**.
   - In the "Working directory: text box" enter the drive and path for your 1-2-3/G program directory, for example **C:\123G**.
   - Select the Add command button at the bottom of the dialog box to confirm this information.

5. Presentation Manager returns you to the Start-Programs window, which now includes 1-2-3/G title (or the name you specified).

OS/2 1.2: Adding 1-2-3/G Title to the Group-Main Window

You can include the 1-2-3/G title in the Group-Main window of OS/2 1.2 using the same method as for OS/2 1.1 except:

1. Open the Group-Main window, if it is not already open. Use the Desktop Manager to do this.

2. Select Program from the Group-Main menu bar. Then select New from the pulldown menu that appears. The New Program dialog box is now displayed.
3. Follow step 4 for OS/2 1.1 above to enter the appropriate information in the New Program dialog box. When you're finished, select the Add command button.
4. Presentation Manager returns you to the Group-Main window, which now includes the 1-2-3/G title (or the name you specified) along with 1-2-3/G's icon.

Adding Fonts

One of the major advantages of using Presentation Manager is that you can install fonts that control the type size and style for the numbers, letters, and symbols displayed on your screen. Once fonts are installed, you can use them in various applications to control the appearance of your data. For example, in Chapter 3 of this book, you learned how to use 1-2-3/G's Range Attributes Font and Worksheet Global Attributes Font commands to format the display of data in your worksheets with different fonts.

When you run 1-2-3/G's INSTALL.EXE program, your C:\OS2\DLL directory is searched to detect the presence of three installed fonts: HELV (Helvetica), COURIER (Courier), and TIMES (Times Roman). (See Chapter 3 for a complete discussion of what these fonts look like.) If these fonts have not been installed, INSTALL.EXE allows you to install them. However, if these fonts have been installed already, INSTALL.EXE does not prompt you install them.

You can also install additional fonts beyond those offered by 1-2-3/G or by Presentation Manager, provided you have those fonts available on your hard disk or on a separate floppy disk. However, you must use Presentation Manager's facilities to do this. Furthermore, the procedure for installing fonts varies depending upon the version of OS/2 you have, Version 1.1 or Version 1.2. A description of how to install fonts in OS/2 version 1.1 and Version 1.2 follows.

OS/2 1.1: Adding Fonts

Use the following procedure to install additional fonts in OS/2 1.1:

1. Open the Start Programs window, if it is not already open. Use the Task Manager to do this.
2. In the Start Programs window, select Group from the Start Programs menu bar. Then choose Utility Programs from the pulldown menu that appears.
3. The Utility Programs names are now displayed in the Start Programs window. Select Control Panel. The Control Panel dialog box is now

displayed. Select Installation from the Control Panel menu bar and choose Add font from the pulldown menu that appears.

4. An "Add New Font" dialog box is now displayed. In the text box, specify the drive and directory that contains the fonts you want to install (this is usually drive A:). Insert the disk that contains the fonts into drive A:, or enter the full path of the directory containing the fonts, for example **C:\OS2\DLL**. Select ENTER.
5. Another "Add New Font" dialog box is now displayed. All available fonts in the specified path are shown in the list box. Select a font name. Then select the Add command button. A third "Add New font" dialog box is now displayed showing the path to the C:\OS2\DLL directory in which the fonts will be installed. Select Yes to accept this path and install the font(s) you've selected. The font is copied to the C:\OS2\DLL directory and you are returned to the Control Panel.
6. Press ALT-F4 to close the Control Panel. Presentation Manager returns you to the Start Programs window.

Note

To use the font(s) you just installed, you must restart your computer. To do this, press CTRL-ALT-DEL.

OS/2 1.2: Adding Fonts

To install additional fonts in OS/2 1.2, use the following steps:

1. Activate the Desktop Manager window. (The Group-Main window is usually the active window.)
2. Select Utilities from the Desktop Manager window and then select Control Panel from the Utilities list box.
3. Select Installation from the Control Panel menu followed by "Add font" from the pulldown menu that appears.
4. An "Add New Font" dialog box is now displayed. In the text box, specify the drive and directory that contains the fonts you want to install (this is usually drive A:). Insert the disk that contains the fonts into drive A:, or enter the full path of the directory containing the fonts, for example **C:\OS2\DLL**. Select ENTER.
5. Another "Add New Font" dialog box is now displayed. All available fonts in the specified path are shown in the list box. Select a font name. Then select the Add command button. A third "Add New font" dialog box is

now displayed showing the path to the C:\OS2\DLL directory in which the fonts will be installed. Select Yes to accept this path and install the font you've selected. The font is copied to the C:\OS2\DLL directory and you are returned to the Control Panel window.

6. Press ALT-F4 to close the Control Panel. Presentation Manager returns you to the Group-Utilities window.

Note

> To use the font(s) you just installed, you must restart your computer. To do this, press CTRL-ALT-DEL.

Adding Printer Drivers

To print from within OS/2, you must install a printer driver capable of driving your specific printer. (Printer drivers are program files that tell OS/2 how to interact with your specific printer.) Once that printer driver is installed for OS/2, you can print your worksheets and graphs from within 1-2-3/G.

When you install 1-2-3/G, a series of Lotus-supplied printer driver files are copied to your 1-2-3/G program directory in compressed form. These printer driver files include drivers for various Hewlett-Packard (HP) Laserjet, Epson, and PostScript printers. During the installation of 1-2-3/G, you are prompted whether you want to install printer divers. If you type "Y" in response to this prompt, INSTALL.EXE displays a list of printer driver names for your selection. (You can also decline to install a printer driver by selecting "No Printer".) Once you select a driver, you are then prompted for both a description for the driver and the default port you want to assign the printer to. Once you make these selections, the appropriate printer driver file is expanded and copied to your C:\OS2\DLL directory. An entry for the driver is also made in your OS2.INI file.

To install a second printer or change printer drivers, you have two options. On the one hand, you can run the INSTALL.EXE program again and specify an additional printer driver or change the current one. Alternatively, you can use Presentation Manager to add or change a printer driver. However, before you use Presentation Manager to install a printer driver provided by 1-2-3/G, you must run 1-2-3/G's INFLATE.EXE program to decompress the file for that driver and copy it to your C:\OS2\DLL directory.

Using the INFLATE.EXE Program

As mentioned, when you installed 1-2-3/G, a series of Lotus-supplied printer drivers were copied to your 1-2-3/G program directory in compressed form. To install a printer driver without using INSTALL.EXE, you must

- Decompress the driver using the INFLATE.EXE program.

- Install the driver using the OS/2 Control Panel.

The following procedure shows you how to use the INFLATE.EXE program:

1. From the Start Programs (OS/2 1.1) or Group-Main (OS/2 1.2) window, select either the OS/2 full-screen or windowed command prompt.
2. Make sure your current directory is the 1-2-3/G program directory (usually C:\123G). For example, if your program directory is C:\123G, type **CD\123G** and press ENTER.
3. Run the INFLATE Utility to decompress the printer driver. (This utility should be in the 1-2-3/G program directory. If it is not, copy it from you original Drivers disk.) Type **INFLATE** *printer-driver* **C:\OS2\DLL**, where *printer driver* is one of the Lotus-supplied printer drivers listed in Table A-1. For example, enter **INFLATE EPSON.D!V C:\OS2\DLL**, which decompresses the EPSON.D!V printer driver and copies it to the C:\OS2\DLL directory as EPSON.DRV. Note that the Epson printer driver is automatically renamed during the process. This is not the case with the PostScript printer driver. You'll need to use the REN command to rename this file to PSCRIPT.DRV.
4. Press ALT-ESC to return to the Start Programs or Group-Main window.
5. Refer to the documentation that came with your copy of OS/2 for information on how to install a printer driver in Presentation Manager.

CHANGING WORKSHEET GLOBAL DEFAULT SETTINGS

You can use the Worksheet Global Default command to turn the undo feature on and off. You can also use this command to stop auto-executing macros from running when you load the worksheet files containing them. In addition, you can use this command to specify the character set format you want 1-2-3/G to use when opening and saving 1-2-3 Release 2 (.WK1) files. Each of these global default settings is discussed in more detail in the sections that follow.

When you select the Worksheet Global Default command, 1-2-3/G displays the dialog box shown in Figure A-1. If you change any settings in the Worksheet

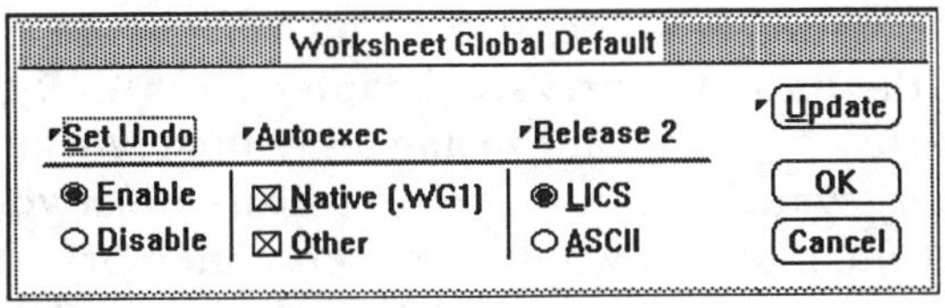

FIGURE A-1 Worksheet Global Default dialog box

TABLE A-1 1-2-3/G Compressed Printer Drivers

Compressed Hewlett-Packard printer drivers*

LASERJET.D!V	HPPCLE.P!M	HPPCLM.P!M	HPPCLT.P!M
GENERIC.D!L	HPPCLF.P!M	HPPCLN.P!M	HPPCLU.P!M
HPADDF.D!L	HPPCLG.P!M	HPPCLP.P!M	HPPCLV.P!M
HPPCLA.P!M	HPPCLH.P!M	HPPCLQ.P!M	HPPCLY.P!M
HPPCLB.P!M	HPPCLJ.P!M	HPPCLR.P!M	HPPCZ1.P!M
HPPCLC.P!M	HPPCLK.P!M	HPPCLS1.P!M	HPPCLZ2A.P!M
HPPCLD.P!M	HPPCLL.P!M	HPPCLS2.P!M	

*The above HP drivers will not function in OS/2 Version 1.1.

Compressed Epson printer drivers

EPSON.D!V	EPSON.H!P	EPSONDAT.D!L

Compressed PostScript printer drivers**

PSCRIPT.1!1	PSCRIPT.1!2

**A PostScript printer driver is not automatically renamed after using the INFLATE utility. After you decompress a PostScript printer driver using the INFLATE utility, you need to rename a PostScript printer driver to PSCRIPT.DRV.

Global Default dialog box and select the OK command button or press ENTER, those changes affect files that are opened during the current session only. On the other hand, if you select the Update command button, 1-2-3/G also saves the settings changes you make for future sessions.

Turning Undo On and Off

As you know, 1-2-3/G includes an undo feature (accessed through the Edit Undo command or by pressing ALT-BACKSPACE) that allows you to undo many of the commands and operations you perform in 1-2-3/G. (For more information on the undo feature, see Chapter 1.) Initially, the undo feature is enabled (on). However, in some instances, you may want to turn it off. For example, you may want to turn the undo feature off if you are using a very large worksheet file and you want to conserve memory.

To turn off the undo feature, select the Worksheet Global Default command. 1-2-3/G displays the dialog box in Figure A-1. Select "Set Undo" and select the Disable option button. (To turn the undo feature back on again, select the Enable option button.) To complete the command, press ENTER or select the OK command button.

Caution

> If you select the Update command button to complete the Worksheet Global Default Set Undo Disable command, you disable undo for future 1-2-3/G sessions. Instead, you may wish to select the OK command button or press ENTER so that undo is only affected for the current session.

The Autoexec Option

The Worksheet Global Default Autoexec command allows you to specify whether an auto-executing (\0) macro is automatically run when you load a worksheet file. (See Chapter 10 for details on auto-executing macros.) The Autoexec option offers two check boxes, Native and Other. The Native check box controls auto-executing macros for 1-2-3/G worksheet files. If you remove the X from this box, auto-executing macros will *not* be executed for 1-2-3/G worksheet files. The Other check box controls auto-executing macros for 1-2-3 Release 2 (.WK1) and Release 3 (.WK3) files that you load into 1-2-3/G. If you remove the X from this box, auto-executing macros in those files will *not* be executed. As you can see in Figure A-1, the default setting for both the Native and Other options is on (boxes checked).

The Release 2 Option

Use the Worksheet Global Default Release 2 option to specify the character set format 1-2-3/G uses when you open, retrieve, or save Release 2 files. You can choose from LICS or ASCII. If you select LICS (the default) 1-2-3/G uses the Lotus International Character Set. On the other hand, if you select ASCII, 1-2-3/G uses the ASCII character set.

CHANGING USER SETTINGS

You can further customize 1-2-3/G by using the User Settings command. This command is available from either the Utility menu or the Desktop Control menu. Whichever method you use to select the command, 1-2-3/G displays a menu with the following four options:

Option	Allows you to specify
Preferences	Save Options Keystroke compatibility Function key bar display Dialog marker display
Directories	Paths to the working, file template, backup, and temporary directories
Startup	Tool and file opened when you start 1-2-3/G
International	Date, time, number, and currency formats Date, time, number, and currency separators Currency symbol and placement Function argument separator Character set (code page) Data sort options Unit of measurement (inches or millimeters) for column widths, row heights, and print margins

Each of these options is discussed in more detail below.

The User Settings Preferences Command

When you select the Utility User Settings Preferences command, 1-2-3/G displays the dialog box shown in Figure A-2. You can use the options in this dialog box to control any of the following:

- How 1-2-3/G saves files.
- Specify that certain keys function as prescribed by Presentation Manager or function as they do in 1-2-3 Release 3.
- Display the function key bar.
- Display dialog box markers.

When you make a settings change in the Utility User Settings Preferences dialog box, select OK or press ENTER to save those changes for the current

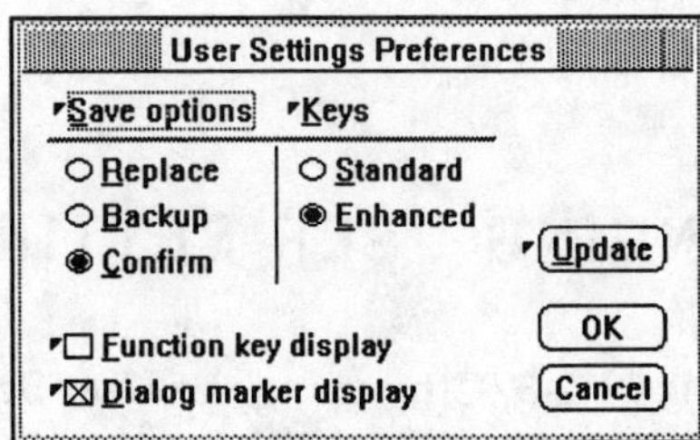

FIGURE A-2 The Utility User Settings Preferences dialog box

session only. To save those changes for future 1-2-3/G sessions as well, select the Update command button.

The Save Options

You can specify how 1-2-3/G saves a file by using the Save options shown in the Utility User Settings Preferences dialog box. You can select from Replace, Backup, or Confirm.

Caution

> You must select the Confirm option if you want macros created in Release 2.2 and 3 to work properly in 1-2-3/G.

THE REPLACE OPTION If you choose the Replace option button from the "Save options" section, 1-2-3/G overwrites the last copy of the file to have been saved when you use the File Save command. The Save Window dialog box containing the Cancel, Replace, and Backup command buttons is not displayed. For example, suppose you are editing the file CASH.WG1, which you have previously saved. If you select the File Save command and accept the filename CASH.WG1, 1-2-3/G simply saves the file. The Save Window dialog box is not displayed and no backup copy is created. If you have made a mistake in the file, you are pretty much out of luck, unless you correct the error to the file in memory and resave the file. (You cannot use the undo feature to reverse the File Save command.)

THE CONFIRM OPTION When you choose the Confirm option (the default) from the "Save options" section, 1-2-3/G displays the Save Window dialog for the File Save command if it finds that an earlier copy of the file you wish to save already exists on the disk. This dialog box contains Cancel, Replace, and Backup command buttons that allow you to specify the following for the File Save command:

- **Cancel:** Cancels the File Save command.
- **Replace:** Replaces the file on disk with the file you specified.
- **Backup:** Copies the previously saved version of the file to the default backup directory. The new version of the file in memory is then saved on disk in place of the original version.

THE BACKUP OPTION If you choose the Backup option button from the Utility User Settings Preferences dialog box, 1-2-3/G automatically creates a backup file when you use the File Save command. This causes 1-2-3/G to copy the original version of the file on disk to the default backup directory. If a previous backup copy has been made, the new backup copy is saved on top of that file. The file in memory is then saved in the original file's disk location. 1-2-3/G does not display the Save Window dialog box, however. Therefore, you cannot cancel the File Save command. However, a backup copy of the file now exists. If you later notice an error in the file, you can always retrieve the backup copy.

The Keys Option

You can use the Keys option in the Utility User Settings Preferences dialog box to specify keyboard compatibility. You can choose Standard, which maintains keyboard compatibility with Presentation Manager, or you can choose Enhanced to specify 1-2-3 Release 3 keyboard compatibility.

The Enhanced option primarily affects the use of the keyboard with dialog boxes—specifically the behavior of the ESC and ENTER keys. For example, ESC can be used to move the focus of a dialog box up one level; or, if the focus is already at the first level, pressing ESC cancels the dialog box. ENTER can be used to move the focus of a dialog box down one level; or, if the focus is already at the last level, pressing ENTER confirms the dialog box.

Caution

> If you select Standard, existing 1-2-3/G macros may not run properly.

Function Key Display

You can use the "Function key display" check box in the User Settings Preferences dialog box to turn the function key display on or off. The default setting is off (box unchecked), as shown in Figure A-2. If you turn this option on (click on the box, or press F to select this option), the Function Key bar is displayed at the bottom of the 1-2-3/G desktop. The Function Key bar displays the first 10 function keys, as well as the functions each key performs—for example, EDIT or GOTO. You can click on any function key to execute its function, just as if you pressed the function key on the keyboard. See Chapter 1 for more information on 1-2-3/G's function keys.

Dialog Marker Display

The "Dialog marker display" check box in the User Settings Preferences dialog box turns the display of dialog box markers on or off. As you know, dialog box markers are small triangles that are located to the left of items in a dialog box when you can select them by typing their underlined letter. For example, in Figure A-2, dialog markers appear next to these options: Save options, Keys, Update, Function key display, or Dialog marker display.

As you can see in Figure A-2, the default setting for "Dialog marker display" is on (box checked). That way, dialog box markers are always displayed to the left of a dialog box item when you select it by typing its first letter. If you turn off the "Dialog marker display" check box, 1-2-3/G will no longer display dialog markers.

The User Settings Directories Command

The User Settings Directories command allows you to change the default directories used by 1-2-3/G. When you select this command, 1-2-3/G displays the dialog box shown in Figure A-3.

In addition to the program directory, 1-2-3/G uses four other directories, as follows:

- Working directory
- File template directory
- Backup directory
- Temporary directory

The role of each of these directories is explained in the sections that follow.

To change a default directory, use the mouse or keyboard to select the text box for that directory. Then type the drive and path for the directory you want to use. To save the change for the current session, select the OK command button or press ENTER. To save the setting for future 1-2-3/G sessions as well, select the Update command button.

When you specify a directory in the User Setting Directories dialog box, keep the following in mind:

- The directory must already exist.
- If you are running 1-2-3/G on a network, you must have write access to a directory you specify.
- Avoid specifying the root directory for your primary drive. This directory contains important system files that should be stored separately for protection purposes.

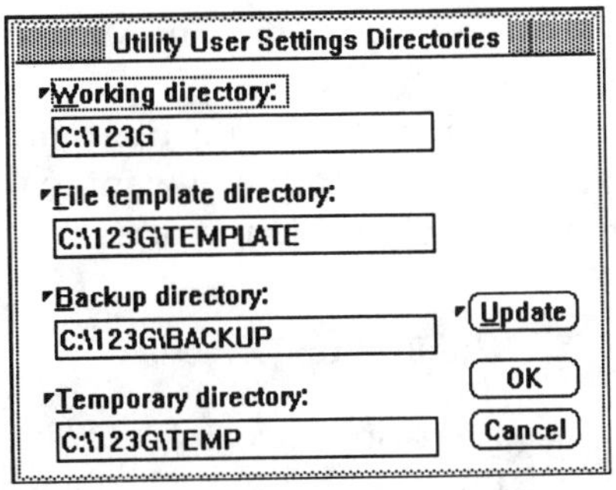

Utility User Settings Directories

Working directory:
C:\123G

File template directory:
C:\123G\TEMPLATE

Backup directory:
C:\123G\BACKUP

Temporary directory:
C:\123G\TEMP

Update
OK
Cancel

FIGURE A-3 **The Utility User Settings Directories dialog box**

The Working Directory

The working directory is the default directory 1-2-3/G uses when retrieving and saving worksheet, graph, or desktop files. The path to this directory appears in the "File name" text box for the File Open, File Retrieve, and File Save commands. For more information about these commands, see Chapter 5, "File Management."

When you install 1-2-3/G, the name C:\123G\WORK is suggested for the default working directory. You can accept this name or specify the name of another directory. If the directory does not exist, 1-2-3/G will create it.

You can override the setting for the default working directory by using the File Directory command. When you specify a directory with this command, 1-2-3/G uses that directory until you change it.

Note

> Your working directory must be different from your backup directory. If the two are the same, 1-2-3/G will not allow you to create backup files.

The File Template Directory

1-2-3/G uses the File template directory to store template files. Template files are used as models for creating new files with the File New command. The new file gets its data and settings from the template file. The default name for this directory is usually C:\123G\TEMPLATE. In this directory, 1-2-3/G stores two files, DEFAULT.WG1 and DEFAULT.GPH, that are used as templates for creating all new files. The name of one of these files appears in the "File template" text box when you select the File New command. You can accept the appropriate DEFAULT file for use as a template or you can specify the path and name of another existing file. See Chapter 5, "File Management," for more about the File New command.

You can use any directory you want as a file template directory. Simply specify the drive and path to the directory you want to use in the "File template directory" text box of the User Settings Directories dialog box.

The Backup Directory

The backup directory is used to store backup files. The name of this directory is usually C:\123G\BACKUP. At least, 1-2-3/G suggests this name when you install the product on your hard disk. However, you can use any directory you want as a backup directory.

To change the current backup directory, select the Utility User Settings Directories command and select the "Backup directory" text box. In that box, type the drive and path to the directory you want to use as a backup directory and select OK or Update to complete the User Settings Directories command.

To create backup files, you use the File Save command. When you use this command to save an existing file, 1-2-3/G displays the Save Window dialog box, which contains Cancel, Replace, and Backup command buttons. If you select Backup, 1-2-3/G will copy the old version of the file on disk to the default backup directory. The new version of the file in memory will then be saved in the old file's disk location.

There are two exceptions to this, however. If you have previously selected the Utility User Setting Preferences Save options Backup command discussed earlier (see "The Save Options" under "The User Settings Preferences Command"), 1-2-3/G will automatically create a backup file whenever you use the File Save command. Or, if you previously selected the Utility User Settings Save options Replace command, the original file on disk is automatically replaced when you use the File Save command. In this instance, you are not given an opportunity to create a backup file.

Note

> Don't fall into the trap of specifying the same directory as both a backup and a working directory. If you do this, 1-2-3/G will not allow you to create backup files.

Temporary Directory

The Temporary directory contains files 1-2-3/G creates during its operation. Occasionally, 1-2-3/G needs to create temporary files to support such features as printing or undo. However, these files are deleted when you end the current work session.

The name of the temporary directory is usually C:\123G\TEMP. However, you can use any directory you want as a temporary directory. To change the current temporary directory, select the Utility User Settings Directories command and select the "Temporary directory" text box. In that box, type the drive and path to the directory you want to use as a Temporary directory and select OK or Update to complete the User Settings Directories command.

The User Settings Startup Command

You can use the User Settings Startup command to specify the type of tool and file that 1-2-3/G will open each time you begin a work session. The User

Settings Startup command is available from either the Utility menu or the Desktop Control menu. When you select this command, 1-2-3/G displays the dialog box shown in Figure A-4.

The three command buttons located in the upper-left corner of the User Settings Startup dialog box determine the type of file 1-2-3/G opens at the beginning of each session. These command buttons perform the following functions:

- **Restore:** Causes 1-2-3/G to record the status of the desktop—the files that are open and their window positions—when you ended your last work session. Those same files are opened the next time you start 1-2-3/G and their windows are positioned in the same way. Thus the desktop is "restored" just as you left it. Use this option when you want to pick up where you left off.
- **New File:** Allows you to specify the type of file (worksheet or graph) that is opened when you start 1-2-3/G. When you select this command button, 1-2-3/G activates the "Tool name" list box. From this list box, select the type file (Worksheet or Graph) you want 1-2-3/G to open each time you start the program.
- **Old file:** Allows you to specify an existing worksheet, graph, or desktop file that 1-2-3/G will open each time you start the program. When you select this option, 1-2-3/G activates the "File name" text box and its associated list box and the "Drives" options buttons. In the "File name" text box, 1-2-3/G shows the path to the current working directory followed by the extension *.*. This causes 1-2-3/G to list all the files in the current working directory in the list box below. Select the name of the file you want 1-2-3/G to open each time you start the program.

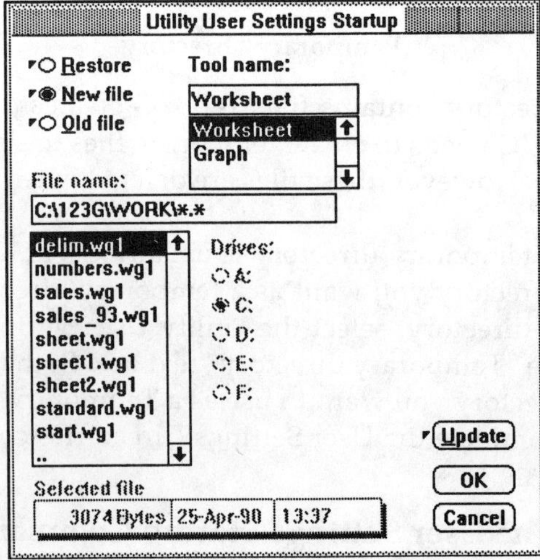

FIGURE A-4 **The Utility User Settings Startup dialog box**

Once you select from Restore, New file, or Old file, complete the User Settings Startup command by selecting the Update command button. This saves any settings you may have made for future 1-2-3/G sessions.

The "New file" option button is the default for the User Settings Startup command. Further, the default selection in the "Tool name" list box is Worksheet. These two default selections cause 1-2-3/G to display a new worksheet file each time you start the program.

As mentioned, when you select the "Old file" option button, 1-2-3/G activates the "File name" text box and its associated list box and "Drives" options buttons. In the "File name" text box, 1-2-3/G displays the path to the default working directory (set with User Settings Directories) followed by a *.* extension. This causes 1-2-3/G to display the files in the working directory in the list box below. You can then make your selection from that list box. However, you can also select from a list of files in other directories by using any of the following techniques:

- Modify the drive and path in the "File name" text box and press ENTER. 1-2-3/G displays the files in the directory you specified in the list box below.
- Select the parent directory [displayed as two dots (..) from the "File name" list box]. This causes 1-2-3/G to move one level closer to the root directory and display filenames and subdirectory names in that directory.
- Select another "Drives" option (for example, A, B, C, D, and so on). 1-2-3/G displays the files in the current directory of the drive you select.
- Type the drive, path, and filename of an existing file in the "File name" text box. 1-2-3/G will then open that file each time you start the program.

The User Settings Startup command can be useful as a convenience feature, but you can also use it to control the use of 1-2-3/G. For example, imagine you are preparing a worksheet file for use by others. In that file, you can create an auto-executing (\0) macro (see auto-executing macros in Chapter 10). You can then use the "Old file" option for the User Settings Startup command to specify that the file be automatically opened when you start 1-2-3/G. That way, 1-2-3/G comes up under the control of your macro.

The User Settings International Command

The User Settings International command allows you to specify various default settings for 1-2-3/G. This command is available from either the Utility menu or the Desktop Control menu. When you select the User Settings International command, 1-2-3/G displays the dialog box shown in Figure A-5.

Briefly, the User Settings International dialog in Figure A-5 allows you to specify the following default settings:

- Date, time, currency (and comma), and number formats.
- Date, time, currency (and comma), and number separators.

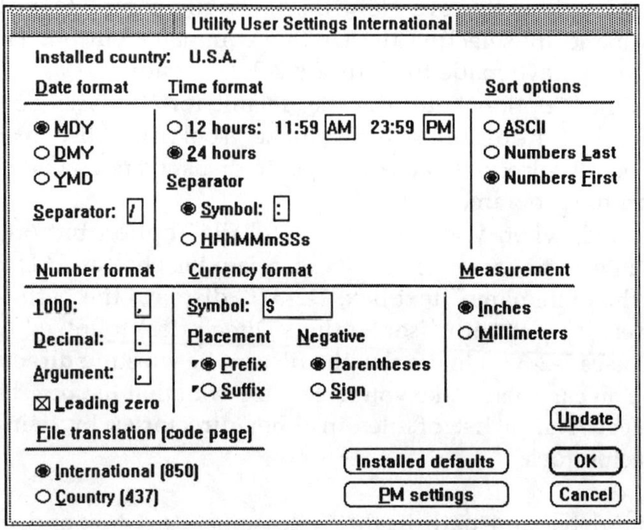

Utility User Settings International

Installed country: U.S.A.

Date format | Time format | Sort options

MDY / DMY / YMD
Separator: /

12 hours: 11:59 AM 23:59 PM
24 hours
Separator
Symbol: :
HHhMMmSSs

ASCII / Numbers Last / Numbers First

Number format | Currency format | Measurement

1000: ,
Decimal: .
Argument: ,
Leading zero

Symbol: $
Placement: Prefix / Suffix
Negative: Parentheses / Sign

Inches / Millimeters

File translation (code page)
International (850)
Country (437)

Installed defaults | PM settings | Update | OK | Cancel

FIGURE A-5 The User Settings International dialog box

- An argument separator for functions, macros, range, and collection addresses.
- A Character set (code page) for use with the File Import and Print File commands.
- A default sort sequence for the Data Sort command.
- Unit of measurement (inches or millimeters) for column widths, row heights, and print margins.

When you make a settings change in the User Settings International dialog box, you can save that setting in one of two ways. On the one hand, if you select the OK command button at the lower right of the dialog box, 1-2-3/G will use the settings you specified for the current session only. On the other hand, if you select the Update command button, 1-2-3/G will use the settings both for the current session and for future sessions.

Installed Country: Controlling 1-2-3/G Default Values

During installation of 1-2-3/G, you are prompted to select a country driver. The driver you select affects the default character set, sort order, date, time, number, and currency formats used by 1-2-3/G. You can choose from 17 country driver files. However, most American users choose the U.S.A. country driver file.

The country driver file you selected is displayed after "Installed country" label in the upper-left corner of the dialog box in Figure A-5. In this case U.S.A. is displayed, indicating the U.S.A. driver has been installed. If you want to use another country driver file, you must run the INSTALL.EXE file as described at the beginning of this chapter and select the name of that driver.

To a large degree, the country driver you select affects the default settings displayed in the User Settings International dialog box. If you change the default settings and then decide you want to return to using the original default settings, there are two selections you can use, "Installed defaults" and "PM settings". Both are located in the lower-right corner of the User Settings International dialog box. The "Installed defaults" selection restores *all* default settings to those of the country driver file you specified when you installed 1-2-3/G. For example, the default U.S.A. settings are shown in Figure A-5.

On the other hand, the "PM settings" option restores *only* the Time format, Number format, Date format, and Currency format sections of the User Settings International dialog box to match the default settings for Presentation Manager, not the country driver. The remaining selections in the User Settings International dialog box are not affected. To modify the settings for Presentation Manager, you can use the Presentation Manager Control Panel. See your Presentation Manager documentation for more details on this.

Date Format

The "Date format" section of the User Settings International dialog box allows you to change the display of Date 4 (YY/MMo/DD) and Date 5 (MMo/DD) date formats. This affects the Range Format Date and Worksheet Global Format Date commands in the Worksheet Tool, and the Settings Number Format command in the Graph Tool.

If you make a selection from the "Date format" section of the User Settings International dialog box, existing entries that are formatted as Date 4 or Date 5 are updated for the change. For example, suppose you have entered the date May 1, 1990 as @DATE(90,5,1) in a cell and formatted that cell with the Range Format Data/Time 4 or 5 command. The following table shows the impact that making a selection from the "Date format" section will have on the display of that entry:

Date Format Selection	D4 format	D5 format
MDY (U.S. Default)	05/01/90	05/01
DMY	01/05/90	01/05
YMD	90/05/01	05/01

DATE FORMAT SEPARATOR You can also use the "Date format" "Separator" option to change the separator displayed between the month, day, and year components of dates. In the adjacent text box, you can type a **/** (slash, the U.S. default), **-**(hyphen), or **.** (period). For example, suppose you enter the function @DATE(90,5,1) and format that cell as Date 4. If you enter a **-** (hyphen) in the Separator box, the date in that cell is now displayed as 05–01–90.

Time Format

You can use the "Time format" section of the User Settings International dialog box to control the display of time formats, specifically Date/Time 6 (HH:MMi:SS AMPM), Date/Time 7 (HH:MMi AMPM), Date/Time 8 (HH:MMi:SS), and Date/Time 9 (HH:MMi). This affects the Range Format Date/Time or Worksheet Global Format Date/Time commands, and the Settings Number Format command in the Graph Tool. (It also affects the time of creation in 1-2-3/G file listings.)

The "Time format" section offers two options, "12 hours" and "24 hours." The *12* hours option displays time in a 12-hour format. The 24 hours option (U.S. default) displays the time in a 24-hour format, more commonly known as military time.

If you select the "12 hours" option, 1-2-3/G prompts you to specify abbreviations that differentiate the first 12 hours of a day from the second 12 hours of a day. As shown in Figure A-5, the default setting AM shown in the box after 11:59 is used for the first 12 hours, while the default PM in the box after 23:59 designates the second 12 hours in a day. Actually, you can enter any abbreviation you wish.

For example, suppose you enter B for your AM abbreviation and Z for your PM abbreviation. If you enter the time 2:30 PM in a cell as @TIME(14,30,0) or 2:30 PM, it is displayed for the different time formats as follows:

Time Format Selection	AM Abbr.	PM Abbr.	Time Format D6	D7	D8	D9
12 hours	B	Z	2:30:00 Z	2:30 Z	2:30:00 Z	2:30 Z
24 hours (default)			2:30:00 Z	2:30 Z	14:30:00	14:30

Any cells in your worksheet or graph already time formatted automatically display this new time format. Notice that when the *12*-hour option is selected, even the D8 and D9 formats display the PM abbreviation Z.

TIME FORMAT SEPARATOR The "Time format" "Separator" option in the User Settings International dialog box allows you to select the separator between the hours, minutes, and seconds components in time displays. You can select from two different options. On the one hand, you can use the "Symbol" option to specify a symbol between the components of a formatted time. On the other hand, the HHhMMmSSs option displays a letter for each separator in a time.

If you select the Symbol option, you can enter any of the following time separator symbols in the Symbol box:

Time Format Separator Symbol	
: (colon)	(U.S. default)
. (period)	
, (comma)	

Any cells in your worksheet or graph that are already time formatted now display the new time separator. For example, if you enter a , (comma) in the Separator box, the time 2:30:00 PM is now displayed as 2,30,00 PM.

If you select the HHhMMmSSs option, 1-2-3/G uses alphabetic separators between each component of a time, but *only* for the Date/Time 8 and Date/Time 9 time formats. An **h** separator designates the hours, **m** the minutes, and **s** the seconds. For example, if the time 5:30 AM is entered in a cell and the *H*HhMMmSSs option is chosen, this time is displayed as follows:

Separator Option	Time Format Selection	D6	Time Format D7	D8	D9
HHhMMmSSs	12 hours	05:30:00 AM	05:30 AM	05h30m00s AM	05h30m AM
HHhMMmSSs	24 hours	05:30:00 AM	05:30 AM	05h30m00s	05h30m

As shown above, only the Date/Time 8 and Date/Time 9 time formats display the alphabetic separators **h**, **m**, and **s**. However, when you select HHhMMmSSs, the D6 and D7 formats display the U.S. default separator : even when the "Symbol" box contains another separator.

Number Format

You can use the "Number format" option in the User Settings International dialog box to specify how numbers in your worksheet are displayed. Using this option, you can specify any of the following:

- A thousands separator.
- A decimal separator.
- An argument separator for functions and macros, as well as range and collection addresses.
- Whether a leading 0 precedes a decimal value that has been formatted as Currency or Comma.

NUMBER FORMAT 1000 AND DECIMAL SEPARATORS Use the Number format 1000 option to specify your thousands separator. In the 1000 box, enter any of the following:

Thousand Separator	Number Displayed as
, (comma) (U.S. default)	2,000
. (period)	2.000
' (apostrophe)	2'000
blank space	2 000

Any cells in your worksheet or graph using the Currency or Comma format automatically display the new thousand separator. For example, if you enter a , (comma) in the 1000 box, the value 2000 is displayed as 2,000.

Note

1-2-3/G displays an error message if you try to use the same thousand separator and decimal separator. The U.S. default decimal separator is . (period). So make sure you change the decimal separator first if you want your thousand separator to be a . (period).

To specify a decimal separator, select the "Number format" "Decimal" option, and type any of the following symbols as a decimal separator:

Decimal Separator	Number Displayed as
. (period) (U.S. default)	2.5
, (comma)	2,5

NUMBER FORMAT ARGUMENT SEPARATOR The "Number format" "Argument" option of the User Settings International dialog box affects the argument separator for @functions, macros, and range or collection addresses.

To specify a new argument separator, select the "Argument" option, and specify any one of the following argument separators in the adjacent text box:

Argument Separator	Function Entered as	Range or Collection Address Entered as	Macro Entered as
, (comma) (default)	@TIME(2,30,0)	A1..A5,B1..B2	{TONE 100,500}
. (period)	@TIME(2.30.0)	A1..A5.B1..B2	{TONE 100.500}
; (semicolon)	@TIME(2;30;0)	A1..A5;B1..B2	{TONE 100;500}

Note

> 1-2-3/G displays an error message if you try to use the same symbol as both an argument separator and decimal separator. The U.S. default decimal separator is . (period). Therefore, make sure you change the decimal separator first if you want your argument separator to be a . (period).

Note

> The ; semicolon is the "international" argument separator. 1-2-3/G always interprets this argument separator correctly, regardless of the separator you specify using the "Number format" "Argument" option.

LEADING ZERO The "Leading zero" check box in the "Number format" section of the User Settings International dialog box affects the display of numbers that are less than one and have been formatted as Currency or Comma. For example, numbers that are less than one and formatted as Currency are normally displayed with a leading zero to the left of the decimal, such as $0.25. However, if you remove the X from the "leading zero" check box, $0.25 becomes $.25.

Currency Format

The "Currency format" section of the User Settings International dialog box determines how numbers formatted as currency are displayed. Using this option, you can specify any of the following:

- The currency symbol used with Currency formats.
- The placement of the currency symbol.
- How negative numbers are displayed for Currency and Comma formats.

Changing the Currency Format Symbol

Use the "Symbol" text box in the Currency format section to specify the currency symbol you want 1-2-3/G to display. 1-2-3/G uses the symbol you specify when you format a range or worksheet with the Range Format Currency and Worksheet Global Format Currency commands. This also affects the Settings Number Format command in the Graph Tool.

Initially, the default U.S. currency symbol, $, is displayed in the "Symbol" box. However, you can enter another currency designation in this box that is up to five characters in length. You can also enter another currency symbol that is not designated on the U.S keyboard, such as £ (the British pound sign) using either of the following methods:

- Use a compose sequence. Press COMPOSE (ALT-F1) and enter the compose sequence for the character. For the British pound sign, enter **L=**. The £ sign appears in the Symbol box.
- Press the ALT key and enter the corresponding code-page number for the character. (For both the U.S default code page, 850, and the U.S. backup code page, 437, the British pound sign corresponds to code number 156.) First, select NUM LOCK. Then press ALT, and keeping that key depressed, type **156** on your numeric keypad. The £ sign appears in the Symbol box.

Any values in your worksheet that use a Currency format now display the British pound sign, £, instead of the U.S. dollar sign.

Note

For other compose sequences and character codes, see "1-2-3/G Character Set" in Appendix B of this book.

Currency Symbol Placement

You can use the "Currency format" "Placement" option in the User Settings International dialog box to control the positioning of the currency symbol in relation to a value. You can select from either of the following options:

Placement Option	Value Displayed As
Prefix (U.S. default)	$1
Suffix	1$

Any values in your worksheet or graph using a Currency format are automatically updated and display a currency symbol in the placement you specify.

Currency Format Negative

Use the "Currency format" "Negative" option to control the way negative numbers in Currency or Comma format are displayed. This setting affects the Range Format Currency and Worksheet Global Format Currency commands. It also affects the Settings Number Format command in the Graph Tool. When you select "Currency Format" "Negative," you can then select from either of the following options:

Negative Option	Currency Formatted Value Displayed As
Parentheses (U.S. default)	($1.00)
Sign	-$1.00

When you make a "Negative" option selection, existing values in your worksheets or graphs that are formatted as Currency are immediately updated to reflect your selection.

Caution

Before you use User Settings International Currency format Negative Parentheses, make sure you reset the Worksheet Global Format (Parens) or Range Format (Parens) setting to the default. If you use the Range Format (Parens) Yes command before you select this setting, Comma and Currency formatted values display two sets of parentheses such as (($1.00)). Also, if you use the Worksheet Global Format (Parens) Yes command, then select this setting, all negative values regardless of the format display two sets of negative parentheses.

Measurement

You can use the Measurement section of the User Settings International dialog box to specify the unit of measurement for 1-2-3/G. You can choose from Inches (the default) or Millimeters. The choice you make affects the following:

- **Column widths:** Set with the Worksheet Global Column Units Absolute command or the Worksheet Column Units Absolute command.
- **Row heights:** Set with the Worksheet Row command or the Worksheet Global Row command.
- **Print margins:** Set with File Print Options Margins command or the Print Printer Options Margins command

For example, suppose the cell pointer is in row 1 and you select the Worksheet Row Set height command. You then enter 1 in the "Set height" text box. Immediately to the right of this text box, 1-2-3/G displays "inch," and it interprets your entry as "1 inch." However, imagine that you now select the Utility User Settings International Measurement Millimeters command. The height of Row 1 does not change. But, if you select the Worksheet Row command again, the "Set height" text box contains the value 25.411 followed by "mm" (millimeters). In addition, if you use your mouse to change the height of a row, the Control Line displays the height of the row in millimeters when you click your mouse button.

Sort Options

The "Sort options" section of the User Settings International dialog box allows you to specify a sort sequence for the Data Sort command. You can choose from any of the following sort options:

Sort Option Selection	Sorts
ASCII	According to the code-page value for each character (Case is honored)
Numbers Last	Labels that contain letters before cells that contain numbers (Case is ignored)
Numbers First (Default)	Labels that contain numbers before cells that contain letters (Case is ignored)

The *ASCII* option sorts your data based on the code-page number assigned to each character. This can be particularly handy if you want 1-2-3/G to sort labels that begin with upper-case letters ahead of labels that begin with lower-case letters. Otherwise, 1-2-3/G ignores case when sorting labels. As you'll see in Appendix B, each character used in 1-2-3/G is assigned a code-page number. The letter "A" is assigned the number 65 and the letter "a" is assigned number 97. Therefore, the letter "A" is sorted before the letter "a."

File Translation (Code Page)

The "File translation" option specifies the code page 1-2-3/G uses when text files are imported or exported (printed) using the File Import and Print File commands. When you import a text file with File Import, that text file must use the same character code set as specified by the "File translation" option. Otherwise, the characters from the text file may appear corrupted when they arrive in 1-2-3/G. Conversely, when you write to a text file with the Print File command, that file must use the same character set as the "File Translation" option or the characters in the text file may appear corrupted.

The "File translation" section of the User Settings International dialog box offers two options, "International (850)" and "Country (437)." The "International (850)" refers to the IBM Multilingual Character set (code page 850), which is the default character set used by 1-2-3/G. However, this character set does not include many of the Greek letters and other common mathematical characters, such as pi. Therefore, 1-2-3/G provides access to a secondary code page, code page 437, which corresponds to the IBM Extended ASCII character set.

1-2-3/G cannot display characters using the code page 437 character set. It is only capable of converting code page 437 characters to code page 850 characters for the File Import command. Conversely, it can convert code page 850 characters to code page 437 characters for the File Print command.

The 1-2-3/G Character Set

1-2-3/G uses the IBM PC Multilingual code-page 850 character set to store, display, and print your data. This character set includes characters and symbols that are commonly used in the English language as well as in 18 other European languages. The characters included in the code-page 850 character set are shown in Figures B-1, B-2, and B-3 of this appendix.

Although many of the characters in the code-page 850 character set appear on your keyboard, many do not. Obviously, you can produce those characters that do appear on your keyboard by simply pressing the appropriate key. However, you can also produce those in the code-page 850 character set that do not appear on your keyboard. In fact, that is what this appendix is about.

Each character in the code-page 850 character set is assigned a sequential number, 1 through 255. In Figures B-1, B-2, and B-3, the code-page value for each character is shown immediately to the left of the character.

USING CODE-PAGE VALUES

You can use a character's code-page value to produce that character, even though it may not appear on your keyboard. You can do this in one of the following two ways:

- You can use the @CHAR function followed by the appropriate code-page value. For example, suppose you want to produce the Japanese Yen symbol (code-page value 190, Figure B-2) in the current worksheet cell. To do this, simply type **@CHAR(190)** and press ENTER.

1-2-3/G — Ready

File Edit Worksheet Range Copy... Move... Print Graph Data Utility Quit... Help

A:B1 @CHAR(+A1)

CODE850.WG1

A	A	B	C	D	E	F	G	H	I	J	K	L
1	1	☺	18	↕	35	#	52	4	69	E	86	V
2	2	☻	19	‼	36	$	53	5	70	F	87	W
3	3	♥	20	¶	37	%	54	6	71	G	88	X
4	4	♦	21	§	38	&	55	7	72	H	89	Y
5	5	♣	22	▬	39	'	56	8	73	I	90	Z
6	6	♠	23	↨	40	(	57	9	74	J	91	[
7	7	•	24	↑	41	)	58	:	75	K	92	\
8	8	◘	25	↓	42	*	59	;	76	L	93	]
9	9	○	26	→	43	+	60	<	77	M	94	^
10	10	◙	27	←	44	,	61	=	78	N	95	_
11	11	♂	28	∟	45	-	62	>	79	O	96	`
12	12	♀	29	↔	46	.	63	?	80	P	97	a
13	13	♪	30	▲	47	/	64	@	81	Q	98	b
14	14	♫	31	▼	48	0	65	A	82	R	99	c
15	15	☼	32		49	1	66	B	83	S	100	d
16	16	►	33	!	50	2	67	C	84	T	101	e
17	17	◄	34	"	51	3	68	D	85	U	102	f

FIGURE B-1 Code-page 850 character set

1-2-3/G — Ready

File Edit Worksheet Range Copy... Move... Print Graph Data Utility Quit... Help

A:B18

CODE850.WG1

A	A	B	C	D	E	F	G	H	I	J	K	L
20	103	g	120	x	137	ë	154	Ü	171	½	188	╝
21	104	h	121	y	138	è	155	ø	172	¼	189	¢
22	105	i	122	z	139	ï	156	£	173	¡	190	¥
23	106	j	123	{	140	î	157	Ø	174	«	191	┐
24	107	k	124	|	141	ì	158	×	175	»	192	└
25	108	l	125	}	142	Ä	159	ƒ	176	░	193	┴
26	109	m	126	~	143	Å	160	á	177	▒	194	┬
27	110	n	127	⌂	144	É	161	í	178	▓	195	├
28	111	o	128	Ç	145	æ	162	ó	179	│	196	─
29	112	p	129	ü	146	Æ	163	ú	180	┤	197	┼
30	113	q	130	é	147	ô	164	ñ	181	Á	198	ã
31	114	r	131	â	148	ö	165	Ñ	182	Â	199	Ã
32	115	s	132	ä	149	ò	166	ª	183	À	200	╚
33	116	t	133	à	150	û	167	º	184	©	201	╔
34	117	u	134	å	151	ù	168	¿	185	╣	202	╩
35	118	v	135	ç	152	ÿ	169	®	186	║	203	╦
36	119	w	136	ê	153	Ö	170	¬	187	╗	204	╠

FIGURE B-2 Code-page 850 charcter set (continued)

1-2-3/G — Ready

File Edit Worksheet Range Copy... Move... Print Graph Data Utility Quit... Help

A:B18

CODE850.WG1

A	A	B	C	D	E	F	G	H	I	J	K	L	M
39	205	═	222	Ì	239	´							
40	206	╬	223	▀	240	-							
41	207	¤	224	Ó	241	±							
42	208	ð	225	ß	242	‗							
43	209	Đ	226	Ô	243	¾							
44	210	Ê	227	Ò	244	¶							
45	211	Ë	228	õ	245	§							
46	212	È	229	Õ	246	÷							
47	213	ı	230	µ	247	¸							
48	214	Í	231	þ	248	°							
49	215	Î	232	Þ	249	¨							
50	216	Ï	233	Ú	250	·							
51	217	┘	234	Û	251	¹							
52	218	┌	235	Ù	252	³							
53	219	█	236	ý	253	²							
54	220	▄	237	Ý	254	■							
55	221	¦	238	¯	255								

FIGURE B-3 Code-page 850 character set (continued)

- You can also use the ALT key to produce a code-page 850 character. To do this, press the NUM LOCK key to activate the numeric keypad. Then press the ALT key and hold it down. Finally, type the code-page value for the character and release the ALT key.

For example, to produce the Japanese Yen symbol (code-page value 190, Figure B-2), press NUM LOCK and type **ALT-190** and release the ALT key.

USING COMPOSE SEQUENCES

You can also produce code-page 850 characters by using COMPOSE sequences. To do this, press COMPOSE (ALT-F1) and then type the appropriate symbols for the code-page 850 character from Table B-1. (You can cross reference the code-page values in Table B-1 to the code-page values in Figures B-1, B-2, and B-3.) When you're finished press ENTER. For example, suppose you want to enter the Japanese Yen symbol (code-page 190, Table B-1) in the current cell by using a COMPOSE sequence. To do this, press COMPOSE (ALT-F1) and type **Y=**. 1-2-3/G displays the Yen symbol in the Control Line. To confirm the entry and place it in the current cell, press ENTER.

Note

Not all code-page 850 characters have COMPOSE sequence characters. Those that do appear in Table B-1.

TABLE B-1 COMPOSE Sequence Characters

Code-Page Value	Compose Sequence	Character Description
20	!P or !p	Paragraph symbol
21	SO or so	Section symbol
27	mg	Left arrow
30	ba	Solid triangle
31	ea	Solid triangle, inverted
35	++	Number sign
64	AA or aa	At sign
91	((	Open bracket
92	//	Backslash
93	))	Close bracket
94	vv	Circumflex
123	(-	Open curly brace
124	^/	Bar
125	)-	Closed curly brace
126	--	Tilde
128	C,	C cedilla, uppercase
129	u"	u umlaut, lowercase
130	e'	e acute, lowercase
131	a^	a circumflex, lowercase
132	a"	a umlaut, lowercase
133	a'	a grave, lowercase
134	a*	a ring, lowercase
135	c,	c cedilla, lowercase
136	e^	e circumflex, lowercase
137	e"	e umlaut, lowercase
138	e'	e grave, lowercase
139	i"	i umlaut, lowercase
140	i^	i circumflex, lowercase
141	i'	i grave, lowercase
142	A"	A umlaut, uppercase

(continued)

TABLE B-1 COMPOSE Sequence Characters (*cont.*)

Code-Page Value	Compose Sequence	Character Description
143	A*	A ring, uppercase
144	E′	E acute, uppercase
145	ae	ae dipthong, lowercase
146	AE	AE dipthong, uppercase
147	o^	o circumflex, lowercase
148	o"	o umlaut, lowercase
149	o‘	o grave, lowercase
150	u^	u circumflex, lowercase
151	u‘	u grave, lowercase
152	y"	y umlaut, lowercase
153	O"	O umlaut, uppercase
154	U"	U umlaut, uppercase
155	o/	o slash, lowercase
156	L= l= L- or l-	British pound sign
157	O/	O slash, uppercase
158	xx or XX	Muliplication sign
159	ff	Guilder
160	a′	a acute, lowercase
161	i′	i acute, lowercase
162	o′ o	o acute, lowercase
163	u′	u acute, lowercase
164	n~	n tilde, lowercase
165	N~	N tilde, uppercase
166	a_ or A_	Feminine ordinal indicator
167	o_ or O_	Masculine ordinal indicator
168	??	Question mark, inverted
169	RO ro R0 or r0	Registered trademark
170	-]	End of line symbol/Logical NOT
171	12	One half
172	14	One quarter
173	!!	Exclamation point, inverted
174	<<	Left angle quotes
175	>>	Right angle quotes
181	A′	A acute, uppercase
182	A^	A circumflex, uppercase
183	A‘	A grave, uppercase
184	CO or co	Copyright sybmol
189	c| c/ or C|	Cent sign
190	Y= y= Y- or y-	Yen sign
198	a~	a tilde, lowercase
199	A~	A tilde, uppercase

TABLE B-1 COMPOSE Sequence Characters (*cont.*)

Code-Page Value	Compose Sequence	Character Description
207	XO xo X0 or x0	International currency sign
208	d-	Icelandic eth, lowercase
209	D-	Icelandic eth, uppercase
210	E^	E circumflex, uppercase
211	E"	E umlaut, uppercase
212	E‘	E grave, uppercase
213	i <space>	i without dot, lowercase
214	I’	I acute, uppercase
215	I^	I circumflex, uppercase
216	I"	I umlaut, uppercase
221	/ <space>	Vertical line, broken
222	I‘	I grave, uppercase
224	O’	O acute, uppercase
225	ss	German sharp, lowercase
226	O^	O circumflex, uppercase
227	O‘	O grave, uppercase
228	o~	o tilde, lowercase
229	O~	O tilde, uppercase
230	/u	Micro sign (Greek mu, lowercase)
231	p-	Icelandix thorn, lowercase
232	P-	Icelandix thorn, uppercase
233	U’	U acute, uppercase
234	U^	U circumflex, uppercase
235	U‘	U grave, uppercase
236	y’	y acute, lowercase
237	Y’	Y acute, uppercase
238	^-	Overline character
240	-=	Hyphenation symbol
241	+-	Plus or minus sign
242	__ or ==	Double underscore
243	34	Three quarters sign
246	:-	Division symbol
247	,,	Cedilla accent
248	^0	Degree symbol
250	^.	Center dot
251	^1	One superscript
252	^3	Three superscript
253	^2	Two superscript

INDEX

A

B

E

F

G

H

I

N

O

P

Q

R

S

T

U

X

Y

Z